WORLD RESOURCES

1996–97

WORLD RESOURCES

1996–97

A joint publication by

The World Resources Institute

**The United Nations
Environment Programme**

**The United Nations
Development Programme**

The World Bank

New York   Oxford
Oxford University Press
1996

The cover shows an inner city area in Buenos Aires, Federal District, Argentina.
Photo by James P. Blair, National Geographic Society Image Collection.

The World Resources Institute, the United Nations Environment Programme, the United Nations Development Programme, and the World Bank gratefully acknowledge permission to reprint from the following sources:

Part I:
Figure 1.3, Table 4.2, Figure 5.1, and Table 6.1, The World Bank; Box 3.1, Figure 1, *Scientific American*; Box 3.2, Figure 1, National Academy of Sciences; Figure 3.2, Asian Development Bank.

Part II:
Box 7.1, Figure 1, The World Bank; Figure 8.4, United Nations Development Programme; Figure 8.6, Figure 8.7, and Table 8.1, World Health Organization; Table 9.1, Figure 10.3, Figure 10.4, Table 10.3, Table 10.4, and Figure 13.1, Food and Agriculture Organization of the United Nations; Table 11.1, United Nations Environment Programme; Box 12.1, Figure 1, British Petroleum; Table 13.2 and Table 13.3, Population Action International; Figure 14.3 and Figure 14.4, Intergovernmental Panel on Climate Change.

Printed in the United States of America on recycled paper.

Oxford University Press

Oxford   New York   Toronto
Delhi   Bombay   Calcutta   Madras   Karachi
Kuala Lumpur   Singapore   Hong Kong   Tokyo
Nairobi   Dar es Salaam   Cape Town
Melbourne   Auckland

and associated companies in
Berlin   Ibadan

Copyright © 1996 by the World Resources Institute

Oxford is a registered trademark of Oxford University Press

ISBN 0-19-521160-X
ISBN (PBK) 0-19-521161-8
Library of Congress Cataloging Number: 86-659504
ISSN 0887-0403

World Resources is a biennial publication of the World Resources Institute, 1709 New York, Ave., N.W., Washington, DC, 20006

Printing (last digit): 9 8 7 6 5 4 3 2 1

Contents

Preface   vii

Executive Summary   ix

Part I The Urban Environment

1   Cities and the Environment   1
    *Forces driving urbanization; urban environmental problems; economic costs
    of environmental degradation; urban poverty; challenges to governments*

2   Urban Environment and Human Health   31
    *Physical and social threats to human health; differences among cities;
    socioeconomic inequities and health*

3   Urban Impacts on Natural Resources   57
    *Land conversion; depletion of natural resources; disposal of urban wastes;
    threats to coastal ecosystems*

4   Urban Transportation   81
    *Urban transportation trends; impacts (congestion, pollution, accidents,
    social inequities); managing travel demand and supply*

5   Urban Priorities for Action   103
    *Strategic choices: water and sanitation; water resources management;
    solid waste management; indoor and outdoor air pollution; land use planning*

6   City and Community: Toward Environmental Sustainability   125
    Involving local governments; community initiatives; cities and sustainable development

    Appendix A. Urban Data Tables   149
        A.1 Urban Indicators, 1975–2025
        A.2 Access to Safe Drinking Water and Sanitation, 1980–95
        A.3 Air Pollution in Selected Cities, 1989–94
        A.4 India: City Indicators, 1993

Part II Global Conditions and Trends and Data Tables

7   Basic Economic Indicators   159
    Measuring economic progress; economic growth and the environment
        7.1 Gross National and Domestic Product Estimates, 1983–93
        7.2 Official Development Assistance and External Debt Indicators, 1981–93
        7.3 World Commodity Indexes and Prices, 1975–94

8   **Population and Human Development**   **173**

Trends in population and health; focus on emerging infectious diseases
    8.1 Size and Growth of Population and Labor Force, 1950–2025
    8.2 Trends in Births, Life Expectancy, Fertility, and Age Structure, 1970–95
    8.3 Mortality and Nutrition, 1970–95
    8.4 Education and Child Health, 1970–93

9   **Forests and Land Cover**   **201**

State of the world's tropical and temperate forests; focus on Russia and Suriname
    9.1 Land Area and Use, 1981–93
    9.2 Forest Resources, 1981–90
    9.3 Wood Production and Trade, 1981–93

10   **Food and Agriculture**   **225**

Trends in global agricultural production; getting food to those who need it
    10.1 Food and Agricultural Production, 1982–94
    10.2 Agricultural Inputs, 1981–93
    10.3 Livestock Populations and Grain Consumed as Feed, 1982–94
    10.4 Food Trade and Aid, 1981–93

11   **Biodiversity**   **247**

Coastal ecosystems and marine biodiversity under stress; pressures and policies
    11.1 National and International Protection of Natural Areas, 1994
    11.2 Globally Threatened Species: Mammals, Birds, and Higher Plants, 1990s
    11.3 Globally Threatened Species: Reptiles, Amphibians, and Fish, 1990s
    11.4 Marine Biodiversity

12   **Energy and Materials**   **273**

Energy trends; projections of future energy demand; available energy resources
    12.1 Commercial Energy Production, 1973–93
    12.2 Energy Consumption, 1973–93
    12.3 Reserves and Resources of Commercial Energy, 1993
    12.4 Production, Consumption, and Reserves of Selected Metals, 1980–94
    12.5 Industrial Waste in Selected Countries

13   **Water and Fisheries**   **295**

Marine fishing trends and managing water resources
    13.1 Freshwater Resources and Withdrawals
    13.2 Wastewater Treatment
    13.3 Marine Fisheries, Yield and State of Exploitation
    13.4 Marine and Freshwater Catches, Aquaculture, and Fish Consumption

14   **Atmosphere and Climate**   **315**

Trends in carbon dioxide emissions; costs and benefits of stabilizing greenhouse gas emissions
    14.1 CO_2 Emissions from Industrial Processes, 1992
    14.2 Other Greenhouse Gas Emissions, 1991
    14.3 Atmospheric Concentrations of Greenhouse and Ozone-Depleting Gases, 1970–94
    14.4 World CO_2 Emissions from Fossil Fuel Consumption and Cement Manufacture, 1950–92
    14.5 Common Anthropogenic Pollutants, 1980–93
    14.6 Inventories of National Greenhouse Gas Emissions, 1990

Acknowledgments   **339**

Index   **347**

World Resources Database Index   **363**

Preface

The *World Resources* series is published to meet the critical need for accessible, accurate information on environment and development. Wise management of natural resources and protection of the global environment are essential to achieve sustainable economic development and hence to alleviate poverty, improve the human condition, and preserve the biological systems on which all life depends.

World Resources 1996–97 is the seventh report in the series. Recent reports were prepared by the World Resources Institute (WRI) in collaboration with the United Nations Environment Programme (UNEP) and the United Nations Development Programme (UNDP). For this report, UNEP and UNDP have become full partners with WRI and have been joined by the World Bank. We believe that this new partnership will significantly strengthen our efforts to make this series the most objective and up-to-date report of conditions and trends in the world's natural resources and in the global environment.

Part I of this volume devotes six chapters to the urban environment in support of the June 1996 United Nations' Habitat II Conference in Istanbul, Turkey. Urbanization is a major global trend with a complex variety of impacts. It can have many positive effects, such as improvements in productivity and access to services. As we examine in the first three chapters, however, it can also have a wide variety of adverse impacts on both people and the environment. Many of the most difficult urban issues cut across political, economic, and institutional boundaries; one such issue is transportation, which we examine in Chapter 4. The concluding chapters look at priority areas for improv-ing the urban environment and at community-based approaches.

Part II continues the tradition of examining in each volume basic conditions and trends and key issues in each of the major resource categories, from agriculture to water resources to atmosphere and climate. Many of these chapters focus particularly on future trends; a brief review of these issues can be found in the Executive Summary. In a change that should make the report easier to use, the core data tables from the World Resources Database are now also found in Part II, at the end of each relevant chapter. Additional information and data can be found in the *Human Development Report,* which is published annually by UNDP, and in the World Bank's *World Development Report.*

In an effort to make an expanded set of data accessible to policymakers, scholars, and nongovernmental organizations, WRI also publishes on diskette the *World Resources* Database—expanded to include additional countries, variables, and where possible, a 20-year data set.

The audience for the *World Resources* series has steadily expanded, with English, Spanish, French, Arabic, German, Japanese, and Chinese editions now in print, as well as an Indian edition, which is published in English but printed in New Delhi. *A Teacher's Guide to World Resources* is also available to make the series accessible and useful to teachers and students.

We commend the *World Resources* staff for its efforts in assembling and analyzing this unique collection of information and for producing the volume in a timely fashion. The Editorial Advisory Board, chaired by Dr. M.S. Swaminathan, provided active advice and support at all stages of the project. Similarly, the senior advisors for the special section on the urban environment provided invaluable assistance.

We wish to thank the U.S. Agency for International Development for its support of the urban chapters; the Inter-American Development Bank for support of the Spanish edition; the Netherlands Ministry of Foreign Affairs for assistance in distribution of the report; and the Swedish International Development Authority and the U.S. Environmental Protection Agency for support to expand and strengthen the *World Resources* Database.

Jonathan Lash
President
World Resources Institute

Elizabeth Dowdeswell
Executive Director
United Nations Environment Programme

James Gustave Speth
Administrator
United Nations Development Programme

James D. Wolfensohn
President
The World Bank

Executive Summary

This volume devotes special attention to the urban environment, a major focus of Habitat II—the United Nations Conference on Human Settlements—scheduled for June 1996 in Istanbul, Turkey. Urban environmental conditions are important to the health and quality of life of a city's inhabitants and can impose significant costs on economic and social development. The impact of urban areas on the surrounding environment is also an issue of growing concern. More than half of humankind will live in urban areas by the end of the century, and 60 percent by 2020. In most nations, cities generate a majority of the economic activity, ultimately consume most of the natural resources, and produce most of the pollution and waste. Thus, urban environmental issues, although often overlooked, are important both locally and on national and global scales. Neglect of these issues could compromise larger economic, social, and environmental goals in both developed and developing countries.

This volume also surveys a number of current trends in the global environment and their implications for the future. Most of these trends show worsening environmental problems, suggesting that many national and international environmental goals will not be met without extensive policy reform and significant changes in current practices and strategies. On the positive side, however, this volume also reports a significant environmental milestone, the partial phaseout of production of ozone-depleting chemicals.

THE URBAN ENVIRONMENT

Cities embody the diversity and energy of human pursuits. They are in many ways remarkable engines of economic and social progress. Cities offer employment opportunities, entertainment and other amenities, and potential efficiencies not found elsewhere, as well as advantages in the delivery of education, health, and other social services. On average, urban dwellers have higher incomes and live healthier, easier lives than their rural counterparts, although these advantages are often not shared by all urban inhabitants.

But cities also play a central role in degrading the physical environment and in shaping the social environments in which most of the world's people will soon live. Dysfunctional urban environments have high costs, making more difficult the economic growth needed to improve living standards and helping to perpetuate inequities. The developed world is already largely urbanized. In the developing world, the rapid urbanization now under way will increasingly concentrate both population and economic growth in cities—as much as 90 percent of future population growth and a major share of future economic growth—intensifying the problems of the urban environment. (Chapter 1.)

In recent decades, urban areas in developed countries have made major progress in cleaning up local environmental problems, but they remain significant contributors to regional and global environmental

Urban Population Growth
(population in billions)

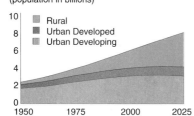

In the developing world, the rapid urbanization now under way will increasingly concentrate both population and economic growth in cities, intensifying the problems of the urban environment.

World Motor Vehicle Ownership
(vehicles in millions)

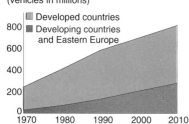

burdens. At the same time, the urban social environment in developed countries—which includes factors such as violence and drug abuse—poses major threats to human health and productivity. In developing countries, urban areas often have huge populations living in poverty and facing the same urban social threats that confront residents of cities in the developed regions. Disparities among different income groups are often more extreme in cities of the developing world. In many cases, for example, overall improvement in urban health indicators masks a widening split between the poor and the well-to-do. The problems of the urban poor are similar to those of the rural poor—lack of access to clean water, sanitation, and adequate housing—compounded by overcrowding and exposure to industrial wastes and urban air pollution. (Chapter 2.)

Burgeoning cities are expanding into fragile ecosystems—nearly 40 percent of cities larger than 500,000 are located on the coast. Cities sometimes deplete nearby areas of water and firewood, rendering them less capable of supporting rural populations and thus adding to the pressures for urban migration. Air pollution already exceeds health standards in many megacities in developing countries. Sewage and industrial effluents are released into waterways with minimal or no treatment, threatening human health and aquatic life. Some urban environmental problems such as access to safe drinking water improve with economic growth, while others tend to worsen. Thus in the absence of policy reform, stronger institutions, and enlightened political leadership, economic and population growth in developing countries in the near term may lead to a deterioration of the urban environment, both physical and social. Stresses on the global environment from urban activities are also likely to accelerate. A major share of greenhouse gas emissions already comes from the use of fossil fuels in wealthy urban areas, especially in the developed countries. (Chapter 3.)

Transportation issues illustrate how environmental, social, and economic factors interact in the urban environment. Transportation demand and motor vehicle ownership are concentrated in urban areas, and energy use for transportation is rising faster than that for any other sector. Motor vehicles in turn are a primary cause of congestion and local air pollution, which are posing a growing threat to economic productivity and human health. Yet the dispersed form of many urban areas makes motor vehicles virtually essential. It also contributes to social inequities, for example, limiting access to jobs and other opportunities for those who cannot afford vehicles or requiring long trips by public transit or on foot. (Chapter 4.)

Priorities for Action

Three issues emerge as particularly critical: water supply and sanitation and water resource management, solid waste management, and air pollution. In each area, there are compelling economic, social, and environmental rationales for change. Successful efforts, however, are likely to require significant changes in urban practices and strategies.

Improving access to clean water and sanitation, for example, has been cited as "the single most effective means of alleviating human distress." Past experience shows the need for a shift away from centralized systems and toward more flexible, community-oriented strategies. In hopes of cutting the costs of solid waste management while improving service, many cities are experimenting with public-private partnerships and informal, community-based approaches. Focusing on pollution prevention and on energy conservation, in part by fixing distorted prices and using other novel economic tools, is likely to be central to reducing air pollution. Underlying many urban environmental problems—from congestion and air pollution to the lack of affordable housing to urban decay—are land use patterns and practices. More effective land use planning is critical to improving access to urban services for the poor and to reducing resource consumption and improving the quality of life in more affluent communities. (Chapter 5.)

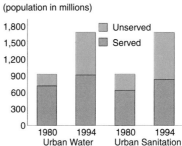

Access to Water and Sanitation in Urban Areas
(population in millions)

Community-Based Strategies

Beyond the immediate priorities for improving the urban environment lies the need to strengthen local governments, to implement new approaches to alleviating poverty and supporting communities, and to develop more environmentally friendly cities. Virtually all of the policies needed to improve the urban environment require more effective urban governance. That will require not only strengthened governments but also the involvement of many other actors in the urban environment—including the poor and the private sector. Community-based approaches are essential if urban services are to reach those who need them and if there is to be broad-based support for needed changes in strategies and practices. The sheer size of urban populations and economies means that cities must lead the way toward more environmentally sustainable practices for the world as a whole. (Chapter 6.)

Virtually all of the policies needed to improve the urban environment require more effective urban governance, including the involvement of both the poor and the private sector.

IMPLICATIONS OF CURRENT GLOBAL TRENDS

Population Growth

Current population trends are cause for both optimism and concern. Some developing countries are moving rapidly toward population stability. But other countries are experiencing rapid population growth, usually accompanied by high levels of poverty, limited progress for women, and high levels of internal and international migration. Overall, the world population is increasing by more than 86 million people every year. Such rapid growth places enormous pressure on natural resources, urban infrastructure and services, and governments at all levels, especially in the poorest countries where growth is most rapid.

Global population will continue to grow for many decades to come, reflecting the demographic inertia of countries in which a large fraction of the population has not yet reached child-bearing age. In the U.N. medium popu-

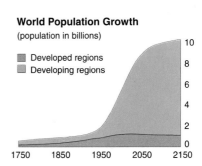

World Population Growth
(population in billions)

Rapid population growth places enormous pressure on natural resources, urban infrastructure and services, and governments at all levels.

lation projection, world population reaches about 10 billion by the middle of the next century before gradually leveling off. Much of that growth occurs in the next few decades and is concentrated in a few regions, such as Africa and Asia. In these projections, fertility is assumed to decline from current levels in developing regions of the world. Projected fertility rates cannot be taken for granted, however; policies that influence fertility rates—provision of family planning services, alleviation of poverty, and improvements in education, health care, and economic opportunities, especially for women—can have a marked effect on future population levels. (Chapter 8.)

Freshwater Supplies

One environmental consequence of growing populations is increasing pressure on natural resources. Demand for water is growing rapidly as populations and industrial activity expand and irrigated agriculture (the largest use) continues to increase. From 1940 to 1990, for example, withdrawals of freshwater from rivers, lakes, and underground aquifers increased by a factor of four. Many current patterns of water withdrawals are clearly unsustainable, such as pumping from subsoil aquifers at rates far greater than they are recharged. Water shortages are already critical in some regions, posing obstacles to continued development and threats to freshwater habitats.

The future availability of water for human use depends on how water resources are managed; water can, in principle, be reused many times. Future pressures on water resources can thus be seen as a measure of the management challenge that water-short regions will face. According to one estimate, between 1 billion and 2.4 billion people (13 to 20 percent of the projected world population) will live in water-scarce countries by 2050. Africa and parts of western Asia appear particularly vulnerable. Policies that improve the efficiency of water use, avoid waste, and preserve supplies (by controlling water pollution and maintaining watersheds) can markedly extend the availability of scarce supplies. Particularly important are more efficient irrigation systems, appropriate water pricing and removal of harmful subsidies, upgrading and improved maintenance of urban water distribution systems, control or treatment of industrial wastewater and urban sewage effluents, and cooperative management of shared watersheds and river basins. (Chapter 13.)

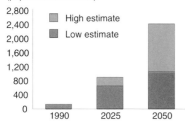

Population Subject to Water Scarcity
(population in millions)

High estimate
Low estimate

Even if global food supplies are adequate, the inability of poor nations to pay for food imports and of poor families to buy food means that many people will continue to go hungry.

Food Security

Water scarcity has a direct impact on food security. Indeed, many countries facing water scarcity may not be able to support irrigated agriculture at levels necessary to feed future populations from domestic agricultural activities. Soil erosion and degradation, especially in fragile tropical and subtropical environments, also threaten the continued productivity of agricultural lands. Overfishing threatens to damage fisheries and lower future harvests, denying many developing regions an important source of protein.

These trends may put severe strains on the world's ability to increase global food production in parallel with population growth. Nonetheless, most recent assessments suggest that global food production—the supply end of the equation—has the capability to keep pace with rising global demand.

There is less optimism about the prospects for reducing undernutrition and improving food security. Even if global food supplies are adequate, the inability of poor nations to pay for food imports, along with an inadequate distribution infrastructure and the inability of poor families to buy food, means that many people will continue to go hungry. For 1990 to 1992, the U.N. Food and Agriculture Organization (FAO) identified 27 countries as having low or critical food security indexes. In sub-Saharan Africa, for example, FAO projects that the number of undernourished people could rise from 175 million to some 300 million by 2010.

Food trade is projected to nearly double between 1990 and 2010, but trade and food aid may not fill the food security gap. Policies that strengthen agricultural research and extension systems, promote sustainable intensification and more sophisticated management of agricultural resources, and develop more effective agricultural markets in developing countries could play a major role in helping these countries to meet their own food needs. Policies that increase rural employment and access to land and credit and that strengthen the capacity of developing country governments can also have an important indirect impact on food security. (Chapter 10.)

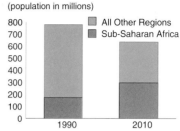

Estimated Chronic Undernutrition
(population in millions)

Energy and Climate

Energy use is already high in the developed countries and is increasing rapidly in many developing countries as they industrialize. Three different studies of future energy demand conclude that global energy use is virtually certain to rise considerably in coming decades. These studies find plausible increases in the range of 34 to 44 percent by 2010 and 54 to 98 percent by 2020. The projected growth is concentrated in Asia (a 100 percent increase from 1990 to 2010) and Latin America (a 50 to 77 percent increase over the same period). Moreover, most of the expanded production will come from fossil energy sources—coal, oil, and natural gas—in the absence of specific policies to alter market incentives. The so-called "new renewables" such as solar, wind, and farm-grown energy crops are expected to provide only 2 to 4 percent of global energy supplies from 1990 to 2020 if current practices and strategies continue.

These projections imply that local and regional air pollution is likely to increase significantly in rapidly developing regions and that global emissions of greenhouse gases will increase as well, greatly increasing the risk and potential impact of global climate change. Emissions of carbon dioxide from industrial activity climbed 38 percent during the 20 years prior to 1990 and are expected to rise another 30 to 40 percent by 2010.

These projected trends make clear that significant changes will be required in energy strategies and practices in all major regions of the world to

Three different studies conclude that global energy use—and emissions of greenhouse gases—is virtually certain to rise considerably in coming decades.

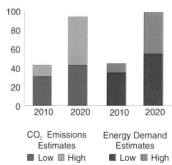

Projected Increases in CO_2 Emissions and Energy Demand
(percent increase from 1990)

About 60 percent of the global population lives within 100 kilometers of the coastline. And about half the world's coastal ecosystems appear to be at significant risk from development.

stabilize global emissions of greenhouse gases. Even greater efforts and, almost certainly, a transition to nonfossil energy sources will be required to eventually reduce emissions and hence stabilize atmospheric concentrations, the ultimate goal of the Global Climate Convention. Policies that encourage more efficient use of energy, that tax energy-based pollution or provide market incentives for the introduction of renewable energy sources, and that facilitate use of the best available technologies for energy consumption and production are well known, if not always easy to implement. Given the growing scientific consensus on global climate change—reflected in the finding by the Intergovernmental Panel on Climate Change that there is "a discernible human influence on global climate"—these policies deserve far greater attention. (Chapters 12 and 14.)

Critical Ecosystems at Risk

Coastal habitats, some of the richest storehouses of marine biodiversity, provide one example of how critical ecosystems are increasingly threatened. About 60 percent of the global population lives within 100 kilometers of the coastline, drawing heavily on coastal and marine habitats for food, building sites, transportation, recreational areas, and waste disposal. According to a new study by the World Resources Institute, 51 percent of the world's coastal ecosystems appear to be at significant risk of degradation from development-related activity. Europe, with 86 percent of its coastline at high or medium risk, and Asia, with 69 percent in these categories, are the regions most threatened by degradation. Worldwide, nearly three fourths of marine protected areas within 100 kilometers of continents or major islands appear to be at risk. (Chapter 11.)

Forest losses are continuing at a rapid rate. A new FAO study shows that fully 20 percent of all tropical natural forest cover was lost from 1960 to 1990. Temperate forest cover, too, has declined, primarily in developing countries. Natural forest cover declined 8 percent in developing countries during the 1980s, although this loss was partially offset by new forest plantations and growth in wooded areas outside forests.

Forest losses in developing countries echo earlier deforestation in developed countries. North America has lost an estimated 20 percent of its original forest cover; the countries of the former Soviet Union, 35 percent; and Europe, 60 percent. Many remaining undisturbed forests are at risk from logging, and fragmentation of forest cover is widespread. Air pollution and fire suppression practices have also contributed to declining forest health.

There is still no international consensus on how to protect forests, nor is it clear that the world community is ready to move forcefully toward managing forests on a sustainable basis. Many efforts are under way to explore policy instruments in areas such as forest management and trade in forest products; others are focusing on improving information about forests and developing greater consensus about appropriate practices. (Chapter 9.)

Percent of Coastlines at Risk
(percent)

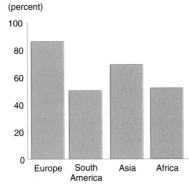

Forest losses are continuing at a rapid rate, and there is still no international consensus on how to protect forests.

Part I
The Urban Environment

1. Cities and the Environment

The world is in the midst of a massive urban transition unlike that of any other time in history. Within the next decade, more than half of the world's population, an estimated 3.3 billion, will be living in urban areas—a change with vast implications both for human well-being and for the environment (1). As recently as 1975, just over one third of the world's people lived in urban areas. By 2025, the proportion will have risen to almost two thirds (2).

The most rapid change is occurring in the developing world, where urban populations are growing at 3.5 percent per year, as opposed to less than 1 percent in the more developed regions (3). Cities are also reaching unprecedented sizes—Tokyo, 27 million; Sao Paulo, Brazil, 16.4 million; Bombay, India, 15 million—placing enormous strains on the institutional and natural resources that support them (4).

Historically, cities have been driving forces in economic and social development. As centers of industry and commerce, cities have long been centers of wealth and political power. They also account for a disproportionate share of national income. The World Bank estimates that in the developing world, as much as 80 percent of future economic growth will occur in towns and cities (5). Nor are the benefits of urbanization solely economic. Urbanization is associated with higher incomes, improved health, higher literacy, and improved quality of life. Other benefits of urban life are less tangible but no less real: access to information, diversity, creativity, and innovation.

Yet along with the benefits of urbanization come environmental and social ills, some of staggering proportions. These include a diversity of problems, from lack of access to clean drinking water, to urban air pollution, to greenhouse gas emissions. Although urban environmental problems defy easy categorization, they can be grouped into two broad classes: those associated with poverty and those associated with economic growth or affluence. The two often coexist within the same city.

Some of the worst problems, in terms of human suffering, occur in the poorest cities of the developing world. Especially where population growth is rapid, local governments are unable to provide for even the most basic needs of their citizens. Throughout the developing world, the urban poor live in life-threatening conditions. At least 220 million urban dwellers lack access to clean drinking water; more than 420 million do not have access to the simplest latrines (6). Between one and two thirds of the solid waste generated is not collected (7). It piles up on streets and in drains, contributing to flooding and the spread of disease. The problems of urban poverty exact an enormous toll in largely preventable deaths and diseases.

Environmental problems are also severe in those developing world cities experiencing rapid economic growth. Economic growth brings needed revenues to cities, but, if proper safeguards are not in place, it all too often occurs at the expense of environmental quality. More than 1.1 billion people live in urban areas where air pollution levels exceed healthful levels (8). In cities across the world, domestic and industrial effluents are released to waterways with minimal or no treatment, threatening both human health and aquatic life. These cities still harbor huge populations of the urban poor who are shut off from the benefits of economic growth. Many live in vast squatter settlements, where they are exposed both to the hazards resulting from economic growth, such as industrial emissions, and to the hazards that accompany poverty.

Worlds apart. *Cities are diverse, as are their environmental problems. In poor communities and cities, such as this newly colonized region of La Paz, Bolivia (left), the worst problems tend to be associated with lack of adequate water, sanitation, and garbage services. By contrast, wealthier cities, such as New York City (right), contribute a disproportionate share of greenhouse gas emissions.*

In the wealthiest cities of the developed world, environmental problems are related not so much to rapid growth as to profligate resource consumption. An urban dweller in New York consumes approximately three times more water and generates eight times more garbage than does a resident of Bombay (9) (10). The massive energy demand of wealthy cities contributes a major share of greenhouse gas emissions.

This special section of *World Resources 1996–97* examines the range of environmental problems and the forces contributing to them in cities of both the developed and the developing world. It then explores the nature of the environmental challenge facing the world's cities. The most immediate and pressing challenge is to improve environmental conditions for the urban poor in the developing world. Given the constraints of rapid population growth and limited financial resources, different strategies will be needed from those previously used in cities in developed regions; these approaches will involve not only technological advances but also efforts to address urban poverty.

A second, and related, challenge is for cities to reconcile the often-competing demands of economic growth and environmental protection. For cities in developed countries, that means reducing their excessive consumption of natural resources and its toll on the global commons. Such strategies are equally important for cities in the developing countries, if they are to avoid the problems of affluence so prominent in the developed world.

Though sobering, these challenges are not insurmountable. Because of their concentrated form and efficiencies of scale, cities offer major opportunities to reduce energy demand and minimize pressures on surrounding lands and natural resources. If cities can harness the energy and creativity of their citizens and build on the inherent advantages that urbanization provides, they can, in fact, be part of the solution to the global problems of poverty and environmental degradation.

URBAN GROWTH PATTERNS

Between 1990 and 2025, the number of people who live in urban areas is expected to double to more than 5 billion people (11). Almost all of this growth—a staggering 90 percent—will occur in the countries of the developing world (12). (See Figure 1.1.)

In the developed world, the most rapid urban growth took place over a century ago. By 1995, more than 70 percent of the population in both Europe and North America was living in urban areas (13). Urban growth continues, although at a much slower rate on average than in previous decades. Much of the population shift now under way involves movement away from concentrated urban centers to vast, sprawling metropolitan regions or to small- and intermediate-size cities. Some of the most rapidly growing cities are in the southwestern United States—but because this growth is fueled largely by urban-to-urban migration, it does not affect the overall level of urbanization.

In the developing world, Latin America and the Caribbean constitute the most urbanized region—with more than 70 percent of its population living in urban areas in 1995 (14). Rapid urban growth is continuing especially in small- and intermediate-size cities (15). By contrast, Africa and Asia are now only about 30 to 35 percent urban (16). It is in these regions that the most explosive growth is under way, at roughly 4 percent per year. This trend is projected to continue for several

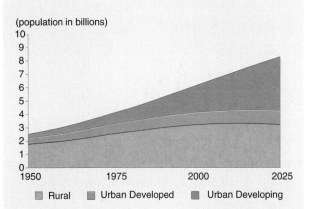

Figure 1.1 Urban Population Growth, 1950–2025

(population in billions)

Source: United Nations (U.N.) Population Division, *World Urbanization Prospects: The 1994 Revision* (U.N., New York, 1995), pp. 86–101.
Note: Urban developed regions include North America, Japan, Europe, and Australia and New Zealand; urban developing regions include Africa, Asia (excluding Japan), Latin America and the Caribbean, and Oceania (excluding Australia and New Zealand). The European successor states of the former Soviet Union are classified as developed regions, while the Asian successor states are classified as developing regions.

decades. Both Asia and Africa are expected to be about 54 percent urban by 2025 (17). (See Figure 1.2.)

In some respects, the patterns of urban growth in developing countries today are not much different from what occurred a century ago in Europe and North America. Many of the forces driving urbanization today are the same—chief among them the shift of jobs from agriculture to industry and services and the concentration of economic opportunities in urban areas. And

Figure 1.2 Regional Trends in Urbanization, 1970–2025

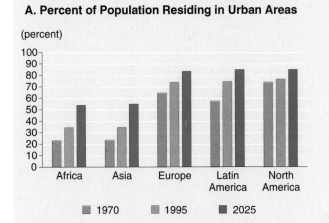

A. Percent of Population Residing in Urban Areas

(percent)

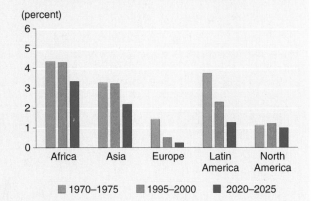

B. Average Annual Urban Growth Rates

(percent)

Source: United Nations (U.N.) Population Division, *World Urbanization Prospects: The 1994 Revision* (U.N., New York, 1995), Table A.2, pp. 78–85, and Table A.6, pp. 110–113.

Box 1.1 Abidjan: A Portrait of the African Urban Experience

Mark Edwards/Still Pictures

Shantytown. As in many African cities, unplanned settlements on the outskirts of Abidjan are mushrooming, and increasing numbers of the urban poor are crowding into makeshift housing.

Although initially a small lagoon village, Abidjan, Cote d'Ivoire, emerged as a prominent urban center in 1891 when the French chose it as the hub of railway lines linking the Atlantic Coast with Niger (1). For much of the 20th Century, the city flourished as a main harbor and seat of trade. Since the region's economic downturn, however, Abidjan's prosperity has faded, and the city is now faced with growing urban poverty and deteriorating environmental conditions.

In some ways, Abidjan is not representative of urban centers in Africa. On a continent where most urban areas are no more than large villages, Abidjan had an estimated population of 2.8 million in 1995, making it the third largest city in sub-Saharan Africa (2). Unlike many cities in Africa, which are primarily market centers, Abidjan has a rela-

tively large industrial base. In addition, Cote d'Ivoire has benefited from a stable political history: Felix Houphouet Boigney ruled the country for the first 33 years after independence, stepping down only in December 1993 to Konan Bedie (3). His regime stands in marked contrast to those in countries such as Angola, now entering its third decade of civil war, and Rwanda, torn apart by ethnic strife (4).

In other ways, however, Abidjan is grimly representative of the urban crisis emerging across the African continent (5). Abidjan's problems mirror those of cities as disparate as Nairobi, Kenya; Lusaka, Zambia; Kinshasa, Zaire; and Dakar, Senegal. These and other cities are confronting rampant urban population growth, a breakdown in urban services such as water and sanitation, a deterioration in urban environmental

quality, the AIDS epidemic, and growing social tensions—problems rendered all the more intractable by the extensive poverty of the region.

In part, the urban crisis in Africa can be attributed to the region's poor macroeconomic performance. Cote d'Ivoire's gross domestic product, which grew at an average rate of 9.2 percent between 1975 and 1979, plunged to negative levels in 1980 and continued to decline by an average of 1 percent between 1986 and 1993 (6). Within Abidjan itself, average household income declined nearly 25 percent between 1985 and 1988 (7). In recent years, this trend seems to have been accentuated by the effects of structural adjustment, which has had a greater negative impact on urban dwellers than on rural residents (8) (9).

Yet, despite its economic woes, Abidjan—like many other African cities—continues to grow at phenomenal rates. The rapid urbanization sweeping the continent seems unlikely to slow soon; fertility rates remain high in both rural and urban areas. Migration has also played a dominant role in Abidjan's growth. According to 1988 census data, 37 percent of the population of Abidjan is foreign born (10). Recent growth rates have dropped to about 5 percent, compared with 12 percent in previous decades; still, an additional 400 urban dwellers are added each day (11). Growth has been fastest on the urban fringe, while the Plateau (the colonial center and business district) has lost residents (12).

This rapid growth has far outpaced the government's ability to provide urban services. The number of people without access to piped water grew from 800,000 in 1988 to almost 1 million in 1993—roughly 38 percent of the population (13). Around 30 percent of the population is serviced by sewers, 55

although cities of the developing world are growing at least twice as fast today as those of the developed world, these rates are not unprecedented. A number of European and U.S. cities sustained very rapid growth in the early 20th Century, as fast as that now under way in the developing countries (18).

What is unprecedented now, however, is the absolute scale of the change, in terms of the number of countries

undergoing rapid urbanization, the number of cities worldwide that are growing rapidly, and the sheer number of people involved (19). Roughly 150,000 people are added to the urban population of developing countries every day (20). Because of the huge population base in developing countries, even a relatively slow rate of urban growth can mean an enormous increase in absolute numbers. Given the huge size of the world's popu-

percent is served by septic tanks and latrines, and 15 percent must resort to open defecation. Most wastewater finds its way to the city's lagoons, which are highly polluted. Municipal, industrial, and hazardous wastes are combined before disposal, increasing the dangers for scavengers working at the site (14).

Deteriorating quality of life has had adverse impacts on health, such as a marked increase since 1978 in citywide mortality rates for infants. Conditions are the worst for the very poor in Abidjan. In the shantytowns, mortality rates for children are almost five times as high as in the richer districts (15).

Health infrastructure has also suffered from neglect. While Abidjan has the highest concentration of trained health personnel in the country, there are still only 2 doctors and 5 paramedics per 10,000 inhabitants. Costs of medicine and health care are prohibitive for the majority of the population. The need for health care is becoming more urgent in the face of the AIDS epidemic. In Abidjan, an estimated 10 percent of adults carry the virus. One study of records at city morgues showed that AIDS-related illness is already the leading cause of adult deaths in Abidjan (16).

As bleak as the picture seems, however, several projects involving communities and nongovernmental organizations are demonstrating that improvements in living conditions are possible without great financial outlays.

Some of the most promising strategies in Abidjan and elsewhere are those that link economic opportunity with environmental improvements. In Abidjan, an innovative trash collection scheme in the community of Alladjan not only helped remove garbage along the coastline but also provided steady employment for community members (17). Other programs, such as the Mathare Slum Upgrading Scheme in Nairobi, are community-led projects designed to improve housing conditions and provide dwellers with communal toilets and piped water (18). In Accra, Ghana, the development of urban market gardens has improved nutrition and created employment and supplementary income for the poor, in addition to providing 90 percent of the city's fresh vegetables (19). In Ndola, Zambia, Habitat's training program has helped residents start microenterprises such as brick-making, not only providing income but also producing high-quality building materials at lower prices than normally available (20).

References and Notes

1. Koffi Attahi, "Planning and Management in Large Cities: A Case Study of Abidjan, Cote d'Ivoire," in *Metropolitan Planning and Management in the Developing World: Abidjan and Quito* (United Nations Centre for Human Settlements, Nairobi, Kenya, 1992), pp. 35–36.

2. United Nations (U.N.) Population Division, *World Urbanization Prospects: The 1994 Revision* (U.N., New York, 1995), pp. 132–139.

3. Howard W. French, "Abidjan Journal: No More Paternalism: But Public Executions?" *New York Times* (May 15, 1995), p. A4.

4. John Darnton, "Africa Tries Democracy, Finding Hope and Peril," *New York Times* (June 21, 1994), p. A9.

5. Richard E. Stren and Rodney R. White, eds., *African Cities in Crisis: Managing Rapid Urban Growth* (Westview Press, Boulder, Colorado, and London, 1989), pp. 1–312.

6. The World Bank, *African Development Indicators 1994–95* (The World Bank, Washington, D.C., 1995), p. 33.

7. Atelier d'Architecture d'Urbanisme et de Topographie, *Profil Environmental d'Abidjan, Volume 1*, draft paper (The World Bank, Washington, D.C., August 1993), p. 22.

8. Lionel Demery, "Cote d'Ivoire: Fettered Adjustment," in *Adjustment in Africa: Lessons from Country Case Studies*, Ishrat Husain and Rashid Faruqee, eds. (The World Bank, Washington, D.C., 1994), pp. 116, 122.

9. Caroline O.N. Moser, Alicia J. Herbert, and Roza E. Makonnen, *Urban Poverty in the Context of Structural Adjustment: Recent Evidence and Policy Responses* (The World Bank, Washington, D.C., 1993), p. 123.

10. Philippe Antoine and Aka Kouame, "Cote d'Ivoire," in *Urbanization in Africa: A Handbook*, James D. Tarver, ed. (Greenwood Press, Westport, Connecticut, 1994), p. 143.

11. *Op. cit.* 2, pp. 133, 145.

12. *Op. cit.* 7, p. 10.

13. Josef Leitmann, "Urbanization and Environment in Sub-Saharan Africa: An Input to the Post-UNCED Urban Axis," draft paper (The World Bank, Washington, D.C., 1995), p. 18.

14. *Ibid.*, pp. 19–20.

15. *Op. cit.* 10, p. 154.

16. Erik Eckholm and John Tierney, "AIDS in Africa: A Killer Rages On," *New York Times* (September 16, 1990), p. A14.

17. Cooperative Housing Foundation (CHF), *Partnership for a Livable Environment* (CHF, Washington, D.C., 1992), p. 26.

18. Wachira Kigotho, "Nairobi: Slum Upgrading in Mathare," *The Urban Age*, Vol. 3, No. 2 (The World Bank, Washington, D.C., June 1995), pp. 13–14.

19. A.J. Annorbah-Sarpei, "Urban Market Gardens: Accra," Urban Environment–Poverty Case Study Series (The Mega Cities Project, New York, and the Center for Community Studies, Action & Development, Accra, 1994), p. 20.

20. United Nations Centre for Human Settlements (Habitat), *Community Participation in Zambia: The Danida/UNCHS Training Programme* (Habitat, Nairobi, Kenya, 1992), p. 39.

lation, even at these somewhat reduced rates of growth the urban population will continue to increase dramatically, slowing down significantly only well into the 21st Century (21).

Although rates of growth vary dramatically from region to region and city to city, growth is generally most pronounced in two contexts: in the poorest regions and in those regions that are undergoing rapid economic growth. Each has vastly different implications for the urban environment and quality of life. In the least developed countries, urban growth rates are among the highest in the world, at nearly 5 percent per year (22). Between 1990 and 1995, some of these countries—Burkina Faso, Mozambique, Nepal, and Afghanistan, to cite a few—were experiencing even higher urban growth rates—more than 7 percent per year (23).

Box 1.2 The Challenge of Environmental Deterioration in Jakarta

Worst of both worlds. In Jakarta, glass and chrome skyscrapers have sprouted up among traditional kampung villages. While the city must increasingly grapple with problems of air pollution and industrial wastes, residents in these settlements still face threats from polluted water and inadequate housing.

Jakarta, Indonesia, embodies many of the contradictory forces at play in rapidly industrializing megacities of the world. These "engines of growth," as they are so commonly called, play a vital role in national economic development. Yet at the same time, worsening environmental problems threaten economic prosperity and human health. In Jakarta, city officials have begun to grapple with these problems in earnest.

Like many megacities, Jakarta is the country's center of government, finance, commerce, and education. The city is leading the country's incredible economic growth—Indonesia's gross domestic product (GDP) increased 5.7 percent per year between 1980 and 1992 (1). As much as 7 percent of Indonesia's GDP, 17 percent of domestic industrial production, and 61 percent of its banking and financial activities are concentrated in the metropolis (2). Per capita income in Jakarta is 70 percent higher than the national average (3).

With economic growth, Jakarta has made major strides in improving overall health and quality of life in the city. In 1989, mortality rates for infants were lower for the city than for the country as a whole, 31.7 per 1,000 live births compared with 58 nationally (4). Combined male and female life expectancy was 66.5 years compared with 62 years nationally (5).

Yet economic growth has had its costs, most notably in the form of increased pollution. As with many other megacities, Jakarta faces a serious problem of air pollution. Ambient levels of particulate matter exceed health standards at least 173 days per year. Vehicle emissions constitute the most important source of harmful pollutants (44 per-

cent of particulates, 89 percent of hydrocarbons, 73 percent of nitrogen oxides, and 100 percent of lead). As the demand for motor vehicles rises with economic growth, attendant pollution is likely to worsen (6). The residential sector also contributes about 41 percent of particulate matter, largely from the burning of solid waste by households and by refuse recyclers; industry contributes the greatest share of sulfur oxides (63 percent) (7).

Jakarta's air pollution is associated with high levels of respiratory disease. Respiratory tract infections, for example, account for 12.6 percent of mortality in Jakarta—more than twice the national average (8). Ambient lead levels, which regularly exceed health standards by a factor of 3 or 4 (9), are associated with increased incidence of hypertension, coronary heart disease, and IQ losses in children (10).

Jakarta's water quality is suffering under the combined strain of domestic and industrial pollution. The backbone of the sanitation system is still an open ditch system that serves as a conduit for all wastewater. While this system may have been adequate for a city of less than half a million—the size of the city when the system was planned—it cannot cope with the wastes of the current 11.5 million residents (11). In 1989, an estimated 200,000 cubic meters of wastewater per day, largely untreated, was disposed of into the city's waterways (12) (13). Domestic wastewater is estimated to contribute 80 percent of surface water pollution, although industrial discharges are a growing concern. In some areas, groundwater is polluted with nitrates and microorganisms from domestic waste and toxics leached from industrial landfills.

Water pollution has impacts on both human health and aquatic life. Diarrhea is responsible for 20 percent of deaths for children under age 5 in Jakarta (14). Organic pollution has also contributed

Local governments are often strapped for cash and do not have the resources to provide even the most basic environmental services for their residents. In 1994, some 30 percent of African urban residents were not served by municipal water services in any form (24). (See Box 1.1.)

Growth rates are also extremely high in the rapidly industrializing cities, located mostly in Southeast Asia and Latin America. Cities in these regions offer several advantages over rural villages, having both more numerous job opportunities and superior infrastructure and living conditions. Even so, infrastructure facilities,

to the decline of coral reefs within Jakarta Bay (15) (16). In the Angke estuary in Jakarta Bay, the mercury content in commercial fish species far exceeds World Health Organization guidelines for human consumption (17).

Jakarta's aquifer is also suffering from overextraction and salinization. At least 30 percent of Jakarta's population relies on the aquifer for water. Because the city lacks a system for registering and controlling water extraction, more water is withdrawn than is naturally recharged. Parts of the city have sunk 30 to 70 centimeters in the past 15 years due to land subsidence (18). Urban expansion into the water catchment areas southwest and southeast of Jakarta is further threatening the aquifer.

For Jakarta's 1.4 million poor, however, the greatest environmental threats still occur at the household and neighborhood level. One recent survey found that in the poorest wealth quintile, 31 percent of households have neither a piped water connection nor access to a private well, compared with 12 percent for the city as a whole (19). In addition, the poorest households were less likely to have neighborhood waste collection and more likely to share toilets and have problems with flies both near the toilet and in food-handling areas (20).

Jakarta officials have taken a number of steps to reverse environmental degradation. One of the most successful programs has been the Kampung Improvement Project, which has improved living conditions for more than 3.5 million people. The program has been duplicated in 200 cities throughout Indonesia (21). In partnership with local communities, the government identifies priority actions such as water supply networks, which include a standpipe for each 25 to 35 families. Other improvements include paved footpaths with side drains, sanitary facilities, garbage carts and waste collection stations, and public health centers. Funding comes primarily from the government and donor agencies, although in some cases community members match these investments. The communities themselves are responsible for operation and maintenance of the facilities (22).

To protect natural resources, the government passed a 1992 "spatial planning" law designed to restrict development in environmentally sensitive areas. The government has also been actively trying to set emission standards for cars and to introduce unleaded gasoline. Already 2,000 taxis and buses in Jakarta run on compressed natural gas, and planners hope to expand the program to 50,000 vehicles nationally (23). The *Prokasih* (Clean River Program), a cooperative agreement between local communities and the government of Jakarta, has managed to reduce the pollution of the Ciliwung River within just 3 years, from 1989 to 1992, although much remains to be done (24). For Jakarta, continued investment in environmental management is crucial if it hopes to contain and even reverse environmental deterioration.

References and Notes

1. The World Bank, *World Development Report 1994* (Oxford University Press, New York, 1994), p. 164.

2. Giles Clarke, Suhaid Hadiwinoto, and Josef Leitmann, "Environmental Profile of Jakarta," draft paper (The World Bank, Washington, D.C., 1991), pp. 1, 7.

3. *Ibid.*, p. 7.

4. Other data sources show very different numbers for infant mortality rates. The Demographic Health Survey places the national Indonesia infant mortality rate at 74.2 per 1,000, with 44.9 per 1,000 for Jakarta. The World Bank reports a national infant mortality rate at 64 per 1,000. However, in all cases, data suggest that infant mortality in Jakarta is lower than in rural Indonesia.

5. *Op. cit.* 2, p. 35.

6. The World Bank, *Indonesia Environment and Development: Challenges for the Future* (The World Bank, Washington, D.C., 1994), p. 73.

7. *Ibid.*

8. *Op. cit.* 6, p. 81.

9. Bart Ostro, "Estimating the Health Effects of Air Pollutants: A Method with an Application to Jakarta," Policy Research Working Paper No. 1301 (The World Bank, Washington, D.C., 1994), p. 44.

10. *Ibid.*, p. 47.

11. United Nations (U.N.), *World Urbanization Prospects: The 1994 Revision* (U.N., New York, 1995), p. 135.

12. K.C. Sivaramakrishnan, *Metropolitan Management* (The World Bank, Washington, D.C., 1986), p. 197.

13. *Op. cit.* 6, p. 70.

14. *Op. cit.* 2, p. 35.

15. Tommy Firman and Ida Ayu Indira Dharmapatni, "The Challenges to Sustainable Development in Jakarta Metropolitan Region," *Habitat International*, Vol. 18, No. 3 (1994), p. 88.

16. *Op. cit.* 6, p. 91.

17. *Op. cit.* 6, p. 91.

18. John McBeth, "Water Peril: Indonesia's Urbanization May Precipitate a Water Crisis," *Far Eastern Economic Review* (June 1, 1995), p. 62.

19. Charles Surjadi *et al.*, *Household Environmental Problems in Jakarta* (Stockholm Environment Institute, Stockholm, Sweden, 1994), p. 26.

20. *Ibid.*, p. 59.

21. The Jakarta Regional Development Planning Board, *Jakarta Our City: Improvement in the Standard of Living* (The Jakarta Regional Development Planning Board, Jakarta, Indonesia, 1985), p. 3.

22. John Silas, "Government-Community Partnerships in Kampung Improvement Programmes in Surabaya," *Environment and Urbanization*, Vol. 4, No. 2 (October 1992), pp. 35–36.

23. Sheila Tefft, "In Search of Solutions for a Polluted Jakarta," *Christian Science Monitor* (September 19, 1994), p. 10.

24. *Op. cit.* 15, p. 91.

such as road networks and wastewater treatment plants, lag far behind what is needed. The result is congested city streets, mounting air and water pollution, and other citywide problems. In addition, although many urban dwellers in these wealthier cities live in comfortable dwellings with piped water and weekly garbage pick-ups, vast numbers of poor people still live in illegal settlements with conditions nearly as dismal as those in the poorest cities. Thus, residents of these cities face the "worst of both worlds": the environmental problems associated with economic growth and the yet unsolved problems of sanitation (25). (See Box 1.2.)

Box 1.3 What Is an Urban Area?

By the year 2010, well over 3.7 billion people will be classified as urban dwellers—more people than inhabited the world just four decades earlier [1]. While some of these urban dwellers will be living in such megacities as Sao Paulo, Brazil, and Shanghai, China, the majority will live in a kaleidoscope of settlements: from large industrial cities to small mercantile towns and villages.

While the term "urban area" is typically used as a synonym for "city," the two are not the same. All cities are urban areas, but not all urban areas are cities. "Urban" is a statistical concept defined by a country's government. A city, on the other hand, is more than just large numbers of people living in close proximity to one another; it is a complex political, economic, and social entity. Cities around the world symbolize their nation's identity and political strength. Cities are also centers of economic production, religion, learning, and culture.

Because each country sets its own definition of "urban," there is a bewildering array of definitions around the world. Governments of small or relatively rural countries may simply declare one or more settlements urban, regardless of size or function [2]. In many countries, the definition is based on a threshold number of inhabitants; when the population of a region exceeds a certain threshold, that region is considered urban [3]. This threshold ranges from a few hundred, as in Peru and Uganda, to more than 10,000, as in Italy and Senegal [4]. Other governments base their definition on a combination of criteria, such as population density, political function, or predominant activity of the region.

These definitional differences can skew international comparisons. If the Indian government adopted Peru's definition of urban, India would suddenly become one of Asia's more urbanized nations [5]. This, in turn, would change the regional urbanization levels for South Asia [6].

Even within countries, the definition of urban may vary. In 1990, the World Bank reported that China's urbanization level jumped from 18 to 50 percent between 1965 and 1988 [7]. While some of this urban growth could be attributed to economic growth and migration, it is largely explained by the government adopting a new definition of urban in 1986, which included many agrarian communities. Since 1986, China has again changed the definition to be more accurate—in 1990, China's population was considered 26.21 percent urban [8].

Defining urban is further complicated by the dynamic nature of cities. In both developed and developing countries, urban activity tends to move beyond established urban boundaries. Depending on the boundary used, Tokyo's 1990 population could range from 8.2 million people (in the 23 wards of the central city) to 39.2 million people (in the National Capital Region) [9]. At night, Tokyo's central city population may actually be much lower, as commuters leave the downtown area for their suburban homes.

For all these reasons, comparisons of urbanization levels, urban growth rates, or city size may be highly misleading [10]. In addition, while the United Nations' urban population figures used in this report are the most extensive international data set available, they should nevertheless be viewed only as best estimates.

References and Notes

1. United Nations (U.N.) Population Division, *World Urbanization Prospects: The 1994 Revision* (U.N., New York, 1995), p. 87.

2. Jorge E. Hardoy and David Satterthwaite, "Urban Change in the Third World: Are Recent Trends a Useful Pointer to the Urban Future?" *Habitat International*, Vol. 10, No. 3 (1986), p. 34.

3. *Ibid.*

4. *Op. cit.* 1, pp. 40, 45–46, 48–49.

5. *Op. cit.* 2.

6. *Op. cit.* 2.

7. The World Bank, *World Development Report 1990* (Oxford University Press, New York, 1990), p. 238.

8. United Nations (U.N.) Economic and Social Commission for Asia and the Pacific, *State of Urbanization in Asia and the Pacific, 1993* (U.N., New York, 1993), p. 2-2.

9. Roman Cybriwsky, "Tokyo," *Cities,* Vol. 10, No. 1 (February 1993), p. 3.

10. United Nations Centre for Human Settlements (Habitat), *An Urbanizing World: Global Report on Human Settlements 1996* (Oxford University Press, Oxford, United Kingdom, and New York, 1996), p. 1-18.

The rapid growth rates of many cities in developing countries, combined with their huge population bases, are pushing cities to unprecedented sizes. In contrast to earlier in the century, most of the world's giant urban agglomerations are now and will continue to be in the developing world.

One commonly used metric for measuring urban growth is the "megacity," defined as a city with a population exceeding 8 million. In 1950, just two such megacities existed: New York, with a population of 12.3 million, and London, with 8.7 million [26]. By 1990, there were 21 megacities, 16 of them in the developing world [27]. In 2015, there will be 33 megacities, 27 in the developing world [28].

Any such rankings and comparisons, however, must be approached with caution, because the population of a given city depends on how its boundaries are chosen—for instance, whether the historic city boundary or the boundaries of the extended metropolitan region are used [29]. (See Box 1.3.)

Table 1.1 shows the world's 25 largest cities and their recent growth rates. With a few notable exceptions, such as Dhaka, Bangladesh, and Lagos, Nigeria, the annual growth rates of many of these were relatively modest during the early 1990s, although it is unclear how much of this apparent slowdown is due to the dispersion of the population to areas right outside official boundaries [30].

Table 1.1 The World's Twenty-Five Largest Cities, 1995

	Population (millions)	Average Annual Growth Rate 1990–95 (percent)
Tokyo, Japan	26.8	1.41
Sao Paulo, Brazil	16.4	2.01
New York, United States of America	16.3	0.34
Mexico City, Mexico	15.6	0.73
Bombay, India	15.1	4.22
Shanghai, China	15.1	2.29
Los Angeles, United States of America	12.4	1.60
Beijing, China	12.4	2.57
Calcutta, India	11.7	1.67
Seoul, Republic of Korea	11.6	1.95
Jakarta, Indonesia	11.5	4.35
Buenos Aires, Argentina	11.0	0.68
Tianjin, China	10.7	2.88
Osaka, Japan	10.6	0.23
Lagos, Nigeria	10.3	5.68
Rio de Janeiro, Brazil	9.9	0.77
Delhi, India	9.9	3.80
Karachi, Pakistan	9.9	4.27
Cairo, Egypt	9.7	2.24
Paris, France	9.5	0.29
Metro Manila, Philippines	9.3	3.05
Moscow, Russian Federation	9.2	0.40
Dhaka, Bangladesh	7.8	5.74
Istanbul, Turkey	7.8	3.67
Lima, Peru	7.5	2.81

Source: United Nations (U.N.) Population Division, *World Urbanization Prospects, 1994 Revision* (U.N., New York, 1995), Table A.12, pp. 132–139, and Table A.14, pp. 143–150.

Table 1.2 Population in Cities with More Than 1 Million Residents, by Region, 1950–2015

Region	Total Population in All Cities with More Than 1 Million Residents (population in millions)			
	1950	1970	1990	2015
Africa	3	16	59	225
Latin America	17	57	118	225
Asia	58	168	359	903
Europe	73	116	141	156
North America	40	78	105	148

Source: United Nations (U.N.) Population Division, *World Population Prospects: 1994 Revision* (U.N., New York, 1995), pp. 12, 14–17.

settlements can swell to huge proportions—becoming cities unto themselves. These "unintended" cities, as they have been called, may be technically within the boundaries of a metropolitan area but are beyond the service domain or taxation reach of the local government (34).

Along with population growth have come changes in the physical dimensions of cities as they sprawl into wider regions. Sometimes called "extended metropolitan regions" or "functional urban regions," these include smaller urban centers and even rural areas outside of the urban core whose populations and activities are clearly part of the functioning of the city (35).

This phenomenon of urban sprawl has been especially manifest in the United States. The traditional downtown has been replaced by urban regions such as Silicon Valley in California, where enterprises are concentrated along major roads and highways, transforming the urban landscape into a string of "100-mile cities." In the developing world, many cities remain compact because infrastructure and labor are still concentrated in city centers and transportation and communications systems are less developed (36). Yet cities such as Sao Paulo, Mexico City, Jakarta, and Bombay are all experiencing increasing decentralization. While some expansion results from the suburbanization of high-income groups, a large share can be attributed to attempts by low-income groups to escape the high land prices in the city's core. The speed of this decentralization and its spatial configuration vary greatly from city to city (37).

Sprawl is not concomitant with rapid population growth, however, although it may seem that way in North America. Whereas Bangkok, Thailand, Manila, Philippines, and Jakarta have spread like cities in North America, Shanghai, China, and Seoul, Republic of Korea, remain much more compact. The densities in parts of Shanghai and Calcutta, India, range between 800 and

Many intermediate-size cities may actually be growing faster on average than the largest cities, at rates well over 5 percent per year. As a result, there is a proliferation of what have been called "million cities" (with populations of between 1 million and 10 million) (31). (See Table 1.2.) By 2015, there will be 516 of these cities, compared with only 270 in 1990. Small cities, home to more than half of the world's urban dwellers in 1990, are also experiencing extremely rapid population growth (32). These cities are often especially affected by inadequate investment in environmental infrastructure or services, because many countries direct their resources to the larger urban centers.

Some of the most rapid urban growth is occurring in distinct parts of cities—either within the official urban area or on the periphery. The urban fringe of Jakarta, Indonesia, for instance, is growing much faster than the city itself—in some areas at nearly 18 percent per year (33). Spontaneous, or squatter, settlements in particular tend to grow much faster than the rest of the city. These

Table 1.3 Urban Versus Rural Demographics and Health in Kenya, 1993

	Urban Residents (percent)	Rural Residents (percent)
Household population with no education		
Female (6 years and above)	13.5	29.1
Male (6 years and above)	7.0	18.2
Household possessions and amenities		
Radio	67.7	48.1
Television	22.0	2.4
Electricity	42.5	3.4
Drinking water piped to residence	55.8	10.7
Flush toilet	44.9	1.6
Health of children		
Mortality rate of children under age 5[a]	75.4	95.6
Infant mortality rate[a]	45.5	64.9
Percent of children between 12 and 23 months with all vaccinations	80.9	78.3
Underweight[b]	12.8	23.5
Maternal health		
Women receiving tetanus toxoid during pregnancy	92.9	88.8
Women receiving prenatal care from a health provider[c]	97.6	94.5
Women receiving delivery care from a health provider[c]	77.6	39.2
Total fertility rate	3.4	5.8

Source: Institute for Resource Development, Demographic and Health Survey Data Archive, Columbia, Maryland.

Notes:

a. Deaths per 1,000 live births. Mortality rates by characteristics such as place of residence are based on the last 10 years prior to the survey in order to ensure sufficient sample size. Mortality rates are based on a minimum of 500 live births.

b. Underweight is defined as the percentage of children whose height-for-age, weight-for-age, weight-for-height z-score is below −2 standard deviations from the median of the International Reference Population (WHO/CDC/NCHS).

c. Doctor, nurse, or trained midwife.

1,000 people per hectare, and in Bangkok and Seoul between 300 and 400, as compared with 70 or even fewer in most North American cities (38). As is discussed in Chapter 3, "Urban Impacts on Natural Resources," urban form has important environmental implications.

WHAT FUELS URBAN GROWTH?

Cities are growing because they provide, on average, greater social and economic benefits than do rural areas. (See Table 1.3.) The higher capital investment caused by urbanization brings health and social benefits that could be achieved in rural areas only at far greater costs. The data are sparse and not always reliable, but access to drinking water, sanitation, health services, and educational opportunities is often dramatically higher in urban areas overall than in rural areas. As a result, life expectancy is usually significantly higher and infant mortality significantly lower in urban areas overall than in rural areas (39) (40). These benefits, however, often do not extend to the poorest groups within a city, as is described below.

Urbanization and Economic Growth

The steady increase in the level of urbanization worldwide since the 1950s also reflects, to a large degree, the enormous changes in the nature and scale of economic activity worldwide. Urban growth is inextricably linked with economic growth, although it is not entirely clear which fuels which. Aggregate and per capita incomes tend to be higher in more urbanized regions of the world (41).

Cities provide a natural locus for economic growth. Commerce and industry concentrate in cities because of the economies of scale they offer. "Cities are extraordinarily efficient," notes one commentator. They "optimize the use of human and mechanical energy, they allow for fast, cheap transportation, they provide flexible, highly productive labor markets. They facilitate a diffusion of products, ideas, and human resources between urban, suburban, exurban, and rural spaces" (42). In a self-perpetuating cycle, commerce and industry in turn attract the ancillary services needed to support them. Such interdependencies give urban areas a clear competitive advantage for industry and commerce; few industries can survive elsewhere (43).

The efficiency inherent in urban areas translates into major gains in productivity. In developing countries, urban areas produce as much as 60 percent of total gross national product with just one third of the population (44). These economies of agglomeration, as they are often called, are especially important when a city's economic base rests on manufacturing. Yet cities have held their allure, even flourished, when the economic base shifts from manufacturing to services such as finance and banking, as it has in much of the developed world. Despite predictions that cities would be rendered obsolete by advances in global telecommunications, for instance, the opposite has happened.

Indeed, many scholars argue that such economic changes are giving rise to a new class of "world cities" that are the nerve centers of an increasingly global economy (45). And it is not just New York, Paris, Tokyo, Los Angeles, or other powerhouses of the developed world that dominate this global scene. Cities as diverse as Berlin, Sao Paulo, Beijing, Bangkok, Mexico City, and Budapest, Hungary, are emerging as world powers in their own right. Transformed into "transnational spaces for economic activity" (46), these world cities have more in common with each other than with cities within their regions or nations.

While these trends can bring enormous prosperity to certain locales, they also increase social and economic inequities. Globalism's sweep is far from uniform. As Barcelona, Spain, and Singapore flourish, other cities, especially old industrial or port cities such as Detroit and Liverpool, United Kingdom, are left further and further behind. Disparities also increase among cities in the same country. Sao Paulo, for instance, has emerged as a major business and financial center at the expense of Rio de Janeiro, once the most important city in Brazil (47). Within cities as well, globalism exacerbates inequalities, as the disparities widen among the incomes of high- and low-wage workers.

The environmental implications of these economic changes are significant. As cities compete with one another to attract manufacturing and other services, the bargaining chips are sometimes cheap labor and lax environmental concerns. Thus, globalization may well lead to greater environmental deterioration and aggravate existing inequities of income and access to basic services (48).

Migration and Natural Population Increase

In addition to economic activity, major demographic forces underlie urban growth. In the earlier waves of industrialization, rapid urban growth was largely fueled by rural-to-urban migration. In the developing world today, however, the natural increase of the urban population is at least as important as migration (49). The high rate of natural increase in these cities, however, does tend to follow migration, because most migrants are of reproductive age. Another contributor to urban growth is the reclassification of city boundaries, which can result in dramatic changes in urban size (50).

The importance of migration varies considerably by region, and migration flows in all directions, not just rural to urban. In some countries, rural-to-rural flows may be of a larger scale than rural to urban (51). What is often overlooked is the role of migration in the growth of cities in the developed world, where fertility rates are relatively low. In the United States, much of urban change now under way stems from the movement of people from one city to another (52).

Figures on rural-to-urban migration are notoriously difficult to pin down, but it is believed to account for between 40 and 60 percent of annual urban population growth in the developing world (53). Migration is expected to be a major factor in the coming years in regions with large rural populations, especially those where rural poverty is rampant, as in Africa and parts of Asia.

Despite the dual role of natural increase and migration, many countries still tend to view urban growth as a "problem" of migration alone. Concerned about burgeoning populations, a number of governments in both the developed and the developing world have adopted policies to restrict the flow of migrants to cities. Few policies, however, have met with success.

Throughout the developing world, the factors driving rural-to-urban migration are complex. Migrants are not only pulled toward cities by the prospect of jobs and higher incomes, they are also pushed out of rural areas by such factors as poverty, lack of land, declining agricultural work, war, and famine. The *favelas* (squatter settlements) of Rio cannot be understood without reference to the *latifundia* land system in rural Brazil, which is characterized by large landholdings concentrated in the hands of a few. In many instances, the decision to move to an urban area is part of a complex household survival strategy, in which families minimize risk by placing members in different labor markets (54). Nor is migration always permanent; many migrants circulate between urban areas and their rural home (55). Considerable diversity also exists among migrants themselves, for instance, in their age and education (56).

Various studies suggest that the vast majority of migrants feel that relocation to the city has improved their situation, even if not as much as they might have hoped (57). In New Delhi, India, a survey of poor migrants from rural areas found that their incomes were 2.5 times greater than they had been in the village, primarily because they could find about twice as many days of work in the city (58).

Other migrants, however, are unable to find work or are forced to take ill-paying or hazardous jobs. Unable to generate enough income to meet their basic needs for food and shelter, they join the ranks of the urban poor.

Employment Opportunities

Unemployment is a significant problem in most cities in developing countries, because the formal economies of Africa, Asia, and Latin America are unable to absorb the enormous influx of workers. Given the urbanization rates these cities are now experiencing, the demand for new jobs will be intense: Starting in 1990, it is estimated that an additional 35 million jobs per year will be required to provide employment to all new labor force participants (59).

As a result, a substantial number of the developing world's urban poor make their living through subsistence activities or informal jobs—namely, production and exchange outside of the formal market. These jobs run the gamut from providing services such as garbage collection and domestic help, to providing goods such as food and building materials in small stores, to small-scale clothing manufacturing. Informal jobs make up an estimated 75 percent of urban employment in many countries in sub-Saharan Africa and between 30 and 50 percent in Latin America (60) (61).

Debate on the role of the so-called informal sector in national economies is rampant (62) (63). Until recently, informal jobs have been viewed as disconnected from the "real" economy of a city, yet evidence suggests that informal jobs are well integrated and contribute directly to the urban economy as a whole (64). In addition, seemingly informal jobs often have direct ties to a city's formal enterprises. For instance, scavengers in Hanoi, Viet Nam, obtain and clean chicken bones that end up in pharmacies in Italy as high-priced calcium supplements (65).

With some exceptions, however, informal jobs tend to pay less well than formal ones and offer little security or benefits. In Latin America, incomes from informal jobs were on average at least 40 percent below those earned in formal employment; in the 13 countries studied, the average income received by those employed in informal jobs was well below official poverty lines (66).

URBAN POVERTY

Historically, poverty has been concentrated in rural areas. Yet as the bulk of the world's population shifts from rural to urban areas, poverty is becoming an increasingly urban phenomenon. The World Bank estimates that in 1988 approximately one quarter of the developing world's absolute poor were living in urban areas (67). By the year 2000, half of the developing world's absolute poor will be in urban areas (68). Several factors, including structural adjustment programs, economic crises, and massive rural-to-urban migration, have contributed to an increasing number of urban poor since the 1980s (69).

Urban poverty is especially pronounced in Latin America. In this region, the absolute number of urban poor already surpasses the number of rural poor (70). Between 1970 and 1990, the number of urban poor increased from 44 million to 115 million, while the number of rural poor increased from 75 million to 80

million (71). In Asia, large decreases in the proportion of the population living in poverty were reported for the rapidly growing economies, such as Malaysia, the Republic of Korea, and Indonesia (72). However, South Asia is expected to continue to house a large share of the world's urban poor (73).

Reliable data are lacking on the scale and intensity of urban poverty in Africa, although the proportion of the population living below the poverty line is likely to have grown because of the region's poor macro-economic performance (74). The incidence of rural poverty is still significantly higher than that of urban poverty, but that difference appears to be narrowing (75).

Poverty has also risen steeply in the countries of Central and Eastern Europe as they struggle with the transition toward a market economy (76). Cities that relied heavily on industrial production are experiencing record numbers of unemployed as factories shut down and production is curtailed (77).

In North America and industrial Europe, most of the population, and thus most of the poverty, has been concentrated in urban areas since the beginning of the century (78). The characteristics of urban poverty, however, are changing. As the manufacturing base of many cities has declined and the middle class has fled to the suburbs, urban poverty has become concentrated in the inner cities and among ethnic minorities, especially in North America. (See Box 1.4.)

In developed regions as well, unemployment is a primary factor contributing to urban poverty. However, in contrast with cities in the developing world, the growth in urban unemployment in cities in developed regions is the result of a combination of slow macro-economic growth, technological change, export of manufacturing jobs, and increases in the female labor force (79). As manufacturing jobs are transported to other regions, few opportunities are left for inner-city poor, who tend to be geographically isolated in the urban core and are often unable to reach jobs in the suburbs. Especially in inner cities, the mismatch between the education levels of the residents and the levels needed for the locally available jobs greatly contributes to poverty. (See Box 1.5.) In New York City, 33,209 new jobs were created between 1980 and 1990—nearly a 10 percent increase—but 162,739 manufacturing jobs were lost during that same period (80).

Available poverty figures are likely to underestimate the extent of urban poverty, because global data are scarce. The issue is complicated by the fact that definitions of poverty differ from country to country. In addition, absolute poverty figures describe households whose incomes fall below a set level, usually determined

Box 1.4 Sharing Responsibility for Inner-City Problems

Protecting the environment has usually meant halting the encroachment of development in pristine areas. And environmental protection has most often been defined as something outside of, and mostly unrelated to, the concerns and interests of our cities (1).

Those of us who have been grappling with the problems of U.S. cities have been concerned with jobs, housing, and transportation. We have been concerned with public services—schools, fire protection, law enforcement. With the exception perhaps of air pollution, environmental concerns have been too often perceived as a luxury reserved for the suburbs.

At the same time, the poor, especially poor minority U.S. residents, have become increasingly concentrated in inner cities. Once the anchors of the United States' industrial manufacturing base, inner cities are now paying the price of years of environmental abuse. Businesses have moved to the suburbs or overseas and plants have been shut down, leaving behind "brown-fields"—empty buildings on contaminated lots that no one wants to develop. This legacy of industrial pollution contributes to the poverty in these communities by impeding revitalization; it leads to communities that literally cannot sustain themselves.

Clearly, environmental concerns are critical to the future of our urban communities. Today in the United States, as in other countries, many of us are wrestling with the concept of "sustainable communities," trying to develop new ways to integrate environmental concerns with issues of economic and social equity.

The U.S. experience has shown all too clearly that while social and economic divisions are inevitable, they are potentially devastating when they become spatially fixed in urban settings. When poor people become concentrated in precisely defined geographic areas, their problems are sure to grow almost exponentially. We have experienced this first-hand in our most populous cities, where the concentration of mostly minority poor in inner cities has been accompanied by soaring unemployment, increased and prolonged welfare dependency, rising crime, and public health problems too numerous to mention.

There has been an unfortunate tendency in this country to blame these problems on the urban poor. But it is the sheer number of poor people and the density of poverty that have eviscerated these communities and turned them into places where there are few viable businesses and no job base—where there is virtually no chance to lift yourself and your children to a better life.

Spatial separation by income and ethnic group can spur environmental degradation. When better-off people abandon communities, they also abandon their stake in the physical well-being of those places. Thus, places where the poor and politically dispossessed live inevitably become places where environmental problems are too easily ignored—where sewage systems break down, where water purification is inadequate, where vermin infest garbage-filled lots and invade dwellings, where children eat lead paint from walls in deteriorating apartment buildings.

We are beginning to understand in the United States that withdrawal from the cities is no answer. Middle- and upper-income families may flee to the suburbs, but the problems of the inner city are sure to follow them.

The problems of the inner city may follow in the form of increased public outlays for welfare assistance, indigent health care, and public safety, draining scarce resources from other needs—schools, parks, libraries. And they may follow in the form of expanding concentric waves of crime, drugs, and violence that spill over into neighboring areas, eroding their stability and threatening other, more removed areas in turn.

Evidence has shown that there is a direct correlation between the economic health of greater metropolitan areas and the economic health of central cities. When central cities flourish, surrounding communities flourish as well. Where central city economies stagnate and decline, the economies of surrounding greater metropolitan areas suffer. Yet most cities remain politically divided from their surrounding communities.

Part of the solution to the problems our cities face is to think of governance in terms of broader regional or metropolitan-wide units. Here in the United States, that requires greater acceptance of mutual responsibility by local governments and increased cooperation across traditional jurisdictional lines. For example, in the seven-county Minneapolis–St. Paul region in Minnesota, 188 municipalities have been pooling property tax revenues since 1971. They have been redistributing those revenues to achieve greater parity in resources among jurisdictions. The city of Minneapolis, which was once a net revenue recipient, is now the region's largest net revenue generator.

No amount of enlightened regional governance, however, can succeed unless we reduce concentrations of poverty. We must dismantle the barriers that separate poor minority people from the rest of society. Those people who live in these isolated urban pockets must be enabled to move into the wider community where they can find jobs and gain access to better services. At the same time, these distressed communities must be restored as places where people of all ethnic groups and income levels can choose to live—because there is decent housing, because the streets are safe, because the schools are good, because there are jobs, parks, libraries, and other amenities that make urban living attractive. In a diverse community where everyone has a stake, environmental concerns are addressed and the quality of life improves.

—*Henry Cisneros*

Henry Cisneros is Secretary of the U.S. Department of Housing and Urban Development, Washington, D.C.

References and Notes

1. Box is excerpted from a speech presented at the Second Annual World Bank Conference on Environmentally Sustainable Development, September 19, 1994, Washington, D.C.

by how much money would hypothetically be required to buy a basket of basic goods and services. Poverty lines, however, are often set unrealistically low. In some countries, the poverty line is set at the same level for both urban and rural areas, not taking into account the higher costs of living in cities.

Nor can poverty be adequately described as just a lack of economic resources or access to basic needs. Poverty also involves *relative* deprivation or inequality in access to income and material goods and services—and in most countries, income inequalities are wider in the city than in the countryside. Another shortcoming of income-based measures of poverty is that they do not describe the numbers of people who hover just above the poverty line and who can easily be thrown into poverty by any number of setbacks, such as the loss of a job or sudden illness [81].

Certain groups within cities—in particular, women, children, the elderly, migrants, and minorities—are more likely to face pressures that either contribute to or exacerbate conditions of poverty [82] [83]. Women face a number of social barriers that limit their access to income-earning opportunities. In many countries in the developing world, for instance, girls and women still do not receive the same amount of schooling as do men [84]. Within poor households, girls and women often receive less food than males and income-earning adults [85]. In countries where women do not have the right to own property or gain access to credit, sudden loss of a partner or job can leave the household without any means to stay afloat.

Children are also especially vulnerable to poverty. According to World Bank estimates, in the year 2000, half of the children born in urban areas in developing countries will be in poor families [86]. Child poverty is strongly self-perpetuating. Poor children are more likely to be underweight and malnourished and to suffer ill health and earlier death than their wealthier counterparts [87]. Many poor households rely on child labor for survival, yet this work is often at the expense of schooling and the health of the child, making it difficult for the next generation to escape from poverty. An increasing number of children are also facing new dangers associated with homelessness and street life—an estimated 100 million children struggle for survival daily on city streets [88] [89].

Households headed by women tend to be disproportionately poor, and their proportion appears to be growing, especially in large urban areas [90] [91]. In poor households in the developing world, women often take on the triple role of income earning, child rearing, and household management [92]. When women must spend a significant proportion of their time collecting water or fuel, they have less time available for income-earning activities. However, the increase in female-headed households has positive aspects as well. Poor households may be better off when headed by women than men [93]. Numerous studies have shown that women and children in female-headed households tend to have better diets than those in male-headed households of similar incomes, and children are less likely to be withdrawn from school at an early age [94].

Environmental Implications of Urban Poverty

The urbanization of poverty has implications for the urban environment and quality of life. For one, the urban poor bear the greatest burden of urban environmental risks because of the situations in which they are forced to live—whether in the sprawling squatter settle-

Mark Edwards/Still Pictures

Relative deprivation. In most countries, income inequalities are more apparent in the city than in the countryside. In Nairobi (above) and other cities, the poor often live alongside the wealthy.

ments of developing world cities or in the blighted urban centers of Europe and North America.

Throughout the cities of the developing world, anywhere from 30 to 60 percent of a city's population lives in substandard housing (95). Unable to afford even the lowest-cost housing, many of the poor build their own makeshift shelters out of cardboard, plywood, or scraps of metal. Overcrowding increases the risks of airborne infections and accidents. Many poor neighborhoods are often unserved by water and sanitation facilities and garbage collection. In some cases, local governments are unable to pay for extending services to these regions; in others, they are reluctant to do so because such action might be seen as conferring legal status on what they consider illegal settlements (96). Whatever the reason, the lack of services increases the risk of intestinal infections and other communicable diseases (97). In Manila, mortality rates for infants are three times higher in the slums than in the rest of the city, rates of tuberculosis are nine times higher, and three times as many children suffer from malnutrition (98).

The urban poor are also forced to make trade-offs between affordable housing and environmental safety and protection (99). Squatter settlements are often located on land no one wants—whether on flood plains or on steep hillsides, where they are vulnerable to flooding and mudslides.

Proximity to industrial facilities, often the result of the desire of the poor to live near places of employment, poses another set of risks. The 1984 accident at the Union Carbide factory in Bhopal, India, caused 2,988 deaths and at least 100,000 injuries, affecting mostly residents of the shantytowns near the chemical factory (100).

The poor also contribute to local environmental degradation, mainly because the city fails to provide them with the necessary services. If solid waste is not collected, for instance, people must dispose of their own garbage and often do so in inappropriate dumping areas (101). Denied access to suitable land for housing, families may settle in protected areas of the city, on fragile ecosystems such as wetlands (102). Disposal of human wastes from the over-water settlements in cities such as Salvador, Brazil, and Manila can be a major source of water contamination (103). When low-income groups engage in environmentally degrading activities, however, it is usually because they have no alternative (104) (105).

The poor are understandably reluctant to invest heavily in improving the household or neighborhood environment since they could be evicted at any given time (106). As is described in Chapter 5, "Urban Priorities for Action," and Chapter 6, "City and Community: Toward Environmental Sustainability," however, once

given housing security, these same individuals often become substantial agents for environmental improvement.

Similar trends are evident for the poor who reside in many of the thriving cities of developed regions. Although the environmental health threats they face pale in comparison with those experienced by their counterparts in developing regions, their burden is excessive nonetheless when compared with circumstances of the wealthier residents of the same city.

Many of the urban poor lack access to safe and affordable housing. Extended families crowd into one-bedroom apartments, often with rodent infestations, gas leaks, and broken heaters. In the United States, elevated blood lead levels, often from dilapidated apartment buildings with peeling lead-based paint and poor ventilation, threaten the well-being of more than 1.7 million children. The most vulnerable are low-income minority children in central cities (107). Cold, damp homes impair the health of poor urban dwellers. In Britain, hypothermia results in approximately 30,000 to 60,000 excess winter deaths each year, especially among the poor and elderly who live in poor-quality housing (108). As is discussed in Chapter 2, "Urban Environment and Human Health," some of the major threats to the health and well-being of the urban poor are emerging from the social environment of cities.

In the United States, studies emerging from the new field of "environmental justice" suggest that hazardous waste sites, incinerators, and polluting industries are disproportionately located near poor and minority communities, whether urban or rural, although these studies are controversial (109). Methodological differences aside, there is little doubt that poor people and minorities are far more likely than their wealthier counterparts to live in blighted neighborhoods near industrial sites, exposed to a variety of pollutants.

URBAN ENVIRONMENTAL PROBLEMS

As centers of population and human activities, cities consume natural resources from both near and distant sources. They also generate waste that is disposed of both inside and outside the city. In the process, urban areas generate environmental problems over a range of spatial scales: the household and workplace, the neighborhood, the city, the wider region, and the globe (110).

Urban environmental problems also create a range of social impacts. They may impair human health, cause economic and other welfare losses, or damage the ecosystems on which both urban and rural areas depend. Most urban environmental problems entail all three of

Box 1.5 Detroit Battles Long-Term Effects of Suburban Flight

In 1915, Henry Ford's Model T automobile rolled off the first moving assembly line and catapulted Detroit, Michigan, into international renown as the birthplace of modern industrial production. The assembly line revolutionized manufacturing. When Ford announced that workers would make $5.00 for an 8-hour shift—in contrast to the standard wage of $2.75 for a 10-hour shift in the countryside—crowds of eager workers lined up outside factory doors (1). Detroit's population quadrupled in only 20 years, from 285,704 in 1900 to well over 1 million by 1921 (2) (3). By 1950, Detroit's population was almost 2 million. Inspired by post–World War II boom times, city planners were building roads and houses for a city of 8 million (4).

Forty-five years later, however, Detroit's population is again hovering around the 1 million mark. Ironically, the automobile is now at the heart of a new urban transition: one of suburban flight. In 1911, one writer aptly observed that the city had "the possibility of almost unlimited expansion, with easy access to places of labor. It is significant that practically all the automobile factories, which have been built within the last five years, are located on the outskirts, where before there were great tracts of vacant land" (5).

This suburban flight has brought along with it a new set of urban problems, far different from those Detroit faced at the dawn of the Automobile Age. In 1920, with waves of migrants seeking jobs in the new automobile industry, the city lacked adequate shelter for more than 30,000 families.

Current statistics are a stark contrast. In the past two decades, Detroit has lost 32 percent of its population. The suburban exodus of jobs and workers has trapped Detroit in a downward economic spiral, leaving the local government without sufficient funds to manage the city. In addition, the percentage of poor has more than doubled, from 14.9 percent in 1970 to 32.4 percent in 1990 (6). Infant mortality rates, though far below their 1920 level, are three times higher in Detroit (21 per 1,000 live births) than in the neighboring suburb of Warren (7 per 1,000) (7). The murder rate has risen steadily, from 32.7 per 100,000 population in 1970, to 45.7 in 1980, to 59.3 in 1991 (8) (9) (10).

Detroit also faces its share of urban environmental problems. Neighborhoods are lined by abandoned buildings and garbage. One of the most pressing problems is the emergence of "brownfield" sites—land and buildings contaminated by previous industrial activity that now stand empty. While the presence of brownfields does not translate into human exposure to toxics or land contamination per se, it does detract from the economic value of the land. Companies are hesitant to invest in the land because of expensive cleanup regulations.

Further exacerbating the chasm between inner city and suburb is the lack of an adequate public transportation system. Before World War II, most factories were located along railroad lines, and workers' homes were clustered near train stations. As motor vehicles became less expensive, however, industries began to use trucks instead of trains to move materials. Freeway con-

struction allowed plants to be located at greater distances from materials (11). Today, the lack of public transportation facilities limits job opportunities for inner city residents. Four in ten Detroit residents between the ages of 18 and 65 do not have a car and are unable to reach the jobs located primarily in the suburbs (12).

Many other cities in both the United States and the United Kingdom face similar problems of suburban flight and industrial downsizing. While in 1950, 60 percent of the U.S. urban population lived in central cities and 40 percent in the suburbs, by 1990, the proportions were reversed—60 percent lived in the suburbs and 40 percent in central cities (13). Yet many of these cities have managed to temper the negative impacts of these trends through new partnerships with the private sector, with neighboring suburbs, or through community leadership. Newark, New Jersey, for example, has actively recruited recycling industries to the city, promoting economic development and jobs at available sites zoned only for industrial use (14). The city of Leicester, England, is using a grant from the national government to clean up vacant land in the city center and is broadening the city's economy with the addition of a new research science park (15). Jacksonville, Florida, has consolidated its city and county governments enabling the city to share resources within the region (16).

Detroit, however, has failed to attract new businesses, such as banking or other service industries. Attempts at establishing metropolitan-wide planning have failed, and political decisionmaking often breaks down into debates be-

these impacts, either directly or indirectly. For example, urban air pollution has a direct impact on human health, increasing the incidence of respiratory disease. Its impact on the economy is mainly indirect, arising largely from productivity losses due to ill health (111).

Determinants of Urban Environmental Problems

Environmental problems vary from city to city and region to region and are influenced by such variables as

a city's size and rate of growth, income, local geography, climate, and institutional capabilities. Especially where local governments are weak or underfinanced, rapid economic or population growth can exacerbate these problems. Environmental management tends to be more difficult in very large cities. For one, the financial resources needed to provide services to tens of millions of people are daunting. Compounding the difficulty is the fact that the largest cities often are made up of many local jurisdictions with overlapping responsibilities (112) (113).

tween the white suburbs and the black inner city. Whereas in 1950, politics were dominated by a strong Democratic party and active labor unions, the active engagement of civil society in government is sorely lacking [17].

The election of a new mayor in 1994 has brought some hope to the city. Spurred by the belief that the city government cannot tackle Detroit's ills on its own, the mayor's office is working to facilitate partnerships with community members and private businesses. In addition, Detroit recently won a $100 million urban redevelopment grant from the national government to encourage new businesses to move to the central city [18].

The zone marked for renewal encompasses the far east side of Detroit, through the Woodward corridor and into southwest Detroit [19]. Median family income in the zone is under $10,000 a year, and 47 percent of residents live below the poverty line [20]. The redevelopment proposal covers a range of activities from job training to building renovation to classes on parenthood [21]. By the year 2005, Mayor Dennis Archer hopes to create 5,800 new jobs in the area [22]. Cooperative ventures between banks, schools, and auto companies are expected to pump an additional $1.9 billion into the community over the next 10 years and generate at least 3,275 more jobs [23].

References and Notes

1. Arthur M. Woodford, *Detroit: American Urban Renaissance* (Continental Heritage, Inc., Tulsa, Oklahoma, 1979), p. 91.

2. United States (U.S.) Bureau of the Census, *Statistical Abstract of the United States, 1915,* 38th edition (U.S. Government Printing Office, Washington, D.C., 1916), p. 40.

3. *Op. cit.* 1, p. 106.

4. Ed Hustoles, "City Life, Scenes, Feelings," in *Detroit Lives,* Robert H. Mast, ed. (Temple University Press, Philadelphia, 1994), pp. 156–157.

5. Myron E. Adams, "Detroit—A City Awake," *Survey* (August 5, 1911), as reprinted in *Detroit Perspectives: Crossroads and Turning Points,* Wilma Wood, ed. (Wayne State University Press, Detroit, Michigan, 1991), p. 289.

6. United States (U.S.) Bureau of the Census, *Poverty in the United States 1992* (U.S. Government Printing Office, Washington, D.C., 1992), p. 46.

7. Office of the State Registrar and Division of Health Statistics, "Table 7: Infant Deaths, Live Births and Infant Death Rates: Selected Michigan Cities, 1992 and 1993," unpublished data (Michigan Department of Public Health, Grand Rapids, Michigan, 1993).

8. United States (U.S.) Bureau of the Census, *Statistical Abstract of the United States, 1972,* 93rd edition (U.S. Government Printing Office, Washington, D.C., 1972), p. 145.

9. United States (U.S.) Bureau of the Census, *Statistical Abstract of the United States, 1981,* 102nd edition (U.S. Government Printing Office, Washington, D.C., 1981), p. 175.

10. United States (U.S.) Bureau of the Census, *Statistical Abstract of the United States, 1993,* 113th edition (U.S. Government Printing Office, Washington, D.C., 1993), p. 195.

11. Episcopal Diocese of Michigan, "The Emerging Pattern: A Regional Perspective," as reprinted in *Detroit Perspectives: Crossroads and Turning Points,* Wilma Wood, ed. (Wayne State University Press, Detroit, Michigan, 1991), pp. 544–545.

12. United States (U.S.) Bureau of the Census, *County and City Data Book: 1994* (U.S. Government Printing Office, Washington, D.C., 1994), pp. 758, 764.

13. David Rusk, "Thinking Regionally, Stretching Central Cities," in *The State of the American Community: Empowerment for Local Action,* Robert H. McNulty, ed. (Partners for Livable Communities, Washington, D.C., 1994), pp. 42–43.

14. Newark Public Information Office (NPIO), "City of Newark to Attract Recycling Businesses to 'Planet Newark,'" press release (NPIO, Newark, New Jersey, June 13, 1994), pp. 1–3.

15. Department of the Environment, *City Challenge: Partnerships Regenerating England's Urban Areas* (United Kingdom Department of the Environment, London, 1994), p. 12.

16. *Op. cit.* 13, pp. 48–49.

17. Hank V. Savitch and Paul Kantor, "Urban Mobilization of Private Capital: A Cross-National Comparison," Occasional Paper Series No. 3 (Woodrow Wilson International Center for Scholars, Washington, D.C., 1994), p. 20.

18. John Lippert and Roger Chesley, "Just a Modest $2.2-Billion Proposal," *Detroit News and Free Press* (November 13, 1994), p. 1F.

19. *Ibid.*

20. *Op. cit.* 18, p. 4F.

21. Sam Walker, "Detroit Battles Decay, Joblessness in Ultimate U.S. Test of Renewal," *Christian Science Monitor* (February 9, 1995), p. 18.

22. *Op. cit.* 18.

23. *Op. cit.* 21.

Income

One of the most important determinants of a city's environmental problems is its income level. As the wealth of a city grows, many types of environmental degradation first increase and then eventually diminish. Other environmental problems increase with wealth. (See Figure 1.3.)

The income level at which a city undergoes these changes differs widely. Vastly different environmental conditions can be found in cities of comparable wealth. Policies, as well as demography and geography, can make an enormous difference.

In poor cities, and particularly their poor neighborhoods, the most threatening environmental problems are usually those close to home [114]. The dangers of exposure to environmental risks are high, especially for women and children. Inadequate household water supplies are typically more crucial to people's well-being than polluted waterways. There is often more exposure to air pollution in smoky kitchens than outdoors. Waste accumulating, uncollected, in the neighborhood poses more serious problems than the waste at the city dumps. Human excreta is frequently the most critical pollutant, and unsanitary conditions in the home and neighborhood are generally more of a threat to health than industrial pollution.

These problems, so prevalent in cities in the developing world, stem from myriad causes, including the inability or unwillingness of local governments to provide for basic needs of citizens—which in turn stems from a lack of revenue-generating capacity. Another key factor is the poor's lack of access to suitable land for housing.

As income increases, urban households and cities as a whole consume far more resources, such as energy, water, and building materials—and generate far more of certain types of wastes. Yet the rich devote part of their wealth to measures that protect them from environmental hazards. The problems close to home are the first to improve as wealth increases, generally because they are the most threatening and require cooperation on only a relatively small scale. However, while these improvements reduce personal exposure, they often simply shift the problem elsewhere. Waterborne sewage systems, for example, reduce personal exposure to fecal material. However, if sewage is discharged without treatment, it can lower the quality of a city's waterways and strain water supplies. Electricity is a clean fuel where it is used, but electric power plants can be an important source of ambient air pollution.

Thus, even as household and neighborhood environmental problems recede from prominence for a growing number of a city's population, citywide and regional problems, such as ambient air pollution, water pollution, and hazardous waste generation, may increase. These problems tend to be severe in rapidly industrializing cities of the developing world and in the transition economies of Central and Eastern Europe, where industrial activity often occurs without adequate concern for its environmental implications. (See Box 1.6.) Lack of investment in urban infrastructure, such as increased road networks and sewage treatment plants, and weak environmental protection laws with lax enforcement, exacerbate these problems.

In high-income cities, such as those in Europe and North America, many of the worst city-level problems have been addressed. For instance, many cities in the developed world have improved the quality of their ambient air and water over the past decades. A wealthy city can more easily afford the public finance and administration needed to regulate the more perceptible forms of pollution.

But while the ambient environment of high-income cities may actually be more benign in terms of the health impacts of pollution, these cities exert a far greater toll on the regional and global environment. The resources consumed and greenhouse gases emitted to support even the cleanest cities in developed countries are, on a per capita basis, far greater than those associated with the poorer cities of developing regions. Indeed, the largest per capita urban contributors to global environmental problems are the wealthy, living preponderantly in the urban areas of the developed world.

Not confronted with the direct impacts of their activities on the global environment, wealthy cities and countries tend to have fewer incentives to address them. In manufacturing, for example, relatively little progress has been made in introducing "clean" production in the broadest sense of the term or in shifting from the linear material flows that characterize most modern technologies to the closed cycles that many advocate (115). As with global warming, the costs are often seen as too uncertain or too distant to compel action now.

In its broad outlines, the transition summarized above suggests an association among a city's wealth, its environment, and the health of its citizens. Generally, the poor create environmental problems for themselves and their neighbors, while the wealthy create problems for a wider public.

Natural Features

The natural features of a city and its surroundings—its geography, topography, and climate—are also critical determinants of the nature of its environmental problems. Climate, for instance, determines which disease vectors can thrive. London has been spared from malaria not because of its wealth but because it is too cold for the mosquito vector to survive. Mexico City and Los Angeles are especially plagued by air pollution not only from the number of cars per capita—associated with income—but also because they are bounded by mountains that prevent dispersal of air pollutants. Cities in cold regions often confront air pollution problems stemming from energy use for domestic heating, especially where low-quality coal is used, as in northern China and Eastern Europe (116).

When natural features are combined with the level and type of economic activity, they can be used to predict which types of problems are likely to be severe in different types of cities (117). For example, air pollution problems tend to rise with temperature extremes. In cold areas, more fuel is used for heating; in warm, sunny areas, contributions to ozone formation increase owing to the release of hydrocarbons and nitrogen oxides, particularly from motor vehicle fuel. Air pollution also rises with income level because, as is described above, levels of car use, industrial production, and fuel consumption are higher in wealthier cities.

Figure 1.3 Environmental Indicators at Different Country Income Levels, 1980s

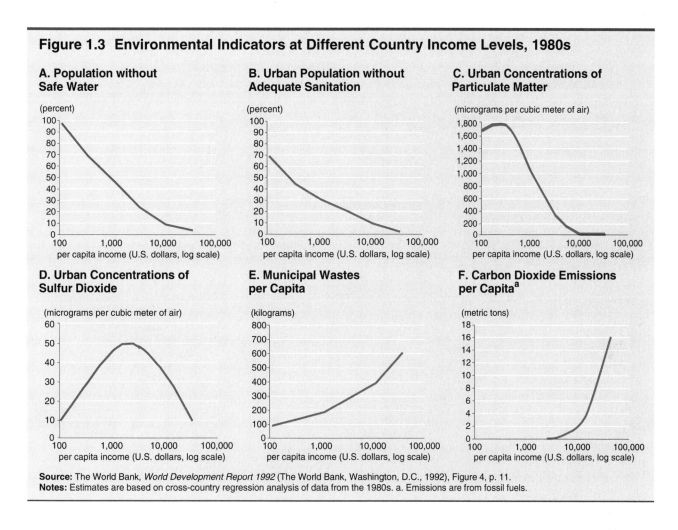

A. Population without Safe Water

(percent)

B. Urban Population without Adequate Sanitation

(percent)

C. Urban Concentrations of Particulate Matter

(micrograms per cubic meter of air)

D. Urban Concentrations of Sulfur Dioxide

(micrograms per cubic meter of air)

E. Municipal Wastes per Capita

(kilograms)

F. Carbon Dioxide Emissions per Capita[a]

(metric tons)

per capita income (U.S. dollars, log scale)

Source: The World Bank, *World Development Report 1992* (The World Bank, Washington, D.C., 1992), Figure 4, p. 11.
Notes: Estimates are based on cross-country regression analysis of data from the 1980s. a. Emissions are from fossil fuels.

The Brown Agenda

Although most of the world's population will soon be living in developing world cities, the environmental problems most prominent in these cities have often been conspicuously absent from the global environmental agenda. Indeed, over the past two decades the global agenda has shifted away from local and regional problems such as air pollution and inadequate water supplies toward vast global concerns such as ozone depletion, climate change, and the loss of biological diversity (118).

Aware of this disconnect between the "green" agenda and the problems confronting cities, a number of researchers, international donor agencies, and nongovernmental organizations over the past few years have advocated a renewed focus on the "brown" agenda—that is, the problems of pollution, poverty, and environmental hazards in cities (119) (120) (121). As one scholar noted, "The adverse effects of household airborne and water-carried wastes on child mortality and female life expectancy are of no less global proportion

than, say, the destruction of tropical forests, and in immediate human terms, they may be the most urgent of all worldwide environmental problems" (122). This is not to argue for less attention to global concerns, but for the recognition that urban and global concerns are intertwined and must both be addressed. This section focuses on the "brown" problems so prominent in many of the world's cities.

Water and Sanitation

One of the greatest threats to human health in the developing world is the lack of adequate water and sanitation services. The International Drinking Water Supply and Sanitation Decade brought significant progress—the number of urban residents with access to an adequate water supply increased by approximately 80 percent—but those gains were overshadowed by rapid population growth. In 1994, at least 220 million people still lacked a source of potable water near their homes (123). (See Table 1.4.)

Box 1.6 Pollution and Health in the Transition Economies

One of the primary challenges for urban areas in transition economies is to clean up the pollution resulting from decades of uncontrolled industrial production (1). Since World War II, these countries have promoted heavy industry, a resource-intensive and highly polluting economic sector. The lack of sufficient environmental regulations and incentives to conserve resources, increase production efficiency, or reduce waste and pollution has greatly exacerbated environmental degradation.

Since 1989, the region's economic downturn has led to reductions in both industrial production and pollution. Industrial production in Bulgaria, for example, fell by more than 50 percent between 1989 and 1992 (2). Annual mean sulfur dioxide concentrations in Prague, Czech Republic; Bratislava, Slovakia; and Warsaw, Poland, declined by 50 percent between 1985 and 1990 (3).

Despite such declines in industrial emissions, however, both short-term and long-term sulfur dioxide exposure in the region still regularly exceeds World Health Organization guidelines (4). New threats to air quality are emerging as well, such as rising emissions of

lead and nitrogen oxides as more people gain access to cars. Between 1986 and 1993, per capita car ownership increased by 34 percent in Hungary and 64 percent in Poland (5) (6). Many cars are old and inefficient. In Katowice, for instance, 75 percent of lead emissions come from cars that are 10 to 30 years old and still burn leaded fuel (7).

Recent evidence suggests that the region's pollution is one of several factors adversely affecting human health, although exact cause-and-effect relationships remain unclear. In contrast to usual demographic trends, life expectancies in Poland's urban areas are lower than in rural areas; pollution is also concentrated in urban areas (8). In the Czech Republic, life expectancies in urban regions affected by heavy air pollution are significantly lower than for the country as a whole (9).

In several cities, especially mining towns, ambient lead levels are high (10). Exposure to even low doses of lead can cause subtle brain damage and learning problems in children. Average blood levels among exposed children in Central and Eastern Europe are often greater than 15 micrograms per deciliter and

sometimes exceed 40 micrograms per deciliter, especially in city centers with heavy car traffic (11). By comparison, in Vancouver, Canada, where unleaded gasoline is mandated, average blood levels among 2- to 3-year-olds is roughly 5.3 micrograms per deciliter.

High levels of air pollution have also been linked with acute and chronic illnesses such as asthma and bronchitis, as well as increased mortality. In Krakow, Poland, an epidemiological study showed an increase in lung cancer risk among residents of the city center; in the past, especially, the central area was heavily polluted by the extensive burning of coal to heat buildings and homes (12).

At the same time, urban residents in the region are facing increasing risks from crumbling infrastructure and deteriorating health services. Throughout the region, there has been a resurgence of "poverty diseases" such as diphtheria, tuberculosis, and hepatitis, providing graphic evidence of the decline in sanitary conditions, hygiene, and nutrition (13). Housing stock in particular has suffered from neglect. In Russian cities, 20 percent of the housing stock

These statistics probably underestimate the actual number of people inadequately served. Definitions of what constitutes an adequate amount of safe drinking water and sanitation vary from country to country. Although many governments classify the existence of a water tap within 100 meters of a house as "adequate," such a tap does not guarantee that the individual household will be able to secure enough water for good health. Communities of 500 inhabitants or more are often served by one tap (124). Communal taps often function only a few hours each day, so residents must wait in long lines to fill even one bucket. For example, in Lucknow, India, a city with almost 2 million people, water is available only 10 hours each day (125). In smaller cities, the situation can be much worse. In Rajkot, India, for example, a city with a population of 600,000, the piped water runs for only 20 minutes each day (126). Households cannot obtain sufficient water for washing, laundry, and personal hygiene if it takes too long to fetch and if the water has to be carried long distances.

Statistics on national coverage also hide inequalities within a city. Although 80 percent of high-income

urban residents in the developing world have a house-connected water supply, only 18 percent of low-income residents do (127). In many cities in developing countries, per capita water availability in marginal settlements can be anywhere from 3 to 10 times less than in better-off neighborhoods (128) (129) (130). Those without access to a safe water supply must buy water from vendors at costs of anywhere from 4 to 100 times higher than the cost of water from a piped city supply (131). In Lima, Peru, a poor family pays more than 20 times what a middle-class family pays for water (132).

The proportion of the urban population covered by sanitation services is even smaller. More than 420 million urban residents do not have access to even the simplest latrine (133). Many resort instead to open defecation on land or in waterways. As with the statistics on adequate water, estimates of the number unserved are probably low because they do not reflect the actual functioning or use of the facilities.

These figures also hide considerable inequalities among the rich and poor. In developing countries, 8 percent of urban low-income dwellers have a house

lacks running water, sewerage, and central heating (14).

In response, many municipalities are implementing broad-based strategies to curb industrial pollution. In Katowice, for example, the Minister of Environmental Protection, in cooperation with local officials, prepared a list of the most polluting industries and ordered them to reduce emissions. Katowice has also expanded its air quality monitoring system, which is now the most extensive in Poland (15).

Novokuznetsk, Russia, has forged a partnership with the U.S. city of Pittsburgh to exchange information about the links between pollution and health and to learn from its experiences in tackling industrial pollution (16).

References and Notes

1. The term "transition economies" lacks a formal definition, but is used here to include the successor states of the former Soviet Union (Armenia, Azerbaijan, the Republic of Belarus, the Republic of Estonia, the Republic of Georgia, the Republic of Kazakhstan, the Kyrgyz Republic, the Republic of Latvia, the Republic of Lithuania, the Republic of Moldova, the Rus-sian Federation, the Republic of Tajikistan, the Republic of Turkmenistan, Ukraine, and the Republic of Uzbekistan) and the countries of Central Europe (Albania, Bulgaria, the Czech Republic, Hungary, Poland, Romania, and the Slovak Republic).

2. Janusz Cofala, "Energy Reform in Central and Eastern Europe," *Energy Policy,* Vol. 22, No. 6 (June 1994), p. 490.

3. European Environment Agency, *Europe's Environment: The Dobris Assessment,* David Stanners and Philippe Bourdeau, eds. (European Environment Agency, Copenhagen, Denmark, 1995), p. 268.

4. *Ibid.*

5. Motor Vehicle Manufacturers' Association (MVMA) of the United States, *MVMA Motor Vehicle Facts & Figures '86* (MVMA, Detroit, Michigan, 1986), p. 37.

6. American Automobile Manufacturers' Association (AAMA), *Motor Vehicle Facts & Figures '95* (AAMA, Washington, D.C., 1995), p. 47.

7. Jerzy Borkiewicz *et al.,* "Environmental Profile of Katowice," draft paper (The World Bank, Washington, D.C., 1991), p. 9.

8. Clyde Hertzman, *Environment and Health in Central and Eastern Europe* (The World Bank, Washington, D.C., 1995), p. ix.

9. *Ibid.*

10. *Op. cit.* 3, p. 269.

11. *Op. cit.* 8, pp. 20–25.

12. *Op. cit.* 3, p. 302.

13. United Nations Children's Fund (UNICEF) International Child Development Centre, *Crisis in Mortality, Health, and Nutrition,* Economies in Transition Studies Regional Monitoring Report No. 2 (UNICEF, Florence, Italy, 1994), p. 54.

14. *Op. cit.* 3, p. 274.

15. Wojciech Beblo, "Katowice, Poland: Industrial Air Pollution and the Air Protection Program," in *The Human Face of the Urban Environment, Proceedings of the Second Annual World Bank Conference on Environmentally Sustainable Development,* Ismail Serageldin, Michael Cohen, and K.C. Sivaramakrishnan, eds. (The World Bank, Washington, D.C., September 19–21, 1994), pp. 66–69.

16. Viktor Zinovievich Koltun, Institute for Advanced Training of Doctors, Novokuznetsk, Russia, 1994 (personal communication).

sewer connection, compared with 62 percent of urban high-income dwellers (134). Low-income families often share latrines with 100 or more other community members, and long lines or overflowing tanks deter residents from using them at all.

Poor sanitation poses health hazards through several routes—including direct exposure to feces near homes, contaminated drinking water, ingestion of fish from polluted waters, and ingestion of produce that has been fertilized by wastewater. Inadequate access to water and sanitation facilities is the main cause for the intestinal diseases, transmitted by feces, that are so prevalent in developing countries. Two of these diseases, diarrhea and intestinal worm infections, account for an estimated 10 percent of the total burden of disease in developing countries (135).

An estimated 2 million fewer children would die from diarrheal diseases each year if all people had access to adequate water and sanitation facilities, according to the World Bank (136). Diarrheal diseases alone killed more than 3 million children in 1993 and cause some 1.8 billion episodes of illness annually (137).

Wastewater Disposal

In the developing world, it is estimated that more than 90 percent of sewage is discharged directly into rivers, lakes, and coastal waters without treatment of any kind (138). Of India's 3,119 towns and cities, only 8 have full wastewater collection and treatment facilities; 209 have partial treatment facilities (139). Even in higher-income countries such as Chile, where sanitation services are relatively well developed, domestic wastewater is still the main threat to water quality. Santiago has only one small pilot wastewater treatment plant, which processes a mere 4 percent of the city's wastewater; the rest is dumped into the rivers that run through the city (140).

Disposal of domestic wastewater remains a problem, although by no means as severe, in wealthier regions as well. In member countries of the Organisation for Economic Co-Operation and Development (OECD), approximately one third of the population is still not served by wastewater treatment plants (141). Many older U.S. cities have outmoded sewer systems that collect wastewater and storm water together, so that when rainfall is heavy, untreated wastewater is released through overflow drains (142).

Indoor Air Pollution

Indoor air pollution from burning of low-quality fuels, such as charcoal or animal dung, has been largely considered a rural problem. Yet many urban residents of the developing world rely on biomass fuels for cooking and heating. In many smaller urban centers in Asia and Africa, between 50 and 90 percent of domestic energy supplies come from these materials (143). Exposure tends to be highest for women and young children, who often spend many hours indoors and cooking over open fires; indeed, they face greater exposure to pollutants from indoor than outdoor air (144).

Data are scarce on the number of people affected by indoor air pollution, especially urban residents, but in 1992 the World Bank identified indoor air pollution as one of the four most critical global environmental problems (145). Indoor air pollution contributes to acute respiratory infections in young children and chronic lung diseases and cancer in adults (146). Acute respiratory infections, principally pneumonia, are the chief killers of young children in developing countries, accounting for an estimated 10 percent of the total burden of disease. Smoke contributes to acute respiratory infections that cause an estimated 4 million deaths annually among infants and children (147) (148).

Urban Air Pollution

Worldwide, more than 1.1 billion people live in urban areas with unhealthful air (149), exposed to a cocktail of pollutants released from industrial, energy, and vehicular sources. Air pollution is particularly severe in megacities such as Beijing, Seoul, Mexico City, and Cairo, Egypt, each of which exceeds WHO guidelines for at least two of the pollutants that WHO monitors (150). In Mexico City, suspended particulate matter from vehicles and others sources contributes to 6,400 deaths each year, and 29 percent of all children have unhealthy blood lead levels (151). The World Bank estimates that if particulate levels alone were reduced to WHO guidelines, between 300,000 and 700,000 premature deaths per year could be avoided globally (152). That is the equivalent of roughly 2 to 5 percent of all deaths in urban areas that have excessive levels of particulates. In addition, chronic coughing in urban children under age 14 could be reduced by half, or about 50 million cases

Table 1.4 Urban Water and Sanitation Coverage, 1994

Service	Africa	Asia and Pacific	Middle East	Latin America
Water				
Percent of population covered	68.9	80.9	71.8	91.4
Percent served by				
House connection	65	48.4	89.7	92
Public standpost	26	24	9.3	3.3
Other	9	27.6	0	4.7
Sanitation				
Percent of population covered	53.2	69.8	60.5	79.8
Percent served by				
House connection to sewer/septic system	53.0	42.7	100.0	91.2
Pour-flush latrine	3.0	43.1	0	2.1
Ventilated improved pit latrine	13.6	2.7	0	0.9
Simple pit latrine	22.4	8.5	0	5.4
Other	2.6	3.0	0	0.4

Source: G. Watters, Health and Environment, World Health Organization, Geneva, 1995 (personal communication).

annually, reducing the chance that these children will face permanent respiratory damage (153). Improving urban air quality should also reduce the incidence of chronic and infectious respiratory diseases.

Urban air quality in the more developed countries has generally improved over the past two decades, largely from advances in controlling emissions from stationary sources such as power plants. Rising motor vehicle use, in part reflecting the increasingly sprawling form of many cities, now poses the greatest threat to air quality (154) (155) (156). By contrast, urban air quality has generally deteriorated throughout the developing world and the formerly socialist economies. The reasons are increasing power generation, rising industrial activity, and rising motor vehicle use—especially of poorly maintained vehicles that use leaded fuel (157).

Air quality seems likely to worsen with rapid urban growth unless rigorous pollution control measures are put into effect. In many cities in developing countries, motor vehicle use per capita is relatively low, so cars are still a minor contributor to air pollution. Car ownership, however, is sparked by both increasing incomes and urbanization and is expected to skyrocket. In 1990, the global vehicle fleet (excluding two- and three-wheel vehicles) totaled some 580 million, but this will grow to an estimated 816 million vehicles by 2010 (158). Most of this growth will occur in the developing countries and in Central and Eastern Europe.

Lead is particularly hazardous to human health, and cars that still rely on leaded gasoline account for up to 95 percent of airborne lead pollution in cities in developing countries (159). The World Bank projects that under an "unchanged practices" scenario, lead emissions could increase fivefold from 1990 to 2030 (160).

Even with efficiency reforms and pollution abatement measures, lead emissions would not disappear until after 2010 (161).

For many cities in developing countries, such as Cairo and Bangkok, ambient lead levels of 1.5 micrograms per cubic meter are common (162) (163) (164). In contrast, lead levels typically range from 0.2 to 0.8 micrograms per cubic meter in most North American and European cities (165). Along roads with high traffic density, lead levels tend to be especially high (166). Residents of the numerous informal settlements that are located next to major roads are thus subject to high levels of exposure.

Urban air pollution not only impairs human health but also damages crops, vegetation, and man-made structures, including historic monuments. These effects are more difficult to quantify. However, acid rain and transported air pollutants from automobiles and heavy industry have contributed to the decline of forest tracts downwind of urban areas (167) (168). As is noted above, cities are also among the major contributors to regional and global atmospheric pollution. (See Chapter 3, "Urban Impacts on Natural Resources.")

Solid and Hazardous Wastes

Cities generate tremendous amounts of solid waste, and those amounts increase with income. In cities of the developing world, an estimated 20 to 50 percent of the solid waste generated remains uncollected, even though up to one half of local operational expenditures often goes toward waste collection (169) (170). In Guatemala City, for instance, just 65 percent of municipal waste is collected; the rest is disposed of in unofficial locations in the metropolitan region (171). In low-income or squatter settlements, garbage collection is often nonexistent, either because these settlements fall outside "official" service areas or because trucks are unable to maneuver along narrow, unpaved streets. Uncollected domestic waste is the most common cause of blocked urban drainage channels in Asian cities, increasing the risk of flooding and vectorborne diseases (172). In some cities, refuse is often mixed with human excrement, which facilitates the spread of disease, especially among children and wastepickers.

In most OECD countries, 100 percent of the urban population is serviced by municipal waste collection (173). However, with their higher consumption levels, they confront ever-increasing mounds of garbage. Since 1980, the generation of municipal waste per capita has increased in all OECD countries except Germany (174) (175). Despite massive recycling and incineration projects, Tokyo is unable to cope with the more than 22,000

Mark Edwards/Still Pictures

Scarce resource. Inadequate water supplies make hygiene difficult and increase the risk of infectious disease in poor communities. Above, a woman in Bombay washes utensils in an open drain.

metric tons of garbage generated each day; as a result, officials are building islands of waste in Tokyo Bay, which threaten both the shipping and the fishing industry (176).

Even if collected, municipal wastes remain a problem in many cities in developing countries. Municipal solid waste sites often handle both domestic and industrial wastes, including hazardous wastes. Without proper disposal, toxic chemicals can leach into water supplies. Few data exist on the composition of hazardous waste streams in developing countries. The OECD has compiled rough estimates of the volumes of industrial and hazardous wastes generated worldwide, yet no such data exist on their disposal (177). Effluents from chemical production, pulp and paper factories, mining industries, and leather and tanning processes are playing an increasing role in environmental pollution. If current trends are any indication, the volume of toxic heavy metals generated in countries such as China, India, the Republic of Korea, and Turkey could reach levels comparable to those of France and the United Kingdom within 15 years (178).

The lack of emissions standards or enforcement of regulations in many developing nations compounds pollution problems. Illegal dumping and improper disposal of toxic and hazardous wastes are common. In addition, industrial activity in the developing world tends to be concentrated in relatively few locations, often close to city centers (179). Three quarters of all Thai factories dealing with hazardous chemicals are located within Bangkok's metropolitan area and the neighboring provinces. This includes five of Thailand's seven lead smelting plants and more than 90 percent of its chemical, dry-cell battery, paint, pharmaceutical, and textile manufacturing plants (180). The concentration of people close to these industries increases the risks of exposure.

Exposures can be severe in the case of industrial accidents or dumping. Even so, they tend to be localized, in contrast to the citywide problems of air and water pollution (181). The health effects of hazardous wastes remain controversial, yet are generally believed to pose a far smaller threat than those associated with biological pathogens in the urban environment (182). In the developed world, where the most egregious exposures to hazardous wastes have largely been remedied, concern is mounting about exposures to even minute levels of toxic wastes (183) (184).

ECONOMIC COSTS OF URBAN ENVIRONMENTAL DEGRADATION

In addition to their toll on human health and natural resources, urban environmental problems exact economic costs as well, some direct, some indirect. All told, these problems can significantly undermine the productivity that urbanization fosters. Some of these costs are relatively simple to calculate, such as the medical costs of treating pollution-related illnesses. But the majority prove far more problematic.

Environmental problems that affect human health, for instance, are often measured in terms of lost worker productivity. But economic losses encompass more than losses in productivity or output as conventionally measured. A loss of a working day due to pollution-caused health problems is an economic cost, but so is ill health unrelated to work loss, as well as the loss of an amenity such as the pleasure of a natural area, or lost leisure time spent in traffic jams. Valuing health symptoms and risks of mortality in economic terms is especially controversial because it rests on assumptions about the value of a human life.

A handful of studies in recent years give an indication of the economic losses incurred by urban environmental degradation. In Mexico City, economic damages due to the health impacts of air pollution are estimated at $1.5 billion per year. Particulates are estimated to cause 12,500 extra deaths and 11.2 million lost workdays per year, both due to respiratory illnesses. Because of excessive exposure to lead, about 140,000 children suffer a reduction in IQ and agility—with implications for adult productivity (185). Problems of inadequate infrastructure show up in direct economic costs as well. In Jakarta, households spend more than $50 million per year to boil water for drinking—an amount equal to 1 percent of the city's gross domestic product (186).

Even more vexing is gauging the monetary costs of the impact of cities on surrounding ecosystems. Yet they, too, appear to be substantial. Ozone damage to U.S. crops, for example, is estimated to cost several billion dollars per year (187). Often the economic value of the services ecosystems provide are apparent only after they have been lost. In East Calcutta, for instance, the filling of 4,000 hectares of lagoons and wetlands not only resulted in an annual loss of some 25,000 metric tons of fish but also caused local flooding after the rains (188) (189). More difficult still to capture in monetary terms are the amenity losses associated with urban environmental degradation—for instance, the pleasure that is lost when a view is degraded or a pristine beach is spoiled.

Impacts on human health and degradation of the natural resource base combine to undermine a city's economic productivity. In addition to the increased cost of treating illness, health problems reduce productivity through lost workdays, lost educational opportunities, and shorter working lives (190). When the natural resources in the surrounding area are exhausted or degraded, cities must draw on them from further away, at increasing cost.

The productivity of cities also depends on a reliable and well-maintained urban infrastructure. When women have to devote considerable amounts of their time to fetching water from distant standpipes or disposing of household wastes, they have less time for income-earning activities. For business as well, dependable supplies of power and water, communications, and transportation networks can raise output and lower production costs. Infrastructure shortages, or intermittent failures in delivery, by contrast, can exact severe economic losses (191).

One notable example of infrastructure failure is congestion. Congested city streets slow the movement of goods and services and generally increase the price of doing business in cities. Not only does traffic congestion allocate time to unproductive waiting, but it also results in inefficient fuel use and worsening air pollution. Indirectly, congestion also reduces productivity by adding to workers' stress and aggravation.

The costs of congestion are significant; however, as with all cost estimates, they vary widely according to the assumptions used to calculate them. The cost of traffic congestion in Bangkok, for instance, varies from $272 million to more than $1 billion per year, depending on the value imputed to time stuck in traffic (192). Conservative estimates for losses due to congestion in a number of Asian cities are shown in Table 1.5 (193). In the United States, estimates of the cost of congestion (from traffic delays and wasted fuel) in urban areas range between $35 billion and $48 billion (194) (195) (196). Other estimates suggest that the United States loses roughly 2 percent of its gross national product to congestion and that the United Kingdom loses about 5 percent (197).

CONFRONTING THE URBAN ENVIRONMENTAL CHALLENGE

The enormous toll urban environmental problems exact—in terms of losses to human health and quality of life, natural resources, and economic productivity—makes a compelling case for action.

On a global scale, the most urgent challenge is to provide for the basic needs of the urban poor and thereby alleviate the toll of human misery associated with degraded urban environments. (See Chapter 2, "Urban Environment and Human Health.") Throughout the cities of the developing world, meeting this challenge will entail activities ranging from providing fundamental urban services such as water and sanitation and garbage collection to reforming land tenure policies. Much is to be gained from encouraging income-generating activities, such as waste recycling, that simultaneously improve livelihoods and the local environment. By doing so, cities can capitalize on what has been called the "incidental greening" of cities—the efforts of the poor to manage their environments (198). Equally important is the recognition and support of the rights of the poor to know the risks to which they are exposed, to determine their priorities, and to meet their own needs through community initiatives.

Table 1.5 Estimated Losses Due to Traffic Jams, Selected Cities

City	Annual Cost of Time Delay (million US$)	Percent of Regional Gross National Product
Bangkok	272	2.1
Hong Kong	293	0.6
Jakarta	68	0.9
Kuala Lumpur	68	1.8
Manila	51	0.7
Seoul	154	0.4
Singapore	305	1.6

Source: Euisoon Shin *et al.,* "Valuing the Economic Impacts of Environmental Problems: Asian Cities," Urban Management Programme Discussion Paper (draft) (The World Bank, Washington, D.C., 1992), p. 139, as cited in J. David Foster, *The Role of the City in Environmental Management: 1994 Edition* (U.S. Agency for International Development, Washington, D.C., 1994), p. 20.

Even in the developed world, addressing the linkage between poverty and the environment should be a top concern. Although such basic health threats as feces-contaminated water have long been addressed, even for the poor in high-income cities, problems in the urban social environment are posing an increasing threat to human health and well-being and, ultimately, to social stability.

A second and related challenge for cities worldwide is to develop strategies to reconcile economic growth with environmental protection. Some of the worst examples of environmental degradation can now be found in and around the rapidly industrializing cities of the developing world, where economic growth is proceeding without adequate concern for its environmental impact. These cities need to find ways to both encourage economic development and provide for the increasing demands of citizens for energy, water, and other resources—in ecologically sound ways. For higher-income cities in North America and Europe, the priority is to reduce their excessive draw on the world's natural resources. Global problems such as greenhouse gas emissions will worsen if policies are not enacted to curb the excessive resource consumption of urbanites in developed regions.

Fortunately, the dynamism and creativity that cluster in cities provide a source for solutions to these problems. Cities tend to devote a higher percentage of funds to environmental protection than do rural areas (199). The concentration of population and activities in cities offers important economies of scale that can reduce not only the unit cost of providing services such as education or health care, but also the cost of providing vital infrastructure. Similarly, enforcing environmental regulations and collecting taxes are easier in

Box 1.7 Designing Sustainable Solutions for Cities

Hyderabad, India, where I serve as commissioner of the Municipal Corporation, has had the distinction of being one of the fastest-growing cities in India during the past decade. The population has increased from 3.2 million in 1985 to 5.2 million in 1995. It is said that in 1591, Muhammed Quli Qutab Shahi, the founder of Hyderabad, prayed that the city would be filled with a population as numerous as the fish in the rivers. His wish seems to have come true.

As managers of rapidly growing urban areas, our primary challenge, and the ultimate challenge, is not to allow events to overtake us but to plan for and manage growth in order to ensure a sustainable city of tomorrow. When discussing sanitation, we should be looking not only at conveyances for removing sewage but also at low-cost technologies for latrines. Or, when focused on questions related to a city's water supply, we should be linking distribution systems with issues of conservation, recycling, and the protection of water sources.

Designing sustainable solutions also requires us to look at the spatial scale of each urban environmental problem. Deciding whether an environmental problem is limited to specific households or affects the entire city, or whether it is a regional, national, or even global problem, allows one to define the necessary infrastructure and services needed to address the problem. An understanding of scale also helps to clarify which government departments should be involved in providing the solution.

For example, the impacts of inadequate garbage collection are greater and more immediate at the household and community level. Garbage, then, is one area that can be addressed at the local level. In Hyderabad, people place their garbage in communal bins located around the city; these bins are then emptied by the municipality. However, the city began receiving complaints that garbage was not being removed from the bins regularly. Garbage was overflowing or being dumped illegally on the streets and in drains. The bins were constantly being moved, further hindering collection efforts.

Hyderabad decided to involve the community in solving the problem. In one pilot neighborhood, the city helped residents form an association that would be in charge of the garbage bins. In addition to picking a permanent location for the bin, the association appointed one person to go from house to house to collect garbage and deposit it in the central bins. The city paid this person 5 rupees (US$0.13) per household per month, and the residents' association matched that amount. This amount is much smaller than what it would cost for the Corporation to operate its own door-to-door collection service. Since the success of the initial test neighborhood, 170 neighborhoods have set up residents' associations to manage garbage removal.

On the other hand, problems such as traffic congestion require more complex, comprehensive actions. The impacts are many—time delays leading to losses in productivity, wasted fuel, pollution, and accidents—and transcend the boundaries of the city. Policy actions would have to be undertaken at a higher level, modifying road networks and land use patterns, increasing the diversity of transport options, and increasing the costs of owning and driving a motor vehicle.

However we define our urban environmental problems, whether they are simple or complex, common to the whole region or confined to one neighborhood, the challenge is primarily a human one.

—*Rachel Chatterjee*

Rachel Chatterjee is commissioner of the Hyderabad Municipal Corporation in Hyderabad, India.

---

urban areas than in dispersed rural areas (200). The job creation potential of cities can be critical in reducing poverty.

In other ways as well, cities have the potential to be far more environmentally benign than most are now. As described in Chapter 3, "Urban Impacts on Natural Resources," the spatial concentration of humans and their activities can minimize pressures on surrounding lands and natural resources. Compact cities such as Saarbrucken, Germany, and Copenhagen, Denmark, use approximately half as much energy on a per capita basis as sprawling, low-density cities such as Minneapolis, Minnesota, and Denver, Colorado, in the United States (201). Well-designed cities can channel development away from wetlands and other sensitive areas. By integrating land use and transportation planning, cities can reduce both congestion and pollution. (See Chapter 4, "Urban Transportation.")

But these benefits of urbanization will not be realized without the concerted efforts of the stakeholders involved—national, regional, local governments, the private sector, international agencies, communities, and citizens. Achieving this will require changes in governance, from improving the formal regulatory and financing bodies of national and local governments to finding new ways to encourage the full participation of civil society.

Environmental management is complicated by issues of jurisdictional complexity. By their very nature, urban environmental problems often require strategies that span jurisdictions and sectors. This is true whether the issue is delivering water and sanitation services to low-income communities or protecting coastal ecosystems from environmental degradation. (See Box 1.7.) Without adequate solid waste management, urban drainage systems will not work, because garbage is the most common cause of blockage (202). Similarly, strategies to reduce air pollution will not work without addressing both stationary and mobile sources of emissions. Some of the most promising approaches to reducing coastal pollution are targeted at the entire watershed that feeds into the basin—often stretching over many thousands of square kilometers.

Yet, in both developed and developing countries, responsibilities for urban environmental management tend to be fragmented among different agencies and jurisdictions. The problem is especially pronounced in huge metropolitan regions, which often spread across multiple jurisdictions—in the case of Mexico City, 42 in all (203). In addition, lines of responsibility and authority are sometimes blurred among the many actors. Municipal authorities, for instance, tend to focus on the environmental concerns of local communities, such as garbage collection, while paying little attention to problems that affect adjacent municipalities or cities located downwind or downstream (204).

Problems of jurisdictional complexity are compounded in cities in developing countries, where local governments may lack both the institutional and the financial resources needed to be effective environmental managers. In the name of decentralization, local governments have been saddled with additional responsibilities for environmental management, but these often come without the necessary autonomy. In many cities of the developing world, the local capacity to generate revenues, through, for example, property taxes or user charges, is rudimentary. This inability to raise funds contributes to the failure of local authorities to properly operate and maintain those environmental facilities they do have, such as wastewater treatment plants (205).

As is described in Chapter 6, "City and Community: Toward Environmental Sustainability," strengthening local governments will be critical to improving the urban environment in the developing world. Equally important is an informed citizenry that demands environmental quality and holds governments accountable. Indeed, some of the most innovative strategies for improving the urban environment are emerging from the bottom up, from neighborhoods and communities that have the most at stake, be they in Karachi, Pakistan, or the Bronx, New York. This special section of *World Resources 1996–97* describes some of the ongoing efforts to create more livable, humane, and ecologically sound cities.

References and Notes

1. United Nations (U.N.) Population Division, *World Urbanization Prospects: The 1994 Revision* (U.N., New York, 1995), p. 87.

2. *Ibid.*, pp. 86–87, 102–103.

3. *Op. cit.* 1, p. 27.

4. *Op. cit.* 1, pp. 132, 135.

5. Carl Bartone *et al.*, "Toward Environmental Strategies for Cities: Policy Considerations for Urban Environmental Management in Developing Countries," Urban Management Programme Policy Paper No. 18 (The World Bank, Washington, D.C., 1994), pp. 9–10.

6. G. Watters, Health and Environment, World Health Organization, Geneva, 1995 (personal communication).

7. Jorge E. Hardoy, Diana Mitlin, and David Satterthwaite, *Environmental Problems in Third World Cities* (Earthscan, London, 1992), p. 58.

8. Dietrich Schwela, "Public Health Implications of Urban Air Pollution in Developing Countries," paper presented at the Tenth World Clean Air Congress, Erjos, Finland, May 28–June 2, 1995 (World Health Organization, Geneva, 1995).

9. World Resources Institute, *The 1994 Information Please Environmental Almanac* (Houghton Mifflin Company, Boston, 1994), pp. 205, 209.

10. National Institute of Urban Affairs (NIUA), *Urban Environmental Maps: Delhi, Bombay, Vadodara, Ahmedabad* (NIUA, New Delhi, India, 1994), pp. 2.21–2.22.

11. *Op. cit.* 1.

12. *Op. cit.* 1, p. 27.

13. *Op. cit.* 1, pp. 81, 85.

14. *Op. cit.* 1, pp. 91, 107.

15. Jorge Gavidia, "Housing and Land in Large Cities of Latin America," in *Enhancing the Management of Metropolitan Living Environments in Latin America* (United Nations Centre for Regional Development, Nagoya, Japan, 1994), p. 19.

16. *Op. cit.* 1, pp. 87, 89, 103, 105.

17. *Op. cit.* 1, pp. 87, 89, 103, 105.

18. United Nations Centre for Human Settlements (Habitat), *An Urbanizing World: Global Report on Human Settlements 1996* (Oxford University Press, Oxford, United Kingdom, and New York, in press), p. 1-27.

19. *Ibid.*, pp. 1-27–1-28.

20. *Op. cit.* 1, p. 27.

21. Nick Devas and Carole Rakodi, "The Urban Challenge" in *Managing Fast Growing Cities*, Nick Devas and Carole Rakodi, eds. (Longman Group, Essex, United Kingdom, and John Wiley & Sons, Inc., New York, 1993), p. 2.

22. *Op. cit.* 1, p. 23.

23. *Op. cit.* 1, pp. 110–111.

24. *Op. cit.* 6.

25. A. Rossi-Espagnet, G.B. Goldstein, and I. Tabibzadeh, "Urbanization and Health in Developing Countries: A Challenge for Health for All," *World Health Statistics Quarterly*, Vol. 44, No. 4 (1991), p. 208.

26. *Op. cit.* 1, pp. 4, 6.

27. *Op. cit.* 1, p. 167.

28. *Op. cit.* 1, p. 6.

29. *Op. cit.* 18, pp. 1-16–1-17.

30. *Op. cit.* 18, pp. 1-19, 1-21.

31. *Op. cit.* 18, p. 1-16.

32. *Op. cit.* 1, p. 10.

33. The World Bank, *Indonesia Environment and Development: Challenges for the Future* (The World Bank, Washington, D.C., 1994), p. 117.

34. K.C. Sivaramakrishnan, "Changes in the Urban Landscape: From Habitat I to Habitat II, Issues of Governance: Local Realities," draft paper prepared for the Woodrow Wilson International Center for Scholars, May 16, 1995, p. 2.

35. *Op. cit.* 18, p. 1-18.

36. *Op. cit.* 18, p. 1-22.

37. Alain Bertaud, "Land Resources: Differing Perspectives on the Shape of Future Cities—Overview," in *The Human Face of the Urban Environment, Proceedings of the Second Annual World Bank Conference on Environmentally Sustainable Development,* Ismail Serageldin, Michael A. Cohen, and K.C. Sivaramakrishnan, eds., The World Bank, Washington, D.C., September 19–21, 1994, p. 235.

38. *Op. cit.* 34, p. 1.

39. D.R. Phillips and Y. Verhasselt, eds., *Health and Development* (Routledge, New York, 1994).

40. Institute for Resource Development, Demographic and Health Surveys, data compiled from 59 country surveys conducted between 1984 and 1994, Columbia, Maryland.

41. The World Bank, *Urban Policy and Economic Development: An Agenda for the 1990s* (The World Bank, Washington, D.C., 1991), p. 18.

42. Hank V. Savitch and Hyung-Ki Ahn, "Change Since Habitat I: A Paradigmatic Inquiry," paper presented at the Woodrow Wilson International Center for Scholars, Washington, D.C., February 28, 1995, p. 8.

43. *Op. cit.* 21, p. 25.

44. Per Ljung and Catherine Farvacque, "Addressing the Urban Challenge: A Review of World Bank FY87 Water Supply and Urban Development Operations," Report INU-13 (The World Bank, Washington, D.C., 1988), as cited in George E. Peterson, G. Thomas Kingsley, and Jeffrey P. Telgarsky, *Urban Economies and National Development* (U.S. Agency for International Development Office of Housing and Urban Programs, Washington, D.C., 1991), p. 17.

45. Saskia Sassen, *Cities in a World Economy* (Pine Forge Press, Thousand Oaks, California, 1994), p. xiv.

46. *Ibid.*

47. *Op. cit.* 45, p. 5.

48. *Op. cit.* 34, p. 4.

49. *Op. cit.* 18, p. 1-24.

50. Terence G. McGee and C.J. Griffiths, "Global Urbanization: Towards the Twenty-First Century," in *Population Distribution and Migration,* draft proceedings of the United Nations Expert Meeting on Population Distribution and Migration, Santa Cruz, Bolivia, January 18–22, 1993 (United Nations, New York, August 1994), pp. 61, 63.

51. *Op. cit.* 18, p. 1-24.

52. *Op. cit.* 18, pp. 1-24–1-25.

53. *Op. cit.* 50, p. 60.

54. *Op. cit.* 21, p. 24.

55. Mike Parnwell, *Population Movements and the Third World* (Routledge, London, 1993), pp. 18–24.

56. *Op. cit.* 18, p. 1-24.

57. Josef Gugler, "Overurbanization Reconsidered," in *The Urbanization of the Third World,* Josef Gugler, ed. (Oxford University Press, Oxford, United Kingdom, 1988), p. 83.

58. *Op. cit.* 55, p. 87.

59. George E. Peterson, G. Thomas Kingsley, and Jeffrey P. Telgarsky, *Urban Economies and National Development* (U.S. Agency for International Development Office of Housing and Urban Programs, Washington, D.C., 1991), p. 7.

60. The World Bank, *World Development Report 1995: Workers in an Integrating World* (The World Bank, Washington, D.C., 1995), p. 35.

61. United Nations Economic Commission for Latin America and the Caribbean (ECLAC), *Social Panorama of Latin America, 1994* (ECLAC, Santiago, Chile, 1994), p. 25.

62. Nick Devas, "Evolving Approaches," in *Managing Fast Growing Cities: New Approaches to Urban Planning and Management in the Developing World,* Nick Devas and Carole Rakodi, eds. (Longman Group, Essex, U.K., 1993), pp. 77–78.

63. A.S. Oberai, *Population Growth, Employment and Poverty in Third-World Mega-Cities: Analytical and Policy Issues* (St. Martin's Press, New York, 1993), pp. 62–67.

64. G. Shabbir Cheema, "The Challenge of Urban Management: Some Issues," in *Urban Management: Policies and Innovations in Developing Countries,* G. Shabbir Cheema, ed. (Praeger, Westport, Connecticut, and London, 1993), p. 12.

65. Michael Douglass, Chairman, Department of Urban and Regional Planning, University of Hawaii at Manoa, Honolulu, Hawaii, 1995 (personal communication).

66. *Op. cit.* 61.

67. The World Bank, *Structural Adjustment and Sustainable Growth: The Urban Agenda for the 1990s* (The World Bank, Washington, D.C., 1990), p. 3, as cited in United Nations Development Programme (UNDP), *The Urban Environment in Developing Countries* (UNDP, New York, 1992), p. 16.

68. The World Bank, *Structural Adjustment and Sustainable Growth: The Urban Agenda for the 1990s* (The World Bank, Washington, D.C., 1990), p. 5, as cited in United Nations Development Programme (UNDP), *The Urban Environment in Developing Countries* (UNDP, New York, 1992), p. 16.

69. Ellen Wratten, "Conceptualizing Urban Poverty," *Environment and Urbanization,* Vol. 7, No. 1 (April 1995), p. 11.

70. *Op. cit.* 61, p. 157.

71. *Op. cit.* 61, p. 157.

72. *Op. cit.* 18, p. 3-25.

73. Yeu-Man Yeung, "Past Approaches and Emerging Challenges," in *The Urban Poor and Basic Infrastructure Services in Asia and the Pacific,* Vol. 1, Proceedings of the Regional Seminar, Manila, Philippines, January 22–28, 1991 (Asian Development Bank and Economic Development Institute, Manila, Philippines, 1991), p. 35.

74. *Op. cit.* 18, p. 3-26.

75. United Nations Development Programme (UNDP), *Cities, People, & Poverty: Urban Development Cooperation for the 1990s* (UNDP, New York, 1991), p. 19.

76. United Nations Children's Fund (UNICEF) International Child Development Centre, "Crisis in Mortality, Health, and Nutrition," Economies in Transition Studies Regional Monitoring Report No. 2 (UNICEF, Florence, Italy, 1994), p. 3.

77. *Ibid.*

78. *Op. cit.* 69, pp. 19–21.

79. Michael Cohen, "The Hypothesis of Urban Convergence: Are Cities in the North and South Becoming More Alike?" draft paper, February 22, 1995, Washington, D.C., p. 2.

80. John D. Kasarda, "Cities as Places Where People Live and Work: Urban Change and Neighborhood Distress," in *Interwoven Destinies,* Henry Cisneros, ed. (W.W. Norton & Company, New York, 1994), p. 83.

81. Philip Amis and Carole Rakodi, "Urban Poverty: Issues for Research and Policy," *Journal of International Development: Policy, Economics and International Relations,* Vol. 6, No. 5 (September–October 1994), p. 630.

82. *Ibid.*

83. *Op. cit.* 60, pp. 43–45.

84. United Nations (U.N.) Development Programme (UNDP), *Human Development Report 1995* (Oxford University Press, Oxford, United Kingdom, and New York, 1995), pp. 66–68.

85. Caroline O.N. Moser, Alicia J. Herbert, and Roza E. Makonnen, "Urban Poverty in the Context of Structural Adjustment: Recent Evidence and Policy Responses," Transportation, Water, and Urban Development Department Discussion Paper No. 4 (The World Bank, Washington, D.C., 1993), p. 22.

86. United Nations Development Programme (UNDP), *The Urban Environment in Developing Countries* (UNDP, New York, 1992), p. 16.

87. *Ibid.,* p. 18.

88. *Op. cit.* 25, p. 205.

89. Depending on the definition used, estimates of the number of street children range from 10 million to 100 million. UNICEF has accepted 100 million as a reasonable estimate, using a definition that encompasses children who are sent into the streets by their parents to find income-earning opportunities, children who voluntarily break ties with their family or see them only infrequently, and orphans.

90. Caroline Moser, *Gender Planning and Development: Theory, Practice and Training* (Routledge, New York, 1993), p. 17.

91. United Nations (U.N.), *The World's Women 1970–1990: Trends and Statistics* (U.N., New York, 1991), p. 17.

92. *Op. cit.* 85, p. 4.

93. *Op. cit.* 18, p. 1-13.

94. *Op. cit.* 18, p. 1-13.

95. David Satterthwaite, "Health and Environmental Problems in the Cities of Developing Countries," in *Population Distribution and Migration, Proceedings of the United Nations (U.N.) Expert Meeting on Population Distribution and Migration, Santa Cruz, Bolivia, 18–22 January 1993* (U.N., New York, August 1994), p. 183.

96. Michael Douglass, "The Political Economy of Urban Poverty and Environmental Management: Access, Empowerment and Community Based Alternatives," *Environment and Urbanization,* Vol. 4, No. 2 (October 1992), pp. 15–16.

97. The World Bank, *World Development Report 1993: Investing in Health* (The World Bank, Washington, D.C., 1993), p. 90.

98. United Nations Development Programme, *Human Development Report 1990* (Oxford University Press, New York, 1990), p. 86.

99. Tim Campbell, "Environmental Dilemmas and the Urban Poor," in *Environment and the Poor: Development Strategies for a Common Agenda,* H. Jeffrey Leonard, ed. (Overseas Development Council, Washington, D.C., 1989), p. 177.

100. United Nations Environment Programme, *Environmental Data Report* (Basil Blackwell, Oxford, United Kingdom, 1991), p. 288.

101. Patricia McCarney, "Urban Research in the Developing World: Four Approaches to the Environment of Cities," in *Urban Research in the Developing World: Towards an Agenda for the 1990s,* Richard Stren, ed. (University of Toronto, Toronto, 1994), p. 41.

102. Janis D. Bernstein, "Land Use Considerations in Urban Environmental Management," Urban Management Programme Discussion Paper No. 12 (The World Bank, Washington, D.C., 1994), p. 17.

103. *Op. cit.* 99.

104. *Op. cit.* 101.

105. Porus Olpadwala and William W. Goldsmith, "The Sustainability of Privilege: Reflections on the Environment, the Third World City, and Poverty," *World Development,* Vol. 20, No. 4 (1992), p. 630.

106. *Op. cit.* 96.

107. Debra J. Brody *et al.,* "Blood Lead Levels in the U.S. Population: Phase 1 of the Third National Health and Nutrition Examination Survey (NHANES III, 1988 to 1991)," *Journal of the American Medical Association,* Vol. 272, No. 4 (July 27, 1994), p. 277.

108. Rodney R. White, *Urban Environmental Management: Environmental Change and Urban Design* (John Wiley & Sons, Chichester, United Kingdom, 1994), pp. 71, 73.

109. For further reading on environmental justice, see Robert D. Bullard, *Dumping in Dixie: Race, Class, and Environmental Quality* (Westview Press, Boulder, Colorado, 1994), United Church of Christ Commission for Racial Justice, *Toxic Wastes and Race in the United States: A National Report on the Racial and Socio-Economic Characteristics of Communities with Hazardous Waste Sites* (United Church of Christ, New York, 1987), and Bunyan Bryant and Paul Mohai, eds., *Race and the Incidence of Environmental Hazards: A Time for Discourse* (Westview Press, Boulder, Colorado, 1992).

110. Carlos A. Linares, Daniel A. Seligman, and Daniel B. Tunstall, "Developing Urban Environmental Indicators in Third World Cities," draft final report presented to U.S. Agency for International Development (World Resources Institute, Washington, D.C., April 26, 1993), p. 5.

111. *Ibid.,* pp. 5–6.

112. *Op. cit.* 5, p. 22.

113. Ellen Brennan, "Mega-City Management and Innovation Strategies: Regional Views," in *Mega-City Growth and the Future,* Roland J. Fuchs *et al.,* eds. (United Nations University Press, New York, 1994), p. 250.

114. Gordon McGranahan, "Household Environmental Problems in Low-Income Cities: An Overview of Problems and Prospects for Improvement," *Habitat International,* Vol. 17, No. 2 (1993), p. 105.

115. *Op. cit.* 108, pp. 1–14.

116. *Op. cit.* 5, p. 16.

117. *Op. cit.* 110, p. 16.

118. *Op. cit.* 101, p. 9.

119. Among the international organizations working on the brown agenda are The World Bank, the United Nations Centre for Human Settlements (Habitat), the United Nations Development Programme, and the U.S. Agency for International Development.

120. The number of research institutions focusing on the brown agenda are too numerous to cover here, but include institutions such as the University of Toronto, Centre for Urban and Community Studies; the Department of City and Regional Planning, University of Wales, Cardiff; the National Institute of Urban Affairs, New Delhi, India; the International Institute for Environment and Development, Buenos Aires, Argentina; and the Mazingira Institute, Nairobi, Kenya.

121. For a partial listing of nongovernmental organizations working on the brown agenda, see United Nations Centre for Human Settlements (Habitat), *Directory of Non-Governmental Organizations in the Field of Human Settlements* (Habitat, Nairobi, Kenya, 1993). The journal *Environment and Urbanization* also regularly publishes profiles of nongovernmental organizations working on human settlements.

122. *Op. cit.* 99, p. 173.

123. *Op. cit.* 6.

124. *Op. cit.* 7, pp. 43–45.

125. P.K. Roy, "Lucknow: Slow Death of a Water Source," *The Hindu Survey of the Environment 1994* (May 31, 1994), pp. 119–122.

126. Arunkumar Bhatt, "Rujkot: Chronic Scarcity," *The Hindu Survey of the Environment 1994* (May 31, 1994), pp. 113–117.

127. World Health Organization (WHO) and United Nations Children's Fund (UNICEF) Joint Water Supply and Sanitation Monitoring Programme, *Water Supply and Sanitation Sector Monitoring Report 1993* (WHO and UNICEF Joint Monitoring Programme, New York and Geneva, 1993), Figure 1, pp. 10, 18.

128. United Nations (U.N.) Economic and Social Commission for Asia and the Pacific, *State of Urbanization in Asia and the Pacific 1993* (U.N., New York, 1993), p. 2-45.

129. Carolyn Stephens *et al., Environment and Health in Developing Countries: An Analysis of Intra-Urban Differentials Using Existing Data* (London School of Hygiene & Tropical Medicine in collaboration with Fundacao SEADE, and Ghana Ministry of Environment, London, 1994), pp. 23, 57.

130. National Research Council, Academia de la Investigacion Cientifica, A.C., and Academia Nacional de Ingenieria, A.C., *Mexico City's Water Supply: Improving the Outlook for Sustainability* (National Academy Press, Washington, D.C., 1995), p. 56.

131. John Briscoe, "When the Cup Is Half Full: Improving Water and Sanitation Services in the Developing World," *Environment,* Vol. 35, No. 4 (1993), p. 10.

132. *Ibid.*

133. *Op. cit.* 6.

134. *Op. cit.* 127, Figure 2, pp. 11, 19.

135. *Op. cit.* 97.

136. The World Bank, *World Development Report 1992: Development and the Environment* (The World Bank, Washington, D.C., 1992), p. 49.

137. World Health Organization (WHO), *The World Health Report 1995: Bridging the Gaps* (WHO, Geneva, 1995), p. 10.

138. *Op. cit.* 131, p. 15.

139. Carter Brandon and Ramesh Ramankutty, "Toward an Environmental Strategy for Asia," World Bank Discussion Paper No. 224 (The World Bank, Washington, D.C., 1993), p. 49.

140. The World Bank, *Chile, Managing Environmental Problems: Economic Analysis of Selected Issues* (The World Bank, Washington, D.C., December 1994), p. 9.

141. Organisation for Economic Co-Operation and Development (OECD), *Environmental Indicators* (OECD, Paris, 1994), p. 49.

142. National Research Council, Committee on Wastewater Management for Coastal Urban Areas, *Managing Wastewater in Coastal Urban Areas* (National Academy Press, Washington, D.C., 1993), pp. 32, 61–62.

143. Douglas F. Barnes *et al.,* "Urban Energy Transitions, Poverty, and the Environment: Understanding the Role of the Urban Household Energy in Developing Countries," draft

paper (The World Bank, Washington, D.C., September 1994), p. 15.

144. *Op. cit.* 97, p. 91.

145. *Op. cit.* 97, p. 91.

146. Kirk R. Smith and Youcheng Liu, "Indoor Air Pollution in Developing Countries," in *Epidemiology of Lung Cancer,* Jonathan M. Samet, ed. (Marcel Dekker, Inc., New York, 1994), pp. 154–163.

147. *Op. cit.* 136, p. 52.

148. *Op. cit.* 137, Table 5, pp. 18–19.

149. *Op. cit.* 8.

150. World Health Organization and United Nations Environment Programme, *Urban Air Pollution in Megacities of the World* (Blackwell Reference, Oxford, United Kingdom, 1992), p. 39.

151. *Op. cit.* 5, p. 11.

152. *Op. cit.* 136, p. 52.

153. *Op. cit.* 136, p. 52.

154. *Op. cit.* 141, p. 75.

155. Jacqueline Aloisi de Larderel, "The Risks of Exposure: The Challenge of Urban Air Pollution—Overview," in *The Human Face of the Urban Environment, Proceedings of the Second Annual World Bank Conference on Environmentally Sustainable Development,* Ismail Serageldin, Michael A. Cohen, and K.C. Sivaramakrishnan, eds. (The World Bank, Washington, D.C., September 19–21, 1994), p. 60.

156. Organisation for Economic Co-Operation and Development (OECD) and European Conference of Ministers of Transport (ECMT), *Urban Travel and Sustainable Development* (ECMT and OECD, Paris, 1995), pp. 33–63.

157. *Op. cit.* 97, p. 96.

158. Asif Faiz and Surhid Gautam, "Motorization, Urbanization, and Air Pollution," discussion paper (The World Bank, Washington, D.C., 1994), p. 8.

159. *Op. cit.* 136, p. 124.

160. *Op. cit.* 136, p. 18.

161. *Op. cit.* 136, p. 18.

162. Alliance to End Childhood Lead Poisoning and Environmental Defense Fund, *The Global Dimensions of Lead Poisoning: An Initial Analysis* (Alliance to End Childhood Lead Poisoning, Washington, D.C., 1994), p. 26.

163. United States Agency for International Development (U.S.AID), *Comparing Environmental Health Risks in Cairo, Egypt, Vol. II: Technical Annexes,* draft paper (U.S.AID, Washington, D.C., 1994), p. A-3.

164. United States Agency for International Development (U.S.AID), *Ranking Environmental Health Risks in Bangkok, Thailand, Vol. II: Technical Appendices* (U.S.AID, Washington, D.C., December 1990), p. A-8.

165. *Op. cit.* 162.

166. *Op. cit.* 162.

167. John L. Innes, *Forest Health: Its Assessment and Status* (CAB International, Oxon, United Kingdom, 1993), p. 42.

168. William M. Ciesla and Edwin Donaubauer, *Decline and Dieback of Trees and Forests: A Global Overview,* Forestry Paper No. 120 (Food and Agriculture Organization of the United Nations, Rome, 1994), p. 61.

169. *Op. cit.* 95, p. 184.

170. *Op. cit.* 5, p. 26.

171. Gail Rothe and Eduardo Perez, "Planning for Urban Environmental Health Programs in Central America," WASH Field Report No. 420 (United States Agency for International Development, Washington, D.C., October 1993), p. 16.

172. Yok-shiu F. Lee, "Urban Planning and Vector Control in Southeast Asian Cities," *Kaohsiung Journal of Medical Science,* Vol. 10 (1994), p. S-44.

173. United Nations Environment Programme, *Environmental Data Report 1993–94* (Blackwell Publishers, Oxford, United Kingdom, 1993), p. 331.

174. The small decline in arisings in Germany can be explained by the increase in the separate collection of recyclable materials such as glass and paper.

175. *Op. cit.* 141, p. 93.

176. Eugene Linden, "Megacities," *Time,* Vol. 141, No. 2 (January 11, 1993), p. 36.

177. *Op. cit.* 173, p. 332.

178. *Op. cit.* 136, p. 55.

179. *Op. cit.* 7, pp. 63–64.

180. *Op. cit.* 7, p. 64.

181. *Op. cit.* 136, p. 55.

182. *Op. cit.* 7, p. 22.

183. Cheryl Simon Silver and Dale S. Rothman, "Toxics and Health: The Potential Long-Term Effects of Industrial Activity," a report on "A Workshop on the Effects of Industrial Activity on Human and Ecosystem Health," The 2050 Project, Yulee, Florida, May 19–20, 1994, p. 41.

184. U.S. Environmental Protection Agency (EPA) Office of Air Quality, "EPA Air Quality Trends," EPA-4S4/F-95 003 (EPA, Washington, D.C., September 1995), p. 12.

185. *Op. cit.* 5, p. 103.

186. *Op. cit.* 5, p. 42.

187. *Op. cit.* 184, p. 8.

188. *Op. cit.* 128, p. 5-28.

189. United Nations Economic and Social Commission for Asia and the Pacific (ESCAP), *State of the Environment in Asia and the Pacific, 1990* (ESCAP, Bangkok, Thailand, 1992), p. 71.

190. *Op. cit.* 5, p. 2.

191. The World Bank, *World Development Report 1994: Infrastructure for Development*

(The World Bank, Washington, D.C., 1994), pp. 25–26.

192. J. David Foster, *The Role of the City in Environmental Management: 1994 Edition* (U.S. Agency for International Development, Washington, D.C., 1994), p. 19.

193. Euisoon Shin *et al.,* "Valuing the Economic Impacts of Environmental Problems: Asian Cities," Urban Management Programme Discussion Paper, working draft (The World Bank, Washington, D.C., 1994), p. 139.

194. Apogee Research, Inc., "The Costs of Transportation: Final Report," prepared for The Conservation Law Foundation (March 1994), p. 12.

195. David Schrank, Shawn Turner, and Timothy Lomax, "Trends in Urban Roadway Congestion—1982 to 1991, Volume 1: Annual Report," Research Report 1131-6, Vol. 1 (Texas Transportation Institute, College Station, Texas, 1994), p. 32.

196. Richard Arnott and Kenneth Small, "The Economics of Traffic Congestion," *American Scientist,* Vol. 82, No. 5 (September/October 1994), p. 446.

197. James J. MacKenzie, Roger C. Dower, and Donald D.T. Chen, *The Going Rate: What It Really Costs to Drive* (World Resources Institute, Washington, D.C., 1992), pp. 18–19.

198. Christine Furedy, "Incidental Greening—Saving Resources in Asian Cities," in *Green Cities: Ecologically Sound Approaches to Urban Space,* David Gordon, ed. (Black Rose Books, Montreal, 1990), pp. 43–54, as cited in Patricia McCarney, "Urban Research in the Developing World: Four Approaches to the Environment of Cities," in *Urban Research in the Developing World: Towards an Agenda for the 1990s,* Richard Stren, ed. (University of Toronto, Toronto, 1994), p. 22.

199. *Op. cit.* 192, p. 3.

200. David Satterthwaite, "The Preventable Disease Burden in Cities," *Environment and Urbanization,* Vol. 5, No. 2 (October 1993), p. 5.

201. Ralph Torrie, "Findings and Policy Implications from the Urban CO_2 Reduction Project," International Council for Local Environmental Initiatives (ICLEI) Paper (ICLEI, Toronto, January 1993), p. 7.

202. *Op. cit.* 172.

203. Exequiel Ezcurra and Marisa Mazari-Hiriart, "Are Mega-Cities Viable? A Cautionary Tale from Mexico City," *Environment,* Vol. 38, No. 1 (January/February 1996), p. 11.

204. *Op. cit.* 113.

205. *Op. cit.* 5, p. 34.

2. Urban Environment and Human Health

Urbanization is one of the major social changes sweeping the globe, especially in developing countries, where urban growth rates are the most intense. Soon, a majority of the world's people will be living in urban environments quite unlike the rural settings that have been home to most of human society to date. Urbanization brings fundamental changes in the ways people live—in the number of people they see, in the places they work, and often in the quality of the water they drink, the air they breathe, and the housing in which they live.

Such changes have profound implications—both positive and negative—for the health of city residents. On the one hand, urbanization and economic development have brought dramatic improvements in health, largely because of environmental improvements and, in part, increased access to health services. Health statistics show that in the more highly urbanized countries, people tend to have the longest life expectancies and children under age 5 tend to have the lowest rates of mortality (1). Even within countries, urban-rural comparisons of indicators such as infant mortality and vaccination coverage show that there are significant advantages in urban areas. (See Table 2.1.)

However, urbanization can also have many negative influences on human health. For much of the world, growth in urban populations is synonymous with growth in urban poverty, both in absolute and in relative terms (2). Increasingly, cities are becoming the world's starkest symbol of the maldistribution of resources, both physical and societal. These inequalities have serious impacts on the health of urban dwellers everywhere, but especially in the fast-growing towns and cities in the developing world.

This chapter examines these negative impacts of urbanization and the urban environment on human health, particularly in the developing world. Indisputable evidence ties ill health to deficiencies in the physical environment, including inadequate water and sanitation, flimsy, overcrowded housing, air pollution, uncollected garbage, and dangerous workplaces. In poor cities of the developing world, infectious and parasitic diseases related to these deficiencies continue to exact an enormous toll on human health.

Now there is increasing evidence of the role of social factors—including alienation, high rates of unemployment, ethnic tensions, and urban poverty—in influencing health as well. The effects of the urban social environment are by no means independent of physical conditions; they are interrelated. The political and economic structures within a city fundamentally determine the distribution of and access to the physical, biological, and social benefits that cities provide. In other words, the poorest groups within a city face the greatest exposure to physical and biological threats and have the least access to protective services.

These social factors affect health indirectly, through changes in behavior. But the urban social environment also contains direct health threats, such as urban violence, drug abuse, and depression and other psychosocial illnesses. These problems are of increasing importance in cities across the globe. Indeed, throughout the developed world, physical threats have largely

Table 2.1 Comparison of Urban-Rural Health Statistics, Selected Countries, 1991–94

Indicator	Kenya Urban	Kenya Rural	Senegal Urban	Senegal Rural	Bolivia Urban	Bolivia Rural	Bangladesh Urban	Bangladesh Rural	Indonesia Urban	Indonesia Rural
Mortality rate for children under 5 (deaths per 1,000 live births)	75.4	95.6	101.8	184.2	104.0	162.0	114.3	153.2	83.7	116.4
Percent of children between 12 and 23 months with all vaccinations	80.9	78.3	64.9	40.4	44.4	28.4	70.4	57.5	65.2	40.9
Total fertility rate	3.4	5.8	5.1	6.7	3.8	6.3	2.7	3.5	2.6	3.2
Percent of females over age 6 with no education	13.5	29.1	50.6	88.7	11.1	33.0	34.0	50.0	15.5	28.7

Source: Institute for Resource Development, Demographic and Health Survey Data Archive, Columbia, Maryland.
Note: Data are for the following years: Kenya, 1993; Senegal, 1992; Bolivia, 1994; Bangladesh, 1993; and Indonesia, 1991.

receded and social factors are emerging as the greatest threats to public health.

For these reasons, the term *environment* is defined here to include not just the physical elements associated with the built environment but social factors as well. (See Box 2.1.) This chapter examines, in particular, evidence linking socioeconomic inequities in cities with inequities in health. First, the chapter describes how health problems stemming from the urban environment vary dramatically from city to city, depending in large part on a city's developmental status or wealth. Next, it examines the dramatic differences between rich and poor within the same city. The chapter then explores in greater detail how elements of both the physical environment and the social environment interact to increase the burden of ill health.

Attention to the social factors that affect the health of urban dwellers is relatively new. Past analyses have tended to focus on elements of the physical environment, usually in isolation. If policies to improve health are to succeed, they must recognize the interconnections between physical and societal factors and strive for an integrated approach. In short, simply providing better physical facilities such as improved sanitation and water supply—although essential—is not enough to address the serious health problems that plague urban residents.

HEALTH PROFILES OF URBAN DWELLERS

Differences Among Cities

Urban residents in developing countries have a far greater burden of premature death and disease than do their counterparts in developed countries, reflecting broadly their relative poverty and inadequate access to basic services and opportunities. Yet, even within those broad categories of developed and developing countries, cities differ widely in their health profiles. Profiles depend broadly on several factors: the mix of environmental risks faced (physical, biological, and social), the proportion of the population facing different risks, the demographic profile of the city and of groups within it, and access to health services. All of these tend to shift with development and increasing wealth.

Since the mid-19th Century, when improvements in the handling of urban water and sewage began to take hold, the burden of communicable diseases has steadily declined throughout many cities in the developed world. The major causes of death are now chronic and degenerative diseases—primarily heart disease and cancer—that are related to such social factors as diet, stress, and lifestyle. And, recently, violence and accidents have become increasingly significant causes of death in cities.

This shift from communicable to noncommunicable diseases has been described as the "epidemiological transition" or the "health transition" (3). This transition, which is not unique to urban areas but which typically occurs first and fastest there, is related to several factors. One is exposure to the risk factors for disease, which change as countries urbanize and develop. Access to effective health services is clearly a second major factor (4). Finally, the aging of the population, which is in turn related to mortality and fertility rates, is also a critical determinant, since the incidence of chronic and degenerative diseases typically increases with age (5).

Signs of this health transition are now apparent throughout cities of the developing world. In some cities, especially the economically advanced ones, heart disease and cancer are emerging as major causes of death, as they already have in the developed world. Indeed, in cities as diverse as Sao Paulo, Brazil; Cape Town, South Africa; and Accra, Ghana, heart disease

Box 2.1 Can We Improve Neighborhood Quality in Neglected U.S. Cities?

Webster's New World Dictionary defines the word environment as "all the conditions, circumstances, and influences surrounding and affecting the development of an organism or group of organisms" (1). In other words, everything we see, smell, feel, or hear as soon as we walk outside our home is our neighborhood environment. This includes not only trees and sidewalks but noisy neighbors, litter in the street, abandoned houses, and polluted air.

In policymaking, however, the United States, like many other nations, has a much narrower definition of environment. In local, state, and national government, environmental problems are equated with air, land, and water pollution. Crime is left to the criminal justice system; blight is the responsibility of housing, community development, police, and firefighting organizations; traffic noise, congestion, and access are left to departments of transportation.

The U.S. Environmental Protection Agency's narrow environmental mandate has not prevented the agency and its state progeny from improving the environment. Nationally, despite substantial increases in population, production, and consumption, emissions into the air, land, and water have decreased (2)(3)(4). But this single-agency mandate does not work for inner-city neighborhoods, which face a multitude of hazards.

The inner-city neighborhood of East Elizabeth, New Jersey, exemplifies the array of problems facing declining U.S. cities. Residents confront deafening noise from Newark Airport, the 10th busiest airport in the United States, located just 1.6 kilometers away. The New Jersey Turnpike, the most heavily trafficked road in the United States, runs directly through the community.

The largest petrochemical complex on the East Coast, which, according to toxic release inventory data, is the seventh largest waste-producing site and eighth largest emitter of toxins in New Jersey, is located on the southwest boundary of the neighborhood. The site of a former hazardous waste incinera-

tor that exploded in 1980 still stands vacant, surrounded by a 2.4-meter-high chain link fence. The neighborhood also contains clusters of abandoned buildings and numerous littered lots. Police warn visitors not to venture into public housing projects located in the center of East Elizabeth because the area is said to be the local epicenter of illegal drug activity.

When surveyed, the citizens of East Elizabeth, as well as local government experts, recognize that there are multiple sources of environmental risk. They also say that solving one or even two of these risks is insufficient to substantially improve neighborhood quality (5)(6).

At this time, however, the U.S. government does not assess the cumulative risk of living in neighborhoods with crime and other behavioral hazards, severe physical blight, and multiple forms of pollution. Experts well-versed in air pollution modeling and epidemiological studies have neither the mandate nor the skills to assess risk from other pollution problems.

Furthermore, crime, uncontrolled dogs and rats, abandoned and unsafe buildings, and various forms of antisocial behavior and physical decay are not included with pollution in risk assessments. As a result, mitigation efforts tend to be piecemeal and uncoordinated and thus unlikely to markedly reduce the risk these neighborhoods face.

I cannot offer a realistic and simple solution to the multiple environmental problems of these neighborhoods. However, if efforts to rehabilitate our cities are to succeed, we must redefine the concept of environment in a way that matches the realities in multiple-hazard neighborhoods—in a way that is closer to Webster's definition. We cannot set priorities for action unless we understand the full extent of the risks these communities face. For now, those best equipped to set priorities are the residents and local officials who live and work in these neighborhoods.

It is also clear that no single agency can play the heroic knight. The agencies responsible for environment, criminal justice, housing, transportation, and

other areas must contribute both individually and collectively—along with businesses and communities—to finding ways to improve the environment and quality of life in multiple-hazard neighborhoods.

—*Michael Greenberg*

Michael Greenberg is a professor of urban studies and community health at the Edward J. Bloustein School of Planning and Public Policy of Rutgers University, New Brunswick, New Jersey.

References and Notes

1. David Guralnik, ed., *Webster's New World Dictionary,* second edition (Simon and Schuster, New York, 1980), p. 468.

2. Paul Portney, ed., *Public Policy for Environmental Protection* (Resources for the Future, Washington, D.C., 1992), pp. 7–25, 275–289.

3. Richard Smith, Richard Alexander, and M. Gordon Wolman, "Water Quality Trends in the Nation's Rivers," *Science,* Vol. 235 (1987), pp. 1607–1615.

4. J.G. Calvert, *et al.,* "Achieving Acceptable Air Quality: Some Reflections on Controlling Vehicle Emissions," *Science,* Vol. 261, No. 5117 (1993), pp. 37–39.

5. Michael Greenberg and Dona Schneider, "Hazardous Waste Site Remediation, Neighborhood Change, and Neighborhood Quality," *Environmental Health Perspectives,* Vol. 102, No. 6/7 (1994), pp. 542–547.

6. Michael Greenberg and Dona Schneider, *Environmentally Devastated Neighborhoods: Perceptions, Policies, and Realities* (Rutgers University Press, New Brunswick, New Jersey, 1996).

Figure 2.1 Causes of Death in Three Cities

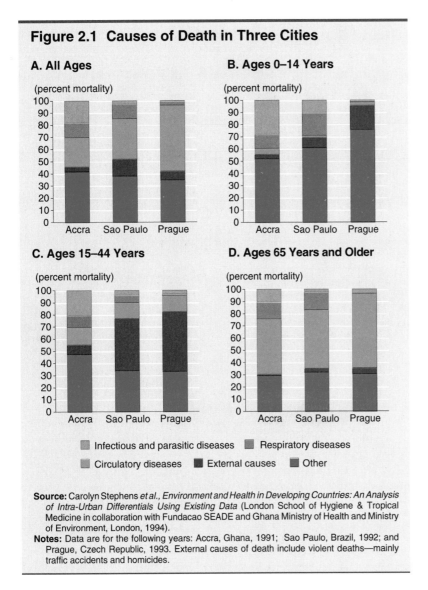

A. All Ages

(percent mortality)

B. Ages 0–14 Years

(percent mortality)

C. Ages 15–44 Years

(percent mortality)

D. Ages 65 Years and Older

(percent mortality)

■ Infectious and parasitic diseases   ■ Respiratory diseases
■ Circulatory diseases   ■ External causes   ■ Other

Source: Carolyn Stephens *et al., Environment and Health in Developing Countries: An Analysis of Intra-Urban Differentials Using Existing Data* (London School of Hygiene & Tropical Medicine in collaboration with Fundacao SEADE and Ghana Ministry of Health and Ministry of Environment, London, 1994).
Notes: Data are for the following years: Accra, Ghana, 1991; Sao Paulo, Brazil, 1992; and Prague, Czech Republic, 1993. External causes of death include violent deaths—mainly traffic accidents and homicides.

in developing countries, the burden of communicable diseases, related to poverty, combines with risks of chronic diseases, associated with social conditions, to create a double burden of ill health (16).

These changing patterns of health in urban areas can be seen by examining data on the causes of death in three very different cities: Accra, Sao Paulo, and Prague, Czech Republic. (See Figure 2.1.) The health profile depicted for each urban center reflects not only the impact of environmental health policies pursued in the past but also the importance of the demographic mix in particular urban centers.

In both Prague and Sao Paulo, two economically advanced cities, the proportion of deaths attributable to infectious and parasitic diseases is now extremely low for the overall population (0.3 percent in Prague and 4 percent in Sao Paulo) (17) (18). To a great extent, these statistics illustrate the level of wealth of each urban center and the relative success of past initiatives for improving urban health conditions. Both Prague and Sao Paulo have made efforts to provide comprehensive water and sanitation coverage, along with vaccination programs for preventable infections and basic health services.

In Accra, the picture is somewhat different: infections (largely diarrheal diseases, malaria, and measles) account for 18 percent of all deaths (19). Limited access to basic water and sanitation facilities explains part of the profile within Accra. Yet, demographic factors are also important. Of the three cities, Accra contains the largest proportion of children under age 5, and young children are most vulnerable to the risk of death from infections.

Respiratory diseases are significant in all three cities, accounting for 12 percent of all deaths in Accra and Sao Paulo and 3.5 percent in Prague (20) (21).

In both Accra and Sao Paulo, diseases of the circulatory system are the primary cause of death in the population as a whole (24 and 33 percent of all deaths, respectively) (22). In Prague, as in most developed cities, the proportion is even higher (54 percent). Accidents and violence emerge as more important than infections or respiratory conditions in both Prague and Sao Paulo (23) (24).

and cancer are now leading causes of death, just as they are in London and Washington, D.C. (6) (7) (8) (9). Violence has now reached epidemic proportions in some urban centers in South America as well as North America (10) (11) (12) (13) (14) (15).

The health transition, however, is by no means complete in most cities in the developing world. In fact, the image of a smooth transition from communicable to noncommunicable diseases as development progresses does not seem to fit the evolving health profiles of these cities, many of which are struggling with high incidences of both types of problems.

Although data on overall causes of death in urban areas of the developing world are sparse, they present a general picture of urban populations in developing countries suffering the "worst of both worlds" in their mortality profiles. In other words, for residents of cities

Differences Within Cities

Perhaps as striking as differences among cities is the variation in health among different groups within the same city. This variation within cities flies in the face of conventional wisdom about the effect of urbanization on health. Until the late 1970s and early 1980s, urbanization was viewed as a consistently positive force for improved health, largely because it resulted in better access to health services.

Comparisons of average urban health figures with average rural figures suggest that this is so, but such comparisons conceal gross health inequalities within the urban population (25) (26) (27). In many cities in developing countries, evidence now suggests that health conditions for the urban poor are sometimes worse than they are for their rural counterparts (28) (29) (30). (See Figure 2.2.)

In the developing world, mortality rates are significantly higher for children in squatter areas of cities than for children living in nonsquatter areas (31). For example, in Tondo, a large squatter settlement in Manila, Philippines, infant mortality rates are nearly three times greater than those in nonsquatter sections of the city. In addition, the incidence of diarrhea in Tondo (adults and children) is two times higher and the incidence of tuberculosis is nine times higher than in wealthier sections of Manila (32).

In interpreting environmental health differentials, it is important to keep in mind that poor people in general tend to be more vulnerable, both physically and economically. With their greater levels of exposure to poor sanitation, overcrowded conditions, inadequate nutrition, social stresses, and environmental pollutants and their limited access to health care, they are more likely both to get sick and to remain sick. Moreover, the economic consequences of illness tend to be more serious among the poor, often undermining the already fragile finances of the household. The financial loss that occurs when an income earner is ill or when medical bills must be paid can help create a cycle of poverty and chronic ill health (33).

Nor are the health differentials between wealthy and poor confined to the developing world. In cities in developed countries as well, the poor show disproportionately high rates of death and disease for a range of problems. For example, in New York City, children in overcrowded poor households in the Bronx have a

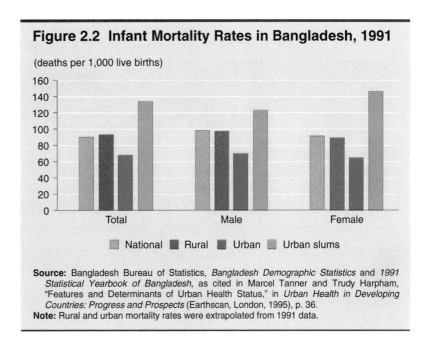

Figure 2.2 Infant Mortality Rates in Bangladesh, 1991

(deaths per 1,000 live births)

Legend: National, Rural, Urban, Urban slums

Categories: Total, Male, Female

Source: Bangladesh Bureau of Statistics, *Bangladesh Demographic Statistics* and *1991 Statistical Yearbook of Bangladesh,* as cited in Marcel Tanner and Trudy Harpham, "Features and Determinants of Urban Health Status," in *Urban Health in Developing Countries: Progress and Prospects* (Earthscan, London, 1995), p. 36.
Note: Rural and urban mortality rates were extrapolated from 1991 data.

fivefold greater risk of contracting tuberculosis than their better-off neighbors (34). In London, there are two-fold health differences in rates of heart disease, tuberculosis, and other respiratory diseases between those living in poor areas and their wealthier neighbors (35). Similar patterns can be discerned in social risks too. In Kansas City, Missouri, in the central part of the United States, African-American adolescents (12- to 16-year-olds), who tend to live in poorer areas, have a 13-fold greater risk of injury from firearms than white adolescents (541 compared with 42 per 100,000 persons per year) (36).

Urban violence tends to concentrate in particular areas of cities and towns. In a 1990 study, mortality rates among African Americans in Harlem were found to be the highest in New York City—and 50 percent higher than those of all African Americans. The study's authors conclude that the mortality rates among people in Harlem justify classifying Harlem as a natural disaster area. Survival analysis showed that men in Harlem were less likely than men in Bangladesh to reach age 65 (37). Data on the distribution of violence within cities in the developing world are sparse. In Cape Town, however, homicides account for 19 percent of deaths in the black community, but just 8 percent of deaths in the city as a whole (38).

The Special Vulnerability of Children and Women

Even among the poor, certain groups are more susceptible to both biological and social risks than others. The very young and the very old, for instance, tend to be more susceptible to infectious diseases and are more likely to die if they do become ill.

Mark Edwards/Still Pictures

At risk. Poor women and children are especially vulnerable to both physical and social threats in the urban environment. Above, a homeless woman and child in Calcutta.

Studies show that the increased health risks that impoverished children face in cities can be significant. Children are exposed to a barrage of infectious agents and toxic contaminants during play, at meals, and at school or other communal activities (39). Intestinal disorders such as severe diarrhea, caused by a variety of bacteria, viruses, and parasites, are among the most prevalent and serious health risks to children exposed to poor sanitation or contaminated water supplies. Of the 5 million children who are estimated to die annually of diarrheal diseases in the developing world, the majority come from poor urban families (40).

Respiratory infections, which are the second most common cause of death among children in the developing world (41), also pose a particular risk to children in urban settings, with overcrowding and air pollution—both indoors and outdoors—being two significant contributors to this risk. Overcrowded conditions increase the levels of exposure to infected individuals,

which facilitates the more rapid dissemination of respiratory diseases (42).

Indoor and outdoor air pollutants can damage children's lung tissues, predisposing them to viral or bacterial infections. There is also evidence that urban environmental factors associated with lower-income settings can aggravate, and perhaps even initiate, childhood asthma. These factors include indoor pollutants from cooking fires, coal-fired heaters, secondhand cigarette smoke, and other sources, as well as allergens associated with dust mites and cockroaches (43) (44) (45).

Infant and child death in poor settlements is often not simply the result of a discrete disease but the outcome of a series of health problems. This typically involves an interplay of malnutrition, a variety of infectious diseases, and, possibly, exposure to chemical pollutants. Lack of health care increases vulnerability.

Social factors, too, can be important in increasing the health risks that urban children face. Adolescents seem to be particularly affected by inadequate urban social environments. Data from some cities in North and South America suggest striking, age-specific problems with homicides among young men and boys. In public health terms, violence now overshadows infectious diseases as a cause of death among older children in some urban environments (46) (47). For example, violence—mostly homicides—accounted for 86 percent of all deaths of boys ages 15 to 19 in Sao Paulo in 1992 and more than half of all deaths among 5- to 14-year-old boys (48).

Urban women also face increased health risks, largely because of their social and economic roles, which expose them to greater numbers of environmental hazards. Women are usually responsible for taking care of sick children, increasing their direct exposure to disease-causing organisms. They usually take primary responsibility for obtaining water and washing laundry—activities that can be hazardous where sanitation is poor, washing facilities are inadequate, and water supplies are contaminated (49). As the household food preparer, urban women in the developing world are often exposed to very high levels of smoke from cookstoves, which also put them at risk of receiving burns.

Physiological factors also play a part in making women's health more vulnerable. Women are particularly at risk during pregnancy and after childbirth, being more vulnerable to some chemical toxins and more susceptible to certain diseases, such as malaria (50) (51).

The kinds of employment that women have access to often put them at risk as well. Many urban women in developing countries work in small-scale industries where toxic chemicals are often used without adequate safeguards. Piecework done at home, such as fabricating sandals or articles of clothing, is a common source of income among urban women and can involve the use of dangerous adhesives and other flammable or toxic materials (52). Risks to women due to chemical exposure, repetitive motion, or stress are high even in many modern urban industries such as microelectronics and large-scale garment manufacturing, where women make up a high percentage of the work force (53). Prostitution, with its predominantly urban focus, is associated with a host of health risks, from sexually transmitted diseases such as AIDS and gonorrhea to physical abuse.

Social factors are especially important contributors to the increased health vulnerability that urban women experience. Violence against women—within and outside of the home—has been increasingly recognized as a prime threat to women's health in both the developed and the developing world (54). Although this is by no means a strictly urban phenomenon, its incidence is high in cities and may be increased by psychosocial factors such as stress associated with poor urban housing, inadequate income, and lack of equal opportunity to employment or education, although the precise links between these stresses and violence are not well defined (55).

THE URBAN PHYSICAL ENVIRONMENT AND HEALTH

A century and a half ago, average urban mortality rates in European cities were often far higher than those in the surrounding rural areas (56). Bad sanitation, which then referred to a range of poorly understood environmental health hazards rather than just disposal of excreta, was increasingly seen as being responsible for this urban disadvantage. Prominent scientists studied sanitary conditions and health, and reformers in urban centers around the world discussed both the technical and the moral aspects of urban sanitary reform.

In many ways, the so-called sanitary revolution that resulted from these reforms was the environmental movement of the 19th Century. As in environmental discussions today, one of the most heated debates was about the appropriate role for government and whether attempts to impose sanitary improvements constituted an infringement on what would now be called the private sector. Eventually, the reformers won. One reason is that, although the health problems were far worse in poor areas, the wealthy were also at risk. Politicians even worried that the military strength of their nations was being undermined by urban health problems (57). The politically powerful gradually accepted the fact that

the threat from these unhealthful urban conditions was indeed public and required a public response.

The environmental concerns of the world's wealthy have moved on, and international attention has followed suit. Now, comparisons of average urban and rural mortality rates do not display the same urban disadvantage, even in countries where urban sanitation is poor. However, as illustrated in the previous section, averages hide gross disparities in the health status of urban dwellers. Many city residents face environmental conditions roughly comparable to those that shocked the bourgeoisie in the 19th Century. Although the environmental health burden for the urban poor, now mostly in the developing countries, may not be as high as it once was, in poor neighborhoods inadequacies in the physical environment remain the most important causes of urban ill health globally (58).

Shared standpipe. *Limited access to water supplies greatly increases the risk of disease. In Favela Rocinha, one of the largest shantytowns in Rio de Janeiro, Brazil, hundreds of poor families share a public tap.*

Box 2.2 ASHA Works To Improve Health in Delhi

Many health problems of the urban poor arise from the poverty and the degraded environment in which they live. However, conventional health delivery systems in most cities provide curative services to people, whereas environmental improvements or social services are the responsibility of different government departments. Because these departments tend to work in isolation, they seldom make a coordinated effort to improve the quality of life of the poor. Even existing health care systems are often beyond the reach of the poor because of cost, inconvenient locations, and overcrowded conditions (1).

In Delhi, India, a local nongovernmental organization, Action for Security Health for All (ASHA), has spent the past 6 years trying to improve the health of poor residents through community-based programs that address both poverty and the environment. The challenge is daunting: more than 1 million of Delhi's residents live in *jhuggie* shelters, temporary structures made of mud, thatch, plastic, and other discarded objects. *Jhuggies* are small and devoid of ventilation or natural light; many are susceptible to fire, dust, smoke, and noise pollution. The streets of *jhuggie* settlements are heaped with garbage, attracting dogs, pigs, flies, and

mosquitos. One study found that although latrines were available in 46 percent of the settlements, most were poorly maintained, and nearly 41 percent of the residents still defecated in the open. *Jhuggies* are often located near garbage dumps, power plants and factories, and roads, exposing residents to risks from chemical residues, toxic wastes, and car exhaust fumes.

Not surprisingly, *jhuggie* residents—particularly women and children—are especially prone to respiratory and waterborne diseases. The infant mortality rate in *jhuggie* settlements is 100 per 1,000 live births, compared with 40 per 1,000 live births for the city as a whole. Roughly 40 percent of children under age 2 have not received all immunizations; 40 percent of women and children suffer severe malnutrition; just 17 percent of pregnant women receive at least three prenatal checkups; and 80 percent of all deliveries are conducted by untrained midwives.

ASHA began in 1988 as an emergency health clinic in a slum in south Delhi to deal with a serious cholera epidemic. During this period, the clinic staff observed that although treatments were effective in curing patients, the incidence of disease remained unaffected. Indeed,

there were repeated recurrences of preventable illnesses. Realizing that the community's health problems were intricately linked to poverty, pollution, and environmental degradation, ASHA began to focus on a broader approach to dealing with health, directing its efforts toward improving the environment, empowering women, increasing the literacy rate, and educating residents about the links between environment and health.

ASHA began by forging a partnership with the public agency responsible for delivering services to squatter settlements. Acting as mediator between the public agency and community members, ASHA managed to get the government to implement site and service improvement projects. ASHA also helped community members form cooperatives. The cooperative objectives were to improve local environmental conditions by acquiring land rights and establishing long-term leases, providing home improvement loans, maintaining and repairing common spaces, and extending coverage of basic services such as water and sanitation facilities and roads.

These initial efforts were marred by difficulties. The site and service upgrading schemes had mixed results as news

Most of the following discussion centers on the physical environmental conditions that pose a large risk to health and also on the question of who bears the burden. In poor cities, and particularly poor neighborhoods, the most threatening environmental problems are usually those in the household or neighborhood as opposed to the broader city (59). Inadequate household water supplies are typically more damaging than polluted waterways to the health of urban residents. Exposure to air pollution may be higher in smoky kitchens than outdoors. Uncollected waste in neighborhoods poses more of a threat than waste at the city dump. (See Box 2.2.)

The wealthy, by contrast, can avoid some of these local threats by buying better houses in safer neighborhoods or buying water from safer sources. However, many environmental problems, such as air pollution and lead contamination, are spread over large areas, and it is difficult for households or individuals to buy their way out.

In one of the few attempts to compare systematically the environmental health risks in low-income neighborhoods with those of a city as a whole, a recent study of Quito, Ecuador, found that all inhabitants faced a high risk from microbial food contamination and outdoor air pollution, whereas the inhabitants of low-income neighborhoods also faced a high risk from bad water and sanitation, indoor air pollution, and occupational hazards (60). Roughly, the better-off citizens of Quito could do little to avoid buying locally marketed foods or breathing the air outdoors.

Although the aggregate health effects of such city-wide problems are typically less than those associated with poor sanitation or other problems affecting poor households, the more articulate and politically influential members of the public often perceive them as the more important health threat. The result is that resources are often devoted disproportionately to addressing these problems relative to their public health impact.

of slum improvement attracted additional settlers and increased land market values, displacing the original residents. Local power struggles arose over access to the improved facilities, and the cooperatives ultimately dissolved after ASHA decided to withdraw from the daily tasks of running them.

Through this experience, however, ASHA learned that women play a far greater role than men in managing households and the community. Women's health is a decisive factor in the well-being of their families; thus, they have a much larger stake in improving the living conditions in the community. A clear disadvantage of the first cooperative structure was that it had excluded women from an active role in community decisionmaking.

In response, ASHA helped form Mahila Mandals within some of the Delhi *jhuggies*. Mahila Mandals are community-based women's groups that meet once a week to talk about community issues and that also serve as a forum for health education sessions, income-earning activities, and loans. ASHA acts as a facilitator, helping to inform the community about relevant government policies and serving as a communication link to the formal system.

Recognizing that women play a key role as health care providers, ASHA set up a training program for female community health workers called *basti sevikas*. Selected through a process of community consultation and aptitude testing, *basti sevikas* are trained to provide basic health care treatment for colds, fevers, coughs, and diarrhea, and for more serious diseases such as malaria, scabies, and worms. Each *sevika* is responsible for 200 families and charges a small fee for visits. *Basti sevikas* also provide health education about environment-related issues such as hand washing and boiling water, encourage pregnant women to go for prenatal care, and maintain health records for households in the settlements. In exchange, the *basti sevikas* also receive a monthly honorarium.

The use of *basti sevikas* has proved to be an effective way of improving health care delivery to the urban poor. By selecting women from the community, ASHA ensures that health care is available to the community at all times. *Basti sevikas* reduce the load on the formal health care system by taking care of illnesses not requiring the attention of a doctor or hospital. Although the *basti sevikas* charge a small fee for their services, they are much

more affordable than formal medical care for the urban poor.

Even now, ASHA's work is not obstacle free. Factors such as heavy workloads, resistance from husbands and families, and personal inhibitions prevent women from participating in Mahila Mandals. Residents resist paying fees to *basti sevikas* because they are not formally trained. Still, by approaching health care at the community level and encouraging residents to take charge of their environments, ASHA has helped to improve the health of many *jhuggie* residents. Between 1988 and 1993, ASHA increased its reach from 1 slum and 4,000 people to 21 slums and about 115,000 people. Empirical data are lacking, but a community survey shows that through ASHA's programs, child morbidity and malnutrition have decreased, residents are more likely to seek treatment for minor ailments, and overall environmental conditions in the slums have improved.

References and Notes

1. This box was taken from Pratibha Mehta, "Action for Securing Health for All," Mega-Cities Urban Environmental Poverty Case Study Series (Mega-Cities Project and National Institute for Urban Affairs, New York and New Delhi, India, 1994), pp. 1–40.

Even in cities that have excellent water systems, relatively clean air, and most other features typically associated with environmental health, there are serious health hazards that fall heavily on the poor. As described below, many of these involve more social than physical threats to health: stress, depression, chemical dependency, and violence. Others, however, such as crowding, clearly have a physical aspect.

The following discussion distinguishes environmental health problems both by their scale of impact (for instance, at the household and neighborhood levels or the city and regional levels) and by the principal environmental medium through which people are affected (air, water, food, and pests) or proximate cause (e.g., traffic accidents). However, there is no truly satisfactory way to classify environmental health hazards, which do not respect boundaries, either physical or conceptual. That, in part, defines the challenge of environmental management: it is not possible to deal with each problem in isolation.

Household and Neighborhood Problems

Water and Sanitation

Various diarrheal and other diseases are spread via the fecal-oral route, and this route is far better traveled where water supplies and sanitary conditions are inadequate. Although contaminated water can carry many infectious agents, it can nonetheless be a critical tool in maintaining good hygiene. Washing, even with water that might be better not to drink, can help curb diseases spread by the fecal-oral route as well as a variety of other health problems ranging from scabies to louse-borne typhus.

Better sanitation can lead to less contact with fecal material at defecation sites and less indirect exposure via water, insects, food, or human carriers. Given the number of illnesses and deaths attributed globally to diarrhea, it seems fair to say that human feces remain one of the world's most hazardous pollutants and that related water and sanitation inadequacies still constitute one of the world's most serious health problems.

In many poor urban neighborhoods in the developing world, other hazards contribute to the burden of diseases spread by the fecal-oral route as well. Indeed, the boundaries between water, sanitation, food contamination, insects, and solid waste problems are blurred. Although it is difficult to determine which routes are the most important, the most common technological interventions involve providing new facilities both for supplying water and for sanitation. Epidemiological studies have consistently shown that improving access to such facilities can reduce the incidence of diarrheal disease substantially—more than 20 percent, according to a recent review (61).

In the developed world, these problems were solved, or were at least displaced, by providing indoor piped water and flush toilets to virtually all urban residents. The same is true for the wealthy in developing countries. For the poor majority, however, comprehensive technological solutions like these are unrealistic. Neither low-income residents nor their financially strapped governments can afford anything like complete coverage with indoor plumbing.

In cities of the developing world, households without indoor piping often obtain their water from a number of sources, such as overcrowded or distant communal standpipes, expensive private water vendors, or heavily polluted wells or open waterways. Those without flush toilets may end up using pit latrines, pan latrines, or latrines located over ponds, streams, drains, or open sewers—all of which demand far more rigorous hygiene behavior than is required for the more standardized technologies of the wealthy.

Technical improvements are an important part of the solution, and there has been some success with relatively simple but more hygienic latrines (62). For example, the "ventilated improved pit" latrine developed in Zimbabwe is designed to eliminate flies and odors while providing a more hygienic and comfortable facility. Overcrowding, however, combined with poor maintenance, can and often does defeat such design improvements. Public latrines are difficult to manage and, when overused, can become public health hazards—less hygienic and convenient for the user than defecation in the open. Even when private latrines are available, sharing them among several families seems to increase sanitation problems (63).

Poorly treated or untreated wastes released into open waterways can also have health impacts on water users downstream. Although the overall burden on health is relatively small, it can be quite severe locally. During a cholera epidemic, for example, the ingestion of seafood contaminated by sewage can be an important transmission route.

Housing

The quality of housing is a significant factor affecting health. Case studies in many larger cities in the developing world show that as much as 30 to 60 percent of the urban population lives in substandard housing, although this percentage may be less in smaller cities (64). Housing quality extends beyond the availability of water or sanitation facilities. Overcrowding, dampness, inadequate insulation from the extremes of heat and cold, pest infestation, noise, dust, inadequate drainage, and insufficient ventilation all contribute to the health risks associated with substandard housing. Women and children, many of whom spend considerable time in the house, are especially subject to these hazards (65).

Overcrowding is particularly common among poor urban residents, many of whom live in cheap boarding houses or tenements. In Delhi, India, a case study of a typical two-story tenement found 518 people (constituting 106 separate households) living in 49 rooms, allowing approximately 1.5 square meters per person (66). Overcrowding can aid the transmission of a variety of infectious diseases, particularly airborne respiratory diseases such as colds, pneumonia, and tuberculosis (67). Overcrowded conditions, where privacy is an unaccustomed luxury, can also be detrimental to mental health, adding stress and contributing to depression and other psychosocial disorders (68).

Also contributing to the psychological burden of inadequate housing for many is insecure tenure. Fear of eviction is a common worry among most low-income tenants or residents in illegal settlements and causes considerable stress (69).

Food Contamination

Food, like water, can transmit infectious diseases and harmful chemicals. Infectious bacteria can multiply in food, and some of the bacteria and fungi that grow on food produce toxins. The major health burden arising from food contamination is almost certainly its contribution to the diarrhea and dysentery that figure so highly in the illness and premature death of children in the developing world.

However, the extent to which food contamination is involved in the spread of these diseases is poorly understood. Epidemiological studies give little indication of the relative importance of food contamination, and one of the few attempts to estimate indirectly the share of diarrhea involving food contamination gives a strikingly wide range of 15 to 70 percent (70). Even so, it is safe to say that microbial food contamination is a health problem that is more severe in poor countries than in wealthy ones, although some kinds of contamination, such as salmonella, may be more common in the latter.

Food handling and storage practices are critical factors in food contamination, and the dangers of contamination are heightened where water and sanitation are inadequate. Washing hands before food preparation and avoiding contact between food and flies are two obvious examples of preventive measures in the home. They are also practices that are easier, although less important, in homes with good water and sanitation facilities.

Contamination can also occur during transport or processing, before the food is purchased, which is difficult for the consumer to monitor. Finally, urban consumption patterns can contribute to food contamination problems. In a study of Monrovia, Liberia, it was found that most poor urban households stored cooked food, and 63 percent of the stored food samples were heavily contaminated with enterobacteria (81 percent for baby foods) (71). On the other hand, rural households were less inclined to store cooked food, and only 39 percent of their food samples were contaminated (72).

In wealthy countries, complex regulations and inspection procedures help to control food-handling practices at the point of sale in restaurants and markets. However, in poor countries, such regulations are often too costly to enforce. Informal means of avoiding bad food provide an important alternative to regulation. For example, the economic lure of future sales and the psychology of personal contact can induce a vendor to avoid selling contaminated food to regular customers. However, such informal mechanisms are generally less effective in an urban context. In any case, measures that help to prevent food spoilage are likely to be far more effective than measures that attempt to stop spoiled food from being sold.

Pests

Rats, fleas, and the bubonic plague firmly established pests in the annals of urban environmental health. Even today, a minor outbreak of plague can quickly make international headlines. (See Box 2.3.) However, for most wealthy urbanites of the developed world, diseases transmitted by pests are no longer a major concern. And in urban areas in the developing world, mosquitos and flies are far more important health threats than rats or fleas.

Neither mosquitos nor flies are particularly urban. Indeed, there is a far greater variety of habitats and species of these insects in rural areas. In addition, the opportunities for controlling such disease vectors are generally greater in urban areas. However, some types of disease-bearing mosquitos and flies have adapted well to particular urban habitats and find themselves relatively free of competition (73).

The *Aedes aegypti* mosquito breeds in small containers, such as flower vases and water drums, and has been carried from its East African home to every tropical continent, often following the used tire trade. Its Asian relative, *Aedes albopictus*, is now using the same trick and has recently invaded North and South America, the Mediterranean, and West Africa. Both of these species transmit dengue, a disease of increasing importance in Latin America and Southeast Asia. (See Chapter 8, "Population and Human Development.")

In African and Indian cities, malaria is the most prevalent mosquito-borne disease and is often a prime cause of hospital admissions and deaths, particularly among children. In Accra, for instance, malaria accounted for more than 40 percent of reported illnesses at outpatient facilities from 1987 to 1990 (74). In both regions, urbanization has created important new breeding sites. In India, for instance, the *Anopheles stephensi* mosquito breeds in overhead water storage tanks.

Just as urban mosquito problems are intimately linked to water, urban fly problems are linked to waste. Various families of flies have adapted to the opportunities of urban ecology. The most obvious health risk is that they provide a shortcut on the fecal-oral route, although the extent of their contribution is still not clear. The housefly, along with several other species, is a filth feeder and breeder. Given poor sanitation, some flies are likely to be in contact with human feces and later land on human food, drink, or skin. Piles of garbage increase fly populations. Open food preparation and food storage areas provide opportunities for flies to land on food.

Some diseases are transmitted by mites, face flies, or other pests that thrive in dwellings or neighborhoods (75). Chagas' disease is carried by triatomine bugs, leishmaniasis by sand flies, schistosomiasis by snails, scabies by mites, and yaws by face flies. Globally, these diseases are less serious urban health problems than those spread by mosquitos or the fecal-oral route diseases transmitted by flies. In many locations, however, they can be critical problems.

Some of the measures used to control insects and other pests indoors create their own environmental health threats. Mosquito coils and other substances burned to repel insects cause air pollution. Indoor spraying with aerosols and pump sprays exposes residents to potentially damaging pesticides. There may well be

Box 2.3 The Black Death Revisited: India's 1994 Plague Epidemic

In September 1994, nearly 30 years after the last urban outbreak of plague in India, plague struck Surat, a city in the western part of India (1). The Surat outbreak, which killed 56 people nationwide, did not have the devastating impact originally feared, but it did generate considerable anxiety worldwide while also exacting a heavy economic toll in India (2) (3). It also served as a chilling reminder of how rapid urbanization and deterioration of the urban environment can bring people into contact with forgotten disease vectors.

Plague has long been a scourge of cities. The disease, caused by the bacterium *Yersinia pestis*, is best known for its role in the Black Death that swept across Europe and Asia in the Middle Ages, killing roughly one fourth of the population of Western Europe—an estimated 20 million people. Yet, its roots may be more ancient still: as early as 1190 BC, Homer referred to a plague-like disease that was associated with the movement of rats into populated areas (4).

The last major epidemic occurred early in the 20th Century in India, where it killed more than 10 million people (5). By the 1970s, although a number of small outbreaks continued to occur around the world, plague as an urban health threat had been largely relegated to the past. Or so the world thought until the Surat outbreak.

Two Types of Plague

Bubonic plague—the form of plague that ravaged Europe—is transmitted to people through the bite of an infected flea. In urban areas, rats are the primary source of plague-infected fleas. In parts of Asia, Africa, South America, and the United States, wild rodent populations are persistently infected with the plague organism, serving as a natural reservoir for the disease.

However, the outbreak of plague that occurred in Surat was pneumonic plague—a highly contagious form of the disease that kills 100 percent of its victims if left untreated. Pneumonic plague is caused by the same disease organism that causes bubonic plague, but it infects the lungs rather than the lymph system. Since the disease invades the lungs, it can be transmitted to others in close physical contact through exhaled sputum droplets. Crowding and poor sanitation can provide ideal conditions for the spread of this type of plague (6) (7).

Because it is so contagious, and thus easily portable from one location to the next, the pneumonic plague outbreak in Surat caused panic both locally and internationally. In Surat, hysteria followed reports of the rapid and painful deaths of seven people on September 21 and the preliminary diagnosis of plague.

The fear of an epidemic was so intense among Surat residents that within 4 days, one quarter of the populace had fled the city. This exodus fueled anxiety throughout India, with the fear that plague might be transported far and wide by Surat refugees. On September 25, the government brought in a Rapid Action Force of police to stem the exodus and to prevent frightened patients from abandoning the hospitals where they were being treated.

Fortunately, the Surat outbreak was diagnosed quickly, and widespread treatment with tetracycline was begun. About half a million capsules of tetracycline were distributed in Surat alone. The death rate dropped dramatically, from roughly 10 each day from September 21 to 23 to none at all after September 28 (8). Not a single case was confirmed in Bombay, the nearest large city.

Why an Epidemic?

Why did plague reemerge in an urban setting after many years of relative quiescence? Evidence points to two principal factors: the squalid conditions in much of Surat and the occurrence of two recent natural disasters in the area. Both of these factors contributed to bringing a plague-infected rat population into contact with the human population of Surat. Even though pneumonic plague does not require rats and fleas for its transmission among humans, the Surat rat population is regarded as the original source of the infection.

A year before the plague incident, an earthquake measuring 6.4 on the Richter scale hit the adjacent state of Maharashtra, killing at least 10,000 people and causing extensive damage (9). Researchers believe that the disturbances and resettlement associated with the earthquake helped bring the wild ro-

---

cases in which the health damage caused by using such measures outweighs their sometimes minimal effect on the spread of pest-borne disease.

Air Pollution from Domestic Sources

For much of the 20th Century, air pollution has been identified with urban smog or smoke spewing forth from factory chimneys. In wealthy countries, these images can seem outdated amid discussions of invisible pollutants. In the developing world, however, smoky household fires probably constitute the largest air-pollution health hazard, with women and children being the principal victims.

Studies of personal exposure and indoor air pollution levels indicate that although there is considerable vari-

ation, many users of smoky fuels are exposed to disturbingly high levels of particulates and other pollutants (76). Rough data suggest that, on average, indoor air pollution tends to be a problem that is worse in rural environments than in urban environments. However, in the homes of the urban poor, especially those in small towns, particulate concentrations are likely to be higher than urban averages and to exceed those of rural households.

Three major health risks have been associated with the domestic use of polluting fuels (77). First, by irritating the respiratory passages and perhaps through other means, pollution from domestic fuels may facilitate the spread of acute respiratory infection, a major killer of children under age 5 in poor countries (78). Second,

dent population inhabiting the forested area near Surat into contact with the domestic rat population, introducing the disease into the local rat population in the process.

Surat's sanitation problems then helped the rat population grow dramatically. Surat, a city of 2.2 million, generates close to 1,250 metric tons of garbage each day, 250 metric tons of which remain uncollected. To make matters worse, floodwaters inundated the city during the 1994 monsoon, particularly in low-lying slum areas near the river. Surat residents complain that nothing was done to remove the great piles of rubbish that remained after the floodwaters receded, offering an ideal habitat for rats.

LESSONS LEARNED

An international response followed in the aftermath of the Surat plague outbreak. The World Health Organization (WHO) announced plans to establish a Disease Intelligence Unit that will function independently when such outbreaks occur to help diagnose the problem quickly. In addition, WHO asked the International Civil Aviation Organization to tighten its health controls at all international airports and to strengthen quarantine measures that seem to have lapsed since the eradication of smallpox.

India has also taken steps to prepare for future plague incidents. In response to the outbreak, medical school course work has been revised to address

plague in greater detail. The National Institute for Communicable Disease's plague research unit has been modernized to make diagnosis easier. In addition to activating plague control units all over the country, the national government plans to set up a more sophisticated national surveillance system (10).

This reemergence of plague is a striking reminder that infectious diseases have not been defeated. Malaria has consolidated its strength as a major killer, although it had almost disappeared a few decades ago. Cholera and tuberculosis are donning new faces with drug-resistant strains.

By comparison, the health toll of the Surat plague was relatively minor. It killed just 56 people, whereas the malaria epidemic in Rajasthan in 1994 killed nearly 300 people (11). By any other name, the plague probably would not have caused the kind of panic that it did during this outbreak.

In financial terms, however, the plague's toll was much greater, costing the Indian economy in excess of $600 million. More than 45,000 people canceled their travel plans to India, and the country's hotel occupancy rate dipped to 20 to 60 percent. Many countries stopped air and ship traffic to India altogether. In total, exports from the country suffered a $420 million loss (12).

References and Notes

1. John W. Anderson, "Plague Deaths Recede in Stricken Indian City," *Washington Post* (September 27, 1994), p. A10.

2. Centers for Disease Control and Prevention, "Update: Human Plague—India, 1994," *Morbidity and Mortality Weekly Report*, Vol. 43, No. 41 (October 21, 1994), p. 761.

3. Molly Moore, "Plague Turns India into Region's Pariah: Outbreak of Disease Hurts Tourism, Trade," *Washington Post* (October 2, 1994), pp. A29, A33.

4. Institute of Medicine, *Emerging Infections: Microbial Threats to Health in the United States*, Joshua Lederberg *et al.,* eds. (National Academy Press, Washington, D.C., 1992), pp. 16–17.

5. *Ibid.,* p. 16.

6. Tom Post *et al.,* "The Plague of Panic," *Newsweek* (October 10, 1994), pp. 40–41.

7. "The Old Enemy," *The Economist* (October 1, 1994), pp. 40–41.

8. J.C. Gandhi, "Plague Outbreak in Surat, Gujarat," presentation at the World Health Organization Interregional Meeting on Prevention and Control of Plague, New Delhi, India, March 1995.

9. V.K. Saxena *et al.,* "Earthquake in Maharashtra: Impact Assessment on Communicable Diseases Potential," *Journal of Basic and Applied Medicine*, Vol. 2, No. 1 (1993), p. 77.

10. Government of India, *Report of the Technical Advisory Committee on Plague* (Government of India, Delhi, India, 1995).

11. World Health Organization, "India Malaria," *Weekly Epidemiological Record*, Vol. 69, No. 43 (October 28, 1994), p. 321.

12. Kai Friese, "The Morning After," *India Today* (October 31, 1994), pp. 30–39.

long-term exposure may contribute to chronic lung diseases such as chronic bronchitis, emphysema, and asthma, which are significant health problems among adult women. Third, long-term exposure is a risk factor for cancer.

As with inadequate water supplies and sanitation, the extent of ill health actually caused by exposure to domestic smoke is difficult to determine. Cancer and chronic respiratory problems are likely to be the consequence of long-term or past exposures, which are hard to assess. There are many other risk factors for respiratory infection—crowding, poor ventilation, malnutrition, poor sanitation, and lack of immunization—and they tend to be interrelated (79). Other sources of domestic air pollution may relate to respiratory illness as well,

such as mosquito coils, waste burning, and tobacco smoking. Generally, the women and children who are more exposed to air pollution from domestic fires are also likely to be more exposed to other environmental hazards, which could also account for ill health.

Household fuel choice in the developing world is often described as an energy ladder, with dirty fuels such as crop residues and firewood at the bottom. These are followed by charcoal, kerosene, liquid propane gas, and finally, electricity (80). Generally, the higher up the ladder, the less polluting the fuel. The cleaner and more convenient fuels such as kerosene, liquid propane, and electricity are usually favored by wealthy households.

Although wood and crop wastes are less common in cities, charcoal and coal are fairly common. Charcoal is

Mark Edwards/Still Pictures

Smoky fuels. Unable to afford clean fuels, the urban poor are exposed to high levels of pollutants from the burning of firewood, coal, and other biomass fuels.

widely used by poor and even middle-class households in African towns and cities and, to a lesser extent, households in Asian and Latin American urban areas. In terms of respirable particulates, which probably represent the major health risk of these fuels, charcoal is considerably less polluting than wood, although carbon monoxide exposure may be higher (81). Coal emissions are heavily dependent on the type of coal, but they can be relatively high in both particulates and carbon monoxide (82). Studies of coal use in China have produced some of the most convincing evidence of a link between domestic fuel use and cancer (83).

Some indoor air pollution problems are specifically urban. A large number of domestic users of smoky fuels can create a neighborhood air pollution problem and can even contribute to citywide air pollution problems, as has happened in Beijing. Studies in South Africa indicate that whether the neighborhood is electrified, and perhaps even whether the school is located in an electrified neighborhood, can make a significant difference in the level of children's exposure to particulates (84). Exposure to pollution from domestic fires therefore seems to be yet another factor that cannot be easily controlled by individual households in an urban setting.

Although smoke and other combustion products are perhaps the most damaging of indoor air pollution, they are not the only source. Formaldehyde, chloroform, and other organic chemicals emitted by building materials or furnishings, asbestos fibers from insulation materials, and radon are other significant pollutants. These may be of particular concern in office buildings or other urban institutional settings that have restricted or closed-loop ventilation systems, giving rise to the so-called sick building syndrome (85) (86).

Solid Waste

Most domestic solid waste is not a direct threat to health, although it is safer to avoid it. Compared with industrial waste, it contains few hazardous chemicals. However, fecal matter is often mixed with domestic waste, especially where disposable diapers are used or sanitary facilities are scarce. If solid waste is kept in closed containers and removed regularly, as is usually the case in wealthy neighborhoods in developing and developed countries, the health risks to local residents are minimal.

Problems of waste disposal are most severe in poor cities in developing countries. Door-to-door waste collection is too expensive for many households or municipalities to afford, and in any case, the streets of many poor neighborhoods are too narrow for vehicles. Collection points can easily become small garbage dumps, especially when collection is intermittent. In many poor countries, public budgets have been under great pressure in recent years, and waste collection is often among the services to suffer most (87) (88). Solid waste often creates one of the most visible environmental problems in low-income communities.

The two groups most directly exposed to solid waste are children and wastepickers in low-income neighborhoods in cities in developing countries. Accumulated garbage, however, can also contribute indirectly to neighborhood environmental health problems by providing food or breeding sites for flies and other pests.

Citywide Problems

Although the environmental threats people are exposed to in their homes and neighborhoods tend to pose the greatest health risks, some citywide problems pose significant risks as well. These include occupational exposures, ambient air pollution, traffic accidents, and exposure to lead. Box 2.4 explores which types of problems tend to be most severe—household or city-wide—by wealth and city size.

Occupational Exposures

Hazards in the workplace can be a significant addition to the health burdens that urban life imposes. These can include contact with a wide range of toxic substances and communicable diseases, unsafe machinery, unhealthful noise levels, inadequate lighting or ventilation, and extremes of heat or cold. These hazards are often made worse by a lack of protective clothing or equipment (89).

In many developing countries, the problem of occupational hazards is compounded by the lack of any sick pay or compensation for workplace injuries, as well as a lack of adequate occupational health care (90). In developing nations in Asia and Africa, less than 25 percent of the work force is thought to have access to any kind of occupational health service (91). In addition, appropriate occupational health standards have been neither universally adopted nor enforced.

Occupational exposures are thought to be widely underdiagnosed and underreported and therefore to be a greater problem than government statistics sometimes indicate (92). For example, researchers found that the number of health-impaired workers at a single Mexican steel mill was roughly twice the number officially recorded for the whole of Mexico in 1988; the researchers reported that more than 80 percent of the mill workers were exposed to extreme heat, noise, and toxic dust (93).

The most common occupational diseases include respiratory diseases caused by particulates such as asbestos, silicon, and cotton; metal poisoning from lead; pesticide poisoning; hearing loss from excessive noise; and skin diseases due to chemical exposures (94) (95). In some instances, disease rates among exposed workers can be very high. In asbestos factories in Bombay, India, one third of workers suffered from asbestos-related lung disease, according to a 1983 report (96).

Health hazards in the workplace may be exacerbated by malnutrition or the burden of chronic diseases that workers already suffer from, both of which may lower resistance to toxic insults or infectious diseases encountered at work. For example, nonalcoholic liver disease is widespread among Africans and Asians and may make workers who suffer from it less able to detoxify the poisons that they encounter in the workplace (97).

Hazards may also be intensified by climatic conditions, such as hot and humid weather, which make it more difficult to convince workers to use protective clothing such as respirators or aprons. Long working hours, frequently demanded by employers in the developing world or opted for by the workers themselves for financial reasons, can play a part in increasing exposures to chemical toxins or increasing accident rates due to fatigue (98).

Occupational hazards are a particular problem in small-scale or home-based industries. Small enterprises make up a surprisingly large percentage of the industrial base in many nations. For example, small-scale industries with fewer than 50 employees constitute more than 40 percent of all industries in Southeast Asia. However, conditions in these settings are often much worse than those in larger industries, with poorer physical facilities, less money available to buy safe machinery or safety equipment, and a lower priority given to worker protection and safe operating procedures (99) (100).

Small workshops and informal or home-based enterprises are often the worst in terms of occupational exposures, frequently making use of toxic chemicals without the proper equipment or precautions and sometimes spreading contaminants into the home environment. For example, automobile mechanics and gas vendors in many urban settings are routinely exposed to benzene, a gasoline additive, and suffer high rates of anemia and other diseases associated with benzene exposure (101). In Jamaica, workers in small enterprises that repair and recycle lead-acid batteries often suffer from lead contamination, which can also affect their customers and families (102).

Ambient Air Pollution

In those cities with high air pollution levels and a combination of geography and weather that prevents pollutants from dispersing, ambient air pollution can pose a significant health risk to rich and poor alike. That risk is compounded in cities where air pollution regulations or enforcement is weak. Worldwide, an estimated 1.1 billion urban residents are exposed to particulate or sulfur dioxide levels in excess of the guidelines set by the World Health Organization (WHO) (103).

Although air pollution traditionally has been linked to industrial emissions, motor vehicles have now become a major source of pollution in many cities. The problem is particularly pronounced in cities with large numbers of poorly maintained vehicles and widespread use of leaded gasoline, which is still common in Latin America, Asia, and Eastern Europe.

Studies confirm the ill effects of outdoor air pollution on health. Pollution at the levels typically found in the air of large cities has been implicated in both acute and chronic illnesses, such as asthma and chronic bronchitis. Those most vulnerable are children, the elderly, cigarette

Box 2.4 Household Environmental Problems, Wealth, and City Size

Very large cities are often portrayed as environmental disasters, offering the worst of health conditions. Certainly, these so-called megacities suffer from serious citywide health threats such as air pollution. But there is evidence that household-level problems such as sanitation or indoor air pollution, which pose the most direct threat to human health, are actually less of a problem in megacities than in many of the smaller and poorer urban settlements.

Recent studies of Accra, Ghana (1), Jakarta, Indonesia (2), and Sao Paulo, Brazil (3), confirm that bigger is not necessarily worse. Sao Paulo (9.6 million population) is larger and wealthier than Jakarta (8.2 million population), which in turn is larger and wealthier than Accra (1.2 million population) (4). Even Accra can be considered relatively large, since about two thirds of the urban population in developing countries live in cities of less than 1 million residents.

When researchers compared a series of household environmental indicators (e.g., the availability of piped water or the presence of flies in the kitchen) in Accra, Jakarta, and Sao Paulo, the household conditions improved based on the relative wealth of the city. In all cases, household conditions were better in Sao Paulo than in Jakarta, and better in Jakarta than in Accra. (See Table 1.) Other detailed household statistics also confirm this trend. The most obvious explanation is the relative wealth of the three cities.

Indeed, as indicated in Table 2, similar patterns can be observed by looking across different neighborhoods of Accra. The wealthy neighborhoods of Accra seem to have roughly the same access to water and sanitation as the Sao Paulo average, whereas the middle-class neighborhoods are roughly comparable to the Jakarta average.

Table 1 Household Environmental Indicators in Accra, Jakarta, and Sao Paulo, 1991–92

Indicator	Percent of Sample Households		
	Accra	Jakarta	Sao Paulo
No water source at residence	46	13	5
Share toilets with more than 10 households	48	14–20	<3
No home garbage collection	89	37	5
Wood or charcoal as main cooking fuel	76	2	0
Flies observed in kitchen	82	38	17

Source: Gordon McGranahan and Jacob Songsore, "Wealth, Health, and the Urban Household: Weighing Environmental Burdens in Accra, Jakarta, Sao Paulo," *Environment,* Vol. 36, No. 6 (July–August 1994), p. 9.
Note: In both Accra, Ghana, and Sao Paulo, Brazil, 1,000 households were surveyed; in Jakarta, Indonesia, the sample was 1,055 households.

Table 2 Household Environmental Indicators in Poor, Middle-Class, and Wealthy Neighborhoods of Accra, 1991–92

Indicator	Percent of Sample Households		
	Poor	Middle-Class	Wealthy
No water source at residence	55	15	4
Share toilets with more than 10 households	60	17	2
No home garbage collection	94	77	55
Wood or charcoal as main cooking fuel	85	44	30
Flies observed in kitchen	91	56	18

Source: Stockholm Environment Institute and University of Ghana households survey, unpublished data, 1991–92.
Note: The sample was drawn from the greater Accra metropolitan area and included 790 poor households, 160 middle-class households, and 50 wealthy households.

References and Notes

1. George Benneh *et al., Environmental Problems and the Urban Household in the Greater Accra Metropolitan Area (GAMA)—Ghana* (Stockholm Environment Institute, Stockholm, Sweden, 1993).

2. Charles Surjadi *et al., Household Environmental Problems in Jakarta* (Stockholm Environment Institute, Stockholm, Sweden, 1994).

3. Pedro Jacobi, *Environmental Problems Facing the Urban Household in the City of Sao Paulo, Brazil* (Stockholm Environment Institute, Stockholm, Sweden, 1994).

4. These population figures differ from those reported in United Nations (U.N.) Population Division, *World Urbanization Prospects: 1994 Revision* (U.N., New York, 1994). As discussed in Chapter 1, "Cities and the Environment," city population figures can differ dramatically depending on the administrative boundaries used. To maintain the consistency of this health study, these population figures instead of those published by the U.N. are being used.

smokers, and those who already have respiratory difficulties. Most research has concentrated on particulate matter, sulfur dioxide, and nitrogen oxides. The most dangerous pollutants appear to be small particles under 10 microns in diameter, which can be easily breathed into the lungs (104) (105). These arise mostly from motor vehicle exhaust, coal-fired power plants and boilers, and certain manufacturing industries.

Recent studies give strong evidence of the relationship between particulate air pollution and premature death (106) (107). One U.S. study that followed some 550,000 people in 151 cities over 7 years found that residents of the most polluted cities have a 15 to 17 percent higher risk of premature death from all causes than residents of the least polluted cities (108) (109). Since the late 1970s, epidemiological data from cities in the United States have consistently suggested that air pollution kills—primarily through respiratory or cardiovascular disease—about 30,000 to 60,000 people per year, accounting directly for 2 to 3 percent of all deaths (110) (111).

Such results have been replicated in urban areas in other countries as well. Studies in the Czech Republic and in Poland, parts of which suffer from very high pollutant levels, suggest that, as in the United States, 2 to 3 percent of all deaths there could be attributed to air pollution (112) (113). A similar study in Jakarta, Indonesia, where concentrations of particulates are also very high, estimates that reducing airborne particulates to the level recommended by WHO could prevent 1,400 deaths, about 2 percent of annual deaths in the city (114) (115).

Although these data suggest that air-pollution-related deaths are only a modest contributor to urban mortality rates, the role of air pollution in causing ill health among urbanites is much wider. For example, in Jakarta, researchers estimated that compliance with WHO guidelines could prevent some 600,000 asthma attacks and 125,000 cases of bronchitis in children each year (116).

Traffic Accidents

An estimated 885,000 people per year lose their lives in traffic accidents, according to WHO (117). The majority of traffic accidents (70 percent) occur in the low-and middle-income countries of the developing world, even though private vehicle usage is markedly lower there than in wealthier nations (118). The differences in risk per vehicle are dramatic: in several African countries, fatality rates exceed 100 per 10,000 registered vehicles, compared with fewer than 4 in Western Europe. In Kenya, 40 percent of road accidents happen in cities and 60 percent occur in rural areas.

The rate of fatal injuries per registered vehicle has climbed 300 percent since 1968 in Africa, whereas it has dropped slightly in the developed world (119). One reason for the higher fatality rate is that each incident frequently affects many people, for example, when an accident involves an overcrowded bus. Inadequate safety standards are another contributor to high fatality rates.

In developing countries, pedestrians account for about 40 percent of deaths from traffic accidents, compared with 20 percent in developed countries (120). A major reason for this is the concentration of different road users jostling for space on crowded city roads. (See Chapter 4, "Urban Transportation.")

Exposure to Lead

Lead is ubiquitous in the urban environment. Emissions from vehicles burning leaded gasoline constitute an

important source of dispersed lead in many urban areas. Industrial emissions, particularly from smelters and battery recycling plants, are also a significant source.

Humans are exposed via the inhalation of contaminated air, ingestion of contaminated water and foods, and, especially among children in North America, ingestion of lead-based paint. Contact with and ingestion of contaminated soil provide another important route of exposure, particularly among children. Serious occupational exposures occur among adults involved in metal industries, electronics industries, construction trades, and battery manufacturing.

The adverse effects of lead on health have been recognized for centuries. Lead's principal threat, other than acute lead poisoning, is neurological damage in children. A 1988 study in Mexico City, where ambient lead levels are high because of the use of leaded gasoline, found that more than one quarter of newborns had blood lead levels high enough to impair neurological and motor-physical development (121).

Studies conducted in North America, Western Europe, and Australia report that elevated levels of exposure to lead in infancy cause intellectual impairment, although quantifying this impairment is still somewhat controversial (122). Children with elevated dentine lead levels are reported to have a deficit in intelligence scores, speech, and language processing skills compared with children with low lead levels (123). A 1990 study in Bangkok, Thailand, a city heavily polluted with lead, suggested that 30,000 to 70,000 children risked a loss of four or more IQ points because of high lead levels, and many more risked lesser reductions in intelligence (124).

Moreover, it has been suggested that exposure to high lead levels in childhood may be associated with dropping out of high school, reading disability, absenteeism, and neurodevelopmental deficits later in life (125). Some studies have also linked increases in blood lead levels in adults with elevated blood pressure, although this finding has not been borne out in all studies (126) (127).

The findings of neurological impairment in children sparked the effort in the 1970s and 1980s to reduce lead levels in gasoline and other sources in the United States and Europe—an effort that has resulted in lower ambient and blood lead levels in these areas. Blood lead concentrations in the United States, for instance, have dropped substantially since the late 1970s, when the use of leaded fuel was phased out. Many countries in developing regions, however, have yet to enact such regulations, and the risk of exposure to lead remains dangerously high.

THE URBAN SOCIAL ENVIRONMENT AND HEALTH

Although overcrowding, air pollution, uncollected garbage, and other deficiencies in the physical environment frequently represent the most obvious manifestations of urban environmental health problems, cities must deal concurrently with the less visible problems of the urban social environment. Although debate continues, it is likely that differentials in mortality among urban residents from noncommunicable diseases such as heart disease and cancer are related to the social rather than the physical environment within cities.

The contribution of the urban social environment to ill health is increasingly recognized in the developed world, where many physical risks have been largely addressed. For instance, the recent Helsinki Declaration on Action for Environment and Health in Europe emphasizes that the exceptionally high levels of unemployment (especially among young people) caused by economic and technological changes can have adverse effects on physical and mental health. The declaration also warns that a lack of action on these issues, when combined with already unacceptable levels of deprivation and squalor in many places, could threaten "the very cohesion of society" (128).

Recognition of the role of social factors in public health is slower in poorer cities in the developing world, where physical risks still constitute a major health threat. Even so, socially related health problems are assuming increasingly large proportions. As is the case with physical risks in the urban environment, it is the poorest groups who are the most severely affected.

Socioeconomic Status

As is clear from earlier sections, socioeconomic status is the most obvious social factor involved in determining the health risk that an urban resident faces, because it largely determines his or her exposure to physical environmental threats and to amenities such as adequate housing. It is no surprise that access to sanitation and running water, for example, is closely related to income and education levels. In Sao Paulo, Brazil, districts with the lowest income and literacy rates had five times lower per capita consumption of water than districts with the highest income and literacy rates (129).

Housing conditions in the developed world are different from those in developing countries, but the general pattern—that more socially deprived groups are more exposed to poor living conditions—holds true. In England, for example, the proportion of households reporting damp spots and molds, both of which are implicated in the development of asthma in children, is strongly related to their social class (130).

The urban social environment, however, also influences health in less obvious ways. The higher rates of socially related health conditions among the disadvantaged are often traced to risk behaviors such as smoking or drinking, which, in turn, are often responses to social or economic stress. For instance, in the United Kingdom, rates of smoking, drinking, and, in some cases, drug abuse are higher among unemployed adults, and these behaviors contribute to the higher rates of heart disease found among the unemployed (131).

Both heart disease and cancer used to be considered diseases of affluence, because they are linked with behaviors such as sedentary lifestyle, stress, and diets high in fat and sodium that are typically associated with the wealthy. Yet, recent data suggest that mortality rates from chronic disease in both developing and developed nations are highest among the poor (132).

Social Marginalization

Urban areas are often diverse ethnically, culturally, and economically. Residence time in the city also varies widely, from longtime residents to recent immigrants. The close interaction and interdependence of these diverse groups within cities and towns can enhance social cohesion. Conversely, diversity in urban populations can lead to social stress, alienation or disenfranchisement of some groups, and feelings of insecurity by individuals or communities within the overall society. All of these contribute to what is known as social marginalization.

Groups in cities can become marginalized in economic terms or through cultural differences from dominant groups. The two tend to work together: particular cultural groups in cities may be disadvantaged in terms of access to education and employment opportunities. Increasingly, social marginalization is believed to exact a toll on human health, largely through behavioral changes such as seeking relief through smoking or alcohol or substance abuse.

Studies in Seattle, Washington, in the United States, suggest the consequence of social and economic marginalization for Native Americans and Alaska Natives in urban areas. Both groups have much higher death rates from injuries and alcohol-related causes than urban whites or rural Native Americans and Alaska Natives. Both groups also have a higher incidence of having babies with low birth weights. Tobacco and alcohol use, adolescent pregnancy, and inadequate prenatal care are linked to low birth weight (133).

Relative Inequality

Although absolute poverty is obviously a critical factor affecting a person's access to the goods and opportunities essential for a healthy, productive life, increasing evidence suggests that relative poverty, or relative inequality, may be just as important (134). Relative inequality or social deprivation is more broadly defined than absolute poverty, encompassing not only the lack of economic resources but also the inability to acquire the same amenities and types of services that typically accrue to other, more privileged, members of society (135).

Relative inequality refers to the way in which a person sees himself or herself in relation to neighbors or other groups in society. It implies that the social meanings attached to inferior facilities, job opportunities, or other privations are just as important as exposure to the facility or the job itself in determining health (136).

Intriguing evidence to support the notion of relative inequality as a major determinant of health comes from recent studies suggesting that it is countries with the narrowest gap between rich and poor that enjoy the best national health—not those that spend the most money per capita on health in absolute terms (137).

Differential rates of urban violence, described earlier, have also been linked to relative deprivation. This is perhaps not so surprising, since rich and poor often live and interact closely within cities, making the differences between them obvious to each group.

Accra and Sao Paulo

The importance of social environmental factors in urban health is borne out by data on differential mortality among different socioeconomic groups in Sao Paulo, Brazil, and Accra, Ghana. Sao Paulo is a relatively wealthy city of more than 9.6 million people, whereas Accra is a rapidly developing city of 1.3 million people (138) (139).

Figure 2.3 Age-Adjusted Mortality Rates by Socio-Environmental Zones in Accra and Sao Paulo, 1991–92

A. Accra[a]

(deaths per 10,000 population)

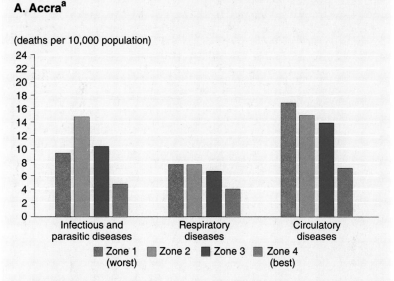

Zone 1 (worst)   Zone 2   Zone 3   Zone 4 (best)

B. Sao Paulo[b]

(deaths per 10,000 population)

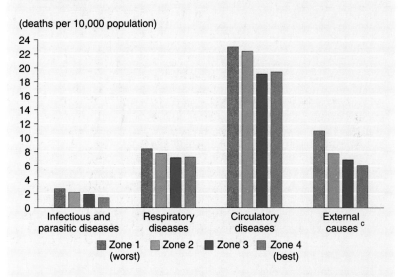

Zone 1 (worst)   Zone 2   Zone 3   Zone 4 (best)

Source: Carolyn Stephens *et al., Environment and Health in Developing Countries: An Analysis of Intra-Urban Differentials Using Existing Data* (London School of Hygiene & Tropical Medicine in collaboration with Fundacao SEADE and Ghana Ministry of Health and Ministry of Environment, London, 1994).

Notes:
a. Data for Accra, Ghana, are for 1991. In Accra, residential areas were grouped into zones using three indicators: household income, population density, and age/ethnicity of the community and community dwellings. Zone 1 represented a high-density, indigenous sector; zone 2 represented a high-density, low-class sector; zone 3 represented a medium-density, indigenous sector; and zone 4 represented a middle- to high-class, low-density sector.
b. Data for Sao Paulo, Brazil, are for 1992. In Sao Paulo, an index that ranked the 56 districts and subdistricts of the city was constructed to form four zones with equal numbers of districts and subdistricts in each zone by level of education, income, per capita water supply, access to sewage facilities, and population density.
c. External causes of death include violent deaths—mainly traffic accidents and homicides.

Box 2.5 Community Perceptions of Urban Health Risks

Understanding how a community perceives health risks such as polluted water, inadequate drainage, or lack of garbage collection is essential to designing effective programs to address those problems. Individuals perceive risks to their health through a lens derived from their cultural, economic, societal, and educational backgrounds and respond accordingly. For example, a squatter in a slum in Calcutta, India, might happily boil water collected at a public tap rather than move to a house with piped water that was located far from job opportunities; a middle-class family in Los Angeles would probably make a very different choice.

Until recently, these differences in how people view and respond to risks were not part of formal health risk analysis, which has traditionally relied on statistical correlations between exposure to risks and the incidence of various illnesses. Now, health planners are beginning to realize that using such objective measures of risk to design public health projects without accounting for how the affected community itself views the health risk being addressed is a recipe for failure.

CASE STUDY: INDORE'S DRAINAGE IMPROVEMENT PROJECT

The importance of incorporating community perceptions into project planning can be seen in the case of a public project designed to relieve flooding in the slums of Indore, India. The majority of Indore's 183 slums are located on the banks of canals and rivers that crisscross the city and on land located in the city's flood plain. Monsoon waters frequently flood these communities, submerging city streets and destroying homes.

Residents of the slums are well aware of the health risks associated with this flooding. Although they might not know the epidemiological details of pollution and contagion, they are all too familiar with the symptoms that they suffer. The names given to different floodwaters illustrate their perception of health risks. Each type of water has its own name. Dirty water that is contaminated with feces is known as *Ganda pani* and is seen as the worst kind of water, containing "small unseen insects" *(kitanuh)* responsible for causing stomach problems and other illnesses. Even wading through such water is recognized to be unhealthful. On the other hand, *Maila pani* (dirty water without excreta) is unpleasant to walk through, but not dangerous. *Pineh ka pani* is water that is clean enough to be used for drinking.

For these poor communities, however, the advantages of their location—close to the city center, with easy access to jobs, low land costs, and strong community ties—far outweigh the health risks associated with flooding and contact with dirty water. In addition, although city planners view the flooding only as a recurring problem, local residents associate flooding with heavy rain and good crop yields, leading to a positive perception of flooding.

In designing a project to improve health conditions in 157 of Indore's squatter settlements, city planners identified flooding as a major health risk and constructed closed drainage channels in an effort to reduce flooding and upgrade sanitary conditions. Despite these improvements, many community members now perceive flooding problems to be worse than before.

One important source of their dissatisfaction is that the new drainage system has reduced the ability of the community to apply its own risk reduction strategies, thus increasing economic losses from the flooding. Because the drains are closed, residents can no longer predict the severity of the approaching flood. With the previous open drains, community members would adjust their level of flood response depending on rainfall intensity and the volume of water that they could see in the open drains.

In light floods, structural adaptations including high internal shelving, raised storage platforms for valuables, and electricity connections at head height were enough to minimize damage. Food supplies, electronics, and mattresses were moved to ceiling-level platforms for safety.

When community members anticipated severe floods, all valuable possessions were moved to higher ground. Children, the elderly, and livestock were evacuated first, while clothes and uten-

---

Case studies in these two cities examined differences in mortality from circulatory diseases, infectious and parasitic diseases, and respiratory diseases among different socioeconomic groups across all age groups. In Sao Paulo, the study was extended to include external causes (homicides and traffic accidents) because they account for a significant share of deaths. Consistently, the disadvantaged have higher rates of mortality than their better-off neighbors from both infectious diseases and socially related conditions such as heart disease.

In these studies, the cities were divided into four zones, from worst to best, according to several indicators of poverty and environmental quality. The indicators included income, education, age and ethnicity of the community, per capita water supply, access to sewage facilities, and population density. (See Figure 2.3.)

As Figure 2.3A shows, in Accra, age-adjusted rates of mortality from circulatory diseases were more than two times higher for the 46 percent of the city's population in the worst zone compared with the mortality rates in the most affluent zone. Mortality from infectious and parasitic diseases was likewise about twice as high in the worst zone as in the best zone, as was mortality from respiratory diseases (140).

sils were generally moved last. Unable to implement these coping strategies with the new drainage system, residents fear they may now lose many of the valuables on which they depend for their livelihood.

Residents also believe that the closed system does not drain as effectively as their previous open system. Unlike the open sewers, which were wider, the closed sewers are easily blocked by plastic bags and other trash. Water backups flood the area, in some cases affecting houses that were previously outside the flood-prone area. In addition, because residents can no longer see the water flowing, they do not have confidence that it is draining adequately. Finally, the open drains had the added benefit of washing away rubbish and excreta, which now remain on the streets.

INCORPORATING COMMUNITY PERCEPTIONS INTO HEALTH SOLUTIONS

Can risks to health from environmental hazards be reduced in a way that integrates community perceptions and priorities? Some recent efforts to address the health problems surrounding solid waste collections argue that this approach can succeed.

Although the "formal" urban planner considers municipal garbage a health and environmental hazard, many of the poor who earn their livings as scavengers look upon urban waste as an economic resource from which marketable products can be derived. In cities throughout the developing world, scavengers collect waste such as plastic, paper, glass, tin cans, and bones, contributing greatly to garbage collection and recycling efforts in the city.

Of course, scavenging is hazardous employment. It is poverty driven, undertaken by the most vulnerable people—often women and children. In the process of sorting through trash, scavengers expose themselves to serious health hazards such as injuries from broken glass and cans and are disproportionately exposed to disease-carrying pests that breed in garbage.

Nonetheless, implementing a modern garbage collection and recycling system in many cities in the developing world is infeasible and would take jobs from those who need them most. Thus, city officials are starting to realize that this "informal" approach to waste has its benefits. Rather than trying to eliminate scavenging, governments are working with nongovernmental organizations and community groups in an effort to reduce the health risks to scavengers and to make scavenging more profitable. For example, in Cairo, Egypt, wastepickers have built special areas where they can sort waste, rather than bring the waste into their homes, as they did previously. In Manila, Philippines, wastepickers are given masks, gloves, and boots to help protect them from injuries.

Two lessons emerge from these examples. First, for many urban dwellers in developing countries, health is a luxury they cannot afford because their immediate economic survival is at stake. Aware of their limited options, they design innovative ways to try to optimize their conditions. The slum dwellers in Indore, for instance, have developed intricate strategies that attempt to minimize the economic damage done by flooding. These can be very effective in reducing vulnerability to natural and man-made risks.

Second, it is clear that a better understanding of the cultural perceptions of community members can help in the design of local programs that both reduce risks to health and respect the choices of the people living in these cities. The challenge now lies in developing a reliable means of ascertaining community views on local health risks and incorporating them into the planning of environmental health interventions.

—Anton Baare and Rajesh Patnaik

Anton Baare is a social anthropologist with Nordic Consulting Group in Taastrup, Denmark, and Rajesh Patnaik is a research fellow in social anthropology in the Anthropology Department of Andhra University in Visakhapatnam, India.

In Sao Paulo, while the overall rate of mortality from infectious and parasitic diseases was much lower than that in Accra, the same differential exists between the affluent and the disadvantaged, with those living in the worst zone being nearly twice as likely to die from such an infectious or parasitic disease. The differential in mortality rates from heart disease between affluent and disadvantaged in Sao Paulo was much smaller than that in Accra. It was still significant, however, as was the differential for respiratory diseases. In Sao Paulo, the death rates from accidents and homicides were also nearly twice as high in the worst zones of the city as in the best zone (141).

These studies indicate that for urban adults living in poor conditions within Accra and Sao Paulo, the health risk of communicable diseases appears to be compounded by high risks of circulatory diseases and, in Sao Paulo, by epidemic rates of traumatic health problems such as accidents and homicides. Such findings suggest the complex nature of health impacts inflicted by the "web of insecurity" (142) entailed in the deprivation of many cities of the developing world.

Both cities are clearly caught in an incomplete health transition, with chronic and infectious diseases coexisting, and the disadvantaged most subject to this dual risk.

MULTISECTORAL STRATEGIES FOR IMPROVING THE HEALTH OF URBAN DWELLERS

The complex determinants of urban health and the linkages among them underscore the magnitude of the health challenge in urban areas. Throughout the developing world, the burden of death and disease related to the urban environment is great. In terms of global impact, the most pressing need is to improve the health of the urban poor in their local environments. In cities of the developing world, this will entail both technological improvements—chief among them, providing water and sanitation and reducing exposure to air pollutants—and, equally important, institutional reforms. (See Chapter 5, "Urban Priorities for Action.") In the more developed cities, technological reforms are of lesser importance; the fundamental problems appear to be those of social justice.

Improving health and quality of life will require a significant departure from the piecemeal approach that has dominated urban management since the 19th Century, in which each problem is considered in isolation. Most discussions of urban environmental management still resort to a listing of priority problems, as if each exists independently. But the past few years have seen an increasing recognition that the problems of cities cannot be adequately dealt with by using Victorian approaches (143). In other words, even though providing water or shelter can make an enormous difference, neither alone is sufficient to alleviate the burden of ill health.

Recognizing the synergistic factors affecting the quality of life of the urban poor, some cities in the developing world have devised integrated strategies, sometimes called "slum and squatter improvement projects" (144). These projects tend to incorporate diverse municipal agencies, often under an umbrella structure, that work with communities to improve local infrastructure such as water and sanitation services, along with providing health programs, preschool education, and income-generating schemes. To the extent that these projects are proactive in addressing urban poverty and achieving coordinated action, they represent a step forward in urban planning.

However, there are many obstacles to multisectoral strategies for improving urban health. Chief among them is the difficulty of integrating disciplines as diverse as engineering, medicine, social welfare, and economics. Multisectoral approaches to urban environmental management pose a major challenge to both local governments and international lending agencies, which must coordinate responses and overcome the political divisions within cities.

To succeed, any strategy must address the actual concerns of the community affected, which may not match the priorities of the government or the development agency sponsoring the project. (See Box 2.5.) It has also become clear that any successful attempt to address the health concerns of the urban poor must acknowledge the central role that women play in environmental management around the home, and therefore in their families' health. Difficulties aside, an integrated, equity-driven approach appears to be essential if we are to achieve adequate quality of life in an increasingly urban world.

This chapter was written by Carolyn Stephens of the London School of Hygiene & Tropical Medicine (LSHTM), Gordon McGranahan of the Stockholm Environment Institute, Martin Bobak (LSHTM and the University College London Medical School), Antony Fletcher (LSHTM), and Giovanni Leonardi (LSHTM). Box 2.3 was written by Subhadra Menon, a correspondent in New Delhi, India.

References and Notes

1. D.R. Phillips and Y. Verhasselt, eds., *Health and Development* (Routledge, New York, 1994).

2. Ellen Wratten, "Conceptualizing Urban Poverty," *Environment and Urbanization,* Vol. 7, No. 1 (April 1995), p. 11.

3. National Research Council, *The Epidemiological Transition: Policy and Planning Implications for Developing Countries* (National Academy Press, Washington, D.C., 1993), p. 1.

4. *Ibid.,* p. 2.

5. *Op. cit.* 3, p. 5.

6. Pan American Health Organization (PAHO), *Health Conditions in the Americas,* Vol. 2 (PAHO, Washington, D.C., 1994), p. 77.

7. Carolyn Stephens *et al., Environment and Health in Developing Countries: An Analysis of Intra-Urban Differentials Using Existing Data* (London School of Hygiene & Tropical Medicine in collaboration with Fundacao SEADE and Ghana Ministry of Health and Ministry of Environment, London, 1994), p. 52.

8. Medical Officer of Health, *Annual Report: Cape Town, 1992* (Ministry of Health, Cape Town, South Africa, 1992), p. 10.

9. *Op. cit.* 7, p. 14.

10. Paulo Pinheiro, "Reflections on Urban Violence," *The Urban Age,* Vol. 1, No. 4 (1993), p. 3.

11. Arif Hasan, "Karachi and the Global Nature of Urban Violence," *The Urban Age,* Vol. 1, No. 4 (1993), pp. 1–4.

12. Mademba Ndiaye, "Dakar: Youth Groups and the Slide Towards Violence," *The Urban Age,* Vol. 1, No. 4 (1993), p. 7.

13. Rodrigo Guerrero, "Cali's Innovative Approach to Urban Violence," *The Urban Age,* Vol. 1, No. 4 (1993), pp. 12–13.

14. Jose Carvalho de Noronha, "Drug Markets and Urban Violence in Rio de Janeiro: A Call for Action," *The Urban Age,* Vol. 1, No. 4 (1993), p. 9.

15. Pan American Health Organization, "Violence: A Growing Public Health Problem in the Region," *Epidemiological Bulletin,* Vol. 11, No. 2 (1990) pp. 1–7.

16. A. Rossi-Espagnet, G.B. Goldstein, and I. Tabibzadeh, "Urbanization and Health in Developing Countries: A Challenge for Health for All," *World Health Statistics Quarterly,* Vol. 44, No. 4 (1991), p. 208.

17. *Op. cit.* 7.

18. Czech Statistical Office, Computerized records of deaths in the Czech Republic in 1993 (Czech Statistical Office, Prague, Czech Republic, 1994). Compiled by Martin Bobak, University College of London, 1995.

19. *Op. cit.* 7, p. 14.

20. *Op. cit.* 7, pp. 14, 52.

21. *Op. cit.* 18.

22. *Op. cit.* 7, pp. 14, 52.

23. *Op. cit.* 18.

24. *Op. cit.* 7.

25. Trudy Harpham and Carolyn Stephens, "Urbanization and Health in Developing Countries: From the Shadows into the Spotlight," *Tropical Diseases Bulletin,* Vol. 88, No. 8 (1991), pp. 1–35.

26. *Op. cit.* 16, pp. 186–247.

27. Jorge E. Hardoy, Sandy Cairncross, and David Satterthwaite, eds., *The Poor Die Young: Housing and Health in Third World Cities* (Earthscan, London, 1990), pp. 1–309.

28. Trudy Harpham, Tim Lusty, and Patrick Vaughan, eds., *In the Shadow of the City: Community Health and the Urban Poor* (Oxford University Press, Oxford, U.K., 1988), pp. 1–237.

29. World Health Organization (WHO), Commission on Health and Environment, *Report of the Panel on Urbanization* (WHO, Geneva, 1992), pp. 51–54.

30. World Health Organization (WHO), *The Urban Health Crisis: Strategies for Health for All in the Face of Rapid Urbanization* (WHO, Geneva, 1993), pp. 1–4.

31. The World Bank, *World Development Report 1993: Investing in Health* (The World Bank, Washington, D.C., 1993), p. 40.

32. *Op. cit.* 29, p. 55.

33. Jane Pryer, "The Impact of Adult Ill-Health on Household Income and Nutrition in Khulna, Bangladesh," *Environment and Urbanization,* Vol. 5, No. 2 (1993), pp. 35–49.

34. E. Drucker *et al.,* "Childhood Tuberculosis in the Bronx, New York," *Lancet,* Vol. 343, No. 8911 (June 11, 1994), pp. 1482–1485.

35. Megan Landon, "Intra-Urban Health Differentials in London," Master's thesis, London School of Hygiene & Tropical Medicine, London, 1994, pp. 1–33.

36. Denise M. Dowd *et al.,* "Pediatric Firearm Injuries, Kansas City, 1992: A Population-Based Study," *Pediatrics,* Vol. 94, No. 6 (December 1, 1994), p. 867.

37. Colin McCord and Harold Freeman, "Excess Mortality in Harlem," *New England Journal of Medicine,* Vol. 322, No. 3 (January 18, 1990), pp. 173–177.

38. *Op. cit.* 8, p. 13.

39. United Nations Children's Fund (UNICEF), *Environment, Development and the Child* (UNICEF, New York, 1992), pp. 19–44.

40. *Op. cit.* 29, p. 67.

41. World Health Organization (WHO), *The World Health Report 1995: Bridging the Gaps* (WHO, Geneva, 1995), p. 9.

42. *Op. cit.* 29, p. 74.

43. David Bates, "The Effects of Air Pollution on Children," *Environmental Health Perspectives,* Vol. 103, Supplement 6 (September 1995), pp. 49–51.

44. Ruth Etzel, "Indoor Air Pollution and Childhood Asthma: Effective Environmental Interventions," *Environmental Health Perspectives,* Vol. 103, Supplement 6 (September 1995), pp. 55–57.

45. Floyd Malveaux and Sheryl Fletcher-Vincent, "Environmental Risk Factors of Childhood Asthma in Urban Centers," *Environmental Health Perspectives,* Vol. 103, Supplement 6 (September 1995), pp. 59–61.

46. "Homicide Deaths by Age & Percent by Firearms, New York City, 1993," *Bulletin of the New York Academy of Medicine,* Vol. 72, No. 1 (Summer 1995), p. 152.

47. *Op. cit.* 15, pp. 2–3.

48. *Op. cit.* 7, p. 54.

49. David Satterthwaite, "The Impact on Health of Urban Environments," *Environment and Urbanization,* Vol. 5, No. 2 (October 1993), p. 107.

50. *Ibid.,* pp. 106–108.

51. Jacqueline Sims, ed., *Women, Health, and Environment: An Anthology* (World Health Organization, Geneva, 1994), pp. 24–26.

52. Jorge Hardoy, Diana Mitlin, and David Satterthwaite, *Environmental Problems in Third World Cities* (Earthscan, London, 1992), pp. 50–51.

53. *Op. cit.* 51, pp. 126–135.

54. United Nations Development Programme, *Human Development Report 1995* (Oxford University Press, New York, 1995), p. 7.

55. *Op. cit.* 49, pp. 99–100.

56. Paul Bairoch, *Cities and Economic Development: From the Dawn of History to the Present* (Mansell Publishing, London, 1988).

57. Ann-Louise Shapiro, *Housing the Poor of Paris, 1850–1902* (University of Wisconsin Press, Madison, Wisconsin, 1985).

58. *Op. cit.* 31, p. 90.

59. Gordon McGranahan, "Household Environmental Problems in Low-Income Cities: An Overview of Problems and Prospects for Improvement," *Habitat International,* Vol. 17, No. 2 (1993), pp. 105–121.

60. Gustavo Arcia *et al.,* "Environmental Health Assessment: A Case Study Conducted in the City of Quito and the County of Pedro Moncayo, Pichincha Province, Ecuador," Field Report No. 401 (Water and Sanitation for Health Project, Arlington, Virginia, 1993).

61. Stephen A. Esrey *et al.,* "Health Benefits from Improvements in Water Supply and Sanitation: Survey and Analysis of the Literature on Selected Diseases," Technical Report No. 66 (Water and Sanitation for Health Project, Arlington, Virginia, 1990).

62. Gehan Sinnatamby, "Low Cost Sanitation," in *The Poor Die Young: Housing and Health in Third World Cities,* Jorge E. Hardoy, Sandy Cairncross, and David Satterthwaite, eds. (Earthscan, London, 1990), p. 133.

63. William Hogrewe, Steve D. Joyce, and Eduardo A. Perez, *The Unique Challenges of Improving Peri-Urban Sanitation,* Water and Sanitation for Health Technical Report No. 86 (U.S. Agency for International Development, Washington, D.C., July 1993), pp. 44–47.

64. *Op. cit.* 29, pp. 41–43.

65. *Op. cit.* 29, pp. 41–47.

66. *Op. cit.* 29, p. 42.

67. *Op. cit.* 29, p. 44.

68. Siobhan Hair, ed., *Glasgow's Health: Women Count* (Glasgow Healthy City Project, Glasgow, Scotland, 1994), pp. 8–9.

69. *Op. cit.* 29, p. 47.

70. Stephen A. Esrey and Richard G.A. Feachem, *Interventions for the Control of Diarrhoeal Diseases Among Young Children: Promotion of Food Hygiene,* Document WHO/CDD/89.30 (World Health Organization, Geneva, 1989), pp. 1–22.

71. Kare Molbak *et al.,* "Bacterial Contamination of Stored Water and Stored Food: A Potential Source of Diarrhoeal Disease in West Africa," *Epidemiology and Infection,* Vol. 102, No. 2 (1989) pp. 309–316.

72. *Ibid.*

73. Jo Lines *et al.,* "Trends, Priorities and Policy Directions in the Control of Vector-Borne Diseases in Urban Environments," *Health Policy and Planning,* Vol. 9, No. 2 (1994), p. 113.

74. George Benneh *et al., Environmental Problems and the Urban Household in the Greater Accra Metropolitan Area (GAMA)—Ghana* (Stockholm Environment Institute, Stockholm, Sweden, 1993), p. 75.

75. C.J. Schofield *et al.,* "The Role of House Design in Limiting Vector-Borne Disease," in *The Poor Die Young: Housing and Health in Third World Cities,* Jorge E. Hardoy, Sandy Cairncross, and David Satterthwaite, eds. (Earthscan, London, 1990), p. 190.

76. Kirk R. Smith, "Fuel Combustion, Air Pollution Exposure, and Health: The Situation in Developing Countries," *Annual Review of Energy and the Environment,* Vol. 18 (1993), p. 529.

77. B.H. Chen *et al.,* "Indoor Air Pollution in Developing Countries," *World Health Statistics Quarterly,* Vol. 43, No. 3 (1990), pp. 128–134.

78. *Op. cit.* 41.

79. Stephen Berman, "Epidemiology of Acute Respiratory Infections in Children of Developing Countries," *Reviews of Infectious Diseases,* Vol. 13, Supplement 6 (May–June 1991), pp. S454–S460.

80. Kirk R. Smith *et al.,* "Air Pollution and the Energy Ladder in Asian Cities," *Energy,* Vol. 19, No. 5 (May 1, 1994), p. 587.

81. Anders Ellegard and Hans Egneus, "Health Effects of Charcoal and Woodfuel Use in Low-Income Households in Lusaka, Zambia," Energy, Environment and Development Series 14 (Stockholm Environment Institute, Stockholm, Sweden, 1992), pp. 3–4.

82. Kirk R. Smith and Yoncheng Liu, "Indoor Air Pollution in Developing Countries," in *Epidemiology of Lung Cancer,* Jonathan M. Samet, ed. (Marcel Dekker, Inc., New York, 1994), p. 154.

83. *Ibid.,* p. 163.

84. Aletta P.S. Terblanche *et al.,* "Exposure to Air Pollution from Transitional Household Fuels in a South African Population," *Journal of Exposure Analysis and Environment Epidemiology,* Vol. 3, Supplement 1 (1993), p. 150.

85. *Op. cit.* 49, p. 93.

86. World Resources Institute in collaboration with the United Nations Environment Programme and the United Nations Development Programme, *World Resources 1992–93* (Oxford University Press, New York, 1992), p. 195.

87. Richard N. Andrews *et al., Guidelines for Improving Wastewater and Solid Waste Management,* Water and Sanitation for Health Technical Report No. 88 (U.S. Agency for International Development, Washington, D.C., August 1993), p. 1.

88. Carl Bartone *et al.,* "Private Sector Participation in Municipal Solid Waste Service: Experiences in Latin America," *Waste Management and Research,* Vol. 9 (1991), p. 498.

89. Choon-Nam Ong, Jerry Jeyaratnam, and David Koh, "Factors Influencing the Assessment and Control of Occupational Hazards in Developing Countries," *Environmental Research,* Vol. 60, No. 1 (January 1, 1993), pp. 112–123.

90. *Op. cit.* 52, p. 49.

91. *Op. cit.* 89, p. 114.

92. Dean Baker and Philip Landrigan, "Occupational Exposures and Human Health," in *Critical Condition: Human Health and the Environment,* Eric Chivian *et al.,* eds. (MIT Press, Cambridge, Massachusetts, 1993), pp. 71–73.

93. *Op. cit.* 52, p. 49.

94. *Op. cit.* 52, p. 49.

95. *Op. cit.* 92, pp. 74–77.

96. *Op. cit.* 52, pp. 49–50.

97. *Op. cit.* 89, pp. 113–114.

98. *Op. cit.* 89, pp. 116–117.

99. *Op. cit.* 89, p. 114.

100. *Op. cit.* 52, p. 50.

101. *Op. cit.* 89, p. 115.

102. *Op. cit.* 52, p. 50.

103. Dietrich Schwela, "Public Health Implications of Urban Air Pollution in Developing Countries," paper presented at the 10th World Clean Air Congress, Erjos, Finland, May 28–June 2, 1995), p. 1.

104. C. Arden Pope III *et al.,* "Respiratory Health and PM-10 Pollution: A Daily Time Series Analysis," *American Review of Respiratory Disease,* Vol. 144, No. 3 (September 1, 1991), p. 668.

105. Douglas W. Dockery *et al.,* "An Association Between Air Pollution and Mortality in Six U.S. Cities," *New England Journal of Medicine,* Vol. 329, No. 24 (December 9, 1993), p. 1753.

106. *Ibid.*

107. C. Arden Pope III *et al.,* "Particulate Air Pollution as a Predictor of Mortality in a Prospective Study of U.S. Adults," *American Journal of Respiratory and Critical Care Medicine,* Vol. 151, No. 3 (March 1995), p. 669–674.

108. *Ibid.,* p. 669.

109. *Op. cit.* 105, p. 1758.

110. *Op. cit.* 107, p. 672.

111. Philip J. Hilts, "Studies Say Soot Kills up to 60,000 in U.S. Each Year," *New York Times* (July 19, 1993), p. A1.

112. Marek Jakubowski, "Ambient Air Pollution and Health Effects," in *Air Pollution in Central and Eastern Europe: Health and Public Policy* (Management Sciences for Health, Boston, 1991).

113. Martin Bobak and Richard G.A. Feachem, "Air Pollution and Mortality in Central and Eastern Europe: An Estimate of the Impact," *European Journal of Public Health,* Vol. 5 (1995), pp. 82–86.

114. Bart Ostro, "Estimating the Health Effects of Air Pollutants: A Method with an Application to Jakarta," Policy Research Working Paper No. 1301 (The World Bank, Washington, D.C., 1994), p. 47.

115. Bart Ostro, Chief, Air Toxicology and Epidemiology Unit, California Environmental Protection Agency, Berkeley, California, 1995 (personal communication).

116. *Op. cit.* 114.

117. *Op. cit.* 41, p. 35.

118. G.D. Jacobs, "Road Safety in the Developing World," in *Health at the Cross-Roads: Urban Health and Transport Policy,* T. Fletcher and T. McMichael, eds. (London School of Hygiene & Tropical Medicine, London, in press), p. 1.

119. *Ibid.*

120. *Op. cit.* 118, p. 11.

121. *Op. cit.* 49, p. 93.

122. Peter Baghurst *et al.,* "Environmental Exposure to Lead and Children's Intelligence at the Age of Seven Years," *New England Journal of Medicine,* Vol. 327, No. 18 (1992), pp. 1279–1284.

123. Herbert Needleman *et al.,* "Deficits in Psychologic and Classroom Performance of Children with Elevated Dentine Lead Levels," *New England Journal of Medicine,* Vol. 300, No. 13 (1979), pp. 689–695.

124. U.S. Agency for International Development (U.S. AID), Office of Housing and Urban Programs, *Ranking Environmental Health Risks in Bangkok, Thailand,* Vol. 2, *Technical Appendices* (U.S. AID, Washington, D.C., December 1990), p. E-15.

125. Herbert Needleman *et al.,* "The Long-Term Effects of Exposure to Low Doses of Lead in Childhood: An 11-Year Follow-Up Report," *New England Journal of Medicine,* Vol. 322, No. 2 (1990), pp. 83–88.

126. J.A. Staessen *et al.,* "Hypertension Caused by Low-Level Lead Exposure: Myth or Fact?," *Journal of Cardiovascular Risk* (1994), pp. 87–97.

127. James Pirkle *et al.,* "The Relationship Between Blood Lead Levels and Blood Pressure and Its Cardiovascular Risk Implications," *American Journal of Epidemiology,* Vol. 121, No. 2 (1985), pp. 246–258.

128. "The Declaration on Action for Environment and Health in Europe," adopted by the Second European Conference on Environment and Health, Helsinki, Finland, June 20–22, 1994, as cited in *Environmental Policy and Law,* Vol. 25, No. 1–2 (1995), p. 79.

129. *Op. cit.* 7, p. 57.

130. Claire N. Packer, Sarah Stewart-Brown, and Sarah E. Fowle, "Damp Housing and Adult Health: Results from a Lifestyle Study in Worcester, England," *Journal of Epidemiology and Community Health,* Vol. 48, No. 6 (1994), pp. 555–559.

131. *Op. cit.* 35.

132. Richard Feachem *et al.,* "Adult Mortality: Levels, Patterns and Causes," in *The Health of Adults in the Developing World,* Richard Feachem *et al.,* eds. (The World Bank, Washington, D.C., 1992).

133. D.C. Grossman *et al.,* "Health Status of Urban American Indians and Alaska Natives: A Population-Based Study," *Journal of the American Medical Association,* Vol. 271, No. 11 (March 16, 1994), pp. 845–850.

134. Richard G. Wilkinson, "The Epidemiological Transition: From Material Scarcity to Social Disadvantage?," *Daedalus: Journal of the American Academy of Arts and Sciences,* Vol. 123, No. 4 (Fall 1994), pp. 67–68.

135. *Op. cit.* 2, p. 14.

136. *Op. cit.* 134, pp. 71–72.

137. *Op. cit.* 134, p. 69.

138. *Op. cit.* 7, pp. 10, 51.

139. These population figures differ from those reported in United Nations (U.N.) Population Division, *World Urbanization Prospects: 1994 Revision* (U.N., New York, 1994). As discussed in Chapter 1, "Cities and the Environment," city population figures can differ dramatically depending on the administrative boundaries used. In order to maintain the consistency of this health study, these population figures instead of those published by the U.N. are being used.

140. *Op. cit.* 7, p. 42.

141. *Op. cit.* 7, pp. 63–66.

142. *Op. cit.* 16, pp. 186–245.

143. Maggie Black, *Mega-Slums: The Coming Sanitary Crisis* (WaterAid, London, 1994), p. 18.

144. Carolyn Stephens and Trudy Harpham, *Slum Improvement: Health Improvement? A Review of Issues in Health Planning for the Urban Poor of Developing Countries,* Department of Public Health and Policy Publication No. 1 (London School of Hygiene & Tropical Medicine, London, 1991).

3. Urban Impacts on Natural Resources

Sometime around the year 2025, 8 billion people will be living on the planet (1). These people will require land, energy, water, and food, regardless of whether they live in cities or in rural villages. As their incomes rise, they will consume greater quantities and varieties of goods and, in the process, will generate greater quantities of wastes.

How this population growth and economic expansion will affect the environment has been a matter of debate for some time, but now there is a new dimension. By 2025, the majority of the world's population, some 5 billion people, will be living in urban areas (2)—a transformation that is bound to change the nature and scale of humanity's impact on the environment.

Cities are inextricably linked with the economic shift from an agrarian society to one based on manufacturing and services. Thus, disentangling the impacts of urban growth from those of economic growth and industrialization is difficult and perhaps impossible.

Still, urban settlements, with their dense agglomerations of people and economic activities, put different pressures on the environment than do rural settlements. These differences are more pronounced in the developing world because rural settlements there are still primarily traditional villages, where buildings are made of local materials and residents are still largely dependent on their own resources for their livelihood (3). The distinction is less clear in the developed world, where rural and urban residents alike tend to benefit from the same modern goods and services, such as piped water, paved roads, electricity, and telecommunications (4).

Urban areas affect the environment through three major routes: the conversion of land to urban uses, the extraction and depletion of natural resources, and the disposal of urban wastes. As cities expand, prime agricultural land and habitats such as wetlands and forests are transformed into land for housing, roads, and industry. The nexus of people and economic activity (including manufacturing, services, and commerce) in cities requires resources far in excess of what the local area can supply, so cities must draw their essential supplies of food, fuel, and water from distant places. The concentration of wastes in cities is much higher than that in the countryside, reflecting both the sheer number of people living in a relatively small area and their greater levels of consumption. As a result, urban wastes may quickly overtax the ability of local ecosystems to assimilate them.

The scale of urban consumption and waste generation—and the negative impacts associated with them—varies dramatically from city to city, depending in large part on a city's wealth and size. Not surprisingly, the highest levels of resource use and waste generation tend to occur in the wealthiest cities and among the wealthier groups within cities (5) (6). Thus, wealthy cities contribute disproportionately to global environmental problems, such as depletion of natural resources and emissions of greenhouse gases.

By contrast, per capita resource use and levels of waste generation tend to be quite low among the urban poor. Predominantly poor cities thus tend to pose minimal threats to the global environment, but their local impacts can be severe. The urban poor, lacking an alternative place to live, often establish informal settlements in ecologically fragile areas. When these settlements are unserved by sewers or garbage collection services, wastes accumulate and degrade land and local watersheds.

Yet cities of all types also offer important opportunities for protecting the environment. With proper planning, dense settlement patterns can reduce pressures on land from population growth and can also provide opportunities to increase energy efficiency. Recycling becomes more feasible because of the large quantities of materials and the number of large and small industries that can benefit from it (7). And although high densities may exacerbate pollution problems, developing the infrastructure required to manage wastes may be easier and more cost-effective in an urban setting (8) (9).

Urbanization may help improve the environment in indirect ways as well. Birth rates are three to four times lower in urban areas than in rural areas, thereby reducing environmental pressures from population growth (10). Cities provide opportunities to educate residents about environmental issues and mobilize residents around these issues. In addition, per capita expenditures on environmental protection are higher in urban areas, both in absolute terms and as a percentage of the gross national product (11). Many cities are also taking an active role in environmental management, from developing local strategies to protect regional biodiversity and natural resources to joining forces in an effort to reduce global greenhouse gas emissions (12) (13).

To the extent possible, this chapter concentrates on environmental issues that arise directly from urbanization and urban activities rather than the broader set of environmental pressures linked to economic growth and industrialization. In many cases, however, a city's environmental impacts are as much a product of development as they are of urbanization, and the two cannot be teased apart. Although industrial pollution is generated as a result of activities performed to satisfy broad consumer demand—not just urban demand—the impacts are often concentrated around or downwind of cities. Cities per se are not responsible for the rise in greenhouse gas emissions, but the higher consumption patterns linked with urban lifestyles may be—and urban policies could do much to reduce those emissions.

Another difficulty in gauging the full impact of urban areas on the natural environment lies in the still-rudimentary understanding of complex ecological processes. Although abundant research has linked pollution pressures to damage to aquatic or terrestrial life, the total impacts on ecosystems are difficult to measure, so studies are often more descriptive than quantitative.

When evaluating the impacts of urban activities on human health, for instance, the endpoints can be measured in terms of illness and death rates. Few equivalent measures exist for assessing the health of ecosystems.

Few attempts have been made to look at the overall impacts of cities on the environment, as opposed to the more specific impacts of a particular sector such as transportation (14). In the past few years, a number of researchers have begun looking at the issue of cities and sustainable development—in other words, how cities can meet development needs with lower draws per capita on environmental capital (15) (16) (17). In a similar vein, recent attempts have been made to calculate a city's "ecological footprint"—the amount of productive land needed to sustain a city's population and its consumption levels (18) (19). Further research in this area is warranted because the shift toward a predominately urban world appears inevitable. Understanding the environmental impacts of urban areas may provide useful insights into how urban growth can be channeled in positive ways to help reduce humanity's pressures on the global environment.

This chapter provides an overview of how urban areas and related activities affect the environment through land conversion, the extraction and depletion of natural resources, and the disposal of urban wastes. The chapter then takes an in-depth look at the combined impacts of urban areas through two case studies of coastal ecosystems. Although only one of many ecosystem types, coastal ecosystems are especially threatened by urban development and land-based pollution. Already, 40 percent of all cities with a population of 500,000 or greater are located on tidal estuaries or the open coastline. The damage to these ecosystems is worrisome because coastal ecosystems are some of the most productive on the planet. Although the ecosystems of the coastal zone occupy just 8 percent of the global surface, they are responsible for some 26 percent of all biological production, according to one estimate (20).

These case studies vividly illustrate the extent of damage caused by multiple impacts and the need for integrated approaches to addressing urban environmental problems. Further policies for mitigating adverse effects on natural resources and maximizing urban advantages are explored in Chapter 5, "Urban Priorities for Action."

LAND CONVERSION

Although cities represent a dramatic transformation of the natural landscape, the total amount of land dedicated to urban uses is small—just 1 percent of Earth's total land surface, according to several estimates (21). Overall, far more natural lands are lost to agricultural activities, forestry, and grazing than to urbanization.

Urbanization may actually help to reduce the scale and severity of environmental impacts on land from population growth. High residential densities can reduce land pressures in countries experiencing rapid population growth. Households in villages and rural areas in the Republic of Korea, for example, consume six times more land per capita for residential purposes than households in Seoul (22).

Although the amount of land converted to urban uses may be small globally, a trend is emerging in both developed and developing countries: cities from Los Angeles to Jakarta, Indonesia, are rapidly expanding outward, consuming ever greater quantities of land (23). This urban sprawl, characterized by low-density development and vacant or derelict land, leads to the wasteful use of land resources, higher infrastructure costs, and excessive energy consumption and air pollution because of the greater use of motorized transport. Many criticize urban sprawl for aesthetic reasons as well.

The United States provides an apt example. Urban population growth there has slowed to less than 1.3 percent per year (24), yet urban development continues to encroach on surrounding lands as residents abandon inner cities and move to the suburbs. The total amount of land dedicated to urban uses increased from 21 million hectares in 1982 to 26 million hectares in 1992. In one decade, 2,085,945 hectares of forestland, 1,525,314 hectares of cultivated cropland, 943,598 hectares of pastureland, and 774,029 hectares of rangeland were converted to urban uses (25).

Land pressures are even greater in developing countries with high rates of urban population growth. The physical size of cities in developing countries is expected to double between 1980 and 2000 (26). Around certain cities, urban land expansion is occurring even faster. In Sao Paulo, Brazil, the urban core grew from an area of

Steep slopes. *Unable to afford housing, the poor are often forced to settle on land unsuitable for development, such as the hillsides on the outskirts of Rio de Janeiro, which are vulnerable to landslides and erosion.*

180 square kilometers in 1930 to more than 900 square kilometers in 1988. (See Figure 3.1.) The metropolitan region is even larger, covering an astounding 8,000 square kilometers (27). Prime agricultural land and forestland have been converted to urban uses, and development is beginning to move onto steep slopes, which include some of the region's last remaining reserves of natural vegetation (28). Urban expansion is also threatening the local watershed: an estimated 1 million squatters now live in protected watershed areas, and wetlands located next to rivers are covered by streets and housing (29).

The example of Sao Paulo shows that it is not necessarily the scale of urban land conversion that is so important as the type of land being lost. Where a city is located is a major determinant of its environmental impact, and—for historical reasons—cities are often located on prime agricultural land or valuable ecosystems near rivers, lakes, or coasts.

Estimates suggest that 476,000 hectares of arable land in developing countries is being transformed annually to urban uses (30). To compensate for this loss of land, crop production on the remaining lands may become more intense and potentially more environmentally damaging (31). Urban development can push agriculture to less suitable land, with unintended results. In Canada, for instance, replacing the food production from 1 hectare of prime Ontario farmland lost to urban growth requires about 3 hectares of prairie land, thus increasing the rate of land conversion overall (32). As agriculture moves farther from the city, the transportation of food to the city incurs added energy and pollution costs (33). For countries with little unused arable land, such as China and Egypt, the loss of productive farmland may threaten food security (34). For most rapidly developing cities, however, the loss of agricultural land may not constitute a serious problem, because in part it reflects the lower value of agricultural land relative to that of urban land (35).

A greater long-term threat than the loss of agricultural land may be urban encroachment onto fragile ecosystems as a result of intense land use pressures and poor land use planning (36). Squatter settlements are commonly found on steep hillsides vulnerable to landslides and soil erosion, on water catchment areas, on protected lands, and on land subject to flooding or tidal inundation. Although the poor are aware that their settlements lie in precarious locations, the lack of alternative land for housing leaves them no choice. The impacts are twofold: damage to the local environment and threats to the health and well-being of the residents who live there. In Rio de Janeiro, Brazil, *favela* dwellers (residents of squatter settlements) who live on the steep slopes surrounding the city disturb the natural vegetation and destabilize the hillside soils, leading to intensified mudslides that claim hundreds of lives and that leave thousands of people homeless each year (37).

Natural areas are also sacrificed to formal urban development, such as residential estates, industry, and tourism (38). Forests, wetlands, and other ecosystems serve important functions—for instance, species habitat or flood control—but these benefits can seem "intangible" compared with the benefits of urban development.

Urban land use planning can help guide urban development away from vulnerable ecosystems. Such policies will not work, however, unless cities also provide adequate land for housing, for industries and commerce, and for public infrastructure and buildings. Given the scarcity of urban land, important trade-offs will have to be made in land allocation to balance environmental protection with economic development and to meet the basic needs of the poor (39).

Converting the Coasts

Coastal ecosystems, including wetlands, tidal flats, saltwater marshes, mangrove swamps, and the flora and fauna that depend on them, are especially threatened by urban land conversion (40). (See Table 3.1.) Already, coastal urban centers are home to almost 1 billion people worldwide and are experiencing unprecedented growth (41). Much of this growth will take place in developing nations; even now, growth rates in many coastal cities in the developing world substantially exceed those in surrounding rural regions (42). Even in developed countries such as the United States, some of the highest levels of urban growth are occurring in small coastal cities (43). Accordingly, urban impacts along the coasts stand to increase markedly in the years ahead.

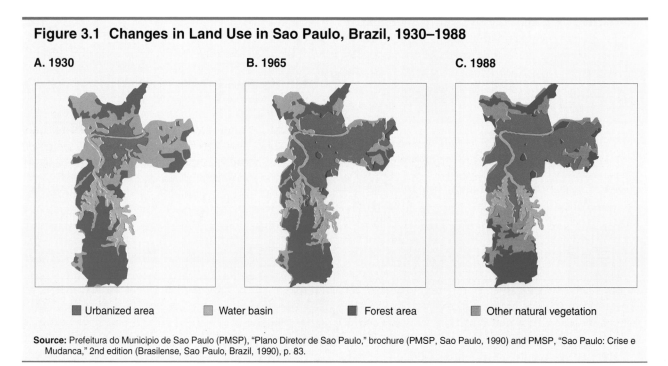

Figure 3.1 Changes in Land Use in Sao Paulo, Brazil, 1930–1988

A. 1930   B. 1965   C. 1988

■ Urbanized area   ■ Water basin   ■ Forest area   ■ Other natural vegetation

Source: Prefeitura do Municipio de Sao Paulo (PMSP), "Plano Diretor de Sao Paulo," brochure (PMSP, Sao Paulo, 1990) and PMSP, "Sao Paulo: Crise e Mudanca," 2nd edition (Brasilense, Sao Paulo, Brazil, 1990), p. 83.

In coastal cities, the higher value placed on shoreline locations increases the economic incentives to develop there. Thus, as coastal cities grow and expand, original coastal habitat is increasingly converted to other uses. Land conversion activities range from draining and filling of marshes and other wetlands to constructing homes or resorts on beaches or dunes, to building seawalls, to undertaking large-scale reclamation projects that extend the shoreline into the sea.

According to a recent study by the World Resources Institute, roughly half of the world's coasts are threatened by development-related activities (44). (See Chapter 11, "Biodiversity.") In Singapore, for instance, demand for land is so great that the island nation has added 6,000 hectares to its land area by filling along the shoreline, increasing its area some 10 percent from what it was three decades ago (45). Along the San Francisco Bay, the most highly urbanized estuary in the United States, filling has reduced the areal extent of the bay by one third in the past 150 years (46).

Double threat. As people move toward the coast in unprecedented numbers, beaches and other coastal ecosystems are threatened by both urbanization and tourism.

In addition to habitat loss, shoreline development can intensify coastal erosion, alter the hydrology of estuaries, and otherwise disrupt natural processes. For instance, beaches, sand dunes, marshes, mangrove swamps, barrier islands, and reefs all act as physical barriers against storm damage. When these buffers are lost to development, the coast is more vulnerable to erosion. The protective structures typically built to dissipate storm energy in turn can disrupt the normal processes by which sand is replenished, leading to fur-

Table 3.1 Distribution of Cities with More Than 500,000 Residents in Coastal and Noncoastal Areas, 1995

	Number of Cities					
	500,000 to 1 Million Residents		1 Million to 10 Million Residents		More Than 10 Million Residents	
Region	Coastal	Noncoastal	Coastal	Noncoastal	Coastal	Noncoastal
World	124	214	108	159	6	2
Africa	12	31	13	14	0	0
Asia	61	102	59	88	5	1
North America	8	12	4	4	0	0
Central America	6	9	3	8	0	1
South America	17	10	12	10	1	0
Europe	16	20	8	15	0	0
Former Soviet Union	4	30	4	20	0	0
Oceania	1	0	5	0	0	0

Sources: Compiled by the World Resources Institute from the following: World Cities Population Database (Birkbeck College, University of London, London, 1990); United Nations (U.N.) Population Division, *Urban Agglomerations as Assessed in 1994* (U.N., New York, 1994); United Nations Environment Programme and World Health Organization, *Urban Air Pollution in Megacities of the World* (Blackwell Publishers, Oxford, U.K., 1992).
Notes: City population data are standardized to a common year (1995). Urban agglomeration data reported by the United Nations often include several cities within a defined agglomeration. In this table, these agglomerations have been subdivided into their smaller administrative units. Therefore, the number of cities of a certain population may not correspond to United Nations urban population data used elsewhere in this report.

ther erosion in adjacent areas (47) (48) (49). Expansion of the port in Tangiers, Morocco, has altered the coastal profile and modified local current patterns; as a result, nearby beaches are now eroding at a rate of 5 meters per year (50).

Cities have been a particular locus of coastal wetland conversion because marshes, mangroves, or other wetlands are apt to line the estuaries and bays where most coastal cities are located. Of the estimated 80,940 hectares of coastal marshes that originally fringed San Francisco Bay, for instance, 80 percent have been lost to development (51).

Wetlands serve as spawning grounds for many aquatic species as well as habitat for waterfowl and other wildlife. In addition, they filter out many waterborne pollutants and provide extensive flood protection. Often, however, the importance of urban wetlands is apparent only after their services have been lost. In East Calcutta, India, 4,000 hectares of lagoons and swamps that had been used to raise fish were filled to provide home sites for 100,000 middle-class families, resulting in an estimated annual loss of 25,000 metric tons of fish and contributing to local flooding problems (52) (53). Even if wetlands are not immediately filled or drained, they frequently suffer from proximity to developed areas, acting as a receptacle for city wastes and runoff that may overwhelm their natural absorptive capacity or disturb their hydrology.

EXTRACTION AND DEPLETION OF NATURAL RESOURCES

Cities require vast quantities of resources to run—both for urban inhabitants and for the economic activities that are clustered there. In contrast to rural communities, which are immediately dependent on the land that supports them, urban communities are rarely confronted with the impacts of their resource consumption—advanced transportation networks allow resources to be tapped from distant hinterlands. Rich cities, in particular, draw on resources far from their boundaries.

The demand for supplies for cities is much greater and more complex than ever before. These supplies range from such basics as water, fuel, sand, and wood, to minerals such as aluminum and steel, to advanced plastics and synthetic materials. For instance, urban expansion creates demands for construction materials such as clays, sand, gravel, and crushed rock to make concrete, cement, and road stone (54). In Aligarh City, India, approximately 1,000 cubic meters of soil is brought into the city each day, altering natural drainage channels and increasing the level of flooding of large areas in the region (55). In Jakarta, Indonesia, 1.2 million cubic meters of wood, mainly from the nearby rural islands of Kalimantan and Sumatra, is imported to the metropolitan region each year (56). The process of resource extraction can also have negative environmental impacts, altering natural habitats, increasing land degradation, and indirectly leading to pollution, such as in mining discharges or saline intrusion into aquifers.

The range of inputs that sustain city life is enormous, and a discussion of all of these inputs is beyond the scope of this report. However, a discussion of two resources—water and energy—illustrates how the scale of urban demand can deplete local resource stores.

Energy Resources

Patterns of Energy Use

Urbanization has a profound effect on the amount and type of energy consumed. Along with population growth, economic development, and industrialization, urbanization is one of the principal forces driving the global increase in energy demand (57) (58). (See Chapter 12, "Energy and Materials.") Although traditional rural societies rely heavily on human and animal energy and on nearby wood for fuel, today's urban societies are characterized by their reliance on fossil fuels and electricity. These different patterns of energy use lead to different environmental impacts.

In the developing world, per capita energy consumption remains low. For many urban dwellers, especially in smaller cities in Africa and Asia, a large share of energy needs are still met by biomass fuels (59) (60). As these countries urbanize, however, demand for energy increases and traditional, bulky fuels such as wood or charcoal are replaced by oil and electricity (61) (62). Energy consumption tends to be greater in urban areas in the developing world as urban households acquire more appliances, such as irons, televisions, and refrigerators (63). Urban dwellers are more likely to travel to work via energy-intensive modes of transportation, and food and other materials consumed in urban areas must be transported across greater distances (64). Urban manufacturing and industry are more energy intensive than traditional farming (65). Building the urban infrastructure necessary to support the high population densities in cities requires energy not typically expended in traditional rural settlements (66) (67) (68).

By contrast, per capita energy use in urban areas of the developed world tends to be lower than that in rural areas (69). Part of the reason is that industries are no longer located strictly in cities (70), but much has to do with the efficiencies of scale possible in cities. For example, attached housing and apartment buildings require less energy for heating and cooling, and mass transit requires less energy than transport by personal car (71). Far greater amounts of energy would be required to provide similar services to dispersed rural populations than to concentrated urban populations.

Impacts of Resource Extraction

In the developing world, biomass fuels provide between 25 and 90 percent of domestic energy supplies, especially in smaller urban centers (72). Although urban consumption of wood as fuel is neither the primary use for forest products nor the major cause of forest loss globally, local impacts on nearby forests can be severe. Even in cities with low levels of per capita consumption of biomass fuels—Bangkok, Thailand, and Manila, Philippines, for example—the large number of people concentrated in a small area can place considerable total demand on forest resources (73).

The growth in demand for wood resources around cities has caused deforestation around some urban centers reaching 100 kilometers and more. In India between 1960 and 1986, the closed forest cover around 18 urban centers decreased between one fifth and two thirds (74). In Africa, urban regions are now experiencing rapid rates of deforestation (75), as in the peri-urban region of Ouagadougou, Burkina Faso, and the subhumid wooded savannah around Dar es Salaam, Tanzania (76). Deforestation also contributes to a variety of indirect environmental impacts, including soil degradation, water siltation, and the loss of indigenous plant and animal species (77). However, since forests are a renewable resource, proper management can help mitigate the impacts; indeed, in some cases the scarcity of fuelwood has led to additional tree planting (78).

As a fuel source, charcoal is often preferred over wood because of its compact size. However, pressures on forests can intensify when urban households switch from wood to charcoal because charcoal is produced at low conversion efficiencies from wood (79) (80). In Senegal, for example, charcoal production accounts for the clearing of between 18,000 and 33,000 hectares per year, or between 11 and 20 percent of total estimated annual deforestation (81). This percentage of annual deforestation can be attributed primarily to urban resource demands, since in urban areas charcoal accounts for 91 percent of wood-based fuels compared with 8 percent in the rural areas (82).

As cities increase their reliance on fossil fuels and electric power, pressure on surrounding forests de-

creases but new problems emerge, often at considerable distances from the city itself. The environmental impacts of, for example, coal mining and oil and gas drilling and transport can be severe (83). In Katowice, Poland, for example, local coal mines are causing water and land degradation. In 1992, Katowice's coal mines discharged more than 4,800 metric tons of salt into the Vistula River each day, leading to major declines in aquatic life (84) (85). About 20,000 hectares of land in the region are degraded (up from 9,500 hectares in 1975) by mining excavations, tunnels, land subsidence, waste dumps, and flooded areas. Each year, 500 to 600 hectares of additional land is degraded; in 1988, only 74 hectares was reclaimed (86) (87).

Water Resources

Many countries, including those with enormous amounts of available water, face urban water supply problems (88). Local water shortages are especially acute in the world's megacities, although they are also appearing in smaller urban agglomerations such as Dakar, Senegal; Lima, Peru; La Rioja, Spain; and Lucknow, India.

The growing demand for water, along with poor water resource management and mounting pollution levels, contributes to water supply problems in and around cities. Although municipal water use accounts for less than one tenth of the world's overall water use (89), urbanization increases the per capita demand for water for domestic purposes. Part of this growth in demand can be attributed to better access to water supplies in cities than in rural areas. Industrial demand for water also rises. As the number of people in urban areas grows, so does the demand for food and, hence, for irrigation in agricultural areas close to the city. These pressures can quickly result in demands for water that surpass local water supplies.

Poor urban water management practices exacerbate local water shortages. Where water rights are not clearly defined, users may claim supplies well in excess of their needs to deal with future uncertainties. Water is usually priced much lower than the actual cost of securing, treating, and distributing it (in part because of government subsidies), leaving little incentive for households and industries to conserve water. Inefficient water systems are another major source of water loss. In many cities in the developing world, leaky pipes and illegal connections waste between 20 and 50 percent of public water supplies (90) (91). (See Figure 3.2.) In developed countries, aging infrastructure is contributing to similar problems. In the United Kingdom, as much as 25 percent of all water used may be lost because of leakage (92).

Box 3.1 Water: The Challenge for Mexico City

Mexico City's struggle to secure enough water is a good example of how urban growth can quickly outstrip the natural resources of a region and lead to environmental degradation. Sprawling over 3,773 square kilometers (1), the city is home to more than 15.6 million people (2). The city's location—in a high, naturally closed basin—uniquely challenges water provision. The absence of an adequate nearby surface water source means that the city must depend largely on the local groundwater source, or import water from several hundred kilometers away. However, the high elevation of the valley makes water importation an expensive alternative (3). In addition, continued urban growth and poor system financing have limited the government's ability to expand service coverage, repair leaks, and provide wastewater treatment (4).

The largest problem, however, is the depletion of Mexico City's aquifer. Today, almost 72 percent of the city's water supply comes from the aquifer that underlies the metropolitan area (5). The groundwater level is sinking by about 1 meter each year (6) (7). Although overdrafting of the aquifer has been occurring at least since the early 1900s, the problem has intensified recently. From 1986 to 1992, the water level of the aquifer showed a net lowering of 6 to 10 meters in the heavily pumped zones (8).

Because of this overextraction, Mexico City is suffering from severe land subsidence. (See Figure 1.) In part, the city's location is to blame, because the clay soils in the region are especially sus-

Figure 1 Subsidence in the Center City Area of Mexico City Due to Groundwater Extraction, 1935–85

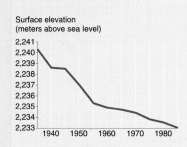

Surface elevation
(meters above sea level)

Source: National Research Council, Academia de la Investigacion Cientifica, A.C., and Academia Nacional de Ingenieria, A.C., *Mexico City's Water Supply: Improving the Outlook for Sustainability* (National Academy Press, Washington, D.C., 1995), p. 70.

ceptible to dewatering and compaction (9). Over the past 100 years, the central area of the Mexico City Metropolitan Area (MCMA) has fallen by an average of 7.5 meters. Neighborhood children mark their height on well casings to see whether they are growing faster than the ground is sinking (10). The result has been extensive damage to the city's infrastructure, including building foundations and the sewer system (11). The city is also especially vulnerable to flooding. In 1900, the bottom of Texcoco Lake was 3 meters lower than the average level of the city center. By 1974, the lake

bottom was 2 meters higher than the city (12). Expensive drainage channels have been built, but flooding remains a problem during heavy rainfall (13).

The aquifer is also at risk from contamination and faces expensive and difficult cleanup. Currently, 90 percent of the municipal and industrial liquid wastes from MCMA are discharged untreated into the sewer systems (14). Industries generate an estimated 3 million metric tons of hazardous wastes per year, of which more than 95 percent are process effluents or treated effluents discharged directly into the municipal sewage system (15). In many areas, this wastewater travels in unlined drainage canals (16). There is the potential that pollutants may leak into the underlying soil and leach through fractures (from land subsidence) into the aquifer, contaminating the water supply (17). Other identified threats to the groundwater include hazardous wastes illegally dumped in landfills, pesticides, and saline intrusion (18) (19).

Demand for water in the region continues to grow. Overall, 94 percent of MCMA's residents are serviced by either a piped water connection or a standpipe (20), but coverage varies widely. In Tlalpan in 1990, for example, 14 percent of homes did not have access to any form of public water supply (21). Mexico City's urban periphery is growing quickly, and providing adequate supplies of water to these residents poses a further challenge. Average per capita water use is still far below that of developed countries, indicating the potential for increased demand. The Federal Dis-

---

Water scarcity is closely linked to water quality. Freshwater lakes and rivers provide affordable and easily accessible water, but uncontrolled discharges of domestic sewage and industrial effluents have left many urban rivers heavily polluted and their water unsafe for use. Consequently, cities must search for water supplies well beyond their boundaries (93).

Other cities rely on groundwater, but many of them are withdrawing water from aquifers faster than natural rates of replenishment, leading to salinization and subsidence. (See Box 3.1.) Saline intrusion is common in almost all coastal cities, from Jacksonville, Florida, to Dakar, Senegal, to the Chinese cities of Dalian, Qingdao, Yantai, and Beihai (94) (95) (96). Land subsidence can

cause structural damage to buildings and roads and can contribute to urban flooding. For Bangkok, which overdraws water from its aquifer by a conservative estimate of 0.6 million to 0.8 million cubic meters per day, the compacting of underlying soils has led to land subsidence ranging from 5 to more than 10 centimeters per year throughout the region (97). To alleviate this land subsidence, Bangkok would have to reduce its groundwater extraction rate by at least one half—a formidable challenge because water demand is expected to grow rapidly in the coming decades (98).

Water shortages and conflicts among urban, industrial, and agricultural users may become especially severe in parts of India, China, and the Middle Eastern

trict uses 364 liters per capita per day [22], compared with New York City, which uses 680 liters per capita per day [23].

Mexico is actively pursuing new solutions to meet these demands and to protect the environment. Aggressive efforts are under way to protect the aquifer recharge areas from urban encroachment [24]. Officials are attempting to institute new pricing systems that would ensure that the full cost of urban water use includes the cost of developing sewage systems and wastewater treatment facilities. Currently, only $0.10 is collected per cubic meter of water, even though the marginal cost of supplying water to MCMA is estimated at about $1.00 per cubic meter [25]. In 1991, the MCMA began a new rate structure that charges more per cubic meter as consumption levels increase. The goal is to provide metered industries with the incentive to conserve water, eventually leading to full cost recovery—an ambitious goal. Now only 53 percent of the users are metered, and not all meters function properly. To achieve full metering, several million additional meters would have to be installed at a cost of roughly $100 each [26].

Some more modest conservation efforts are already showing success. Water utilities are making routine repairs part of their overall strategy, and more than 3,800 leaks in the MCMA distribution system are fixed each month. In 1989, the Federal District initiated a program for retrofitting large office and apartment buildings with low-flow toilets that use only 6 liters of water per flush; older models use 16 liters [27]. By 1996, this program alone is expected to reduce water consumption by 4.3 cubic meters per second within the Federal District [28]. (Total water consumption in the MCMA is approximately 60 cubic meters per second [29].) The State of Mexico recently began a similar program.

Despite these efforts, the financial and environmental costs of supplying water to Mexico City are expected to increase as demand continues to outstrip supplies in the near term [30].

References and Notes

1. National Research Council, Academia de la Investigacion Cientifica, A.C., and Academia Nacional de Ingenieria, A.C., *Mexico City's Water Supply: Improving the Outlook for Sustainability* (National Academy Press, Washington, D.C., 1995), p. 6.

2. United Nations (U.N.) Population Division, *World Urbanization Prospects: The 1994 Revision* (U.N., New York, 1994), Table 1, p. 4.

3. *Op. cit.* 1, p. 7.

4. *Op. cit.* 1, p. 1.

5. *Op. cit.* 1, p. 1.

6. *Op. cit.* 1, p. 17.

7. For a detailed discussion of these calculations, see I. Herrera-Revilla *et al.*, "Diagnostico del Estado Present de las Aguas Subteraneas de la Ciudad de Mexico y Determinacion de sus Condiciones Futuras," and AIC-ANIAC, "El Agua y la Ciudad de Mexico," both of which are cited in National Research Council, Academia de la Investigacion Cientifica, A.C., and Academia Nacional de Ingenieria, A.C., *Mexico City's Water Supply: Improving the Out-*

look for Sustainability (National Academy Press, Washington, D.C., 1995).

8. *Op. cit.* 1, pp. 12–13.

9. *Op. cit.* 1, pp. 6–7.

10. *Op. cit.* 1, pp. 13–14.

11. *Op. cit.* 1, p. 14.

12. *Op. cit.* 1, p. 14.

13. *Op. cit.* 1, p. 14.

14. *Op. cit.* 1, p. 40.

15. *Op. cit.* 1, p. 41.

16. M. Mazari and M.D. Mackay, "Potential Groundwater Contamination by Organic Compounds in the Mexico City Metropolitan Area," *Environment, Science, and Technology,* Vol. 27, No. 5 (1993), as cited in National Research Council, Academia de la Investigacion Cientifica, A.C., and Academia Nacional de Ingenieria, A.C., *Mexico City's Water Supply: Improving the Outlook for Sustainability* (National Academy Press, Washington, D.C., 1995), p. 39.

17. *Op. cit.* 1, p. 40.

18. *Op. cit.* 1, p. 41.

19. *Op. cit.* 1, p. 44.

20. *Op. cit.* 1, p. 20.

21. *Op. cit.* 1, p. 58.

22. *Op. cit.* 1, p. 20.

23. World Resources Institute, *The 1994 Information Please Environmental Almanac* (Houghton Mifflin Company, Boston, 1994), p. 209.

24. *Op. cit.* 1, p. 53.

25. *Op. cit.* 1, p. 55.

26. *Op. cit.* 1, pp. 55, 65.

27. *Op. cit.* 1, pp. 63–64.

28. *Op. cit.* 1, p. 64.

29. *Op. cit.* 1, p. 21.

30. *Op. cit.* 1, p. 70.

nations. Much of sub-Saharan Africa is likely to face similar pressures, although data for the region are scarce. Already struggling with uneven distribution of water resources and local water scarcity, the urban populations of these regions are expected to double in less than 25 years [99].

In India, total demand for water is projected to nearly double by 2025. Although agriculture will still claim the bulk of water supplies, demand is growing fastest in the urban and industrial sectors and is projected to climb 135 percent over the next 40 years [100]. Already in Hyderabad, India, the need for irrigation water during low-flow years is in direct conflict with the need for water within the city itself. Similar conflicts are emerging in China, where about 300 cities already experience water shortages [101].

URBAN WASTES

The increased levels of consumption characteristic of the populations of urban areas lead to the generation of copious quantities of wastes. The impacts of this pollution are experienced both locally and at great distances from the source. Domestic and industrial discharges contaminate air, land, and water with nutrients and toxics. In turn, degraded air, land, and water harm flora and fauna.

Figure 3.2 Percent of Water Supply Unaccounted for in Selected Asian Cities, 1990–91

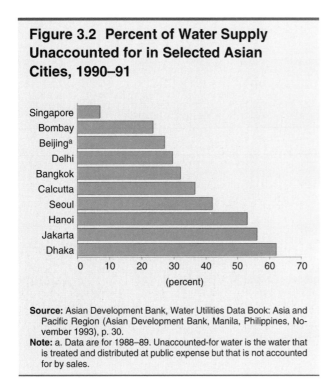

Source: Asian Development Bank, Water Utilities Data Book: Asia and Pacific Region (Asian Development Bank, Manila, Philippines, November 1993), p. 30.

Note: a. Data are for 1988–89. Unaccounted-for water is the water that is treated and distributed at public expense but that is not accounted for by sales.

Much of this pollution stems from economic growth and industrialization rather than urbanization per se. Cities, however, concentrate these wastes in one place, straining the ability of local ecosystems to assimilate them. Wetlands, for example, can render small quanti-

ties of domestic sewage harmless, yet they are no match for vast quantities of urban sewage. Urbanization itself reduces the assimilative capacity of the environment by removing vegetation, slowing the flows of air and water, generating heat, and reducing the infiltration capacity of the land (102).

This section looks at only a few aspects of pollution: air pollution, especially the formation of urban ozone; municipal solid waste; and water pollution, in particular, the problem of urban sewage.

Urban Air Pollution

Despite the potential for energy efficiency in cities, urban energy demand and fossil fuel consumption continue to grow. Already, the concentrations of airborne pollutants in and around cities far exceed those in rural areas. In addition to their toll on human health (see Chapter 2, "Urban Environment and Human Health"), these air pollutants can damage terrestrial and aquatic ecosystems. Not all of this damage can be attributed to urban activities. Nonetheless, sources of emissions are concentrated in or around urban areas—especially in developing countries, where industries still tend to be located in cities. In addition, combustion of the fossil fuels used for urban transportation is playing an ever greater role in air pollution problems. (See Box 3.2 and Chapter 4, "Urban Transportation.")

Air quality standards are typically set with human health in mind, but some forms of ecosystem damage can occur at far lower levels. Table 3.2 compares health-based standards with the levels at which ecosystem damage has been documented. In most northern European cities, for example, sulfur dioxide concentrations rarely exceed World Health Organization guidelines, yet sulfur deposition still exceeds the levels at which ecosystem damage can occur. In fact, some efforts to reduce the health effects of urban air pollution in developed countries have actually increased damage to ecosystems. The tall smokestacks built to disperse pollutants in cities such as New York, Philadelphia, and Pittsburgh in the United States ultimately contributed to the acidification of lakes in the Adirondack Mountains (103). In most developed countries, however, stringent pollution control laws and new technologies have reduced sulfur emissions dramatically since the 1950s.

Table 3.2 Comparison of World Health Organization (WHO) Guidelines Versus Critical Levels of Atmospheric Pollutants Known To Cause Ecosystem Damage

Pollutant	WHO Guidelines (micrograms per cubic meter)		Critical Level for Ecosystem[a] (micrograms per cubic meter)
	1 hour	24 hours	
Sulfur dioxide[b]	350	125	10[c]–20[d,e] 30[d,f]
Nitrogen oxides	400	150	30[g]
Ozone	150–200	100–120 (8 hours)	80[f,h]

Sources: 1. United Nations Environment Programme and World Health Organization, Urban Air Pollution in Megacities of the World (Blackwell Publishers, Oxford, U.K., 1992), pp. 222, 225–226. 2. The Swedish NGO Secretariat on Acid Rain, "Environmental Factsheet No. 6: Critical Loads," Acid News, No. 2 (April 19, 1995), pp. 4–5.

Notes: a. Critical levels are defined as the concentration of pollutants in the atmosphere above which direct adverse effects on receptors, such as plants, ecosystems, or materials, may occur, according to present knowledge. b. Guideline values for combined exposure to sulfur dioxide and suspended particulate matter. These may not apply to situations in which only one of the components is present. c. Annual mean. d. Both annual and half-year mean. e. Forest ecosystems and natural vegetation. f. Agricultural crops. g. Maximum annual mean. h. Threshold concentration. Critical levels are now expressed as cumulative exposure over a threshold concentration, using the formula x parts per billion (ppb) (2 micrograms per cubic meter = 1 ppb) for y hours above the baseline ppb.

In China, where urban use of high-sulfur coal for cooking and domestic heating is common, urban emissions of sulfur dioxide—a precursor to acid rain—may double or even triple over the next two or three decades (104). Already, damage to aquatic and terrestrial ecosystems has been documented downwind from most Chinese cities. In the Wanxian District downwind from the city of Chongqing, 26 percent of a 65,000-hectare pine forest has died, at least in part because of air pollution. Extensive soil acidification in the region has caused damage to farm produce and a drop in harvest yields (105).

Julio Etchart/Reportage/Still Pictures

Inversion layer. Bounded by mountains that prevent dispersal of air emissions, Mexico City has some of the worst air pollution in the world.

Urban Ozone

Whereas in most regions of the world problems related to acid deposition stem more from industrialization than urbanization, ground-level ozone—which damages both human health and vegetation—is a distinctly urban problem. The combination of cars, pollutants, and meteorological conditions unique to cities is key to ozone formation. Ozone levels seem certain to increase as the number of cars (a primary source of the pollutants that produce ozone) in cities continues to climb. (See Chapter 4, "Urban Transportation.")

Urban ozone is a particularly difficult problem to address because no one polluter actually emits it. Ozone is produced when nitrogen oxides, carbon monoxide, and hydrocarbons react with sunlight, a process that takes 8 to 10 hours. In addition to cars, other sources include the production and use of organic chemicals, the use of natural gas, municipal waste disposal, and wastewater treatment plants.

The greatest damage to ecosystems from urban ozone often occurs many kilometers from the city itself, although inversion layers can trap ozone within city limits and cause health problems there as well. Plumes downwind of large North American cities can have ozone concentrations of between 70 and 200 parts per billion, often over distances of several hundred kilometers (106) (107). Ozone concentrations as low as 40 parts per billion can injure plant leaves, whereas exposure to concentra-

tions of 60 to 100 parts per billion for several hours is sufficient to cause significant plant, tree, and crop damage (108). Once injured by ozone, plants are more susceptible to insect attack, root rot, and other diseases.

In the United States, ozone is responsible for most of the crop yield losses from air pollutants (109). In addition, ozone has been implicated in the declines in the numbers of ponderosa and Jeffrey pines in the San Bernardino National Forest east of Los Angeles, where daytime average ozone concentrations of 100 parts per billion are typical during the summer months, and in the white pine in the eastern United States, downwind from the urban industrial centers in New York and New Jersey (110).

The decline in the numbers of trees near Los Angeles sends an important message to other expanding cities. Without policy interventions, ozone will become a problem for virtually all mid-latitude cities where motor vehicle traffic is increasing. Forest damage associated with ozone is already apparent around Santiago, Chile, and Mexico City (111) (112). In Asia and the Pacific, ozone damage is likely to be occurring in forests downwind from Tokyo and Osaka in Japan; Beijing, China; Seoul, Republic of Korea; Taipei, Taiwan; Delhi, India; and Karachi, Pakistan (113) (114).

Greenhouse Gas Emissions

Although the upswing in fossil fuel consumption is not due solely to urbanization, there is no doubt that major

Box 3.2 Los Angeles Copes with Air Pollution

In the past two decades, in the face of sustained population and economic growth, air quality in the Los Angeles area has improved dramatically. (See Figure 1.) From 1955 to 1992 the peak level of ozone declined sharply from 680 to 300 parts per billion. Smog levels in the early 1990s were the lowest on record (1).

Despite these gains, the citizens of Los Angeles suffer from the worst air pollution in the United States. Pollution reaches unhealthful levels on roughly half the days each year—as opposed to 279 days in 1976—causing irritation for many and illness for some (2) (3). A 1991 study found that those living in areas where particulate pollution exceeded government standards for 42 days per year or more had a 33 percent greater risk of contracting bronchitis and a 74 percent greater risk of contracting asthma (4).

Several ingredients contribute to the city's air pollution problems, including a bowl-like setting, abundant sunshine that drives photochemical reactions, low average wind speeds, and rapid growth in the numbers of people, cars, and factories. From 1950 to 1990, the region's population grew from 4.8 million to 14 million; the vehicle population jumped from 2.3 million to 10.6 million (5).

In an effort to improve air quality, state and regional agencies are implementing a stringent and innovative pollution control effort that targets industry, transportation, and consumers. The political arrangements have evolved over many decades.

As early as the 1940s and 1950s, pollution levels in the city were bad enough to prompt public outrage and political action. The *Los Angeles Times* published dozens of editorials demanding action to reduce smog, and several efforts were started to study the chemistry of the atmosphere above Los Angeles (6). By the mid-1970s, each of the four counties that make up the metropolitan region—Los Angeles, Orange, and parts of Riverside and San Bernardino counties—had its own pollution control program. But it was already apparent that local programs would not be able to solve problems that were regional in nature.

In response, the California legislature in 1976 created the South Coast Air Quality Management District and gave it jurisdiction over much of the air quality throughout the four counties. The District was given responsibility for sta-

tionary sources of air pollution, which include about 31,000 businesses ranging from large power plants to small gas stations and which account for about 40 percent of the area's pollution (7). Also under the District's purview are consumer products, such as house paint, charcoal lighter fluid, and products containing solvents. The District's air quality plans must be approved by the California Air Resources Board (CARB) and then by the U.S. Environmental Protection Agency. CARB also was given jurisdiction over mobile sources of pollution such as cars, trucks, and buses (8).

The region has used a variety of strategies to curb air pollution. For example, programs were initiated to recover vapors that escape when gas or other petroleum products are transferred and to eliminate industrial solvents, which play a major role in the formation of ozone. To help combat the region's continuing growth, officials in 1976 issued "new source" regulations requiring industries to use the cleanest technology available for any expansion or new construction (9).

Even so, if Los Angeles is to meet federal health standards by 2010, more stringent requirements will be needed. Hydrocarbon emissions must be cut by about 80 percent, nitrogen oxides by 70

Figure 1 Number of Days Ozone Exceeded 200 Parts Per Billion in the Los Angeles Area, 1980 and 1991

A. 1980

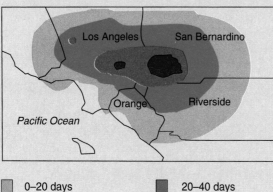

B. 1991

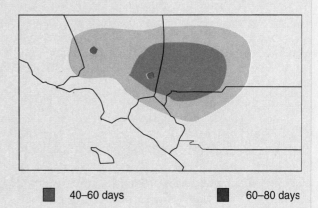

0–20 days   20–40 days   40–60 days   60–80 days

Source: James M. Lents and William J. Kelly, "Clearing the Air in Los Angeles," *Scientific American,* Vol. 269, No. 4 (October 1993), p. 36.
Note: A 1-hour average of 200 parts per billion represents a Stage 1 alert according to criteria established by the South Coast Air Quality Management District and the State of California.

percent, sulfur oxides by 62 percent, and particulates by 20 percent. The benefits will be immense; meeting the federal standards for ozone and particulates could provide $9.4 billion in health benefits every year (10). The penalties for not meeting this target could be severe, however, including the possible loss of millions of dollars in federal money for highway and mass transit construction. The California Clean Air Act also requires steady progress—emissions reductions of 5 percent per year—until the standards are met (11).

To meet the 2010 deadline, the District has devised an elaborate two-stage air quality management plan, relying on both current technologies and some that do not yet exist. The first stage includes some 135 different measures, all using existing technologies that can be adopted by 1996. For example, electric companies will install new burners and catalysts that will cut nitrogen oxide emissions. Reformulated charcoal lighter fluid will help cut pollution from backyard barbecues. Manufacturing plants and construction companies are using newly formulated paints, solvents, and adhesives that minimize pollution.

The second stage will take advantage of technologies that are just entering the commercial market, such as a new house paint that does not release hydrocarbons and automobile engines that run on methanol, natural gas, or other alternative fuels. The District has invested over $40 million in seed money to support new technologies (12).

To ease the financial burden for the business community, the District has provided free technical assistance and has offered loans for the purchase of pollution control equipment. The program also enables firms to adopt the least expensive ways to cut nitrogen and sulfur emissions to meet standards. In the first multipollutant emissions trading effort for an urban area, businesses can either reduce emissions themselves or buy emissions credits from companies that have reduced their emissions below the standards (13).

In 1987, the District implemented a carpooling program that by 1994 had increased the average number of persons per vehicle by 13 percent since the program's inception. The ride share program was expensive for businesses, however, costing about $110 per employee, or $17,421 per metric ton of pollution reduced. In April 1995, the District revised the program by allowing firms to voluntarily substitute emissions reduction measures. Alternatives include scrapping old, high-polluting cars and trucks to earn emissions credits, using remote vehicle sensing equipment to identify high-polluting employee vehicles and earning credits for repair of the vehicles, or paying $110 per employee per year into an air quality escrow account, which would be used for other programs such as the purchase of clean-fuel school buses. Some of the alternatives provide substantial savings to businesses. For example, old vehicle scrapping costs $2,755 to $6,102 per metric ton of pollution reduced, which amounts to a 65 to 84 percent reduction in the cost of the program (14).

Perhaps the most ambitious plan to cut automotive emissions was a 1990 statewide mandate that required that 2 percent of all passenger vehicles sold in the state by 1988 be emission free, increasing to 5 percent in 2001 and 10 percent in 2003 (15). For more than 5 years, the mandate has been driving technology advancement in electric cars (16). However, in December 1995, the California Air Resources Board decided to ease the mandate and proposed suspending current requirements for zero emission vehicles until 2003 (17), citing technology constraints as the major concern. Yet some believe the Board is submitting to pressure from the auto and oil industries (18).

Promoting widespread penetration of electric vehicles will be complicated by other factors as well. The current price for most such vehicles is $25,000 and up, which is too expensive for the average U.S. buyer. Conventional lead-acid batteries take up to 8 hours to recharge and must be changed every 2 to 3 years at a cost of $2,000. Most prototypes have a limited range of 96 to 121 kilometers. Research is under way on batteries that provide twice the cruising range and can be recharged in an hour or two, though such batteries currently are twice the price of lead-acid cells (19). Southern California Edison is developing an elaborate network of recharging stations in Los Angeles, but few other power companies in the United States are making similar plans (20).

References and Notes

1. James M. Lents and William J. Kelly, "Clearing the Air in Los Angeles," *Scientific American*, Vol. 269, No. 4 (October 1993), p. 32.

2. South Coast Air Quality District Governing Board, *Final 1994 Air Quality Management Plan: Meeting the Clean Air Challenge* (South Coast Air Quality Management District and Southern California Association of Governments, Diamond Bar, California, 1994), pp. 2-1 to 2-5.

3. *Ibid.*, p. 2-1.

4. *Op. cit.* 1, p. 38.

5. *Op. cit.* 1, p. 32.

6. *Op. cit.* 1, p. 33.

7. *Op. cit.* 2, pp. 1–5.

8. South Coast Air Quality Management District, "Introducing AQMD," March 1994 (public information brochure).

9. *Op. cit.* 1, pp. 35, 37.

10. *Op. cit.* 1, pp. 38–39.

11. *Op. cit.* 2, pp. 6-1 to 6-22.

12. *Op. cit.* 1, pp. 38–39.

13. *Op. cit.* 1, pp. 38–39.

14. South Coast Air Quality Management District, "Air Quality Officials Approve Major Overhaul of Rideshare Rule," April 14, 1995 (press release).

15. Marla Cone, "State Panel Puts Electric Car Mandate in Reverse," *Los Angeles Times,* (December 22, 1995), p. A1.

16. *Ibid.*

17. Electric Transportation Coalition, "California Air Resources Board Proposes to Suspend ZEV Mandates Until 2003 and to Institute a '*Cal/Big 7*' Technology Development Partnership," memorandum from Kateri Callahan, Executive Director, Electric Transportation Coalition, to Board of Directors and Members, Washington, D.C., December 27, 1995, p. 1.

18. Marla Cone, "Air Panel Bending Under Pressure," *Los Angeles Times* (December 20, 1995), p. A3.

19. Gary Lee, "California Recharges Electric Car Development," *Washington Post* (April 18, 1995), pp. A1, A8.

20. *Ibid.*

Figure 3.3 Comparison of Per Capita Solid Waste Generation and Percent of Waste Collected, Selected Cities

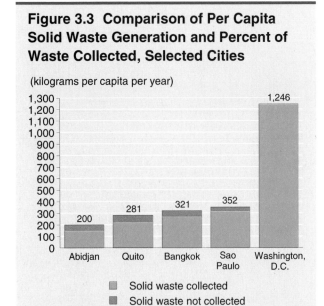

(kilograms per capita per year)

■ Solid waste collected
■ Solid waste not collected

Sources: 1. Abidjan, Cote d'Ivoire: Joseph Leitmann, "Urbanization and Environment in Sub-Saharan Africa: An Input to the Post-UNCED Urban Axis," draft paper (The World Bank, Washington, D.C., 1995), pp. 14, 20. 2. Quito, Ecuador: Gustavo Arcia *et al., Environmental Health Assessment: A Case Study Conducted in the City of Quito and the County of Pedro Moncayo, Pichincha Province, Ecuador,* WASH Reprint, Field Report No. 401 (U.S. Agency for International Development, Washington, D.C., 1993), p. 46. 3. Bangkok, Thailand: United Nations (U.N.) Economic and Social Commission for Asia and the Pacific, *State of Urbanization in Asia and the Pacific 1993* (U.N., New York, 1993), p. 2-55. 4. Sao Paulo, Brazil: Josef Leitmann, "Environmental Profile of Sao Paulo," draft paper (The World Bank, Washington, D.C., 1991), p. 10. 5. Washington, D.C.: World Resources Institute, *The 1994 Information Please Environmental Almanac* (Houghton Mifflin Company, Boston, 1994), p. 205.

metropolitan areas have the greatest concentrations of population, industry, and energy use, and hence the largest amount of pollution and the highest greenhouse gas emissions. (See Chapter 14, "Atmosphere and Climate.") One recent study estimates that almost 40 percent of total carbon dioxide emissions from North America come from 50 metropolitan areas (115). Although this should be considered only a rough approximation, it demonstrates the need for policy interventions to reduce urban output of greenhouse gases. In developing countries especially, the rapid growth in energy demand in urban areas (i.e., from electricity and transportation) is projected to greatly increase greenhouse gas emissions (116) (117) (118). Global warming is predicted to cause a rise in sea level, placing coastal cities at risk (119).

Solid Waste

Solid waste generation, both municipal and industrial, continues to increase worldwide in both absolute and per capita terms (120). Wealth is a primary determinant of how much solid waste a city produces. Wealthy cities

such as Los Angeles and New York are vast producers of solid waste, whereas per capita solid waste generation is still low in cities such as Calcutta, India, and Accra, Ghana. (See Figure 3.3.) As per capita incomes increase in cities in the developing world, the quantity of solid waste will likely grow in tandem. With increased wealth, the composition of wastes changes from primarily biodegradable organic materials to plastics and other synthetic materials, which take much longer to decompose. When solid waste is not collected and disposed of efficiently and effectively, it pollutes and degrades land and water resources. Managing the volume of solid waste can pose a major challenge for city governments, from ensuring that all waste within city boundaries is collected, to reducing health impacts, to acquiring vacant land sites for landfills.

In developing countries, the environmental impacts of improper solid waste disposal are especially severe. In many cities, only 30 to 50 percent of solid waste is collected; the rest is either burned or dumped in unregulated landfills. Uncontrolled disposal of urban waste into water bodies, open dumps, and poorly designed landfills is a principal cause of surface water and groundwater contamination. In Manila, the biggest solid waste dump is Balut, Tondo, which receives approximately 650 metric tons of solid waste each day. This dump site has reclaimed 34 hectares of Manila Bay and has created an enormous mountain of refuse towering 40 meters above sea level (121).

Many cities dispose of household wastes along with industrial wastes, exacerbating pollution problems. In China, for example, most toxic solid wastes are disposed of in the municipal waste stream without treatment (122), leading to contamination of soils and water bodies with heavy metals such as mercury, chromium, lead, and arsenic. These toxics can threaten or destroy marine life (123) (124).

Disposal of solid waste in legal landfills, as is the norm throughout the United States and Europe, averts many of these problems. If the landfills are not properly managed, however, runoff and leachates can contaminate surface water and groundwater supplies. Landfills are also becoming increasingly expensive, owing to the rising costs of construction and operation (125). Incineration, which can greatly reduce the amount of incoming municipal solid waste, is the second most common method of disposal in developed countries (126). However, incinerator ashes may contain hazardous materials, including heavy metals and organic compounds such as dioxin (127) (128). Recycling plays a large role in solid waste management, especially in cities in developing countries, and should be encouraged not only to reduce the need to dispose of vast amounts of waste but also to protect new raw materials from extraction and use. (See Chapter 5, "Urban Priorities for Action.")

Water Pollution

Water pollution probably began with the foundation of the first cities 7,000 years ago along the major river systems of the Tigris-Euphrates and Indus (129). Cities have long used rivers, lakes, and coastal waters as receptacles for diluting and dispersing wastes. The natural processes of water flow help to break down wastes and render them harmless. Ever-increasing urban populations and

Urban sewage. Throughout the developing world, some 90 percent of sewage is released untreated, usually to a water body. In Mexico City, untreated sewage pouring into a drainage canal (above) pollutes the municipal water supply and contaminates crops grown in the suburbs, where wastewater is used for irrigation.

their growing amounts of wastes, however, have over-taxed the natural recycling capabilities of local rivers and lakes. In cities close to coasts, untreated sewage and industrial effluents flow into the sea and damage beaches and inshore waters.

Although there has been significant progress in controlling water pollution in developed nations over the past three decades, pollution has continued to rise in most cities in the developing world and remains high around cities in the transition economies of Russia and Central Europe, posing a threat to human health and to the health of aquatic ecosystems. In some areas, entire estuaries and even international water bodies such as the Mediterranean Sea and the Caribbean are affected.

Urban-generated pollution comes from both localized and dispersed, or point and nonpoint, sources. Major point sources include municipal sewage, industrial outfalls, and air emissions from power plants and heavy industries. Nonpoint sources include silt from earth-moving activities; storm runoff from roads, home gardens, and industrial sites; infiltration from aquifers contaminated with sewage or industrial chemicals; and automobile emissions.

Of the many problems associated with urban effluents, nutrient loading, or eutrophication, of local waters is one of the most serious (130). Nutrients are essential plant foods, but excessive amounts can cause radical plant growth—often massive algal blooms—that blocks

the sunlight that other organisms need. As plants die and decompose, the dissolved oxygen in bottom waters is depleted—a condition that is deadly for fish and other aquatic life (131). Those fish and other mobile species that can survive may nonetheless lose critical habitat, their food supplies may be disrupted, or they may be forced into shallow areas where they are subject to increased predation (132) (133) (134) (135).

Nutrients come from several sources, including run-off from upstream agricultural and urban areas, particularly silt, and air emissions. Atmospheric deposition is thought to be responsible for about one third of the nitrogen in the Chesapeake Bay, which is surrounded by several large urban populations (136). The biggest single source of nutrient loading in urban waters, however, is human waste. Even after conventional wastewater treatment to remove much of the organic material and pathogens, human waste still contains copious amounts of nitrogen and phosphorus—the primary ingredients in fertilizers.

Nutrient enrichment problems are especially severe in urban estuaries, where water flushing is minimal and inputs, often from numerous cities, are large (137) (138). The Baltic Sea, for instance, receives the effluents of more than 70 million people and related industries in dozens of cities. Since 1980, it has manifested increasing symptoms of eutrophication, with a lengthening list of biological effects, from declining lobster and cod catches to increasing numbers of nuisance algal blooms (139) (140) (141). Without a major restructuring of how urban wastewaters are handled, nutrient loads in waters seem certain to rise as urban populations increase and agricultural production expands to feed urban residents (142) (143).

Urban Sewage

Given its sheer volume, sewage is a major threat to local urban waters, as well as one of the most vexing problems for urban managers charged with its safe disposal. Not only is sewage the major source of nutrients in urban waters but it also poses a significant risk to health from such sewage-borne pathogens as the cholera bacterium, hepatitis viruses, salmonellae, and shigellas (144) (145) (146).

Most of the world's sewage is still disposed of untreated. In developing countries, 90 percent or more is released without treatment of any kind—usually to a water body, whether a river, a lake, or an ocean (147) (148). Even in many developed countries, only a portion of the sewage receives conventional treatment (149).

In countries where a higher percentage of sewage is treated, building the infrastructure to collect and treat wastewater has required a concerted and costly national effort, and pollution episodes still occur (150). Many older cities still have outmoded sewer systems that collect sewage and storm water together, so that when rainfall is heavy, the capacity of the treatment plant is overwhelmed and untreated wastewater is released through overflow drains (151).

Increasingly, fisheries are being damaged or destroyed by the volume of urban sewage (152) (153). Major declines in fish catches have been documented in rivers and estuaries around cities in India, China, Venezuela, and Senegal (154). In Manila, two rivers carry vast quantities of the city's sewage into Manila Bay; fishery yields there declined by 39 percent from 1975 to 1988 (155). In addition, fecal coliform counts in most urban rivers in developing countries far exceed health standards. For the urban population that relies on these rivers as a source of drinking water and food, this poses severe health risks. The Tiete River downstream from Sao Paulo, Brazil, is heavily contaminated by the city's wastes, yet it is still used as drinking water by several rural communities in the interior of Sao Paulo state and as a source of irrigation for nearby vegetable farms (156).

Even the release of treated effluents to waters is not without environmental repercussions, because these effluents are a prime source of nutrients and subsequent eutrophication. The chemicals used in wastewater treatment can also have toxic effects. Chlorine, for example, is both toxic to aquatic organisms in its own right and can also combine with some organic compounds in the effluent to form organochlorines such as chloroform and various chloramines, which may be carcinogenic or directly toxic. Moreover, conventional treatment results in the accumulation of large quantities of sewage sludge, which often contains heavy metals and other contaminants and which can have a variety of toxic effects if it is disposed at sea (157).

Industrial Pollutants

Especially in the developing world, industry is concentrated in urban centers, resulting in severe water pollution problems in most large cities. Major sources of water pollution include chemical-intensive industries such as tanneries, metal plating operations, pulp mills, and refineries. Typical contaminants include organochlorines such as polychlorinated biphenyls (PCBs) and dioxins, pesticides, grease and oil from automobiles and shipping traffic, acids and caustics, heavy metals such as cadmium and lead, sewage sludge, and a long list of synthetic organic compounds.

Urban runoff is another source of industrial pollutants. A 1990 study found that a single year's runoff from the Washington, D.C., metropolitan area carried with it 3.8 million to 19 million liters of oil, 180 metric tons of zinc, 29 metric tons of copper, and 10 metric tons of lead (158). For some pollutants, urban runoff rivals or exceeds the output from industrial sources and sewage treatment plants and is often much more difficult to track and control (159).

Industrial releases of toxics have declined in many cities thanks to stringent pollution control measures (160) (161). On a global basis, however, toxic effluents are still a major threat to urban waters, particularly in many developing countries where industrial growth is rapid (162) (163). In Jakarta Bay in Indonesia, where untreated industrial wastes are discharged by some 30,000 small industries such as batik factories, heavy metal accumulations are alarmingly high. In fact, shrimp taken from Jakarta Bay have levels of mercury contamination second only to those of shrimp taken from Minamata Bay in Japan (164).

Cleaning up contaminated sediments is extremely difficult and costly. In the United States, where sediment cleanup is being contemplated at a number of harbor sites, costs are estimated at from $143 per kilogram of PCBs removed in easily accessible areas to more than $6,600 per kilogram for more dispersed contamination. Such costs mean that, once contaminated, most sediments are likely to remain so for years, despite the effects on the local environment (165).

INTEGRATED APPROACHES TO PROTECT THE RESOURCE BASE

The true impacts of urban activities on natural resources cannot be captured with a media-specific approach—in other words, looking first at air pollution and then water. Natural resources are linked, so that the degradation of one resource affects not only the resource itself but also a wider resource base in and around the urban area (166). In Tetuoan, Morocco, for instance, peri-urban deforestation not only destroys local habitat but also increases soil erosion, which in turn leads to heavy siltation in downslope water reservoirs; 50 percent of the Nakhla Reservoir has already been lost. The construction of new dams to meet urban water demands has in turn reduced river flows, affecting riverine habitats and wildlife and reducing the capacity of the rivers to process sewage wastes (167).

As the Tetuoan example makes clear, strategies for environmental management need to consider the entire ecosystem and the range of insults it experiences. Integrated coastal zone management (ICZM) is one such strategy. Its premise is that a coastal ecosystem must be considered as a whole, even though it may be subject to an array of dissimilar threats and under the control of many separate governments. ICZM is also a participatory planning process that seeks to involve all the affected parties—from city residents, to industries, to the different levels of state and city governments—so that the problems at hand and the possible options for addressing them are widely understood and the choices for action are broadly supported (168) (169) (170) (171).

This approach relies on scientific assessments to help define the scope of impacts, the natural tolerances of ecosystems to stress, and the benefits, costs, and trade-offs of control options. Even after a management choice is made—perhaps to treat sewage to remove some but not all nutrients—scientific monitoring is used to evaluate the impact of this action, which may then prompt further action in the next planning cycle. In this way, ICZM evolves as environmental conditions and the attitudes of the stakeholders change (172) (173).

The two profiles presented below provide a more comprehensive view of the variety of impacts that urban areas can have on coastal ecosystems, from land conversion, to land-based pollution, to urban use effects. The Chesapeake Bay profile illustrates how an integrated approach to environmental management has begun to pay off. The Hong Kong profile dramatically illustrates the range and severity of pressures on urban coastal waters and the difficulty of addressing them in the context of rapid industrial development.

Courtesy of Chesapeake Bay Program

Stem the tide. *An erosion control project on the Chesapeake Bay uses mats of Bay grass staked directly into the sand at the shoreline to slow wave action and restore habitat.*

Chesapeake Bay: Regional Mitigation Efforts Bearing Fruit

The effort to reverse the decline of the Chesapeake Bay, the largest estuary in the United States, represents both the promise and the difficulty of a regional approach to coastal zone management. In 1983, Maryland, Virginia, Pennsylvania, and the District of Columbia—all of which are part of the watershed of the Chesapeake Bay—entered into a formal partnership with the federal government to restore the Bay, which has suffered serious degradation from more than 300 years of heavy exploitation and pollution (174).

In the years since the Chesapeake Bay Agreement was signed, specific restoration goals have been wedded to a comprehensive set of actions designed to improve water quality, restore aquatic habitats, regulate development, restrict overexploitation of the Bay's resources, and develop a monitoring program to check the progress of these efforts. This Chesapeake Bay Program has resulted in measurable improvements in the Bay's health. The health of the Bay remains quite threatened, however, and aggressive action is required if the recovery is to continue (175).

The Chesapeake Bay is both extensive and ecologically complex. Stretching nearly 322 kilometers in length, with a shoreline of some 11,263 kilometers (176), the Bay is fed by 48 major rivers that drain a combined watershed of 165,760 square kilometers. This gives rise to a range of physical environments and salinity regimes as fresh water and saltwater mix, creating conditions that support more than 2,500 species of plants and animals. The traditional productivity of the Bay has meant employment to thousands of crabbers, oystermen, and fishers, and has been one of the main attractions for the Bay region's flourishing tourist industry (177).

The productivity of the Bay, however, has been badly compromised by overuse, pollution, and habitat conversion. The very size of its watershed makes the Chesapeake vulnerable to human activities over a vast area. By far the most serious threat to the health of the Chesapeake today is the tremendous influx of the nutrients nitrogen and phosphorus from both urban and agricultural sources throughout its watershed. Whereas forest previously covered 95 percent of the watershed, agriculture now accounts for about 30 percent of the land use and is the largest source of nutrient pollution. Urban development, which covers about 10 percent of the watershed, is close behind as a source of nutrient pollution and is growing quickly. The situation is worsened by suburban sprawl, which causes the loss of wetlands and riparian forest cover, both of which, in their natural states, provide important nutrient buffers (178).

Damage to the Bay from nutrient pollution became evident in the 1960s and 1970s and provides a classic example of progressive eutrophication. At first, extensive algal blooms appeared and the Bay's clarity declined. Eutrophication in turn led to a serious decline in sea grasses and other submerged vegetation, whose loss affected the numerous species that used the vegetation as habitat. Finally, a buildup of organic matter in the depths led to a progressive decrease in dissolved oxygen levels in extensive reaches of the Bay, leaving anoxic dead zones along much of the bottom and stressing many of the organisms in shallower areas (179) (180) (181).

In addition to nutrient enrichment, other pressures on the Bay include industrial effluents and urban runoff, which have left toxic contaminants such as heavy metals, pesticides, and chlorinated hydrocarbons in sediments. Overharvesting of fish and shellfish resources has contributed to the demise of important species such as striped bass, oysters, and shad and may currently be stressing the blue crab fishery—the last major commercial fishery in the Bay. Waterfowl populations have also diminished substantially as shallow water habitats and wetlands have declined (182) (183).

In the mid-1970s and 1980s, the U.S. government undertook an extensive research program to sort out the factors contributing to the Bay's decline. The research revealed the central role of nutrient pollution, providing an essential basis for developing a recovery plan. Later modeling studies indicated that nutrients would need to be cut some 40 percent from 1985 levels for the Bay to recover. In 1987, this 40 percent reduction goal was officially adopted as a centerpiece of the Chesapeake Bay Program (184) (185).

As it stands today, the Chesapeake Bay Program is the most ambitious attempt at integrated coastal zone management in the United States. The program grew out of extensive discussion and negotiation among all interested parties—including state and federal representatives, industries, local governments, environmental and sporting groups, and private citizens—and now has wide public and private support (186).

Achieving that consensus was impressive, considering that more than 1,600 separate communities in three states and the District of Columbia surround the Bay and its tributaries. A regional executive council coordinates the program, receiving oversight and direction from a citizen's advisory committee, a scientific and technical advisory committee, and a committee of local government representatives. State governments and the federal government have lent legal and financial support as well as enforcement powers and monitoring capabilities (187) (188).

Although goals for nutrient reduction and habitat restoration have been set for the Bay as a whole, more detailed goals have also been developed for each of the 10 major tributaries. The actual actions taken to achieve these goals vary widely depending on the location and the nature of the local threats. They include efforts to encourage better methods of farming and timber harvesting throughout the Chesapeake watershed, management of fish and shellfish harvests, stream revegetation and marshland restoration, regulation and monitoring of toxic releases from industry, and mitigation of the effects of shoreline development through such means as vegetative buffer zones, setback requirements, and other zoning restrictions (189) (190) (191) (192) (193).

The results to date have been impressive. Phosphorus levels declined 16 percent from 1985 to 1992 through the use of a combination of bans on phosphorus-containing detergents, upgrades in municipal sewage treatment plants, and soil erosion controls and nutrient management on agricultural land (194). Progress in controlling nitrogen levels has come more slowly, but it is still significant, despite the increasing population in the watershed (195). These gains in nutrient control have led to dramatic improvements in the abundance of submerged vegetation, which increased 75 percent from 1978 to 1993 (196). The striped bass population has rebounded, thanks in part to improved habitat and strict limits on fishing (197).

Even so, a significant effort will be required to meet the goals of a 40 percent reduction in nutrients and a significant improvement in habitat quality throughout the Bay—especially since the area's population is expected to grow nearly 20 percent over the next 25 years (198). So far, the Chesapeake Bay Program has proved to be a flexible mechanism for improving the quality of the Chesapeake Bay, and area leaders are hopeful that the gradual improvement in the Bay's condition will fire public enthusiasm for the difficult steps ahead (199) (200).

Hong Kong: A Study in Multiple Impacts

Pressures on Hong Kong waters are far greater than those on the Chesapeake, and reversing them promises to be even more difficult. Hong Kong is the most densely populated urban center in the world. The Hong Kong conurbation consists of several adjacent cities on the Kowloon Peninsula and nearby Hong Kong Island. It is home to 6.1 million people and more than 200,000 large and small industries whose byproducts flow into two major and several smaller marine embayments (201).

Located in the subtropical climes of the South China Sea, Hong Kong waters once boasted productive coral reefs and mangrove stands and yielded abundant catches of fish and shellfish. However, extensive reclamation projects along the Hong Kong shoreline, massive pollution of the harbor areas, and heavy fishing pressures both in nearby coastal waters and in the more distant waters of the South China Sea have exacted a major toll (202) (203).

Because much of the Hong Kong coast is rather steep, reclamation has played a major role in accommodating

Courtesy of Deborah Farmer

Troubled waters. Adjacent to one of the most densely populated urban centers in the world, Hong Kong's harbors face multiple insults from sewage, industrial wastes, and land reclamation.

urban growth. Filled land now accounts for more than 25 percent of the urban land area, and seawalls armor much of the reclaimed shore. This has radically altered Hong Kong's shoreline ecology, eliminating most mangroves and reducing the diversity of shoreline habitat (204).

Aside from the direct destruction of intertidal, seabed, and coral communities, extensive reclamation around both Victoria and Tolo harbors—Hong Kong's two main harbors—has restricted tidal flushing in the harbor areas, exacerbating the already severe pollution problems there (205). Construction of new airport and port facilities has required some 500 million cubic meters of sand fill, most of which has been obtained by suction dredging from inshore waters. Dredging has stirred up clouds of silt that settle on nearby sea grass beds and coral communities, significantly reducing their original extent (206) (207).

Raw sewage from some 3.6 million people flows into Victoria Harbor, giving rise to severe effects from nutrient loading. Despite generally good water circulation in the harbor, water quality continues to decline. Fecal coliform levels from sewage contamination, for instance, are extremely high, and shellfish contaminated with human pathogens such as salmonellae, shigellas, and hepatitis viruses are common (208). In 1988, a hepatitis epidemic involving nearly 1,400 people was traced to the consumption of contaminated shellfish (209). Dissolved oxygen levels have steadily declined in harbor waters, and some areas where water circulation is poor suffer from permanent or intermittent anoxic conditions. In nearby Tolo Harbor, a smaller embayment with very restricted flow that receives the effluents of 1 million people, conditions are much worse and anoxic waters are much more extensive (210).

Further toxic insult to the harbor areas comes from industrial wastes—solvents, oils, acids, heavy metals, tannery wastes, and other compounds—most of which have been, until recently, discharged through the sewer system. Agricultural chemicals and animal wastes from nearby farms also find their way into the waters around Hong Kong. Shipping traffic is heavy in Victoria Harbor, bringing with it associated hydrocarbon pollution. As a result, the coastal waters are significantly contaminated with trace metals such as cadmium and organochlorines such as dichlorodiphenyltrichloroethane (DDT) (211) (212).

Marine life in Victoria and Tolo harbors has reacted predictably. Severe pollution has resulted in long-term changes in community structure, species abundance, and species diversity of the bottom-dwelling organisms, intertidal organisms, coral communities, and fish. Toxic algal blooms, products of the persistent eutrophication also known as red tides, are common in Tolo Harbor. In 1977, 2 such red tides occurred, but in the peak year of 1988, the number rose to 38. The incidence has declined somewhat with improvements in wastewater treatment (213) (214) (215) (216).

Hong Kong authorities are trying to mitigate these pollution problems in several ways. Already in place are a number of laws that restrict effluent discharges from industry and ships and that regulate the dumping of dredge spoils and sewage sludge at sea (217). Local authorities have constructed a chemical waste treatment plant, and efforts are being made to collect and process animal wastes as well (218).

To address the largest threat to its aquatic environment—sewage—Hong Kong has launched a three-phase project. The first phase, now under way, involves reconstruction of urban sewer lines. The second phase will involve construction of a large sewage treatment facility on a former island in Victoria Harbor. The final phase will be construction of a marine outfall to transport treated wastes well beyond the harbor waters. Marine experts warn, however, that until the marine outfall is built—which is not scheduled for another decade or so—excessive nutrient loading from sewage will continue to degrade Hong Kong's urban waters (219).

To better meet the growing environmental challenges, the Hong Kong government is moving toward integrated coastal zone management. The planning department has issued maps that broadly identify regions where development should be concentrated and is now compiling a database on the physical and biological characteristics of the coastal zone for use in future planning efforts (220).

At the same time, however, continued expansion of the Hong Kong urban zone threatens to degrade coastal areas to the east of the urban core where environmental stresses have previously been light. In response, efforts are under way to establish several marine parks and reserves to afford some protection to these eastern waters, where coral reefs and other components of the marine community are still healthy (221) (222).

To the west, Hong Kong lies adjacent to one of the most rapidly developing areas of China. Chinese authorities have already commenced port construction, and proposals are in hand for construction of an automobile manufacturing plant and other heavy industrial facilities in nearby coastal areas. These potential threats give weight to the argument that regional coastal planning is urgently needed to avoid catastrophic declines in coastal ecosystems not just in Hong Kong but along the entire southern coast of China (223).

References and Notes

1. United Nations (U.N.) Population Division, *World Urbanization Prospects: The 1994 Revision* (U.N., New York, 1995), p. 103.

2. *Ibid.*, p. 87.

3. Ian Douglas, "Human Settlements," in *Changes in Land Use and Land Cover: A Global Perspective*, William B. Meyer and B.L. Turner II, eds. (Cambridge University Press, Cambridge, U.K., 1994), p. 155.

4. *Ibid.*, pp. 154–155.

5. Jorge E. Hardoy, Diana Mitlin, and David Satterthwaite, *Environmental Problems in Third World Cities* (Earthscan, London, 1992), p. 10.

6. Gordon McGranahan and Jacob Songsore, "Wealth, Health, and the Urban Household: Weighing Environmental Burdens in Accra, Jakarta, and Sao Paulo," *Environment*, Vol. 36, No. 6 (July/August 1994), pp. 4–8.

7. *Op. cit.* 5, p. 16.

8. *Op. cit.* 5, p. 33.

9. U.S. Agency for International Development (U.S. AID) Office of Environment and Urban Programs, *The Role of the City in Environmental Management*, 1994 edition (U.S. AID, Washington, D.C., 1994), p. 3.

10. *Ibid.*, p. 5.

11. *Op. cit.* 9.

12. Joseph Poracsky and Michael C. Houck, "The Metropolitan Portland Urban Natural Resource Program," in *The Ecological City: Preserving and Restoring Urban Biodiver-*

sity, Rutherford H. Platt, Rowan A. Rowntree, and Pamela C. Muick, eds. (The University of Massachusetts Press, Amherst, Massachusetts, 1994), pp. 251–268.

13. International Council for Local Environmental Initiatives (ICLEI), "Cities for Climate Protection: An International Campaign to Reduce Urban Emissions of Greenhouse Gases," ICLEI paper (ICLEI, Toronto, 1993).

14. Development agencies are now beginning to sponsor studies on the impacts of urbanization on the surrounding natural resource base. See, for example, U.S. Agency for International Development (U.S. AID), *The Impact of Urbanization on Natural Resources: Tetouan, Morocco* (U.S. AID, Washington, D.C., 1992).

15. *Op. cit.* 5, n.p.

16. Rodney R. White, *Urban Environmental Management: Environmental Change and Urban Design* (John Wiley & Sons, Chichester, U.K., 1994).

17. Richard Stren, Rodney White, and Joseph Whitney, eds., *Sustainable Cities: Urbanization and the Environment in International Perspective* (Westview Press, Boulder, Colorado, 1992).

18. William E. Rees, "Ecological Footprints and Appropriated Carrying Capacity: What Urban Economics Leaves Out," *Environment and Urbanization,* Vol. 4, No. 2 (October 1992), pp. 121–130.

19. Carl Folke, Jonas Larsson, and Julie Sweitzer, "Renewable Resource Appropriation by Cities," Beijer Discussion Paper Series No. 61 (Beijer International Institute of Ecological Economics, Stockholm, Sweden, 1995).

20. P.M. Holligan and H. de Boois, *Land-Ocean Interactions in the Coastal Zone (LOICZ) Science Plan,* International Geosphere Biosphere Programme (IGBP) Global Change Report No. 25 (IGBP, Stockholm, Sweden, 1993), as cited in John Pernetta and Danny Elder, *Cross-Sectoral, Integrated Coastal Area Planning (CICAP): Guidelines and Principles for Coastal Area Development* (World Conservation Union, Gland, Switzerland, 1993), p. 27.

21. Arnulf Grubler, "Technology," in *Changes in Land Use and Land Cover: A Global Perspective,* William B. Meyer and B.L. Turner II, eds. (Cambridge University Press, Cambridge, U.K., 1994), p. 323.

22. Alain Bertaud, "Overview," in *The Human Face of the Urban Environment, Proceedings of the Second Annual World Bank Conference on Environmentally Sustainable Development,* Ismail Serageldin, Michael A. Cohen, and K.C. Sivaramakrishnan, eds. (The World Bank, Washington, D.C., September 19–21, 1994), p. 234.

23. *Op. cit.* 3, p. 162.

24. *Op. cit.* 1, p. 113.

25. Data from the 1992 National Resources Inventory, U.S. Department of Agriculture Soil Conservation Service, Washington, D.C., 1995.

26. United Nations Centre for Human Settlements, *Global Report on Human Settlements 1986* (Oxford University Press, Oxford, U.K., 1987), p. 130.

27. Celso N.E. Oliveira and Josef Leitmann, "Sao Paulo," *Cities,* Vol. 11, No. 1 (1994), p. 10.

28. United Nations (U.N.), *Population Growth and Policies in Mega-Cities: Sao Paulo* (U.N., New York, 1993), p. 16.

29. *Ibid.*

30. U.S. Agency for International Development (U.S. AID), "Urbanization in the Developing Countries," interim report to Congress (U.S. AID, Washington, D.C., 1988), as cited in Euisoon Shin *et al.,* "Valuing the Economic Impacts of Environmental Problems: Asian Cities," Urban Management Program Discussion Paper, draft (The World Bank, Washington, D.C., 1994), p. 3.

31. World Resources Institute in collaboration with the United Nations Environment Programme and the United Nations Development Programme, *World Resources 1994–95* (Oxford University Press, New York, 1994), p. 71.

32. *Op. cit.* 3, p. 162.

33. Donald W. Jones, "How Urbanization Affects Energy-Use in Developing Countries," *Energy Policy,* Vol. 19, No. 7 (September 1991), p. 622.

34. David E. Dowall and Giles Clark, "Making Urban Land Markets Work," draft paper prepared for the Urban Management Programme, The World Bank, as quoted in Janis D. Bernstein, "Land Use Considerations in Urban Environmental Management," Urban Management Programme Discussion Paper No. 12 (The World Bank, Washington, D.C., 1994), p. 25.

35. Janis D. Bernstein, "Land Use Considerations in Urban Environmental Management," Urban Management Programme Discussion Paper No. 12 (The World Bank, Washington, D.C., 1994), p. 26.

36. *Ibid.,* p. 12.

37. *Op. cit.* 35, p. 17.

38. *Op. cit.* 35, p. 13.

39. *Op. cit.* 35.

40. Donald W. Field *et al., Coastal Wetlands of the United States: An Accounting of a Valuable National Resource* (National Oceanic and Atmospheric Administration in cooperation with the U.S. Fish and Wildlife Service, Washington, D.C., 1991), pp. 1–13.

41. *Op. cit.* 31, Table 22.6, pp. 354–355.

42. *Op. cit.* 1, pp. 114–117, 143–150.

43. William H. Frey and Alden Speare, Jr., "The Revival of Metropolitan Population Growth in the United States: An Assessment of Findings from the 1990 Census," *Population and Development Review,* Vol. 18, No. 1 (March 1992), p. 135.

44. Dirk Bryant *et al.,* "Coastlines at Risk: An Index of Potential Development-Related Threats to Coastal Ecosystems," World Resources Institute (WRI) Indicator Brief (WRI, Washington, D.C., 1995), p. 1.

45. Chia Lin Sien, *Singapore's Urban Coastal Area: Strategies for Management,* Association of Southeast Asian Nations/United States Coastal Resources Management Project Technical Publications Series 9 (The International Center for Living Aquatic Resources Management, Manila, Philippines, 1992), p. 17.

46. San Francisco Estuary Project Management Committee, *San Francisco Estuary Project: Comprehensive Conservation and Management Plan* (San Francisco Estuary Project, San Francisco, 1992), p. 52.

47. Matthew Auer, *Urban Impacts on the Coastal Zones of Developing Countries: Problem Identification and Recommendations for Mitigations* (U.S. Agency for International Development, Washington, D.C., 1991), p. 6.

48. University of Rhode Island Coastal Resources Center (URICRC)/U.S. Agency for International Development, *Central America's Coasts: Profiles and an Agenda for Action* (URICRC, Narragansett, Rhode Island, 1992), p. 7.

49. *Op. cit.* 47, pp. 6–7.

50. Mediterranean Environmental Technical Assistance Program, *Tangiers: Municipal Environmental Audit and Strategy* (Commission of the European Communities/United Nations Development Programme/World Bank, Washington, D.C., 1993), p. 2.

51. David Salvesen, *Wetlands: Mitigating and Regulating Development Impacts,* 2nd ed. (The Urban Land Institute, Washington, D.C., 1994), p. 21.

52. United Nations (U.N.) Economic and Social Commission for Asia and the Pacific, *State of Urbanization in Asia and the Pacific, 1993* (U.N., New York, 1993), p. 5–28.

53. United Nations (U.N.) Economic and Social Commission for Asia and the Pacific, *State of the Environment in Asia and the Pacific, 1990* (U.N., Bangkok, Thailand, 1992), p. 71.

54. *Op. cit.* 3, p. 162.

55. Centre for Science and Environment and the International Institute for Environment and Development, funded by Overseas Development Administration (ODA), *Aligarh Environment Study* (ODA, London, 1995), p. 64.

56. Metropolitan Environmental Improvement Program, "The Environmental Profile of Jakarta 1990," draft paper (The World Bank, Washington, D.C., 1991), p. 12.

57. *Op. cit.* 31, p. 171.

58. U.S. Congress, Office of Technology Assessment (OTA), *Energy in Developing Countries* (OTA, Washington, D.C., 1991), p. 11.

59. *Ibid.,* p. 16.

60. Douglas F. Barnes *et al.,* "Urban Energy Transitions, Poverty, and the Environment:

Understanding the Role of the Urban Household Energy in Developing Countries," draft paper (The World Bank, Washington, D.C., 1994), p. 15.

61. Richard H. Hosier, "Editor's Introduction: Urban Energy and the Environment in Africa," *Energy Policy*, Vol. 21, No. 5 (May 1993), p. 435.

62. *Op. cit.* 33, p. 621.

63. Josef Leitmann, "Energy-Environment Linkages in the Urban Sector," Urban Management Programme Paper No. 2 (The World Bank, Washington, D.C., April 1991), p. 1.

64. *Op. cit.* 33, p. 621.

65. *Op. cit.* 33, p. 621.

66. *Op. cit.* 58, pp. 29–30.

67. *Op. cit.* 33, p. 621.

68. Jyoti Parikh and Vibhooti Shukla, "Urbanization, Energy Use and Greenhouse Effects in Economic Development: Results from a Cross-National Study of Developing Countries," *Global Environmental Change*, Vol. 5, No. 2 (1995), pp. 88–89.

69. Ralph Torrie, "Findings and Policy Implications from the Urban CO_2 Reduction Project" (The International Council for Local Environmental Initiatives, Toronto, January 1993), p. 7.

70. *Ibid.*

71. *Op. cit.* 69.

72. *Op. cit.* 60, p. 85.

73. *Op. cit.* 60, p. 87.

74. B. Bowonder, S.S.R. Prasad, and N.V.M. Unni, "Dynamics of Fuelwood Prices in India," *World Development*, Vol. 16, No. 10 (1988), p. 1218. For greater detail on this study, see also World Resources Institute in collaboration with the United Nations Environment Programme and the United Nations Development Programme, *World Resources 1994–95* (Oxford University Press, New York, 1994), p. 93.

75. *Op. cit.* 60, p. 91.

76. Josef Leitmann, "Urbanization and Environment in Sub-Saharan Africa: An Input to the Post-UNCED Urban Axis," draft paper (The World Bank, Washington, D.C., February 1995), p. 16.

77. *Op. cit.* 60, p. 80.

78. Terrence G. Bensel, "Rural Woodfuel Production for Urban Markets: Problems and Opportunities in the Cebu Province, Philippines," *Pacific and Asian Journal of Energy*, Vol. 5, No. 1 (1994), p. 10.

79. Jesse C. Ribot, "Forestry Policy and Charcoal Production in Senegal," *Energy Policy*, Vol. 21, No. 5 (May 1993), p. 559.

80. *Op. cit.* 60, p. 99.

81. *Op. cit.* 79, p. 561.

82. *Op. cit.* 79.

83. *Op. cit.* 31, p. 8.

84. Organisation for Economic Co-Operation and Development (OECD) Group on Environmental Performance, *Environmental Per-*formance Review of Poland: Main Report* (OECD, Paris, October 1994), p. 89.

85. Jerzy Borkiewicz *et al.,* "Environmental Profile of Katowice," draft paper (The World Bank, Washington, D.C., 1991), p. 10.

86. *Op. cit.* 84.

87. *Op. cit.* 85, p. 11.

88. Vaclav Smil, *Global Ecology: Environmental Change and Social Flexibility* (Routledge, London, 1993), p. 66.

89. *Op. cit.* 31, p. 346.

90. Yok-shiu F. Lee, "Urban Water Supply and Sanitation in Developing Countries," in *Metropolitan Water Use Conflicts in Asia and the Pacific*, James E. Nickum and K. William Easter, eds. (Westview Press, Boulder, Colorado, 1994), p. 30.

91. Nonphysical losses, such as illegal connections or malfunctioning meters, can also account for a large share of public water losses.

92. Ian Douglas, Professor of Physical Geography, University of Manchester, Manchester, U.K., 1995 (personal communication).

93. Ismail Serageldin, "Water Supply, Sanitation, and Environmental Sustainability: The Financing Challenge," a keynote address to The Ministerial Conference on Drinking Water and Environmental Sanitation: Implementing Agenda 21 (The World Bank, Washington, D.C., March 1994), p. 6.

94. National Research Council, *Ground Water Quality Protection: State and Local Strategies* (National Academy Press, Washington, D.C., 1986), pp. 48–49.

95. Andre Potworowski, "A Taste of Salt," *IDRC Reports*, Vol. 18, No. 4 (October 1990), p. 10.

96. China National Environmental Protection Agency (NEPA), *Report on the State of the Environment in China 1994* (NEPA, Beijing, 1995), p. 6.

97. Ruangdej Srivardhana, "Water Use Conflicts in Bangkok Metropolitan Region, Thailand," in *Metropolitan Water Use Conflicts in Asia and the Pacific*, James E. Nickum and K. William Easter, eds. (Westview Press, Boulder, Colorado, 1994), p. 137.

98. *Ibid.*

99. *Op. cit.* 1, pp. 87, 89.

100. Carter Brandon and Ramesh Ramankutty, "Toward an Environmental Strategy for Asia," World Bank Discussion Paper No. 224 (The World Bank, Washington, D.C., 1993), p. 140.

101. Bureau of Territorial Planning and Regional Economics, China National Planning Commission, Planning Bureau, China National Environmental Protection Agency, and Chinese Academy of Geological Information, "Major Environmental Problems in China," *Chinese Environment and Development*, Vol. 4, No. 4 (Winter 1993–1994), p. 28.

102. Euisoon Shin *et al.,* "Valuing the Economic Impacts of Environmental Problems: Asian Cities," Urban Management Program Dis-cussion Paper, draft (The World Bank, Washington, D.C., 1994), p. 75.

103. Joan P. Baker *et al.,* "Biological Effects of Changes in Surface Water Acid-Base Chemistry, NAPAP Report 13," in National Acid Precipitation Assessment Program (NAPAP), *Acid Deposition: State of Science and Technology*, Vol. 2 (NAPAP, Washington, D.C., 1990), p. 13-329.

104. Per Elvingson, "Acidification Looming as Industry Expands," *Acid News*, No. 2 (April 1995), p. 10.

105. Environmental Information Center, *Energy Demand Forecast and Environmental Impact in China* (Environmental Information Center, Tokyo, March 1994), p. 55.

106. National Research Council, *Rethinking the Ozone Problem in Urban and Regional Air Pollution* (National Academy Press, Washington, D.C., 1991), p. 99.

107. *Ibid.*

108. David J. Roser and Alistair Gilmour, *Acid Deposition and Related Air Pollution: Its Current Extent and Implications for Biological Conservation in Eastern Asia and the Western Pacific* (World Wide Fund for Nature International, Gland, Switzerland, May 1995), p. 100.

109. Walter W. Heck, "Assessment of Crop Losses from Air Pollutants in the United States," in *Air Pollution's Toll on Forests and Crops*, James J. MacKenzie and Mohamed T. El-Ashry, eds. (Yale University Press, New Haven, Connecticut, 1989), p. 300.

110. U.S. Congress, Office of Technology Assessment (OTA), "Urban Ozone and the Clean Air Act: Problems and Proposals for Change," staff paper (OTA, Washington, D.C., April 1988), pp. 45–47.

111. John L. Innes, *Forest Health: Its Assessment and Status* (CAB International, Oxon, U.K., 1993), p. 42.

112. William M. Ciesla and Edwin Donaubauer, "Decline and Dieback of Trees and Forests: A Global Overview," Forestry Paper No. 120 (Food and Agriculture Organization of the United Nations, Rome, 1994), p. 61.

113. *Op. cit.* 108, pp. 57–59.

114. United Nations Environment Programme and the World Health Organization, *Urban Air Pollution in Megacities of the World* (Blackwell Publishers, Oxford, U.K., 1992), p. 122.

115. Doug Gatlin, ed., *Climate Change Policy Workbook for Local Leaders* (The Climate Institute, Washington, D.C., 1995), pp. 9–10.

116. Intergovernmental Panel on Climate Change (IPCC), "IPCC Synthesis Report" (July 29, 1995 draft) (World Meteorological Organization/United Nations Environment Programme, Geneva, 1995), p. 29.

117. International Energy Agency, *World Energy Outlook, 1995* (Organisation for Economic Co-Operation and Development, Paris, 1995), p. 266.

118. Asif Faiz and Surhid Gautam, "Motorization, Urbanization, and Air Pollution," discussion paper (The World Bank, Washington, D.C., 1994), p. 19.

119. *Op. cit.* 16, pp. 35–36.

120. United Nations Environment Programme (UNEP), *Environmental Data Report 1993–94* (UNEP, Nairobi, Kenya, 1994), p. 329.

121. *Op. cit.* 53, p. 126.

122. *Op. cit.* 101, p. 34.

123. David Misitano, Edmundo Casillas, and Craig Haley, "Effects of Contaminated Sediments on Viability, Length, DNA, and Protein Content of Larval Surf Smelt, *Hypomesus pretiosus*," *Marine Environmental Research,* Vol. 37 (1994), pp. 1–2.

124. Susanne Sami, Mohamed Faisal, and Robert Huggett, "Effects of Laboratory Exposure to Sediments Contaminated with Polycyclic Aromatic Hydrocarbons on the Hemocytes of the American Oyster *Crassostrea virginica*," *Marine Environment Research*, Vol. 35 (1993), p. 131.

125. World Wildlife Fund (WWF) and The Conservation Foundation, *Getting at the Source: Strategies for Reducing Municipal Solid Waste* (WWF, Washington, D.C., 1991), p. 6.

126. *Op. cit.* 120, p. 336.

127. *Op. cit.* 125.

128. U.S. Congress, Office of Technology Assessment, *Facing America's Trash: What Next for Municipal Solid Waste?* (U.S. Government Printing Office, Washington, D.C., 1989), p. 226.

129. Michael Meybeck, Deborah Chapman, and Richard Helmer, eds., *Global Freshwater Quality: A First Assessment* (United Nations Environment Programme and World Health Organization, Geneva, 1989), p. 42.

130. National Research Council, Committee on Wastewater Management for Coastal Urban Areas, *Managing Wastewater in Coastal Urban Areas* (National Academy Press, Washington, D.C., 1993), pp. 178, 261.

131. *Ibid.,* pp. 177–179.

132. *Op. cit.* 130, pp. 177–179.

133. Susanne Baden *et al.,* "Effects of Eutrophication on Benthic Communities Including Fish: Swedish West Coast," *Ambio,* Vol. 19, No. 3 (1990), pp. 113–122.

134. Charles Officer *et al.,* "Chesapeake Bay Anoxia: Origin, Development, and Significance," *Science,* Vol. 223 (1984), pp. 26–27.

135. Gail Mackiernan, ed., "Dissolved Oxygen in the Chesapeake Bay: Processes and Effects," Maryland Sea Grant Publication No. UM-SG-TS-87-03 (University of Maryland, College Park, Maryland, 1987), pp. 139–145.

136. Thomas R. Fisher and Robert D. Doyle, "Nutrient Cycling in Chesapeake Bay," in *Dissolved Oxygen in the Chesapeake Bay: Processes and Effects,* Gail B. Mackiernan, ed. (Maryland Sea Grant College, College Park, Maryland, 1987), pp. 49–54.

137. Rutger Rosenberg *et al.,* "Marine Eutrophication Case Studies in Sweden," *Ambio,* Vol. 19, No. 3 (1990), p. 107.

138. Scott W. Nixon, "Marine Eutrophication: A Growing International Problem," *Ambio,* Vol. 19, No. 3 (1990), p. 1.

139. *Op. cit.* 133.

140. *Op. cit.* 137, pp. 102–107.

141. Mati Kahru, Ulrich Horstmann, and Ove Rud, "Satellite Detection of Increased Cyanobacteria Blooms in the Baltic Sea: Natural Fluctuation or Ecosystem Change?," *Ambio,* Vol. 23, No. 8 (1994), p. 469.

142. Scott W. Nixon, "Coastal Marine Eutrophication: A Definition, Social Causes, and Future Concerns," *Ophelia: International Journal of Marine Biology,* Vol. 41 (March 1995), p. 214.

143. *Op. cit.* 138.

144. *Op. cit.* 130, pp. 23–26.

145. *Op. cit.* 53, p. 60.

146. *Op. cit.* 130, pp. 203–214.

147. John Briscoe, "When the Cup Is Half Full: Improving Water and Sanitation Services in the Developing World," *Environment,* Vol. 35, No. 4 (1993), p. 15.

148. Carl Bartone, "Water Quality and Urbanization in Latin America," *Water International,* Vol. 15 (1990), p. 3.

149. *Op. cit.* 147, p. 29.

150. *Op. cit.* 93, p. 9.

151. *Op. cit.* 130, pp. 32, 61–62.

152. *Op. cit.* 130, pp. 23–26.

153. *Op. cit.* 53, p. 60.

154. *Op. cit.* 5, p. 116.

155. *Op. cit.* 102, p. 103.

156. Danilo J. Anton, *Thirsty Cities: Urban Environments and Water Supply in Latin America* (International Development Research Centre, Ottawa, 1993), p. 71.

157. *Op. cit.* 130, pp. 177, 346.

158. Environmental Defense Fund (EDF) in collaboration with the World Wildlife Fund (WWF), *How Wet Is a Wetland?: The Impacts of the Proposed Revisions to the Federal Wetlands Manual* (EDF/WWF, Washington, D.C., 1992), p. 74.

159. Robert Adler, "Reauthorizing the Clean Water Act: Looking to Tangible Values," *Water Resources Bulletin,* Vol. 30, No. 5 (1994), p. 802.

160. Thomas O'Connor, *Mussel Watch: Recent Trends in Coastal Environmental Quality* (National Oceanic and Atmospheric Administration, Washington, D.C., 1992), p. 26.

161. Shinsuke Tanabe *et al.,* "Persistent Organochlorines in Japanese Coastal Waters: An Introspective Summary from a Far East Developed Nation," *Marine Pollution Bulletin,* Vol. 20, No. 7 (1989), pp. 344–351.

162. *Op. cit.* 53, pp. 56–57.

163. David Phillips and Shinsuke Tanabe, "Aquatic Pollution in the Far East," *Marine Pollution Bulletin,* Vol. 20, No. 7 (1989), pp. 297, 300–302.

164. *Op. cit.* 52, p. 5-19.

165. Thomas Grigalunas and James Opaluch, "Managing Contaminated Marine Sediments," *Marine Policy* (October 1989), p. 321.

166. U.S. Agency for International Development (U.S. AID), "The Impact of Urbanization on Natural Resources: Tetouan, Morocco," working paper (U.S. AID, Washington, D.C., May 1992), p. 3-1.

167. *Ibid.,* p. 3-3.

168. Stephen Olsen and Lynne Hale, "Coasts: the Ethical Dimension," *People and the Planet,* Vol. 3, No. 1 (1994), pp. 29–31.

169. *Op. cit.* 130, pp. 74–87.

170. Stephen Olsen, "Will Integrated Coastal Management Programs Be Sustainable: The Constituency Problem," *Ocean and Coastal Management,* Vol. 21 (1993), pp. 201–225.

171. The World Bank, *The Noordwijk Guidelines for Integrated Coastal Zone Management* (The World Bank, Washington, D.C., 1993), pp. 1–10.

172. *Op. cit.* 130, pp. 74–87.

173. *Op. cit.* 168.

174. Chesapeake Bay Program, *The State of the Chesapeake Bay, 1995* (U.S. Environmental Protection Agency, Washington, D.C., 1995), p. i.

175. Chesapeake Regional Information Service, "Chesapeake Bay Program: A Citizen's Guide" (Chesapeake Regional Information Service, Richmond, Virginia, undated pamphlet).

176. Timothy Hennessey, "Governance and Adaptive Management for Estuarine Ecosystems: The Case of Chesapeake Bay," *Coastal Management,* Vol. 22 (1994), p. 123.

177. *Op. cit.* 175.

178. *Op. cit.* 174, pp. 5–19.

179. K. Price *et al.,* "Nutrient Enrichment of Chesapeake Bay and Its Impact on the Habitat of Striped Bass: A Speculative Hypothesis," *Transactions of the American Fisheries Society,* Vol. 114 (1985), pp. 97, 100–105.

180. *Op. cit.* 134, pp. 22–27.

181. *Op. cit.* 174, pp. 16–32.

182. *Op. cit.* 174, pp. 20–21, 31–42.

183. Karl Blankenship, "Blue Crab Survey Raises Questions About Stock's Health," *Bay Journal,* Vol. 5, No. 1 (March 1995), p. 1.

184. *Op. cit.* 176, pp. 123–138.

185. *Op. cit.* 174, pp. 14–19.

186. *Op. cit.* 176, pp. 123–138.

187. *Op. cit.* 176, p. 131.

188. Glen Eugster, U.S. Environmental Protection Agency, Chesapeake Bay Program Office, Annapolis, Maryland, April 1995 (personal communication).

189. *Op. cit.* 174, pp. 1–39.

190. State of Maryland, Office of the Governor, *Financing Alternatives for Maryland's Tributary Strategies: Innovative Financing Ideas for Restoring the Chesapeake Bay* (State of Maryland, Annapolis, 1995), pp. 11–59.

191. Chesapeake Bay Program Office, *Achieving the Chesapeake Bay Nutrient Goals: A Synthesis of Tributary Strategies for the Bay's Ten Watersheds* (U.S. Environmental Protection Agency, Annapolis, Maryland, 1994), pp. 1–17.

192. Jenny Lynn Plummer, "Establishing Vegetative Buffers on Existing Lots: A Policy for Mitigating Impacts to Coastal Resources," *Coastal Management*, Vol. 22 (1994), pp. 427–430.

193. Chesapeake Bay Program, *Chesapeake Bay Program: A Work in Progress* (Chesapeake Bay Program Office, Annapolis, Maryland, 1994), p. 38.

194. Chesapeake Bay Program, *Environmental Indicators: Measuring Our Progress* (Chesapeake Bay Program Office, Annapolis, Maryland, 1995), p. 20.

195. *Op. cit.* 191, p. 8.

196. *Op. cit.* 174, pp. 22–23.

197. *Op. cit.* 174, pp. 31–32.

198. *Op. cit.* 174, pp. 10–11.

199. M. Elizabeth Gillelan, U.S. National Marine Fisheries Service, National Oceanic and Atmospheric Administration Chesapeake Bay Office, Annapolis, Maryland, March 1995 (personal communication).

200. *Op. cit.* 188.

201. Brian Morton, "Pollution of the Coastal Waters of Hong Kong," Marine Pollution Bulletin, Vol. 20, No. 7 (1989), pp. 312–313.

202. *Ibid.,* pp. 310–312.

203. Brian Morton, "Hong Kong's Coral Communities: Status, Threats and Management Plans," *Marine Pollution Bulletin*, Vol. 29, Nos. 1–3 (1994), p. 82.

204. *Op. cit.* 201, p. 312.

205. *Op. cit.* 201, p. 312.

206. *Op. cit.* 203, pp. 77–78.

207. S.Y. Lee, "Grave Threats to Seagrass," *Marine Pollution Bulletin*, Vol. 28, No. 4 (1994), p. 196.

208. *Op. cit.* 201, pp. 313, 316.

209. *Op. cit.* 53, p. 84.

210. *Op. cit.* 201, pp. 313–314.

211. David Phillips, "Trace Metals and Organochlorines in the Coastal Waters of Hong Kong," *Marine Pollution Bulletin,* Vol. 20, No. 7 (1989), p. 326.

212. *Op. cit.* 201.

213. *Op. cit.* 201, pp. 313–316.

214. Brian Morton, Department of Ecology and Biodiversity, The University of Hong Kong, Hong Kong, November 1995 (personal communication).

215. *Op. cit.* 53, p. 85.

216. Brian Morton, "Hong Kong," Chapter 14 in *Coastal Management in the Asia-Pacific Region: Issues and Approaches,* Kenji Hotta and Ian M. Dutton, eds. (Japan International Marine Science and Technology Federation, Tokyo, 1995), p. 204.

217. *Op. cit.* 203, p. 80.

218. *Op. cit.* 214.

219. *Op. cit.* 214.

220. *Op. cit.* 214.

221. *Op. cit.* 203, pp. 80–83.

222. *Op. cit.* 216, pp. 204–205.

223. *Op. cit.* 214.

4. Urban Transportation

The rapid urbanization occurring across much of the globe means not only that more people than ever before will be living and working in cities but also that more people and more goods will be making more trips in urban areas, often over longer distances. How cities—especially the rapidly growing cities of the developing world—meet this burgeoning demand for urban travel has implications for the environment, the economic efficiency, and the livability of these areas.

Cities have traditionally responded to travel demand by expanding the transportation supply. In much of the developed world, that has meant building more roads to accommodate an ever-growing number of vehicles, thereby creating a new urban form: the sprawling metropolis. Motor vehicles offer undeniable advantages such as speed and convenience; indeed, during the early stages of development, motor vehicles are vital to economic growth (1). However, the costs of increasing dependence on cars in the world's cities are becoming all too apparent. These include expensive road building and maintenance; clogged, congested streets that undermine economic productivity; high levels of energy consumption, with its attendant economic and environmental costs; worsening air and noise pollution; traffic accidents; and social inequities that arise when the poor find transportation services increasingly unaffordable.

These problems are evident to varying degrees in cities across the globe and threaten to become particularly acute in the developing world, where urban populations are growing rapidly and demand for motor vehicles is expected to skyrocket. Bangkok, Thailand, for example, is already plagued with notoriously high levels of air pollution and congestion, even though motor vehicle ownership per capita is low (72 vehicles for every 1,000 residents) compared with that in many developed cities (where ownership averages about 500 per 1,000 residents) (2). Even so, 300 to 400 more vehicles are being added to the streets of Bangkok every day (3). Will rapidly growing cities such as Surabaya, Indonesia, and Manila, Philippines, follow in Bangkok's footsteps, or will they be able to implement sound transportation policies to avoid the problems of gridlock and pollution (4)?

The high costs associated with urban transportation are not inevitable. Indeed, considerable opportunity exists to design more efficient transportation systems and, in the process, create more livable cities. A critical step for developed and developing countries alike is to move toward managing urban travel demand rather than simply increasing the supply—in particular, by reducing or averting overreliance on the privately owned car.

In cities in the developing world, the greatest transportation challenge is to improve the mobility of urban residents and the efficiency of transportation systems. In many of these cities, motor vehicle ownership is still low and land use patterns are still evolving rapidly. These cities have the option of avoiding the mistakes made in the developed world and designing urban transportation systems that facilitate walking, bicycling, and public transportation. However, doing so will not be easy. To alter the current path toward motorization could be as politically difficult in developing countries as it is in the more developed world. Nevertheless, given the dramatic growth of the world's motor vehicle fleet, especially in developing countries and countries in transition, the case for precautionary action to limit car use in cities is strong (5).

In the developed world, many cities are already heavily dependent on cars and have a fixed urban form that would be difficult and expensive to alter. For these cities, the challenge is to improve existing transportation systems and manage urban growth more effectively, in part by increasing the efficiency of existing road networks and providing attractive alternatives to the car. Improving the efficiency and cleanliness of existing vehicles can also help reduce fuel consumption and air pollution.

URBAN TRANSPORTATION TRENDS

The transportation-related problems of many of today's cities stem from a number of interrelated factors. Growing urban populations and increasing household incomes have led to a rise in car ownership, which in turn has created a greater propensity for travel and a demand for more roads. Increasing business and industrial activity has sent more service vehicles onto city streets and has produced more freight traffic. The dispersed form of many cities has also resulted in a demand for more roads, which translates into longer journeys, more congestion, and yet more fuel consumption and pollution (6).

Growth in Motor Vehicle Ownership

The number of motor vehicles worldwide could grow from 580 million in 1990 to 816 million (excluding motorized two- and three-wheel vehicles) by 2010, according to recent estimates (7) (8). The forces driving this level of growth range from demographic factors (urbani-

zation, increasing population, and smaller households), to economic factors (higher incomes and declining car prices), to social factors (increased leisure time and the status associated with vehicle ownership), to political factors (powerful lobbies and governments that view the automobile industry as an important generator of economic growth) (9).

Most of the world's vehicles are now concentrated in the wealthier regions of the world. In 1993, member countries of the Organisation for Economic Co-Operation and Development (OECD) had 70 percent of the world's automobiles (10) (11). At the high end of the countries is the United States, where 58 percent of households own two or more cars and 20 percent own three or more (12). Car ownership rates are highest there, at 561 per 1,000 residents in 1993; the average for OECD countries, excluding the United States, is 366 cars per 1,000 residents (13). (See Figure 4.1.) In all OECD countries, car ownership continues to rise steadily, and there is little sign, as was once expected, of "market saturation" (14).

In the developing world, car ownership rates are far lower—ranging in 1993 from an average of about 68 cars per 1,000 residents in Latin America and the Caribbean to 29 cars per 1,000 residents in East Asia and the Pacific, to about 14 cars per 1,000 residents in Africa (15). Yet, it is in the developing countries and the transition economies (16) that the greatest increases in the number of motor vehicles are expected (17). (See Figure 4.2.) Growth rates will be particularly high in East Asia and the Pacific (18).

Most of the growth in motor vehicle fleets in the developing world will be concentrated in urban areas. Primary cities draw the largest concentration of vehicles; in Iran, the Republic of Korea, Kenya, Mexico, and Thailand, about 50 percent of the country's automobiles are in the capital city (19) (20). Santiago, Chile, had nearly 90 automobiles per 1,000 residents in 1991, almost 70 percent higher than the national average (21).

In much of Asia, most of the growth in the vehicle fleet results from increases in the numbers of motorized two-wheel and three-wheel vehicles. Such vehicles are more affordable than cars for large segments of the population and often serve as a stepping-stone to car ownership. In Thailand, Malaysia, Indonesia, and

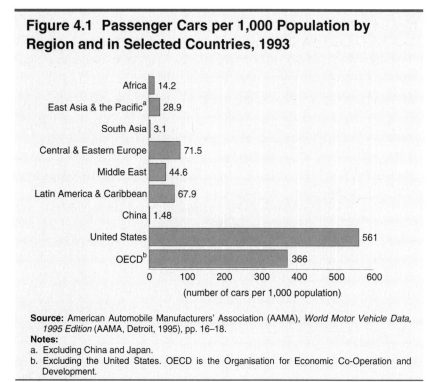

Figure 4.1 Passenger Cars per 1,000 Population by Region and in Selected Countries, 1993

Africa	14.2
East Asia & the Pacific[a]	28.9
South Asia	3.1
Central & Eastern Europe	71.5
Middle East	44.6
Latin America & Caribbean	67.9
China	1.48
United States	561
OECD[b]	366

(number of cars per 1,000 population)

Source: American Automobile Manufacturers' Association (AAMA), *World Motor Vehicle Data, 1995 Edition* (AAMA, Detroit, 1995), pp. 16–18.
Notes:
a. Excluding China and Japan.
b. Excluding the United States. OECD is the Organisation for Economic Co-Operation and Development.

Taiwan, for instance, two and three wheelers make up more than 50 percent of all motor vehicles (22). The number of two- and three-wheel vehicles is expected to grow most rapidly in China and India and in other densely populated, low-income countries. In India, for example, motorcycle ownership is increasing by 17 percent annually (23).

Transportation Choices and Income

Income levels greatly influence which transportation mode people use and the number of trips they make. Walking is the primary means of transportation in Nairobi, Kenya, for example, because of the relatively high cost of public transportation. Only the highest income groups, roughly the top 10 percent, use privately owned cars in that city (24).

In general, as incomes rise, there is a marked increase in vehicle ownership (25). For those who can afford the upfront costs of buying them, cars provide a fast, convenient, and relatively inexpensive mode of travel. However, increased automobile ownership leads to increased travel. In London, a household without a car makes about three trips per day, whereas a household with a car makes more than five with the two additional trips being entirely new trips or trips replacing those formerly made by foot or bicycle. Trips by public transportation drop accordingly (26).

Increased wealth also means more car travel in the form of both new trips, primarily social and leisure, and longer trips (27). In some countries, the number of trips is growing faster than the number of cars. In the United States, for example, between 1983 and 1990, the number of cars increased by 14 percent, while the number of vehicle trips grew by 25 percent and the number of vehicle miles traveled grew by 40 percent (28) (29). These trends have implications for the developing countries as well, especially those experiencing rapid economic growth.

Urban Form

The form of a city greatly influences—and is influenced by—travel patterns. The dense urban cores of many European and Japanese cities, for example, en-

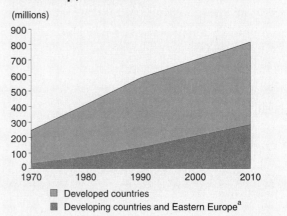

Figure 4.2 World Motor Vehicle Ownership, 1970–2010

(millions)

- Developed countries
- Developing countries and Eastern Europe[a]

Source: Asif Faiz and Surhid P. Gautam, "Motorization, Urbanization, and Air Pollution," discussion paper (The World Bank, Washington, D.C., September 1994), p. 8.
Note: a. Eastern Europe includes the former Eastern bloc countries except East Germany.

able residents to make 30 to 60 percent of all trips by walking and cycling (30). The dispersed urban form of Australian and U.S. cities, by contrast, encourages reliance on the car. Even within the United States, a greater share of work trips are made by cars in sprawling cities such as Phoenix and Houston than in denser cities such as New York and San Francisco (31). (See Table 4.1.)

An increasing number of cities worldwide seem to be developing at a scale that increases reliance on the privately owned automobile. Dispersion is taking place in many different types of cities, from dense, centralized European

Table 4.1 Urban Density and Transportation Patterns, Selected U.S. Cities, 1990

City	Density (number of people per hectare)	Average Number of Cars per Household	Percent of Journeys to Work by Means of Transport[a]		
			Drive Alone	Car Pool	Public Transportation[b]
New York	92	0.6	24.0	8.5	53.4
San Francisco	60	1.1	38.5	11.5	33.5
Chicago	47	1.0	46.3	14.8	29.7
Boston	46	0.9	40.1	10.5	31.5
Los Angeles	29	1.5	65.2	15.4	10.5
Portland, Oregon	14	1.4	65.0	12.9	11.0
Houston	12	1.5	71.7	15.5	6.5
Phoenix	9	1.6	73.7	15.1	3.3

Source: U.S. Bureau of the Census, *Country and City Data Book: 1994* (U.S. Government Printing Office, Washington, D.C., 1994), pp. 650–837.
Notes:
a. Includes workers age 16 and over.
b. Includes bus or trolley bus, streetcar or trolley car, subway or elevated train, railroad, ferryboat, or taxicab.

Mark Edwards/Still Pictures

Urban sprawl. *Heavy reliance on private cars and low-density urban form have created sprawling cities, especially in the United States and Australia. Here, an aerial view of Perth, Australia.*

change is occurring at a slightly slower pace (37). The same is true for some large, middle-income cities of the developing world, such as Sao Paulo, Brazil (38).

Decentralization of people and activities results in two contradictory effects: commuter journeys, many of which now occur from suburb to suburb, are shortened, but most of them are made by privately owned car rather than public transportation (39). Most transit and road systems were developed to facilitate suburb-to-city, rather than suburb-to-suburb, commuting. As a result, suburban roadways are often as congested as urban roadways.

ones such as Madrid, Paris, and Zurich, to rapidly industrializing capitals such as Seoul, Republic of Korea, and Buenos Aires, Argentina, to those experiencing rampant urban growth, such as Bombay, India (32). Cars are not the sole cause of urban expansion—factors such as population growth and land markets also play a role—but cars do make expansion feasible (33).

In the more developed regions of the world, the historical central business district, once the primary destination of commuters and easily serviced by public transportation, is being rendered obsolete by changing manufacturing practices (34). Whereas traditional manufacturing depended on centralized workplaces and transportation schemes, advanced technology has rendered modern industry more flexible. As a result, job opportunities have shifted to the suburbs.

Dispersed urban land development patterns have been particularly manifest in North America, where land is abundant, the transportation costs for individuals are low, and the economy has become dominated by service and technology-based industries such as software development and entertainment. In the United States, by 1980 only 9 percent of the metropolitan population worked in the central city and only 3 percent of suburbanites commuted downtown (35). In addition, travel has become relatively inexpensive compared with land, so households have an incentive to buy lower-priced housing at the urban periphery, even though living there requires much more travel (36). Similar patterns can be found in many European cities, but the

As cities continue to become dispersed, the cost of building and operating public transportation systems is becoming prohibitive. Furthermore, the dispersed residential pattern makes public transportation systems less convenient for the average commuter (40). In New York, despite 10 years of investment, public transit ridership declined from 4.8 million per day in 1980 to 4.3 million per day in 1992 (41).

In much of the developing world, unplanned and uncoordinated land development has led to rapid expansion of the urban periphery. Poorer residents are often isolated in outlying areas without access to affordable and convenient public transportation (42).

IMPACTS OF URBAN TRANSPORTATION TRENDS

These urban transportation trends are exacting significant costs in cities in both the developed and the developing world. One is simply the direct financial cost of providing and maintaining the transportation infrastructure. Investing in the transportation infrastructure is essential for economic growth, increasing productivity and quality of life (43). Especially in the poorest developing countries, where the length of paved roadway per one million residents is 25 times less than that in developed countries, improving the transportation infrastructure is a key factor in providing access to jobs and establishing rural and urban trade links (44). However, inefficient operations and inadequate maintenance are translating into large financial expenditures without the expected benefits. In sub-Saharan Africa, for example, roads valued at almost $13 billion have eroded because of a lack of maintenance (45).

Transportation's environmental and social costs, although perhaps less quantifiable, are no less important, because they degrade quality of life and undermine urban productivity. These impacts include congestion, energy consumption, local and global air pollution, noise pollution, traffic accidents, and social inequities.

Congestion

Congestion is perhaps the most visible manifestation of the failures in urban transportation planning. It undermines the central purpose of the automobile: ready access to people, goods, and services. Clogged city streets exact a major toll on economic productivity and exacerbate air and noise pollution.

In many cities in Japan, India, China, and Indonesia, peak period (rush hour) speeds in city centers consistently declined throughout the 1980s to the point that today traffic creeps along at less than 10 kilometers per hour (46). Perhaps the most notorious example is Bangkok, where peak period traffic speeds in the city center declined by an average of 2 kilometers per hour per year in the second half of the 1980s. As a result, an average car in Bangkok is estimated to spend the equivalent of 44 days per year stuck in traffic (47).

In developed countries, congestion afflicts large and small cities alike. A study of cities in OECD countries found that in virtually every city, speeds in the central business district have declined dramatically since 1970 (48). In the central business district of cities as diverse as Manchester, United Kingdom; Milan, Italy; Utsunomiya, Japan; and Trondheim, Norway, morning peak period speeds were 20 kilometers per hour or less in 1990 (49).

Congestion is frequently the result of an insufficient road network, and thus even a relatively few vehicles can cause intense gridlock (50). Yet, expanding the road network is rarely an adequate solution. In many cities in the developing world, such improvements are beyond a city's financial resources. In addition, road construction requires vacant land; in very dense cities such as Bangkok and Shanghai, China, additional road construction would require destroying existing buildings and/or displacing informal settlements. More important, any increase in road capacity tends to be quickly swamped by new travel.

Mark Edwards/Still Pictures

Gridlock. In cities of both the developed and the developing world, average traffic speeds have declined dramatically since the 1970s and 1980s. In Bangkok, above, an average car is estimated to spend the equivalent of 44 days per year stuck in traffic.

Energy Consumption and Air Pollution

Transportation requires huge amounts of energy. Globally, 20 percent of all energy produced is used for transportation. Of this, between 60 and 70 percent goes toward moving people, and the rest toward moving freight (51) (52). In OECD countries, transportation uses an even larger share: about 31 percent of all energy used in 1991 (53). Transportation is heavily oil dominated; about half of the world's oil is consumed in the transportation sector (54).

Energy consumption in the transportation sector is expected to grow in both the developed and the developing world (55). From 1971 to 1992, worldwide energy use in the transportation sector grew on average 2.7 percent per year, faster than industry or other energy end use sectors (56) (57). This energy consumption contributes to both local and global air pollution and presents an economic burden, especially in countries that import energy resources. (See Chapter 12, "Energy and Materials.")

Indeed, motor vehicles produce more air pollution than any other single human activity (58). Nearly 50 percent of global carbon monoxide, hydrocarbon, and nitrogen oxide emissions from fossil fuel combustion come from gasoline- and diesel-powered engines (59). In city centers, especially on highly congested streets, traffic can be responsible for as much as 90 to 95 percent of the ambient carbon monoxide levels, 80 to 90 percent of the nitrogen oxides and hydrocarbons, and a large portion of the particulates, posing a significant threat to human health and natural resources (60). (See Table 4.2.) (See Chapter 2, "Urban Environment and Human Health," and Chapter 3, "Urban Impacts on Natural Resources.")

In the cities of the developed world, car emissions pose the greatest threat to air quality. In the United States in 1993, transportation sources were responsible for 77 percent of carbon monoxide emissions, 45 percent of nitrogen oxides, 36 percent of volatile organic compounds, and 22 percent of particulates (61). In the European Union, pollution control measures have been initiated over the past 20 years to reduce nitrogen dioxide levels, but these measures have been offset by increases in the numbers of vehicles on the road (62). In the United Kingdom, for example, average concentrations of nitrogen dioxide increased by 35 percent from 1986 to 1991, mainly as the result of increased emissions by motor vehicle traffic (63).

In the developing world, automotive air pollution is mostly a problem in large cities with high levels of traffic, such as Mexico City, Bangkok, and Lagos, Nigeria. In other cities, power plants, factories, and other stationary sources still constitute the greatest threat to air quality. However, even in some smaller urban centers such as Peshawar, Pakistan, and Kathmandu, Nepal, air pollution from motor vehicles is becoming an increasing problem (64).

Motor vehicles are also a significant factor in lead emissions. An estimated 80 to 90 percent of lead in ambient air is derived from the combustion of leaded gasoline. Recognizing the health threat, most developed countries have reduced the lead content of gasoline over the past decade. Unleaded gasoline has been in-

troduced in most Latin American countries, Malaysia, Singapore, Taiwan, and the Republic of Korea, although in most cities of the developing world, ambient lead levels still greatly exceed the health standard of 1 microgram per cubic meter (65). In Cairo, for example, ambient lead levels of 1.5 micrograms per cubic meter are common (66) (67). Lead levels tend to be especially high along roads with heavy traffic density (68).

The impacts of motor vehicle emissions extend far beyond the local area. The transportation sector is the most rapidly growing source of greenhouse gas emissions—that is, emissions of chemicals that have the potential to contribute to global warming (69). These include carbon dioxide, chlorofluorocarbons, nitrous oxide, and carbon monoxide (70). In 1990, about 22 percent of carbon dioxide emissions from fossil fuel use came from the transportation sector (71). OECD countries are responsible for about 70 percent of greenhouse gas emissions attributed to transportation (72). However, the share of emissions from developing countries is expected to rise in the future because of the growing sizes of their motor vehicle fleets and their use of less efficient fuel-burning technologies (73) (74).

Noise Pollution

Traffic noise—from the constant drone of passing cars and trucks to the sound of screeching tires, blaring horns, radios, and car alarms—is extensive in urban areas.

Table 4.2 Contribution of Motor Vehicles to Urban Air Pollutant Levels in Selected Cities, 1980s and 1990s

City	Year	Percent Attributable to Motor Vehicles				
		Carbon Monoxide	Hydro-carbons	Nitrogen Oxides	Sulfur Dioxide	Suspended Particulate Matter
Athens	1990	100	79[a]	76	8	13[b]
Beijing	1989	39	75	46	X	X
Bombay	1992	X	X	52	5	24
Budapest	1987	81	75	57	12	X
Cochin, India	1993	70	95	77	X	X
Colombo, Sri Lanka	1992	100	100	82	94	88
Delhi	1987	90	85	59	13	37
Lagos, Nigeria[c,d]	1988	91	20	62	27	69
Los Angeles	1990	98	62	84	68	11[e]
Mexico City	1990	97	53	75	22	35
Santiago	1993	95	69	85	14	11
Sao Paulo	1990	94	89	92	64	39

Sources:
1. Asif Faiz, Kumares Sinha, and Surhid P. Gautam, *Air Pollution from Motor Vehicles: Characteristics, Trends, and Impacts,* A World Bank Report (mimeo), The World Bank, Washington, D.C., 1995.
2. South Coast Air Quality Management District, *Appendix II-B: Air Quality Trends, 1976–1993* (South Coast Air Quality Management District, Los Angeles, 1994), p. 7.

Notes: a. Applies to road transport only; values listed under hydrocarbons represent volatile organic compounds. b. Includes smoke. c. Percent shares apply to all transportation modes. d. Does not include biomass. e. Directly emitted particulates less than 10 microns (PM10). X = not available.

Noise pollution can damage human hearing and affect psychological well-being, as well as decrease property values (75). An estimated 100 million people in OECD countries are exposed to traffic noise in excess of 65 dB(A) (higher than the 55dB(A) considered acceptable) (76). Although data for developing countries are scarce, data collected along heavily traveled roads in Bombay, India, indicate sound levels of 65 to 85 dB(A) (77).

Traffic Accidents

In 1993, an estimated 885,000 people died in traffic accidents (78). The majority of these deaths were in the developing world, and traffic accident deaths are a leading cause of death among people in economically active age groups (79). In India, for example, roadway death rates (road deaths per 1,000 vehicles) are 18 times higher than those in Japan, amounting to 60,000 fatalities per year (80). In general, urban traffic and pedestrian accidents form a higher proportion of accidents in developing countries than in developed countries (81).

Each year in the European Union, 55,000 people are killed, 1.7 million are injured, and 150,000 are permanently disabled as a result of traffic accidents (82). In the former East Germany after the opening of the Berlin Wall, the sudden increase in automobile use is cited as a primary factor in the doubling of traffic fatalities between 1989 and 1991 (83).

Social Inequities

The dispersed patterns of many of today's cities, made possible by the availability of motor vehicles, contribute to social inequities as well—chiefly, limited access to jobs by the urban poor as well as proportionately higher travel costs. These problems exist in cities in both the developed and the developing world, although the causes and symptoms are somewhat different.

In the United States, suburban flight has left the urban poor concentrated in city centers far from jobs, stores, and entertainment services that have relocated to the periphery as well. Unable to afford cars, many poorer dwellers in the city center must rely on public transportation that rarely adequately serves the suburbs. This has played an important role in limiting job and income opportunities (84). In Detroit, for example, about 40 percent of the central-city population does not have a car, yet most of the new jobs in the region are in outlying suburbs (85) (86).

In cities with large segments of low-income groups in squatter settlements at the periphery of the urban area, similar forms of isolation and inaccessibility exist because opportunities for employment, advanced education, recreation, and shopping are often located in wealthier areas in the city center. In Santiago, Chile, the poorest residents tend to live on the urban periphery. The majority of their trips are over long distances, and they must travel by relatively inconvenient modes, either by public transportation or on foot. For those in the richest sections of the city, the majority of trips are over shorter distances and are made by privately owned automobile (87). In Sao Paulo, poor people can spend 2 hours or more traveling between home and work (88). Similar disparities exist in many Asian and African cities.

Members of poorer households also tend to spend a larger percentage of their income on travel than do members of wealthier households (89). In household budgets, the cost of the breadwinner's trip to work is usually the top priority, which sometimes means that trips for schooling or health services must be sacrificed (90). In Dar es Salaam, Tanzania, many residents cannot afford bus fares, and even a bicycle costs, on average, about four times the monthly minimum wage (91). Thus, access to affordable transportation services can greatly improve the welfare of many poor families.

MOVING FORWARD: KEY STRATEGIES AND TOOLS

Faced with rising transportation demand and growing negative impacts, urban areas require new approaches to addressing their transportation needs. Cities cannot continue to expand their urban transportation systems forever. Although some expansion is necessary, the economic, social, and environmental costs of doing so are prohibitive. Instead, cities need to reexamine urban transportation demand and devise new strategies that provide maximum access at a minimum total cost.

A number of policy tools are available to reduce excessive travel demand and create more sustainable transportation systems, from road pricing to increasing the efficiency of existing systems, to expanding public transit. Most of these tools will have a limited impact if they are used in isolation. Instead, improving urban transportation systems will require a combination of policies that reinforce each other and help to avoid adverse side effects (92).

Managing Travel Demand

Land Use

Perhaps the greatest opportunity to reduce the negative impacts of current transportation systems is to influence land development patterns. An integrated land use and transportation strategy can increase the accessibility of jobs, shops, and other facilities without increasing the need to travel by car.

Many urban planning models have proposed ways to reduce reliance on the automobile. Some point to the compact city as the ideal, where high densities facilitate walking or bicycling and buses or subways are cost-effective alternatives. The mixed land use model, where homes, jobs, and stores are clustered together, can reduce car trips and address the problem of deserted central business districts at night. Other models present the ideal form as many small, self-sufficient urban centers linked by a public transportation system. Greenbelts, greenways, and urban growth boundaries—large tracts of land on which urban development is prohibited—are heralded as effective means of protecting farmland and preventing urban sprawl (93) (94) (95). Unfortunately, these measures are neither easy to implement nor guaranteed to succeed.

Nevertheless, evidence linking urban form and transportation demand is compelling. Various studies suggest that in cities with relatively high residential densities and a balance of jobs and housing, people travel less, make shorter trips, and walk and bicycle more often. In the United Kingdom, for example, national survey data show that travel varies according to density. Travel demand quickly rises as density falls below 15 people per hectare and falls sharply as density exceeds 50 people per hectare (96). However, evidence is not sufficient to recommend an optimal density or settlement pattern. Comparative studies are generally limited by data constraints and confounding factors such as fuel prices, levels of automobile ownership, and cultural values (97).

Furthermore, textbook solutions rarely translate into real-life successes. London and Seoul, famous for their greenbelts, are facing new transportation challenges as urban development extends beyond those boundaries and workers commute even longer distances to downtown jobs (98) (99). In Delhi, India, mixed land uses and high population densities are the norm, yet the city is faced with congestion, air pollution, and limited transportation options for its poor people. (See Box 4.1.) Efforts to manipulate urban form are further complicated by issues of land ownership and market forces. Additionally, an integrated strategy requires coordination between the transportation and land use sectors across an entire metropolitan region—something that is not easily achieved (100) (101).

Still, cities that have managed to integrate transportation and land use are reaping the benefits. Curitiba, Brazil, is a notable example. By channeling urban growth along public transit routes, the city has managed to reduce privately owned car use, despite having the second highest per capita car ownership rate in Brazil (one car for every three people). On a typical workday, more than 70 percent of all commuters (1.3 million people) travel by bus. As a result, Curitiba's gasoline use per capita is 25 percent lower than that of eight comparable Brazilian cities, and the city has one of Brazil's lowest rates of ambient air pollution (102). Portland, Oregon, is using an integrated transportation and land use strategy in an attempt to head off the problems of sprawl and inner-city decay typical of many U.S. cities. (See Box 4.2.) The importance of linking transportation and land use is discussed in detail in Chapter 5, "Urban Priorities for Action."

Full-Cost Pricing

One of the major factors contributing to urban transportation problems is that people do not pay for the full costs of their travel. Motorists rarely pay enough taxes to support the investments needed to construct and repair roads. Nor do car or gasoline prices reflect less tangible costs such as the negative health effects of automotive air pollution or productivity losses incurred by traffic delays.

These costs are substantial. At a national level in the United States, various studies suggest that motor vehicle use imposes on society estimated external costs of more than $300 billion (103) (104) (105). In urban areas, where negative impacts are concentrated, the cost per vehicle distance traveled is probably higher. Although much has been written in recent years about estimating the unpaid costs of travel, estimates of the full costs vary significantly, are subject to much dispute, and should be considered only rough approximations.

Moving toward recovering these costs would help to reduce uneconomical travel and would spread trips across longer periods of the day. These improvements could lead to a reduction in congestion, an increase in the use of public transit, and, perhaps in the long run, more efficient land use patterns (106). In OECD countries, raising the costs of car travel may be a more effective way to reduce car use and its related problems than improving public transportation service or lowering fares (107).

Although it is unlikely that drivers will ever pay the full costs of transportation by car, several policy tools can be used to at least recover some of these costs, ranging from road pricing to gasoline taxes, to increased fees for parking. These can be key elements in a strategy for managing travel demand.

Road Pricing. Road pricing entails charging drivers directly for using roads through a variety of techniques, such as the use of tolls, area licensing schemes, and electronic road pricing. To be most effective, a road pricing scheme should cover all important roads throughout an urban area, and the charge should vary according to demand, with higher prices charged during peak periods, as is the case for electric utilities or telephone service. The goal is to encourage people to use alternate modes of transportation or to drive during off-peak periods.

Designing such a system, however, is complicated administratively, technically, and politically. In addition, road pricing will not succeed if cities do not offer attractive alternative transportation options (108). Accordingly, despite the demonstrated advantages of road pricing, few cities have implemented such schemes.

Most practical applications have been a type of area pricing, in which drivers must pay to enter a specific area. Perhaps the most well-known of these is Singapore's area licensing scheme, which seeks to reduce traffic into the city center by charging low-occupancy vehicles a fee when they enter the area. To enter the restricted area, a car must display a special window sticker, for which a fee is also charged. Since its inception in 1975, the plan has both reduced congestion and stimulated the use of public transportation, at modest cost. The city is replacing the current system with an electronic scheme. Cameras mounted on overhead gateways will automatically deduct entry fees from stored value cards mounted on vehicle dashboards. The fee will be determined by both location and time of day (109).

In OECD countries, road pricing is being considered seriously, although in most places it is still only in the testing phase. A "smart" card, which automatically imposes a charge when a vehicle is stalled in traffic, is being tried in Cambridge, United Kingdom, to reduce congestion (110). In the Norwegian cities of Oslo, Bergen, and Trondheim, electronic toll-collecting systems (initially designed to raise revenue for new road construction) may have the added benefit of reducing traffic in the city center (111).

In the developing world, the widespread introduction of electronic road pricing may not be feasible because of both the up-front costs of the technology and the potential difficulty of enforcement. Yet, road pricing can be cost effective—particularly in middle-income cities of the developing world, where motor vehicle use is increasing rapidly—because it can offset or delay costly expansion of the road system. Government officials in Santiago, Chile, are planning to implement a road pricing scheme (112).

Road pricing can have unintended impacts, however. For instance, it runs the risk of encouraging travel on roads on which a fee is not required, increasing congestion there and precipitating urban growth in new suburban areas. Road pricing must be examined for its equity impacts as well. By raising the price of travel, peak period pricing may squeeze poorer drivers off the road while allowing those who can afford it to drive on a more efficient road system. In San Francisco, the Bay Bridge Congestion Pricing pilot project proposed a way to overcome this problem by using existing low-income targeting mechanisms (in this case, an electric utility program that offers rebates to the poor) to provide discounts for poorer drivers (113). Alternatively, the funds generated could be used to reduce transit fares and improve transit service in low-income areas.

Taxes and Pollution Fees. In addition to road pricing, other variable transportation charges to recover the full costs of transportation have been suggested. In practice, there is already an array of taxes on motor vehicles in most countries, ranging from purchase taxes on new vehicles to fuel taxes. Governments have long used fuel taxes as a means of raising revenue for road building and maintenance. Recently, however, some countries have begun to consider taxation as a means to reduce vehicle use, conserve energy, and reduce carbon dioxide emissions (114). Hungary, for instance, introduced an environmental tax on fuel in 1992 as well as a road maintenance fee (115).

Fuel taxes can be an important policy tool in efforts to change travel behaviors. The direct impact of fuel prices on the level and pattern of transportation demand has been vividly illustrated over the past 20 years by the effects of increases in world oil prices on the overall volume of transport, on the search for improved efficiencies in the use of traditional fuel sources, and on the development of alternative fuel technologies (116). The high cost of fuel in Japan and Europe has led people in those countries to drive less and to drive more fuel-efficient cars than their counterparts in the United States (117). Reducing fuel subsidies and increasing fuel taxes could help improve vehicle efficiencies in developing countries as well (118).

Pollution fees, which increase with the amount of pollution produced by a vehicle, or vehicle-miles-of-travel (VMT) fees also can be used to recover some of the true costs of car transportation. Such fees can be collected at annual vehicle inspections and can be based on odometer readings. Research suggests that a VMT fee of $0.03 per kilometer imposed in Southern California could reduce automobile trips and

Box 4.1 The Indian Transportation Paradigm

Conventional urban transportation planning, as defined in the developed world, has been applied to Indian cities such as Delhi for more than 35 years. Delhi's Master Plan includes numerous "district centers" that provide residential, shopping, commercial, and recreational facilities (1). By some measures, the Master Plan has succeeded: Delhi has high population densities and mixed land use patterns, resulting in short trips, many of which are made by walking, nonmotorized vehicles, or public transportation. Private car ownership is low (2) (3) (4) (5). In that regard, Delhi would seem to be a textbook example of integrated land use and transportation planning.

Even so, air pollution, congestion, and traffic fatalities are terrible and continue to worsen. The World Health Organization has classified Delhi as one of the 10 most polluted cities in the world (6). Congestion in Delhi seems to be worsening, despite local road improve-

ment programs. Average speeds during peak periods range from 10 to 15 kilometers per hour in central areas and from 25 to 40 kilometers per hour on arterial streets (7). Delhi's traffic fatalities in 1993 were more than double those of all other major Indian cities combined (8).

What accounts for this mismatch between the Master Plan and the reality of growing transportation problems? Much of it can be traced to attempting to apply solutions for cities in the developed world to a city in a developing country, with its very different vehicle mix and socioeconomic conditions.

DELHI'S VEHICLE MIX

Traditional urban transportation models are designed to handle a homogeneous mix of passenger cars, trucks, and buses all moving at the same speed, but in Delhi, cars, trucks, and buses must compete for space with two- and three-wheel motorized vehicles as well as camels, ele-

phants, stray cattle, bullock-carts, rickshaws, and handcarts (9). In fact, cars do not even constitute the majority of the city's 2,097,000 vehicles (10); motor scooters and motorcycles account for nearly 70 percent of registered vehicles. Another 4 percent are locally designed three-wheel scooter rickshaws; the rest are taxis, public buses, and trucks (11).

The city's estimated 1,500,000 two- and three-wheel vehicles are heavy contributors to local pollution (12) (13). As a class, these vehicles emit higher levels of hydrocarbons than cars, trucks, or buses. Three-wheel scooter rickshaws also emit significant amounts of carbon monoxide (14). Because they are a low-cost alternative to the city's overcrowded public transportation services, the number of two- and three-wheel vehicles on Delhi streets continues to grow. Since the 1980s, sales of such vehicles have increased by nearly 20 percent per year (15).

Variations in vehicle size, rate of acceleration, and speed mean that often the best way to advance through the road network is to dart laterally from lane to lane to optimize the available space. The sudden braking and change of direction that are required in this type of traffic reduce overall vehicle speeds, increase the chance of accidents, and adversely affect fuel consumption and emission rates (16).

Because there is no formal segregation of vehicles in Delhi and no enforcement of speed limits, nonmotorized vehicles such as bicycles and carts tend to segregate themselves naturally onto the curb lanes on two- and three-lane roads. However, there is still a considerable safety risk (17). Pedestrians, bicyclists, and motorcyclists make up more than 80 percent of Delhi's road fatalities (18). One third of the pedestrian fatalities involve Delhi's buses, which are vastly overcrowded; many deaths occur when passengers forced to ride on running boards or hanging onto the outside of the vehicles are thrown off or struck; many passengers are also struck when boarding or leaving buses.

DELHI'S SOCIOECONOMIC MIX

Many of Delhi's transportation-related problems have arisen because planners

Competing needs. In Delhi and other Indian cities, motor scooters, animal-drawn carts, and pedestrians compete with cars and buses for roadspace, leading to worsening congestion and traffic fatalities.

Jorgen Schytte/Still Pictures

failed to provide for the wide range of socioeconomic levels and especially the extent of poverty within the city.

Few people in Delhi can afford the cost of private motorized transportation, even for the journey to work. Instead they must rely on public transportation. Even the slightest increase in the cost of public transportation can be a hardship. A recent survey indicated that nearly 60 percent of the respondents found the minimum cost of commuting to work on public transportation (less than $0.06 per trip) to be unacceptable [19] [20]. A ride on public transportation—even at the lowest minimum fare—can consume 20 to 30 percent of a family's income for the lowest income groups. A large percentage of low-income people travel long distances and spend 30 to 60 minutes on one-way travel [21].

In response to both the cost of transportation within the city and the long working hours, many of Delhi's poor have no choice but to establish unauthorized settlements in substandard housing on public land near their places of employment. In 1991, an estimated 1.3 million people resided in these *jhuggi-jhopri* settlements [22].

In the mid-1970s, government officials made a conscious effort to relocate the *jhuggi-jhopri* settlements to the outer areas of the city where new developments had been planned. Because few jobs are available on the urban periphery, however, residents in these areas now must commute long distances across the city in search of employment [23].

Many of Delhi's poor work in the so-called informal sector as street vendors or as operators of pavement shops and car or motor scooter repair shops along roadways. Government officials call these services "encroachments" and complain that they reduce road capacity. However, they are an integral part of the urban landscape, providing a variety of services at low cost and at locations where demand for these services is high. As a result, they continue to multiply along the arterial roads of the city.

FINDING NEW SOLUTIONS

The transportation planning tools of the developed world are not adequate to address the urban traffic mix and socioeconomic patterns characteristic of cities such as Delhi. The challenge for Delhi and similar cities is to accommodate this complexity rather than to try to minimize it or wish it away.

Given Delhi's socioeconomic mix, much of the population will be unable to afford cars or even public transportation for some time to come. Meanwhile, bicycles and pedestrians continue to share the roads with cars, where they impede traffic and are exposed to a high risk of accidents. Requests to provide separate facilities for nonmotorized transport are typically met with the argument that scarce resources cannot be wasted for a mode that is going to disappear in the future. However, if Delhi and similar cities were to consider facilities for nonmotorized transport as an integral part of a program to enhance road capacity, then the investment could be justified. Not only are lanes designed for bicycle traffic less expensive to build than roadways, but they also will divert pedestrians and slow-moving vehicles from the roadway, increasing the efficiency of car and bus transport.

By accommodating the needs of all of its citizens—including the poorest ones—for safe and affordable transport, cities such as Delhi can create an equitable and environmentally friendly transportation system.

—*Geetam Tiwari*

Geetam Tiwari is a visiting fellow at the Tata Energy and Resources Institute, Arlington, Virginia, and is a member of the faculty of the Interdisciplinary Applied Systems Research Programme at the Indian Institute of Technology, Delhi.

References and Notes

1. Delhi Development Authority, *Master Plan for Delhi: Perspective 2001* (Vikas Minar, Delhi, India, August 1990), pp. 13–17.
2. *Ibid.*, pp. 6–7.
3. *Op. cit.* 1, p. 8.
4. Tata Energy and Resources Institute (TERI), *Impact of Road Transportation Systems on Energy and Environment: An Analysis of Metropolitan Cities in India* (TERI, New Delhi, India, May 1993), p. 40.
5. *Ibid.*, p. 46.
6. World Health Organization and United Nations Environment Programme, *Urban Air Pollution in Megacities of the World* (Blackwell Publishers, Oxford, U.K., 1992), pp. 99–106.
7. *Op. cit.* 4, p. 36.
8. "Better Traffic Policing Urged," *Indian Express,* Delhi, India (February 26, 1994).
9. National Institute of Urban Affairs (NIUA), *Urban Environmental Maps: Delhi, Bombay, Vadodara, Ahmedabad* (NIUA, New Delhi, India, 1994), p. 1.44.
10. R.A. Shaik, "Transportation in India: Current Issues and Problems," paper presented at the 74th Annual Meeting of the Transportation Research Board, National Academy of Sciences, Washington, D.C., January 1995, Table 2.
11. *Op. cit.* 4, p. 28.
12. *Op. cit.* 4, p. 28.
13. *Op. cit.* 4, Table 4.38, p. 78.
14. Indian Institute of Petroleum (IIP), *State of the Art Report on Vehicle Emissions* (IIP, Dehradun, India, 1985).
15. *Op. cit.* 4, p. 30.
16. F.M.A. Karim, G. Tiwari, and A. Kanda, "Simulation of Heterogeneous Traffic Stream," draft research report, World Health Organization Collaborating Center for Injury Prevention and Control (Indian Institute of Technology, Delhi, India), p. 10.
17. Udesh Jha, "Studies of Heterogeneous Traffic Flows for Planning Facilities" (Department of Civil Engineering, Indian Institute of Technology, Delhi, India, 1995).
18. Delhi Traffic Police, "First Information Report: June 1993–July 1994" (Delhi Police Department, Delhi, India, 1994).
19. Central Road Research Institute (CRRI), *Mobility Levels and Transport Problems of Various Population Groups* (CRRI, New Delhi, India, 1988), p. 32.
20. Based on the exchange rate on December 7, 1995.
21. *Op. cit.* 19, n.p.
22. Mita Sharma, "Delhi Profile: Transport and Environment," Research Paper No. 8 (The Times Research Foundation, Calcutta, India, September 1992), p. 3.
23. *Op. cit.* 19, Table 5.17, p. 48.

Box 4.2 Setting Limits Pays Off in Portland, Oregon

Portland, Oregon, is often considered one of the most livable and best-planned cities in the United States (1). During the 1960s and 1970s, however, Portland faced problems similar to those of many other urban areas in the United States. Urban sprawl was leading to extensive suburban development, while the downtown area was plagued with decaying buildings, vacant lots, and social problems. Heavy car use was increasing levels of congestion, noise, and air pollution (2). Yet, Portland has largely managed to reverse these trends through integrated land use and transportation planning.

A key component of Portland's success was a statewide land use law establishing urban growth boundaries around metropolitan areas. With only a finite supply of land available for urban expansion, Portland was forced to find ways to encourage development within the urban boundary limits (3).

To encourage revitalization of the downtown area, a segment of downtown roadway was replaced with an urban park, a limit was placed on the allowable number of downtown parking spaces, and road construction projects were scrapped in favor of new transit lines. Then, zoning regulations were established to encourage high residential densities along transit corridors (4) (5). At the same time, the city improved the existing bus system and is planning to offer bus service within walking distance of all neighborhoods (6).

Partly as a result of these measures, the number of jobs in downtown Portland has increased by 30,000 since the 1970s, with only a scant increase in traffic; in addition, 40 percent of commuters to the downtown area use public transportation (7). The number of days per year on which carbon monoxide levels violated federal health standards has dropped from 100 to zero (8).

The metropolitan population is continuing to expand at 3.6 percent per year, and future growth threatens to undermine these advances (9). To guard against that possibility, both city residents and the government are exploring alternative urban development options. In response to public opposition to a planned bypass freeway, One Thousand Friends of Oregon initiated a program known as Making the Land Use–Transportation–Air Quality Connection, which advocates clustering mixed use communities around regional rail stations to reduce reliance on automobiles (10). Portland's regional government has developed the Region 2040 project to study how future metropolitan growth can be accommodated without further extending the urban boundaries (11).

Despite these efforts, travel in the Portland region will still be mainly by car, with its associated impacts (12). Nevertheless, by encouraging high-density development along transit routes and by limiting urban sprawl, Portland is showing that at least some reductions in car use are possible.

References and Notes

1. Kevin Kasowski, "Portland's Urban Growth Boundary," *The Urban Ecologist,* Spring 1994 (Urban Ecology, Oakland, California, 1994), p. 1.
2. Organisation for Economic Co-Operation and Development (OECD) and the European Conference of Ministers of Transport (ECMT), *Urban Travel and Sustainable Development* (OECD and ECMT, Paris, 1995), p. 217.
3. *Op. cit.* 1.
4. Judith Corbett, "Portland's Livable Downtown: From Auto-Dependence to Pedestrian Independence," in *Surface Transportation Policy Project Resource Guide* (Surface Transportation Policy Project, Washington, D.C., 1992), p. 2.
5. *Op. cit.* 2.
6. *Op. cit.* 4, p. 1.
7. *Op. cit.* 2.
8. Keith A. Bartholomew, *A Tale of Two Cities* (One Thousand Friends of Oregon, Portland, 1993), p. 4.
9. U.S. Bureau of the Census, *Statistical Abstract of the United States 1993*, 113th edition (U.S. Government Printing Office, Washington, D.C., 1993), p. 39.
10. *Op. cit.* 2.
11. Metro Council, *Metro 2040 Growth Concept* (Metro Council, Portland, Oregon, December 1994).
12. *Op. cit.* 2, p. 218.

Livable city. *Portland has made the downtown area more friendly to pedestrians through the development of an urban park and a "fare free" transit mall. The light rail metro system connects the downtown with neighboring suburbs.*

Courtesy of IIEC

automotive air pollution by an estimated 11 percent and could increase public transit ridership (119).

Objections to higher taxes and fees are numerous. One concern is that they would hurt low-income families, who already spend proportionately more of their income on transportation. In addition, taxes do not influence when a car is used, so they may have little effect on congestion. Some analysts suggest that fuel taxes may become less effective in reducing travel demand as cars become more fuel efficient. However, the major barrier to implementation is political opposition. People tend to view these measures simply as additional unwelcome taxes. Overcoming this barrier will require educating the public about the full costs of their current travel decisions, as well as about how the new revenues will be used to improve the urban transportation system.

Parking Controls. Raising the price of parking in certain areas can also deter the use of privately owned cars. If high parking costs raise the price of commuting to work, for example, workers will be more inclined to look for cheaper alternatives, either in the form of public transportation or carpooling.

This is especially true in the United States, where parking has traditionally been heavily subsidized. In downtown Los Angeles, for example, employer-paid parking increases drive-alone commuting by an estimated 44 percent. It also increases the total distance traveled as well as fuel consumption by 33 percent per employee (120). If, instead, employers were to offer workers a commuter stipend that could be used on any travel alternative in lieu of free or reduced-cost parking, one study found that drive-alone commuting would decrease by an estimated 20 percent and vehicle distance traveled would decrease by 17 percent (121).

Higher parking prices, however, can have the unintended effects of increasing illegal parking or increasing the length of trips (e.g., the additional time spent looking for parking places), thereby worsening congestion. Parking controls are most effective when they are used as part of a more comprehensive program and when strict enforcement is possible (122).

Traffic Bans

Instead of pricing signals, many cities have tried to use outright traffic bans to manage travel demand. Bans in the form of license number restrictions have been tried in Athens, Mexico City, and Santiago as a means of reducing the number of cars in the city and thereby reducing congestion and air pollution (123). Although these bans have been somewhat effective, many households bought a second car or switched license plates to meet their mobility needs. In Athens, the number of households with two cars increased, and motorists who were not allowed to enter the city center drove around the city to get to their destination, thereby increasing the length of their trips while also increasing emissions (124). In addition, the cars bought for use on off-days are often cheap, second-hand vehicles, which tend to be more polluting (125).

Improving the Transportation Supply

Even though mechanisms such as road pricing may be able to reduce travel demand, there is still a considerable need to expand the transportation infrastructure in many rapidly growing urban regions, particularly in the developing world. In many urban areas, the transportation infrastructure—including roads, sidewalks, crosswalks, and railways—is seriously deficient. Poor road surfaces lead to safety hazards, congestion, and premature vehicle aging, as well as increased fuel consumption, pollution, and maintenance costs.

The challenge, however, is to expand and improve the transportation supply in such a way that the automobile is only one part of the transportation system rather than the focus. Tools for discouraging the overreliance on privately owned cars will not work unless people are given fast and efficient transportation alternatives—whether bus, light rail, subway, walking, or cycling. Indeed, travel patterns in a city mirror that city's commitment to providing roads, parking, and transit service (126).

Table 4.3 Capacity, Cost, and Emissions of Various Transportation Modes

Mode of Transport[a]	Persons per Hour per Lane	Total Cost per Passenger Kilometer[b] (US$)	Total Emissions per Passenger Kilometer[c] (grams)
Walking	1,800	Negligible	0
Bicycle	1,500	X	0
Motorcycle	1,100	X	27.497[d]
Car	500–800	0.12–0.24	18.965
Bus			
Mixed traffic	10,000–15,000	0.02–0.05	1.02
Bus-only lane	15,000–20,000	0.02–0.05	0.89
Separate busway	30,000	0.05–0.08	X
Light rail transit, surface exclusive	20,000–36,000	0.10–0.15	
Coal			4.3520
Gas			0.1876
Fuel oil			0.6261
Rapid rail transit			
Surface (coal)	50,000	0.10–0.15	4.9651
Elevated (gas)	70,000	0.12–0.20	0.2307
Underground (fuel oil)	70,000	0.15–0.25	0.7102

Sources:
1. United Nations Centre for Human Settlements (Habitat), *Transportation Strategies for Human Settlements in Developing Countries* (Habitat, Nairobi, Kenya, 1984), p. 25.
2. The World Bank, *Urban Transport* (The World Bank, Washington, D.C., 1986), p. 53.
3. Asif Faiz *et al.*, "Automotive Air Pollution: Issues and Options for Developing Countries," Working Paper No. 492 (The World Bank, Washington, D.C., August 1990), Table 20, p. 43.

Notes:
a. Assumes high-occupancy rates and efficient operation.
b. Includes capital costs, vehicle operating costs, and interest.
c. Includes carbon monoxide, hydrocarbons, nitrogen oxides, sulfur oxides, aldehydes, and suspended particulates.
d. Includes two-stroke engines only.
X = not available.

Public Transit Expansion

For cities in need of expanding their transportation supply, developing a mass transit system, with its effective use of space and lower per-passenger pollution levels, should be a priority option. (See Table 4.3.) From buses that provide flexible and low-cost transportation to subways, cities have a wide array of choices. The options best suited to a particular city depend on a number of factors, including urban form, density, and wealth.

Buses. In most cities, efficient bus systems can be both affordable and effective. Buses can carry as many as 80 passengers during the peak period (and trams can carry even more), yet they take up the space of no more than two privately owned cars (127). Indeed, buses are the transportation choice of a majority of city dwellers in developing countries, especially the urban poor. In 1980, an estimated 600 million trips per day were being made in buses in cities in the developing world; that figure will double by the year 2000 (128).

Yet, despite its vital role, bus service in many places falls far short of demand; systems are often severely overstretched, uncomfortable, and unreliable. Potential passengers increasingly turn to other modes of transportation (especially as incomes rise and cars become an option) or are forced to walk long distances. Buses also tend to be noisy and polluting. Regular maintenance can help improve their safety and reduce emissions. In some cities, buses have been retrofitted with engines that run on compressed natural gas (129).

As long as buses run on the same congested streets as other vehicles, they will never be an attractive alternative for those who can afford a car. An effective way to increase bus ridership is to give buses priority in traffic. A dedicated bus lane (assuming high-occupancy rates and efficient operation) can move twice as many people per hour as buses operating in mixed traffic and 40 times as many people per hour as cars (130). By giving buses priority over car traffic, more people will turn to buses as a fast and efficient alternative (131). Many European cities, including Zurich and Helsinki, Finland, have designed systems that give priority to buses and trolleys at intersections (132).

In Abidjan, Cote d'Ivoire, a system combining exclusive bus lanes with a high-speed bus network has enjoyed considerable success. It not only cut bus trip times in half and relieved congestion, but also enabled the government to postpone planned infrastructure investments of US$120 million between 1981 and 1984 (133). One of the most effective bus systems is in Curitiba, Brazil, where the integration of guided land development and a public transportation network created conditions that naturally promote bus use (134).

In Canada, the city of Ottawa, Ontario, is developing an extensive busway system rather than a subway system because of its comparatively low cost and flexibility in serving low- to medium-density urban areas. In addition to exclusive bus lanes, the city is considering a bus tunnel in part of the city center and will promote the use of alternative fuels, including compressed natural gas and electricity, to help alleviate related emissions problems. The system has been designed so that it could be converted to rail transit if warranted (135).

Rail Transit. Well-planned and well-used light rail systems can move more people than can buses. Light rail systems also consume less energy than buses and, depending on the power source, emit fewer pollutants (136). Light rail systems, such as trams and trolleys, although slower than heavy rail systems, can carry 6,000 people per hour in mixed traffic and up to 36,000 people per hour with five- or six-car trains, exclusive rights-of-way, and grade-separated intersections (137). Light rail systems have certain drawbacks, including system inflexibility and expensive track maintenance (138). However, in the dense cities of Asia, light rail is becoming increasingly attractive and viable (139).

Rapid rail transit, such as subways, often appear to be the ideal solution to clogged city streets. These rail systems promise high mobility, can be built under valuable urban land, and, because they emit relatively few pollutants, are an environmentally attractive alternative. Yet, construction and operating costs are huge and often prove to be excessively burdensome on city budgets (140). For example, a dedicated underground rail system cost $40 million per kilometer in Santiago, Chile, $64 million in Osaka, Japan, and $117 million in Caracas, Venezuela. In comparison, a surface light rail system in Tunis, Tunisia, cost only $29 million per kilometer (141).

Cities should resist the temptation to pursue flashy advanced technology solutions when lower-cost approaches such as buses might be adequate. A phased approach—first identifying transport corridors well in advance of city growth and then upgrading services from dedicated busways to light rail and finally, perhaps, to a subway system—may be the best way to ensure the development of economically and financially sound transit systems (142).

Improving Existing Public Transit Services

Opportunities also exist to improve and upgrade existing public transit systems. One option is to privatize and deregulate bus services. Competition among private bus companies can improve bus services and reduce costs. In Colombo, Sri Lanka, for example, deregulation allowed small bus owners to compete with the public bus company, substantially improving service coverage and quality (143).

At the same time, a completely deregulated and competitive public transport market can have pitfalls. Private companies may concentrate services in areas with high densities and high-income neighborhoods, leaving the poor on the urban periphery without adequate services (144). In Santiago, Chile, the complete deregulation of the bus system in the 1980s resulted in large numbers of poorly maintained buses clogging the main streets, contributing to pollution and endangering riders. To correct these problems, the city recently adopted a comprehensive scheme of auctioning downtown routes. Companies must be able to comply with emissions, safety, frequency, and cost requirements before they can be granted rights to various routes. By promoting competition in the market in this way, buses are cleaner, fares are lower, and service is more uniform (145).

Informal transit services that cater especially to the needs of the poor, such as the *jeepneys* in Manila or the *kabu-kabus* in Lagos, Nigeria, are an important part of transportation systems in developing country cities. In Ankara, Turkey, *dolmus* minibuses have been operating for 40 years, providing about 29 percent of transport trips. These vehicles, which operate without timetables, provide more frequent services than municipal buses. Their small size allows them to maneuver more easily on narrow, winding streets (146). In Africa, similar informal transit services fill a critical need for the urban poor (147). However, these informal services are often polluting and tend to contribute to congestion. They also reflect the failure of public transportation to meet the needs of city residents. Integrating these services into the formal transportation network and improving the safety and efficiency of the vehicles could improve transportation options for the poor.

Improvements in public transportation services may also attract new users. In many Western European cities, including Paris, Zurich, and Hanover, Germany, integration of fares and services across transit modes (e.g., bus to rail) has made public transportation use easy and competitive with the automobile in terms of travel time and comfort (148). Although improvements to public transportation systems bring in more passengers, they tend to have only a limited effect on the use of privately owned cars, and thus on congestion and emissions, even if transit travel is increased substantially. The majority of new public transportation users tend to be former pedestrians, cyclists, or car passengers (149).

Making Cities Friendly to Pedestrians and Nonmotorized Vehicles

In the automobile age, nonmotorized transportation is often given short shrift. However, if properly promoted and encouraged, bicycles and walking can provide access to shopping, schools, and work. For cities plagued by serious traffic congestion and air pollution, nonmotorized transport can be an important alternative to relying on private vehicles and can serve as a link in an integrated public transportation system. (See Box 4.3.)

Bicycling and walking are often the only means of transportation available to the poor in many urban areas—particularly in Asia. Indeed, more than half of the world's 800 million bicycles are estimated to be in Asia, with more than 300 million in China alone (150). However, many cities have imposed constraints on nonmotorized modes of travel, particularly cycle rickshaws, claiming that they cause congestion or unfairly exploit human labor (151). In other cities, lack of access to credit inhibits the greater use of nonmotorized vehicles. Many people are unable to save enough money to buy a bicycle (152). Yet, if their use is encouraged, nonmotorized vehicles can provide the mobility needed to improve the economic welfare of the poor. In addition, they can boost public transportation services by serving as a link between outlying settlements and public transit routes. It is common to see thousands of bicycles parked outside train stops in cities in India and China (153).

In China, 50 to 80 percent of urban trips are by bicycle. The government has actively promoted bicycle commuting by offering subsidies to those bicycling to work. It has also accelerated bicycle production and has allocated extensive urban street space to bicycle traffic (154). In Havana, Cuba, an ambitious government program to encourage bicycle use prompted by the country's petroleum crisis has helped to reduce car traffic by 35 percent and bus traffic by 50 percent. One of every three trips in the city is made by bicycle. In addition to subsidies and bike lane construction, the city has reduced car speeds on the most heavily traveled roads to improve safety conditions (155). Other important steps in making bicycles an attractive alternative include separated road space so that nonmotorized vehicles do not have to compete with and disrupt traffic and regular maintenance of bike and pedestrian routes.

In developed countries, far fewer people depend on bicycles and walking as their primary mode of transportation. In the United States and Australia, for example, only 5 percent of all trips involve cycling or walking (156). For these modes of transportation to become more widely used, cities will have to promote them by improving safety conditions for bicyclists and pedestrians, providing bicycle parking, and creating links with public transportation. Denmark and the Netherlands have perhaps done the most to promote bicycle use, although local culture and flat landscapes have played important

Box 4.3 Nonmotorized Transportation: What's To Become of Bicycles and Pedestrians?

My work has brought me into contact with a number of local governments interested in forming a new and integrated vision of urban development—one that focuses on improving general accessibility in the urban sector and that includes nonmotorized transportation as an essential component of a sustainable transportation agenda. Lately, I have come to the conclusion that it is very ineffective to try to convince cities to invest in nonmotorized transportation programs in the context of a broader urban transportation reform. It is clear that merely building bike paths and pedestrian walkways will not solve any city's transportation problems. Unless cities recognize that nonmotorized vehicles and pedestrians need to be a vital part of an integrated urban transportation system, the value of this option is lost.

Sao Paulo, Brazil, with its 15 million metropolitan area residents and 4.5 million privately owned cars, recently announced plans to construct 300 kilometers of bike paths and lanes. Although this is an ambitious program, there have been few attempts to coordinate these efforts with those of other city departments. For example, a massive road construction program is being conducted concurrently, and officials in the city's traffic engineering division contend that they need every single centimeter of road space for automobiles. They even admit that, if it were possible to do so, they would steal sidewalk space for motorized traffic as well.

I sometimes wonder whether the current interest in nonmotorized transportation is really only wishful thinking on the part of environmentally minded city officials. Basically, nonmotorized transportation suffers from the fact that urban development and transportation policies have heretofore catered to the needs of motorized vehicles. Almost without exception, over the past 40

years governments have neglected all other forms of transportation in favor of an automobile-oriented infrastructure. This is true even in developing countries, where rates of car ownership have been low.

This is not to say that nonmotorized transportation is an easy remedy for the urban transportation stalemate. We have to be realistic about the bicycle in the context of today's increasingly global and westernized urban landscapes. There are obvious limitations; bicycles are an effective alternative to cars and public transport only for distances up to about 6 or 7 kilometers (1).

In cities in developing countries, the pattern that is often seen is one in which residents abandon nonmotorized vehicles as soon as motorbikes or cars become economically feasible—as evidenced in China, India, and Indonesia (2). One wonders whether this will also happen in Cuba, where more than 1 million bicycles were imported from China in 1990 to combat a host of transportation problems (3) (4).

The Netherlands is often used as an example of a country where walking and bicycling are well integrated into daily life, and rightfully so. Bicycles, however, have been a part of Dutch culture for more than a century, and even with the government's intense support, bicycle use has been decreasing while motor vehicle use has rapidly been increasing (5).

Transportation policy is more than a discussion about the effectiveness of various transportation modes. Planners can agree that a sustainable city should be bicycle and pedestrian friendly, but the central question is how are cities to move from the present situation to an urban transportation vision that includes nonmotorized vehicles?

Cities need to begin to develop programs that will curtail car use and pro-

mote an integrated, environmentally sustainable urban transportation system with a clearly defined place for nonmotorized vehicles. Transferring the real cost of driving to car users instead of continuing to subsidize car ownership is an important concept to consider. In addition, instead of continuing to expand road networks to meet the spiraling demand, cities need to find ways to reduce existing as well as future travel demand.

Let's stop preaching to one another about technology modes, fuel efficiency, and other subsidiary issues. More important than technology is the vision!

—*Ricardo Neves*

Ricardo Neves is the president of the Institute of Technology for the Citizen in Rio de Janeiro, Brazil.

References and Notes

1. Organisation for Economic Co-Operation and Development (OECD) and the European Conference of Ministers of Transport (ECMT), *Urban Travel and Sustainable Development* (OECD and ECMT, Paris, 1995), p. 86.

2. Peter Midgley, "Urban Transport in Asia: An Operational Agenda for the 1990s," World Bank Technical Paper No. 224 (The World Bank, Washington, D.C., 1994), pp. 14–15.

3. H. Valdes, "NMT: The Situation in Cuba," in *Proceedings of the International Seminar on Sustainable Transportation Strategies and Development,* Report of the Earth Summit (Global Forum, Rio de Janeiro, Brazil, 1992).

4. Manuel Alepuz, "Bicycles Overtake Bus Travel in Havana," *The Urban Age,* Vol. 2, No. 1 (Fall 1993), p. 16.

5. Ministry of Transport, Public Works and Water Management, *Second Structure Plan for Traffic and Transport* (Ministry of Transport, Public Works and Water Management, The Hague, the Netherlands, 1991).

roles in maintaining the popularity of the bicycle in those countries. Despite already high levels of bicycle use, the Dutch national transportation plan aims to increase the amount of cycling by 30 percent by 2010 by providing new bicycle routes, parking at railway stations and bus and tram stops, and additional safety measures (157). Extensive bicycle paths have also been introduced in several cities in Canada and Australia (158). In Seattle, all 1,250 buses in the metropolitan transit system are now equipped with bicycle racks (159).

Reducing Vehicle Pollution

At the same time that cities try to discourage car use and shift the travel load to other alternatives, they can also take a number of steps to improve air quality by reducing vehicle emissions. This can be achieved by cleaning up the fuels that vehicles burn, promoting the design and market penetration of new vehicle technologies, and improving the performance of the existing vehicle fleet.

Cleaner Fuels

Alternative fuels, including compressed natural gas, liquid petroleum gas, and ethanol, are receiving increased attention as potential pollution reducers (160). Compressed natural gas, already being used in countries such as Canada, Italy, and New Zealand, is an abundant fuel and can be particularly useful in reducing emissions of particulates (161). In Brazil, an ambitious government initiative in support of ethanol reduced the share of gasoline used for transportation from 56 percent in 1971 to 23 percent in 1992 (162). By 1983, 90 percent of all new cars ran on alcohol (163). As a result of this change in the fuel mix, energy efficiency in the transportation sector grew significantly between 1971 and the mid-1980s (164) (165). Recently, alcohol shortages and poor road and car maintenance have begun to threaten the potential benefits of the program (166).

A high priority for developing countries is to reduce the lead content in gasoline. Besides being a direct health threat, lead in gasoline prevents the use of catalytic converters on gas-burning engines; catalytic converters help limit vehicle emissions of hydrocarbons, carbon monoxide, and nitrogen oxides (167).

The costs of eliminating lead from gasoline and of eliminating older vehicles have made it difficult for lower-income countries to switch to unleaded gasoline. In Bangkok, however, the government has supported the introduction of unleaded gasoline through a tax subsidy. By taxing unleaded fuel less than leaded fuel, the government made it cost-effective for local refineries to produce unleaded gasoline. In January 1996, use of unleaded gasoline became mandatory (168).

Mark Edwards/Still Pictures

Alternate routes. Copenhagen has discouraged private car use by making streets safe and convenient for bicycles and pedestrians. Denmark's national plan aims to increase the use of cycling by 30 percent by 2010.

New Vehicle Technologies

Opportunities also exist to improve the efficiency and cleanliness of motor vehicles. One promising alternative is the adoption of motor vehicles that run on electricity, powered by fuel cells, hydrogen, or some combination thereof. Zero emission vehicles, while having no effect on congestion, could greatly improve air quality, improving health and the quality of urban life (169). Although some cities and countries have begun to replace public buses with electric models, the wide-scale adoption of electric vehicles remains uncertain. In California, an ambitious mandate requiring that 2 percent of all cars sold in the state in 1998 be emission free was recently amended due to political pressure and reservations about the current performance capabilities of electric vehicles (170). (See Chapter 3, "Urban Impacts on Natural Resources.") In the developing world, the high costs of these technologies make it unlikely that most residents will be able to afford them for many years to come.

Vehicle Inspection and Maintenance

Older vehicles account for a disproportionate share of air pollution. A badly maintained older vehicle can emit 100 times the pollutants of a properly maintained modern vehicle (171). In Los Angeles, one study estimated that pre-1971 cars, which accounted for only 3 percent of the total vehicle miles traveled, were responsible for 50

Courtesy of IIEC

Healthy commutes. In cities such as Seattle, Washington, and Portland, Oregon, buses are equipped with bicycle racks to increase the distance that commuters can cover by both bicycle and public transit.

percent of total hydrocarbon emissions (172). Effective inspection and maintenance programs can reduce emissions from old vehicles and ensure that new vehicles remain in good condition. According to U.S. data, a well-run inspection and maintenance program can reduce the carbon monoxide and hydrocarbon emissions of an individual vehicle by up to 25 percent (173).

Such programs are especially critical in developing countries and countries in transition, because much of the vehicle fleet is composed of older and generally more polluting cars. In Jakarta, Indonesia, for example, two thirds of the privately owned cars are 5 years old or older (174).

However, inspection and maintenance programs face financial, administrative, political, and enforcement barriers. Beyond that, the results of such programs can be mixed. California recently found that only about 50 percent of the repairs arising from inspections were effective in reducing emissions (175).

Singapore, Taiwan, Thailand, India, the Philippines, Chile, and Mexico have all implemented at least rudimentary inspection and maintenance programs (176). Quezon City, Philippines, began an Auto Anti-Smoke-Belching Campaign in 1993. After a 6-month "benign phase" that educated the public about the health hazards of air pollution and the need to reduce auto emissions, the program moved into its "malevolent phase." Two teams randomly tested about 200 vehicles on city streets each day. The owners of vehicles that failed the test (about 65 percent) were fined, had their licenses and registrations taken away, and were given 24 hours to have their vehicles fixed. More than 95 percent of vehicles passed the second test (177).

Another effective mechanism that can be used to reduce vehicle emissions is to accelerate the disposal of old and inefficient vehicles. In Budapest, Hungary, the city government will exchange public transportation passes for Trabants and Wartburgs, two brands of automobiles that are highly polluting but widely used in the city because of their low cost. For each Trabant, the city awards four year-long passes; for each Wartburg, six year-long passes are issued. In addition, the program will buy these cars for a price higher than the going market rate if the money is used as part of a down payment on a new, more efficient vehicle. So far, an estimated 2,000 Trabants and Wartburgs have been taken off the streets of Budapest (178).

Two-wheel vehicles pose an even greater air pollution challenge, especially in Asia. Two wheelers are responsible for a majority of respirable particulates in the air of many Asian cities (179). Given the sheer number of two-wheel vehicles in Asian cities, imposing strict emissions standards is difficult. However, emissions reductions are possible at modest cost by switching from two-stroke to four-stroke engines or by installing catalytic converters. In most cases, the initial increased cost is offset by improvements in fuel economy (180).

Putting It All Together

Each city faces its own mix of transportation problems, and each city will require its own combination of policies to address them. Heavily car-dependent cities, such as those in the United States, face significant challenges. Extensive land use changes, however desirable, are difficult to implement. Given the extent of the existing transportation infrastructure—and the expense implicit in expanding it further—these cities must focus on maximizing the access that their current systems provide and on improving the efficiency and cleanliness of existing vehicle fleets (181). Still, these strategies need not preclude longer-term goals of increasing densities in cities.

Cities in less developed regions of the world, where urban form is not strongly focused on the automobile, have perhaps the greatest opportunity to ensure that future development patterns effectively manage the demand for transportation. For these cities, the key issue is anticipating the growing demand for access and addressing it before an irreversible commitment is made to an unsustainable lifestyle and urban form (182). Yet, they also have the fewest financial, technical, and institutional resources. Historically, measures to address the environmental impacts of the transportation sector are not introduced until well after the impacts have become acute. For example, Bangkok, London, and Tokyo did not begin to address automobile emissions until residents perceived that the air pollution situation was dire (183).

Perhaps the greatest single barrier to effectively solving transportation problems, regardless of city size and location, is the fact that the responsibility for urban transportation systems resides with many different entities. Typically, one institution is responsible for air quality management, another is in charge of traffic management and enforcement, a third manages public transportation, and a fourth manages the infrastructure. This fragmentation can be further complicated by the existence of several municipal and political structures as well as the presence of various politically influential transportation providers (e.g., taxi commissions, public transport associations, automobile clubs, and freight carriers).

The proper institutional structures will depend on the specific political and institutional context of a metropolitan region. However, without clear lines of authority and strong coordination, any attempts to improve urban transportation systems will inevitably fall short.

This chapter was written by Christopher Zegras of the International Institute for Energy Conservation, Washington, D.C.

References and Notes

1. Zmarak Shalizi and Jose C. Carbajo, "Transport-Related Air Pollution Strategies: What Lessons for Developing Countries?," discussion paper (The World Bank, Washington, D.C., September 1994), p. 16.

2. Philip Sayeg *et al.*, *Assessment of Transportation Growth in Asia and Its Effects on Energy Use, the Environment, and Traffic Congestion: Case Study of Bangkok, Thailand* (International Institute for Energy Conservation, Washington, D.C., 1992), p. 23.

3. *Ibid.*

4. Paul Barter *et al.*, "The Challenge of Southeast Asia's Rapid Motorisation: Kuala Lumpur, Jakarta, Surabaya and Manila in an International Perspective," paper presented at the Asian Studies Association of Australia Biennial Conference 1994, Environment, State, and Society in Asia: The Legacy of the Twentieth Century, hosted by the Asia Research Centre, Murdoch University, Perth, Western Australia, Australia, July 13–16, 1994, p. 21.

5. Organisation for Economic Co-Operation and Development (OECD) and the European Conference of Ministers of Transport (ECMT), *Urban Travel and Sustainable Development* (OECD and ECMT, Paris, 1995), p. 31.

6. The World Bank, *Urban Transport* (The World Bank, Washington, D.C., 1986), p. viii.

7. Asif Faiz and Surhid Gautam, "Motorization, Urbanization, and Air Pollution," discussion paper (The World Bank, Washington, D.C., 1994), p. 8.

8. Michael P. Walsh, "Motor Vehicle Pollution Control: An Increasingly Critical Issue for Developing Countries," discussion paper (The World Bank, Washington, D.C., 1994), p. 7.

9. *Op. cit.* 7, p. 1.

10. The OECD member countries are Australia, Austria, Belgium, Canada, Denmark, Finland, France, Germany, Greece, Iceland, Ireland, Italy, Japan, Luxembourg, Mexico, the Netherlands, New Zealand, Norway, Portugal, Spain, Sweden, Switzerland, Turkey, the United Kingdom, and the United States. Mexico became a member in May 1994. Any discussion of OECD data prior to 1994 does not include data for Mexico.

11. American Automobile Manufacturers' Association (AAMA), *World Motor Vehicle Data, 1995 Edition* (AAMA, Detroit, 1995), pp. 16–18.

12. *Op. cit.* 5, p. 35.

13. *Op. cit.* 11.

14. *Op. cit.* 5, p. 35.

15. *Op. cit.* 11.

16. The term "transition economies" lacks a formal definition, but is used here to include the successor states of the former Soviet Union (Armenia, Azerbaijan, the Republic of Belarus, the Republic of Estonia, the Republic of Georgia, the Republic of Kazakhstan, the Kyrgyz Republic, the Republic of Latvia, the Republic of Lithuania, the Republic of Moldova, the Russian Federation, the Republic of Tajikistan, the Republic of Turkmenistan, Ukraine, and the Republic of Uzbekistan) and the countries of Central Europe (Albania, Bulgaria, the Czech Republic, Hungary, Poland, Romania, and the Slovak Republic).

17. Yannis Karmokolias, *Automotive Industry Trends and Prospects for Investment in Developing Countries*, Discussion Paper No. 7 (International Finance Corporation, The World Bank, Washington, D.C., 1990), p. 4.

18. John Lawson, Director, DRI/McGraw-Hill, London, 1994 (personal communication), as cited in O. Tunali, "Auto Production on the Rise," in *Vital Signs 1995: The Trends That Are Shaping Our Future* (Worldwatch Institute, Washington, D.C., 1995), p. 82.

19. *Op. cit.* 7, p. 7.

20. M.E. Omwenga, S. Obiero, and J. Malombe, "Nairobi Action Plan for Urban Mobility and Non-Motorized Transport," in *Proceedings of the SSATP Seminar on Urban Mobility and Non-Motorized Transport in Sub-Saharan Africa* (Africa Technical Department, The World Bank, Nairobi, Kenya, 1994), p. 4.

21. Secretaria Ejecutiva de la Comision de Planificacion de Inversiones en Infraestructura de Transporte (SECTRA), *Encuesta Origen Destino de Viajes del Gran Santiago: 1991* (SECTRA, Santiago, Chile, 1991), Table 7, p. 20.

22. *Op. cit.* 7, p. 4.

23. Peter Midgley, *Urban Transport in Asia: An Operational Agenda for the 1990s*, World Bank Technical Paper No. 224 (The World Bank, Washington, D.C., 1994), p. 15.

24. *Op. cit.* 20, p. 2.

25. *Op. cit.* 6, p. 6.

26. *Op. cit.* 5, p. 36.

27. *Op. cit.* 5, p. 39.

28. U.S. Department of Transportation, Federal Highway Administration, *The 1990 Nationwide Personal Transportation Survey: Summary of Travel Trends* (Office of Highway Information Management, Washington, D.C., 1992), p. 6.

29. U.S. Department of Transportation, Federal Highway Administration, *The 1990 Nationwide Personal Transportation Survey: Travel Behavior Issues in the 1990s* (Office of Highway Information Management, Washington, D.C., 1992), p. 11.

30. Michael Replogle, "Non-Motorized Vehicles in Asian Cities," World Bank Technical Paper No. 162, Asia Technical Department Series (The World Bank, Washington, D.C., 1992), p. xi.

31. U.S. Bureau of the Census, *County and City Data Book: 1994* (U.S. Government Printing Office, Washington, D.C., 1994), pp. 650–837.

32. *Op. cit.* 5, p. 29.

33. *Op. cit.* 5, p. 42.

34. United States (U.S.) Congress, Office of Technology Assessment (OTA), *Saving Energy in U.S. Transportation: Summary*, OTA-ETI-590 (OTA, Washington, D.C., 1994), p. 6.

35. *Ibid.*

36. Anthony Downs, *Stuck in Traffic: Coping With Peak-Hour Traffic Congestion* (The Brookings Institution, Washington, D.C., and the Lincoln Institute of Land Policy, Cambridge, Massachusetts, 1992), p. 101.

37. *Op. cit. 5*, p. 42.

38. United Nations (U.N.), *Population Growth and Policies in Mega-Cities: Sao Paulo* (U.N., New York, 1993), p. 10.

39. Peter Hall, "Can Cities Be Sustainable?," in *The Human Face of the Urban Environment, Proceedings of the Second Annual World Bank Conference on Environmentally Sustainable Development*, Ismail Serageldin, Michael Cohen, and K.C. Sivaramakrishnan, eds. (The World Bank, Washington, D.C., September 19–21, 1994), p. 34.

40. Mark Derr, "Beyond Efficiency," *Atlantic Monthly*, Vol. 275, No. 1 (January 1995), p. 90.

41. *Ibid.*, p. 91.

42. Janis D. Bernstein, "Land Use Considerations in Urban Environmental Management," Urban Management Programme Discussion Paper No. 12 (The World Bank, Washington, D.C., 1994), p. 26.

43. The World Bank, *World Development Report 1994: Infrastructure for Development* (Oxford University Press, New York, 1994), p. 14.

44. *Ibid.*, p. 26.

45. *Op. cit. 43*, p. 27.

46. *Op. cit. 23*, p. 16.

47. *Op. cit. 23*, p. 16.

48. *Op. cit. 5*, p. 185.

49. *Op. cit. 5*, p. 188.

50. *Op. cit. 4*, p. 10.

51. World Energy Council, *Energy for Tomorrow's World: The Realities, the Real Options, and the Agenda for Achievement* (Kogan Page, London, and St. Martin's Press, New York, 1993), p. 51.

52. International Energy Agency, *World Energy Outlook, 1995* (Organisation for Economic Co-Operation and Development, Paris, 1995), p. 248.

53. *Op. cit. 5*, p. 67.

54. *Op. cit. 52*, p. 245.

55. *Op. cit. 52*, pp. 252–253.

56. *Op. cit. 52*, p. 245.

57. *Op. cit. 51*.

58. World Resources Institute in collaboration with the United Nations Environment Programme and the United Nations Development Programme, *World Resources 1992–93* (Oxford University Press, New York, 1992), p. 203.

59. S.B. Saville, "Automotive Options and Air Quality Management in Developing Countries," *United Nations Environment Programme Industry and Environment*, Vol. 16, No. 1–2 (January–June 1993), p. 32.

60. *Op. cit. 7*, p. 20.

61. U.S. Environmental Protection Agency (U.S. EPA), *National Air Quality and Emissions Trends Report, 1993* (U.S. EPA, Washington, D.C., 1994), pp. 2, 6, 46, 52.

62. Commission of the European Communities, *The State of the Environment in the European Community: Overview*, Vol. 3 (Commission of the European Communities, Brussels, Belgium, 1992), p. 15.

63. U.K. Department of the Environment, *The UK Environment* (U.K. Department of the Environment, London, 1992), p. 17.

64. *Op. cit. 7*, pp. 20–21.

65. Asif Faiz, Kumares Sinha, and Surhid Gautam, "Air Pollution Characteristics and Trends," discussion paper (The World Bank, Washington, D.C., 1994), p. 25.

66. Alliance to End Childhood Lead Poisoning and Environmental Defense Fund, *The Global Dimensions of Lead Poisoning: An Initial Analysis* (Alliance to End Childhood Lead Poisoning, Washington, D.C., 1994), p. 26.

67. U.S. Agency for International Development (U.S.AID), "Comparing Environmental Health Risks in Cairo, Egypt: Vol. 1," draft paper (U.S.AID, Washington, D.C., 1994), p. III-8.

68. *Op. cit. 66*.

69. Intergovernmental Panel on Climate Change, *IPCC Synthesis Report*, July 29, 1995, draft (World Meteorological Organization/United Nations Environment Programme, Geneva, 1995), p. 29.

70. *Op. cit. 7*, p. 19.

71. *Op. cit. 69*.

72. *Op. cit. 52*, p. 266.

73. *Op. cit. 52*, p. 266.

74. *Op. cit. 7*, p. 19.

75. *Op. cit. 5*, p. 66.

76. "Transport and the Environment: Facts and Figures," *United Nations Environment Programme Industry and Environment*, Vol. 16, No. 1–2 (January–June 1993), p. 5.

77. National Institute of Urban Affairs (NIUA), *Urban Environmental Maps: Delhi, Bombay, Vadodara, Ahmedabad* (NIUA, Delhi, 1994), p. 2.27.

78. World Health Organization (WHO), *The World Health Report 1995: Bridging the Gaps* (WHO, Geneva, 1995), p. 19.

79. Alan Ross and Mukami Mwiraria, "Review of World Bank Experience in Road Safety," technical paper (Infrastructure and Urban Development Department, The World Bank, Washington, D.C., March 1992), p. 4.

80. The World Bank, *India Transport Sector: Long Term Issues*, Report No. 13192-IN (Infrastructure Operations Division, Country Department II, The World Bank, Washington, D.C., 1995), p. iv.

81. *Op. cit. 79*, p. 1.

82. *Op. cit. 5*, p. 52.

83. John Pucher, "Modal Shift in Eastern Germany: Transportation Impacts of Political Change," *Transportation*, Vol. 21, No. 1 (1994), p. 15.

84. Martha N. Alt, *Does Access to Jobs Affect Employment Rates and Incomes of Inner-City Residents?* (Earth Island Institute, San Francisco, December 1991), p. 9.

85. *Op. cit. 31*, pp. 759, 764.

86. Robert H. Mast, ed., *Detroit Lives* (Temple University Press, Philadelphia, 1994), p. 4.

87. *Op. cit. 21*, pp. 25, 37.

88. Ian Thomson, "The Transportation Systems of Latin American Cities: How They Might Better Serve the Needs of the Poor," in *Enhancing the Management of Metropolitan Living Environments in Latin America*, United Nations Centre for Regional Development (UNCRD) Research Report Series No. 1 (UNCRD, Nagoya, Japan, 1994), p. 41.

89. *Op. cit. 84*.

90. Ian Thomson, "Improving Urban Transport for the Poor," in *CEPAL Review 49* (United Nations Economic Commission for Latin America and the Caribbean, Santiago, Chile, April 1993), p. 140.

91. T. Rwebangira and J. Nnuma, "Dar es Salaam Action Plan for Urban Mobility and Non-Motorized Transport," in *Proceedings of the SSATP Seminar on Urban Mobility and Non-Motorized Transport in Sub-Saharan Africa* (Africa Technical Department, The World Bank, Nairobi, Kenya, 1994), p. 4.

92. *Op. cit. 5*, pp. 13–14.

93. Peter Newman, "Policies to Influence Urban Travel Demand," paper presented to the Organisation for Economic Co-Operation and Development (OECD) Project Group on Urban Travel and Sustainable Development (OECD, Paris, May 1992), pp. 19–27.

94. *Op. cit. 5*, pp. 89–91.

95. Peter Newman and Jeffrey Kenworthy, *Cities and Automobile Dependence: An International Sourcebook* (Gower Publishing Company, Aldershot, U.K., 1989), pp. 109–122.

96. Royal Commission on Environmental Pollution, *Transport and the Environment* (Her Majesty's Stationery Office, London, 1994), p. 149.

97. William P. Anderson, Pavlos S. Kanaroglou, and Eric J. Miller, "Urban Form, Energy, and the Environment: A Review of Issues, Evidence, and Policy," draft paper (McMaster University, Hamilton, Ontario, Canada, 1994), p. 18.

98. *Op. cit. 5*, p. 99.

99. Kyung-Hwan Kim, "Controlled Development and Densification: Seoul, Korea," in *The Human Face of the Urban Environment, Proceedings of the Second Annual World Bank Conference on Environmentally Sustainable Development*, Ismail Serageldin, Michael Cohen, and K.C. Sivaramakrishnan, eds. (The World Bank, Washington, D.C., September 19–21, 1994), p. 247.

100. *Op. cit.* 97, p. 1.

101. Ralph Gakenheimer, "Land Use/Transportation Planning: New Possibilities for Developing and Developed Countries," Transportation Quarterly (Eno Transportation Foundation, Lansdowne, Virginia, April 1993), p. 322.

102. Jonas Rabinovitch, "Curitiba: Towards Sustainable Urban Development," *Environment and Urbanization*, Vol. 4, No. 2 (October 1992), p. 66.

103. Douglass Lee, "Full Cost Pricing of Transportation" (National Transportation Systems Center, U.S. Department of Transportation, Cambridge, Massachusetts, March 1995), p. 16.

104. United States (U.S.) Congress, Office of Technology Assessment, *Saving Energy in U.S. Transportation*, OTA-ETI-589 (U.S. Government Printing Office, Washington, D.C., 1994), p. 108.

105. Todd Litman, *Transportation Cost Analysis* (Victoria Transport Policy Institute, Victoria, British Columbia, Canada, 1995).

106. *Op. cit.* 103, pp. 25–26.

107. *Op. cit.* 5, p. 158.

108. *Op. cit.* 6, pp. 8–9.

109. International Council for Local Environmental Initiatives (ICLEI), "Limiting Automobile Use Through Integrated Transportation Demand Management: Republic of Singapore," Case Study No. 38 (ICLEI, Toronto, Canada, 1995), pp. 3–5.

110. *Op. cit.* 5, p. 113.

111. *Op. cit.* 5, p. 118.

112. Pilar Pezoa, "Telepeaje, el Gran Cobrador," *La Nacion* (March 14, 1995, Santiago, Chile), p. 3.

113. Metropolitan Transportation Commission (MTC), "Bay Bridge Congestion Pricing Demonstration Project" (MTC, Oakland, California, January 1995).

114. *Op. cit.* 5, p. 113.

115. Clean Air Action Group, *Characteristics of the Road Transport in Hungary and the Attack of Western Capital Interested in Motorization*, Karoly Kiss, ed. (Talento Foundation, Budapest, Hungary, July 1992), pp. 84–85.

116. David Throsby, "Ecologically Sustainable Development and the Transport Sector," *United Nations Environment Programme Industry and Environment*, Vol. 16, No. 1–2 (January–June 1993), p. 17.

117. Lee Schipper *et al.,* "Fuel Prices, Automobile Fuel Economy, and Fuel Use for Land Travel, Preliminary Findings from an International Comparison," draft paper (University of California, Davis, California, 1994), p. 2.

118. The World Bank, *World Development Report 1992: Development and the Environment* (The World Bank, Washington, D.C., 1992), pp. 124–125.

119. Michael Cameron, *Efficiency and Fairness on the Road: Strategies for Unsnarling Traffic in Southern California* (Environmental Defense Fund, Oakland, California, 1994), p. 29.

120. Donald C. Shoup and Richard W. Willson, "Commuting, Congestion and Pollution: The Employer-Paid Parking Connection," Working Paper No. 120 (University of California Transportation Center, Berkeley, California, 1992), p. i.

121. *Ibid.,* p. 21.

122. *Op. cit.* 6, p. 11.

123. Mia Layne Birk and P. Christopher Zegras, *Moving Toward Integrated Transport Planning: Energy, Environment, and Mobility in Four Asian Cities* (International Institute for Energy Conservation, Washington, D.C., 1993), p. 79.

124. *Op. cit.* 1, p. 13.

125. *Op. cit.* 123.

126. *Op. cit.* 93, p. 9.

127. *Op. cit.* 6, p. 15.

128. *Op. cit.* 6, p. 20.

129. *Op. cit.* 123, p. 68.

130. *Op. cit.* 6, Table A-6, p. 53.

131. *Op. cit.* 93, pp. 13–14.

132. *Op. cit.* 5, p. 107.

133. *Op. cit.* 6, p. 17.

134. Jonas Rabinovitch and John Hoehn, "A Sustainable Urban Transportation System: the 'Surface Metro' in Curitiba, Brazil," Working Paper No. 19 (Department of Agricultural Economics, Michigan State University, East Lansing, Michigan, 1995), p. 1.

135. Mohammed Nisar and Ata M. Khan, "Transitway: An Innovation in Public Transportation," *ITE Journal* (Institute of Transport Engineers, Washington, D.C., July 1992), pp. 35–36.

136. Asif Faiz *et al.,* "Automotive Air Pollution: Issues and Options for Developing Countries," Working Paper No. 492 (Infrastructure and Urban Development Department, The World Bank, Washington, D.C., August 1990), p. 43.

137. *Op. cit.* 6, p. 34.

138. *Op. cit.* 123, p. 71.

139. *Op. cit.* 4.

140. *Op. cit.* 6, p. 31.

141. *Op. cit.* 6, p. 52.

142. *Op. cit.* 1.

143. *Op. cit.* 43, p. 58.

144. Jonas Rabinovitch, Senior Consultant, United Nations Development Programme, New York, 1995 (personal communication).

145. Stephen Hall, P. Christopher Zegras, and Henry Malbran Rojas, "Transportation and Energy in Santiago, Chile," *Transport Policy*, Vol. 1, No. 4 (1994), p. 239.

146. United Nations Centre for Human Settlements (Habitat), *Provision of Travelway Space for Urban Public Transport in Developing Countries* (Habitat, Nairobi, Kenya, 1993), p. 83.

147. Tunji Bolade, "Urban Transport in Lagos," *The Urban Age*, Vol. 2, No. 1 (Fall 1993), p. 7.

148. *Op. cit.* 5, pp. 104, 108.

149. *Op. cit.* 5, p. 87.

150. *Op. cit.* 23, p. 1.

151. *Op. cit.* 30, p. 42.

152. *Op. cit.* 30, p. xii.

153. *Op. cit.* 30, p. 37.

154. *Op. cit.* 30, p. 42.

155. Manuel Alepuz, "Bicycles Overtake Bus Travel in Havana," *The Urban Age*, Vol. 2, No. 1 (Fall 1993), p. 16.

156. *Op. cit.* 93, p. 3.

157. *Op. cit.* 5, pp. 109–110.

158. *Op. cit.* 5, p. 110.

159. Todd Litman, Director, Victoria Transport Policy Institute, Victoria, British Columbia, Canada, 1995 (personal communication).

160. Office of Technology Assessment (OTA), *Saving Energy in U.S. Transportation: Summary* (OTA, Washington, D.C., 1994), p. 26.

161. James J. MacKenzie, *The Keys to the Car: Electric and Hydrogen Vehicles for the 21st Century* (World Resources Institute, Washington, D.C., 1994), p. 24.

162. *Op. cit.* 52, p. 132.

163. *Op. cit.* 52, p. 284.

164. *Op. cit.* 52, p. 133.

165. Alcohol is 20 to 40 percent more efficient than gasoline depending on whether it is used in pure form or in a mixture with gasoline (gasohol). The use of diesel as a truck fuel also contributed to gains in efficiency.

166. *Op. cit.* 52, p. 133.

167. Michael P. Walsh, "Motor Vehicle Pollution Control: An Increasingly Critical Issue for Developing Countries," discussion paper (The World Bank, Washington, D.C., 1994).

168. *Op. cit.* 123, p. 94.

169. *Op. cit.* 161, p. 2.

170. Electric Transportation Coalition, "California Air Resources Board Proposes to Suspend ZEV Mandates until 2003 and to Institute a 'Cal/Big 7' Technology Development Partnership," memorandum from Kateri Callahan, Executive Director, Electric Transportation Coalition, to Board of Directors and Members, Washington, D.C., December 27, 1995, p. 1.

171. *Op. cit.* 59, p. 33.

172. *Op. cit.* 50, p. 33.

173. *Op. cit.* 136, p. 63.

174. Sujana Royat, "Toward Affordable and Environmentally Sound Urban Transport Management: The Case of Jakarta," draft paper presented at the International Symposium on Sustainable Urban Development Strategies in the 21st Century: Urban Transport and the Motorized Society (United Nations Center for Regional Development, Sagamihara, Japan, June 4–8, 1994), p. 3.

175. Michael Walsh, Consultant, Virginia, July 1995 (personal communication).

176. Christopher S. Weaver, Asif Faiz, and Michael Walsh, "Emission Control Measures for In-Use Vehicles," discussion paper (The World Bank, Washington, D.C., September 1994), pp. 28–30.

177. International Council for Local Environmental Initiatives (ICLEI), *Manual on the Operational Guidelines for the Implementation of OPLAN Clean Air Metro Manila* and ICLEI Site Visit to Quezon City, Philippines (ICLEI, Toronto, February 1995), n.p.

178. *Op. cit.* 176, p. 38.

179. Lit-Mian Chan and Christopher S. Weaver, *Motorcycle Emission Standards and Emission Control Technology* (The World Bank, Washington, D.C., 1994), p. 1.

180. *Ibid.,* p. 2.

181. Martin Wachs, "Learning from Los Angeles: Transport, Urban Form, and Air Quality," working paper (University of California Transportation Center, Berkeley, California, May 1993), p. 9.

182. *Op. cit.* 1.

183. Yoshitsugu Hayashi *et al.,* "Urbanization, Motorization and the Environment Nexus: An International Comparative Study of London, Tokyo, Nagoya, and Bangkok" in *Memoirs of the School of Engineering,* Vol. 46, No. 1 (Nagoya University, Nagoya, Japan, October 1994), p. 58.

5. Urban Priorities for Action

Many of the environmental problems outlined in the previous chapters—and their impacts on health, ecosystems, and economic productivity— result from political and economic factors rather than from the process of urbanization itself (1). Intermittent or inadequate water supplies, for example, are rarely due to true freshwater shortages; more often, they can be attributed to misguided priorities, inappropriate pricing, or poor management. Urban sprawl is driven less by the need for more urban land and more by zoning regulations, land speculation, and political interests.

Even with strong political will, improving the management of urban environmental problems is far from easy. Governments face a host of factors that hinder their ability to respond to urban environmental problems. In the developed and developing world alike, local government mandates are expanding, adding new tasks such as industrial pollution control to the traditional responsibilities of water and sanitation provision. Often these mandates have not been matched with appropriate control over revenues and budget allocations. In addition, many governments lack the technical knowledge or the staff to adequately enforce environmental regulations. The relentless pace of urban growth in many cities exacerbates these problems, far outstripping the capacity of governments to manage and respond to demands for infrastructure and urban services.

Yet the picture is not all bleak. Many innovative and effective approaches to environmental management have been or are being undertaken by cities around the world. A few broad lessons emerge. First and foremost, it is increasingly apparent that local governments cannot tackle urban environmental problems alone. Coping with urban problems will require that responsibilities be shared and actions taken by a host of actors, including national governments, local governments, nongovernmental organizations (NGOs), communities, the private sector, international donors, and other external support agencies. Future urban environmental management should place a high priority on strengthening the institutional capacity of local administrators to develop and maintain these partnerships.

Second, in the face of growing responsibilities and limited funds, cities must make strategic choices about which problems to tackle first. Setting priorities by assessing the scale of impact and the cost as well as the ease of the solution is an important component of good management. (See Box 5.1.) Here again, local groups should be involved in identifying the key problems and their causes, as well as the capabilities of the community to address the problems (2). Urban managers will also need reliable and recent data on environmental conditions. Most data on urban environmental conditions comes from a few large cities—Mexico City, Sao Paulo, Jakarta, New York, and Bombay—yet these cities represent only a fraction of the urban areas worldwide.

At the same time, attention must be given to cost-effective technologies, greater economic efficiency, and cost recovery (3). Charging the full cost of water production and supply, for instance, can be a powerful incentive for conservation, just as charging the full cost of driving can be. (See Chapter 4, "Urban Transportation.") In addition, improving the maintenance and efficiency of existing facilities can save money and reduce or delay the need for large investments in new facilities. Emphasis on pollution prevention is sorely needed; it is often more efficient to prevent pollution in the first place—through cleaner manufacturing processes, for instance—than to pay to clean it up later.

Box 5.1 Ranking Bangkok's Urban Environmental Problems

The rapid economic growth of Bangkok, Thailand, has generated levels of pollutants and traffic congestion that carry significant costs in terms of both health and productivity. A recent World Bank study attempts to assess the magnitude of these costs and considers how to manage these problems with minimal damage to Bangkok's economy (1).

COSTS OF POLLUTION

The World Bank study identifies air pollution from particulates and lead, surface water pollution due to microbiological contamination, and traffic congestion as Bangkok's most serious urban environmental problems and indicates that even moderate reductions in air pollution and congestion could provide significant benefits. Reducing ambient concentrations of key pollutants by 20 percent from current levels, for example, would provide health benefits estimated at between $400 million and $1.6 billion for particulates and between $300 million and $1.5 billion for lead. For congestion, the study estimates that a 10 percent reduction in peak-hour trips would provide benefits of about $400 million annually.

The study did not consider benefits from reducing microbiological contamination of water, because discharges are primarily from households and therefore are not closely linked to economic growth.

Current trends in air pollutants show an alarming situation both for particulates and for lead. From 1983 to 1992, concentrations of particulates were up at all six monitoring stations in Bangkok; annual standards have been violated at every station in every year since 1988. Ambient lead concentrations have never been particularly high in

Clearing the air. In Bangkok, reducing congestion and air pollution could improve both economic productivity and human health. Along clogged streets, air pollution is so severe that traffic police wear protective masks.

Bangkok (and have decreased since the introduction of low-lead and unleaded gasoline), but the study argues that lead emissions may nevertheless be a significant source of exposure in Bangkok. Blood lead levels of children and adults are among the highest in the world. A study of 82 infants during 1989–90 found average lead levels of 18.5 micrograms per deciliter, nearly twice the level that the U.S. Centers for Disease Control and Prevention considers dangerous.

COST-EFFECTIVE SOLUTIONS

The World Bank study found that the Bangkok economy operates quite efficiently and that there are therefore few opportunities for "win-win" initiatives that would improve environmental quality without slowing economic growth. There are nevertheless some cost-effective initiatives that deal with the highest-priority problems.

In the area of energy-related air pollution, the study recommends managing demand and imposing emissions stand-

ards and taxes. Demand-side management initiatives include the use of energy-efficient lighting and appliances for residential and commercial users, improved building designs, and the use of more energy-efficient motors and production processes in the industrial sector.

One way to reduce particulate emissions would be to devise incentives to reduce the use of lignite, a fuel that emits more particulates and sulfur dioxide than hard coal or fuel oil. Emissions standards that require new power plants to be fitted with low-sulfur control or combustion technologies and precipitators or a switch to hard coal (instead of lignite) and an increase in taxes on lignite also would be relatively cost-effective.

In the area of traffic congestion, the study recommends efforts both to reduce congestion and to reduce emissions from vehicles. Cost-effective programs include efforts to phase out lead in gasoline and to reduce the sulfur content of diesel fuel. Another priority is emissions standards for two-stroke motorcycles, which would reduce emissions (by 90 percent for particulates) to the level of four-stroke motorcycles. Higher taxes on transport fuels also could help restrain the growth of private transportation. Congestion problems also could be reduced by expanding flexible work hours, upgrading bus services, and improving traffic management.

References and Notes

1. Box is based on The World Bank, *Thailand: Mitigating Pollution and Congestion Impacts in a High-Growth Economy* (The World Bank, Washington, D.C., 1994).

Finally, cities will have to rely on a diverse range of policy tools, from economic and regulatory instruments (to address specific problems such as air or water pollution) to broader planning strategies (such as land use planning and community involvement). (See Box 5.2.)

The following sections examine how cities are addressing some of the most critical urban environmental problems: inadequate water supply and poor sanitation, water pollution, outdoor and indoor air pollution, and solid waste. The list of policy options discussed here is

by no means exhaustive; rather, it is intended to give a sense of the diversity of approaches being tried in cities across the globe. Nor should any one solution be considered a panacea for all cities; each has its own unique circumstances. After reviewing economic and regulatory instruments, the chapter then looks at land use planning as a broader approach to addressing environmental concerns. Chapter 6, "City and Community: Towards Environmental Sustainability," explores in greater detail the longer-term issues of strengthening the capacities of local governments and communities as urban environmental managers.

PRIORITIES FOR ACTION: WATER AND SANITATION

Cities across the globe confront problems related to water supply and use. For many cities of the developing world, the top environmental priority remains improving access to clean water and sanitation. As the World Bank concluded in 1992, doing so would be the single most effective means of alleviating human distress (4). When services were improved in cities in developed countries in the 19th and 20th Centuries, health improved dramatically. (See Figure 5.1.) In both the developing and the developed world, there is also a critical need to use water more efficiently and to intensify efforts to stop the deterioration of aquatic environments caused by municipal and industrial effluents.

Improving Access to Water and Sanitation

Despite nearly $100 billion in investments, the International Drinking Water and Sanitation Decade of the 1980s fell far short of meeting its goal of water and sanitation for all (5). During the decade, the number of urban people in the developing world with access to adequate water increased by about 80 percent, and the number of urban people with adequate sanitation facilities increased by about 50 percent. The rapid rise in urban populations offsets these gains, however, and in 1994 more than 220 million urban dwellers (13 percent of the developing world's urban population) still did not have access to a safe and reliable water source, while more than 420 million (25 percent of the developing world's urban population) did not have access to sanitation services (6).

Although the Decade did not meet its goals, it did bring into focus the magnitude of the health problems associated with inadequate water and sanitation services and highlight the need to find new strategies to improve coverage. Indeed, the program's greatest achievement, by some counts, may have been the transformation in thinking that accompanied it (7) (8).

Broadly, four key lessons emerged from the Decade: first, systems should respond to local demands and should be as simple, sturdy, and inexpensive as possible; second, the involvement of the community and households—particularly women—in system design and maintenance is a crucial component to a project's success; third, governments need to improve the efficiency and sustainability of system operation and mainte-

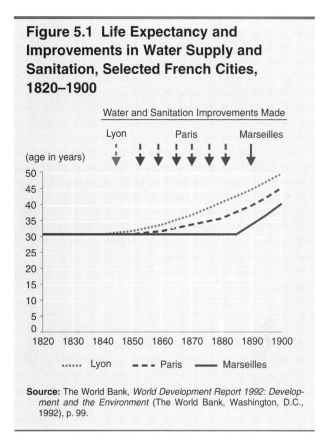

Figure 5.1 Life Expectancy and Improvements in Water Supply and Sanitation, Selected French Cities, 1820–1900

Source: The World Bank, *World Development Report 1992: Development and the Environment* (The World Bank, Washington, D.C., 1992), p. 99.

nance; and fourth, water should be treated as an economic commodity paid for by users (9).

Despite a surprising degree of consensus on these points, many governments and donor agencies have yet to move beyond rhetoric to implementation, according to some critics (10). Translating the lessons into practice poses many challenges (11). However, much progress is being made.

Adopting Appropriate Technology and Standards

The Decade made clear that the high-cost water and sanitation systems adopted throughout the developed world—with centralized systems built and maintained by subsidized public agencies—will not work in the developing world. The number of people unserved is far too great, and city coffers far too small, to provide all residents with piped water and flush toilets in their houses. Whereas some parts of a city, such as the urban core, may be covered by conventional sewerage, other areas, particularly low-income settlements on the urban periphery, would be much better served by lower-cost alternatives (12).

Evidence of the success of low-cost solutions can be found in cities around the world, from large-scale programs for pour-flush latrines or ventilated improved pit

---

Box 5.2 Forging a Combined Approach to Urban Pollution Control

Cities have a wide array of tools at their disposal to tackle environmental problems. Regulatory tools, such as legal restrictions on the quantity of pollutants a factory can discharge or minimum air and water quality standards, have been particularly effective in curbing pollution in the developed world. Their effectiveness relies on good monitoring and enforcement capabilities—capabilities that are in their infancy in many of the developing nations where urban growth pressures and pollution problems are greatest (1) (2).

Making the regulatory approach more effective and affordable in developing cities will require a more flexible approach in setting such regulations, taking into account local pollutant loads, the characteristics of nearby water bodies and air basins, and the community's water and air quality goals. In many cases, policies are set by national governments and do not reflect local needs. For instance, water quality standards may not be strict enough to protect

some coastal urban waters with poor circulation from pollution damage and may be too strict for other better-flushed waters, resulting in expensive overcontrol (3). Giving local governments the authority to set their own environmental standards can have positive benefits (4). In Osaka, Japan, environmental standards for air, water, soil pollution, noise, and vibration are in some cases stricter than national standards (5).

Economic instruments can also be powerful tools for modifying behavior, often at less cost than regulatory instruments. Thus, making use of economic instruments such as effluent taxes, sewer fees, and tradable discharge or emission permits can help cities lessen the rigidity and expense of the regulatory, or command-and-control, approach. These market-based strategies do not specify the use of any particular pollution control technology; rather, they give polluters the flexibility and incentive to find the most cost-efficient

means of achieving pollution control targets. Economic instruments tend to be underutilized and are particularly promising for developing cities that can least afford high regulatory costs (6).

Pollution taxes, which are levied on the basis of the quantity of pollutants released, provide a direct financial disincentive for excessive pollution. They can be especially useful where government budgets for environmental programs are limited—a situation that describes most cities—because they provide a revenue source that can be tapped to fund enforcement efforts (7). While pollution taxes are in fairly common use today even in developing countries, they are often set too low to have the desired effect (8) (9). Furthermore, these instruments rely on strict monitoring and enforcement to be effective, just as traditional regulatory approaches do, so they are not a shortcut to pollution control. In fact, they are more likely to work hand-in-hand with traditional

---

latrines to community groups implementing small-bore sewer schemes. Each solution is unique, tailored to local conditions and needs, but most rely on locally manufactured hardware (e.g., plumbing, sanitary sheds, or concrete caps for pit latrines) and the efforts of community members to install, maintain, and manage the systems (13). Systems using lower-level standard technologies can be effective and much less expensive, at only one tenth to one twentieth of the cost of a conventional sewage system. Most of the lowest-cost systems require far less water, and once they are installed can be upgraded gradually (14).

One of the greatest barriers to installing low-cost alternatives is political opposition to what is considered "low technology." In many developing countries, there is still a tendency on the part of governments and funding agencies to insist on standards that are higher than necessary, sometimes doubling the cost of service delivery (15). In Cartagena, Colombia, for example, officials proposed a conventional sewage system even though a high water table, impermeable soils, and land levels well below the city sewer mains caused pipes to sink and necessitated pumping wastewater uphill to city sewer mains. Once local officials were persuaded that the lower standards of technology were not "illegal," a system that uses a septic tank to remove biosolids and

that transports liquid wastes in small-diameter pipes was installed at one third the cost of a conventional system. The system has been operating successfully for more than 10 years (16).

Condominial sewers have also proved to be a cost-effective alternative, and versions have been installed in low-income neighborhoods in northeast Brazil, Pakistan, and Yemen (17). Condominial sewers use a radically different layout, with smaller and shallower feeder sewers running from toilet to toilet through each backyard. The wastewater of an entire block discharges into the main trunk line at a single point rather than having to connect each house to the main trunk. (See Figure 5.2.)

The Orangi Pilot Project in Karachi, Pakistan, illustrates the successes possible with low-cost sanitation alternatives. The community adopted a sewage system that filters biosolids into a tank and therefore uses smaller pipes and flatter gradients in the streets. The system cost one tenth of what it would have cost to install conventional sewerage. Most of the funds were invested by the community; even now the tanks and sewers are paid for and managed by groups of households. The municipality is responsible only for the construction and maintenance of the main trunk drains (18) (19). (See Chapter 6, "City and Community: Toward Environmental Sustainability.")

command-and-control approaches (10) (11).

Izmir, Turkey, provides an example of a combined approach to pollution control using both effluent standards and an economic instrument—a sewer charge. In attempting to address industrial pollution, national effluent standards were adapted to local conditions and set out in a municipal ordinance. The Izmir Water and Sewerage Authority was charged with monitoring and policing the ordinance, and, through threats of factory closures and fines, has prompted a number of larger industries to build pretreatment facilities for their wastes. The municipality also assesses a sewer charge based on the volume of industrial wastes discharged into the sewer system, the idea being to motivate industries to treat their effluents themselves to the point that they can be discharged to surface waters rather than dumped into the sewer system. Although in their infancy, these programs seem to have achieved some success so far (12).

Few tools available to city managers will work without institutional ability to enforce the regulations, or without the staff to collect fees and taxes (13) (14).

References and Notes

1. Robert Adler, "Reauthorizing the Clean Water Act: Looking to Tangible Values," *Water Resources Bulletin*, Vol. 30, No. 5 (1994), p. 803.

2. Janis D. Bernstein, *Alternative Approaches to Pollution Control and Waste Management*, Urban Management and the Environment, Report No. 3 (The World Bank, Washington, D.C., 1993), pp. 5–8.

3. *Op. cit.* 2.

4. Brendan Barrett, "Integrated Environmental Management—Experience in Japan," *Journal of Environmental Management*, Vol. 40, No. 1 (January 1994), p. 20.

5. *Ibid.*, p. 21.

6. The World Bank, *World Development Report 1992: Development and the Environment* (The World Bank, Washington, D.C., 1992), p. 13.

7. Gunnar Eskeland and Emmanuel Jimenez, "Curbing Pollution in Developing Countries," *Finance and Development*, Vol. 28, No. 1 (March 1991), pp. 15–18.

8. Carter Brandon and Ramesh Ramankutty, *Toward an Environmental Strategy for Asia*, World Bank Discussion Paper No. 224 (The World Bank, Washington, D.C., 1993), p. 76.

9. *Op. cit.* 7.

10. *Op. cit.* 2, pp. 10–26.

11. William Tuohy, "Neglect of Market Incentives in Local Environmental Planning: A Case Study in the National Estuary Program," *Coastal Management*, Vol. 22 (1994), pp. 82–83.

12. Janis D. Bernstein, "Alternative Approaches to Pollution Control and Waste Management: Regulatory and Economic Instruments," Urban Management Programme Discussion Paper No. 3 (The World Bank, Washington, D.C., 1993), pp. 30–34.

13. *Op. cit.* 8, p. 78.

14. *Op. cit.* 7.

Low-cost systems are not foolproof, however. Most rely on the active participation of community members in maintaining the pipes. While this reduces the utility's operating costs, if the community and organizational aspects are missing, the technology will work poorly (20).

Involving the Community

Community involvement in water and sanitation projects is key to their success. Not only must communities be taught how to maintain and operate systems, they also must be consulted to determine what type of system best suits local conditions. Women, the major users of a system, can provide valuable advice about the design and management of a water and sanitation system. Failure to involve the community can lead to inefficient systems. In Nicaragua, for example, new latrines were not used by women because their feet could be seen from outside, denying them the customary privacy (21). In contrast, when women are taught to maintain handpumps or otherwise manage collective water systems, they often perform better than men because they are less likely to migrate, more accustomed to voluntary work, and can be better trusted to administer funds (22). Involving communities has other benefits as well, such as greater community acceptance of a new system and correspondingly increased willingness to pay for a system and help maintain it (23).

In Chinautla, an informal settlement in Guatemala City, Guatemala, community members asked the municipal water enterprise to install a single-source water tank, even though such units are typically used only temporarily. The community believed that this was the best solution to its water supply needs, and each family built its own pipe to the central source. The local community association receives one large bill from the water company, and one resident chosen by the community manages the billing and the collection of fees from each household. While the cost of the single-source water tank per family is more than for families directly connected to the city's water supply network, it is still far less than what they had been paying for water from private vendors. This system is being replicated in other settlements in Guatemala (24).

Improving Operation and Maintenance

National and international agencies have placed far too much emphasis on the construction of new facilities at the expense of improving operation and maintenance of existing installations (25). In Mexico City, for example, 50 percent (7 out of 14) of the wastewater plants are

Figure 5.2 Conventional Versus Condominial Wastewater Collection Systems

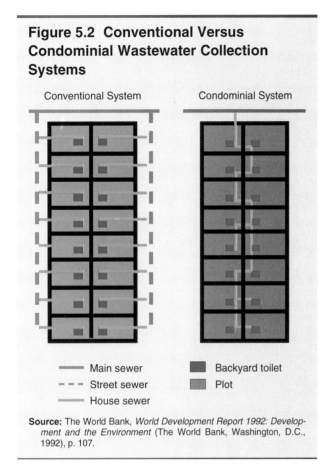

Conventional System   Condominial System

——— Main sewer   ▉ Backyard toilet
- - - Street sewer   ▉ Plot
——— House sewer

Source: The World Bank, *World Development Report 1992: Development and the Environment* (The World Bank, Washington, D.C., 1992), p. 107.

operated at less than their designed flow capacity and treat only about 7 percent of the city's total wastewater (26) (27). The generally poor performance of public water and sewage utilities in developing countries leaves ample room for improvement and is a major factor contributing to the high cost of these services (28).

In many cities, about half of the water that is treated and distributed at public expense is not accounted for. In Manila, Philippines, for instance, 58 percent of water is unaccounted for, as opposed to 8 percent in Singapore. For Latin America as a whole, such water losses cost between $1 billion and $1.5 billion in forgone revenue each year (29).

As much as one half of the water not accounted for is due to unrecorded usage or illegal taps. For example, in Caracas, Venezuela, approximately 30 percent of water connections are not registered (30). Reducing such losses is cheaper than reducing leakages, provided the utility has a sufficient number of trained staff. Major strategies include installing, promptly servicing, and recalibrating meters; updating and reviewing consumer records to estimate consumption when meters are unserviceable; and streamlining bureaucratic procedures to assist customers to make new legal connections.

Reductions in unaccounted-for water can allow investments in new works to be deferred or at least reduced in scope, with significant savings. In addition, by improving the system of meter reading and billing or by detecting and charging for illegal connections, revenue can be greatly increased to pay for water treatment and distribution as well as operation and maintenance. For example, in urban areas in Thailand in the 1980s, each 10 percent of unaccounted-for water saved was estimated to immediately generate an additional $8 million per year from the 3.5 million people served (31).

Cost Recovery

With better cost recovery, utilities in developing countries could improve the quality and availability of water, potentially even in low-income areas. Water supply projects require huge capital investments, yet cities are faced with decreases in funds for urban water supply purposes and burgeoning urban populations. In developing countries, consumers pay only about 35 percent of the costs of supplying water, according to a recent analysis of World Bank–financed projects (32). Recovering a greater percentage of these costs could provide city managers with funds to expand coverage in new areas or to maintain and improve existing facilities.

Drinking water, however, is a basic human need, and sufficient water for good hygiene is a prerequisite of public health. With these considerations in mind, governments have historically subsidized the cost of water. Unfortunately, these subsidies rarely reach the urban poor; instead, they most often benefit the better-off consumers with house connections. In many cases, the poor are actually paying more than their wealthier counterparts for less reliable service. Water from vendors costs substantially more (and may be of poorer quality) than piped water in the same areas. Indeed, the poor may pay as much as 30 percent of their income for water, while the well-to-do pay less than 2 percent (33).

Evidence exists that poor urban residents want and are willing to pay for on-plot—if not in-house—water supplies of reasonable reliability. Unlike some other environmental amenities that benefit the public at large, it is the individual household that receives most of the benefits of piped water. The prevailing assumption is that households are willing to pay about 3 to 5 percent of their income for access to clean water, yet actual studies reveal that some are willing to pay considerably more, some less (34) (35).

The 1980s saw a widespread commitment to adopting more cost-recovery programs, especially among donor organizations. Yet most cities still do not achieve full cost recovery in water supply operations, and equity concerns remain. There is no guarantee, for example, that a financially motivated utility will invest the additional funds in low-income neighborhoods rather than high-income suburbs. Furthermore, the debate concerning how much to charge and to whom and whether water supply tariffs should cover only operation and maintenance costs or should also generate resources for future investment is far from over.

Promoting Water Conservation

For most cities, extending water supply coverage to current residents is challenge enough. Yet cities are also facing pressures to expand their municipal water supplies; demand for municipal water could grow by a factor of five or more over the next four decades (36). Many cities already face critical water shortages and high costs of supply.

The usual response is to increase supplies through expensive investments in new public infrastructure. Yet evidence suggests that cities can also manage the demand for water by reducing wasteful use (through pricing and conservation efforts) and by preventing pollution. A comprehensive strategy would include improving the operation and maintenance of water supply systems, removing subsidies and price distortions that encourage waste, and public education (37). Demand management is a particularly attractive option for cities in the developed world, where per capita water consumption is many times that in the developing world. Recycling, especially of industrial wastewater, is another attractive strategy, providing companies with a cost-effective and reliable source of water and at the same time protecting the environment (38).

In Boston, impending costs of supplying water to the city led officials to implement a Long Range Water Supply Program (LRWSP) to cut down on water use. Between 1988 and 1993, LRWSP reduced the average daily demand for water from 1.2 million to 0.9 million cubic meters (39). The program focused on detecting and repairing leaks, metering, retrofitting showerheads and toilets with more efficient technologies, protecting water sources from pollution, and building support for the program among city residents through outreach and education. These reductions eliminated the need to develop new supplies—saving hundreds of millions of dollars—and the water system is operating within its safe yield for the first time in 20 years (40).

In developing countries, several cities have been implementing demand management programs. In Mexico City, for instance, the water utility implemented a new rate structure that charges more per cubic meter as consumption levels increase. It is hoped that this measure will provide metered industries with incentive to conserve water (41). In Sao Paulo, Brazil, the imposition of effluent charges induced reductions in water demand between 42 and 62 percent at three industrial plants (42).

A study in Beijing showed that a combination of strategies could reduce industrial water consumption by about one third, at a cost substantially less than that of investing in new supplies. The measures included increased recycling of cooling water in manufacturing; recycling of cooling water in power plants; and wastewater recycling. Similarly, about 15 percent of domestic consumption could be saved through measures such as improved efficiency in public facilities, a leakage reduction program, recycling of cooling water used in air conditioning, and installation of water-efficient flush toilets (43).

Reducing Water Pollution

By reducing water pollution, cities can reap the double benefit of effectively increasing the water supply while lessening the deterioration of the aquatic environment. As the "pollution shadow" spreads, cities must go further afield to find clean water, which significantly increases the costs of water supply. Shanghai, China, for instance, moved its water intakes 40 kilometers upstream at a cost of $300 million because of the degradation of river water quality around the city (44) (45).

Of all the pollutants, urban sewage may be the worst offender in near-urban waters, although industrial pollutants can be a major source. In addition, up to half of the contaminants reaching urban waters come from nonpoint sources, such as urban runoff. Controlling urban runoff, although difficult, is essential if cities are to mitigate their impacts on nearby water bodies.

Preventing pollution in the first place may be the best long-term solution. One study in Santiago, Chile, found that although full wastewater treatment would cost about $78 million annually, the economic and health benefits resulting from pollution prevention could justify this investment (46). (See Box 5.3.)

Urban Sewage

In cities of the developing world, only a fraction of urban sewage is treated, even in cities in middle-income countries. Buenos Aires, Argentina, for instance, treats only 2 percent of its wastewater (47). The costs of collecting and treating urban sewage—typically, about $1,500 per household for collection and primary treatment—are prohibitive for many developing countries. Costs are higher still to meet the additional treatment requirements of most developed countries (48).

Box 5.3 Costs and Benefits of Water and Air Pollution Controls in Santiago

The metropolitan region of Santiago, Chile, must cope with significant air and water pollution problems. But do the economic costs of pollution merit large investments in pollution controls? A recent analysis by the World Bank found significant benefits from investments in both water and air pollution controls (1).

Sanitation services in Santiago are well developed—most urban households have access to potable water and adequate sewerage—but the disposal of collected wastewater is inadequate. Except for a small pilot plant that treats about 4 percent of the city's wastewater, most sewage is dumped untreated into open watercourses.

Contaminated surface water has been used to irrigate about 130,000 hectares of farmland, including about 7,000 hectares used to grow vegetables for raw consumption, resulting in high rates of typhoid, hepatitis, and a 1991 outbreak of cholera in Chile.

In response to the cholera outbreak, Chilean authorities imposed a series of emergency measures: a ban on vegetables grown with wastewater irrigation and restrictions on selling irrigated vegetables and fruits outside of Santiago; stepped-up water quality monitoring; chlorination of irrigation water in canals; a public information campaign about the risks of eating raw vegetables; and a ban on serving raw vegetables in restaurants.

These measures helped control the cholera outbreak and significantly reduced the incidence of typhoid and hepatitis. Typhoid cases, which averaged over 3,500 per year from 1985 to 1990, dropped to under 500 in 1991; hepatitis cases dropped to 1,430 cases in 1992, from more than 4,000 per year before. From 1985 to 1991, 45 to 70 percent of all typhoid cases in Santiago were attributable to wastewater irrigation; in 1992 only two cases—less than 1 percent of all cases—were traced to wastewater irrigation.

By their nature, however, these measures rely on the cooperation of farmers and the public, as well as the political will to continue monitoring, enforcement, and outreach. Already, public vigilance and inspections have lapsed as the threat of cholera fades from memory. Recognizing that the only long-term and guaranteed solution is wastewater treatment, the World Bank conducted a cost-benefit analysis to determine to what extent investment in full wastewater treatment is justified on the basis of public health considerations.

The World Bank study found that full wastewater treatment would cost about $78 million annually. However, annual benefits could range from one third to almost all of the cost of treatment, with the wide range resulting from different assumptions about the probability of a cholera epidemic occurring under current conditions. These numbers greatly understate the true benefits, because they do not include the health costs of other gastroenteric diseases such as

---

Even in the United States, where major investments in sewers and treatment plants have already been made, the costs for completing and rehabilitating the existing infrastructure are calculated at $108 billion, and this does not reflect the full costs of removing nutrients from the effluent stream (49). In the United Kingdom, the cost of infrastructure needed to meet the new European water quality standards is estimated at $60 billion over the next decade, or about $1,000 per resident (50).

Lower-cost treatment options are clearly needed. These options should have some capability to remove nutrients as well as accomplish more traditional treatment goals. Alternatives range from modern marine outfalls that transport sewage into deep waters to the use of new low-maintenance equipment such as fine screens and special biological filters. New approaches to natural treatment systems such as sedimentation ponds and artificial wetlands with nutrient-scrubbing plants are promising for cities where sufficient land is still available (51) (52) (53) (54).

Another promising approach involves the reuse of municipal wastewater. Biosolids can be separated out, composted, and reused as fertilizer, for instance, while the treated effluent can be used to irrigate landscaping or crops or to feed aquaculture ponds. Effluent can also be used to recharge groundwater supplies, an approach that may be especially important in areas where saltwater intrusion into coastal aquifers has become a problem because of overdrafting of local groundwater supplies (55) (56) (57).

In Kochcice, Poland, a duckweed pond is being used to treat wastewater from 3,000 residents, at a cost far lower than that of a new wastewater treatment plant. The duckweed pond processes the wastewater, resulting in water quality at the outlet that is higher than Polish surface water standards require. Additionally, the biomass produced is harvested twice a year and used as feed for livestock (58). In Calcutta, India, 680,000 cubic meters of wastewater is discharged daily into 12,000 hectares of nearby wetlands. The wetlands are used for fish production, and the treated water is reused for irrigation. The *E. coli* count of the water entering the wetlands is about 10 million organisms per milliliter, whereas the treated effluent has an *E. coli* count of 10 to 100 per milliliter (59).

Innovative technologies alone will not suffice, however. Especially in the developing world, there is a critical need to develop the institutional capacity to plan, finance, and efficiently operate and maintain conventional wastewater treatment systems. For many cities, the volume of waste is too large, and the purification capability of wetlands too small, to rely solely on these

hepatitis and diarrhea, the amenity values of improved coastal water quality, the impact on fish and shellfish production, or the value of water-use rights for Santiago's treated effluents. Nor does the study consider the impact of future outbreaks of cholera or typhoid on the growth of fruit exports or on tourism.

Santiago suffers from significant emissions of particulates (e.g., PM-10, or particles less than 10 microns in diameter), sulfur oxides (SO_x), nitrogen oxides (NO_x), volatile organic compounds (VOCs), and carbon monoxide (CO). Vehicles account for about 85 percent of NO_x emissions, 69 percent of VOCs, and 94 percent of CO. Vehicles, industrial boilers, and residential wood-burning all contribute to emissions of particulates (in addition to street dust, a sizable component that was not fully assessed in the study). Industrial boilers account for more than half of SO_x emissions, with vehicles accounting for another one fourth. Particulates are by far the most serious pollutant. It is esti-

mated that a 1-metric-ton reduction in PM-10 emissions would yield health benefits more than 10 times those resulting from similar reductions in all other pollutants combined.

Out of a short list of pollution reduction measures, the World Bank study selected four as part of a control strategy: emissions standards for light-duty gasoline vehicles; a requirement that new trucks be equipped with diesel engines meeting 1991 U.S. emissions standards; the use of compressed natural gas for buses in place of diesel engines; and the conversion of wood-burning industrial sources to distillate fuel. The study then developed a dispersion model to simulate the strategy's impact on air quality, particularly in heavily populated and highly polluted areas. The study also used a model to estimate the improvements in public health resulting from the air quality improvements; a valuation of health benefits in terms of fewer lost work-days; and a cost-benefit comparison. The study concluded that

the benefits of the control strategy would outweigh costs by a factor of 1.7 and that investing $50 million to $100 million in pollution controls would be cost-effective. Because these estimates are considered conservative, it is likely that substantially larger investments would also be cost-effective. For example, the health valuation accounts only for lost productivity and treatment costs, while the estimate of health effects considers only acute effects and not cumulative and long-term effects.

References and Notes

1. Box is based on The World Bank Environment and Urban Development Division, *Chile—Managing Environmental Problems: Economic Analysis of Selected Issues*, Report No. 13061-CH (The World Bank, Washington, D.C., 1994), pp. viii, x–xi, 39–41, 50–59, 83–85, 96–98.

methods of treatment. In addition, where wastewater also contains industrial wastes, new threats emerge from the bioaccumulation of heavy metals and other chemicals in fish and crops.

Industrial Effluents

Cities are using a variety of regulatory and economic instruments to reduce industrial water pollution. Effluent charge systems, for example, impose fees on industrial facilities according to the quantity or quality of pollutants discharged. These systems are often more economical than regulatory mechanisms to induce firms to reduce pollution loads (60). The Netherlands has an effective water pollution charge system that provides a strong incentive for industries to reduce pollution. From 1969 to 1980, it is estimated that 50 to 70 percent of the pollution reduction in 14 industrial sectors was due to effluent charges (61).

Where possible, cities should encourage the separation of industrial wastewaters from domestic wastewater streams. Separate treatment of industrial wastes—or pretreatment before they are discharged to sewers—removes heavy metals and other toxics so that they do not contaminate domestic biosolids and wastewater that will be recycled. Separation and pretreatment also fa-

cilitate pollutant monitoring as well as the recycling of industrial wastewater, which reduces industrial water demand and the volume of wastewater discharged.

PRIORITIES FOR ACTION: SOLID WASTE MANAGEMENT

The growing volume of waste spawned by the consumption inherent in city life is a formidable challenge to cities in developing and developed countries alike. For low-income cities, the main solid waste problem is how to extend collection services to the poor—often 50 percent of the population is without service. Improving efficiency in these cities is key, because waste management often accounts for 30 to 50 percent of operational budgets, yet collects only 50 to 80 percent of the refuse generated (62) (63). In middle-income and high-income cities, collection often reaches 95 to 100 percent of the population, but disposing of ever greater quantities of waste emerges as the key challenge (64) (65).

The traditional approach to solid waste management—that municipal governments handle all aspects of collection, transport, and disposal—has been at best a mixed success in both developed and developing countries. The search for more efficient and economical solid waste collection programs has taken cities in several directions, most notably toward new partnerships with communities or the private sector and toward new types of economic policy instruments, such as recycling credits (payment to a recycler), landfill disposal levies (taxes at the landfill site designed to reduce the amount of waste being landfilled), and product charges (a packaging tax to discourage overpackaging).

Informal Waste Collection

In the developing world, the municipal system handles only a minor fraction of the wastes generated in a city. In many cities, especially in Asia, more wastes are dealt with by a vast network of urban wastepickers (66). These wastepickers provide clear environmental and economic benefits to the city: saving resources through recycling raw materials, reducing the costs of waste disposal, allowing for the production of cheaper goods from recycled materials, and creating much-needed jobs (67).

Wastepickers are often highly organized and can account for a large share of waste collection. In Indonesian cities, estimates suggest that wastepickers reduce total urban refuse by one third (68). In Bangalore, India, street and dump pickers gather an estimated 500 metric tons of post-consumer wastes daily, compared with only 37 metric tons gathered by municipal workers (69).

In addition, many businesses depend on regular supplies of waste materials from the wastepickers. In Dar es Salaam, Tanzania, one study found that small-scale industries received 50 to 65 percent of their raw materials from wastepickers working landfill sites (70). The finished products ranged from buckets to kerosene cookers. More generally, steel, paper, and glass producers in developing countries are heavily dependent on recycled material inputs.

Yet in most cases, wastepicking is driven by abject poverty. For many, the only access to many of the resources they need for housing, clothing, fuel, and work comes from the waste materials of the more affluent (71). Socially ostracized, wastepickers—many of whom are women and children—usually work in squalid, unhealthful conditions for long hours and low returns (72).

With the increasing recognition of the value of informal waste collection to urban functioning, efforts are now under way in a number of cities to integrate these activities into the formal urban economy and to minimize the health and safety risks of waste collection for those whose livelihood depends on it. Many of these efforts are driven by NGOs or community-based organizations and face the organizational and financial difficulties common to voluntary efforts. As a result, few projects have led to citywide programs, and many have not survived even on a small scale (73) (74).

However, some efforts have shown a measure of success. In Belo Horizonte, Brazil, and Bandung, Indonesia, for example, wastepickers are being organized into "unions" or "cooperatives" (75) (76) (77). Cooperatives can improve the efficiency of collection by pooling financial resources (e.g., by using community loans to upgrade collection equipment) and by giving wastepickers a greater political voice. Unions can appeal to the municipality to allow them access to recyclables within the city and the city's dump sites. In a few cities, these groups take on social roles as well, lobbying for improved sanitation facilities and schools.

In Madras, India, one organization worked with scavengers to integrate them into the city's door-to-door waste collection service (78) (79). Wastepickers collect

Meager living. At Manila's Smoky Mountain, a child sorts through garbage for items to recycle. For many poor families, wastepicking is an important source of income, but much needs to be done to reduce health threats.

Nigel Dickinson/Still Pictures

wastes from households and either deliver them to municipal vehicles or deposit them at transfer points, with households paying a fee for this service. In other cities, the collectors can trade the recyclables for extra income, and the organics can be taken for small-scale composting. In still others, wastepickers have been given picks, gloves, and boots to provide protection from cuts and exposure to pathogens (80). However, wastepicking remains a hazardous occupation.

New Partnerships and the Private Sector

Opportunities exist to improve the efficiency of municipal solid waste collection services. Given the limited financial and administrative resources of local governments in developing countries, there is a great deal of speculation about whether privatization, which has generally worked well in North America and Europe, can be adapted to poorer cities (81). Solid waste collection services by the private sector are from 20 to 48 percent less costly than public services and can be a great improvement in terms of efficiency and quality (82).

However, privatization should not be considered a panacea. Private companies may only be interested in servicing high-income areas of the city, where service charges can be higher and where the value of reclaimed or recycled materials is higher. In addition, without a proper regulatory structure and competition, private companies may not have incentives to provide the best services or to dispose of wastes according to environmental regulations.

The ideal arrangement may be a mix of public and private services—that is, contracting out the collection of solid waste in some zones of the city while retaining public service to the remaining zones (83). This system can make city operations more cost-effective while still allowing the city the ability to take over solid waste collection if a private contractor fails. In the United States, the city of Phoenix is divided into zones for solid waste collection. The city's department of public works retains jurisdiction over two zones and competes with private companies for 7-year contracts to service the other zones. The contract is awarded to the lowest bidder; so far the city has won about half of the contracts. After a decade of competitive bidding, the city estimated that cost savings amounted to $11 million, and cost avoidance (from lower costs of contracts won back by the city) amounted to $9 million (84).

Similar arrangements have also been successful in developing country cities. Seoul, Republic of Korea; Kuala Lumpur, Malaysia; and Bangkok, Thailand, for example, all maintain some form of public solid waste collection service while privatizing some parts of the city (85). In Kuala Lumpur, the city provides detailed guidance to bidders, including estimates of the daily amount of garbage to be picked up and the likely number of workers needed. The city also makes certain that each contractor's offer is sufficient to ensure satisfactory service and a profit for the contractor, but it reserves the right to terminate contracts at any time should service be unsatisfactory (86).

Reducing Waste Generation

In developed countries, the volume of municipal waste generated far exceeds that in developing countries, and the costs of disposal are becoming increasingly burdensome for strapped city budgets. Many cities are trying to find new ways to provide incentives for residents to reduce waste generation and increase recycling. Variable garbage can rates or pay-per-bag systems have been very effective in reducing solid waste generation at minimal cost to the city. In Perkasie, Pennsylvania, for example, the introduction of per-bag fees led to reductions in the volume of solid waste by more than 50 percent; the cost of solid waste disposal fell by 30 to 40 percent (87).

Other cities are fostering businesses with innovative recycling projects. In Berkeley, California, a company called Urban Ore combs the city's trash for products and materials it can clean up or repair and then sell. In Chicago, another company repairs car tires or reprocesses them into products ranging from snowblower blades to conveyor rollers (88).

Paying more for garbage disposal or intensifying recycling efforts is only a small portion of what needs to be done, however. Reducing the amount of waste generated will require fundamental changes in how countries value and use resources (89).

PRIORITIES FOR ACTION: AIR POLLUTION

For health, environmental, and economic reasons, strategies to reduce air pollution are critical in many cities of the developed and, especially, the developing world. Ambient air pollution emanates from three major sources—energy generation, industry, and transportation—all of which tend to increase with economic growth. Strategies to cope with automobile-related air pollution, which constitutes the fastest growing component of urban air problems, are discussed in Chapter 4, "Urban Transportation."

At the most basic level, addressing urban air problems requires an understanding of the air basin in which the city is situated and the pollution sources that affect it. Forming or participating in an air basin management district or other regional regulatory body is often the best way for cities to develop this understanding and to coordinate basinwide efforts to control pollution, including the drafting and enforcement of ambient air quality standards. (See Chapter 3, "Urban Impacts on Natural Resources.") Developing a local air monitoring capability is essential to both policymaking and enforcement efforts. In Bombay, for example, citywide air monitoring since 1969 has provided an extensive database that is used to assess both daily air quality and regional pollution trends (90).

In many cities in the developing world, however, the most critical health threat stems from exposure to indoor air pollution. Reducing this threat requires a different set of strategies.

Addressing Indoor Air Pollution

For many city residents, air pollution from indoor smoke, usually from biomass fuels, poses a greater health risk than outdoor air pollution. (See Chapter 2, "Urban Environment and Human Health.") The optimal strategy to reduce the exposure of lower-income residents to indoor air pollutants is to facilitate their switch from dirty fuels, for example, by providing clean-burning gas or by establishing programs to make kerosene stoves more affordable. However, for many poor residents of areas without access to city services, this transition to higher-priced fuels will not be possible for some time. For this population, the most promising interim measures are the distribution of improved cookstoves and the fostering of improved house design with better ventilation.

Programs to design and disseminate cleaner-burning stoves have been under way for many years in countries such as China, India, Kenya, and Nepal. However, most stove programs are designed to improve efficiency, not reduce air pollution. One of the most successful urban stove projects has been the Kenya Ceramic Jiko initiative. More than 500,000 stoves have been distributed since the mid-1980s. The stove is a modification of the traditional stove that can be built locally from easily accessible materials and that burns charcoal more efficiently (91). Despite the program's apparent success, penetration of this new stove was limited to middle-class neighborhoods in Nairobi. In addition, ensuring the quality of the new stoves has been difficult.

In higher-income residences and commercial buildings, in both developing and developed countries, indoor pollutants are more likely to come from cigarette smoking, unvented or improperly vented stoves or heaters, airborne contaminants such as asbestos or molds

and fungi, and the release of gases from construction materials and furnishings such as rugs and upholstery.

Several strategies are available to address indoor pollution in higher-income settings. Smoking indoors and in public places can be discouraged through public information campaigns alerting residents to the dangers of secondhand smoke. To minimize combustion products indoors, city environmental managers can establish programs to check home heaters and stoves to ensure proper venting and maintenance. Local ordinances can be enacted to restrict the use of asbestos insulation and fireproofing in new construction. And building codes can direct attention to the provision of adequate ventilation, particularly in new commercial buildings with closed-loop heating and cooling systems.

Reducing Energy Sector Emissions

Cutting emissions from the energy sector, particularly coal- or oil-fired power plants, is critical to controlling outdoor air pollution in many urban areas. Unfortunately, many of the factors determining energy sector pollution—such as the price of energy, the siting of state-owned power plants, the level of investment in new technologies or alternative energy sources, and the privatization of local utilities to improve their capitalization and management—are frequently determined at a national or state level. Nonetheless, cities often have considerable influence over how local utilities are run and over the energy consumption patterns of city residents.

Reducing pollution from coal- and oil-fired power plants can come via three routes: upgrading the generating efficiency and pollution-control capabilities of the plants themselves so that they emit fewer pollutants; cleaning up fuels, either by cleaning the coal before burning or by switching to cleaner-burning natural gas; or reducing the demand for power through energy conservation. (See Promoting Energy Conservation, below.) Attention to proper operation and maintenance procedures is required in any case to keep the performance of power plants from declining over time—an acute problem in many developing countries.

These same strategies of retrofitting with new technology and cleaning up or switching fuels can also be applied at the building or individual household level to cut energy-related emissions within neighborhoods. Replacing or installing pollution control devices on aging coal-fired boilers in commercial and residential buildings in temperate zone cities can increase efficiency and decrease pollutants; converting them to gas can reduce their impact on local air problems still more.

In cities where coal is used to fire individual coal stoves, as in many Chinese and Eastern European cities, upgrading the quality of coal used for such heating can bring immediate and significant air quality benefits to neighborhoods. For example, use of coal briquettes—formed from pulverized, washed coal—can improve combustion efficiency in home heaters by 20 to 30 percent and reduce carbon monoxide emissions by 70 percent and particulate emissions by 60 percent. Adding a sulfur absorbent to briquettes can cut sulfur dioxide emissions by about half. Again, where possible, converting residential heating to gas provides further pollution relief. Recognizing this, but committed to using its huge coal reserves, China is building several coal gasification plants to provide gas for urban residential use (92).

Promoting Energy Conservation

While energy policies are generally considered to be the responsibility of national governments, cities are in a position to help lower energy consumption. Cities can use several tools in their quest to lower energy demand, the first being a vigorous public education campaign on the need for and benefits of energy conservation and the options available to residential and commercial energy users. Such options include the use of more efficient appliances and lighting fixtures, and, in cooler climates, the installation of weatherstripping and insulation.

The Urban CO_2 Reduction Project, sponsored by the International Council for Local Environmental Initiatives, is a network of 14 cities that are working together to develop local strategies to reduce energy consumption and carbon dioxide emissions. The goal of the project is to show that emission reductions are possible without harming the city's economic productivity. A preliminary study in the city of Toronto showed that the city could reduce per capita emissions of carbon dioxide by 33 percent at net economic savings even without considering the additional benefits of local job creation and the stimulation of new manufacturing industries (93).

Policies adopted by the 14 cities range from economic instruments to regulations to broader strategies such as land use planning and improving public transportation. To achieve its target of 25 percent emission reductions, Hanover, Germany, has proposed the following measures (among others): switching fuels for electricity generation, retrofitting municipal buildings, strengthening energy performance standards in the building codes for new buildings, modifying land use patterns, and improving waste management. Copenhagen, Denmark, has proposed a local energy tax and utility rate reform to reduce energy consumption (94).

The Urban CO_2 Reduction Project shows that simple technical fixes such as insulating pipes and repairing leaks in the steam heating systems in residential buildings can translate into reduced energy use (95) (96). For cities in developing countries, reducing energy consumption may not be a top priority, yet in rapidly growing cities where new construction is high, the potential for cutting future energy needs through efficiency standards in building codes is large (97). Building in energy efficiency during initial construction is almost always less costly than retrofitting, and the energy saved—and the power plant emissions prevented—can be substantial.

Encouraging Pollution Prevention

One of the most promising tacks to reducing industrial emissions is to prevent pollution in the first place. Pollution prevention focuses on designing cleaner production processes and material handling procedures. This approach follows a natural hierarchy of industrial

Jorgen Schytte/Still Pictures

Smokestacks. *High urban demand for energy contributes to both ambient air pollution and greenhouse warming. Cities can play a critical role in reducing both energy consumption and industrial pollution.*

waste management options. First, reduce pollutants at the source as much as possible. Second, recycle or reuse as much as possible of the pollutants or wastes that are produced despite these efforts. Third, treat, detoxify, or destroy what remains. And fourth, only as a last resort release pollutants to the surrounding environment (98).

The central rationale for this approach is economic: preventing pollution at the source both reduces pollution control costs and increases the efficiency of production, because fewer materials are lost as waste. Preventing pollution can also be a powerful marketing and public relations tool in areas where environmental awareness has increased and environmental health concerns have made their way onto urban agendas.

Cities can be important catalysts and partners in pollution prevention, mostly by helping to educate both the private sector and the public about the advantages of cleaner manufacturing. Developing and helping to administer information clearinghouses that offer details on alternative technologies and their successful application in other industries are prime means of facilitating a change to cleaner industrial processes. City governments can foster a stronger environmental ethic among local industries by conducting public "green performance" ratings of manufacturing facilities, by encouraging industrial managers to publicly commit to pollution-reduction targets, and by offering awards for exemplary environmental performance.

Cities can enlist the support of the public through education campaigns that make clear the unseen costs of pollution and that encourage consumers to "buy green." Enacting public disclosure laws that force local industries to reveal their annual pollution emissions can also prod local firms to improve their environmental records, lest they acquire a reputation for being insensitive to local citizens and the environment. Such disclosure laws have been quite effective in altering corporate behavior in some developed countries. Encouraging local nongovernmental organizations to act as watchdogs for industrial pollution problems has also proved effective in many instances (99) (100).

PRIORITIES FOR ACTION: LAND USE

Underlying virtually all urban environmental problems is the issue of land use, from the lack of affordable housing, to congestion and pollution from motor vehicles, to inner cities marred by abandoned buildings. Indeed, urban form and land use patterns within a city are critical determinants of environmental quality (101). This connection implies that land use planning could be

used to improve the urban environment by directing urban growth in certain ways.

Translating potential into policy and then into reality has proved difficult, however. In part, the problem lies with defining the ideal urban form. While high-density cities can reduce the need for transportation, and thereby problems of energy consumption and pollution, without adequate infrastructure they may facilitate the transmission of communicable diseases and increase congestion (102) (103). In contrast, low-density cities are land intensive but may provide other amenities such as open space. Within a city, a dense cluster of industries may be especially hazardous if located near a residential neighborhood or a coastal estuary, yet dispersing them throughout the city could increase the need for transportation and may hinder pollution control efforts (104).

Even more vexing has been the relative failure of governments to successfully guide urban form, even with detailed master plans and regulatory systems. Land use planning is notoriously difficult. In most cities, governments and/or private landowners are unwilling to relinquish control of land because it provides a source of cash income and political power (105) (106) (107). Furthermore, there are no "decisionmakers" deciding on the shapes of cities; city form is determined by the interaction of countless decisions by individuals, households, and businesses on the one hand, and a variety of government interventions designed to influence or control those decisions on the other (108). Regulatory tools can have unintended impacts. In the United States, minimum plot sizes, initially intended to prevent urban expansion, have achieved just the opposite by requiring each house to occupy its own large lot (109). In cities in developing countries, zoning and regulations have the unintended effect of putting the land out of the financial reach of the majority of residents.

Government intervention in land markets is nonetheless warranted to meet the land needs of the urban poor and to protect land on which settlement would have irreparable environmental consequences, such as water catchment areas (110). This section explores how land use planning can improve urban environmental quality. Prescriptions for better urban land use are not the same for all cities. In cities in developing countries, land use issues must still focus on improving access to serviced urban land for the poor, for it is at this level that the greatest toll on the environment and human health is being taken. How cities choose to allocate and direct this land, however, can have an impact on future environmental conditions. In developed countries, land use issues should focus on reducing resource consumption and improving the quality of urban life.

Land for Housing

In many parts of the world, one of the main ways in which the poor have obtained access to land has been through informal settlement, particularly of fringe areas and hazardous land. The squatter settlements of the urban poor are a consistent feature of developing country cities—from New Delhi, India, to Caracas, Venezuela (111). (See Figure 5.3.) This process of land acquisition and shelter provision is often illegal, but in many cases it is the only option because governments are unable to provide sufficient serviced land for housing. Public housing projects fall far short of demand and often benefit middle-class rather than poor households (112).

As described in Chapter 1, "Cities and the Environment," informal settlements are rarely serviced by water or sanitation facilities or basic garbage collection. As long as land rights remain unclear, governments will be unwilling to service these areas, even though in many cases these settlements are so large that the government has no intention of dismantling them. And as long as residents face the threat of eviction, they will be unwilling to invest in their homes (113).

Traditional policy responses have been to regard this lack of infrastructure as the responsibility of public works departments. A land-based strategy, however, suggests that a more effective way to improve the environmental conditions in these settlements is to grant legal land tenure, either in the form of outright transfer of land ownership to tenants or through long-term leases and residential rights. Experience has shown that with security of tenure, the poor will build and invest to improve the quality of their own housing (114) (115). In Ouagadougou, Burkina Faso, for example, the government adjusted the land allocation process in an effort to curb urban sprawl and limit the growth of illegal settlements. Not only did the number of legalized lots increase dramatically (60,000 plots of land between 1984 and 1989), the regularization of land title led to the mobilization of local citizens and resources in support of other public services such as water supplies and schools (116). As urban land becomes more scarce, however, it will become progressively more difficult for the poor to obtain land and housing in this manner (117).

In addition to granting land tenure, several other redistribution mechanisms have been tried to allocate serviced land to the urban poor, including land sharing, land banking, and land readjustment. Few of these efforts have been successful. Land readjustment (also known as land consolidation or land pooling) has been somewhat effective in Taiwan, the Republic of Korea, Japan, Colombia, and India. The government (or other public authority) pools land from many private land-

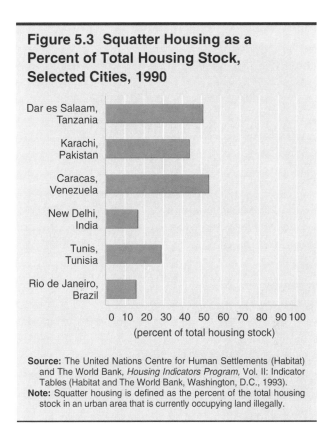

Figure 5.3 Squatter Housing as a Percent of Total Housing Stock, Selected Cities, 1990

Source: The United Nations Centre for Human Settlements (Habitat) and The World Bank, *Housing Indicators Program*, Vol. II: Indicator Tables (Habitat and The World Bank, Washington, D.C., 1993).
Note: Squatter housing is defined as the percent of the total housing stock in an urban area that is currently occupying land illegally.

owners and installs public infrastructure and then retains part of the land for public use (either for housing for the poor or to sell to finance the cost of the infrastructure). The remaining land is returned to its original owners, who now own a smaller portion of land but at a higher value (118).

Protecting Land Resources

Using land use tools to guide the siting of housing and industry away from environmentally sensitive areas can greatly improve environmental quality in cities. This is critical, for example, at the fringes of coastal urban areas, where development can result in rapid deterioration of the nearby coastal environment as untreated wastes, erosion, and uncontrolled access to biological resources take their toll (119).

Zoning, building codes, permits, and economic instruments such as taxes and fees are common tools used by governments to protect fragile areas and to prevent the unnecessary conversion of rural land to urban uses. These tools can be used to control densities, to separate land uses, and to directly protect natural areas (120). In Costa Rica, for example, urban development is restricted in a 200-meter-wide marine and terrestrial zone along the coastline (121). Economic instruments such as taxes on vacant land can encourage owners of land ripe

Squatter settlement. *Lack of affordable land for housing leads to the development of informal settlements, like this one in La Paz, Bolivia. When granted land tenure, many residents will upgrade housing on their own.*

Caracas, for example, 67 percent of the land area occupied by *barrios* is unsuitable for housing because of geological instability and frequent landslides. Yet this unstable terrain is home to more than 550,000 people (127). Restricting these areas from development will have little effect if other housing options are not available.

City planners can reduce the health impacts of pollution and the costs of abatement through strategic decisions on the siting and density of urban industries. In many cities, industrial sites often abut residential neighborhoods or are located in environmentally sensitive areas where the negative effects of pollutants will be most pronounced. Judicious use of industrial zoning laws can help relieve this problem by relocating heavy industries out of the urban center and into industrial parks. In Turkey, the government provides subsidized credits for relocating industries to industrial parks, where existing infrastructure is better equipped to deal with wastes than in other parts of the city (128).

Often, clustering facilities in this way can lead to significant savings by allowing collective treatment of industrial wastes in a shared treatment plant. One such collective treatment facility, in Surabaya, Indonesia, is fully supported by the effluent charges collected from users, and is able to treat the wastes it uses thoroughly enough that its effluent can be reused by the industries it serves, helping them save on water costs (129).

Clustering facilities can be a particularly effective way of addressing the needs of smaller businesses that lack the knowledge or financial means to treat their own wastes. In some cases, it may be necessary to underwrite part or all of the costs of relocating lower-income firms to special cluster sites and constructing common treatment facilities for their wastes (130).

Broader Strategies: Urban Form and Environment

In addition to directing development away from fragile lands, land use planning has the potential to address problems of resource consumption and pollution by

for development to build on it, thereby reducing vacant land within city boundaries and limiting the extent of urban sprawl (122).

Zoning laws or regulations that ban urban development in specific regions of the city—such as greenbelts, green ways, and urban growth boundaries—can preserve open space and shape the form of the city. Although few examples of successful greenbelts exist to date, interest is growing in many cities. In older developed cities, from Manchester, United Kingdom, to Philadelphia, large plots of inner city land, known as "brownfields," lie abandoned as companies and industries move to undeveloped land in suburban and rural communities (123). For these cities, urban containment policies would restrict outward sprawl and encourage growth and redevelopment in existing urban areas. In the United Kingdom, for example, the combination of stringent greenbelt policies and funding incentives is leading to the regeneration of many city centers (124).

Without regional coordination, however, these containment policies are rarely successful. Greenbelts or urban growth boundaries can increase land prices in the city and encourage sprawl beyond them, as in the case of Seoul (125). In addition, political will and citizen activism in favor of greenbelts need to be strong to fend off proposals that request boundary changes (126).

Furthermore, ecologically sensitive areas are impossible to protect from urban encroachment if people and industries are not given alternative land options. In

manipulating urban densities. Numerous negative impacts are associated with low-density settlements. They are often land intensive and are characterized by high infrastructure costs, greater reliance on private transportation with its attendant energy consumption and pollution, high domestic energy use due to the lack of shared insulation, and poor recycling rates due to large collection costs.

A compact city with a concentration of jobs and housing in a central location is typically described as the most resource-efficient city form, using minimal land resources and saving energy through multistory buildings and reduced need for travel (131). Debate continues, however, on the optimal density needed to produce these desired effects. Even in cities in developing countries, where densities tend to be comparatively high, large tracts of vacant land within the city exist that could be developed at high densities before expanding outward. In Karachi, Pakistan, for example, where overall city density approaches 4,000 people per square kilometer (132), more than 4,800 hectares of land within the city boundary lies vacant (133).

As cities grow to unprecedented sizes, however, the centralized city model becomes less tenable. First, while development along major lines of transportation to and from the center of the city tends to be high density, the areas between these "fingers" develop at low densities as the region attracts more people and businesses. Second, concentrating several million people (and all the economic activities that support them) in a central city can lead to severe congestion. Recent studies suggest that a more efficient urban form may be multinucleated urban regions, where many small, dense nodes—satellite towns, new towns, edge cities—are linked together by transportation infrastructure (134).

In Berkeley, California, a proposed land use plan adopts this "nodal" vision rather than a centralized model for future urban growth. By redeveloping existing neighborhoods at higher densities, the centers will become increasingly compact and surrounding land can be reclaimed as open space. Within each of these neighborhoods, zoning laws will require a combination of jobs, housing, and entertainment, all within walking distance (135).

Integrated Land Use and Transportation

Studies on whether high densities should be concentrated in one centralized location or in many smaller nodes for maximum energy efficiency remain inconclusive (136). What is clear, however, is that neither strategy will provide benefits unless closely coordinated with transportation infrastructure. Indeed, transportation infrastructure development may be far more influential in determining where development will take place than land use planning (137). The development of toll roads connecting Jakarta, Indonesia, with the nearby towns of Tangerang, Bekasi, and Bogor has had a tremendous impact on the physical growth of Jakarta, intensifying housing and industrial development far from the city itself and greatly increasing car traffic (138). In contrast, in Curitiba, Brazil, where development was channeled along bus lines, car use is much lower (139). (See Box 5.4.)

Directing urban growth along public transportation lines can greatly increase transit ridership and reduce energy consumption. Recently, a number of large cities—Portland, Oregon; Stockholm, Sweden; Toronto; Vienna, Austria; and Copenhagen, Denmark—have all attempted to concentrate high-density residential development near public transit stations (140). Without coordination of land use and transportation planning at the outset, chances are that cities will develop increasingly car-dependent forms. In the Netherlands, for example, the new town of Zoetermeer did not qualify for a railway connection until there were 50,000 inhabitants; by then, car infrastructure was already in place and car-dependent travel patterns had been established (141).

The different nature of the transportation and land use sectors and general lack of institutional coordination between them have limited the success of efforts to integrate the two in practice (142). The effect of land use policies on travel demand is also likely to depend on the adoption of economic instruments that increase the real costs of car travel. Otherwise, people may still choose their car over other modes of transportation. (See Chapter 4, "Urban Transportation.")

Institutional Needs for Improved Land Use

In addition to the constraints to successful land use planning mentioned above, one of the key roadblocks in developing countries is poor institutional capacity to manage urban land. Most cities in developing countries lack the information to carry out land use strategies. Urban maps are 20 to 30 years old and lack any description of entire sections of cities, particularly the burgeoning peri-urban regions (143). Conflicting approaches to land management—a formal statutory system (often left over from colonial rule), an informal system, and an indigenous system—come together within the confined space of a city (144). In addition, excessive and poorly coordinated regulations, inappropriate pricing and taxation, and land speculation all perpetuate land use problems. Improving land management in these cities is a crucial first step. Only then will

Box 5.4 Integrated Transportation and Land Use Planning Channel Curitiba's Growth

Curitiba, Brazil, has received international acclaim as a city that works—a good example of sustainability and exemplary urban planning. In 1950, however, all trends indicated that Curitiba was likely to become yet another city overwhelmed by rapid population growth and urban environmental prob-

lems. From 1950 to 1990, Curitiba mushroomed from a town of 300,000 to a metropolis of about 2.3 million (1). Migrants, pushed from the land as the result of agricultural mechanization, flocked to the city and settled in squatter housing at the urban periphery. Rivers and streams were converted into artifi-

cial canals without consideration for natural drainage channels, contributing to frequent flooding in the city center (2).

How did Curitiba manage to turn itself into a positive example for cities in both developed and developing countries? In part, the city's success can be attributed to strong leadership. Realizing that a static master plan would not be adequate to deal with the dynamic nature of urban problems, city officials focused on developing simple, flexible, and affordable solutions that could be realized at the local level and adapted to changing conditions. In addition, the government promoted a strong sense of public participation. Officials were encouraged to look at problems, talk to the people, discuss the main issues, and only then reach for the pen. This process provides insights that are seldom self-evident at the drawing table (3). One of the key actors in Curitiba's success over the past 25 years has been Jaime Lerner, who served as mayor three times, from 1970 to 1974, from 1979 to 1983, and from 1989 to 1992.

The most important unifying feature of Curitiba's success is its emphasis on integrating transportation and land use planning. The key concept was to channel the city's physical expansion away from the central city and along five linear corridors or axes. (See Figure 1.) Each axis is built around a central or "structural" road that has exclusive lanes for express buses, for local traffic, and for high-speed car traffic flowing in and out of the city. Zoning laws encourage high-density commercial development along these transport corridors, while land away from the corridors is zoned at low densities. The central city, where traffic congestion and noise have

Figure 1 Curitiba Integrated Transportation Network

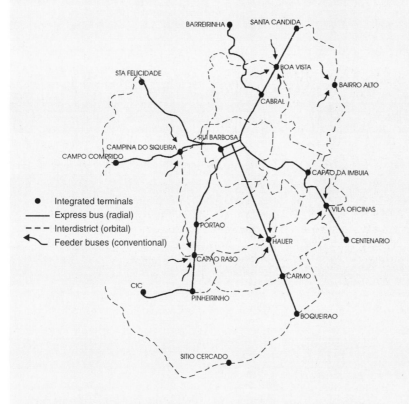

• Integrated terminals
— Express bus (radial)
- - - Interdistrict (orbital)
⌒← Feeder buses (conventional)

Source: Jonas Rabinovitch and John Hoehn, "A Sustainable Urban Transportation System: the 'Surface Metro' in Curitiba, Brazil," The Environmental and Natural Resources Policy and Training (EPAT) Project Working Paper No. 19 (EPAT/ The Midwest Universities Consortium for International Activities, Inc., University of Wisconsin, Madison, Wisconsin, May 1995), p. 18.

cities be able to begin to resolve conflicting demands for the use and protection of land.

It is also becoming increasingly apparent that mitigating urban environmental impacts will depend on the cooperation of local and regional governments on land use issues. Yet to date few mechanisms exist to facilitate such cooperation. One such strategy is regional land use

planning, now being tried in a few developed and developing world cities. Although each city has different needs and goals, the broad tenets of regional planning are similar. First, high priority is given to environmental values. Land is recognized as being valuable in its natural state and is not simply seen as raw material for urbanization. Second, rather than trying to fix problems

been greatly reduced, has been returned to pedestrians.

As a result of these efforts, the bus system is used by more than 1.3 million passengers each day. Twenty-eight percent of direct-route bus users previously traveled in their cars (4). Despite having the second highest per capita car ownership rate in Brazil, Curitiba's gasoline use per capita is 30 percent below that of eight comparable Brazilian cities, and air pollution levels are among the lowest in Brazil (5).

The city also uses zoning and economic incentives to preserve cultural districts and to protect natural areas. Strong land use legislation and incentives have increased the ratio of available green area per inhabitant from 0.5 square meters in 1970 to 50 square meters in 1992 (6). Beginning in the late 1960s, the city set aside strips of land and prohibited them from development. In 1975, the remaining river basins were protected by stringent legislation and turned into urban parks (7). By protecting natural drainage channels, the city avoided the need for substantial new investments in flood control, and costly flooding has become a thing of the past.

Curitiba has also managed to avoid problems common to other developing cities, such as land that remains vacant while ownership disputes are settled, lengthy waits for development permits, and inefficient property tax collection. The city maintains a detailed land inventory that allows city hall to deliver information quickly to citizens about the building potential of any plot in the city. The system is constantly updated as the city expands (8).

Curitiba has found other low-cost solutions to urban problems. In 1989, faced with growing mounds of garbage, the city was ready for a large-scale recycling plant. But such a plant was beyond city resources. Instead, the city launched an innovative "Garbage That Is Not Garbage" program. The program relied on households to separate garbage for the city, significantly cutting municipal costs. A campaign was also developed to educate children about the importance of recycling, turning them into "secret agents inside each home"; now more than 70 percent of households participate in the recycling program. In all, two thirds of the city's trash is recycled, more than 100 metric tons daily (9).

In slums where streets are too narrow for garbage trucks to enter, the city found a way to get the garbage to come to the trucks. The "Garbage Purchase" program allows residents to trade filled garbage bags for bus tokens, parcels of surplus food, and school notebooks. The food and vouchers cost no more than hiring trash collectors to go into the slums, and provide the added benefit of improving nutrition as well as public transit ridership among the poor. An estimated 35,000 families have benefited from this program (10).

In all its projects, the city emphasizes low-cost programs that help people to help themselves. Instead of huge city outlays for row upon row of housing projects, the city provides architects and loans, encouraging people to build their own homes. Old public buses are converted into mobile schools for low-income families and are able to go to a different neighborhood each day of the week (11).

The lesson to be learned from Curitiba is that creativity can substitute for financial resources. Any city, rich or poor, can draw on the skills of its residents to tackle urban environmental problems. What may not be transferable is the will to change, political commitment, and leadership that Curitiba has enjoyed over the past 25 years.
—*Jonas Rabinovitch*

Jonas Rabinovitch is a Senior Urban Development Advisor for the United Nations Development Programme in New York.

References and Notes

1. Jonas Rabinovitch and Josef Leitmann, "Environmental Innovation and Management in Curitiba, Brazil," Urban Management Program Working Paper Series No. 1 (The World Bank, Washington, D.C., June 1993), Table 1-1, p. 2.
2. *Ibid.*, pp. 2, 37–38.
3. *Op. cit.* 1, pp. 8–16.
4. Jonas Rabinovitch, "Curitiba: Towards Sustainable Urban Development," *Environment and Urbanization*, Vol. 4, No. 2 (October 1992), p. 66.
5. *Ibid.*, pp. 65–66.
6. Jonas Rabinovitch and John Hoehn, "A Sustainable Urban Transportation System: the 'Surface Metro' in Curitiba, Brazil," The Environmental and Natural Resources Policy and Training (EPAT) Project Working Paper No. 19 (EPAT/The Midwest Universities Consortium for International Activities, Inc., University of Wisconsin, Madison, Wisconsin, May 1995), p. 37.
7. *Op. cit.* 1, p. 38.
8. *Op. cit.* 1, p. 28.
9. *Op. cit.* 4, pp. 67–68.
10. *Op. cit.* 1, pp. 34–36.
11. *Op. cit.* 1, p. 47.

after damage is done, efforts are made to anticipate and prevent environmental damage in the first place. Assessment of impacts, including an assessment of the possible cumulative effects of urban development, should precede and guide land use decisions. Finally, to the extent possible, planning efforts should encompass ecosystem-based units such as watersheds (145).

This chapter was written by Mike Douglass of the Department of Urban and Regional Planning at the University of Hawaii at Manoa, Honolulu, Hawaii, and Yok-shiu F. Lee of the Program on Environment, East-West Center, Honolulu.

References and Notes

1. Jorge Hardoy, Diana Mitlin, and David Satterthwaite, *Environmental Problems in Third World Cities* (Earthscan, London, 1992), pp. 17, 23.

2. Carl Bartone *et al.,* "Toward Environmental Strategies for Cities: Policy Considerations for Urban Environmental Management in Developing Countries," Urban Management Programme Policy Paper No. 18 (The World Bank, Washington, D.C., 1994), p. 5.

3. *Ibid.,* p. 7.

4. The World Bank, *World Development Report 1992: Development and the Environment* (The World Bank, Washington, D.C., 1992), p. 5.

5. World Health Organization (WHO), *The International Drinking Water Supply and Sanitation Decade* (WHO, Geneva, 1992), p. 8.

6. G. Watters, Health and Environment, World Health Organization, Geneva, 1995 (personal communication).

7. Maggie Black, *Mega-Slums: The Coming Sanitary Crisis* (WaterAid, London, 1994), p. 18.

8. Sandy Cairncross, *Sanitation and Water Supply: Practical Lessons from The Decade* (The World Bank, Washington, D.C., 1992), p. 1.

9. *Op. cit.* 7, p. 19.

10. *Op. cit.* 7, p. 19.

11. *Op. cit.* 7, p. 15.

12. *Op. cit.* 4, pp. 106–107.

13. Gehan Sinnatamby, "Low Cost Sanitation," in *The Poor Die Young,* Jorge E. Hardoy, Sandy Cairncross, and David Satterthwaite, eds. (Earthscan, London, 1990), pp. 127–157.

14. *Op. cit.* 1, p. 130.

15. John Pickford, "Training and Human Resource Development in Water Supply and Sanitation," *Water International,* Vol. 16, No. 3 (1991), p. 174.

16. Tova Maria Solo, Eduardo A. Perez, and Steven D. Joyce, "Constraints in Providing Water and Sanitation Services to the Urban Poor," Water and Sanitation for Health Project (WASH) Technical Report No. 85 (WASH, Washington, D.C., March 1993), p. 8.

17. William Hogrewe, Steven D. Joyce, and Eduardo A. Perez, "The Unique Challenges of Improving Peri-Urban Sanitation," Water and Sanitation for Health Project (WASH) Technical Report No. 86 (WASH, Washington, D.C., July 1993), p. 45.

18. *Op. cit.* 7, p. 21.

19. "Orangi Pilot Project," *Environment and Urbanization,* Vol. 7, No. 2 (October 1995), pp. 228–230.

20. J.C.R. de Melo, "Sistemas Condominiais de Esgotos," *Engenharia Sanitaria,* Vol. 24, No. 2 (1985), pp. 237–238, as cited in John Briscoe, "When the Cup Is Half Full: Improving Water and Sanitation Services in the Developing World," *Environment,* Vol. 35, No. 4 (May 1993), p. 32.

21. United Nations International Research and Training Institute for the Advancement of Women, "Women, Water, and Sanitation," in *Women and the Environment: A Reader,* Sally Sontheimer, ed. (Monthly Review Press, New York, 1991), p. 123.

22. *Op. cit.* 4, p. 113.

23. Yok-shiu F. Lee, "Rethinking Urban Water Supply and Sanitation Strategy in Developing Countries in the Humid Tropics: Lessons from the International Water Decade," East-West Center Reprints, Environment Series No. 9 (East-West Center, Honolulu, 1993), p. 553.

24. Lair Espinosa and Oscar A. Lopez Rivera, "UNICEF's Urban Basic Services Programme in Illegal Settlements in Guatemala City," *Environment and Urbanization,* Vol. 6, No. 2 (October 1994), p. 19.

25. Dennis B. Warner and Louis Laugeri, "Health for All: The Legacy of the Water Decade," *Water International,* Vol. 16, No. 3 (1991), pp. 135–141.

26. National Research Council, Academia de la Investigacion Cientifica, A.C., and Academia Nacional de Ingenieria, A.C., *Mexico City's Water Supply: Improving the Outlook for Sustainability* (National Academy Press, Washington, D.C., 1995), pp. 32–33.

27. Exequiel Ezcurra and Marisa Mazari-Hiriart, "Are Mega-Cities Viable? A Cautionary Tale from Mexico City," *Environment,* Vol. 38, No. 1 (January/February 1996), p. 14.

28. Ismail Serageldin, "Water Supply, Sanitation and Environmental Sustainability: The Financing Challenge," keynote address to the Ministerial Conference on Drinking Water and Environmental Sanitation: Implementing Agenda 21 (The World Bank, Washington, D.C., March 1994), p. 10.

29. *Ibid.*

30. *Op. cit.* 28.

31. *Op. cit.* 23, p. 550.

32. *Op. cit.* 4, pp. 103–104.

33. D.A. Okun, "The Value of Water Supply and Sanitation in Development: An Assessment," *American Journal of Public Health,* Vol. 78, No. 11 (1988), pp. 1463–1467.

34. D. Whittington *et al.,* "Household Demand for Improved Sanitation Services in Kumasi, Ghana: A Contingent Valuation Study," *Water Resources Research,* Vol. 29, No. 6 (1993), pp. 1539–1560.

35. David Pearce, Director, CESERGE, University College, London, December 1995 (personal communication).

36. John Briscoe, "When the Cup Is Half Full: Improving Water and Sanitation Services in the Developing World," *Environment,* Vol. 35, No. 4 (May 1993), p. 10.

37. *Op. cit.* 4, p. 100.

38. *Op. cit.* 36, p. 13.

39. Massachusetts Water Resources Authority (MWRA), "MWRA Long Range Water Supply Program," Progress Briefing (MWRA, Boston, Massachusetts, March 9, 1994), p. 1.

40. Stephen A. Estes-Smargiassi, "Living Within Our Means: A Successful Demand-Side Water Resources Plan for Boston," paper prepared for the Massachusetts Water Resources Authority (MWRA) (MWRA, Boston, 1994), p. 2.

41. *Op. cit.* 26, p. 56.

42. *Op. cit.* 4, p. 102.

43. *Op. cit.* 4, p. 103.

44. *Op. cit.* 4, p. 101.

45. *Op. cit.* 28, p. 9.

46. The World Bank Environment and Urban Development Division, *Chile—Managing Environmental Problems: Economic Analysis of Selected Issues,* Report No. 13061-CH (The World Bank, Washington, D.C., 1994), p. 83.

47. *Op. cit.* 28, p. 2.

48. *Op. cit.* 28, p. 12.

49. United States General Accounting Office (GAO), *Water Pollution: Information on the Use of Alternative Wastewater Treatment Systems,* Report No. RCED-94-109 (GAO, Washington, D.C., 1994), p. 2.

50. *Op. cit.* 28, p. 9.

51. National Research Council, Committee on Wastewater Management for Coastal Urban Areas, *Managing Wastewater in Coastal Urban Areas* (National Academy Press, Washington, D.C., 1993), pp. 309–327.

52. Carl Bartone, "Water Quality and Urbanization in Latin America," *Water International,* Vol. 15 (1990), pp. 8–14.

53. *Op. cit.* 49, pp. 13–31.

54. Rodney Fujita, "New Approaches to Wastewater Treatment," Study Paper (Environmental Defense Fund, New York, 1993), p. 1.

55. *Op. cit.* 51, pp. 314–317.

56. *Op. cit.* 52, pp. 12–14.

57. Takashi Asano, "Reusing Urban Wastewater—An Alternative and a Reliable Water Resource," *Water International,* Vol. 19 (1994), pp. 36–42.

58. Janusz Niemczynowicz, "Urban Water Pollution in Developing Countries," *Water Resources Journal,* No. 24 (December 1994), p. 18.

59. United Nations Economic and Social Commission for Asia and the Pacific (ESCAP), *State of the Environment in Asia and the Pacific, 1990* (ESCAP, Bangkok, Thailand, 1990), p. 234.

60. Janis D. Bernstein, "Alternative Approaches to Pollution Control and Waste Management: Regulatory and Economic Instruments," Urban Management Programme Discussion Paper No. 3 (The World Bank, Washington, D.C., 1993), pp. 10–11.

61. *Ibid.*, p. 33.

62. *Op. cit.* 2, p. 26.

63. Carl Bartone, Transport, Water and Urban Development Department, The World Bank, Washington, D.C., 1995 (personal communication).

64. United Nations Environment Programme, *Environmental Data Report 1993–94* (Blackwell Publishers, Oxford, U.K., 1993), p. 331.

65. *Op. cit.* 63.

66. Christine Furedy, "Solid Wastes in the Waste Economy: Socio-Cultural Aspects," paper presented at the Workshop on "The Waste Economy," National Institute for Scientific and Technical Forecasting, University of Toronto, and International Development Research Centre, Hanoi, Viet Nam, August 22–25, 1994, p. 3.

67. *Ibid.*

68. Christine Furedy, "Social Aspects of Solid Waste Recovery in Asian Cities," *Environmental Sanitation Reviews*, No. 30 (Asian Institute of Technology, Bangkok, Thailand, December 1990), p. 17.

69. *Op. cit.* 66, p. 15.

70. Michael Yhdego, "Scavenging Solid Wastes in Dar es Salaam, Tanzania," *Waste Management and Research*, Vol. 9 (1991), p. 263.

71. *Op. cit.* 68, p. 4.

72. *Op. cit.* 66, p. 7.

73. Christine Furedy, "Garbage: Exploring Non-Conventional Options in Asian Cities," *Environment and Urbanization*, Vol. 4, No. 2 (October 1992), p. 52.

74. *Op. cit.* 1, p. 135.

75. *Op. cit.* 66, p. 6.

76. Local Initiative Facility for Urban Environment (LIFE), "LIFE Small Project Status Report—Latin America and the Caribbean," (United Nations Development Programme, New York, August 23, 1995), p. 5.

77. Hasan Poerbo, "Urban Solid Waste Management in Bandung: Towards an Integrated Resource Recovery System," *Environment and Urbanization*, Vol. 3, No. 1 (April 1991), p. 63.

78. *Op. cit.* 73, p. 49.

79. *Op. cit.* 66, p. 6.

80. *Op. cit.* 66, p. 7.

81. Yok-shiu F. Lee, "An Overview of Solid Waste Management Privatization Experiences in Asia and the Pacific," East-West Center Paper (East-West Center, Honolulu, 1992), p. 5.

82. *Ibid.*

83. *Op. cit.* 81, p. 22.

84. Sandra Cointreau-Levine, "Private Sector Participation in Municipal Solid Waste Services in Developing Countries, Vol. 1: The Formal Sector," Urban Management Programme Discussion Paper No. 13 (The World Bank, Washington, D.C., 1994), p. 18.

85. *Op. cit.* 81, pp. 21–22.

86. *Op. cit.* 81, pp. 9–10.

87. *Op. cit.* 60, p. 55.

88. John E. Young and Aaron Sachs, "The Next Efficiency Revolution: Creating a Sustainable Materials Economy," Worldwatch Paper No. 121 (Worldwatch Institute, Washington, D.C., September 1994), p. 46.

89. World Wildlife Fund (WWF) and The Conservation Foundation, *Getting at the Source: Strategies for Reducing Municipal Solid Waste* (WWF, Washington, D.C., 1991), p. 3.

90. Metropolitan Environmental Improvement Program, "Air Quality Management in Sri Lanka," Intercountry Study No. 1 (The World Bank, Washington, D.C., 1993), p. 22.

91. United Nations Centre for Human Settlements (Habitat), *Application of Biomass-Energy Technologies* (Habitat, Nairobi, Kenya, 1993), p. 41.

92. Robert Perlack and Milton Russell, "Energy and Environmental Policy in China," *Annual Review of Energy and the Environment*, Vol. 16 (1991), pp. 220–221.

93. L.D. Danny Harvey, "Tackling Urban CO_2 Emissions in Toronto," *Environment*, Vol. 35, No. 7 (September 1993), p. 19.

94. *Ibid.*

95. *Op. cit.* 93.

96. U.S. Congress, Office of Technology Assessment (OTA), *Energy Efficiency Technologies for Central and Eastern Europe*, OTA-E-562 (OTA, Washington, D.C., 1993), p. 69.

97. International Institute for Energy Conservation (IIEC), "Superwindow Technology Leads to Super Savings," *E-Notes*, Vol. 2, No. 4 (IIEC, Washington, D.C., November 1992), p. 4.

98. World Resources Institute in collaboration with the United Nations Environment Programme and the United Nations Development Programme, *World Resources 1994–95* (Oxford University Press, New York, 1994), p. 219.

99. *Ibid.*, pp. 218–219.

100. Carter Brandon and Ramesh Ramankutty, "Toward an Environmental Strategy for Asia," World Bank Discussion Paper No. 224 (The World Bank, Washington, D.C., 1993), pp. 79–80.

101. *Op. cit.* 2, p. 13.

102. Yok-shiu F. Lee, "Urban Planning and Vector Control in Southeast Asian Cities," *Kaohsiung Journal of Medical Science*, Vol. 10 (1994), p. S39.

103. *Op. cit.* 2, p. 13.

104. *Op. cit.* 2, p. 13.

105. United Nations Centre for Human Settlements (Habitat), *Evaluation of Experience with Initiating Enabling Shelter Strategies* (Habitat, Nairobi, Kenya, 1991), p. 18.

106. Catherine Farvacque and Patrick McAuslan, "Reforming Urban Land Policies and Institutions in Developing Countries," Urban Management Program Policy Paper No. 5 (The World Bank, Washington, D.C., 1992), p. 51.

107. *Ibid.*, p. 18.

108. Nick Devas, "Evolving Approaches," in *Managing Fast Growing Cities: New Approaches to Urban Planning and Management in the Developing World*, Nick Devas and Carole Rakodi, eds. (Longman Group, Essex, U.K., and John Wiley & Sons, Inc., New York, 1993), p. 63.

109. Marcia D. Lowe, "Shaping Cities," in *State of the World 1992*, Lester Brown, ed. (Worldwatch Institute, Washington, D.C., 1992), p. 121.

110. *Op. cit.* 108, pp. 75–76.

111. *Op. cit.* 105.

112. *Op. cit.* 105.

113. Michael Douglass, "The Political Economy of Urban Poverty and Environmental Management: Access, Empowerment and Community Based Alternatives," *Environment and Urbanization*, Vol. 4, No. 2 (October 1992), pp. 15–16.

114. *Op. cit.* 102, pp. S45–S46.

115. U.S. Agency for International Development (U.S. AID), *Regularizing the Informal Land Development Process, Vol. 2: Discussion Papers* (U.S. AID, Washington, D.C., 1991), p. ix.

116. Sylvy Jaglin, "Why Mobilize Town Dwellers?—Joint Management in Ouagadougou (1983–1990)," *Environment and Urbanization*, Vol. 6, No. 2 (October 1994), pp. 113–114.

117. *Op. cit.* 108, p. 83.

118. Michael Mattingly, "Urban Management Intervention in Land Markets," in *Managing Fast Growing Cities: New Approaches to Urban Planning and Management in the Developing World*, Nick Devas and Carole Rakodi, eds. (Longman Group, Essex, U.K., and John Wiley & Sons, New York, 1993), p. 122.

119. Stephen Olsen, Director, Coastal Resources Management Center, University of Rhode Island, Narragansett, Rhode Island, March 1995 (personal communication).

120. Janis D. Bernstein, "Land Use Considerations in Urban Environmental Management," Urban Management Programme Discussion Paper No. 12 (The World Bank, Washington, D.C., 1994), p. 67.

121. *Ibid.*

122. Carole Rakodi and Nick Devas, "Conclusions: Assessing the New Approaches," in *Managing Fast Growing Cities: New Approaches to Urban Planning and Management in the Developing World*, Nick Devas

and Carole Rakodi, eds. (Longman Group, Essex, U.K., and John Wiley & Sons, Inc., New York, 1993), p. 277.

123. Donald T. Iannone, "Redeveloping Urban Brownfields," *Landlines,* Vol. 7, No. 6 (Lincoln Institute of Land Policy, Cambridge, Massachusetts, November 1995), p. 1.

124. United Kingdom (U.K.) Department of the Environment, *City Challenge: Partnerships Regenerating England's Urban Areas* (U.K. Department of the Environment, London, 1994), pp. 1–32.

125. Kyung-Hwan Kim, "Controlled Development and Densification: Seoul, Korea," in *The Human Face of the Urban Environment, Proceedings of the Second Annual World Bank Conference on Environmentally Sustainable Development,* Ismail Serageldin, Michael Cohen, and K.C. Sivaramakrishnan, eds. (The World Bank, Washington, D.C., September 19–21, 1994), p. 248.

126. Jim Sayer, "Green Edges for Healthy Cities," *The Urban Ecologist: The Journal of Urban Ecology* (Spring 1994), p. 4.

127. Virginia Jimenez Diaz, "Landslides in the Squatter Settlements of Caracas: Towards a Better Understanding of Causative Factors," *Environment and Urbanization,* Vol. 4, No. 2 (October 1992), p. 84.

128. *Op. cit.* 120, p. 73.

129. *Op. cit.* 100, pp. 78–79.

130. *Op. cit.* 100, pp. 78–79.

131. Michael Replogle, "Best Practices in Transportation Modeling for Air Quality Planning," paper prepared for the Environmental Defense Fund (Environmental Defense Fund, Washington, D.C., December 1991), p. 12.

132. United Nations Development Programme (UNDP), *Human Development Report 1994* (UNDP, New York, 1994), p. 173.

133. *Op. cit.* 105.

134. William P. Anderson, Pavlos S. Kanaroglou, and Eric J. Miller, "Urban Form, Energy, and the Environment: A Review of Issues, Evidence, and Policy," *Urban Studies,* Vol. 33, No. 1 (1996), forthcoming.

135. Mark Roseland, *Toward Sustainable Communities: A Resource Book for Municipal and Local Governments* (National Round Table on the Environment and the Economy, Ottawa, Canada, 1992), pp. 38–39.

136. For a literature review of comparisons of urban form and energy use, see William P. Anderson, Pavlos S. Kanaroglou, and Eric J. Miller, "Urban Form, Energy, and the Environment: A Review of Issues, Evidence, and Policy," *Urban Studies,* Vol. 33, No. 1 (1996), forthcoming.

137. *Op. cit.* 108, p. 88.

138. Tommy Firman and Ida Ayu Indira Dharmapatni, "The Challenges to Sustainable Development in Jakarta Metropolitan Region," *Habitat International,* Vol. 18, No. 3 (1994), p. 83.

139. Jonas Rabinovitch and Josef Leitmann, "Environmental Innovation and Management in Curitiba, Brazil," Urban Management Program Working Paper Series No. 1 (The World Bank, Washington, D.C., June 1993), p. 2.

140. Organisation for Economic Co-Operation and Development (OECD) and European Conference of Ministers of Transport (ECMT), *Urban Travel and Sustainable Development* (OECD and ECMT, Paris, 1995), p. 88.

141. Organisation for Economic Co-Operation and Development (OECD), *Environmental Policies for Cities in the 1990s* (OECD, Paris, 1990), p. 31.

142. *Op. cit.* 134.

143. Ellen Brennan, "Mega-City Management and Innovation Strategies: Regional Views," in *Mega-City Growth and the Future,* Roland J. Fuchs *et al.,* eds. (United Nations University Press, Tokyo, 1994), p. 238.

144. *Op. cit.* 106, pp. 36–37.

145. Ronald L. Doering *et al., Planning for Sustainability: Towards Integrating Environmental Protection into Land-Use Planning* (Royal Commission of the Future of the Toronto Waterfront, Toronto, 1991), pp. 67–68.

6. City and Community: Toward Environmental Sustainability

anaging environmental resources during this era of global urbanization is one of the greatest challenges facing the world's cities. With the fastest urban growth occurring in the cities of the developing world, the impact of urban and industrial growth on the environment is no longer limited to a handful of rich countries. It is rapidly becoming a problem shared around the world. In addition, the growing problem of urban poverty is a serious confounding factor in the effort to manage the urban environment and provide essential urban services.

The previous chapter outlines a range of policy options for tackling many of the direct environmental threats facing the world's cities. None of these policies will work, however, if there are insufficient administrative legal resources, or insufficient political will and public support to implement these policies effectively (1). Meeting this urban challenge will require the concerted actions of everyone with a stake in the world's cities—governments at all levels, nongovernmental organizations (NGOs), private enterprises, communities, and citizens.

First among these actors must be government. A powerful argument remains for a strong government role in environmental management (2). Governments are needed to plan for growth, to regulate polluting activities, to harmonize competing uses of the urban environment, and to address questions of equity that purely market-oriented approaches miss.

In efforts to improve the urban environment, local governments are especially critical. Local governments are responsible for most aspects of environmental management at the city level, from the provision of urban infrastructure and land use planning to local economic development and pollution control. To properly fill this role, local governments must develop their capabilities far beyond their current levels. In both the developing and the developed world, local governments are under severe stress from rapid urban change—either population growth or decline—fiscal pressures, growing demand for services, and increasing pollution. They often have neither the mandate nor the money or resources to cope with their mounting problems. This is especially true in the developing world, where urban growth is most rapid and governments tend to be underfunded and institutionally weak.

Equally important is the need to build on the efforts of low-income communities to improve their own environments. Community mobilization is by no means a substitute for government intervention; government action is essential in tackling the interconnected problems of poverty and environmental degradation. But the potential for communities to help themselves can be a major force for change. Indeed, over the past three decades, most urban "success" stories have involved projects that have incorporated community action, from the Orangi Pilot Project in Karachi, Pakistan, to the Zabbaleen in Cairo, Egypt.

Table 6.1 Structure of Political Accountability in Major Cities in Developing Countries

City	Mayor	Council
Bombay, India	Directly elected	Temporarily dissolved
Jakarta, Indonesia	Appointed by government	Directly elected, no legislative power
Mexico City (federal district), Mexico	Appointed by government	Directly elected, no legislative power
Sao Paulo, Brazil	Directly elected	Directly elected at large, legislative power
Seoul, Republic of Korea	Appointed by government	Directly elected, no legislative power
Lagos, Nigeria	Directly elected	Elected
Shanghai, China	Elected by council	Elected

Source: The World Bank, *Better Urban Services: Finding the Right Incentives* (The World Bank, Washington, D.C., 1995), p. 39.

As described in the previous chapters, some of the most severe environmental degradation is occurring in cities of the developing world, with the poorest citizens being the most severely affected. This is where the most concerted action for urban environmental improvement is needed. For that reason, this chapter focuses primarily on the developing world, examining the challenges facing local governments and strategies for enhancing their capacity as managers of the urban environment. It then looks at strategies for empowering and encouraging low-income communities and giving them access to the resources they need to improve their own lives. Community mobilization is by no means limited to cities in developing countries, however. This chapter also describes related initiatives in developed country cities such as New York City and Chattanooga, Tennessee. Finally, it concludes by examining the vital role that cities must play in achieving the goals of sustainable development.

STRENGTHENING LOCAL GOVERNMENTS IN DEVELOPING COUNTRIES

Local governments play a central role in managing the urban environment. They usually bear primary responsibility for urban infrastructure and land use planning and are often directly involved in the provision of basic water, sanitation, and garbage disposal services.

Given the difficulty and variety of these many functions, strong institutional capacity—including adequate funding, efficient organization, clear lines of authority, and qualified personnel—is necessary if local governments are to be effective environmental managers. Unfortunately, such capacity is too often lacking. In many developing countries, local governments cannot provide basic urban services, let alone regulate and enforce environmental legislation [3]. In Europe and North America, when air pollution became severe, the legal, regulatory, and financial structures to implement environmental management already existed. The basic in-

frastructure was already in place. In contrast, many cities in developing countries are facing new pollution threats with weak institutional structures, inadequate capital budgets, backlogs in providing basic infrastructure, and economies far less able to generate the needed capital [4].

Part of the problem is that, until recently, most governments in developing countries were centralized, often authoritarian, regimes [5]. In the late 1960s and 1970s, many central governments established national housing authorities, urban development corporations, and national land use planning authorities to control urban development as newly independent regimes sought to consolidate their power [6]. These institutions were believed to be better equipped to handle urban development and infrastructure investment because of their much wider powers and greater financial resources compared with those of existing local authorities.

However, as the numbers of these institutions grew, confusion over levels of authority, overlapping responsibilities, and vested political interests grew in parallel. Metropolitan authorities would construct large, expensive infrastructure and then transfer the management responsibilities to local authorities, who had neither the financial nor the technical resources to operate or maintain it. In addition, metropolitan institutions, accountable to the central government, lacked adequate avenues for public participation [7].

As a result of these and other factors, by the late 1980s, a distinct trend toward decentralization emerged, with a majority of central governments transferring some degree of political power back to local units of government [8]. Yet, the scale and extent of this decentralization have varied enormously. In many Latin American countries, for instance, decentralization has meant a shift from a centrally appointed mayor to one directly elected by the public [9]. In some countries in Africa, by contrast, decentralization appears to have occurred only in name. The central government continues to appoint municipal officials and control local spending decisions [10] [11]. In short, decentralization has not always resulted in a real devolution of power to local municipalities, nor has it necessarily increased the electoral accountability or fiscal autonomy of local authorities (12). (See Table 6.1.)

The reluctance of central governments to delegate full financial resources and functional responsibilities to municipalities is understandable in political terms (13). Furthermore, there is no guarantee that local governments will perform any better than central governments. Good local leadership goes far beyond financial resources and technical skills (14). For example, strong political will is needed to impose a new property tax, and all too often, municipal leaders find it easier to ignore the needs of the city's poor than to raise the taxes of the city's wealthier constituents (15). Despite these difficulties, a number of local authorities have already begun to address urban environmental problems. (See Box 6.1.)

In other cities, however, there remains a distinct need to build a foundation for urban planning and governance at the local level (16). Doing so will require enhancing local revenue resources for planning and management and rapidly building the technical and professional competences of local government personnel (17). In this era of increasing responsibilities, it will also require forming partnerships with other actors, including other cities and the private sector.

Generating Revenue

Although local governments in developing countries often have levels of responsibility for services and infrastructure comparable to those of local governments in developed countries, their revenue bases are generally much smaller—about one hundredth or less, according to one estimate (18). Indeed, in some of the poorer developing nations, local governments must function on annual budgets equivalent to only a few U.S. dollars per capita, which severely restricts their ability to fund services or expand infrastructure (19).

Low revenue bases result from many factors, not the least of which is the failure of central governments to transfer to local governments financial resources along with management responsibilities. In most developing countries, local capacities for revenue generation are rudimentary and dependence on central governments

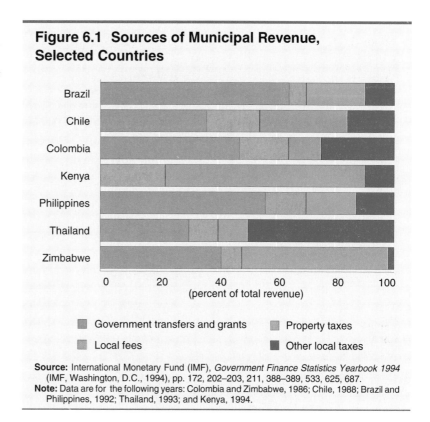

Figure 6.1 Sources of Municipal Revenue, Selected Countries

Source: International Monetary Fund (IMF), *Government Finance Statistics Yearbook 1994* (IMF, Washington, D.C., 1994), pp. 172, 202–203, 211, 388–389, 533, 625, 687.
Note: Data are for the following years: Colombia and Zimbabwe, 1986; Chile, 1988; Brazil and Philippines, 1992; Thailand, 1993; and Kenya, 1994.

for financial assistance is high (20). (See Figure 6.1.) Studies show that an average of 90 percent of public revenues is collected and spent by national governments in developing countries, compared with about 65 percent in high-income countries (21).

Attention to urban finance is crucial if cities are to adequately discharge their duties as urban environmental managers. Strategies to increase urban financial resources begin with basic reform, allowing municipalities to initiate, determine the rate of, and better administer taxes—be they property taxes, special taxes such as business taxes or motor vehicle registration taxes, local surcharges on national taxes, or user fees and service charges for government-funded programs (22).

One critical area of reform is improving property tax collection. Although property taxes are a common form of local taxation, in many cities they generate little revenue compared with other local taxes such as automobile or income taxes (23). Difficulties in assessing property values, keeping assessments current, and enforcing compliance have made tax administration a burden on municipalities. Also, exemptions to such taxes made for political reasons or to attract development can erode the tax base or distribute the tax burden inequitably. Moreover, tax rates and exemption policies are often set by the central government, so changes in these

A CONTRIBUTION BY THE EARTH COUNCIL

Box 6.1 Cities Take Action: Local Environmental Initiatives

Action at the local level is essential if the host of urban environmental challenges are to be met and cities are to become more livable and sustainable in the long term. Realizing this, many cities have begun local environmental initiatives or embarked on ambitious planning processes to guide their future development. The best of these efforts are consultative in their design and action, involving input from residents, civic organizations, nongovernmental organizations (NGOs), businesses, and labor unions. A few of these initiatives are profiled below (1).

Local voices. In Cajamarca, Peru, decentralized governments have given community members a voice in urban environmental planning.

Courtesy of ICLEI

DEVELOPING A LOCAL AGENDA 21

Agenda 21, the plan of action developed in Rio de Janeiro, Brazil, at the United Nations Conference on Environment and Development (UNCED), recognizes the importance of local authorities in planning for sustainable development. Local authorities often oversee planning, maintain infrastructure, establish environmental regulations, assist in implementing national policies, and are pivotal in rallying the public to support environmental objectives.

Agenda 21 challenges each local authority to work with its citizens, local organizations, and private enterprises in adopting a "Local Agenda 21." Through consultation and consensus building, local authorities are encouraged to formulate strategies that reflect the environ-mental goals of the community.

Since 1992, approximately 1,200 local authorities in 33 countries have established Local Agenda 21 campaigns.

The focus of these Local Agenda 21 campaigns is on the process itself—mobilizing community resources and commitments, setting clear targets, maintaining accountability, and measuring concrete progress—rather than on the community environmental plan that results. Yet, these plans incorporate many of the elements necessary to reduce urban impacts on health and the environment, such as the provision of basic services, conservation of resources, and pollution prevention.

Cajamarca, Peru, is one of the many cities that has successfully developed a Local Agenda 21. Cajamarca ranks among the poorest communities in the world. In 1993, the infant mortality rate was 94.7 per 1,000 live births, 82 percent higher than the Peruvian national average and 30 percent higher than the average for low-income countries. The Kilish River, a source of drinking water for many of the region's poor, has been contaminated by mining operations and untreated sewage. Farming on the steep Andean hillsides, overgrazing, and the cutting of trees for fuel have resulted in severe soil erosion, exacerbating flooding problems and threatening the livelihoods of the area's rural population.

In 1993, the provincial municipality of Cajamarca, which governs the entire province, initiated an extensive Local Agenda 21 planning effort with two main components. First, Cajamarca City was divided into 12 neighborhood councils and the surrounding countryside was divided into 64 "minor populated centers" (MPCs), each with its own elected mayors and councils. This dramatic decentralization of government power meant that local government decisions would better reflect the needs of the province's many small and remote communities.

Second, a committee was established to develop a Provincial Sustainable Development Plan. It consisted of representatives from the province's different jurisdictions, NGOs, the private sector, and key constituency groups. The committee established six "theme boards" in the areas of education; natural resources and agriculture; production and employment; cultural heritage and tourism; urban environment; and women's issues, family, and population. After gathering local input from the various regions, each board developed a strategic plan for its particular area.

The initiatives proposed by these groups reflect the different concerns of the constituents. In the rural communities, the plan included initiatives for items such as terracing on steep hillsides, seed banks, and woodworking training centers. Water delivery systems were considered a top priority. Farmers' concerns about mining pollution resulted in plans for more rigorous environmental assessments and a new tax system.

The urban board, in contrast, drew up a strategy that included development of health services, a refuse collection program, and a park improvement program. The urban board is also considering the creation of an ecological belt and a land use plan that will guide the city's expansion.

In many cities, developing local indicators to measure progress is a key component of the Local Agenda 21 process. The region of Hamilton-Wentworth in Canada is at the forefront of these efforts. Local officials used an extensive public consultation process including focus groups, questionnaires, and community meetings to design indicators that are now being used to assess progress toward tangible goals.

TACKLING URBAN ENVIRONMENTAL PROBLEMS

Municipal authorities are also making great strides in improving urban environmental quality. Initiatives address a broad range of problems, from providing basic services such as water and sanitation in Quito, Ecuador, to conserving biodiversity in Durban, South Africa, to reducing car emissions in Quezon City, Philippines. These programs prove that huge sums of money and advanced technologies are not always necessary to make localized improvements.

In Graz, Austria, the challenge was to find a way to reduce pollution from small businesses (automobile and machine production, shoe manufacturing, brewing) without undermining their economic viability. In 1991, the city initiated a partnership with the Institute for Chemical Engineering at the Graz University of Technology to work with a sample group of small businesses. The initial participants included three printing companies, a large vehicle repair shop, and a wholesale coffee roaster and chain store company.

After an initial training session, each company set up a project team to develop a cleaner production program. The Institute helped the companies to review new technologies and a variety of other waste management measures based on the major waste streams of each company. Identified measures were classified according to their economic payback. For example, the small print shops had 54 technically feasible management options for waste minimization and pollution prevention. Twenty-four percent would be profitable in 1 year, 30 percent would be profitable within 2 years, and 15 percent would be economically neutral.

As an additional economic incentive, companies that achieve a threshold reduction in wastes and emissions are awarded an "ECOPROFIT Label" that they can use for marketing purposes for 1 year. After 1 year, companies need to achieve further waste reduction to continue to display the label. The biggest incentive, however, is direct cost savings: production costs for participating companies have been reduced by as much as 60 percent.

Since the project's inception, approximately 40 firms have participated, and the volume of toxic and solid wastes generated by these companies has been reduced by more than 50 percent.

Many local governments are also realizing the role that cities play in regional and global environmental problems. Cities are banding together under the auspices of various associations to tackle problems such as regional water pollution (as in the Mediterranean). Partnerships among cities also transfer information and technology concerning approaches and solutions to common urban problems.

One of these partnerships is the CO_2 Reduction Program coordinated by the

International Council for Local Environmental Initiatives (ICLEI). More than 100 local authorities from 27 countries have joined an International Cities for Climate Protection Campaign. Participants pledge to meet and exceed the requirements of the Framework Convention on Climate Change by reducing carbon dioxide emissions by up to 20 percent by 2005. As part of this initiative, ICLEI worked with 14 cities to develop comprehensive local action plans to reduce carbon dioxide emissions.

LESSONS LEARNED

These examples represent only a fraction of the various efforts of local authorities. However, they illustrate several key points. First, despite the seemingly overwhelming challenges, local governments are not stagnant. Many are making great strides in addressing urban problems through partnerships with local businesses, NGOs, and even other cities. Second, a crucial component of successful urban planning consists of public participation and consensus building. Third, although most policy analyses assume a top-down approach in trying to introduce pollution regulations or carbon dioxide emission reductions, these problems can also be addressed from a decentralized, community-based perspective.

Finally, urban development failures of the past decades demonstrate that local governance cannot be replaced by international infrastructure programs, the relocation of central government agencies to secondary cities, the establishment of

Pollution control. In Quezon City, Philippines, impromptu road inspections help to control vehicle emissions.

parastatal service companies, private companies, or NGOs. Without strong local governments, policies will not reflect local priorities, programs will not be responsive to local conditions, budgets will not reflect local realities, the actions of different sectors will not be coordinated, and communities will lack the consistent voice they need in national and international policy processes.

—*Jeb Brugmann*

Jeb Brugmann is the Secretary General of the International Council of Local Environmental Initiatives, Toronto, Canada. This contribution was commissioned by the Earth Council, San Jose, Costa Rica.

References and Notes

1. Box is drawn from case studies published by the International Council for Local Environmental Initiatives, Toronto.

rates and policies—even to compensate for inflation or to correct inequities—can be difficult to achieve (24).

Maximizing the potential of property taxes for local revenue generation will require both changes in local tax structures and improved assessment and collection procedures. This will not be easy. The basic data on which property taxes are based are lacking in most cities. Disputes over land ownership, outdated city maps, and land transactions that occur outside formal market structures all complicate tax collection. Rapid urban growth on the peripheries of these cities exacerbates the difficulties because new settlements must be constantly incorporated into city records if the tax base is to reflect the physical growth of the city (25).

In the area of improving compliance, some relatively simple measures can result in significant tax revenue increases. Delhi, India, for example, increased its property tax collections by 96 percent in 1 year through a combination of measures, including providing discounts for early payments, centralizing collection points for tax payments, freezing bank accounts for defaulters, and requiring taxpayers to pay taxes before appeals against their assessments can be considered (26).

Another valuable source of revenue for city governments is the introduction of user fees for environmental services such as water and sewerage (27). Few local governments have either the institutional capability or the legal authorization to set and collect user fees (28) (29). In Bangkok, for example, the allowable charge for garbage collection is set by Thailand's central government, although it is the city that must provide these services. As a result, city officials can charge only US$5.95 per household for garbage collection, even though it costs them US$9.83 (30) (31). Even when local governments do have the authority to set user fees, these fees still typically fall far below the actual costs of providing services, as described in Chapter 5, "Urban Priorities for Action."

Attempts to increase the financial base of local governments must also include reforming the direct transfer of funds from central to local governments. These transfers, which occur through such mechanisms as grants, subsidies, and other payments, are currently one of the largest sources of local funds in the developing world. In many cases, however, they are subject to political manipulation, are not targeted well, are irregular in their timing, or do not take into account local circumstances or priorities (32) (33).

Building Professional Capacity

More revenue does not in itself guarantee a more effective local government (34). In addition to adequate fund-

ing, effective urban environmental management requires personnel with appropriate managerial, technical, and financial skills. Key skills span a wide range: the drafting of legislation and regulations, environmental monitoring and enforcement, and cost accounting, to name just a few (35).

In many developing countries, there is a severe shortage of trained personnel. Lack of training, low wages, and limited career opportunities present serious obstacles to attracting and keeping effective urban managers (36). In Indonesia, a recent study found that the average length of training related to urban management and finance among more than 700,000 local officials averaged only about 2 hours per year. Accordingly, the Indonesian government plans to establish regional centers for local personnel training (37).

Building the capacities of environmental professionals in local government will require a greater commitment to training and technical assistance programs at a variety of levels (38). National governments can play a part in enhancing local professional capacity both by providing grant money to support local training efforts and by establishing national technical assistance programs specifically directed at municipal employees. In Brazil, a team of trained officials from the central government was sent on a temporary basis to local government offices to advise municipal urban managers and help them upgrade the analytic and technical capabilities of their staffs. Eventually, it evolved into a permanent extension service known as the Brazilian Institute of Municipal Administration (39). In Malaysia, regional centers that offer course work in local planning, budgeting, and other skills have been established for local government professionals (40).

Partnerships with Other Actors

Whereas governments have historically provided the bulk of urban services themselves, the scope of problems facing today's cities are too large and city coffers are too small for local governments to handle them alone. Instead, local governments will need to capitalize on the resources available to them, be they private companies providing capital and jobs, NGOs providing information and grassroots mobilization, or communities themselves.

In recent years, there has been a trend toward the privatization of public services (41). Awarding contracts for environmental services to private companies offers potential cost savings. Where competition and adequate accountability to municipal managers exist, privatization may net substantial savings without degrading the quality of service. This has been the case with garbage disposal service in Buenos Aires, Argentina, where private firms under municipal contract are able to offer high-quality collection services more efficiently than the city itself can (42). For such partnerships to be effective, however, cities must execute appropriate oversight (43).

Partnerships between industry and government can also be productive. Such partnerships can stimulate development of cleaner manufacturing processes and energy technologies for local use or can encourage the adaptation of off-the-shelf technologies to local circumstances (44).

Some of the most valuable relationships that governments can cultivate are with NGOs and community groups. These organizations can determine the special circumstances and needs of neighborhoods, plan appropriate projects to address those needs, mobilize funding, and generally bridge the gap between government and the affected community. Partnerships do not just happen, however. To foster them, city governments must actively promote the involvement of outside groups in environmental planning and decisionmaking.

Taking Charge

In many cities and towns in the developing world, municipal governments are already involved in urban improvements, establishing participatory planning processes and marshaling their political and economic clout to strengthen local authority over environmental management. In 1992, citizen protests about the basin's deteriorating air quality prompted Mexico City officials to create the Metropolitan Commission for the Protection of Air Quality (45). The local government has played an active role in urban air quality control, removing polluting industrial facilities from the city, restricting private automobile use, developing and bringing cleaner vehicle fuels to the market, planting trees, and investing heavily in public transit infrastructure (46). To pay for these initiatives, the municipality has established its own direct and flexible financing arrangements with foreign banks and governments.

In 1994, the city of Quito, Ecuador, took a similar course and achieved the passage of national legislation to establish the Metropolitan District of Quito. This legislation provided the municipality with control over all aspects of environmental policy, land use regulation, transportation planning, and organizational design of the municipal government. Having established a local government with sufficient power to plan its own future, the mayor then proceeded to decentralize the municipal administration into three geographic zones. Each zone has its own local office responsible for formulating new service delivery strategies for its area. One

of the primary objectives of decentralization was to put the municipal government in closer touch with the community and to facilitate a higher level of citizen participation in planning urban services, especially with the barrio associations in the city's long-underserved south zone (47).

Other municipalities such as Porto Alegre and Santos, Brazil, have established democratic planning and budgeting procedures using the input of citizen councils, each representing a specific population group or urban service issue (48).

A COMMUNITY-LEVEL APPROACH TO ENVIRONMENTAL MANAGEMENT

Governments and others sometimes underestimate the ability of low-income communities to contribute to solving the environmental problems that plague them. For one, the magnitude of urban environmental problems—inadequate sewerage, flooding, air pollution, and ground subsidence—are often seen as being too vast for communities to address. Furthermore, communities, especially poor ones, are seen as lacking the organizational capacity or financial resources to either construct community infrastructure or manage environmental services such as water pumps or public toilets (49).

Evidence from successful community efforts counters these beliefs. Although it is true that many environmental problems such as air pollution and flooding require a citywide or even a regionwide approach, many individual projects carried out at the community level can contribute to a solution. Numerous examples have shown that under supportive conditions, neighborhoods and communities can manage lanes, waterways, and waste disposal systems. In community after community, households have joined together to improve drainage, construct roads and lanes for access, clear land of refuse, or create open spaces where children can play. (See Box 6.2.)

Poverty and the Urban Economy

If governments and other actors are to pursue more supportive policies and actions toward low-income communities, they must begin by adjusting their perceptions of poverty and its relation to the urban economy. First, these actors must abandon the notion that accelerating economic growth in the city will necessarily "cure" urban poverty or reverse environmental deterioration. In fact, although economic growth and structural change in the economy have raised general standards of living in many countries, there has been no

Box 6.2 The Orangi Pilot Project, Karachi, Pakistan

For well over a decade, a nongovernmental organization (NGO) called the Orangi Pilot Project (OPP) has demonstrated that, when community interest and resources are mobilized, low-income settlements can greatly improve their own access to environmental services, health care, and employment.

Located on the northwest periphery of Karachi, Orangi is the largest of the city's approximately 650 low-income settlements, known as *katchi abadi* (1). Orangi was first developed in 1963 as a government township of 500 hectares, but migrants flooded into the settlement after the 1971 war that led to the creation of Bangladesh, swelling the settlement to more than 3,200 hectares. The ethnically diverse population of laborers, skilled workers, shopkeepers, clerks, and white-collar workers now numbers about 800,000, living in 94,000 houses (2). The average family income is estimated to be 1,500 rupees per month (about US$59), but spans a range from under 500 rupees per month (US$18) to more than 25,000 rupees per month (US$980) (3) (4).

OPP's approach is based on the conviction that people organized in small groups can help themselves, and that if social and economic organizations within a community are strengthened, services and material conditions—such as sanitation, schools, clinics, and job training—will begin to improve, as will employment opportunities (5).

In Orangi, OPP organized residents into groups of 20 to 40 families living along the same lane, with the thought that these families will generally know and trust each other. This principle of small-scale organization, along with careful research on the needs and capabilities of the community and the use of appropriate technology, has governed OPP's community development strategy.

OPP started its work in Orangi in 1980 with a low-cost sanitation program and spent the next 4 years working with all segments of the community to build trust and confidence that OPP was going to be a permanent part of the community.

Once the sanitation program had gained momentum, OPP gradually developed other community efforts, including a basic health and family planning program, a credit program for small family enterprises, a low-cost housing upgrade program, a program to assist in upgrading physical and academic conditions at schools, a women's work center program, and a rural development program.

Each program was introduced only after a thorough analysis of community needs and identification of the most important community actors. Each program has periodically been reevaluated and modified to respond to changes within the community. Three of these programs are profiled here.

LOW-COST SANITATION

Until 1981, Orangi had only primitive forms of sewage disposal and drainage. Convinced that it was possible for low-income people to install their own sanitation systems at an affordable cost, OPP began to use the organizational capabilities of the local leadership in each lane to adapt and implement simple sanitation technologies.

The greatest initial obstacle was the Orangi residents' expectation that the government would supply a sewer system without charge. Only when all efforts to petition the government for services had been exhausted was OPP able to work with the community to develop alternative solutions.

Although poor, Orangi residents were motivated to pay for improvements to sewage systems because their houses represented a significant investment. Health concerns were another major motivator; mothers in particular saw a clear connection between unsanitary conditions and disease. Homeowners were willing to assume responsibility for constructing and maintaining in-house latrines, sewer lines in the lanes, and secondary or collector drains, performing between 80 and 90 percent of the work needed to build the system. The Karachi government would then be responsible for the provision of the main drains and treatment plants (6).

OPP personnel prepared models and other visual aids to demonstrate how the sewer system would be laid out. They drew up instruction sheets and posters for each lane to ensure that decentralized construction planning nonetheless resulted in a coherent and workable system. Each lane selected its own lane manager, who formally applied to OPP for assistance, collected money, received tools, and organized the work (7).

OPP was able to drastically reduce the cost of construction by simplifying designs and standardizing parts. The cost of a sanitary latrine inside the house and the underground sewerage line in the lane was 1,000 rupees (US$90) per household—about one fifth the cost of similar improvements built by the city government (8) (9).

Each lane depended on its own small septic tank until the system reached the critical mass required to install secondary drains. Although this represented a gamble on the future expansion of the system and was discouraged by international development experts, OPP believed that only such a decentralized approach would empower residents to build their own sewage infrastructure. When the system successfully reached the scale required to integrate the lane systems into an overall community system, the lane septic tanks were covered over and did not become the sanitation "time bombs" predicted by outside experts.

Waste from the Orangi sewers runs into open waterways that flow to the sea. These waterways are overburdened by waste from Orangi and from Karachi in general and still tend to overflow during heavy rains. The main sewers required to prevent this flooding are the responsibility of the Karachi authorities. OPP has developed designs for main sewers and is lobbying the Karachi Municipal Corporation to build them.

Under OPP guidance, between 1981 and 1993 Orangi residents installed sewers serving 72,070 of 94,122 houses (10). To achieve this, community members spent more than US$2 million of their own money, and OPP invested about US$150,000 in research and extension of new technologies (11).

HEALTH AND FAMILY PLANNING FOR LOW-INCOME WOMEN

Research conducted by OPP showed that Orangi residents suffered high incidences of typhoid, malaria, dysentery, diarrhea, and scabies, as well as high rates of infant and maternal mortality. Surveys revealed that Orangi residents spent a substantial portion of their income on curative health care, but paid little attention to preventive measures. Therefore, in 1984, OPP began a pilot program to provide health education and family planning information to poor women.

Realizing that conventional clinics were ineffective because traditional gender segregation made it difficult to reach women through such a public facility, OPP introduced mobile health training teams, consisting of female doctors, health educators, and social organizers. These teams contacted groups of women through selected activist families in their neighborhoods, providing a more discreet and effective source of health education.

OPP also developed a system in which the neighborhood health activist delivered medical and birth control supplies. An intimate neighbor, the health activist was a permanent and confidential source of supply for the members of her group. The health activist also arranged for women to receive intrauterine devices or tubal ligations from the mobile health team.

Originally, these health and family planning services were targeted to 3,000 low-income families in Orangi. A survey of the targeted families demonstrates the effectiveness of the program: more than 95 percent of the children are immunized, 44 percent of the families practice birth control, epidemic diseases are controlled, and hygiene and nutrition have improved (12). Infant mortality fell from 130 per 1,000 live births in 1982 to 37 in 1991 (13). In 1991, OPP revised its model to reach out to a larger number of families. OPP introduced a 3-month health curriculum that covered the prevention of diseases common in Orangi, methods of family planning, and improved nutrition and hygiene.

PROGRAM FOR WOMEN'S EMPLOYMENT

OPP initiated its program to develop Women's Work Centers (WWCs) in 1984, beginning with a survey of employment patterns in Orangi. The survey revealed that the rising costs of living forced wives and daughters in Orangi to work to supplement family income (14).

In its program, OPP chose to address the largest category of women's employment, which is stitching clothing for contractors in Karachi. Women stitchers in Orangi complete piecework bound for export to international markets. The system of contracting for this piecework was exploitative both financially and socially. Male contractors paid women substandard wages, often mistreating and sexually harassing them.

Eliminating the contractor, OPP set up WWCs that deal directly with suppliers and customers. The WWCs, located in family homes in the neighborhood, were lent machinery and supplies by OPP and were assisted in contacting clients. The families running WWCs were allowed to charge only minimal overhead and were required to earn most of their income through their own piecework. Reduced costs enabled the WWCs to pay a fair wage to the workers. The WWC daily wage was 20 rupees (US$0.80), compared with the standard daily wage of 15 rupees (US$0.60). WWC managers tended to be women and to treat the women workers fairly, since they were also neighbors and friends.

Initially, the WWCs required substantial financial and managerial support from OPP. Over time, however, WWC managers learned to weed out untrustworthy suppliers and customers, to motivate their workers, and to increase quality control. WWCs, operating as supportive community organizations rather than exploitative contractors, have proven more efficient and reliable than traditional contractors. Clients in Karachi actually prefer to use WWCs because of their greater productivity, and individual workers prefer to work for WWCs because of their higher wages.

By the sixth year of the program, the WWCs had become self-sustaining. OPP continues to provide loans for the creation of new WWCs, but these are paid back with interest (15).

AN ONGOING ROLE

OPP's approach to community development offers a model of how communities can assume responsibility for services formerly considered the responsibility of government. In none of these programs did OPP see its role as the provider of a

particular service. Rather, the community provided the service to itself, with appropriate assistance from OPP.

This approach to community development demonstrates the flexibility required for successful NGO intervention in low-income urban settlements. OPP worked methodically and sequentially, developing its organizational and technical capabilities in each particular problem area before moving on to address another. As a result, each OPP project can stand on its own. Taken together, however, these projects demonstrate the effective long-term role that an NGO can play by working in a single community on an ongoing basis.

—*Akhtar Badshah*

Akhtar Badshah is Director of Programs for the Mega-Cities Project in New York.

References and Notes

1. Arif Hasan, *Sealing-Up of the OPP's Low-Cost Sanitation Program* (Orangi Pilot Project—Research Training Institute, Karachi, Pakistan, 1993), p. 1.

2. Arif Hasan, "Replicating the Low-Cost Sanitation Programme Administered by the Orangi Pilot Project in Karachi, Pakistan," in *The Human Face of the Urban Environment, Proceedings of the Second Annual World Bank Conference on Environmentally Sustainable Development,* Ismail Serageldin, Michael A. Cohen, and K.C. Sivaramakrishnan, eds. (The World Bank, Washington, D.C., September 19–21, 1994), p. 152.

3. The exchange rate in 1995 was US$1 = Rs. 25.45.

4. Akhter Hameed Khan, *Orangi Pilot Project Programs* (Orangi Pilot Project–Research Training Institute, Karachi, Pakistan, 1994), p. 3.

5. *Op. cit.* 2, p. 150.

6. *Op. cit.* 4, p. 7.

7. "Orangi Pilot Project," *Environment and Urbanization,* Vol. 7, No. 2 (October 1995), p. 229.

8. *Ibid.,* p. 228.

9. *Op. cit.* 2, p. 151.

10. *Op. cit.* 2, p. 151.

11. *Op. cit.* 2, p. 151.

12. *Op. cit.* 4, p. 24.

13. *Op. cit.* 2, p. 151.

14. *Op. cit.* 7, p. 233.

15. *Op. cit.* 7, p. 233.

Courtesy of Cooperative Housing Foundation

Community action. *In Honduras, community members play an active role in building shelters and latrines. By using local construction materials and relying on labor from the community, environmental improvements can be made at a much smaller cost than public provision of these services.*

instance of poverty taking care of itself in any city via economic growth or market forces alone (50) (51).

Not only is poverty a persistent feature of societies at all levels of per capita income, but accelerated economic growth brings its own forms of environmental crises, social dislocation and alienation, and heightened social and economic inequities that the market has not displayed any capacity to resolve (52) (53). (See Chapter 2, "Urban Environment and Human Health.") Thus, environmental improvements for poor neighborhoods cannot simply wait for better economic times but must be an integral part of the strategy for economic development within the city (54).

Especially in the developing world, governments must also accept that environmental factors are closely interwoven with crucial economic factors such as employment. This is particularly true in poor neighbor-

hoods, where a substantial share of income is generated in the home and neighborhood itself. One of the most consistent findings about urban squatter settlements is that the strongest motivation for continuing to live in them, despite the environmental degradation, is access to the variety of economic activities found nearby (55).

In circumstances in which the community itself is the locus of substantial employment, an improved living environment can generate important new economic opportunities. For example, in many low-income settlements where environmental infrastructure such as pathways and covered drainage channels have been constructed, these improvements have led to a proliferation of commercial enterprises—food stalls, beauty salons, and general stores—where few existed before (56) (57).

An important corollary is the fact that improving the environment within low-income communities contributes directly to the health of the urban economy (58). Too often, the poor are assumed to contribute to an undifferentiated "informal sector" that is mistakenly presumed to have no linkages to the rest of the urban, national, or international economy. In reality, this informal sector is integrated into and contributes directly to the urban economy as a whole (59) (60). The informal sector supplies goods (recycled materials, tools, small machines) and services (repairs, transport, sales) to the agricultural, livestock, fishing, and forestry sectors as well as to other businesses within the city (61) (62).

Such interconnections underscore the critical need to address community problems in an integrated fashion that deals with both income generation and environmental management.

Elements of Success in Community Management

Several lessons have emerged from studies of how poor urban households and their communities cope with environmental problems. Taken together, these can be a basis for rethinking how governments, NGOs, and the international development community can best augment rather than undermine grassroots environmental management efforts.

Integrating Environment and Livelihood at the Household Level

Often, through no choice of their own, low-income households are *de facto* managers of the local environment (63). Many of their daily activities revolve around using and managing natural resources such as water and fuelwood. The ability of poor households to manage these resources and reduce their exposure to environmental degradation (either by boiling water or by removing garbage from their communities) is largely determined by how much effort they must expend on other necessities, such as earning sufficient income or securing access to health care and education.

The size and composition of a household are critical to its ability to manage the environment. The poorest of poor households are those with only one adult or parent who cannot perform the many tasks needed to sustain basic levels of existence (64). When a large share of effort and time is spent on basic survival, it is less likely that significant attention will be given to environmental management. Poor women in the *barrios* of Latin America, for example, spend up to 80 to 90 hours per week earning cash and buying or otherwise obtaining essentials such as water, food, clothing, and transportation (65). Expecting them to manage a community sewage system is unrealistic.

Households do not live in isolation, however. Where community-oriented sentiment is strong, a poorer household often looks to neighbors, friends, and relatives in the community for help. Studies also show that households negotiate issues such as responsibility for cleaning neighborhood streets or securing fuel, as well as how resources within a community will be distributed.

These findings suggest two strategies for improving environmental conditions. First, it is possible to build on community networks as a means of mobilizing labor (as in the Orangi Pilot Project), as a way to reduce costs of basic goods (as in Cali, Colombia), or as a mechanism to improve the efficiency of service delivery. In Buenos Aires, for example, the government has been building on community networks to improve its distribution of food aid through its Programa Alimentario Integral y Solidario (PAIS) plan. Under the PAIS plan, begun in 1989, groups of 20 to 100 residents form multifamily kitchens; these kitchens then receive a subsidy from the government to purchase food themselves (66). This form of distribution proved to have several advantages over the previous system, which distributed boxes of food to individual households. By forming a pool, the families in the kitchen are able to buy food in bulk at reduced prices. More importantly, the families are able to decide for themselves how to spend the subsidy. By 1994, 6,700 multifamily kitchens were operating in Buenos Aires (67).

Second, one of the best avenues for improving household environmental management lies in combining it with income-generating activities. This can be done through activities based directly on environmental management, such as recycling, or indirectly, through programs that create community-based enterprises that enable household members simultaneously to earn incomes and to obtain essentials, such as clean water, food, construction materials, and health care (68) (69).

The experience of the Zabbaleen in Cairo illustrates the potential of this approach. An ethnic group living in several large settlements, the Zabbaleen have long earned their incomes through wastepicking. This informal means of waste collection provides a substantial benefit to the local government by reducing the amount of solid waste that needs to be officially collected. Yet, the health and productivity of the Zabbaleen are threatened by the environmental conditions in which they live and work. In the early 1980s, for instance, most settlements had no water supply, sewerage, or electricity. Residents made a living by sorting garbage, often within their homes, greatly increasing the risk of illness from disease vectors as well as injuries from broken glass and metal.

Starting in the 1980s, several international and local groups began working with the Zabbaleen, establishing programs to improve environmental conditions in the settlement and to facilitate the collection and recycling of garbage. A small industries project, for example, gave loans to families to buy machines that can convert garbage such as rags and plastics into useful secondary materials. This not only has reduced direct contact with the garbage, but also has increased income because the materials fetch a much higher price than the rags would. The construction of local compost plants has given residents the ability to recycle organic wastes as well, creating new employment opportunities and reducing the amount of garbage left on the streets (70).

In Mexico City, the squatters of El Molino have also combined environmental management and income-earning opportunities. Household wastewater, garbage, and sewage are conducted by above-ground rubber tubing into a "sirdo," an alternative system for recycling organic wastes. The sirdo dries and filters wastes, producing water clean enough for aquaculture and community gardens and fertilizer that is sold for profit (71).

Household Stability and Community Membership

Essential services such as water supply, sanitation, and garbage collection in low-income settlements are not readily provided by individual action. Nor do increases in individual family income necessarily lead to improvements in neighborhood living conditions. Instead, these are neighborhood and community issues requiring collective action (72). However, if people do not feel a sense of security in their households or that they are members of a community, they are not likely to devote their energies to improving environmental conditions.

Courtesy of Diana Page

Competing roles. *Many poor women work within the home or neighborhood, where they juggle competing demands of jobs, childcare, and household management.*

to improve the quality of their own housing (76) (77). (See Box 6.3.)

The Role of Women in Environmental Management

In low-income communities, women are invariably the principal managers of local environmental resources. They are responsible for keeping the house and the neighborhood clean, disposing of household garbage, and obtaining fuel and water, among other things. Women also play a critical, if largely unrecognized, role in community planning and management. They seek to ensure the provision and maintenance of such basic collective services as water, health care, and education. Women also come together to confront and solve common problems such as inadequate housing or infrastructure (78) (79).

First and foremost, security comes from land and housing tenure. In many squatter settlements, however, the status of residency is uncertain. Official policies often declare these settlements illegal, which means that residents are subject to eviction without warning (73). On the other hand, at least in selected areas, governments have given implicit recognition to such communities by providing them with basic services, limited infrastructure, and even quasi-government officials (74) (75).

Even though land or housing tenure affords a sense of stability in a community, it is the perception of being able to stay on the land rather than having the legal right to occupy the land that often matters the most. This perception can arise from other indications of continuity, such as the length of time that the community has existed, the extent of government investment in community infrastructure and services, or whether previous efforts to avoid eviction have been successful.

Although perceptions of stability appear to be more important than the legality of land occupation, this should not be taken to mean that land security issues can be ignored. To the contrary, one of the most critical needs in cities is a coherent land titling process for the poor and low-income communities. The long-term stability of low-income communities depends on the ability of households to gain clear title to land for housing. (See Chapter 5, "Urban Priorities for Action.")

When given security of tenure and clearer legal bases for property ownership, the poor will build and invest

Yet, in many instances, women are given little voice in decisionmaking (80). Local authorities and planners rarely consult with women or work with them as equal partners. The consequences of not including women in community decisionmaking range from inappropriate infrastructure designs to poorly coordinated services. There are innumerable examples of projects to install toilets, water pumps, and wash basins in which no attempt was made to consult women or understand what would be culturally acceptable or practical for them. In the Yucatan, Mexico, squat-plate latrines built on the recommendations of engineers were rejected by women who preferred pour-flush latrines, even though this necessitated carrying water (81).

Consequently, involving women in community projects has two very real benefits. First, tapping into women's knowledge can greatly improve the likelihood of a program's success. Second, improving the urban environment can translate into direct benefits to women's health and thus to the overall sustenance of the household. Where women have been given access to credit, a voice in decisionmaking, and educational and employment opportunities, substantial improvements in living conditions have been documented.

In Nairobi, Kenya, for example, female-headed households in the Kayole/Soweto slums east of the city have made tremendous progress in improving their living conditions. Since 1988, the Muungano Women's Group (comprising women living in Soweto) has been working with the African Housing Board to improve the economic status of its members as well as the health and education of children in the slum. The Muungano Group currently has more than 1,000 members who pay about US$2—roughly a full day's salary—to join the group (82).

Loans from the African Housing Board have allowed the women to establish a factory that produces building materials that can be used for members' homes or sold on the open market. A carpentry workshop makes doors and windows for homes as well as for the day-care center and provides 10 permanent jobs for Muungano women. A revolving fund has also been created for continued construction of new houses and improvement of older dwellings (83).

In addition, a self-help health initiative has begun to show some results. By 1993, some 670 families had been trained by community health trainees who are funded by the African Housing Board. Those families that receive the training in turn have the responsibility of working with five other families. Learning about the link between malaria and standing water, for instance, has enabled some families to take measures to protect themselves (84).

In many cities, women are also forming their own professional or organizational networks to help improve conditions for the urban poor. In 1990, an NGO based in Kathmandu, Nepal, and composed of professional women, known as Women in Environment, began an environmental awareness campaign in Balaju, a squatter settlement on the west bank of Nepal's Bishnumati River. At the time, some 70 families lived in the settlement amid piles of solid waste and untreated sewage. By providing simple materials such as buckets (for waste collection) and water standpipes, the NGO helped to improve environmental conditions in the neighborhood (85).

Involving women does not mean that the whole burden of community management should be placed on them. Governments, planners, and even NGOs often make unrealistic assumptions about how much energy, time, and money women can spend in communal or individual self-help programs to improve their environment. Case studies of communal housing projects from Harare, Zimbabwe, to Kingston, Jamaica, to Cordoba, Spain, demonstrate that women who are the sole income earners and childcare providers often do not have the time, skills, or money to invest substantially in community management (86) (87) (88).

Community Organization

Community-based efforts depend largely on the ability of different voices to come together toward a common goal. Most poor communities have some form of organized leadership resulting either from long-standing cultural and religious institutions or from families who have resided in the community for many years. A strong leader can serve as a focal point for discussion and decisionmaking, for mediation of conflicts among community members, and for pooling and reallocating resources within the community (89). A community leader can also serve as a go-between, linking the local community to the city at large. However, leaders can also be exclusive and elitist, without much community support. In such cases, successful community mobilization is unlikely.

Community mobilization often emerges from a sense of shared destiny—often, a sense of economic deprivation and limited alternatives. In San Miguel Teotongo, Mexico, for example, the local population originally rallied together in an effort to persuade the government to recognize the legality of the settlement, forming a community-based organization called Union de Vecinos de San Miguel Teotongo (UVST) in 1982. In 1992, the settlement was finally incorporated into Mexico City's formal master plan, an important step toward ensuring tenure and service provision (90). Although originally created to achieve tenure, UVST has since expanded into other community actions, such as improving water and sanitation services (91). Box 6.4 describes how a community in the United States mobilized around housing security as well.

In other situations, social stratification, ethnic or religious differences, or even political skepticism can hinder efforts to build community cohesion. Evidence suggests that communities that are unable to develop consensus or that have leadership without community support are the least likely to be able to manage their internal affairs, including their environmental resources (92). In these cases, NGOs can help mobilize residents or strengthen existing leadership functions and roles in the community. Local governments can also help foster organization by explicitly recognizing the rights of communities to organize.

Partnerships with NGOs

In many cities where local governments have failed to represent their constituencies or deliver basic needs, NGOs have come to play a critical role in community development (93). They have been principal sources in both mobilizing community resources and building coalitions to create linkages among communities and wider

Box 6.3 Housing Program for Cali's Poor Encourages Self-Help

During the time that I served as mayor of Cali, Colombia, from 1992 to 1994, I tried to design programs for the city's poor that supported people's basic desire to improve their living conditions. Many of these concepts grew out of my work as president of the Carvajal Foundation, a well-known philanthropic organization that has developed a number of programs to support small businesses and community initiatives in low-income settlements.

Cali, a city of 1.7 million inhabitants, is Colombia's second largest city; the city is known throughout Colombia for the civic-mindedness of its citizens and business community (1). Located in a rich agricultural valley, Cali is an industrial and commercial center.

Although overall environmental quality in the city is good, many of Cali's citizens reside in illegal squatter settlements in conditions of extreme poverty where services such as schools and primary health care are lacking. Because these communities have sprung up on government-owned or privately owned land without the required permits, they also lack basic services such as water, sewers, electricity, roads, and garbage collection.

One such district is Aguablanca, a settlement of 350,000 residents covering 1,500 hectares. Aguablanca attracted large numbers of people looking for a better place to live after a series of natural disasters and political upheavals in the 1980s (2).

In providing development assistance to the residents of Aguablanca, the Carvajal Foundation's strategy was to observe what people were doing to improve their living conditions and what obstacles they faced. Most of Aguablanca's housing consisted of shacks illegally constructed by the residents. Building a

house or even improving an existing structure was very expensive. Residents could only buy construction materials at nearby locations where prices were high because there were many intermediaries between the manufacturer and the final retailer (3).

To assist the residents, the Carvajal Foundation built a warehouse in the middle of the squatter area to provide space for manufacturers to sell their construction materials directly to residents at wholesale prices (4).

In the beginning, convincing manufacturers to sell their goods in Aguablanca was difficult because they thought that the low-income residents would not have money. However, the poor did have some money, and they had it in cash, which was attractive to the merchants because they did not have to sell on credit. To profit, however, the merchants had to be open on weekends and holidays, when the residents could shop.

In addition to providing space, the Foundation provided insurance and agreed to handle the money to alleviate merchants' fears of handling large sums of cash in the Aguablanca district. The Foundation charged a commission of about 2 percent to cover operating costs.

Once people had access to construction materials, they usually hired friends to build their houses. But, because few people understood basic building concepts, they often purchased the wrong types of materials or used them incorrectly. For example, residents typically built foundations of reinforced concrete with far more load-bearing capacity than their modest structures required. Their money then ran out and the building stopped.

The Foundation approached a local school of architecture and invited stu-

dents to come up with a sound, simple, modular house design that would enable the Carvajal Foundation to provide residents with the full plans needed to complete their houses (5). In this scheme, residents could start with a single space and a bathroom and then expand into a fully developed house as resources allowed. The basic starter house was 17 square meters; the fully developed house was 90 square meters. Designs for a house with a workshop and a house with a small store were also developed.

Eager to involve government agencies in this effort, the Foundation also convinced the city to approve the building plans and to set up a small office at the warehouse where residents could obtain building permits. Having preapproved building plans and easily obtainable permits was a valuable incentive for residents to build legal, affordable structures.

The government-owned Central Mortgage Bank also opened an office in Aguablanca and encouraged residents to open savings accounts and obtain construction loans for their homes. Residents could make a down payment of 50,000 pesos (US$600) and then take out a 10-year loan. The monthly payment for a basic single-space house with bathroom was 20,000 pesos (US $250), which is less than the normal rent in the district.

Families interested in building their own homes were (and continue to be) invited to a workshop that covered everything from financing to construction. Each family sat down with a financial advisor who helped them evaluate their financial resources and decide how much space they could afford to complete initially. They were trained in how to read blueprints and how to

political processes. They have played key roles in helping slum dwellers resist eviction and negotiate land settlements, in gaining basic human and political rights for the poor, and in establishing community organizations (94).

Many countries have thousands of NGOs with rich experience in promoting community participation in urban development. Many types of NGOs exist, how-

ever, and not all of them actually work toward empowering communities (95). Many governments severely limit the role of such organizations to small-scale, charitable activities rather than allow open advocacy of, for example, squatters' rights.

Many international NGOs still tend to focus on global and rural environmental issues and rarely on cities or the needs of low-income urban communities.

build foundations, walls, and roofs, as well as in plumbing and wiring.

Banks give families a 60-day grace period during which they do not have to make payments on their loans, so families work hard to complete their houses during this period to avoid having to continue to pay rent after they have begun repaying their loans. Through this process, families learn how to budget for the house and control their cash flow.

The success of the Carvajal Foundation's original program inspired a private developer to develop 3,000 lots in another part of the city. Nearly 11,000 families applied for the program, and 2,500 lots were sold in the first week.

In 1992, the city of Cali adopted the same model and launched a program, the Cuidadela Desepaz, for 28,000 minimum-wage families. About 3,000 lots were developed by the municipality to relocate families from high-risk areas; the remaining lots are being developed by the private sector (both nonprofit and for-profit) (6).

MICROENTERPRISE SYSTEMS

The Foundation discovered that the food costs of the poor in Aguablanca were more than those of people in many other, more prosperous areas of the city, partly because grocery stores were not purchasing goods efficiently. The Foundation offered management training to grocery store owners and established wholesale food outlets. To participate, a grocery store owner had to agree to attend a simple, 30-hour course on accounting, marketing and sales, and investment project analysis.

Once food sellers completed the training process, they could buy directly from these outlets. This meant that for the first time, they could buy their stock at the best wholesale prices. As soon as

the program went into effect, retail prices went down by as much as 15 or 20 percent. Merchants were making higher profits, because, as part of the training, the Foundation suggested that merchants use a markup of about 10 percent, instead of the 3 to 4 percent that they had been charging.

The Foundation has developed a training course for entrepreneurs (7). Because many informal entrepreneurs have only 1 to 2 years of primary schooling, the courses emphasized basic business skills. The program covers topics such as sales and marketing, administration, accounting, cost estimation and investment analysis, handling personnel, and quality control (8). Individual counseling was provided to help entrepreneurs set up account records and transfer other skills that they had learned to their individual businesses. The Foundation also provided loans to entrepreneurs if they needed them.

The combination of training, individual counseling, and credit reduced the failure rate of many small businesses to about 5 to 10 percent. Individual counseling and direct training have been provided to 22,000 Colombian entrepreneurs in microenterprises. Thirty percent have received US$3.9 million in small loans. According to estimates by the Carvajal Foundation, about 20,000 new jobs have been created in Cali through this program (9).

In addition, the Foundation has trained volunteers from the community to educate families in the importance of proper nutrition, prenatal care, and immunization (10). Success can be seen through the reduction in the infant mortality rate from 70 per 1,000 live births in 1983 to 26.2 per 1,000 live births in 1993. Seventy percent of the population has access to health services in Aguablanca; vaccination programs cover 90

percent of the children under the age of 1 year and 75 percent of the children under the age of 5 years.

—*Rodrigo Guerrero*

Rodrigo Guerrero is a regional advisor on health and violence at the Pan American Health Organization in Washington, D.C. In addition to serving as mayor of Cali, and President of the Carvajal Foundation, he is also a physician.

References and Notes

1. Tatiana Gutierrez and Elizabeth Olson, "The Role of Intersectoral Links in the Socioeconomic Development of Cali, Colombia," paper presented at the Conference on Cali: The Entrepreneurial Spirit, School of International and Public Affairs, Columbia University, New York, March 21–24, 1994.

2. World Health Organization (WHO), "La Funcion de Los Centros de Salud en el Desarrollo de los Sistemas Urbanos de Salud," Serie de Informes Tecnicos No. 827 (WHO, Geneva, 1992).

3. Luis Fernando Cruz, "Fundacion Carvajal; The Carvajal Foundation," *Environment and Urbanization*, Vol. 6, No. 2 (October 1994), p. 178.

4. *Ibid.,* pp. 178–179.

5. *Op. cit.* 3, p. 179.

6. Instituto de Vivienda de Cali (INVICALI), "Veintiun Mesos de Gestion Responsable," Informe del Gerente a la Junta Directiva del Instituto de Vivienda de Cali (INVICALI, Cali, Colombia, December 1994).

7. United Nations Children's Fund (UNICEF), "The Urban Poor and Household Food Security," *Urban Examples*, Volume No. 19 (UNICEF, New York, 1994), pp. 20–23.

8. *Op. cit.* 3.

9. *Op. cit.* 3.

10. *Op. cit.* 3, p. 181.

Yet, when they do, they can make a tremendous difference. In Tegucigalpa, for instance, the Honduran office of the Cooperative Housing Foundation (CHF), a Washington-based NGO, began an urban sanitation program in 1991. With the support of the United Nations Children's Fund, the government of Honduras had already begun to provide piped water to the households. CHF's role was to ensure that this water was put to good use. CHF made loans to households to install latrines, water tanks, showers, taps, and sinks in residents' homes. CHF, with the assistance of local NGOs, works with women to decide what type of latrine they desire: a pour-flush latrine, a dry-compost latrine, or an improved ventilated pit latrine. Depending on their needs and ability to pay, women are given a loan that can range from $250 to $750 and that must be repaid in 3

Urban renewal. Redeveloping vacant land by creating urban parks and plazas can help return green space to inner cities, providing natural spaces for people to gather and for businesses to prosper.

to 5 years. More than 1,700 households have benefited from the improvements (96).

Community Credit Programs

The lack of financial resources is a major obstacle in fostering community-based development. However, many experiences show that, once they are organized, communities can and will begin to contribute their own financial resources and will repay loans. A common feature of many successful programs is the principle of group responsibility, which is often accomplished by organizing borrowers into small-scale subgroups within the community. (See Box 6.5.)

Environmental Education

Surveys in many countries show that relationships between environmental pollution and human health are often poorly understood. Simple acts such as washing hands, which can significantly break poor environment–poor health cycles, are not practiced. Modest programs, such as poster or radio campaigns, and working with leaders or designated community environmental health specialists can begin to address these issues.

SETTING PRIORITIES

A key element in the many efforts under way to create better communities and cities, from Cajamarca, Peru, to

Chattanooga, Tennessee, in the United States, is citizen involvement in deciding which problems to tackle and how they should be tackled. This is the case in grassroots efforts led by communities and NGOs and in government initiatives such as Local Agenda 21, as well as those instituted with the help of international groups, whether they are NGOs such as the Habitat International Coalition or donor agencies such as the United Nations, the World Bank, and the World Health Organization. (See Box 6.6.)

In poor cities in the developing world, these exercises generally focus on identifying the worst environmental threats to health. A range of techniques is being used to identify priorities, and some of these are more participatory and inclusive than others. Some emphasize data collection in concert with public consultations; others focus more on consensus building to reach environmental goals.

There is no agreement on which approaches work best. As the Urban Management Programme (UMP) found, the priorities determined by public consultations may be very different from those identified by rapid scientific assessments. (The UMP, a joint program of the United Nations Development Programme, the Habitat International Coalition, and the World Bank, is involved in developing environmental action plans in a number of cities.) In Sao Paulo, Brazil, for example, limited green space was identified as a high priority in the consultation process but did not even make it onto the data-based problem ranking (97). (See Table 6.2.) The outcomes of both of these processes are largely dependent on who is involved; a poor family may have a quite different set of priorities than a rich one. Even in the data collection process, the biases of those collecting and interpreting the data may be a factor.

Furthermore, questions remain about whether and how these exercises can best be translated into action. Priority-setting studies provide valuable information but may have limited impact if they ignore public sentiment or the particular political, financial, and institutional context of a city. They may be less effective if

Box 6.4 Citizen Participation Leads to Better Plan for the Bronx, New York

In the summer of 1992, residents of the downtrodden Melrose Commons neighborhood in New York City's South Bronx discovered that the city was planning to revitalize the neighborhood and that many homes were slated for demolition.

As it turned out, the City Planning Department had been working on the plan since 1985, but with little community participation. Like so many other such plans, the "revitalization" would displace many community residents from their homes, apartments, and businesses.

A few residents were outraged that members of the community who had stayed through thick and thin would be rewarded for their fortitude with the loss of their homes. They were also frustrated that the plan was developed by people who did not live in or know the neighborhood.

At a series of public forums held by the Bronx Center, a community-based volunteer planning effort for a 300-block section of the Bronx that encompasses Melrose Commons, long-time residents angrily denounced the plan.

Stung by the public reaction, the leaders of the Bronx Center and the Bronx borough president actively encouraged Melrose Commons residents to get organized and involved in the revision of the plan. The Bronx Center provided the services of two community organizers, and a longtime resident provided office space. Two architects donated their services to the group, known as the Nos Quedamos (We're Staying) Committee. (1).

In 1 year, the group had 168 meetings and each week sent out about 250 faxes to city officials. The original plan was withdrawn by the city, and the Nos Quedamos Committee became the focal point of a revised plan.

The residents' insights produced many significant changes. City planners had envisioned the center of the community as being in the south, but residents said the center was actually in the northeast quadrant, where many people lived. The original plan called for an 8,000-square-meter park in the middle of the project, but residents thought that such a park would be indefensible and would immediately become a haven for drug addicts and criminals. The revised

plan includes a variety of more defensible spaces for different ages and different purposes (2).

The original city plan proposed a middle-income community with 4,000 units of small, attached houses over 30 blocks. The plan developed by the Nos Quedamos Committee envisioned a low- to mid-rise mixed-income residential community with about 1,500 new dwelling units, 80 rehabilitated units, 16,250 square meters of commercial retail and office space, and 18,600 square

Courtesy of Urban Assembly

meters of space in community structures.

One key to the plan was the use of six- to eight-story mixed-use buildings with stores at the street level and apartments above. Residents felt that such buildings would provide enough people on the streets and in the stores to help make the neighborhood safe (3).

Another key was to minimize the displacement of residents. Under the original plan, about 78 families and 80 businesses were to be moved out of the area; under the new plan, about 55 families and 51 businesses would have to move, but most would be given top priority for new homes and stores within the community.

By mid-1994, the new plan had been approved by two local community boards, the Bronx borough president's office, the New York City Planning Commission and various other city agencies, and the City Council. But many of the designs for housing developments in the proposal do not fit into any current government housing programs, so it could take a decade or

more for the entire project to be completed.

The Nos Quedamos Committee has identified a first phase of the project that encompasses an eight-block area. The development includes proposed six- to eight-story mixed-use buildings, four-story townhouses, two-family homes, restoration of existing residential buildings, off-street parking, a 4,000-square-meter park, and various other open spaces for community gardens and children's recreation. The area includes all

We are staying. In the Bronx, local leaders helped convince city officials that community input is crucial to the success of plans to redevelop decaying urban neighborhoods.

of the building types proposed for the larger development and can thus serve as a model for subsequent development. Most of the land is city owned, which will minimize the need to acquire privately owned sites.

The work of the Bronx Center has attracted the attention of community activists, public officials, business leaders, professionals and academics from many cities in the United States and abroad, and international institutions such as the World Bank.

References and Notes

1. David Gonzalez, "Revolution of People Power Wells Up in the Bronx," *New York Times* (July 8, 1993), p. B1.
2. Mervyn Rothstein, "A Renewal Plan in the Bronx Advances," *New York Times* (July 10, 1994), p. 1R.
3. *Ibid.*

Participatory planning. In Chattanooga, Tennessee, citizens, leaders, and planners were all given a chance to pick up a pen and help redesign 140 hectares of underutilized land.

those most affected (the poor) are not given the means to articulate their needs. Political support, timing, and an emphasis on cost-effective solutions are also important if these processes are to be translated into tangible improvements.

In the wealthier cities of the developed world, priority setting can take on a different guise. Rather than focus on life-threatening environmental problems, some communities have the luxury of thinking about the future. In numerous cities across North America, for instance, communities are using public forums to develop a vision of the future and then decide upon collaborative strategies for getting there.

Indeed, the experience of Chattanooga, Tennessee, shows how large-scale community participation can add extra impetus to a city restoration program. Only three decades ago, air pollution in Chattanooga was so bad that drivers often had to switch on headlights in the middle of the day. Tuberculosis cases were three times the national average.

The city's political, business, and environmental leaders, along with the community as a whole, all played a role in the turnaround. The city's political leaders cracked down on air pollution in response to the requirements of the 1970 federal Clean Air Act. Meeting the new law's health standards meant requiring local industries to install air pollution control equipment. But the requirements also provided local economic stimulus, generating some $40

million locally in spending on air pollution control equipment and a new local manufacturer of air pollution "scrubbers."

The city's business and political leaders also saw improvements in the city's environment as a marketing opportunity that could attract new businesses and new investments. The city's electric buses are made by a new local firm that has also received orders from cities in several other states. The city wants to transform a decrepit old industrial area, the South Central Business District, into a new mixed-use community of neighborhoods and environmentally pristine businesses, which would allow employees to live near their workplaces.

Environmental improvements gained further community support in 1984 during the Vision 2000 project, which brought some 1,700 members of the community together over 20 weeks to talk about their vision of the city in the year 2000. The meetings resulted in 34 concrete goals, which in turn generated some 223 city projects. The projects included the construction of the Tennessee River Park, the Tennessee Aquarium, and a commitment to upgrade the city's substandard housing. By 1992, 85 percent of the goals had been met. Some $739 million was invested in the city, of which about two thirds came from private sources. By 1993, the community was ready to start all over again, launching ReVision 2000.

Table 6.2 Methods for Establishing Environmental Priorities, Sao Paulo, Brazil

Problem Priority	Consultation Process[a]	Data-Based and Criteria-Based Problem Ranking[b]
High	Substandard housing Lack of urban infrastructure for the poor Settlement of risk-prone areas Limited green space	Surface water Environmental hazards Forest/agriculture Hazardous waste Poor sanitation
Medium	Inadequate sewage treatment Water supply not protected Flooding	Ambient pollution Solid waste Noise pollution Coastal pollution Indoor pollution
Low	Vehicular air pollution Poor transportation management	Rural ecosystems Cultural property

Source: Josef Leitmann, "Rapid Urban Environmental Assessment: Lessons from Cities in the Developing World, Volume 1: Methodology and Preliminary Findings," Urban Management Programme Discussion Paper No. 14 (The World Bank, Washington, D.C., 1993), p. 33.

Notes:

a. A public forum that reaches a consensus on priority issues. This process does not necessarily reflect public opinion but is based on participation by interested stakeholders.

b. Using data collected during the rapid urban environmental assessment phase, urban problems are ranked according to the scale of their health impact, economic losses, impact on the urban poor, irreversibility, unsustainability of resource consumption, and degree of local support.

Box 6.5 Nigeria's Community Banks: A Capital Idea

With a small loan, many low-income workers and craftspersons in Africa could expand their informal businesses enough to provide some security for their families. However, it is difficult, if not impossible, for most people to obtain a bank loan because few have holdings, such as land, houses, or livestock, that could be used as collateral to secure a loan. Without such leverage, a large segment of the population is consigned to persistent poverty.

A popular alternative in Nigeria is the community banking program, in which one's honor and standing in the community can take the place of collateral in securing a loan. The principal function of collateral is to ensure that the applicant does not renege on the commitment to repay the loan by the due date. In Nigeria, in places where strong community ties exist, a peer sanction system has been used to ensure correct behavior in credit transactions. The community's basic system of trust creates a climate in which residents can pool their money and then loan it to one another.

Although primarily designed to deliver credit to the rural population, Nigeria's community banking program has been launched in urban areas with large numbers of poor persons whose livelihoods depend on informal jobs. More than 35 percent of Nigeria's community banks are in urban areas—with one fifth of these in the Lagos metropolitan area. Most urban community banks are located close to urban markets, where they cater largely to the credit needs of market women, food sellers and wholesalers, drivers, and mechanics, many of whom, although not well-to-do, own some small shares in the bank.

The first community bank in Nigeria was commissioned in 1990 in Tudun Wada, in the Kaduna Local Government Area of Kaduna State. Within 3 years, some 879 community banks had been established throughout the country. Currently, 1,052 community banks are in operation in Nigeria.

To establish a community bank, a community must provide all of its own banking equipment—a building, safes, office furniture, ultraviolet lights for de-tecting forged currencies, and so forth—as well as a minimum working capital of about 250,000 Naira (US$11,000). Communities raise funds for the bank in much the same way as they finance other cooperative efforts such as building a school, a clinic, or a church. This entails mobilizing everyone with strong ties to the community, including sons and daughters living abroad, to pay a charge or make a donation. This sense of ownership by the community has contributed to the program's success.

The community is also responsible for appointing a board of directors and staff for the bank. According to its charter, a community bank must be owned primarily by a community development association, although overseas relatives and collectives such as trade associations, farmers' unions, market women's organizations, cooperative societies, social clubs, and corporate bodies can also be shareholders.

The only government involvement is a National Board of Community Banks, which develops, monitors, and provides provisional licensing for these banks. The National Board can provide a community bank with a matching loan equivalent to its working capital after it has been operating successfully for 3 months. The matching loan must be paid back within 5 years. Community banks may apply for a final license issued by the Central Bank of Nigeria. After receiving a final license, a community bank can apply to the Nigeria Deposit Insurance Corporation to have its customers' deposits insured against a bank failure.

By December 1993, community banks had mobilized more than N2 billion (US$90 million) nationwide—more than half of this as savings deposits. Total assets had risen to more than N3.2 billion (US$145 million), and loans and advances of nearly N750 million (US$34 million) have been made. Some 40 percent of the loans and advances were for commercial activities. Manufacturing accounted for more than 18 percent of loans, agriculture and forestry accounted for 17 percent, and transportation accounted for 8 percent.

Most loans are for less than N5,000 (US$200).

The community bank program has far exceeded the country's expectation. The annual general meeting of these banks has become something of a community festival, with drums welcoming the community members, who often come out in their Sunday best. The chairmen and board members of the banks have acquired local respectability and feel a deep sense of accomplishment in the changes they are bringing to the economic fortunes of their neighbors.

At a few community banks, some minor problems that required intervention by the National Board have arisen. A more serious problem, however, has been the exposure of some community banks to the crisis in the financial sector of the economy. This has particularly affected those community banks that had placed funds in distressed banks and finance houses in Nigeria.

It is still too early to make a definitive statement of how much community banks have contributed to resolving the problems of urban poverty. Examples of specific loans, however, illustrate the potential of these types of credit arrangements for improving people's lives. For instance, an unemployed young man got a loan of N7,500 (US$340) from the Obeiudu Community Bank in Uromia, Edo State, to buy a maize grinder. Because he paid in cash, he got a discount that enabled him to buy a wheelbarrow as well. He employed another young man to use the wheelbarrow to help market women and customers to move their goods around. With money earned from that activity, he was able to pay back the first loan and to take out another one to buy a second maize grinder. When he paid back that loan, he took out yet another one to buy a portable electric generator, and he has not looked back.

—*Akin L. Mabogunje*

Akin L. Mabogunje is a chairman of the Development Policy Center in Ibadan, Nigeria. He formerly served as Chairman of the National Board for Community Banks in Nigeria.

Box 6.6 International Urban Environment Programs

There is growing recognition among agencies that their role should be one of institutional strengthening—helping cities identify their worst problems and develop local means to address them. To this end, many of the multilateral and bilateral programs dealing with the urban environment are focusing on research, capacity building, and information exchange, as well as trying to find new ways to foster participation by local communities and political leaders in the process of assessing environmental problems and developing priorities for action.

One of these programs is the Urban Management Programme (UMP), which is funded jointly by the United Nations Development Programme (UNDP) and a number of bilateral agencies. The UMP is executed by the United Nations Centre for Human Settlements (Habitat) with the World Bank as an associate agency. The program focuses on five areas: urban land management, the provision and maintenance of urban infrastructure, municipal finance, the alleviation of urban poverty, and the protection of the urban environment.

Since 1990, the UMP has helped cities define broad environmental strategies and build the capacity to manage urban problems (1). The program is operationally decentralized (with four regional offices in Accra, Ghana; Kuala Lumpur, Malaysia; Quito, Ecuador; and Cairo, Egypt) and attempts to bring together the creative expertise of the international assistance community.

The Metropolitan Environmental Improvement Program (MEIP), a UNDP-funded effort managed by the World Bank, focuses on environmental improvements in Asian cities. MEIP works in cities such as Beijing, China; Bombay, India; Colombo, Sri Lanka; and Kathmandu, Nepal (2). MEIP assists member cities in the development of environmental management strategies and action plans, the strengthening of the institutional and legislative framework for environmental planning and enforcement, the identification and mobilization of resources for high-priority investment projects, the promotion of community-led efforts to improve the environment, and the sharing of information among member cities.

UNDP's Public-Private Partnerships Programme promotes the collaboration between the government and private companies, with the participation of nongovernmental organizations (NGOs) and the scientific-academic community, in the provision of city services such as water and sanitation and waste management. The objective of the program is to help foster communication between local authorities and the private sector at various levels, creating concrete opportunities for technology dissemination and investments that can produce social, economic, and environmental benefits.

UNDP also has created the Local Initiative Facility for Urban Environment (LIFE) program, which is an attempt by the international community to provide direct support to local groups working to improve the urban environment. A committee composed of a diverse group of local people looks for proposed projects that involve collaborative action among NGOs, community-based organizations, local authorities, and, potentially, the private sector (3).

The Sustainable Cities Programme, which was launched by Habitat and the United Nations Environment Programme in 1990, focuses on capacity building at city, country, regional, and global levels. In individual cities, the program uses broad-based consultation processes to mobilize local resources for the development of environmental strategies and the implementation of priority projects. More broadly, the program promotes the sharing of information among cities in different regions of the world and also marshals technical and financial resources from bilateral and multilateral sources. Demonstration activities are under way in cities in 20 countries, including Chile, China, Egypt, Ghana, Mozambique, Poland, and Tunisia (4).

In 1986, the World Health Organization devised the Healthy Cities Project to serve as a forum for city officials, NGOs, and others to exchange ideas about a wide range of issues, including traffic, housing, tobacco use, AIDS, and mental health (5). Initially limited to Europe, the project has since become an international movement involving hundreds of cities around the world. There are 3 international and 17 national networks, including programs in Australia, Canada, and the United States (6).

The International Council for Local Environmental Initiatives, which is formally affiliated with the International Union of Local Authorities is the international environmental agency for local authorities, working directly with municipalities to develop tools and management approaches for environmental protection and to implement local versions of the Agenda 21, the plan of action developed at the United Nations Conference on Environmental Development (the Earth Summit) (7).

Numerous NGOs are also forming information exchange networks. The Habitat International Coalition, for example, is a coalition formed by over 200 NGOs from 56 countries working on housing or related issues (8). Other networks include the Asian Coalition for Housing Rights, the Arab NGO Network, and the Center for African Settlement Studies and Development.

References and Notes

1. Carl Bartone *et al.,* "Toward Environmental Strategies for Cities: Policy Considerations for Urban Environmental Management in Developing Countries," Urban Management Programme Paper No. 18 (The World Bank, Washington, D.C., 1994), p. 83.

2. The Metropolitan Environmental Improvement Program (MEIP), *MEIP Progress Report 1993* (The World Bank, Washington, D.C., 1993), p. 1.

3. United Nations Development Programme (UNDP), "Local Initiative Facility for Urban Environment (LIFE): Report on the Global Advisory Committee and Donor Workshop: First Year Review and Strategic Planning" (UNDP, New York, 1994), pp. i, 3.

4. United Nations Centre for Human Settlements (Habitat), *Sustainable Human Settlements Development: Implementing Agenda 21* (Habitat, Nairobi, Kenya, 1994), p. 9.

5. Joan M. Twiss, "California Healthy Cities Project: Piloting Community-Based Health Promotion Statewide," National Civic Review (Spring/Summer 1992), pp. 105–106.

6. *Ibid.,* p. 105.

7. *Op. cit.* 1, p. 84.

8. "Habitat International Coalition," *Environment and Urbanization,* Vol. 2, No. 1 (April 1990), pp. 105–112.

Although the process was somewhat *ad hoc*, it nevertheless was driven by an underlying consensus in the late 1960s and 1970s that the city was failing, both economically and environmentally. What drove the process ahead was a tacit agreement between business leaders and the community at large about the value of environmental improvements; in addition, there was strong community support resulting from the Vision 2000 process (98).

CITIES AND SUSTAINABLE DEVELOPMENT

Many of these same ideas about citizen participation and community mobilization are embodied in the broader concept of "sustainable cities," which has garnered increasing attention over the past few years—especially but not exclusively in the developed world. As yet, however, there is little agreement about what constitutes a "sustainable city" or whether, in fact, such an entity is possible in the narrow sense of the word. A narrow focus on sustainable cities, for instance, can lead to the idea that cities should only draw on natural resources from within the immediate region, which seems increasingly at odds with the globalization of the world economy.

Some commentators have argued persuasively that a more useful framework is to focus instead on the role of cities in sustainable development (99) (100). Here, "sustainable development" is defined as meeting the needs of the present without undermining the resource and ecological base for future generations. This definition is in keeping with that used in *Our Common Future*, the report of the World Commission on Environment and Development (also known as the Brundtland Commission) (101) (102).

Cities are clearly central to meeting the goals of sustainable development. The majority of the world's population will soon live in towns and cities. World-wide, city-based producers and consumers already account for most of the renewable and nonrenewable resource consumption and waste generation (103).

Many of the priority actions called for in this report have been focused on the first part of the equation: meeting the current needs of the urban poor. As previous chapters have made clear, this involves not just providing physical necessities such as food, fuel, and water but adequate livelihoods and other social, cultural, health, and political needs as well.

In wealthier cities, the second part of the equation, sustainable development, assumes increasing importance, and the priority actions center on reducing both excessive consumption of natural resources and the burden of wastes on the global environment. As described in Chapter 5, "Urban Priorities for Action," such initiatives include reducing fossil fuel consumption, for example, through energy conservation and more efficient transportation systems, and reducing the amount of waste through pollution prevention.

These longer-term ecological concerns are relevant to cities in the developing world as well, for as they grow and prosper, their consumption of resources and generation of wastes will rise accordingly unless actions are taken now to promote the efficient use of resources and the minimization of waste (104). The challenge for all cities is to seek new management approaches that both provide for the needs of urban residents and protect the environmental resources on which human life depends.

This chapter was written by Mike Douglass of the Department of Urban and Regional Planning at the University of Hawaii at Manoa, Honolulu, Hawaii, and Yok-shiu F. Lee of the Program on Environment, East-West Center, Honolulu.

References and Notes

1. Nick Devas and Carole Rakodi, "The Urban Challenge," in *Managing Fast Growing Cities: New Approaches to Urban Planning and Management in the Developing World,* Nick Devas and Carole Rakodi, eds. (Longman, Essex, U.K., and John Wiley & Sons, New York, 1993), pp. 31–33.

2. *Ibid.*

3. Carl Bartone *et al.,* "Toward Environmental Strategies for Cities: Policy Considerations for Urban Environmental Management in Developing Countries," Urban Management Programme Policy Paper No. 18 (The World Bank, Washington, D.C., 1994), pp. 33–34.

4. Jorge E. Hardoy, Diana Mitlin, and David Satterthwaite, *Environmental Problems in Third World Cities* (Earthscan, London, 1992), p. 213.

5. William Dillinger, "Decentralization and Its Implications for Urban Service Delivery," Urban Management Programme Discussion Paper No. 16 (The World Bank, Washington, D.C., 1994), p. 8.

6. Nick Devas, "Evolving Approaches," in *Managing Fast Growing Cities: New Approaches to Urban Planning and Management in the Developing World,* Nick Devas and Carole Rakodi, eds. (Longman, Essex, U.K., and John Wiley & Sons, New York, 1993), p. 90.

7. *Ibid.,* p. 91.

8. *Op. cit.* 5.

9. *Op. cit.* 5.

10. *Op. cit.* 5, p. 9.

11. Patricia McCarney, Mohamed Halfani, and Alfredo Rodriguez, "Towards an Understanding of Governance," in *Urban Research in the Developing World, Volume Four: Perspectives on the City,* Richard Stren and Judith Kjellberg Bell, eds. (Centre for Urban & Community Studies, University of Toronto, Toronto, 1995), p. 122.

12. *Op. cit.* 5.

13. *Op. cit.* 4, pp. 163–164, 207.

14. *Op. cit.* 11.

15. *Op. cit.* 4, pp. 28–29, 213.

16. *Op. cit.* 11, p. 100.

17. *Op. cit.* 11, p. 104.

18. *Op. cit.* 4, p. 162.

19. Silvina Arrossi *et al., Funding Community Initiatives* (Earthscan, London, 1994), p. 23.

20. William Dillinger, "Urban Property Tax Reform: Guidelines and Recommendations," Urban Management Programme Tool No. 1 (The World Bank, Washington, D.C., 1992), p. 38.

21. *Op. cit.* 5, p. 16.

22. *Op. cit.* 5, pp. 2–3.

23. *Op. cit.* 5, p. 19.

24. Miroo Desai Brewer, "Meeting the Needs of the Urban Poor: Financing Environmental Infrastructure and Services in Asian Cities,"

Master's thesis, University of Hawaii, Honolulu, 1995, pp. 22–26.

25. *Op. cit.* 20, p. 11.

26. *Op. cit.* 24, p. 24.

27. G. Shabbir Cheema, "The Challenge of Urban Management: Some Issues," in *Urban Management: Policies and Innovations in Developing Countries,* G. Shabbir Cheema, ed. (Praeger, Westport, Connecticut, and London, 1993), p. 7.

28. *Op. cit.* 5, pp. 26–27.

29. *Op. cit.* 24, pp. 45–70.

30. Ksemsan Suwarnarat and Watana Luanratana, "Waste Management and the Need for Public Participation in Bangkok," *Regional Development Dialogue,* Vol. 14, No. 3 (1993), pp. 68–69.

31. The exchange rate on February 13, 1996, was US$1.00 = 25.23 Baht.

32. *Op. cit.* 5, pp. 28–31.

33. *Op. cit.* 24, pp. 26–30.

34. *Op. cit.* 27, p. 8.

35. *Op. cit.* 3, pp. 49–51.

36. *Op. cit.* 27, p. 8.

37. Mike Douglass, Indira Dharmapatni, and Apradicio Laquin, *Framework for the Urban Policy Action Plan: Repelita VI* (Bappenas, Government of Indonesia, Jakarta, 1994).

38. *Op. cit.* 3, p. 50.

39. *Op. cit.* 3, p. 51.

40. Mike Douglass, Department of Urban and Regional Planning, University of Hawaii, Honolulu, 1996 (personal communication).

41. *Op. cit.* 6, p. 98.

42. *Op. cit.* 3, p. 56.

43. *Op. cit.* 3, p. 56.

44. *Op. cit.* 3, p. 57.

45. Exequiel Ezcurra and Marisa Mazari-Hiriart, "Are Mega-Cities Viable? A Cautionary Tale from Mexico City," *Environment,* Vol. 38, No. 1 (January/February 1996), p. 30.

46. *Op. cit.* 3, pp. 103–104.

47. International Council for Local Environmental Initiatives (ICLEI), "Community-Based Service Delivery: Quito, Ecuador," Case Study No. 21 (ICLEI, Toronto, Canada, 1994).

48. Jeb Brugmann, Secretary General, International Council for Local Environmental Initiatives, Toronto, Canada, 1995 (personal communication).

49. Mike Douglass, "The Political Economy of Urban Poverty and Environmental Management in Asia: Access, Empowerment, and Community Based Alternatives," *Environment and Urbanization,* Vol. 4, No. 2 (October 1992), p. 13.

50. *Op. cit.* 6, p. 94.

51. Michael Douglass, "Urban Poverty in Asia: A Summary of Issues and Policy Recommendations," discussion paper (Department of Urban and Regional Planning, University of Hawaii, Honolulu, 1995), p. 5.

52. *Op. cit.* 6, p. 94.

53. *Op. cit.* 49, p. 15.

54. *Op. cit.* 49, p. 15.

55. *Op. cit.* 4, p. 53.

56. Orathai Ard-am and Kusol Soonthorndhada, "Household Economy and Environmental Management in Bangkok: The Cases of Wat Chonglom and Yen-ar-kard," *Asian Journal of Environmental Management,* Vol. 2, No. 1 (1994), pp. 37–48.

57. Mike Douglass and Malia Zoghlin, "Sustaining Cities at the Grassroots: Livelihood, Environment and Social Networks in Suan Phlu, Bangkok," *Third World Planning Review,* Vol. 16, No. 2 (1994), pp. 171–200.

58. Janice E. Perlman, "Mega-Cities: Global Urbanization and Innovation," in *Urban Management: Policies and Innovations in Developing Countries,* G. Shabbir Cheema, ed. (Praeger, Westport, Connecticut, and London, 1993), pp. 47–48.

59. John Friedmann, *Empowerment: The Politics of Alternative Development* (Blackwell, Cambridge and Oxford, U.K., 1992), pp. 43–45, 49–51, 96–101.

60. *Op. cit.* 27, p. 12.

61. Ministry of Foreign Affairs, "Urban Poverty Alleviation," Sectoral Policy Document of Development Cooperation No. 5 (Minister for Development Cooperation, The Hague, Netherlands, 1994), p. 41.

62. Michael Yhdego, "Scavenging Solid Wastes in Dar es Salaam, Tanzania," *Waste Management Research,* Vol. 9 (1991), p. 263.

63. *Op. cit.* 49, pp. 13–14.

64. United Nations (U.N.) Economic and Social Commission for Asia and the Pacific, *State of Urbanization in Asia and the Pacific 1993* (U.N., New York, 1993), pp. 4-17–4-21.

65. *Op. cit.* 59.

66. The Mega-Cities Project and the Center for Urban and Regional Studies with The Foundation on Contemporary Studies, "The PAIS Plan: Food, Organization and Self-Employment for the Poor: Buenos Aires," Urban Environment-Poverty Case Study Series (Mega-Cities Project, New York, 1994), p. 10.

67. *Ibid.,* p. 12.

68. *Op. cit.* 49, p. 23.

69. Hasan Poerbo, "Urban Solid Waste Management in Bandung: Towards an Integrated Resource Recovery System," *Environment and Urbanization,* Vol. 3, No. 1 (April 1991), pp. 60–69.

70. The Mega-Cities Project and Environmental Quality International, "Zabbaleen Environmental and Development Program: Cairo," Urban Environment-Poverty Case Study Se-

ries (Mega-Cities Project, New York, 1994), pp. 1–42.

71. *Op. cit.* 58, p. 47.

72. Yok-shiu F. Lee, "Community-Based Urban Environmental Management: Local NGOs as Catalysts," *Regional Development Dialogue*, Vol. 15, No. 2 (Autumn 1994), p. 158.

73. Joel Audefroy, "Eviction Trends Worldwide—and the Role of Local Authorities in Implementing the Right to Housing," *Environment and Urbanization*, Vol. 6, No. 1 (April 1994), pp. 10–16.

74. Beatriz Cuenya *et al.*, "Land Invasions and Grassroots Organization: The Quilmes Settlements in Greater Buenos Aires, Argentina," *Environment and Urbanization*, Vol. 1, No. 2 (October 1990), pp. 61–73.

75. Michael Mattingly, "Urban Management Intervention in Land Markets," in *Managing Fast Growing Cities: New Approaches to Urban Planning and Management in the Developing World*, Nick Devas and Carole Rakodi, eds. (Longman, Essex, U.K., and John Wiley & Sons, New York, 1993), p. 108.

76. Yok-shiu F. Lee, "Urban Planning and Vector Control in Southeast Asian Cities," *Kaohsiung Journal of Medical Science*, Vol. 10 (1994), pp. S45–S46.

77. U.S. Agency for International Development (U.S. AID), *Regularizing the Informal Land Development Process*, Vol. 2: Discussion Papers (U.S. AID, Washington, D.C., 1991), p. ix.

78. Caroline O.N. Moser, *Gender Planning and Development: Theory, Practice & Training* (Routledge, London and New York, 1993), pp. 15–36.

79. Judith Kjellberg Bell, "Women, Environment and Urbanization: A Guide to the Literature," *Environment and Urbanization*, Vol. 3, No. 2 (October 1991), pp. 92–103.

80. Pamela L. Sayne, "Food for Thought: Making Women Visible," *Environment and Urbanization*, Vol. 3, No. 2 (October 1991), p. 47.

81. United Nations International Research and Training Institute for the Advancement of Women (INSTRAW), "Women, Water and Sanitation," in *Women and the Environment: A Reader*, Sally Sontheimer, ed. (Monthly Review Press, New York, 1991), p. 123.

82. African Housing Fund, "African Housing Fund Progress Report for Project KE-003: Kayole Soweto, July 1992–June 1993" (African Housing Fund, Nairobi, Kenya, 1993), pp. 2–39.

83. Rebecca Katumba, "A New Life for the Squatters of Soweto," *Community Builders Bulletin*, Vol. 1, No. 2 (African Housing Fund, Nairobi, Kenya, 1990), pp. 6–8.

84. *Op. cit.* 82.

85. Kamala Dhungel, "Women in Environment Implement a Squatter Settlement Improvement Project," in *Partners in Life: Proceedings of the Global Assembly of Women and the Environment*, November 4–8, 1991, Miami, Florida, Waafas Ofusu-Amaah and Wendy Phileo, eds. (WorldWIDE Network in collaboration with the United Nations Environment Programme, Washington, D.C., 1992), p. 127.

86. Ann Schlyter, *Women Householders and Housing Strategies: The Case of Harare, Zimbabwe*, Research Report SB:26 (The National Swedish Institute for Building Research, Stockholm, Sweden, 1992).

87. Ann H. May and David K. May, "Community Planning in Developing Nations: Land Use Planning, User Participation, and Appropriate Technologies," in *Shelter, Women and Development: First and Third World Perspectives*, Hemalata C. Dandekar, ed. (George Wahr Publishing Co., Ann Arbor, Michigan, 1993), pp. 208–214.

88. Ana Falu and Mirina Curutchet, "Rehousing the Urban Poor: Looking at Women First," *Environment and Urbanization*, Vol. 3, No. 2 (October 1991), pp. 23–38.

89. *Op. cit.* 57, pp. 186–189.

90. Eugenia Castro, Elvia Flores, and Gustavo Romero, "Plan Urbano Ecologico San Miguel Teotongo," in *Taller de Experiencias en Procesos Participativos de Problemas Urbanos y Ambientales* (Cuaderno de Trabajo, Mexico, January 1994).

91. *Ibid.*

92. *Op. cit.* 57, pp. 186–189.

93. *Op. cit.* 72.

94. *Op. cit.* 4, pp. 146–151, 209–211.

95. *Op. cit.* 72, pp. 165–167.

96. Theresa A. Kilbane, Country Director, Cooperative Housing Foundation–Honduras, speech given at Cooperative Housing Foundation, Worldwide Conference 1995, May 23–25, 1995, Washington, D.C.

97. Josef Leitmann, "Rapid Urban Environmental Assessment: Lessons from Cities in the Developing World, Vol. 1: Methodology and Preliminary Findings," Urban Management Programme Discussion Paper No. 14 (The World Bank, Washington, D.C., 1993), pp. 32–35.

98. Steve Lerner, "Brave New City? Chattanooga, Belle of the 'Sustainable Communities' Ball," *The Amicus Journal*, Vol. 17, No. 1 (Spring 1995), pp. 22–28.

99. *Op. cit.* 4, pp. 171–201.

100. Rodney White and Joseph Whitney, "Cities and the Environment: An Overview," in *Sustainable Cities: Urbanization and the Environment in International Perspective*, Richard Stren, Rodney White, and Joseph Whitney, eds. (Westview Press, Boulder, Colorado, 1992), pp. 8–51.

101. *Op. cit.* 4, p. 172.

102. World Commission on Environment and Development, *Our Common Future* (Oxford University Press, Oxford, U.K., 1987), p. 8.

103. *Op. cit.* 4, p. 171.

104. *Op. cit.* 4, p. 189.

Appendix A. Urban Data Tables

Assembling comparable data on the world's urban places has been surprisingly difficult. Despite the importance of cities as home to more than 45 percent of the world's people, data that characterize the urban experience are unexpectedly sparse.

Those data sets that do exist are scattered among the international statistical agencies according to their topical mandates. For example, the United Nations Population Division makes estimates of urban demographic parameters (and contrasts them to the rural experience) and estimates population in the world's largest cities. The United Nations Environment Programme (UNEP) and the World Health Organization (WHO) monitor air pollution in about 50 of the world's cities under their Global Environmental Monitoring System. WHO also provides urban/rural estimates of access to safe drinking water and sanitation services, while the United Nations Children's Fund (UNICEF) provides similar data on access to health services. Yet these few global data efforts are not designed to provide an integrated or comprehensive view of the urban experience.

Even within cities, topical responsibility can make it difficult to find data. Some kinds of useful data (e.g., measures of the economic importance of a city or urban/rural migration rates) are simply never collected. Urban areas are often spread across many jurisdictions, and, consequently, no one agency is responsible for collecting and reporting data on any given topic for the whole. Different administrative units might have noncontiguous but overlapping areas, further compounding the confusion. In the United States, for example, port authorities can include parts of many cities (e.g., the San Diego Bay area) and even parts of separate states (e.g., the New York Port Authority). Difficulties in creating comprehensive, international data sets are exacerbated by differences among countries in the definition of what constitutes an urban place and in the priority assigned to data collection, given specific local or national needs. Most national and international programs that promise globally comparable urban data sets have not yet produced any publishable findings.

The United Nations Centre for Human Settlements (Habitat) is the only international institution with a specific mandate to assemble information on urban areas. While recognizing the limitations of definition, comparability, and comprehensiveness, Habitat has nonetheless set out to develop a set of indicators on the world's cities that "would create a substantially enhanced capacity to make an accurate description of shelter and urbanization conditions." Habitat's efforts to compile these data, while fraught with difficulties, have begun to bear fruit as countries such as India begin to assemble new data sets. (See Data Table A.4.)

Once developed, a common set of urban indicators would be enormously valuable both locally and internationally. Such indicators would provide a global context for local problems, helping local leaders determine which of their problems are unique and which they share with other cities. Ideally, such a shared data set would result in increased communication and the sharing of local solutions to common problems. A common set of urban indicators might also promote the collection, sharing, and integration of data and information within cities.

Local policymakers need information to make wise management decisions. In addition, policymakers at regional, national, and international levels need information on urban issues to set priorities, allocate resources, and help construct solutions to urban problems.

Data Table A.1 Urban Indicators, 1975–2025

	Urban Population (000)			Percent Urban			1990-95 Urban Growth Rates	1990-95 Rural Growth Rates	Number of Cities Greater Than 750,000 Population {a}	Dependency Ratio (Dependent population, ages <15 and >65, as a percent of the potential labor force, ages 15 to 65)		People in Absolute Poverty (percent) 1980-1990		
	1975	1995	2025	1975	1995	2025				Urban	Rural	Total	Urban	Rural
WORLD	1,538,346	2,584,454	5,065,334	38	45	61	2.5	0.8	369	X	X	X	X	X
AFRICA	104,123	250,276	804,239	25	34	54	4.4	2.0	35	X	X	X	X	X
Algeria	6,460	15,591	33,675	40	56	74	3.8	0.5	1	44	46	23	20	25
Angola	1,087	3,569	14,799	18	32	56	6.3	2.6	1	X	X	X	X	65
Benin	620	1,691	6,344	20	31	52	4.6	2.5	0	49	51	X	X	65
Botswana	91	418	1,651	12	28	55	7.0	1.7	0	33	55	43	30	55
Burkina Faso	394	2,809	14,376	6	27	66	11.2	0.3	0	43	49	X	X	90
Burundi	118	480	2,853	3	8	21	6.6	2.7	0	43	50	84	55	85
Cameroon	2,022	5,938	19,504	27	45	67	4.9	1.2	2	44	50	37	15	40
Central African Rep	693	1,301	3,745	34	39	59	3.4	1.9	0	49	49	X	X	90
Chad	627	1,362	4,970	16	21	39	3.6	2.5	0	42	50	54	30	56
Congo	504	1,523	4,347	35	59	77	4.9	0.6	1	46	51	X	X	80
Cote d'Ivoire	2,168	6,211	23,611	32	44	64	5.0	2.4	1	49	54	X	30	X
Egypt	16,877	28,170	60,519	43	45	62	2.6	1.9	3	39	45	23	21	25
Equatorial Guinea	61	169	547	27	42	69	5.9	0.4	0	46	48	67	60	70
Eritrea	256	607	2,511	12	17	36	4.4	2.4	0	X	X	X	X	X
Ethiopia	3,061	7,371	37,929	10	13	30	4.7	2.7	1	44	50	60	X	63
Gabon	195	660	1,877	31	50	70	4.7	1.2	0	40	43	X	X	41
Gambia, The	91	286	1,022	17	26	49	6.2	3.1	0	47	47	X	X	85
Ghana	2,955	6,333	21,934	30	36	58	4.3	2.3	1	45	50	42	20	54
Guinea	676	1,981	8,039	16	30	53	5.8	2.0	1	48	51	X	X	70
Guinea-Bissau	100	238	882	16	22	45	4.4	1.6	0	X	X	X	X	75
Kenya	1,775	7,817	32,616	13	28	51	6.8	2.5	1	41	54	52	10	55
Lesotho	128	473	1,973	11	23	47	6.2	1.8	0	44	45	54	50	55
Liberia	488	1,366	4,674	30	45	65	4.6	2.3	0	49	51	20	X	23
Libya	1,491	4,649	11,951	61	86	93	4.3	(1.1)	2	48	50	X	X	X
Madagascar	1,253	4,003	17,378	16	27	50	5.8	2.3	0	X	X	43	21	50
Malawi	402	1,505	7,083	8	14	32	6.2	3.1	0	X	X	82	25	90
Mali	1,000	2,909	12,277	16	27	50	5.7	2.3	0	48	51	54	27	60
Mauritania	278	1,224	3,255	20	54	73	5.4	(0.3)	0	46	51	X	X	80
Mauritius	388	453	856	43	41	58	1.2	1.1	0	30	34	8	X	12
Morocco	6,520	13,071	26,917	38	48	66	3.1	1.2	2	38	47	37	28	45
Mozambique	905	5,481	21,468	9	34	61	7.4	0.3	1	45	50	59	40	65
Namibia	186	576	1,939	21	37	64	5.9	1.0	0	42	51	X	X	X
Niger	507	1,558	8,160	11	17	36	5.6	2.9	0	X	X	X	X	35
Nigeria	14,676	43,884	146,948	23	39	62	5.2	1.7	2	46	52	40	21	51
Rwanda	175	483	2,367	4	6	15	4.2	2.5	0	44	53	85	30	90
Senegal	1,643	3,512	10,505	34	42	62	3.7	1.7	1	48	47	X	X	70
Sierra Leone	620	1,632	5,136	21	36	59	4.8	1.2	0	X	X	X	X	65
Somalia	1,164	2,382	9,760	21	26	46	2.5	0.9	1	X	X	60	X	70
South Africa	12,314	21,073	48,673	48	51	69	2.9	1.6	6	35	48	X	X	X
Sudan	3,033	6,915	27,075	19	25	46	4.4	2.1	1	44	48	X	X	85
Swaziland	67	267	933	14	31	57	6.2	1.4	0	33	52	48	45	50
Tanzania	1,602	7,230	30,344	10	24	48	6.1	2.0	1	44	53	58	10	60
Togo	373	1,276	4,906	16	31	52	4.8	2.5	0	46	50	X	X	30
Tunisia	2,797	5,093	9,784	50	57	74	2.8	0.9	1	37	44	17	20	15
Uganda	933	2,670	13,818	8	13	29	5.8	3.1	1	45	52	X	X	80
Zaire	6,860	12,766	52,129	30	29	50	3.9	2.9	1	52	51	70	X	90
Zambia	1,686	4,071	11,467	35	43	60	3.5	2.6	1	50	52	64	47	80
Zimbabwe	1,202	3,619	10,874	20	32	55	5.0	1.5	1	36	53	X	X	60
EUROPE	453,668	535,052	597,660	67	74	83	0.6	(1.0)	79	X	X	X	X	X
Albania	794	1,285	2,661	33	37	57	1.8	0.4	0	32	40	X	X	X
Austria	4,034	4,424	5,651	52	56	68	0.7	0.6	1	32	34	X	X	X
Belarus, Rep	4,714	7,215	8,361	50	71	84	1.1	(2.9)	1	X	X	X	X	X
Belgium	9,298	9,809	10,236	95	97	98	0.4	(2.5)	1	X	X	X	X	X
Bosnia and Herzegovina	1,172	1,695	3,102	31	49	69	(2.5)	(6.1)	0	X	X	X	X	X
Bulgaria	5,017	6,201	6,450	58	71	83	0.4	(2.4)	1	31	40	X	X	X
Croatia, Rep	1,924	2,896	3,428	45	64	81	1.4	(2.6)	0	X	X	X	X	X
Czech Rep	5,780	6,736	8,096	58	65	76	0.1	(0.3)	1	32	36	X	X	X
Denmark	4,140	4,414	4,577	82	85	90	0.3	(0.4)	1	33	32	X	X	X
Estonia, Rep	968	1,118	1,181	68	73	83	(0.2)	(1.5)	0	33	39	X	X	X
Finland	2,745	3,225	4,129	58	63	76	1.0	(0.4)	1	31	35	X	X	X
France	38,481	42,203	50,055	73	73	82	0.5	0.4	4	34	37	X	X	X
Germany	63,866	70,616	70,310	81	87	92	0.8	(1.2)	16	31	36	X	X	X
Greece	5,003	6,817	7,806	55	65	79	1.2	(1.0)	2	31	37	X	X	X
Hungary	5,560	6,541	7,393	53	65	79	0.3	(1.9)	1	32	34	X	X	X
Iceland	189	246	321	87	92	95	1.3	(1.1)	0	35	39	X	X	X
Ireland	1,704	2,043	2,740	54	58	71	0.5	0.0	1	34	39	X	X	X
Italy	36,394	38,101	39,895	66	67	76	0.0	0.1	6	X	X	X	X	X
Latvia, Rep	1,618	1,863	1,943	65	73	83	(0.4)	(2.0)	1	33	39	X	X	X
Lithuania, Rep	1,842	2,667	3,213	56	72	84	0.9	(2.3)	0	32	40	X	X	X
Macedonia, former Yugoslav Rep	847	1,294	1,914	51	60	74	1.8	0.1	0	X	X	X	X	X
Moldova, Rep	1,376	2,293	3,647	36	52	71	1.9	(1.3)	0	X	X	X	X	X
Netherlands	12,070	13,801	15,105	88	89	93	0.8	0.2	2	X	X	X	X	X
Norway	1,842	2,667	3,213	68	73	82	0.7	(0.2)	0	33	44	X	X	X
Poland, Rep	18,850	24,853	32,565	55	65	78	0.9	(1.1)	5	32	38	X	X	X
Portugal	2,515	3,496	5,374	28	36	55	1.1	(0.7)	1	30	34	X	X	X
Romania	9,809	12,650	15,499	46	55	71	0.5	(1.3)	1	30	38	X	X	X
Russian Federation	89,168	111,736	118,705	66	76	86	0.4	(1.7)	16	X	X	X	X	X
Slovak Rep	2,191	3,146	4,451	46	59	74	1.2	(0.7)	0	X	X	X	X	X
Slovenia, Rep	738	1,236	1,445	42	64	79	1.8	(2.1)	0	X	X	X	X	X
Spain	24,765	30,292	31,886	70	76	85	0.5	(0.7)	2	31	34	X	X	X
Sweden	6,778	7,296	8,583	83	83	88	0.5	0.5	1	36	39	X	X	X
Switzerland	3,534	4,379	5,762	56	61	74	1.5	0.4	1	31	35	X	X	X
Ukraine	28,564	36,099	40,195	58	70	83	0.7	(1.9)	7	X	X	X	X	X
United Kingdom	49,896	52,119	57,375	89	89	93	0.4	(0.4)	4	35	37	X	X	X
Yugoslavia, Fed Rep	3,905	6,134	8,479	43	57	74	2.6	(0.2)	1	30	35	X	X	X

	Urban Population (000)			Percent Urban			1990-95 Urban Growth Rates	1990-95 Rural Growth Rates	Number of Cities Greater Than 750,000 Population {a}	Dependency Ratio (Dependent population, ages <15 and >65, as a percent of the potential labor force, ages 15 to 65)		People in Absolute Poverty (percent) 1980-1990		
	1975	1995	2025	1975	1995	2025				Urban	Rural	Total	Urban	Rural
NORTH & CENTRAL AMERICA	235,306	331,761	507,609	57	68	79	1.8	0.4	64	X	X	X	X	X
Belize	67	101	231	50	47	60	2.3	3.0	0	X	X	X	X	65
Canada	17,548	22,593	32,018	76	77	84	1.2	1.1	5	32	35	X	X	X
Costa Rica	814	1,702	3,843	41	50	69	3.5	1.4	1	36	43	29	24	34
Cuba	5,977	8,389	10,882	64	76	86	1.5	(1.1)	1	31	36	X	X	35
Dominican Rep	2,289	5,051	8,890	45	65	80	3.3	(0.3)	2	38	43	55	45	70
El Salvador	1,651	2,599	6,015	40	45	62	2.7	1.8	0	41	48	51	20	75
Guatemala	2,211	4,404	13,389	37	41	62	3.9	2.2	1	44	50	71	66	74
Haiti	1,069	2,266	7,076	22	32	54	4.0	1.2	1	42	45	76	65	80
Honduras	969	2,482	6,870	32	44	64	4.5	1.8	0	42	50	37	14	55
Jamaica	888	1,314	2,319	44	54	70	1.5	(0.3)	0	34	42	X	X	80
Mexico	36,948	70,535	117,222	63	75	86	2.8	(0.0)	8	39	44	30	23	51
Nicaragua	1,220	2,787	7,072	50	63	78	4.8	2.1	1	48	51	20	21	19
Panama	839	1,401	2,620	49	53	70	2.4	1.2	1	35	43	42	21	65
Trinidad and Tobago	637	938	1,511	63	72	84	1.9	(0.8)	0	38	44	X	X	39
United States	159,069	200,695	281,179	74	76	85	1.3	0.2	43	34	36	X	X	X
SOUTH AMERICA	137,578	249,331	406,679	64	78	88	2.5	(0.8)	31	X	X	X	X	X
Argentina	21,029	30,463	43,083	81	88	93	1.6	(1.3)	4	37	42	16	15	20
Bolivia	1,975	4,505	10,370	42	61	79	4.1	0.0	1	41	46	60	30	86
Brazil	66,065	126,599	204,791	61	78	89	2.7	(1.4)	14	36	44	47	38	73
Chile	8,101	11,966	17,684	78	84	89	1.8	0.9	0	36	41	X	X	25
Colombia	14,434	25,526	41,532	61	73	84	2.4	(0.3)	4	35	43	42	40	45
Ecuador	2,926	6,698	13,456	42	58	76	3.5	0.5	2	38	46	56	40	65
Guyana	220	302	668	30	36	59	2.4	0.1	0	33	38	X	X	60
Paraguay	1,045	2,613	6,476	39	53	72	4.3	1.2	0	38	48	35	19	50
Peru	9,319	17,175	30,653	61	72	84	2.6	0.3	1	37	45	32	13	75
Suriname	163	213	418	45	50	70	2.3	(0.0)	0	X	X	X	X	57
Uruguay	2,349	2,877	3,491	83	90	95	0.9	(2.1)	1	37	33	13	10	29
Venezuela	9,911	20,281	33,791	78	93	97	2.8	(3.5)	4	38	47	31	28	58
ASIA	592,282	1,197,970	2,718,435	25	35	55	3.3	0.8	154	X	X	X	X	X
Afghanistan, Islamic State	2,040	4,026	18,059	13	20	40	7.7	5.4	1	43	43	53	18	60
Armenia	1,780	2,473	3,783	63	69	80	1.8	0.6	1	X	X	X	X	X
Azerbaijan	2,930	4,216	7,194	52	56	71	1.7	0.6	1	X	X	X	X	X
Bangladesh	7,108	22,034	78,430	9	18	40	5.3	1.5	3	X	X	78	X	86
Bhutan	39	105	597	3	6	19	4.8	1.0	0	X	X	X	X	90
Cambodia	731	2,123	8,567	10	21	44	6.2	2.2	0	44	45	X	X	X
China	160,047	369,492	831,880	17	30	55	4.0	(0.0)	51	28	36	9	X	13
Georgia, Rep	2,432	3,190	4,544	50	58	74	1.0	(1.0)	1	X	X	X	X	X
India	132,272	250,681	629,757	21	27	45	2.9	1.6	34	36	41	40	33	42
Indonesia	26,259	69,992	167,393	19	35	61	4.5	0.1	9	34	39	25	20	27
Iran, Islamic Rep	15,278	39,716	92,491	46	59	75	3.6	1.3	5	47	53	X	X	30
Iraq	6,765	15,258	36,435	61	75	85	3.2	0.4	1	45	52	X	X	30
Israel	2,994	5,098	7,308	87	91	94	3.9	3.1	1	38	40	X	X	X
Japan	84,409	97,120	103,190	76	78	85	0.4	(0.2)	8	29	36	X	X	X
Jordan	1,438	3,887	10,107	55	71	84	5.9	2.6	1	45	50	16	14	17
Kazakhstan, Rep	7,374	10,218	16,257	52	60	75	1.2	(0.5)	1	X	X	X	X	X
Korea, Dem People's Rep	9,356	14,650	25,094	56	61	75	2.4	1.2	1	X	X	X	X	20
Korea, Rep	16,947	36,572	50,987	48	81	94	2.9	(5.7)	6	28	31	5	5	4
Kuwait	844	1,501	2,765	84	97	99	(6.3)	(13.0)	1	X	X	X	X	X
Kyrgyz Rep	1,250	1,847	4,079	38	39	57	2.1	1.4	0	X	X	X	X	X
Lao People's Dem Rep	344	1,060	4,316	11	22	45	6.1	2.2	0	48	48	X	X	85
Lebanon	1,849	2,622	4,154	67	87	94	4.1	(1.4)	0	39	44	X	X	15
Malaysia	4,616	10,814	22,942	38	54	73	3.9	0.8	1	39	45	16	8	22
Mongolia	704	1,468	2,926	49	61	76	3.0	0.6	0	X	X	X	X	X
Myanmar	7,282	12,188	35,759	24	26	47	3.3	1.8	1	38	42	35	X	40
Nepal	649	2,996	13,959	5	14	34	7.1	2.0	0	44	46	60	51	61
Oman	53	285	1,983	6	13	33	7.8	3.7	0	X	X	X	X	6
Pakistan	19,733	48,742	161,579	26	35	57	4.4	2.0	8	44	48	28	26	29
Philippines	15,294	36,614	77,622	36	54	74	4.2	(0.1)	2	38	45	54	40	64
Saudi Arabia	4,257	14,339	37,618	59	80	88	2.9	(0.6)	2	X	X	X	X	X
Singapore	2,263	2,848	3,355	100	100	100	1.0	0.0	1	29	0	X	X	X
Sri Lanka	2,998	4,108	10,660	22	22	43	2.2	1.0	0	33	37	39	15	46
Syrian Arab Rep	3,352	7,676	23,311	45	52	70	4.3	2.6	2	48	54	X	X	54
Tajikistan, Rep	1,223	1,964	5,881	36	32	50	2.9	2.9	0	X	X	X	X	X
Thailand	6,244	11,787	28,756	15	20	39	2.5	0.8	1	28	36	30	17	34
Turkey	16,651	42,598	79,102	42	69	87	4.4	(2.5)	5	36	43	X	X	14
Turkmenistan, Rep	1,198	1,839	4,067	48	45	61	2.3	2.3	0	X	X	X	X	X
United Arab Emirates	330	1,600	2,700	65	84	91	3.4	(0.9)	0	30	36	X	X	X
Uzbekistan, Rep	5,465	9,430	22,300	39	41	59	2.6	2.0	1	X	X	X	X	X
Viet Nam	9,021	15,479	46,135	19	21	39	3.1	2.0	2	36	44	54	X	60
Yemen, Rep	1,147	4,877	19,674	16	34	58	8.0	3.6	0	X	X	X	X	X
OCEANIA	15,389	20,063	30,712	72	70	75	1.5	1.7	6	X	X	X	X	X
Australia	11,943	15,318	21,852	86	85	89	1.3	1.9	5	33	34	X	X	X
Fiji	212	319	692	37	41	60	2.2	1.1	0	X	X	X	X	20
New Zealand	2,552	3,077	4,011	83	86	92	1.5	(0.4)	1	X	X	X	X	X
Papua New Guinea	326	690	2,431	12	16	32	3.6	2.0	0	X	X	73	10	75
Solomon Islands	17	65	323	9	17	38	6.5	2.7	0	X	X	X	X	60

Sources: United Nations Population Division and United Nations Development Programme.
Notes: a. Cities greater than 750,000 population as assessed in 1990.
World and regional totals include countries not listed. 0 = zero or less than half of the unit of measure. X = not available or indeterminate; negative numbers are shown in parentheses.
For additional information, see Sources and Technical Notes.

Data Table A.2 Access to Safe Drinking Water and Sanitation, 1980–95

	Access to Safe Drinking Water (percent)		Access to Sanitation Services (percent)		Urban Household Access to Safe Drinking Water Sources (percent of all households)				Urban Household Access to Sanitation Services (percent of all households)			
	Urban	Rural	Urban	Rural	House or Yard Pipe	Public Standpipe	Borehole and Pump	Other	House to Sewer	Septic System	Wet Latrine	Other
WORLD												
AFRICA												
Algeria	X	X	X	X	X	X	X	X	X	X	X	X
Angola	69.0	15.0	26.0	9.0	45.0	18.0	4.0	2.0	8.0	8.0	0.0	10.0
Benin	41.0	43.0	60.0	4.0	X	X	X	X	X	X	X	X
Botswana	100.0	88.0	100.0	85.0	X	X	X	X	X	X	X	X
Burkina Faso	52.9	75.0	50.0	10.0	23.0	30.0	0.0	0.0	X	X	X	X
Burundi	92.0	49.0	74.0	50.0	30.0	62.0	0.0	0.0	X	X	X	X
Cameroon	42.0	45.0	X	X	X	X	X	X	X	X	X	X
Central African Rep	18.0	18.0	X	X	8.0	7.0	1.0	0.0	X	X	X	X
Chad	48.0	17.0	72.0	7.0	10.0	28.0	0.0	10.0	0.0	2.0	0.0	71.0
Congo	92.0	2.0	X	2.0	X	X	X	X	X	X	X	X
Cote d'Ivoire	59.0	81.0	100.0	41.0	59.0	0.0	0.0	0.0	87.0	13.0	0.0	0.0
Egypt	82.0	50.0	23.0	6.0	X	X	X	X	X	X	X	X
Equatorial Guinea	88.0	100.0	100.0	15.0	13.2	X	36.1	38.7	87.0	13.0	X	X
Eritrea	X	X	X	X	X	X	X	X	X	X	X	X
Ethiopia	70.0	11.0	97.0	7.0	X	X	X	X	X	X	X	X
Gabon	90.0	50.0	X	X	X	X	X	X	X	X	X	X
Gambia, The	91.6	50.8	50.0	29.0	42.0	50.0	0.0	0.0	11.0	17.0	0.0	23.0
Ghana	70.0	49.0	64.0	33.0	45.8	6.7	10.0	7.5	0.0	20.0	0.0	45.0
Guinea	61.0	62.0	17.8	1.1	61.0	0.0	0.0	0.0	0.0	17.8	0.0	0.0
Guinea-Bissau	38.0	57.0	24.0	19.0	35.4	0.0	0.0	0.0	1.2	8.0	0.0	15.6
Kenya	67.0	49.0	63.9	78.6	X	X	X	X	X	X	X	X
Lesotho	57.0	57.0	3.0	44.0	31.0	26.8	0.0	0.0	1.6	2.4	0.0	0.0
Liberia	58.0	8.0	49.0	4.0	29.8	1.6	0.0	26.6	2.0	20.0	0.0	28.0
Libya	100.0	80.0	100.0	85.0	X	X	X	X	X	X	X	X
Madagascar	83.0	10.0	49.2	3.6	X	X	X	X	X	X	X	X
Malawi	52.0	44.0	89.0	60.0	35.4	14.6	1.0	1.0	15.0	0.0	0.0	75.0
Mali	36.0	38.0	99.0	24.0	17.6	14.4	4.8	1.2	7.2	6.8	0.0	86.0
Mauritania	84.0	89.0	34.0	X	X	X	X	X	X	X	X	X
Mauritius	95.0	95.0	98.0	97.0	95.0	0.0	0.0	0.0	42.0	41.0	4.0	12.0
Morocco	98.0	14.0	66.5	17.9	X	X	X	X	X	X	X	X
Mozambique	17.0	40.0	70.0	4.6	9.5	8.2	0.0	0.3	13.0	7.0	0.0	48.0
Namibia	87.0	42.0	76.0	41.0	72.0	14.2	0.8	0.0	69.3	0.0	0.0	7.7
Niger	46.0	55.0	69.0	4.0	29.0	14.0	3.0	0.0	0.0	3.0	0.0	67.0
Nigeria	63.0	26.0	51.0	29.0	32.7	24.2	3.6	2.5	0.0	35.0	0.0	16.5
Rwanda	84.0	67.0	88.0	17.0	X	X	X	X	X	X	X	X
Senegal	84.0	28.1	92.1	40.0	54.1	30.0	0.9	0.0	25.4	0.0	50.0	11.1
Sierra Leone	58.0	21.0	55.0	31.0	X	X	X	X	X	X	X	X
Somalia	50.0	29.0	41.0	5.0	X	X	X	X	X	X	X	X
South Africa	X	X	X	X	X	X	X	X	X	X	X	X
Sudan	66.0	43.0	85.8	14.0	31.9	12.8	0.0	21.3	2.6	12.6	0.0	70.2
Swaziland	41.0	44.0	78.0	35.0	37.2	3.8	0.0	0.0	37.0	42.0	0.0	0.0
Tanzania	75.0	46.0	76.0	77.0	X	X	X	X	X	X	X	X
Togo	74.0	58.0	12.2	20.0	30.1	42.5	0.2	1.2	0.0	4.1	0.4	7.7
Tunisia	100.0	89.0	98.0	93.0	93.3	4.3	0.4	2.0	55.0	35.0	2.3	6.0
Uganda	47.0	32.0	73.6	57.8	X	X	X	X	X	X	X	X
Zaire	37.0	23.0	20.8	3.6	X	X	X	X	X	X	X	X
Zambia	64.0	27.0	67.0	25.0	X	X	X	X	X	X	X	X
Zimbabwe	95.0	80.0	95.0	22.0	X	X	X	X	X	X	X	X
EUROPE												
Albania	100.0	95.0	100.0	100.0	X	X	X	X	X	X	X	X
Austria	100.0	100.0	100.0	100.0	X	X	X	X	X	X	X	X
Belarus, Rep	100.0	100.0	100.0	100.0	X	X	X	X	X	X	X	X
Belgium	100.0	100.0	100.0	100.0	X	X	X	X	X	X	X	X
Bosnia and Herzegovina	100.0	X	X	X	X	X	X	X	X	X	X	X
Bulgaria	100.0	96.0	100.0	100.0	X	X	X	X	X	X	X	X
Croatia, Rep	100.0	X	X	X	X	X	X	X	X	X	X	X
Czech Rep	100.0	100.0	100.0	100.0	X	X	X	X	X	X	X	X
Denmark	100.0	100.0	100.0	100.0	X	X	X	X	X	X	X	X
Estonia, Rep	100.0	100.0	100.0	100.0	X	X	X	X	X	X	X	X
Finland	99.0	90.0	90.0	90.0	X	X	X	X	X	X	X	X
France	100.0	100.0	100.0	100.0	X	X	X	X	X	X	X	X
Germany	100.0	100.0	X	X	X	X	X	X	X	X	X	X
Greece	100.0	95.0	100.0	95.0	X	X	X	X	X	X	X	X
Hungary	100.0	95.0	100.0	100.0	X	X	X	X	X	X	X	X
Iceland	100.0	100.0	100.0	100.0	X	X	X	X	X	X	X	X
Ireland	100.0	100.0	100.0	100.0	X	X	X	X	X	X	X	X
Italy	100.0	100.0	100.0	100.0	X	X	X	X	X	X	X	X
Latvia, Rep	100.0	100.0	100.0	100.0	X	X	X	X	X	X	X	X
Lithuania, Rep	100.0	100.0	100.0	100.0	X	X	X	X	X	X	X	X
Macedonia, former Yugoslav Rep	100.0	X	X	X	X	X	X	X	X	X	X	X
Moldova, Rep	100.0	100.0	100.0	100.0	X	X	X	X	X	X	X	X
Netherlands	100.0	100.0	100.0	100.0	X	X	X	X	X	X	X	X
Norway	100.0	100.0	100.0	100.0	X	X	X	X	X	X	X	X
Poland, Rep	94.0	82.0	82.0	82.0	X	X	X	X	X	X	X	X
Portugal	97.0	90.0	100.0	95.0	X	X	X	X	X	X	X	X
Romania	100.0	90.0	100.0	95.0	X	X	X	X	X	X	X	X
Russian Federation	100.0	100.0	100.0	100.0	X	X	X	X	X	X	X	X
Slovak Rep	100.0	100.0	100.0	100.0	X	X	X	X	X	X	X	X
Slovenia, Rep	100.0	X	X	X	X	X	X	X	X	X	X	X
Spain	100.0	100.0	100.0	100.0	X	X	X	X	X	X	X	X
Sweden	100.0	100.0	100.0	100.0	X	X	X	X	X	X	X	X
Switzerland	100.0	100.0	100.0	100.0	X	X	X	X	X	X	X	X
Ukraine	100.0	100.0	100.0	100.0	X	X	X	X	X	X	X	X
United Kingdom	100.0	100.0	100.0	100.0	X	X	X	X	X	X	X	X
Yugoslavia, Fed Rep	100.0	X	X	X	X	X	X	X	X	X	X	X

	Access to Safe Drinking Water (percent)		Access to Sanitation Services (percent)		Urban Household Access to Safe Drinking Water Sources (percent of all households)				Urban Household Access to Sanitation Services (percent of all households)			
	Urban	Rural	Urban	Rural	House or Yard Pipe	Public Standpipe	Borehole and Pump	Other	House to Sewer	Septic System	Wet Latrine	Other
NORTH & CENTRAL AMERICA												
Belize	96.0	82.0	24.2	88.9	X	X	X	X	16.1	8.1	0.0	0.0
Canada	100.0	100.0	X	X	X	X	X	X	X	X	X	X
Costa Rica	88.0	99.0	99.4	98.2	83.6	0.0	0.0	1.4	96.0	0.0	0.0	3.4
Cuba	88.0	99.0	71.3	51.3	X	X	X	X	X	X	X	X
Dominican Rep	74.0	67.0	93.0	71.0	X	X	X	X	X	X	X	X
El Salvador	78.0	37.0	92.0	59.0	67.9	10.1	0.0	0.0	61.0	5.0	0.0	26.0
Guatemala	92.0	43.0	72.0	52.0	X	X	X	X	X	X	X	X
Haiti	37.0	23.0	41.8	16.2	X	X	X	X	X	X	X	X
Honduras	81.0	53.0	88.2	53.2	58.0	6.7	16.3	0.0	49.5	0.0	0.0	38.7
Jamaica	96.0	46.0	14.0	X	X	X	X	X	X	X	X	X
Mexico	91.0	62.0	85.5	25.0	X	X	X	X	X	X	X	X
Nicaragua	81.0	27.0	32.0	X	X	X	X	X	X	X	X	X
Panama	100.0	100.0	100.0	73.2	98.6	0.0	0.0	1.4	50.0	18.1	0.0	31.9
Trinidad and Tobago	100.0	88.0	100.0	92.0	X	X	X	X	X	X	X	X
United States	X	X	X	X	X	X	X	X	X	X	X	X
SOUTH AMERICA												
Argentina	73.0	17.0	100.0	29.0	X	X	X	X	X	X	X	X
Bolivia	78.0	22.0	62.9	17.5	39.0	39.0	0.0	0.0	36.2	12.7	X	13.9
Brazil	85.0	31.0	84.0	32.0	X	X	X	X	36.2	12.7	0.0	0.0
Chile	94.0	37.0	84.8	6.0	94.0	0.0	0.0	0.0	84.8	0.0	0.0	0.0
Colombia	88.0	48.0	73.2	36.8	74.7	0.0	0.0	13.3	73.2	0.0	0.0	0.0
Ecuador	82.0	55.0	86.0	34.2	76.2	4.5	0.0	1.3	60.8	0.0	16.5	8.7
Guyana	90.0	51.0	100.0	84.0	83.0	0.0	0.0	7.0	0.0	36.0	0.0	64.0
Paraguay	61.0	9.0	31.0	60.0	X	X	X	X	X	X	X	X
Peru	74.4	23.6	62.0	9.3	74.4	0.0	0.0	0.0	62.0	0.0	0.0	0.0
Suriname	82.0	56.0	64.0	36.0	X	X	X	X	X	X	X	X
Uruguay	100.0	5.0	60.0	65.0	X	X	X	X	X	X	X	X
Venezuela	80.0	75.0	97.0	72.0	86.1	0.0	0.0	0.0	X	X	X	X
ASIA												
Afghanistan, Islamic State	39.0	4.9	27.6	1.2	7.3	11.7	10.2	9.8	5.0	18.0	0.0	3.0
Armenia	100.0	100.0	100.0	100.0	X	X	X	X	X	X	X	X
Azerbaijan	100.0	100.0	100.0	100.0	X	X	X	X	X	X	X	X
Bangladesh	100.0	88.8	44.4	27.7	18.9	9.5	69.9	1.7	0.0	0.0	27.0	16.0
Bhutan	75.0	54.0	89.6	17.9	75.0	0.0	0.0	0.0	70.0	10.0	4.0	4.0
Cambodia	X	X	X	X	X	X	X	X	X	X	X	X
China	93.0	89.0	70.0	6.0	X	X	X	X	0.0	0.0	70.0	0.0
Georgia, Rep	100.0	100.0	100.0	100.0	X	X	X	X	X	X	X	X
India	85.0	79.0	70.0	12.0	44.1	24.1	16.8	0.0	26.0	27.0	0.0	17.0
Indonesia	78.0	54.0	78.0	39.0	21.6	10.3	16.9	29.1	0.0	58.0	0.0	20.0
Iran, Islamic Rep	89.0	77.0	82.9	36.5	X	X	X	X	X	X	X	X
Iraq	50.0	30.0	40.0	25.0	X	X	X	X	X	X	X	X
Israel	100.0	97.0	99.0	95.0	X	X	X	X	X	X	X	X
Japan	100.0	85.0	X	X	X	X	X	X	X	X	X	X
Jordan	91.8	82.8	41.1	1.7	X	X	X	X	X	X	X	X
Kazakhstan, Rep	100.0	100.0	100.0	100.0	X	X	X	X	X	X	X	X
Korea, Dem People's Rep	100.0	100.0	100.0	100.0	X	X	X	X	X	X	X	X
Korea, Rep	100.0	100.0	100.0	12.0	X	X	X	X	X	X	X	X
Kuwait	100.0	X	100.0	X	X	X	X	X	X	X	X	X
Kyrgyz Rep	100.0	100.0	100.0	100.0	X	X	X	X	X	X	X	X
Lao People's Dem Rep	40.0	39.0	96.0	12.0	34.3	2.9	0.7	2.1	0.0	38.0	44.0	15.0
Lebanon	99.0	99.0	89.0	89.5	96.0	0.0	0.0	4.0	81.0	9.0	X	X
Malaysia	96.0	66.0	94.0	94.0	X	X	X	X	X	X	X	X
Mongolia	100.0	58.0	100.0	47.0	X	X	X	X	X	X	X	X
Myanmar	36.0	39.0	45.0	40.5	14.8	19.4	1.8	0.0	3.0	17.0	21.0	5.0
Nepal	66.0	41.0	69.0	16.0	37.4	0.0	28.6	0.0	0.0	45.0	9.0	16.0
Oman	97.0	50.0	97.0	68.0	X	X	X	X	X	X	X	X
Pakistan	77.0	52.0	62.0	19.0	X	X	X	X	X	X	X	X
Philippines	93.0	77.0	87.0	67.0	45.0	16.0	29.0	3.0	X	X	X	X
Saudi Arabia	100.0	74.0	100.0	30.0	X	X	X	X	X	X	X	X
Singapore	100.0	X	99.0	X	X	X	X	X	X	X	X	X
Sri Lanka	87.0	47.0	83.0	62.0	60.0	11.0	7.0	9.0	1.0	77.0	0.0	5.0
Syrian Arab Rep	92.0	78.0	100.0	100.0	80.4	11.6	0.0	0.0	100.0	0.0	0.0	0.0
Tajikistan, Rep	100.0	100.0	100.0	100.0	X	X	X	X	X	X	X	X
Thailand	67.0	85.0	84.0	86.0	X	X	X	X	X	X	X	X
Turkey	100.0	70.0	95.0	90.0	X	X	X	X	X	X	X	X
Turkmenistan, Rep	100.0	100.0	100.0	100.0	X	X	X	X	X	X	X	X
United Arab Emirates	100.0	100.0	100.0	77.0	X	X	X	X	X	X	X	X
Uzbekistan, Rep	100.0	100.0	100.0	100.0	X	X	X	X	X	X	X	X
Viet Nam	53.0	32.0	44.0	16.0	35.1	X	X	X	0.0	30.0	10.0	5.0
Yemen, Rep	X	X	X	X	X	X	X	X	X	X	X	X
OCEANIA												
Australia	100.0	100.0	100.0	100.0	X	X	X	X	X	X	X	X
Fiji	100.0	100.0	99.0	99.0	88.3	0.0	0.0	11.7	18.0	50.0	28.0	4.0
New Zealand	100.0	82.0	95.0	88.0	X	X	X	X	X	X	X	X
Papua New Guinea	84.0	17.0	95.0	12.0	X	X	X	X	X	X	X	X
Solomon Islands	82.0	58.0	73.0	2.0	X	X	X	X	X	X	X	X

Sources: World Health Organization and United Nations Children's Fund.
Notes: All of the former constituent republics of the Soviet Union were given the same 100 percent coverage of water and sanitation services as occurred in the former Soviet Union.
All successor countries to the former Yugoslavia were given the same 100 percent coverage as occurred in Yugoslavia.
Percent served by specific sources or services need not sum to total served. 0 = zero or less than half the unit of measure; X = not available or indeterminate.
For additional information, see Sources and Technical Notes.

Data Table A.3 Air Pollution in Selected Cities, 1989–94

		Suspended Particulate Matter		Smoke		Sulfur Dioxide		Lead	
		Site Years	Mean (micrograms)	Site Years	Mean (micrograms)	Site Years	Mean (micrograms)	Site Years	Mean (micrograms)
AFRICA									
Egypt	Cairo	X	X	12	55.2	12	41.7	X	X
EUROPE									
Finland	Helsinki	6	47.1	X	X	3	8.7	X	X
Germany	Frankfurt	5	36.8	X	X	5	23.2	X	X
Poland	Jarczew	X	X	9	48.2	8	18.9	X	X
	Wroclaw	X	X	6	67.4	6	125.4	X	X
Portugal	Lisbon	7	105.7	X	X	5	35.5	7	0.4
Spain	Madrid	X	X	9	41.9	9	16.3	X	X
Yugoslavia	Zagreb	8	72.1	X	X	12	39.1	3	0.4
NORTH AMERICA									
Canada	Hamilton	10	49.6	X	X	5	19.3	6	0.0
	Montreal	2	43.1	X	X	4	19.6	X	X
	Toronto	7	58.4	X	X	5	17.7	4	0.0
	Vancouver	6	34.9	X	X	4	17.1	4	0.0
United States	Los Angeles	6	49.0	X	X	X	X	6	0.1
	New York City	9	61.6	X	X	11	37.5	10	0.0
SOUTH AMERICA									
Brazil	Sao Paulo	2	36.4	10	43.0	10	36.6	X	X
Venezuela	Caracas	X	X	2	24.0	2	24.3	X	X
ASIA									
China	Beijing	8	362.7	X	X	8	88.6	X	X
	Guangzhou	8	169.7	X	X	8	45.5	X	X
	Shanghai	8	225.2	X	X	8	63.3	X	X
	Shenyang	8	356.9	X	X	8	131.5	X	X
	Xian	8	444.9	X	X	8	50.0	X	X
Hong Kong	Hong Kong	9	82.4	X	X	X	X	9	57.7
Iran, Islamic Rep	Tehran	10	263.2	11	112.1	11	139.5	1	0.0
Japan	Osaka	16	44.0	X	X	16	67.9	X	X
	Tokyo	12	49.9	X	X	12	70.0	X	X
Pakistan	Lahore	1	405.5	X	X	X	X	X	X
Thailand	Bangkok	2	171.4	X	X	2	1,224.1	2	7.5
OCEANIA									
New Zealand	Auckland	X	X	4	4.0	4	3.5	X	X
	Christchurch	3	20.5	X	X	4	13.8	X	X

Sources: World Health Organization and the United Nations Environment Programme.
Notes: These data are the most recent available, dating from 1989 to 1994. Large numbers of observation years are due to multiple sites in a city over several years.
X = not available. For additional information, see Sources and Technical Notes.

Data Table A.4 India: City Indicators, 1993

Indicator	Bombay	Delhi	Madras	Bangalore	Lucknow	Varanasi	Hubli-Dharwad	Mysore	Gulbarga	Bhiwandi	Tumkur
Population											
Population (million)	10.26	8.96	5.65	4.47	1.80	1.08	0.68	0.70	0.33	0.57	0.19
Growth Rate (%)	2.04	3.19	2.11	4.14	4.04	2.27	2.33	3.64	2.75	22.88	4.04
Average Household Size	4.80	4.97	4.70	4.82	5.71	7.50	5.61	5.24	6.09	5.21	5.09
Female Headed (%)	14.10	9.00	13.42	17.42	6.40	6.20	12.47	14.40	8.19	7.10	14.85
Below Poverty Line (%)	17.00	17.00	18.50	12.00	22.00	28.27	12.82	5.51	17.44	2.69	24.60
Household Income Distribution (Quintile Boundaries US$)											
I Quintile (poorest 20%)	374	290	347	385	291	268	284	373	258	X	287
II Quintile	620	679	531	670	482	426	698	746	660	X	433
III Quintile	939	1,082	772	1,144	762	634	845	1,176	1,052	X	641
IV Quintile	1,553	1,496	1,492	1,437	1,331	1,230	1,473	1,511	1,435	X	923
V Quintile (richest 20%)	2,497	3,292	2,781	2,487	2,181	2,084	2,009	2,372	1,951	X	1,761
Household Connections (%)											
Water	54.74	57.00	33.87	47.30	32.68	39.65	37.62	37.90	26.68	51.43	31.23
Sewage	51.43	39.60	37.17	35.34	30.00	73.35	37.37	90.00	13.92	14.69	0.00
Electricity	89.61	70.30	81.91	81.80	76.25	85.66	74.11	83.01	78.16	94.87	87.44
Telephone	18.00	30.80	18.31	16.34	11.71	21.91	7.42	15.28	10.19	10.22	8.41
Access to Potable Water	96.39	91.50	59.90	80.89	88.21	84.53	88.70	89.94	90.41	85.72	86.20
Miscellaneous											
Informal Employment (%)	68.10	66.67	60.60	32.21	48.00	48.96	30.73	31.12	27.35	77.94	63.17
Automobiles (per 1,000 pop.)	50.91	205.41	101.82	130.23	129.70	85.27	48.73	122.59	59.91	14.47	84.85
House Price to Income Ratio	3.53	7.00	7.88	10.79	4.76	5.11	3.70	7.48	4.04	0.27	6.36
Floor Area per Person (sq.m.)	3.49	6.88	6.22	9.48	5.51	4.53	6.22	11.83	6.11	2.41	7.38
Social Development											
Crime Rate -- Murder (per 1,000 pop.)	0.14	0.04	0.02	0.04	0.04	0.04	0.02	0.09	0.10	X	0.02
Crime Rate -- Theft (per 1,000 pop.)	1.68	1.64	0.68	1.73	1.38	0.23	0.95	0.79	1.19	X	0.46
Classroom Size -- Primary	48	39	30	32	20	43	47	21	44	60	29
Classroom Size -- Secondary	31	42	61	36	57	54	31	16	24	33	22
Hospital Beds (people per bed)	398.00	372.00	137.00	270.00	460.00	372.00	721.00	156.00	209.00	924.00	486.00
Infant Mortality (per 1,000 live births)	23.02	19.00	18.23	7.94	47.00	55.00	21.44	X	30.29	25.70	20.62
Annual per Capita Solid Waste (metric tons)	0.20	0.44	0.29	0.16	0.31	0.14	0.15	0.26	0.13	0.10	0.13
Solid Waste Collected (%)	90.00	76.92	90.00	96.00	73.66	87.50	89.08	60.00	74.24	40.00	50.00

Source: Society for Development Studies.
Note: X = not available. For additional information, see Sources and Technical Notes.

Sources and Technical Notes

Data Table A.1
Urban Indicators, 1975–2025

Sources: Urban population, percent urban, urban growth rates, and rural growth rates: United Nations (U.N.) Population Division, *Urban and Rural Areas, 1950–2025 (The 1994 Revision)*, on diskette (U.N., New York, 1995); number of cities over 750,000: United Nations (U.N.) *U.N. World Urbanization Prospects: The 1994 Revision* (Sales No. E.95.XIII.12, U.N., New York, 1995) Tables A1, A2, A6, A7, and A17; urban and rural dependency ratios: United Nations (U.N.) Population Division, *Urban and Rural Areas by Sex and Age: The 1992 Revision* (U.N., New York, 1993); and people in absolute poverty: United Nations Development Programme, *Human Development Report 1994* (Oxford University Press, New York, 1994).

As part of its biennial revision of population projections, the Population Division of the United Nations Department for Economic and Social Information and Policy Analysis prepares a number of data sets of global population estimates and projections. The most recent *Population Prospects* was revised in 1994. This table includes data from two data sets created as part of that 1994 revision and one data set from the 1992 revision. Population data in these data sets are estimates based on population censuses and surveys. See the Sources and Technical Notes for Data Table 8.1 for further information. All projections are for the medium-case scenario.

Urban population and *percent urban* refer to the midyear population of areas defined as urban in each of the countries of the world. These definitions vary slightly from country to country. Rural is defined as "not urban." *Urban growth rates* and *rural growth rates* include the effects of urban-rural migration.

Number of cities greater than 750,000 population is the number of cities in each country (as defined by each country) that had a population of 750,000 or more in 1990. There are only 369 such cities in the world.

Urban dependency ratio is defined here as the ratio of the urban population under 15 years and over 65 years of age compared with the urban population between the ages of 15 and 65. The *rural dependency ratio* is defined similarly. For the purposes of this indicator, this latter age group is defined as the economically active population upon which younger and older people depend. In reality, some people under the age of 15 and over the age of 65 are economically active everywhere, and some people between the ages of 15 and 65 are economically dependent on others.

People in absolute poverty is derived from a host of country studies and may not be strictly comparable.

Data Table A.2
Access to Safe Drinking Water and Sanitation, 1980–95

Sources: World Health Organization (WHO) and the United Nations Children's Fund (UNICEF), *WHO/UNICEF Joint Water Supply and Sanitation Monitoring Programme*, unpublished data (WHO, Geneva, 1995); WHO, *The International Drinking Water Supply and Sanitation Decade: End of Decade Review (as at December 1990)* (WHO, Geneva, August 1992); WHO, *Global Strategy for Health for All: Monitoring 1988–1989: Detailed Analysis of Global Indicators* (WHO, Geneva, May 1989); WHO, *The International Drinking Water Supply and Sanitation Decade: Review of Mid-Decade Progress (as at December 1985)* (WHO, Geneva, September 1987); WHO, *The International Drinking Water Supply and Sanitation Decade: Review of National Progress (as at December 1983)*; WHO, *The International Drinking Water Supply and Sanitation Decade: Review of National Baseline Data: December 1980* (WHO, Geneva, 1984); and WHO, unpublished data (WHO, Geneva, July 1991).

WHO collected data on drinking water and sanitation from national governments in 1980, 1983, 1985, 1988, and 1990 using questionnaires completed by public health officials, WHO experts, and resident representatives of the United Nations Development Programme, and most recently collected these data for 1994 in support of a monitoring system for WHO/UNICEF's Child Summit. These data are for a variety of developing countries and often include information on the percent of the urban population served by specific sources of water or specific sanitation systems. Urban and rural populations were defined by each national government and might not be strictly comparable.

WHO defines reasonable *access to safe drinking water* in an urban area as access to piped water or a public standpipe within 200 meters of a dwelling or housing unit. In rural areas, reasonable access implies that a family member need not spend a "disproportionate" part of the day fetching water. "Safe" drinking water includes treated surface water and untreated water from protected springs, boreholes, and sanitary wells. Definitions of safe water and appropriate access to sanitation

and health services vary depending upon location and condition of local resources.

Urban areas with *access to sanitation services* are defined as urban populations served by connections to public sewers or household systems such as pit privies, pour-flush latrines, septic tanks, communal toilets, and other such facilities. Rural populations with access were defined as those with adequate disposal such as pit privies, pour-flush latrines, and so forth. Application of these definitions may vary, and comparisons can therefore be misleading.

Data Table A.3
Air Pollution in Selected Cities, 1989–94

Source: World Health Organization (WHO)/United Nations Environment Programme, and the Global Environment Monitoring System (GEMS)/AIR Monitoring Project, unpublished data (U.S. Environmental Protection Agency, Research Triangle Park, North Carolina, 1995).

These data should be used with care. Because different methods and procedures may have been used in each country, the best comparative data may be time trends within a country. GEMS/AIR sponsors a network of air pollution monitoring sites in more than 50 cities worldwide. These data are based on reports from those sites of observations made between 1989 and 1994 (exact years vary by city). Air quality in selected cities is given for the number of *site years* (number of sites multiplied by the number of years of operation in recent years) for *suspended particulate matter*, *smoke*, and *sulfur dioxide* (SO_2), and *lead*. These data are presented as the annual *mean* for each pollutant during the years of observation.

The health effects of *suspended particulate matter* (SPM) are in part dependent on the chemical makeup and biological activity of the particles. Heavy metal particles or hydrocarbons condensed onto dust particles can be especially toxic. There are two commonly used methods to measure SPM: high-volume gravimetric sampling and smoke shade methods. Gravimetric sampling determines the mass of particulates in a given volume of air. Smoke shade methods relate the reflectance of a stain left on filter paper that has had ambient air drawn through it to the concentration of particulates in the air. Smoke shade data cannot be used interchangeably with gravimetrically determined mass measurements because the smoke shade measurement is predominantly an indication of dark material in the air, which may not be proportional to the total weight of suspended matter. High-volume data may be twice as large as concurrent smoke shade results. This table includes both gravimetrically determined *suspended particulate matter* measurements and smoke shade measurements. The WHO recommends exposures of less than 60 to 90 micrograms per cubic meter per day for total suspended particles and 40 to 60 micrograms per day for smoke. Many cities exceed the WHO guidelines on an average basis. SPM arises from numerous anthropogenic and natural sources. Among the anthropogenic sources are combustion, industrial and agricultural practices, and the formation of sulfates from SO_2 emissions.

WHO recommends that SO_2 exposures should not exceed an average of 40 to 60 micrograms per cubic meter over the course of a year. Many cities in Asia far exceed this level on an average basis. This is of particular concern for young children and people at risk of respiratory illness. Exposure, along with acute respiratory illness, could lead to chronic respiratory illness later in life. SO_2 is created by both natural and anthropogenic activities. Anthropogenic sources include fossil fuel combustion and industrial activities. High levels of SO_2 and SPM may cause respiratory problems among adults and children and may also result in illness in the lower respiratory tract, primarily in children. In the atmosphere, SO_2 oxidizes and, with moisture, becomes sulfuric acid. This acid precipitation, made more acidic by the simultaneous addition of nitric acid, can have effects far distant from its source and has been implicated in declines in forests in North America and Europe, negative effects on soils and crops, and the deterioration of architectural treasures.

Lead emissions are almost all anthropogenic. Alkyl lead, an antiknock additive to ordinary gasoline, accounts for 60 percent of global emissions and up to 90 percent in individual countries. Children are especially vulnerable to lead poisoning, which affects heme biosynthesis and the nervous system. The WHO guidelines call for annual average concentrations of less than 0.5 to 0.1 micrograms per cubic meter.

Data Table A.4
India: City Indicators, 1993

Source: Society for Development Studies (SDS) *India: City Indicators Programme* (Society for Development Studies, New Delhi, India, January 1996).

The India City Indicators Programme of the Society for Development Studies (SDS) is a collaborative effort between the government of India, various state governments, the United Nations Conference on Human Settlements (Habitat), and the United States Agency for International Development to develop inputs to India's national report for the upcoming United Nations Habitat II Conference. Assembling these indicators, and harmonizing them, across cities was no small accomplishment. The 11 cities studied were selected to represent the variety of urban processes found within India. In most cases, the data collection and statistical infrastructure necessary to measure these indicators are nonexistent. In these cases, SDS used other data to estimate these indicators.

Population data, including *growth rates,* are derived from the Census of India, and the estimates of state census offices, projected, where necessary, to estimate city populations. It is not always clear whether other indicators collected relate to the exact city boundaries used to estimate population.

Household data including the *average household size,* the percent of *female headed* households, and *floor area per person* are estimated from both Census of India data and the quinquennial National Sample Survey also carried out by the government of India, and if necessary from other data (see *Source* for further information).

Household income distribution was estimated from survey data obtained from state parastatals for megacities and quick surveys for smaller cities. The number of households *below poverty line* was estimated from the number of applications for assistance received by cities. There is a strong possibility of undercounting.

Data on *household connections* were obtained from the state parastatal or local government providing water, sewer, telephone, and electrical connections. Illegal connections are not included but are believed significant.

Access to potable water includes other sources than household connections.

Estimates of the percent engaged in *informal employment* were made based upon projected total employment and growth in the formal sector as well as information from local, state, and national agencies. *Crime rate* data were obtained from local police departments and are only as complete as the reporting allows. Data on the number of *automobiles* were derived from studies at research centers as well as new estimates. Data on *hospital beds* are part of a good public health infrastructure database held by governmental authorities, but private hospitals are poorly represented. *Classroom size* is an essential parameter derived from local government information on enrollment. *Infant mortality* is derived from death registrations and is believed to be strongly understated. Estimates of *annual per capita solid waste* emissions and *solid waste collected* were obtained from local government authorities.

Part II
Global Conditions and Trends
and Data Tables

7. Basic Economic Indicators

How we measure economic progress is important, because inaccurate or misleading indicators can create distorted impressions and lead to bad policy or investment decisions. Thus, it is useful to recognize the limitations of frequently used economic indicators and to consider various indicators to gain a more complete picture, especially when making international comparisons. This chapter considers and compares two alternative ways of expressing standard indicators of economic activity and economic growth; the result is revealing and contradicts widely held perceptions about the relative scale and growth of economic activity in different regions of the world.

Standard indicators of economic activity do not necessarily measure real economic progress—indeed, they can suggest progress where there is none—because they omit or misrepresent many important economic activities. This chapter therefore presents recent preliminary work toward a radically different set of economic indicators that could eventually provide better guidance to policymakers. It also considers some aspects of economic inequalities among nations—inequalities whose trends raise important questions about the nature and sustainability of global economic progress.

Finally, this chapter considers the controversial subject of the relationship between economic growth and the environment. Does economic growth lead to improvements in environmental quality or to greater environmental deterioration? Can environmental degradation impair economic growth? According to a number of recent empirical studies, the answer depends both on the level of per capita income and on the type of environmental impact examined. Although simple correlations between economic growth and environmental conditions must be used cautiously, these relationships, when combined with per capita income trends, suggest that many forms of degradation will increase in the coming decades in the absence of explicit policy interventions by governments. Other evidence suggests that some environmental damage will be irreversible and may thus hinder future economic growth.

MEASURING ECONOMIC PROGRESS

The size of a nation's economy is traditionally denoted by its yearly *gross domestic product* (GDP)—the value of all final goods and services produced within its borders—and by *gross national product* (GNP)—GDP plus *net income* from abroad. *Per capita GDP* and *GNP* are often used as a measure of an average resident's economic well-being.

These indicators are frequently used as yardsticks of economic progress and as a basis for international comparisons. They are nonetheless widely recognized as incomplete and misleading in several important respects: they ignore nonmarket economic activity, such as household work; they include government services at cost rather than measuring the actual value to society; and they say nothing about the distribution of economic benefits within a society. Moreover, the national income accounts, on which GDP and GNP are based, do not take into account the degradation and depletion of natural resources when calculating income (1) (2).

These accounts also say nothing about the accumulation or degradation of human and social capital—social wealth in the form of human knowledge, stable families, and productive social organizations—that underpins much economic activity. Economic activities that produce a gain by depleting the national stock of natural

Box 7.1 National Wealth and Genuine Saving

A number of attempts have been made to construct indicators of progress that are more relevant to sustainable development than conventional economic indicators. These include the United Nations Development Programme's Human Development Index and the Genuine Progress Indicator (1)(2). Recently, the World Bank has also proposed two new indicators, wealth and genuine saving (3).

The Bank's estimates of the wealth of nations go well beyond the sources of wealth traditionally considered. They include estimates of natural capital (the value of land, water, timber, and subsoil assets), human capital (the value represented by people's productive capacity), and economic capital (produced assets such as buildings and equipment) and amount to a kind of balance sheet on a nation's primary assets. The importance of including natural and human capital in a measure of national wealth is that these quantities may be significantly larger than produced assets. According to preliminary Bank estimates, natural assets exceeded the value of produced assets in 81 of 190 countries examined (4). The value of human resources exceeded the value of produced assets in virtually every country, and in many countries exceeded the value of both

produced assets and natural capital. Overall, produced assets account for barely 16 percent of global wealth; natural capital accounts for 20 percent; and human capital accounts for the rest, although the proportions vary among those developing countries dependent on exporting raw materials, other developing countries, and high-income countries (5). (See Figure 1.)

If these preliminary estimates (admittedly based on shortcut methods) are even roughly correct, then modest declines in natural capital due to resource depletion or degradation could overwhelm increases in produced assets measured by conventional economic measures. Indeed, natural resource accounting studies suggest that is exactly what happened in some countries during periods of rapid deforestation (6). Under such circumstances, conventional economic indicators would give the wrong policy signals, since they suggest that national wealth is increasing rather than decreasing.

Increases in the stock of total wealth, defined in this broad way, could come either from a pattern of economic activity that resulted in genuine saving (an increase in the overall total of produced, natural, and human capital) or from increases in the value of existing

assets. The genuine saving indicator measures net flows to the combined stock of produced and natural capital—in effect, production (gross fixed-capital formation) less consumption, depletion, or degradation of produced and natural capital and damages from carbon dioxide emissions. It does not as yet explicitly account for flows to a nation's stock of human resources. A pattern of economic activity that resulted in genuine saving could be a critical first step to improving a country's overall stock of wealth.

To produce preliminary estimates of genuine saving, the Bank took into account both conventional production as well as the extraction or harvest of natural resources and damages from carbon dioxide emissions (used as a proxy for all pollution damages caused by fossil fuel use). It calculated these estimates for each country and summarized the results for major regions of the world (7). Genuine saving appears to have increased markedly over the past decade in East Asia and is low but positive in South Asia. However, genuine saving has been sharply negative since the late 1970s in sub-Saharan Africa. Genuine saving in Latin America and the Caribbean, by this measure, has been low and fluctuating (8).

Figure 1 Differences in Composition of Wealth Between High-Income and Developing Countries

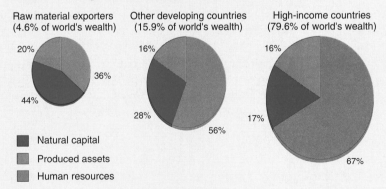

Raw material exporters (4.6% of world's wealth)

20% 36% 44%

Other developing countries (15.9% of world's wealth)

16% 28% 56%

High-income countries (79.6% of world's wealth)

16% 17% 67%

- ■ Natural capital
- ▨ Produced assets
- ▤ Human resources

Source: The World Bank, *Monitoring Environmental Progress: A Report on Work in Progress* (The World Bank, Washington, D.C., 1995), p. 63.
Note: Developing countries here are divided between raw material exporters (63 countries dependent on exporting raw materials to earn foreign exchange) and other developing countries (100 countries). The remaining 29 countries are classified as high-income countries.

References and Notes

1. United Nations Development Programme (UNDP), *Human Development Report 1995* (UNDP, New York, 1995).

2. Clifford Cobb, Ted Halstead, and Jonathan Rowe, "If the GDP is Up, Why is America Down?," *The Atlantic Monthly*, Vol. 276, No. 4 (October 1995), p. 59.

3. The World Bank, *Monitoring Environmental Progress: A Report on Work in Progress* (The World Bank, Washington, D.C., 1995), pp. 53–66.

4. The World Bank, "World Bank Develops New System to Measure Wealth of Nations," press release (The World Bank, Washington, D.C., September 17, 1995).

5. *Op. cit.* 3, pp. 61–63.

6. Tropical Science Center and World Resources Institute, *Accounts Overdue: Natural Resources Depreciation in Costa Rica* (World Resources Institute, Washington, D.C., 1991).

7. *Op. cit.* 3.

8. *Op. cit.* 3, pp. 54–56.

or human capital—by cutting forests or shutting schools and using the money earned or saved to buy arms, for example—would increase the GDP, even though the society might ultimately be the poorer and have a less promising economic future. Thus, these conventional indicators of economic activity can misrepresent the long-term sustainability of a nation's economy. Growth in GDP is not necessarily the same as real economic progress, even though it may be an important component of that progress.

Efforts to create economic indicators that can send more accurate policy signals are therefore important, even though initial attempts are likely to be controversial. One such effort, recently published in preliminary form by the World Bank, proposes two new indicators: wealth and genuine saving (3). The wealth measure extends the concept of national economic wealth (traditionally measured in produced assets such as equipment and buildings) to encompass human and natural wealth as well. The second indicator, genuine saving, measures the net of the annual flows that increase the stock of wealth (broadly defined) and the flows that decrease it (such as natural resource depletion). A positive genuine saving number would reflect net additions to the overall stock of produced and natural capital (and, potentially, human capital) and thus is, the Bank suggests, a more meaningful measure of the productive potential that a nation is leaving for future generations than are conventional economic indicators. (See Box 7.1.) Indeed, preliminary calculations of a limited form of the new indicator suggest that, for a significant number of developing countries, the genuine saving indicator is negative, meaning that the current pattern of economic activity in those countries is actually decreasing national wealth (4).

PURCHASING POWER PARITY

In making international comparisons, GDP and GNP (as conventionally calculated) have an additional—and purely economic—limitation, namely, that market exchange rates for a nation's currency often do not reflect that currency's true purchasing power at home. Recently, it has become possible to compare national currencies based on *purchasing power parity* (PPP)—in effect, how much of a common "market basket" of goods and services each currency can purchase locally, including goods and services that are not traded internationally. (See Box 7.2.) The use of PPP currency values can dramatically change prevalent notions about a country's place in the world economy.

Consider, for example, the standard of living as measured by average per capita GDP in Japan and the United States. Market-based exchange rates represent the standard of living in Japan as having been higher than that in the United States since the early 1980s, when Japan's per capita GDP (measured in dollars) surpassed the U.S. per capita GDP. PPP-based currency values, however, provide a different perspective, suggesting that the U.S. standard of living is still significantly higher. (See Figures 7.1A and 7.1B.)

Reports of very rapid economic growth in China since the early 1980s have attracted international interest and investment. Market-based exchange rates give a growth rate averaging nearly 9 percent per year over the 1983–93 period. With PPP-based currency values, however, China's GDP growth rate for the same period is about 5 percent (5) (6). India, in fact, shows a growth rate slightly higher than that of China for the same period, when calculated with PPP figures. (See Data Table 7.1.) Nonetheless, these PPP figures also indicate that China's economy is already much larger than conventional GDP figures suggest—larger than that of Germany and nearly as large as that of Japan.

Examples such as these illustrate how important the choice of indicators and calculation methods can be in shaping perceptions. Increasingly, international organizations are using PPP-based measures of economic activity in international comparisons. All figures given in the remainder of this chapter are PPP-based, unless otherwise noted.

ECONOMIC INEQUALITY

Using PPP-based currency values to compare national incomes usually produces lower GDP figures in wealthy countries and higher GDP figures in poorer nations, compared with market-based exchange rates. Likewise, per capita incomes in virtually all developing countries are significantly higher when compared on the basis of purchasing power parity than when compared with market-based exchange rates. But even with this "compression" of differences between rich and poor, income remains unequally distributed across nations.

In 1992, per capita GDP ranged from $504 in Chad to $23,220 in the United States. The global *average* per capita income for that year was $5,336—about that of Fiji and Belize. (See Data Table 7.1.) However, the *median* value was closer to China's $1,800.

In 1992, the poorest half of the world's people accounted for less than 15 percent of global GDP. Conversely, the 15 percent with the highest incomes accounted for over 50 percent of global GDP.

Box 7.2 Purchasing Power Parity

For international comparisons, economic indicators are converted from local currencies into a common currency, such as dollars. Traditionally, market exchange rates are used to make these conversions. In theory, exchange rates adjust through the action of the market so that the local currency prices of a group of identical goods and services represent equivalent value in every nation. In practice, however, such adjustments can lag far behind rapidly changing economic circumstances. Government actions, such as currency controls, influence over interest rates, import tariffs, and export subsidies, may further distort the accuracy of market-based exchange rates at any given time. Moreover, many goods and services are not traded in international commerce; market-based exchange rates may not reflect the relative values of such goods, even in theory. Thus, international comparisons based on market exchange rates can greatly over- or understate the value of a nation's economic activity.

An alternative approach is based on estimates of the purchasing power of different currencies, rather than their market exchange rates. On the basis of comparisons of prices and expenditures for several hundred goods and services by the International Comparison Project (ICP) in a large number of participating countries, the relative values of local currencies are adjusted to reflect purchasing power parity (PPP) or equivalence. In effect, the PPP currency values reflect the number of units of a country's currency required to buy the same quantity of comparable goods and services in the local market as one U.S. dollar would buy in an average country. The average country is based on a composite of all participating countries, so no single country acts as the base country (1)(2)(3). The ICP estimates, made for benchmark years, have been extended in the *Penn World Table* for nonbenchmark years and countries (4) (5) (6) (7). The most recent version (Mark 5.6) was completed in 1994 and includes data through 1992 (8) (9).

Just how dramatically exchange rate and PPP currency values can differ is shown by an amusing, yet enlightening piece of analysis, *The Economist*'s Big Mac™ index. For the past several years, that publication has calculated PPP equivalents for the local price of a McDonald's Big Mac hamburger and compared these to market exchange rates to estimate how overvalued or undervalued major currencies are compared to the U.S. dollar. The most recent analysis indicates that the U.S. dollar is 50 percent undervalued against the Japanese yen and nearly 100 percent overvalued against the Chinese yuan(10).

The World Bank now presents estimates of national gross domestic product (GDP) and per capita GDP converted to a common currency using PPP equivalents, in addition to values converted using market exchange rates (11). The International Monetary Fund uses country weights based on PPP-based GDP for aggregating growth rates and other economic indicators(12)(13). Such comparisons using PPP-based con-

---

Will this unequal distribution of income even out over time? Many developing economies are growing more rapidly than the more mature economies of developed nations. From 1983 to 1992, average GDP growth for the nations constituting the poorest half of the global population was 4.6 percent annually, versus 3.2 percent for the richer half. The nations where the poorest half lives did improve their share of global GDP slightly over the 1983–92 period, from 12.5 percent to 13 percent. Because of rapidly expanding populations in many developing nations, however, this rising income had to be divided among many more people. Average per capita GDP growth was only 2.7 percent annually in nations constituting the poorest half of the global population (7).

Thus, despite higher economic growth rates in many poorer countries, the actual gap in per capita incomes between rich and poor countries has widened in recent decades. Consider differences between China and India, the largest developing economies, and Japan and the United States, the largest industrial economies.

Between 1970 and 1992, the absolute difference in per capita GDP between China and Japan (measured in constant 1985 International dollars) more than doubled—from $6,611 in 1970 to over $13,612 in 1992. (See Figure 7.2.) Differences between China and the United States also increased by more than 30 percent over this same period. Similar conclusions are reached in looking at the relative growth of India versus Japan and the United States. Such trends imply that the world is becoming economically more unequal, with the absolute value of per capita incomes rising more rapidly in rich countries than in poor countries, at least for the time being.

These trends stem from the already large gaps in per capita GDP and the relatively low average incomes in many developing countries, such that even rapid percentage GDP growth in poor countries cannot add annual increments of per capita income as large as those in rich countries. To the extent that sustainable development on a global scale requires more equitable growth and ultimately more equitable distributions of income, the current trends are in the wrong direction.

ECONOMIC GROWTH AND THE ENVIRONMENT

Environmental considerations have not played any central role in national and international economic policy. To the extent that economic planners have focused on

version rates tend to give results qualitatively similar to the Big Mac example: GDP values measured in dollars tend to be higher for developing countries than market-based exchange rates (i.e., their currencies are undervalued), while some developed countries' currencies appear to be overvalued relative to the U.S. dollar. (See Data Table 7.1.) From a PPP perspective, the developing world's share of economic activity is larger than is reflected in market-based exchange rates (although market-based measures may be more relevant for some purposes, such as assessing trade potential).

References and Notes

1. Dale S. Rothman, "Three Essays on Environmental Economics," Ph.D. dissertation, Cornell University, Ithaca, New York, 1993, pp. 39–41.
2. World Resources Institute in collaboration with the United Nations Environment Programme, and the United Nations Development Programme, *World Resources 1994–95* (Oxford University Press, New York, 1994), pp. 255–257, 264.
3. The World Bank, *Purchasing Power of Currencies: Comparing National Incomes Using ICP Data* (Socio-Economic Data Division, International Economics Department, The World Bank, Washington, D.C., 1993).
4. Irving B. Kravis, Alan Heston, and Robert Summers, *International Comparisons of Real Product and Purchasing Power* (Statistical Office of the United Nations and The World Bank, The Johns Hopkins University Press, Baltimore, Maryland, 1978).
5. Irving B. Kravis, Alan Heston, and Robert Summers, *World Product and Income: International Comparisons of Real Gross Product* (Statistical Office of the United Nations and The World Bank, The Johns Hopkins University Press, Baltimore, Maryland, 1982).
6. Robert Summers et al., *The Penn World Table (Mark 5.6)*, on diskette (University of Pennsylvania, Philadelphia, December 1994). Methodology and table described in Robert Summers and Alan Heston, "The Penn World Table (Mark 5): An Expanded Set of International Comparisons, 1950–1988," *Quarterly Journal of Economics*, Vol. 106, No. 2 (1991), pp. 327–368.
7. Robert Summers and Alan Heston, "The Penn World Table (Mark 5): An Expanded Set of International Comparisons, 1950–1988," Quarterly Journal of Economics, Vol. 106, No. 2 (1991), p. 327.
8. *Op. cit.* 6.
9. *Op. cit.* 7.
10. "Big MacCurrencies," *The Economist*, Vol. 355, No. 7910 (April 15–21, 1995), p. 74.
11. The World Bank, *World Development Report 1994: Infrastructure for Development* (Oxford University Press, New York, 1994), Technical Notes, pp. 230–233.
12. International Monetary Fund (IMF), "Revised Weights for the World Economic Outlook," World Economic Outlook (IMF, Washington, D.C., 1993), pp. 116–119.
13. A.M. Gulde and M. Schulze-Chattas, *Aggregation of Economic Indicators Across Countries: Exchange Rate versus PPP Based GDP Weights* (International Monetary Fund, Washington, D.C., 1992).

environmental questions, the assumption in recent years has often been that "economic growth and economic liberalization (including the liberalization of international trade) are, in some sense, good for the environment" [8]. Such assertions depend partly on the idea that consumer preferences and the structure of the economy change as a country develops, that development brings more modern and often cleaner technologies, and that growing and richer economies can more easily invest in environmental improvements. Countries in the early stages of development, according to this argument, inevitably focus first on improving their physical infrastructure, basic production, and other forms of material wealth, ignoring pollution and accepting some degradation in the quality of the environment.

The hypothesis is that, in the past, there has been an empirical relationship—in the shape of an inverted "U" curve—between per capita income and some measures of environmental degradation. Such relationships, known as environmental Kuznets curves, have been investigated for a wide variety of environmental indicators [9] [10] [11] [12] [13] [14] [15]. In effect, such curves suggest that economic growth in a given country will lead to worse environmental degradation until a "turning point" in per capita income, but then will lead to improved environmental conditions.

The upshot of a number of such studies is that some environmental indicators (especially access to clean water, urban sanitation, and urban air quality) do indeed show improvement with increased income, with or without an initial period of deterioration [16] [17]. Other indicators, however, show continued worsening as incomes rise (especially carbon dioxide emissions and municipal waste per capita). The turning point at which environmental improvement begins varies from study to study and indicator to indicator, but falls most often in the range of incomes typical of middle-income countries [18]. Most environmental conditions that do improve with economic growth are those that have local impact and abatement costs that are relatively inexpensive in terms of money and changes in lifestyle. Environmental problems that improve only at higher income levels (or that continue to worsen as incomes rise) generally create impacts that affect only a few people (e.g., solid waste) or that occur either outside the local area or in the future (e.g., the contributions of carbon dioxide emissions to climate change) [19].

Criticism of efforts to construct environmental Kuznets curves focuses on several points. Such efforts

Figure 7.1 Comparing Per Capita Gross Domestic Product in Japan and the United States

A. Using Market-Based Exchange Rates

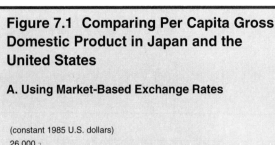

(constant 1985 U.S. dollars)

B. Using Purchasing Power Parity

(constant 1985 International dollars)

Sources:
1. Robert Summers *et al., The Penn World Table (Mark 5.6),* on diskette (University of Pennsylvania, Philadelphia, December 1994). Methodology and table described in Robert Summers and Alan Heston, "The Penn World Table (Mark 5): An Expanded Set of International Comparisons, 1950–1988,"*Quarterly Journal of Economics,* Vol. 106, No. 2 (1991), pp. 327–368.
2. The World Bank, *World Tables,* on diskette (The World Bank, Washington, D.C., 1995).

Figure 7.2 Per Capita Gross Domestic Product in Constant 1985 International Dollars

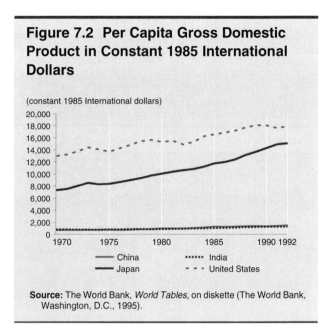

(constant 1985 International dollars)

Source: The World Bank, *World Tables,* on diskette (The World Bank, Washington, D.C., 1995).

developing countries, an experience that developing countries are unlikely to be able to replicate (20). Some studies have also focused primarily on pollution problems and say little about the degradation or depletion of the natural resources on which many of the poorest segments of populations in developing countries depend in a direct way for their livelihood and day-to-day sustenance (21). Thus, correlations between economic growth and environmental improvement or degradation must be used cautiously; any general claim that economic growth leads to environmental improvement must be heavily qualified.

A number of these studies note that turning points in the relationship between economic growth and environmental quality do not just happen, but result largely from explicit policy actions (22) (23). They do not imply that societies can automatically grow their way out of environmental problems nor that economic liberalization and other policies that promote economic growth can substitute for environmental policies (24).

Forecasts or projections of environmental quality developed from these empirical studies, despite their limitations, paint an alarming picture for the near future. In effect, they suggest that if these correlation curves and the hypothesis on which they rest are correct, economic growth will worsen rather than improve the world's environmental conditions (25) (26) (27). Pollution emissions and forest destruction are likely to increase significantly, according to such forecasts; stabilization and cleanup or restoration will occur only some decades later—if at all. One study, for example, projects some improvement in *global* forest cover after

assume that environmental degradation will not damage prospects for future economic growth, despite evidence that some kinds of degradation are effectively irreversible—destruction of habitat critical to the maintenance of fisheries' breeding stocks, for example, as well as severely eroded lands or carbon dioxide accumulations that will persist in the atmosphere for centuries. The correlation curves ignore the possibility that some of the pollution reductions in developed countries may have come from transferring heavy industries to

the year 2016, but sees a continued decline in *tropical* forest cover throughout the period studied (1990–2025) (28). A second study forecasts rising emissions of all pollutants until at least the middle of the next century or, under different assumptions, throughout the next century (29).

Countries containing a large majority of the world's population will have average incomes below the estimated Kuznets turning points for some time to come. Thus, economic growth in these countries could be expected to increase pollution. Globally, these projected increases would more than cancel out any reduction of pollution in more developed countries (and the environ-

mental Kuznets curves predict increases rather than reductions for carbon dioxide emissions even in rich countries).

Projections are not destiny, but such measures do serve fair warning that more vigorous efforts and policy interventions will be necessary to avoid the widespread degradation forecast by these means.

Dale Rothman of the University of British Columbia in Vancouver, formerly of the World Resources Institute, provided the background analysis for this chapter.

References and Notes

1. Robert Repetto *et al.*, *Wasting Assets: Natural Resources in the National Income Accounts* (World Resources Institute, Washington, D.C., 1989).

2. Ernest Lutz and Salah El-Serafy, "Environmental and Resource Accounting: An Overview," in *Environmental Accounting for Sustainable Development*, Yusuf J. Ahmad, Salah El-Serafy, and Ernest Lutz, eds. (The World Bank, Washington, D.C., 1989).

3. The World Bank, *Monitoring Environmental Progress: A Report on Work in Progress* (The World Bank, Washington, D.C., 1995), pp. 53–66.

4. *Ibid.*, pp. 54–56.

5. According to the *Penn World Table (Mark 5.6)* (Robert Summers *et al.*, *The Penn World Table (Mark 5.6)*, on diskette (University of Pennsylvania, Philadelphia, December 1994)), there is considerable uncertainty in PPP values for China. The values reported in this new edition of the Table reflect, among other extensive adjustments, a downward adjustment in growth rates of up to 40 percent, to reflect artificially high growth rates (or understated inflation rates) in China's official economic statistics.

6. Robert Summers *et al.*, *The Penn World Table (Mark 5.6)*, on diskette (University of Pennsylvania, Philadelphia, December 1994). Methodology and table described in Robert Summers and Alan Heston, "The Penn World Table (Mark 5): An Expanded Set of International Comparisons, 1950–1988," *Quarterly Journal of Economics*, Vol. 106, No. 2 (1991), pp. 327–368.

7. Estimated by the World Resources Institute from data available from the World Bank, *World Tables*, on diskette (The World Bank, Washington, D.C., 1995).

8. Kenneth Arrow *et al.*, "Economic Growth, Carrying Capacity, and the Environment," *Science*, Vol. 268, No. 5210 (April 28, 1995), pp. 520–521.

9. Theodore Panayotou, *Empirical Tests and Policy Analysis of Environmental Degrada-tion at Different Stages of Economic Development*, Working Paper (International Labour Office, Technology and Environment Program, United Nations, Geneva, 1993).

10. Thomas M. Selden and Daqing Song, "Environmental Quality and Development: Is There a Kuznets Curve for Air Pollution Emissions?" *Journal of Environmental Economics and Management*, Vol. 27, No. 2 (1994), p. 147.

11. Maureen Cropper and Charles Griffiths, *The Interaction of Population Growth and Environmental Quality* (The World Bank, Washington, D.C., 1994).

12. Gene M. Grossman and Alan B. Krueger, *Economic Growth and the Environment* (National Bureau of Economic Research, Cambridge, Massachusetts, 1994).

13. Gene M. Grossman, "Pollution and Growth: What Do We Know?" in *The Economics of Sustainable Development*, Ian Goldin and L. Alan Winters, eds. (Cambridge University Press, New York, 1995), p. 19.

14. Nemat Shafik and Sushenjit Bandyopadhyay, *Economic Growth and Environmental Quality: Time Series and Cross-Country Evidence* (The World Bank, Washington, D.C., 1992).

15. Nemat Shafik, "Economic Development and Environmental Quality: An Econometric Analysis," *Oxford Economic Papers*, Vol. 46 (1994), p. 757.

16. *Op. cit.* 14.

17. *Op. cit.* 15.

18. The World Bank defines *low-income economies* as those countries with a per capita GNP of $675 or less in 1992, *middle-income economies* as those with a per capita GNP of more than $675 but less than $8,356 in 1992, and *high-income economies* as those with a per capita GNP of $8,356 or more in 1992.

19. *Op. cit.* 12.

20. David I. Stern, Michael S. Common, and Edward B. Barbier, *Economic Growth and Environmental Degradation: A Critique of the Environmental Kuznets Curve* (Department of Environmental Economics and Environmental Management, University of York, York, U.K., 1994).

21. *Op. cit.* 8.

22. *Op. cit.* 12, pp. 19–20.

23. *Op. cit.* 14, pp. 23–24.

24. *Op. cit.* 8.

25. *Op. cit.* 10, pp. 156–160.

26. *Op. cit.* 20, pp. 12–15.

27. Douglas Holtz-Eakin and Thomas M. Selden, *Stoking the Fires? CO_2 Emissions and Economic Growth* (National Bureau of Economic Research, Cambridge, Massachusetts, 1992), pp. 14–21.

28. *Op. cit.* 20, pp. 13–14.

29. *Op. cit.* 10, p. 160.

Data Table 7.1 Gross National and Domestic Product Estimates, 1983–93

	Gross National Product (GNP) 1993 {a}		Gross Domestic Product (GDP) — Exchange Rate Based (GDP) 1993 {b}		Gross Domestic Product (GDP) — Purchasing Power Parity (PPP) 1992 {c}		Average Annual Growth Rate (percent) {d}			Distribution of GDP, 1993 (percent)		
	Total (million US$)	Per Capita (US$)	Total (million US$)	Per Capita (US$)	Total (million Int$)	Per Capita (Int$)	GNP 1983-93	GDP 1983-93	PPP 1983-93	Agriculture	Industry	Services
WORLD												
AFRICA												
Algeria	47,565	1,780	49,762	1,862	80,271	3,076	0.8	1.0	1.6	13	43	43
Angola	X	X	X	X	6,947	3,076 e	X	X	3.7 f	X	X	X
Benin	2,187	430	2,125	418	5,948	1,245 g	2.5	2.6	1.2 h	36	13	51
Botswana	3,909	2,790	3,813	2,722	4,202	3,406 e	9.6	8.8	6.4 f	6	47	47
Burkina Faso	2,932	300	2,815	288	6,183	651	3.2	3.2	3.3	44 i	20 i	37 i
Burundi	1,085	180	948	157	4,149	710	3.8	3.8	4.5	52	21	27
Cameroon	10,268	820	11,082	885	13,667	1,122	(1.9)	(2.2)	(0.4)	29	25	47
Central African Rep	1,262	400	1,233	391	1,950	634	0.4	0.8	0.8	50	14	36
Chad	1,262	210	1,197	199	2,955	504	4.2	4.2	5.3	44	22	35
Congo	2,321	950	2,385	976	6,012	2,538	0.7	0.5	1.0	11	35	53
Cote d'Ivoire	8,389	630	9,298	698	16,882	1,315	(0.8)	(0.4)	(0.6)	37	24	39
Egypt	37,246	660	39,357	697	125,842	2,274	4.0	2.9	2.1	18	22	60
Equatorial Guinea	159	420	157	413	X	X	3.5 j	3.4 j	X	47	26	27
Eritrea	X	X	488	X	X	X	X	X	X	13	21	66
Ethiopia	X	100	X	X	17,245	405 k	X	X	0.1 l	60	10	29
Gabon	4,995	4,960	5,420	5,383	3,943	3,983	0.3	1.3	(0.2)	8	45	47
Gambia, The	365	350	361	346	940	1,019 i	4.3	3.2	5.1 m	28	15	58
Ghana	7,072	430	6,084	370	19,921	1,249	4.7	4.7	5.4	48	16	36
Guinea	3,153	500	3,172	503	3,694	604	4.2 j	3.7 j	3.5	24	31	45
Guinea-Bissau	247	240	241	235	832	827	5.2	5.0	2.4	45	19	36
Kenya	6,844	270	5,539	219	29,024	1,176	3.7	4.0	4.5	29	18	54
Lesotho	1,263	650	759	390	1,942	1,027	2.4	6.0	2.5	10	47	43
Liberia	1,313	560 n	1,397	596 n	2,272	1,001 k	(0.6) m	(1.4) m	(1.7) l	X	X	X
Libya	26,840	6,125 e	24,734	5,645 e	36,531	9,649 o	(4.2) f	(5.0) f	X	X	X	X
Madagascar	3,048	220	3,352	242	10,148	757	1.3	1.4	0.5	34	14	52
Malawi	2,104	200	1,974	188	6,092	607	3.0	2.7	5.1	39	18	43
Mali	2,736	270	2,662	263	6,737	708 g	3.6	3.3	3.2 h	42	15	42
Mauritania	1,081	500	947	438	2,282	1,083	2.2	2.1	1.5	28	30	42
Mauritius	3,306	3,030	3,280	3,006	8,672	8,025	7.0	6.5	6.6	10	33	57
Morocco	26,983	1,040	26,635	1,027	70,474	2,777	3.3	3.6	4.1	14	32	53
Mozambique	1,359	90	1,467	97	13,369	898	3.1	4.5	(0.2)	33	12	55
Namibia	2,659	1,820	2,508	1,716	4,596	3,231	4.9	3.3	2.8	10	27	63
Niger	2,309	270	2,220	260	4,711	629 e	0.6	0.3	(0.5) f	39	18	44
Nigeria	31,579	300	31,593	300	115,579	1,132	5.1	4.6	1.2	34	43	24
Rwanda	1,586	210	1,494	198	7,071	961	1.1	1.1	2.1	41	21	38
Senegal	5,927	750	5,770	730	10,601	1,411 g	2.6	2.4	2.4 h	20	19	61
Sierra Leone	670	150	732	164	3,984	914	(0.1)	1.4	0.0	38 g	16 g	46 g
Somalia	1,134	131 i	996	115 i	8,849	1,040 e	2.0 p	2.7 p	2.8 f	65 i	9 i	26 i
South Africa	118,184	2,980	117,433	2,961	150,608	3,885	1.2	1.0	1.4	5	39	56
Sudan	10,589	493 o	13,326	621 o	18,304	725 g	X	X	0.9 h	34 q	17 q	50 q
Swaziland	1,047	1,190	1,038	1,179	2,259	2,950 e	4.0	3.9	4.1 f	12	39	50
Tanzania	2,522	90	2,373	85	15,912	663 r	4.0	4.9	8.2 s	56	14	30
Togo	1,321	340	1,249	322	2,517	669	1.2	0.8	2.4	49	18	33
Tunisia	14,889	1,720	14,634	1,691	32,192	3,807	3.7	3.7	3.7	18	31	51
Uganda	3,245	180	3,236	179	11,504	654	3.9	3.8	(1.2)	53	12	35
Zaire	9,574	264 e	9,920	274 e	19,049	526 e	2.1 p	(0.5) t	2.6 f	X	X	X
Zambia	3,396	380	3,685	412	7,360	877 g	1.4	1.3	1.0 h	34	36	30
Zimbabwe	5,584	520	5,635	525	15,419	1,479	2.8	2.9	2.3	15	36	48
EUROPE												
Albania	1,152	340	707	211 q	X	X	X	(3.2) t	X	40 q	13 q	47 q
Austria	184,829	23,510	182,067	23,159	132,669	16,989	2.7	2.6	2.7	2 q	35 q	62 q
Belarus, Rep	29,240	2,870	27,545	2,704	62,594	6,130 i	1.8	1.8	X	17	54	29
Belgium	217,537	21,650	210,576	20,957	181,190	18,091	2.6	2.4	2.8	2 i	30 i	68 i
Bosnia and Herzegovina	X	X	X	X	X	X	X	X	X	X	X	X
Bulgaria	10,112	1,140	10,369	1,169	60,299	6,774	(1.4)	(0.8)	2.5	13	38	49
Croatia, Rep	X	X	11,688	2,591	X	X	X	X	X	11	30	58
Czech Rep	27,902	2,710	31,613	3,070	X	X	(1.5) u	(1.5) u	1.3 m	6	40	54
Denmark	138,049	26,730	135,998	26,333	96,579	18,730	1.7	1.7	1.8	4 q	27 q	69 q
Estonia, Rep	4,780	3,080	5,092	3,281	9,906	6,326 g	(4.5)	(4.5)	X	8	29	63
Finland	97,624	19,300	83,794	16,566	78,627	15,619	1.1	1.4	1.7	5 q	31 q	64 q
France	1,292,556	22,490	1,251,689	21,779	1,043,232	18,232	2.2	2.2	2.5	3	29	69
Germany	1,901,131	23,560	1,910,761	23,679	1,315,229	20,197	X	X	X	1 g	38 g	61 g
Greece	76,599	7,390	73,182	7,060	91,259	8,877 g	1.8	1.8	2.4 h	18 q	32 q	50 q
Hungary	34,204	3,350	38,099	3,732	59,327	5,780	0.1	(1.2)	(1.1)	6	28	66
Iceland	6,570	24,950	6,076	23,075	4,253	16,324	2.3	2.2	2.4	12 g	28 g	60 g
Ireland	45,928	13,000	47,677	13,495	43,187	12,259	4.2	4.5	4.0	8 g	10 g	82 g
Italy	1,133,287	19,840	991,386	17,356	954,749	16,724	2.3	2.4	2.6	3 q	32 q	65 q
Latvia, Rep	5,248	2,010	4,601	1,762	18,246	6,891 g	(3.9)	(2.5)	X	15	32	53
Lithuania, Rep	4,900	1,320	4,335	1,168	18,637	5,025 g	(4.8)	(4.8)	X	21	41	38
Macedonia, former Yugoslav Rep	1,702	820	1,704	821	X	X	X	X	X	X	X	X
Moldova, Rep	4,672	1,060	4,292	974	17,875	4,085 g	(3.8)	(3.8)	X	35	48	18
Netherlands	320,120	20,950	309,227	20,237	263,549	17,373	2.6	2.7	2.8	4	X	X
Norway	111,628	25,970	103,419	24,060	73,148	17,094	2.4	2.4	2.1	3 g	35 g	62 g
Poland, Rep	86,565	2,260	85,853	2,241	187,577	4,907	0.6	0.1	0.1	6	39	55
Portugal	89,848	9,130	85,665	8,705	95,107	9,638 i	4.2	3.6	5.6 m	6 i	38 i	56 i
Romania	25,948	1,140	25,969	1,141	48,388	2,130	(4.8)	(5.0)	2.9 f	21	40	40
Russian Federation	347,896	2,340	329,233	2,214	1,223,573	8,320 g	(2.4)	(2.4)	X	9 q	51 q	39 q
Slovak Rep	10,360	1,950	11,076	2,085	X	X	(1.2) u	(1.2) u	X	7	44	49
Slovenia, Rep	12,571	6,490	11,974	6,182	X	X	X	X	X	6	36	58
Spain	536,547	13,590	478,582	12,122	511,794	12,986	3.4	3.4	4.2	5 i	35 i	61 i
Sweden	215,013	24,740	185,289	21,320	158,987	18,387	1.2	1.4	1.7	2 q	31 q	67 q
Switzerland	252,197	35,760	232,161	32,919	150,960	21,631	1.9	2.1	2.5	X	X	X
Ukraine	113,928	2,210	109,078	2,116	296,347	5,768 g	(1.2)	(1.2)	X	35	47	18
United Kingdom	1,045,994	18,060	941,424	16,255	941,413	16,302	2.2	2.3	2.7	2 q	33 q	65 q
Yugoslavia, Fed Rep	X	X	X	X	X	X	2.9 f	2.9 f	(1.3) m	X	X	X

| | Gross National Product (GNP) 1993 {a} | | Gross Domestic Product (GDP) | | | | Average Annual Growth Rate (percent) {d} | | | Distribution of GDP, 1993 (percent) | | |
| | | | Exchange Rate Based (GDP) 1993 {b} | | Purchasing Power Parity (PPP) 1992 {c} | | | | | | | |
	Total (million US$)	Per Capita (US$)	Total (million US$)	Per Capita (US$)	Total (million Int$)	Per Capita (Int$)	GNP 1983-93	GDP 1983-93	PPP 1983-93	Agriculture	Industry	Services
NORTH & CENTRAL AMERICA												
Belize	500	2,450	524	2,568	1,142	5,739	7.3	7.3	6.4	19	28	53
Canada	574,786	19,970	546,349	18,982	596,557	20,970	2.4	2.4	3.0	3 i	32 i	65 i
Costa Rica	7,031	2,150	7,577	2,317	14,403	4,522	5.0	4.4	4.2	15	26	59
Cuba	X	X	X	X	43,907	4,266 o	X	X	X	X	X	X
Dominican Rep	9,278	1,230	9,510	1,261	21,555	2,918	3.4	3.0	2.3	15	23	62
El Salvador	7,282	1,320	7,625	1,382	12,286	2,274	2.8	2.6	2.2	9	25	66
Guatemala	11,032	1,100	11,309	1,128	28,135	2,888	2.8	2.8	3.0	25	19	55
Haiti	3,158	477 g	1,455	211	6,794	1,069 e	(1.5)	(1.6)	0.3 f	39	16	46
Honduras	3,201	600	3,343	627	9,274	1,792	3.1	3.5	3.1	20	30	50
Jamaica	3,472	1,440	3,825	1,587	7,273	3,053 g	1.1	2.9	1.8 h	8	41	51
Mexico	324,997	3,610	343,472	3,815	692,795	7,867	2.4	2.0	3.6	8	28	63
Nicaragua	1,399	340	1,800	437	5,669	1,542 i	(4.1)	(2.6)	(3.6) m	30	20	50
Panama	6,599	2,600	6,565	2,587	10,208	4,102	1.4	1.1	0.2	10	18	72
Trinidad and Tobago	4,895	3,830	4,670	3,654	12,679	10,145 g	(1.8)	(1.4)	(1.6) h	3	43	55
United States	6,378,873	24,740	6,259,899	24,279	5,925,080	23,220	2.5	2.6	2.6	X	X	X
SOUTH AMERICA												
Argentina	243,877	7,220	255,595	7,567	191,699	5,921 i	1.8	1.4	(0.9) m	6	31	63
Bolivia	5,369	760	5,382	762	14,288	2,066	3.0	2.4	1.5	X	X	X
Brazil	458,504	2,930	507,353	3,242	754,804	4,912	2.6	2.2	2.3	11 g	37 g	52 g
Chile	43,816	3,170	45,639	3,302	85,948	6,326	7.5	6.8	6.3	X	X	X
Colombia	49,955	1,400	54,076	1,516	148,368	4,254	3.9	4.0	4.0	16 q	35 q	50 q
Ecuador	13,176	1,200	14,304	1,303	36,685	3,420	3.1	2.7	1.9	12	38	50
Guyana	286	350	326	400	1,135	1,426 i	(0.3)	0.1	(1.7) m	30 g	38 g	32 g
Paraguay	7,099	1,510	6,825	1,452	12,116	2,655	3.3	3.6	3.4	26	21	53
Peru	34,100	1,490	41,061	1,794	58,791	2,620	(0.6)	(0.5)	(0.7)	11	43	46
Suriname	489	1,180	420	1,015	1,102	2,787 e	0.8	0.9	(4.3) f	22	24	54
Uruguay	12,061	3,830	13,144	4,174	21,087	6,736	3.9	3.0	3.3	9	27	64
Venezuela	59,393	2,840	59,995	2,869	172,419	8,449	3.1	3.1	2.9	5	42	53
ASIA												
Afghanistan, Islamic State	X	X	X	X	X	X	X	X	X	X	X	X
Armenia	2,462	660	2,190	587	16,477	4,750 g	(6.7)	(6.7)	0.0	48	30	22
Azerbaijan	5,390	730	4,992	676	27,016	4,257 g	(5.2)	(5.2)	X	22 q	52 q	26 q
Bangladesh	25,345	220	23,977	208	215,385	1,908	4.0	3.9	5.5	30	18	52
Bhutan	X	X	239	X	1,118	870 o	8.2	6.4	X	41	29	30
Cambodia	X	X	1,996	206	X	X	5.6 v	5.6 v	X	47	14	38
China	X	X	425,611	361	2,141,180	1,838	X	8.9	4.7	19	48	33
Georgia, Rep	3,159	580	2,994	550	24,388	4,495 g	(10.9)	(10.9)	X	58	22	20
India	269,460	300	250,966	279	1,437,124	1,633	5.0	5.1	5.2	31	27	41
Indonesia	138,492	740	144,707	773	478,799	2,601	5.9	5.8	5.0	19	39	42
Iran, Islamic Rep	134,174	2,159 q	113,171	1,821 q	258,602	4,161	1.6	1.7	1.7	21	36	43
Iraq	42,725	2,363 i	52,833	2,923 i	54,787	3,347 n	(14.9) h	(14.9) h	(9.0) m	X	X	X
Israel	72,653	13,920	69,739	13,362	64,245	12,783	4.7	4.5	4.2	X	X	X
Japan	3,919,529	31,490	4,214,204	33,857	2,473,223	19,920	4.1	4.0	4.3	2 q	41 q	57 q
Jordan	4,881	1,190	5,190	1,265	13,241	4,039 i	0.1	1.2	1.1 m	8	26	66
Kazakhstan, Rep	26,445	1,560	24,728	1,459	82,590	4,929 g	(2.1)	(2.1)	X	29 g	42 g	30 g
Korea, Dem People's Rep	X	X	X	X	60,990	3,067 o	X	X	X	X	X	X
Korea, Rep	338,044	7,660	330,830	7,497	415,320	9,565 g	9.0	8.7	9.6 h	7	43	50
Kuwait	34,120	19,360	22,402	12,711	17,557	8,561 e	(2.1)	2.0 s	(0.4) f	0	55	45
Kyrgyz Rep	3,902	850	3,915	853	14,959	3,372 g	0.6	0.6	X	43 g	35 q	22 g
Lao People's Dem Rep	1,289	280	1,334	290	7,592	1,753 g	4.7 u	4.7 u	3.9 w	51	18	31
Lebanon	X	X	7,535	1,955	X	X	X	X	X	X	X	X
Malaysia	59,808	3,140	64,450	3,384	133,586	7,191	6.7	6.5	6.2	X	X	X
Mongolia	904	390	1,093	471	5,319	2,443 i	X	X	3.7 x	21	46	33
Myanmar	X	X	55,224	1,238	31,582	772 e	(0.1)	(0.1)	1.0 f	63	9	28
Nepal	3,954	190	3,748	180	24,586	1,240 e	4.9	4.9	3.8 /	43	21	36
Oman	9,640	4,850	11,686	5,879	13,975	8,650	5.8	5.4	2.6 f	3 q	53 q	44 q
Pakistan	52,805	430	51,825	422	214,098	1,793	4.8	5.7	5.0	25	25	50
Philippines	55,080	850	54,068	834	137,734	2,172	2.6	2.1	2.4	22	33	45
Saudi Arabia	133,275	7,953 q	124,163	7,410 q	143,679	9,390 e	2.5 t	3.1 t	(1.6) f	6 i	50 i	43 i
Singapore	55,380	19,850	55,153	19,769	46,213	16,736	6.9	6.9	6.1	0	37	63
Sri Lanka	10,738	600	10,472	585	49,170	2,783	3.9	3.8	2.8	25	26	50
Syrian Arab Rep	15,582	1,219 g	18,061	1,413 g	63,326	4,955 g	0.8 h	1.9 h	2.6 h	30 g	23 g	48 g
Tajikistan, Rep	2,710	470	2,520	437	14,475	2,783 i	(3.0)	(3.0)	X	33 g	35 g	32 g
Thailand	122,515	2,110	124,862	2,150	286,533	5,018	8.9	8.8	7.8	10	39	51
Turkey	177,003	2,970	174,167	2,922	285,592	4,893	4.2	4.8	5.1	15	30	55
Turkmenistan, Rep	5,418	1,416 q	5,267	1,376 q	16,556	4,527 i	1.9 t	1.9 t	X	32 g	31 g	37 g
United Arab Emirates	38,727	21,430	35,405	19,592	25,381	15,784 e	1.6	(0.4) p	0.5 f	2	57	40
Uzbekistan, Rep	21,204	970	20,425	934	72,104	3,334 i	1.4	1.4	X	23	36	41
Viet Nam	12,125	170	12,834	180	39,838	665 o	X	6.6 u	X	29	28	42
Yemen, Rep	X	X	12,616	956	30,305	2,769 e	X	X	9.7 f	21	24	55
OCEANIA												
Australia	307,967	17,500	289,390	16,444	321,126	18,500	2.7	2.8	2.8	3 q	29 q	67 q
Fiji	1,623	2,130	1,684	2,210	3,973	5,288	2.9	2.8	3.6 m	18 q	20 q	62 q
New Zealand	43,941	12,600	43,699	12,530	53,395	15,502	1.0	1.1	0.8	7 g	26 g	67 g
Papua New Guinea	4,644	1,130	5,091	1,239	7,923	1,972	3.2	3.7	1.4	26	43	31
Solomon Islands	262	740	246	718 q	789	2,639 r	5.0	5.4 t	7.7 s	X	X	X

Sources: The World Bank, United Nations Population Division, and Penn World Tables.

Notes: a. Current U.S. dollars (Atlas Methodology). b. Current 1993 U.S. dollars. c. Current 1992 international dollars (Int$). d. Constant $. e. Data are for 1989. f. Data are for 1983-89. g. Data are for 1991. h. Data are for 1983-91. i. Data are for 1990. j. Data are for 1986-93. k. Data are for 1986. l. Data are for 1983-86. m. Data are for 1983-87. n. Data are for 1987. o. Data are for 1985. p. Data are for 1983-90. q. Data are for 1992. r. Data are for 1988. s. Data are for 1983-88. t. Data are for 1983-92. u. Data are for 1983-88. v. Data are for 1987-93. w. Data are for 1984-91. x. Data are for 1984-90. 0 = zero or less than half the unit of measure; X = not available; negative numbers are shown in parentheses.
For additional information, see Sources and Technical Notes.

Data Table 7.2 Official Development Assistance and External Debt Indicators, 1981–93

	Average Annual Official Development Assistance (ODA) (million US$) {a}		ODA as a Percentage of GNP {a}	1993 ODA Per Capita (US$){a}	Total External Debt (million US$)		Disbursed Long-Term Public Debt (million US$) % of GNP		Debt Service as a Percentage of: Exports of Goods and Services	Current Borrowing	Current Borrowing Per Capita (US$)
	1984-86	1991-93	1991-93	(US$){a}	1981-83	1991-93	1991-93	1991-93	1991-93	1991-93	1991-93
WORLD											
AFRICA											
Algeria	80	(6)	(0.0)	(0)	17,461	26,923	25,259	50.5	72.5	135.1	260.7
Angola	117	308	X	29	X	9,233	7,504	NA	6.9	63.0	39.3
Benin	104	275	13.5	57	626	1,401	1,332	65.3	5.7	32.1	19.0
Botswana	101	126	3.3	90	205	641	634	16.7	1.2	87.9	74.9
Burkina Faso	223	444	15.6	48	359	1,053	987	34.6	7.5	25.7	15.5
Burundi	157	271	22.8	40	238	1,016	949	80.0	35.9	42.7	15.4
Cameroon	190	594	5.6	44	2,668	6,431	5,255	49.6	18.7	82.3	40.5
Central African Rep	119	175	13.6	55	249	854	763	59.5	7.4	20.3	21.4
Chad	154	245	19.3	38	189	692	635	50.0	5.5	11.7	16.9
Congo	96	125	5.0	53	1,841	4,880	3,992	160.1	16.0	93.6	88.3
Cote d'Ivoire	146	719	8.4	58	8,633	18,230	10,618	124.7	33.1	141.6	60.5
Egypt	1,784	3,644	10.0	38	28,703	40,721	36,174	99.0	15.8	149.6	27.7
Equatorial Guinea	18	59	41.0	139	111	259	216	149.5	5.6	22.6	33.1
Eritrea	X	X	X	20	X	X	X	X	X	X	X
Ethiopia	X	1,126	X	22	1,285	4,419	4,230	X	13.7	27.4	7.6
Gabon	72	105	2.1	82	1,017	3,933	3,024	60.5	11.4	251.1	96.8
Gambia, The	68	101	28.7	86	198	380	339	96.2	8.7	79.4	36.7
Ghana	265	707	10.2	38	1,553	4,383	3,150	45.5	25.3	74.7	24.4
Guinea	157	416	14.1	66	1,350	2,716	2,516	85.0	13.9	41.6	39.7
Guinea-Bissau	66	108	44.0	95	162	667	613	250.2	15.6	18.4	31.4
Kenya	435	913	11.7	35	3,415	6,947	5,030	64.5	31.4	129.3	21.4
Lesotho	94	138	12.0	73	112	475	444	38.9	5.2	49.7	33.0
Liberia	107	134	X	44	907	1,934	1,086	X	X	1,833.3	0.3
Libya	(43)	27	X	5	X	X	X	X	X	X	X
Madagascar	236	396	14.0	27	1,879	4,520	3,934	139.5	22.1	77.6	10.6
Malawi	157	532	26.4	48	851	1,733	1,604	79.6	23.9	61.9	16.5
Mali	365	423	16.3	37	902	2,610	2,477	95.7	6.4	33.7	10.1
Mauritania	203	250	23.1	156	1,128	2,192	1,895	175.2	20.8	80.2	60.6
Mauritius	40	47	1.5	24	563	1,028	756	25.0	7.6	123.1	113.5
Morocco	513	982	3.6	29	12,211	21,532	20,374	75.2	26.5	149.0	60.0
Mozambique	413	1,240	96.4	78	X	5,055	4,429	344.4	16.6	39.2	10.5
Namibia	X	161	6.3	106	X	X	X	X	X	X	X
Niger	258	365	15.2	41	976	1,656	1,299	54.2	24.2	94.9	10.0
Nigeria	42	267	0.8	3	14,543	32,655	29,959	89.9	18.7	435.3	6.7
Rwanda	186	359	18.6	48	219	872	803	41.6	14.0	27.2	9.3
Senegal	410	604	10.4	63	1,870	3,652	2,945	50.7	14.9	101.4	27.4
Sierra Leone	74	148	21.2	47	605	1,301	689	98.9	13.7	41.5	13.2
Somalia	405	576	X	99	1,229	2,466	1,913	X	X	4.0	0.5
South Africa	X	X	X	7	X	X	X	X	X	X	X
Sudan	905	627	X	17	7,003	16,160	9,066	X	3.4	20.5	4.3
Swaziland	30	54	5.4	67	212	242	235	23.8	3.5	199.7	16.9
Tanzania	579	1,126	41.5	34	3,341	7,334	6,599	243.2	35.8	72.2	11.5
Togo	133	175	11.9	26	949	1,333	1,135	76.9	8.3	92.7	11.1
Tunisia	189	348	2.5	29	3,812	8,498	7,245	52.2	21.4	116.9	137.8
Uganda	181	651	17.4	31	871	2,985	2,499	66.8	81.2	69.5	13.6
Zaire	362	307	X	4	5,168	11,025	8,996	X	X	63.4	3.7
Zambia	345	931	28.8	98	3,697	7,006	4,792	148.2	37.8	139.8	35.7
Zimbabwe	256	563	9.4	47	1,774	3,870	2,806	47.0	30.7	92.6	61.6
EUROPE											
Albania	X	307	X	61	X	627	121	NA	5.1	9.6	15.7
Austria	(209)	(549)	(0.3)	(69)	X	X	X	X	X	X	X
Belarus, Rep	X	197	0.6	13	X	383	X	X	X	2.8	17.0
Belgium	(476)	(836)	(0.4)	(80)	X	X	X	X	X	X	X
Bosnia and Herzegovina	X	X	X	X	X	X	X	X	X	X	X
Bulgaria	X	198	1.7	15	X	12,125	9,898	83.3	7.6	145.0	25.3
Croatia, Rep	X	X	X	X	X	989	X	X	X	224.2	12.4
Czech Rep	X	185	0.7	12	2,341	7,539	X	X	3.2	94.4	132.3
Denmark	(528)	(1,311)	(1.0)	(259)	X	X	X	X	X	X	X
Estonia, Rep	X	54	1.0	27	X	71	X	X	0.9	22.2	21.2
Finland	(234)	(643)	(0.6)	(70)	X	X	X	X	X	X	X
France	(4,296)	(7,857)	(0.6)	(138)	X	X	X	X	X	X	X
Germany	X	(7,142)	(0.4)	(86)	X	X	X	X	X	X	X
Greece	15	43	0.1	4	X	X	X	X	X	X	X
Hungary	X	365	1.1	19	10,239	23,123	19,044	58.1	37.4	117.3	370.8
Iceland	X	X	0.0	X	X	X	X	X	X	X	X
Ireland	(45)	(74)	(0.2)	(23)	X	X	X	X	X	X	X
Italy	(1,545)	(3,504)	(0.3)	(53)	X	X	X	X	X	X	X
Latvia, Rep	X	40	0.5	12	X	97	X	X	X	8.6	16.1
Lithuania, Rep	X	53	0.7	16	X	110	X	X	X	2.0	15.0
Macedonia, former Yugoslav Rep	X	X	X	X	X	289	X	X	X	2,700.0	0.1
Moldova, Rep	X	X	0.0	3	X	109	X	X	X	5.5	9.8
Netherlands	(1,381)	(2,598)	(0.8)	(165)	X	X	X	X	X	X	X
Norway	(637)	(1,155)	(1.1)	(236)	X	X	X	X	X	X	X
Poland, Rep	X	1,658	2.1	27	X	49,201	X	X	8.8	178.0	20.6
Portugal	113	(254)	(0.3)	(25)	13,230	32,627	22,049	27.1	13.6	90.6	651.0
Romania	X	299	1.0	9	9,859	3,380	1,257	4.4	5.8	39.6	33.1
Russian Federation	X	1,525	0.4	14	4,757	76,430	64,138	14.8	11.1	56.6	69.4
Slovak Rep	X	92	0.8	12	473	2,854	X	X	5.1	104.2	96.1
Slovenia, Rep	X	X	X	X	X	641	X	X	X	130.8	56.0
Spain	(172)	(1,331)	(0.3)	(31)	X	X	X	X	X	X	X
Sweden	(890)	(2,115)	(0.9)	(203)	X	X	X	X	X	X	X
Switzerland	(337)	(932)	(0.4)	(112)	X	X	X	X	X	X	X
Ukraine	X	407	0.3	6	X	1,379	1,304	1.0	X	19.0	7.2
United Kingdom	(1,566)	(3,117)	(0.3)	(50)	X	X	X	X	X	X	X
Yugoslavia, Fed Rep	X	X	X	X	20,341	14,693	X	X	X	439.0	43.1

	Average Annual Official Development Assistance (ODA) (million US$) {a}		ODA as a Percentage of GNP {a}	1993 ODA Per Capita (US$){a}	Total External Debt (million US$)		Disbursed Long-Term Public Debt (million US$)	% of GNP	Debt Service as a Percentage of: Exports of Goods and Services	Current Borrowing	Current Borrowing Per Capita (US$)
	1984-86	1991-93	1991-93		1981-83	1991-93	1991-93	1991-93	1991-93	1991-93	1991-93
NORTH & CENTRAL AMERICA											
Belize	20	26	5.5	150	77	175	156	33.3	7.7	88.0	114.7
Canada	(1,650)	(2,497)	(0.4)	(82)	X	X	X	X	0.0	X	X
Costa Rica	231	138	2.2	30	3,713	3,962	3,222	50.5	18.9	194.2	81.7
Cuba	703	35	X	4	X	X	X	X	X	X	X
Dominican Rep	163	44	0.5	0	2,581	4,580	3,746	44.5	8.3	261.9	16.0
El Salvador	316	369	5.7	73	1,438	2,151	2,034	31.2	15.5	78.2	61.1
Guatemala	94	203	2.1	21	1,536	2,843	2,214	22.4	18.1	208.2	18.2
Haiti	154	137	X	18	511	764	618	NA	2.2	105.3	1.7
Honduras	281	331	10.7	62	1,891	3,614	3,258	104.9	31.5	96.7	69.5
Jamaica	172	134	3.7	45	2,864	4,396	3,699	103.8	24.1	194.7	135.9
Mexico	160	332	0.1	4	85,757	115,604	75,278	25.7	30.4	154.7	135.4
Nicaragua	300	607	47.8	78	3,169	10,740	8,842	695.4	65.2	102.9	59.5
Panama	65	114	1.9	31	3,893	6,674	3,800	62.9	19.6	710.2	26.3
Trinidad and Tobago	10	3	0.1	2	1,230	2,326	1,713	34.9	15.7	245.4	173.6
United States	(9,226)	(10,897)	(0.2)	(38)	0	X	X	X	X	X	X
SOUTH AMERICA											
Argentina	59	291	0.2	8	41,737	69,213	50,006	26.0	38.8	112.6	164.1
Bolivia	232	584	11.5	80	3,539	4,169	3,631	71.2	44.2	113.6	47.6
Brazil	154	62	0.0	2	90,757	123,721	84,777	19.0	24.0	111.7	56.2
Chile	13	148	0.4	13	16,969	19,239	9,505	24.9	22.6	148.7	136.4
Colombia	71	159	0.3	3	10,145	17,236	13,523	29.0	33.6	203.8	51.7
Ecuador	140	241	2.0	22	7,655	12,953	9,906	81.8	28.4	195.9	47.6
Guyana	28	111	42.2	131	1,014	1,919	1,716	654.7	11.1	126.8	93.1
Paraguay	56	129	2.0	29	1,287	1,766	1,445	22.8	21.8	320.8	26.6
Peru	306	528	1.7	24	10,213	20,447	15,614	50.2	38.4	178.1	41.3
Suriname	10	68	13.0	193	X	X	X	X	X	X	X
Uruguay	12	82	0.8	38	2,704	6,689	4,494	41.8	39.5	129.2	209.0
Venezuela	(15)	41	0.1	2	34,194	36,453	25,875	45.1	20.2	165.3	104.5
ASIA											
Afghanistan, Islamic State	263	314	X	13	X	X	X	X	X	X	X
Armenia	X	24	0.6	14	X	50	48	1.1	X	1.5	12.9
Azerbaijan	X	X	X	3	X	12	12	0.2	X	X	X
Bangladesh	1,302	1,703	6.9	12	4,965	13,331	12,417	50.0	16.6	77.6	6.4
Bhutan	27	62	X	41	1	85	84	X	4.9	104.7	4.0
Cambodia	136	205	X	33	X	398	239	X	5.5	894.4	0.2
China	719	2,777	0.5	3	7,922	70,876	59,236	10.9	10.9	60.7	12.5
Georgia, Rep	X	14	0.2	6	X	216	X	X	0.9	8.1	10.0
India	1,728	2,228	0.8	2	27,350	88,621	76,786	27.3	29.5	114.1	8.1
Indonesia	662	1,999	1.6	11	26,042	83,128	50,201	40.1	31.7	109.5	57.6
Iran, Islamic Rep	19	147	X	2	6,400	14,915	4,220	X	5.1	86.0	17.9
Iraq	40	291	X	9	X	X	X	X	X	X	X
Israel	1,712	1,694	2.5	241	X	X	X	X	X	X	X
Japan	(4,583)	(11,121)	(0.3)	(90)	X	X	X	X	X	X	X
Jordan	599	551	12.5	63	2,727	7,314	7,062	160.2	17.7	146.4	89.6
Kazakhstan, Rep	NA	44	0.1	1	X	558	X	X	X	3.0	6.3
Korea, Dem People's Rep	93	12	NA	1	X	X	X	X	X	X	X
Korea, Rep	(21)	8	0.0	(1)	36,913	43,698	23,700	7.5	8.0	95.7	176.9
Kuwait	(831)	324	1.3	215	X	X	X	X	X	X	X
Kyrgyz Rep	NA	NA	NA	10	X	103	X	X	X	1.4	7.3
Lao People's Dem Rep	127	172	15.3	45	423	1,926	1,895	169.3	7.0	19.7	17.7
Lebanon	75	130	NA	49	741	1,576	340	X	6.9	528.8	8.9
Malaysia	249	199	0.4	5	13,361	20,369	13,782	26.1	7.4	145.7	126.2
Mongolia	621	106	NA	54	0	252	211	X	7.2	37.0	33.4
Myanmar	353	132	NA	2	2,027	5,219	4,888	X	3.8	117.5	1.6
Nepal	245	419	10.3	18	361	1,862	1,800	44.4	8.4	41.9	7.8
Oman	76	47	0.5	36	1,067	2,805	2,377	23.8	6.6	160.8	186.2
Pakistan	870	1,169	2.3	8	11,373	24,361	18,794	37.7	23.4	96.7	18.2
Philippines	613	1,420	2.8	23	23,136	33,275	26,046	51.1	24.2	141.2	46.4
Saudi Arabia	(3,081)	1,009	NA	31	X	X	X	X	X	X	X
Singapore	31	17	0.0	8	X	X	X	X	X	X	X
Sri Lanka	507	718	7.4	35	2,581	6,581	5,736	59.0	12.3	86.5	29.1
Syrian Arab Rep	751	73	X	0	6,542	19,311	16,167	X	7.0	54.6	49.1
Tajikistan, Rep	X	X	X	4	X	17	X	X	X	X	1.4
Thailand	484	704	0.6	11	12,331	40,462	13,802	12.7	15.2	120.4	97.2
Turkey	255	803	0.5	8	19,759	57,850	40,625	25.3	30.6	109.9	134.0
Turkmenistan, Rep	X	X	X	2	X	3	X	X	X	X	0.8
United Arab Emirates	(91)	321	0.8	130	X	X	X	X	X	X	X
Uzbekistan, Rep	X	X	X	0	X	250	X	X	X	6.6	8.1
Viet Nam	1,473	359	X	4	X	23,397	21,135	X	12.7	127.7	4.6
Yemen, Rep	290	286	X	X	2,413	6,322	X	X	8.8	91.5	X
OCEANIA											
Australia	(759)	(1,006)	(0.3)	(54)	X	X	X	X	X	X	X
Fiji	35	57	3.7	81	404	343	232	15.2	9.1	232.9	46.4
New Zealand	(61)	(98)	(0.2)	(28)	X	X	X	X	X	X	X
Papua New Guinea	281	381	9.2	74	1,560	3,211	1,547	37.6	29.2	117.3	143.5
Solomon Islands	23	45	18.6	158	29	109	96	39.4	5.6	191.9	15.7

Sources: Organisation for Economic Co-Operation and Development, the World Bank, and United Nations Population Division.

Notes: a. For ODA, flows to recipients are shown as positive numbers; flows from donors are shown as negative numbers (in parentheses).
0 = zero or less than half the unit of measure; X = not available. For additional information, see Sources and Technical Notes.
For additional information, see Sources and Technical Notes.

Commodity Indexes (based on constant prices with 1990 = 100) {a}

	1975	1980	1983	1984	1985	1986	1987	1988	1989	1990	1991	1992	1993	1994
Petroleum	101	224	187	183	173	78	89	68	82	100	83	78	69	63
NONFUEL COMMODITIES	167	175	149	154	134	115	105	117	114	100	93	86	86	102
Total Agriculture	180	193	162	173	147	128	111	116	112	100	96	89	93	113
Total Food	224	193	152	157	126	95	95	113	114	100	97	94	93	98
-Cereals	258	187	158	153	130	95	87	107	118	100	100	95	88	93
-Fats and Oils	228	206	195	232	165	108	114	140	126	100	102	105	105	115
-Other Foods	203	187	113	98	92	85	84	93	102	100	91	84	85	86
Beverages	183	257	226	264	241	242	153	148	122	100	92	75	80	137
Raw Materials	119	145	127	128	103	87	102	95	102	100	97	92	104	115
-Timber	92	110	92	101	86	79	90	84	98	100	102	107	144	143
Metals and Minerals	118	132	118	109	102	81	88	120	118	100	87	81	70	77
Fertilizers	350	179	141	144	130	110	106	114	112	100	100	90	79	85

Commodity Prices (in constant 1990 US$ per unit measure) {a}

		1975	1980	1983	1984	1985	1986	1987	1988	1989	1990	1991	1992	1993	1994
Cocoa (New York & London)	kg	2.76	3.62	3.05	3.52	3.29	2.56	2.25	1.66	1.31	1.27	1.17	1.03	1.05	1.27
Coffee (other mild arabicas)	kg	3.19	4.81	4.19	4.68	4.71	5.31	2.82	3.18	2.52	1.97	1.83	1.32	1.47	3.02
Tea (World)	kg	3.06	3.10	3.35	5.08	2.89	2.38	1.92	1.88	2.13	2.03	1.80	1.88	1.76	1.67
Rice (Thailand)	mt	803.32	602.78	398.42	370.25	314.75	260.20	259.35	316.26	338.13	287.18	307.61	269.61	254.24	325.94
Grain Sorghum (U.S.)	mt	247.57	179.03	185.32	174.74	150.15	101.98	81.98	103.36	111.83	103.90	102.84	96.39	93.25	94.77
Maize (U.S.)	mt	264.60	174.03	195.68	199.56	163.56	108.28	85.25	112.17	117.74	109.30	105.09	97.80	96.13	98.13
Wheat (U.S.)	mt	329.77	239.90	226.50	223.69	198.00	142.05	127.13	152.36	178.71	135.52	125.89	141.84	132.05	136.62
Sugar (World)	kg	1.00	0.88	0.27	0.17	0.13	0.16	0.17	0.24	0.30	0.28	0.19	0.19	0.21	0.24
Beef (U.S.)	kg	2.94	3.83	3.51	3.34	3.13	2.59	2.69	2.64	2.71	2.56	2.61	2.30	2.46	2.13
Lamb (New Zealand)	kg	3.15	4.01	2.78	2.82	2.69	2.69	2.45	2.53	2.45	2.66	2.28	2.45	2.74	2.72
Bananas (Any Origin)	mt	545.80	526.39	616.98	542.58	554.37	471.82	411.49	501.68	577.40	540.90	547.46	443.81	417.17	400.99
Oranges (Mediterranean)	mt	504.42	542.50	536.98	517.18	580.76	486.65	513.51	475.76	470.33	531.10	509.78	458.95	407.24	375.05
Copra (Philippines)	mt	567.04	628.75	713.67	1,042.73	562.68	243.51	347.97	417.63	367.37	230.70	280.23	356.87	278.15	380.78
Coconut Oil (Phil. & Indonesia)	mt	870.58	935.83	1,050.22	1,695.45	860.06	367.12	497.75	592.65	545.72	336.50	423.68	541.84	423.96	554.29
Groundnut Meal (Any Origin)	mt	309.73	333.75	329.50	274.74	214.29	203.96	182.43	219.83	210.35	184.80	146.87	146.03	158.29	153.59
Groundnut Oil (Nigeria)	mt	1,898.23	1,193.06	1,022.88	1,492.95	1,319.24	703.34	563.06	619.41	818.16	963.70	875.54	572.14	695.93	933.17
Linseed (Canada)	mt	747.62	487.56	398.82	437.91	399.42	257.14	190.23	308.47	364.50	314.00	204.74	197.97	214.68	215.82
Linseed Oil (Any Origin)	mt	1,550.54	968.60	696.97	840.56	915.45	517.99	353.44	547.69	799.79	709.00	430.05	372.68	421.69	417.34
Palm Kernels (Nigeria)	mt	457.96	479.17	525.61	763.58	414.72	175.53	203.83	280.17	265.05	188.00	215.26	215.76	216.57	X
Palm Oil (Malaysia)	mt	960.62	810.42	721.44	1,070.19	730.32	317.68	386.26	458.76	370.01	289.80	331.70	369.14	355.70	482.14
Soybeans (U.S.)	mt	486.50	411.39	405.14	414.24	326.53	257.11	243.24	318.47	290.39	246.80	234.44	220.92	240.21	229.77
Soybean Oil (Any Origin)	mt	1,369.47	828.47	758.27	1,063.14	833.82	422.74	376.13	485.83	456.18	447.00	444.03	402.35	452.37	561.66
Soybean Meal (U.S.)	mt	342.92	363.89	342.16	289.57	228.86	228.68	228.60	280.69	259.66	200.20	192.86	191.74	196.02	175.57
Fish Meal (Peru)	mt	542.04	700.00	651.80	547.72	408.16	396.79	431.31	570.83	431.26	412.20	467.51	451.69	343.50	343.37
Cotton (Index)	kg	2.57	2.84	2.67	2.62	1.92	1.31	1.86	1.47	1.77	1.82	1.64	1.20	1.21	1.61
Burlap (U.S.)	meter	0.49	0.50	0.42	0.54	0.50	0.31	0.30	0.32	0.33	0.31	0.30	0.27	0.25	0.28
Jute (Bangladesh)	mt	820.80	427.78	434.82	779.44	849.71	333.84	363.51	388.25	394.19	408.30	372.14	299.79	257.37	272.14
Sisal (East Africa)	mt	1,282.90	1,062.66	809.72	858.19	766.76	635.43	576.32	578.11	689.91	715.00	655.37	474.39	579.27	552.23
Wool (New Zealand)	kg	6.06	6.39	5.23	5.40	5.19	4.09	5.08	6.08	5.65	4.07	3.46	3.69	2.84	3.55
Rubber (Malaysia)	kg	1.24	1.98	1.53	1.41	1.11	1.00	1.11	1.24	1.02	0.86	0.81	0.81	0.78	1.03
Logs (Malaysia)	cm	131.19	271.54	198.14	230.19	177.45	171.30	227.22	210.77	201.26	177.19	187.36	196.54	367.05	280.61
Plywood (Philippines)	sheet	2.69	3.80	3.31	3.33	3.07	3.38	4.49	3.76	3.70	3.55	3.64	3.57	6.23	5.49
Sawnwood (Malaysia)	cm	368.14	507.08	437.84	450.51	402.77	329.05	310.92	321.72	445.51	524.20	461.74	481.34	506.70	710.28
Tobacco (India)	mt	3,606.19	3,194.44	3,230.22	2,922.17	2,842.57	2,348.58	2,083.33	2,036.73	1,996.83	1,964.00	2,158.51	2,307.69	1,977.40	1,746.35
Coal (U.S.)	mt	X	59.86	64.03	71.37	67.93	54.26	40.77	38.93	42.77	41.67	40.61	38.09	35.78	33.28
Crude Petroleum (spot)	bbl	23.08	51.21	42.67	41.93	39.63	17.74	20.43	15.44	18.84	22.88	18.95	17.84	15.86	14.50
Gasoline (Europe)	mt	266.09	497.43	369.62	378.25	372.01	180.49	192.82	165.77	202.85	252.30	218.95	X	X	X
Fuel Oil (Europe)	mt	137.36	235.93	235.29	262.16	220.70	90.86	112.00	71.24	91.18	98.60	75.14	X	X	X
Aluminum (Europe)	mt	1,763.27	2,022.22	2,070.50	1,837.00	1,517.49	1,421.51	1,762.39	2,676.81	2,060.19	1,639.00	1,274.17	1,176.64	1,072.55	1,347.43
Bauxite (Jamaica)	mt	55.96	57.25	49.91	46.49	43.73	34.61	29.27	31.79	36.34	34.40	33.11	30.02	X	X
Copper (London)	mt	2,736.73	3,030.56	2,290.50	2,022.47	2,066.18	1,698.15	2,007.32	2,730.01	3,007.81	2,661.50	2,288.45	2,139.92	1,801.39	2,105.31
Lead (London)	kg	0.92	1.26	0.61	0.65	0.57	0.50	0.67	0.69	0.71	0.81	0.55	0.51	0.38	0.50
Tin (London)	kg	15.21	23.30	18.69	17.96	16.82	7.62	7.51	7.40	9.01	6.09	5.47	5.72	4.86	4.99
Zinc (New York)	kg	1.64	1.06	1.10	1.35	1.14	0.93	0.90	1.30	1.75	1.51	1.09	1.16	0.96	0.99
Iron Ore (Brazil)	mt fe	38.27	39.01	41.73	38.40	38.72	32.46	27.59	24.66	27.98	30.80	32.53	29.64	26.50	23.24
Manganese Ore (India)	10 kg	3.05	2.18	2.18	2.10	2.06	1.70	1.49	1.54	2.13	3.36	3.77	3.45	2.76	X
Nickel (Canada)	mt	10,111.06	9,053.75	6,723.45	6,978.41	7,141.55	4,797.53	5,486.71	14,457.82	14,053.01	8,864.10	7,980.04	6,567.76	4,984.39	5,784.51
Phosphate Rock (Morocco)	mt	148.23	64.86	53.09	56.24	49.42	42.27	34.91	37.78	43.08	40.50	41.59	39.17	31.07	30.11
Diammonium Phosphate (U.S.)	mt	537.61	308.61	264.03	277.68	246.36	190.61	195.61	206.19	182.47	171.40	169.18	136.17	121.57	157.66
Potassium Chloride (Canada)	mt	179.87	160.97	108.35	122.91	122.45	85.04	77.70	91.82	104.44	98.10	106.51	105.13	101.15	96.46
Triple Superphosphate (U.S.)	mt	446.90	250.00	194.24	192.36	176.38	149.57	155.41	165.79	152.06	131.82	130.25	113.26	105.40	120.54
Urea (Any Origin)	mt	438.05	308.47	194.82	251.54	198.69	132.26	131.31	162.64	139.60	157.00	168.30	131.61	100.52	134.96

Source: The World Bank.
Notes: a. The World Bank Price Index for the Primary Commodities (revised April 1995).
kg = kilogram; mt = metric ton; cm = centimeter; bbl = barrel; fe = iron. 0 = zero or less than half the unit of measure; X = not available.
For additional information, see Sources and Technical Notes.

Sources and Technical Notes

Data Table 7.1
Gross National and Domestic Product Estimates, 1983–93

Sources: 1993 Gross national product (GNP), gross domestic product (GDP), annual growth rates of GNP and GDP, and distribution of GDP: derived from the World Bank, *World Tables 1995* on diskette (World Bank Software, Washington, D.C., 1995). Population figures for calculations: United Nations (U.N.) Population Division *Annual Populations, 1950–2050 (The 1994 Revision),* on diskette (U.N., New York, 1993). Total and per capita purchasing power parity (PPP), GDP, and average annual growth rates of same: derived from Robert Summers *et al., The Penn World Table,* Mark 5.6 (University of Pennsylvania, Philadelphia, December 1994).

Data for years prior to 1993 (1992 for PPP) have been converted to 1993 U.S. dollars (US$) (1992 international dollars (Int $) for PPP) using deflators derived from U.S. data.

Gross national product is the sum of two components: the GDP and net factor income from abroad. GDP is the final output of goods and services produced by the domestic economy, including net exports of goods and nonfactor services. Net factor income from abroad is income in the form of overseas workers' remittances, interest on loans, profits, and other factor payments that residents receive from abroad, less payments made for factor services (i.e., labor and capital). Most countries estimate GDP by the production method. This method sums the final outputs of the various sectors of the economy (e.g., agriculture, manufacturing, and government services), from which the value of the inputs to production have been subtracted.

GNP estimates at current purchaser values (market prices) in U.S. dollars are calculated using *The World Bank Atlas* methodology. GNP estimates in local currencies were converted to U.S. dollars using a 3-year average exchange rate, adjusted for domestic and U.S. inflation. The *Atlas* method of averaging 3 years of exchange rates smoothes fluctuations due to the currency market and provides a more reliable measure, over time, of GNP than do estimates based on a single year's exchange rate.

The *gross domestic product* estimates at purchaser values (market prices) are in 1993 U.S. dollars (based on 1993 exchange rates), and are the sum of GDP at factor cost (value added in the agriculture, industry, and services sectors) and indirect taxes, less subsidies.

These estimates are in accord with the United Nations System of National Accounts.

Per capita estimates of GNP and GDP for 1993 are calculated using United Nations Population Division data.

Total and per capita purchasing power parity are GDP estimates based on the purchasing power of currencies rather than on current exchange rates. The estimates are a blend of extrapolated and regression-based numbers, using the results of the International Comparison Programme (ICP) as modified and extended by the Penn World Tables. (See Box 7.2 for additional information.)

The ICP benchmark studies are (essentially) multilateral pricing exercises. Intercountry price comparisons are reported in six phases: 1970, 1973, 1975, 1980, 1985, and 1990. Another benchmark study is under way with 1993 as the reference year. PPP studies recast traditional national accounts through special price collections and the disaggregation of GDP by expenditure components. ICP details are reported by national statistical offices, and the results are coordinated by the United Nations Statistical Division, assisted by other agencies, particularly the Statistical Office of the European Communities and the Organisation for Economic Co-Operation and Development. Sixty-four countries participated in ICP Phase V. The next round of ICP surveys for 1993 is expected to cover more than 80 countries.

International dollar values, which are different from U.S. dollar values of GNP or GDP, are obtained using special conversion factors that equalize the purchasing powers of different currencies. This conversion factor, the PPP, is defined as the number of units of a country's currency required to buy the same amounts of goods and services in the domestic market as $1 would buy in the "average" country. The average price index thus equalizes dollar prices in every country so that cross-country comparisons of GDP based on them reflect differences in quantities of goods and services free of price-level differentials. This procedure is designed to bring cross-country comparisons in line with cross-time real-value comparisons that are based on constant price series. PPP estimates tend to lower per capita GDPs in industrialized countries and raise per capita GDPs in developing countries.

The *average annual growth rates* of GNP, GDP, and PPP-based GDP are least-squares calculations of productivity growth based on constant price GNP, GDP, and PPP data. That is, the GNP, GDP, and PPP-based GDP estimates have been adjusted to exclude inflation.

The *distribution of GDP* is calculated using current local currency units provided in the *World Tables 1995. Agriculture* includes agricultural and livestock production and services, logging, forestry, fishing, and hunting. *Industry* comprises mining and quarrying; manufacturing; construction; and electricity, gas, and water. *Services* include wholesale and retail trade; transport, storage, and communications; banking, insurance, and real estate; public administration and defense; ownership of dwellings; and others. The *distribution of GDP* does not always add up to 100 percent due to rounding.

Although considerable effort has been made to standardize economic data according to the United Nations System of National Accounts, care should be taken in interpretation. Intercountry and intertemporal comparisons using economic data involve complicated technical problems that are not easily resolved; therefore, readers are urged to read these data as characterizing major differences between economies rather than as precise, quantitative measurements.

Data Table 7.2
Official Development Assistance and External Debt Indicators, 1981–93

Sources: Official development assistance (ODA): Organisation for Economic Co-Operation and Development (OECD), *Development Co-Operation* (OECD, Paris, 1984, 1986, 1987, 1988, 1989, 1990, 1991, 1992, 1993, and 1994); *Geographical Distribution of Financial Flows to Developing Countries 1981/84, 1983/86, 1984/87, 1986/89, 1988/91* (OECD, Paris, 1986, 1988, 1989, 1991, and 1993); and *Geographical Distribution of Financial Flows to Aid Recipients 1989–93.* ODA as a percentage of gross national product (GNP) was calculated using the World Bank, *The World Bank Atlas* (The World Bank, Washington, D.C., 1992). Population figures for per capita estimates of ODA and current borrowing: United Nations (U.N.) Population Division, *Annual Populations, 1950–2050 (The 1994 Revision),* on diskette (U.N., New York, 1995). External debt, disbursed long-term public debt, debt service, and current borrowing: The World Bank, *World Debt Tables 1994–95,* on diskette (The World Bank, Washington, D.C., 1995).

Net *average annual official development assistance* (in current U.S. dollars) is the net amount of disbursed grants and concessional loans given or received by a country. Grants include gifts of money, goods, or services for which no repayment is required. A concessional loan has a grant element of 25 percent or more. The grant element is the amount by which the face value of the loan exceeds its present market value because of below-market interest rates, favorable maturity schedules, or repayment grace periods.

ODA contributions are shown as negative numbers (in parentheses); receipts are shown as positive numbers. Data for donor countries include contributions made directly to developing countries and through multilateral institutions.

ODA sources include the development assistance agencies of OECD and the Organization of Petroleum Exporting Countries members, as well as other countries. Grants and concessional loans to and from multilateral development agencies are also included as contributions and receipts. OECD gathers ODA data through questionnaires and reports from countries and multilateral agencies. Only limited data are available on ODA flows among developing countries.

The GNP data used to calculate *ODA as a percentage of GNP* were *Atlas* GNP estimates. For full comparability of these ratios, the GNP figures should be at current prices and calculated using single-year exchange rates, like the ODA figures.

The *1993 ODA per capita* estimates are calculated using 1993 ODA estimates in current dollars and United Nations Population Division population data.

The World Bank operates the Debtor Reporting System (DRS), which compiles reports supplied by 116 of its member countries. Countries submit detailed reports on the annual status, transactions, and terms of the long-term external debt of public agencies and of publicly guaranteed private debt. Additional data are drawn from the World Bank, the International Monetary Fund (IMF), regional development banks, government lending agencies, and the Creditor Reporting System (CRS). The CRS is operated by OECD to compile reports from the members of its Development Assistance Committee.

Total external debt (current U.S. dollars) includes long-term debt outstanding, private nonguaranteed debt outstanding, use of IMF credit, and short-term debt. A long-term debt is an obligation with a maturity of at least one year that is owed to nonresidents and is repayable in foreign currency, goods, or services. Long-term debt is divided into long-term public debt and long-term publicly guaranteed private debt. A short-term debt is a public or publicly guaranteed private debt that has a maturity of one year or less. This class of debt is especially difficult for countries to monitor. Only a few countries supply these data through the DRS; the World Bank supplements these data with creditor-country reports, information from international clearinghouse banks, and other sources to derive rough estimates of short-term debt.

Use of IMF credit, which refers to all drawings on the Fund's General Resources Account, is converted to U.S. dollars by applying the average special-drawing-right exchange rate in effect for the year being calculated.

A private debt is an external obligation of a private debtor that is not guaranteed by a public entity. Data for this class of debt are less extensive than are those for public debt, and are included in the total when available.

A *disbursed long-term public debt* is an outstanding public or publicly guaranteed long-term debt. A public debt is an obligation of a national or subnational government or its agencies and autonomous bodies. A publicly guaranteed debt is an external obligation of a private debtor guaranteed for repayment by a public entity.

Long-term public debt as a percentage of GNP is calculated using the disbursed long-term public debt and the *Atlas* GNP estimates. Again, for full comparability, the GNP estimates should be at current prices and using single-year exchange rates, like the long-term public debt data.

Total *debt service* (in foreign currencies, goods, and services) comprises interest payments and principal repayments made on the disbursed long-term public debt and private, nonguaranteed debt, IMF debt repurchases, IMF charges, and interest payments on short-term debt.

Exports of goods and services are the total value (current prices in U.S. dollars) of goods and nonfactor services sold to the rest of the world. *Current borrowing* is the total long-term debt disbursed during the specified years. *Current borrowing per capita* was calculated using the United Nations Population Division data noted previously.

Debt data are reported to the World Bank in the units of currency in which they are payable. The World Bank converts these data to U.S. dollars using the IMF par values, central rates, or the current market rates, where appropriate. Debt service data are converted to U.S. dollars at the average exchange rate for the given year. Comparability of data among countries and years is limited by variations in methods, definitions, and comprehensiveness of data collection and reporting.

ODA figures are derived from the annual questionnaire completed by each Development Assistance Committee member country; for nonmembers, values are based on information published by governments or provided directly to the OECD by them.

External debt data pertain only to those countries within the DRS, which focuses on low- and middle-income economies. Many economies are not represented within the system. Estimates that are presented may not be comprehensive because of different reporting frameworks. These data do not account for the term structure and the concessionality mix of debt, which can lead to a misrepresentation of a country's underlying solvency.

Data Table 7.3
World Commodity Indexes and Prices, 1975–94

Source: The World Bank, unpublished data (The World Bank, Washington, D.C., July 1995).

Price data are compiled from major international marketplaces for standard grades of each commodity. For example, maize refers to No. 2, yellow, FOB (free on board) U.S. gulf ports. The 1990 U.S. constant dollar figures were derived by converting current average monthly prices in local currencies to U.S. dollars using average monthly exchange rates. These average monthly dollar figures were then averaged to produce an average annual dollar figure, which was adjusted to 1990 constant dollars using the manufacturing unit value index. This index is a composite price index of all manufactured goods exported by the G-5 countries (the United States, the United Kingdom, France, Germany, and Japan) to developing countries.

The aggregate price indexes have the following components:

1. *Petroleum*
2. *Nonfuel commodities*: individual commodities listed under items 4–12, below.
3. *Total agriculture*: total food, beverages, and raw materials.
4. *Total food*: cereals, fats and oils, and other foods.
5. *Cereals*: maize, rice, wheat, and grain sorghum.
6. *Fats and oils*: palm, coconut, and groundnut oils; soybeans; soybean oil; and soybean meal.
7. *Other foods*: sugar, beef, bananas, and oranges.
8. *Beverages*: coffee, cocoa, and tea.
9. *Raw materials*: cotton, jute, rubber, tobacco, and timber.
10. *Timber*: logs and sawnwood.
11. *Metals and minerals*: copper, tin, nickel, aluminum, iron ore, lead, and zinc.
12. *Fertilizers*: phosphate rock and triple superphosphate.

The commodity prices reported here are specific to the markets named. The commodities themselves are often defined more specifically than is suggested in the table (e.g., lamb (New Zealand), frozen whole carcasses, wholesale price, Smithfield market, London).

8. Population and Human Development

Traditional demographic statistics can help provide an understanding of the human condition and future global change. Global population trends, for example, are an important indicator of future demand for water, food, and energy. Life expectancy and child mortality trends are important indicators of human well-being.

In recent years, led notably by the United Nations Development Programme's *Human Development Report*, attempts have been made to draw a more complete picture of the human condition, that is, to forecast whether the millions of people added to the population every year will be rich or poor, healthy or sick, educated or illiterate. An important component of this bigger picture concerns equity—among races, genders, nations, and regions—and the changing nature of opportunities for people.

This chapter begins with a brief discussion of global demographic conditions and population trends. It then touches on a few of the broader issues of human development, looking particularly at global health trends.

POPULATION TRENDS

Current global population estimates and projections for the future give rise to both optimism and concern. On the one hand, populations in developed and transition economies are growing relatively slowly or, in some cases, are actually falling (1). Furthermore, some developing countries are moving rapidly toward population

stability. On the other hand, population growth continues at high levels in many developing countries—usually accompanied by high levels of poverty, limited progress for women, and high levels of internal and international migration.

Overall, the world population is still increasing by more than 86 million people annually (2). (See Data Table 8.1.) By the year 2025, the world population is projected to total about 8.3 billion people, or about 45 percent more than the estimated current population of 5.7 billion. By 2050, the global population could be about 10 billion people. Most of this growth will occur in developing countries (3). (See Figure 8.1.)

The actual global population could vary considerably from this estimate and depends on a multitude of factors, including the level and pattern of future fertility and mortality, the effectiveness and extent of family planning programs, the impact of economic growth on poverty, and trends in the status of women.

Long-term projections to 2150 show a wide range of possible global population outcomes, with the differences largely being due to differing assumptions about future trends in fertility rates. (See Figure 8.2.) The predicted global population range in 2050—7.9 billion to 11.9 billion—suggests that effective programs and economic progress in the poorest nations could substantially affect global population totals (4).

The most critical indicator of demographic stability is the point at which a nation's fertility rate will drop to the "replacement level" of about two children per woman. The total fertility rate refers to the average number of children a woman would have in her lifetime

Figure 8.1 Trends and Projections in World Population Growth, 1750–2150

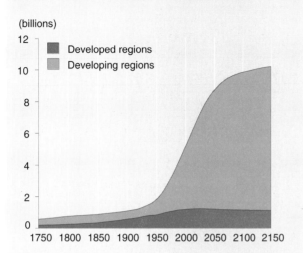

Sources:
1. United Nations (U.N.) Population Division, *Long-Range World Population Projections: Two Centuries of World Population Growth, 1950–2150* (U.N., New York, 1992), p. 22.
2. Carl Haub, Director of Information and Education, Population Reference Bureau, Washington, D.C., 1995 (personal communication).
Note: Projections are based on the U.N. medium variant. See Figure 8.2.

Figure 8.2 Long-Range Population Projections on the Basis of Different Fertility Rates, 1990–2150

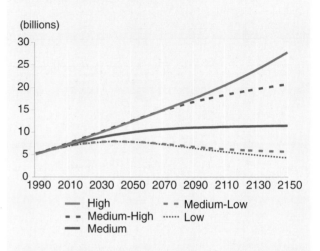

Source: United Nations (U.N.) Population Division, *Long-Range World Population Projections: Two Centuries of Population Growth, 1950–2150* (U.N., New York, 1992), p. 14.
Note: Under the medium fertility rate projection, which assumes that the fertility rate ultimately will stabilize at a replacement level of about 2.06, the global population could reach about 10 billion in 2050, and 11.5 billion in 2150, and could ultimately stabilize at about 11.6 billion shortly after 2200.

Under a medium-high rate, with the fertility rate stabilizing at 2.17 children (5 percent higher than the replacement level), the world population could be nearly 21 billion by 2150. At a high fertility stabilization rate (2.5 children), the world population could reach 28 billion by 2150.

If fertility stabilized at 5 percent below the replacement level, the world population could peak at 7.8 billion in 2050 and then fall to 5.6 billion by 2150; under an even lower assumption (1.7 children), population could peak at 7.8 billion in 2050 and then fall to 4.3 billion in 2150.

on the basis of fertility rates in a given year. When the total fertility rate drops to about 2, it means that each couple is replacing itself without adding to the size of the future population. (Data Table 8.2 shows United Nations (U.N.) estimates of the total fertility rate for the 1990–95 period. The U.N. also has devised estimates of the fertility rate for 1995–2000. Since the current situation is probably somewhere in between these two estimates, the U.N.'s *State of World Population 1995* calculates midpoint estimates for 1995. Those numbers are used here.)

Fertility rates have generally been declining since the 1960s. Worldwide, total fertility is currently estimated to be about 3. In developed countries, the fertility rate has declined from about 2.8 in the early 1950s to about 1.7 today. For developing countries as a whole, it has dropped from 6.2 in 1960 to about 3.4 today. In the poorest developing countries, however, it is still about 5.6 (5).

Reaching replacement-level fertility does not mean that population growth levels off immediately. Even with fertility below the replacement level, countries with large numbers of couples in their reproductive years will continue to grow for some time because of "demographic momentum"; that is, each woman is having fewer children, but many more women are giving birth.

Two other demographic trends are especially noteworthy. First, the world's population is becoming more urban. (See Chapter 1, "Cities and the Environment.") Urbanization is an important factor in the demographic transition to lower fertility rates. When people move into cities, they have more job opportunities, their incomes tend to increase, and they have greater access to health and education facilities. As a result of these and other factors, their fertility tends to decline. Higher proportions of the global population living in urban areas should therefore help bring down fertility rates.

Second, the world's population is aging. The world's population currently is growing at a rate of about 1.5 percent per year (6), but because of past levels of high fertility coupled with declining mortality rates, the population over age 65 is increasing at an annual rate of 2.7 percent. The most rapid changes are in the developing world, where the population over age 65 may grow by as much as 400 percent in some countries over the next 30 years. There will also be a dramatic rise in the number of people over age 80 (7).

A long life is not necessarily a healthy life, however—a point of concern for those charged with providing health care and other services to aging populations. Elderly people are heavy users of health services; in some countries where elderly people make up only 10 percent of the population, they use 30 percent of the health services (8). As the next century approaches, more elderly people will be dependent on fewer people of working age as the source of funding for their care and security. The additional health resources required to treat a growing population of elderly people could also mean that fewer resources will be available to prevent acute and chronic illness in the general population.

Regional Differences in Population

Distinctions between developed and developing countries do not adequately capture the current regional diversity of the demographic outlook. (See Figure 8.3.) Between 1995 and 2025, for example, many countries in Central Europe and the former Soviet Union—including Belarus, Bulgaria, Hungary, Romania, the Russian Federation, and Ukraine—are projected to lose population. The population of the Russian Federation is projected to decline by about 6 percent, from the current 147 million to 138.5 million by 2025. The populations of developed countries such as Japan, Germany, Denmark, Greece, Italy, Spain, and Portugal also are projected to decline over the next three decades. Among the developed countries, the biggest exception to this trend is the United States, whose population is projected to grow from the current 263 million to about 331 million (9).

In contrast, the population of Africa is projected to double between 1995 and 2025, from 728 million to 1.49 billion, whereas the population of Asia could grow from the current 3.46 billion to 4.96 billion, or more than 40 percent (10).

The decline in fertility in the developing countries as a whole has been dramatic. The most impressive progress has occurred in East and Southeast Asia and in Latin America. In China, the world's most populous nation at 1.2 billion, the fertility rate is now estimated to be 2.0, a level that, if it holds, will significantly restrain future population growth. Even with this low fertility rate,

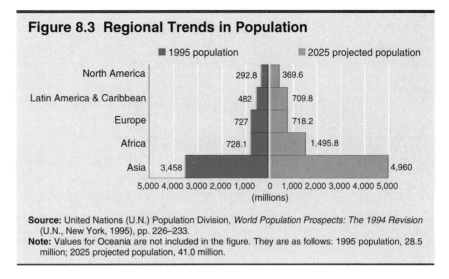

Figure 8.3 Regional Trends in Population

■ 1995 population   ■ 2025 projected population

Region	1995 population	2025 projected population
North America	292.8	369.6
Latin America & Caribbean	482	709.8
Europe	727	718.2
Africa	728.1	1,495.8
Asia	3,458	4,960

5,000 4,000 3,000 2,000 1,000   0   1,000 2,000 3,000 4,000 5,000
(millions)

Source: United Nations (U.N.) Population Division, *World Population Prospects: The 1994 Revision* (U.N., New York, 1995), pp. 226–233.
Note: Values for Oceania are not included in the figure. They are as follows: 1995 population, 28.5 million; 2025 projected population, 41.0 million.

demographic momentum is projected to propel China's population to 1.5 billion by 2025. The fertility rates of South Korea and Singapore are also below the replacement level, and that of Thailand—at 2.1—is nearly there. Indonesia has made tremendous progress; the fertility rate is estimated to be 2.8. In Latin America, only Cuba and a few small Caribbean islands have fertility rates below the replacement level, but many nations—Jamaica, Argentina, Brazil, Chile, Colombia, and Uruguay—have fertility rates well below 3 (11).

In India, the fertility rate decline stalled at about 4 in the early 1980s, but the latest U.N. estimate of 3.8 is positive news for that nation (12). Even more encouraging are the findings of the India National Family Health Survey 1992–93, not yet incorporated into U.N. estimates, which indicate a total fertility rate of 3.4 (13).

It is in the least developed countries, particularly in sub-Saharan Africa, where the demographic outlook is most troubling. The region's total fertility rate was 6.6 in 1960 and was still 6.5 in the early 1990s (14). The average fertility rate for eastern, middle, and western Africa is about 6.2 (15).

There is a continuing debate about the relative impact of various factors on fertility rates. Bangladesh, for example, has used active family planning to achieve a substantial decline in its fertility rate without rapid economic growth or much progress in women's education. In Latin America, on the other hand, government family planning programs have not been as active but the fertility rate has nonetheless declined sharply (16).

The availability and use of contraceptives can also have an impact on fertility rates. In the past 30 years, contraceptive use has increased rapidly, growing in developing countries from about 14 percent in 1960–65 to about 57 percent today. In developed countries, the

Figure 8.4 Gender and Opportunity, Selected Indicators, 1994

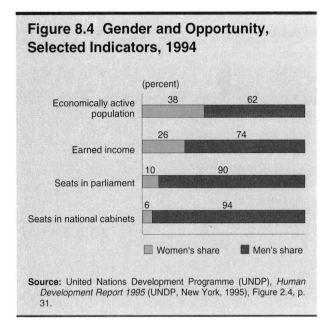

(percent)

	Women's share	Men's share
Economically active population	38	62
Earned income	26	74
Seats in parliament	10	90
Seats in national cabinets	6	94

☐ Women's share   ■ Men's share

Source: United Nations Development Programme (UNDP), *Human Development Report 1995* (UNDP, New York, 1995), Figure 2.4, p. 31.

prevalence of contraceptive use is estimated to be about 70 perce it (17).

Continuing global efforts to expand family planning programs and to invest in human development are likely to have a huge payoff. There is growing consensus that investments in women's education, for example, can provide women with the information they need to control their fertility. Furthermore, lengthening the time that girls spend in school tends to increase the median age of marriage, which delays childbearing and reduces population growth momentum in the future. The combined effect of these and other policies could substantially moderate future population expansion (18).

Family planning costs are about $2 to $3 per capita annually, but the cost is more than made up by the money saved on health, education, and other government programs. The United Nations estimates that family planning and reproductive health programs in de /eloping countries will require $11 billion in 1995, rising to $17 billion in 2015. Equalizing girls' school enrollment with that of boys would cost perhaps $6.5 billion annually; universal primary education in developing countries would cost much more—about $100 billion per year by the year 2000 (19).

HUMAN DEVELOPMENT TRENDS

Human development emphasizes human well-being as the end product of development and pays particular attention to issues of equity, poverty, and gender.

The concept has been advanced since 1990 by the *Human Development Report*. The centerpiece of the

report is the Human Development Index, an aggregate indicator that is based on national levels of life expectancy, educational attainment, and real gross domestic product, now measured in purchasing power parity dollars. (See Chapter 7, "Basic Economic Indicators.")

The 1995 report focuses on gender issues and the struggle for women's rights and notes that progress is being made worldwide (20). For example, female life expectancy has increased 20 percent faster than male life expectancy over the past two decades, and fertility rates have fallen by one third. Women's literacy in developing countries increased from 54 percent of the male rate in 1970 to 74 percent in 1990, whereas combined female primary and secondary school enrollments increased from 67 percent of the rate for males in 1970 to 86 percent in 1990. Girls' combined primary and secondary school enrollments in East Asia (83 percent) and Latin America (87 percent) are approaching the levels in developed countries (97 percent) (21).

Still, much remains to be done. Although many women are increasing their skills through education, economic opportunities for women remain limited. Of the 1.3 billion people living in poverty, 70 percent are women. Female participation in the labor force was estimated to be 40 percent in 1990, up just 4 percentage points since 1970. In the 55 countries with comparable data, women's wages are only three fourths those of men in the nonagricultural sector (22).

Women also have made limited progress in breaking into the ranks of political and economic decisionmakers. Only about one in seven administrators and managers in developing countries is a woman. Worldwide, only 10 percent of parliamentary seats and 6 percent of cabinet positions are held by women (23). (See Figure 8.4.)

The 1995 report includes a gender-related development index that ranks 130 countries in terms of gender disparities. The Nordic countries (Sweden, Finland, Norway, and Denmark), which have adopted women's empowerment as conscious national policies, score the highest. Several developing countries and territories score fairly high, including Barbados, Hong Kong, the Bahamas, Singapore, Uruguay, and Thailand. The report also includes a gender empowerment measure, which ranks countries according to women's share of seats in parliament, their numbers in the managerial and professional ranks, and their share of national income. The Nordic countries again score the highest (24).

World Conference on Women

Women's empowerment was the principal subject of the Fourth World Conference on Women, held in Beijing in September 1995. The Conference's final declaration, although not binding on governments, does give women's issues new visibility. Some governments pledged to redirect their national budgets toward programs for women, although few governments made large new financial commitments. The final declaration's key provisions include the following:

- Women have the right to decide freely all matters related to their sexuality and childbearing.

- The systematic rape of women in wartime is a crime, and perpetrators should be tried as war criminals.

- Genital mutilation of girls, attacks on women because their dowries are too small, domestic battering, and sexual harassment at work are all violations of human rights.

- Girls are discriminated against throughout the world, often before birth in cultures where more value is placed on boys.

- Access to credit is critical to the empowerment of women. Governments and international lending institutions should support banking services for low-income women.

- Governments should guarantee women equal rights to inherit.

- The family is the basic unit of society and should be strengthened, protected, and supported. Women must not suffer discrimination because they are mothers (25).

Trends in Life Expectancy

Increasing life expectancy is an important indicator of social progress in both developed and developing nations. According to the latest estimates compiled by the World Health Organization, between 1980 and 1993, overall life expectancy increased from 61 to about 65 years (26). In developed regions, life expectancy is estimated to be 71.2 years for males and 78.6 years for females; in less-developed regions, these values are 62.4 and 65.3, respectively; and in the least-developed regions, these values are 51.5 and 53.6, respectively (27). Between the least-developed (43 years) and the most-developed (78 years) nations, the gap in life expectancy is some 35 years. That gap could widen even further, to 37 years, by the year 2000 (28).

In 45 developing countries with a total population of nearly 850 million people (15 percent of the global population), life expectancy at birth has not even reached 60 years (29). It is noteworthy, however, that life expectancy at birth is strongly influenced by mortality among the youngest members of the population. Of the population that survives beyond age 5, a surprising number live beyond age 60.

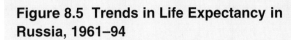

Figure 8.5 Trends in Life Expectancy in Russia, 1961–94

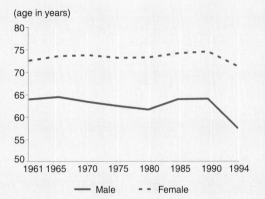

Sources:
1. Jacob Nell and Kitty Stewart, "Death in Transition: The Rise in the Death Rate in Russia Since 1992," Innocenti Occasional Papers, Economic Policy Series, No. 45 (United Nations Children's Fund International Child Development Center, Florence, Italy, 1994), p. 38.
2. Figures for life expectancy in 1994 provided by Carl Haub, Director of Information and Education, Population Reference Bureau, Washington, D.C., 1995 (personal communication).

The trend toward generally increasing life expectancy has been shattered in many nations in recent years. The most dramatic examples are in the countries of the former Soviet Union, in 15 sub-Saharan African nations severely afflicted by acquired immune deficiency syndrome (AIDS), and, to a lesser extent, in the transition economies of Central Europe.

Life Expectancy in Russia

One of the most dramatic reversals of life expectancy has occurred in Russia. From a peak of 65.1 years in 1987 (widely associated with the implementation of a national antialcohol policy), life expectancy for males in Russia fell to 62 in 1992, continued downward to 59 in 1993 (30), and then in 1994 fell even further, to 57.3 (31). Life expectancy for women in Russia declined from a peak of 74.6 years in 1986–87 to 71.1 in 1994. The gap in life expectancy between men and women widened from about 10 years in 1989 to nearly 14 years in 1994 (32) (33). (See Figure 8.5.)

Trends in crude death rates show a similarly tragic pattern, rising from 10.7 per 1,000 in 1989 to 15.6 per 1,000 in 1994 (34). Roughly one third of these deaths can be attributed to population growth and the aging of the Russian population, but the rest is due to other factors (35).

Statistics show that the rise in mortality is predominantly a rise in male mortality, primarily among the working-age population. It is mainly due to diseases of the heart and circulatory system plus other external causes such as alcohol poisoning, suicide, and murder (36). For example, between 1992 and 1993, the number of people dying from heart disease and related circulatory diseases jumped 17 percent, from 646 to 760 deaths per 100,000 people. For the first 6 months of 1994, the rate increased even further, to 863 per 100,000 (37).

Similarly, deaths from external causes are up sharply, increasing 30 percent in 1992–93. Notably, many more of these deaths occur among the population in the northern and northwestern industrial regions and in eastern Siberia and the Far East, where life is generally colder and bleaker and economic prospects are usually poor. Alcohol is likely to be a major contributing factor in nearly all such deaths (38). Russians also are heavy smokers; in the late 1980s, tobacco was estimated to be an associated cause of death for 40 percent of deaths among middle-aged male Russians (39).

It is generally assumed that much of the blame lies with the difficult living conditions in Russia. For many Russians, the economic transition has meant unemployment or a new job at less pay. Rampant inflation also has undermined the salaries of those who remain employed. Between 1991 and 1992, the number of people living in extreme poverty increased from 2.5 to 23.2 percent (40). By 1992, average pensions had fallen to about half of their 1989 value, while wages were about two thirds of their value in 1989 (41). All of these changes have created great psychological as well as economic stress.

Furthermore, it is widely acknowledged that Russia's health care system has badly deteriorated. For example, infant mortality rose from 17.6 per 1,000 live births in 1990 to 20.05 by 1993, an increase of nearly 14 percent (42).

Part of the problem stems from a breakdown in preventive health care programs. Rubella, for instance, can lead to the transfer of genetic mutations from a pregnant mother to a fetus. With the help of rubella vaccinations, the rate of rubella in the United States averaged just 427 cases per year from 1985 to 1989. In Russia, however, where access to the vaccine has dwindled, there were 360,470 cases in 1994, nearly triple the total of 128,000 in 1993 (43) (44).

Many Russian scientists suspect that environmental contamination over many decades also may help explain the current situation. In particular, they think that the cumulative effects of toxic waste from chemical plants, pesticides from farming, and radiation—from test sites, waste dumps, and the Chernobyl nuclear accident—could be factors in the surge in illnesses and birth defects (45).

Other statistics suggest a link between environmental conditions and low birth weights. In several regions with high pollution levels, low birth weights occur in 6.8 to 11.3 percent of all births—rates that are three to five times higher than those in regions with low pollution levels (46).

Life Expectancy in Other Countries

Russia is not the only nation where life expectancy is heading in the wrong direction. Life expectancy also appears to be declining in most of the other newly independent nations of the former Soviet Union. In Moldova, for example, the death rate increased 12 percent from 1993 to 1994.

In the central Africa region, the impact of AIDS has been so devastating that life expectancy apparently is declining in many nations there as well. The impact is particularly severe in 15 nations: Benin, Burkina Faso, Burundi, the Central African Republic, Congo, Cote d'Ivoire, Kenya, Malawi, Mozambique, Rwanda, Tanzania, Uganda, Zaire, Zambia, and Zimbabwe. According to U.N. estimates, in this group of nations, life expectancy with the continued presence of the AIDS pandemic is estimated to reach 49.6 years by 2000–2005. In the absence of AIDS, the U.N. estimates life expectancy would be 57.1 years, or fully 7.5 years longer. In some countries the gap is even greater: 10.3 years in Uganda, 10.7 years in Kenya, 13.2 years in Zambia, and 14.8 years in Zimbabwe. In all these countries, life expectancy is expected to fall or improve only marginally during the period from 1990–95 to 2000–2005 (47).

GLOBAL HEALTH TRENDS

A key component of human development is health. Broad indicators of human health show that significant progress has been made over the past few decades. Yet the conditions in many developing countries remain difficult—especially for the poorest groups. Furthermore, new outbreaks of infectious diseases pose potentially significant new medical challenges.

Although they are probably generally accurate, the numbers reported here should be treated with some caution. According to the World Health Organization (WHO), which compiled the most recent estimates in *The World Health Report 1995: Bridging the Gaps*, the majority of nations "still experience great difficulty in obtaining valid and timely data on many indicators." Official statistics are often not comparable to those from other countries and can be incomplete or out-of-date (48). The incidence of diseases reported here is based on cases officially reported to WHO, but there may be large differences between the officially reported total and the actual total.

Infant Mortality

WHO estimates that, between 1980 and 1993, infant mortality declined by 25 percent and, as mentioned earlier, life expectancy increased by 4 years (49). However, such successes are somewhat offset by the fact that each year 3 million babies born in developing countries do not survive for more than 1 week (50). Many of the world's people are at the bottom of the health care pyramid, where incomes are low, access to safe drinking water and sanitation is limited, and disease and disability are inevitable. These inequities exist not just among regions or countries but also among populations within countries. Most urban areas, in developed and developing countries alike, contain large numbers of people who are unemployed, elderly, or beyond the reach of basic social and health services. In the inner-city areas of many developed countries, for example, immunization rates are below those in the developing world. (See Chapter 2, "Urban Environment and Human Health.")

Main Causes of Death

Worldwide, about 51 million people died in 1993. Globally, the biggest killers were infectious and parasitic diseases, which account for nearly one third of the total, and diseases of the circulatory system, which account for another one fifth. (See Figure 8.6.)

Causes of death differ dramatically between developed and developing countries. In the developed countries, where residents usually receive adequate medical care and life expectancy is generally over 70, chronic diseases have become the big killers. Diseases of the circulatory system, including primarily heart disease and cerebrovascular diseases such as stroke, accounted for 46.7 percent (5.4 million) of the total of 11.7 million deaths in 1993. Cancer is second, accounting for 21.6 percent (2.5 million) of all deaths (51). (See Figure 8.7.)

Heart Disease

Heart disease is associated with factors such as smoking, diet, blood pressure, and cholesterol. There are remarkably sharp differences in the incidence of heart disease among different groups. For example, a study of 75,000 episodes in 1985–87 found that the likelihood of heart

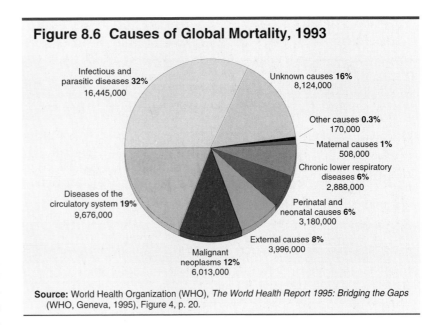

Figure 8.6 Causes of Global Mortality, 1993

Infectious and parasitic diseases **32%** 16,445,000

Unknown causes **16%** 8,124,000

Other causes **0.3%** 170,000

Maternal causes **1%** 508,000

Chronic lower respiratory diseases **6%** 2,888,000

Perinatal and neonatal causes **6%** 3,180,000

External causes **8%** 3,996,000

Malignant neoplasms **12%** 6,013,000

Diseases of the circulatory system **19%** 9,676,000

Source: World Health Organization (WHO), *The World Health Report 1995: Bridging the Gaps* (WHO, Geneva, 1995), Figure 4, p. 20.

attack was 12 times higher among men in North Karelia (Finland) than in Beijing and 9 times higher among women in Glasgow (United Kingdom) than in Catalonia (Spain) (52).

Cancer

Of the 6 million cancer deaths in 1993 in all countries, lung cancer accounted for more than 1 million deaths and was the single biggest killer, followed by stomach cancer, which accounted for 734,000 deaths. Female breast cancer claimed more than 250,000 lives worldwide. Other cancers that were responsible for a quarter million deaths include mouth, esophageal, liver, and colon cancer (53).

Cancer is expected to take an increasing toll on human life. WHO estimates that, by the year 2000, cancer deaths will total about 7.2 million, including about 4 million cancer deaths among males and 3.2 million deaths among females. WHO estimates that almost two thirds of new cancers over the next 25 years will occur in the developing world (54).

Cancer and circulatory diseases killed nearly as many people in developing countries in 1993 as in developed nations. But they accounted for only about one fifth of the total of 39 million deaths in the developing world (55).

Infectious Diseases

Although infectious diseases account for only about 1 percent of deaths in developed countries, they are still the major killer in the developing world, accounting for a staggering 16.3 million deaths, or 41.5 percent of all deaths, in those nations in 1993 (56).

In many cases, the most deadly diseases are also the most familiar, and as long as access to health care remains limited and sanitation is poor, they are likely to remain so. (See Table 8.1.) For example, although they are among the most highly manageable and curable of infectious diseases, diarrheal diseases, whether they were caused by a virus, a bacterium, or a parasite, claimed the lives of 3 million children in the developing world in 1993 (57). Tuberculosis (TB), an ancient scourge that scientists suspect was first introduced in humans around 5000 BC (58), currently kills 52,000 people each week (59), and the numbers appear to be growing, especially in Africa. The human immunodeficiency virus (HIV) and TB are a particularly lethal combination: HIV damages the immune system and hastens the development of TB into a life-threatening disease, whereas TB can hasten the progress of HIV infection into AIDS. Even though TB has been on the decline in many areas for more than 30 years, drug-resistant strains have become increasingly prevalent—a phenomenon that is occurring with other diseases as well.

Malaria accounts for 2 million deaths annually, half in children under 10, with another 400 million clinical bouts of malaria. Most of these are in Africa. The remaining cases are concentrated in India, Brazil, Sri Lanka, Afghanistan, Viet Nam, and Colombia. Although the area of the world where malaria is a problem has shrunk, malaria control is now more difficult and drug resistance is a growing problem (60). Cholera, which afflicted 377,000 people and caused 7,000 deaths in 1993, has become endemic in Africa, Latin America,

and Asia (61). Dengue and yellow fever also are spreading. In addition, although these old foes stubbornly persist and continue to kill millions of people a year, "new" or previously unknown infectious diseases are also appearing (see below). As these and other data make manifestly clear, the war against infectious disease is far from won.

True, there have been some success stories. Smallpox has been eradicated. Polio has now been declared eradicated in the Americas, and WHO believes that it will be eradicated globally by the year 2000. Those may be the exceptions, however.

Although the goal once may have been a decisive victory in the war against infectious diseases, many public health officials have concluded that in the face of nature's complex interdependencies, eliminating most communicable diseases will be impossible. Rather than wiping out all infectious diseases, success has come to be defined as being able not only to respond rapidly to disease threats as they arise but also to anticipate their onset and alter the situations that promote their spread (62).

EMERGING AND REEMERGING INFECTIOUS DISEASES

If the public needed a reminder that a deadly, infectious disease could emerge at any moment, they got one in the spring of 1995. Reports began trickling out of the city of Kikwit, Zaire, that the local hospital was being

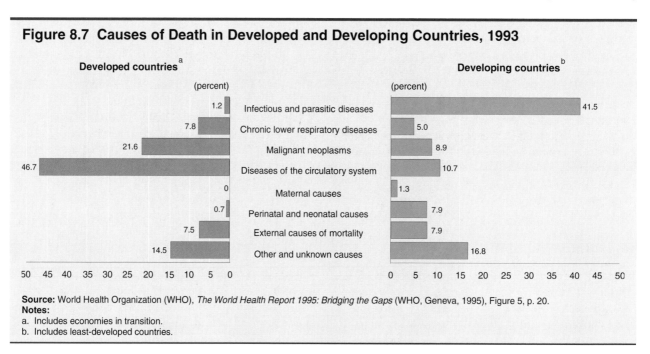

Figure 8.7 Causes of Death in Developed and Developing Countries, 1993

Developed countries[a] (percent)	Cause	Developing countries[b] (percent)
1.2	Infectious and parasitic diseases	41.5
7.8	Chronic lower respiratory diseases	5.0
21.6	Malignant neoplasms	8.9
46.7	Diseases of the circulatory system	10.7
0	Maternal causes	1.3
0.7	Perinatal and neonatal causes	7.9
7.5	External causes of mortality	7.9
14.5	Other and unknown causes	16.8

Source: World Health Organization (WHO), *The World Health Report 1995: Bridging the Gaps* (WHO, Geneva, 1995), Figure 5, p. 20.
Notes:
a. Includes economies in transition.
b. Includes least-developed countries.

swamped with cases of hemorrhagic fever. Both WHO in Geneva and the Centers for Disease Control and Prevention (CDC) in Atlanta sent teams of experts to evaluate the outbreak, but even as the teams were arriving in Kikwit, blood samples that had been sent to the CDC confirmed that the illness was caused by the Ebola virus (63).

Although extremely deadly, the Ebola virus is not easily transmitted. Close contact with blood or other body fluids appears to be necessary. The CDC and WHO teams trained local health workers in proper infection control procedures, including the use of masks and gloves, and the need to sterilize needles and surgical instruments. Local Red Cross workers warned people not to perform a traditional burial ritual, which would expose them to infected body fluids. After several nervous weeks, WHO officials appeared confident that the epidemic was under control, although nearly 250 people died in the outbreak (64). Health officials were especially relieved that the epidemic did not spread to Kinshasa, the capital city of 4 million less than 250 kilometers away.

But it certainly could have. The Ebola virus outbreak appears to have begun in the winter of 1994–95, but it was not recognized until several months later. The illness has an incubation period of up to 3 weeks, although it may often be 1 week or less. During this time, the patient has no symptoms. It is easy enough to imagine a truck driver or riverboat captain becoming infected and bringing the disease into the capital before showing any symptoms and then swiftly spreading the disease to others. If the disease had not been recognized promptly when the patients began showing symptoms and were therefore most infectious, the capital could easily have had a public health disaster on its hands. And the disease could even conceivably have spread to other parts of the world via air travel.

The illness caused by the Ebola virus is just one of a number of new diseases such as hantavirus and cholera that has emerged in recent years or that has "reemerged" in a new location or a more dangerous form. This phenomenon has sparked alarm among health officials worldwide. Although new diseases like that caused by the Ebola virus capture headlines, the death toll from the latest outbreak fortunately remained in the hundreds.

Factors That Contribute to Emergence

What are the factors that lead to the emergence of new threats from infectious disease? Infectious disease experts generally identify six factors: environmental change and disturbances to the balance of natural habitats, human demographics and behavior, international

Table 8.1 Estimated Deaths from Infectious and Parasitic Diseases, 1993

Disease/Condition	Number of Deaths[a] (thousands)
Acute lower respiratory infections under age 5	4,110
Diarrhea under age 5, including dysentery	3,010 [b]
Tuberculosis	2,709
Malaria	2,000
Measles	1,160
Hepatitis B	933
AIDS	700
Whooping cough	360
Bacterial meningitis	210
Schistosomiasis	200
Leishmaniasis	197
Congenital syphilis	190
Tetanus	149
Hookworm diseases	90
Amoebiasis	70
Ascariasis (roundworm)	60
African trypanosomiasis (sleeping sickness)	55
American trypanosomiasis (Chagas' disease)	45
Onchocerciasis (river blindness)	35
Meningitis	35
Rabies	35
Yellow fever	30
Dengue/dengue hemorrhagic fever	23
Japanese encephalitis	11
Foodborne trematodes	10
Cholera[c]	6.8
Poliomyelitis	5.5
Diphtheria	3.9
Leprosy	2.4
Plague	0.5
Total	**16,445**

Source: World Health Organization (WHO), *The World Health Report 1995: Bridging the Gaps* (WHO, Geneva, 1995), Table 5, p. 18.
Notes:
a. Estimates for some diseases may contain cases that have also been included elsewhere.
b. Deaths from dysentery are estimated at 450,000.
c. Officially reported figures only.

travel and commerce, complications of modern medicine, microbial adaptation and change, and the breakdown of public health measures (65).

Environmental Change

Some emerging diseases are associated with environmental changes that occur with economic or agricultural development or changes in land use patterns (66). Certainly, the development and growth of cities often fueled by an influx of migrants can foster the establishment of a new infection in a population. Once established in a crowded urban area, a disease can easily take root and can be extremely difficult to eradicate. Other human activities that disturb natural ecosystems,

Box 8.1 Implications of Climate and Ecosystem Change for Infectious Diseases

PROGRESSIVE WARMING

The latest estimate of the Intergovernmental Panel on Climate Change is that global mean temperatures are likely to rise at a rate of about 0.3° C per decade (1). Although many aspects of climate change science are not fully understood, there is a growing consensus that progressive warming is caused by increasing concentrations of greenhouse gases (principally carbon dioxide, methane, and chlorofluorocarbons) in the atmosphere.

Such a change could have numerous implications for future patterns of infectious disease. Even subtle changes in temperature can have significant effects on the vectors—mosquitos, flies, snails, and rodents—that transmit infectious diseases. The *Aedes aegypti* mosquito—one of the prime carriers of dengue and yellow fever—has extended its range to both higher latitudes and higher altitudes. For the first time, the mosquito has moved into the mountainous regions of many nations, including Costa Rica, Colombia, India, and Kenya (2). In eastern Africa, a slight increase in winter temperatures could extend the mosquito's habitat above 2,500 meters and threaten urban populations such as Nairobi in Kenya and Harare in Zimbabwe.

In Rwanda, temperatures increased greatly between 1961 and 1990, reaching a peak in 1987. In the mid-1980s, malaria became established in areas where it had previously been rare or absent. Among people in high-altitude zones, the incidence of malaria was up more than 500 percent. Studies indicate that high temperatures and large amounts of rainfall accounted for 80 percent of the difference in the monthly incidence (3).

Global climate change models suggest that warming could lead to an increase in the number of malaria cases from the current 400 million annually to about 500 million annually by the year 2100. With a 3° C increase in global mean temperatures by 2100, however, there would be a substantial geographical widening of the malaria zone and a likely increase of an additional 50 million to 80 million cases (4).

ENSO EVENTS AND OTHER CLIMATE FLUCTUATIONS

Many malaria epidemics and other vectorborne disease outbreaks seemingly are linked to climate fluctuations associated with El Nino/Southern Oscillation (ENSO) events. Such events, which usually last about 12 months, tend to increase the severity of both droughts and wet periods. La Nina episodes have a reverse pattern of climate anomalies.

Wherever El Nino/La Nina events cause extended heavy rainfall, outbreaks of vectorborne disease are likely to accompany the event. For example, in southern Africa, a wet summer (La Nina) in 1974 produced an epidemic of West Nile fever. An unusually severe Indian monsoon in 1973 (La Nina) led to an epidemic of Japanese encephalitis. In Latin America, a 1982–83 El Nino event led to heavy rains and flooding and subsequently to major epidemics of malaria in Ecuador, Peru, and Bolivia (5).

Warming conditions and El Nino events also can have important effects on disease-carrying rodent populations. The hantavirus outbreak in the southwestern United States has been linked to a 6-year drought followed by an El Nino event that caused heavy rains in the region. (See the discussion of hantavirus elsewhere in this chapter.)

Climate fluctuations also may have played a part in India's 1994 plague outbreak. In the summer months prior to the outbreak, temperatures reached 69° C, causing widespread animal deaths and creating hot-air columns that drew in moisture-laden maritime air that contributed to an unusually long (3-month) monsoon period. Subsequent flooding created conditions that were ideal for the plague outbreak (6).

HIGHER OCEAN TEMPERATURES

The rapid growth of marine algal blooms is prompted by many factors, including nutrient-rich wastewater runoff and declining fish stocks. Another factor is climate-induced warmer sea surface temperatures, which increase algal growth by augmenting photosynthesis and shift the community of organisms toward more toxic species such as those that produce red tides (7).

including road-building, logging, and irrigation projects, can also bring humans into new areas while displacing microbes that must then seek out new hosts. Changes in local climate, such as drier, wetter, or warmer periods, can extend the range of mosquitos and other disease vectors (67) (68). (See Box 8.1.)

Hantavirus. Hantavirus, one of the newest emerging diseases, causes different symptoms—such as hemorrhagic fever, abdominal pain, or respiratory infection—depending on the strain of the virus. It appears in areas where litter and trash abound and rats and mice nest (69). More than 100,000 cases have been reported in China. The disease is also found elsewhere in Asia and in Scandinavia, the Balkan region, much of Europe, and recently in the United States (70).

The recent hantavirus outbreak in the southwestern United States has been linked to a change in ecological conditions. The strain that hit New Mexico in 1993 causing a frequently lethal respiratory infection was transmitted by inhalation of airborne droplets of rodent urine and feces (71). Between 1992 and 1993, an unusually wet and mild winter led to increased adult rat and mouse survival and, in turn, an increased rodent population in the spring. As competition forced the rodents beyond their normal habitat in search of food, human contact with infected animals (and, hence, with the virus) also increased (72).

For the United States as a whole, as of June 1995, the CDC had confirmed 110 cases in 23 states; 50.9 percent of these were fatal. Now that tests that can diagnose hantavirus infection are available, it is clear that infection is more widespread than was initially expected and that the virus has probably been around for a long time (73).

Researchers have linked cholera outbreaks to coastal plankton blooms. A quiescent form of cholera is found in a wide range of surface marine life. Under certain conditions, when waters are rich in nitrogen and phosphorus and temperatures are relatively high, blooms develop and cholera comes out of its quiescent state and becomes infectious. This process apparently was an important factor in the outbreak of cholera in South America in 1991 and in recent outbreaks in Bangladesh (8).

Higher ocean temperatures are associated with many other types of toxic algal blooms that have implications for human health. In 1987, warm eddies of the Gulf Stream came unusually close to Prince Edward Island in Canada. The warm waters carried pennate diatoms producing domoic acid, which killed five people and caused 156 cases of amnesic shellfish poisoning (9).

CHANGES IN BIODIVERSITY

Changes in biodiversity and habitat also have many implications for human health and disease. For example, changes in the balance between predators and prey can allow populations of disease-carrying animals to multiply rapidly. In the northeastern United States, the clearing of land for agriculture in the 18th and 19th Centuries depleted the deer population as well as the wolf population, their chief predator. When agricultural activity shifted to the Midwest in

the 20th Century, northeastern forests regenerated and the deer population rebounded, but the wolf population did not. Deer, which carry the tick that is the host for Lyme disease, are currently abundant in the Northeast (10).

The likelihood that many bird populations are diminishing both in diversity and absolute numbers also has important implications for disease, since many birds feed on disease vectors such as mosquitos. For example, eastern equine encephalitis, which is deadly in about 30 percent of cases, was recently isolated from a mosquito in Polk County, Florida, where bird habitat has been severely disrupted (11) (12).

References and Notes

1. International Panel on Climate Change, "The Social Costs of Climate Change: Greenhouse Damage and the Benefits of Control," Chapter 6 in Second Assessment Report, Working Group III (April 1995 draft) (World Meteorological Organization/United Nations Environment Programme, Geneva, 1995), p. 9.

2. Richard Stone, "If the Mercury Soars, So May Health Hazards," *Science*, Vol. 267, No. 5199 (February 17, 1995), pp. 957–958.

3. Michael E. Loevinsohn, "Climatic Warming and Increased Malaria Incidence in Rwanda," *The Lancet*, Vol. 343 (March 19, 1994), pp. 714–717.

4. *Op. cit.* 2, p. 958.

5. Neville Nicholls, "El Nino–Southern Oscillation and Vector-Borne Disease," in

Health and Climate Change (The Lancet Ltd., London, 1994), p. 22.

6. Paul R. Epstein, "Climate Change Played a Role in India's Plague," Letter to the Editor, Sunday News of the Week in Review, *New York Times* (November 13, 1994), p. E14.

7. Paul R. Epstein, "Emerging Diseases and Ecosystem Instability: New Threats to Public Health," *American Journal of Public Health*, Vol. 85, No. 2 (February 1995), pp. 168–172.

8. Paul R. Epstein *et al.*, "Marine Ecosystem Health: Implications for Public Health," *Annals of the New York Academy of Sciences*, Vol. 737 (December 1994), pp. 13–23.

9. Paul R. Epstein, Timothy E. Ford, and Rita R. Colwell, "Marine Ecosystems," *The Lancet*, Vol. 342, No. 8881 (November 13, 1993), pp. 1,216–1,219.

10. Richard Levins *et al.*, "The Emergence of New Diseases," *American Scientist*, Vol. 82, No. 1 (January–February 1994), pp. 52–60.

11. Paul R. Epstein, "Review of *Biodiversity: The Diversity of Life*, by Edward O. Wilson," in *Journal of the American Medical Association*, Vol. 269, No. 15 (April 21, 1993), pp. 2,006–2,007.

12. Many of the references cited here can be found in Paul R. Epstein, "Health Implications of Climate Variability and Change," a report prepared for the Climate Research Committee, National Academy of Sciences, Washington, D.C. (May 1995).

Rift Valley Fever. Some infectious diseases have been linked to the ecological changes brought about by dam construction; dams change the water flow and can cause water to puddle and serve as breeding sites for mosquitos. In Senegal, the construction and activation of Diama Dam are believed to have led to the introduction of Rift Valley fever, a disease never before seen in the region. Surprisingly, one third of inhabitants were found to have antibodies to the virus. Still, near the village of Keur Macene upstream from the dam, a 1987 epidemic caused 244 human deaths and more than 1,200 illnesses, as well as spontaneous abortions in sheep and cattle (74).

Malaria. Habitat disruption can play a role in the resurgence of malaria, which is transmitted by *Anopheles* mosquitos. In southern Honduras, erosion from grazing and farming coupled with a severe increase in

temperature between 1972 and 1990 forced many Hondurans into recently deforested regions in the north. The new migrants tended to be nonimmune to malaria. The surge in population, coupled with heavy rains, caused the number of malaria cases in the northern region to jump from 20,000 in 1987 to an expected 90,000 in 1993 (75) (76).

Warm, wet weather can lead to the establishment of new breeding sites, which may have been a factor in the recent episodes of malaria in Houston, Texas.

Human Demographics and Behavior

Human activity plays a critical role in the spread of disease. Changes in the size, density, or distribution of human populations contribute significantly to the transmission of infections. An influx of large numbers of people can produce overcrowding and inadequate supplies of safe water, which in turn leads to problems in hygiene—a combination that is ideal for the spread of infectious diseases. The increasing incidence of poverty worldwide underlies the resurgence of diseases such as tuberculosis and diphtheria.

Dengue. Dengue virus, which is now the most important and fastest growing insect-borne viral infection in the world, is transmitted primarily by the *Aedes aegypti* mosquito (77). The mosquito vector that transmits dengue multiplies in any small pool of stagnant water, especially in discarded automobile tires or other detritus that results from life in overcrowded urban areas. The disease, also known as "break-bone fever," produces severe headaches and disabling pain in muscles and joints. A far more serious form of the disease, hemorrhagic dengue fever or dengue shock syndrome, has a 40 to 50 percent fatality rate if it is left untreated (78).

In 1993, some 23,000 deaths from dengue and 560,000 cases of dengue were officially reported to WHO (79), a substantial increase over previous years. During the 1960s, dengue typically averaged about 30,000 cases per year; from 1985 through 1989, nearly 1 million cases were reported (80). However, even these numbers are likely to be underestimates: for every confirmed case of dengue, officials suspect that there are four additional cases that have either not been reported or have been misdiagnosed (81). In poor urban areas in the tropics, where mosquito-control programs are sparse or nonexistent, dengue is becoming an enormous problem. In Southeast Asia, dengue hemorrhagic fever (and dengue shock syndrome) is one of the leading causes of hospitalization and death among children (82). In many parts of Latin America, dengue has reached epidemic proportions, even though the disease was believed to have been nearly eradicated in the 1960s. In addition, hemorrhagic dengue fever is increasing in incidence (83). Brazil has been hardest hit, with 88,039 confirmed cases of dengue and 105 cases of hemorrhagic dengue fever in the first 9 months of 1995. The year's unusually long wet season and high number of hurricanes are believed to be contributing to the severity of the epidemic, providing fertile breeding grounds for the *Aedes aegypti* mosquito (84).

AIDS. Researchers believe that the virus responsible for AIDS was transported in Africa by the movement of infected people from rural areas to rapidly expanding urban areas (85), helped along by the paving of the Kinshasa Highway across central Africa (86). Sexual activity and substance abuse were the primary human activities responsible for the spread of the disease (87).

Through 1994, WHO had received reports of 1,025,073 AIDS cases from around the world, but it is likely that there are three times that many unreported cases (88). As of late 1994, WHO estimated that 18 million adults have been infected with HIV (89).

The disease is spreading most rapidly in Africa and Asia. In Thailand, HIV infection is spreading quickly via sexual contact, yet it was virtually unknown in that country in 1987. In India, infection rates have tripled since 1992. In sub-Saharan Africa, the part of the world worst affected, the prevalence of HIV infection already exceeds 10 percent in a few countries (90).

In addition, children are bearing a growing burden from the AIDS pandemic. It is estimated that by the year 2000 more than 5 million children will be infected with HIV (91).

In the United States, the disease initially escaped detection because of its long incubation period. The slow response of the federal government in educating the population about the spread of the disease may also have fueled the epidemic (92).

Tuberculosis. TB, which for decades was on the decline, now kills more people each year than any other infectious disease, accounting for 3 million deaths in 1993, more than 5 percent of all deaths globally (93).

WHO expects about 8.8 million new TB cases in 1995, with some 80 percent of victims being in the economically active group of individuals from 15 to 49 years of age (94). About 2 billion people, mostly poor people in developing countries, carry the causative organism of TB, *Mycobacterium tuberculosis;* up to 10 percent of those people will develop the active form of the disease, usually as a result of a weakening of the immune system through malnutrition, old age, cancer, or AIDS (95).

Active TB is contagious, but transmission (via airborne droplets) usually occurs only after prolonged contact in a closed environment. Drug treatment is relatively cheap and can cure the disease, but the treatment requires people to take the drugs for at least 6 months without interruption. Many patients stop taking the drugs after a few weeks, thus risking a recurrence and the likelihood of becoming infected with a drug-resistant strain.

In the United States, the prevalence of drug-resistant strains of *M. tuberculosis* has grown from 1 to 2 percent in the early days of drug treatment to 3 to 5 percent in the 1960s. By the 1990s in New York City, 33 percent of *M. tuberculosis* strains were resistant to at least one drug and 19 percent were resistant to two or more drugs (96). The resistance problem is certain to spread along with the spread of the disease.

The number of people suffering from both TB and AIDS is on the rise. WHO estimates that in Asia alone during the next 10 years, the number of people expected to die from AIDS and TB together is greater than the combined populations of Tokyo, Beijing, Singapore, and Yokohama (97).

International Travel and Commerce

Travel has long helped to spread infectious diseases, especially for easily transmissible viruses such as that which causes smallpox. Concerns have heightened dramatically now that it is easy to get from one end of the world to the other in less than 48 hours. For diseases such as malaria that require a local population of *Anopheles* mosquitos to transmit the disease to humans, travel to regions outside that vector's range does not present a threat. The same cannot be said, however, for diseases such as TB and influenza that are transmitted through person-to-person contact (98).

In September 1994, reports of a pneumonic plague outbreak in Surat, India, set off an international panic. Indians fled the areas where the disease had been reported, and more than 45,000 people canceled their plans to travel to India (99). Pneumonic plague is spread primarily through coughing and sneezing, so the disease could easily have been carried to other parts of the world by air travel. However, many believe the scale of the panic was unjustified—the 56 deaths and 272 confirmed plague cases are comparable to those resulting from recent outbreaks of plague in other areas of the world (100). (See Chapter 2, "Urban Environment and Human Health.")

Other infectious and parasitic diseases take advantage of modern travel without even having to rely on human hosts for transport. For example, a shipment of old tires from Japan to the southern United States, which carried thousands of mosquito eggs, allowed the dengue vector to become established in a new location.

Complications of Modern Medicine

Although modern medicine and hospitals provide relief from suffering, they can also bring an increase in the incidence of disease and the potential for the appearance of new diseases.

Hospital-Acquired Infections. A hospital by its very nature provides a large pool of sick people with increased vulnerability to infection. About 5 percent of patients who enter acute-care hospitals acquire infections from their hospitalization, and the incidence of drug-resistant strains of the most common of these so-called nosocomial infections (e.g., *Staphylococcus aureus* and coagulase-negative staphylococci) is on the rise (101). Infections can be transmitted from staff to patients, from visitors to patients, and from patients to other patients.

Many invasive procedures performed in hospitals, including surgeries such as hip replacements that involve inserting a foreign body, catheterization, transfusion, or even organ transplantation, create opportunities for nosocomial infections to develop.

Infection control programs in many long-term-care facilities such as nursing homes are also often ineffective and allow infections to be transmitted rapidly among a population whose immunity has already been compromised by age or chronic illness. Standards to control the spread of infection among children in schools and daycare facilities are also difficult to maintain.

Drug Resistance. Because bacteria reproduce so rapidly, mutant strains are constantly arising. In the laboratory, it is easy enough to create strains of bacteria that are resistant to a particular antibiotic simply by looking for mutant strains that are able to survive in the presence of that drug. The same thing will ultimately happen inside people, and the indiscriminant use of antibiotics hastens the process. Bacterial resistance is already an enormous problem in U.S. hospitals (102).

Microbial Adaptation and Change

Like other organisms, bacteria and viruses undergo spontaneous mutations. Through this process, viruses can evolve rapidly into new variants that can reinfect previously infected people or produce a slightly different strain to which the exposed population has not developed an immunity. Mutation also allows some microbes to develop resistance to the drugs previously used to control them (see above).

Influenza Virus. The influenza virus has found a unique way to persist and cause disease. Most new strains of the disease arise in Southeast Asia, where ducks, pigs, and farmers live in close proximity. Scientists theorize that pigs can be infected by both a human influenza virus and an avian influenza virus. The two viruses then exchange genetic material and a new strain of virus is established (103). These new forms have the potential to cause widespread and frequently fatal diseases; they have arisen periodically and have caused global pandemics. An influenza virus epidemic in 1918 killed 500,000 people in the United States alone; smaller outbreaks occurred in that country in 1957 and 1968 (104).

Without effective antiviral drugs, the only way to fight influenza is with a vaccine. But producing vaccines targeted at a new strain takes time, and most experts agree that another global pandemic of influenza is inevitable (105).

Breakdown in Public Health Measures

Vaccinations and proper hygiene have helped to provide protection against infectious disease. When a breakdown in public health or sanitation measures occurs, it provides opportunistic organisms with an ideal breeding ground and the chance to reach large numbers of people. Societal disruptions such as wars, economic collapse, or natural disasters can rapidly destroy public health protection systems and bring on disease (106).

Waterborne Illnesses. In areas where populations are rapidly expanding beyond the capacity of the local water supply, waterborne infections can be expected to create serious outbreaks of disease. Bacteria, viruses, and parasites can all thrive in untreated or inadequately treated water sources and are often carried into a water system by contaminated feces. In 1993, the United States experienced one of the largest outbreaks of waterborne disease ever reported. An estimated 403,000 people in the Milwaukee, Wisconsin, area were stricken with cryptosporidiosis, a parasitic infection that causes severe diarrhea and is found increasingly in unfiltered raw water. Of the 44,000 people who sought medical attention in the city, more than 4,000 had to be hospitalized. City public health officials surmise that heavy rains, snowmelt, and runoff from nearby farms may have overloaded the city's water treatment plants (107). *Cryptosporidia* are resistant to chlorine and must be removed from water supplies by mechanical filtration.

Cholera. In 1991, inadequate sanitation brought on an epidemic of cholera in South America for the first time in almost a century. The bacterium that causes cholera, *Vibrio cholerae,* is believed to have been introduced in Lima, Peru, through the past dumping of bilge water into the city's harbor from ships arriving from the Far East (108). An El Nino/Southern Oscillation event in 1991, which warmed coastal and inshore waters, may have stimulated the growth of a plankton harboring the cholera bacterium (109). The bacteria then contaminated fish and shellfish, which were consumed by the local population. In addition, inadequately treated wastewater permitted the bacteria to enter the municipal drinking water supply, and the disease spread rapidly. By 1991, there were 366,056 reported cases of the disease and 3,894 deaths (110).

Worldwide and only on the basis of officially reported figures, there were 6,800 deaths from cholera in 1993, about one quarter occurring in Africa. The dramatic outbreak of cholera in the refugee camps of Goma, Zaire, in the summer of 1994 demonstrates how quickly the disease can spread in situations of massive overcrowding without adequate safe drinking water and sanitation. Cholera can almost always be treated with oral rehydration therapy (111).

Measles. Infectious diseases also tend to regain lost ground when populations become complacent and disease prevention measures—such as immunization programs—begin to falter. In the United States, after a long decline, the number of measles cases started to rise in the late 1980s when there was a drop in the number of children being vaccinated against the disease. By 1990, when immunization rates had slumped to only 70 percent, more than 26,000 cases were reported. In 1991, reported cases were down sharply in the United States, a development that researchers estimate is due in part to a concerted effort by public health officials to increase the number of children vaccinated (112).

Diphtheria. A recent resurgence of diphtheria has occurred in parts of Central Europe and the former Soviet Union. This resurgence is presumed to be the result of decreasing immunization coverage, intermittent vaccine supplies, and large-scale population movements—all in the wake of political and economic upheavals that have interfered with once-normal prevention measures. The number of reported cases rose from 1,200 in 1990 to 15,210 in 1993 (113).

A Guarded Prognosis

Understanding the factors that cause outbreaks of disease makes it easier for global health professionals to marshal their resources; however, in recent years, global programs to detect, investigate, and control infectious diseases as well as prevent further outbreaks have been unable to keep up with the problem. Many of the global health community's most important tools have become ineffective.

Disease Surveillance

Funding shortages have severely hampered disease research and tracking programs (114). Infectious disease laboratories were established around the world many years ago to detect spots where unusual clusters of disease are present. However, in recent years, the number of facilities actively involved in gathering information has declined. In addition, many countries lack the expertise to spot early warning signs that a disease such as that caused by the Ebola virus or the hantavirus is on the rise. And often, even if the knowledge is there, it is not widely applied. International communications are better today, but they are still inadequate to provide rapid early warnings of new disease outbreaks. Multinational organizations such as WHO and the Pan American Health Organization are focal points for global surveillance programs, but they are only as good as the information provided to them. Frequently, developing countries do not have individuals with the medical expertise to recognize an emerging health threat. International health agencies are also hindered by a lack of cooperation and difficulties in getting information to and from remote sites in many developing countries. Improving this situation will require funds that seem to be in chronically short supply.

To a certain extent, it may be possible, using only existing resources, to improve global disease surveillance. One suggestion is to focus existing resources on detecting clusters of new or unusual disease syndromes. In addition, all countries could pool certain resources, such as the biosafety level-4 containment facilities of the CDC, where new pathogenic agents could safely be studied. Global health bodies should also review the ways in which they respond to disease outbreaks (115).

Drug Development

Vaccines have reduced or eliminated death and illness caused by 20 different infectious diseases, but providing the benefits of vaccines to the populations that need them is usually expensive. Immunization and antibiotics are highly specific for the diseases they fight, and thus in most cases they are expensive to produce. Bringing a new drug to market involves extensive research and testing and can cost from $10 million to $100 million (116).

It is not surprising, then, that drug manufacturers are not always eager to develop new antibiotics, antiviral agents, or vaccines to treat infectious diseases. Such products are not always profitable, especially if the

market for the drug is small or the countries where the disease is rampant would be hard-pressed to pay for expensive new drugs.

The drug azidothymidine (AZT) has been found to reduce the risk of a mother transmitting HIV to her baby by almost 70 percent. However, poorer countries cannot afford AZT, let alone the health care services needed to ensure that women get the appropriate doses throughout their pregnancies (117). Still, WHO and other groups are working hard to develop low-budget strategies to make these drugs available to those who need them.

The key to responding to emerging infectious diseases lies only partly with researchers. More vaccines and better therapies will certainly have an effect. But certain basic measures should not be overlooked. These include making sure people have access to clean water and adequate sanitation, making sure that the vaccines that do exist are administered to people who need them, and providing basic health care to all people so that a small problem with disease does not suddenly become an epidemic in a vulnerable population.

Another part of the solution is considering health along with development. Any intervention that changes the local ecology—new cities, new roads, and new industry—brings with it a health cost. That health cost must be figured into the true cost of the project if future suffering is to be alleviated.

Joe Palca of National Public Radio in Washington, D.C., wrote the section on emerging and reemerging infectious diseases in this chapter.

References and Notes

1. The term "transition economies" lacks a formal definition, but is used here to include the successor states of the former Soviet Union (Armenia, Azerbaijan, the Republic of Belarus, the Republic of Estonia, the Republic of Georgia, the Republic of Kazakhstan, the Kyrgyz Republic, the Republic of Latvia, the Republic of Lithuania, the Republic of Moldova, the Russian Federation, the Republic of Tajikistan, the Republic of Turkmenistan, Ukraine, and the Republic of Uzbekistan) and the countries of Central Europe (Albania, Bulgaria, the Czech Republic, Hungary, Poland, Romania, and the Slovak Republic).

2. United Nations Population Fund (UNFPA), The State of World Population 1995 (UNFPA, New York, 1995), p. 16.

3. *Ibid.*, pp. 16–17, 67.

4. *Op. cit.* 2, pp. 1–2.

5. *Op. cit.* 2, p. 67.

6. Carl Haub, Director of Information and Education, Population Reference Bureau, Washington, D.C., 1995 (personal communication).

7. World Health Organization (WHO), *The World Health Report 1995: Bridging the Gaps* (WHO, Geneva, 1995), pp. 37–38.

8. *Ibid.*, pp. 38–39.

9. United Nations (U.N.) Population Division, *World Population Prospects: The 1994 Revision* (U.N., New York, 1995), pp. 232–233.

10. *Ibid.*, pp. 226–229.

11. *Op. cit.* 2, pp. 67–70.

12. Eduard Bos, Demographer/Population Specialist, The World Bank, Washington, D.C., 1995 (personal communication).

13. International Institute for Population Sciences, *National Family Health Survey: Introductory Report* (International Institute for Population Sciences, Bombay, India, 1994), p. 29.

14. *Op. cit.* 6.

15. *Op. cit.* 2, pp. 67–68.

16. *Op. cit.* 12.

17. *Op. cit.* 2, pp. 53–54.

18. John Bongaarts, "Population Policy Options in the Developing World," *Science*, Vol.

263, No. 5148 (February 11, 1994), pp. 771–776.

19. Joseph Speidel, "Population Policy for the 21st Century: Setting Priorities, Paying for Programs," paper presented at the Third Session of the Preparatory Committee for the International Conference on Population and Development, United Nations, New York, April 4, 1994, pp. 13–14.

20. United Nations Development Programme, *Human Development Report 1995* (Oxford University Press, New York, 1995), p. iii.

21. *Ibid.*, p. 3.

22. *Op. cit.* 20, p. 4.

23. *Op. cit.* 20, p. 4.

24. *Op. cit.* 20, pp. 2–4.

25. Patrick E. Tyler, "Forum on Women Agrees on Goals," *New York Times* (September 15, 1995), p. A1.

26. *Op. cit.* 7, p. 1.

27. *Op. cit.* 2, p. 63.

28. *Op. cit.* 7, pp. 1–2.

29. *Op. cit.* 7, pp. 47–48.

30. Jacob Nell and Kitty Stewart, "Death in Transition: The Rise in the Death Rate in Russia Since 1992," Innocenti Occasional Papers, Economic Policy Series, No. 45 (United Nations Children's Fund International Child Development Centre, Florence, Italy, 1994), p. 38.

31. *Op. cit.* 6.

32. *Op. cit.* 30, p. 38.

33. *Op. cit.* 6.

34. *Op. cit.* 6.

35. United Nations Children's Fund (UNICEF) International Child Development Centre, *Crisis in Mortality, Health and Nutrition,* Economies in Transition Studies Regional Monitoring Report No. 2 (UNICEF, Florence, Italy, 1994), p. 43.

36. *Op. cit.* 30, p. 9.

37. *Op. cit.* 30, p. 39.

38. *Op. cit.* 30, p. 28.

39. *Op. cit.* 30, p. 29.

40. *Op. cit.* 35, p. 3.

41. *Op. cit.* 30, p. 18.

42. *Op. cit.* 30, p. 50.

43. Michael Specter, "Plunging Life Expectancy Puzzles Russia," *New York Times* (August 2, 1995), p. A1.

44. Murray Feshbach, "Uniqueness of the Environmental and Health Atlas of Russia," in *Environmental and Health Atlas of Russia,* Murray Feshbach *et al.,* eds. (Paims Publishing House, Moscow, 1995), p. xix.

45. *Op. cit.* 43.

46. *Op. cit.* 44.

47. *Op. cit.* 9, pp. 55–57.

48. *Op. cit.* 7, p. 97.

49. *Op. cit.* 7, p. 1.

50. *Op. cit.* 7, pp. 4–5.

51. *Op. cit.* 7, pp. 18–20.

52. *Op. cit.* 7, p. 31.

53. *Op. cit.* 7, p. 32.

54. *Op. cit.* 7, p. 32.

55. *Op. cit.* 7, pp. 20, 31–32.

56. *Op. cit.* 7, pp. 18–20.

57. *Op. cit.* 7, p. 10.

58. Michael D. Iseman, "Evolution of Drug-Resistant Tuberculosis: A Tale of Two Species," in *Infectious Diseases in an Age of Change: The Impact of Human Ecology and Behavior in Disease Transmission,* Bernard Roizman, ed. (National Academy Press, Washington, D.C., 1995), p. 136.

59. *Op. cit.* 7, p. 21.

60. *Op. cit.* 7, pp. 12, 23–24.

61. *Op. cit.* 7, p. 23.

62. Richard Levins *et al.,* "The Emergence of New Diseases," *American Scientist,* Vol. 82, No. 1 (January–February 1994), p. 52.

63. Centers for Disease Control and Prevention, "Update: Outbreak of Ebola Viral Hemorrhagic Fever, Zaire, 1995," *Morbidity and Mortality Weekly Report,* Vol. 44, No. 20 (May 26, 1995), p. 339.

64. "Ebola Hemorrhagic Fever," *World Health Organization Weekly Epidemiological Record,* Vol. 70, No. 4 (August 25, 1995), p. 241.

65. Institute of Medicine, *Emerging Infections: Microbial Threats to Health in the United States,* Joshua Lederberg, Robert E. Shope, and Stanley C. Oaks, Jr., eds. (National Academy Press, Washington, D.C., 1992), p. 47.

66. Stephen S. Morse, "Regulating Viral Traffic," *Issues in Science and Technology,* Vol. 7, No. 1 (Fall 1990), p. 84.

67. Mary E. Wilson, "Anticipating New Diseases," *Current Issues in Public Health,* Vol. 1 (1995), pp. 90–94.

68. *Op. cit.* 65, pp. 1–2.

69. James W. LeDuc *et al.,* "Hantaan (Korean Hemorrhagic Fever) and Related Rodent Zoonoses," in *Emerging Viruses,* Stephen S. Morse, ed. (Oxford University Press, New York, 1993), p. 153.

70. *Ibid.,* pp. 149–158.

71. Stephen S. Morse, "Factors in the Emergence of Infectious Diseases," *Journal of Emerging Infectious Diseases,* Vol. 1, No. 1 (January 1995), pp. 7–15.

72. *Ibid.*

73. Mary E. Wilson, Chief, Division of Infectious Diseases, Mount Auburn Hospital, Cambridge, Massachusetts, 1995 (personal communication).

74. *Op. cit.* 65, p. 72.

75. J. Almendares *et al.,* "Critical Regions: A Profile of Honduras," in *Health and Climate Change* (The Lancet, London, 1994), pp. 29–31.

76. Richard Stone, "If the Mercury Soars, So May Health Hazards," *Science,* Vol. 267, No. 5200 (February 17, 1995), pp. 957–958.

77. *Op. cit.* 7, p. 24.

78. Tod Robberson, "Dengue Fever Epidemic Spreads Despite Latin American Efforts," *Washington Post* (October 20, 1995), p. A22.

79. *Op. cit.* 7, Table 5, p. 18.

80. *Op. cit.* 65, pp. 30, 49–50.

81. *Op. cit.* 78.

82. *Op. cit.* 65, p. 50.

83. Thomas P. Monath, Vice-President, Research & Medical Affairs, OraVax, Cambridge, U.K., 1995 (personal communication).

84. *Op. cit.* 78.

85. *Op. cit.* 65, p. 55.

86. Anne Platt, "The Resurgence of Infectious Diseases," *World Watch,* Vol. 8, No. 4 (July–August 1995), p. 28.

87. *Op. cit.* 65, pp. 54–55.

88. "Statistics from the World Health Organization: Cumulative AIDS Cases Reported to the World Health Organization as of 29 December 1994," *AIDS,* Vol. 9, No. 4 (April 1995), p. 410.

89. "Acquired Immunodeficiency Syndrome (AIDS)—Data as of 31 December 1994," *World Health Organization Weekly Epidemiological Record,* Vol. 70, No. 2 (January 13, 1995), p. 3.

90. *Op. cit.* 7, pp. 29–30.

91. *Op. cit.* 7, p. 13.

92. *Op. cit.* 65, p. 56.

93. *Op. cit.* 65, p. 31.

94. *Op. cit.* 7, p. 21.

95. *Op. cit.* 7, pp. 21–22.

96. *Op. cit.* 58, p. 137.

97. *Op. cit.* 7, p. 22.

98. Mary E. Wilson, "Travel and the Emergence of Infectious Diseases," *Emerging Infectious Diseases,* Vol. 1, No. 2 (April–June 1995), pp. 39–46.

99. Subhadra Menon, Correspondent, New Delhi, India, 1995 (personal communication).

100. John Ward Anderson, "Plague Subsiding in India: International Isolation Unfair, Officials Say," *Washington Post* (October 8, 1994), p. A23.

101. M. N. Swartz, "Hospital-Acquired Infections: Diseases with Increasingly Limited Therapies," in *Infectious Diseases in an Age of Change: The Impact of Human Ecology and Behavior in Disease Transmission,* Bernard Roizman, ed. (National Academy Press, Washington, D.C., 1995), pp. 130–131.

102. *Ibid.,* pp. 116–119.

103. *Op. cit.* 65, pp. 86–87.

104. *Op. cit.* 65, pp. 18–19.

105. In anticipation of that, the United States is currently preparing an influenza pandemic preparedness plan with a comprehensive control and prevention program that relies mainly on vaccination. Joel G. Breman, Deputy Director, Division of International Train-

ing and Research, John E. Fogarty International Center for Advanced Study in the Health Sciences, National Institutes of Health, Washington, D.C., 1995 (personal communication).

106. *Op. cit.* 65, pp. 106–107.

107. Centers for Disease Control and Prevention, "Addressing Emerging Infectious Disease Threats: A Prevention Strategy for the United States: Execuive Summary," *Morbid-*

ity and Mortality Weekly Report, Vol. 43, No. RR-5 (April 15, 1994), p. 4.

108. *Op. cit.* 65, p. 107.

109. Walter V. Reid, "Biodiversity and Health: Prescription for Progress," *Environment,* Vol. 37, No. 6 (July–August 1995), p. 36.

110. *Op. cit.* 65, p. 107.

111. *Op. cit.* 7, p. 23.

112. *Op. cit.* 65, pp. 109–110.

113. *Op. cit.* 86, p. 31.

114. Kathleen Day, "Budget Cuts Slow Agencies Fighting New Bacteria Strains," *Washington Post* (June 27, 1995), pp. A1, A6.

115. *Op. cit.* 65, p. 135.

116. Tim Beardsley, "Better Than a Cure," *Scientific American,* Vol. 272, No. 1 (January 1995), p. 90.

117. "Bringing AZT to Poor Countries," *Science,* Vol. 269, No. 5224 (August 4, 1995), p. 624.

	Population (millions)				Average Annual Population Change (percent)			Average Annual Increment to the Population (thousands)			Average Annual Growth of the Labor Force (percent)	
	1950	1990	1995	2025	1980-85	1990-95	2000-05	1980-85	1990-95	2000-05	1981-90	1991-2000
WORLD	2,519,748	5,284,832	5,716,426	8,294,341	1.7	1.6	1.4	80,396	86,319	87,270		
AFRICA	223,967	632,669	728,074	1,495,772	2.9	2.8	2.6	14,627	19,081	22,690		
Algeria	8,753	24,935	27,939	45,475	3.1	2.3	2.0	629	601	650	4.1	3.5
Angola	4,131	9,194	11,072	26,619	2.6	3.7	3.1	197	376	431	1.6	2.9
Benin	2,046	4,633	5,409	12,252	2.9	3.1	2.8	106	155	191	2.1	2.4
Botswana	389	1,276	1,487	2,980	3.5	3.1	2.7	34	42	50	3.7	3.2
Burkina Faso	3,654	8,987	10,319	21,654	2.5	2.8	2.5	184	266	307	2.0	2.0
Burundi	2,456	5,503	6,393	13,490	2.8	3.0	2.6	124	178	204	2.3	2.5
Cameroon	4,466	11,526	13,233	29,173	2.8	2.8	2.8	263	341	465	2.2	2.4
Central African Rep	1,314	2,927	3,315	6,360	2.3	2.5	2.3	56	78	89	1.5	1.8
Chad	2,658	5,553	6,361	12,907	2.3	2.7	2.5	108	162	192	1.6	2.5
Congo	808	2,232	2,590	5,677	2.8	3.0	2.6	51	72	83	2.2	2.4
Cote d'Ivoire	2,776	11,974	14,253	36,817	3.9	3.5	3.2	348	456	576	2.8	2.5
Egypt	21,834	56,312	62,931	97,301	2.6	2.2	1.7	1,200	1,324	1,256	2.6	2.7
Equatorial Guinea	226	352	400	798	7.2	2.6	2.4	19	10	12	X	X
Eritrea	1,140	3,082	3,531	7,043	2.5	2.7	2.5	63	90	108	2.0	2.2
Ethiopia	18,434	47,423	55,053	126,886	2.5	3.0	2.9	954	1,526	1,987	2.2	2.3
Gabon	469	1,146	1,320	2,697	4.0	2.8	2.5	36	35	39	2.4	1.5
Gambia, The	294	923	1,118	2,102	3.0	3.8	2.4	21	39	33	X	X
Ghana	4,900	15,020	17,453	37,988	3.6	3.0	2.8	421	487	609	2.8	2.8
Guinea	2,550	5,755	6,700	15,088	2.2	3.0	2.9	105	189	239	1.8	2.4
Guinea-Bissau	505	964	1,073	1,978	1.9	2.1	2.1	16	22	27	X	X
Kenya	6,265	23,613	28,261	63,360	3.6	3.6	3.0	650	930	1,042	3.2	3.0
Lesotho	734	1,792	2,050	4,172	3.1	2.7	2.6	45	52	64	2.4	2.4
Liberia	824	2,575	3,039	7,240	3.2	3.3	3.1	65	93	119	2.4	2.6
Libya	1,029	4,545	5,407	12,885	4.4	3.5	3.2	149	172	222	3.9	3.5
Madagascar	4,229	12,571	14,763	34,419	3.2	3.2	3.1	314	438	570	2.5	2.8
Malawi	2,881	9,367	11,129	22,348	3.2	3.5	2.0	213	352	257	3.7	2.1
Mali	3,520	9,212	10,795	24,575	2.9	3.2	2.9	210	317	394	2.7	2.8
Mauritania	825	2,003	2,274	4,443	2.6	2.5	2.5	43	54	68	2.5	3.1
Mauritius	493	1,057	1,117	1,481	1.0	1.1	1.1	10	12	13	2.2	1.6
Morocco	8,953	24,334	27,028	40,650	2.4	2.1	1.6	487	539	478	3.1	3.1
Mozambique	6,198	14,187	16,004	35,139	2.3	2.4	2.8	289	363	577	0.7	2.2
Namibia	511	1,349	1,540	3,049	2.7	2.7	2.5	30	38	47	2.4	2.8
Niger	2,400	7,731	9,151	22,385	3.4	3.4	3.2	204	284	371	2.7	2.7
Nigeria	32,935	96,154	111,721	238,397	2.9	3.0	2.7	2,209	3,113	3,765	2.2	2.4
Rwanda	2,120	6,986	7,952	15,797	3.2	2.6	2.5	179	193	239	2.9	2.6
Senegal	2,500	7,327	8,312	16,896	2.8	2.5	2.6	167	197	263	2.2	2.2
Sierra Leone	1,944	3,999	4,509	8,690	2.0	2.4	2.3	69	102	123	1.5	1.9
Somalia	3,072	8,677	9,250	21,276	3.2	1.3	3.0	232	115	348	1.7	1.5
South Africa	13,683	37,066	41,465	70,951	2.5	2.2	2.1	775	880	1,007	2.9	2.7
Sudan	9,190	24,585	28,098	58,388	2.8	2.7	2.6	556	703	898	2.8	3.1
Swaziland	264	744	855	1,647	3.0	2.8	2.6	18	22	27	X	X
Tanzania	7,886	25,600	29,685	62,894	3.2	3.0	2.6	643	817	956	2.8	2.5
Togo	1,329	3,531	4,138	9,377	2.9	3.2	2.9	83	121	152	2.3	2.5
Tunisia	3,530	8,080	8,896	13,290	2.6	1.9	1.5	175	163	154	3.2	2.7
Uganda	4,762	17,949	21,297	48,056	2.8	3.4	2.7	398	670	717	2.5	2.6
Zaire	12,184	37,436	43,901	104,639	3.2	3.2	3.0	938	1,293	1,651	2.4	2.5
Zambia	2,440	8,150	9,456	19,130	3.6	3.0	2.4	225	261	274	3.8	3.3
Zimbabwe	2,730	9,903	11,261	19,631	3.3	2.6	2.0	253	272	267	3.2	2.0
EUROPE	548,711	721,734	726,999	718,203	0.4	0.2	0.0	2,676	1,053	17		
Albania	1,230	3,289	3,441	4,668	2.1	0.9	1.1	58	30	41	2.7	1.5
Austria	6,935	7,705	7,968	8,262	0.0	0.7	0.2	2	53	18	0.9	0.6
Belarus, Rep	7,798	10,212	10,141	9,903	0.7	(0.1)	(0.1)	66	(14)	(12)	0.5	0.1
Belgium	8,639	9,951	10,113	10,407	0.0	0.3	0.1	1	32	14	0.4	0.2
Bosnia and Herzegovina	2,661	4,308	3,459	4,474	1.0	(4.4)	0.2	42	(170)	11	1.6	0.2
Bulgaria	7,251	8,991	8,769	7,768	0.2	(0.5)	(0.4)	20	(44)	(37)	0.3	(0.2)
Croatia, Rep	3,850	4,517	4,495	4,234	0.4	(0.1)	(0.1)	19	(4)	(6)	0.3	0.1
Czech Rep	8,925	10,306	10,296	10,622	0.0	(0.0)	0.1	4	(2)	11	0.1	0.6
Denmark	4,271	5,140	5,181	5,081	(0.0)	0.2	(0.0)	(2)	8	(1)	0.6	0.1
Estonia, Rep	1,101	1,575	1,530	1,422	0.8	(0.6)	(0.3)	11	(9)	(5)	0.6	(0.2)
Finland	4,009	4,986	5,107	5,407	0.5	0.5	0.3	24	24	13	0.7	0.3
France	41,829	56,718	57,981	61,247	0.5	0.4	0.2	258	253	132	0.8	0.6
Germany	68,376	79,365	81,591	76,442	(0.2)	0.6	(0.1)	(127)	445	(83)	0.7	0.2
Greece	7,566	10,238	10,451	9,868	0.6	0.4	0.0	58	43	1	0.9	0.5
Hungary	9,338	10,365	10,115	9,397	(0.2)	(0.5)	(0.3)	(26)	(50)	(29)	(0.8)	0.3
Iceland	143	255	269	337	1.1	1.1	0.9	3	3	3	X	X
Ireland	2,969	3,503	3,553	3,882	0.9	0.3	0.4	30	10	16	0.6	1.2
Italy	47,104	57,023	57,187	52,324	0.1	0.1	(0.2)	67	33	(87)	0.7	0.1
Latvia, Rep	1,949	2,671	2,557	2,335	0.6	(0.9)	(0.5)	16	(23)	(11)	0.4	(0.7)
Lithuania, Rep	2,567	3,711	3,700	3,816	0.9	(0.1)	0.1	31	(2)	2	1.0	0.1
Macedonia, former Yugoslav Rep	1,230	2,046	2,163	2,571	1.4	1.1	0.7	26	23	16	1.5	1.1
Moldova, Rep	2,472	4,362	4,432	5,130	1.0	0.3	0.5	41	14	22	0.7	0.8
Netherlands	10,114	14,952	15,503	16,276	0.5	0.7	0.3	70	110	47	1.3	0.5
Norway	3,265	4,241	4,337	4,719	0.3	0.5	0.3	13	19	15	0.9	0.6
Poland, Rep	24,824	38,119	38,388	41,542	0.9	0.1	0.3	326	54	103	0.2	0.9
Portugal	8,405	9,868	9,823	9,685	0.3	(0.1)	(0.0)	28	(9)	(4)	0.4	0.3
Romania	16,311	23,207	22,835	21,735	0.5	(0.3)	(0.2)	105	(74)	(41)	(0.2)	0.8
Russian Federation	103,283	147,913	147,000	138,548	0.7	(0.1)	(0.2)	910	(183)	(268)	0.4	0.2
Slovak Rep	3,463	5,256	5,353	6,014	0.7	0.4	0.4	33	19	24	0.9	1.1
Slovenia, Rep	1,473	1,918	1,946	1,825	0.5	0.3	(0.1)	10	6	(2)	0.5	0.5
Spain	28,009	39,272	39,621	37,571	0.5	0.2	(0.0)	186	70	(8)	1.2	0.7
Sweden	7,014	8,559	8,780	9,751	0.1	0.5	0.3	8	44	30	0.5	0.4
Switzerland	4,694	6,834	7,202	7,786	0.7	1.1	0.5	43	74	34	1.3	0.7
Ukraine	37,024	51,637	51,380	48,715	0.4	(0.1)	(0.2)	191	(51)	(90)	0.2	0.1
United Kingdom	50,616	57,411	58,258	61,476	0.1	0.3	0.2	58	169	98	0.5	0.3
Yugoslavia, Fed Rep	7,131	10,156	10,849	11,478	0.7	1.3	0.4	65	139	40	X	X

	Population (millions)				Average Annual Population Change (percent)			Average Annual Increment to the Population (thousands)			Average Annual Growth of the Labor Force (percent)	
	1950	1990	1995	2025	1980-85	1990-95	2000-05	1980-85	1990-95	2000-05	1981-90	1991-2000
NORTH & CENTRAL AMERICA	219,633	423,658	454,229	615,549	1.3	1.4	1.1	5,097	6,114	5,492		
Belize	69	189	215	386	2.6	2.6	2.3	4	5	6	X	X
Canada	13,737	27,791	29,463	38,266	1.1	1.2	0.9	270	334	295	1.5	1.0
Costa Rica	862	3,035	3,424	5,608	2.9	2.4	1.8	72	78	73	3.1	2.6
Cuba	5,850	10,598	11,041	12,658	0.8	0.8	0.5	78	89	54	2.5	1.2
Dominican Rep	2,353	7,110	7,823	11,164	2.3	1.9	1.4	136	143	126	3.3	2.6
El Salvador	1,940	5,172	5,768	9,735	0.9	2.2	2.0	43	119	135	1.3	2.8
Guatemala	2,969	9,197	10,621	21,668	2.8	2.9	2.7	209	285	350	2.9	3.4
Haiti	3,261	6,486	7,180	13,128	1.8	2.0	2.1	102	139	173	1.5	1.6
Honduras	1,380	4,879	5,654	10,656	3.2	3.0	2.5	123	155	172	3.6	3.7
Jamaica	1,403	2,366	2,447	3,301	1.6	0.7	1.0	36	16	26	2.2	1.7
Mexico	27,740	84,511	93,674	136,594	2.4	2.1	1.5	1,694	1,833	1,597	3.1	2.6
Nicaragua	1,109	3,676	4,433	9,079	2.8	3.7	2.8	85	151	154	2.4	4.7
Panama	860	2,398	2,631	3,767	2.1	1.9	1.4	43	47	42	2.8	2.5
Trinidad and Tobago	636	1,236	1,306	1,808	1.4	1.1	1.1	16	14	16	1.6	1.8
United States	152,271	249,924	263,250	331,152	0.9	1.0	0.8	2,142	2,665	2,227	1.1	1.0
SOUTH AMERICA	111,690	293,131	319,790	462,664	2.1	1.7	1.4	5,301	5,332	5,172		
Argentina	17,150	32,547	34,587	46,133	1.5	1.2	1.1	442	408	416	1.2	1.7
Bolivia	2,714	6,573	7,414	13,131	1.9	2.4	2.2	108	168	189	2.4	2.4
Brazil	53,444	148,477	161,790	230,250	2.2	1.7	1.4	2,751	2,663	2,517	2.2	2.1
Chile	6,068	13,154	14,262	19,775	1.6	1.6	1.2	187	222	195	2.5	1.8
Colombia	11,946	32,300	35,101	49,359	2.1	1.7	1.3	591	560	526	2.8	2.3
Ecuador	3,387	10,264	11,460	17,792	2.7	2.2	1.7	228	239	230	2.9	2.8
Guyana	423	796	835	1,141	0.8	0.9	1.1	6	8	10	X	X
Paraguay	1,351	4,317	4,960	9,017	3.3	2.8	2.3	111	129	134	3.2	2.8
Peru	7,632	21,588	23,780	36,692	2.4	1.9	1.7	439	438	466	2.7	2.6
Suriname	215	400	423	599	1.2	1.1	1.1	4	5	5	X	X
Uruguay	2,239	3,094	3,186	3,691	0.6	0.6	0.6	19	18	18	0.6	0.9
Venezuela	5,094	19,502	21,844	34,775	2.5	2.3	1.8	409	468	460	3.1	2.8
ASIA	1,402,725	3,186,446	3,457,957	4,959,987	1.9	1.6	1.4	52,331	54,302	53,473		
Afghanistan, Islamic State	8,958	15,045	20,141	45,262	(2.0)	5.8	2.7	(309)	1,019	759	(1.0)	6.4
Armenia	1,362	3,352	3,599	4,724	1.0	1.4	1.0	32	49	39	1.1	1.3
Azerbaijan	2,890	7,117	7,558	10,106	1.6	1.2	1.0	100	88	78	2.1	1.7
Bangladesh	41,783	108,118	120,433	196,128	2.2	2.2	2.0	2,067	2,463	2,874	2.7	2.9
Bhutan	734	1,544	1,638	3,136	2.1	1.2	2.3	28	19	45	1.9	1.4
Cambodia	4,346	8,841	10,251	19,686	3.0	3.0	2.3	213	282	284	2.5	2.3
China	554,760	1,155,305	1,221,462	1,526,106	1.4	1.1	0.8	14,260	13,231	10,543	2.2	1.2
Georgia, Rep	3,726	5,418	5,457	6,122	0.8	0.1	0.4	41	8	21	1.0	0.3
India	357,561	850,638	935,744	1,392,086	2.2	1.9	1.6	15,866	17,021	17,040	2.0	1.9
Indonesia	79,538	182,812	197,588	275,598	2.1	1.6	1.3	3,275	2,955	2,884	2.5	2.1
Iran, Islamic Rep	16,913	58,946	67,283	123,549	4.4	2.7	2.5	1,932	1,667	1,991	3.9	2.9
Iraq	5,158	18,078	20,449	42,656	3.3	2.5	2.8	462	474	713	3.7	3.5
Israel	1,258	4,660	5,629	7,808	1.8	3.8	1.3	71	194	84	2.1	3.3
Japan	83,625	123,537	125,095	121,594	0.7	0.3	0.1	806	312	159	1.1	0.5
Jordan	1,237	4,259	5,439	12,039	5.4	4.9	3.0	182	236	211	5.1	4.8
Kazakhstan, Rep	6,756	16,670	17,111	21,748	1.1	0.5	0.8	175	88	149	1.4	1.1
Korea, Dem People's Rep	9,726	21,774	23,917	33,386	1.7	1.9	1.3	326	429	337	3.6	2.0
Korea, Rep	20,357	42,869	44,995	54,418	1.4	1.0	0.8	536	425	394	2.5	1.6
Kuwait	152	2,143	1,547	2,805	4.5	(6.5)	2.5	69	(119)	48	5.5	(2.3)
Kyrgyz Rep	1,749	4,362	4,745	7,128	2.0	1.7	1.5	75	77	82	2.1	2.1
Lao People's Dem Rep	1,755	4,202	4,882	9,688	2.3	3.0	2.6	78	136	153	1.8	2.2
Lebanon	1,443	2,555	3,009	4,424	(0.0)	3.3	1.5	(0)	91	49	0.7	3.2
Malaysia	6,110	17,891	20,140	31,577	2.6	2.4	1.7	383	450	406	2.8	2.7
Mongolia	761	2,177	2,410	3,827	2.8	2.0	1.9	49	47	52	2.9	2.9
Myanmar	17,832	41,813	46,527	75,564	2.1	2.1	1.9	745	943	1,011	1.7	1.8
Nepal	7,974	19,253	21,918	40,693	2.6	2.6	2.4	420	533	626	2.4	2.5
Oman	456	1,751	2,163	6,094	4.8	4.2	3.7	59	82	107	4.5	3.7
Pakistan	39,513	121,933	140,497	284,827	3.7	2.8	2.7	3,438	3,713	4,657	3.6	3.0
Philippines	20,988	60,779	67,581	104,522	2.5	2.1	1.8	1,270	1,360	1,384	2.3	2.3
Saudi Arabia	3,201	16,048	17,880	42,651	5.5	2.2	3.1	609	366	720	6.6	2.1
Singapore	1,022	2,705	2,848	3,355	1.2	1.0	0.6	29	29	19	1.8	0.8
Sri Lanka	7,678	17,225	18,354	25,031	1.7	1.3	1.1	259	226	221	1.5	1.7
Syrian Arab Rep	3,495	12,348	14,661	33,505	3.5	3.4	3.2	329	463	599	3.6	4.1
Tajikistan, Rep	1,558	5,287	6,101	11,792	2.8	2.9	2.5	121	163	184	3.2	3.2
Thailand	20,010	55,583	58,791	73,584	1.8	1.1	0.9	882	642	554	2.3	1.3
Turkey	20,809	56,098	61,945	90,937	2.5	2.0	1.5	1,181	1,169	1,070	2.6	2.0
Turkmenistan, Rep	1,212	3,657	4,099	6,650	2.4	2.3	1.9	72	88	91	2.9	2.9
United Arab Emirates	70	1,671	1,904	2,958	6.1	2.6	1.8	73	47	39	4.3	1.8
Uzbekistan, Rep	6,376	20,420	22,843	37,678	2.6	2.2	2.0	435	485	527	3.0	2.9
Viet Nam	29,954	66,689	74,545	118,151	2.2	2.2	1.9	1,237	1,571	1,614	2.7	2.7
Yemen, Rep	4,316	11,311	14,501	33,676	3.1	5.0	3.1	276	638	562	4.0	5.1
OCEANIA	12,612	26,428	28,549	41,027	1.5	1.5	1.3	354	424	415		
Australia	8,219	16,888	18,088	24,667	1.4	1.4	1.1	214	240	215	1.9	1.4
Fiji	289	726	784	1,161	2.0	1.5	1.5	13	12	13	X	X
New Zealand	1,908	3,360	3,575	4,376	0.8	1.2	0.8	27	43	31	1.3	1.3
Papua New Guinea	1,613	3,839	4,302	7,532	2.2	2.3	2.1	71	93	109	1.8	1.9
Solomon Islands	90	320	378	844	3.5	3.3	3.1	9	12	15	X	X

Sources: United Nations Population Division and International Labour Office.

Notes: World and regional totals include countries not listed here.
0 = zero or less than half the unit of measure; X = not available; negative numbers are shown in parentheses.
For additional information, see Sources and Technical Notes.

Data Table 8.2 Trends in Births, Life Expectancy, Fertility, and Age Structure, 1970–95

	Crude Birth Rate (births per 1,000 population)		Life Expectancy at Birth (years)		Total Fertility Rate		Percentage of Population in Specific Age Groups					
							1975			1995		
	1970-75	1990-95	1970-75	1990-95	1970-75	1990-95	<15	15-65	>65	<15	15-65	>65
WORLD	30.9	25.0	57.9	64.7	4.5	3.1	36.9	57.5	5.6	31.5	62.0	6.5
AFRICA	46.5	41.9	46.0	52.8	6.6	5.8	44.8	52.2	3.1	44.0	52.8	3.2
Algeria	48.0	29.1	54.5	67.1	7.4	3.9	47.6	48.2	4.2	38.7	57.7	3.6
Angola	49.0	51.3	38.0	46.5	6.6	7.2	44.2	52.9	3.0	47.1	50.0	2.9
Benin	49.4	48.7	40.0	47.6	7.1	7.1	44.8	51.6	3.6	47.4	49.7	2.8
Botswana	48.6	37.1	53.2	64.9	6.6	4.9	50.1	47.8	2.1	43.2	54.3	2.4
Burkina Faso	47.8	46.8	41.2	47.4	6.4	6.5	44.0	53.3	2.8	44.9	52.0	3.1
Burundi	44.0	46.0	44.0	50.2	6.8	6.8	45.5	51.1	3.5	46.3	50.8	3.0
Cameroon	45.3	40.7	45.8	56.0	6.3	5.7	43.4	53.1	3.6	44.0	52.4	3.6
Central African Rep	43.1	41.5	43.0	49.4	5.7	5.7	40.6	55.5	3.9	42.7	53.4	4.0
Chad	44.6	43.7	39.0	47.5	6.0	5.9	41.7	54.7	3.6	43.4	53.0	3.6
Congo	46.1	44.7	46.7	51.3	6.3	6.3	44.4	52.2	3.5	45.6	51.0	3.4
Cote d'Ivoire	51.1	49.9	45.4	51.0	7.4	7.4	45.8	51.8	2.4	49.1	48.2	2.6
Egypt	38.4	29.3	52.1	63.6	5.5	3.9	40.0	55.8	4.2	38.0	57.8	4.2
Equatorial Guinea	42.4	43.5	40.5	48.0	5.7	5.9	40.0	55.6	4.4	43.3	52.8	4.0
Eritrea	46.1	43.0	44.3	50.4	6.2	5.8	44.6	52.9	2.5	44.0	53.1	2.9
Ethiopia	49.3	48.5	41.0	47.5	6.8	7.0	45.8	51.6	2.6	46.4	50.8	2.9
Gabon	30.9	37.3	45.0	53.5	4.3	5.3	32.3	61.9	5.8	39.2	55.1	5.8
Gambia, The	49.2	43.7	37.0	45.0	6.5	5.6	42.0	54.9	2.9	41.3	55.8	2.9
Ghana	45.8	41.7	50.0	56.0	6.6	6.0	45.4	51.9	2.7	45.3	51.8	2.9
Guinea	51.6	50.6	37.3	44.5	7.0	7.0	45.3	52.0	2.6	47.1	50.3	2.6
Guinea-Bissau	41.4	42.7	36.5	43.5	5.4	5.8	38.1	58.2	3.8	41.7	54.2	4.1
Kenya	52.9	44.5	51.0	55.7	8.1	6.3	49.1	47.2	3.7	47.7	49.4	2.9
Lesotho	42.4	36.9	50.4	60.5	5.7	5.2	41.7	54.8	3.6	42.1	53.9	4.0
Liberia	48.1	47.3	47.5	55.4	6.8	6.8	44.0	52.3	3.7	46.0	50.4	3.7
Libya	49.0	41.9	52.9	63.1	7.6	6.4	46.0	51.7	2.2	45.4	52.0	2.6
Madagascar	47.2	43.9	46.5	56.5	6.6	6.1	44.7	52.4	2.9	46.1	51.1	2.8
Malawi	56.6	50.5	41.0	45.6	7.4	7.2	47.2	50.6	2.2	46.7	50.5	2.7
Mali	51.0	50.8	38.5	46.0	7.1	7.1	46.0	51.5	2.5	47.4	50.0	2.5
Mauritania	45.0	39.8	43.5	51.5	6.5	5.4	43.3	53.8	3.0	43.1	53.7	3.2
Mauritius	26.1	20.8	62.9	70.2	3.3	2.4	39.7	57.6	2.8	27.7	66.4	5.8
Morocco	45.6	29.1	52.9	63.3	6.9	3.8	47.2	49.2	3.7	36.1	59.8	4.1
Mozambique	45.7	45.2	42.5	46.4	6.5	6.5	43.8	53.0	3.1	44.7	52.0	3.2
Namibia	42.5	37.0	48.8	58.8	6.0	5.3	42.9	53.7	3.4	41.9	54.4	3.7
Niger	59.8	52.5	39.0	46.5	8.1	7.4	46.4	51.2	2.4	48.4	49.2	2.4
Nigeria	46.3	45.4	43.5	50.4	6.5	6.5	44.9	52.6	2.5	45.6	51.7	2.8
Rwanda	52.9	44.1	44.6	47.3	8.3	6.6	48.2	49.4	2.4	46.0	51.5	2.5
Senegal	49.2	43.0	40.3	49.3	7.0	6.1	44.8	52.4	2.8	44.6	52.5	2.9
Sierra Leone	48.9	49.1	35.0	39.0	6.5	6.5	42.5	54.4	3.1	44.2	52.8	3.0
Somalia	50.1	50.2	41.0	47.0	7.0	7.0	45.4	51.6	3.0	47.5	49.8	2.7
South Africa	39.6	31.2	53.9	62.9	5.5	4.1	40.9	55.2	3.8	37.3	58.3	4.4
Sudan	47.0	39.8	43.7	53.0	6.7	5.7	44.4	52.8	2.7	43.8	53.3	2.9
Swaziland	47.5	38.5	47.3	57.5	6.5	4.9	45.6	51.5	2.9	43.0	54.4	2.7
Tanzania	49.6	43.1	46.5	52.1	6.8	5.9	47.9	49.8	2.3	45.9	51.6	2.6
Togo	45.6	44.5	45.5	55.0	6.6	6.6	44.2	52.7	3.1	45.7	51.1	3.2
Tunisia	37.1	25.6	55.6	67.8	6.2	3.2	43.8	52.7	3.5	34.9	60.7	4.4
Uganda	50.3	51.8	46.5	44.9	6.9	7.3	47.4	50.1	2.5	48.8	48.8	2.4
Zaire	47.7	47.5	46.1	52.0	6.3	6.7	45.3	52.0	2.8	48.0	49.1	2.9
Zambia	49.1	44.6	47.3	48.9	6.9	6.0	46.5	50.9	2.6	47.4	50.2	2.4
Zimbabwe	48.6	39.1	51.5	53.7	7.2	5.0	49.0	48.4	2.6	44.1	53.1	2.8
EUROPE	15.6	11.6	70.8	72.9	2.1	1.6	23.7	64.8	11.4	19.2	67.0	13.8
Albania	31.9	23.8	67.7	72.0	4.7	2.9	39.9	55.6	4.5	31.4	63.1	5.5
Austria	13.7	11.9	70.6	76.2	2.0	1.5	23.2	61.9	14.9	17.8	67.3	14.9
Belarus, Rep	15.8	12.0	71.5	69.8	2.2	1.7	25.6	64.5	10.0	21.6	65.8	12.6
Belgium	13.6	12.1	71.4	76.4	1.9	1.6	22.2	63.9	13.9	17.8	66.4	15.8
Bosnia and Herzegovina	21.3	13.4	67.4	72.4	2.6	1.6	30.9	63.7	5.5	22.2	70.0	7.8
Bulgaria	16.2	10.3	71.2	71.2	2.2	1.5	22.0	67.1	10.9	18.3	67.1	14.5
Croatia, Rep	15.0	11.3	69.6	71.4	2.0	1.7	21.5	67.5	11.0	19.1	68.2	12.8
Czech Rep	17.3	12.9	70.0	71.3	2.2	1.8	22.3	64.8	12.9	19.4	68.1	12.5
Denmark	14.6	12.5	73.6	75.3	2.0	1.7	22.6	64.0	13.4	17.2	67.6	15.2
Estonia, Rep	15.4	11.0	70.5	69.3	2.2	1.6	21.8	66.0	12.2	20.6	66.6	12.8
Finland	13.2	13.1	70.7	75.7	1.6	1.9	22.0	67.4	10.6	19.1	66.8	14.1
France	16.3	12.9	72.4	76.9	2.3	1.7	23.9	62.6	13.5	19.6	65.5	14.9
Germany	11.4	9.9	71.0	76.0	1.6	1.3	21.5	63.6	14.8	16.1	68.7	15.2
Greece	15.9	9.9	72.3	77.6	2.3	1.4	23.9	63.9	12.2	16.7	67.4	15.9
Hungary	15.7	11.7	69.3	69.0	2.1	1.7	20.3	67.0	12.6	18.1	67.9	14.0
Iceland	21.0	17.6	74.3	78.2	2.8	2.2	30.3	61.0	9.2	24.5	64.3	11.2
Ireland	22.1	14.7	71.3	75.3	3.8	2.1	31.2	57.8	11.0	24.4	64.3	11.2
Italy	16.1	9.8	72.1	77.5	2.3	1.3	24.2	63.7	12.0	15.1	68.9	16.0
Latvia, Rep	14.4	11.5	70.1	69.1	2.0	1.6	21.1	66.2	12.7	20.6	66.1	13.3
Lithuania, Rep	16.6	13.5	71.3	70.4	2.3	1.8	25.5	63.4	11.1	21.9	66.0	12.2
Macedonia, former Yugoslav Rep	23.8	15.5	67.5	71.8	3.0	2.0	30.7	63.1	6.1	24.4	67.5	8.2
Moldova, Rep	18.5	16.0	64.8	67.6	2.6	2.1	28.9	64.3	6.8	26.4	64.4	9.3
Netherlands	15.4	13.0	74.0	77.4	2.0	1.6	25.3	63.9	10.8	18.4	68.4	13.2
Norway	16.8	14.2	74.4	76.9	2.3	1.9	23.8	62.5	13.7	19.5	64.7	15.9
Poland, Rep	17.8	13.2	70.4	71.1	2.3	1.9	24.0	66.4	9.5	22.9	66.1	11.0
Portugal	19.5	12.0	68.0	74.6	2.8	1.6	27.9	62.2	9.9	18.8	67.0	14.1
Romania	19.3	11.3	69.0	69.9	2.6	1.5	25.2	65.2	9.6	20.4	67.7	11.8
Russian Federation	15.2	10.9	68.2	67.6	2.0	1.5	23.3	67.8	8.9	21.1	66.9	12.1
Slovak Rep	19.7	14.3	70.0	70.9	2.5	1.9	26.2	64.3	9.6	22.9	66.3	10.8
Slovenia, Rep	16.7	10.5	69.8	72.6	2.2	1.5	23.7	65.3	11.0	18.3	69.2	12.4
Spain	19.5	9.7	72.9	77.6	2.9	1.2	27.6	62.4	10.0	16.5	68.6	14.9
Sweden	13.6	14.1	74.7	78.2	1.9	2.1	20.7	64.2	15.1	19.0	63.7	17.3
Switzerland	14.2	12.6	73.8	78.0	1.8	1.6	22.4	65.0	12.6	17.7	68.1	14.2
Ukraine	14.9	11.4	70.1	69.4	2.0	1.6	23.0	66.5	10.5	20.1	65.9	14.0
United Kingdom	14.5	13.5	72.0	76.2	2.0	1.8	23.3	62.7	14.0	19.6	65.0	15.5
Yugoslavia, Fed Rep	18.5	14.2	68.8	72.0	2.4	2.0	24.6	66.2	9.2	22.0	66.6	11.4

	Crude Birth Rate (births per 1,000 population)		Life Expectancy at Birth (years)		Total Fertility Rate		Percentage of Population in Specific Age Groups					
							1975			1995		
	1970-75	1990-95	1970-75	1990-95	1970-75	1990-95	<15	15-65	>65	<15	15-65	>65
NORTH & CENTRAL AMERICA	**22.8**	**20.2**	**68.6**	**74.1**	**3.1**	**2.5**	**31.2**	**60.5**	**8.4**	**27.0**	**63.5**	**9.8**
Belize	40.2	34.7	67.6	73.6	6.3	4.2	47.0	48.5	4.5	42.3	53.5	4.2
Canada	16.0	15.1	73.1	77.4	2.0	1.9	26.1	65.4	8.4	20.8	67.3	11.8
Costa Rica	31.5	26.3	68.1	76.3	4.3	3.1	42.2	54.4	3.4	35.0	60.4	4.7
Cuba	26.7	16.9	70.9	75.3	3.6	1.8	37.3	55.9	6.7	22.9	68.2	8.9
Dominican Rep	38.8	27.0	59.9	69.6	5.6	3.1	45.3	51.6	3.0	35.1	60.9	4.0
El Salvador	42.8	33.5	58.7	66.4	6.1	4.0	45.9	51.2	2.9	40.7	55.2	4.1
Guatemala	44.6	38.7	54.0	64.8	6.5	5.4	45.7	51.5	2.8	44.3	52.2	3.5
Haiti	38.6	35.3	48.5	56.6	5.8	4.8	41.1	54.3	4.6	40.2	55.9	3.9
Honduras	46.9	37.1	54.1	67.7	7.1	4.9	48.0	49.4	2.6	43.8	53.1	3.1
Jamaica	32.5	21.7	68.6	73.6	5.0	2.4	45.2	49.0	5.8	30.8	62.6	6.6
Mexico	42.4	27.7	62.9	70.8	6.4	3.2	46.3	49.8	3.9	35.9	59.9	4.2
Nicaragua	47.2	40.5	55.3	66.7	6.8	5.0	48.0	49.5	2.5	46.0	50.9	3.1
Panama	35.6	25.0	66.4	72.8	4.9	2.9	42.9	52.9	4.3	33.4	61.4	5.2
Trinidad and Tobago	27.0	20.9	65.7	71.6	3.5	2.4	38.0	57.0	4.9	32.3	62.0	5.7
United States	15.7	15.9	71.3	76.0	2.0	2.1	25.2	64.3	10.5	22.0	65.3	12.6
SOUTH AMERICA	**32.9**	**24.8**	**60.7**	**68.5**	**4.6**	**3.0**	**39.5**	**56.3**	**4.3**	**32.7**	**61.8**	**5.5**
Argentina	23.4	20.4	67.2	72.1	3.2	2.8	29.2	63.2	7.6	28.7	61.8	9.5
Bolivia	45.2	35.7	46.7	59.4	6.5	4.8	43.0	53.5	3.4	40.6	55.6	3.8
Brazil	33.6	24.6	59.8	66.3	4.7	2.9	40.1	56.2	3.7	32.3	62.5	5.2
Chile	27.5	21.9	63.5	73.8	3.6	2.5	37.0	57.7	5.3	29.5	63.8	6.6
Colombia	32.6	24.0	61.7	69.3	4.7	2.7	43.1	53.4	3.5	32.9	62.6	4.5
Ecuador	40.6	28.3	58.9	68.8	6.0	3.5	43.8	52.1	4.0	36.4	59.2	4.4
Guyana	35.0	25.1	60.0	65.2	4.9	2.6	44.1	52.2	3.7	32.2	63.7	4.0
Paraguay	36.6	33.0	65.6	70.0	5.7	4.3	44.3	52.2	3.5	40.3	55.9	3.8
Peru	40.5	27.3	55.5	66.0	6.0	3.4	43.2	53.2	3.5	35.1	60.8	4.1
Suriname	34.6	25.3	64.0	70.3	5.3	2.7	47.8	48.6	3.8	35.0	60.0	5.0
Uruguay	21.1	17.1	68.8	72.5	3.0	2.3	27.7	62.7	9.6	24.4	63.3	12.3
Venezuela	35.1	27.4	66.0	71.7	4.9	3.3	43.3	53.6	3.1	36.2	59.7	4.1
ASIA	**33.9**	**25.2**	**56.3**	**64.8**	**5.1**	**3.0**	**39.9**	**55.9**	**4.2**	**32.0**	**62.7**	**5.3**
Afghanistan, Islamic State	51.6	50.2	38.0	43.5	7.1	6.9	43.8	53.9	2.4	40.8	56.4	2.8
Armenia	22.3	20.7	72.5	72.6	3.0	2.6	34.3	59.8	5.8	29.6	63.0	7.4
Azerbaijan	27.0	22.5	69.0	70.6	4.3	2.5	40.0	54.4	5.6	31.8	62.3	5.9
Bangladesh	48.5	35.5	44.9	55.6	7.0	4.4	45.9	50.5	3.6	39.5	57.5	3.1
Bhutan	41.6	39.6	40.7	50.7	5.9	5.9	39.9	56.8	3.2	41.1	55.5	3.5
Cambodia	39.9	43.5	40.3	51.6	5.5	5.3	41.6	55.6	2.8	44.9	52.4	2.6
China	28.3	18.5	63.2	68.5	4.8	2.0	39.5	56.1	4.4	26.4	67.5	6.1
Georgia, Rep	18.7	15.9	69.2	72.8	2.6	2.1	28.4	63.1	8.5	23.7	64.8	11.4
India	38.2	29.1	50.3	60.4	5.4	3.8	39.8	56.4	3.8	35.2	60.2	4.6
Indonesia	38.2	24.7	49.3	62.7	5.1	2.9	42.0	54.8	3.2	33.0	62.7	4.3
Iran, Islamic Rep	44.1	35.5	55.9	67.5	6.5	5.0	45.4	51.3	3.3	43.5	52.6	3.9
Iraq	47.4	38.1	57.0	66.0	7.1	5.7	46.6	50.9	2.5	43.6	53.5	3.0
Israel	27.4	21.2	71.6	76.5	3.8	2.9	32.9	59.4	7.8	29.1	61.4	9.5
Japan	19.2	10.1	73.3	79.5	2.1	1.5	24.3	67.8	7.9	16.2	69.6	14.1
Jordan	50.0	38.9	56.6	67.9	7.8	5.6	47.2	50.0	2.8	43.3	54.0	2.7
Kazakhstan, Rep	25.9	19.8	64.4	69.6	3.5	2.5	34.6	59.7	5.7	29.8	63.2	7.0
Korea, Dem People's Rep	35.8	24.1	61.5	71.1	5.7	2.4	45.1	51.7	3.1	29.1	66.3	4.6
Korea, Rep	28.8	16.4	62.6	71.1	4.1	1.7	37.7	58.6	3.6	23.6	70.8	5.6
Kuwait	44.4	24.2	67.3	74.9	6.9	3.1	44.4	54.0	1.6	39.8	58.5	1.7
Kyrgyz Rep	31.1	29.0	63.1	69.0	4.7	3.7	39.9	54.2	5.9	37.1	57.1	5.8
Lao People's Dem Rep	44.4	45.2	40.4	51.0	6.2	6.7	42.1	55.3	2.7	44.8	52.2	3.0
Lebanon	32.1	26.9	65.0	68.5	4.9	3.1	41.2	53.9	5.0	34.1	60.4	5.5
Malaysia	34.7	28.8	63.0	70.8	5.2	3.6	42.1	54.2	3.7	38.0	58.1	3.9
Mongolia	41.5	27.6	53.8	63.7	5.8	3.6	43.7	53.4	2.9	38.0	58.5	3.4
Myanmar	39.9	32.5	49.8	57.6	5.8	4.2	40.7	55.4	3.8	37.4	58.5	4.1
Nepal	45.6	39.2	43.3	53.5	6.3	5.4	42.3	54.5	3.2	42.4	54.2	3.4
Oman	49.6	43.6	49.0	69.6	7.2	7.2	44.6	52.5	2.7	47.5	49.9	2.6
Pakistan	47.5	40.9	50.6	61.5	7.0	6.2	45.5	51.6	3.0	44.3	52.7	3.0
Philippines	38.4	30.4	57.8	66.3	5.5	3.9	43.6	53.8	2.7	38.3	58.3	3.4
Saudi Arabia	47.6	35.1	53.9	69.7	7.3	6.4	44.3	52.7	3.0	41.9	55.4	2.7
Singapore	21.2	15.9	69.5	74.8	2.6	1.7	32.8	63.1	4.1	22.7	70.5	6.7
Sri Lanka	28.9	20.7	65.0	71.9	4.0	2.5	39.4	56.6	4.1	30.7	63.5	5.8
Syrian Arab Rep	46.6	41.1	57.0	67.1	7.7	5.9	48.5	47.8	3.7	47.3	49.9	2.8
Tajikistan, Rep	39.7	36.8	63.4	70.2	6.8	4.9	45.4	49.9	4.7	43.1	52.6	4.3
Thailand	35.1	19.4	59.6	69.0	5.0	2.1	44.9	52.1	3.0	28.3	66.7	5.0
Turkey	34.5	27.3	57.9	66.5	5.0	3.4	40.1	55.4	4.5	33.9	61.1	5.0
Turkmenistan, Rep	37.1	31.9	60.6	65.0	6.2	4.0	43.5	52.1	4.5	39.5	56.4	4.2
United Arab Emirates	33.0	23.2	62.5	73.8	6.4	4.2	28.1	69.7	2.0	31.3	67.0	1.7
Uzbekistan, Rep	35.7	31.5	64.1	69.2	6.0	3.9	43.3	51.1	5.5	39.9	55.6	4.4
Viet Nam	37.6	30.7	50.3	65.2	5.9	3.9	43.7	52.3	4.0	37.5	57.7	4.9
Yemen, Rep	53.2	49.4	42.1	50.2	7.6	7.6	50.9	46.5	2.6	46.7	50.9	2.4
OCEANIA	**23.9**	**19.2**	**66.6**	**73.0**	**3.2**	**2.5**	**31.1**	**61.5**	**7.5**	**26.0**	**64.4**	**9.5**
Australia	19.6	14.8	71.7	77.6	2.5	1.9	27.6	63.7	8.7	21.6	66.8	11.6
Fiji	32.5	23.7	65.1	71.5	4.2	3.0	39.9	57.5	2.6	34.6	61.5	3.8
New Zealand	20.8	17.3	71.7	75.5	2.8	2.2	30.0	61.3	8.7	23.4	65.3	11.3
Papua New Guinea	41.0	33.4	47.7	55.8	6.1	5.1	42.0	54.9	3.1	39.5	57.5	2.9
Solomon Islands	47.2	37.5	62.0	70.4	7.2	5.4	47.9	48.9	3.2	44.2	52.9	2.9

Source: United Nations Population Division.
Notes: World and Regional Totals include countries not listed here.
0 = zero or less than half the unit of measure.
For additional information, see Sources and Technical Notes.

Data Table 8.3 Mortality and Nutrition, 1970–95

	Crude Death Rate (per 1,000 population)		Infant Mortality Rate (per 1,000 live births)		Under-5 Mortality Rate (per 1,000 live births)			Maternal Mortality Rate (per 100,000 live births)	Wasting (percentage of children under age 5)	Stunting (percentage of children under age 5)	Calories Available (as percentage of need)	Total Expenditure on Health (as percentage of GDP)
	1970-75	1990-95	1970-75	1990-95	1960	1980	1993	1980-92	1980-91	1980-91	1988-90	1990
WORLD	11.7	9.3	93	64								
AFRICA	19.2	13.7	131	93								
Algeria	15.4	6.4	132	55	243	145	68	140 a	6	18	123	7.0
Angola	26.0	19.2	173	124	345	261	292	X	X	X	80	X
Benin	25.7	17.8	136	86	310	176	144	160	X	X	104	4.3
Botswana	13.6	6.6	88	43	170	94	56	250	X	44	97	X
Burkina Faso	24.6	18.2	173	130	318	218	175	810	13	29	94	8.5
Burundi	20.2	15.7	137	102	255	193	178	X	6 a	48 a	84	3.3
Cameroon	19.5	12.2	119	63	264	173	113	430	3	24	95	2.6
Central African Rep	21.8	16.7	132	102	294	202	177	600	X	X	82	4.2
Chad	24.9	18.0	166	122	325	254	206	960	X	X	73	6.3
Congo	18.9	14.9	95	84	220	125	109	900	5	27	103	X
Cote d'Ivoire	19.4	15.1	129	92	300	180	120	X	9	17	111	3.3
Egypt	16.3	8.1	150	67	258	180	59	270	3	24	132	2.6
Equatorial Guinea	24.1	18.0	157	117	316	243	X	X	X	X	X	X
Eritrea	19.7	15.2	136	105	X	X	204	X	X	X	X	X
Ethiopia	22.9	18.0	154	119	294	260	204	560 a	8 a	64 a	73	3.8
Gabon	20.2	15.5	132	94	287	194	154	190	X	X	104	X
Gambia, The	26.7	18.8	179	132	375	278	X	X	X	X	X	X
Ghana	15.8	11.7	107	81	215	157	170	1,000	7	31	93	3.5
Guinea	26.8	20.3	177	134	337	276	226	800	X	X	97	3.9
Guinea-Bissau	26.7	21.3	183	140	336	290	235	700 a	X	X	97	X
Kenya	17.3	11.7	98	69	202	112	90	170 a	6	33	89	4.3
Lesotho	19.3	10.0	130	79	204	173	156	X	5	26	93	X
Liberia	19.6	14.2	182	126	288	235	217	X	3 a	37 a	98	X
Libya	14.8	8.1	117	68	269	150	100	70 a	X	X	140	X
Madagascar	19.0	11.8	172	93	364	216	164	570	5	51	95	2.6
Malawi	23.5	20.0	191	143	365	290	223	400	5	49	88	5.0
Mali	25.4	19.1	203	159	400	310	217	2,000	11 a	24 a	96	5.2
Mauritania	21.5	14.4	142	101	321	249	202	X	16	57	106	X
Mauritius	7.0	6.6	55	18	84	42	22	99	16	22	128	X
Morocco	15.7	8.1	122	68	215	145	59	330	2	23	125	2.6
Mozambique	21.7	18.5	168	148	331	269	282	300	X	X	77	5.9
Namibia	16.8	10.5	113	60	206	114	79	370 a	9	28	X	X
Niger	25.2	18.9	167	124	320	320	320	700	16	32	95	5.0
Nigeria	20.2	15.4	111	84	204	196	191	800	9	43	93	2.7
Rwanda	20.5	16.7	142	110	191	222	141	210	4	48	82	3.5
Senegal	23.9	16.0	122	68	303	221	120	600	9	22	98	3.7
Sierra Leone	29.2	25.2	193	166	385	301	284	450	9 a	35	83	2.4
Somalia	23.6	18.5	155	122	294	246	211	1,100	X	X	81	1.5
South Africa	13.8	8.8	76	53	126	91	69	84 a	X	X	128	5.6
Sudan	19.8	13.1	110	78	292	210	128	550	14	32	87	3.3
Swaziland	18.0	10.7	133	75	233	151	X	X	X	X	X	X
Tanzania	18.5	13.6	125	85	249	202	167	340 a	6	47	X	4.7
Togo	19.4	12.8	129	85	264	175	135	420	5 a	30 a	99	4.1
Tunisia	12.3	6.4	120	43	244	102	36	70	3 a	18 a	131	4.9
Uganda	18.5	19.2	116	115	218	181	185	550	2	45	93	3.4
Zaire	18.9	14.5	127	93	286	204	187	800	5 a	43 a	96	2.4
Zambia	18.0	15.1	100	104	220	160	203	150	5	40	87	3.2
Zimbabwe	15.1	12.0	93	67	181	125	83	X	1 a	29 a	94	6.2
EUROPE	10.1	11.2	25	12								
Albania	6.9	5.8	58	30	151	57	41	X	X	X	107	X
Austria	12.8	10.8	24	7	43	17	8	8	X	X	133	8.5 a
Belarus, Rep	8.8	11.6	21	16	X	X	22	X	X	X	X	X
Belgium	12.1	10.9	19	6	35	15	10	3	X	X	149	8.1 a
Bosnia and Herzegovina	6.9	7.0	51	15	X	X	X	X	X	X	X	X
Bulgaria	9.7	12.7	26	14	70	25	19	9	X	X	148	5.4 a
Croatia, Rep	10.5	11.8	27	9	X	X	X	X	X	X	X	X
Czech Rep	13.4	13.1	20	9	X	X	10	X	X	X	X	X
Denmark	10.0	12.0	12	7	25	10	7	3	X	X	135	7.0 a
Estonia, Rep	11.0	12.9	21	16	X	X	23	X	X	X	X	X
Finland	9.5	10.3	12	5	28	9	5	11	X	X	113	8.9 a
France	10.6	9.8	16	7	34	13	9	9	X	X	143	9.1 a
Germany	12.4	11.6	21	6	40	16	7	5	X	X	X	9.1 a
Greece	8.6	9.8	34	10	64	23	10	5	X	X	151	4.8 a
Hungary	11.8	14.6	34	15	57	26	15	15	X	X	137	6.0 a
Iceland	7.0	7.0	12	5	22	9	X	X	X	X	X	8.3 a
Ireland	11.0	9.0	18	7	36	14	7	2	X	X	157	8.0 a
Italy	9.8	9.9	26	8	50	17	9	4	X	X	139	8.3 a
Latvia, Rep	11.4	13.2	21	14	X	X	26	X	X	X	X	X
Lithuania, Rep	8.9	11.3	22	13	X	X	20	X	X	X	X	X
Macedonia, former Yugoslav Rep	7.8	7.3	74	27	X	X	X	X	X	X	X	X
Moldova, Rep	10.2	10.5	37	25	X	X	36	X	X	X	X	X
Netherlands	8.3	8.8	12	7	22	11	8	10	X	X	114	8.7 a
Norway	10.0	10.9	12	8	23	11	8	3	X	X	120	8.4 a
Poland, Rep	8.3	10.5	27	15	70	24	15	11	X	X	131	5.1 a
Portugal	10.5	10.5	45	10	112	31	11	10	X	X	136	6.2 a
Romania	9.4	11.1	40	23	82	36	29	72	X	X	116	3.9 a
Russian Federation	9.1	12.4	28	21	X	X	31	X	X	X	X	X
Slovak Rep	10.6	10.6	24	12	X	X	18	X	X	X	X	X
Slovenia, Rep	10.2	10.8	22	8	X	X	X	X	X	X	X	X
Spain	8.3	9.0	21	7	57	16	9	5	X	X	141	6.5 a
Sweden	10.4	11.3	10	5	20	9	6	5	X	X	111	8.8 a
Switzerland	9.0	9.4	13	6	27	11	8	5	X	X	136	8.0 a
Ukraine	9.2	13.2	22	16	X	X	25	X	X	X	X	X
United Kingdom	11.7	11.4	17	7	27	14	8	8	X	X	130	6.6 a
Yugoslavia, Fed Rep	9.3	9.6	47	20	X	X	X	X	X	X	X	X

	Crude Death Rate (per 1,000 population)		Infant Mortality Rate (per 1,000 live births)		Under-5 Mortality Rate (per 1,000 live births)			Maternal Mortality Rate (per 100,000 live births)	Wasting (percentage of children under age 5)	Stunting (percentage of children under age 5)	Calories Available (as percentage of need)	Total Expenditure on Health (as percentage of GDP)
	1970-75	1990-95	1970-75	1990-95	1960	1980	1993	1980-92	1980-91	1980-91	1988-90	1990
NORTH & CENTRAL AMERICA	9.2	7.8	35	19								
Belize	7.3	4.8	52	33	X	X	X	X	X	X	X	X
Canada	7.4	7.6	16	7	33	13	8	5	X	X	122	9.9 a
Costa Rica	5.8	3.7	53	14	112	29	16	36	2	8	121	X
Cuba	6.6	6.8	38	12	50	26	10	39	1	X	135	X
Dominican Rep	9.9	5.6	94	42	152	94	48	X	1	19	102	3.7
El Salvador	10.9	7.1	99	46	210	120	60	X	5	30	102	5.9
Guatemala	13.4	7.7	95	48	205	136	73	200	1 a	58 a	103	3.7
Haiti	17.8	11.9	135	86	270	195	130	600	9 a	40 a	89	7.0
Honduras	13.4	6.1	104	43	203	100	56	220	2	34	98	4.5
Jamaica	8.2	6.2	42	14	76	39	13	120	3	9	114	X
Mexico	9.2	5.3	68	36	141	81	32	110	6	22	X	3.2
Nicaragua	12.7	6.8	100	52	209	143	72	X	1	22	99	8.6
Panama	7.5	5.3	43	25	104	31	20	60	6	22	98	X
Trinidad and Tobago	7.7	6.1	42	18	73	40	21	110	4 a	5 a	114	X
United States	9.2	8.8	18	9	30	15	10	8	X	X	138	13.3 a
SOUTH AMERICA	9.7	7.1	84	48								
Argentina	9.0	8.2	48	24	68	41	27	140	X	X	131	4.2
Bolivia	19.0	10.2	151	75	252	170	114	600	2 a	38 a	84	4.0
Brazil	9.7	7.5	91	58	181	93	63	200	2	16	114	4.2
Chile	8.9	5.7	69	16	138	35	17	35	1 a	10 a	102	4.7
Colombia	8.6	6.0	73	37	132	59	19	200	3	17	106	4.0
Ecuador	11.5	6.2	95	50	180	101	57	170	2	34	105	4.1
Guyana	10.3	7.1	79	48	126	88	X	X	X	X	X	X
Paraguay	7.2	5.5	55	38	90	61	34	300	0	17	116	2.8
Peru	12.8	6.9	110	64	236	130	62	300	1	37	87	3.2
Suriname	7.5	5.8	49	28	96	52	X	X	X	X	X	X
Uruguay	10.1	10.3	46	20	47	42	21	36	X	16	101	4.6
Venezuela	6.5	4.7	49	23	70	42	24	X	2	6	99	3.6
ASIA	11.4	8.4	98	65								
Afghanistan, Islamic State	26.0	21.8	194	163	360	280	257	640	X	X	72	X
Armenia	5.7	6.5	22	21	X	X	33	X	X	X	X	X
Azerbaijan	6.9	6.4	35	28	X	X	52	X	X	X	X	X
Bangladesh	20.8	11.7	140	108	247	211	122	600	16 a	65 a	88	3.2
Bhutan	22.6	15.3	178	124	324	249	197	1,310	4	56	128	X
Cambodia	22.5	14.3	181	116	217	330	181	500	X	X	96	X
China	6.3	7.2	61	44	209	65	43	95	4 a	32 a	112	3.5
Georgia, Rep	9.2	8.9	33	19	X	X	28	X	X	X	X	X
India	15.8	10.0	132	82	236	177	122	460	X	65 a	101	6.0
Indonesia	17.3	8.4	114	58	216	128	111	450	X	X	121	2.0
Iran, Islamic Rep	14.5	6.7	122	36	233	126	54	120	X	X	125	2.6
Iraq	14.6	6.7	96	58	171	83	71	120	3	22	128	X
Israel	7.1	6.9	23	9	39	19	9	3	X	X	125	4.2 a
Japan	6.6	7.6	12	4	40	11	6	11	X	X	125	6.8 a
Jordan	14.4	5.5	82	36	149	66	27	48 a	3	19	110	3.8
Kazakhstan, Rep	9.2	7.5	50	30	X	X	49	X	X	X	X	X
Korea, Dem People's Rep	8.3	5.3	47	24	120	43	32	41	X	X	121	X
Korea, Rep	8.9	6.2	38	11	124	18	9	26	X	X	120	6.6
Kuwait	5.0	2.1	43	18	128	35	13	6	3	12	X	X
Kyrgyz Rep	10.4	6.9	59	35	X	X	58	X	X	X	X	X
Lao People's Dem Rep	22.7	15.2	145	97	233	190	141	300	11	40	111	2.5
Lebanon	9.3	7.1	48	34	91	62	40	X	X	X	127	X
Malaysia	8.8	5.1	42	13	105	42	17	59	X	X	120	3.0
Mongolia	13.1	7.4	98	60	185	112	78	200	2 a	26 a	97	X
Myanmar	16.1	11.1	122	84	237	146	111	460	X	X	114	X
Nepal	21.1	13.3	153	99	279	177	128	830	14 a	69 a	100	4.5
Oman	20.0	4.8	145	30	300	95	29	X	X	X	X	X
Pakistan	17.7	9.3	140	91	221	151	137	500	9	50	99	3.4
Philippines	10.2	6.4	71	44	102	70	59	100	6	37	104	2.0
Saudi Arabia	16.9	4.7	105	29	292	90	38	41	X	X	120	4.8
Singapore	5.1	5.7	19	6	40	13	6	10	4 a	11 a	136	1.9
Sri Lanka	8.1	5.8	56	18	130	52	19	80	18	36	101	3.7
Syrian Arab Rep	12.1	5.8	88	39	201	73	39	140	X	X	126	2.1
Tajikistan, Rep	9.8	6.1	74	48	X	X	83	X	X	X	X	X
Thailand	9.3	6.1	65	37	146	61	33	50	6 a	22 a	103	5.0
Turkey	11.6	7.4	138	65	217	141	84	150	X	X	127	4.0
Turkmenistan, Rep	10.3	7.6	78	57	X	X	89	X	X	X	X	X
United Arab Emirates	9.9	2.7	57	19	240	64	21	X	X	X	X	X
Uzbekistan, Rep	9.2	6.2	63	41	X	X	66	X	X	X	X	X
Viet Nam	14.3	8.0	106	42	219	105	48	120	7	60	103	2.1
Yemen, Rep	22.1	15.5	184	119	X	X	X	X	X	X	X	X
OCEANIA	9.6	7.8	41	27								
Australia	8.5	7.4	17	7	24	13	8	3	X	X	124	8.6 a
Fiji	6.2	4.5	45	23	97	42	X	X	X	X	X	X
New Zealand	8.4	8.4	16	9	26	16	9	13	X	X	131	7.7 a
Papua New Guinea	17.1	10.7	100	68	248	95	95	900	X	X	114	4.4
Solomon Islands	9.2	4.4	61	27	X	X	X	X	X	X	X	X

Sources: United Nations Population Division, United Nations Children's Fund, and the World Bank.

Notes: a. Indicates data that refer to years or periods other than those specified in the column heading, that differ from the standard definition, or that refer to only part of a country.
0 = zero or less than half the unit of measure; X = not available.
For additional information, see Sources and Technical Notes.

| | Adult Female Literacy (percent) | | Adult Male Literacy (percent) | | Gross Primary School Enrollment (as percentage of age group) | | | | Births Attended by Trained Personnel (percent) | ORT{a} Use (percent) | Low-Birth-Weight Infants (percent) | Percentage of 1-Year-Olds Fully Immunized in 1993 Against: {b} | | | | Contraceptive Prevalence (percent) Any/Modern |
| | | | | | Female | | Male | | | | | | | | | |
	1970	1990	1970	1990	1960	1993	1960	1993	1990	1993	1990	TB	DPT	Polio	Measles	Method
WORLD	X	69	X	82	71	93 c	91	104 c								
AFRICA	X	40	X	62	31	66 c	53	79 c								
Algeria	12	41	39	68	37	97	55	112	15	27 c	9	87	73	73	69	47/43
Angola	7	29	16	56	14	79	30	86	15	48 c	19	53	30	28	47	X
Benin	4	19	17	42	15	46	39	92	45	28	X	88	75	72	67	9/1
Botswana	31	55	60	78	43	118	38	112	78	64	8	50	57	57	60	33/32
Burkina Faso	2	7	13	26	5	30	12	47	42	15	21 c	72	47	47	42	8/4
Burundi	7	19	30	45	10	62	33	75	19	49	X	75	63	64	61	9/1
Cameroon	18	44	47	70	37	81	77	94	64	84	13	41	33	33	33	16/4
Central African Rep	5	41	21	60	11	62	50	99	66	24 c	15	90	60	60	69	X
Chad	12	29	36	57	4	37	29	78	15	15 c	X	34	13	13	19	X
Congo	21	59	49	78	X	X	X	X	X	67 c	16	63	60	60	55	X
Cote d'Ivoire	6	24	25	44	22	58	62	80	50	16 c	14 c	53	50	50	52	3/1
Egypt	18	34	47	60	52	89	79	105	41	34	10	95	89	89	89	46/45
Equatorial Guinea	29	61	65	86	54	X	92	X	X	40 c	X	X	X	X	X	X
Eritrea	X	X	X	X	X	41	X	52	X	X	X	37	28	28	23	X
Ethiopia	9	21	24	41	3	19	9	26	14	68	16	46	28	28	22	4/3
Gabon	14	45	39	68	X	X	X	X	80	25 c	X	97	66	66	65	X
Gambia, The	7	20	28	48	10	57	21	81	X	51	X	X	X	X	X	X
Ghana	17	46	45	71	31	69	58	82	59	44 c	17	70	48	47	50	20/10
Guinea	6	18	25	45	9	30	27	61	25	82	21	76	55	55	57	X
Guinea-Bissau	17	36	43	63	15	43	35	77	27	26	20	92	45	45	46	X
Kenya	27	62	59	82	29	91	62	92	54	69 c	16	95	85	85	76	33/27
Lesotho	34	57	62	78	109	105	73	90	40	42	11	98	80	76	77	23/19
Liberia	7	18	27	49	13	X	40	X	58	15 c	X	X	X	X	X	6/6
Libya	11	54	57	84	18	110	70	110	76	80 c	X	91	91	91	89	X
Madagascar	43	73	56	88	57	72	74	75	56	26	10	82	64	64	52	17/5
Malawi	20	37	58	69	26	78	50	86	55	50	20	96	92	92	92	13/7
Mali	4	17	11	32	5	24	13	38	32	41	17	77	46	46	51	5/1
Mauritania	17	24	37	47	3	62	12	76	40	54 c	11	84	44	44	49	3/1
Mauritius	55	75	76	85	90	106	96	107	85	0	9	87	88	89	84	75/49
Morocco	9	26	33	52	28	63	69	90	31	14	9	91	86	86	83	42/36
Mozambique	6	18	26	52	43	51	71	69	25	60	20	66	49	49	62	X
Namibia	X	X	X	X	48	141	43	138	68	75	12	92	73	79	71	29/26
Niger	1	5	11	18	3	22	8	37	15	17	15	34	20	20	20	4/2
Nigeria	11	39	32	61	31	83	54	105	37	80	16	43	29	29	34	6/4
Rwanda	18	44	45	65	29	73	65	75	26	36	17	94	85	85	81	7/5
Senegal	7	19	24	39	18	50	37	66	46	27	11	69	52	52	46	X
Sierra Leone	5	14	22	40	15	39	30	57	25	60 c	17	79	63	63	67	X
Somalia	1	14	5	36	2	X	6	X	2 c	78 c	16	31 c	18 c	18 c	30 c	X
South Africa	68	79	72	80	X	110	X	111	X	X	X	66	79	79	85	50/48
Sudan	9	28	33	53	11	48	29	62	69	47	15	61	51	51	49	9/6
Swaziland	44	71	53	74	X	116	X	123	X	85 c	X	X	X	X	X	X
Tanzania	21	49	55	75	16	69	33	71	53	83 c	14	92	82	81	79	10/7
Togo	10	30	36	61	25	81	64	122	54	33	20	75	53	53	48	12/3
Tunisia	17	56	42	73	43	113	88	123	69	22	8	81	98	98	89	50/40
Uganda	22	44	53	70	18	X	39	X	38	45	X	99	73	74	73	5/3
Zaire	28	61	61	83	32	58	89	78	X	46	15	43	29	29	33	8/2
Zambia	32	65	64	82	40	81	61	87	51	90	13	88	64	62	62	15/9
Zimbabwe	58	77	75	88	65	114	82	123	70	82	14	79	69	69	73	43/36
EUROPE	X	97	X	99	107	102 c	107	102 c								
Albania	X	X	X	X	86	97	102	95	99	X	7	82	96	98	76	0
Austria	X	X	X	X	104	103	106	103	X	X	6	97	90	90	60	71/56
Belarus, Rep	X	96	X	99	X	95	X	96	X	X	X	94	86	91	96	X
Belgium	99	X	99	X	108	100	111	99	100	X	6	X	85	100	77	79/75
Bosnia and Herzegovina	X	X	X	X	X	X	X	X	X	X	X	X	X	X	X	X
Bulgaria	X	97	94	99	92	84	94	87	100	X	6	99	97	99	92	76/8
Croatia, Rep	X	95	X	99	X	87	X	87	X	X	X	X	X	X	X	X
Czech Rep	X	X	X	X	X	100	X	99	X	X	X	98	99	99	97	69/46
Denmark	X	X	X	X	103	99	103	98	100	X	6	X	88	95	81	78/72
Estonia, Rep	X	100	X	100	X	83	X	84	X	X	X	99	79	84	74	X
Finland	X	X	X	X	95	100	100	100	100	X	4	99	99	100	99	80/78
France	98	X	99	X	143	105	144	107	94	X	5	78	89	92	76	80/64
Germany	X	X	X	X	X	97	X	96	99	X	X	84	75	90	70	75/72
Greece	76	93	93	98	101	107	104	106	97	X	6	56	54	77	76	X
Hungary	98	98	98	X	100	95	103	95	99	X	9	99	100	100	100	73/62
Iceland	X	X	X	X	X	98	X	102	X	X	X	X	X	X	X	X
Ireland	X	X	X	X	112	106	107	105	X	X	4	X	65	63	78	X
Italy	99	X	99	X	109	99	112	98	X	X	5	6	95	98	50	78/32
Latvia, Rep	X	99	X	100	X	82	X	83	X	X	X	91	79	83	80	X
Lithuania, Rep	X	98	X	99	X	90	X	59	X	X	X	98	92	97	94	X
Macedonia, former Yugoslav Rep	X	X	X	X	X	87	X	88	X	X	X	87	70	94	96	X
Moldova, Rep	X	94	X	99	X	77	X	78	X	X	X	96	87	97	92	X
Netherlands	X	X	X	X	104	98	105	95	100	X	X	X	97	97	95	80/77
Norway	X	X	X	X	100	99	100	99	X	X	4	95	96	93	94	76/72
Poland, Rep	97	X	99	99	107	97	110	98	100	X	X	94	98	98	96	75/26
Portugal	65	X	78	89	129	127	132	131	90	X	5	92	94	93	99	66/33
Romania	X	95	96	98	95	84	101	85	100	X	7	99	98	92	91	57/14
Russian Federation	X	97	X	99	X	107	X	107	X	X	X	86	62	69	83	21/13
Slovak Rep	X	X	X	X	X	101	X	101	X	X	X	91	99	99	96	74/41
Slovenia, Rep	X	X	X	X	X	97	X	97	X	X	X	X	X	X	X	X
Spain	86	X	94	97	116	105	106	104	96	X	4	X	84	85	83	59/38
Sweden	X	X	X	X	96	100	95	100	100	X	5	14	99	99	95	78/71
Switzerland	X	X	X	X	118	90	118	88	99	X	5	X	89	95	83	71/65
Ukraine	X	97	X	99	X	59	X	74	X	X	X	93	88	89	90	X
United Kingdom	X	X	X	X	92	112	92	111	100	X	7	75	92	95	92	81/78
Yugoslavia, Fed Rep	X	89	X	X	X	73	X	72	X	X	X	X	X	X	X	55/12

	Adult Female Literacy (percent)		Adult Male Literacy (percent)		Gross Primary School Enrollment (as percentage of age group)				Births Attended by Trained Personnel (percent)	ORT{a} Use (percent)	Low-Birth-Weight Infants (percent)	Percentage of 1-Year-Olds Fully Immunized in 1993 Against: {b}				Contraceptive Prevalence (percent) Any/Modern
					Female		Male									
	1970	1990	1970	1990	1960	1993	1960	1993	1990	1993	1990	TB	DPT	Polio	Measles	Method
NORTH & CENTRAL AMERICA	X	X	X	X	97	103 c	100	108 c								
Belize	X	X	X	X	X	106	X	109	X	92	X	X	X	X	X	47/42
Canada	X	X	X	X	105	103	108	105	99	X	6	85	85	85	85	73/70
Costa Rica	87	89	88	94	92	105	94	106	93	78	6	97	86	87	82	75/65
Cuba	78	94	85	95	110	104	109	104	90	80 c	8	97	99	97	93	70/67
Dominican Rep	66	80	70	80	74	99	75	95	92	37	16	84	57	82	99	56/52
El Salvador	52	67	61	71	56	80	59	79	66	45	11	79	79	79	86	53/48
Guatemala	36	45	51	60	39	78	48	89	51	24	14	46	75	77	71	23/19
Haiti	20	38	28	44	39	51	50	54	20	20 c	15	48	30	30	24	10/9
Honduras	51	69	57	70	67	112	68	111	81	70	9	95	94	95	94	47/35
Jamaica	73	87	66	79	79	112	78	111	82	10	11	99	91	93	72	62/57
Mexico	70	85	80	90	75	110	80	114	77	87	12	97	94	95	93	53/45
Nicaragua	56	65	58	63	59	105	57	101	73	40	15	94	78	94	83	49/45
Panama	78	88	80	89	86	102	89	106	96	70	10	91	81	83	83	58/54
Trinidad and Tobago	89	X	95	98	108	94	111	94	98	75	10	X	81	78	87	53/44
United States	99	X	99	X	X	106	X	107	99	X	7	X	83	72	83	74/69
SOUTH AMERICA	X	X	X	X	67	109 c	71	106 c								
Argentina	92	96	93	96	99	107	99	108	87	80	8	96	79	80	95	X
Bolivia	46	71	71	88	43	97	70	106	55	63 c	12	84	81	83	81	45/18
Brazil	65	81	72	82	56	109	58	117	95	63 c	11	98	75	66	84	66/57
Chile	87	94	89	94	86	98	87	99	98	90	7	97	94	94	93	X
Colombia	79	89	82	90	74	120	74	118	94	40	10	94	83	85	94	66/55
Ecuador	70	86	79	90	75	124	82	125	84	89	11	99	76	79	73	53/42
Guyana	88	96	94	98	99	105	110	111	X	31 c	X	X	X	X	X	X
Paraguay	76	89	86	93	94	110	106	114	66	52	8	95	79	80	96	48/35
Peru	60	80	83	93	74	117	98	121	52	31 c	11	87	84	86	75	59/33
Suriname	76	89	88	94	106	125 c	113	129 c	X	63	X	X	X	X	X	X
Uruguay	93	97	92	96	117	108	117	109	96	96	8	99	88	88	80	X
Venezuela	73	89	80	91	99	96	98	94	69	80	9	82	69	75	63	49/38
ASIA	X	60	X	79	64	97 c	95	111 c								
Afghanistan, Islamic State	3	11	25	42	2	16	14	46	9	26 c	20	60	34	34	42	2/2
Armenia	X	97	X	99	X	93	X	87	X	X	X	88	85	92	93	X
Azerbaijan	X	96	X	99	X	87	X	91	X	X	X	94	71	70	84	X
Bangladesh	12	23	36	47	31	86	80	100	5	26	50	95	74	74	71	45/37
Bhutan	9	23	31	51	0	19 c	5	31 c	7	85	X	93	84	85	68	X
Cambodia	23	22	X	48	48	X	85	X	47	6 c	X	57	35	36	37	X
China	36	68	67	87	90	116	131	120	94	22	9	93	95	95	94	83/80
Georgia, Rep	X	98	X	99	X	X	X	X	X	X	X	63	45	45	58	X
India	18	34	48	62	44	91	83	113	33	37 c	33	92	90	90	82	41/36
Indonesia	44	75	69	88	58	112	78	116	32	78	14	94	89	93	90	50/47
Iran, Islamic Rep	X	56	X	74	28	101	59	109	70	85 c	9	99	99	99	96	65/45
Iraq	15	38	44	66	36	83	94	98	50	70 c	15	79	82	82	81	14/10
Israel	X	93	X	97	97	95	99	94	99	0	7	X	92	91	96	X
Japan	99	X	99	X	102	102	103	102	100	X	6	85	87	90	66	64/57
Jordan	34	73	73	91	X	X	X	X	87	53	7	X	95	95	88	35/27
Kazakhstan, Rep	X	96	X	99	X	86	X	86	X	X	X	93	76	69	91	X
Korea, Dem People's Rep	X	X	X	X	X	X	X	X	100	85	X	99	90	99	99	X
Korea, Rep	80	95	94	99	94	102	108	100	89	X	9	94	97	95	89	79/70
Kuwait	45	72	65	78	99	65	132	65	99	10 c	7	3	98	98	93	35/32
Kyrgyz Rep	X	96	X	99	X	X	X	X	X	X	X	96	88	91	94	X
Lao People's Dem Rep	18	39	45	65	20	92	43	123	X	55	18	42	25	26	46	X
Lebanon	73	88	87	94	105	114	112	117	45	45 c	10	4	87	87	65	53/23
Malaysia	44	74	69	87	79	93	108	93	87	47 c	10	99	89	89	80	48/31
Mongolia	52	73	75	87	80	100	80	95	99	65	10	84	80	79	84	X
Myanmar	60	75	84	88	53	106	60	110	57	37	16	80	73	73	71	17/14
Nepal	4	11	24	37	3	90	19	134	6	14	X	X	X	X	X	23/22
Oman	X	X	X	X	X	82	X	87	60	72	10	95	97	97	95	9/8
Pakistan	9	21	31	46	11	30	39	59	35	59 c	25	87	74	74	71	12/9
Philippines	83	93	86	94	93	109	98	112	53	59	15	90	88	89	87	40/25
Saudi Arabia	21	44	49	69	3	75	32	80	90	90	7	94	93	94	92	X
Singapore	61	83	87	95	101	103	120	106	100	X	7	99	89	92	89	X
Sri Lanka	71	85	88	93	95	105	107	106	94	76	25	86	91	91	89	62/40
Syrian Arab Rep	21	49	61	82	39	99	89	111	61	95 c	11	91	90	90	86	36/28
Tajikistan, Rep	X	96	X	99	X	88	X	91	X	X	X	69	82	74	97	X
Thailand	70	91	86	96	88	97	97	99	71	65	13	98	92	92	86	66/64
Turkey	40	69	73	90	58	96	90	104	77	20	8	63	79	79	74	63/34
Turkmenistan, Rep	X	97	X	99	X	X	X	X	X	X	X	98	99	99	98	X
United Arab Emirates	40	76	61	77	X	108	X	112	99	81 c	6	98	90	90	90	X
Uzbekistan, Rep	X	96	X	98	X	79	X	80	X	X	X	89	58	51	91	X
Viet Nam	65	87	82	95	74	108	103	114	95	52	17	94	91	91	93	53/38
Yemen, Rep	X	X	X	X	X	X	X	X	X	6 c	X	X	X	X	X	X
OCEANIA	X	93	X	96	109	110 c	110	112 c								
Australia	X	X	X	X	103	107	103	108	99	X	X	X	95	72	86	76/72
Fiji	67	86	79	92	X	129	X	130	X	100	X	X	X	X	X	X
New Zealand	X	X	X	X	106	101	110	102	99	X	6	20	81	68	82	70/62
Papua New Guinea	33	51	60	78	15	69	24	82	20	51	23	65	37	35	30	X
Solomon Islands	X	X	X	X	X	87	X	102	X	60	X	X	X	X	X	X

Sources: United Nations Children's Fund; United Nations Educational, Scientific and Cultural Organization; and the World Health Organization.

Notes: a. Oral Rehydration Therapy. b. Figures refer to BCG, diphtheria-pertussis-tetanus (third dose), oral poliovirus (third dose), and measles vaccine.
c. Most recent year with data (other than the year specified in the column heading), differing from the standard definition, or referring to only part of a country.
0 = zero or less than half the unit of measure; X = not available. For additional information, see Sources and Technical Notes.

Sources and Technical Notes

Data Table 8.1

Size and Growth of Population and Labor Force, 1950–2025

Sources: United Nations (U.N.) Population Division, *Annual Populations (The 1994 Revision)*, on diskette (U.N., New York, 1993); International Labour Office (ILO), *1995 World Labour Report* (ILO, Geneva, 1995).

Population refers to the midyear population. Most data are estimates based on population censuses and surveys. All projections are for the medium-case scenario. (See the following discussion.) The *average annual population change* takes into account the effects of international migration.

Many of the values in Data Tables 8.1–8.3 are estimated using demographic models based on several kinds of demographic parameters: a country's population size, age and sex distribution, fertility and mortality rates by age and sex groups, growth rates of urban and rural populations, and the levels of internal and international migration.

Information collected through recent population censuses and surveys is used to calculate or estimate these parameters, but accuracy varies. The United Nations Population Division compiles and evaluates census and survey results from all countries. These data are adjusted for overenumeration and underenumeration of certain age and sex groups (e.g., infants, female children, and young males), misreporting of age and sex distributions, and changes in definitions, when necessary. These adjustments incorporate data from civil registrations, population surveys, earlier censuses, and, when necessary, population models based on information from socioeconomically similar countries. (Because the figures have been adjusted, they are not strictly comparable to the official statistics compiled by the United Nations Statistical Office and published in the *Demographic Yearbook*.)

After the figures for population size and age/sex composition have been adjusted, these data are scaled to 1990. Similar estimates are made for each 5-year period between 1950 and 1990. Historical data are used when deemed accurate, also with adjustments and scaling. However, accurate historical data do not exist for many developing countries. In such cases, the Population Division uses available information and demographic models to estimate the main demographic parameters. Projections are based on estimates of the 1990 base-year population. Age- and sex-specific mortality rates are applied to the base-year population to determine the number of survivors at the end of each 5-year period. Births are projected by applying age-specific fertility

rates to the projected female population. Births are distributed by an assumed sex ratio, and the appropriate age- and sex-specific survival rates are applied. Future migration rates are also estimated on an age- and sex-specific basis. Combining future fertility, mortality, and migration rates yields the projected *population size*, *average annual population change*, and *average annual increment to the population*.

Assumptions about future mortality, fertility, and migration rates are made on a country-by-country basis and, when possible, are based on historical trends. Four scenarios of population growth (high, medium, low, and constant) are created by using different assumptions about these rates. For example, the medium-case scenario assumes medium levels of fertility—an assumption that may vary among countries. Refer to the source for further details. While projections may be of questionable quality, U.N. demographic models are based on surveys and censuses with well-understood qualities, which makes these data fairly reliable.

The labor force includes all people who produce economic goods and services. It includes all employed people (employers, the self-employed, salaried employees, wage earners, unpaid family workers, members of producer cooperatives, and members of the armed forces), and the unemployed.

The ILO determines the *average annual growth of the labor force* by multiplying the activity rates of age/sex groups (the economically active fraction of an age/sex group) by the number of people in those groups. Estimates of activity rates are based on information from national censuses and labor force surveys. The ILO adjusts national labor force statistics when necessary to conform to international definitions. The growth of age/sex groups is provided to the ILO by the United Nations Population Division.

Data Table 8.2

Trends in Births, Life Expectancy, Fertility, and Age Structure, 1970–95

Source: United Nations (U.N.) Population Division, *Demographic Indicators, 1950–2050 (The 1994 Revision)*, on diskette (U.N., New York, 1995).

The *crude birth rate* is derived by dividing the number of live births in a given year by the midyear population. This ratio is then multiplied by 1,000.

Life expectancy at birth is the average number of years that a newborn baby is expected to live if the age-specific mortality rates

effective at the year of birth apply throughout his or her lifetime.

The *total fertility rate* is an estimate of the number of children an average woman would have if current age-specific fertility rates remained constant during her reproductive years.

The *percentage of population in specific age groups* shows a country's age structure: 0–14, 15–65, and over 65 years. It is useful for inferring dependency, needs for education and employment, potential fertility, and other age-related factors. For additional details on data collection, estimation, and projection methods, refer to the sources or to the Technical Notes for Data Table 8.1.

Data Table 8.3

Mortality and Nutrition, 1970–95

Sources: Crude death rate and infant mortality rate data: United Nations (U.N.) Population Division, *Demographic Indicators 1950–2050 (The 1994 Revision)*, on diskette (U.N., New York, 1995). Under-5 mortality rate, maternal mortality rate, wasting, stunting, and per capita average calories available as a percentage of need: United Nations Children's Fund (UNICEF), *State of the World's Children 1995* (UNICEF, New York, 1995). Total expenditure on health as a percentage of GDP: The World Bank, *World Development Report 1993* (Oxford University Press, New York, 1993).

The *crude death rate* is derived by dividing the number of deaths in a given year by the midyear population and multiplying by 1,000.

The *infant mortality rate* is the probability of dying by exact age 1, multiplied by 1,000. The United Nations Population Division provides this cohort measure.

The *under-5 mortality rate* is the probability of dying by exact age 5, multiplied by 1,000. UNICEF provides this cohort measure, which is derived from *Child Mortality Since the 1960s—A Database for Developing Countries* (U.N., New York, 1992) and from infant mortality estimates provided by the United Nations Population Division. The mix is the result of a move from modeled estimates to estimates based on a periodically updated child mortality database. Nonetheless, this variable should not be compared to the United Nations Population Division's infant mortality rate, which is derived from population models—where otherwise not available.

The *maternal mortality rate* is the number of deaths from pregnancy- or childbirth-related causes per 100,000 live births. A maternal death is defined by the World Health Organization (WHO) as the death of a woman while pregnant or within 42 days of termination of pregnancy from any cause related to or aggravated by the pregnancy, including abortion. Most official maternal mortality rates are underestimated because of underreporting, incorrect classification, and unavailable cause of death information. In some countries, over 60 percent of women's deaths are registered without a specified cause. Maternal deaths are highest among women of ages 10–15 years, over 40 years, and in women with five or more children. Data are provided to UNICEF by WHO and refer to a single year between 1980 and 1990. Data for a few countries are outside the range of years indicated. The models used for deriving estimates of maternal mortality are relatively new. In addition, in many cases it is difficult to estimate the number of maternal deaths outside a hospital setting.

Wasting indicates current acute malnutrition and refers to the percentage of children under 5 whose weight-for-height is below minus 2 standard deviations from the median of the reference population, as defined by the U.S. National Center for Health Statistics (NCHS).

Stunting, an indicator of chronic undernutrition, refers to the percentage of children under 5 whose height-for-age is below minus 2 standard deviations from the median of the reference population. NCHS, among others, has found that healthy children in one country differ little, as a group, in terms of weight and height from healthy children in other countries. WHO has accepted the NCHS weight-for-age and weight-for-height standards; however, a number of countries still use local reference populations, and the estimates provided may utilize a number of sources, not solely or primarily the WHO database. Children with low weight-for-age are at a high risk of mortality. Data on wasting and stunting, provided to UNICEF by WHO, refer to a single year between 1980 and 1993. Data for wasting and stunting are generally good if derived from recent national household surveys, such as the Demographic and Health Surveys, but are not good if they are old or from local subnational studies.

The average *calories available (as percentage of need)* are calories from all food sources: domestic production, international trade, stock draw-downs, and foreign aid. The quantity of food available for human consumption, as estimated by the Food and Agriculture Organization of the United Nations (FAO), is the amount that reaches the consumer. The calories actually consumed may be lower than the figures shown, depending on how much is lost during home storage, preparation, and cooking, and how much is fed to pets and domestic animals or discarded. Estimates of daily caloric requirements vary for individual countries according to the population's age distribution and estimated level of activity.

Total expenditure on health (as percentage of GDP) includes both public and private expenditures based on official exchange rates. Expenditures are for all health-related activities including disease prevention, health promotion, rehabilitation, health care, family planning activities, nutrition activities, and food and emergency aid specifically for health. These estimates include spending on hospitals, health centers, and clinics. Estimates for member countries of the Organisation for Economic Co-Operation and Development (OECD) were provided to the World Bank by OECD, while estimates for other countries were derived from national sources, data from the International Monetary Fund on governmental expenditures, special World Bank studies, and the Social Security Division of the International Labour Office.

Data Table 8.4
Education and Child Health, 1970–93

Sources: Adult literacy: United Nations (U.N.) Educational Scientific and Cultural Organization (UNESCO), *Statistics on Adult Illiteracy: Preliminary Results of the 1994 Estimations and Projections* (UNESCO Division of Statistics, *Statistical Issues (STE-16),* (October 1994, Paris), and personal communication. Primary school enrollment: UNESCO, *Trends and Projections of Enrollment by Level of Education, by Age, and by Sex, 1960–2025* (as assessed in 1993) (UNESCO, Division of Statistics (BPE-94/WS.1), Paris, December 1993). Births attended by trained personnel, ORT use, low-birth-weight infants, and percentage of 1-year-olds fully immunized in 1991 against TB, DPT, polio, and measles: World Health Organization (WHO), *The World Health Report 1995* (WHO, Geneva, 1995). Contraceptive prevalence: United Nations Population Fund (UNFPA), *The State of World Population 1995* (UNFPA, New York, 1995).

Adult female and male literacy rates refer to the percentage of people over the age of 15 who can read and write. UNESCO recommends defining as illiterate "a person who cannot with understanding both read and write a short, simple statement about his or her everyday life." This concept is widely accepted, but its interpretation and application vary. It does not include people who, though familiar with the basics of reading and writing, do not have the skills to function at a reasonable level in their own society. Actual definitions of adult literacy are not strictly comparable among countries. Literacy data for 1990 were, for the majority of countries, projected from past census figures, using 1994 United Nations Population Division estimates of age group size and country populations.

The *gross primary school enrollment (as percentage of age group)* data for females and males are provided by UNESCO. These data entail two reference years, 1960 and 1993. UNESCO defines the primary school enrollment ratio as the total enrollment, regardless of age, divided by the population of the age group that corresponds to this specific level of education. Primary education is level 1 of the International Standard Classification of Education, and its principal function is to provide the basic elements of education, such as those provided by elementary and primary schools. Intercountry comparisons should be made cautiously, because regulations for this level are extremely flexible. Even intracountry time comparisons should be made with care, as 1960 and 1993 estimates could be based on different assumptions.

The *percentage of births attended by trained personnel* includes all health personnel accepted by national authorities as part of the health system. The types of personnel included vary by country. Some countries include traditional birth attendants and midwives; others, only doctors.

ORT (oral rehydration therapy) use refers to administration of oral rehydration salts or appropriate household solutions to children (under 5 years old) to combat diarrheal diseases leading to dehydration or malnutrition.

The *percentage of low-birth-weight infants* refers to all babies weighing less than 2,500 grams at birth. WHO has adopted the standard that healthy babies, regardless of race, should weigh more than 2,500 grams at birth. These data are provided by UNICEF and WHO, and refer to a single year between 1980 and 1990.

Immunization data show the *percentage of 1-year-olds fully immunized in 1993 against:* TB (tuberculosis), DPT (diphtheria), pertussis (whooping cough), and tetanus, third dose, polio (oral poliovirus, third dose), and measles. Almost all country data refer to the immunization situation in 1993.

Contraceptive prevalence is the level of current contraceptive use of any method/modern methods among couples in which the woman is of childbearing age. Among the contraceptive methods used are: sterilization, oral and injectable contraceptives, condoms, intrauterine devices, vaginal barriers (including diaphragms, cervical caps, and spermicides), and traditional methods (including rhythm, withdrawal, abstinence, douching, and folk remedies). Many of these surveys were national surveys or were conducted as part of the World Fertility Survey, Contraceptive Prevalence Survey, or Demographic and Health Survey. All data were collected after 1975, and 80 percent date from between 1987 and 1994.

9. Forests and Land Cover

Humans have left an impressive mark on the world's lands over the past several centuries. With the dramatic growth in world population, from roughly 1 billion in 1800 to well over 5 billion today, pressures on the land have greatly increased. The need for greater food production has led to a massive increase in cropland. By the early 1990s, almost 40 percent of Earth's land surface had been converted to cropland and permanent pasture. This conversion has occurred largely at the expense of forests and grassland.

Land transformation continues today, yet the extent of the change is still not known precisely. The most dramatic changes are occurring in developing countries, where it is estimated that in just three decades—1960 to 1990—fully one fifth of all natural tropical forest cover was lost. Although the forested area seems to have stabilized in developed countries, it is nevertheless only a portion of what was once there. For example, according to a recent estimate, only about 40 percent of Europe's estimated original forest cover remains (1).

Even as deforestation continues, however, understanding of the value of forests—as regulators of global climate, as repositories of species and potentially valuable new products, as conservators of soil and water resources—is growing rapidly. This increased knowledge has spawned a wide-ranging debate within a variety of international institutions, yet it is still not clear that the world community is ready to forcefully move toward managing forests on a sustainable basis.

STATE OF THE WORLD'S FORESTS

Global forest, woodland, and scrub cover declined by 2 percent during the 1980s, according to a 1995 report by the Food and Agriculture Organization of the United Nations (FAO). The report, "Forest Resources Assessment 1990: Global Synthesis," provides the first complete estimate of 1990 forest cover and changes in forest cover over the preceding decade (2). (See Figure 9.1.)

Although forest conversion is not an active problem in developed countries, forest degradation in these regions remains significant. In Europe, forests and woodlands are now probably less than half of their original extent. The world's few remaining stands of undisturbed temperate forests—in Canada, the United States, and elsewhere—continue to be harvested. Pollution threatens many forests and woodlands, including those in Europe and Russia.

In developing countries, deforestation rates within the tropics increased steadily from 1960 to 1990 (3).

This chapter discusses the complete results of the FAO Forest Resources Assessment 1990, which was published in several stages, culminating in the Synthesis report mentioned above. Earlier editions of the *World Resources* report (1992–93 and 1994–95) provided details on the FAO assessments of forests in tropical developing countries and temperate developed countries. This edition incorporates this information with new data from the Synthesis report on the state of global forests and of forests located in temperate developing countries (4). Each country is classified by FAO as either tropical, temperate developing, or temperate developed. (See Figure 9.2.)

In assessing the state of the world's forests, several characteristics warrant consideration, including the extent and distribution of forest cover, the condition of remaining wooded areas, and changes in the extent and condition of forests. These issues are discussed in more detail in the following sections.

Figure 9.1 Percent of Land Area Under Forest Cover, by Country, 1990

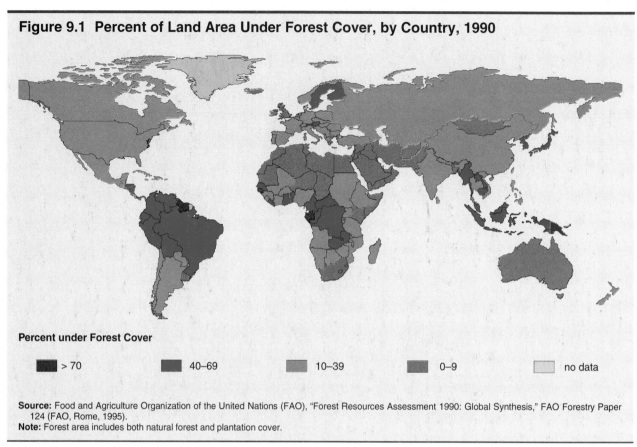

Percent under Forest Cover

> 70   40–69   10–39   0–9   no data

Source: Food and Agriculture Organization of the United Nations (FAO), "Forest Resources Assessment 1990: Global Synthesis," FAO Forestry Paper 124 (FAO, Rome, 1995).
Note: Forest area includes both natural forest and plantation cover.

Figure 9.2 FAO Forest Regions, by Country, 1990

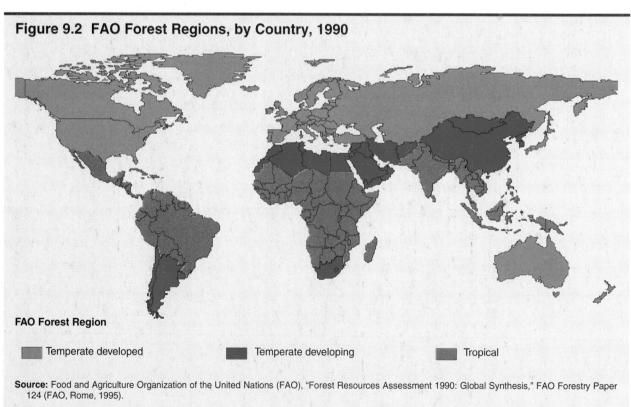

FAO Forest Region

Temperate developed   Temperate developing   Tropical

Source: Food and Agriculture Organization of the United Nations (FAO), "Forest Resources Assessment 1990: Global Synthesis," FAO Forestry Paper 124 (FAO, Rome, 1995).

Table 9.1 Summary Results from the 1990 FAO Assessment, by Region

| | Forest and Other Wooded Land | | Forest Area | | | | | |
| | | | Total Forest Area[a] | | Natural Forest | | Plantation Forest | |
Region	Extent, 1990 (000 ha)	Percent Change, 1981–90	Extent, 1990 (000 ha)	Percent Change, 1981–90	Extent, 1990 (000 ha)	Percent Change, 1981–90	Extent, 1990 (000 ha)	Percent Change, 1981–90
All tropical countries	**2,727,999**	–3.6	**1,792,030**	–7.1	**1,761,228**	**–8.1**	**30,802**	**146.7**
Tropical Africa	1,083,826	–2.2	529,818	–7.0	527,697	–7.2	2,121	75.0
Tropical Asia and Oceania	452,908	–4.3	338,025	–6.7	315,391	–11.1	22,634	188.7
Tropical Latin America and Caribbean	1,191,265	–4.5	924,187	–7.2	918,140	–7.5	6,047	76.0
All temperate developing countries	**328,665**	**0.8**	**217,884**	**2.4**	**180,240**	**–4.5**	**37,644**	**57.0**
Temperate Africa	52,850	–7.2	15,267	–4.2	12,972	–9.4	2,295	41.0
Temperate Asia and Oceania	207,362	5.3	159,334	5.2	125,704	–3.4	33,630	58.3
Temperate Latin America	68,453	–5.3	43,283	–4.7	41,564	–6.2	1,719	55.0
All temperate developed countries	**2,063,565**	**–0.0**	**1,432,457**	**X**	**X**	**X**	**X**	**X**
All temperate countries	**2,392,230**	**0.1**	**1,650,341**	**X**	**X**	**X**	**X**	**X**
World	**5,120,227**	**–1.9**	**3,442,369**	**X**	**X**	**X**	**X**	**X**

Source: Food and Agriculture Organization of the United Nations (FAO), "Forest Resources Assessment 1990: Global Synthesis," FAO Forestry Paper 124 (FAO, Rome, 1995), p. ix and Annex 1, pp. 18–21.
Notes:
a. Includes natural forests and plantation forests. Total forest is not strictly comparable between developed and developing nations, because of differences in classification. The term "forest" includes all lands with a minimum tree crown cover of 10 percent in developing regions and 20 percent in developed regions.
X = not available.

Changes in the Extent and Distribution of Global Forest Cover

In 1990, forest and other wooded land covered 5.1 billion hectares, about 40 percent of the Earth's land area. (See Table 9.1.) This figure includes 3.4 billion hectares of forest, which is defined by FAO as land with a minimum tree crown cover of 20 percent in developed countries and 10 percent in developing countries. Forests consist of natural forests, which are composed largely of native tree species, and plantation forests. The remaining 1.7 billion hectares consisted of other woody vegetation such as open woodland, scrubland and brushland, and areas under shifting cultivation (5).

The FAO definition of deforestation refers to the conversion of forest to other uses such as cropland and shifting cultivation. Forests that have been logged and left to regenerate are not included (6). By using that definition, the world's forest and other wooded land area declined by 2 percent—or 100 million hectares, an area about the size of Egypt—from 1980 to 1990.

Almost all of the change occurred in tropical countries, where forest and other wooded land area declined by 3.6 percent. (See Table 9.1 and Figure 9.3.)

In developed countries, forest and other wooded land area declined by less than 0.04 percent during that same period (7). This figure does not include changes in cover in the countries of the former Soviet Union, where two other studies report very different estimates suggesting that there was a net increase of either 10.6 million or 22.6 million hectares (8). (See Box 9.1.) If the lower estimate is included in the total for developed countries, the forest and other wooded land area increased slightly from 1980 to 1990.

The 2 percent global net loss of forest and other wooded land area masks more significant declines in natural forest cover alone. The FAO 1990 Assessment estimates natural forest change only for developing regions; data were not available for developed countries. In developing countries, natural forest cover declined 8 percent (163 million hectares) during the 1980s. On a net basis, however, total forest and other wooded

Figure 9.3 Estimated Annual Deforestation Rates, by Country, 1980–90

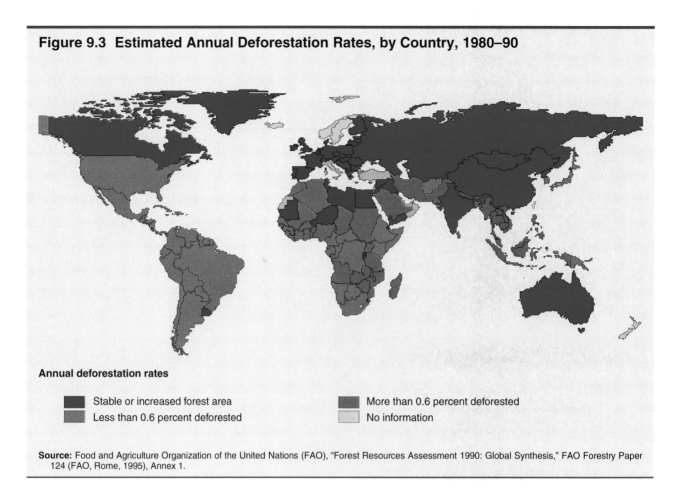

Annual deforestation rates

- Stable or increased forest area
- Less than 0.6 percent deforested
- More than 0.6 percent deforested
- No information

Source: Food and Agriculture Organization of the United Nations (FAO), "Forest Resources Assessment 1990: Global Synthesis," FAO Forestry Paper 124 (FAO, Rome, 1995), Annex 1.

land area in developing countries declined by only 98.7 million hectares. The loss of natural forest cover was offset by new plantation cover totaling 31.9 million hectares and by a 32.1-million-hectare increase in other wooded area, mostly former natural forests (9).

The FAO 1990 Assessment is based on data compiled from national inventory reports and adjusted to a common set of definitions. Many uncertainties about the reliability of the data exist, however. For details on the methodology and notes about data quality, refer to the Technical Note to Data Table 9.2.

Regional results from the FAO study are presented in the next two sections of this chapter. Unless otherwise stated, the source and notes for these data are presented in Data Table 9.2.

Temperate Forests

Globally, temperate forest and other wooded land covered 2.4 billion hectares in 1990. The total area increased from 1980 (by 0.1 percent) because of a significant increase in plantation area (10).

Most of this temperate cover is located in the sparsely populated northern forests of Canada and the Russian Federation, where forest cover increased slightly from 1980 to 1990. The United States, which had about 12 percent of the world's temperate forest and other wooded land in 1990, lost 1.1 percent of its total forest cover during the same period. This loss, totaling about 3.2 million hectares, was offset by net gains in forest and other wooded land within most other developed countries (11).

Because the northern forests of Russia and Canada are so extensive, the global figure for the change in temperate forest area masks declines of 4.5 percent in the smaller area of natural temperate forests in developing countries during the 1980s. In percentage terms, the steepest declines in temperate natural forest cover took place in regions where little historical cover remains. Both North Africa and the Middle East, which have undergone centuries of deforestation, lost 11 percent of their remaining natural forest cover during the 1980s. Natural forest cover in these regions now averages less than 1 percent of the total land area (12).

China's 162 million hectares of temperate forest are about half of the temperate forest and other wooded land located in all developing countries. China's total includes 102 million hectares of natural forest. Natural forest cover in China declined by just under 4 percent between 1980 and 1990 (13).

Although the temperate forest cover within developed regions appears to have stabilized, the forest area that remains within many countries is a fraction of what it was before human settlement. According to an unpublished 1995 study by the Institute for Sustainable Development (ISD), North America may have lost 20 percent of its original forest cover, and the countries of the former Soviet Union may have lost about 35 percent. These figures mask much higher estimated rates of loss within the nonboreal forests of these regions (14).

Original (prehistoric) forest cover is difficult to estimate because humans have long influenced vegetation patterns across landscapes by repeated burning (to create forage for livestock and game) and clearing of land for agricultural use. In addition, natural climate changes over recent centuries have to some extent altered the distribution of the world's forests and woodlands.

Crude estimates or indicators of historical forest loss can be derived by comparing the current distribution of forests with the *potential* forest area (areas where, given current rainfall, soil type, and related geophysical characteristics, forest vegetation could be expected to be supported in the absence of human activity). ISD compared FAO estimates of 1990 forest and other wooded land cover with mapped data on potential forest and woodland cover to produce the estimates of changes in historical forest cover discussed above (15).

Tropical Forests

Tropical forests (including plantations) make up just over half of the world's forest cover (about 1.8 billion hectares in 1990). The FAO 1990 Assessment revealed the extent and loss of six categories of tropical forest ecosystems. Rainforests are the most prevalent forest type in the tropics, covering almost 714 million hectares in 1990 (16). (For details on forest changes by ecological zone, see *World Resources 1994–95*, p. 132.)

According to FAO data, the world lost 450 million hectares of its tropical forest cover between 1960 and 1990. Asia lost almost one third of its tropical forest cover during that period, whereas Africa and Latin America each lost about 18 percent (17).

Although deforestation rates within all regions of the tropics have climbed steadily over the past three decades, the total area deforested per decade has declined in Asia and appears to have stabilized in Africa. This has not been the case in Latin America, where increasingly more forest area was converted to other uses—primarily agricultural—from 1960 to 1990 (18). These pressures are continuing. (See Box 9.2.)

During the 1980s, the world lost 8 percent of its natural tropical forest cover. Regional deforestation rates were highest in Asia, where 11 percent of this cover was lost between 1980 and 1990. (See Figure 9.4.) Globally, forests and other wooded areas in the tropics declined by a more modest 3.6 percent during the 1980s. (See Table 9.1.)

Table 9.2 Plantation Area Within Tropical and Temperate Developing Regions, 1980–90

Region	Plantation Area, 1980 (000 ha)	Plantation Area, 1990 (000 ha)	Annual Change (000 ha)	Percent Change, 1980–90	Degree to Which Plantation Establishment Offset Deforestation, 1980–90 (percent)
Africa	**2,839**	**4,416**	**158**	**55.5**	3.7
Tropical	1,212	2,121	91	75.0	2.2
Temperate	1,627	2,295	67	41.1	49.9
Asia and Oceania	**29,080**	**56,264**	**2,718**	**93.5**	**62.2**
Tropical	7,839	22,634	1,480	188.7	37.7
Temperate	21,241	33,630	1,239	58.3	278.4
Latin America and Caribbean	**4,543**	**7,765**	**322**	**70.9**	**4.2**
Tropical	3,435	6,047	261	76.0	3.5
Temperate	1,109	1,719	61	55.0	22.2
All tropical countries	**12,486**	**30,802**	**1,832**	**146.7**	**11.9**
All temperate developing countries	**23,977**	**37,644**	**1,367**	**57.0**	**160.0**
All developing countries	**36,462**	**68,445**	**3,198**	**87.7**	**19.6**

Source: Food and Agriculture Organization of the United Nations (FAO), "Forest Resources Assessment 1990: Global Synthesis," FAO Forestry Paper 124 (FAO, Rome, 1995), Annex 1, pp. 18–21.
Notes: Plantation cover for all temperate developed countries is included under "Total Forest Area" in Table 9.1. Totals may not add due to rounding.

Box 9.1 Are Russia's Forests Threatened?

The Russian Federation contains the largest forest area of any nation in the world—an estimated 750 million to 771 million hectares (1) (2) (3) (4). Yet the future of this resource is threatened by ineffective management policies, uncertain property rights, deteriorating forest conditions caused by pollution and other factors, the prospect of increasingly massive cutting in Siberia, and the possible cutting of remaining undisturbed forests in European Russia.

Russian forests represent a unique range of ecosystem types including more than 70 percent of the world's boreal forest—coniferous woodlands that survive some of the harshest winter climates on Earth (5). Siberian forests—the bulk of the national total—are a huge source of living carbon, which, if released through cutting and burning, could contribute significantly to global warming. Some of the largest tracts of pristine temperate forest remaining in the world are also found in the Russian Far East. These forests are home to highly endangered species such as the Amur leopard and the Siberian tiger (6) (7).

No data are available for Russia alone, but for the former Soviet Union as a whole it is estimated that forests and wooded land increased by about 3 percent (22.6 million hectares) between 1978 and 1988. Other estimates by the Food and Agriculture Organization of the United Nations (FAO) suggest that the increase may have been about half this total (8).

Although the total area of forests seems to be stable or increasing slightly, wide areas of Russia's forests appear to be degraded. During the 1930s and 1940s, the Soviets cut timber from the Ural region to support industrial growth, but paid little attention to replanting or other aspects of forest management (9). Today, most remaining wooded areas in the Ural region are heavily degraded, and only one quarter of the original forest cover remains in the southern portion of the Urals (10).

Pollution also contributes to forest degradation. For example, air pollution from huge nickel smelters in the Arctic city of Norilsk has killed 350,000 hectares of forest and has damaged another 140,000 hectares. The Norilsk plant emits 2.3 million metric tons of sulfur dioxide every year, five times the total sulfur emissions of Sweden (11). Industrial emissions are blamed for killing off 1 million hectares of forestland, whereas the 1986 Chernobyl nuclear power plant accident contaminated 4 million hectares of forests located within Russia, Belarus, and Ukraine (12) (13).

Logging is another significant source of degradation. About 65 percent of Siberia's forests are located in the permafrost zone and are particularly sensitive to disturbance. Logging exposes frozen soils to sunlight, and once the top layer of permafrost melts, these areas often convert to swamps, making reforestation impossible. Forests in mountain areas also are prone to soil erosion when tree cover is removed (14) (15).

PROSPECTS FOR SIBERIA

Since the 1950s, the government has made a concerted effort to develop Siberia's timber, mineral, oil, and gas resources. Planting has lagged well behind the rate of cutting, and plantation survival rates have been low (16). It is estimated that logging contributed to a 10 to 20 percent reduction in growing stock in Siberia from 1966 to 1988 (17).

Overall, Russian timber exports have declined in recent years, in part because of Russia's painful political and economic transition and a breakdown of supply and production links within the former Soviet Union. Furthermore, under the old regime there was relatively little investment in new processing and logging technologies (18).

A lack of infrastructure and outmoded extraction practices have been the primary limitations on cutting within Siberian forests. Only one third of the region is accessible to commercial logging operations (19). New road-building projects, however, primarily in the Russian Far East, could open up previously inaccessible forests to industrial logging for new Pacific markets. The proposed Nelma-Sukpai Road in the Russian Far East, for example, would feed a new log port at Nelma and bisect the roadless Samarga River watershed, opening up 800,000 hectares of untouched forests to logging (20).

In addition, Japanese, U.S., and other trading companies are seeking to expand their operations into new regions as the demand for raw logs begins to grow (21) (22) (23). The potential demand for lumber in Asian markets alone is huge. For example, the total amount of roundwood imported into China increased by almost 40 percent from 1973 to 1993 (24). FAO projects that both China and Japan will remain major net importers of wood products through 2010 and that the Russian Federation could be one of the top global suppliers (25).

Until recently, U.S. markets were closed to Russian roundwood imports because of concerns over the introduction of new pest species into U.S. forests. However, new rules were enacted by the U.S. Department of Agriculture in August 1995 lifting the ban on the import of raw logs. Under these regulations, Russian raw logs must be sterilized to kill pests prior to reaching U.S. shores. These regulations have been challenged by environmental groups as being too weak (26).

A 1989 agreement with the Hyundai Corporation of the Republic of Korea has led to large-scale clear-cutting in the Primorsky region, one of the most unique and biologically diverse temperate forests in the world (27) (28). Only a fraction of the proposed harvest has been realized, however, and Hyundai is now reportedly considering pulling out of the region (29).

These ventures often provide few benefits to local economies. The Hyundai venture employed Chinese loggers rather than local people to work the forest. In addition, multinational corporations prefer to export raw logs rather than process timber within the country, which would provide jobs in Siberian mills (30).

IS SUSTAINABLE DEVELOPMENT LIKELY?

International investors increasingly prefer trade agreements that rely on increased domestic production to boost Russian timber exports. These have included barter deals with companies in Japan, Korea, and the United States in which the companies provide logging equipment and technology to modernize the logging industry in exchange for timber. Modernization of the timber industry could improve efficiency within the forestry sector; in the past, up to half of all cut logs were left on the ground, and perhaps 20 percent of the extracted wood was wasted during the milling process (31). However, some environmentalists are worried that new technology will lead to increased logging of steep slopes and areas previously untouched because of the inefficiency of existing harvesting equipment (32).

It remains to be seen whether Russia will develop its timber industry in a sustainable fashion. Several recent events suggest otherwise. The 1993 Federal Forest Legislation failed to clarify property rights issues or establish mechanisms that would permit public participation and oversight of the leasing of forestland for logging and other management decisions (33) (34). Management agencies, strapped for resources and lacking clear jurisdiction over forest areas, find it difficult to balance conflicting environmental and economic development concerns (35) (36). In 1994, Roslesprom—the state-controlled holding company responsible for government shareholdings in the forest sector—released its 10-year forestry development plan, which called for more than a doubling of 1994 logging rates within European Russia, potentially jeopardizing some of the few remaining undisturbed forests within the region (37).

Russia's forests face an uncertain future. The absence of long-term conservation incentives, effective management policies, and clear property rights provides encouragement for uncontrolled timber exploitation. Increased demand for raw logs, coupled with declining supplies in other parts of the world, will continue to increase pressure to log Siberian and Russian Far Eastern forests. If, however, development proceeds cautiously, the government may have time to build the new institutional and legal structures that are needed to better manage this nation's vast and invaluable forest resources.

References and Notes

1. O.N. Krankina and R.K. Dixon, "Forest Management in Russia: Challenges and Opportunities in the Era of Perestroika," *Journal of Forestry,* Vol. 90, No. 6 (June 1992), p. 30.

2. Kit Prins and Alex Korotkov, "The Forest Sector of Economies in Transition in Central and Eastern Europe," *Unasylva,* Vol. 45, No. 179 (1994), p. 5.

3. Food and Agriculture Organization of the United Nations (FAO), "Forest Resources Assessment 1990: Global Synthesis," FAO Forestry Paper 124 (FAO, Rome, 1995), pp. 12–17.

4. Anjali Acharya, "Plundering the Boreal Forests," *World Watch* (May/June 1995), pp. 24–27.

5. Kullervo Kuusela, "The Boreal Forests: An Overview," *Unasylva,* Vol. 43, No. 170 (1990), p. 3.

6. World Wildlife Fund (WWF), *Conserving Russia's Biological Diversity* (WWF, Washington, D.C., 1994), pp. i, 120.

7. Antony Scott and David Gordon, "The Russian Timber Rush," *The Amicus Journal,* Vol. 14, No. 3 (Fall 1992), p. 15.

8. *Op. cit.* 3, p. 17.

9. *Op. cit.* 1, pp. 29–30.

10. *Op. cit.* 6, p. 65.

11. Roger Olsson, "The Taiga—Treasure or Trash?" *Taiga News,* No. 7 (October 1993), p. 6.

12. *Op. cit.* 1, p. 33.

13. *Op. cit.* 2, p. 8.

14. Anatoly Shvidenko and Sten Nilsson, "What Do We Know About the Siberian Forests?," *Ambio,* Vol. 23, No. 7 (1994), p. 396.

15. *Op. cit.* 7, p. 17.

16. *Op. cit.* 14, p. 401.

17. *Op. cit.* 14, p. 400.

18. D. Lipman, "The Russian Forest Industry during the Transitional Period," *Unasylva,* Vol. 45, No. 179 (1994), pp. 19–20.

19. *Op. cit.* 14, pp. 402–403.

20. "Forestry," *Russian Forest Update,* Vol. 5, No. 4 (April 1995), p. 11.

21. "Siberian Wood," in *The Taiga Trade—A Report on the Production, Consumption and Trade of Boreal Wood Products* (The Taiga Reserve Network, 1995), p. 57.

22. David Gordon and Sarah Lloyd, "Russia May Irradiate Logs for Export to U.S. Mills," *Earth Island Journal* (Winter 1994–95), n.p.

23. Divish Petrof, "Siberian Forests Under Threat," *The Ecologist,* Vol. 22, No. 6 (1992), pp. 268–269.

24. Food and Agriculture Organization of the United Nations (FAO), *FAOSTAT-PC,* on diskette (September 4, 1995).

25. Nikos Alexandratos, ed., *World Agriculture: Towards 2010, An FAO Study* (John Wiley and Sons, Chichester, U.K., and Food and Agriculture Organization of the United Nations, Rome, 1995), pp. 222–223.

26. "Lawsuit Challenges Pest Treatment of Log Imports," *The Register-Guard* (November 15, 1995, Eugene, Oregon), p. 2C.

27. David Gordon and Bill Pfeiffer, "Hyundai Hacking Siberia's Forests," *Earth Island Journal,* Vol. 7, No. 4 (Fall 1992), p. 18.

28. *Op. cit.* 6, pp. 117–120.

29. David Gordon, Co-Director, Siberian Forests Protection Project, Pacific Environment and Resources Center, Sausalito, California, 1995 (personal communication).

30. *Op. cit.* 7, pp. 16–17.

31. *Op. cit.* 23.

32. David Gordon, "U.S. Venture Must Protect Russian Taiga," *The Oregonian* (Wednesday, January 18, 1995), p. B09

33. *Op. cit.* 14, p. 403.

34. Alexei Grigoriev, "Russia's New Forestry Act: Leaving the Door Wide Open for Ruthless Exploitation," *Taiga News,* No. 5 (March 1993), p. 2.

35. *Op. cit.* 1, pp. 32–33.

36. *Op. cit.* 14, p. 403.

37. Alexei Grigoriev, "Development Program Launched," *Taiga News,* No. 12 (February 1995), pp. 4–5.

Box 9.2 For Sale: Suriname's Forests

One of the world's few remaining large blocks of pristine rainforest—covering 80 percent of the South American country of Suriname—is up for sale. Between 1993 and 1995, the Suriname government began negotiations with several Asian timber conglomerates to make 25 to 40 percent of the country's land area (7 million to 12 million hectares) available for logging. The government reportedly plans to sell off these forests at a fraction of their potential value, and likely at considerable future environmental and social cost, to provide a short-term fix for its desperate economic situation (1). As of December 1995, none of these agreements had been signed, however, and considerable controversy continues in the National Assembly.

In many areas of the world, forests shrink as growing rural populations move in to clear new land for agriculture. Such pressures do not seem significant in Suriname. The country's total population of about 400,000 is growing at a rate of less than 2 percent per year. (See Data Table 8.1.) Annual deforestation during the 1980s averaged

just 0.1 percent, one eighth of the average rate in the tropics during this period (2).

What threatens Suriname's forests is a fiscal crisis: with growing unemployment and a 500 percent annual inflation rate, the government is looking for new sources of income to offset declining revenues from its bauxite mining industry, currently the major source of export earnings. Timber consortiums from Malaysia, Indonesia, and China have offered investment packages of more than $500 million (almost equal to the country's total annual gross domestic product) for access to remote, untouched forests in the country's interior. Most of the profits would go to the companies. A recent World Resources Institute (WRI) study on forest policy in Suriname found that the government would lose between 41 and 86 percent of potential revenue from logging, depending on how honestly companies report their profits (3).

This offer of economic relief comes with hidden social and environmental costs. The forest areas proposed for logging concessions are inhabited by thou-

sands of indigenous people who make a subsistence living within the forest. Experience in other countries suggests that many of these people would lose their homes and their way of life if tribal lands are opened up to such development (4).

Suriname's forests are also home to a rich array of plant and animal species. A consortium of conservation and pharmaceutical interests is exploring Suriname's little-studied forests, looking for wild species useful in combating cancer and other diseases. Large-scale logging puts biodiversity at risk and forces the forfeiture of other benefits, including the potential for ecotourism development, a major source of revenue in nearby countries with rainforests, such as Costa Rica and Belize. Logging would give rise to other environmental costs, for example, the siltation of watersheds, changes in local climate, and soil erosion—a particular risk given that much of the forest concessions are located in areas with hilly terrains (5).

With suitable management practices on the part of the logging companies and careful planning on the part of the

Plantation Cover

Plantations partially compensate for the loss of forest resources from conversion and degradation, but they generally are less diverse and tend to be less resistant than natural forests to pests and natural disturbances (19). The FAO Synthesis report provides new figures on plantation establishment in temperate developing countries and revised data for tropical countries (20). No data were available for developed countries.

FAO estimates that during the 1980s total plantation cover almost doubled in developing countries. The total area planted, however, was only one fifth of the total area of natural forest converted to other uses (21). According to the FAO 1990 Assessment, plantation cover in developing countries increased by 88 percent from 1980 to 1990 (by 32 million hectares). Rates of plantation establishment during this period were much higher in tropical Asia and the Pacific (189 percent), Africa (75 percent), and Latin America and the Caribbean (76 percent) than in the temperate countries of these regions. (See Table 9.2.) As a result of a massive tree-planting program in China, afforestation actually exceeded deforestation in the 1980s in Asia and the Pacific.

Changes in Global Forest Condition

Forest condition can be measured in several ways, including the following:

- the degree of degradation, as measured by the extent of fragmentation and biomass removal;

- the degree of naturalness, or the extent to which recent human activity has modified forest structure and species composition;

- the intensity of forest management, which aims to develop the potential production of the site as fully as economic considerations permit; and

- the relative health of the tree species within a forest.

The condition of the world's forests has not been assessed comprehensively because degradation, naturalness, and forest health are difficult to observe and quantify on a regional and global scale. Forest degradation in the tropics is a significant concern because of the substantial losses of biomass and habitat fragmentation not reflected in estimates of deforestation (22). In temperate forests, the loss of remaining undisturbed areas, fragmentation, and the declining health of forest systems are major threats to forest condition (23) (24).

government, the social and economic costs could be reduced. Neither appear to be likely outcomes, however, if the proposed timber agreements go ahead as planned. Several of the timber consortiums bidding on concessions have poor environmental track records and a history of unscrupulous business practices (6). This has included, according to one report, bribing members of Suriname's parliament to secure their votes on current logging proposals (7). The government's land use planning laws are inadequate and are often ignored. In addition, Suriname's Forest Service currently lacks the capacity to adequately monitor loggers' compliance with new concession agreements. The government may actually lose money on the proposed deal once the costs of building a monitoring capacity are factored in (8).

Suriname's case illustrates the institutional, economic, and policy failures that leave forests vulnerable in a number of tropical and temperate countries of the world (9). Deforestation and tighter controls on cutting in some countries have limited the number of

new areas that national and international timber concerns can turn to for the continued supply of cheap wood. Forests in countries with ailing economies, weak institutions, and inadequate forest protection laws are particularly vulnerable to exploitation.

The WRI report recommends that Suriname revamp its forestry sector development policies to institute new bidding and taxation practices so that the country captures more of the return from the harvest of its timber. It suggests that the government impose controls to minimize environmental damage and social disruption from logging. These moves would yield higher long-term profits to the country and could also reduce the total area opened to timber exploitation (10).

International assistance is needed in the short term to implement these changes, to develop alternative sources of income from forest areas, and to meet Suriname's immediate cash needs (11). The solution to Suriname's forest crisis—should the government and the international donor community respond appropriately—could provide a

development model for other countries where cash-strapped governments are contemplating selling off their forests to meet short-term economic needs.

References and Notes

1. Nigel Sizer and Richard Rice, *Backs to the Wall in Suriname: Forest Policy in a Country in Crisis* (World Resources Institute, Washington, D.C., 1995), p. 1.

2. Food and Agriculture Organization of the United Nations (FAO), "Forest Resources Assessment 1990: Tropical Countries," FAO Forestry Paper 112 (FAO, Rome, 1993), Annex 1, Table 4.

3. *Op. cit.* 1, pp. 1, 15.

4. *Op. cit.* 1, pp. 6, 17

5. *Op. cit.* 1, pp. 6, 9, 21.

6. *Op. cit.* 1, pp. 1, 11.

7. Gary Lee, "Proposal to Log Suriname's Rain Forest Splits the Needy Nation," *The Washington Post* (May 13, 1995), p. A1.

8. *Op. cit.* 1, pp. 7–10.

9. *Op. cit.* 1.

10. *Op. cit.* 1, pp. 21–29.

11. *Op. cit.* 1, pp. 34–36.

Forest degradation affects species composition in a number of ways. It can endanger individual species survival, for example, through the unsustainable logging of mahogany trees in the tropics. Fragmentation of habitats can leave patches of forest that are too small to support populations of plants and animals dependent on forest ecosystems and can create a habitat for weedy species. Degradation can also produce adverse changes in local microclimates and can make native species more vulnerable to predators and disturbances such as drought and pest infestations (25).

Temperate Forests

Intensive logging practices, air pollution, fire suppression practices, and the spread of new pest species and diseases affect the condition and health of forests in many temperate regions. A 1992 report on temperate forests of the world found that undisturbed forests in North America, Chile, Eastern Europe and the Baltic countries, northern Russia, China, Australia, and parts of Nepal and Bhutan are especially at risk from logging (26). Declining areas of old-growth forest and fragmen-

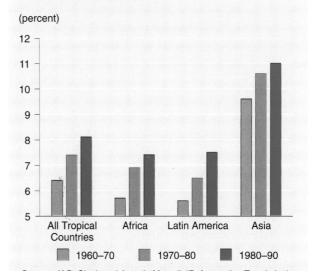

Figure 9.4 Estimated Rate of Tropical Deforestation, 1960–90

(percent)

Source: K.D. Singh and Antonio Marzoli, "Deforestation Trends in the Tropics: A Time Series Analysis," paper presented at the World Wildlife Fund Conference on the Potential Impact of Climate Change on Tropical Forests, San Juan, Puerto Rico, April 1995, pp. 8–9.

Figure 9.5 European Forests Either Moderately or Severely Defoliated or Dead, by Country, 1994

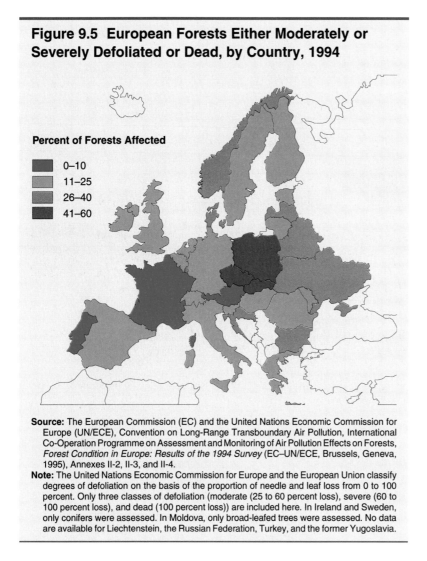

Percent of Forests Affected

- 0–10
- 11–25
- 26–40
- 41–60

Source: The European Commission (EC) and the United Nations Economic Commission for Europe (UN/ECE), Convention on Long-Range Transboundary Air Pollution, International Co-Operation Programme on Assessment and Monitoring of Air Pollution Effects on Forests, *Forest Condition in Europe: Results of the 1994 Survey* (EC–UN/ECE, Brussels, Geneva, 1995), Annexes II-2, II-3, and II-4.
Note: The United Nations Economic Commission for Europe and the European Union classify degrees of defoliation on the basis of the proportion of needle and leaf loss from 0 to 100 percent. Only three classes of defoliation (moderate (25 to 60 percent loss), severe (60 to 100 percent loss), and dead (100 percent loss)) are included here. In Ireland and Sweden, only conifers were assessed. In Moldova, only broad-leafed trees were assessed. No data are available for Liechtenstein, the Russian Federation, Turkey, and the former Yugoslavia.

tation of the remaining forest cover are also serious issues (27).

Most of the forests of Europe, North Africa, and the Middle East were cleared centuries ago. Similar patterns of deforestation have occurred within the past few hundred years in eastern North America, Australia, and New Zealand (28). In some cases, cleared areas have been abandoned so that forests can naturally regenerate or they have been converted to plantations, and forests are returning to these areas. In Europe, for example, forest area has been increasing since 1950. Forests also are returning along the East Coast of the United States (29) (30).

Most of the woodland areas in Europe and North America—with the exception of the northernmost boreal forests—consist of secondary growth and plantations. In unmanaged natural forests, periodic natural disturbances such as fire create a heterogeneous landscape with tree stands of different ages (31). Management practices such as fire suppression have helped create a

more uniform forest cover in many temperate countries, with wooded landscapes dominated by single-age stands. Plantation areas are also uniform, with only a handful of tree species (32). Although uniform forests are often high in timber productivity, they harbor less diversity than undisturbed forests and are generally more vulnerable to fire, windstorms, disease, and other naturally occurring events (33).

The regenerated forests of temperate regions are often quite different from the original forests. Studies of the reforested areas of the northeastern United States show changes in tree species composition and smaller tree sizes compared with those of the historical forest cover. There are also high numbers of introduced (exotic) plant species. Other changes include high proportions of threatened and endangered native species and repeated infestations of introduced tree pests (34) (35).

Forest health is also an issue in Europe. A 1994 assessment of forests in 29 countries found that 26.4 percent of the trees surveyed suffered from moderate to severe defoliation. (See Figure 9.5.) This continues a trend that has been observed through annual assessments since 1986. Although it is difficult to determine the cause of this damage, air pollution is believed to have played a significant role (36).

Tropical Forests

The FAO Synthesis report includes new estimates on how forest cover is changing within the tropics. That study, based on analyses of satellite imagery for two time periods and covering 10 percent of the entire tropical forest region, provides a picture of how forests in the region are being cleared or degraded (37).

FAO found that more than 7 percent of the 1980 forest area underwent change during the period from 1980 to 1990 (38). Of this change, less than half represented conversion to other land uses (42 percent to permanent agriculture and 3 percent to plantations), while more than half represented changes in forest "condition," ranging from moderate forms of degradation (loss of forest density or increase of "disturbance," such as long fallow shifting cultivation) to severe forms of degradation (reduction to shrublike formations or short fallow shifting cultivation). (See Figure 9.6.) The latter represent the most common degradation pattern, accounting for about one quarter of all forest cover changes. (In the FAO study, however, these severe forms of degradation are considered "deforestation to other wooded land.") Fragmentation represents the second most common form of degradation, representing some 12 percent of total forest change (39).

The FAO imagery study also sheds some light on the underlying causes of forest conversion and degradation in different tropical regions of the world. In Africa, almost 70 percent of forest changes in the 1980s occurred through the degradation of closed forest to open and fragmented forest and areas marked by shifting cultivation with short fallow periods (40). This suggests that rural population pressure—through subsistence farming, grazing, and wood extraction (for fuelwood and building materials)—is the primary agent behind forest change (41).

In Latin America, about 60 percent of forest change during the 1980s occurred because of the direct conversion of forest to other land types, primarily as a result of large-scale projects to settle and develop forested regions. In Asia, forest change occurred as a result of an increase in shifting cultivation and the establishment of agricultural and other plantations, suggesting that both rural population pressure and planned development are the primary agents of deforestation in this region (42) (43).

FOREST POLICY INSTRUMENTS

The often contentious debate at the Earth Summit—the 1992 United Nations Conference on Environment and Development (UNCED)—over forests and the resultant UNCED Forest Principles (44) have moved discussions on forest issues to a new level. Although no comprehensive, internationally binding agreement exists on the loss of global forest cover, consensus has been reached on several important issues, including the role of forests in maintaining biological diversity and climate, the criteria and indicators for sustainable forest management, the driving forces behind deforestation, and the need for cross-sectoral policy frameworks to confront deforestation.

The UNCED Conventions and Forests

Two major UNCED agreements, the Convention on Biological Diversity and the Framework Convention on Climate Change, recognize the broader role that forests play in the maintenance of global ecosystems. Scientists

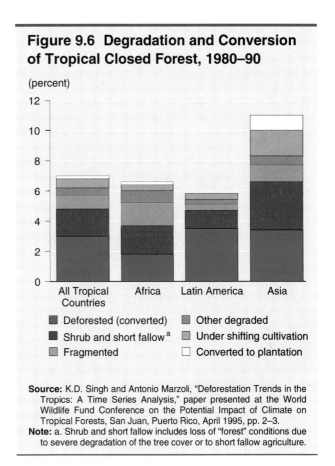

Figure 9.6 Degradation and Conversion of Tropical Closed Forest, 1980–90

(percent)

Legend: Deforested (converted), Shrub and short fallow[a], Fragmented, Other degraded, Under shifting cultivation, Converted to plantation

Source: K.D. Singh and Antonio Marzoli, "Deforestation Trends in the Tropics: A Time Series Analysis," paper presented at the World Wildlife Fund Conference on the Potential Impact of Climate on Tropical Forests, San Juan, Puerto Rico, April 1995, pp. 2–3.
Note: a. Shrub and short fallow includes loss of "forest" conditions due to severe degradation of the tree cover or to short fallow agriculture.

believe that forests—particularly moist tropical forests, which are experiencing the fastest rate of loss—harbor the majority of the world's species. Forests also are a significant repository of carbon, which can affect global climate change (45).

While there have been proposals to expand the Biodiversity Convention to address forest loss, there is still no consensus among the signatory countries. In the context of the Climate Change Convention, however, forests have become a factor in joint implementation agreements because of their important role in regulating Earth's temperature. When two countries enter into a joint implementation agreement, one country pays another to either reduce its emissions of greenhouse gases or to absorb them through sequestration; in this way, the two countries can then collectively claim the overall reduction. Joint implementation has not been achieved, however, nor have agreements on a scale large enough to reverse the trends of forest loss or global warming been reached. (See Chapter 14, "Atmosphere and Climate.") Under both of these Conventions, nations are likely to continue to develop potential mechanisms to support forest-related activities over the next several years.

Criteria and Indicators for Sustainable Management of Forests

Perhaps the most significant areas of agreement regarding forests since the Earth Summit have been on the definition of the criteria and indicators for sustainable forest management. In 1990, the International Tropical Timber Organization (ITTO) became the first intergovernmental body to produce criteria and guidelines for the sustainable management of tropical forests. Following the renegotiation of the International Tropical Timber Agreement (ITTA) in 1994, timber-producing countries were able to extract an agreement from timber-consuming countries that they, too, would comply with ITTO's Target 2000, the year by which all forest products should come from sustainably managed forests. (See section on Trade and Forests, below.)

Three separate processes that emerged after the ITTA negotiation include the Pan-European Helsinki process, the non-European Montreal process (both of which focus on boreal and temperate forests), and the Tarapoto declaration of the Amazon Treaty Organization regarding Amazonian forests. Each covers a broad range of general guidelines for the sustainable management of forests. Similar exercises are also being planned under the aegis of FAO for Central America and Africa (46) (47).

Despite these advances, it remains to be seen whether the ITTO producer countries can be convinced that the timber-consuming developed countries are really willing (and able) to apply these criteria to their domestic forests and not just to tropical forests.

World Commission on Forests and Sustainable Development

The independent World Commission on Forests and Sustainable Development (WCFSD) received a formal mandate from the InterAction Council of Former Heads of State and Government. WCFSD does not plan to produce a specific international instrument. Rather, it hopes to generate consensus and resolve conflict on the dual role of forests in preserving natural habitats and promoting socioeconomic development; on the linkages between data, science, and policy; and on the importance of cooperation between developed and developing countries in determining priorities on forest issues (48) (49).

A number of working panels are being created to supplement WCFSD. These panels will address the sustainable and equitable use and management of forest resources; trade and the environment; and financial mechanisms, international agreements, and the roles of international institutions (50) (51).

Intergovernmental Panel on Forests

The WCFSD process is designed to be complementary to that of the Open-End Ad Hoc Intergovernmental Panel on Forests (IPF), approved during the third session of the United Nations Commission on Sustainable Development. The Commission on Sustainable Development created IPF to generate consensus and propose actions for the implementation of UNCED's forest-related agreements at the national and international levels. Such agreements could cover a multitude of issues, including cross-sectoral linkages; the transfer of financial and technological resources through international cooperation; scientific research, global forest assessment, and criteria and indicators for sustainable forest management; trade and environment in relation to forest products and services; and the roles of international organizations, multilateral institutions, and legal instruments (52).

IPF has a challenging task ahead; its scope of work is broad and complex and is to be completed on a tight time line over the course of four meetings between late 1995 and mid-1997. Nonetheless, as the highest international body to ever address forest issues, IPF's recommendations are likely to set the agenda for forest policy and international development aid for the next several years (53).

Trade and Forests

Several independent initiatives have been launched by governments, nongovernmental organizations (NGOs), and private-sector forest proponents—sometimes in concert with one another—to influence markets for sustainably produced forest goods and services.

CITES Monitoring and Protection

The Convention on International Trade in Endangered Species of Wild Fauna and Flora (CITES), which became effective in 1975 and now has 128 member countries, is a binding international treaty regulating trade in wildlife and plants to help protect species threatened with extinction.

Commercially important timber species were not listed in CITES until 1992, when international trade in Brazilian rosewood (*Dalbergia nigra*) was banned (54). Trade in more than a dozen other timber species is either banned or strictly controlled (55).

In 1994, a contentious battle erupted between the signatory countries over the proposed listing of mahogany (*Swietenia macrophylla*). The proposal was defeated and further resulted in the delisting of several African timber species (56). As a result, the Timber Working

Group was established to examine the relationship of CITES to the international timber trade (57).

It remains to be seen whether CITES can be used to more actively monitor timber species or whether it will be limited to implementation only after there is scientific consensus that a botanical species is indeed threatened with extinction.

International Tropical Timber Agreement

The International Tropical Timber Agreement (ITTA) of 1983 is a binding agreement governing the trade of tropical timbers and, by extension, tropical forests.

When the ITTA was renegotiated in 1994 after it expired, many criticized the secretariat for focusing too much on individual projects of questionable quality rather than on issues relevant to the broader trade, environment, and policy reform goals of the agreement. Furthermore, many argued that a renegotiated ITTA should include binding requirements for reaching Target 2000 and significant new funding to assist producer countries in achieving Target 2000 and should be expanded to include all timbers, including temperate and boreal sources (58). In the end, the agreement's scope was not expanded and Target 2000 remained a nonbinding agreement. The consuming countries did, however, commit themselves to a parallel but separate effort for the sustainable management of temperate and boreal forests (see Criteria and Indicators, above). Unfortunately, the new agreement has yet to be ratified by a sufficient number of member countries. Major unresolved issues include the agreement's continuing "double standard" problem, since it has not expanded its scope to all forests; the ability of ITTO's project approach to grapple with needed policy reforms; and, ultimately, ITTO's ability to promote sustainability within the tropical timber trade (59).

Forest Stewardship Council

Given the frustrations and spotty performance of intergovernmental agreements, several concerned NGOs and private-sector groups have launched voluntary efforts to harness market forces to promote trade in forest products from well-managed forests. However, many critics seriously question the ability of timber certification programs to effect more sustainable practices, largely because the market has not proved willing to bear the additional costs (60). One prominent initiative that has emerged in this area is the Forest Stewardship Council (FSC).

FSC is an assembly of NGOs, industry representatives, scientists, and indigenous peoples established in 1993 to promote the environmentally appropriate, socially beneficial, and economically viable management of the world's forests. It is governed by a nine-member board of environmental, social, and economic representatives elected by the membership. In 1994, FSC adopted a set of principles and criteria for the sustainable management of forests, as well as guidelines on how to conduct field inspections and verify the chain of custody of certified forest products as they travel from the forest to the store shelf (61).

In 1995, FSC developed a rigorous framework for the evaluation, accreditation, and monitoring of organizations that issue certification claims in the marketplace (62), as well as guidelines for developing regional forest management standards and a protocol for endorsing national certification initiatives. National initiatives based on the FSC guidelines are under development in more than 12 countries, ranging from Brazil to Sweden to Indonesia (63). Although FSC had 4 years of extensive consultations worldwide, some industry associations and governments criticize it as being anti-industry and having overly inflexible principles as well as being too driven by a "green" agenda and too dependent on unproven auditors (64). Nonetheless, as the first international program endorsed by major retailers to ensure public confidence in marketing claims (particularly in Western Europe), it will set the tone for how sustainability is measured in forestry operations and in the verification of "green" claims.

Trade and Noneconomic Values of Forests

A vexing question for all trade initiatives is whether they can shift the trade and environment debate away from inherent conflicts and toward natural complementarity. Trade liberalization and environmental objectives share a common goal—to use available resources more efficiently (65). To the extent that regulatory interventions can pull ecological, social, and cultural values into the marketplace, such actions will promote more efficient resource use. Conversely, trade liberalization measures that inhibit the recognition of these values in the marketplace and that in effect pass the associated costs on to society are undesirable. Just as environmental objectives should be pursued with the least restrictive impacts on trade possible, trade liberalization objectives that result in the least amount of environmental damage should also be pursued (66). The success of these trade instruments also depends on their ability to capture the incremental costs of one country delivering environmental benefits to others, as well as on the development of mechanisms that reconcile economic development with global environmental goals between countries (67).

References and Notes

1. Bruce A. Wilcox and Kristin Duin, "Global Forest Assessment: Current (1990)—Potential Forest Cover Difference as a Global Environmental Indicator," draft report (Institute for Sustainable Development, Menlo Park, California, September 1995), Table 1.

2. Food and Agriculture Organization of the United Nations (FAO), "Forest Resources Assessment 1990: Global Synthesis," FAO Forestry Paper 124 (FAO, Rome, 1995), p. ix.

3. K.D. Singh and Antonio Marzoli, "Deforestation Trends in the Tropics: A Time Series Analysis," paper presented at the World Wildlife Fund Conference on Potential Impact of Climate Change on Tropical Forests, San Juan, Puerto Rico, April 1995, pp. 8–9.

4. All developed countries, including the countries of the former Soviet Union, Israel, and Australia, are considered *temperate developed* countries. *Temperate developing* countries include all countries of North Africa and the Middle East, Lesotho, Swaziland, South Africa, China, Korea, Mongolia, Argentina, Uruguay, and Chile. All other countries are *tropical* countries.

5. *Op. cit.* 2, p. 7.

6. *Op. cit.* 2, Annex 2, p. 43.

7. *Op. cit.* 2, Annex 1, Table 4, p. 17.

8. *Op. cit.* 2, p. 17.

9. *Op. cit.* 2, p. 8 and Annex 1, pp. 17–21.

10. *Op. cit.* 2, Annex 1, Table 4, pp. 19–21.

11. *Op. cit.* 2, Annex 1, p. 17.

12. *Op. cit.* 2, p. 21.

13. *Op. cit.* 2, Annex 1, p. 20.

14. *Op. cit.* 1.

15. *Op. cit.* 1, pp. 1–2.

16. World Resources Institute in collaboration with the United Nations Environment Programme and the United Nations Development Programme, *World Resources 1994–95* (Oxford University Press, New York, 1994) p. 308.

17. *Op. cit.* 3, p. 8.

18. *Op. cit.* 3, p. 9.

19. Reed Noss and Allen Cooperrider, *Saving Nature's Legacy: Protecting and Restoring Biodiversity* (Island Press, Washington, D.C., 1994), pp. 190–192, 197.

20. FAO's current country-level data for plantations have been adjusted downward to include estimated survival rates. See Sources and Technical Notes for Data Table 9.2.

21. *Op. cit.* 2, Annex 1, Table 4, pp. 17–21.

22. Food and Agriculture Organization of the United Nations (FAO), "Forest Resources Assessment 1990: Tropical Countries," FAO Forestry Paper 112 (FAO, Rome, 1993), pp. 52–53.

23. Nigel Dudley, *Forests in Trouble: A Review of the Status of Temperate Forests Worldwide* (World Wide Fund for Nature, Gland, Switzerland, 1992), pp. 67, 159.

24. William Alverson, Walter Kuhlmann, and Donald Waller, *Wild Forests: Conservation Biology and Public Policy* (Island Press, Washington, D.C., 1994), pp. 92–93.

25. *Ibid.*, p. 93.

26. *Op. cit.* 23, p. 11.

27. Jerry Franklin, "Structural and Functional Diversity in Temperate Forests," in *Biodiversity*, E.O. Wilson, ed. (National Academy Press, Washington, D.C., 1988), pp. 166–167.

28. *Op. cit.* 23, p. 22.

29. Alexandre Korotkov and Tim Peck, "Forest Resources of the Industrialized Countries: An ECE/FAO Assessment," *Unasylva*, Vol. 44, No. 174 (1993), pp. 23–24.

30. Bill McKibben, "An Explosion of Green," *The Atlantic Monthly*, Vol. 275, No. 4 (April 1995), p. 63.

31. *Op. cit.* 19, p. 179.

32. *Op. cit.* 19, p. 192.

33. *Op. cit.* 19, pp. 195, 197.

34. Stephen Trombulak, "The Northern Forest: Conservation Biology, Public Policy, and a Failure of Regional Planning," *Endangered Species Update*, Vol. 11, No. 12 (1994), pp. 7–8.

35. *Op. cit.* 30, p. 70.

36. The European Commission (EC) and the United Nations Economic Commission for Europe (UN/ECE), Convention on Long-Range Transboundary Air Pollution, International Co-Operative Programme on Assessment and Monitoring of Air Pollution Effects on Forests, *Forest Condition in Europe: Results of the 1994 Survey* (EC–UN/ECE, Brussels, Geneva, 1995), pp. 21, 102.

37. The satellite scenes used were obtained on various dates because of the difficulty in obtaining quality, cloud-free images for large regions for any one point in time. Images of each sample site were taken roughly 10 years apart, with the latest scene taken close to 1990.

38. The results produced by the Forest Resources Assessment 1990 Project consisted of transition matrices of nine-by-nine land cover classes, which allowed a detailed analysis of land cover changes. The changes are grouped into seven main categories: "deforestation to other land cover" (conversion to permanent agriculture or pasture, with total loss of woody biomass), "deforestation to other wooded land" (loss of "forest" condition due to severe degradation of the tree cover or to short fallow agriculture), "fragmentation" (from continuous forest cover to isolated forest patches), "degradation" (reduction of forest canopy from

closed to open), "forest affected by shifting cultivation" (presence of long fallow shifting cultivation), "amelioration" (increase of forest density or decrease of disturbance) and "conversion to plantation." Apart from the first and last change categories, which represent land use conversions, all others can be considered changes in forest condition.

39. K.D. Singh, Project Coordinator, Forest Resources Assessment Project, Food and Agriculture Organization of the United Nations, Rome, 1995 (personal communication).

40. *Ibid.*

41. *Op. cit.* 2, p. 38.

42. *Op. cit.* 39.

43. *Op. cit.* 2, pp. 38–39.

44. "Non-Legally Binding Authoritative Statement of Principles on the Management, Conservation and Sustainable Development of All Types of Forests," United Nations Conference on Environment and Development, Rio de Janeiro, Brazil, June 1992.

45. Nigel Sizer, "Opportunities to Save and Sustainably Use the World's Forests Through International Cooperation," WRI Issues and Ideas (World Resources Institute, Washington, D.C., 1994), p. 7.

46. *Ibid.*, pp. 8–10.

47. Pro Tempore Secretariat, Amazon Cooperation Treaty, "Tarapoto Proposal on Criteria and Indicators of Sustainability for the Amazon Forests," (Amazon Treaty Organization, Lima, Peru, February 25, 1995).

48. World Commission on Forests and Sustainable Development, "Note by the Secretariat," First Meeting of the World Commission on Forests and Sustainable Development, Woods Hole Research Center, Woods Hole, Massachusetts, June 1995.

49. World Commission on Forests and Sustainable Development, "Forests and Sustainable Development: An Issues Paper," First Meeting of the World Commission on Forests and Sustainable Development, Woods Hole Research Center, Woods Hole, Massachusetts, June 1995.

50. R.A. Houghton, The Woods Hole Research Center, Woods Hole, Massachusetts, June 1995 (personal communication).

51. Woods Hole Research Center, "World Commission on Forests Concludes Its First Meeting" (Woods Hole Research Center, Woods Hole, Massachusetts, 1995), p. x.

52. "Report of the First Session of the CSD Intergovernmental Panel on Forests: 11–15 September 1995," *Earth Negotiations Bulletin*, Vol. 13, No. 3 (September 18, 1995), pp. 1–12.

53. "Rome Statement on Forestry," First Ministerial Meeting on Forestry, Food and Agriculture Organization of the United Nations, Rome, March 1995.

54. Convention on International Trade in Endangered Species (CITES) Secretariat, "The CITES Timber Working Group: An Opportunity to Resolve Issues Related to Listing Timber Species in the CITES Appendices," *Tropical Forest Update,* Vol. 5, No. 3 (September 1995), p. 4.

55. International Tropical Timber Organization (ITTO), "What Is CITES: An International Convention Explained," *Tropical Forest Update,* Vol. 5, No. 3 (September 1995), p. 3.

56. Morten Bjorner, "Two Views on the Role of CITES: From the Timber Trade," *Tropical Forest Update,* Vol. 5, No. 3 (September 1995), p. 5.

57. *Op. cit.* 54.

58. Richard G. Tarasofsky, "Developing the Current International Forests Regime: Some Legal and Policy Issues," discussion paper, World Conservation Union (IUCN), IUCN Environmental Law Centre, Bonn, Germany, April 1995, p. 7.

59. Nigel Sizer, "Opportunities to Save and Sustainably Use the World's Forests Through International Cooperation," WRI Issues and Ideas (World Resources Institute, Washington, D.C., 1994), p. 6.

60. Bruce Cabarle *et al.,* "Certification Accreditation: The Need for Credible Claims," *Journal of Forestry,* Vol. 93, No. 4 (April 1995), pp. 12–16.

61. Forest Stewardship Council (FSC), "FSC Principles and Criteria for Natural Forest Management" and "FSC Guidelines for Certifiers" (FSC, Oaxaca, Mexico, 1994).

62. Forest Stewardship Council (FSC), "FSC Manual for Evaluation and Accreditation of Certification Bodies" (FSC, Oaxaca, Mexico, 1994).

63. *Op. cit.* 58.

64. Bruce Cabarle, Chair of Forest Stewardship Council and Director of Forestry and Land Use, World Resources Institute, Washington, D.C., 1995 (personal communication).

65. Robert Repetto, "Trade and Environment Policies: Achieving Complementarities and Avoiding Conflicts," *World Resources Institute Issues and Ideas* (World Resources Institute, Washington, D.C., 1993), p. 1.

66. *Ibid.*

67. Uttam Dabholkar, Principal Officer, Global Environment Facility, The World Bank, Washington, D.C., 1995 (personal communication).

Data Table 9.1 Land Area and Use, 1981–93

	Land Area (000 hectares)	Population Density 1995 (per 1,000 hectares)	Domesticated Land as a % of Land Area {a}	Cropland 1991-93	Cropland % Change Since 1981-83	Permanent Pasture 1991-93	Permanent Pasture % Change Since 1981-83	Forest and Woodland 1991-93	Forest and Woodland % Change Since 1981-83	Other Land 1991-93	Other Land % Change Since 1981-83
WORLD {b}	**13,098,404**	**436**	**38**	**1,450,834**	**1.3**	**3,364,537**	**3.6**	**4,168,956**	**(3.6)**	**4,114,077**	**(0.5)**
AFRICA	**2,963,611**	**246**	**35**	**187,357**	**5.8**	**853,049**	**1.2**	**760,576**	**(3.1)**	**1,162,630**	**(0.3)**
Algeria	238,174	117	16	7,938	7.0	30,752	(3.2)	3,969	(9.5)	195,516	(0.5)
Angola	124,670	89	26	3,483	2.5	29,000	0.0	51,917	(3.1)	40,270	(3.9)
Benin	11,062	489	21	1,877	4.1	442	0.0	3,407	(12.0)	5,337	(7.3)
Botswana	56,673	26	46	420	5.0	25,600	0.0	26,500	0.0	4,153	0.5
Burkina Faso	27,360	377	35	3,564	23.5	6,000	0.0	13,800	0.0	3,996	17.0
Burundi	2,568	2,489	89	1,357	3.9	915	0.5	85	0.0	211	26.3
Cameroon	46,540	284	19	7,033	1.2	2,000	0.0	35,900	0.0	1,607	5.2
Central African Rep	62,298	53	8	2,015	2.9	3,000	0.0	46,700	0.0	10,583	0.5
Chad	125,920	51	38	3,239	2.8	45,000	0.0	32,400	0.0	45,281	0.2
Congo	34,150	76	30	170	11.6	10,000	0.0	21,120	(0.9)	2,860	(6.4)
Cote d'Ivoire	31,800	448	53	3,703	16.7	13,000	0.0	7,080	(24.4)	8,017	(21.9)
Egypt	99,545	632	8	2,760	11.7	4,934	12.7	31	0.0	91,820	0.9
Equatorial Guinea	2,805	143	12	230	0.0	104	0.0	1,297	0.1	1,174	0.1
Eritrea	10,100	350	60	1,280	X	1,600	X	2,000	X	5,220	93.5
Ethiopia	110,100	500	53	13,930	0.0	44,825	(1.0)	26,950	(3.4)	24,395	(5.8)
Gabon	25,767	51	20	459	1.5	4,700	0.0	19,900	(0.5)	708	(12.7)
Gambia, The	1,000	1,118	27	180	13.0	90	0.0	280	0.0	450	4.6
Ghana	22,754	767	41	4,320	23.4	5,000	0.0	7,943	(8.0)	5,491	2.4
Guinea	24,572	273	25	730	2.4	5,500	0.0	14,480	(3.9)	3,862	(14.6)
Guinea-Bissau	2,812	382	50	340	13.7	1,080	0.0	1,070	0.0	322	12.7
Kenya	56,914	497	45	4,517	5.5	21,300	0.0	16,800	0.0	14,297	1.7
Lesotho	3,035	675	76	320	10.4	2,000	0.0	80	(4.8)	635	4.1
Liberia	9,675	314	63	374	0.9	5,700	0.0	1,707	(13.2)	1,894	(13.6)
Libya	175,954	31	9	2,167	3.5	13,300	0.8	840	35.1	159,647	0.2
Madagascar	58,154	254	47	3,104	3.3	24,000	0.0	23,200	0.0	7,850	1.3
Malawi	9,408	1,183	38	1,697	22.1	1,840	0.0	3,700	(1.1)	2,171	12.3
Mali	122,019	88	27	2,270	10.6	30,000	0.0	6,907	(3.9)	82,843	(0.1)
Mauritania	102,522	22	38	207	6.2	39,250	0.0	4,413	(2.1)	58,652	(0.1)
Mauritius	203	5,502	56	106	(0.9)	7	0.0	44	(24.1)	46	(32.6)
Morocco	44,630	606	69	9,781	15.9	20,900	0.0	8,290	6.0	5,659	32.0
Mozambique	78,409	204	60	3,163	2.7	44,000	0.0	14,053	(7.7)	17,192	(6.3)
Namibia	82,329	19	47	662	0.5	38,000	0.0	18,030	(1.8)	25,637	(1.3)
Niger	126,670	72	10	3,605	1.5	8,913	(3.4)	2,500	0.8	111,652	(0.2)
Nigeria	91,077	1,227	79	32,368	6.1	40,000	0.0	11,400	(20.3)	7,309	(14.1)
Rwanda	2,467	3,223	66	1,167	8.5	453	(15.2)	550	(4.8)	297	(5.8)
Senegal	19,253	432	28	2,350	0.0	3,100	0.0	10,467	(4.4)	3,336	(14.5)
Sierra Leone	7,162	630	38	540	5.6	2,203	(0.1)	2,043	(2.9)	2,376	(1.4)
Somalia	62,734	147	70	1,032	2.2	43,000	0.0	16,000	6.7	2,702	37.8
South Africa	122,104	340	77	13,177	(0.1)	81,378	(0.0)	8,200	0.0	19,349	(0.1)
Sudan	237,600	118	52	12,950	3.6	110,000	12.2	44,340	(6.1)	70,310	13.6
Swaziland	1,720	497	73	191	35.4	1,070	(6.5)	118	15.7	341	(2.5)
Tanzania	88,359	336	44	3,500	19.2	35,000	0.0	33,500	(14.4)	16,359	(31.0)
Togo	5,439	761	48	2,430	3.0	200	0.0	933	(8.5)	1,876	(0.9)
Tunisia	15,536	573	52	4,897	2.2	3,525	5.1	664	18.8	6,451	5.9
Uganda	19,965	1,067	43	6,763	13.4	1,800	0.0	5,503	(7.7)	5,898	5.8
Zaire	226,705	194	10	7,893	2.9	15,000	0.0	173,860	(1.7)	29,952	(9.6)
Zambia	74,339	127	47	5,271	2.2	30,000	0.0	28,727	(2.3)	10,341	(5.5)
Zimbabwe	38,685	291	20	2,864	3.4	4,856	0.0	8,800	(7.4)	22,165	(2.7)
EUROPE {c}	**2,269,180**	**320**	**X**	**136,757**	**(2.7)**	**80,794**	**(5.6)**	**158,219**	**1.4**	**808,204**	**0.2**
Albania	2,740	1,256	41	702	(0.8)	424	4.7	1,050	2.3	564	6.6
Austria	8,273	963	42	1,509	(5.6)	1,978	(2.2)	3,228	(1.0)	1,557	(10.8)
Belarus, Rep	20,760	488	45	6,255	(1.7)	3,128	(6.2)	7,009	(5.2)	4,369	(16.0)
Belgium {d}	3,282	3,205	52	1,007	30.6	691	(9.4)	700	0.4	885	18.9
Bosnia and Herzegovina	5,100	678	38	1,007	X	1,067	X	2,100	X	927	450.4
Bulgaria	11,055	793	55	4,267	2.8	1,878	(7.4)	3,875	0.5	1,035	(1.5)
Croatia, Rep	5,592	804	43	1,415	(13.2)	1,247	(21.2)	2,081	2.3	849	(59.5)
Czech Rep	7,728	1,332	54	3,293	X	873	X	2,629	X	933	728.3
Denmark	4,243	1,221	65	2,549	(3.3)	206	(14.9)	445	(9.7)	1,043	(16.3)
Estonia, Rep	4,227	362	34	1,146	15.2	312	(6.8)	1,986	19.2	783	57.2
Finland	30,461	168	9	2,560	2.1	116	(23.6)	23,198	(0.5)	4,587	(2.3)
France	55,010	1,054	55	19,297	1.6	11,023	(12.8)	14,884	2.0	9,806	(10.4)
Germany	34,927	2,336	50	12,009	(3.7)	5,274	(11.0)	10,700	4.0	6,943	(10.1)
Greece	12,890	811	68	3,506	(11.2)	5,253	(0.0)	2,620	0.0	1,510	(29.4)
Hungary	9,234	1,095	66	5,077	(4.2)	1,165	(9.2)	1,726	6.1	1,266	(19.2)
Iceland	10,025	27	23	6	(20.8)	2,274	0.0	120	0.0	7,625	(0.0)
Ireland	6,889	516	81	926	(12.2)	4,691	0.5	320	(0.8)	951	(11.1)
Italy	29,406	1,945	55	11,915	(3.7)	4,284	(15.7)	6,769	6.2	6,438	(13.2)
Latvia, Rep	6,205	412	41	1,715	(1.3)	822	9.0	12,507	(5.6)	(8,839)	7.8
Lithuania, Rep	4,551	813	77	3,043	(3.6)	459	(15.1)	1,980	1.0	(930)	18.9
Macedonia, former Yugoslav Rep	2,543	851	51	663	X	636	X	1,002	X	242	952.3
Moldova, Rep	3,297	1,344	79	2,202	(0.4)	378	8.0	421	74.3	296	67.5
Netherlands	3,392	4,570	59	922	12.0	1,065	(10.1)	343	15.9	1,061	2.4
Norway	30,683	141	3	888	5.8	120	18.4	8,330	0.0	21,344	0.3
Poland, Rep	30,442	1,261	61	14,694	(0.9)	4,043	(0.6)	8,779	0.9	2,926	(2.7)
Portugal	9,195	1,068	44	3,169	0.7	839	0.1	3,293	12.3	1,894	20.2
Romania	23,034	991	64	9,974	(5.3)	4,820	8.7	6,681	1.8	1,559	(3.5)
Russian Federation	1,699,580	86	12	133,141	(1.8)	77,985	(6.8)	778,512	1.9	709,941	0.9
Slovak Rep	4,808	1,113	51	1,623	X	825	X	1,990	X	370	1,198.3
Slovenia, Rep	2,012	967	43	302	X	559	X	1,018	X	133	1,412.8
Spain	49,944	793	60	19,897	(2.9)	10,281	(2.7)	15,970	2.4	3,796	(13.6)
Sweden	41,162	213	8	2,779	(5.8)	573	(18.9)	28,000	0.1	9,809	(2.9)
Switzerland	3,955	1,821	40	449	9.1	1,279	(20.5)	1,185	12.7	1,042	(15.3)
Ukraine	57,935	887	72	34,458	(2.9)	7,471	6.6	10,278	36.4	5,728	37.9
United Kingdom	24,160	2,411	71	6,442	(7.7)	11,112	(1.6)	2,424	12.0	4,182	(11.0)
Yugoslavia, Fed Rep	X	X	X	7,730	(1.4)	6,352	(0.6)	9,120	(1.4)	(23,202)	1.2

	Land Area (000 hectares)	Population Density 1995 (per 1,000 hectares)	Domesticated Land as a % of Land Area {a}	Cropland 1991-93	% Change Since 1981-83	Permanent Pasture 1991-93	% Change Since 1981-83	Forest and Woodland 1991-93	% Change Since 1981-83	Other Land 1991-93	% Change Since 1981-83
NORTH & CENTRAL AMERICA {e}	**2,178,176**	**209**	**29**	**271,300**	**(0.9)**	**362,033**	**0.1**	**854,897**	**5.7**	**689,945**	**6.3**
Belize	2,280	94	5	57	7.5	48	9.1	2,100	0.0	75	10.7
Canada	922,097	32	8	45,523	(1.3)	27,933	(3.3)	494,000	11.6	354,640	14.0
Costa Rica	5,106	671	56	530	3.5	2,337	9.1	1,570	(5.2)	670	19.1
Cuba	10,982	1,005	57	3,337	3.8	2,970	11.4	2,403	(9.2)	2,273	8.0
Dominican Rep	4,838	1,617	30	1,449	1.4	2	0.0	608	(3.7)	2,780	(0.1)
El Salvador	2,072	2,784	65	731	0.8	610	0.0	104	(18.8)	627	(2.9)
Guatemala	10,843	980	41	1,817	2.3	2,534	91.8	5,271	17.4	1,221	166.6
Haiti	2,756	2,605	51	908	1.3	495	(2.3)	140	0.0	1,212	(0.0)
Honduras	11,189	505	32	1,904	7.7	1,511	0.7	6,000	0.0	1,774	8.3
Jamaica	1,083	2,259	44	219	(4.8)	257	0.0	184	(4.5)	423	(4.7)
Mexico	190,869	491	52	24,727	0.2	74,499	0.0	48,700	4.1	42,943	4.6
Nicaragua	11,875	373	57	1,272	1.0	5,483	9.7	3,223	(24.3)	1,896	(28.4)
Panama	7,443	353	29	658	15.0	1,487	10.9	3,260	(18.0)	2,038	(23.8)
Trinidad and Tobago	513	2,546	26	121	3.4	11	0.0	235	3.1	146	7.6
United States	957,311	275	45	187,776	(1.2)	239,172	(0.4)	286,400	(2.0)	243,963	(3.8)
SOUTH AMERICA	**1,752,925**	**182**	**34**	**104,567**	**1.6**	**495,884**	**3.9**	**846,721**	**(4.1)**	**305,753**	**(5.2)**
Argentina	273,669	126	62	27,200	0.0	142,033	(0.7)	50,900	0.0	53,536	(1.8)
Bolivia	108,438	68	27	2,373	11.1	26,517	(1.7)	58,000	0.0	21,549	(1.1)
Brazil	845,651	191	28	50,560	0.3	185,767	6.8	488,833	(4.8)	120,491	(10.3)
Chile	74,880	190	24	4,293	0.3	13,583	3.7	16,500	0.0	40,504	1.2
Colombia	103,870	338	44	5,450	4.2	40,567	4.8	49,633	(5.8)	8,220	(12.1)
Ecuador	27,684	414	18	3,012	20.2	2,091	(0.0)	15,600	0.6	6,981	8.7
Guyana	19,685	42	9	496	0.2	1,230	0.5	16,413	0.3	1,546	3.3
Paraguay	39,730	125	60	2,258	19.3	21,600	30.6	12,983	(32.5)	2,888	(28.6)
Peru	128,000	186	24	3,630	0.7	27,120	0.0	84,800	(0.1)	12,450	(0.2)
Suriname	15,600	27	1	68	24.4	21	6.8	15,000	0.8	511	26.4
Uruguay	17,481	182	85	1,304	(6.8)	13,520	(0.6)	930	0.0	1,727	(10.5)
Venezuela	88,205	248	25	3,912	4.1	17,783	2.8	29,828	(8.2)	36,682	(5.5)
ASIA {c}	**3,089,163**	**1,119**	**X**	**470,322**	**2.9**	**799,881**	**12.9**	**533,087**	**(1.9)**	**958,376**	**9.1**
Afghanistan, Islamic State	65,209	309	58	8,054	0.0	30,000	0.0	1,900	0.0	25,255	0.0
Armenia	2,840	1,267	X	X	X	X	X	X	X	2,840	0.0
Azerbaijan	8,610	878	49	2,000	2.0	2,233	(4.1)	960	(12.5)	3,417	(5.7)
Bangladesh	13,017	9,252	79	9,703	6.1	600	0.0	1,896	(12.2)	818	36.3
Bhutan	4,700	349	9	133	6.7	272	2.5	3,100	20.4	1,194	45.3
Cambodia	17,652	581	25	2,367	47.9	1,967	239.1	11,667	(11.3)	1,652	40.0
China	932,641	1,310	X	95,975	(3.3)	X	X	X	X	836,666	(0.4)
Georgia, Rep	6,970	783	43	993	0.3	2,033	(9.8)	2,717	(6.1)	1,227	(32.2)
India	297,319	3,147	61	169,547	0.6	11,533	(4.1)	68,330	1.4	47,909	3.0
Indonesia	181,157	1,091	24	30,993	19.2	11,776	(1.3)	111,258	(3.7)	27,130	2.1
Iran, Islamic Rep	163,600	411	38	18,057	22.1	44,000	0.0	11,400	0.0	90,143	3.6
Iraq	43,737	468	22	5,450	0.1	4,000	0.0	192	0.0	34,095	0.0
Israel	2,062	2,730	28	435	4.8	145	12.7	124	12.7	1,358	3.7
Japan	37,652	3,322	14	4,511	(6.6)	656	9.8	25,187	(0.0)	7,299	(3.7)
Jordan	8,893	612	13	404	18.4	791	0.1	70	6.6	7,628	0.9
Kazakhstan, Rep	266,980	64	83	35,328	(1.6)	186,452	(1.0)	9,600	(6.5)	35,600	(8.6)
Korea, Dem People's Rep	12,041	1,986	17	2,010	4.5	50	0.0	2	0.0	9,979	0.9
Korea, Rep	9,873	4,557	22	2,072	(4.9)	91	43.9	7,370	0.0	340	(23.1)
Kuwait	1,782	868	8	5	150.0	137	2.0	6,464	(1.4)	(4,824)	1.8
Kyrgyz Rep	19,130	248	54	1,387	(3.9)	8,943	(1.7)	2	0.0	8,798	(2.4)
Lao People's Dem Rep	23,080	212	7	807	11.6	800	0.0	703	(11.3)	20,770	(0.0)
Lebanon	1,023	2,941	31	306	2.7	10	0.0	2,819	2.3	(2,112)	(3.4)
Malaysia	32,855	613	15	4,880	0.4	27	0.0	20,347	(1.8)	7,601	(4.6)
Mongolia	156,650	15	81	1,399	11.1	124,800	1.1	13,750	(9.4)	16,701	0.6
Myanmar	65,755	708	16	10,061	(0.1)	359	(0.7)	32,397	0.9	22,938	1.2
Nepal	13,680	1,602	32	2,354	1.5	2,000	4.2	5,750	4.4	3,576	9.9
Oman	21,246	102	5	62	49.6	1,000	0.0	X	X	20,184	0.1
Pakistan	77,088	1,823	34	22,890	12.4	5,000	0.0	3,470	14.5	45,728	6.5
Philippines	29,817	2,267	35	9,177	3.8	1,277	17.1	13,600	13.4	5,764	37.0
Saudi Arabia	214,969	83	58	3,719	75.7	120,000	41.2	1,800	36.7	89,450	41.5
Singapore	61	46,689	X	1	(84.2)	X	X	3	0.0	57	(9.4)
Sri Lanka	6,463	2,840	36	1,903	2.1	439	0.0	2,126	21.4	1,995	20.7
Syrian Arab Rep	18,378	798	75	5,770	0.8	8,018	(4.0)	679	37.9	3,911	(2.5)
Tajikistan, Rep	14,270	428	31	836	(7.2)	3,507	1.1	535	7.8	9,391	0.1
Thailand	51,089	1,151	42	20,775	9.4	797	17.2	13,557	(13.8)	15,960	(1.7)
Turkey	76,963	805	52	27,583	0.6	12,378	22.6	20,199	0.0	16,803	14.6
Turkmenistan, Rep	48,810	84	77	1,462	(39.1)	36,274	0.8	4,000	(10.4)	7,074	(16.0)
United Arab Emirates	8,360	228	3	39	36.0	200	0.0	3	0.0	8,118	0.1
Uzbekistan, Rep	42,540	537	63	4,728	4.6	22,183	(5.9)	1,323	(42.5)	14,306	(15.1)
Viet Nam	32,549	2,290	22	6,607	0.4	328	7.9	9,639	(8.8)	15,975	(5.5)
Yemen, Rep	52,797	275	33	1,481	1.1	16,065	0.0	2,000	(33.3)	33,251	(3.0)
OCEANIA	**845,349**	**34**	**57**	**51,619**	**4.3**	**430,738**	**(3.7)**	**199,962**	**24.4**	**163,030**	**15.2**
Australia	764,444	24	60	46,579	3.8	416,567	(3.7)	145,000	36.8	156,298	15.9
Fiji	1,827	429	24	257	42.8	174	34.1	1,185	0.0	211	57.6
New Zealand	26,799	133	65	3,831	9.4	13,577	(5.3)	7,377	3.6	2,014	(8.3)
Papua New Guinea	45,286	95	1	412	11.1	81	(17.3)	42,000	0.0	2,793	0.9
Solomon Islands	2,799	135	3	57	8.2	39	0.0	2,450	(3.5)	253	(33.9)

Sources: Food and Agriculture Organization of the United Nations, the United Nations Population Division and other sources.

Notes: a. Domesticated land is the sum of cropland and permanent pasture. b. Does not include Antarctica. c. Regional land use totals do not include countries of the former Soviet Union.
d. Includes Luxembourg. e. Includes Greenland. Regional totals include countries not listed.
0 = zero or less than half the unit of measure; X = not available; negative numbers are shown in parentheses.
For additional information, see Sources and Technical Notes.

Data Table 9.2 Forest Resources, 1981–90

	Forest and Other Wooded Land		Forest Area — Total Forest		Forest Area — Natural Forest		Plantation		Other Wooded Land		Annual Logging of Closed Broadleaf Forest, 1981-90 (000 ha)		
	1990 Extent (000 ha)	Annual % Change (1981-90)	1990 Extent (000 ha)	Annual % Change (1981-90)	1990 Extent (000 ha)	Annual % Change (1981-90)	1990 Extent (000 ha)	Annual % Change (1981-90)	1990 Extent (000 ha)	Annual % Change (1981-90)	Extent 1990	% of Closed Forest	% That Is Primary Forest
WORLD	5,120,227	(0.19)	3,442,369	X	X	X	X	X	1,677,719	X	X	X	X
AFRICA	1,136,676	(0.24)	545,085	(0.70)	540,669	(0.73)	4,416	5.55	591,591	0.22	X	X	X
North Africa	11,137	(0.62)	6,905	(0.28)	5,655	(1.11)	1,250	6.82	4,232	(1.11)	X	X	X
Algeria	3,945	X	2,039	(0.88)	1,554	(1.96)	485	6.08	1,906	X	X	X	X
Egypt	34	X	34	1.97	0	X	34	1.97	0	X	X	X	X
Libya	846	X	400	3.79	190	X	210	10.98	446	X	X	X	X
Morocco	5,744	X	3,864	(0.42)	3,543	(0.69)	321	4.26	1,880	X	X	X	X
Tunisia	569	X	569	0.92	368	(1.48)	201	12.58	0	X	X	X	X
West Sahelian Africa	105,956	(0.27)	40,941	(0.64)	40,766	(0.68)	175	49.95	65,015	(0.02)	6	0.2	78
Burkina Faso	13,813	X	4,436	(0.65)	4,416	(0.67)	20	12.73	9,377	X	0	0.0	0
Cape Verde	78	X	16	7.78	6	0.00	10	23.33	62	X	X	X	X
Chad	32,450	X	11,438	(0.72)	11,434	(0.72)	4	7.78	21,012	X	0	0.0	81
Gambia, The	286	X	98	(0.75)	97	(0.76)	1	0.00	188	X	0	1.1	0
Guinea-Bissau	2,162	X	2,022	(0.73)	2,021	(0.73)	1	0.00	140	X	5	0.6	90
Mali	28,791	X	12,158	(0.79)	12,144	(0.80)	14	143.85	16,633	X	0	0.0	0
Mauritania	4,536	X	556	0.03	554	0.00	2	101.11	3,980	X	0	0.1	0
Niger	10,442	X	2,562	0.03	2,550	0.00	12	17.91	7,880	X	0	0.0	0
Senegal	13,400	X	7,656	(0.52)	7,544	(0.64)	112	118.00	5,744	X	0	0.0	5
East Sahelian Africa	161,048	(0.38)	65,983	(0.80)	65,450	(0.83)	533	7.03	95,065	(0.07)	4	0.1	65
Djibouti	1,320	X	22	0.00	22	0.00	0	X	1,298	X	X	X	X
Ethiopia {a}	41,991	X	14,354	(0.18)	14,165	(0.27)	189	17.49	27,637	X	0	0.0	92
Kenya	16,816	X	1,305	(0.39)	1,187	(0.55)	118	1.58	15,511	X	2	0.6	86
Somalia	15,945	X	758	(0.36)	754	(0.36)	4	0.00	15,187	X	1	0.6	0
Sudan	68,955	X	43,179	(0.99)	42,976	(1.01)	203	7.58	25,776	X	0	0.0	0
Uganda	16,023	X	6,366	(0.92)	6,346	(0.92)	20	0.00	9,657	X	1	0.1	61
West Africa	149,764	(0.06)	55,919	(0.94)	55,607	(0.96)	312	4.72	93,845	0.56	312	2.0	47
Benin	11,497	X	4,961	(1.22)	4,947	(1.23)	14	6.67	6,536	X	0	0.3	57
Cote d'Ivoire	18,952	X	10,967	(0.96)	10,904	(0.99)	63	10.04	7,985	X	85	7.6	34
Ghana	18,013	X	9,608	(1.24)	9,555	(1.26)	53	2.47	8,405	X	11	0.7	19
Guinea	17,484	X	6,696	(1.14)	6,692	(1.15)	4	5.81	10,788	X	9	0.5	87
Liberia	6,632	X	4,639	(0.52)	4,633	(0.52)	6	1.03	1,993	X	79	1.7	87
Nigeria	65,654	X	15,785	(0.68)	15,634	(0.71)	151	3.23	49,869	X	127	2.3	31
Sierra Leone	6,969	X	1,895	(0.60)	1,889	(0.61)	6	3.45	5,074	X	1	0.2	0
Togo	4,566	X	1,370	(1.31)	1,353	(1.39)	17	23.33	3,196	X	1	0.3	47
Central Africa	296,704	(0.19)	204,238	(0.52)	204,113	(0.53)	125	16.12	92,466	0.64	571	0.4	90
Cameroon	35,905	X	20,366	(0.56)	20,350	(0.57)	16	29.02	15,539	X	333	4.5	89
Central African Rep	46,753	X	30,568	(0.40)	30,562	(0.41)	6	1,190.00	16,185	X	3	0.0	93
Congo	25,285	X	19,902	(0.15)	19,865	(0.16)	37	21.73	5,383	X	78	0.4	89
Equatorial Guinea	2,719	X	1,829	(0.37)	1,826	(0.37)	3	0.00	890	X	5	0.3	88
Gabon	19,966	X	18,256	(0.60)	18,235	(0.60)	21	5.79	1,710	X	126	0.7	93
Zaire	166,076	X	113,317	(0.60)	113,275	(0.61)	42	16.67	52,759	X	26	0.0	95
Tropical Southern Africa	346,896	(0.21)	146,609	(0.82)	145,869	(0.84)	740	8.14	200,287	0.30	9	0.1	38
Angola	77,198	X	23,194	(0.69)	23,074	(0.70)	120	0.88	54,004	X	1	0.0	5
Botswana	26,561	X	14,262	(0.51)	14,261	(0.51)	1	0.00	12,299	X	X	X	X
Burundi	1,314	X	325	2.49	233	(0.57)	92	59.43	989	X	0	0.0	0
Malawi	3,724	X	3,612	(1.12)	3,486	(1.31)	126	12.42	112	X	0	0.0	0
Mozambique	55,881	X	17,357	(0.72)	17,329	(0.72)	28	5.38	38,524	X	1	0.0	40
Namibia	26,296	X	12,569	(0.33)	12,569	(0.33)	0	X	13,727	X	X	X	X
Rwanda	946	X	252	1.81	164	(0.24)	88	9.43	694	X	1	0.4	5
Tanzania	68,497	X	33,709	(1.13)	33,555	(1.15)	154	12.52	34,788	X	2	0.2	77
Zambia	60,337	X	32,349	(1.00)	32,301	(1.01)	48	7.78	27,988	X	5	0.2	34
Zimbabwe	26,144	X	8,981	(0.62)	8,897	(0.64)	84	1.98	17,163	X	0	0.2	14
Temperate Southern Africa	41,712	(0.74)	8,361	(0.53)	7,317	(0.79)	1,044	1.82	33,351	(0.79)	X	X	X
South Africa	41,543	X	8,208	(0.55)	7,243	(0.80)	965	1.91	33,335	X	X	X	X
Swaziland	146	X	146	0.05	74	0.00	72	0.10	0	X	X	X	X
Insular Africa	23,457	(0.37)	16,127	(0.75)	15,892	(0.78)	235	1.69	7,331	0.62	20	0.3	31
Comoros	41	X	11	(3.13)	11	(3.13)	0	X	30	X	X	X	X
Madagascar	23,225	X	15,999	(0.76)	15,782	(0.79)	217	1.65	7,226	X	20	0.3	31
Mauritius	44	X	12	1.32	3	0.00	9	1.84	32	X	X	X	X
ASIA	657,361	X	489,466	X	X	X	X	X	167,895	X	X	X	X
Temperate and Middle East Asia	252,339	X	192,386	0.68	X	X	33,566	5.80	59,953	(1.71)	X	X	X
Afghanistan, Islamic State	2,614	X	1,199	(0.03)	1,191	(0.03)	8	0.00	1,415	X	X	X	X
China	162,029	X	133,799	0.59	101,968	(0.38)	31,831	5.58	28,230	X	X	X	X
Iran, Islamic Rep	11,437	X	1,737	(1.38)	1,658	(1.65)	79	16.33	9,700	X	X	X	X
Iraq	192	X	83	0.00	69	0.00	14	0.00	109	X	X	X	X
Israel	124	X	102	X	X	X	X	X	22	X	X	X	X
Japan	24,718	(0.02)	24,158	X	X	X	X	X	560	X	X	X	X
Jordan	173	X	51	0.28	28	(2.00)	23	5.75	122	X	X	X	X
Korea, Dem People's Rep	7,370	X	6,170	1.43	4,700	0.00	1,470	11.00	1,200	X	X	X	X
Korea, Rep	6,291	X	6,291	(0.02)	6,291	(0.02)	0	X	0	X	X	X	X
Lebanon	144	X	78	(0.71)	65	(0.85)	13	0.00	66	X	X	X	X
Mongolia	13,741	X	9,406	0.00	9,406	0.00	0	X	4,335	X	X	X	X
Saudi Arabia	902	X	202	(1.85)	201	(1.86)	1	0.00	700	X	X	X	X
Syrian Arab Rep	484	X	245	2.85	118	(2.76)	127	36.01	239	X	X	X	X
Turkey	20,199	0.02	8,856	X	X	X	X	X	11,343	X	X	X	X
Yemen	1,921	X	9	0.00	9	0.00	0	X	1,912	X	X	X	X
South Asia	100,164	0.63	77,762	0.66	63,931	(0.79)	13,831	29.84	22,402	0.52	62	0.2	17
Bangladesh	1,472	X	1,004	(2.02)	769	(3.28)	235	10.89	468	X	15	2.5	7
Bhutan	3,168	X	2,813	(0.54)	2,809	(0.55)	4	11.05	355	X	2	0.2	79
India	82,648	X	64,959	1.15	51,729	(0.62)	13,230	32.13	17,689	X	42	0.1	18
Nepal	5,751	X	5,079	(0.90)	5,023	(0.98)	56	32.11	672	X	X	X	X
Pakistan	3,128	X	2,023	(2.64)	1,855	(2.93)	168	3.33	1,105	X	X	X	X
Sri Lanka	3,998	X	1,885	(1.00)	1,746	(1.33)	139	7.64	2,113	X	3	0.2	3

| | Forest and Other Wooded Land | | Forest Area | | | | | | Other Wooded Land | | Annual Logging of Closed Broadleaf Forest, 1981-90 (000 ha) | | |
| | | | Total Forest | | Natural Forest | | Plantation | | | | | | |
	1990 Extent (000 ha)	Annual % Change (1981-90)	1990 Extent (000 ha)	Annual % Change (1981-90)	1990 Extent (000 ha)	Annual % Change (1981-90)	1990 Extent (000 ha)	Annual % Change (1981-90)	1990 Extent (000 ha)	Annual % Change (1981-90)	Extent 1990	% of Closed Forest	% That Is Primary Forest
Continental South and East Asia	**123,400**	**(0.81)**	**77,484**	**(1.36)**	**75,239**	**(1.49)**	**2,245**	**7.77**	**45,916**	**0.29**	**304**	**0.5**	**76**
Cambodia	13,724	X	12,170	(0.97)	12,163	(0.97)	7	0.00	1,554	X	3	0.0	88
Lao People's Dem Rep	21,436	X	13,177	(0.89)	13,173	(0.89)	4	5.38	8,259	X	9	0.1	94
Myanmar	49,774	X	29,091	(1.16)	28,856	(1.22)	235	49.51	20,683	X	198	0.7	90
Thailand	14,968	X	13,264	(2.68)	12,735	(2.88)	529	12.55	1,704	X	37	0.5	45
Viet Nam	23,499	X	9,782	(0.83)	8,312	(1.42)	1,470	5.00	13,717	X	58	1.2	45
Insular South East Asia	**181,458**	**(0.77)**	**141,834**	**(1.01)**	**135,425**	**(1.25)**	**6,409**	**11.12**	**39,624**	**0.21**	**1,721**	**1.5**	**85**
Indonesia	145,108	X	115,674	(0.71)	109,549	(1.00)	6,125	11.82	29,434	X	1,223	1.4	86
Malaysia	22,248	X	17,664	(1.81)	17,583	(1.84)	81	35.00	4,584	X	455	2.6	85
Philippines	13,640	X	8,034	(2.82)	7,831	(2.88)	203	0.00	5,606	X	41	0.5	62
Singapore	4	X	4	0.00	4	0.00	0	X	0	X	X	X	X
THE AMERICAS	**2,009,006**	**(0.31)**	**1,424,206**	**(0.49)**	**959,704**	**(0.74)**	**7,765**	**7.09**	**584,801**	**0.17**	**X**	**X**	**X**
Temperate North America	**749,289**	**(0.04)**	**456,737**	**X**	**X**	**X**	**X**	**X**	**292,552**	**(0.11)**	**X**	**X**	**X**
Canada	453,300	0.00	247,164	X	X	X	X	X	206,136	X	X	X	X
United States	295,989	(0.11)	209,573	X	X	X	X	X	86,416	(0.35)	X	X	X
Central America and Mexico	**158,034**	**(0.50)**	**68,289**	**(1.39)**	**68,097**	**(1.40)**	**192**	**16.13**	**89,745**	**0.32**	**90**	**0.4**	**65**
Costa Rica	1,569	X	1,456	(2.44)	1,428	(2.57)	28	132.86	113	X	34	2.6	27
El Salvador	890	X	127	(1.85)	123	(2.06)	4	37.06	763	X	X	X	X
Guatemala	9,465	X	4,253	(1.58)	4,225	(1.61)	28	16.67	5,212	X	3	0.1	50
Honduras	6,054	X	4,608	(1.94)	4,605	(1.95)	3	101.11	1,446	X	2	0.1	19
Mexico	129,057	X	48,695	(1.21)	48,586	(1.22)	109	9.29	80,362	X	4	0.0	94
Nicaragua	7,732	X	6,027	(1.69)	6,013	(1.71)	14	143.85	1,705	X	45	0.9	92
Panama	3,266	X	3,123	(1.70)	3,117	(1.71)	6	14.00	143	X	3	0.1	71
Caribbean Subregion	**50,989**	**(0.10)**	**47,447**	**(0.22)**	**47,138**	**(0.25)**	**309**	**11.31**	**3,543**	**1.90**	**42**	**0.1**	**73**
Belize	2,117	X	1,998	(0.24)	1,996	(0.24)	2	0.00	119	X	3	0.2	5
Cuba	3,262	X	1,960	(0.19)	1,715	(0.92)	245	12.29	1,302	X	3	0.2	8
Dominican Rep	1,530	X	1,084	(2.43)	1,077	(2.46)	7	7.54	446	X	0	0.0	61
Guyana	18,755	X	18,424	(0.09)	18,416	(0.10)	8	171.82	331	X	9	0.0	91
Haiti	139	X	31	(1.91)	23	(3.95)	8	256.67	108	X	1	7.7	11
Jamaica	653	X	254	(5.08)	239	(5.29)	15	6.20	399	X	1	0.4	91
Suriname	15,093	X	14,776	(0.08)	14,768	(0.09)	8	4.41	317	X	11	0.1	94
Trinidad and Tobago	236	X	168	(1.75)	155	(1.93)	13	1.21	68	X	3	1.8	4
Nontropical South America	**68,453**	**(0.53)**	**43,283**	**(0.47)**	**41,564**	**(0.62)**	**1,719**	**5.51**	**25,170**	**(0.62)**	**X**	**X**	**X**
Argentina	50,936	X	34,436	(0.57)	33,889	(0.59)	547	0.91	16,500	X	X	X	X
Chile	16,583	X	8,033	(0.07)	7,018	(0.79)	1,015	11.61	8,550	X	X	X	X
Uruguay	933	X	813	0.12	657	(0.15)	156	1.44	120	X	X	X	X
Tropical South America	**982,242**	**(0.47)**	**808,450**	**(0.68)**	**802,905**	**(0.71)**	**5,545**	**7.24**	**173,792**	**0.71**	**2,445**	**0.4**	**90**
Bolivia	57,977	X	49,345	(1.12)	49,317	(1.12)	28	5.44	8,632	X	12	0.0	71
Brazil	671,921	X	566,007	(0.58)	561,107	(0.61)	4,900	6.63	105,914	X	1,982	0.5	93
Colombia	63,231	X	54,190	(0.62)	54,064	(0.64)	126	23.96	9,041	X	108	0.2	94
Ecuador	15,576	X	12,007	(1.65)	11,962	(1.66)	45	4.85	3,569	X	152	1.3	96
Paraguay	19,256	X	12,868	(2.38)	12,859	(2.38)	9	35.00	6,388	X	49	1.8	19
Peru	84,844	X	68,090	(0.37)	67,906	(0.38)	184	9.21	16,754	X	89	0.1	85
Venezuela	69,436	X	45,943	(1.13)	45,690	(1.16)	253	19.16	23,493	X	54	0.1	39
EUROPE	**174,340**	**0.11**	**140,197**	**X**	**X**	**X**	**X**	**X**	**34,143**	**0.58**	**X**	**X**	**X**
Albania	1,449	0.01	1,046	X	X	X	X	X	403	X	X	X	X
Austria	3,877	0.38	3,877	X	X	X	X	X	0	X	X	X	X
Belgium	620	0.32	620	X	X	X	X	X	0	X	X	X	X
Bulgaria	3,683	0.22	3,386	X	X	X	X	X	298	X	X	X	X
Czechoslovakia (former)	4,491	0.04	4,491	X	X	X	X	X	0	X	X	X	X
Denmark	466	0.22	466	X	X	X	X	X	0	X	X	X	X
Finland	23,373	0.02	20,112	X	X	X	X	X	3,261	X	X	X	X
France	14,154	0.06	13,110	X	X	X	X	X	1,044	X	X	X	X
Germany	10,735	0.46	10,490	X	X	X	X	X	245	X	X	X	X
Greece	6,032	0.01	2,512	X	X	X	X	X	3,520	X	X	X	X
Hungary	1,675	0.51	1,675	X	X	X	X	X	0	X	X	X	X
Iceland	123	X	0	X	X	X	X	X	123	X	X	X	X
Ireland	429	1.26	396	X	X	X	X	X	33	X	X	X	X
Italy	8,550	X	6,750	X	X	X	X	X	1,800	X	X	X	X
Luxembourg	88	0.12	85	X	X	X	X	X	3	X	X	X	X
Netherlands	334	0.31	334	X	X	X	X	X	0	X	X	X	X
Norway	9,565	X	8,697	X	X	X	X	X	868	X	X	X	X
Poland, Rep	8,672	0.06	8,672	X	X	X	X	X	0	X	X	X	X
Portugal	3,102	0.47	2,755	X	X	X	X	X	347	X	X	X	X
Romania	6,265	0.00	6,190	X	X	X	X	X	75	X	X	X	X
Spain	25,622	0.00	8,388	X	X	X	X	X	17,234	X	X	X	X
Sweden	28,015	X	24,437	X	X	X	X	X	3,578	X	X	X	X
Switzerland	1,186	0.59	1,130	X	X	X	X	X	56	X	X	X	X
United Kingdom	2,380	1.13	2,207	X	X	X	X	X	173	X	X	X	X
Yugoslavia (former)	9,454	0.38	8,371	X	X	X	X	X	1,083	X	X	X	X
U.S.S.R. (former)	**941,530**	**0.01**	**754,958**	**X**	**X**	**X**	**X**	**X**	**186,572**	**X**	**X**	**X**	**X**
Belarus, Rep	6,256	0.46	6,016	X	X	X	X	X	240	X	X	X	X
Ukraine	9,239	0.27	9,213	X	X	X	X	X	26	X	X	X	X
OCEANIA	**200,971**	**(0.02)**	**88,254**	**X**	**X**	**X**	**X**	**X**	**112,717**	**X**	**X**	**X**	**X**
Australia	145,613	0.00	39,837	X	X	X	X	X	105,776	X	X	X	X
Fiji	859	X	853	0.17	775	(0.44)	78	18.26	6	X	X	X	X
New Zealand	7,472	X	7,472	X	X	X	X	X	0	X	X	X	X
Papua New Guinea	42,115	X	36,030	(0.30)	36,000	(0.30)	30	9.61	6,085	X	57	0.2	93
Solomon Islands	2,455	X	2,410	(0.18)	2,394	(0.19)	16	2.12	45	X	X	X	X

Sources: Food and Agriculture Organization of the United Nations and the United Nations Economic Commission for Europe.

Notes: a. Ethiopia includes Eritrea. Subregional totals may include countries not listed.
0 = zero or less than half the unit of measure; X = not available; numbers in parentheses indicate increase in forest area.
For additional information, see Sources and Technical Notes.

| | Roundwood Production | | | | | | Processed Wood Production | | | | Paper Production | | Avg. Annual Net Trade in Roundwood {a} | |
| | Total | | Fuel and Charcoal | | Industrial Roundwood | | Sawnwood | | Panels | | | | | |
	(000 cubic meters) 1991-93	Percent Change Since 1981-83	(000 cubic meters) 1991-93	Percent Change Since 1981-83	(000 cubic meters) 1991-93	Percent Change Since 1981-83	(000 cubic meters) 1991-93	Percent Change Since 1981-83	(000 cubic meters) 1991-93	Percent Change Since 1981-83	(000 cubic meters) 1991-93	Percent Change Since 1981-83	(000 cubic meters) 1981-83	1991-93
WORLD	3,411,547	15	1,855,709	19	1,555,838	10	441,589	2	128,838	28	247,320	44		
AFRICA	539,683	32	480,752	34	58,931	13	8,219	8	1,593	(1)	2,558	33	(4,130)	(4,216)
Algeria	2,305	33	2,006	32	298	41	13	0	50	0	91	(13)	X	X
Angola	6,382	31	5,483	32	899	26	5	(38)	11	(68)	0	(100)	X	X
Benin	5,374	35	5,075	35	299	45	25	178	X	X	X	X	X	X
Botswana	1,399	36	1,312	36	86	36	X	X	X	X	X	X	X	X
Burkina Faso	9,254	30	8,836	30	418	29	2	0	X	X	X	X	X	X
Burundi	4,484	34	4,431	34	53	44	3	200	X	X	X	X	X	X
Cameroon	14,483	35	11,490	37	2,993	28	481	(0)	78	7	5	0	(428)	(732)
Central African Rep	3,628	16	3,185	22	443	(12)	63	(3)	2	(84)	X	X	X	X
Chad	4,164	25	3,569	25	595	26	2	100	X	X	X	X	X	X
Congo	3,438	45	2,155	34	1,283	70	53	(23)	36	(50)	X	X	X	X
Cote d'Ivoire	13,370	13	10,498	46	2,872	(38)	606	(12)	229	40	X	X	(2,254)	(323)
Egypt	2,352	27	2,243	27	109	28	X	X	76	110	203	67	232	74
Equatorial Guinea	613	16	447	2	166	88	10	(43)	7	400	X	X	X	X
Eritrea {b}	X	X	X	X	X	X	X	X	X	X	X	X	X	X
Ethiopia {b}	44,937	28	43,227	29	1,711	1	12	(77)	9	(36)	5	(46)	0	0
Gabon	4,345	39	2,712	41	1,633	37	32	(70)	140	(26)	X	X	X	X
Gambia, The	948	17	927	16	21	26	1	0	X	X	X	X	X	X
Ghana	16,965	16	15,512	13	1,453	63	407	71	60	(7)	X	X	X	X
Guinea	4,359	35	3,792	36	567	28	66	(27)	0	(100)	X	X	(13)	(15)
Guinea-Bissau	572	3	422	0	150	15	16	0	X	X	X	X	X	X
Kenya	37,324	41	35,513	41	1,811	38	185	26	52	133	148	124	(8)	0
Lesotho	635	30	635	30	X	X	X	X	X	X	X	X	X	X
Liberia	6,000	41	5,040	34	960	86	411	132	8	85	X	X	(236)	(234)
Libya	646	2	536	0	110	16	31	0	X	X	6	20	45	(1)
Madagascar	8,600	33	7,793	37	807	0	235	1	5	275	5	7	X	X
Malawi	9,730	57	9,235	57	496	46	44	26	17	108	X	X	X	X
Mali	5,955	35	5,575	35	380	37	13	117	X	X	X	X	X	X
Mauritania	13	30	8	33	5	25	X	X	X	X	X	X	X	X
Mauritius	15	(54)	2	(90)	13	30	5	40	0	X	X	X	1	16
Morocco	2,296	38	1,426	28	869	58	83	(37)	34	(67)	106	10	213	376
Mozambique	15,980	12	15,022	13	958	(0)	21	(56)	4	22	2	(17)	(5)	(7)
Namibia	X	X	X	X	X	X	X	X	X	X	X	X	X	X
Niger	5,292	38	4,965	38	326	38	2	X	X	X	X	X	X	X
Nigeria	114,704	35	106,441	38	8,263	5	2,723	2	109	(48)	63	373	(59)	(49)
Rwanda	5,647	10	5,392	11	255	(4)	27	248	2	0	X	X	X	X
Senegal	4,953	34	4,281	33	672	40	23	109	X	X	X	X	X	X
Sierra Leone	3,227	26	3,106	28	121	(18)	9	(56)	X	X	X	X	X	X
Somalia	8,761	28	8,655	28	106	19	14	0	0	(100)	X	X	0	0
South Africa	19,747	(1)	7,146	1	12,601	(2)	1,792	8	350	(11)	1,735	25	(72)	(1,066)
Sudan	24,108	34	21,877	34	2,231	32	3	(68)	2	0	3	(67)	X	X
Swaziland	2,297	3	560	0	1,737	4	103	(1)	8	14	X	X	(199)	0
Tanzania	34,911	42	32,849	40	2,062	74	156	72	15	150	25	X	(0)	(9)
Togo	1,265	80	1,072	90	192	38	3	100	X	X	X	X	0	(1)
Tunisia	3,324	26	3,169	25	155	42	10	222	102	61	67	150	33	40
Uganda	15,099	35	13,103	35	1,996	36	64	180	4	160	3	X	0	0
Zaire	43,252	48	40,101	49	3,151	34	105	1	28	(8)	2	0	(62)	(111)
Zambia	13,778	44	12,952	43	826	70	106	137	81	1,513	3	(23)	9	(4)
Zimbabwe	8,033	17	6,269	12	1,764	35	250	42	79	103	86	33	(9)	(6)
EUROPE {c}	319,100	(5)	50,672	(7)	268,428	(4)	76,383	(10)	34,710	12	68,233	36	15,668	13,669
Albania	2,556	10	1,556	(3)	1,000	39	382	91	16	33	44	450	X	X
Austria	13,759	(0)	2,860	102	10,899	(12)	7,015	13	1,896	54	3,214	87	2,651	5,205
Belarus, Rep	10,714	X	819	X	9,895	X	1,619	X	525	X	221	X	X	X
Belgium {d}	4,412	X	550	X	3,862	X	1,204	X	2,503	X	1,176	X	2,615	1,424
Bosnia and Herzegovina	X	X	X	X	X	X	X	X	X	X	X	X	0	(2)
Bulgaria	3,599	(26)	1,695	(2)	1,904	(39)	564	(62)	268	(55)	188	(57)	340	(101)
Croatia, Rep	2,131	X	710	X	1,421	X	671	X	90	X	X	X	X	(270)
Czech Rep	10,306	X	996	X	9,310	X	2,650	X	739	X	656	X	X	(1,425)
Denmark	2,245	(24)	493	35	1,752	(32)	688	(17)	294	(1)	330	16	(962)	(80)
Estonia, Rep	2,293	X	928	X	1,365	X	300	X	140	X	42	X	X	X
Finland	37,663	(6)	3,320	(0)	34,343	(6)	7,111	(10)	1,044	(30)	9,304	52	3,882	5,144
France	43,617	15	10,450	0	33,167	20	10,181	13	3,514	26	7,652	48	(1,176)	(2,421)
Germany	36,245	X	3,795	X	32,450	X	13,295	X	9,067	X	12,998	X	X	(5,825)
Greece	2,726	2	1,502	(21)	1,224	56	354	2	372	(1)	508	84	213	102
Hungary	5,094	(21)	2,310	(19)	2,784	(23)	717	(41)	387	0	335	(28)	406	(945)
Iceland	X	X	X	X	X	X	X	X	X	X	X	X	17	13
Ireland	1,795	115	50	15	1,745	121	465	96	244	578	36	17	(376)	(385)
Italy	9,240	6	4,750	12	4,490	0	1,797	(23)	3,670	51	5,951	31	5,047	6,719
Latvia, Rep	3,515	X	700	X	2,815	X	593	X	190	X	28	X	X	X
Lithuania, Rep	X	X	X	X	X	X	X	X	200	X	50	X	X	(187)
Macedonia, former Yugoslav Rep	X	X	X	X	X	X	X	X	X	X	X	X	X	X
Moldova, Rep	X	X	X	X	X	X	X	X	X	X	X	X	X	X
Netherlands	1,397	55	156	65	1,241	54	400	47	105	(10)	2,851	71	177	40
Norway	10,516	7	934	19	9,582	6	2,329	(1)	564	(7)	1,812	34	653	749
Poland, Rep	18,314	(19)	2,975	5	15,339	(22)	3,822	(42)	1,666	(12)	1,128	(4)	(975)	(981)
Portugal	11,409	42	598	7	10,811	45	1,176	(45)	1,085	106	904	69	(150)	(43)
Romania	12,110	(45)	2,396	(45)	9,714	(45)	2,384	(49)	835	(46)	359	(56)	(30)	62
Russian Federation	244,488	X	56,738	X	187,750	X	46,685	X	6,909	X	5,115	X	X	(11,098)
Slovak Rep	5,003	X	521	X	4,482	X	80	X	X	X	X	X	X	(374)
Slovenia, Rep	1,470	X	314	X	1,157	X	422	X	327	X	407	X	X	(106)
Spain	15,216	7	1,990	3	13,226	7	2,784	13	2,361	28	3,458	29	237	1,800
Sweden	59,907	17	4,424	0	55,483	18	12,110	9	912	(41)	8,503	39	3,525	4,266
Switzerland	4,571	7	825	(11)	3,746	11	1,554	(14)	856	33	1,299	43	236	(189)
Ukraine	X	X	X	X	X	X	X	X	X	X	X	X	0	2
United Kingdom	6,197	50	263	88	5,934	48	2,139	32	1,907	201	5,115	56	(193)	377
Yugoslavia, Fed Rep	X	X	X	X	X	X	X	X	X	X	X	X	940	(299)

| | Roundwood Production | | | | | | Processed Wood Production | | | | Paper Production | | Avg. Annual Net Trade in Roundwood {a} | |
| | Total | | Fuel and Charcoal | | Industrial Roundwood | | Sawnwood | | Panels | | | | | |
	(000 cubic meters) 1991-93	Percent Change Since 1981-83	(000 cubic meters) 1991-93	Percent Change Since 1981-83	(000 cubic meters) 1991-93	Percent Change Since 1981-83	(000 cubic meters) 1991-93	Percent Change Since 1981-83	(000 cubic meters) 1991-93	Percent Change Since 1981-83	(000 cubic meters) 1991-93	Percent Change Since 1981-83	(000 cubic meters) 1981-83	1991-93
NORTH & CENTRAL AMERICA	730,441	20	155,803	7	574,637	24	165,733	39	38,264	19	94,943	31	(17,551)	(25,723)
Belize	188	48	126	41	62	63	14	(25)	X	X	X	X	(1)	(2)
Canada	172,703	20	6,834	18	165,869	20	56,044	41	6,538	38	16,900	28	(1,215)	601
Costa Rica	4,168	25	3,134	32	1,034	10	661	63	65	32	19	24	1	2
Cuba	3,142	(5)	2,531	(10)	611	18	130	22	149	130	78	(20)	X	X
Dominican Rep	982	4	976	4	6	(18)	0	X	X	X	9	0	42	2
El Salvador	6,362	17	6,216	17	146	30	70	60	X	X	17	6	X	X
Guatemala	11,263	21	11,142	22	121	(34)	78	(36)	16	161	14	(26)	4	1
Haiti	6,052	21	5,813	22	239	0	14	0	X	X	X	X	0	0
Honduras	6,298	21	5,672	39	626	(28)	362	(28)	13	77	X	X	X	X
Jamaica	539	819	385	4,178	154	211	27	11	0	(100)	4	(74)	2	18
Mexico	22,940	22	15,449	25	7,491	16	2,696	49	645	(10)	2,828	45	21	(210)
Nicaragua	3,569	7	3,269	33	300	(66)	69	(80)	5	(70)	X	X	2	0
Panama	1,018	9	910	23	109	(45)	30	(43)	18	45	28	(35)	3	6
Trinidad and Tobago	65	(20)	22	10	43	(30)	46	65	X	X	X	X	5	3
United States	491,000	19	93,300	(2)	397,700	26	105,489	38	30,816	16	75,045	31	(16,406)	(26,191)
SOUTH AMERICA	362,400	26	243,585	20	118,815	39	26,411	17	4,287	21	8,344	50	(738)	(7,611)
Argentina	11,660	18	4,447	(12)	7,214	49	1,298	22	326	(15)	972	28	7	(1,002)
Bolivia	1,530	15	1,377	28	153	(40)	208	146	55	622	0	(100)	0	(1)
Brazil	268,879	22	191,166	21	77,713	24	18,628	13	2,552	2	5,051	54	(14)	(443)
Chile	29,066	117	8,979	58	20,087	161	3,117	107	492	267	537	68	(760)	(6,005)
Colombia	20,619	22	16,936	21	3,683	31	813	(0)	177	45	582	53	0	(1)
Ecuador	7,435	(4)	4,218	(25)	3,218	55	892	(14)	220	128	150	354	X	X
Guyana	175	(15)	14	(11)	161	(15)	12	(83)	2	X	X	X	(28)	(9)
Paraguay	8,502	25	5,396	23	3,106	29	313	(52)	127	79	13	0	X	X
Peru	8,031	3	6,981	8	1,050	(21)	511	(3)	32	(45)	327	42	1	1
Suriname	149	(40)	19	37	131	(45)	42	(31)	7	(69)	X	X	(27)	(2)
Uruguay	4,015	40	3,034	16	981	290	248	356	7	(49)	80	85	1	(129)
Venezuela	2,086	74	954	56	1,132	94	312	20	292	130	633	29	106	13
ASIA {c}	1,122,978	20	849,658	21	273,320	18	99,785	6	39,094	99	63,606	108	34,702	48,013
Afghanistan, Islamic State	7,327	20	5,683	24	1,644	10	400	0	1	0	X	X	0	(3)
Armenia	X	X	X	X	X	X	X	X	X	X	X	X	X	X
Azerbaijan	X	X	X	X	X	X	X	X	X	X	X	X	X	X
Bangladesh	31,751	26	31,021	28	730	(23)	79	(56)	9	(10)	97	(9)	X	X
Bhutan	1,460	8	1,333	25	127	(54)	35	518	13	X	X	X	X	X
Cambodia	6,782	38	5,726	31	1,057	86	127	195	2	0	0	X	X	X
China	291,046	22	196,149	22	94,897	21	21,702	(6)	11,819	367	20,757	173	9,929	6,449
Georgia, Rep	X	X	X	X	X	X	X	X	X	X	X	X	X	X
India	282,384	22	257,813	22	24,571	15	17,460	32	442	19	2,505	86	3	571
Indonesia	185,426	26	146,342	22	39,084	45	8,471	38	10,359	325	2,206	589	(4,871)	(1,466)
Iran, Islamic Rep	7,405	11	2,511	7	4,894	13	177	8	304	262	200	156	118	41
Iraq	153	19	103	30	50	0	8	0	3	50	13	(54)	X	X
Israel	113	(4)	13	18	100	(7)	X	X	177	16	209	69	X	X
Japan	34,110	6	372	(36)	33,738	7	27,267	(14)	8,228	(8)	28,380	61	42,255	46,485
Jordan	11	32	7	62	4	0	X	X	X	X	20	247	X	X
Kazakhstan, Rep	X	X	X	X	X	X	X	X	X	X	X	X	X	(25)
Korea, Dem People's Rep	4,783	9	4,183	11	600	0	280	0	X	X	80	0	71	(89)
Korea, Rep	6,485	(23)	4,491	(27)	1,994	(14)	3,584	13	1,634	4	5,410	195	5,916	9,327
Kuwait	X	X	X	X	X	X	X	X	X	X	X	X	21	58
Kyrgyz Rep	X	X	X	X	X	X	X	X	X	X	X	X	X	X
Lao People's Dem Rep	4,681	42	4,132	34	549	158	231	998	13	192	X	X	X	X
Lebanon	487	3	479	7	8	(70)	10	(67)	46	0	42	(7)	16	30
Malaysia	52,906	31	9,157	30	43,750	32	9,249	43	3,288	145	531	810	(18,369)	(15,681)
Mongolia	1,063	(56)	535	(60)	528	(49)	173	(63)	3	(17)	X	X	(233)	(1,352)
Myanmar	22,566	20	18,715	24	3,851	4	308	(56)	16	4	12	23	(233)	(1,352)
Nepal	19,595	30	18,975	31	620	11	620	182	X	X	13	550	X	X
Oman	X	X	X	X	X	X	X	X	X	X	X	X	10	(0)
Pakistan	27,019	45	24,379	37	2,640	214	1,497	495	80	54	214	194	25	79
Philippines	39,137	12	35,149	27	3,988	(46)	631	(48)	433	(35)	484	79	(1,637)	256
Saudi Arabia	X	X	X	X	X	X	X	X	X	X	X	X	227	89
Singapore	160	X	160	X	X	X	27	(89)	361	(38)	85	132	633	(218)
Sri Lanka	9,247	11	8,588	13	659	(3)	5	(81)	10	(32)	26	28	(181)	(16)
Syrian Arab Rep	74	62	23	21	52	91	9	0	27	0	1	(67)	73	(1)
Tajikistan, Rep	X	X	X	X	X	X	X	X	X	X	X	X	X	X
Thailand	37,619	10	34,854	15	2,765	(32)	910	(2)	611	168	1,138	249	(167)	1,466
Turkey	15,317	(29)	9,750	(35)	5,567	(15)	5,133	15	1,121	146	924	93	(41)	1,539
Turkmenistan, Rep	X	X	X	X	X	X	X	X	X	X	X	X	X	X
United Arab Emirates	X	X	X	X	X	X	X	X	X	X	X	X	0	36
Uzbekistan, Rep	X	X	X	X	X	X	X	X	X	X	X	X	X	X
Viet Nam	33,008	25	28,407	24	4,601	31	861	120	39	26	116	158	39	(193)
Yemen, Rep	X	X	X	X	X	X	X	X	X	X	X	X	X	X
OCEANIA	44,140	25	8,748	11	35,392	29	5,827	1	1,766	48	2,803	31	(8,248)	(13,521)
Australia	19,860	17	2,896	38	16,964	14	3,028	(8)	901	9	2,007	39	(5,745)	(6,470)
Fiji	307	31	37	48	270	29	108	25	17	58	X	X	(2)	(230)
New Zealand	15,110	51	50	0	15,060	51	2,527	14	802	134	796	13	(1,093)	(4,685)
Papua New Guinea	8,188	9	5,533	0	2,655	36	117	(6)	46	142	X	X	X	X
Solomon Islands	468	(9)	138	26	330	(18)	16	(4)	0	(100)	X	X	X	X

Source: Food and Agriculture Organization of the United Nations.

Notes: a. Imports of roundwood are shown as positive numbers; exports are shown as negative numbers (in parentheses). b. Ethiopia includes Eritrea. c. Regional totals do not include countries of the former Soviet Union. d. Includes Luxembourg. World and regional totals include countries not listed.
0 = zero or less than half the unit of measure; X = not available; negative numbers are shown in parentheses.
For additional information, see Sources and Technical Notes.

Sources and Technical Notes

Data Table 9.1
Land Area and Use, 1981–93

Sources: Land area and use: Food and Agriculture Organization of the United Nations (FAO), *FAOSTAT-PC*, on diskette (FAO, Rome, 1995); United States Central Intelligence Agency (CIA), *The World Factbook 1994* (CIA, Washington, D.C., 1994); population density: calculated from FAO land area data and population figures provided by United Nations (U.N.) Population Division, *Interpolated National Populations (The 1994 Revision)*, on diskette (U.N., New York, 1994).

Land area and *land use* data are provided to FAO by national governments in response to annual questionnaires. FAO also compiles data from national agricultural censuses. When official information is lacking, FAO prepares its own estimates or relies on unofficial data. Several countries use definitions of total area and land use that differ from those used in this chapter. Refer to the sources for details.

FAO often adjusts the definitions of land use categories and sometimes substantially revises earlier data. For example, in 1985, FAO began to exclude from the cropland category land used for shifting cultivation but currently lying fallow. Because land use changes can reflect changes in data-reporting procedures along with actual land use changes, apparent trends should be interpreted with caution.

Land use data are periodically revised and may change significantly from year to year. For the most recent land use statistics, see the latest *FAO Production Yearbook*.

Land area data are for 1993. They exclude major inland water bodies, national claims to the continental shelf, and Exclusive Economic Zones. (See Chapter 11, "Biodiversity," Data Table 11.4, Marine Biodiversity.)

The *population density* and *land use* figures for the world refer to the six inhabited continents. Population density was derived by using the population figures for 1995 published by the United Nations Population Division and land area data for 1993 from FAO. Although the population figures were published in 1994, actual censuses and estimates were made in prior years. For additional information on population and methodology, see the Technical Notes to Data Table 8.1, Size and Growth of Population and Labor Force, 1950–2025, in Chapter 8, "Population and Human Development."

Domesticated land as a percent of land area provides a crude indicator of the degree to which national landscapes have been heavily

modified through agricultural use. Domesticated land, as defined here, is a sum of FAO's "cropland" and "permanent pasture" land use categories. This indicator may overestimate or underestimate the actual degree to which a country's land area has been modified. Permanent pasture, for example, may include a significant proportion of rangeland in some countries, while consisting largely of heavily modified pasturelands in others. Domesticated land area does not include built-up lands or plantation forests, the latter constituting a major portion of heavily modified land area in many countries of the world.

Cropland includes land under temporary and permanent crops, temporary meadows, market and kitchen gardens, and temporary fallow. Permanent crops are those that do not need to be replanted after each harvest, such as cocoa, coffee, fruit, rubber, and vines. It excludes land used to grow trees for wood or timber.

Permanent pasture is land used for 5 or more years for forage, including natural crops and cultivated crops. This category is difficult for countries to assess because it includes wildland used for pasture. In addition, few countries regularly report data on permanent pasture. As a result, the absence of a change in permanent pasture area (e.g., 0 percent change for many African and Asian countries) may indicate differences in land classification and data reporting rather than actual conditions. Grassland not used for forage is included under *other land*.

Forest and woodland includes land under natural or planted stands of trees, as well as logged-over areas that will be reforested in the near future. These data are not comparable with forest and other wooded land data presented in Data Table 9.2.

Other land includes uncultivated land, grassland not used for pasture, built-on areas, wetlands, wastelands, and roads.

Data Table 9.2
Forest Resources, 1981–90

Sources: Food and Agriculture Organization of the United Nations (FAO), Forest Resources Division, *Forest Resources Assessment 1990: Global Synthesis* (FAO, Rome, 1995); FAO, Forest Resources Division, *Forest Resources Assessment 1990: Tropical Countries* (FAO, Rome, 1993); United Nations Economic Commission for Europe (UN/ECE) and FAO, *The Forest Resources of the Temperate Zones. Volume I: General Forest Resource Information* (UN/ECE–FAO, Geneva, 1993).

The FAO and UN/ECE–FAO used slightly different definitions in their assessments, each adapting its definitions to the respective forest ecosystem (forests in tropical and temperate developing countries versus forests in temperate developed countries). For this reason, these data are not strictly comparable between temperate developed countries (which include the former Soviet Union but not China) and the remaining countries of the world. FAO defines a *natural forest* in tropical and temperate developing countries as a forest composed primarily of indigenous (native) tree species. Natural forests include closed forest, where trees cover a high proportion of the ground and where grass does not form a continuous layer on the forest floor (e.g., broadleaved forests, coniferous forests, and bamboo forests), and open forest, which FAO defines as mixed forest/grasslands with at least 10 percent tree cover and a continuous grass layer on the forest floor. Natural forests in tropical and temperate developing countries encompass all stands except plantations and include stands that have been degraded to some degree by agriculture, fire, logging, and other factors. For all regions, trees are distinguished from shrubs on the basis of height. A mature tree has a single well-defined stem and is taller than 7 meters. A mature shrub is usually less than 7 meters tall.

UN/ECE–FAO defines a forest as land where tree crowns cover more than 20 percent of the area. Also included are open forest formations; forest roads and firebreaks; small, temporarily cleared areas; young stands expected to achieve at least 20 percent crown cover upon maturity; and windbreaks and shelterbelts exceeding 0.5 hectare in size. Under this definition, forest land in temperate developed countries includes both natural forest and plantation.

Total forest consists of all forest area for temperate developed countries, and the sum of natural forest and plantation area categories for tropical and temperate developing countries.

Plantation refers to forest stands established artificially by afforestation and reforestation for industrial and nonindustrial usage. Reforestation does not include regeneration of old tree crops (through either natural regeneration or forest management), although some countries may report regeneration as reforestation. Many trees are also planted for nonindustrial uses, such as village wood lots. Reforestation data often exclude this component. The data presented here reflect plantation survival rate as estimated by FAO. Plantation extent differs from figures presented in *World Resources 1994–95*, which did not include an adjustment for estimated survival rate.

The category *other wooded land* encompasses forest fallows (closed and open forests) and shrubs in tropical countries. In the temperate zone, other wooded land consists of open woodland and scrub, shrub, and brushland. The category also includes wooded areas used for rangeland, but excludes orchards, wood lots under 0.5 hectare, and tree hedgerows.

Annual change figures in parentheses (negative change) reflect net deforestation, which is defined as the "clearing of forest lands for all forms of agricultural uses (shifting cultivation, permanent agriculture and ranching) and for other land uses such as settlements, other infrastructure and mining." In tropical countries, this entails clearing that reduces tree crown cover to less than 10 percent. As defined here, deforestation does not include other alterations, such as selective logging (unless the forest cover is permanently reduced to less than 10 percent), that can substantially affect forests, forest soil, wildlife and its habitat, and the global carbon cycle. Positive annual change figures reflect net afforestation within a country or region.

Annual logging of closed broadleaf forest provides averages of the total area of *primary* (undisturbed) and thus secondary (previously logged) forest logged each year. Note that many "primary" forests are essentially old secondary forests.

Data for tropical and temperate developing countries are based on FAO's 1990 Forest Resources Assessment Project. This project provided a consistent estimate of developing country forest extent and rates of forest area change between 1981 and 1990 by using a model to adjust baseline forest inventory data from each country to a common year (1990). Existing forest inventory data on national and subnational scales were carefully reviewed, adjusted to a common set of classifications and concepts, and finally combined in a database. FAO used a geographic information system to integrate statistical and map data for this purpose. The model used forest area adjustment functions that correlated the share of forest cover for each subnational unit to population density and growth, initial forest extent, and ecological zone. This relation is expressed through the differential equation $dY/dP = b_1 \times Y^{b_2} - b_3 \times Y$, where Y is the percentage of nonforest area, P is the natural log of (1 + population density), and b_1, b_2, and b_3 are the model parameters. The shape of the respective adjustment curves differed for each ecological zone; for example, there was a logistic function for the wet zones and an inverted j-function for the dry zones.

The reliability of these modeled estimates hinges partly on the quality of the primary data sources feeding into the model. FAO assessed the quality and appropriateness of the national forestry inventories and their contribution to the reliability of the reported state and change assessments. The variation in quality, comprehensiveness, and timeliness of the forest information is tremendous, and acute information deficits in regard to forest resources can easily be highlighted. Whereas good forest resources data are hard to find for Africa, better data are available for Latin America, and the best information obtainable is that for Asia.

Although there were forest cover estimates for two periods for 136 of the 143 developing countries assessed (97 percent), forest data, on average, were almost 10 years old. Refer to the Technical Notes to Chapter 19, "Forests and Rangelands," in *World Resources 1994–95*, for details on forest cover and change data quality for the tropical countries.

Although the forest change model allowed standardization of country data to a common baseline, a number of additional factors may have contributed to discrepancies in forest area and change estimates for specific countries. Potential forest cover estimates for dry forests and the related adjustment function are of unknown reliability; and for some countries, socioeconomic factors may have played a larger role in deforestation—for example, livestock projects in Central America and resettlement schemes in Indonesia. FAO acknowledged these shortcomings implicitly and noted that country estimates are "not intended to replace the original country information which remain a unique source of reference."

Because of the shortcomings of the FAO methodology, readers are encouraged to refer to those country inventories that use satellite data or extensive ground data for estimates of forest cover and deforestation. Data for several independent country assessments are presented in the Technical Notes to Chapter 19, "Forests and Rangelands," in *World Resources 1994–95*.

The 1980 forest extent estimates for tropical and temperate developing countries presented in this data table are taken from the 1990 assessment and therefore are not comparable with estimates for that year presented in previous editions of *World Resources*. Past estimates were taken from two earlier FAO studies on forest extent. FAO's 1980 assessment covered 76 tropical developing countries and used subnational statistical data on population and socioeconomic variables, maps on vegetation and ecofloristic zones, forest survey data, and remote-sensing images to determine forest area. In many cases, FAO

adjusted data to fit common definitions and to correspond to the baseline year of 1980. FAO's *1988 Interim Report* expanded the country coverage of the 1980 assessment to 53 more developing countries (covering the whole developing world and overseas territories of developed countries), keeping 1980 as the reference year. In that document, FAO evaluated the overall reliability of data on closed forest areas and deforestation rates for the original 76 developing countries. The 1990 assessment incorporated previously unavailable baseline inventory data to improve on 1980 country estimates.

The UN/ECE–FAO 1990 survey of temperate zone countries covers all forests in the 32 countries of the ECE region (Europe, North America, and the former Soviet Union), as well as forests in Japan, Australia, and New Zealand. Data for this study were obtained mainly from official sources in response to a questionnaire, although there are estimates by experts in some countries. Recent ECE and FAO publications, country reports, official articles, and estimates by the professional staff conducting the study are also included. Most data refer to the period around 1990, although data for Belgium are based on 1980 figures, data for Iceland cover 1970–85, and estimates for several other countries are from the mid-to-late 1980s.

Data Table 9.3
Wood Production and Trade, 1981–93

Source: Food and Agriculture Organization of the United Nations (FAO), *FAOSTAT-PC*, on diskette (FAO, Rome, April 1995).

Total roundwood production refers to all wood in the rough, whether destined for industrial or fuelwood uses. All wood felled or harvested from forests and trees outside the forest, with or without bark, round, split, roughly squared, or in other forms such as roots and stumps, is included.

Fuel and charcoal production covers all rough wood used for cooking, heating, and power production. Wood intended for charcoal production, pit kilns, and portable ovens is also included.

Industrial roundwood production comprises all roundwood products other than fuelwood and charcoal: sawlogs, veneer logs, sleepers, pitprops, pulpwood, and other industrial products.

Processed wood production includes sawnwood and panels. *Sawnwood* is wood that has been sawn, planed, or shaped into products such as planks, beams, boards, rafters, or railroad ties. Wood flooring is excluded. Sawnwood generally is thicker than 5 millimeters. *Panels* include all wood-based panel commodities such as veneer sheets, plywood, particle board, and compressed or noncompressed fiberboard.

Paper production includes newsprint, printing and writing paper, and other paper and paperboard.

Average annual net trade in roundwood is the balance of imports minus exports. Trade in roundwood includes sawlogs and veneer logs, fuelwood, pulpwood, other industrial roundwood, and the roundwood equivalent of trade in charcoal, wood residues, and chips and particles. All trade data refer to both coniferous and nonconiferous wood. Imports are usually on a cost, insurance, and freight basis. Exports are generally on a free-on-board basis.

FAO compiles forest products data from responses to annual questionnaires sent to national governments. Data from other sources, such as national statistical yearbooks, are also used. In some cases, FAO prepares its own estimates. FAO continually revises its data using new information; the latest figures are subject to revision.

Statistics on the production of fuelwood and charcoal are lacking for many countries. FAO uses population data and country-specific, per capita consumption figures to estimate fuelwood and charcoal production. Consumption of nonconiferous fuelwood ranges from a low of 0.0016 cubic meter per capita per year in Jordan to a high of 0.9783 cubic meter per capita per year in Benin. Consumption was also estimated for coniferous fuelwood. For both coniferous and nonconiferous fuelwood, the per capita consumption estimates were multiplied by the number of people in the country to determine national totals.

10. Food and Agriculture

Discussions about the future of global agriculture take place in an unusual context: production is generally growing and is likely to continue to grow, but globally, the rate of growth is slowing. At the same time, about 90 million people are being added to the world's population every year, putting more pressure on the world's food production system.

In the face of these declining growth rates, many experts are concerned about the capacity of the world agricultural system to continue to increase production over the coming decades to feed an ever-larger world population. Other experts worry not so much about the growth potential of global production as they do about the poorest countries of Africa and Asia and the continuing prevalence of chronic undernutrition in those regions. A further concern is whether there are ways to increase production while at the same time reducing environmental and resource damage.

Differences among regions and between rich and poor are an important subplot to this story. In two regions, sub-Saharan Africa and South Asia, food security and undernutrition problems seem relatively intractable. In both regions, population growth is still relatively high and poverty is persistent.

RECENT TRENDS

Production and Trade

Figure 10.1 shows the essential success story of global agriculture: steady growth in the production of most food crops from 1961 to 1994. The latest country-by-country data are provided in Data Table 10.1.

The success has not been shared equally, however, as shown in Figure 10.2, which depicts per capita food production trends. Africa's food production has risen steadily; since 1961, total food production has more than doubled (1). As the per capita trend indicates, however, it has not been fast enough to keep up with population growth.

A notable recent development is the drop in production in the nations of the former Soviet Union. Compared with a peak production year in 1989, production in 1994 was down fully 40 percent (2). But 1994 was a particularly disastrous year in the region, and production for that year may not say much about future trends. Other regions—notably, Asia and to a lesser extent Latin America—have experienced tremendous success in both absolute and per capita terms.

Agricultural commodities have been a major component of many developing countries' trade, yet in the aggregate, countries that depend on such exports have not been rewarded. The prices of most agricultural commodities have fallen globally over the past 15 years. Developing countries must rely on shipping larger volumes of commodities to maintain their export earnings. In sub-Saharan Africa, the total value of agricultural exports in current U.S. dollars fell by an average of 4.6 percent from 1980 to 1985 and by 1.1 percent per year from 1986 to 1992 (3). Declining returns from exports have contributed to a rapid worsening of the region's external debt (4).

An important point in the debate about future prospects concerns the question of production trends over the past few decades and particularly the question of slowing growth in production. From 1961 to 1992, the growth of world agricultural production slowed, dropping from 3 percent annually in the 1960s to 2.3 percent per year in the 1970s and to 2 percent during the 1980–92 period. The trend is similar for world cereals production (5). (See Figure 10.3.)

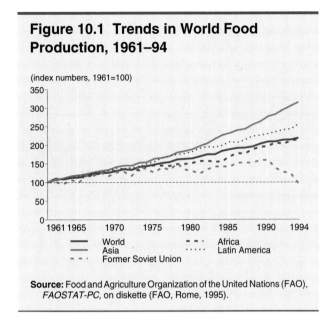

Figure 10.1 Trends in World Food Production, 1961–94

(index numbers, 1961=100)

World   Africa
Asia   Latin America
Former Soviet Union

Source: Food and Agriculture Organization of the United Nations (FAO), *FAOSTAT-PC,* on diskette (FAO, Rome, 1995).

Figure 10.2 Trends in Per Capita Food Production, 1961–94

(index numbers, 1961=100)

World   Africa
Asia   Latin America
Former Soviet Union

Source: Food and Agriculture Organization of the United Nations (FAO), *FAOSTAT-PC,* on diskette (FAO, Rome, 1995).

Production trends are most critical, however, in those developing countries characterized by high economic dependence on agriculture (i.e., with more than one third of the economically active population engaged in agriculture), low levels of per capita food supplies, and a limited ability to import more food. About 62 of the 93 principal developing countries are in this category (6). For these countries (excluding China), growth rates in recent years have actually been higher than those in earlier periods. (See Figure 10.4.) Recent production trends in the most vulnerable developing countries do not seem noticeably worse than they were in the late 1960s and early 1970s. They remain, however, grossly inadequate to meet the needs of the current and future populations in those nations and to help generate the

additional income among the poor necessary to dramatically reduce chronic undernutrition.

Yields

The causes of production gains in developing countries in the past few decades—often subsumed under the term "Green Revolution"—include the introduction of modern varieties of rice, wheat, and maize in combination with the more intensive use of inputs such as fertilizers, water, and pesticides.

There are large regional differences in the adoption of modern varieties. China's rice and maize crops, for example, are almost entirely planted to modern varieties. On the other hand, modern varieties have not been widely adopted in areas prone to drought or in rice crop areas with poor water control. Diffusion also is slower in areas with poor infrastructure or market access, as is the case with many regions in sub-Saharan Africa or the hillside systems of Latin America and Asia. For developing countries as a whole, as of 1990–91, nearly three fourths of rice and wheat crop areas and more than half of all maize croplands were planted to modern varieties (7).

Although some exceptions exist, most of the growth in production in developing countries is a result of the higher yields generated by the Green Revolution. As shown in Table 10.1,

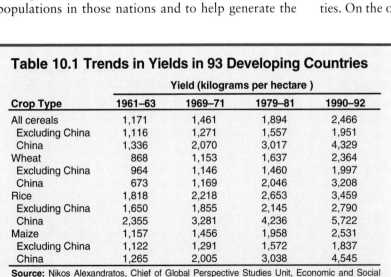

Table 10.1 Trends in Yields in 93 Developing Countries

Crop Type	Yield (kilograms per hectare)			
	1961–63	1969–71	1979–81	1990–92
All cereals	1,171	1,461	1,894	2,466
Excluding China	1,116	1,271	1,557	1,951
China	1,336	2,070	3,017	4,329
Wheat	868	1,153	1,637	2,364
Excluding China	964	1,146	1,460	1,997
China	673	1,169	2,046	3,208
Rice	1,818	2,218	2,653	3,459
Excluding China	1,650	1,855	2,145	2,790
China	2,355	3,281	4,236	5,722
Maize	1,157	1,456	1,958	2,531
Excluding China	1,122	1,291	1,572	1,837
China	1,265	2,005	3,038	4,545

Source: Nikos Alexandratos, Chief of Global Perspective Studies Unit, Economic and Social Department, Food and Agriculture Organization of the United Nations, Rome, 1995 (personal communication, based on data from *FAOSTAT-Mainframe*).

increases in the yields of the major cereals in developing countries have been substantial, even when excluding the effects of China's astounding yield increases.

Because so much of the recent success is due to increases in yields, a vital question for the future is whether such increases will continue and at what rates. Table 10.2 shows the growth rates in the yields of the major cereals over the past few decades; since China's performance has such a bearing on the trends, the table also shows the trends for all developing countries excluding China.

The table confirms that although total yields have increased, yield growth rates in developing countries have slowed for all cereals. The results tend to be skewed by China's performance, however, especially its dramatic yield increases during the 1960s. For all other countries, growth rates in the yields of rice and wheat have climbed steadily over the past three decades, whereas growth rates in the yields of maize have declined.

Food Aid

Food aid plays a major part in meeting food needs in parts of Africa and elsewhere. In the early 1990s, the ratio of food aid to total cereal imports in developing countries was in the 7 to 10 percent range, yet it could drop to as low as 5.4 percent in 1994–95 if total cereal imports in developing countries continue to rise (8).

The frequency and scale of humanitarian crises requiring the international community to provide food aid have increased substantially in recent years. The number of people affected by disasters (both natural and political) rose from about 44 million in 1985 to more than 175 million in 1993, whereas the number of people officially receiving protection and assistance from the United Nations rose from 1 million in 1970 to 17 million in 1993 (9).

The rapid increase in the number of crises has led to a substantial shift in priorities. For example, in 1986, the World Food Programme allocated 75 percent of its resources to development projects, but by 1993–94 more than 85 percent of its resources were going to emergencies and refugee needs. Food aid for relief operations rose to 4.5 million metric tons in 1993–94, up substantially from less than 1 million metric tons in 1979–80 (10).

All told, the global redistribution of food by public-sector agencies amounted to a record 17 million met-

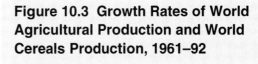

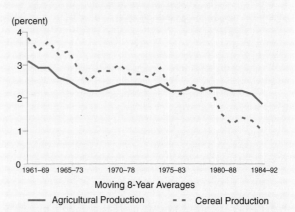

Figure 10.3 Growth Rates of World Agricultural Production and World Cereals Production, 1961–92

Moving 8-Year Averages

—— Agricultural Production - - - Cereal Production

Source: Nikos Alexandratos, ed., *World Agriculture: Towards 2010, An FAO Study* (John Wiley and Sons, Chichester, U.K., and Food and Agriculture Organization of the United Nations, Rome, 1995), p. 39.

ric tons in 1993; about 25 percent went to Somalia, Rwanda, and other countries in sub-Saharan Africa, whereas about 41 percent went to Central Europe and the countries of the former Soviet Union (11). The amount of food redistributed in 1993 is still far short of the total need; it is estimated that 24 million to 27 million metric tons would have been needed in 1993 to raise the per capita global caloric intake to recommended minimum levels. In 1994, total food aid was about 14 million metric tons (12).

Africa remains the continent most seriously affected by food shortages. Fifteen countries in the region are

Table 10.2 Trends in Growth Rates in Yields of Wheat, Rice, and Maize in 93 Developing Countries, 1961–92

Crop Type	Growth (percent)		
	1961–70	1970–80	1980–92
All cereals	2.8	2.6	2.1
Excluding China	1.5	2.1	1.9
China	6.0	3.7	2.9
Wheat	3.7	3.5	3.2
Excluding China	2.0	2.5	2.8
China	7.8	5.4	3.7
Rice	2.5	1.7	2.1
Excluding China	1.3	1.5	2.2
China	4.9	2.5	2.3
Maize	3.0	2.9	2.2
Excluding China	1.7	1.6	1.3
China	6.2	4.2	3.3

Source: Nikos Alexandratos, Chief of Global Perspective Studies Unit, Economic and Social Department, Food and Agriculture Organization of the United Nations, Rome, 1995 (personal communication, based on data from *FAOSTAT-Mainframe*).

Figure 10.4 Growth Rates of Agricultural Production in High-Dependence Developing Countries, 1961–92

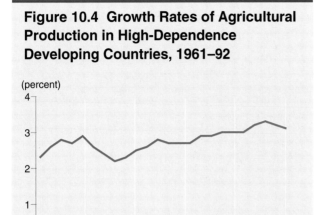

(percent)

Moving 8-Year Averages

—— Agricultural Production

Source: Nikos Alexandratos, ed., *World Agriculture: Towards 2010, An FAO Study* (John Wiley and Sons, Chichester, U.K., and Food and Agriculture Organization of the United Nations, Rome, 1995), p. 43.
Notes: Data for China are excluded from the data presented here. Of the 93 principal developing countries, 31 have relatively "low" dependence on agriculture for employment and income. Most of these countries have less than one third of their economically active population in agriculture. These countries have a total population of 730 million people, which is about one fifth of the total population in developing countries. The remaining 62 "high-dependence" countries have more than one third of their economically active population in agriculture. Per capita food supplies average 2,370 calories per day, with the majority of countries nearer the 2,000 calorie level. All of these countries depend heavily on their own agriculture both to produce food and to provide income.

facing exceptional food emergencies (13). Of the 27 countries with household food security problems, 22 are in sub-Saharan Africa (14). (See Figure 10.5.)

FUTURE GLOBAL CEREAL PRODUCTION: FEAST OR FAMINE?

Numerous attempts have been made in recent years to grapple with the question of whether global food production can keep up with population growth and reduce undernutrition in the next few decades. Whether they are positive or negative in outlook, most studies agree that the key issues include the potential for expanding cropland area and irrigated cropland area, for increasing yields, and for improving efficiency. Other scholars emphasize the importance of resource conservation and alternative production models that are less environmentally damaging than the conventional high-input approach.

The Food and Agriculture Organization of the United Nations (FAO) has published a study on the food production outlook through the year 2010 (15). The

World Bank has produced a similar study, although it does not represent the formal position of the Bank on these issues (16). In addition to the World Bank and FAO analyses, other studies have looked at food production potential over a longer time frame. The International Food Policy Research Institute (IFPRI), which is part of the Consultative Group on International Agricultural Research (CGIAR), recently published a study of food production potential through the year 2020 (17). A previous World Bank study examined the issue through the year 2030 (18). Vaclav Smil, a geographer and China scholar at the University of Manitoba, Canada, has made some rough estimates through the year 2050 (19). Although acknowledging the many obstacles to future food production increases, these studies generally support the FAO forecast that production increases can accommodate effective demand and rising world population, although they are much less sanguine about reducing undernutrition. A proviso in most of the forecasts is that continuing substantial investments in agricultural research are essential.

Lester Brown and Hal Kane are much more pessimistic about future food production. They argue that food production will be constrained by the shrinking backlog of unused agricultural technology, by the approaching limits to the biological productivities of fisheries and rangelands, by the increasing scarcity of water (see Chapter 13, "Water") and the declining effectiveness of additional fertilizer applications, and generally by social disintegration in many developing countries (20). Ian Carruthers argues that the fragile tropical and subtropical environments in many developing countries will be unable to sustain further food production increases, and that prospects for production increases are much better in temperate zone nations such as the United States, Australia, and Europe. Carruthers believes that temperate zone countries will increasingly export food to developing countries in exchange for labor-intensive manufactured goods (21). Other scholars emphasize the significance of soil erosion as a major threat to the sustainability and productive capacity of agriculture (22).

As with many predictions about the future, there are wide differences in outlook. Many factors help explain these differences. Slight differences in population growth assumptions, for instance, can lead to substantial differences in outcomes. There is uncertainty about the extent to which past agricultural performance is a useful guide to future performance; if yields were x over the past two decades, does this mean they will continue to be x over the next two decades? New cereal varieties have played a big role in the success of the past few decades, but it is hard to say whether the pace of new

Figure 10.5 Developing Countries with Low or Critical Food Security Indexes, 1990–92

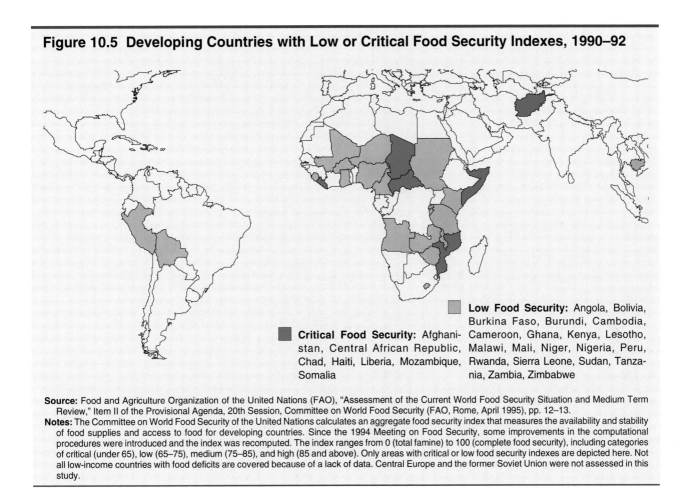

Critical Food Security: Afghanistan, Central African Republic, Chad, Haiti, Liberia, Mozambique, Somalia

Low Food Security: Angola, Bolivia, Burkina Faso, Burundi, Cambodia, Cameroon, Ghana, Kenya, Lesotho, Malawi, Mali, Niger, Nigeria, Peru, Rwanda, Sierra Leone, Sudan, Tanzania, Zambia, Zimbabwe

Source: Food and Agriculture Organization of the United Nations (FAO), "Assessment of the Current World Food Security Situation and Medium Term Review," Item II of the Provisional Agenda, 20th Session, Committee on World Food Security (FAO, Rome, April 1995), pp. 12–13.
Notes: The Committee on World Food Security of the United Nations calculates an aggregate food security index that measures the availability and stability of food supplies and access to food for developing countries. Since the 1994 Meeting on Food Security, some improvements in the computational procedures were introduced and the index was recomputed. The index ranges from 0 (total famine) to 100 (complete food security), including categories of critical (under 65), low (65–75), medium (75–85), and high (85 and above). Only areas with critical or low food security indexes are depicted here. Not all low-income countries with food deficits are covered because of a lack of data. Central Europe and the former Soviet Union were not assessed in this study.

innovations will continue unabated. (See Box 10.1.) Environmental degradation has clearly had a significant effect on agricultural production in many regions; will such degradation get worse under the pressures of population growth and further intensification of production? Finally, models cannot predict the future of the world economy with much confidence.

These caveats notwithstanding, most studies indicate that over the next few decades global food production can continue to increase to meet "effective" demand, that is, the level of demand that corresponds to purchasing power irrespective of food needs. This is not likely to be the case in sub-Saharan Africa and South Asia, however. These regions are likely to experience regional production shortages, food distribution problems, and famines. In addition, given the millions of people who lack the money to buy all the food they need, it is even more doubtful that growth in purchasing power will be adequate to raise per capita food consumption to levels comparable to those needed to eliminate undernutrition.

Growing more cereals in the United States or in other developed countries will not meet the food needs of many of the poor in developing countries. To improve the food security of this group, ways must be found to help farmers grow more of their own food. Many of these nations remain primarily rural and heavily dependent on the agricultural economy. Boosting domestic food production would thus be doubly positive, increasing both food supplies and the incomes of many of the poor.

The FAO forecast may be somewhat toward the optimistic end of the range of studies on future food production. Because the study provides a consistent data set, the FAO numbers are used in most of the following discussion.

Sources of Food Production Growth

There is a broad consensus that yield increases will continue to be the key component of future growth in food production. FAO estimates that increased yields will account for 66 percent of production growth through the year 2010 in developing countries, with arable land expansion accounting for an additional 21 percent and increased cropping intensity (fewer fallow

Box 10.1 New Varieties and Agricultural Research

Many new cultivars are in the pipeline at the centers of the Consultative Group on International Agricultural Research (CGIAR). For example, the transfer of hybrid rice varieties from China to tropical Asia proved difficult because of their susceptibility to disease, but the International Rice Research Institute (IRRI) has developed hybrids that provide a 15 to 25 percent boost in yields (1). Meanwhile, progress in hybrid rice seed production has lowered the cost of seed and has greatly increased the area where hybrids would be profitable (2).

IRRI has reported a breakthrough in the development of a rice variety that goes well beyond the current potential of modern varieties of 10 metric tons per hectare. The first generation has the potential to achieve yields of 12 metric

tons per hectare. Experience has shown, however, that the actual yield boost in farmers' fields rarely comes close to the yield boost in test plots. IRRI also is working on varieties that are better adapted to rainfed and upland rice ecosystems and other varieties with enhanced resistance to pests (3).

Researchers at the Centro Internacional de Mejoramiento de Maiz y Trigo (CIMMYT) in Mexico have developed varieties of maize that are tolerant of acid soil and drought conditions, yielding 40 percent more grains than conventional varieties under the same conditions (4). CIMMYT also has developed new varieties for lowland tropical environments that yield at least 25 percent more grain than existing cultivars. Agricultural research is vital to future

gains in productivity, yet financial support is dwindling both for CGIAR and for national systems (5).

References and Notes

1. Consultative Group on International Agricultural Research (CGIAR) Secretariat, "Current CGIAR Research Efforts and Their Expected Impact on Food, Agriculture, and National Development," draft paper (CGIAR, Washington, D.C., March 1994), p. 35.
2. Nikos Alexandratos, ed., *World Agriculture: Towards 2010, An FAO Study* (John Wiley and Sons, Chichester, U.K., and Food and Agriculture Organization of the United Nations, Rome, 1995), p. 179.
3. *Op. cit.* 1.
4. *Op. cit.* 1, p. 28.
5. *Op. cit.* 1, p. 4.

periods or more than one crop per year on a field) providing 13 percent of the projected increase (23). (See Table 10.3.)

Global gross agricultural production will continue to grow over the next two decades; however, it is projected to grow at a slower rate (1.8 percent per annum) than it did in the previous 20 years (24). According to FAO, the slowdown in the growth of production will be due in part to slowing rates of population growth and an increasing saturation in demand for food, especially in developed countries. Inadequate income growth in countries with low levels of consumption will also be a factor (25).

Table 10.3 Estimated Sources of Growth in Crop Production and Total Land Use, Developing Countries, Excluding China, 1988–90 to 2010

Region	Percent Contribution		
	Increased Yield	Arable Land	Cropping Intensity
Developing countries	66	21	13
Sub-Saharan Africa	53	30	17
Near East/North Africa	71	9	20
East Asia	61	32	7
South Asia	82	4	14
Latin America/ Caribbean	53	28	19

Source: Nikos Alexandratos, ed., *World Agriculture: Towards 2010, An FAO Study* (John Wiley and Sons, Chichester, U.K., and Food and Agriculture Organization of the United Nations, Rome, 1995), p. 170.

Expanding Cropland

All told, developing countries (excluding China) have about 2.5 billion hectares of land on which rainfed crops could achieve reasonable yields. About 760 million hectares currently are used in crop production, but only about 600 million hectares are harvested in an average year; in any given year, some lands are fallow and are not harvested (26). China is thought to have roughly 125 million hectares of cropland (the admittedly understated official total is 96 million hectares), but the total has been shrinking for some time and is likely to continue to decline.

FAO estimates that by the year 2010, the 760 million hectares of land currently in crop production in developing countries (excluding China) could increase by 12 percent to 850 million hectares. Of these 850 million hectares, 720 million hectares could be harvested in a given year—an increase of about 21 percent—because of greater cropping intensities (27). (See Figure 10.6.)

Some experts are much less optimistic about the potential for further cropland expansion in the next few decades. They believe that the potential for further expansion of cropland area is rapidly disappearing in most regions (28). The potential to expand cropland is limited by many factors, including environmental costs and the cost of developing the infrastructure in remote areas. (See Box 10.2.) Furthermore, undeveloped areas usually are not prime cropland, so yields will generally be less than average (29).

Over the past three decades, the expansion of cropland area has been significant in two regions: sub-

Saharan Africa and Latin America. Indeed, sub-Saharan Africa stands out as the only region in the world where the expansion of cropland area contributed nearly as much as yield increases to the growth of cereal production during the 1961–90 period. In Latin America over the same period, expansion of cropland area accounted for nearly one third of production gains (30).

There remain relatively large areas of sub-Saharan Africa and Latin America that are potentially cultivable. In each of these regions, FAO estimates that expansion of arable land will contribute about 30 percent to the increase in crop production (47 percent including greater cropping intensity) (31). Most of the expansion of cropland area projected by FAO will be in maize and other coarse grains, which are more prominent crops in these regions (32).

At least 45 percent of the potential cropland in sub-Saharan Africa and Latin America is under forest or is in protected areas (33); about 72 percent of the potential cropland suffers from soil and terrain constraints (34). Conversion would entail high financial and ecological costs, including the loss of biodiversity, increased carbon dioxide emissions, and significantly decreased carbon storage capacity (35) (36).

Asia has more than 50 percent of the world's population, but two thirds of its potentially arable land is already under cultivation; the main exceptions are Indonesia and Myanmar. South Asia's agricultural land is almost totally developed; land expansion is likely to account for only about 4 percent of production growth through 2010 (37).

Expanding Irrigation

Estimates of the world's total irrigated land vary but usually range between 225 million and 250 million hectares. Irrigated land accounted for more than 50 percent of the increase in global food production from the mid-1960s to the mid-1980s and currently accounts for about one third of total production. Irrigation promotes higher crop yields and also allows multiple cropping, which dramatically increases production (38) (39). About 60 percent of the world's total irrigated land is in Asia, mostly in India, China, and Pakistan. Africa and South America have 5 and 4 percent of the world's total irrigated land, respectively (40).

FAO predicts that irrigated land in developing countries (excluding China) will expand at a rate of 0.8 percent annually, which is much slower than the 2.2 percent annual increase experienced during the 1970s and the 1.9 percent annual increase in the 1980s. About two thirds of the expansion will be in Asia. Even with this slower growth rate, more than half of the increment

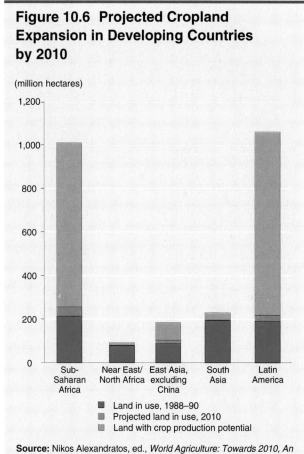

Figure 10.6 Projected Cropland Expansion in Developing Countries by 2010

(million hectares)

- ■ Land in use, 1988–90
- ▨ Projected land in use, 2010
- ▨ Land with crop production potential

Source: Nikos Alexandratos, ed., *World Agriculture: Towards 2010, An FAO Study* (John Wiley and Sons, Chichester, U.K., and Food and Agriculture Organization, Rome, 1995), pp. 162–163.

in crop production between now and 2010 will come from irrigated land, according to the FAO model (41).

The rate at which cropland is brought under irrigation is declining, mainly because of the increasing cost of irrigation (both development and maintenance), the growing competition for water uses, and the decline in both real agricultural and food prices. Irrigation's environmental and health impacts also may inhibit further expansion. Salinization and waterlogging problems from improper irrigation techniques reduce crop yields, constraining future gains in production. Furthermore, it is increasingly costly to avoid or reverse the accretion of silt in dams and reservoirs and of the salt in already irrigated soil (42).

Increasing Yields

Yields of maize, rice, and wheat doubled between 1961 and 1991 in developing countries as a whole. The most extraordinary gains occurred in Asia, where wheat yields rose from 0.7 to 2.6 metric tons per hectare. In China, rice yields jumped from 2.3 to 5.7 metric tons

Box 10.2 Agriculture and the Environment

Agricultural growth will put additional pressures on land and water resources. The Food and Agriculture Organization of the United Nations (FAO) estimates that roughly half of the 90 million hectares that could be converted to crop production by the year 2010 in developing countries (excluding China) is currently in forest. This represents a significant potential loss of carbon storage capacity and of biodiversity resources. FAO also projects an expansion of 6 million hectares in dry land areas, which are mostly rangeland. This could increase grazing pressure on the remaining pastures or displace livestock to even more marginal lands (1).

Land conversion for aquaculture, although involving a small amount of land, still may threaten unique areas such as mangrove swamps. In some areas, wetlands also are being converted to croplands. As demand for irrigation water increases, the overextraction of groundwater—already a serious problem in the Near East and in parts of South Asia—will likely worsen. This in turn often leads to salinization, which can seriously reduce yields and may ultimately render the land unusable (2) (3).

Soil erosion presents another potentially significant constraint, particularly in the tropics, where soil fertility is concentrated near the surface. Erosion also has important downstream effects, such as the siltation of reservoirs.

Agriculture also is a significant contributor to anthropogenic sources of greenhouse gases, contributing about 70 percent of the total amount of methane (largely through rice cultivation) and about 90 percent of all nitrous oxide (4).

References and Notes

1. Nikos Alexandratos, ed., *World Agriculture: Towards 2010, An FAO Study* (John Wiley and Sons, Chichester, U.K., and Food and Agriculture Organization of the United Nations, Rome, 1995), pp. 351–352.

2. *Ibid.,* pp. 353–355.

3. Pacific Institute for Studies in Development, Environment and Security and the Stockholm Environment Institute, *Water in Crisis*, Peter H. Gleick, ed. (Oxford University Press, New York, 1993), pp. 6–7.

4. *Op. cit.* 1, pp. 362–363.

---

per hectare, whereas maize yields increased from 1.2 to 4.6 metric tons per hectare (43). In Africa, maize, rice, and wheat yields have been poor, especially compared with those in Asia and Latin America. Between 1961 and 1991, maize yields in Asia rose from 1.2 to 3.4 metric tons per hectare, whereas maize yields in Africa rose from about 0.8 to 1.2 metric tons per hectare (44).

From 1988–90 to 2010, cereal yields in developing countries (excluding China) are projected to increase by about 1.4 percent per year, according to FAO. (This does not include increases due to greater cropping intensity.) FAO's model assumes a substantial slowdown in the rate of yield increases for all of the major cereals: the average yearly growth in wheat yields, for example, is forecast to fall from 2.8 percent in 1970 to 1990 to 1.6 percent from 1988–90 to 2010; similarly, annual growth in rice yields is expected to drop from 2.3 percent to 1.5 percent (45). (See Table 10.4.) Wheat yields could rise by 40 percent to nearly 2.7 metric tons per hectare by 2010, whereas rice yields (for irrigated, naturally flooded, and rainfed lands) could increase by 37 percent to 3.8 metric tons per hectare by 2010 (46).

Part of FAO's cautious optimism about continuing yield increases is based on the existing wide disparities in yields among countries. For example, rice yields on irrigated land vary from 1 to 10 tons per hectare; today's average yield of 3.7 metric tons per hectare is well below the 6.7 metric tons per hectare achieved by the best-performing countries (47). Similarly, average yields of wheat and maize on irrigated land are only about half the yields achieved by the best-performing countries (48). Thus, there is considerable room for further improve-

ment by farmers currently achieving less-than-peak yields, according to the FAO model.

Although FAO predicts that, on average, increased yields will contribute about 66 percent to future crop production growth, they project that yield increases will make the strongest contribution in South Asia (82 percent) and much smaller contributions in Latin America and Africa (53 percent) (49).

Brown and others argue that the dramatic gains in yields achieved over the past three decades are not likely to be repeated, since more and more of the world's farmers are already using varieties with the highest genetic yield potential. Furthermore, they note that rice yields at experiment stations in Asia have been stagnant for many years (50).

Minimizing Soil Degradation

Fertilizer consumption is expected to increase in all developing regions. In South Asia, for example, FAO projects an increase from the 1988–90 level of 69 kilograms of fertilizer per hectare to 138 kilograms by the year 2010, or an average annual growth of 3.4 percent (51).

In sub-Saharan Africa, relatively little cropland is fertilized, so the average amount of fertilizer used per hectare in 1988–90 was estimated at just 11 kilograms. FAO projects increases of about 3.3 percent per year, but that would still mean an average rate of use of just 21 kilograms per hectare by the year 2010 (52). Many reasons are cited for Africa's lagging fertilizer consumption, including shortages of foreign exchange that limit imports; prohibitively high prices, especially for landlocked countries dependent on imports; and inefficient distribution systems (53). Low-cost options, such as the use of organic fertilizers, could be a practical alternative for the region's subsistence farmers.

In many areas, the lack of inputs—combined with inherently fragile characteristics of the land, shortening of fallow periods, and continuous cropping—create conditions in which nutrients are steadily lost and production declines. Soil nutrient mining can ultimately result in the lowering of crop yields. Crop production measures to replenish soil nutrients include the use of organic and mineral fertilizers, leguminous crops, and nitrogen-fixing algae (54). Aside from the primary nutrients, other secondary nutrients and micronutrients are depleted in the course of crop production. This depletion may cause lower yields even with the application of chemical fertilizer and cropping measures that essentially replenish primary nutrients. Deficiencies in micronutrients such as zinc, iron, and copper are reported in India, which partly explains the decline in demonstration plot yields despite growing chemical fertilizer use (55). Nutrient mining also is a serious problem in parts of Africa, where livestock manure is in short supply and the use of mineral fertilizer is seldom economical (56).

A survey of soil degradation (GLASOD) by the International Soil Reference and Information Center estimated that 9 million hectares worldwide are extremely degraded, with original biotic functions fully destroyed, and 1.2 billion hectares—10 percent of the Earth's vegetated surface—are at least moderately degraded.

Worldwide, faulty agricultural practices account for 28 percent of the degraded soils, including about one fourth of the degraded soils in Africa and Asia and nearly two thirds of the degraded soils in North America. Causes include shortening of the fallow period during shifting cultivation (shifting cultivation is the clearing of land—usually by fire—followed by phases of cultivation and a fallow period), cultivating hillsides without adequate erosion control measures, leaving soil exposed during fallow periods, and insufficient drainage of irrigation water. Overgrazing by livestock is another significant cause of land degradation, accounting for nearly half of all land degradation in Africa. (See *World Resources 1992–93*, pp. 111–118.)

The impact on production is difficult to determine. For example, the study classified 10 to 49 percent of the land in six U.S. states (Illinois, Iowa, Kansas, Nebraska, and North and South Dakota) as moderately degraded because of agriculturally induced water and wind erosion. Over the past 40 years, however, land degradation has been masked by other yield-boosting factors such as higher inputs (57).

In many other regions, such as the rainfed areas of Africa and South Asia, inputs have played a lesser role and the relative impact of degradation certainly seems to be greater. One promising new development is the United Nations Convention to Combat Desertification, which could provide some new impetus for the management of croplands in the dryland areas of Africa. The Convention, which is expected to enter into force by 1997, calls for the development of national action programs that encourage diversification in agriculture, promote the use of drought-resistant crops and the

Table 10.4 Production, Yield, and Area by Major Cereal Crop, Developing Countries, Excluding China, 1969–71 to 2010

Crop Type	1969–71	1988–90	2010	1970–90	1988–90 to 2010
	Production (million metric tons)			Growth (percent)	
Wheat	67	132	205	3.8	2.1
Rice (paddy)	177	303	459	3.0	2.0
Maize	70	112	196	2.7	2.7
Other cereals	67	84	135	1.3	2.3
Total	**381**	**631**	**995**	**2.8**	**2.2**
	Yields (kilograms per hectare)				
Wheat	1,150	1,900	2,660	2.8	1.6
Rice (paddy)	1,855	2,775	3,810	2.3	1.5
Maize	1,300	1,790	2,470	1.8	1.5
Other cereals	730	940	1,210	1.3	1.2
Total	**1,270**	**1,910**	**2,560**	**2.2**	**1.4**
	Harvested Area (million hectares)				
Wheat	58	70	77	0.9	0.5
Rice (paddy)	95	109	120	0.8	0.5
Maize	54	63	80	0.9	1.2
Other cereals	92	89	112	0.0	1.0
Total	**299**	**331**	**389**	**0.6**	**0.8**

Source: Nikos Alexandratos, ed., *World Agriculture: Towards 2010, An FAO Study* (John Wiley and Sons, Chichester, U.K., and Food and Agriculture Organization of the United Nations, Rome, 1995), p. 169.
Note: Other cereals include barley, millet, sorghum, rye, oats, buckwheat, quinoa, triticale, and canary seed.

application of integrated dry land farming systems, and ensure the more integrated and sustainable management of agricultural and pastoral lands (58).

Improving Agronomic Practices

Crop production can also be increased by applying appropriate farming techniques. Optimizing the timing and density of planting and seeding has raised corn yields by as much as 2.5 metric tons per hectare and soybean yields by 1 additional metric ton per hectare (59). In marginal wheat production areas of Africa, every 1-day delay in sowing after the optimal sowing date can result in a sizable reduction in grain yield. Seedbed preparation also can be critical in areas prone to waterlogging.

Timing operations to achieve maximum yields of one crop may have opportunity costs elsewhere on the farm, however. For example, in northern Nigeria, cotton yields can be increased significantly through earlier planting, but cotton then competes with food crops for labor at a critical time of year. Thus, farmers continue to plant later, even though this reduces their cotton yield, in order to give greater priority to their food crops (60).

Timing improvements depend on a well-informed corps of agricultural extension officers or some similar type of educational programs for farmers, which are not always available in many developing countries.

Improving the Efficiency of Water Use

Instead of expanding the area of irrigated cropland, it may often be more cost-effective to rehabilitate existing cropland areas or implement price reforms to improve the efficiency of water use (61). In many cases, less than 50 percent of irrigation water is utilized by crops, while the rest is lost through seepage from unlined canals, evaporation and runoff from poorly applied water, and poor management that fails to deliver water at the right time in the proper amounts (62). Water is used inefficiently not only because of management problems but also because it is usually priced below its true value. Current water prices in many countries do not even cover the cost of delivery (63).

Water-use efficiency improvements could result in expansion of the area of irrigated cropland or an increase in crop yields, or both (64). Such gains, however, can require significant investments in both infrastructure and institutional reform and can depend on crucial investments in agricultural education. More expensive irrigation improvements include pressurized systems, portable sprinklers, center pivots, moving lines, and drip systems (65).

With the many constraints that limit the expansion of irrigation, improvements to rainfed cropland—about

84 percent of total cropped land—are important to future food production (66). There are many opportunities in this area: for example, techniques that increase soil moisture around the root zone can improve yields and reduce production risks (67).

Reducing Postharvest Losses

Reducing postharvest losses provides another opportunity to improve yields. The actual magnitude of crop losses after harvest is not well known. One study estimates total global marketing and distribution losses at 8 percent (68); other estimates are higher, often in the range of about 10 percent for developed countries such as the United States and about 20 percent for developing countries (69). In Kenya, for example, it is estimated that 24 percent of harvested grains are damaged by molds, fungi, insects, rodents, and other pests; losses are significantly larger in remote areas of the country (70).

Gains can be obtained through better processing and improved storage and distribution facilities (including transportation infrastructure and transport facilities). Improved food storage facilities may also reduce vulnerability to famines and food shortages (71). In developing countries, seemingly minor changes in handling crops such as cereals could result in significant reductions in postharvest losses.

Alternative Models

In recent decades, the formula for increasing production has been to use high-yielding varieties in combination with large amounts of water, synthetic fertilizers, and pesticides to increase yields. This high-input approach has worked, but it has many environmental disadvantages, including the loss of genetic stocks and the deterioration of soil quality.

Some experts are urging farmers to adopt alternative, more environmentally friendly systems that depart from the traditional factorylike approach. Farmers are often taking the lead themselves. In the United States, for example, a group called Practical Farmers of Iowa is doing its own on-farm research and networking to help custom design and implement integrated farming systems (72). CGIAR's international agricultural research centers also are broadening their horizons to include research on food legumes, livestock, agroforestry, farming systems, integrated pest management, improved methods for dealing with soil and climatic stresses, and policy and management issues (73).

In Africa, some experts believe that alternative models that can provide yield growth and do less damage to the environment could be very beneficial.

In areas with high production potential, for example, sustainable intensification strategies include better design and management of irrigation systems to reduce waterlogging; reformed water pricing to reduce excessive use; rotation of other crops with rice to maintain the health of irrigated soils; integrated use of natural predators, more selective use of pesticides, and the use of pest-resistant varieties; improved soil testing and fertilizer application; creation of regionally diversified crop breeding programs; and more farmer education.

In fragile areas, factors such as poor infrastructure, drought risk, and lower yield response undermine the high-input strategy. Alternative strategies include moisture conservation, erosion control, nutrient recycling, and the increased use of mixed farming systems that integrate annual crops with perennial crops, farm trees, and livestock (74).

Food Security: A Continuing Challenge

Many developing countries are faced with a food security crisis now and into the foreseeable future. In many areas, farmers are overwhelmed by unfavorable conditions, poor people are unable to afford food, civil strife is a constant threat, and governments are unable to provide the needed rural infrastructure or agricultural policies that encourage domestic production.

Food security differs fundamentally from food production. Food security means ensuring that all people have physical and economic access to the basic food they need to work and function normally. It can be constrained by availability (inadequate supplies of food, including imports and food aid) and by physical and economic access. Physical access to food can be impeded by poor infrastructure, poor marketing and storage facilities, and civil strife. Economic access has two dimensions: the ability of nations to generate the foreign exchange to pay for food imports and the ability of households to generate the income necessary to buy enough food.

Famines and temporary food deficiencies can result from drought, flood, war, political strife, or poor harvests. Such events are increasing, as discussed earlier.

Chronic undernutrition is a more long-term, intractable food security problem. Current estimates of chronic undernutrition in developing countries and projections for the year 2010 provide a rough guide to the nature of the food security challenge that lies ahead. The bleakest prospects are for sub-Saharan Africa, where the number of undernourished people could rise to some 300 million from an estimated 175 million in 1988–90. Sub-Saharan Africa is projected to have a per capita food supply of 2,170 calories per day—the lowest among all regions—by 2010. In contrast, the developed countries are projected to have a per capita food supply of 3,470 calories per day (75). IFPRI's model, which projects ahead to the year 2020, also envisages little improvement in food security in sub-Saharan Africa, even under a variety of alternative projections of growth, investment, and trade liberalization (76).

South Asia's situation is also difficult. For the region as a whole, FAO projects available calories of 2,450 per capita per day by 2010 and an estimated 195 million people suffering from chronic undernutrition (77). IFPRI predicts that per capita food availability will rise to 2,600 calories per day by 2020, but that the number of malnourished children will only drop to 76 million from the current estimate of 96 million (78).

Population growth rates and undernutrition are generally declining in the rapidly industrializing region of East Asia. FAO estimates that by 2010 the number of undernourished people could be down to 77 million, or just 4 percent of the population. Similarly, in Latin America the proportion of undernourished people could decline from 13 percent in 1988–90 to 6 percent by 2010. For the 93 developing countries studied, chronic undernutrition could drop to 11 percent of the population in 2010 from the 1988–90 figure of 20 percent (79).

Where domestic production falls short of needs, governments will be forced to buy from abroad or seek food aid. The World Bank projects that developing countries could be importing about 15 percent of their grain consumption by 2010 (80). FAO estimates that net imports by the developing countries may increase from 90 million metric tons in 1988–90 to about 160 million metric tons by 2010 (81). Most of the imports will be wheat and coarse grains; rice consumption is expected to be satisfied largely by domestic production. Large increases in grain imports are projected to occur in North Africa, Mexico, Indonesia, India, and China (82).

Trade and aid may not be enough to fill the gap in sub-Saharan Africa. By the year 2000, the region's cereals production shortfall could increase to well above the current net imports of about 10 million tons (83). Yet it is doubtful that the region will be able to generate sufficient foreign exchange to import such large amounts of food or that food aid will be able to make up the gap. South Asia faces a similar, although somewhat less dire, outlook (84).

The developed countries are projected to maintain adequate food levels over the next two decades. In North America and Western Europe, agricultural policies will continue to be used to limit production. A significant increase in world food prices or in demand by developing countries, however, could bring some idled land back into production.

The transition economies of Central Europe and the former Soviet Union provide potential for an expansion of food production (85). The countries in these regions are currently major cereal importers. If policy reforms succeed, these countries could become net exporters (86) (87).

Future Capacity

Most recent attempts to develop hypothetical models of the world's potential to increase food production over the next few decades conclude that the potential is sufficient to meet the growth of effective demand as world population and incomes increase. There is a substantial gap, however, between the world's hypothetical production potential and short-term realities in certain regions, particularly in Africa and South Asia.

As part of its 2020 project, IFPRI developed a vision for the year 2020 of what needs to be done to achieve a world "where every person has economic and physical access to sufficient food to sustain a healthy and productive life, where malnutrition is absent, and where food originates from efficient, effective, and low-cost food and agricultural systems that are compatible with sustainable use and management of natural resources" (88).

IFPRI concluded that sustained action is needed to:

- Strengthen the capacities of developing-country governments to perform their appropriate functions.
- Enhance the productivity, health, and nutrition of low-income people and increase their access to employment and productive assets.
- Strengthen agricultural research and extension systems in and for developing countries.
- Promote sustainable agricultural intensification and sound management of natural resources, with increased emphasis on areas with fragile soils, limited rainfall, and widespread poverty.
- Develop effective, efficient, and low-cost agricultural input and output markets.
- Expand international assistance and improve its efficiency. IFPRI recommends realigning international development assistance to low-income developing countries, primarily in sub-Saharan Africa and South Asia (89).

References and Notes

1. Food and Agriculture Organization of the United Nations (FAO), *FAOSTAT-PC*, on diskette (FAO, Rome, 1995).

2. *Ibid.*

3. The World Bank, *African Development Indicators 1994–95* (The World Bank, Washington, D.C., 1995), p. 236.

4. Akin L. Mabogunje, "The Environmental Challenges in Sub-Saharan Africa," *Environment,* Vol. 37, No. 4 (May 1995), p. 6.

5. Nikos Alexandratos, ed., *World Agriculture: Towards 2010, An FAO Study* (John Wiley and Sons, Chichester, U.K., and Food and Agriculture Organization of the United Nations, Rome, 1995), pp. 38–44.

6. *Ibid.,* p. 41.

7. *Op. cit.* 5, pp. 184–185.

8. Food and Agriculture Organization of the United Nations (FAO), "Assessment of the Current World Food Security Situation and Medium Term Review," Item II of the Provisional Agenda, 20th Session, Committee on World Food Security (FAO, Rome, April 1995), p. 3.

9. Patrick Webb, "A Time of Plenty, A World of Need: The Role of Food Aid in 2020," International Food Policy Research Institute (IFPRI) 2020 Brief No. 10 (IFPRI, Washington, D.C., 1995), p. 2.

10. *Ibid.*

11. *Op. cit.* 9, p. 1.

12. *Op. cit.* 9, p. 1.

13. Food and Agriculture Organization of the United Nations (FAO), *The State of Food and Agriculture 1994* (FAO, Rome, 1994), p. 11.

14. *Op. cit.* 8, pp. 12–13.

15. *Op. cit.* 5, n.p.

16. Donald O. Mitchell and Merlinda D. Ingco, *The World Food Outlook* (The World Bank, Washington, D.C., 1993).

17. Mark W. Rosegrant, Mercedita Agcaoili-Sombilla, and Nicostrato D. Perez, "Global Food Projections to 2020: Implications for Investment," International Food Policy Research Institute (IFPRI) Food, Agriculture, and the Environment, draft discussion paper (IFPRI, Washington, D.C., 1995).

18. Pierre Crosson and Jock R. Anderson, "Resources and Global Food Prospects: Supply and Demand for Cereals to 2030," World Bank Technical Paper No. 184 (The World Bank, Washington, D.C., 1992).

19. Vaclav Smil, "How Many People Can the Earth Feed?," *Population and Development Review,* Vol. 20, No. 2 (June 1994).

20. Lester R. Brown and Hal Kane, *Full House: Reassessing the Earth's Population Carrying Capacity* (W.W. Norton, New York, 1994).

21. Ian Carruthers, "Going, Going, Gone! Tropical Agriculture as We Knew It," *Tropical Agriculture Association Newsletter,* Vol. 13,

No. 3 (U.K.), pp. 1–5, cited in Alex F. McCalla, "Agriculture and Food Needs to 2025: Why We Should Be Concerned," Sir John Crawford Memorial Lecture, International Centers Week (Consultative Group on International Agricultural Research, Washington, D.C., October 1994), pp. 17–19.

22. David Pimentel *et al.,* "Environmental and Economic Costs of Soil Erosion and Conservation Benefits," *Science,* Vol. 267, No. 5201 (February 24, 1995), pp. 1117–1122.

23. *Op. cit.* 5, p. 170.

24. *Op. cit.* 5, p. 80.

25. *Op. cit.* 5, pp. 79–80.

26. *Op. cit.* 5, p. 15.

27. *Op. cit.* 5, pp. 164–165.

28. Per Pinstrup-Andersen and Rajul Pandya-Lorch, "Alleviating Poverty, Intensifying Agriculture, and Effectively Managing Natural Resources," Food, Agriculture, and the Environment Discussion Paper No. 1 (International Food Policy Research Institute, Washington, D.C., 1994), p. 6.

29. *Op. cit.* 18, p. 20.

30. The World Bank, *World Development Report 1992* (The World Bank, Washington, D.C., 1992), p. 135.

31. *Op. cit.* 5, p. 170.

32. *Op. cit.* 5, p. 172.

33. *Op. cit.* 5, p. 152.

34. *Op. cit.* 5, p. 155.

35. *Op. cit.* 16, pp. 50–51.

36. Paul R. Ehrlich *et al.,* "Food Security, Population, and Environment," *Population and Development Review,* Vol. 19, No. 1 (1993), p. 7.

37. *Op. cit.* 5, p. 170.

38. The World Bank and the United Nations Development Programme, *Irrigation and Drainage Research: A Proposal* (The World Bank, Washington, D.C., 1990), pp. 3, 103, cited in Pierre Crosson and Jock R. Anderson, "Resources and Global Food Prospects: Supply and Demand for Cereals to 2030," World Bank Technical Paper No. 184 (The World Bank, Washington, D.C., 1992), p. 45.

39. Henry W. Kendall and David Pimentel, "Constraints on the Expansion of the Global Food Supply," *Ambio,* Vol. 23, No. 3 (1994), p. 200.

40. *Op. cit.* 16, p. 68.

41. *Op. cit.* 5, p. 160.

42. *Op. cit.* 18, pp. 47–53.

43. Nikos Alexandratos, Chief of Global Perspective Studies Unit, Economic and Social Department, Food and Agriculture Organization of the United Nations, Rome, 1995 (personal communication).

44. Per Pinstrup-Andersen, *World Food Trends and Future Food Security* (International Food Policy Research Institute, Washington, D.C., 1994), p. 5.

45. *Op. cit.* 5, p. 90.

46. *Op. cit.* 5, p. 90.

47. *Op. cit.* 5, p. 14.

48. *Op. cit.* 5, p. 174.

49. *Op. cit.* 5, p. 170.

50. *Op. cit.* 20, p. 137.

51. *Op. cit.* 5, p. 192.

52. *Op. cit.* 5, p. 192.

53. *Op. cit.* 5, pp. 189–190.

54. *Op. cit.* 5, pp. 357–358.

55. Robert Repetto, *The Second India Revisited: Population, Poverty and Environmental Stress over Two Decades* (World Resources Institute, Washington, D.C., 1994), p. 38.

56. *Op. cit.* 5, p. 19.

57. *Op. cit.* 18, p. 34.

58. United Nations Environment Programme (UNEP), *United Nations Convention to Combat Desertification,* Text with Annexes (UNEP, Geneva, 1995), pp. 45–46.

59. *Op. cit.* 19, p. 267.

60. Peter Hazell, Director, Environment and Production Technology Division, International Food Policy Research Institute, Washington, D.C., 1995 (personal communication).

61. Food and Agriculture Organization of the United Nations (FAO), *Agriculture: Towards 2010,* 27th Session Conference Proceedings (FAO, Rome, 1993), p. 138.

62. Peter H. Gleick, "An Introduction to Global Fresh Water Issues," in *Water in Crisis,* Peter H. Gleick, ed. (Oxford University Press, New York, 1993), p. 6.

63. *Op. cit.* 19, p. 270.

64. *Op. cit.* 19, p. 270.

65. *Op. cit.* 19, p. 278.

66. *Op. cit.* 5, p. 151.

67. Sandra Postel, "Water and Agriculture," in *Water in Crisis,* Peter H. Gleick, ed. (Oxford University Press, New York, 1993), p. 63.

68. William Bender, independent consultant, Groton, Massachusetts, 1995 (personal communication).

69. David Pimentel, Cornell University College of Agriculture and Life Sciences, Ithaca, New York, 1995 (personal communication).

70. P. Berck and D. Bigman, *Food Security and Food Inventories in Developing Countries* (Cab International, Wallingford, U.K., 1993), p. 19.

71. *Op. cit.* 36, p. 16.

72. Neill Schaller, Associate Director, Henry A. Wallace Institute for Alternative Agriculture, Greenbelt, Maryland, 1995 (personal communication).

73. Consultative Group on International Agricultural Research (CGIAR), *CGIAR Annual Report 1993–1994* (CGIAR, Washington, D.C., 1993), pp. 4–52.

74. Peter Hazell, "Managing Agricultural Intensification," International Food Policy Research Institute (IFPRI) 2020 Brief No. 11 (IFPRI, Washington, D.C., 1995), pp. 1–2.

75. *Op. cit.* 5, p. 84.

76. *Op. cit.* 17, pp. 17–18.

77. *Op. cit.* 5, p. 84.

78. *Op. cit.* 17, pp. 17–20.

79. *Op. cit.* 5, p. 84.

80. *Op. cit.* 16, p. 159.

81. *Op. cit.* 5, p. 8.

82. *Op. cit.* 16, p. 159.

83. Food and Agriculture Organization of the United Nations (FAO), *Food Outlook* (FAO, Rome, August/September 1995), n.p.

84. Peter Hazell, "Prospects for a Well-Fed World," paper prepared for an external panel, appointed by the Oversight Committee of the Consultative Group on International Agricultural Research to prepare A Vision Statement for International Agricultural Research (International Food Policy Research Institute, Washington, D.C., March 31, 1994), p. 6.

85. The term "transition economies" lacks a formal definition, but is used here to include the successor states of the former Soviet Union (Armenia, Azerbaijan, the Republic of Belarus, the Republic of Estonia, the Republic of Georgia, the Republic of Kazakhstan, the Kyrgyz Republic, the Republic of Latvia, the Republic of Lithuania, the Republic of Moldova, the Russian Federation, the Republic of Tajikistan, the Republic of Turkmenistan, Ukraine, and the Republic of Uzbekistan) and the countries of Central Europe (Albania, Bulgaria, the Czech Republic, Hungary, Poland, Romania, and the Slovak Republic).

86. *Op. cit.* 16, pp. 148–149, 152–153.

87. Rod Tyers, *Economic Reform in Europe and the Former Soviet Union: Implications for International Food Markets,* International Food Policy Research Institute (IFPRI) Research Report No. 99 (IFPRI, Washington, D.C., 1995), pp. 1–3.

88. International Food Policy Research Institute (IFPRI), "A 2020 Vision for Food, Agriculture, and the Environment," draft paper (IFPRI, Washington, D.C., June 1995), p. i.

89. *Ibid.,* pp. ii–viii.

Data Table 10.1 Food and Agricultural Production, 1982–94

| | Index of Agricultural Production (1979-81 = 100) | | | | Index of Food Production (1979-81 = 100) | | | | Average Production of Cereals | | Average Yields of Cereals | | Average Yields of Roots and Tubers | |
| | Total | | Per Capita | | Total | | Per Capita | | (000 metric tons) | % Change Since | Kilograms Per Hectare | % Change Since | Kilograms Per Hectare | % Change Since |
	1982-84	1992-94	1982-84	1992-94	1982-84	1992-94	1982-84	1992-94	1992-94	1982-84	1992-94	1982-84	1992-94	1982-84
WORLD	108	130	102	104	108	130	102	105	1,934,117	14	2,791	17	12,290	1
AFRICA	102	135	94	94	102	138	94	95	94,708	41	1,160	10	7,607	17
Algeria	106	179	96	125	105	178	96	125	2,513	76	841	47	9,938	55
Angola	99	105	92	72	101	109	94	75	358	6	363	(24)	3,919	(3)
Benin	112	186	102	126	110	175	100	119	628	59	929	36	9,434	26
Botswana	100	108	90	70	100	108	90	70	33	141	314	43	5,200	(32)
Burkina Faso	107	185	99	132	106	183	99	130	2,494	119	860	55	5,733	(42)
Burundi	101	122	93	84	102	125	94	86	274	22	1,344	23	6,591	(4)
Cameroon	106	111	97	77	106	114	98	79	953	14	1,195	28	5,845	24
Central African Rep	106	132	99	97	105	135	98	99	98	(10)	877	35	3,873	1
Chad	106	134	99	100	100	133	94	99	895	124	651	22	5,189	8
Congo	109	114	100	78	109	114	100	78	27	138	900	40	6,855	(4)
Cote d'Ivoire	101	140	90	86	106	152	95	94	1,413	48	1,024	12	5,914	5
Egypt	107	155	99	112	111	168	102	122	14,722	72	5,921	38	21,961	10
Equatorial Guinea	X	X	X	X	X	X	X	X	X	X	X	X	2,638	(14)
Eritrea	X	X	X	X	X	X	X	X	116	(34)	841	0	2,889	(7)
Ethiopia	99	38	93	28	100	39	94	28	4,563	X	1,346	X	3,647	X
Gabon	103	122	91	79	103	122	91	79	26	93	1,791	(6)	5,420	3
Gambia, The	120	114	111	70	120	110	111	68	101	18	1,218	(6)	3,000	0
Ghana	104	172	94	112	105	173	94	113	1,450	127	1,199	83	6,518	8
Guinea	102	150	96	106	102	148	96	105	1,062	55	838	(4)	7,373	5
Guinea-Bissau	117	144	110	111	118	144	110	111	184	20	1,462	97	7,222	19
Kenya	114	137	102	86	112	139	100	87	2,773	13	1,548	(7)	8,061	20
Lesotho	91	100	83	69	89	100	81	68	164	29	1,038	56	8,000	X
Liberia	109	70	99	46	111	88	101	58	72	(75)	789	(39)	7,637	22
Libya	116	82	101	50	116	82	101	50	273	(17)	635	(9)	7,400	5
Madagascar	106	125	97	82	107	127	97	83	2,620	18	1,936	15	6,570	12
Malawi	106	110	97	65	103	100	95	59	1,306	(10)	958	(18)	3,243	(11)
Mali	109	139	101	94	110	135	101	91	2,221	69	826	5	8,340	2
Mauritania	96	116	89	83	96	116	89	83	155	186	810	71	1,875	(0)
Mauritius	107	119	104	105	107	120	104	106	2	0	X	X	18,333	10
Morocco	111	168	103	125	110	168	103	125	5,224	28	975	7	16,240	12
Mozambique	98	91	91	73	100	94	92	75	608	(5)	430	(14)	3,766	(9)
Namibia	76	105	70	74	77	108	71	76	76	(8)	660	2	7,945	(10)
Niger	93	125	84	82	93	125	84	82	2,210	47	305	(14)	7,456	7
Nigeria	104	197	95	134	104	196	95	134	13,390	45	1,237	(21)	10,259	39
Rwanda	107	110	97	75	106	108	96	74	210	(32)	1,117	(2)	6,455	(20)
Senegal	98	154	91	108	98	153	90	108	965	44	794	27	2,930	(30)
Sierra Leone	108	116	102	87	107	111	101	83	530	(3)	1,181	(13)	4,333	35
Somalia	107	87	96	65	107	87	96	65	260	(38)	443	(27)	10,500	(1)
South Africa	89	95	82	70	88	96	81	71	10,481	22	1,893	50	19,460	46
Sudan	97	127	89	89	93	130	86	91	4,445	123	561	36	2,969	(8)
Swaziland	109	120	100	83	111	119	101	82	67	(17)	1,116	(11)	2,000	4
Tanzania	105	117	95	77	106	118	96	78	3,649	21	1,155	(13)	8,260	(16)
Togo	99	151	91	102	99	144	91	97	552	59	842	0	7,412	43
Tunisia	105	159	97	119	105	159	97	119	1,592	45	1,270	65	13,848	12
Uganda	116	154	106	101	115	155	106	102	1,887	65	1,549	17	6,289	2
Zaire	111	149	101	97	110	149	100	98	1,712	68	872	4	7,921	11
Zambia	101	138	90	89	100	136	90	88	1,179	31	1,611	(1)	5,379	(1)
Zimbabwe	97	113	89	75	93	100	85	66	1,841	14	1,121	31	4,520	(1)
EUROPE	106	105	105	101	106	105	105	101	258,449	(7)	4,099	3	21,202	11
Albania	108	106	102	84	109	110	103	87	601	(41)	2,532	(13)	9,690	36
Austria	109	111	109	106	109	111	109	106	4,403	(15)	5,318	9	25,255	(1)
Belarus, Rep	X	X	X	X	X	X	X	X	6,769	31	2,603	34	12,673	(15)
Belgium {a}	97	143	97	93	97	143	97	93	2,260	1	6,500	16	43,415	8
Bosnia and Herzegovina	X	X	X	X	X	X	X	X	1,225	X	3,177	X	4,770	X
Bulgaria	104	67	103	67	106	73	105	73	6,272	(31)	2,762	(36)	10,370	(5)
Croatia, Rep	X	X	X	X	X	X	X	X	2,561	X	4,126	X	8,073	X
Czech Rep	X	X	X	X	X	X	X	X	6,609	X	4,088	X	19,230	X
Denmark	113	128	113	126	113	128	113	126	7,681	(3)	5,156	12	36,582	10
Estonia, Rep	X	X	X	X	X	X	X	X	685	(27)	1,728	(26)	13,826	(15)
Finland	113	105	111	99	113	105	111	99	3,114	(15)	3,360	10	20,148	17
France	105	105	104	99	105	106	104	99	56,637	11	6,517	23	34,942	18
Germany	107	107	108	104	107	107	108	104	35,566	1	5,588	20	33,555	50
Greece	104	112	102	104	104	105	102	98	4,955	(5)	3,651	10	20,079	16
Hungary	111	83	111	86	111	84	112	87	10,137	(32)	3,630	(29)	16,578	(7)
Iceland	103	84	99	73	103	85	99	74	0	X	X	X	7,667	(39)
Ireland	104	128	101	122	104	128	101	122	1,800	(19)	6,484	18	24,924	11
Italy	102	104	101	102	102	104	101	102	19,500	4	4,739	29	22,705	31
Latvia, Rep	X	X	X	X	X	X	X	X	1,042	(20)	1,768	(4)	13,463	(14)
Lithuania, Rep	X	X	X	X	X	X	X	X	2,398	2	2,028	(11)	11,382	(16)
Macedonia, former Yugoslav Rep	X	X	X	X	X	X	X	X	586	X	2,460	X	9,769	X
Moldova, Rep	X	X	X	X	X	X	X	X	2,206	(10)	2,973	(17)	8,324	(8)
Netherlands	109	125	107	116	108	125	107	115	1,390	2	7,515	11	43,973	17
Norway	107	114	106	108	107	114	106	108	1,227	0	3,488	(8)	25,070	(0)
Poland, Rep	103	101	100	93	103	103	100	95	21,714	(4)	2,574	(7)	15,861	(0)
Portugal	100	110	98	109	100	111	99	110	1,439	11	2,008	60	14,223	72
Romania	109	82	107	80	109	84	107	82	15,098	(21)	2,449	(22)	14,226	(24)
Russian Federation	X	X	X	X	X	X	X	X	92,892	1	1,612	17	10,622	(6)
Slovak Rep	X	X	X	X	X	X	X	X	3,526	X	4,176	X	13,762	X
Slovenia, Rep	X	X	X	X	X	X	X	X	429	X	3,625	X	12,443	X
Spain	107	115	105	110	107	116	105	110	15,765	(1)	2,317	9	19,408	22
Sweden	108	91	108	87	108	91	108	87	4,524	(26)	4,059	1	34,009	25
Switzerland	107	110	105	98	107	110	105	98	1,241	26	6,112	11	43,732	20
Ukraine	X	X	X	X	X	X	X	X	37,045	3	2,958	17	12,029	(2)
United Kingdom	108	106	107	103	108	106	108	103	20,399	(12)	6,609	14	42,015	22
Yugoslavia, Fed Rep	107	X	105	X	107	X	105	X	7,780	X	3,165	X	6,587	X

	Index of Agricultural Production (1979-81 = 100)				Index of Food Production (1979-81 = 100)				Average Production of Cereals		Average Yields of Cereals		Average Yields of Roots and Tubers	
	Total		Per Capita		Total		Per Capita		(000 metric tons)	% Change Since	Kilograms Per Hectare	% Change Since	Kilograms Per Hectare	% Change Since
	1982-84	1992-94	1982-84	1992-94	1982-84	1992-94	1982-84	1992-94	1992-94	1982-84	1992-94	1982-84	1992-94	1982-84
NORTH & CENTRAL AMERICA	99	115	95	97	100	116	96	97	405,147	12	4,227	21	22,169	17
Belize	110	132	102	95	110	132	102	95	26	3	1,510	(17)	X	X
Canada	111	125	108	107	112	126	108	108	49,328	3	2,566	15	27,404	16
Costa Rica	104	146	95	102	101	148	92	104	230	(30)	3,184	47	25,105	263
Cuba	108	82	106	73	108	81	105	72	308	(51)	1,779	(34)	5,024	(13)
Dominican Rep	108	130	101	98	108	141	101	106	581	2	4,301	16	6,308	(9)
El Salvador	88	93	86	76	89	116	87	95	948	49	1,978	15	17,111	21
Guatemala	97	115	89	79	112	145	103	100	1,492	22	1,834	6	4,872	19
Haiti	103	86	98	67	104	87	99	68	397	(5)	936	(10)	3,829	(5)
Honduras	102	139	92	93	101	135	92	90	673	26	1,343	(2)	9,357	(2)
Jamaica	103	120	98	107	102	120	98	106	5	(24)	1,455	(24)	14,151	20
Mexico	107	123	100	91	108	126	101	94	27,207	23	2,708	18	17,188	24
Nicaragua	94	79	86	54	89	95	81	64	562	26	1,682	3	11,700	4
Panama	109	122	102	93	108	120	101	92	334	24	1,778	18	5,889	(20)
Trinidad and Tobago	86	103	83	87	88	106	84	89	23	258	3,091	14	11,000	(0)
United States	98	113	95	100	99	113	96	100	323,029	13	5,092	23	35,553	21
SOUTH AMERICA	106	135	99	105	107	140	100	108	85,456	11	2,475	26	11,891	10
Argentina	107	117	102	97	107	118	102	98	25,123	(23)	2,902	19	17,419	10
Bolivia	96	147	90	112	97	150	91	114	1,006	46	1,462	20	6,465	24
Brazil	106	144	99	112	108	151	101	117	44,323	39	2,256	40	12,439	11
Chile	102	149	97	120	102	151	97	121	2,721	63	4,299	78	15,430	36
Colombia	101	140	95	109	102	145	96	113	3,633	6	2,518	0	12,585	11
Ecuador	101	159	93	115	101	159	93	115	1,787	148	2,133	20	6,549	(37)
Guyana	102	100	99	93	102	101	100	94	281	(1)	3,029	(5)	8,000	28
Paraguay	117	164	106	110	116	169	105	113	920	7	1,986	27	14,164	1
Peru	107	120	X	X	110	125	X	X	1,967	7	2,679	18	8,212	4
Suriname	111	108	108	93	111	108	108	93	234	(19)	3,739	(5)	X	X
Uruguay	110	122	108	113	110	123	108	114	1,467	36	2,690	37	8,747	56
Venezuela	104	142	96	103	104	144	97	104	1,969	40	2,749	39	9,076	6
ASIA	115	160	108	127	114	161	108	127	894,866	23	2,947	22	14,324	3
Afghanistan, Islamic State	X	X	X	X	94	76	100	69	2,541	(29)	1,147	(14)	16,585	10
Armenia	X	X	X	X	X	X	X	X	X	X	X	X	12,292	(17)
Azerbaijan	X	X	X	X	X	X	X	X	1,135	(5)	1,741	(27)	7,763	(6)
Bangladesh	106	131	99	100	106	132	99	101	28,523	25	2,656	26	10,479	0
Bhutan	110	110	103	85	109	110	103	85	106	(38)	1,093	(24)	11,133	56
Cambodia	135	202	126	136	135	196	126	133	2,196	22	1,227	5	8,265	46
China	120	181	115	151	117	181	112	151	401,088	17	4,482	21	15,180	(1)
Georgia, Rep	X	X	X	X	X	X	X	X	415	(29)	1,609	(26)	10,000	(13)
India	114	162	107	124	115	164	107	125	206,608	33	2,062	38	15,751	15
Indonesia	114	173	107	136	115	178	108	140	54,579	36	3,864	16	11,565	24
Iran, Islamic Rep	121	207	107	127	122	211	107	129	16,545	68	1,750	52	18,723	22
Iraq	116	127	106	85	116	127	105	85	2,641	59	883	5	17,475	(7)
Israel	119	115	113	85	121	132	115	97	218	(18)	2,199	0	28,917	(33)
Japan	103	92	101	87	104	96	102	90	13,603	(7)	5,588	1	25,498	6
Jordan	121	234	108	125	120	238	107	127	120	35	1,078	72	23,700	32
Kazakhstan, Rep	X	X	X	X	X	X	X	X	22,526	23	1,037	43	9,685	(1)
Korea, Dem People's Rep	113	112	108	89	113	110	108	87	4,604	(26)	3,195	(17)	12,461	(1)
Korea, Rep	104	112	100	97	105	113	100	98	7,523	(16)	5,815	5	20,271	4
Kuwait	X	X	X	X	X	X	X	X	2	100	X	X	X	X
Kyrgyz Rep	X	X	X	X	X	X	X	X	1,390	18	2,366	2	11,911	(6)
Lao People's Dem Rep	117	158	110	110	117	158	110	110	1,530	27	2,494	50	8,808	(9)
Lebanon	112	196	112	187	113	202	113	192	77	178	1,958	65	20,927	36
Malaysia	117	218	108	156	124	277	115	198	2,085	19	3,026	16	9,697	4
Mongolia	105	97	97	70	106	98	98	70	477	(27)	892	(21)	8,040	(25)
Myanmar	124	135	116	103	125	138	118	105	17,402	16	2,808	(4)	8,927	(1)
Nepal	111	161	102	115	112	164	103	118	5,524	40	1,847	15	7,630	26
Oman	X	X	X	X	X	X	X	X	4	117	1,857	(7)	X	X
Pakistan	111	170	100	109	112	168	101	108	22,748	25	1,894	17	13,229	16
Philippines	103	119	96	89	102	120	95	90	14,523	30	2,229	28	6,841	17
Saudi Arabia	191	555	157	307	192	566	158	313	4,737	406	4,266	56	18,348	45
Singapore	86	45	82	39	86	46	83	39	0	X	X	X	X	X
Sri Lanka	100	98	95	81	102	101	97	84	2,534	6	3,008	7	8,961	(19)
Syrian Arab Rep	113	140	103	89	111	138	101	88	5,136	140	1,417	80	17,708	6
Tajikistan, Rep	X	X	X	X	X	X	X	X	269	(10)	981	(37)	11,947	(25)
Thailand	110	134	104	109	110	125	104	102	23,469	3	2,278	12	13,914	(15)
Turkey	109	134	101	100	110	135	102	101	29,302	14	2,114	10	23,499	41
Turkmenistan, Rep	X	X	X	X	X	X	X	X	1,090	265	2,412	15	10,556	66
United Arab Emirates	X	X	X	X	X	X	X	X	7	24	7,000	24	X	X
Uzbekistan, Rep	X	X	X	X	X	X	X	X	2,231	(11)	1,703	(21)	10,530	11
Viet Nam	116	173	109	130	116	171	109	128	23,378	52	3,343	32	7,677	10
Yemen, Rep	97	133	88	83	97	133	88	83	813	34	1,100	63	14,024	(7)
OCEANIA	103	118	99	97	103	119	99	98	23,115	(10)	1,748	22	11,436	6
Australia	104	122	99	101	103	119	99	99	22,319	(9)	1,709	22	29,000	16
Fiji	102	114	96	96	102	115	96	96	26	24	2,108	4	12,800	11
New Zealand	106	108	104	96	107	118	105	106	765	(20)	5,274	14	25,182	(13)
Papua New Guinea	106	135	100	102	108	139	101	104	3	0	1,500	0	7,218	2
Solomon Islands	115	140	104	90	116	140	104	90	X	X	X	X	18,278	18

Source: Food and Agriculture Organization of the United Nations.

Notes: a. Data for Belgium and Luxembourg are combined under Belgium.
World and regional totals include some countries not listed here.
0 = zero or less than half the unit of measure; X = not available; negative numbers are shown in parentheses.
For additional information, see Sources and Technical Notes.

Data Table 10.2 Agricultural Inputs, 1981–93

	Cropland Total Hectares (000) 1993	Cropland Hectares Per Capita 1993	Cropland Total Hectares (000) 1983	Cropland Hectares Per Capita 1983	Irrigated Land as a Percentage of Cropland 1981-83	Irrigated Land as a Percentage of Cropland 1991-93	Annual Fertilizer Use (kilograms per hectare of cropland) 1983	Annual Fertilizer Use 1993	Tractors Average Number 1991-93	Tractors Percent Change Since 1981-83	Harvesters Average Number 1991-93	Harvesters Percent Change Since 1981-83
WORLD	**1,447,509**	**0.26**	**1,432,735**	**0.31**	**15**	**17**	**88**	**83**	**25,879,371**	**10**	**3,888,353**	**2**
AFRICA	**187,887**	**0.27**	**177,907**	**0.34**	**6**	**7**	**19**	**21**	**515,884**	**10**	**40,802**	**(32)**
Algeria	7,850	0.29	7,231	0.35	4	7	22	17	91,333	70	9,567	88
Angola	3,500	0.34	3,400	0.45	2	2	3	2	10,297	0	X	X
Benin	1,880	0.37	1,806	0.48	0	0	3	9	137	22	X	X
Botswana	420	0.30	400	0.40	1	0	3	2	6,000	133	95	15
Burkina Faso	3,565	0.36	2,935	0.39	0	1	5	6	134	12	X	X
Burundi	1,360	0.23	1,306	0.29	1	1	2	3	168	53	2	100
Cameroon	7,040	0.56	6,960	0.74	0	0	7	3	503	(21)	X	X
Central African Rep	2,020	0.64	1,970	0.79	0	0	0	1	208	23	19	65
Chad	3,256	0.54	3,150	0.66	0	0	1	1	168	5	17	2
Congo	170	0.07	154	0.08	1	1	10	12	708	4	59	51
Cote d'Ivoire	3,710	0.28	3,219	0.35	1	2	12	15	3,667	15	65	44
Egypt	2,800	0.05	2,478	0.05	100	100	363	357	60,333	33	2,367	10
Equatorial Guinea	230	0.61	230	0.84	0	0	0	0	100	2	X	X
Eritrea	1,280	0.38	X	X	X	1	X	0	850	X	40	X
Ethiopia	13,930	0.27	13,930	0.36	1	1	1	6	X	X	103	X
Gabon	460	0.37	452	0.49	1	1	5	1	1,493	14	X	X
Gambia, The	180	0.17	160	0.23	8	8	15	4	44	2	5	25
Ghana	4,320	0.26	3,500	0.29	0	0	6	1	4,083	12	537	49
Guinea	730	0.12	714	0.15	13	12	0	2	287	43	X	X
Guinea-Bissau	340	0.33	310	0.37	5	5	2	1	19	12	X	X
Kenya	4,520	0.17	4,280	0.23	1	1	20	27	14,000	73	650	50
Lesotho	320	0.16	283	0.19	1	1	16	19	1,850	22	35	16
Liberia	375	0.13	371	0.18	1	1	8	0	334	9	X	X
Libya	2,170	0.43	2,105	0.60	12	22	43	49	34,000	28	3,410	18
Madagascar	3,105	0.22	3,011	0.30	24	34	5	3	2,900	6	150	15
Malawi	1,700	0.16	1,420	0.21	1	1	30	51	1,417	11	X	X
Mali	2,503	0.25	2,053	0.28	0	0	5	10	840	1	49	7
Mauritania	208	0.10	195	0.12	25	24	2	22	336	8	X	X
Mauritius	106	0.10	107	0.11	15	16	254	245	367	9	X	X
Morocco	9,920	0.38	8,330	0.40	15	13	29	29	41,667	33	4,527	14
Mozambique	3,180	0.21	3,080	0.24	2	4	5	1	5,750	0	X	X
Namibia	662	0.45	662	0.59	1	1	0	0	3,133	16	X	X
Niger	3,605	0.42	3,540	0.57	1	2	1	0	179	38	X	X
Nigeria	32,385	0.31	30,670	0.39	3	3	9	16	11,867	25	X	X
Rwanda	1,170	0.15	1,090	0.19	0	0	1	2	90	7	X	X
Senegal	2,350	0.30	2,350	0.39	3	3	11	11	533	16	155	7
Sierra Leone	540	0.13	518	0.15	5	5	2	6	547	33	6	38
Somalia	1,020	0.11	1,015	0.14	15	18	2	0	2,137	16	X	X
South Africa	13,179	0.33	13,169	0.42	9	10	67	64	130,667	(24)	13,333	(67)
Sudan	12,975	0.49	12,558	0.62	14	15	3	5	10,484	6	1,540	63
Swaziland	191	0.24	141	0.23	42	35	123	61	4,433	27	X	X
Tanzania	3,500	0.12	3,130	0.15	4	4	7	14	6,633	(25)	X	X
Togo	2,430	0.63	2,360	0.83	0	0	1	4	370	42	X	X
Tunisia	4,952	0.58	4,967	0.72	5	8	15	22	26,833	2	3,049	18
Uganda	6,770	0.34	6,300	0.44	0	0	0	0	4,667	43	15	36
Zaire	7,900	0.19	7,700	0.26	0	0	1	1	2,427	14	X	X
Zambia	5,273	0.59	5,158	0.81	0	1	13	16	5,983	18	289	7
Zimbabwe	2,876	0.27	2,806	0.36	6	7	55	55	16,067	1	717	10
EUROPE	**136,005**	**0.19**	**140,245**	**0.20**	**10**	**12**	**169**	**116**	**9,791,242**	**6**	**802,272**	**(2)**
Albania	702	0.21	710	0.25	54	52	145	17	9,173	(11)	988	(29)
Austria	1,498	0.19	1,516	0.20	0	0	252	175	348,568	7	24,522	(19)
Belarus, Rep	6,248	0.61	6,360	0.65	3	2	X	136	125,167	(0)	28,667	(9)
Belgium {a}	794	X	771	X	0	0	577	403	0	X	8,373	(10)
Bosnia and Herzegovina	940	0.25	X	X	X	0	X	11 b	205,930	X	400	X
Bulgaria	4,310	0.49	4,141	0.46	29	29	244	54	48,407	(17)	7,754	(14)
Croatia, Rep	1,313	0.29	1,627	0.37	X	0	X	172	4,200	(27)	1,036	(44)
Czech Rep	3,293	0.32	X	X	X	0	X	81	78,000	X	3,933	X
Denmark	2,542	0.49	2,610	0.51	15	17	266	191	157,069	(11)	31,997	(14)
Estonia, Rep	1,143	0.74	991	0.65	0	0	X	57	19,597	X	2,469	X
Finland	2,580	0.51	2,467	0.51	2	2	212	132	233,333	0	42,000	(9)
France	19,439	0.34	19,027	0.35	5	8	307	237	1,460,000	(2)	153,833	4
Germany	12,116	0.15	12,450	0.16	4	4	368	221	1,373,967	(16)	138,994	(22)
Greece	3,494	0.34	3,945	0.40	25	36	162	148	215,750	28	6,250	(3)
Hungary	4,973	0.49	5,292	0.50	3	4	300	40	41,380	(25)	9,145	(26)
Iceland	6	0.02	8	0.03	0	0	X	X	0	X	18	13
Ireland	923	0.26	1,020	0.29	0	0	665	769	167,333	10	5,103	(2)
Italy	11,860	0.21	12,268	0.22	20	23	168	148	1,439,022	23	48,264	24
Latvia, Rep	1,711	0.66	1,736	0.67	0	0	X	56	51,992	X	5,976	X
Lithuania, Rep	3,008	0.81	3,150	0.89	0	0	X	27	47,400	X	9,633	X
Macedonia, former Yugoslav Rep	663	0.31	X	X	X	12	X	18	49,864	X	731	X
Moldova, Rep	2,193	0.50	2,215	0.54	11	14	X	52	53,835	(0)	4,754	6
Netherlands	934	0.06	831	0.06	60	60	821	560	182,000	(0)	5,573	(5)
Norway	890	0.21	849	0.21	9	11	298	229	156,000	9	16,100	(8)
Poland, Rep	14,668	0.38	14,799	0.40	1	1	231	87	1,168,833	54	83,667	72
Portugal	3,160	0.32	3,150	0.32	20	20	71	75	131,158	30	7,967	60
Romania	9,941	0.43	10,555	0.47	23	31	139	39	142,114	(17)	42,727	(2)
Russian Federation	133,900	0.91	135,550	0.96	4	4	X	29	1,283,333	(8)	376,667	(24)
Slovak Rep	1,613	0.30	X	X	X	2	X	50	33,663	X	9,361	X
Slovenia, Rep	301	0.16	X	X	X	1	X	249	69,761	X	1,034	X
Spain	19,656	0.50	20,508	0.54	15	17	71	93	765,769	29	48,860	12
Sweden	2,780	0.32	2,941	0.35	3	4	164	120	165,776	(12)	40,339	(16)
Switzerland	467	0.07	412	0.06	6	5	430	321	114,000	10	4,000	(18)
Ukraine	34,417	0.67	35,500	0.70	6	8	X	39	430,469	0	103,282	7
United Kingdom	6,127	0.11	6,970	0.12	2	2	375	338	500,000	(5)	47,333	(16)
Yugoslavia, Fed Rep	X	X	7,813	0.80	2	X	X	X	X	X	5,392	X

	Cropland				Irrigated Land as a Percentage of Cropland		Annual Fertilizer Use (kilograms per hectare of cropland)		Tractors		Harvesters	
	Total Hectares (000) 1993	Hectares Per Capita 1993	Total Hectares (000) 1983	Hectares Per Capita 1983	1981-83	1991-93	1983	1993	Average Number 1991-93	Percent Change Since 1981-83	Average Number 1991-93	Percent Change Since 1981-83
NORTH & CENTRAL AMERICA	271,447	0.61	273,428	0.71	10	11	90	95	5,831,199	4	849,770	(1)
Belize	57	0.28	53	0.34	4	4	32	114	1,133	30	45	32
Canada	45,500	1.58	46,080	1.82	1	2	49	60	738,050	8	155,000	(3)
Costa Rica	530	0.16	515	0.21	14	23	171	208	6,833	12	1,187	12
Cuba	3,340	0.31	3,215	0.32	25	27	164	52	78,167	18	7,390	7
Dominican Rep	1,450	0.19	1,430	0.23	12	16	39	61	2,347	6	X	X
El Salvador	730	0.13	725	0.16	15	16	113	106	3,427	2	413	22
Guatemala	1,880	0.19	1,785	0.24	5	7	38	87	4,273	5	3,047	11
Haiti	910	0.13	899	0.16	8	8	4	5	228	20	X	X
Honduras	2,015	0.38	1,770	0.45	5	4	16	32	3,921	18	X	X
Jamaica	219	0.09	220	0.10	15	16	58	107	3,077	5	X	X
Mexico	24,730	0.27	24,688	0.34	20	24	60	71	172,000	14	19,333	17
Nicaragua	1,270	0.31	1,267	0.41	6	7	56	21	2,683	14	X	X
Panama	660	0.26	581	0.28	5	5	40	48	5,016	(6)	1,015	(25)
Trinidad and Tobago	122	0.10	118	0.10	18	18	66	51	2,643	6	X	X
United States	187,776	0.73	189,799	0.81	11	11	104	108	4,800,000	3	662,333	(1)
SOUTH AMERICA	102,767	0.33	103,685	0.41	7	9	31	59	1,223,582	22	120,845	15
Argentina	27,200	0.81	27,200	0.92	6	6	5	11	280,000	38	49,600	9
Bolivia	2,380	0.34	2,173	0.38	7	7	4	6	5,333	19	120	(1)
Brazil	48,955	0.31	51,000	0.39	4	6	45	85	733,333	19	47,667	22
Chile	4,257	0.31	4,302	0.37	29	30	18	58	39,727	16	8,733	5
Colombia	5,460	0.16	5,249	0.19	8	10	61	94	36,333	13	2,783	24
Ecuador	3,020	0.28	2,490	0.29	21	18	30	31	8,867	20	777	23
Guyana	496	0.61	495	0.63	25	26	21	24	3,627	3	438	5
Paraguay	2,270	0.48	1,930	0.56	3	3	5	14	16,293	70	X	X
Peru	3,430	0.15	3,650	0.20	32	37	22	44	16,500	6	X	X
Suriname	68	0.16	57	0.16	78	88	162	49	1,320	14	273	24
Uruguay	1,304	0.41	1,376	0.46	6	10	31	72	32,967	(2)	4,677	2
Venezuela	3,915	0.19	3,758	0.23	4	5	41	65	48,833	18	5,767	44
ASIA	468,661	0.14	455,997	0.16	30	34	84	118	5,565,425	38	1,366,519	21
Afghanistan, Islamic State	8,054	0.46	8,054	0.53	31	37	7	5	843	6	X	X
Armenia	X	X	X	X	X	X	X	X	14,615	9	1,864	27
Azerbaijan	2,000	0.27	1,970	0.31	64	58	X	27	35,667	(6)	3,800	(14)
Bangladesh	9,694	0.08	9,131	0.10	19	32	61	98	5,283	12	X	X
Bhutan	134	0.08	127	0.10	24	25	2	1	49	23	X	X
Cambodia	2,400	0.25	1,550	0.22	6	4	3	6	1,365	1	20	0
China	95,975	0.08	99,254	0.10	45	52	184	261	770,295	X	49,357	X
Georgia, Rep	1,000	0.18	990	0.19	43	44	X	54	22,500	(14)	1,367	(11)
India	169,650	0.19	168,520	0.23	24	28	46	73	1,131,395	124	3,067	17
Indonesia	30,987	0.16	26,000	0.16	17	15	58	85	34,660	234	17,467	15
Iran, Islamic Rep	18,150	0.28	15,210	0.34	37	51	68	52	117,333	19	2,750	(5)
Iraq	5,450	0.28	5,450	0.38	32	47	17	52	32,333	(4)	1,933	(22)
Israel	435	0.08	407	0.10	53	42	206	225	25,513	(6)	257	(26)
Japan	4,463	0.04	4,806	0.04	63	63	437	407	2,003,333	26	1,161,667	15
Jordan	405	0.08	347	0.10	11	16	47	34	5,800	21	77	19
Kazakhstan, Rep	34,800	2.05	35,949	2.33	6	6	X	14 b	203,333	(16)	85,667	(26)
Korea, Dem People's Rep	2,000	0.09	1,935	0.10	61	73	409	315	74,667	21	X	X
Korea, Rep	2,055	0.05	2,167	0.05	61	65	331	474	64,644	747	60,999	939
Kuwait	5	0.00	2	0.00	50	40	420	200	107	357	X	X
Kyrgyz Rep	1,420	0.31	1,440	0.38	68	67	X	20	25,133	(8)	3,500	(30)
Lao People's Dem Rep	805	0.17	760	0.22	15	15	1	4	887	24	X	X
Lebanon	306	0.11	298	0.11	29	28	119	118	3,000	0	95	6
Malaysia	4,880	0.25	4,860	0.33	7	7	116	212	12,433	38	X	X
Mongolia	1,401	0.60	1,314	0.73	3	6	12	4 b	11,667	9	2,583	2
Myanmar	10,087	0.23	10,077	0.28	10	10	16	19	10,667	18	49	54
Nepal	2,354	0.11	2,319	0.14	27	37	16	31	4,567	70	X	X
Oman	63	0.03	43	0.03	X	X	32	143	149	43	44	241
Pakistan	21,250	0.16	20,340	0.21	76	80	59	101	279,501	112	1,633	173
Philippines	9,190	0.14	8,880	0.17	15	17	40	61	11,333	22	693	34
Saudi Arabia	3,740	0.22	2,270	0.20	18	12	95	122	2,067	38	657	30
Singapore	1	0.00	6	0.00	X	X	783	5,600	65	29	X	X
Sri Lanka	1,900	0.11	1,869	0.12	29	29	90	111	32,733	25	6	64
Syrian Arab Rep	5,775	0.42	5,607	0.58	10	15	32	65	69,198	88	3,336	18
Tajikistan, Rep	849	0.15	910	0.21	70	75	X	81	35,238	5	1,267	(16)
Thailand	20,800	0.36	19,198	0.39	17	21	25	54	74,870	192	47,964	60
Turkey	27,535	0.46	26,618	0.56	11	13	63	80	724,430	40	11,174	(17)
Turkmenistan, Rep	1,480	0.38	2,100	0.68	48	91	x	97	62,021	57	14,075	25
United Arab Emirates	39	0.02	32	0.03	16	13	140	710	184	11	5	67
Uzbekistan, Rep	4,500	0.21	4,640	0.27	79	92	X	150	178,333	4	7,733	(29)
Viet Nam	6,700	0.09	6,590	0.11	26	28	57	136	36,667	29	X	X
Yemen, Rep	1,481	0.11	1,465	0.16	20	24	X	X	X	X	X	X
OCEANIA	51,500	1.86	49,573	2.09	4	5	35	41	401,469	(5)	60,136	(3)
Australia	46,486	2.64	44,975	2.97	4	4	26	32	315,333	(3)	56,533	(2)
Fiji	260	0.34	185	0.27	1	0	59	56	7,051	43	X	X
New Zealand	3,800	1.09	3,500	1.10	6	7	153	154	75,667	(16)	3,050	(21)
Papua New Guinea	415	0.10	374	0.11	0	0	18	31	1,140	(8)	475	14
Solomon Islands	57	0.16	53	0.21	0	0	0	0	0	X	X	X

Sources: Food and Agriculture Organization of the United Nations and the United Nations Population Division.

Notes: a. Data for Belgium and Luxembourg are combined under Belgium. b. Data are from 1992. World and regional totals might include countries not listed here.
X = not available; negative numbers are shown in parentheses. For additional information, see Sources and Technical Notes.

Data Table 10.3 Livestock Populations and Grain Consumed as Feed, 1982–94

	Cattle		Sheep and Goats		Pigs		Equines		Buffaloes and Camels		Chickens		Grains Fed to Livestock as Percent of Total Grain Consumption	
	Annual Average (000) 1992-94	Percent Change Since 1982-84	Annual Average (000) 1992-94	Percent Change Since 1982-84	Annual Average (000) 1992-94	Percent Change Since 1982-84	Annual Average (000) 1992-94	Percent Change Since 1982-84	Annual Average (000) 1992-94	Percent Change Since 1982-84	Annual Average (millions) 1992-94	Percent Change Since 1982-84	1974	1994
WORLD	1,283,702	3	1,699,921	6	869,872	12	118,215	5	166,949	13	12,638	48	38	38
AFRICA	190,361	8	379,161	15	20,162	90	19,482	13	16,953	7	975	49	6	15
Algeria	1,351	(11)	20,589	17	6	20	504	(34)	120	(16)	77	55	0	22
Angola	3,243	(0)	1,817	14	815	21	6	0	0	X	6	0	0	0
Benin	1,139	30	2,099	1	545	36	7	0	0	X	24	53	0	0
Botswana	2,767	(2)	2,690	190	16	172	191	16	0	X	2	133	0	0
Burkina Faso	4,178	43	12,627	49	540	54	459	23	12	9	18	41	0	2
Burundi	407	(3)	1,260	14	93	35	0	X	0	X	4	33	0	0
Cameroon	4,821	38	7,398	83	1,380	68	51	(10)	0	X	20	119	0	0
Central African Rep	2,752	37	1,478	32	476	48	0	X	0	X	3	50	X	0
Chad	4,548	5	5,176	8	16	60	458	5	577	24	4	33	0	0
Congo	67	(3)	414	50	56	114	0	X	0	X	2	20	0	0
Cote d'Ivoire	1,206	53	2,174	15	393	21	0	X	0	X	26	44	6	3
Egypt	3,006	69	6,485	41	27	22	1,611	(11)	3,408	32	46	24	9	35
Equatorial Guinea	5	25	44	7	5	0	0	X	0	X	0	X	X	X
Eritrea	1,533	4	2,897	5	0	X	0	X	68	(1)	4	20	X	X
Ethiopia	19,633	X	20,500	16	13	X	3,280	(52)	357	(65)	20	(63)	0	0
Gabon	37	511	253	29	165	51	0	X	0	X	3	33	0	0
Gambia, The	405	38	271	(14)	11	0	46	(5)	0	X	1	X	0	0
Ghana	1,410	41	5,599	52	501	30	15	(25)	0	X	12	67	2	3
Guinea	1,640	9	969	9	33	(22)	3	(10)	0	X	14	46	0	0
Guinea-Bissau	473	52	521	35	307	12	7	75	0	X	1	50	0	0
Kenya	11,333	(7)	13,079	(5)	106	14	2	0	812	18	25	43	0	2
Lesotho	638	17	2,659	22	76	34	287	34	0	X	1	0	0	25
Liberia	36	(14)	432	(6)	120	4	0	X	0	X	4	33	0	0
Libya	83	(49)	4,967	(26)	0	X	77	(22)	127	(33)	18	57	0	27
Madagascar	10,284	(0)	2,008	(5)	1,525	20	0	(100)	0	X	30	40	0	0
Malawi	972	6	1,084	28	241	21	2	200	0	X	9	13	0	2
Mali	5,432	(5)	12,608	11	67	33	696	(3)	247	10	23	39	0	2
Mauritania	1,070	(16)	8,100	14	0	X	173	9	1,017	33	4	33	0	0
Mauritius	34	28	102	28	15	44	0	X	0	X	3	33	0	0
Morocco	2,875	18	21,214	34	10	32	1,630	21	36	(40)	82	172	1	26
Mozambique	1,250	(5)	505	9	171	27	20	0	0	X	23	17	0	0
Namibia	2,093	11	4,399	15	18	2	135	13	0	X	2	100	X	X
Niger	1,947	(36)	9,333	(3)	39	16	532	(21)	368	(4)	20	76	0	0
Nigeria	16,244	29	38,651	60	6,305	473	1,215	30	18	0	120	33	0	1
Rwanda	610	(4)	1,498	16	130	12	0	X	0	X	1	0	0	7
Senegal	2,750	22	7,527	141	320	69	845	104	15	156	33	223	0	0
Sierra Leone	357	1	461	4	50	24	0	X	0	X	6	38	0	2
Somalia	4,000	(8)	22,000	(26)	6	(43)	43	(9)	5,900	(4)	2	(22)	41	4
South Africa	12,720	(3)	35,975	(7)	1,511	7	454	0	0	X	41	27	34	33
Sudan	21,650	4	38,773	17	0	X	699	(2)	2,835	2	35	19	0	0
Swaziland	660	5	449	26	31	82	13	(22)	0	X	1	0	0	0
Tanzania	13,296	2	13,206	34	333	87	177	6	0	X	27	48	0	3
Togo	250	5	3,166	142	861	279	5	167	0	X	6	200	0	21
Tunisia	652	10	8,266	32	6	64	366	10	231	32	39	38	12	29
Uganda	5,133	5	5,133	15	887	310	17	6	0	X	20	28	0	0
Zaire	1,649	34	5,175	49	1,145	65	0	X	0	X	35	130	0	0
Zambia	3,200	37	660	60	293	45	2	100	0	X	21	48	6	4
Zimbabwe	4,400	(21)	3,066	94	278	53	128	9	0	X	12	48	13	9
EUROPE	110,006	(17)	149,419	3	170,256	(3)	5,455	(19)	135	(31)	1,297	(1)	62	59
Albania	627	2	3,138	43	90	(56)	187	42	2	0	3	(25)	0	0
Austria	2,432	(5)	369	57	3,750	(5)	62	50	0	X	14	(7)	67	69
Belarus, Rep	6,216	(12)	377	(37)	4,395	(11)	222	(2)	20	X	49	15	X	70
Belgium {a}	3,301	6	174	47	6,836	32	21	(30)	0	X	35	9	56	44
Bosnia and Herzegovina	438	X	724	X	454	X	59	X	1	X	8	X	X	X
Bulgaria	1,011	(43)	5,707	(50)	2,631	(31)	444	(10)	21	(47)	18	(56)	71	55
Croatia, Rep	566	X	613	X	1,264	X	38	X	0	X	13	X	X	X
Czech Rep	2,525	X	309	X	4,426	X	19	X	0	X	27	X	X	62
Denmark	2,126	(25)	90	74	10,693	18	23	(31)	0	X	20	26	82	81
Estonia, Rep	595	(29)	116	(42)	588	(45)	7	X	0	X	4	(43)	X	64
Finland	1,242	(25)	73	(20)	1,322	(9)	49	41	0	X	5	(33)	69	60
France	20,470	(14)	11,573	(19)	12,672	11	367	7	0	X	263	23	66	65
Germany	16,307	(22)	2,492	(28)	26,061	(26)	518	17	0	X	102	(23)	X	60
Greece	618	(22)	15,265	19	1,103	5	203	(49)	1	0	27	(9)	51	52
Hungary	1,194	(38)	1,643	(47)	5,453	(40)	77	(33)	0	X	37	(43)	71	75
Iceland	76	13	500	(31)	21	85	78	49	0	X	0	X	X	X
Ireland	6,244	8	6,044	130	1,419	32	68	(17)	0	X	11	31	66	63
Italy	7,823	(8)	11,730	4	8,352	(6)	381	(13)	89	(17)	159	3	46	48
Latvia, Rep	1,174	(19)	166	(19)	950	(44)	29	(13)	0	X	6	(51)	X	64
Lithuania, Rep	1,849	(22)	61	(34)	1,580	(40)	79	2	0	X	11	(26)	X	63
Macedonia, former Yugoslav Rep	280	X	2,405	X	179	X	63	X	1	X	4	X	X	X
Moldova, Rep	962	(22)	1,361	17	1,468	(21)	53	X	0	X	21	5	X	50
Netherlands	4,766	(12)	2,079	158	13,809	29	65	7	0	X	110	28	65	40
Norway	998	1	2,421	2	752	7	21	39	0	X	4	0	67	66
Poland, Rep	7,853	(31)	1,336	(68)	20,137	17	821	(49)	0	X	55	(16)	67	61
Portugal	1,361	3	6,771	22	1,825	(46)	275	(8)	0	X	27	35	55	58
Romania	3,878	(40)	13,331	(26)	10,023	(24)	775	19	0	X	96	(11)	66	65
Russian Federation	51,934	(12)	50,108	(23)	31,835	(15)	2,571	X	133	X	641	7	X	57
Spain	4,998	(1)	26,949	35	18,227	53	413	(29)	0	X	51	(3)	64	68
Slovak Rep	1,165	X	508	X	2,292	X	0	X	0	X	15	X	X	64
Slovenia, Rep	497	X	31	X	584	X	0	X	0	X	11	X	X	X
Sweden	1,825	(4)	467	7	2,238	(17)	81	42	0	X	13	(3)	77	75
Switzerland	1,743	(10)	477	11	1,693	(19)	56	15	0	X	6	0	60	55
Ukraine	22,597	(12)	7,310	(19)	16,437	(20)	731	(10)	0	X	207	(12)	X	59
United Kingdom	11,688	(11)	29,375	29	7,828	(2)	183	7	0	X	138	14	57	50
Yugoslavia, Fed Rep	1,925	X	2,740	X	3,979	X	84	302	19	X	23	X	57 b	52 b

	Cattle		Sheep and Goats		Pigs		Equines		Buffaloes and Camels		Chickens		Grains Fed to Livestock as Percent of Total Grain Consumption	
	Annual Average (000) 1992-94	Percent Change Since 1982-84	Annual Average (000) 1992-94	Percent Change Since 1982-84	Annual Average (000) 1992-94	Percent Change Since 1982-84	Annual Average (000) 1992-94	Percent Change Since 1982-84	Annual Average (000) 1992-94	Percent Change Since 1982-84	Annual Average (millions) 1992-94	Percent Change Since 1982-84	1974	1994
NORTH & CENTRAL AMERICA	161,223	(9)	32,036	(7)	91,825	1	20,915	(1)	9	13	2,145	37	68	65
Belize	57	14	5	25	26	32	9	0	0	X	1	50	X	X
Canada	11,935	0	697	19	10,846	8	426	12	0	X	103	5	75	76
Costa Rica	1,983	(16)	5	0	247	6	126	1	0	X	14	126	29	51
Cuba	4,567	(11)	420	(11)	1,603	(1)	632	(23)	0	X	25	(0)	0	0
Dominican Rep	2,392	17	702	30	833	168	607	32	0	X	33	37	27	58
El Salvador	1,237	31	20	11	322	(18)	122	6	0	X	4	(8)	21	24
Guatemala	2,181	2	515	(27)	695	14	163	12	0	X	16	12	7	25
Haiti	800	(36)	995	(5)	200	(65)	690	(4)	0	X	5	(25)	0	2
Honduras	2,238	(7)	41	33	597	35	281	9	0	X	11	100	9	47
Jamaica	328	15	443	7	180	(11)	37	(3)	0	X	8	53	0	32
Mexico	30,503	1	16,613	2	17,111	(10)	12,588	1	0	X	300	42	23	38
Nicaragua	1,645	(28)	10	11	538	(10)	302	(6)	0	X	6	27	22	5
Panama	1,434	(2)	5	(17)	292	47	160	20	0	X	8	47	7	39
Trinidad and Tobago	55	(16)	66	15	50	(28)	5	0	9	13	11	19	0	35
United States	99,240	(13)	10,946	(20)	57,918	2	4,719	(9)	0	X	1,580	39	75	68
SOUTH AMERICA	279,363	13	118,854	(0)	50,885	(1)	22,295	11	1,430	101	1,138	51	39	52
Argentina	50,292	(6)	24,767	(24)	2,167	(43)	3,587	10	0	X	64	35	43	51
Bolivia	5,862	14	9,071	(1)	2,277	29	1,036	4	0	X	34	173	17	34
Brazil	152,710	22	32,332	17	32,007	(1)	9,575	13	1,429	101	670	42	47	60
Chile	3,570	(5)	5,256	(21)	1,307	18	531	5	0	X	53	119	22	34
Colombia	25,265	5	3,507	4	2,638	18	3,330	10	0	X	71	108	16	30
Ecuador	4,821	44	1,978	34	2,502	(32)	939	46	0	X	57	70	12	38
Guyana	190	19	209	7	45	(26)	3	0	0	X	11	(13)	4	5
Paraguay	7,962	19	495	4	2,983	180	390	10	0	X	13	8	0	2
Peru	3,965	(4)	13,565	(9)	2,371	5	1,411	4	0	X	64	45	26	38
Suriname	97	74	18	135	37	79	0	X	1	X	6	20	0	0
Uruguay	9,972	(0)	24,614	20	224	(14)	482	3	0	X	9	56	32	13
Venezuela	14,641	29	2,317	37	2,317	(9)	1,007	3	0	X	86	74	33	33
ASIA	402,804	10	700,609	13	470,092	29	43,627	6	147,787	13	5,894	91	8	18
Afghanistan, Islamic State	1,500	(54)	16,350	(17)	0	X	1,524	(13)	265	0	7	0	0	0
Armenia	0	X	781	(64)	82	(69)	12	X	0	X	3	(72)	X	19
Azerbaijan	1,709	(8)	4,913	(9)	126	(37)	38	X	40	X	26	7	X	28
Bangladesh	23,844	7	26,998	132	0	X	0	X	857	68	124	61	0	0
Bhutan	429	26	96	153	74	28	57	33	4	(33)	0	X	X	0
Cambodia	2,508	95	0	X	2,080	144	20	100	812	50	14	105	0	0
China	86,469	53	210,519	18	392,182	29	26,605	9	22,624	15	2,995	129	9	23
Georgia, Rep	1,132	(29)	1,442	(28)	707	(32)	21	X	20	X	19	(3)	X	21
India	192,777	(1)	162,132	11	11,630	14	2,672	29	80,153	10	437	136	1	3
Indonesia	11,298	28	18,197	38	8,357	92	706	15	3,454	35	647	128	2	9
Iran, Islamic Rep	7,000	15	68,700	22	0	X	2,288	(13)	440	13	180	53	11	18
Iraq	1,117	(34)	7,393	(40)	0	X	192	(63)	116	(53)	24	(61)	0	23
Israel	356	17	444	15	100	(11)	11	0	10	(9)	27	(17)	66	60
Japan	4,998	9	60	(22)	10,790	5	27	14	0	X	331	7	39	46
Jordan	41	33	2,553	75	0	X	26	(12)	18	15	76	144	21	54
Kazakhstan, Rep	9,336	4	34,409	(4)	2,610	(9)	1,513	X	170	X	59	18	X	54
Korea, Dem People's Rep	1,310	31	694	19	3,323	33	51	17	0	X	22	24	0	0
Korea, Rep	2,847	29	511	53	5,897	101	6	89	0	X	74	58	7	50
Kuwait	10	(58)	147	(48)	0	X	0	(100)	1	(86)	9	(31)	26	25
Kyrgyz Rep	1,093	9	8,513	(17)	237	(21)	318	X	50	X	13	18	X	46
Lao People's Dem Rep	1,047	109	134	124	1,575	22	29	(21)	1,202	31	9	35	0	0
Lebanon	77	54	706	20	41	81	43	171	1	X	23	0	30	35
Malaysia	713	21	659	63	2,975	45	5	0	189	(24)	105	66	3	46
Mongolia	2,777	17	20,239	5	60	52	2,186	10	435	(25)	0	X	0	0
Myanmar	9,582	3	1,391	6	2,544	(8)	128	(2)	2,113	3	29	(21)	0	0
Nepal	6,343	(6)	6,373	15	614	52	0	X	3,102	20	7	22	0	0
Oman	142	15	882	6	0	X	26	13	94	33	3	200	0	0
Pakistan	17,890	11	67,922	32	0	X	4,208	34	19,731	48	95	63	2	4
Philippines	1,778	(7)	2,564	26	8,068	3	207	9	2,589	(12)	74	13	12	25
Saudi Arabia	202	(29)	11,091	18	0	X	103	(10)	413	16	81	98	5	74
Singapore	0	(100)	1	(57)	167	(79)	0	X	0	X	2	(86)	35	20
Sri Lanka	1,589	(7)	519	(6)	90	14	2	0	879	(4)	9	42	0	0
Syrian Arab Rep	747	(2)	13,661	0	1	X	224	(25)	4	(59)	18	22	3	29
Tajikistan, Rep	1,239	(5)	2,921	(6)	47	(72)	86	X	50	X	4	(41)	X	17
Thailand	6,866	45	286	199	5,007	20	67	247	4,622	(27)	151	72	4	30
Turkey	11,945	(20)	49,580	(26)	10	(14)	1,551	(32)	347	(60)	161	155	22	31
Turkmenistan, Rep	962	37	6,060	34	203	1	46	X	40	X	7	22	X	46
United Arab Emirates	60	96	1,125	99	0	X	0	X	136	93	7	83	0	20
Uzbekistan, Rep	5,226	35	9,376	(2)	525	(25)	269	X	112	X	33	11	X	28
Viet Nam	3,298	68	303	37	14,033	30	134	12	2,951	21	113	48	0	0
Yemen, Rep	1,143	10	6,943	11	0	X	503	(19)	172	17	21	148	0	0
OCEANIA	33,421	6	191,930	(8)	X	X	X	X	X	X	X	X	46	54
Australia	24,225	5	139,915	2	2,726	11	280	(38)	0	X	65	36	46	60
Fiji	312	34	201	16	107	50	43	8	0	X	3	50	0	0
New Zealand	8,456	9	51,730	(26)	424	2	83	(13)	0	X	10	43	50	47
Papua New Guinea	105	(14)	6	50	1,022	12	2	100	0	X	3	50	0	0
Solomon Islands	13	(44)	0	X	55	15	0	X	0	X	0	X	X	X

Sources: Food and Agriculture Organization of the United Nations and the United States Department of Agriculture.
Notes: a. Data for Belgium and Luxembourg are combined under Belgium. b. Data are for the area of the former Yugoslavia.
World and regional totals include some countries not listed here.
0 = zero or less than half the unit of measure; X = not available; negative numbers are shown in parentheses. For additional information, see Sources and Technical Notes.

Data Table 10.4 Food Trade and Aid, 1981–93

	Average Annual Net Trade in Food						Average Annual Donations or Receipts of Food Aid					
	Cereals (000 metric tons)		Oils (metric tons)		Pulses (metric tons)		Cereals				Oils (metric tons)	Milk (metric tons)
							(000 metric tons)		Kg Per Capita			
	1981-83	1991-93	1981-83	1991-93	1981-83	1991-93	1980-82	1990-92	1980-82	1990-92	1990-92	1990-92
WORLD												
AFRICA	20,123	31,328	1,025,867	1,863,785	164,824	459,234	4,371	6,077	9	7	205,935	47,221
Algeria	3,527	5,184	216,258	270,651	98,600	92,986	18	20	1	1	787	978
Angola	289	321	31,191	45,478	25,390	29,994	37	108	5	4	6,895	682
Benin	101	156	15,862	8,317	212	118	8	11	2	2	915	277
Botswana	77	119	3,174	4,474	(120)	1,947	13	3	13	10	561	597
Burkina Faso	69	145	6,430	5,518	(2,772)	(300)	56	57	8	6	2,815	1,277
Burundi	19	24	1,007	832	0	0	10	3	2	2	211	695
Cameroon	133	296	9,885	17,853	(12)	50	8	6	1	1	470	169
Central African Rep	16	30	271	2,331	25	27	2	4	1	1	216	206
Chad	39	64	0	(8)	(179)	0	20	31	4	3	396	920
Congo	69	134	3,020	5,253	18	1,570	2	11	1	1	839	116
Cote d'Ivoire	566	555	72,465	150,677	145	650	1	45	0	0	887	374
Egypt	7,326	7,144	314,631	721,161	98,000	188,387	1,860	1,124	41	32	9,264	2,783
Equatorial Guinea	5	9	0	2,704	0	35	3	4	15	9	5	274
Eritrea	X	X	X	X	X	X	X	13	X	0	X	X
Ethiopia	278	620	3,275	39,484	(34,162)	14,880	176	907	5	4	39,873	6,122
Gabon	42	75	1,503	2,437	36	15	0	0	0	0	0	0
Gambia, The	38	93	(7,651)	4,598	0	0	15	9	22	15	640	35
Ghana	188	369	4,470	3,915	70	973	82	113	7	5	1,644	524
Guinea	112	323	2,018	9,679	0	(385)	32	24	7	5	617	4
Guinea-Bissau	34	72	486	2,242	59	57	25	9	30	25	671	337
Kenya	148	483	91,730	149,079	(45,352)	(36)	129	172	7	5	3,263	565
Lesotho	107	130	0	0	5,193	4,167	36	35	26	19	1,181	486
Liberia	109	150	3,408	4,310	159	5,267	24	146	12	9	7,754	222
Libya	843	2,329	57,859	50,044	18,448	11,384	0	0	0	0	0	0
Madagascar	311	93	12,764	19,151	(2,883)	(7,904)	43	48	5	3	2,885	612
Malawi	(4)	362	519	4,743	(9,808)	8,223	8	358	1	1	5,368	748
Mali	148	118	(4,869)	(891)	22	0	46	37	7	5	949	286
Mauritania	198	310	9,869	154,105	3,637	1,327	73	59	46	35	1,067	814
Mauritius	174	205	18,126	21,843	7,424	9,912	28	7	29	26	34	490
Morocco	2,224	2,901	170,100	177,354	(7,465)	9,842	239	210	12	10	50,734	3,927
Mozambique	299	690	9,387	46,867	9,133	31,381	151	656	12	10	13,227	2,602
Namibia	63	141	0	0	8,367	8,000	0	14	0	0	502	181
Niger	122	138	7,462	13,119	(8,363)	(49,433)	30	48	5	4	1,348	934
Nigeria	1,947	1,203	238,658	65,118	2,386	43	0	0	0	0	3	878
Rwanda	17	49	863	10,625	(797)	2,792	14	34	3	2	2,008	1,065
Senegal	500	587	(36,541)	(37,121)	36	232	99	57	17	13	784	767
Sierra Leone	88	151	720	4,554	58	0	26	37	8	6	1,491	318
Somalia	359	248	19,816	10,710	583	12,333	218	168	31	25	7,628	726
South Africa	(2,551)	1,824	(27,218)	132,541	22,495	64,560	0	0	0	0	0	0
Sudan	102	635	(16,786)	69,570	8,388	30,333	200	426	10	8	11,411	3,758
Swaziland	48	72	0	0	0	0	1	16	1	1	248	240
Tanzania	274	186	4,511	46,206	(35,420)	(17,192)	211	25	11	8	573	1,169
Togo	66	77	415	1,985	548	77	5	11	2	1	1,263	249
Tunisia	1,032	950	11,759	31,438	(6,204)	767	120	179	18	15	3,611	3,303
Uganda	27	(22)	0	13,100	367	(19,737)	41	49	3	2	1,756	1,005
Zaire	399	253	26,837	10,367	133	1,600	81	77	3	2	780	840
Zambia	222	372	8,522	13,105	221	339	117	291	20	14	4,462	311
Zimbabwe	(328)	421	(422)	8,859	908	3,924	6	331	1	1	6,572	238
EUROPE	11,309	(26,553)	968,973	1,113,441	580,815	1,149,822	(1,253)	1,047	(2)	(2)	2,026	NA
Albania	58	477	7,550	26,893	(300)	1,752	0	393	0	0	21,487	X
Austria	(451)	(583)	106,888	97,582	6,138	7,821	(17)	(22)	(2)	(2)	0	NA
Belarus, Rep	X	2,243	X	X	X	X	0	82	0	0	1,833	66
Belgium {a}	2,687	2,658	23,904	(156,495)	68,649	403,580	(38)	(39)	(4)	(4)	0	0
Bosnia and Herzegovina	X	X	X	X	X	X	0	0	0	0	0	0
Bulgaria	(105)	36	(13,453)	17,386	3,941	(15,011)	0	100	0	0	1,335	2,822
Croatia, Rep	X	(178)	X	10,672	X	992	0	0	0	0	0	0
Czech Rep	X	153	X	X	X	(92,261)	0	0	0	0	0	0
Denmark	(248)	(1,921)	53,627	91,322	(16,968)	(178,887)	(16)	(19)	(3)	(3)	(366)	X
Estonia, Rep	X	219	X	3,331	X	140	0	140	0	0	0	0
Finland	503	(795)	1,133	8,227	1,293	2,355	0	0	0	0	(10,434)	(4,729)
France	(19,378)	(30,993)	326,807	31,227	(138,374)	(1,072,512)	(170)	(197)	(3)	(3)	(2,775)	(460)
Germany	5,642	(4,648)	114,199	195,530	119,075	689,258	(172)	(243)	(2)	(2)	(11,661)	(3,479)
Greece	(408)	(715)	(39,411)	(59,189)	10,135	38,228	0	(1)	0	0	0	0
Hungary	(1,417)	(1,881)	(133,450)	(203,448)	(46,177)	(193,482)	0	0	0	0	0	0
Iceland	21	22	1,601	2,687	334	240	0	0	0	0	0	0
Ireland	357	(2)	41,878	58,871	7,722	35,457	(4)	(8)	(1)	(1)	0	(1,000)
Italy	4,361	4,424	337,759	474,278	109,438	412,853	(85)	(138)	(2)	(1)	(22,336)	X
Latvia, Rep	X	57	X	105	X	(818)	0	208	0	0	0	0
Lithuania, Rep	X	327	X	169	X	X	0	227	0	0	0	0
Macedonia, former Yugoslav Rep	X	110	X	6,708	X	(883)	0	0	0	0	0	0
Moldova, Rep	X	104	X	X	X	X	0	24	0	0	0	0
Netherlands	3,454	2,760	(37,406)	(102,670)	248,157	736,787	(68)	(106)	(5)	(5)	(8,786)	(3,101)
Norway	596	254	(383)	19,307	5,720	4,668	(29)	(60)	(7)	(7)	(80)	(218)
Poland, Rep	5,024	703	114,824	68,482	1,171	(153,654)	139	317	4	4	6,843	434
Portugal	3,544	1,793	(35,245)	10,301	11,535	51,073	174	0	18	18	0	0
Romania	552	2,009	(69,683)	21,597	5,983	(533)	0	333	0	0	16,683	1,584
Russian Federation	X	25,554	X	155,481	X	(707)	0	377	0	0	25,557	20,255
Slovak Rep	X	20	X	X	X	X	0	0	0	0	0	0
Slovenia, Rep	X	542	X	X	X	1,486	0	0	0	0	0	0
Spain	5,767	2,365	(411,725)	(351,139)	74,406	546,079	(12)	(31)	(0)	(0)	(403)	0
Sweden	(867)	(921)	48,715	67,248	4,933	5,597	(104)	(127)	(12)	(12)	(14,070)	(101)
Switzerland	1,196	466	54,727	37,265	15,211	9,903	(23)	(70)	(4)	(3)	(370)	(2,823)
Ukraine	X	1,400	X	X	X	X	0	66	0	0	1	0
United Kingdom	(578)	(2,485)	397,880	719,738	79,192	(69,074)	(80)	(160)	(1)	(1)	(1,510)	(24)
Yugoslavia, Fed Rep	X	(915)	11	6,226	X	3,722	0	0	0	0	1,078	0

	Average Annual Net Trade in Food						Average Annual Donations or Receipts of Food Aid					
	Cereals (000 metric tons)		Oils (metric tons)		Pulses (metric tons)		Cereals (000 metric tons)		Cereals Kg Per Capita		Oils (metric tons)	Milk (metric tons)
	1981-83	1991-93	1981-83	1991-93	1981-83	1991-93	1980-82	1990-92	1980-82	1990-92	1990-92	1990-92
NORTH & CENTRAL AMERICA	(118,272)	(98,546)	(650,209)	896,088	(421,975)	(754,560)	(5,504)	(7,602)	(15)	(13)	(289,810)	(1,256)
Belize	6	17	0	147	123	(485)	0	0	0	0	0	0
Canada	(25,386)	(25,702)	(112,419)	(141,114)	(168,752)	(483,287)	(643)	(949)	(26)	(23)	(35,592)	(4,565)
Costa Rica	152	408	3,230	14,085	11,102	2,113	16	42	7	5	183	0
Cuba	2,044	1,655	72,806	121,273	109,628	116,000	0	2	0	0	457	3,734
Dominican Rep	371	811	59,756	88,934	(2,441)	14,940	84	9	14	12	11,247	783
El Salvador	176	325	9,772	34,778	920	7,531	61	99	13	11	8,708	2,905
Guatemala	161	419	9,115	49,721	1,079	5,711	11	177	2	1	3,475	2,144
Haiti	198	362	20,242	60,767	521	18,000	75	54	14	11	3,870	2,636
Honduras	82	190	7,938	(12,396)	(2,190)	(1,203)	32	101	9	6	1,839	1,185
Jamaica	403	440	6,580	11,085	479	1,292	79	231	36	33	1,042	1,214
Mexico	6,391	6,394	82,622	393,243	262,291	(14,735)	0	112	0	0	1,843	5,668
Nicaragua	152	135	14,278	32,017	8,992	3,312	77	113	27	20	29,986	3,031
Panama	85	175	20,279	22,589	6,178	4,576	2	1	1	1	7,721	0
Trinidad and Tobago	237	224	11,591	(700)	12,196	10,403	0	0	0	0	0	0
United States	(103,612)	(84,689)	42,576	664,374	(670,747)	(446,970)	(5,298)	(7,593)	(23)	(21)	(324,590)	(19,992)
SOUTH AMERICA	(7,616)	676	(1,422,461)	(2,774,328)	(11,316)	27,613	190	140	1	1	40,019	11,855
Argentina	(18,460)	(12,493)	(694,282)	(2,606,117)	(149,319)	(226,446)	(42)	(3)	(1)	(1)	0	0
Bolivia	314	348	9,001	(4,744)	1,047	(6,036)	83	231	15	12	2,707	2,217
Brazil	4,475	6,754	(1,182,042)	(673,227)	13,568	112,042	3	12	0	0	25	1,273
Chile	1,332	847	73,215	94,084	(56,451)	(60,648)	21	9	2	2	352	1,147
Colombia	789	1,331	104,932	57,664	63,760	88,283	4	9	0	0	248	113
Ecuador	346	431	34,832	50,412	804	2,649	8	52	1	1	1,084	1,772
Guyana	(31)	(42)	2,686	130	3,839	4,200	2	46	3	3	128	431
Paraguay	61	45	787	(25,201)	63	(1,176)	8	0	2	2	10	1,080
Peru	1,425	1,918	57,284	84,346	9,822	16,598	100	402	6	5	33,596	3,755
Suriname	(71)	(12)	3,596	6,199	2,333	2,333	0	12	0	0	1,833	0
Uruguay	(353)	(311)	(5,330)	9,745	937	3,513	2	7	1	1	37	67
Venezuela	2,547	1,860	194,238	265,050	97,861	91,705	0	0	0	0	0	0
ASIA	69,058	69,333	(651,617)	(2,125,261)	(106,821)	(388,978)	3,525	3,157	1	1	151,007	29,173
Afghanistan, Islamic State	84	172	2,000	3,033	(8,200)	(1,433)	111	86	7	7	918	X
Armenia	X	375	X	X	X	X	0	49	0	0	2,217	1,117
Azerbaijan	X	340	X	X	X	X	0	4	0	0	0	167
Bangladesh	1,541	1,412	126,031	298,636	2,470	71,462	1,074	1,143	12	10	10,193	94
Bhutan	9	36	0	249	0	0	1	4	1	1	408	222
Cambodia	131	65	1,800	0	0	0	124	57	19	14	1,805	0
China	18,134	5,894	93,521	1,747,970	(6,738)	(755,453)	(11)	123	(0)	(0)	2,549	7,803
Georgia, Rep	X	500	X	X	X	X	0	57	0	0	0	33
India	1,336	(179)	1,347,222	241,067	160,845	378,878	328	257	0	0	62,218	10,741
Indonesia	2,272	2,813	(344,622)	(1,566,942)	9,619	53,715	440	48	3	2	580	15
Iran, Islamic Rep	3,849	5,037	280,025	578,378	21,839	22,800	0	63	0	0	1,669	312
Iraq	3,023	1,793	167,262	131,574	49,475	25,667	0	66	0	0	1,831	539
Israel	1,521	2,075	409	32,429	16,738	25,005	14	1	3	3	0	0
Japan	23,965	27,451	258,394	436,721	214,511	197,547	(703)	(419)	(6)	(6)	(322)	(976)
Jordan	543	1,483	16,369	60,685	11,914	24,552	80	330	26	18	2,270	1,145
Kazakhstan, Rep	X	(4,300)	X	X	X	X	0	1	0	0	0	0
Korea, Dem People's Rep	354	1,210	10,717	34,220	0	0	0	0	0	0	0	0
Korea, Rep	6,526	10,719	64,473	315,245	7,729	39,375	431	0	11	10	0	0
Kuwait	331	236	7,103	27,604	8,888	6,872	0	0	0	0	0	0
Kyrgyz Rep	X	773	X	X	X	X	0	30	0	0	0	0
Lao People's Dem Rep	46	24	2,433	1,523	43,500	14,639	2	6	1	0	0	0
Lebanon	535	698	20,818	109,015	38,163	54,121	22	15	8	8	5,608	1,864
Malaysia	1,713	3,115	(2,736,030)	(6,010,144)	38,163	54,121	0	3	0	0	0	0
Mongolia	94	101	0	1,410	X	X	0	15	0	0	0	33
Myanmar	(762)	(231)	32,667	148,313	(82,833)	(355,000)	8	0	0	0	0	0
Nepal	35	25	5,546	27,739	(1,189)	(256)	30	8	2	2	406	682
Oman	159	329	3,437	20,928	1,187	7,937	0	0	0	0	0	0
Pakistan	(749)	720	478,900	991,687	78,007	172,212	257	284	3	2	53,716	0
Philippines	1,195	1,767	(944,154)	(919,811)	3,873	27,905	78	60	2	1	229	2,611
Saudi Arabia	4,758	4,332	120,500	221,346	32,551	42,699	(25)	(4)	(2)	(1)	0	0
Singapore	797	567	4,737	209,699	11,610	29,360	0	0	0	0	0	0
Sri Lanka	687	1,018	(15,561)	28,336	7,438	66,289	200	296	13	11	0	7
Syrian Arab Rep	726	1,255	23,228	41,451	(28,824)	(24,973)	42	19	5	3	1,303	2,321
Tajikistan, Rep	X	500	X	X	X	X	0	24	0	0	0	0
Thailand	(6,155)	(4,707)	42,655	10,256	(211,628)	(102,291)	10	80	0	0	2,005	4
Turkey	(776)	(2,477)	133,512	514,247	(520,957)	(472,574)	0	(15)	0	0	232	12
Turkmenistan, Rep	X	1,120	X	X	X	X	0	1	0	0	100	0
United Arab Emirates	266	330	26,562	49,344	12,245	25,893	0	0	0	0	0	0
Uzbekistan, Rep	X	4,078	X	X	X	X	0	0	0	0	0	0
Viet Nam	605	(1,312)	1,269	13,598	(8,233)	(9,393)	126	76	2	2	1,072	428
Yemen, Rep	X	X	25,224	112,535	X	X	0	0	X	X	0	0
OCEANIA	(12,306)	(12,407)	(31,004)	(23,383)	(60,029)	(527,732)	(382)	(303)	(17)	(14)	0	0
Australia	(12,658)	(13,099)	79,083	150,853	(25,936)	(482,063)	(390)	(303)	(26)	(23)	(1,260)	(613)
Fiji	86	106	(7,839)	2,084	4,178	4,828	5	0	8	7	0	0
New Zealand	12	180	23,214	53,076	(39,046)	(51,376)	0	0	0	0	0	(5)
Papua New Guinea	144	249	(87,012)	(193,198)	65	10	0	0	0	0	0	1
Solomon Islands	5	24	17,043	26,833	18	10	0	0	0	0	0	0

Sources: Food and Agriculture Organization of the United Nations and the United Nations Population Division.

Notes: a. Data for Belgium and Luxembourg are combined under Belgium.
World and regional totals for net trade include some countries not listed here. Totals for food aid do not add because of rounding.
Imports and food aid receipts are shown as positive numbers; exports and food aid donations are shown as negative numbers in parentheses.
0 = zero or less than half the unit of measure; X = not available; negative numbers are shown in parentheses.
For additional information, see Sources and Technical Notes.

Sources and Technical Notes

Data Table 10.1
Food and Agricultural Production, 1982–94

Source: Food and Agriculture Organization of the United Nations (FAO), *FAOSTAT-PC,* on diskette (FAO, Rome, July 1995).

Indexes of agricultural production and *food production* portray the disposable output (after deduction for feed and seed) of a country's agriculture sector relative to the base period 1979–81. For a given year and country, the index is calculated as the disposable average output of a commodity in terms of weight or volume during the period of interest multiplied by the 1979–81 average national producer price per unit. The index represents the total value of the commodity for that period in terms of the 1979–81 price. The values of all crop and livestock products are totaled to yield an aggregated value of agricultural production in 1979–81 prices. The ratio of this aggregate for a given year to that for 1979–81 is multiplied by 100 to obtain the index number.

The multiplication of disposable outputs with the 1979–81 unit value eliminates inflationary or deflationary distortion. However, the base period's relative prices among the individual commodities are also preserved. Especially in economies with high inflation, price patterns among agricultural commodities can change dramatically over time.

The continental and world index values for a given year are calculated by totaling the disposable outputs of all relevant countries for each agricultural commodity. Each of these aggregates is multiplied by a respective 1979–81 average "international" producer price and is then summed to give a total agricultural output value for that region or for the world in terms of 1979–81 prices. This method avoids distortion caused by the use of international exchange rates.

The agricultural production index includes all crop and livestock products originating in each country. The food production index covers all edible agricultural products that contain nutrients. Coffee and tea are excluded.

Average production of cereals includes cereal production for feed and seed. Crop yields (*average yields of cereals* and *average yields of roots and tubers*) are calculated from production and area data. Area refers to the area harvested. Cereals comprise all cereals harvested for dry grain, exclusive of crops cut for hay or harvested green. Roots and tubers cover all root crops grown principally for human consumption; root crops grown principally for feed are excluded.

Data Table 10.2
Agricultural Inputs, 1981–93

Sources: Food and Agriculture Organization of the United Nations (FAO), *FAOSTAT-PC,* on diskette (FAO, Rome, July 1995). Per capita figures: United Nations Population Division, *Interpolated National Populations, 1950–2025 (The 1994 Revision),* on diskette (U.N., New York, 1995).

Cropland refers to land under temporary and permanent crops, temporary meadows, market and kitchen gardens, and temporarily fallow land. Permanent cropland is land under crops that do not need to be replanted after each harvest, such as cocoa, coffee, fruit trees, rubber, and vines. Human population data used to calculate *hectares per capita* are for 1993. For trends in cropland area, see Data Table 9.1.

Irrigated land as a percentage of cropland refers to areas purposely provided with water, including land flooded by river water for crop production or pasture improvement, whether or not this area is irrigated several times or only once during the year.

Annual fertilizer use refers to the application of nutrients in terms of nitrogen (N), phosphate (P_2O_5), and potash (K_2O). The fertilizer year is July 1–June 30; data refer to the year beginning in July.

Tractors generally refer to wheeled and crawler tractors used in agriculture. Garden tractors are excluded. *Harvesters* refer to harvesters and threshers.

Data Table 10.3
Livestock Populations and Grain Consumed as Feed, 1982–94

Sources: Livestock data: Food and Agriculture Organization of the United Nations (FAO), *FAOSTAT-PC,* on diskette (FAO, Rome, July 1995). Feed data: Economic Research Service, United States Department of Agriculture (USDA), *PS&D View,* on-line bulletin board service (USDA, Washington, D.C., 1995).

Data on livestock include all animals in the country, regardless of place or purpose of their breeding. Data on livestock numbers are collected annually by FAO; estimates are made by FAO for countries that either do not report data or only partially report data. *Equines* include horses, mules, and asses. For some countries, data on *chickens* include all poultry. *Grain fed to livestock as percent of total grain consumption* was calculated using USDA grain consumption and feed numbers. Grains include wheat, rice (milled weight), corn, barley, sorghum, millet, rye, oats, and mixed grains. Grain consumption is the total domestic use during the local marketing year of the individual country. It is the sum of feed, food, seed, and industrial uses.

Data Table 10.4
Food Trade and Aid, 1981–93

Sources: Trade and food aid data: Food and Agriculture Organization of the United Nations (FAO), *FAOSTAT-PC,* on diskette (FAO, Rome, July 1995). Population data: United Nations Population Division, *Interpolated National Populations, 1950–2025 (The 1994 Revision),* on diskette (U.N., New York, 1995).

Figures shown for food trade are *net* imports or exports. Exports were subtracted from imports.

Two definitions of trade are used by countries reporting trade data. "Special trade" refers only to imports for domestic consumption and exports of domestic goods. "General trade" encompasses total imports and total exports, including reexports. In some cases, trade figures include goods purchased by a country that are reexported to a third country without ever entering the purchasing country. For information on the definition used by a particular country, see *FAO Trade Yearbook 1994* (FAO, Rome, 1995).

Average annual donations or receipts of food aid are shown as either positive or negative numbers: receipts are shown as positive numbers; donations are expressed as negative numbers. For some countries that are both recipients and donors of food aid, donations were subtracted from receipts.

Trade in *cereals* includes wheat and wheat flour, rice, barley, maize, rye, and oats. Trade in *oils* includes oils from soybeans, groundnuts (peanuts), olives, cottonseeds, sunflower seeds, rape or mustard seeds, linseeds, palms, coconuts, palm kernels, castor beans, and maize, as well as animal oils, fats, and greases (including lard). Trade in *pulses* includes all kinds of dried leguminous vegetables, with the exception of vetches and lupins.

Food aid refers to the donation or concessional sale of food commodities. *Cereals* include wheat, rice, coarse grains, bulgur wheat, wheat flour, and the cereal component of blended foods. Cereal donations or receipts (*kilograms per capita*) are the result of dividing the 3-year averages by the population averages provided by the United Nations Population Division. *Oils* include vegetable oil and butter oil. *Milk* includes skimmed milk powder and other dairy products (mainly cheese).

Food aid data are reported by donor countries and international organizations.

11. Biodiversity

Earth is home to a cornucopia of plants, animals, and other living things. Most birds, mammals, and plants have been identified. Little is known, however, about other orders, such as insects, or about organisms that inhabit poorly explored habitats, such as the deep-sea floor. The current total of all identified species is about 1.7 million, but this number pales next to estimates of the total number of species, which has been put conservatively at close to 14 million by an international group of experts, but could range from 3 million to 111 million species. (See Table 11.1.) Much of this wide range is accounted for by insects, which could number anywhere from 2 million to 100 million species; the working estimate is 8 million species [1].

Many of the world's species are gravely threatened. Various projections suggest that from 1975 to 2015 between 1 and 11 percent of the world's species per decade will be committed to extinction. The causes include introductions of nonindigenous species, habitat destruction, hunting, and deliberate extermination.

Such losses impose profound costs at both a practical and an intangible level. Species diversity provides a host of wild and domestic plant, fish, and animal products used for medicines, cosmetics, industrial products, fuel and building materials, and food, among other things. Species diversity also plays a vital role in the functioning of ecosystems.

This chapter briefly describes the results of the first comprehensive global assessment of biodiversity and of a World Resources Institute study of threats to coastal ecosystems. The balance of the chapter examines the current state of marine biodiversity. Readers are referred to *World Resources 1994–95* and previous editions for details on the state of terrestrial biodiversity and on

measures that have been proposed and, in some cases, are being implemented, to address threats to land-based species and habitats.

NEW BIODIVERSITY ASSESSMENT

The United Nations Environment Programme's (UNEP's) first comprehensive global assessment of biodiversity concludes that between 5 and 20 percent of some groups of animal and plant species could be threatened with extinction in the foreseeable future [2].

Released on November 14, 1995, at the second Conference of the Parties to the Convention on Biological Diversity, UNEP's *Global Biodiversity Assessment* represents an emerging consensus about current trends in biodiversity, about ways to approach the problem, and about possible solutions [3]. About 1,500 scientists participated in the preparation of the report, which was sponsored by the Global Environment Facility.

Although the total number of species remains unknown, the report finds that a reasonable estimate is close to 14 million, of which about 1.7 million have been scientifically described [4].

Aside from its statistical assessment, the report also covers strategies to protect biodiversity. The traditional approach to protecting biodiversity emphasized the separation of ecosystems, species, and genetic resources from human activity through the creation of protected areas, prohibitions on harvesting endangered species, and the preservation of germ plasm in seed banks or cryogenic storage facilities. Scientists now think that it is impossible to shield all genes, species, and ecosystems from human influence. Instead, preservation efforts must include a blend of strategies, including programs to save species by creating controlled environments and

Table 11.1 Estimated Total Numbers of Species, 1995

Species	Number of Described Species[a] (000)	Estimated Numbers of Species[b,c] High (000)	Estimated Numbers of Species[b,c] Low (000)	Working Number[b,d] (000)	Accuracy[e]
Viruses	4	1,000[f]	50	400	Very poor
Bacteria	4	3,000[f]	50	1,000	Very poor
Fungi	72	2,700[f]	200	1,500	Moderate
Protozoa	40	200[f]	60	200	Very poor
Algae	40	1,000[g]	150	400	Very poor
Plants	270	500	300	320	Good
Nematodes	25	1,000[g]	100	400	Poor
Arthropods					
Crustaceans	40	200[g]	75	150	Moderate
Arachnids	75	1,000	300	750	Moderate
Insects	950	100,000	2,000	8,000	Moderate
Molluscs	70	200[g]	100	200	Moderate
Chordates	45	55	50	50	Good
Others	115	800	200	250	Moderate
Total	**1,750**	**111,655**	**3,635**	**13,620**	**Very poor**

Source: United Nations Environment Programme, *Global Biodiversity Assessment* (Cambridge University Press, Cambridge, U.K., 1995), Table 3.1-2, p. 118.

Notes: a. Includes approximate numbers of described species currently recognized. b. The reliability of all estimates is likely to vary greatly. c. Includes estimates of possible species for groups of organisms with more than 20,000 described species and/or estimated to include in excess of 100,000 described species. d. Working numbers are those widely accepted by specialists in each area. e. Accuracy is categorized as within a factor of 2 (good), within a factor of 5 (moderate), within a factor of 10 (poor), or not within an order of magnitude (very poor). f. Higher numbers have been proposed by extrapolating from certain assumptions that have been made with respect to the specificity and loads of parasites in invertebrate hosts. g. Higher numbers have been proposed by extrapolating from the contents of small samples of soil or mud from deep-sea sediment samples.

policies to manage natural environments in ways that minimize adverse impacts on biodiversity.

In the case of agriculture, for example, a growing number of scientists are emphasizing the need for protecting genetic crop resources and agroecosystems in their natural settings. This approach allows for the traditional, dynamic adaptation of plants to the environment.

Similarly, there is a new recognition of the need for more integrated approaches to conservation, including looking at entire ecosystems rather than just some protected areas within those ecosystems.

THREATS TO COASTAL ECOSYSTEMS

Coastal ecosystems, which are one of the richest storehouses of marine biodiversity, are threatened by development-related activities along roughly half of the world's coasts, according to new data compiled by the World Resources Institute (5).

According to the estimate, about 34 percent of the world's coasts are at high potential risk of degradation,

and another 17 percent are at moderate risk. Most of the coastal ecosystems potentially threatened by development are located within northern temperate and northern equatorial zones. Europe, with 86 percent of its coasts at either high or moderate risk, and Asia, with 69 percent of its coasts in these categories, are the regions whose coastal ecosystems are most threatened by degradation (6). (See Figure 11.1 and Table 11.2.)

Coastlines ranked as under a low threat were primarily within desert, subarctic, and arctic regions (7).

The study drew upon digitized map data and defined coastal zones to include the land area within 60 kilometers of the coast and the adjacent nearshore waters. The threat estimates were derived from an index that was based on five indicators:

- *Cities with populations of more than 100,000* captures potential threats from coastal development, sewage, and industrial pollution.

- *Major ports* measures the potential threats from species introductions (through the release of ballast water), the potential for oil spills, and industrial pollution.

- *Population density* measures potential threats from coastal development and pollution.

- *Road density* is an indirect measure of access to coastal resources and coastal development.

- *Pipeline density* measures the potential threat of oil pollution and of spills of other industrial wastes.

Each of the five indicators was given equal weight in the construction of a final index of potential threat to coastal ecosystems. The presence of cities and ports automatically defined those units of the coastal zone as being under a high threat. Units outside of cities and ports were defined as being under a high threat if any one of the three density indicators was high; remaining units were defined as being under a moderate threat if one or more of the density indicators were moderate.

The analysis also considered threats to currently identified national marine protected areas within 100 kilometers of continents and major islands. Within this group, about 59 percent of marine protected areas were found to be at high risk and another 14 percent were

Figure 11.1 Coastal Ecosystems Threatened by Development

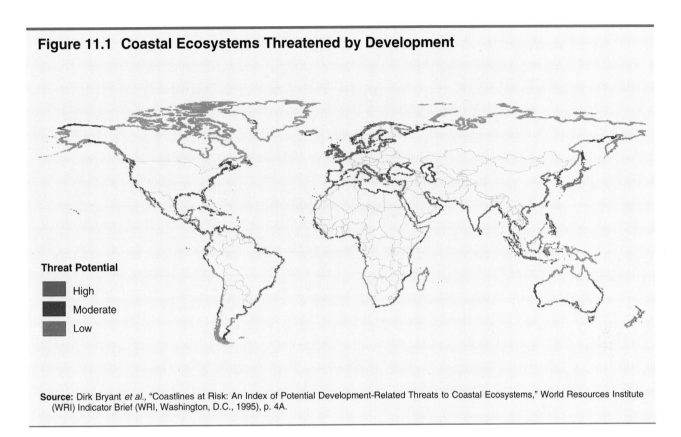

Threat Potential

- High
- Moderate
- Low

Source: Dirk Bryant *et al.*, "Coastlines at Risk: An Index of Potential Development-Related Threats to Coastal Ecosystems," World Resources Institute (WRI) Indicator Brief (WRI, Washington, D.C., 1995), p. 4A.

found to be at moderate risk from development-related activities (8). (See Table 11.3.)

The study notes that there are many limitations in the current estimate. For example, the impacts of fishing, deforestation, and agricultural activity are not covered; human activities beyond 60 kilometers of the coast were not considered; the study did not factor in the relative sensitivities of different ecosystems to disturbance; data quality was better for some regions than for others; data modeling and mapping added additional uncertainty to the results; and pressures may have been underrepresented where they have a cumulative effect.

The current study also was at too coarse a scale to guide national management and planning activities. A second phase of the project would develop a set of more comprehensive, finer-resolution indicators (9).

(For more on the impact of human activity on coastal ecosystems, see Chapter 3, "Urban Impacts on Natural Resources.")

MARINE BIODIVERSITY

Marine ecosystems, and the species within them, provide a number of functions key to human survival and well-being. In addition to contributing fish to the human diet and providing a source of income to millions,

marine species are used as animal feed, fertilizer, clothing, and jewelry and as additives in foods, cosmetics, and other household products. Wetland and estuarine organisms clarify sediment-loaded runoff waters before they reach the sea, and mangroves, coral reefs, seagrasses, and kelp beds prevent coastal erosion by cutting down wave action. Yet, notwithstanding the wide gaps in knowledge, there are many indications that marine biodiversity is in real trouble. The most obvious signs include dramatic declines in many of the world's fish stocks, massive die-offs of seals and dolphins, the appearance of huge blooms of toxic red tides, and the bleaching of coral reefs. In many cases, human activity is clearly the source of these changes. Coastal development, overfishing, pollution, introductions of exotic species to new waters, and other factors all play a major role in jeopardizing marine ecosystems and marine biodiversity.

The balance of this chapter focuses on the state of marine biodiversity and the condition of marine ecosystems; however, freshwater biodiversity is not included in the present discussion.

Much of the evidence of the decline in marine biodiversity is piecemeal and anecdotal; few long-term studies on the status of marine species have been conducted, and no comprehensive global assessments of changes in the extent and conditions of coral reefs, mangroves, and

Table 11.2 Percent of Regional Coastlines Under Low, Moderate, or High Potential Threat, 1995

Region	Percent of Coastline Under Potential Threat[a]		
	Low[b]	Moderate[c]	High[d]
Africa	49	14	38
Asia	31	17	52
North and Central America	71	12	17
South America	50	24	26
Europe	14	16	70
Former Soviet Union	64	24	12
Oceania	56	20	24
World	**49**	**17**	**34**

Source: Dirk Bryant *et al.*, "Coastlines at Risk: An Index of Potential Development-Related Threats to Coastal Ecosystems," World Resources Institute (WRI) Indicator Brief (WRI, Washington, D.C., 1995), pp. 5–6.

Notes: a. Threat ranking depicts potential risk to coastal ecosystems from development-related activities. b. Coastal areas with a population of less than 75 persons per square kilometer, a road network density of less than 100 kilometers of road per square kilometer, and no pipelines known to be present. c. Coastal areas with a population density of between 75 and 150 persons per square kilometer, a road network density of between 100 and 150 kilometers of road per square kilometer, or a pipeline density of between 0 and 10 kilometers of pipeline per square kilometer. d. Coastal areas falling within a city or major port footprint or having a population density exceeding 150 persons per square kilometer, a road network density exceeding 150 kilometers of road per square kilometer, or a pipeline density exceeding 10 kilometers of pipeline per square kilometer.

other marine habitats have been carried out. Enough is known, however, to confirm that dramatic changes in the abundance of habitats and marine species are taking

Table 11.3 Marine Protected Areas Potentially Threatened by Nearby Coastal Development Activity, 1995

Region	Percent of Areas at Risk			Number of Marine Protected Areas	
	Low	Moderate	High	Assessed[a]	Unassessed
Africa	24	8	68	96	17
Asia	14	11	75	286	12
North and Central America	40	12	49	319	69
South America	49	11	40	35	6
Europe	13	12	75	109	13
Former Soviet Union	39	6	56	18	1
Oceania	27	25	48	245	47
World	**26**	**14**	**59**	**1,108**	**182**[b]

Source: Dirk Bryant *et al.*, "Coastlines at Risk: An Index of Potential Development-Related Threats to Coastal Ecosystems," World Resources Institute (WRI) Indicator Brief (WRI, Washington, D.C., 1995), p. 7.

Notes:
a. Includes only marine protected areas with known geographic coordinates located within 100 kilometers of continental and large island coastlines.
b. The world total includes 17 unassessed sites within the Antarctic region.

place, even though in many cases the species may not suffer complete extinction.

Extent and Variety of Marine Species

Little is known about the extent of global biodiversity, and even less is known about what species exist in the world's seas. Of the 1.7 million species cataloged to date, about 250,000 are from marine environments [10] [11].

Although marine ecosystems are probably less diverse than terrestrial environments in terms of total numbers of species, marine ecosystems harbor more varied life forms. Scientists measure this variation in "body architecture" by comparing the range of phyla (major kinds of organisms) found on land and in the sea [12]. For example, it is estimated that 32 of the world's 33 animal phyla are found in marine environments—15 exclusively so [13].

Aquatic organisms in both marine and freshwater habitats have a variety of survival strategies. Filter feeding, for example, is rarely found in land organisms but is characteristic of many species of whales, oysters, clams and mussels, barnacles, corals, sea anemones, sponges, and several fish, including basking and whale sharks [14] [15]. This functional diversity, which is also typified by the wide range of chemicals found within marine organisms, suggests that oceans can be an important source of new biochemical products, including medicines [16]. The medicines derived from marine organisms include antibiotics, anticoagulants, and drugs for treating cancer and heart disease [17]. In addition to being a source of medicinal, food, and industrial products, marine biodiversity provides a range of ecosystem services essential for human survival.

Recent sampling of the deep-sea floor, the least explored region on Earth, has uncovered countless new species. Some experts believe that deep-water habitats could harbor at least 10 million species [18]. Existing data on species distributions indicate, however, that much of the diversity in the oceans occurs within tropical waters and within nearshore habitats. (See Box 11.1.)

Current Trends in Marine Populations and Species

The clearest indication of stress in marine populations is evident in the drastically declining stocks of commercial fish species. In 6 of 11 major fishing regions, more than 60 percent of all commercial fish stocks either have been depleted or are being fished to their limits (19). About 25 percent of stocks for which data are available are either depleted or in danger of depletion, while another 44 percent of fish stocks are being fished at their biological limit (20). (For a detailed discussion of marine fishing trends, see Chapter 13, "Water and Fisheries.")

Relatively few attempts to monitor noncommercial marine populations have been carried out. As a result, it is difficult to gauge the impact of habitat loss and other human pressures on maritime resources (21) (22).

Even with improved monitoring, it will be some time before the full effects of current human activities on marine species can be determined. Species are considered extinct only when they have not been recorded for 50 years. Thus, extinctions occurring today may not be documented until at least 2045. Long-lived species, such as sea turtles, may live for decades on the verge of extinction, even when their populations are too low to permit recovery.

Marine species, because they tend to have broad ranges, were traditionally thought to be less vulnerable than terrestrial species to overharvesting and other pressures (23). There are many exceptions to this rule, however. For example, species with widely distributed populations account for fully one third of documented marine extinctions (24).

Many far-ranging marine species reproduce in small, restricted areas. The harvesting of these species when they are congregated over spawning grounds or the loss of a breeding habitat can severely deplete species and populations. In addition, marine flora and fauna are more susceptible to pollution than terrestrial species because they lack the protective coverings of their land-based counterparts (25).

Declines in marine populations and local species extinctions have two important consequences. The first involves effects on genetic variability within a species. Species exhibiting broad genetic diversity (the range of genetic variability found within the different organisms in a population and between populations of a single species) are more likely to adapt to changing conditions than species with narrow genetic diversity (26). Population declines, by reducing genetic diversity, also reduce the ability of a species to adapt to changing conditions.

Second, these losses can have cascading, unanticipated effects on other species within an ecosystem. Sea otters, for example, play a key role in maintaining highly productive kelp forests by keeping sea urchins, which feed on kelp, in check. The elimination of local populations of sea otters off the Aleutian Islands may have contributed to a proliferation of sea urchins and a subsequent decline in populations of kelp and species dependent on the kelp's habitat (27). The growth of sea urchin populations (as a result of disease and overfishing of predator species) has contributed to similar ecosystem-wide impacts within coral reef communities in the Caribbean (28) (29).

Ecosystem Diversity

Because marine species are a part of specific ecosystems, assessing the condition of ecosystems is a useful indicator of threats to species-level diversity. Furthermore, changes in the extent and condition of these habitats are relatively easy to measure; for example, satellite imagery can be used to measure changes in the extent of mangrove area. The decline of critical habitats implies that species dependent on such areas may also be in jeopardy.

Although they make up a fraction of the total volume of habitable space available to marine species, coastal ecosystems account for almost one third of all marine biological productivity (the amount of living biomass produced within oceans). Estuarine ecosystems, which include mangroves and seagrass beds, are among the most productive ecosystems on Earth (30). Even though they generally occur in tropical waters where productivity is low, coral reefs contain the highest levels of known diversity among marine species (31).

Estuaries, mangroves, and other wetlands serve as nursery areas and habitats for a significant number of marine species. These habitats are often rich in food, and their shallow waters and vegetation provide shelter from predators. Three fourths of the commercial fish catch in U.S. waters, for example, consists of species dependent on estuaries for part or all of their life cycles (32).

Noncoastal areas include a number of unique habitats, including upwellings and ocean vent communities. Ocean areas with upwellings (regions where nutrient-rich currents come to the surface) are marked by high levels of primary productivity and serve as feeding grounds for many important species. One third of the global marine catch is taken from these areas, including many species that are commercially important. Upwellings, which can shift to new locations, cover about 0.1 percent of the world's ocean surface (33).

Ocean vent communities, located around temporary hot springs on the deep-sea floor, are supported by an unusual source of energy. Primary production is based not on photosynthesizing phytoplankton but on bacteria that convert sulfur to energy. Vent communities support tube worms, sea anemones, mussels, shrimp, and a host of other creatures, many of which appear to be endemic to these ecosystems (34) (35).

Box 11.1 Species Richness and Conservation

In the face of uncertain knowledge about the magnitude and location of biodiversity, scientists look for trends or gradients in species richness and patterns of endemism (having a relatively narrow distribution) to determine what areas are most in need of protection. They hope that by focusing conservation efforts on species-rich areas or areas with many threatened and endemic species (hot spots), they can protect much of the flora and fauna that have yet to be discovered.

Because only about 7 percent of the oceans have been sampled, the current state of knowledge regarding species distribution and hot spots is poor (1). However, some trends are apparent: The highest overall diversity occurs in the tropical Indo-Western Pacific, a region that includes waters off the coasts of Asia, East Africa, northern Australia, and the Pacific Islands (2) (3). Within this region, some of the highest levels of marine species richness are found off the coasts of the Philippines, Indonesia, and New Guinea (4). Waters surrounding Polynesia, portions of the Indian Ocean and the Red Sea, and the Caribbean contain areas with high levels of reef fish diversity (coral reef fish make up one quarter of all known marine fish species) (5).

In general, species richness—as in terrestrial ecosystems—increases from the poles to the equator, although this rule does not hold for all taxonomic groups, especially those located in shallower seas. (Seaweeds, for example, are most diverse at midlatitudes.) The total richness of open-water habitats also varies by depth, being much higher along coastal areas than in deep waters (6) (7) (8). In noncoastal areas, species richness is highest on deep-ocean bottoms and at middepths of 2,000 to 3,000 meters on the abyssal plain (flat basins below the continental slope) (9).

Patterns of marine endemism are generally not well known. Most marine species appear to have much larger ranges than terrestrial species because of their life cycles. Many species, including sedentary organisms such as mussels and coral, produce free-floating planktonic larvae. Their young may drift for as little as a few hours or up to 6 months or more—depending on the species—before changing into their adult forms.

This free-floating stage permits these species to disperse well beyond spawning areas (10).

However, endemism does occur within marine communities; it appears to be proportionately higher in areas surrounding isolated oceanic islands and thermal vents (11) (12). Although broad distributions may mean that marine species are less vulnerable to extinction than their terrestrial kin, not all marine species may be as wide-ranging as is currently believed. A recent effort to map the distribution of coral reef fish revealed that of the 950 species whose ranges were mapped (about 23 percent of the total), one third were limited to areas of less than 2,220 square kilometers (13).

Beyond simply looking at areas with high levels of species richness and endemism, several other criteria can be applied to define conservation priorities. These include protecting ecosystem diversity (preserving representative samples of all habitats and unique ecosystems) and conserving areas noted for their high levels of biological productivity (because they are rich fishing areas) as well as areas that serve as breeding grounds and nurseries (such as estuaries and mangroves) for marine species. Many marine species reproduce and spend the early parts of their lives in areas that represent a fraction of their total ranges.

Spawning grounds represent a continuous source of juvenile larvae, which drift with the currents to a broad swath of downstream areas (sinks). Adults of some species migrate upstream to these areas when it is time to reproduce (14). But not all marine organisms migrate, have planktonic larvae, or have well-defined spawning grounds. Protecting the spawning grounds of commercially valuable fish is one useful way to help fish stocks, but that alone will not ensure continued productivity within the fishery as a whole.

Priority areas cannot be conserved solely through the establishment of marine parks and sanctuaries because of the broad ranges and migratory natures of many marine species. Marine protected areas (MPAs) are almost never large enough to protect the critical spawning and feeding grounds of all of the species found within them. Some

ecosystem boundaries (ocean upwellings, for example) can shift with the currents. In addition, protected habitats can be affected by human activities occurring hundreds of kilometers away (for example, oil spills occurring outside MPA boundaries or siltation from poor agricultural practices occurring on adjacent land masses). Thus, a combination of approaches—including protecting habitats and managing surrounding marine and terrestrial areas as integrated units—is needed (see Tools for Protecting Marine Biodiversity, below).

References and Notes

1. Elizabeth Culotta, "Is Marine Biodiversity at Risk?," *Science,* Vol. 263, No. 5149 (February 18, 1994), p. 919.
2. Walter Reid and Kenton Miller, *Keeping Options Alive: The Scientific Basis for Conserving Biodiversity* (World Resources Institute, Washington, D.C., 1989), p. 14.
3. Geerat Vermeij, *Biogeography and Adaptation: Patterns of Marine Life* (Harvard University Press, Cambridge, Massachusetts, 1978), p. 2.
4. *Op. cit.* 2.
5. Don McAllister *et al.,* "Mapping and GIS Analysis of the Global Distribution of Coral Reef Fish on an Equal Area Grid," in *Mapping the Diversity of Nature,* Ronald Miller, ed. (Chapman and Hall, London, 1994), pp. 155, 171.
6. Amanda Vincent and Andrew Clarke, "Diversity in the Marine Environment," *Trends in Ecology and Evolution,* Vol. 10, No. 2 (1995), p. 55.
7. United Nations Environment Programme, *Global Biodiversity Assessment* (Cambridge University Press, Cambridge, U.K., 1995), p. 140.
8. Martin Angel, "Biodiversity of the Pelagic Ocean," *Conservation Biology,* Vol. 7, No. 4 (1993), p. 762.
9. *Op. cit.* 7, p. 141.
10. Elliott A. Norse, ed., *Global Marine Biological Diversity: A Strategy for Building Conservation into Decision Making* (Island Press, Washington, D.C., 1993), pp. 40, 80.
11. *Ibid.,* p. 59.
12. *Op. cit.* 7, p. 181.
13. *Op. cit.* 5, pp. 155, 161, 172.
14. *Op. cit.* 10, p. 62.

Current Conditions in Coastal Ecosystems

Of all marine habitats, coastal ecosystems in general—including reefs, mangroves, seagrass beds, and lagoons—have been the most heavily affected by human activity. Coastal ecosystems within the highly diverse Indo-Western Pacific region have been severely affected, with likely long-term consequences to marine diversity. For example, 60 to 70 percent of reef areas in Southeast Asia, which straddles the Indo-Western Pacific, were ranked in poor condition in a 1992 assessment conducted by the Australian Institute of Marine Science. Coastal habitats within the Caribbean region, also an area with a high level of biodiversity, are under stress from development, pollution, sedimentation, and dredging (36). A 1992 U.S. government assessment of Central American coastal areas found that mangrove destruction was a "priority issue" in five of the seven countries studied. In addition, coastal wetland conversion and degradation were a "priority" in one country and a "significant" problem in four others (37).

This section focuses on coral reefs and mangroves because these are the coastal ecosystems for which the most data are available regarding status and trends.

Coral Reefs

In general, coral reefs are much less resistant to disturbances (both natural and anthropogenic) than other coastal habitats, and as such, they are particularly vulnerable to a range of human pressures (38).

Coral reefs are located along the coasts of 110 tropical countries (39). In at least 93 of these countries, significant portions of the coral reefs have been degraded or destroyed, primarily as a result of pollution; erosion of nearby land areas and subsequent smothering of corals by sediments; mining and dynamiting of corals for building materials; cyanide poisoning (used to stun fish for the aquarium market); and damage from recreational use (40) (41) (42). Overfishing has affected the coral reef areas bordering at least 80 countries (43). A 1992 assessment of global coral reef condition found that 5 to 10 percent of these habitats have been destroyed (44).

These findings have direct implications for overall marine species diversity. Although coral reefs cover an area of less than 0.2 percent of the world's ocean beds, they are the most species-diverse areas of all explored marine habitats, approaching tropical rainforests in their species richness (45). Up to one quarter of all marine species and one fifth (4,500) of known marine fish species live in coral reef ecosystems (46) (47). The loss of reef habitats therefore threatens a disproportionately high percentage of the ocean's biota.

Many coral reef species are important food sources: between 20 and 25 percent of the fish catch in developing countries is taken from coral reef ecosystems (48). These habitats are unique not only for the high numbers of species that seek food and shelter there but also because reefs are the oldest structures in existence created by living creatures, with some approaching 6,000 years in age (49).

Reef biodiversity is highest in the Indo-Western Pacific, which is also thought to have the world's highest overall marine biodiversity. Over half of the world's coral reefs are located within this region. A second reef biodiversity hot spot is located in the tropical Atlantic and includes about 15 percent of the world's total reef area (50). Figure 11.2 provides a breakdown of the world's coral reefs by region.

A study of coral reefs conducted from 1983 to 1991 provides further evidence that these habitats are in trouble. That study found that bleaching occurred within reefs in all tropical oceans of the world during 1983, 1987, and 1991 and that bleaching was correlated with water temperature increases of 1° C or more (51).

Reefs are created by tiny coral-building animals, which live symbiotically with photosynthesizing algae (the algae provide corals with food and oxygen, and the corals provide nutrients and shelter in exchange). Bleaching occurs when corals expel resident algae in response to stress from pollution, sedimentation, or natural localized warming cycles. Analysis of bleaching patterns in the study suggested that a global pattern of local warming events is a likely cause of coral stress, although other factors probably contributed to the bleaching episodes (52) (53).

Corals live in waters that are near the upper limit of their temperature tolerance, and so they are especially vulnerable to even small changes in atmospheric temperature resulting from global warming.

Mangroves

Mangroves line one quarter of the world's tropical coastlines, covering an area of between 190,000 and 240,000 square kilometers (54). Approximately 117 countries and territories have mangrove resources within their borders (55). Figure 11.3 depicts the extent of mangrove cover in the 10 countries with the largest share of the total global mangrove cover.

It is estimated that half of the world's mangroves have been destroyed (56). Table 11.4 presents estimates on the extent of mangrove habitat and the percent lost in selected countries. The Philippines, for example, has lost 70 percent of its original mangrove cover. Human activities contributing to the loss and degradation of

Figure 11.2 Global Coral Cover by Region

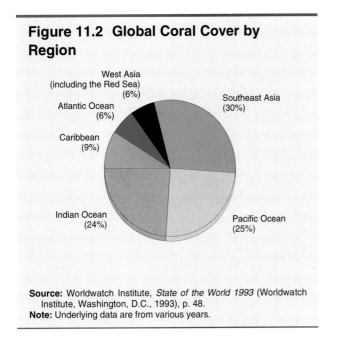

Source: Worldwatch Institute, *State of the World 1993* (Worldwatch Institute, Washington, D.C., 1993), p. 48.
Note: Underlying data are from various years.

mangrove habitat include overharvesting for fuelwood and timber production; land clearing for agriculture and coastal development; mining; pollution; damming of rivers, which alters water salinity; and conversion to shrimp and other aquaculture ponds. In the Indo-Western Pacific region alone, 1.2 million hectares was estimated to have been converted to aquaculture ponds by 1977 (57).

Although they are not particularly species-rich (about 400 species of fish are known to be dependent on mangrove areas), mangrove ecosystems are important nursery areas and habitats for commercially valuable shrimp, prawn, shellfish, and fish species. Mangrove areas have some of the highest levels of productivity recorded among ecosystem types (58).

PRESSURES ON MARINE BIODIVERSITY

An estimated 60 percent of the global population lives within roughly 100 kilometers of the shore. This means that about 3.4 billion people rely heavily on marine habitats and resources for food, building materials, building sites, and agricultural and recreational areas and use coastal areas as a dumping ground for sewage, garbage, and toxic wastes (59). Moreover, much of the remaining noncoastal population is concentrated along rivers and other waterways. Pollution and poor land use practices within these watersheds affect downstream marine habitats because sediments and pollutants are ultimately washed into coastal waters.

Pressures on marine ecosystems include coastal population density and continued population growth, which are accompanied by increased consumer demand for marine products, increased waste disposal, rapid alteration of coastal habitats, uncontrolled industrial pollution, inadequate institutional structures for managing marine resources, lack of property rights and management regimes within international waters, and lack of understanding and awareness of marine ecosystem processes and the effects of human actions on marine biodiversity.

Most of the world's marine ecosystems—particularly nearshore habitats—are stressed by a combination of these factors. The Black Sea, for example, is dying under the weight of pollution and overfishing. Land-based pollution in the form of industrial wastes, sewage, and runoff of pesticides and fertilizers, combined with oil and other wastes from ship traffic, have contaminated the entire basin. Eutrophication has left 90 percent of the Black Sea facing critically low oxygen levels (60). The total fish catch within the region declined by 64 percent between 1986 and 1992 (61). The cost of this damage is estimated at $500 million annually to the fishing and tourism industries alone (62).

The direct factors (pressures) leading to the loss of marine biodiversity can be broken into five categories: habitat loss, intense overexploitation, pollution and sedimentation, species introductions, and climate change.

Habitat Loss

Habitat conversion and degradation are generally thought to be the most significant threats to terrestrial life. Within marine ecosystems, they rank along with overexploitation and pollution as major causes of biodiversity loss (63).

Coastal development contributes to habitat loss in a number of ways. These include conversion of mangroves and other wetlands as a result of urbanization and agricultural expansion, the building of shoreline stabilization structures such as breakwaters, mining, oil drilling, and dredging and filling. These result both in the destruction of wetlands and other habitats and in the degradation of nearby areas (through siltation and changes in water temperature and flow, salinity, and other physical factors).

Damming of rivers and water diversion projects lead to changes in downstream estuarine and marine communities, because interruption of freshwater flow changes the physical environment of such areas and the amount of nutrients that they receive. Completion of the Aswan Dam on the Nile River in 1965 led to the erosion of delta habitats and is considered a factor in the subsequent collapse of eastern Mediterranean fisheries (64). In addition, dams can cut off species access to spawning areas—this includes not only species that live in saltwater and reproduce in rivers (such as salmon) but also freshwater species that breed at sea (such as freshwater eels).

Intense exploitation of marine resources can indirectly lead to habitat loss. For example, trawling disturbs bottom-dwelling communities—both adjacent to shorelines and in deeper coastal waters—as nets scour seabeds and smother burrowing creatures and other species with sediments. Fishing with dynamite and harvesting of corals are major threats to coral reef areas.

Intense Overexploitation

According to a 1995 report, from 1988 to 1991, humans removed about 8 percent of all annual primary production (the total amount of living carbon) within aquatic ecosystems. This figure is lower than the ratio of primary production co-opted for human use in terrestrial systems; however, it masks exceptionally high removal rates within some of the most productive and species-rich ecosystems. For example, more than one fourth of all production occurring within ocean upwellings and tropical marine shelf areas is consumed by humans; in temperate shelf regions, it is about 35 percent (65). Continued exploitation at such levels is leading to changes in species composition, loss of biodiversity (66), and shifts in dominance and survival ability (67).

Much of the global fishing effort is targeted at a few species, located primarily near the top of the food chain. Overexploitation of these species has three effects. First, as discussed earlier, it results in the loss of genetic diversity as fish populations decline. Second, overfishing affects the relative abundance of individual species or the mix of different species within an ecosystem. Often, populations of both the target species and the predators that feed on these species decline and are replaced by stocks of lesser commercial value. Third, depleted fisheries have direct economic impacts, including reduced income (and unemployment) and higher consumer prices (68).

Overfishing affects other marine species, not just fish stocks. Overharvesting, along with habitat degradation, is a key factor that contributed to a 95 percent decline in native Chesapeake Bay oyster populations (69). Overhunting has decimated many marine mammal populations. By 1994, 90 marine mammal species were listed as threatened or endangered (70). Poor management practices, subsidization of the fishing industry, uncontrolled harvests within international waters, and

Figure 11.3 Ten Countries with the Most Extensive Mangrove Area

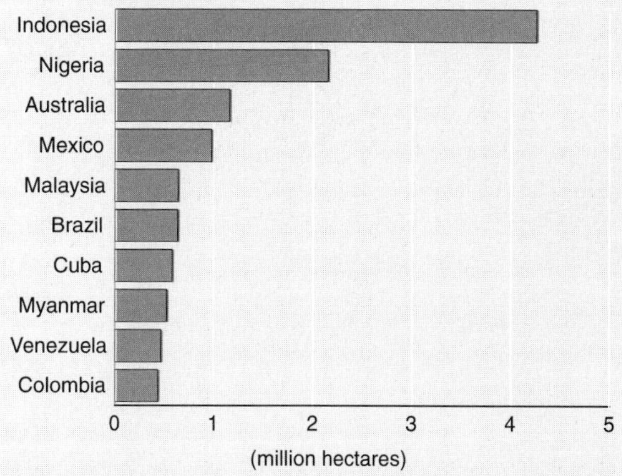

Source: World Conservation Monitoring Centre, *Biodiversity Data Sourcebook* (World Conservation Press, Cambridge, U.K., 1994), pp. 74–98.
Notes: The only countries ranked are those for which data on the extent of mangrove area are available. The total current mangrove area reported for each country is the average of the high and low estimates except for Australia and Myanmar, for which data are based on one estimate. Data are from various years.

destructive and wasteful capture methods are to blame for the overexploitation of most marine species. (See Chapter 13, "Water and Fisheries," for a more detailed discussion of the underlying causes and effects of overfishing.)

Pollution and Sedimentation

Dumping and discharging of pollutants into the sea, oil spills, nutrient- and silt-laden runoff from land and rivers, fallout of chemicals carried by the wind from land-based sources, and noise from ships and other machinery (which disrupts communication among whales and other species) are some of the major contaminants affecting marine species and ecosystems (71). As Figure 11.4 shows, air pollution and runoff and point discharges from the land (and rivers) account for some three fourths of the pollutants entering marine ecosystems.

Contaminants affect marine biodiversity in a number of ways. Untreated sewage, oil, heavy metals, and other wastes may be directly toxic to some marine organisms. Their effects may be instantaneous or cumulative. For example, oil has lethal and almost immediate effects on a wide range of marine life—from algae to seabirds—resulting in death through asphyxiation, poisoning, and, among mammals and birds, loss of the insulating

Table 11.4 Mangrove Extent and Loss, Selected Countries

Region and Country	Current Extent (000 hectares)	Approximate Percent Lost	Period Covered
Asia			
India	100–700	50	1963–77
Peninsular Malaysia	98.3	17	1965–85
Philippines	140+	70	1920s to circa 1990
Singapore	0.5–0.6	20–30+	Preagricultural period to present
Thailand	196.4–268.7	25	1979–87
Viet Nam	200	50	1943 to early 1990s
Latin America			
Puerto Rico	6.5	75	Precolonial to present
Ecuador	117+	30+	Preagricultural to present
Guatemala	16	30+	1965–90
Africa			
Cameroon	306	40	Preagricultural to mid-1980s
Kenya	53.0–61.6	70	Preagricultural to mid-1980s
Guinea-Bissau	236.6	75+	Preagricultural to mid-1980s
Liberia	20	70	Preagricultural to mid-1980s

Sources: 1. Great Barrier Reef Marine Park Authority, The World Bank, and the World Conservation Union, *A Global Representative System of Marine Protected Areas,* Vol. 1, Graeme Kelleher, Chris Bleakley, and Sue Wells, eds. (The World Bank, Washington, D.C., 1995), pp. 16, 109–110. 2. World Conservation Monitoring Centre, *The Conservation Atlas of Tropical Forests: Asia and the Pacific,* Marc Collins, Jeffrey Sayer, and Timothy Whitmore, eds. (Macmillan Press Ltd., London, 1991), pp. 187, 212. 3. J. Honculada Primavera, "Intensive Prawn Farming in the Philippines: Ecological, Social, and Economic Implications," *Ambio,* Vol. 20, No. 1 (1991), p. 29. 4. World Conservation Monitoring Centre, *Biodiversity Data Sourcebook* (World Conservation Press, Cambridge, U.K., 1994), pp. 78, 88, 92, 94. 5. Don Hinrichsen, *Our Common Seas: Coasts in Crisis* (Earthscan Publications Ltd., London, 1990), pp. 55, 91. 6. U.S. Agency for International Development and the Coastal Resources Center, University of Rhode Island, *Central America's Coasts: Profiles and an Agenda for Action* (University of Rhode Island, Narragansett, Rhode Island, 1992), p. 136. 7. John and Cathy MacKinnon, *Review of the Protected Areas System in the Afrotropical Realm* (United Nations Environment Programme and World Conservation Union, Gland, Switzerland, 1986), pp. 195, 211, 214, 217.

Note: Data for current mangrove extent may differ from estimates presented in Data Table 11.4, where alternative sources were used.

functions of feathers and fur, causing hypothermia. Eggs and larvae are particularly sensitive to the toxic effects of pollutants, as are organisms living at the ocean surface and on the seabed, where wastes tend to accumulate [72].

Other contaminants such as radioactive waste, pesticides, and other chemicals have cumulative effects, building up within individuals over time, especially within species high on the food chain. Moreover, various contaminants and physical degradation can act together in a cumulative or synergistic fashion.

Between 1987 and 1991, dolphin and seal die-offs were recorded in the North and Baltic seas, off the eastern coast of the United States, in the Gulf of Mexico, and in the Mediterranean Sea [73]. The carcasses of these animals were found to contain elevated levels of polychlorinated biphenyls (PCBs), dioxins, and other organochlorines, known to accumulate in the blubber (or lipid tissues) of large species and predators at the top of the food chain. These die-offs and an epidemic of tumors observed within green sea turtles have been linked to the cumulative buildup of PCBs and other chemicals that are believed to weaken immune systems, creating a vulnerability to viral infections [74].

Other contaminants can trigger ecosystem-wide changes, resulting in conditions that are inimical to a range of species. Runoff of sewage from cities and of fertilizers from agricultural areas elevates the levels of nutrients within nearshore waters. Certain algal species capitalize on these conditions, undergoing massive population explosions (known as blooms), which, by lowering water clarity and oxygen content, effectively crowd out other taxa in the community [75]. (Algal blooms block the light reaching algae living within corals and other photosynthesizing bottom-dwelling organisms, killing them; then, the decomposition of the bloom algae deoxygenates the water.)

Many bloom species produce toxins. So-called killer blooms have been linked to die-offs of fish, shellfish, and other species that consume or come into contact with toxic algae or that ingest other consumers of those algae [76]. Human health can also be at risk. A 1987 toxic bloom occurring off the Guatemalan coast, for example, indirectly resulted in the death of 26 people and produced serious illness in 200 other individuals who consumed poisoned seafood [77]. Although small-scale blooms (both toxic and nontoxic) are a naturally occurring phenomenon in most regions, the frequency, magnitude, and toxicity of such events appear to have increased dramatically in recent years [78].

Widespread effects are often noted as a result of sedimentation. Soils eroded from deforested areas and poorly managed agricultural lands often end up at sea, reducing light penetration to seagrass bed, coral, and other communities dependent on the productivity of photosynthesizers living on the sea floor. As sediments settle out, they smother bottom-dwelling organisms and affect filter-feeding species.

In a 1990 report, United Nations marine pollution experts estimated that rivers carry volumes of sediment three times higher than the levels that might be found in undeveloped watersheds, testifying to the magnitude of this problem (79).

Nontoxic solid wastes and marine debris cause significant mortality among marine species. For example, plastic bags, fishing lines, and other debris can entangle seals, seabirds, and other organisms, causing slow but sure deaths. Bits of plastic and other man-made materials are regularly ingested by sea turtles and other species, often with fatal consequences. Abandoned fishing nets, lobster pots, and other equipment continue to catch fish and other marine creatures years after the gear is discarded or lost (80).

Species Introductions

For centuries, ships have served as a means by which organisms can hitchhike to new waters (81). Until recently, such transport was limited mainly to animals that attached themselves to or burrowed into the hulls of ocean-going vessels. Now, however, ships carry an enormous variety of exotic species, including both plankton and larger species in larval form, within their ballast water (82). According to one estimate, about 3,000 species are transported in ships around the world each day. This number reflects both the heavy volume of international shipping and the large size (i.e., large volume of ballast water) of modern ships (83).

Accidental introduction of exotic species may be one factor in the apparent spread of toxic blooms; it is also the suspected cause of a disease affecting corals that has recently appeared in waters off the coast of Asia and the Middle East (84) (85). By feeding on or overrunning dominant native species, exotic species can trigger changes in the species mix within ecosystems. For example, an American jellyfish first observed in the Black Sea in 1982 is now one of the most common animals reported in those waters; furthermore, its predation on anchovy stocks contributed to the collapse of the Sea of Azov anchovy fishery (86).

Although there are no documented marine extinctions caused by exotic species, introduced species have played a major role in threatening or leading to the extinction of numerous inland species (87). Even though a species may not be exotic, transfer from one area to another may cause the mixing of genetic stocks and the transmission of disease. For example, a stock enhancement program that transferred the Atlantic salmon from the Baltic Sea to the Norwegian Sea introduced a parasite to the Norwegian Sea that now threatens Norwegian native stocks (88).

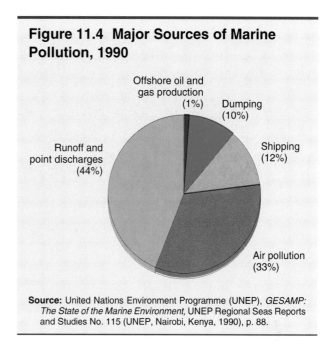

Figure 11.4 Major Sources of Marine Pollution, 1990

Offshore oil and gas production (1%)
Dumping (10%)
Shipping (12%)
Air pollution (33%)
Runoff and point discharges (44%)

Source: United Nations Environment Programme (UNEP), *GESAMP: The State of the Marine Environment,* UNEP Regional Seas Reports and Studies No. 115 (UNEP, Nairobi, Kenya, 1990), p. 88.

Climate Change

Global warming could be a significant threat to marine biodiversity. Among other effects, rising waters (as a result of melting ice caps) could drown coastal mangrove and other wetland habitats. Even if global warming were to proceed at a pace slow enough to permit species to colonize new coastline boundaries, the presence of existing agricultural and urban development with protective bulkheads and dikes would, in many cases, prevent the establishment of new wetland areas (89).

Projected climate change could have other effects, including changes in ocean currents, salinity (due to changes in river flow), and surface temperatures. These would alter the species compositions found within individual ecosystems today, perhaps triggering local and global extinctions in the process (90).

Some evidence exists that local and regional warming episodes may already be affecting marine ecosystems. It is difficult to determine whether these changes are due to natural, cyclical variations in temperature or to a long-term warming trend. As noted above, localized increases in water temperatures are believed to be one of several factors behind recent episodes of global coral bleaching. In a long-term study off the coast of southern California, researchers found an 80 percent decrease in zooplankton density between 1951 and 1993. This decline was linked to increases in ocean surface temperatures of 1.2° to 1.6° C during this time period (91). Other scientists in central California have reported major shifts in bottom-dwelling coastal populations over the past half century.

TOOLS FOR PROTECTING MARINE BIODIVERSITY

Because human activity both nearshore and far up-stream places many marine species at risk, there is a great need for comprehensive far-reaching strategies to conserve marine biodiversity. The overfishing of a single species can certainly affect other, unharvested species within the marine ecosystem. But even such disturbances as deforestation along a river can lead to the degradation of a coral reef or estuary thousands of kilometers away. To be effective, future measures must include not only mechanisms for protecting species (and ecosystems) whose ranges overlap several countries but also mechanisms to protect species within international waters. They should address stresses that originate in one country and yet affect the resources of a neighboring country, and they should be applied to marine ecosystems as a whole rather than just their component parts. Ideally, these mechanisms would take into account the dynamic nature of marine systems (for example, fish harvest quotas that are responsive to natural temporal fluctuations of populations of the stocks in question).

This chapter includes only brief descriptions of a few of the measures available to conserve marine biodiversity. These include establishment of marine protected areas, bioregional management approaches, and negotiation of international agreements for regulating pressures on marine resources.

There are other promising strategies and technologies, including, for example, reducing the proportion of fish that are discarded because they are either of low value or undersized. (See Chapter 13, "Water and Fisheries.") In addition, pollution from agricultural and aquacultural practices could be reduced through, among other things, waste treatment, the integration of farming systems with recycling, use of biological control to reduce reliance on antibiotics, and the proper handling of biodegradable pharmaceutical and feed ingredients (92).

Marine Protected Areas

Since 1986, the World Conservation Union (IUCN) Commission on National Parks and Protected Areas has been promoting the establishment and management of a global system of marine protected areas (MPAs). Some national governments have already established MPAs, and many have identified priorities for protection in documents such as national environmental action plans and national conservation strategies.

MPAs are a relatively new concept; most sites were established only within the past two decades (93). About 1,300 MPAs currently exist, but there is limited information about their effectiveness. An assessment of 383 sites found that about 31 percent were generally achieving their management objectives (94).

In 1995, the Great Barrier Reef Marine Park Authority, the World Bank, and IUCN released the first ever global assessment of MPAs (95). That report reveals that most MPAs are too small to adequately protect the species within them and that many globally unique habitats receive no protection whatsoever. Comparison of these results with data on global protected area systems indicates strongly that, in general, marine ecosystems receive far less protection than their terrestrial counterparts.

On the basis of several criteria, including the economic, social, and scientific importance of the sites, the 1995 study identifies 81 existing and proposed sites as "regional priorities" for future protection (96). These areas, if protected, would help fill gaps in the world's MPA system.

Although the portion of Earth's surface covered by marine areas is more than twice that of terrestrial habitats, only a fraction of the existing global protected area system includes parks with a subtidal component. Almost half of these MPAs are located within Asia and Oceania (258 within Australian and New Zealand waters alone). South America has the least number of protected areas (41 sites) of any geopolitical region. (See Data Table 11.4.)

The 1995 study includes a biogeographic analysis of MPA coverage, looking at the extent to which different habitat types are protected within marine realms. This work required the development of a global classification system, because no one system had been accepted as an international standard. Of the 150 biogeographic zones identified globally, more than one fifth lack protected areas, whereas existing MPAs cover less than 1 percent of the total area of most of these zones (97).

To effectively protect the species within them, MPAs must be much larger than terrestrial parks and reserves. Half of existing MPAs are less than 1,000 hectares in size, an area much too small to encompass the breeding, nursery, and feeding areas of many of the species found within them. (See Figure 11.5.) Recent studies suggest that protected areas on land need to be hundreds of thousands, if not millions, of hectares in size to fully protect viable populations of all of the species found within their borders (98) (99) (100). To acquire that level of protection at sea, MPAs need to be considerably larger than that (101) or need to be part of a multiple MPA system that provides protection for a network of smaller critical areas. Currently, only 2.2 percent of all MPAs exceed 1 million hectares (102). Because of the many external influences that can affect MPAs, these areas also need to be incorporated into an overall scheme of integrated coastal area management (103).

Bioregional Management

Policymakers and managers within a number of countries have begun to move away from a sector-by-sector approach to managing marine resources and toward an integrated, total ecosystem strategy for regulating coastal development, fish harvest, and other factors affecting marine biodiversity. Such an approach, whether on land or at sea, can be used to balance conservation needs with the economic and social demands of people living within coastal zones or adjacent to marine and terrestrial habitats. The concept of bioregional management often includes integrated coastal zone management programs, which have been applied in many areas of the world to regulate coastal development and resource use. These programs offer a means for coordinating the activities of the various government agencies and other institutions charged with coastal zone resource management. (See Chapter 3, "Urban Impacts on Natural Resources.")

Examples of bioregional management vary in scale and focus. Biosphere reserves, for example, are relatively limited in scale and have a strong conservation focus. The reserves encompass one or more strictly protected core areas plus surrounding buffer zones, where limited extractive and development activities are permitted. Ninety of the world's 327 biosphere reserves currently include coastal or marine habitats (104). Bioregional management is also being applied within non-biosphere reserve protected areas, for example, in Australia's 344,000-square-kilometer Great Barrier Reef Marine Park (105), as well as in the 8,898-square-kilometer Florida Keys National Marine Sanctuary in the United States (106).

Large-scale applications include the 10 Regional Seas programs of UNEP. In the regional program that includes the Mediterranean basin, 18 basin countries have worked since 1976 to coordinate development planning, pollution research, and monitoring within the region (107).

The large marine ecosystem (LME) approach to managing marine resources evaluates an individual fish stock by also evaluating the stock's competitors and predators. LMEs are generally at least 200,000 square kilometers in size, and there are currently 49 LMEs on the margins of the world's oceans that cover the most commercially productive marine fisheries.

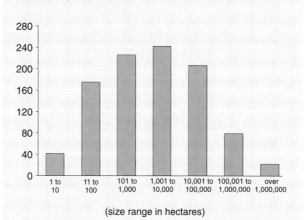

Figure 11.5 Number of Marine Protected Areas by Size Class

(size range in hectares)

Source: Great Barrier Reef Marine Park Authority, The World Bank, and the World Conservation Union, *A Global Representative System of Marine Protected Areas,* Vol. IV, Graeme Kelleher, Chris Bleakley, and Sue Wells, eds. (The World Bank, Washington, D.C., 1995), Table 2, p. 6.
Note: Includes only marine protected areas whose size is known.

The LME bioregional management program could provide a means of integrated fisheries management. However, because LMEs often include the territorial waters of several countries, their use as an effective management tool is dependent on the cooperation of all bordering countries as well as on the existence of regional bodies to coordinate fisheries management activities (108) (109). (See *World Resources 1994–95,* pp. 193–194.)

International Agreements

International treaties provide a means for regulating access to commonly shared resources and for controlling human activities with potentially far-reaching impacts. More than half a dozen international agreements and a series of regional agreements are directly relevant to the conservation of marine biodiversity. These include agreements to regulate pollution resulting from maritime activity, such as the 1978 International Convention on the Prevention of Pollution from Ships (MARPOL) and the 1978 MARPOL Protocol, and agreements to regulate international trade in threatened species, such as the 1973 Convention on International Trade in Endangered Species (CITES). In addition, there are nine UNEP Regional Seas agreements.

Four of the most important recent agreements are described below.

• *The United Nations Convention on the Law of the Sea:* Drafted in 1982 and entered into force in 1994, this treaty establishes national sovereignty over marine resources lying within coastal waters. The greatest rights are exercised within 12 miles of the coast, although lesser controls apply to waters of the 200-mile exclusive economic zone (EEZ). By establishing property rights that apply to the species and habitats found within coastal waters, the treaty provides countries with some incentive to better manage these resources. However, the agreement does not obligate countries to conserve species within waters 12 miles from the coast (110). The convention is notable for its comprehensive coverage of marine resource issues, although many of the provisions regarding the management of these resources are not binding. It also establishes binding procedures for settling disputes over natural resources lying outside of sovereign waters (111).

- *U.N. Conference on Straddling Stocks and Highly Migratory Fish Stocks:* This accord, signed in 1995, will go into force after ratification by at least 30 countries. It regulates the catch of deep-water and migratory species, including tuna, swordfish, and cod stocks. Regulations apply both to international waters and to national EEZs. (See Chapter 13, "Water and Fisheries.")

- *The Convention on Biological Diversity:* This 1992 agreement (ratified in December 1993) is a comprehensive, binding agreement covering the use and conservation of biodiversity (112). It requires countries to develop and implement strategies for sustainable use and protection of biodiversity and provides a forum for continuing international dialogue on biodiversity-related issues through the annual conference of the parties meetings (113). The 1995 meeting dealt with marine biodiversity issues. Because these national obligations apply to waters within EEZs, the Convention extends protection to biodiversity located within the 12-mile limit zones—areas not directly protected under the Law of the Sea (114).

- *The UNEP Conference on Protection of the Marine Environment from Land-Based Activities:* This agreement provides an action plan for controlling pollution, habitat destruction, and other land-based activities affecting coastal and marine ecosystems. Although it is not binding, this agreement would provide a framework for addressing some of the most significant stresses on marine species and ecosystems (115).

References and Notes

1. United Nations Environment Programme, *Global Biodiversity Assessment* (Cambridge University Press, Cambridge, U.K., 1995), p. 118.

2. *Ibid.,* p. 234.

3. *Op. cit.* 1.

4. *Op. cit.* 1.

5. Dirk Bryant *et al.,* "Coastlines at Risk: An Index of Potential Development-Related Threats to Coastal Ecosystems," WRI Indicator Brief (World Resources Institute, Washington, D.C., 1995).

6. *Ibid.,* p. 6.

7. *Op. cit.* 5, p. 4.

8. *Op. cit.* 5, p. 5.

9. *Op. cit.* 5, p. 1.

10. *Op. cit.* 1, pp. 118, 141.

11. *Op. cit.* 12, pp. 149–150.

12. Judith Winston, "Systematics and Marine Conservation," in *Systematics, Ecology, and the Biodiversity Crisis,* Niles Eldredge, ed. (Columbia University Press, New York, 1992), p. 148.

13. Elliott A. Norse, ed., *Global Marine Biological Diversity: A Strategy for Building Conservation into Decision Making* (Island Press, Washington, D.C., 1993), p. 14.

14. *Ibid.*

15. Devin M. Bartley, Fishery Resources Officer, Fisheries Department, Food and Agriculture Organization of the United Nations, Rome, 1995 (personal communication).

16. *Op. cit.* 13, pp. 20–21.

17. Boyce Thorne-Miller and John Catena, *The Living Ocean: Understanding and Protecting Marine Biodiversity* (Island Press, Washington, D.C., 1991), p. 13.

18. *Op. cit.* 1, p. 121.

19. Food and Agriculture Organization of the United Nations (FAO), *The State of World Fisheries and Aquaculture* (FAO, Rome, 1995), Figure 7, p. 11.

20. *Ibid.,* p. 8.

21. Harold Upton, "Biodiversity and Conservation of the Marine Environment," *Fisheries,* Vol. 17, No. 3 (May–June 1992), pp. 20–21.

22. Elizabeth Culotta, "Is Marine Biodiversity at Risk?," *Science,* Vol. 263, No. 5149 (February 18, 1994), p. 919.

23. *Ibid.*

24. Geerat Vermeij, "Biogeography of Recently Extinct Marine Species: Implications for Conservation," *Conservation Biology,* Vol. 7, No. 2 (1993), p. 393.

25. *Op. cit.* 13, p. 43.

26. *Op. cit.* 21, p. 22.

27. Thomas Suchanek, "Temperate Coastal Marine Communities: Biodiversity and Threats," *American Zoologist,* Vol. 34 (1994), p. 108.

28. *Op. cit.* 1, p. 384.

29. Callum M. Roberts, "Effects of Fishing on the Ecosystem Structure of Coral Reefs," *Conservation Biology,* Vol. 9, No. 5 (October 1995), p. 990.

30. Robert Costanza, W. Michael Kemp, and Walter Boynton, "Predictability, Scale and Biodiversity in Coastal and Estuarine Ecosystems: Implications for Management," *Ambio,* Vol. 22, No. 2–3 (1993), pp. 90–91.

31. Great Barrier Reef Marine Park Authority, The World Bank, and the World Conservation Union, *A Global Representative System of Marine Protected Areas,* Vol. I, Graeme Kelleher, Chris Bleakley, and Sue Wells, eds. (The World Bank, Washington, D.C., 1995), p. 30.

32. *Op. cit.* 13, p. 65.

33. *Op. cit.* 31, p. 32.

34. Frederick Grassle, "Hydrothermal Vent Animals: Distribution and Biology," *Science,* Vol. 229 (August 23, 1985), p. 713.

35. *Op. cit.* 17, p. 63.

36. Don Hinrichsen, *Our Common Seas: Coasts in a Crisis* (Earthscan Publications Ltd., London, 1990), p. 55.

37. Gordon Foer and Stephen Olsen, *Central America's Coasts: Profiles and an Agenda for Action* (U.S. Agency for International Development and the University of Rhode Island, Narragansett, Rhode Island, 1992), p. 22.

38. *Op. cit.* 30, p. 91.

39. World Conservation Monitoring Centre (WCMC), *Biodiversity Data Sourcebook* (WCMC, Cambridge, U.K., 1994), pp. 70–98.

40. Peter Weber, "Reviving Coral Reefs," in *State of the World 1993* (Worldwatch Institute, Washington, D.C., 1993), pp. 42, 51.

41. World Conservation Monitoring Centre, *Global Biodiversity: Status of the Earth's Living Resources* (Chapman and Hall, London, 1992), p. 307.

42. Peter Rubec, "The Need for Conservation and Management of Philippine Coral Reefs," *Environmental Biology of Fishes,* Vol. 23, No. 1–2 (1988), p. 145.

43. *Op. cit.* 40, p. 51.

44. *Op. cit.* 40, pp. 46–47.

45. *Op. cit.* 40, p. 43.

46. *Op. cit.* 40, p. 43.

47. *Op. cit.* 31.

48. *Op. cit.* 40, p. 44.

49. *Op. cit.* 1, p. 381.

50. *Op. cit.* 1, p. 381.

51. Thomas Goreau and Raymond Hayes, "Coral Bleaching and Ocean Hotspots," *Ambio,* Vol. 23, No. 3 (May 1994), pp. 176–177.

52. *Ibid.,* pp. 177–179.

53. *Op. cit.* 49, p. 179.

54. *Op. cit.* 31.

55. *Op. cit.* 39.

56. *Op. cit.* 31.

57. *Op. cit.* 41, p. 326.

58. *Op. cit.* 31.

59. *Op. cit.* 36, p. 7.

60. Anne Platt, "Dying Seas," *World Watch* Vol. 8, No. 1 (January/February 1995), pp. 11–12

61. Food and Agriculture Organization of the United Nations (FAO), *Review of the State of World Fishery Resources: Marine Fisheries,* FAO Fisheries Circular No. 884 (FAO, Rome, 1995), p. 82.

62. *Op. cit.* 60, p. 12.

63. *Op. cit.* 13, p. 106.

64. Jeremy Cherfas, "The Fringe of the Ocean—Under Siege from Land," *Science,* Vol. 248, No. 4952 (April 13, 1990), p. 164.

65. D. Pauly and V. Christensen, "Primary Production Required to Sustain Global Fisheries," *Nature,* Vol. 374, No. 6519 (March 16, 1995), p. 257.

66. John Beddington, "The Primary Requirements," *Nature,* Vol. 374, No. 6519 (March 16, 1995), pp. 213–214.

67. John B. Pearce, retired, Northeast Fisheries Science Center, National Marine Fisheries Service, National Oceanic and Atmospheric Administration, U.S. Department of Commerce, Woods Hole, Massachusetts, 1995 (personal communication).

68. *Op. cit.* 21, pp. 20–23.

69. *Op. cit.* 27, p. 105.

70. The World Conservation Union (IUCN), *1994 IUCN Red List of Threatened Animals,* Brian Groombridge, ed. (IUCN, Gland, Switzerland, 1993).

71. *Op. cit.* 13, pp. 113–114, 117–127.

72. *Op. cit.* 13, pp. 119, 123.

73. Janet Raloff, "Something's Fishy," *Science News,* Vol. 146, No. 1 (July 2, 1994), p. 8.

74. *Op. cit.* 74, pp. 8–9.

75. *Op. cit.* 13, pp. 124–125.

76. *Op. cit.* 13, p. 125.

77. Patrick Hughes, "Killer Algae," *Discover,* Vol. 14, No. 4 (April 1993), p. 72.

78. *Op. cit.* 64, p. 163.

79. United Nations Environment Programme (UNEP), *GESAMP: The State of the Marine Environment,* UNEP Regional Seas Reports and Studies No. 115 (UNEP, Nairobi, Kenya, 1990), p. 20.

80. *Op. cit.* 13, pp. 127–129.

81. James Carleton, "Marine Invasions and the Preservation of Coastal Biodiversity," *Endangered Species Update,* Vol. 12, No. 4–5 (1995), p. 2.

82. *Op. cit.* 13, pp. 131–132.

83. *Op. cit.* 81, p. 3.

84. *Op. cit.* 13, p. 132.

85. *Op. cit.* 40, p. 50.

86. *Op. cit.* 81, p. 3.

87. J.E. Williams *et al.,* "Fishes of North America Endangered, Threatened, or of Special Concern—1989," *Fisheries,* Vol. 14, No. 6 (1989), pp. 2–20.

88. W. Folsom *et al.,* "World Salmon Culture," Technical Memo NMFS-F/SPO-3 (National Oceanic and Atmospheric Administration, Silver Spring, Maryland, 1992).

89. *Op. cit.* 13, p. 146.

90. *Op. cit.* 13, pp. 139–147.

91. D. Roemmich and J. McGowan, "Climatic Warming and the Decline of Zooplankton in the California Current," *Science,* Vol. 267, No. 5202 (March 3, 1995), p. 1324.

92. *Op. cit.* 15.

93. *Op. cit.* 13, p. 218.

94. *Op. cit.* 31, pp. 13–15.

95. Great Barrier Reef Marine Park Authority, The World Bank, and the World Conservation Union, *A Global Representative System of Marine Protected Areas,* Vols. I–IV, Graeme Kelleher, Chris Bleakley, and Sue Wells, eds. (The World Bank, Washington, D.C., 1995).

96. *Op. cit.* 31, pp. 4, 18.

97. *Op. cit.* 31, pp. 14, 18.

98. William D. Newmark, "A Land-Bridge Island Perspective on Mammalian Extinctions in Western North American Parks," *Nature,* Vol. 325, No. 6103 (January 27, 1987), pp. 430–432.

99. Reed F.O. Noss, "The Wildlands Project: Land Conservation Strategy" *Wild Earth* (Special Issue 1992), p. 19.

100. J.M. Thiollay, "Area Requirements for the Conservation of Rain Forest Raptors and Game Birds in French Guyana," *Conservation Biology,* Vol. 3, No. 2 (June 1989), pp. 128–137.

101. *Op. cit.* 31, p. 19.

102. *Op. cit.* 31, Table 2, p. 14.

103. *Op. cit.* 15.

104. *Op. cit.* 31, p. 10.

105. Kenton Miller, *Balancing the Scales: Guidelines for Increasing Biodiversity's Chances Through Bioregional Management* (World Resources Institute, Washington, D.C., 1995), p. 41.

106. Charles Ehler and Daniel Basta, "Integrated Management of Coastal Areas and Marine Sanctuaries: A New Paradigm," *Oceanus,* Vol. 36, No. 3 (Fall 1993), pp. 10–11.

107. *Op. cit.* 13, pp. 248–249.

108. Intergovernmental Oceanographic Commission, *Assessment and Monitoring of Large Marine Ecosystems* (United Nations Educational, Scientific and Cultural Organization, Paris, 1993), p. iii.

109. *Op. cit.* 13, pp. 204–205.

110. The World Conservation Union (IUCN), "The Possibilities of International Law and Institutions for Sustainable Use of Marine Biodiversity: Focus on Coral Reef Ecosystems," draft (IUCN, Gland, Switzerland, May 1995), p. 30.

111. *Ibid.,* pp. 28–31.

112. Francoise Burhenne-Guilmin and Lyle Glowka, "An Introduction to the Convention on Biological Diversity," in *Widening Perspectives on Biodiversity,* Anatole Krattiger *et al.,* eds. (The World Conservation Union, Gland, Switzerland, 1994), p. 15.

113. *Ibid.,* pp. 15–16.

114. *Op. cit.* 110, pp. 33–35.

115. *Op. cit.* 110, p. 45.

Data Table 11.1 National and International Protection of Natural Areas, 1994

| | National Protection Systems | | | | | | | | | International Protection Systems {a} | | | | | |
| | All Protected Areas (IUCN categories I-V) | | | Totally Protected Areas (IUCN categories I-III) | | Partially Protected Areas (IUCN categories IV-V) | | % of Protected Areas (IUCN categories I-V) at Least | | Biosphere Reserves | | World Heritage Sites | | Wetlands of Intl. Importance | |
	Number	Area (000 ha)	Percent of Land Area	Number	Area (000 ha)	Number	Area (000 ha)	100,000 ha in Size	1 million ha in Size	Number	Area (000 ha)	Number	Area (000 ha)	Number	Area (000 ha)
WORLD	9,793	959,568	7.1	3,819	510,120	5,974	449,449	11.9	1.6	327	217,710	119	113,400	652	43,267
AFRICA	727	149,541	4.9	301	91,639	426	57,902	26.1	4.7	44	23,198	31	28,654	54	4,400
Algeria	19	11,919	5.0	12	11,801	7	118	10.5	10.5	2	7,276	1	300	2	5
Angola	5	2,641	2.1	1	790	4	1,851	60.0	0.0	0	0	0	0	0	0
Benin	2	778	6.9	2	778	0	0	100.0	0.0	1	880	0	0	0	0
Botswana	9	10,663	18.3	5	9,731	4	932	88.9	33.3	0	0	0	0	0	0
Burkina Faso	12	2,662	9.7	3	489	9	2,173	41.7	8.3	1	19	0	0	3	299
Burundi	3	89	3.2	0	0	3	89	0.0	0.0	0	0	0	0	0	0
Cameroon	14	2,050	4.3	7	1,032	7	1,019	57.1	0.0	3	850	1	526	0	0
Central African Rep	13	6,106	9.8	5	3,188	8	2,918	92.3	23.1	2	1,640	1	1,740	0	0
Chad	9	11,494	9.0	2	414	7	11,080	100.0	22.2	0	0	0	0	1	195
Congo	10	1,177	3.4	1	127	9	1,051	30.0	0.0	2	172	0	0	0	0
Cote d'Ivoire	12	1,993	6.2	10	1,891	2	102	33.3	8.3	2	1,480	3	1,485	0	0
Egypt	12	793	0.8	4	99	8	695	8.3	0.0	2	2,577	0	0	2	106
Equatorial Guinea	0	0	0.0	0	0	0	0	0.0	0.0	0	0	0	0	0	0
Eritrea	0	0	0.0	0	0	0	0	0.0	0.0	0	0	0	0	0	0
Ethiopia	23	6,023	5.5	12	3,040	11	2,982	69.6	0.0	0	0	1	22	0	0
Gabon	6	1,045	3.9	1	15	5	1,030	33.3	0.0	1	15	0	0	3	1,080
Gambia, The	5	23	2.0	3	18	2	5	0.0	0.0	0	0	0	0	0	0
Ghana	9	1,104	4.6	7	1,097	2	7	33.3	0.0	1	8	0	0	6	178
Guinea	3	164	0.7	3	164	0	0	33.3	0.0	2	133	1	13	6	225
Guinea-Bissau	0	0	0.0	0	0	0	0	0.0	0.0	0	0	0	0	1	39
Kenya	36	3,504	6.0	32	3,451	4	52	19.4	2.8	5	1,335	0	0	1	19
Lesotho	1	7	0.2	0	0	1	7	0.0	0.0	0	0	0	0	0	0
Liberia	1	129	1.3	1	129	0	0	100.0	0.0	0	0	0	0	0	0
Libya	6	173	0.1	3	51	3	122	0.0	0.0	0	0	0	0	0	0
Madagascar	36	1,115	1.9	16	740	20	375	2.8	0.0	1	140	1	152	0	0
Malawi	9	1,059	8.9	5	696	4	362	33.3	0.0	0	0	1	9	0	0
Mali	11	4,012	3.2	1	350	10	3,662	54.5	18.2	1	771	1	400	3	162
Mauritania	4	1,746	1.7	3	1,496	1	250	75.0	25.0	0	0	1	1,200	1	1,173
Mauritius	1	4	1.8	0	0	1	4	0.0	0.0	1	4	0	0	0	0
Morocco	11	369	0.8	6	62	5	307	9.1	0.0	0	0	0	0	4	11
Mozambique	1	2	0.0	0	0	1	2	0.0	0.0	0	0	0	0	0	0
Namibia	12	10,218	12.4	6	9,000	6	1,218	50.0	25.0	0	0	0	0	0	0
Niger	5	8,416	6.6	1	220	4	8,196	60.0	20.0	0	0	1	7,736	1	220
Nigeria	19	2,971	3.2	6	2,226	13	745	47.4	0.0	1	0	0	0	0	0
Rwanda	2	327	12.4	2	327	0	0	50.0	0.0	1	15	0	0	0	0
Senegal	9	2,180	11.1	5	1,012	4	1,168	33.3	0.0	3	1,094	2	929	4	100
Sierra Leone	2	82	1.1	0	0	2	82	0.0	0.0	0	0	0	0	0	0
Somalia	1	180	0.3	0	0	1	180	100.0	0.0	0	0	0	0	0	0
South Africa	238	6,970	5.7	55	4,280	183	2,689	2.5	0.4	0	0	0	0	12	228
Sudan	16	9,383	3.7	9	8,514	7	869	43.8	25.0	2	1,901	0	0	0	0
Swaziland	3	40	2.3	0	0	3	40	0.0	0.0	0	0	0	0	0	0
Tanzania	31	13,936	14.7	12	4,100	19	9,836	61.3	9.7	2	2,338	4	7,381	0	0
Togo	11	647	11.4	3	357	8	290	27.3	0.0	0	0	0	0	0	0
Tunisia	6	44	0.3	6	44	0	0	0.0	0.0	4	32	1	13	1	13
Uganda	31	1,909	8.1	7	876	24	1,033	19.4	0.0	1	220	2	132	1	15
Zaire	8	9,917	4.2	8	9,917	0	0	100.0	50.0	3	298	4	5,482	0	0
Zambia	21	6,364	8.5	21	6,364	0	0	52.4	4.8	0	0	1	4	2	333
Zimbabwe	25	3,068	7.9	11	2,704	14	364	24.0	4.0	0	0	2	1,095	0	0
EUROPE {b}	2,923	223,905	8.9	565	157,432	2,358	66,473	7.2	0.5	127	88,767	18	838	411	6,914
Albania	11	34	1.2	6	10	5	24	0.0	0.0	0	0	0	0	0	0
Austria	170	2,081	24.8	1	76	169	2,005	0.6	0.0	4	28	0	0	7	103
Belarus, Rep	11	265	1.3	2	144	9	120	0.0	0.0	2	253	1	88	0	0
Belgium	3	77	2.5	0	0	3	77	0.0	0.0	0	0	0	0	6	8
Bosnia and Herzegovina	5	25	0.5	1	17	4	8	0.0	0.0	0	0	0	0	0	0
Bulgaria	46	370	3.3	31	288	15	82	2.2	0.0	17	25	2	41	4	2
Croatia, Rep	30	392	6.9	11	74	19	318	3.3	0.0	1	150	1	19	4	80
Czech Rep	34	1,067	13.5	6	88	28	979	2.9	0.0	5	363	0	0	9	28
Denmark {b}	114	99,618	44.9	10	98,278	104	1,340	3.5	1.8	1	70,000	0	0	38	1,833
Estonia, Rep	38	412	9.1	8	228	30	184	2.6	0.0	1	1,560	0	0	1	49
Finland	81	2,744	8.1	36	560	45	2,184	11.1	0.0	2	770	0	0	11	101
France	102	5,598	10.2	14	332	88	5,266	20.6	0.0	6	576	2	12	8	426
Germany	497	9,193	25.8	3	37	494	9,156	5.0	0.0	12	1,159	0	0	31	673
Greece	21	221	1.7	10	78	11	143	0.0	0.0	2	9	2	0	11	107
Hungary	53	574	6.2	5	159	48	415	0.0	0.0	5	129	0	0	13	115
Iceland	20	916	8.9	8	219	12	697	10.0	0.0	0	0	0	0	2	58
Ireland	11	47	0.7	5	37	6	10	0.0	0.0	2	9	0	0	21	13
Italy	171	2,275	7.5	12	473	159	1,801	1.2	0.0	3	4	0	0	46	57
Latvia, Rep	45	775	12.0	5	41	40	734	2.2	0.0	0	0	0	0	0	0
Lithuania, Rep	76	625	9.6	9	144	67	481	0.0	0.0	0	0	0	0	4	43
Macedonia, former Yugoslav Rep	16	217	8.4	8	156	8	61	0.0	0.0	0	0	1	38	0	0
Moldova, Rep	3	12	0.4	3	12	0	0	0.0	0.0	0	0	0	0	0	0
Netherlands	85	429	11.5	38	292	47	137	1.2	0.0	1	260	0	0	15	313
Norway	113	5,536	17.1	75	5,054	38	482	9.7	0.9	1	1,555	0	0	14	16
Poland, Rep	111	3,069	9.8	16	155	95	2,914	4.5	0.0	7	164	1	5	5	7
Portugal	24	583	6.3	4	37	20	546	4.2	0.0	1	0	0	0	2	31
Romania	39	1,074	4.5	23	891	16	183	2.6	0.0	3	614	1	547	1	647
Russian Federation	209	70,536	4.1	111	47,166	98	23,371	43.5	5.7	15	9,561	0	0	3	1,168
Slovak Rep	40	1,016	20.7	7	202	33	813	2.5	0.0	4	203	0	0	7	26
Slovenia, Rep	10	108	5.3	1	85	9	23	0.0	0.0	0	0	1	0	1	1
Spain	214	4,246	8.4	10	132	204	4,114	3.7	0.0	13	860	2	55	29	131
Sweden	197	2,982	6.6	52	1,444	145	1,538	3.0	0.0	1	96	0	0	30	383
Switzerland	109	731	17.7	1	17	108	714	0.0	0.0	1	17	0	0	8	7
Ukraine	19	485	0.8	15	312	4	173	0.0	0.0	3	160	0	0	3	211
United Kingdom	168	5,109	20.9	8	32	160	5,078	8.9	0.0	13	44	2	1	73	261
Yugoslavia, Fed Rep	21	347	3.4	9	151	12	195	0.0	0.0	1	200	2	32	2	18

	All Protected Areas (IUCN categories I-V)			National Protection Systems — Totally Protected Areas (IUCN categories I-III)		Partially Protected Areas (IUCN categories IV-V)		% of Protected Areas (IUCN categories I-V) at Least		International Protection Systems {a} — Biosphere Reserves		World Heritage Sites		Wetlands of Intl. Importance	
	Number	Area (000 ha)	Percent of Land Area	Number	Area (000 ha)	Number	Area (000 ha)	100,000 ha in Size	1 million ha in Size	Number	Area (000 ha)	Number	Area (000 ha)	Number	Area (000 ha)
NORTH & CENTRAL AMERICA	2,549	230,199	10.2	1,297	112,100	1,252	118,098	10.7	1.8	74	36,928	23	29,910	61	14,467
Belize	13	323	14.1	6	160	7	163	15.4	0.0	0	0	0	0	0	0
Canada	627	82,358	8.3	347	34,539	280	47,820	14.7	2.7	6	1,050	6	14,993	31	13,020
Costa Rica	28	648	12.7	16	503	12	144	3.6	0.0	2	729	1	585	3	30
Cuba	56	1,154	10.4	18	157	38	997	3.6	0.0	4	324	0	0	0	0
Dominican Rep	17	1,048	21.5	8	564	9	484	17.6	0.0	0	0	0	0	0	0
El Salvador	2	5	0.2	1	3	1	2	0.0	0.0	0	0	0	0	0	0
Guatemala	18	1,333	12.2	12	1,279	6	54	22.2	0.0	2	1,236	1	58	1	48
Haiti	3	10	0.3	2	8	1	2	0.0	0.0	0	0	0	0	0	0
Honduras	43	862	7.7	15	469	28	393	4.7	0.0	1	500	1	500	1	13
Jamaica	1	2	0.1	1	2	0	0	0.0	0.0	0	0	0	0	0	0
Mexico	68	9,854	5.0	41	1,925	27	7,929	16.2	2.9	10	5,393	2	1,068	1	48
Nicaragua	59	903	6.9	6	389	53	514	1.7	0.0	0	0	0	0	0	0
Panama	14	1,326	17.6	13	1,324	1	2	28.6	0.0	1	597	2	804	3	111
Trinidad and Tobago	5	16	3.0	1	2	4	14	0.0	0.0	0	0	0	0	1	6
United States	1,585	130,209	13.3	803	70,639	782	59,570	9.5	1.8	44	27,008	10	11,902	13	1,133
SOUTH AMERICA	706	112,834	6.3	391	67,506	315	45,328	25.1	3.4	27	50,559	11	7,115	20	7,788
Argentina	84	4,372	1.6	65	3,024	19	1,347	14.3	0.0	5	2,410	2	655	3	82
Bolivia	25	9,233	8.4	8	3,774	17	5,459	56.0	16.0	3	435	0	0	1	5
Brazil	272	32,189	3.8	149	20,423	123	11,766	23.5	1.8	2	29,940	1	170	5	4,537
Chile	66	13,725	18.1	32	8,375	34	5,350	25.8	7.6	7	2,407	0	0	1	5
Colombia	80	9,381	8.2	41	9,036	39	345	22.5	2.5	3	2,514	1	72	0	0
Ecuador	15	11,114	39.2	10	3,087	5	8,027	46.7	6.7	2	1,446	2	1,038	2	90
Guyana	1	59	0.3	1	59	0	0	0.0	0.0	0	0	0	0	0	0
Paraguay	20	1,495	3.7	13	1,368	7	127	10.0	0.0	0	0	0	0	0	0
Peru	22	4,176	3.2	15	4,044	7	133	27.3	9.1	3	2,507	4	2,180	3	2,416
Suriname	13	736	4.5	2	87	11	649	15.4	0.0	0	0	0	0	1	12
Uruguay	8	32	0.2	2	15	6	17	0.0	0.0	1	200	0	0	1	435
Venezuela	100	26,322	28.9	53	14,215	47	12,108	35.0	5.0	1	8,700	1	3,000	1	10
ASIA	1,774	141,793	4.4	548	42,525	0	0	11.6	1.1	42	13,513	23	1,736	61	4,559
Afghanistan, Islamic State	6	218	0.3	1	41	5	177	0.0	0.0	0	0	0	0	0	0
Armenia	4	214	7.2	4	214	0	0	25.0	0.0	0	0	0	0	2	492
Azerbaijan	12	191	2.2	12	191	0	0	0.0	0.0	0	0	0	0	1	133
Bangladesh	8	97	0.7	0	0	8	97	0.0	0.0	0	0	0	0	1	60
Bhutan	9	966	20.6	5	725	4	241	33.3	0.0	0	0	0	0	0	0
Cambodia	20	2,998	16.6	7	871	13	2,127	55.0	0.0	0	0	0	0	0	0
China	463	58,082	6.1	4	128	459	57,954	10.4	1.9	10	2,488	5	248	6	587
Georgia, Rep	15	187	2.7	15	187	0	0	0.0	0.0	0	0	0	0	0	0
India	339	14,337	4.4	66	3,874	273	10,463	6.2	0.0	0	0	5	281	6	193
Indonesia	168	18,564	9.7	97	14,397	71	4,167	18.5	3.0	6	1,482	2	298	1	163
Iran, Islamic Rep	67	8,299	5.0	26	2,986	41	5,314	26.9	1.5	9	2,610	0	0	18	1,358
Iraq	0	0	0.0	0	0	0	0	0.0	0.0	0	0	0	0	0	0
Israel	15	308	14.6	1	3	14	305	6.7	0.0	0	0	0	0	0	0
Japan	80	2,758	7.3	37	1,514	43	1,245	10.0	0.0	4	116	2	28	9	83
Jordan	10	290	3.3	1	1	9	289	10.0	0.0	0	0	0	0	1	7
Kazakhstan, Rep	20	988	0.4	9	892	11	96	10.0	0.0	0	0	0	0	2	609
Korea, Dem People's Rep	2	58	0.5	1	44	1	14	0.0	0.0	1	132	0	0	0	0
Korea, Rep	27	693	7.0	5	19	22	674	3.7	0.0	1	37	0	0	0	0
Kuwait	2	27	1.5	1	2	1	25	0.0	0.0	0	0	0	0	0	0
Kyrgyz Rep	5	284	1.4	5	284	0	0	20.0	0.0	1	71	0	0	1	630
Lao People's Dem Rep	0	0	0.0	0	0	0	0	0.0	0.0	0	0	0	0	0	0
Lebanon	1	4	0.3	1	4	0	0	0.0	0.0	0	0	0	0	0	0
Malaysia	51	1,484	4.5	41	903	10	581	9.8	0.0	0	0	0	0	0	0
Mongolia	15	6,168	3.9	14	5,618	1	550	13.3	6.7	1	5,300	0	0	0	0
Myanmar	2	173	0.3	1	161	1	13	50.0	0.0	0	0	0	0	0	0
Nepal	12	1,109	7.9	8	1,014	4	94	33.3	0.0	0	0	2	208	1	18
Oman	28	986	4.6	1	46	27	940	7.1	0.0	0	0	1	0	0	0
Pakistan	55	3,721	4.7	6	882	49	2,839	20.0	0.0	1	31	0	0	9	21
Philippines	27	606	2.0	15	267	12	339	3.7	0.0	2	1,174	1	33	0	0
Saudi Arabia	10	6,201	2.9	2	279	8	5,922	80.0	30.0	0	0	0	0	0	0
Singapore	1	3	4.5	0	0	1	3	0.0	0.0	0	0	0	0	0	0
Sri Lanka	56	796	12.1	25	468	31	328	0.0	0.0	2	9	1	9	1	6
Syrian Arab Rep	0	0	0.0	0	0	0	0	0.0	0.0	0	0	0	0	0	0
Tajikistan, Rep	3	86	0.6	3	86	0	0	0.0	0.0	0	0	0	0	0	0
Thailand	111	7,020	13.7	74	4,336	37	2,684	18.9	0.0	3	26	1	622	0	0
Turkey	49	1,071	1.4	23	417	26	655	2.0	0.0	0	0	2	10	0	0
Turkmenistan, Rep	8	1,112	2.3	8	1,112	0	0	25.0	0.0	1	35	0	0	1	189
United Arab Emirates	0	0	0.0	0	0	0	0	0.0	0.0	0	0	0	0	0	0
Uzbekistan, Rep	10	244	0.5	10	244	0	0	0.0	0.0	0	0	0	0	0	0
Viet Nam	52	1,334	4.0	9	202	43	1,131	1.9	0.0	0	0	1	0	1	12
Yemen, Rep	0	0	0.0	0	0	0	0	0.0	0.0	0	0	0	0	0	0
OCEANIA	1,087	100,282	11.7	701	38,361	386	61,920	9.8	1.4	13	4,745	13	45,147	45	5,139
Australia	889	94,077	12.2	568	32,459	321	61,618	10.3	1.6	12	4,743	11	42,471	39	4,510
Fiji	5	19	1.0	5	19	0	0	0.0	0.0	0	0	0	0	0	0
New Zealand	182	6,067	22.4	122	5,853	60	214	7.7	0.5	0	0	2	2,677	5	39
Papua New Guinea	5	82	0.2	3	7	2	75	0.0	0.0	0	0	0	0	1	590
Solomon Islands	0	0	0.0	0	0	0	0	0.0	0.0	0	0	0	0	0	0

Source: World Conservation Monitoring Centre.

Notes: a. Areas listed often include nationally protected systems. b. Totals include Greenland. World totals exclude Antarctica. World and regional totals include countries not listed here.
0 = zero or less than half the unit of measure; X = not available. For additional information, see Sources and Technical Notes.

	Mammals				Birds				Higher Plants			
	Total Number of Known Species			No. of Species per 10,000 Square km {a}	Total Number of Known Species			No. of Species per 10,000 Square km {a}	Total Number of Known Species			No. of Species per 10,000 Square km {a}
	All Species	Endemic Species	Threatened Species		All Species	Endemic Species	Threatened Species		All Species {b}	Endemic Species	Threatened Species	
WORLD	4,327 c	X	X	X	9,672	X	X	X	270,000 d	X	X	X
AFRICA	X	X	X	X	X	X	X	X	X	X	X	X
Algeria	92	2	11	15	375	1	7	62	3,100	250	145	509
Angola	276	7	16	56	909	13	13	185	5,000	1,260	25	1,017
Benin	188	0	7	85	423	0	1	190	2,000	X	3	899
Botswana	164	0	8	43	550	0	5	144	X	17	4	X
Burkina Faso	147	0	6	49	453	0	1	152	1,100	X	0	369
Burundi	107	0	6	76	596	0	5	425	2,500	X	1	1,783
Cameroon	297	13	21	83	874	8	14	244	8,000	156	74	2,237
Central African Rep	209	2	9	53	662	0	2	169	3,600	100	0	921
Chad	134	1	13	27	532	0	3	107	1,600	X	12	322
Congo	200	2	13	62	569	0	3	177	4,350	1,200	3	1,356
Cote d'Ivoire	230	1	16	73	694	0	11	221	3,517	62	66	1,118
Egypt	98	7	7	21	439	0	10	96	2,066	70	84	452
Equatorial Guinea	184	3	12	131	322	3	4	229	3,000	66	9	2,135
Eritrea	112	0	3	49	537	0	3	236	X	X	X	X
Ethiopia	255	31	21	54	813	28	17	172	6,500	1,000	153	1,378
Gabon	190	2	12	64	629	0	4	213	6,500	X	78	2,197
Gambia, The	108	0	3	104	504	0	1	484	966	X	0	928
Ghana	222	1	12	78	725	1	7	255	3,600	43	32	1,264
Guinea	190	1	13	66	552	0	11	192	3,000	88	35	1,043
Guinea-Bissau	108	0	5	71	319	0	1	209	1,000	12	0	655
Kenya	359	21	16	94	1,068	6	22	280	6,000	265	158	1,571
Lesotho	33	0	2	23	281	0	3	195	1,576	2	7	1,093
Liberia	193	0	13	91	581	1	13	274	2,200	103	1	1,037
Libya	76	5	8	14	323	0	2	59	1,800	134	57	327
Madagascar	105	77	33	27	253	103	28	66	9,000	6,500	189	2,347
Malawi	195	0	6	86	645	0	9	285	3,600	49	61	1,592
Mali	137	0	12	28	622	0	5	127	1,741	11	14	355
Mauritania	61	1	10	13	541	0	3	117	1,100	X	3	239
Mauritius	4	2	3	7	81	9	9	137	700	325	222	1,183
Morocco	105	4	7	30	416	0	11	119	3,600	625	195	1,028
Mozambique	179	1	9	42	678	0	13	160	5,500	219	92	1,294
Namibia	154	3	12	36	609	1	6	142	3,128	X	23	729
Niger	131	0	10	27	482	0	2	98	1,170	X	0	237
Nigeria	274	6	22	62	862	2	8	194	4,614	205	9	1,036
Rwanda	151	0	14	110	666	0	6	484	2,288	26	0	1,662
Senegal	155	0	9	58	610	0	5	228	2,062	26	32	771
Sierra Leone	147	0	12	77	622	0	12	325	2,090	74	12	1,091
Somalia	171	11	12	43	649	10	8	165	3,000	500	57	761
South Africa	247	27	25	51	790	7	16	162	23,000	X	953	4,711
Sudan	267	11	16	43	937	0	9	151	3,132	50	8	506
Swaziland	47	0	4	39	485	0	4	404	2,636	4	41	2,197
Tanzania	322	14	16	72	1,005	19	30	224	10,000	1,122	406	2,229
Togo	196	1	8	110	558	0	1	315	2,000	X	0	1,128
Tunisia	78	1	5	31	356	0	6	142	2,150	X	24	855
Uganda	338	6	15	119	992	3	10	350	5,000	X	6	1,762
Zaire	415	28	23	69	1,096	22	26	181	11,000	1,100	7	1,817
Zambia	229	3	7	55	736	1	10	177	4,600	211	9	1,105
Zimbabwe	270	1	9	81	648	0	7	193	4,200	95	94	1,253
EUROPE	X	X	X	X	X	X	X	X	7,777	X	X	X
Albania	68	0	3	48	306	0	5	216	2,965	24	50	2,093
Austria	83	0	3	41	414	0	3	205	2,950	35	22	1,462
Belarus, Rep	X	0	5	X	X	0	4	X	X	X	0	X
Belgium	58	0	2	40	429	0	3	297	1,400	1	3	969
Bosnia and Herzegovina	X	0	X	X	X	0	2	X	X	X	0	X
Bulgaria	81	0	1	37	374	0	11	169	3,505	320	94	1,584
Croatia, Rep	X	0	X	X	X	0	4	X	X	X	0	X
Czech Rep	X	0	3	X	X	0	5	X	X	X	X	X
Denmark	43	0	1	27	439	0	2	271	1,200	1	6	741
Estonia, Rep	65	0	5	40	330	0	2	201	1,630	X	2	992
Finland	60	0	3	19	425	0	4	133	1,040	X	11	325
France	93	0	5	25	506	9	5	135	4,500	133	117	1,198
Germany	76	0	2	23	503	0	5	155	2,600	6	16	799
Greece	95	2	5	41	398	0	9	170	4,900	742	539	2,091
Hungary	72	0	2	34	363	0	7	174	2,148	38	24	1,029
Iceland	11	0	0	5	316	0	1	146	340	1	1	157
Ireland	25	0	0	13	417	0	1	219	892	X	9	469
Italy	90	3	4	29	490	0	6	159	5,463	712	273	1,776
Latvia, Rep	83	0	4	45	325	0	5	176	1,153	X	0	623
Lithuania, Rep	68	0	4	37	305	0	4	164	1,200	X	0	646
Macedonia, former Yugoslav Rep	X	0	X	X	X	0	X	X	X	X	X	X
Moldova, Rep	68	0	1	46	270	0	6	181	X	X	1	X
Netherlands	55	0	2	36	456	0	3	295	1,170	X	1	758
Norway	54	0	3	17	453	0	3	144	1,650	1	20	524
Poland, Rep	79	0	4	25	421	0	5	135	2,300	3	27	738
Portugal	63	1	6	30	441	2	7	212	2,500	150	240	1,200
Romania	84	0	3	30	368	0	11	129	3,175	41	122	1,116
Russian Federation	X	X	17	X	X	X	35	X	X	X	127	X
Slovak Rep	X	X	3	X	X	X	4	X	X	X	X	X
Slovenia, Rep	69	0	3	55	361	0	3	286	X	X	11	X
Spain	82	4	7	22	506	5	10	139	X	X	896	X
Sweden	60	0	3	17	463	0	4	132	4,916	941	19	1,400
Switzerland	75	0	2	47	400	0	3	251	1,650	1	9	1,033
Ukraine	X	1	4	X	X	0	10	X	2,927	1	16	756
United Kingdom	50	0	1	17	590	1	2	205	1,550	16	28	539
Yugoslavia, Fed Rep	X	X	X	X	X	X	X	X	X	X	X	X

	Mammals				Birds				Higher Plants			
	Total Number of Known Species			No. of Species per 10,000 Square km {a}	Total Number of Known Species			No. of Species per 10,000 Square km {a}	Total Number of Known Species			No. of Species per 10,000 Square km {a}
	All Species	Endemic Species	Threatened Species		All Species	Endemic Species	Threatened Species		All Species {b}	Endemic Species	Threatened Species	
NORTH & CENTRAL AMERICA	X	X	X	X	X	X	X	X	18,849	X	X	X
Belize	125	0	5	95	533	0	1	405	2,750	150	41	2,090
Canada	193	7	6	20	578	3	5	59	2,920	147	649	299
Costa Rica	205	6	8	120	850	7	10	496	11,000	950	456	6,421
Cuba	31	12	10	14	342	22	13	155	6,004	3,229	811	2,714
Dominican Rep	20	0	3	12	254	0	10	151	5,000	1,800	73	2,965
El Salvador	135	0	2	106	420	0	0	329	2,500	17	35	1,956
Guatemala	250	3	5	114	669	1	4	304	8,000	1,171	315	3,638
Haiti	3	0	3	2	220	0	10	157	4,685	1,623	28	3,345
Honduras	173	1	5	78	684	1	4	308	5,000	148	55	2,252
Jamaica	24	3	2	23	262	25	7	254	2,746	923	371	2,662
Mexico	450	140	24	79	1,026	89	34	180	25,000	12,500	1,048	4,382
Nicaragua	200	2	6	86	750	0	3	322	7,000	40	78	3,003
Panama	218	14	11	112	929	8	9	477	9,000	1,222	561	4,618
Trinidad and Tobago	100	1	1	125	433	1	2	540	1,982	236	16	2,470
United States	428	101	22	44	768	70	46	79	16,302	4,036	1,845	1,679
SOUTH AMERICA	X	X	X	X	X	X	X	X	4,958	X	X	X
Argentina	320	47	20	50	976	19	40	153	9,000	1,100	170	1,407
Bolivia	316	20	21	67	1,274	16	27	270	16,500	4,000	49	3,500
Brazil	394	96	45	43	1,635	177	103	176	55,000	X	463	5,935
Chile	91	16	11	22	448	15	15	107	5,125	2,698	292	1,229
Colombia	359	28	24	75	1,695	62	62	355	50,000	1,500	376	10,479
Ecuador	302	23	20	100	1,559	37	50	517	18,250	4,000	375	6,052
Guyana	193	1	7	70	737	0	1	268	6,000	X	47	2,180
Paraguay	305	2	8	90	600	0	22	177	7,500	X	12	2,208
Peru	344	45	29	69	1,678	109	60	338	17,121	5,356	377	3,448
Suriname	180	0	6	72	673	0	1	268	4,700	X	48	1,870
Uruguay	81	1	4	31	365	0	9	141	2,184	40	11	845
Venezuela	305	16	12	69	1,296	42	22	292	20,000	8,000	107	4,510
ASIA	X	X	X	X	X	X	X	X	5,990	X	X	X
Afghanistan, Islamic State	123	1	8	31	460	0	12	116	3,500	800	6	882
Armenia	X	3	1	X	X	0	5	X	X	X	0	X
Azerbaijan	X	0	3	X	X	0	6	X	X	X	1	X
Bangladesh	109	0	16	45	684	0	28	284	5,000	X	24	2,074
Bhutan	99	0	18	59	543	0	12	326	5,446	75	20	3,268
Cambodia	123	0	19	47	429	0	16	165	X	X	7	X
China	394	77	42	41	1,244	67	86	129	30,000	18,000	343	3,112
Georgia, Rep	X	2	3	X	X	0	5	X	X	X	1	X
India	316	44	40	47	1,219	55	71	180	15,000	5,000	1,256	2,216
Indonesia	436	198	57	77	1,531	393	104	271	27,500	17,500	281	4,864
Iran, Islamic Rep	140	5	9	26	502	1	12	93	X	X	1	X
Iraq	81	1	4	23	381	1	11	109	X	X	2	X
Israel	92	3	7	72	500	0	8	391	X	X	38	X
Japan	132	38	17	40	583	21	31	176	4,700	2,000	704	1,418
Jordan	71	0	8	34	361	0	4	175	2,200	X	10	1,069
Kazakhstan, Rep	X	4	9	X	X	0	14	X	X	X	0	X
Korea, Dem People's Rep	X	0	7	X	390	0	16	172	2,898	107	7	1,274
Korea, Rep	49	0	6	23	372	0	19	175	2,898	224	69	1,360
Kuwait	21	0	2	17	321	0	3	265	234	X	0	193
Kyrgyz Rep	X	X	4	X	X	X	5	X	X	X	1	X
Lao People's Dem Rep	172	0	25	61	651	1	23	229	X	X	5	X
Lebanon	54	0	5	53	329	0	5	325	X	X	4	X
Malaysia	286	27	20	90	736	9	31	232	15,000	3,600	510	4,732
Mongolia	134	0	8	25	390	0	11	74	2,272	229	1	429
Myanmar	251	6	20	62	999	4	43	249	7,000	1,071	29	1,742
Nepal	167	1	23	70	824	2	23	344	6,500	315	21	2,716
Oman	56	2	5	20	430	0	5	157	1,018	73	4	371
Pakistan	151	3	10	36	671	0	22	158	4,929	372	12	1,163
Philippines	153	97	22	50	556	183	86	181	8,000	3,500	371	2,604
Saudi Arabia	77	0	6	13	413	0	10	70	1,729	X	6	294
Singapore	45	1	3	113	295	0	6	738	2,000	2	14	5,007
Sri Lanka	88	13	4	47	428	23	11	230	3,000	890	436	1,613
Syrian Arab Rep	X	X	4	X	X	X	6	X	X	X	10	X
Tajikistan, Rep	X	2	6	X	X	0	9	X	X	X	0	X
Thailand	265	7	22	72	915	3	44	249	11,000	X	382	2,999
Turkey	116	1	4	28	418	0	13	99	8,472	2,675	1,827	2,012
Turkmenistan, Rep	X	0	8	X	X	0	9	X	X	X	1	X
United Arab Emirates	25	0	2	12	360	0	4	179	X	X	0	X
Uzbekistan, Rep	X	0	7	X	X	0	11	X	X	X	5	X
Viet Nam	213	7	25	67	761	10	45	240	>7,000	1,260	350	X
Yemen, Rep	66	2	4	18	366	8	12	99	X	135	149	X
OCEANIA	X	X	X	X	X	X	X	X	5,825	X	X	X
Australia	252	198	43	28	751	353	51	84	15,000	14,074	1,597	1,672
Fiji	4	1	4	3	109	26	8	89	1,307	760	72	1,071
New Zealand	10	4	3	3	287	76	45	97	2,160	1,942	236	727
Papua New Guinea	214	57	33	60	708	80	31	200	10,000	X	95	2,821
Solomon Islands	53	19	5	37	223	44	18	157	2,780	30	43	1,959

Source: World Conservation Monitoring Centre.

Notes: a. Values are standardized using a species-area curve. b. Flowering plants only c. Includes cetaceans. d. All vascular plant species. Threatened species data are as of June 1993.
X = not available. For additional information, see Sources and Technical Notes.

Data Table 11.3 Globally Threatened Species: Reptiles, Amphibians, and Fish, 1990s

	Reptiles				Amphibians				Total Number of Known Freshwater Fish Species	
	Total Number of Known Species			Number of Species per 10,000 Square km	Total Number of Known Species			Number of Species per 10,000 Square km		
	All Species	Endemic Species	Threatened Species		All Species	Endemic Species	Threatened Species		All Species	Threatened Species
WORLD	6,900	X	X	X	4,400	X	X	X	X	X
AFRICA	X	X	X	X	X	X	X	X	X	X
Algeria	X	3	0	X	X	0	0	X	X	1
Angola	X	18	5	X	X	22	0	X	X	0
Benin	X	1	2	X	X	0	0	X	X	0
Botswana	157	2	0	41	38	0	0	10	92	0
Burkina Faso	X	3	1	X	X	0	0	X	X	0
Burundi	X	0	0	X	X	2	0	X	X	0
Cameroon	X	19	3	X	X	66	1	X	X	20
Central African Rep	X	0	1	X	X	0	0	X	X	0
Chad	X	1	1	X	X	0	0	X	X	0
Congo	X	1	2	X	X	1	0	X	X	0
Cote d'Ivoire	X	2	4	X	X	3	1	X	X	0
Egypt	83	0	4	18	6	0	0	1	70	1
Equatorial Guinea	X	3	3	X	X	2	1	X	X	0
Eritrea	X	0	0	X	X	0	0	X	X	0
Ethiopia	X	6	2	X	X	32	0	X	X	0
Gabon	X	3	3	X	X	4	0	X	X	0
Gambia, The	X	1	1	X	X	0	0	X	79	0
Ghana	X	1	4	X	X	4	0	X	X	0
Guinea	X	3	3	X	X	3	1	X	X	0
Guinea-Bissau	X	2	3	X	X	1	0	X	X	0
Kenya	187	15	3	49	88	11	0	23	X	X
Lesotho	X	2	1	X	X	1	2	X	8	1
Liberia	62	2	3	29	38	4	1	18	X	0
Libya	X	1	2	X	X	0	0	X	X	0
Madagascar	252	197	10	66	144	143	0	38	40	10
Malawi	124	6	0	55	69	3	0	31	X	0
Mali	16	2	1	3	X	1	0	X	X	0
Mauritania	X	1	3	X	X	0	0	X	X	0
Mauritius	11	8	6	19	0	0	0	0	X	0
Morocco	X	8	1	X	X	1	0	X	X	1
Mozambique	X	5	6	X	62	1	1	15	X	1
Namibia	X	26	2	X	32	1	1	7	102	5
Niger	X	0	0	X	X	0	0	X	X	0
Nigeria	> 135	7	3	0	>109	1	0	0	260	0
Rwanda	X	1	0	X	X	0	0	X	X	0
Senegal	X	1	6	X	X	1	0	X	83	0
Sierra Leone	X	1	3	X	X	2	0	X	X	0
Somalia	193	48	2	49	27	3	0	7	X	1
South Africa	299	81	36	61	95	45	16	19	94	34
Sudan	X	6	2	X	X	1	0	X	X	0
Swaziland	102	1	2	85	40	0	1	33	40	0
Tanzania	245	56	4	55	121	43	0	27	X	X
Togo	X	1	3	X	X	3	0	X	X	0
Tunisia	X	1	1	X	X	0	0	X	X	0
Uganda	149	2	0	53	50	1	0	18	291	X
Zaire	X	33	3	X	X	53	0	X	X	1
Zambia	X	2	1	X	83	1	0	20	X	0
Zimbabwe	153	2	0	46	120	3	0	36	112	0
EUROPE	X	X	X	X	X	X	X	X	X	X
Albania	31	0	2	22	13	0	0	9	39	1
Austria	14	0	0	7	20	0	0	10	60	2
Belarus, Rep	8	0	0	3	10	0	0	4	X	0
Belgium	8	0	0	6	17	0	0	12	X	1
Bosnia and Herzegovina	X	0	X	X	X	0	X	X	X	X
Bulgaria	33	0	1	15	17	0	0	8	X	1
Croatia, Rep	X	0	X	X	X	0	X	X	X	X
Czech Rep	X	0	0	X	X	0	0	X	X	2
Denmark	5	0	0	3	14	0	0	9	41	1
Estonia, Rep	5	0	0	3	11	0	0	7	30	1
Finland	5	0	0	2	5	0	0	2	66	2
France	32	0	2	9	32	3	2	9	53	3
Germany	12	0	0	4	20	0	0	6	71	4
Greece	51	3	4	22	15	0	1	6	98	17
Hungary	15	0	0	7	17	0	0	8	X	1
Iceland	0	0	0	0	0	0	0	0	7	1
Ireland	1	0	0	1	3	0	0	2	25	2
Italy	40	0	3	13	34	7	9	11	45	2
Latvia, Rep	7	0	0	4	13	0	0	7	109	1
Lithuania, Rep	7	0	0	4	13	0	0	7	X	1
Macedonia, former Yugoslav Rep	X	0	X	X	X	0	X	X	X	X
Moldova, Rep	9	0	0	6	13	0	0	9	82	2
Netherlands	7	0	0	5	16	0	0	10	X	1
Norway	5	0	0	2	5	0	0	2	X	2
Poland, Rep	9	0	0	3	18	0	0	6	X	3
Portugal	29	2	0	14	17	0	1	8	28	9
Romania	25	0	1	9	19	0	0	7	87	3
Russian Federation	X	X	3	X	X	X	0	X	X	4
Slovak Rep	X	X	0	X	X	X	0	X	X	2
Slovenia, Rep	21	0	0	17	X	0	2	X	X	0
Spain	53	9	4	15	X	0	3	X	98	13
Sweden	6	0	0	2	25	2	0	7	50	2
Switzerland	14	0	0	9	13	0	1	8	X	3
Ukraine	19	0	0	5	18	0	0	5	48	3
United Kingdom	8	0	0	3	7	0	0	2	36	2
Yugoslavia, Fed Rep	X	X	X	X	X	X	X	X	X	X

	Reptiles				Amphibians				Total Number of Known Freshwater Fish Species	
	Total Number of Known Species			Number of Species per 10,000 Square km	Total Number of Known Species			Number of Species per 10,000 Square km		
	All Species	Endemic Species	Threatened Species		All Species	Endemic Species	Threatened Species		All Species	Threatened Species
NORTH & CENTRAL AMERICA	X	X	X	X	X	X	X	X	X	X
Belize	107	2	5	81	32	1	0	24	63	0
Canada	41	0	0	4	41	0	0	4	177	20
Costa Rica	214	36	7	125	162	34	1	95	130	0
Cuba	102	80	8	46	41	42	0	19	28	0
Dominican Rep	105	22	8	62	35	15	1	21	16	0
El Salvador	73	4	6	57	23	0	0	18	16	0
Guatemala	231	18	9	105	99	28	0	45	220	0
Haiti	102	29	6	73	46	23	2	33	16	0
Honduras	152	12	7	68	56	16	0	25	46	0
Jamaica	36	26	10	35	21	21	4	20	6	0
Mexico	687	368	18	120	285	179	3	50	384	98
Nicaragua	161	5	7	69	59	2	0	25	50	0
Panama	226	25	7	116	164	21	0	84	101	0
Trinidad and Tobago	70	2	5	87	26	2	0	32	76	0
United States	280	71	23	29	233	146	16	24	822	174
SOUTH AMERICA	X	X	X	X	X	X	X	X	X	X
Argentina	220	64	6	34	145	45	5	23	410	1
Bolivia	208	17	4	44	112	26	0	24	389	1
Brazil	468	177	10	51	502	349	1	54	X	8
Chile	72	33	18	17	41	30	20	10	44	27
Colombia	584	106	12	122	585	208	0	123	X	3
Ecuador	374	114	12	124	402	160	0	133	706	0
Guyana	X	2	7	X	X	13	0	X	X	0
Paraguay	120	3	3	35	85	3	0	25	X	0
Peru	298	95	7	60	315	122	0	63	X	0
Suriname	151	0	5	60	95	8	0	38	300	0
Uruguay	X	1	0	X	X	4	0	X	X	0
Venezuela	259	57	10	58	199	116	0	45	X	0
ASIA	X	X	X	X	X	X	X	X	X	X
Afghanistan, Islamic State	103	4	0	26	6	1	0	2	84	0
Armenia	46	1	2	32	6	0	0	4	X	0
Azerbaijan	52	0	1	26	8	0	0	4	X	0
Bangladesh	119	1	17	49	19	0	0	8	X	0
Bhutan	19	2	1	11	24	0	0	14	X	0
Cambodia	82	1	7	32	28	0	0	11	>215	4
China	340	74	8	35	263	154	1	27	686	16
Georgia, Rep	46	0	5	24	11	0	1	6	X	0
India	389	185	21	57	197	120	3	29	X	2
Indonesia	511	298	16	90	270	109	0	48	X	65
Iran, Islamic Rep	164	26	6	30	11	5	0	2	269	2
Iraq	81	1	0	23	6	0	0	2	X	2
Israel	X	1	4	X	X	0	0	X	26	0
Japan	66	27	10	20	52	41	11	16	186	10
Jordan	X	0	0	X	X	0	0	X	26	0
Kazakhstan, Rep	37	0	0	6	10	0	0	2	X	1
Korea, Dem People's Rep	19	1	0	8	14	0	0	6	X	0
Korea, Rep	25	3	0	12	14	2	0	7	130	0
Kuwait	29	0	2	24	2	0	0	2	X	0
Kyrgyz Rep	X	X	0	X	X	X	0	X	X	1
Lao People's Dem Rep	66	1	3	23	37	1	0	13	244	3
Lebanon	X	2	1	X	X	0	0	X	X	0
Malaysia	268	68	10	85	158	57	0	50	449	4
Mongolia	21	0	0	4	8	0	0	2	70	0
Myanmar	203	38	11	51	75	10	0	19	X	1
Nepal	80	3	8	33	36	9	0	15	120	0
Oman	64	9	4	23	X	0	0	X	3	2
Pakistan	172	21	7	41	17	3	0	4	156	0
Philippines	190	153	8	62	63	55	2	21	X	21
Saudi Arabia	84	4	2	14	X	0	0	X	8	0
Singapore	X	0	1	X	X	0	0	X	73	0
Sri Lanka	144	75	9	77	39	21	0	21	65	19
Syrian Arab Rep	X	X	1	X	X	X	0	X	X	0
Tajikistan, Rep	38	0	0	16	2	0	0	1	X	0
Thailand	298	35	11	81	107	17	0	29	>600	11
Turkey	102	4	10	24	18	2	3	4	>152	18
Turkmenistan, Rep	80	2	0	22	2	0	0	1	X	1
United Arab Emirates	37	1	2	18	X	0	0	X	5	0
Uzbekistan, Rep	51	0	0	15	2	0	0	1	X	0
Viet Nam	180	39	8	57	80	27	1	25	X	2
Yemen, Rep	77	31	2	21	X	1	0	X	5	0
OCEANIA	X	X	X	X	X	X	X	X	X	X
Australia	748	596	42	83	205	188	20	23	216	54
Fiji	25	11	6	20	2	2	0	2	X	0
New Zealand	40	36	12	13	3	3	3	1	29	6
Papua New Guinea	280	77	7	79	197	115	0	56	282	49
Solomon Islands	61	10	6	43	17	9	0	12	X	0

Source: World Conservation Monitoring Centre.

Notes: a. Values are standardized using a species-area curve. Threatened species data are as of 1993.
World and regional totals include countries not listed. X = not available. For additional information, see Sources and Technical Notes.

Data Table 11.4 Marine Biodiversity

	Length of Coastline (km)	Maritime Area (000 sq. km) Shelf to 200-Meter Depth	Exclusive Economic Zone	Total Number of Known Coastal Marine Species {a} Fish	Turtles	Mammals Total	Mammals Threatened	Marine Habitats (000 hectares) Mangroves	Coral Reefs	Marine Protected Areas Number	Area (hectares)	Regional Priority Sites {b} (number)
WORLD	X	X	X	X	7	56	15	X	X	1,306	X	73
AFRICA	X	X	X	X	X	X	X	X	X	112	X	9
Algeria	1,183	14	137	X	X	X	X	0	0	2	76,568	0
Angola	1,600	67	606	X	5	3	1	110	NS	3	2,465,200	0
Benin	121	X	27	X	X	2	1	3	X	X	X	X
Cameroon	402	11	15	X	3	2	1	306	NS	1	160,000	0
Cape Verde	965	X	789	108	3	X	X	X	P	X	X	X
Congo	169	9	25	X	3	2	1	2	X	X	X	X
Cote d'Ivoire	515	10	105	X	2	2	1	2	NS	X	X	X
Djibouti	314	X	6	X	2	2	1	P	P	2	X	0
Egypt	2,450	37	174	X	3	2	1	P	P	6	708,300	0
Equatorial Guinea	296	X	283	X	2	2	1	20	P	X	X	X
Eritrea	2,234	X	X	X	2	2	1	P	P	X	X	X
Gabon	885	46	214	X	3	2	1	250	NS	1	200,000	0
Gambia, The	80	X	20	X	2	2	1	66	X	3	18,440	1
Ghana	539	21	218	X	5	2	1	2	NS	X	X	X
Guinea	346	38	71	X	2	2	1	223	X	X	X	X
Guinea-Bissau	274	X	151	X	5	2	1	237	X	1	0	0
Kenya	536	14	118	X	3	2	1	53-62	P	10	79,559	1
Liberia	579	20	230	X	4	2	1	20	NS	X	X	X
Libya	1,770	84	338	X	1	X	1	NP	NP	X	X	X
Madagascar	4,828	180	1,292	X	4	2	1	326	P	1	1,000	0
Mauritania	754	44	154	X	4-5	4	2	P	X	2	1,186,000	1
Mauritius	177	92	1,183	313	X	X	1	P	P	6	8,400	0
Morocco	1,835	62	278	X	3	2	1	NP	NP	3	56,900	0
Mozambique	2,470	104	562	X	5	2	1	85	P	4	1,027,000	2
Namibia	1,489	X	X	X	1	2	0	X	X	X	X	X
Nigeria	853	46	211	X	X	2	1	970-3,328	X	X	X	X
Senegal	531	32	206	X	5	3	1	169	NS	6	84,186	1
Seychelles	491	X	1,349	379	2	X	X	P	P	15	X	0
Sierra Leone	402	26	156	X	3	2	1	100-171	NS	X	X	X
Somalia	3,025	61	783	X	2	2	1	10	P	X	X	X
South Africa	2,881	143	1,553	X	2	9	1	1	P	22	X	0
Sudan	853	22	92	X	2	2	1	P	P	2	X	0
Tanzania	1,424	41	223	X	4	2	1	134	P	7	X	3
Togo	56	1	2	X	3	2	1	P	X	X	X	X
Tunisia	1,143	51	86	X	1	1	X	NP	NP	2	4,480	0
Zaire	37	1	1	X	3	2	1	53	X	1	76,850	0
EUROPE	X	X	X	X	X	X	X	X	X	142	X	27
Albania	418	5	12	X	X	X	X	NP	NP	X	X	X
Belgium	64	3	3	X	X	2	0	NP	NP	1	X	1
Bosnia and Herzegovina	20	X	X	X	X	X	X	NP	NP	X	X	X
Bulgaria	354	12	33	X	X	1	X	NP	NP	X	X	X
Croatia, Rep	5,790	X	X	X	X	X	X	NP	NP	6	40,882	0
Cyprus	648	7	99	96	2	X	X	NP	NP	1	650	0
Denmark	3,379	69	1,464	X	X	3	0	NP	NP	13	X	1
Estonia, Rep	1,393	X	X	X	X	X	0	NP	NP	5	X	1
Finland	1,126	98	98	X	X	3	0	NP	NP	5	X	1
France	3,427	148	3,493	X	3	3	0	NP	NP	11	X	0
Germany	2,389	41	50	X	X	3	0	NP	NP	11	X	4
Greece	13,676	25	505	X	1	X	1	NP	NP	1	100,000	0
Iceland	4,988	134	867	X	X	4	0	NP	NP	2	272	0
Ireland	1,448	126	380	X	X	3	0	NP	NP	1	X	0
Italy	4,996	144	552	X	X	X	1	NP	NP	10	X	0
Latvia, Rep	531	X	X	X	X	X	X	NP	NP	1	X	0
Lithuania, Rep	108	X	X	X	X	X	X	NP	NP	3	X	2
Netherlands	451	85	85	X	X	3	0	NP	NP	4	X	2
Norway	5,832	103	2,025	X	X	9	1	NP	NP	5	X	0
Poland, Rep	491	28	29	X	X	2	0	NP	NP	1	X	0
Portugal	1,693	39	1,774	X	X	2	1	NP	NP	13	X	7
Romania	225	24	32	X	X	X	X	NP	NP	X	X	X
Russian Federation	37,653	X	X	X	X	17	3	NP	NP	12	X	5
Slovenia, Rep	32	X	X	X	X	X	X	NP	NP	2	X	0
Spain	4,964	170	1,219	X	X	2	1	NP	NP	8	X	1
Sweden	3,218	155	155	X	X	4	0	NP	NP	6	X	0
Ukraine	2,782	X	X	X	X	X	X	NP	NP	3	72,013	0
United Kingdom	12,429	492	1,785	X	X	3	0	NP	NP	9	X	2
Yugoslavia, Fed Rep	199	X	X	X	X	X	X	NP	NP	X	X	X
NORTH & CENTRAL AMERICA	X	X	X	X	X	X	X	X	X	385	X	8
Antigua and Barbuda	153	X	X	108	3	X	X	1	3	2	2,500	0
Barbados	97	0	167	270	1	X	X	P	P	1	250	0
Belize	386	X	X	X	3	X	1	73-78	P	2	4,336	0
Canada	90,908	2,903	2,939	X	X	15	2	NP	NP	76	18,193,255	0
Costa Rica	1,290	16	259	X	4	X	1	40-41	P	13	X	1
Cuba	3,735	X	363	320	3	X	1	530-626	P	16	579,634	1
Dominica	148	X	20	105	3	X	1	P	P	2	X	0
Dominican Rep	1,288	18	269	269	4	X	1	9-24	P	7	717,060	2
El Salvador	307	18	92	X	4	X	X	35-45	X	X	X	X
Guatemala	400	12	99	X	4	X	1	16	X	2	57,200	0
Haiti	1,771	11	161	272	3	X	1	18	P	X	X	X
Honduras	820	54	201	X	4	X	1	117-121	P	4	X	0
Jamaica	1,022	40	298	340	3	X	1	11-20	P	4	X	0
Mexico	9,330	442	2,851	X	6	7	3	525-1,420	P	37	X	3
Nicaragua	910	73	160	X	2-3	X	1	60	P	X	X	X
Panama	2,490	57	307	X	5	2	1	171-298	P	3	X	0
Trinidad and Tobago	362	29	77	487	5	2	1	8-9	P	1	650	0
United States {c}	19,924	1,871	9,711	X	5	17	3	190-281	P	183	X	0

	Length of Coastline (km)	Maritime Area (000 sq. km) Shelf to 200-Meter Depth	Maritime Area (000 sq. km) Exclusive Economic Zone	Total Number of Known Coastal Marine Species {a} Fish	Turtles	Mammals Total	Mammals Threatened	Marine Habitats (000 hectares) Mangroves	Coral Reefs	Marine Protected Areas Number	Area (hectares)	Regional Priority Sites {b} (number)
SOUTH AMERICA	X	X	X	X	X	X	X	X	X	41	X	10
Argentina	4,989	796	1,165	X	X	7	0	NP	NP	4	X	0
Brazil	7,491	769	3,168	X	5	4	1	250-1,012	P	15	1,665,552	5
Chile	6,435	27	2,288	X	1	11	2	NP	P	X	X	X
Colombia	2,414	68	603	X	5	2	1	358-501	P	8	192,606	1
Ecuador	2,237	47	1,159	419	3	3	0	162-182	P	4	16,070,101	3
Guyana	459	50	130	X	4	2	1	80-150	X	X	X	X
Peru	2,414	83	1,027	X	2	5	1	5-6	X	2	X	1
Suriname	386	X	101	X	5	2	1	115	X	X	X	X
Uruguay	660	57	119	X	X	4	0	X	X	X	X	X
Venezuela	2,800	88	364	X	3	2	1	250-674	P	8	619,561	0
ASIA	X	X	X	X	X	X	X	X	X	292	X	12
Azerbaijan	X	X	X	X	X	X	1	0	0	X	X	X
Bahrain	161	5	5	133	X	3	1	X	P	X	X	X
Bangladesh	580	55	77	X	3	4	1	410	NP	X	X	X
Brunei	161	X	X	X	3	1	1	7	NS	4	3,780	0
Cambodia	443	X	56	X	2	4	1	10	P	X	X	X
China	14,500	870	1,356	X	1	4	1	20	P	41	X	0
Georgia, Rep	310	X	X	X	X	X	X	NP	NP	X	X	X
India	12,700	452	2,015	X	5	4	1	357	P	11	276,042	4
Indonesia	54,716	2,777	5,409	X	5	4	1	4,251-4,254	P	30	3,739,353	2
Iran, Islamic Rep	3,180	107	156	X	2	4	2	24	P	1	160	0
Iraq	58	1	1	X	X	3	1	X	X	X	X	X
Israel	273	4	23	X	1-2	2	1	X	P	3	1,073	0
Japan	13,685	481	3,861	X	3	9	1	P	P	113	X	0
Jordan	26	X	1	X	X	X	1	X	P	X	X	X
Kazakhstan, Rep	2,909	X	X	X	X	X	1	NP	NP	X	X	X
Korea, Dem People's Rep	2,495	X	130	X	X	X	X	X	X	X	X	X
Korea, Rep	2,413	245	X	X	X	X	X	X	X	6	338,130	0
Kuwait	499	12	12	100	1-2	3	1	X	P	X	X	X
Lebanon	225	4	23	X	X	X	X	X	X	X	X	X
Malaysia	4,675	374	476	X	4	4	1	630-641	P	21	X	2
Myanmar	3,060	229	510	X	3	4	1	518	P	X	X	X
Oman	2,092	61	562	X	4	3	1	2	P	5	33,600	0
Pakistan	1,046	58	319	X	2	3	1	262-283	X	X	X	X
Philippines	22,540	178	1,786	~2,00	2	4	1	232-400	2,700	19	X	1
Qatar	563	24	24	X	1-2	X	X	P	P	X	X	X
Saudi Arabia	2,510	78	186	X	2	3	1	20	P	2	60,200	0
Singapore	193	0	0	292	X	3	1	1	P	1	87	0
Sri Lanka	1,340	27	517	X	5	3	1	9	P	4	X	0
Syrian Arab Rep	193	X	10	X	X	X	X	X	X	X	X	X
Thailand	3,219	258	86	X	3	4	1	196-269	P	15	486,028	2
Turkey	7,200	50	237	X	2	2	1	NP	NP	8	358,250	0
Turkmenistan, Rep	1,768	X	X	X	X	X	1	NP	NP	X	X	X
United Arab Emirates	1,448	59	59	X	X	3	1	3	P	X	X	X
Uzbekistan, Rep	420	X	X	X	X	X	X	X	X	X	X	X
Viet Nam	3,444	328	722	X	2	4	1	P	X	2	30,243	1
Yemen, Rep	1,906	25	584	X	2	2	1	P	P	X	X	X
OCEANIA	X	X	X	X	X	X	X	X	X	301	X	7
Australia	25,760	2,269	4,496	X	6	11	1	1,162	P	244	X	7
Fiji	1,129	2	1,135	407	4	X	X	39	P	X	X	X
Kiribati	1,143	X	X	X	2	X	X	P	P	1	32,100	0
New Zealand	15,134	243	4,833	X	X	6	2	20	P	14	X	0
Papua New Guinea	5,152	X	2,367	665	4-5	3	1	200	P	6	229,490	0
Solomon Islands	5,313	X	1,340	489	4	1	1	64	P	X	X	X

Sources: World Conservation Monitoring Centre, Great Barrier Reef Marine Park Authority, The World Bank, The World Conservation Union, United Nations Office for Ocean Affairs and the Law of the Sea, Food and Agriculture Organization of the United Nations, and other sources.

Notes: a. Includes fish recorded in coastal waters, nesting turtle species, and marine species restricted to coastal habitats. b. Regional priorities as defined by The Great Barrier Reef Marine Park Authority, The World Bank and the World Conservation Union. c. Species and habitat data for Hawaii are not included in United States totals. NS = not significant; P = present; NP = not present. World and regional totals include countries not listed. 0 = zero or less than half the unit of measure. X = not available. For additional information, see Sources and Technical Notes.

Sources and Technical Notes

Data Table 11.1
National and International Protection of Natural Areas, 1994

Source: Protected Areas Data Unit of the World Conservation Monitoring Centre (WCMC), unpublished data (WCMC, Cambridge, U.K., August 1995).

All protected areas combine natural areas in five World Conservation Union, formerly the International Union for Conservation of Nature and Natural Resources (IUCN), management categories (areas of at least 1,000 hectares). *Totally protected areas* are maintained in a natural state and are closed to extractive uses. They encompass the following three management categories:

Category I. Scientific reserves and strict nature reserves possess outstanding, representative ecosystems. Public access is generally limited, with only scientific research and educational use permitted.

Category II. National parks and provincial parks are relatively large areas of national or international significance not materially altered by humans. Visitors may use them for recreation and study.

Category III. Natural monuments and natural landmarks contain unique geological formations, special animals or plants, or unusual habitats.

Partially protected areas are areas that may be managed for specific uses, such as recreation or tourism, or areas that provide optimum conditions for certain species or communities of wildlife. Some extractive use within these areas is allowed. They encompass two management categories:

Category IV. Managed nature reserves and wildlife sanctuaries are protected for specific purposes, such as conservation of a significant plant or animal species.

Category V. Protected landscapes and seascapes may be entirely natural or may include cultural landscapes (e.g., scenically attractive agricultural areas).

Nationally protected areas listed in Data Table 11.1 do not include locally or provincially protected sites, or privately owned areas.

Protected areas at least 100,000 hectares and 1 million hectares in size refer to all IUCN category I–V protected areas that fall within these two classifications. The totals are for single sites, and it is likely that some sites are not contiguous blocks. These data do not account for agglomerations of protected areas that together might exceed 100,000 or 1 million hectares.

International protection systems usually include sites that are listed under national protection systems. *Biosphere reserves* are representative of terrestrial and coastal environments that have been internationally recognized under the Man and the Biosphere Programme of the United Nations Educational, Scientific, and Cultural Organization. They have been selected for their value to conservation and are intended to foster the scientific knowledge, skills, and human values necessary to support sustainable development. Each reserve must contain a diverse, natural ecosystem of a specific biogeographical province, large enough to be an effective conservation unit. For further details, refer to M. Udvardy, *A Classification of the Biogeographical Provinces of the World* (IUCN, Morges, Switzerland, 1975), and to *World Resources 1986,* Chapter 6. Each reserve also must include a minimally disturbed core area for conservation and research and may be surrounded by buffer zones where traditional land uses, experimental ecosystem research, and ecosystem rehabilitation may be permitted.

World heritage sites represent areas of "outstanding universal value" for their natural features, their cultural value, or for both natural and cultural values. The table includes only natural and mixed natural and cultural sites. Any party to the World Heritage Convention may nominate natural sites that contain examples of a major stage of Earth's evolutionary history; a significant ongoing geological process; a unique or superlative natural phenomenon, formation, or feature; or a habitat for a threatened species. Several countries share world heritage sites. These sites, referred to as international heritage sites, are counted only once in continental and world totals.

Any party to the Convention on Wetlands of International Importance Especially as Waterfowl Habitat (Ramsar, Iran, 1971) that agrees to respect a site's integrity and to establish wetland reserves can designate *wetlands of international importance.*

Data Table 11.2
Globally Threatened Species: Mammals, Birds, and Higher Plants, 1990s

Sources: World Conservation Monitoring Centre (WCMC), *Biodiversity Data Sourcebook,* (World Conservation Press, Cambridge, U.K., 1994); WCMC, *Global Biodiversity Status of the Earth's Living Resources* (Chapman and Hall, London, 1992),

and unpublished data (WCMC, Cambridge, U.K., July 1995).

The *total number of known species* may include introductions in some instances. Data on mammals exclude cetaceans (whales and porpoises), except where otherwise indicated. Threatened bird species are listed for countries included within their breeding or wintering ranges. Only flowering plants are listed under total *higher plants* species numbers.

The number of *endemic species* refers to those species known to be found only within the country listed. The number of total endemic plant species listed for each country includes flowering plants, ferns, and conifers and cycads.

Figures are not necessarily comparable among countries because taxonomic concepts and the extent of knowledge vary (for the latter reason, country totals of species and endemics may be underestimates). In general, numbers of mammals and birds are fairly well known, while plants have not been as well inventoried.

The World Conservation Union (IUCN) classifies threatened and endangered species into six categories:

Endangered. "Taxa in danger of extinction and whose survival is unlikely if the causal factors continue operating."

Vulnerable. "Taxa believed likely to move into the Endangered category in the near future if the causal factors continue operating."

Rare. "Taxa with world populations that are not at present Endangered or Vulnerable, but are at risk."

Indeterminate. "Taxa known to be Endangered, Vulnerable, or Rare but where there is not enough information to say which of the three categories is appropriate."

Out of Danger. "Taxa formerly included in one of the above categories, but which are now considered relatively secure because effective conservation measures have been taken or the previous threat to their survival has been removed."

Insufficiently Known. "Taxa that are suspected but not definitely known to belong to any of the above categories."

The number of *threatened species* listed for all countries includes full species that are endangered, vulnerable, rare, and indeterminate, but excludes introduced species, species whose status is insufficiently known, or those known to be extinct. Threatened species data for animals, presented in Data Tables 11.2 and 11.3, reflect estimates presented in the World Conservation Union (IUCN), *1994 IUCN Red List of Threatened Animals* (IUCN, Gland, 1993). Threatened species data for birds are based on a 1994 Birdlife International assessment, using a new threat assessment methodology. A version of this methodology is currently under review for adoption by IUCN.

Number of species per 10,000 square kilometers provides a relative estimate for comparing numbers of species among countries of differing size. Because the relationship between area and species number is nonlinear (i.e., as the area sampled increases, the number of new species located decreases), a species-area curve has been used to standardize these species numbers. The curve predicts how many species a country would have, given its current number of species, if it was a uniform 10,000 square kilometers in size. This number is calculated using the formula: $S = cA^z$, where S = the number of endangered species, A = area, and c and z are constants. The slope of the species-area curve is determined by the constant z, which is approximately 0.33 for large areas containing many habitats. This constant is based on data from previous studies of species-area relationships. In reality, the constant z would differ among regions and countries, because of differences in species' range size (which tend to be smaller in the tropics) and differences in varieties of habitats present. A tropical country with a broad variety of habitats would be expected to have a steeper species-area curve than a temperate, homogenous country because one would predict a greater number of both species and threatened species per unit area. Species-area curves are also steeper for islands than for mainland countries. At present, there are insufficient regional data to estimate separate slopes for each country.

Data Table 11.3
Globally Threatened Species: Reptiles, Amphibians, and Fish, 1990s

Sources: World Conservation Monitoring Centre (WCMC), *Biodiversity Data Sourcebook* (World Conservation Press, Cambridge, U.K., 1994); WCMC, *Global Biodiversity Status of the Earth's Living Resources* (Chapman and Hall, London, 1992), and unpublished data (WCMC, Cambridge, U.K., July 1995 and January 1996).

For definitions of *total species*, *endemic species*, and *threatened species*, refer to the Technical Notes for Data Table 11.2. Threatened marine turtles and marine fish are excluded from country totals. Endangered fish species numbers do not include approximately 250 haplochromine and 2 tilapiine species of Lake Victoria cichlids, since the ranges of these species are undetermined.

The number of species per 10,000 square kilometers provides a relative estimate for

comparing numbers of species among countries of differing size. For details, refer to the Technical Notes for Data Table 11.2.

Data Table 11.4
Marine Biodiversity

Sources: Length of marine coastline: United Nations Office for Ocean Affairs and the Law of the Sea, unpublished data (United Nations, New York, June 1989); U.S. Central Intelligence Agency, *The World Factbook 1994* (U.S. Government Printing Office, Washington, D.C., 1994). Shelf area to 200-meter depth: John P. Albers, M. Devereux Carter, Allen L. Clark *et al.*, *Summary Petroleum and Selected Mineral Statistics for 120 Countries, Including Offshore Areas*, Geological Survey Professional Paper 817 (U.S. Government Printing Office, Washington, D.C., 1973). Exclusive economic zone: United Nations Office for Ocean Affairs and the Law of the Sea, unpublished data (United Nations, New York, June 1989). French Polynesia and New Caledonia: Anthony Bergin, "Fisheries Surveillance in the South Pacific," *Ocean & Shoreline Management*, Vol. 11 (1988), p. 468. Marine species data: World Conservation Monitoring Centre, *Biodiversity Data Sourcebook* (World Conservation Press, Cambridge, U.K., 1994); Thomas Jefferson, Stephen Leatherwood, and Marc Webber, *Marine Mammals of the World* (United Nations Environment Programme and Food and Agriculture Organization of the United Nations, Rome, 1993). Marine protected areas: Great Barrier Reef Marine Park Authority, unpublished data (Canberra, Australia, 1995); Graeme Kelleher, Chris Bleakley, and Sue Wells, eds., *A Global Representative System of Marine Protected Areas*, Vol. I, (The Great Barrier Reef Marine Park Authority, The World Bank, and the World Conservation Union (IUCN), Washington, D.C., 1995).

The United Nations Office for Ocean Affairs and the Law of the Sea compiles information concerning coastal claims from the following sources: the United Nations Legislative Series, official gazettes, communications to the Secretary General, legal journals, and other publications. National claims to maritime zones fall into five categories: territorial sea, contiguous zone, exclusive economic zone (EEZ), exclusive fishing zone, and continental shelf. The extent of the continental *shelf to 200-meter depth* and the *exclusive economic zone* for those countries with marine coastline are presented in the table. Only the potential and not the actual established area of the EEZ is shown.

Under currently recognized international principles, an EEZ may be established by a nation out to 200 nautical miles to claim all

the resources within the zone, including fish and all other living resources; minerals; and energy from wind, waves, and tides. Nations may also claim rights to regulate scientific exploration, protect the marine environment, and establish marine terminals and artificial islands. The EEZ data shown do not reflect the decisions of some countries, such as those in the European Community, to collectively manage fishing zones on EEZs in some areas. When countries' EEZs overlap—such as those of the United States and Cuba, which both have 200-mile EEZs, yet are only 90 miles apart—they must agree on a maritime boundary between them, often a halfway point.

Total number of known coastal marine species includes *fish* recorded within coastal waters, *turtles*—loggerhead, green turtle, leatherback, hawksbill turtle, Kemp's ridley, and olive ridley—recorded to nest along national shorelines; and several categories of *mammal* species: cetaceans (whales, porpoises, and dolphins) restricted to nearshore waters, seals, sea lions, dugongs, manatees, otters, and polar bears.

Threatened coastal marine mammal species includes full species that are listed by the World Conservation Union as endangered, vulnerable, and rare, and those whose status is classified as indeterminate. It excludes species whose status is insufficiently known, and species known to be extinct. For details of these threatened classifications, refer to the Technical Notes to Data Table 11.2. Total and threatened mammal species data do not include a large number of cetacean species that range outside of nearshore waters.

Only two types of *marine habitats* are listed within Data Table 11.4: *mangroves* and *coral reefs*. Information on mangrove and coral reef extent was culled by WCMC from numerous sources; therefore country totals are not comparable as data are for various years, and data quality varies.

Marine protected areas (MPAs) list nationally protected areas with a sub-tidal component. Total area listed may include terrestrial portions of MPA sites. A number of these sites are also internationally protected areas (Ramsar sites, biosphere reserves, and world heritage sites). For further details on protected area classification, refer to the Technical Notes to Data Table 11.1. National and regional totals include all MPAs for which geographic (last/long) coordinates are available. Global totals also include 17 sites in Antarctica, and 16 sites for which geographic coordinates were not available.

MPA data come from a global assessment conducted by the World Bank, IUCN, and The Great Barrier Reef Marine Park Authority of existing protected areas, and priorities for future protection. *Regional priority sites* were selected according to eight criteria: i) biogeographic representativeness (the degree to which sites offer protection to ecosystem types otherwise underrepresented within the global marine protected area network); ii) ecological criteria that relate to size, integrity, and conservation importance; iii) natural-ness; iv) economic importance (e.g., nursery areas for economically important species); v) social importance, such as sites of cultural, historical and educational value; vi) scientific importance; vii) international or national significance (e.g., potential to be listed as a biosphere reserve); and viii) the degree to which it is practical or feasible to create or maintain a protected area within the site, given existing pressures and management and sociopolitical constraints. Proposed regional priority sites are excluded from data presented in this table.

12. Energy and Materials

The growing industrialization of many developing countries is reflected in their rapidly rising consumption of energy. These trends, in turn, are reflected in rising global energy use. Producing additional supplies of energy to meet growing demand, however, often leads to other problems in developing countries. These include raising the huge sums required to finance capital-intensive energy production facilities without diverting capital from other critical development needs, as well as coping with increased levels of pollution and other energy-related environmental degradation.

Policy measures to address these problems are well known, if not always easy to implement. Privatization of energy systems, for example, is one way in which countries are increasingly dealing with the problem of financing. Encouraging more efficient use of energy—by eliminating energy subsidies, for example, and encouraging the development of a more energy-efficient infrastructure—can reduce both the amount of financing required and the pollution generated. Taxing pollution and helping to facilitate use of the best available technologies—in energy-driven equipment such as automobiles and steel mills as well as in energy production facilities such as power plants—can help reduce local and regional environmental burdens. Far more could be done with such policies to reduce energy-related problems in both developed and developing countries. The problem is not in not knowing what to do; rather, it is in finding the necessary political will and creating the required administrative capacity. Given the rate at which the level of energy production is rising, such policies deserve far greater attention.

Even with enlightened policies, however, energy consumption in developing countries—and hence for the world as a whole—is likely to rise significantly in coming decades. That is the conclusion of three different investigations into future energy demand. Moreover, most of the expanded production will come from fossil energy sources—coal, oil, and natural gas. These projections, if they hold true, imply that global emissions of greenhouse gases will also increase significantly, greatly increasing the risk and potential impact of climate change. Ultimately, a transition to nonfossil energy sources—of which renewable energy sources such as wind and solar energy appear to have the best long-range prospects—will be required to eliminate such risks.

This chapter surveys current energy trends, examines studies of future energy demand and the potential for future energy supplies from renewable sources, and considers potential constraints, both environmental and geological, to future energy supplies. Chapter 14, "Atmosphere and Climate," considers the global environmental consequences of the present and future trends discussed here.

ENERGY PRODUCTION AND CONSUMPTION

The long upward trend in global commercial energy production and consumption continued through 1993, the most recent year for which data are available. Global energy production in 1993 reached 338 exajoules (1 exajoule equals 10^{18} joules, or about 163 million barrels of oil)—40 percent greater than that in 1973. (See Data Table 12.1.) Total energy consumption rose to 326 exajoules, fully 49 percent greater than that 20 years earlier. (See Figure 12.1 and Data Table 12.2.)

Figure 12.1 Total Energy Consumption, 1973–93

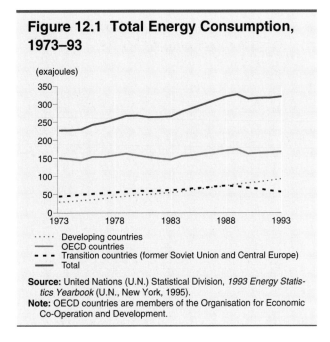

(exajoules)

····· Developing countries
—— OECD countries
- - - Transition countries (former Soviet Union and Central Europe)
—— Total

Source: United Nations (U.N.) Statistical Division, *1993 Energy Statistics Yearbook* (U.N., New York, 1995).
Note: OECD countries are members of the Organisation for Economic Co-Operation and Development.

Figure 12.2 Share of Energy Consumption and Production, 1993

A. Consumption

B. Production

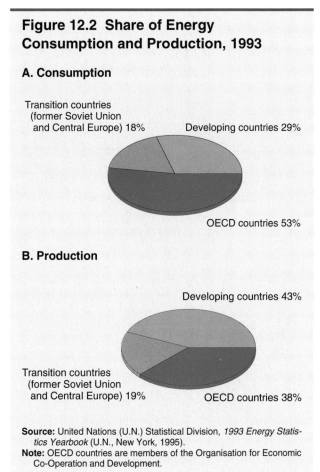

Source: United Nations (U.N.) Statistical Division, *1993 Energy Statistics Yearbook* (U.N., New York, 1995).
Note: OECD countries are members of the Organisation for Economic Co-Operation and Development.

The patterns of energy consumption and production, however, show strong national and regional differences. (See Figures 12.2 and 12.3.) These include the following:

• The countries of the Organisation for Economic Co-Operation and Development (OECD) (1) consumed more than half of all commercial energy in 1993 but produced only slightly more than one third of all commercial energy. These figures emphasize the fact that many developed countries are still heavily dependent on imported energy supplies to fuel their economies. Energy consumption in OECD countries has grown about 30 percent over the past 20 years (2).

• Energy consumption also grew substantially over most of the past two decades in the transition economies, but it has declined recently with the economic disruptions there (3). From 1989 to 1992, energy consumption dropped 17 percent in the former Soviet Union and Central Europe (4), and energy demand in these countries is less than one fifth of global demand.

• Energy consumption in developing countries, on the other hand, has grown rapidly and consistently since 1973, but from a much smaller base than that in the developed world. Although their consumption has increased almost threefold since 1973, developing countries still accounted for less than one third of world energy consumption in 1993, even though they contain the predominant share of the world's population.

Consumption within the developing world varies greatly by region. Asia (excluding Japan), for example,

consumes 60 percent of all energy in the developing world and has accounted for a good deal of the expansion of energy demand in developing countries over the past two decades because of the robust economic growth in nations such as China, India, Korea, Thailand, Taiwan, and Indonesia. Although Africa, the Middle East, and Latin America consume proportionately less energy, growth in energy demand in these regions over the past 20 years has also been very high. The Latin American region, for example, has more than doubled its energy use since 1970, despite the burden of a huge foreign debt. Africa has nearly tripled its consumption since 1970, but energy use in Africa still accounts for only 11 percent of all energy use in the developing world (5). (See Data Table 12.2.)

Even though total energy use has increased greatly in the developing world, rapid population increases have kept per capita energy use in developing nations very low compared with that in the developed world. In many developing nations, much of the increase in energy use has been absorbed in trying to meet the basic needs of industry and to provide minimum services to an expanding populace. Thus, there has been only a modest increase in the quality of energy services (e.g., providing better heating, refrigeration, lighting, and transportation). Although per capita use varies widely from nation to nation, on average, energy use per person is still more than nine times greater in developed countries than in developing countries.

ENERGY RESOURCES

Estimates of world energy reserves have increased significantly over the past 20 years, despite rising levels of consumption. Proved recoverable reserves of petroleum rose 60 percent between 1973 and 1993; those of natural gas rose more than 140 percent (6). If energy consumption were to remain constant at current levels, proved reserves (7) would supply world petroleum needs for 40 years, natural gas needs for 60 years, and coal needs for well over 200 years (8).

Petroleum

Petroleum reserves are of particular importance, given the central role that petroleum plays in world energy supplies and world energy markets. Liquid fuels—primarily petroleum—continue to dominate world commercial energy production, providing 40 percent of the world's commercial energy—some 22 billion barrels per year. Oil dependence varies widely among countries, from nearly 100 percent in several African countries (e.g., Burkina Faso, The Gambia, Senegal, and Sierra Leone) to 35 percent in Canada and 17 percent in China. Oil dominates the international trade in energy because of its ready portability.

Estimates of global petroleum reserves have increased over the past decade (up 43 percent between 1984 and 1994), primarily due to major reevaluations of oil reserves in 1987 and 1989 in the Middle East, where more than 65 percent of the world's oil resources are located (9) (10). Since 1989, however, new discoveries, additions, and revisions have broadly matched the world's production, leaving total reserves basically unchanged (11). (See Box 12.1, Figure 1.) Regionally, however, reserves have been declining in many important energy-consuming nations. For instance, reserves in the former Soviet Union declined by 10 percent between 1984 and 1994 (12) (13). Indeed, the Russian Federation's high-yield oil deposits are 60 to 90 percent depleted, a situation that has contributed to recent cuts in production there (14). In the United States, reserves declined 14 percent between 1984 and 1994 (15).

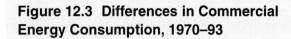

Figure 12.3 Differences in Commercial Energy Consumption, 1970–93

A. OECD Countries

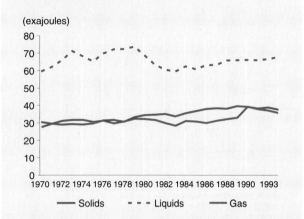

B. Eastern Europe and the Former Soviet Union

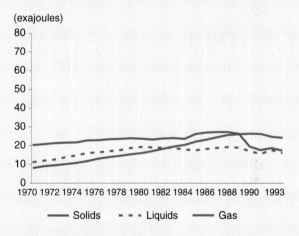

C. All Developing Countries

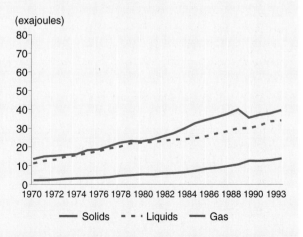

Source: United Nations Statistical Division (UNSTAT), *1993 Energy Statistics Yearbook* (UNSTAT, New York, 1995).

Box 12.1 Petroleum Resources: When Will Production Peak?

Studies of future energy demand, such as those reported in this chapter, are primarily based on economic factors; they do not assume specific physical limits to energy supplies. In contrast, studies of energy resources incorporate both geological and economic factors, and they yield a different perspective.

At present, there is little near-term concern over petroleum supplies; production capacity is ample, and, consequently, oil prices are relatively low. The world's petroleum resources are finite, however, and global production will eventually peak and then start to decline. Just how large total resources will prove to be is unknown, in part because higher oil prices can stimulate further exploration and make feasible the recovery of now marginal deposits. As a result, there is vigorous debate among petroleum geologists, energy economists, oil companies, and other interested parties about the extent of the total resource and, more important, when production might peak.

To further complicate such assessments, the bulk of the world's petroleum resources are heavily concentrated in a few countries, most of which are located in politically unstable regions. (See Figure 1.) Events that could cause short-term interruptions in petroleum supplies cannot be ruled out. A more gradual impact on the world's oil supply might come from underinvestment in production facilities in key oil-producing countries, particularly when petroleum production decisions reflect national policy and not just the demands of the market. New wells, pipe-

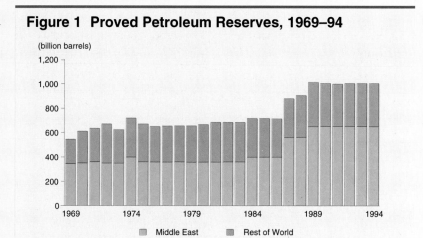

Figure 1 Proved Petroleum Reserves, 1969–94

(billion barrels)

Middle East   Rest of World

Source: British Petroleum (BP), *Statistical Review of World Energy* (BP, London, June 1995), p. 3.
Note: Increases in reserves in 1987 and 1989 were the result of revisions in a few countries, not new discoveries.

lines, and tanker platforms require massive amounts of capital, for which most major oil-exporting countries have other competing demands. The result could be that global oil production capacity would fail to keep up with rising demand.

RESOURCE ESTIMATES

Petroleum geologists estimate minimum and maximum bounds on the amount of oil that will ultimately be produced in a region. Such estimates are based on seismic data, a knowledge of the kinds of basins where oil was originally formed, exploratory drilling, the limits of recovery technology, and, of course, an expected range of oil prices. Given

such estimates, geologists assert, the production history for a region will usually follow a predictable profile, rising until approximately half of the estimated recoverable resource has been produced and then peaking and beginning a decline. U.S. oil production has followed precisely such a pattern, closely resembling some predictions based on geological analysis. Geologists from Petroconsultants S.A., a consulting firm in Geneva, Switzerland, that deals with the collection and analysis of global petroleum data, argue that world oil production will follow a similar pattern.

Petroconsultants has produced a depletion model based on its worldwide

Solid Fuel

Solid fuels (e.g., coal, lignite, and peat) are in relatively abundant supply and are an important component of the world energy mix, making up 27 percent of global commercial energy production. Most solid fuel is consumed in the country where it is produced because of the expense of transport. In China and India, solid fuels dominate the energy mix, accounting for about three quarters of commercial energy production in both countries. Given the rapid economic expansion under way in both countries and their considerable indigenous supplies of coal, consumption of coal is expected to grow particularly rapidly in Asia in the next few decades (16).

Natural Gas

Currently, natural gas is the fossil fuel experiencing the fastest growth in consumption. Natural gas now supplies 23 percent of global commercial energy, and production has risen more than 70 percent in the past 20 years. Even though estimates of global natural gas reserves have been increasing rapidly, there is still less natural gas than petroleum in proved reserves. Russia holds the largest natural gas reserves with 48,160 billion cubic meters in 1993. This represents about one third of the world total and is more than ten times that of natural gas reserves in the United States. Ample reserves are also found in the Middle East. (See Data Table 12.3.)

database. It considers four scenarios of demand and price, with the base case showing a plateau of peak production between 1998 and 2002, followed by a decline (1). More conventional estimates suggest that global production will not peak for another decade or two, somewhere between 2010 and 2025 (2) (3) (4).

Petroconsultants' conclusion depends on two assumptions. First, they assume that government estimates of current reserves, especially in the Middle East, are exaggerated and may include reserves that are neither economically nor technically viable. Second, they believe that most large oil fields have been discovered (5) (6). Petroconsultants' geologists also assert that neither oil prices nor improved technology will influence petroleum exploration and discovery as much as economists suggest. The discoveries of major oil fields in Alaska and the North Sea, for example, were made when prices were relatively low. Oil prices now are relatively high compared with the costs of producing conventional oil, but no new major oil fields have been discovered in recent years (7). Furthermore, the main impact of technology is to accelerate depletion—for example, it would make possible the exploitation of deposits in deeper offshore waters but would add only minor new reserves. Technologies for higher levels of extraction already exist, and higher prices will make them more widely used (8).

In contrast, energy economists generally argue that resource estimates and predictions such as those of Petroconsultants have been made all too frequently in the past, only to be proved wrong. Forecasts of when the "peak" will occur have been continually revised farther into the future (9). In the 1940s, for example, recoverable crude oil resources were estimated at about 600 billion barrels. Today, estimates range as high as 2,300 billion barrels (10). Historically, higher oil prices have led to new oil discoveries and higher levels of production—for example, following the 1973 oil embargo there was an increase in production by countries that were not members of the Organization of Petroleum Exporting Countries.

When the production of oil—which accounts for 40 percent of the world's energy supply—does peak, it does not mean that the world will soon "run out" of petroleum-based fuels. Oil production would continue, although at a declining rate, for many decades after a peak. Other fuels would fill the gap—for example, natural gas or the large reserves of coal, heavy oils, and bitumen that could be used to produce liquid or gaseous substitutes for crude oil (11). The inability of the world's oil producers to supply all of the oil that the market demands, however, would be expected to lead to significant increases in petroleum prices and perhaps in energy prices in general. This development could have significant effects on transportation systems, now largely dependent on oil-based fuels, and might also mean that industrialization in developing countries would take place in an era of expensive energy—in contrast to the generally low energy prices throughout most of the 20th Century.

Such potential consequences explain the interest in—and the intensity of the debate over—when global petroleum production will reach its peak.

References and Notes

1. C.J. Campbell, Independent Petroleum Consultant, Gourdon, France, April 1995 (personal communication).

2. World Energy Council (WEC), *Survey of Energy Resources, 1995* (WEC, London, 1995), pp. 47–50.

3. Energy Information Administration, U.S. Department of Energy, *International Energy Outlook, 1995,* Report No. DOE/EIA-0484(95) (U.S. Government Printing Office, Washington, D.C., 1995), pp. 27–31.

4. C.D. Masters, D.H. Root, and E.D. Attanasi, "Resource Constraints in Petroleum Production Potential," *Science,* Vol. 253, No. 5016 (July 12, 1991), p. 146.

5. C.J. Campbell, "The Depletion of the World's Oil," *Pétrole et Techniques,* No. 383 (October 1993), pp. 5–12.

6. Jean Laherrere, "World Oil Reserves—Which Number to Believe?," *OPEC Bulletin* (February 1995), pp. 9–13.

7. C.J. Campbell, "The Next Oil Price Shock: The World's Remaining Oil and Its Depletion," *Energy Exploration and Exploitation,* Vol. 13, No. 1 (1995), pp. 19–44.

8. L.F. Ivanhoe, "Future World Oil Supplies: There Is a Finite Limit," *World Oil* (October 1995), p. 78.

9. Michael C. Lynch, "Limitations in Forecasting Petroleum Supply," *Geopolitics of Energy* (June 1, 1995), p. 5.

10. *Op. cit.* 7, pp. 23–24.

11. *Op. cit.* 4, p. 151.

Other Energy Sources

Large-scale hydroelectric plants and nuclear power plants are the most important sources of primary electricity—the electricity generated from sources other than fossil-fuel-burning plants. In 1993, primary electricity accounted for just over 10 percent of total commercial energy consumption. Nuclear power provided most of this energy (70 percent); this was followed by hydropower (25 percent). All other sources, including geothermal, wind, and solar energy, supplied about 5 percent of primary electricity.

The present energy-generating capacity of nuclear power is expected to increase slightly between 1995 and 2010 as existing and planned construction comes to completion (17). At current consumption rates, there is about a 41-year supply of uranium reserves to fuel these reactors (18). Proved reserves of uranium have declined in recent years, primarily because of mine closures after an excess supply caused uranium prices to collapse (19).

FUTURE ENERGY DEMAND

Over the years, energy demand has increased in concert with growth in the global economy and the world population. For instance, during the past 50 years, the global economy increased fivefold, the world population doubled, and world energy use tripled. Will these trends continue over the next 50 years?

Anticipating how much energy demand is likely to rise over the coming decades and how that demand is likely to be met—through what combination of oil, gas, coal, nuclear power, or renewable resources—is critical to both government planners and private enterprise. Developing energy policies (government subsidies or energy taxes, for example), determining priorities for energy-related research and development, and gauging the potential for climate change from the buildup of greenhouse gases all require realistic appraisals of possible future energy demand.

Not surprisingly, several different national and international institutions have ongoing efforts to project future energy use. This section reports on modeling efforts by the World Energy Council (WEC), the International Energy Agency (IEA), and the U.S. Department of Energy's (DOE's) Energy Information Administration. By incorporating plausible assumptions about the key determinants of energy supply and demand—for instance, future population growth, future economic growth, changes in energy efficiency, innovations in technology, the sizes of known fuel reserves, and energy pricing—they have attempted to model the magnitude and direction of the change ahead. However, none of these institutions claims to accurately foresee the future; consequently, the scenarios they have constructed should not be taken too literally. (See Box 12.2.)

In their reference scenarios, which use current consumption trends as a basis for future projections, all three organizations predict a substantial increase in energy use over the next 20 to 30 years, even though their scenarios incorporate slightly different assumptions about economic growth and changes in energy efficiency. In WEC's reference case, demand rises more than 50 percent by 2020. IEA and DOE projections, which span a shorter period, show a 34 to 44 percent rise in demand by 2010.

All three models show much of the growth in demand occurring in Asia and Latin America [20]. For example, IEA and DOE projections show at least a doubling of energy use in Asia from 1990 to 2010 and a 50 to 77 percent rise in consumption in Latin America during the same period [21] [22]. The huge increases in energy use in Asia can be attributed in large part to an expected continuation of the current surge of economic growth in India, China, and Southeast Asia. In fact, some observers believe that energy demand in Asia may outstrip even these projected high growth rates [23].

In any case, all three projections foresee that the proportion of the world's energy consumed by the

OECD countries—which has traditionally accounted for a greater share of world energy consumption—will continue to decline as developing nations rapidly expand their energy sectors in the coming decades. In 1970, energy consumption in non-OECD countries represented only one third of world energy consumption, but by 2010 it is expected to account for roughly half of world energy consumption [24] [25].

The modelers expect increases in the production of all forms of energy to meet the increased energy demand that their projections show. Petroleum is expected to remain the dominant energy source over the next three to four decades; this is followed by coal, gas, renewable energy sources, and nuclear power. Natural gas and renewable sources of energy are expected to take a growing share of the energy mix at the expense of petroleum and, in most circumstances, coal. The exact mix of energy sources varies considerably among the different scenarios and also depends on whether governments are assumed to more vigorously support policies that promote energy efficiency and the use of renewable fuels. (See Box 12.2.) In any case, fossil fuels continue to supply at least three quarters of the energy consumed in all of the scenarios, even the most optimistic ones [26] [27] [28].

Future Energy Supplies from Renewable Sources

Most projections of future energy supplies predict that renewable sources will play a small but increasing role in the total energy supply over the next 30 years. Many advocates, however, claim that renewable sources could realistically supply a larger share of world energy needs under the right circumstances.

The use of renewable energy sources is not new. Traditional (noncommercial) biomass fuels—such as fuelwood, charcoal, dung, or straw—already supply more than 10 percent of total global energy needs and a much higher percentage of energy needs in developing nations, albeit with low levels of efficiency and service quality [29].

Large hydropower facilities are also well-established sources of renewable energy, contributing almost 6 percent of world energy in 1990 [30]. The potential for further development of the world's hydroelectric capacity remains high—at least theoretically—especially in China, Brazil, and the former Soviet Union [31]. China, for example, has a known exploitable potential of more than 2 million megawatts, but in 1993 it had an installed capacity of only 60,000 megawatts. (See Data Table 12.3.) Opposition to building large dams, however, is increasing on environmental and social grounds, as witnessed by the long-standing controversy over China's planned Three Gorges Project.

In the long term, the renewable sources with the largest potential for expansion are the so-called new renewables, such as wind energy, geothermal energy, plantation- or farm-grown energy crops, and several forms of solar energy, particularly solar electricity from photovoltaic cells (32). Today, these and other nontraditional forms of renewable energy contribute less than 2 percent of global energy supplies, and their growth will likely be modest without significant efforts to promote them. A detailed study by WEC projects that they will contribute only about 4 percent of global energy supplies by the year 2020 if current policies continue (33).

However, WEC projects that under an "ecologically driven" scenario, which assumes vigorous energy conservation measures and deliberate economic and regulatory incentives to accelerate the penetration of renewable energy sources, these new technologies could contribute as much as 12 percent of global energy by 2020 (34). At present, though, neither public nor private entities are making the investments required for a significant renewable energy future. Even if such investments are forthcoming, experts warn that fossil fuels will still dominate energy markets for years to come. A 21st Century energy supply dominated by fossil fuels has profound implications for future emissions of greenhouse gases and hence for the potential for significant climate change. (See Chapter 14, "Atmosphere and Climate.")

CONSTRAINTS TO ENERGY CONSUMPTION

As the scenarios discussed above suggest, there is a good deal of momentum behind the current and projected growth in global energy demand, particularly in the developing world. Global development necessarily involves expansion of basic infrastructure such as transport systems, housing, and industrial facilities—all significant consumers of energy. Progressively rapid growth in world population is a second and equally fundamental factor driving global energy demand higher.

From the standpoint of available energy supplies, meeting this burgeoning demand seems quite feasible, at least for the next few decades. Substantial global reserves exist for all conventional commercial fuels, although there is some dispute on the availability of oil and, to a lesser extent, natural gas. (See Box 12.1.) Also,

world energy markets are well developed and relatively flexible, and substitutes are available should shortages develop for one fuel or another. Although energy prices are expected to rise gradually, they are not expected to create a major obstacle to increased energy use.

Environmental Costs

Other constraints to the continued expansion of energy consumption do exist, however. Chief among them are the environmental costs of continued reliance on fossil fuels and, to a lesser extent, nuclear fuel. Increased production and use of fossil fuels, especially coal, the most plentiful fossil fuel, could have severe local and regional impacts. Locally, air pollution already takes a significant toll on human health. Acid precipitation and other forms of air pollution can also degrade downwind habitats—especially lakes, streams, and forests—and can damage crops, buildings, and other materials. For example, one recent study warns that, in the absence of sulfur abatement measures, acid depositions in parts of China and South Asia could eventually exceed the critical load for major agricultural crops by a factor of 10 (35).

Without the use of the best available technology and practices, mining leads to land degradation and water pollution, as does the disposal of hazardous coal ash. On a global level, increased burning of fossil fuels will mean an accompanying rise in greenhouse gas emissions, along with the potential adverse impacts of global warming and other climate changes. (See Chapter 14, "Atmosphere and Climate.") Nuclear fuel, too, has obvious environmental costs associated with its production and disposal, although nuclear power produces virtually none of the air pollution and carbon dioxide discharges of fossil fuels.

Lack of Investment Capital

In addition to environmental constraints, shortages of investment capital to build energy production and distribution facilities—from drilling platforms, refineries, and pipelines to power plants, transmission lines, coal-carrying railroads, and dams—may act to restrain global energy consumption, especially in developing nations. The price tag for the energy infrastructure required to meet the development goals of developing countries is estimated in the trillions of dollars over the next two decades—a sum far higher than present investment levels can finance (36).

Already, energy-related investments account for a substantial fraction of the total public investment in the developing world—as much as 40 percent in many nations (37). Continued energy growth and its accompa-

Box 12.2 Projecting Future Energy Use

Projections of energy consumption over the next few decades were reported recently by three organizations: the World Energy Council (WEC), the International Energy Agency (IEA), and the U.S. Department of Energy (DOE).

In making their future energy projections, WEC, IEA, and DOE all used the same projections of population growth, but slightly different assumptions about economic growth and improvements in energy efficiency (as measured by energy intensity—that is, energy used per dollar of gross domestic product). Their choice of geographic units for analysis varied somewhat as well. Small differences in these assumptions can make large differences in both regional and global projections. (See Table 1.)

WORLD ENERGY COUNCIL
SCENARIOS

WEC, an international institution with the goal of promoting the sustainable supply and use of energy, has developed

four energy scenarios that look at energy use to 2020 (1). Because WEC used the input of thousands of energy practitioners, it can be considered a consensus view on many important energy issues.

WEC's *Reference* case assumes a moderate economic growth rate. It assumes substantially increased supplies of natural gas, oil, and coal, with China producing the bulk of the increased coal supply. The Reference case also assumes a slow expansion of nuclear power and "new" renewable energy sources (i.e., solar, wind, nontraditional biomass, and geothermal). Progress in improving energy planning and pricing is presumed to be good. WEC also presumes that know-how and technology are transferred relatively quickly among nations and that improvements in energy efficiency are at a relatively high level (2).

This Reference scenario results in a 54 percent rise in energy use from 1990 levels by 2020, with developing nations ac-

counting for more than four fifths of this additional energy use (3).

In WEC's *Modified Reference* case, the rate of improvement in energy efficiency is assumed to be somewhat slower than that in the Reference case (4). As a result, energy use in 2020 climbs 84 percent over 1990 levels, and carbon dioxide emissions rise 73 percent, showing how crucial a global effort to increase energy efficiency is to keeping energy demand and greenhouse gas emissions down.

WEC also developed a *High Growth* case, which assumes an economic growth rate in developing countries higher than that in the Reference case (5). Energy use in the High Growth scenario rises 98 percent during the period 1990–2020, and carbon dioxide emissions nearly double as well, demonstrating the close relationship between robust economic development and increased energy demand and carbon dioxide emissions, at least as national energy sectors are currently configured.

Table 1 Projections of Energy Consumption

	World Energy Council Scenarios				International Energy Agency Scenarios		U.S. Department of Energy Reference Scenario
	High Growth	Modified Reference	Reference	Ecologically Driven	Capacity Constraints	Energy Savings	
Projection period	1990–2020	1990–2020	1990–2020	1990–2020	1992–2010	1992–2010	1990–2010
Economic growth, percent per year	High	Moderate	Moderate	Moderate	Moderate	Moderate	Moderate
OECD countries	2.4	2.4	2.4	2.4	2.5	2.5	2.3
Former Soviet Union and Central Europe	2.4	2.4	2.4	2.4	2.1	2.1	0.6
Developing countries	5.6	4.6	4.6	4.6	5.3	5.3	2.8–6.1[a]
World	3.8	3.3	3.3	3.3	3.1	3.1	2.7
Percent increase in world energy demand over projection period	98	84	54	30	44	34	36[b]
Percent increase in annual carbon dioxide emissions over 1990 levels	93	73	42	5	42	30	35[c]

Sources: 1. World Energy Council, *Energy for Tomorrow's World: The Realities, the Real Options, and the Agenda for Achievement* (Kogan Page, London, and St. Martin's Press, New York, 1993), p. 76. 2. International Energy Agency, *World Energy Outlook, 1995* (Organisation for Economic Co-Operation and Development, Paris, 1995), pp. 11–18; Table A2, p. 298; Table A5, p. 301; Table A20, p. 321. 3. Energy Information Administration, U.S. Department of Energy, *International Energy Outlook, 1995,* Report No. DOE/EIA-0484(95) (U.S. Government Printing Office, Washington, D.C., 1995), Table 2, p. 7; Table A1, p. 79; Table A9, p. 87.

Notes:

a. Varies by region: Africa, 2.8 percent; Latin America, 3.7 percent; Middle East, 3.9 percent; Asia, 6.1 percent.

b. Range = 22 to 52 percent.

c. Range = 26 to 47 percent.

Finally, WEC developed an *Ecologically Driven* case that examines a world with limited increases in energy demand and the widespread use of the best energy technologies. This scenario was developed to illustrate the far-reaching and immediate actions that are required if annual carbon dioxide emissions by 2020 are to be roughly stabilized at their 1990 levels.

In this Ecologically Driven scenario, WEC makes the same assumptions about economic and population growth as it does for its Reference case, but it assumes very high annual improvements in energy efficiency, a massive transfer of energy-efficient technology to those nations without it, and, consequently, a very low increase in energy demand among developing countries over the next 30 years. In addition, this scenario presumes an accelerated switch to natural gas and renewable energy sources. As a result, total energy use rises only 30 percent between 1990 and 2020 in this scenario. Because of the greater penetration of gas and renewable energy sources in the energy supply, carbon dioxide emissions rise only 5 percent from 1990 levels. WEC stresses that the implementation of such a scenario would require major and unprecedented changes in energy use and energy policy (6).

INTERNATIONAL ENERGY AGENCY SCENARIOS

IEA, a sister organization to the Organisation for Economic Co-Operation and Development (OECD), developed two scenarios that project energy demand to 2010. One is a *Capacity Constraints* case, in which current trends continue to dominate future energy consumption patterns and increasing oil demand strains the world's oil-producing capacity. The second is an *Energy Savings* case that assumes the adoption of a high level of energy-efficiency improvements and energy conservation measures (7).

In IEA's reference scenario (the Capacity Constraints case), the underlying assumptions are that past patterns of consumption will continue, that total energy demand will grow faster than production, and that demand will not be able to be met at current prices. Indeed, the balance of production in this scenario shifts increasingly toward a small number of countries that produce oil at low cost (8). The results of the Capacity Constraints scenario show a 44 percent rise in world energy use from 1992 to 2010 and a concomitant 42 percent rise in carbon dioxide emissions over their 1990 levels.

In its Energy Savings case, IEA examines the issues that would arise if additional energy efficiency improvements were imposed on consumers. Under this case, IEA, like WEC, assumes the same economic and population growth projections that it uses in its Capacity Constraints case. However, it assumes greater improvements in energy efficiencies in most economic sectors (industry, transport, buildings, and agriculture), increased use of renewable energy sources, and generally lower energy prices. These improvements are assumed to occur through the adoption of new consumer behaviors at rapid rates. The Energy Savings case does not rely on new technologies to achieve greater energy efficiency but uses existing, cost-effective technologies (9).

Global energy use rises 34 percent in the Energy Savings scenario and emissions rise about 30 percent, demonstrating the difficulty of cutting energy demand and emissions in the face of global development, even when consumers are cooperative in adopting the best available technologies. In this scenario, energy consumption by OECD countries would fall to less than one quarter of the world's total consumption (10).

U.S. DEPARTMENT OF ENERGY SCENARIO

DOE projections are of interest because they play an important role in national energy planning in the world's largest energy-producing and energy-consuming nation. Instead of alternative cases, the DOE's global forecast presents a *range of sensitivity* that reflects the uncertainties and outcomes of various underlying assumptions (11).

In DOE projections, energy use increases 36 percent (with a possible range of 22 to 52 percent) from 1990 to 2010. Carbon dioxide emissions rise 35 percent (with a possible range of 26 to 47 percent) over the same period (12).

Because DOE projections include a slower economic growth rate for developing nations than IEA projections, the developing world accounts for just 56 percent of the rise in energy use over the projection period—a much lower figure than that forecast by IEA (13).

None of these studies included the possibility of a major course correction in global energy strategies, for example, a concerted international effort to move to renewable and other nonfossil energy sources. Clear evidence of significant—and damaging—changes in climate caused by human activities, for example, could lead to a new global consensus and broad political support for a strengthened Global Climate Convention. Implementation of such a treaty could make available very large sums of money for investment in alternative energy sources. Such an energy transition—still speculative, but not implausible—would markedly alter the demand for fossil fuels.

References and Notes

1. WEC is a global (100 member countries) energy institution that embodies private, governmental, and regional and international organizations. It is supported by its members.

2. World Energy Council, *Energy for Tomorrow's World: The Realities, the Real Options, and the Agenda for Achievement* (Kogan Page, London, and St. Martin's Press, New York, 1993), pp. 76–82.

3. *Ibid.*, p. 80.

4. *Op. cit.* 2, p. 81.

5. *Op. cit.* 2, p. 80.

6. *Op. cit.* 2, pp. 81–82.

7. International Energy Agency, *World Energy Outlook, 1995* (Organisation for Economic Co-Operation and Development, Paris, 1995), pp. 11–17.

8. *Ibid.*, pp. 12–13.

9. *Op. cit.* 7, p. 13.

10. *Op. cit.* 7, p. 17.

11. Energy Information Administration, U.S. Department of Energy, *International Energy Outlook, 1995*, Report No. DOE/EIA-0484(95) (U.S. Government Printing Office, Washington, D.C., 1995), pp. vii–ix, 9, 95.

12. *Ibid.*, pp. 79, 87.

13. *Op. cit.* 11, pp. 15, 17.

nying demand for capital will put additional strain on national budgets and could result in diverting available capital from critical needs such as education and other social services to the energy sector. Although many developing nations are attempting to attract private investment capital to finance energy sector growth by liberalizing utility ownership and regulatory requirements, there is little doubt that limited investment capital will remain a considerable barrier to expanding the energy infrastructure in the future.

Reduced Demand Through Efficiency and National Policies

It is also possible, as indicated earlier, that energy demand could be constrained deliberately through a coordinated international effort to promote energy efficiency and to develop and disseminate renewable energy technologies. In this way, the link between economic growth and increasing energy use could be weakened. This would require a greater commitment by developed nations to finance research into alternative energy sources and to make a comprehensive effort to share new technologies with developing nations. Because the energy sectors in developing nations are on a steep growth curve, prudent investments in energy-efficient infrastructure today could reap big energy savings in the future.

A change in national energy policies could also help to restrain the growth in consumption and would act as a natural complement to enhanced research and technology sharing. Reducing energy subsidies such as oil depletion allowances or subsidized electricity rates, levying energy consumption taxes such as gas taxes, and setting minimum energy-efficiency standards for autos and appliances are some of the ways that energy policies could be modified to encourage energy conservation.

It is important to realize, however, that changing the world's current energy use trajectory will take time. The extended lifetime of energy facilities such as power plants, the length of the research and development cycle and the technology dissemination process, and the momentum in current population growth all weigh heavily against the likelihood of rapid change in current energy use patterns. Thus, even with successful policy reform and a genuine effort to adopt energy-efficient technologies and develop alternative energy sources, global energy use is still nearly certain to rise considerably in the next few decades. Without such measures, however, the growth in consumption will be significantly more rapid and the accompanying levels of air pollution and greenhouse gas emissions will be much higher.

References and Notes

1. The OECD member countries are Australia, Austria, Belgium, Canada, Denmark, Finland, France, Germany, Greece, Iceland, Ireland, Italy, Japan, Luxembourg, Mexico, the Netherlands, New Zealand, Norway, Portugal, Spain, Sweden, Switzerland, Turkey, the United Kingdom, and the United States. Mexico became a member in May 1994. Any discussion of OECD data prior to 1994 does not include Mexico. Developing countries include all countries except for OECD member countries and the former Soviet Union and Central European countries (the transition countries).

2. Energy Information Administration, U.S. Department of Energy, *International Energy Outlook, 1995*, Report No. DOE/EIA-0484(95) (U.S. Government Printing Office, Washington, D.C., 1995), p. 15.

3. The term "transitional economies" lacks a formal definition, but is used here to include the successor states of the former Soviet Union (Armenia, Azerbaijan, the Republic of Belarus, the Republic of Estonia, the Republic of Georgia, the Republic of Kazakhstan, the Kyrgyz Republic, the Republic of Latvia, the Republic of Lithuania, the Republic of Moldova, the Russian Federation, the Republic of Tajikistan, the Republic of Turkmenistan, Ukraine, and the Republic of

Uzbekistan) and the countries of Central Europe (Albania, Bulgaria, the Czech Republic, Hungary, Poland, Romania, and the Slovak Republic).

4. *Op. cit.* 2.

5. *Op. cit.* 2, Table 7, p. 17.

6. British Petroleum (BP), *BP Statistical Review of World Energy, June 1995* (BP, London, 1995), pp. 3, 19.

7. *Proved reserves in place* represent the total resources that are known to exist in specific locations and in specific quantities and qualities. *Proved recoverable reserves* are the fraction of proved reserves in place that can be extracted under present and expected local economic conditions with existing available technology. Additional energy resources, comprising those that cannot currently be recovered economically, are not represented. (See also Sources and Technical Notes.)

8. *Op. cit.* 6, pp. 2, 18, 26. Reserve-to-consumption ratios are not predictions of the number of years remaining, but rather a way to add a comparative factor to reserve estimates. These ratios show how many years known proved reserves would last at current rates of consumption. They do not predict the year of actual depletion.

9. British Petroleum (BP), *BP Statistical Review of World Energy, June 1985* (BP, London, 1985), p. 2.

10. *Ibid.*, pp. 2–3.

11. *Op. cit.* 9, p. 3.

12. *Op. cit.* 9.

13. *Op. cit.* 9, p. 3.

14. A. Konoplyanik, "Russia Struggling to Revive Production, Rebuild Oil Industry," *Oil & Gas Journal*, Vol. 91, No. 31 (August 2, 1993), p. 44.

15. *Op. cit.* 9.

16. International Energy Agency, *World Energy Outlook, 1995* (Organisation for Economic Co-Operation and Development, Paris, 1995), pp. 35–39.

17. *Op. cit.* 2, p. 37.

18. World Energy Council, *Energy for Tomorrow's World: The Realities, the Real Options, and the Agenda for Achievement* (Kogan Page, London, and St. Martin's Press, New York, 1993), pp. 90–91. This is extended to 64 years if uranium resources recoverable at less than $130 per kilogram (not just $80 per kilogram) are taken into account.

19. World Resources Institute in collaboration with the United Nations Environment Programme and the United Nations Develop-

ment Programme, *World Resources 1994–95* (Oxford University Press, New York, 1994), p. 170.

20. Edward Carr, "Energy: The New Prize," *The Economist,* Vol. 331, No. 7868 (June 18, 1994), pp. SS3–SS6.

21. *Op. cit.* 16, pp. 314–316, 318, Tables A14, A15, A16, A18.

22. *Op. cit.* 2, p. 17, Table 7.

23. *Op. cit.* 20.

24. *Op. cit.* 16, pp. 1–2.

25. *Op. cit.* 2, p. 8.

26. *Op. cit.* 16, p. 2.

27. *Op. cit.* 2, p. 5, Table 1.

28. *Op. cit.* 18, p. 296.

29. *Ibid.,* p. 50.

30. *Op. cit.* 28, p. 50.

31. *Op. cit.* 19.

32. World Energy Council, *New Renewable Energy Resources: A Guide to the Future* (Kogan Page, London, 1994), pp. 25–64.

33. *Ibid.,* p. 20.

34. *Op. cit.* 32, p. 44.

35. World Energy Council (WEC) and International Institute for Advanced Systems Analysis (IIASA), *Global Energy Perspectives to 2050 and Beyond* (WEC, London, and IIASA, Laxerburg, Austria, 1995), pp. 82–86.

36. *Op. cit.* 19, pp. 171–172.

37. Mohan Munasinghe, *Electric Power Economics* (Butterworth, London, 1990), p. 5, as cited in U.S. Office of Technology Assessment, *Energy in Developing Countries,* Report OTA-E-486 (U.S. Government Printing Office, Washington, D.C., 1991), p. 35.

| | Total | | Solid | | Liquid | | Gas | | Primary Electricity {a} | | | | | |
| | | | | | | | | | Geothermal & Wind | | Hydro | | Nuclear | |
	Peta-joules 1993	% Change Since 1973	Peta-joules 1993	% Change Since 1973	Peta-joules 1993	% Change Since 1973	Peta-joules 1993	% Change Since 1973	Peta-joules 1993	% Change Since 1973	Peta-joules 1993	% Change Since 1973	Peta-joules 1993	% Change Since 1973
WORLD	337,518	40	91,748	36	134,060	11	78,146	72	1,463	641	8,554	86	23,646	1,365
AFRICA	21,308	50	4,259	155	13,835	14	2,941	797	13	X	182	68	79	X
Algeria	4,584	99	1	162	2,481	16	2,102	1,190	0	X	1	(27)	0	X
Angola	1,066	207	0	X	1,055	209	7	175	0	X	5	102	0	X
Benin	13	X	0	X	13	X	0	X	0	X	0	X	0	X
Botswana	X	X	0	X	X	X	0	X	0	X	0	X	0	X
Burkina Faso	X	X	0	X	X	X	0	X	0	X	0	X	0	X
Burundi	1	3,312	0	X	X	X	0	X	0	X	0	X	0	X
Cameroon	270	6,879	0	X	260	X	0	X	0	X	10	145	0	X
Central African Rep	0	X	0	X	X	X	0	X	0	X	0	74	0	X
Chad	X	X	0	X	X	X	0	X	0	X	0	X	0	X
Congo	365	313	0	X	363	315	0	X	0	X	2	550	0	X
Cote d'Ivoire	18	2,880	0	X	14	X	0	X	0	X	4	385	0	X
Egypt	2,435	546	0	X	2,028	471	376	10,960	0	X	31	66	0	X
Equatorial Guinea	0	X	0	X	X	X	0	X	0	X	0	20	0	X
Eritrea	X	X	0	X	X	X	0	X	0	X	0	X	0	X
Ethiopia	7	494	0	X	X	X	0	X	3	X	4	269	0	X
Gabon	637	89	0	X	631	98	4	(78)	0	X	3	14,100	0	X
Gambia, The	X	X	0	X	X	X	0	X	0	X	0	X	0	X
Ghana	22	58	0	X	0	X	0	X	0	X	22	84	0	X
Guinea	1	256	0	X	X	X	0	X	0	X	1	151	0	X
Guinea-Bissau	X	X	0	X	X	X	0	X	0	X	0	X	0	X
Kenya	21	1,328	0	X	X	X	0	X	10	X	11	646	0	X
Lesotho	X	X	0	X	X	X	0	X	0	X	0	X	0	X
Liberia	1	(7)	0	X	X	X	0	X	0	X	1	(34)	0	X
Libya	3,054	(33)	0	X	2,806	(37)	248	107	0	X	0	X	0	X
Madagascar	1	71	0	X	X	X	0	X	0	X	1	145	0	X
Malawi	3	341	0	X	X	X	0	X	0	X	3	364	0	X
Mali	1	694	0	X	X	X	0	X	0	X	1	506	0	X
Mauritania	0	X	0	X	X	X	0	X	0	X	0	X	0	X
Mauritius	0	X	0	X	X	X	0	X	0	X	0	52	0	X
Morocco	21	(8)	18	29	0	X	1	(63)	0	X	2	(73)	0	X
Mozambique	1	(90)	1	(90)	X	X	0	X	0	X	0	(82)	0	X
Namibia	X	X	0	X	X	X	0	X	0	X	0	X	0	X
Niger	5	X	5	X	X	X	0	X	0	X	0	X	0	X
Nigeria	4,140	(3)	3	(63)	3,935	(8)	191	1,513	0	X	12	121	0	X
Rwanda	1	112	0	X	X	X	0	X	0	X	1	89	0	X
Senegal	X	X	0	X	X	X	0	X	0	X	0	X	0	X
Sierra Leone	X	X	0	X	X	X	0	X	0	X	0	X	0	X
Somalia	X	X	0	X	X	X	0	X	0	X	0	X	0	X
South Africa {b}	4,146	169	4,064	164	X	X	0	X	0	X	3	(1)	79	X
Sudan	3	316	0	X	X	X	0	X	0	X	3	836	0	X
Swaziland	X	X	0	X	X	X	0	X	0	X	0	X	0	X
Tanzania	2	78	0	X	X	X	0	X	0	X	2	95	0	X
Togo	0	X	0	X	X	X	0	X	0	X	0	50	0	X
Tunisia	209	24	0	X	196	21	13	144	0	X	0	21	0	X
Uganda	3	1	0	X	X	X	0	X	0	X	3	(6)	0	X
Zaire	78	365	3	(7)	54	X	0	X	0	X	22	75	0	X
Zambia	38	11	10	(57)	X	X	0	X	0	X	28	154	0	X
Zimbabwe	160	79	154	122	X	X	0	X	0	X	6	(68)	0	X
EUROPE	92,937	192	22,091	6	25,700	1,451	30,702	335	167	79	2,551	95	11,855	1,515
Albania	44	(61)	5	(58)	23	(74)	4	(46)	0	X	12	270	0	X
Austria	263	(18)	18	(66)	50	(54)	57	(38)	0	X	137	X	0	X
Belarus, Rep	122	X	28	X	84	X	10	X	0	X	0	X	0	X
Belgium	470	110	10	(95)	X	X	0	X	0	X	4	76	457	419,177
Bosnia and Herzegovina	14	X	0	X	X	X	0	X	0	X	14	X	0	X
Bulgaria	376	(11)	212	(47)	2	(75)	2	(74)	0	X	7	(7)	152	X
Croatia, Rep	179	X	3	X	90	X	70	X	0	X	16	X	0	X
Czech Rep	1,439	X	1,283	X	5	X	8	X	0	X	6	139	138	X
Denmark	525	17,831	0	X	346	12,071	175	X	4	X	0	14	0	X
Estonia, Rep	121	X	121	X	X	X	0	X	0	X	0	X	0	X
Finland	324	690	59	1,578	X	X	0	X	0	X	49	33	217	X
France	4,746	237	263	(62)	136	52	94	(68)	0	X	244	38	4,017	2,423
Germany	6,178	X	3,675	X	128	X	626	X	4	X	77	X	1,674	X
Greece	352	75	315	63	24	X	4	X	0	X	9	(5)	0	X
Hungary	533	(24)	133	(69)	87	(2)	163	(8)	0	X	1	56	151	X
Iceland	25	186	0	X	X	X	0	X	9	1,027	16	161	0	X
Ireland	152	170	48	(10)	X	X	100	X	1	X	4	54	0	X
Italy	1,226	35	11	(42)	194	318	730	24	132	42	160	8	0	X
Latvia, Rep	14	X	3	X	X	X	0	X	0	X	10	X	0	X
Lithuania, Rep	138	X	0	X	3	X	0	X	0	X	1	X	134	X
Macedonia, former Yugoslav Rep	86	X	82	X	X	X	0	X	0	X	3	X	0	X
Moldova, Rep	1	X	0	X	X	X	0	X	0	X	1	X	0	X
Netherlands	3,112	19	0	X	138	111	2,930	17	6	X	0	X	43	1,111
Norway	6,365	1,778	8	(22)	4,801	7,139	1,127	X	0	X	430	77	0	X
Poland, Rep	3,878	(17)	3,719	(16)	10	(45)	137	(30)	0	X	13	85	0	X
Portugal	35	10	3	(45)	X	X	0	X	1	X	31	23	0	X
Romania	1,345	(40)	318	(27)	279	(53)	702	(40)	0	X	46	74	0	X
Russian Federation	43,550	X	6,309	X	14,815	X	20,497	X	1	X	631	X	1,300	X
Slovak Rep	186	X	44	X	3	X	8	X	0	X	11	X	120	X
Slovenia, Rep	86	X	31	X	0	X	0	X	0	X	11	X	43	X
Spain	1,204	142	427	47	47	47	27	45,963	0	X	93	(29)	612	1,080
Sweden	950	298	10	3,312	0	X	0	X	2	X	271	40	670	4,088
Switzerland	386	136	0	X	X	X	0	X	0	X	132	51	255	550
Ukraine	4,501	X	2,802	X	178	X	662	X	0	X	40	X	821	X
United Kingdom	9,663	105	1,922	(41)	4,210	25,370	2,537	125	8	X	20	63	975	204
Yugoslavia, Fed Rep	347	X	230	X	48	X	33	X	0	X	36	X	0	X

| | Total | | Solid | | Liquid | | Gas | | Primary Electricity {a} | | | | | |
| | | | | | | | | | Geothermal & Wind | | Hydro | | Nuclear | |
	Peta-joules 1993	% Change Since 1973	Peta-joules 1993	% Change Since 1973	Peta-joules 1993	% Change Since 1973	Peta-joules 1993	% Change Since 1973	Peta-joules 1993	% Change Since 1973	Peta-joules 1993	% Change Since 1973	Peta-joules 1993	% Change Since 1973
NORTH & CENTRAL AMERICA	**87,427**	**27**	**21,948**	**59**	**28,029**	**3**	**26,454**	**(1)**	**947**	**1,709**	**2,307**	**41**	**7,746**	**1,068**
Belize	X	X	0	X	X	X	0	X	0	X	0	X	0	X
Canada	13,195	60	1,571	271	4,162	(1)	5,263	88	1	X	1,165	80	1,034	1,307
Costa Rica	14	242	0	X	X	X	0	X	0	X	14	259	0	X
Cuba	43	556	0	X	41	610	1	80	0	X	0	43	0	X
Dominican Rep	6	2,744	0	X	X	X	0	X	0	X	6	2,361	0	X
El Salvador	21	1,227	0	X	X	X	0	X	15	X	6	319	0	X
Guatemala	22	1,820	0	X	15	X	0	X	0	X	7	543	0	X
Haiti	1	153	0	X	X	X	0	X	0	X	1	136	0	X
Honduras	8	519	0	X	X	X	0	X	0	X	8	646	0	X
Jamaica	0	X	0	X	X	X	0	X	0	X	0	(36)	0	X
Mexico	8,067	362	160	52	6,548	510	977	95	237	658,233	94	69	52	X
Nicaragua	20	1,636	0	X	X	X	0	X	19	X	1	(5)	0	X
Panama	8	X	0	X	X	X	0	X	0	X	8	X	0	X
Trinidad and Tobago	470	7	0	X	268	(27)	202	186	0	X	0	X	0	X
United States	65,547	9	20,218	52	16,992	(21)	20,008	(15)	675	1,191	995	0	6,659	1,030
SOUTH AMERICA	**15,355**	**35**	**844**	**360**	**10,468**	**5**	**2,475**	**170**	**0**	**X**	**1,478**	**416**	**89**	**X**
Argentina	2,411	105	4	(64)	1,311	43	925	296	0	X	87	1,506	85	X
Bolivia	164	8	0	X	52	(44)	107	88	0	X	5	96	0	X
Brazil	2,491	296	85	42	1,382	291	173	2,144	0	X	845	357	5	X
Chile	222	26	47	35	44	(42)	67	45	0	X	63	237	0	X
Colombia	1,812	208	591	685	971	137	149	99	0	X	101	281	0	X
Ecuador	784	75	0	X	758	70	5	271	0	X	21	1,219	0	X
Guyana	0	X	0	X	X	X	0	X	0	X	0	X	0	X
Paraguay	113	10,267	0	X	X	X	0	X	0	X	113	16,241	0	X
Peru	325	79	2	153	264	77	18	27	0	X	41	152	0	X
Suriname	15	318	0	X	11	X	0	X	0	X	4	(2)	0	X
Uruguay	26	364	0	X	X	X	0	X	0	X	26	634	0	X
Venezuela	6,990	(13)	114	9,161	5,674	(24)	1,031	115	0	X	171	683	0	X
ASIA	**113,332**	**67**	**37,897**	**162**	**54,936**	**8**	**14,412**	**671**	**337**	**3,675**	**1,894**	**190**	**3,835**	**3,180**
Afghanistan, Islamic State	9	(92)	0	X	0	X	7	(93)	0	X	2	4	0	X
Armenia	11	X	0	X	X	X	0	X	0	X	11	X	0	X
Azerbaijan	714	X	0	X	474	X	231	X	0	X	9	X	0	X
Bangladesh	217	744	0	X	5	2,337	209	759	0	X	3	343	0	X
Bhutan	6	28,471	0	X	X	X	0	X	0	X	6	27,671	0	X
Cambodia	0	X	0	X	X	X	0	X	0	X	0	X	0	X
China	31,359	143	24,045	133	6,080	171	661	184	0	X	546	427	27	X
Georgia, Rep	28	X	0	X	4	X	0	X	0	X	23	X	0	X
India	8,088	233	6,141	211	1,158	284	460	1,838	2	X	254	160	74	500
Indonesia	7,145	148	808	21,781	4,192	50	2,062	3,127	39	X	44	850	0	X
Iran, Islamic Rep	8,448	(35)	43	66	7,310	(41)	1,056	49	0	X	40	212	0	X
Iraq	1,476	(65)	0	X	1,374	(67)	99	110	0	X	2	200	0	X
Israel	1	X	0	X	0	X	1	(48)	0	X	0	X	0	X
Japan	3,466	224	186	(66)	32	25	90	(22)	65	628	380	20	2,719	2,529
Jordan	0	X	0	X	0	X	0	X	0	X	0	X	0	X
Kazakhstan, Rep	4,025	X	2,809	X	961	X	227	X	0	X	27	X	0	X
Korea, Dem People's Rep	2,671	201	2,585	206	X	X	0	X	0	X	86	100	X	X
Korea, Rep	832	145	178	(47)	X	X	0	X	0	X	22	339	634	X
Kuwait	4,329	(34)	0	X	4,155	(36)	174	60	0	X	0	X	0	X
Kyrgyz Rep	66	X	29	X	4	X	1	X	0	X	32	X	0	X
Lao People's Dem Rep	3	248	0	X	X	X	0	X	0	X	3	286	0	X
Lebanon	1	(42)	0	X	X	X	0	X	0	X	1	(55)	0	X
Malaysia	2,167	1,038	8	X	1,307	619	835	17,932	0	X	18	327	0	X
Mongolia	84	138	84	138	X	X	0	X	0	X	0	X	0	X
Myanmar	75	58	1	327	30	(27)	38	853	0	X	5	166	0	X
Nepal	3	934	0	X	X	X	0	X	0	X	3	943	0	X
Oman	1,720	181	0	X	1,621	165	98	X	0	X	0	X	0	X
Pakistan	766	311	61	116	127	818	496	295	0	X	77	485	5	333
Philippines	276	2,801	33	3,312	21	X	0	X	207	X	15	93	0	X
Saudi Arabia	19,171	20	0	X	17,770	11	1,401	7,187	0	X	0	X	0	X
Singapore	X	X	0	X	X	X	0	X	0	X	0	X	0	X
Sri Lanka	14	449	0	X	X	X	0	X	0	X	14	344	0	X
Syrian Arab Rep	1,234	432	0	X	1,134	389	76	X	0	X	24	10,731	0	X
Tajikistan, Rep	70	X	5	X	2	X	2	X	0	X	62	X	0	X
Thailand	678	5,396	170	3,105	155	58,664	339	X	0	X	13	114	0	X
Turkey	779	119	484	144	163	11	7	X	3	X	122	958	0	X
Turkmenistan, Rep	2,430	X	0	X	211	X	2,219	X	0	X	0	X	0	X
United Arab Emirates	5,273	68	0	X	4,378	41	895	2,600	0	X	0	X	0	X
Uzbekistan, Rep	X	X	45	X	170	X	1,529	X	0	X	26	X	0	X
Viet Nam	489	549	173	134	264	X	0	X	22	X	30	1,870	0	X
Yemen, Rep	X	X	0	X	480	X	0	X	0	X	0	X	0	X
OCEANIA	**7,159**	**144**	**4,707**	**162**	**1,091**	**28**	**1,162**	**718**	**57**	**35**	**141**	**48**	**0**	**X**
Australia	6,658	141	4,634	167	1,006	19	959	627	0	X	61	42	0	X
Fiji	1	X	0	X	X	X	0	X	0	X	1	X	0	X
New Zealand	496	193	74	24	85	1,150	203	1,873	57	36	77	51	0	X
Papua New Guinea	2	251	0	X	X	X	0	X	0	X	2	211	0	X
Solomon Islands	X	X	0	X	X	X	0	X	0	X	0	X	0	X

Source: United Nations Statistical Division.

Notes: a. The production of primary electricity was assessed at the equivalent of 100 percent efficiency for hydroelectric and wind generation (at the heat value of electricity: 1 kilowatt hour = 3.6 million joules), at 33 percent efficiency for nuclear power generation, and at 10 percent efficiency for geothermal generation.
b. Data are for the South Africa Customs Union (Botswana, Lesotho, Namibia, South Africa, and Swaziland).
1 petajoule = 1,000,000,000,000,000 joules = 947,800,000,000 Btus = 163,400 "U.N. standard" barrels of oil = 34,140 "U.N. standard" metric tons of coal.
World and regional totals include countries not listed. 0 = zero or less than half of the unit of measure; X = not available or indeterminate; negative numbers are shown in parentheses.
For additional information, see Sources and Technical Notes.

| | Commercial Energy Consumption | | | | | | | | Traditional Fuels | | | | | |
| | Total | | Per Capita | | Per Constant 1987 US$ of GNP | | Imports as a % of Consumption | | Total | | Per Capita | | % of Total Consumption | |
	Peta-joules 1993	% Change Since 1973	Giga-joules 1993	% Change Since 1973	Mega-joules 1993	% Change Since 1973	1973	1993	Peta-joules 1993	% Change Since 1973	Mega-joules 1993	% Change Since 1973	1993	1973
WORLD	325,296	49	59	6	X	X	X	X	19,926	47	3,594	4	6	6
AFRICA	8,805	144	13	41	X	X	(280)	(134)	4,815	76	6,991	0	35	43
Algeria	1,183	387	44	173	18	144	(858)	(274)	19	64	714	(8)	2	5
Angola	26	(30)	3	(51)	X	X	(795)	(3,835)	56	(12)	5,455	(50)	68	63
Benin	7	27	1	(48)	4	(28)	103	(71)	48	67	9,482	(5)	87	84
Botswana	X	X	X	X	0	X	X	X	13	102	9,420	2	100	100
Burkina Faso	8	237	1	150	3	57	100	100	85	62	8,652	(2)	91	96
Burundi	3	241	0	X	2	77	103	100	44	60	7,222	(4)	94	97
Cameroon	36	138	3	41	4	17	90	(639)	114	72	9,130	(2)	76	81
Central African Rep	3	18	1	(23)	3	(2)	97	133	34	67	10,694	4	92	89
Chad	1	(55)	0	X	1	(71)	153	200	35	55	5,900	(0)	97	91
Congo	24	331	10	146	10	67	(1,009)	(1,379)	22	77	8,945	(1)	48	69
Cote d'Ivoire	109	195	8	35	11	115	117	119	103	111	7,723	(1)	49	57
Egypt	1,226	337	20	149	30	36	(25)	(84)	45	59	752	(2)	4	9
Equatorial Guinea	2	184	5	80	13	X	54	100	4	20	11,522	(20)	69	84
Eritrea	X	X	X	X	X	X	X	X	0	X	0	X	X	X
Ethiopia	45	104	1	X	X	X	108	93	414	84	7,984	9	90	91
Gabon	32	(11)	26	(59)	7	(52)	(823)	(1,859)	26	138	21,166	10	45	24
Gambia, The	3	241	3	75	10	59	97	100	9	27	8,579	(38)	75	89
Ghana	67	55	4	(13)	10	10	83	75	152	101	9,213	15	69	64
Guinea	15	35	2	(27)	6	X	98	100	35	43	5,594	(8)	70	69
Guinea-Bissau	3	105	3	18	13	6	100	100	4	11	4,012	(38)	58	72
Kenya	90	87	3	(20)	10	(14)	160	97	344	84	13,049	(11)	79	80
Lesotho	X	X	X	X	0	X	X	X	6	168	3,338	56	100	100
Liberia	5	(74)	2	(84)	X	X	96	100	48	56	17,045	(17)	91	62
Libya	457	722	91	268	X	X	(8,069)	(562)	5	18	1,037	(47)	1	7
Madagascar	15	1	1	(51)	5	(10)	128	93	76	56	5,483	(17)	84	77
Malawi	11	58	1	(29)	8	(20)	93	82	133	198	12,596	39	92	86
Mali	7	96	1	65	3	12	102	100	54	68	5,279	(2)	88	90
Mauritania	39	508	18	267	37	297	105	118	0	58	37	(4)	0	1
Mauritius	21	123	19	74	8	(20)	125	143	17	(13)	15,392	(31)	44	67
Morocco	297	166	11	63	13	19	88	108	14	147	529	57	5	4
Mozambique	14	(63)	1	(74)	7	X	101	114	147	57	9,758	4	91	71
Namibia	X	X	X	X	0	X	X	X	0	X	0	X	X	X
Niger	15	255	2	114	6	175	100	67	47	83	5,484	(3)	76	86
Nigeria	705	420	7	221	19	220	(3,066)	(481)	1,010	82	9,590	3	59	80
Rwanda	7	387	1	186	3	154	71	100	53	16	6,986	(37)	88	97
Senegal	38	112	5	26	8	28	356	126	49	75	6,257	1	57	61
Sierra Leone	6	(46)	1	(75)	10	(59)	84	233	30	49	6,903	(2)	83	64
Somalia	X	X	X	X	X	X	106	X	71	143	7,975	39	100	89
South Africa {a}	3,578	X	79	X	42	X	X	(15)	131	13	3,314	(31)	4	100
Sudan	48	(40)	2	(63)	X	X	101	110	220	78	8,261	1	82	61
Swaziland	X	X	X	X	0	X	0	X	18	111	22,852	19	100	66
Tanzania	30	(21)	1	(61)	6	(56)	112	100	330	135	11,769	25	92	79
Togo	9	92	2	(7)	8	61	102	100	10	139	2,665	34	53	48
Tunisia	218	264	25	125	18	42	(147)	7	31	55	3,593	(2)	12	25
Uganda	16	(5)	1	(37)	2	X	89	81	137	85	6,870	(2)	90	81
Zaire	73	45	2	(15)	X	X	84	4	365	70	8,854	(9)	83	81
Zambia	51	(18)	6	(56)	22	(32)	64	33	130	91	14,536	(2)	72	52
Zimbabwe	208	67	19	(12)	32	1	18	25	70	57	6,513	(16)	25	26
EUROPE	108,523	90	148	73	X	X	59	18	552	(14)	761	(21)	1	1
Albania	43	(11)	13	(38)	X	X	(38)	37	15	(3)	4,485	(34)	26	25
Austria	966	16	123	12	7	(26)	67	75	30	191	3,766	179	3	1
Belarus, Rep	1,249	X	123	X	58	X	X	91	X	X	X	X	X	X
Belgium	1,976	14	197	X	12	(22)	105	90	6	40	557	36	0	0
Bosnia and Herzegovina	29	X	8	X	X	X	X	52	X	X	X	X	X	X
Bulgaria	965	(6)	109	(9)	45	X	63	70	13	29	1,448	26	1	1
Croatia, Rep	263	X	58	X	X	X	X	43	0	X	0	X	0	X
Czech Rep	1,659	X	161	X	54	X	X	18	0	X	0	X	0	X
Denmark	762	(1)	148	(3)	7	(30)	110	31	5	1,178	943	1,141	1	0
Estonia, Rep	214	X	138	X	1	X	X	45	0	X	0	X	0	X
Finland	1,014	54	200	42	12	9	104	63	30	(56)	5,892	(59)	3	9
France	9,153	36	159	23	9	(9)	91	53	101	(2)	1,757	(12)	1	2
Germany	13,724	2	170	X	9	(39)	0	57	0	X	0	X	0	0
Greece	989	123	95	91	19	47	118	74	13	(29)	1,274	(39)	1	4
Hungary	990	3	97	5	47	(16)	41	53	24	(1)	2,319	1	2	2
Iceland	54	68	205	35	10	(10)	87	54	0	X	0	X	0	0
Ireland	428	62	121	40	10	(27)	88	67	0	72	139	50	0	0
Italy	6,749	40	118	34	8	(14)	100	74	48	31	848	26	1	1
Latvia, Rep	187	X	72	X	30	X	X	84	X	X	X	X	X	X
Lithuania, Rep	368	X	99	X	83	X	X	62	X	X	X	X	X	X
Macedonia, former Yugoslav Rep	139	X	66	X	X	X	X	45	0	X	0	X	0	X
Moldova, Rep	234	X	53	X	59	X	X	102	X	X	X	X	X	X
Netherlands	3,306	44	216	26	13	(4)	29	13	2	(250)	150	(232)	0	(0)
Norway	904	61	210	48	10	(20)	54	(588)	9	73	2,198	60	1	1
Poland, Rep	4,056	8	106	(6)	69	X	(12)	4	X	X	X	X	X	X
Portugal	603	140	61	119	12	41	100	106	6	31	573	20	1	3
Romania	1,762	(20)	77	(27)	70	X	4	30	19	(66)	841	(69)	1	3
Russian Federation	30,042	X	203	X	102	X	X	(40)	0	X	0	X	0	X
Slovak Rep	672	X	126	X	53	X	X	74	0	X	0	X	0	X
Slovenia, Rep	194	X	100	X	X	X	X	56	X	X	X	X	X	X
Spain	3,359	72	85	52	10	9	89	78	18	(53)	466	(58)	1	2
Sweden	1,660	20	191	12	10	(8)	89	46	122	(4)	14,062	(10)	7	8
Switzerland	985	34	139	20	5	8	82	57	14	103	2,052	81	1	1
Ukraine	8,058	X	156	X	105	X	X	46	0	X	0	X	0	X
United Kingdom	9,518	10	164	7	13	(21)	53	1	4	27	72	23	0	0
Yugoslavia, Fed Rep	381	X	36	X	X	X	X	17	X	X	X	X	X	X

| | Commercial Energy Consumption | | | | | | | | Traditional Fuels | | | | | |
| | Total | | Per Capita | | Per Constant 1987 US$ of GNP | | Imports as a % of Consumption | | Total | | Per Capita | | % of Total Consumption | |
	Peta-joules 1993	% Change Since 1973	Giga-joules 1993	% Change Since 1973	Mega-joules 1993	% Change Since 1973	1973	1993	Peta-joules 1993	% Change Since 1973	Mega-joules 1993	% Change Since 1973	1993	1973
NORTH & CENTRAL AMERICA	97,154	19	220	(10)	X	X	14	11	1,825	106	4,130	53	2	1
Belize	4	92	20	20	9	(39)	115	100	4	53	18,789	(3)	49	55
Canada	9,198	47	319	12	21	(15)	(26)	(43)	67	96	2,326	53	1	1
Costa Rica	63	115	19	21	10	4	90	79	35	(24)	10,784	(56)	36	61
Cuba	369	26	34	5	X	X	103	96	205	31	18,848	8	36	35
Dominican Rep	148	101	20	30	24	(1)	105	96	25	(25)	3,360	(53)	15	32
El Salvador	72	170	13	90	13	97	99	74	39	5	7,050	(26)	35	58
Guatemala	72	88	7	4	8	6	107	89	104	89	10,335	7	59	59
Haiti	9	64	1	(13)	11	55	97	100	57	35	8,213	(7)	86	88
Honduras	43	120	8	18	8	7	111	81	58	89	10,897	0	57	61
Jamaica	104	(5)	43	(23)	29	(13)	109	100	6	(32)	2,493	(45)	5	7
Mexico	4,941	155	55	66	30	30	15	(57)	248	48	2,755	(9)	5	8
Nicaragua	52	112	13	20	15	165	106	67	39	78	9,450	(2)	43	47
Panama	61	X	24	X	10	9,449	0	89	16	3	6,366	(34)	21	98
Trinidad and Tobago	267	100	209	56	58	55	(164)	(78)	3	(42)	2,210	(55)	1	4
United States	81,751	13	317	(7)	16	(28)	18	21	916	297	3,553	226	1	0
SOUTH AMERICA	10,095	94	33	30	X	X	(104)	(43)	2,748	26	8,888	(17)	21	30
Argentina	2,019	56	60	17	16	14	16	(9)	116	0	3,421	(25)	5	8
Bolivia	86	140	12	56	16	64	(328)	(92)	19	55	2,723	(0)	18	26
Brazil	3,800	120	24	43	13	14	83	46	2,021	20	12,912	(21)	35	49
Chile	539	61	39	17	17	(31)	45	62	84	72	6,050	24	13	13
Colombia	829	95	24	29	18	(11)	(29)	(117)	235	81	6,927	22	22	23
Ecuador	245	305	22	141	18	93	(624)	(208)	74	67	6,757	(1)	23	42
Guyana	15	(38)	18	(46)	38	(38)	102	100	4	(39)	5,355	(46)	23	23
Paraguay	51	350	11	146	11	64	95	(131)	55	59	11,699	(14)	52	75
Peru	314	30	14	(17)	2,276	3	34	(3)	88	7	3,828	(33)	22	25
Suriname	24	(24)	58	(32)	17	(29)	89	75	1	349	2,959	302	5	1
Uruguay	77	(1)	24	(13)	10	(32)	101	69	28	109	8,948	87	27	15
Venezuela	2,083	125	100	27	36	51	(735)	(226)	22	32	1,046	(25)	1	2
ASIA	95,679	185	28	92	X	X	(83)	(9)	9,009	47	2,690	1	9	15
Afghanistan, Islamic State	22	1	1	(32)	X	X	(394)	64	51	31	2,863	9	70	64
Armenia	49	X	14	X	22	X	X	96	0	X	0	X	0	X
Azerbaijan	546	X	74	X	134	X	X	23	0	X	0	X	0	X
Bangladesh	313	417	3	259	14	113	72	33	277	27	2,401	(20)	47	78
Bhutan	2	3,312	1	1,783	6	X	100	(150)	12	79	7,345	21	85	99
Cambodia	7	443	1	456	5	X	100	100	54	21	5,560	(11)	88	97
China	29,679	179	25	110	69	(43)	(1)	(2)	2,018	54	1,687	15	6	11
Georgia, Rep	159	X	29	X	51	X	X	91	X	X	X	X	X	X
India	9,338	258	10	128	27	46	26	21	2,824	58	3,132	4	23	41
Indonesia	2,658	394	14	237	24	46	(418)	(125)	1,465	54	7,642	4	36	64
Iran, Islamic Rep	3,264	227	51	60	18	X	(1,171)	(164)	29	95	446	(5)	1	1
Iraq	933	357	48	142	X	X	(1,949)	(24)	1	(13)	53	(54)	0	1
Israel	505	148	96	54	10	9	50	118	0	0	24	(38)	0	0
Japan	17,505	41	141	24	6	(30)	103	87	10	(37)	78	(45)	0	0
Jordan	147	509	30	104	22	X	119	109	0	108	16	5	0	0
Kazakhstan, Rep	3,381	X	199	X	167	X	X	(16)	0	X	0	X	0	X
Korea, Dem People's Rep	2,925	168	127	84	X	X	4	8	40	33	1,753	(8)	1	3
Korea, Rep	4,504	452	102	325	21	8	71	98	26	(83)	584	(87)	1	16
Kuwait	471	241	265	71	X	X	(4,440)	(798)	0	X	0	X	0	0
Kyrgyz Rep	150	X	33	X	49	X	X	57	0	X	0	X	0	X
Lao People's Dem Rep	5	(32)	1	(61)	3	X	88	40	39	35	8,366	(15)	89	79
Lebanon	121	35	43	29	X	X	113	101	5	9	1,653	5	4	5
Malaysia	996	401	52	206	25	34	11	(114)	90	61	4,686	(3)	8	22
Mongolia	105	170	45	58	X	X	36	19	13	0	5,689	(41)	11	25
Myanmar	71	73	2	41	6	(11)	11	3	193	48	4,324	(4)	73	76
Nepal	19	239	1	121	6	55	91	84	206	88	9,882	12	92	95
Oman	162	3,905	81	1,324	14	704	(13,764)	(957)	0	X	0	X	0	0
Pakistan	1,135	286	9	118	25	24	46	36	296	101	2,228	8	21	33
Philippines	787	97	12	22	20	12	93	84	382	44	5,892	(9)	33	40
Saudi Arabia	2,933	2,037	171	718	X	X	(10,943)	0	0	X	0	X	0	0
Singapore	745	184	267	123	22	(31)	201	202	0	X	0	X	0	0
Sri Lanka	78	71	4	15	9	(33)	159	113	89	45	4,996	6	53	58
Syrian Arab Rep	565	626	41	266	X	X	(168)	(105)	0	8	9	(45)	0	0
Tajikistan, Rep	258	X	45	X	126	X	X	75	0	X	0	X	0	X
Thailand	1,628	426	28	254	18	23	109	63	526	75	9,141	19	24	49
Turkey	1,979	189	33	84	18	13	53	67	96	(63)	1,606	(76)	5	27
Turkmenistan, Rep	555	X	142	X	X	X	X	(327)	X	X	X	X	X	X
United Arab Emirates	1,039	1,992	572	313	X	X	(6,199)	(364)	0	X	0	X	0	0
Uzbekistan, Rep	1,903	X	87	X	132	X	X	(13)	0	X	0	X	0	X
Viet Nam	316	(3)	4	(44)	6	X	73	(48)	251	54	3,516	(1)	44	33
Yemen, Rep	X	X	X	X	X	X	100	X	X	X	X	X	X	X
OCEANIA	4,595	93	166	44	X	X	1	(61)	185	16	6,693	(14)	4	6
Australia	3,917	99	222	53	16	15	(16)	(77)	109	6	6,191	(19)	3	5
Fiji	11	35	15	2	14	(16)	175	109	12	54	15,606	12	52	48
New Zealand	565	76	162	49	14	29	54	15	0	(80)	140	(83)	0	1
Papua New Guinea	33	72	8	9	7	(3)	101	97	60	34	14,550	(15)	64	70
Solomon Islands	2	X	6	16	X	X	109	X	3	121	9,107	11	62	61

Source: United Nations Statistical Division.

Notes: Commercial energy consumption does not include bunkers for aircraft and ships in international transport or additions to stocks.
Imports are net imports (gross imports minus exports) and may exceed consumption due to additions to stocks and use in bunkers.
a. Data are for the South Africa Customs Union (Botswana, Lesotho, Namibia, South Africa, and Swaziland).
1 petajoule = 1,000,000,000,000,000 joules = 947,800,000,000 Btus = 163,400 "U.N. standard" barrels of oil = 34,140 "U.N. standard" metric tons of coal.
1 gigajoule = 1,000,000,000 joules = 947,800 Btus; 1 megajoule = 1,000,000 joules = 947.8 Btus. World and regional totals include countries not listed.
0 = zero or less than half of the unit of measure; X = not available or indeterminate; negative numbers are shown in parentheses.
For additional information, see Sources and Technical Notes.

Data Table 12.3 Reserves and Resources of Commercial Energy, 1993

	Anthracite/Bituminous Coals (million metric tons) 1993		Subbituminous/Lignite Coals (million metric tons) 1993		Crude Oil (million metric tons) 1993	Natural Gas (billion cubic meters) 1993	Uranium (metric tons) Recoverable at Less Than		Hydroelectric (megawatts)	
	Proved Reserves in Place	Proved Recoverable Reserves	Proved Reserves in Place	Proved Recoverable Reserves	Proved Recoverable Reserves	Proved Recoverable Reserves	$80 per kg 1993	$130 per kg 1993	Known Exploitable Potential	Installed Capacity 1993
WORLD	1,087,982	519,358	741,463	512,252	140,676	141,335	1,532,000	698,870	X	612,505
AFRICA	132,951	60,405	1,509	1,267	10,494	10,166	431,570	138,340	X	20,689
Algeria	X	43	X	X	1,183	3,700	26,000	X	287 a	274
Angola	X	X	X	X	736	51	X	X	100,000	322
Benin	X	X	X	X	4	X	X	X	500 a	0
Botswana	7,000	3,500	X	X	X	X	X	X	1 a	0
Burkina Faso	X	X	X	X	X	X	X	X	200 a	30
Burundi	X	X	X	X	X	X	X	X	1,366	36
Cameroon	X	X	X	X	54	110	X	X	115,000	725
Central African Rep	X	X	4	4	X	X	8,000	8,000	2,000 a	22
Chad	X	X	X	X	X	X	X	X	30 a	0
Congo	X	X	X	X	113	77	X	X	50,000	89
Cote d'Ivoire	X	X	X	X	7	14	X	X	14,000	900
Egypt	25	13	X	40	472	706	X	X	3,210 a	2,825
Equatorial Guinea	X	X	X	X	2	37	X	X	2,000 a	X
Eritrea	X	X	X	X	X	X	X	X	X	X
Ethiopia	X	X	14	X	X	23	X	X	162,000	378
Gabon	X	X	X	X	182	14	9,780	4,650	32,500	326
Gambia, The	X	X	X	X	X	X	X	X	X	0
Ghana	X	X	X	X	0	23	X	X	11,550	1,072
Guinea	X	X	X	X	X	X	X	X	26,000	61
Guinea-Bissau	X	X	X	X	X	X	X	X	300	0
Kenya	X	X	X	X	X	X	X	X	30,000	611
Lesotho	X	X	X	X	X	X	X	X	2,000	0
Liberia	X	X	X	X	X	X	X	X	11,000	81
Libya	X	X	X	X	5,931	1,296	X	X	X	0
Madagascar	1,000	X	75	X	X	2	X	X	23,061	130
Malawi	15	2	X	X	X	X	X	X	6,000	146
Mali	X	X	X	X	X	X	X	X	10,000	45
Mauritania	X	X	X	X	X	X	X	X	X	61
Mauritius	X	X	X	X	X	X	X	X	65 a	59
Morocco	134	45	44	X	0	3	X	X	4,000	713
Mozambique	X	240	X	X	X	77	80,620	16,000	72,000	2,081
Namibia	X	X	X	X	X	147	X	X	1,060	249
Niger	X	70	X	X	X	X	159,170	6,650	235 a	0
Nigeria	X	21	338	169	1,693	3,451	X	X	40,000	1,970
Rwanda	X	X	X	X	X	57	X	X	3,000	59
Senegal	X	X	X	X	X	X	X	X	500 a	0
Sierra Leone	X	X	X	X	X	X	X	X	6,800	X
Somalia	X	X	X	X	X	6	0	6,600	50 a	0
South Africa {b}	121,218	55,333	X	X	6	27	144,400	96,440	X	593
Sudan	X	X	X	X	41	86	X	X	1,900	225
Swaziland	1,000	116	X	999	X	X	X	X	400	51
Tanzania	304	200	X	X	X	116	X	X	20,000	339
Togo	X	X	X	X	X	X	X	X	270 a	73
Tunisia	X	X	X	X	45	92	X	X	65 a	79
Uganda	X	X	X	X	X	X	X	X	10,200	155
Zaire	720	88	X	X	25	1	1,800	X	530,000	2,829
Zambia	X	X	69	55	X	X	1,800	X	309,009	2,259
Zimbabwe	1,535	734	965	X	X	X	X	X	19,281	666
EUROPE	114,691	55,765	117,674	70,470	9,569	55,461	331,916	214,116	X	179,398
Albania	X	X	15	X	22	2	X	X	17,000	1,395
Austria	X	X	347	31	15	22	X	X	56,800	11,739
Belarus, Rep	X	X	X	X	X	X	X	X	X	X
Belgium	715	410	X	X	X	X	X	X	500	130
Bosnia and Herzegovina	X	X	X	X	X	X	X	X	X	1,220
Bulgaria	48	13	4,791	2,698	1	2	X	X	2,240	2,150
Croatia, Rep	7	6	38	33	25	35	X	X	X	2,058
Czech Rep	X	X	X	X	2	5	16	6	X	1,144
Denmark {c}	X	X	183	X	101	142	X	X	14	52
Estonia, Rep	X	X	X	X	X	X	X	X	X	X
Finland	X	X	X	X	X	X	0	1,500	22,600	2,550
France	594	113	129	26	20	36	17,080	13,800	101,976	24,810
Germany	44,000	24,000	78,000	43,300	51	341	0	3,000	27,000	4,376
Greece	X	X	5,312	3,000	6	8	300	X	16,000	2,617
Hungary	1,407	596	8,306	3,865	19	97	620	510	4,500	48
Iceland	X	X	X	X	X	X	X	X	64,000	875
Ireland	19	14	X	X	X	15	X	X	194	229
Italy	X	X	75	34	44	270	4,800	X	65,000	17,832
Latvia, Rep	X	X	X	X	X	X	X	X	X	1,503
Lithuania, Rep	X	X	X	X	8	X	X	X	X	111
Macedonia, former Yugoslav Rep	X	X	X	X	X	X	X	X	X	X
Moldova, Rep	X	X	X	X	X	X	X	X	X	X
Netherlands	1,406	497	X	X	16	1,875	X	X	500	36
Norway	X	X	69	4	1,494	2,028	X	X	171,400	27,035
Poland, Rep	64,650	29,100	14,413	13,000	5	124	X	X	12,000	867
Portugal	8	3	38	33	X	X	7,300	1,400	30,500	3,405
Romania	1	1	3,199	3,117	218	445	X	X	40,000	6,253
Russian Federation	X	X	X	X	6,670	48,160	219,600	80,100	X	42,853
Slovak Rep	X	X	447	228	X	8	X	X	X	1,198
Slovenia, Rep	87	X	358	X	X	X	X	1,800	X	820
Spain	1,750	850	950	600	2	19	18,000	23,300	69,100	14,700
Sweden	X	X	4	1	X	X	2,000	2,000	70,000	16,638
Switzerland	X	X	X	X	X	0	X	X	41,000	11,758
Ukraine	X	X	X	X	235	1,172	62,200	86,700	X	4,700
United Kingdom {d}	X	162	1,000	500	605	610	X	X	5,600	1,064
Yugoslavia, Fed Rep	X	X	X	X	11	45	X	X	X	4,101

	Anthracite/Bituminous Coals (million metric tons) 1993		Subbituminous/Lignite Coals (million metric tons) 1993		Crude Oil (million metric tons) 1993	Natural Gas (billion cubic meters) 1993	Uranium (metric tons) Recoverable at Less Than		Hydroelectric (megawatts)	
	Proved Reserves in Place	Proved Recoverable Reserves	Proved Reserves in Place	Proved Recoverable Reserves	Proved Recoverable Reserves	Proved Recoverable Reserves	$80 per kg 1993	$130 per kg 1993	Known Exploitable Potential	Installed Capacity 1993
NORTH & CENTRAL AMERICA	**234,968**	**111,864**	**219,639**	**138,528**	**11,717**	**9,017**	**394,500**	**379,100**	**X**	**151,878**
Belize	X	X	X	X	X	X	X	X	X	0
Canada	6,435	4,509	14,355	4,114	758	2,232	278,000	119,000	614,882	62,725
Costa Rica	X	X	27	X	X	X	X	X	37,000	868
Cuba	X	X	X	X	14	3	X	X	X	49
Dominican Rep	X	X	X	X	X	X	X	X	2,517	376
El Salvador	X	X	X	X	X	X	X	X	4,009	406
Guatemala	X	X	X	X	66	0	X	X	43,370	443
Haiti	X	X	13	X	X	X	X	X	430	70
Honduras	X	X	21	X	X	X	X	X	24,000	483
Jamaica	X	X	X	X	X	X	X	X	335	0
Mexico	1,569	860	732	351	6,906	1,951	4,500	6,100	80,000	8,247
Nicaragua	X	X	X	X	X	X	X	X	6,552	111
Panama	X	X	X	X	X	X	X	X	16,233	552
Trinidad and Tobago	X	X	X	X	73	232	X	X	X	0
United States	226,964	106,495	204,491	134,063	3,900	4,599	112,000	254,000	376,000	77,384
SOUTH AMERICA	**6,225**	**5,649**	**15,298**	**4,548**	**11,608**	**5,430**	**168,390**	**2,400**	**X**	**90,082**
Argentina	X	X	195	130	310	517	4,600	2,400	390,038	7,213
Bolivia	X	1	X	X	17	126	X	X	50,000	380
Brazil	X	X	10,162	2,845	542	137	162,000	X	1,116,900	48,193
Chile	79	31	4,500	1,150	41	110	X	X	162,262	2,431
Colombia	5,449	4,240	411	299	462	212	X	X	418,200	7,759
Ecuador	X	X	30	24	274	108	X	X	180,000	1,497
Guyana	X	X	X	X	X	X	X	X	63,100	4
Paraguay	X	X	X	X	X	X	X	X	39,630	6,490
Peru	X	960	X	100	109	200	1,790	X	412,000	2,507
Suriname	X	X	X	X	11	X	X	X	12,840	290
Uruguay	X	X	X	X	X	X	X	X	6,750	2,331
Venezuela	697	417	X	X	9,842	4,020	X	X	261,700	10,989
ASIA	**403,974**	**133,074**	**160,784**	**95,411**	**97,041**	**52,529**	**9,130**	**52,150**	**X**	**157,779**
Afghanistan, Islamic State	112	66	X	X	X	99	X	X	25,000 a	299
Armenia	X	X	X	X	X	X	X	X	X	750
Azerbaijan	X	X	X	X	157	538 e	X	X	X	1,700
Bangladesh	1,054	X	X	X	1	370	X	X	800 a	230
Bhutan	X	X	X	X	X	X	X	X	X	356
Cambodia	X	X	X	X	X	X	X	X	83,000	0
China {d}	177,600	62,200	108,800	52,300	3,264	1,670	X	X	2,168,304	59,655
Georgia, Rep	X	X	X	X	X	3	X	X	X	1,725
India	196,892	68,047	26,000	1,900	776	686	X	X	205,000	19,843
Indonesia	X	962	X	31,101	759	2,000	0	5,420	709,000	2,169
Iran, Islamic Rep	3,754	193	2,295	X	12,700	20,659	X	X	56,000	1,957
Iraq	X	X	X	X	13,417	3,100	X	X	70,000	910
Israel	X	X	X	X	1	1	X	X	1,600	0
Japan	8,296	804	175	17	8	30	0	6,600	134,750	21,020
Jordan	X	X	X	X	0	28	X	X	87	0
Kazakhstan, Rep	X	X	X	X	723	1,498	X	X	X	3,500
Korea, Dem People's Rep	2,000	300	300	300	X	X	X	X	X	5,000
Korea, Rep	276	183	X	X	X	X	0	31,000	3,467	2,469
Kuwait	X	X	X	X	13,358	1,360	X	X	X	0
Kyrgyz Rep	1,080	X	1,580	812	12	5	X	X	X	2,833
Lao People's Dem Rep	X	X	X	X	X	X	X	X	22,638	235
Lebanon	X	X	X	X	X	X	X	X	1,000	267
Malaysia	15	4	126	X	585	2,150	X	X	59,229	1,439
Mongolia	12,000	X	12,000	X	X	X	X	X	160,000	0
Myanmar	5	2	X	X	7	278	X	X	160,000	288
Nepal	X	X	0	X	X	0	X	X	144,000	249
Oman	X	X	X	X	659	550	X	X	X	0
Pakistan	X	X	X	734	27	646	X	X	85,000	4,732
Philippines	1	0	369	262	33	98	X	X	31,951	2,055
Saudi Arabia	X	X	X	X	35,620	5,260	X	X	X	0
Singapore	X	X	X	X	X	X	X	X	X	0
Sri Lanka	X	X	X	X	X	X	X	X	7,175	1,160
Syrian Arab Rep	X	X	X	X	340	250	X	X	4,500	900
Tajikistan, Rep	X	X	X	X	X	7	X	X	X	4,054
Thailand	X	0	1,422	999	27	175	X	X	8,169	2,459
Turkey	590	162	7,705	6,986	66	11	9,130	9,130	216,000	9,810
Turkmenistan, Rep	X	X	X	X	73	2,860	X	X	X	10
United Arab Emirates	X	X	X	X	12,330	5,794	X	X	X	0
Uzbekistan, Rep	X	X	X	X	X	1,870	X	X	X	1,904
Viet Nam	300	150	12	X	68	105	X	X	6,490	1,864
Yemen, Rep	X	X	X	X	544	429	X	X	X	0
OCEANIA	**66,253**	**45,367**	**51,139**	**45,690**	**248**	**1,065**	**462,000**	**55,000**	**X**	**12,679**
Australia	66,220	45,340	50,600	45,600	199	555	462,000	55,000	25,248	7,189
Fiji	X	X	X	X	X	X	X	X	515	85
New Zealand	33	27	539	90	17	85	X	X	60,000	5,059
Papua New Guinea	X	X	X	X	31	425	X	X	98,000	240
Solomon Islands	X	X	X	X	X	X	X	X	37	0

Sources: World Energy Council and the World Bank.
Notes: a. Technical potential. b. Data are for the South Africa Customs Union (Botswana, Lesotho, Namibia, South Africa, and Swaziland). c. Denmark includes Greenland.
d. China's and the United Kingdom's coal reserves contrast sharply with previous estimates; see Sources and Technical Notes. e. Data from another source; see Sources and Technical Notes.
World totals include countries for which no data are listed here. 0 = zero or less than half of the unit of measure. X = not available.
For additional information, see Sources and Technical Notes.

Data Table 12.4 Production, Consumption, and Reserves of Selected Metals, 1980–94

	Annual Production (000 metric tons)					Annual Consumption (000 metric tons)			
	1980	1985	1990	1994		1980	1985	1990	1994
ALUMINUM {a}									
Australia	27,179.0	31,838.9	40,697.0	41,733.0	United States	4,453.5	4,282.0	4,330.4	5,407.1
Guinea	11,862.0	11,790.0	16,150.0	17,040.0	Japan	1,639.0	1,694.8	2,414.3	2,174.8
Jamaica	12,054.0	6,239.0	10,936.7	11,571.3	China	550.0	630.0	861.0	1,318.0
Brazil	5,538.0	5,846.0	9,875.6	8,280.8	Germany	1,272.3	1,390.9	1,378.5	1,300.0
China	1,500.0	1,650.0	3,655.0	7,260.0	U.S.S.R. {b}	1,850.0	1,750.0	2,790.0	1,185.0
India	1,785.0	2,281.0	5,277.0	5,280.0	France	600.9	586.1	723.0	665.0
Russian Federation {c}	4,600.0	4,600.0	5,500.0	4,000.0	Korea, Rep	87.5	145.6	368.9	557.0
Suriname	4,646.0	3,738.0	3,266.8	3,200.5	Italy	458.0	470.0	652.0	554.0
Venezuela	0.0	0.0	786.0	2,540.0	United Kingdom	550.0	350.4	453.7	477.3
Greece	3,286.0	2,453.0	2,496.0	2,168.0	India	233.8	297.6	433.3	475.3
Ten Countries Total	**72,450.0**	**70,435.9**	**98,640.1**	**103,073.6**	**Ten Countries Total**	**11,695.0**	**11,597.4**	**14,405.1**	**14,113.5**
World Total	**89,220.0**	**84,189.0**	**114,850.8**	**111,024.2**	**World Total**	**15,297.9**	**15,861.5**	**19,251.8**	**20,201.1**
Bauxite, World Reserves 1994 (000 metric tons)				23,000,000	World Reserves Life Index (years)				207
Bauxite, World Reserve Base 1994 (000 metric tons)				28,000,000	World Reserve Base Life Index (years)				252
CADMIUM									
Japan	2.2	2.5	2.5	2.6	Japan	1.1	1.9	4.8	6.6
Canada	1.3	1.7	1.5	2.2	Belgium	1.7	1.9	2.7	2.6
Belgium	1.5	1.3	2.0	1.6	United States	3.9	3.7	3.1	2.2
U.S.S.R. {b}	2.9	3.0	2.4	1.5 d	France	1.2	1.1	1.4	1.5
China	0.3	0.5	1.1	1.3 d	U.S.S.R. {b}	2.4	2.9	2.0	1.0 d
United States	1.6	1.6	1.9	1.1	United Kingdom	1.3	1.4	0.9	0.7
Germany	1.2	1.1	3.0	1.1	Germany	2.2	1.6	0.7	0.7
Australia	1.0	0.9	0.6	0.9	China	0.3	0.4	0.4	0.6 d
Italy	0.6	0.5	0.7	0.6	India	0.1	0.2	0.3	0.4
Korea, Rep	0.4	0.1	0.6	0.6	Korea, Rep	0.2	0.3	0.4	0.4
Ten Countries Total	**13.0**	**13.2**	**16.2**	**13.5**	**Ten Countries Total**	**13.3**	**13.5**	**16.8**	**16.7**
World Total	**18.2**	**19.1**	**20.3**	**18.3** d	**World Total**	**17.0**	**17.6**	**20.3**	**18.3** d
World Reserves 1994 (000 metric tons)				540	World Reserves Life Index (years)				X e
World Reserve Base 1994 (000 metric tons)				970	World Reserve Base Life Index (years)				X e
COPPER									
Chile	1,063.0	1,359.8	1,628.3	2,219.9	United States	1,867.7	1,958.0	2,213.5	2,674.3
United States	1,181.0	1,104.8	1,497.5	1,795.4	Japan	1,158.3	1,226.3	1,446.6	1,374.9
Canada	716.4	738.6	704.5	617.3	Germany	870.8	886.8	854.7	983.1
U.S.S.R. {b}	590.0	600.0	640.0	540.0 d	China	386.0	420.0	528.0	745.7 d
China	115.0	185.0	375.0	432.1	U.S.S.R. {b}	1,300.0	1,305.0	1,140.0	560.0 d
Australia	243.5	259.8	296.0	415.6	France	433.4	397.8	458.8	495.0
Zambia	595.8	452.6	445.0	384.4	Korea, Rep	84.0	206.6	251.6	476.2
Poland	343.0	431.3	384.0	376.8	Italy	388.0	362.0	474.8	467.9
Peru	336.1	391.3	372.8	359.9	Belgium	303.9	309.6	376.0	404.9
Indonesia	59.0	88.7	144.0	333.8	United Kingdom	450.5	346.5	324.7	377.3
Ten Countries Total	**5,242.8**	**5,611.9**	**6,487.1**	**7,475.2**	**Ten Countries Total**	**7,242.6**	**7,418.6**	**8,068.7**	**8,559.3**
World Total	**7,739.0**	**8,088.2**	**8,814.0**	**9,522.6**	**World Total**	**9,374.6**	**9,699.9**	**10,780.2**	**11,084.2**
World Reserves 1994 (000 metric tons)				310,000	World Reserves Life Index (years)				33
World Reserve Base 1994 (000 metric tons)				590,000	World Reserve Base Life Index (years)				62
LEAD									
Australia	397.4	498.0	570.0	523.8	United States	1,094.0	1,141.7	1,275.2	1,374.8
China	160.0	200.0	363.9	376.2	Germany	433.1	440.0	391.8	347.9
United States	550.4	424.4	493.4	374.0	Japan	392.5	394.9	416.4	345.0
Peru	184.5	201.5	187.7	216.7	United Kingdom	295.5	274.3	301.6	267.6
Canada	349.1	268.3	241.3	172.6	Italy	275.0	235.0	258.0	262.2
Mexico	145.5	206.7	174.1	164.4	France	212.8	208.0	254.2	246.7
Kazakhstan {c}	420.0	440.0	245.0	160.0 d	China	210.0	220.0	250.0	214.1
Sweden	72.2	75.9	84.2	112.8	U.S.S.R. {b}	800.0	800.0	380.0	200.0
Namibia	50.2	34.6	19.4	93.1	Korea, Rep	33.0	63.2	147.4	175.1
Morocco	114.8	106.8	66.9	75.7	Mexico	85.1	105.6	118.8	162.0
Ten Countries Total	**2,444.1**	**2,456.2**	**2,445.9**	**2,269.3**	**Ten Countries Total**	**3,831.0**	**3,882.7**	**3,793.4**	**3,595.4**
World Total	**3,448.2**	**3,431.2**	**3,150.3**	**2,764.7**	**World Total**	**4,435.6**	**5,236.6**	**5,676.5**	**5,342.2**
World Reserves 1994 (000 metric tons)				63,000	World Reserves Life Index (years)				23
World Reserve Base 1994 (000 metric tons)				130,000	World Reserve Base Life Index (years)				47
MERCURY									
China	0.7	0.7	1.0	0.7	United States	2.0	1.7	1.2	X
Algeria	0.8	0.8	0.6	0.4	Spain	0.2	0.6	0.8	X
Spain	1.5	0.9	0.0	0.3	Algeria	X	0.2	0.7	X
Kyrgyz Rep	X	X	X	0.3	United Kingdom	0.4	0.3	0.4	X
Finland	0.1	0.1	0.1	0.1	China	0.5	0.4	0.3	X
United States	1.1	0.6	0.6	0.1 d	Brazil	X	0.2	0.3	X
Russian Federation {c}	2.1	2.2	0.8	0.1 d	Germany	0.5	0.3	0.2	X
Tajikistan Rep	X	X	X	0.1	Mexico	X	0.2	0.2	X
Slovak Rep {f}	0.2	0.2	0.1	0.1	Belgium	0.1	0.3	0.1	X
Ukraine	X	X	X	0.1	U.S.S.R. {b}	0.9	X	X	X
Ten Countries Total	**6.5**	**5.5**	**3.3**	**2.1**	**Ten Countries Total**	**4.6**	**4.1**	**4.2**	**X**
World Total	**6.9**	**6.8**	**4.1**	**2.9** d	**World Total**	**6.9**	**7.4**	**6.6**	**X**
World Reserves 1994 (000 metric tons)				130	World Reserves Life Index (years)				45
World Reserve Base 1994 (000 metric tons)				240	World Reserve Base Life Index (years)				83

	Annual Production (000 metric tons)					Annual Consumption (000 metric tons)			
	1980	1985	1990	1994		1980	1985	1990	1994
NICKEL									
U.S.S.R. {b}	154.2	185.1	212.0	243.0 d	Japan	122.0	136.1	164.9	164.9
Canada	184.8	170.0	196.2	150.1	United States	143.1	143.1	124.6	137.3
Indonesia	53.3	40.3	68.6	81.2	Germany	78.1	87.0	88.8	93.9
New Caledonia	86.6	72.4	85.0	73.6	U.S.S.R. {b}	132.0	138.0	115.0	64.0 d
Australia	74.3	85.8	67.0	71.9	Italy	27.1	29.0	27.3	44.6
Dominican Republic	16.3	25.4	28.7	31.6	France	38.4	31.9	44.8	42.2
Cuba	36.6	32.1	40.8	31.0	United Kingdom	22.8	24.8	32.6	38.0
China	10.9	25.0	26.0	30.7	China	18.0	21.0	27.5	26.8
South Africa	25.7	25.0	30.0	30.1	Finland	9.3	14.7	19.0	23.4
Colombia	0.0	15.5	18.4	20.8	Sweden	20.0	17.0	19.4	23.0
Ten Countries Total	**642.7**	**676.6**	**772.7**	**764.0**	**Ten Countries Total**	**610.8**	**642.6**	**663.9**	**829.9**
World Total	**779.7**	**812.6**	**880.3**	**802.5**	**World Total**	**716.7**	**775.2**	**839.6**	**882.0**
World Reserves 1994 (000 metric tons)				47,000	World Reserves Life Index (years)				59
World Reserve Base 1994 (000 metric tons)				110,000	World Reserve Base Life Index (years)				137
TIN									
China	14.6	15.0	35.8	46.0 d	United States	56.4	37.8	37.2	33.5
Indonesia	32.5	21.7	31.7	30.6	Japan	30.9	31.6	33.8	29.4
Peru	1.1	3.8	4.8	20.0	China	12.5	11.5	16.9	26.1
Brazil	6.9	26.5	39.1	17.0	Germany	19.0	17.8	18.6	18.2
Bolivia	27.3	16.1	17.3	16.1	U.S.S.R. {b}	25.0	31.5	24.0	14.5 d
Malaysia	61.4	36.9	28.5	6.5	United Kingdom	9.9	24.8	10.2	10.4
Australia	11.6	6.4	7.4	6.4	Korea, Rep	1.8	2.6	6.9	9.8
U.S.S.R. {b}	36.0	13.5	13.0	5.0 d	France	10.1	6.9	8.1	9.2
Portugal	0.3	0.2	1.3	4.3	Netherlands	5.0	4.5	6.1	7.9
Thailand	33.7	16.9	14.6	3.1	Thailand	0.8	0.6	2.6	5.1
Ten Countries Total	**225.4**	**157.0**	**193.5**	**155.0**	**Ten Countries Total**	**171.4**	**169.6**	**164.4**	**164.1**
World Total	**247.3**	**180.7**	**210.8**	**169.4**	**World Total**	**232.5**	**215.4**	**231.9**	**216.8**
World Reserves 1994 (000 metric tons)				7,000	World Reserves Life Index (years)				41
World Reserve Base 1994 (000 metric tons)				10,000	World Reserve Base Life Index (years)				59
ZINC									
Canada	1,059.0	1,172.2	1,203.2	1,007.3	United States	879.0	962.0	992.0	1,118.3
Australia	495.3	759.1	945.0	945.0 d	Japan	752.0	780.0	814.3	723.1
China	160.0	300.0	619.0	900.0 d	China	259.0	349.0	500.0	611.9
Peru	487.6	523.4	583.9	602.6 d	Germany	474.0	480.0	484.0	531.6
United States	317.1	251.9	543.2	513.1 d	Italy	236.0	218.0	270.0	336.1
Mexico	235.8	275.4	306.7	369.7 d	U.S.S.R. {b}	1,030.0	1,000.0	640.0	330.0 d
Sweden	167.4	216.4	164.1	173.3 d	France	330.0	247.0	284.0	296.7
Kazakhstan {c}	785.0	810.0	550.0	250.0 d	Korea, Rep	68.0	120.0	230.0	264.9
Korea, Dem People's Rep	140.0	180.0	230.0	210.0 d	Belgium	155.0	169.0	177.6	225.0
Ireland	228.7	191.6	166.5	210.0 d	Australia	100.4	86.6	113.9	215.4
Ten Countries Total	**4,075.9**	**4,680.0**	**5,311.6**	**5,181.0**	**Ten Countries Total**	**4,283.4**	**4,411.6**	**4,505.8**	**4,653.0**
World Total	**6,064.4**	**6,125.0**	**7,158.2**	**6,895.1** d	**World Total**	**6,283.0**	**6,552.0**	**6,696.0**	**6,950.3**
World Reserves 1994 (000 metric tons)				140,000	World Reserves Life Index (years)				20
World Reserve Base 1994 (000 metric tons)				330,000	World Reserve Base Life Index (years)				48
IRON ORE									
China	68,072.0	80,000.0	168,300.0	234,660.0 d	China	120,394.0	140,354.0	193,471.0	222,771.0 g
Brazil	114,726.7	128,251.0	152,300.0	151,000.0 d	U.S.S.R. {b}	197,840.0	203,760.0	199,679.0	168,938.0 g
Australia	95,529.4	97,447.0	110,508.0	120,534.0 d	Japan	108,693.0	102,215.0	39,642.0	113,783.0 g
Russian Federation {c}	244,702.6	247,639.0	236,000.0	75,000.0 d	United States	90,832.0	64,679.0	38,140.0	63,039.0 g
Ukraine	X	X	105,866.0	70,000.0 d	Brazil	18,383.0	36,419.0	38,004.0	44,965.0 g
India	41,934.4	42,545.0	54,579.0	61,000.0 d	Germany	50,072.0	45,204.0	43,809.0	41,350.0 g
United States	70,726.8	49,533.0	56,408.0	55,651.0 d	Korea, Rep	9,675.0	11,709.0	22,798.0	32,001.0 g
Canada	48,751.7	39,502.0	34,855.0	30,568.0 d	France	37,875.0	26,606.0	24,256.0	20,199.0 g
South Africa	26,310.3	24,414.0	30,291.0	29,385.0 d	Belgium	15,756.0	13,353.0	20,262.0	17,975.0 g
Macedonia, former Yugoslav Rep	X	X	X	20,000.0 d	United Kingdom	9,326.0	15,176.0	14,753.0	15,826.0 g
Ten Countries Total	**710,753.9**	**709,331.0**	**949,107.0**	**847,798.0**	**Ten Countries Total**	**658,846.0**	**659,475.0**	**634,814.0**	**740,847.0**
World Total	**890,924.3**	**860,640.0**	**984,048.0**	**988,797.0** d	**World Total**	**890,924.3**	**860,640.0**	**979,047.0**	**970,422.0** g
World Reserves 1994 (000 metric tons)				150,000,000	World Reserves Life Index (years)				152
World Reserve Base 1994 (000 metric tons)				230,000,000	World Reserve Base Life Index (years)				233
STEEL, CRUDE									
Japan	111,396.9	105,281.0	110,339.0	99,600.0 d	U.S.S.R. {b}	150,330.0	157,161.0	152,556.0	131,865.0 h
United States	101,456.7	80,069.0	89,726.0	88,793.0 d	Japan	79,007.0	73,377.0	99,032.0	99,149.0 h
China	37,120.8	46,721.0	66,100.0	88,680.0 d	United States	114,433.0	105,593.0	105,335.0	93,325.0 h
Russian Federation {c}	147,943.5	154,670.0	154,414.0	58,000.0 d	China	43,005.0	71,428.0	68,419.0	71,042.0 h
Germany	51,147.0	48,350.0	43,891.0	37,600.0 d	Germany	44,631.0	39,995.0	39,550.0	39,088.0 h
Korea, Rep	8,558.5	13,539.0	23,125.0	33,000.0 d	Italy	26,764.0	21,880.0	28,489.0	26,593.0 h
Ukraine	X	X	52,646.0	30,500.0 d	Korea, Rep	6,100.0	11,310.0	21,480.0	26,190.0 h
Italy	26,501.1	23,789.0	25,439.0	25,701.0 d	India	10,900.0	14,400.0	21,700.0	20,300.0 h
Brazil	15,338.9	20,456.0	20,567.0	25,000.0 d	France	20,159.0	14,812.0	18,076.0	16,588.0 h
India	10,384.0	12,185.0	15,313.0	18,500.0 d	United Kingdom	16,050.0	14,350.0	16,690.0	14,600.0 h
Ten Countries Total	**509,847.4**	**505,060.0**	**548,914.0**	**505,374.0**	**Ten Countries Total**	**511,379.0**	**524,306.0**	**571,327.0**	**538,740.0**
World Total	**713,813.1**	**718,131.0**	**771,373.0**	**725,129.0** d	**World Total**	**718,921.0**	**720,568.0**	**773,383.0**	**732,002.0** h

Sources: U.S. Bureau of Mines, World Bureau of Metal Statistics, and International Iron and Steel Institute.
Notes: a. Production refers to bauxite, consumption to aluminum. b. Data refer to all components of the former U.S.S.R.
c. Data are for the country named for 1994 only. Data for prior years are for the former U.S.S.R. d. Data are for 1993. e. A production reserve ratio would be misleading because production data include secondary metals. f. Slovak Rep data for years prior to 1994 refer to Czechoslovakia in its entirety. g. Data are for 1992.
h. Data are for 1991. The world reserves life index equals world reserves estimated for 1994 divided by world production for 1994.
The world reserve base life index equals the world reserve base estimated for 1994 divided by world production for 1994.
0 = zero or less than half the unit of measure; X = not available. For additional information, see Sources and Technical Notes.

Data Table 12.5 Industrial Waste in Selected Countries

	Year of Estimate	Waste Generated from Surface Treatment of Metals and Plastics (metric tons)	Biocide Production (metric tons)	Waste (metric tons)			Waste from Production and Use of (metric tons)			
				Oil	Containing PCBs	Clinical and Pharmaceutical	Photographic Materials	Organic Solvents	Paints and Pigments	Resins and Latex
Austria	1990	14,731	450	60,300	81	8,254	1,400	27,253	15,000	X
Canada	1985	186,200	4,500	367,000	120,000	X	X	262,000	72,700	74,000 a
Czechoslovakia (former)	1987	2,561,174	183	565,764	X	X	X	20,723	13,875	131,519
Finland	1987	1,813	361	35,684	1,789	97	547	7,384	5,787	2,123
France	1990	X	X	409,000	17,000 b	X	X	285,000 b	X	X
Germany, Fed Rep	1987	219,527	X	859,456	10,537	X	X	454,489	225,525	867,015
Greece	1990	X	X	25,000	1,800	1,500	X	21,000	6,000	150
Hungary	1989	12,000	10,300	455,000	134	X	X	49,000	11,000	X
Ireland	1991	7,000	5	1,000 c	X	X	X	12,500	X	45,000
Japan	1985	8,877,000 d	X	3,672,000 d	X	X	X	X	X	2,894,000
Luxembourg	1990	22,200	5	3,900	480	356	29	284	540	X
Netherlands	1990	22,000	1,800	279,000	400	1,000	21,000	69,000	25,000	20,000
New Zealand	1990	3,030	1,100	18,151	4	2,770	451	3,690	29,381	12,892
Norway	1988	8,000	400	55,000	2,000 e	X	6,000	9,000	16,000	X
Poland	1990	X	X	41,400	X	X	X	X	175,900	X
Portugal	1989	X	X	16,473	703	X	X	X	X	X
Spain	1990	X	X	320,000	2,200	X	X	5,400	X	X
United States {f}	1990	1,982,379	13,216	4,960,000	5,015,060	2,800,000	X	70,000,000	693,833	41,000,000

Source: Organisation for Economic Co-Operation and Development.

Notes: a. Data for resins and latex are from 1987; PCB waste includes 6,500 metric tons in storage. b. Data for PCBs and organic solvents are from 1989.
c. Waste oil is only lubricating oil; data for organic solvents include miscellaneous chemical wastes.
d. Waste oil includes waste solvents; waste generated from the surface treatment of metals is total waste metals; data for resins and latex refer to plastics and rubber.
e. Data for PCBs refer to 1987. f. Data are from 1989 through 1991; PCB data are from a survey and do not represent total PCB waste; organic solvents include all organic chemicals; resins and latex refer to plastics and rubber. X = not available.
For additional information, see Sources and Technical Notes.

Sources and Technical Notes

Data Table 12.1
Commercial Energy Production, 1973–93

Source: United Nations Statistical Division (UNSTAT), *1993 Energy Statistics Yearbook* (UNSTAT, New York, 1995).

Energy data are compiled by UNSTAT, primarily from responses to questionnaires sent to national governments, supplemented by official national statistical publications and by data from intergovernmental organizations. When official numbers are not available, UNSTAT prepares estimates based on the professional and commercial literature.

Total production of commercially traded fuels includes solid, liquid, and gaseous fuels and primary electricity production. *Solid* fuels include bituminous coal, lignite, peat, and oil shale burned directly. *Liquid* fuels include crude petroleum and natural gas liquids. *Gas* includes natural gas and other petroleum gases. *Primary electricity* is valued differently depending on its source. Wind, tidal, wave, solar, and hydroelectric power generation are expressed as the energy value of electricity (1 kilowatt hour = 3.6 million joules). Nuclear and geothermal power generation are valued on a fossil-fuel-avoided basis rather than on an energy-output basis. For example, a nuclear power plant that produces 1,000 kilowatt-hours of electricity provides the equivalent heat of 0.123 metric ton of coal. However, more than 0.123 metric ton of coal would be required to produce 1,000 kilowatt-hours of electricity. Much of the energy released from coal combustion (or from a nuclear or geothermal plant) in a power plant is used in the mechanical work of turning dynamos or is lost in waste heat, so less energy is embodied in the final electricity than in the initial coal. The efficiency of a thermal electric plant is the ratio between the amount of final electricity produced and the initial energy supplied. Although this rating varies widely from country to country and from plant to plant, UNSTAT and other international energy organizations use a standard factor of 33 percent efficiency to estimate the fossil fuel value of nuclear electricity and 10 percent efficiency to estimate the fossil fuel value of geothermal energy. Electricity production data generally refer to gross production. Data for the Dominican Republic, Finland, France (including Monaco), Mexico, the United States, Zambia, and Zimbabwe refer to net production. Gross production is the amount of electricity produced by a generating station before consumption by station auxiliaries and transformer losses within the station are deducted. Net production is the amount of electricity remaining after these deductions. Typically, net production is 5 to 10 percent less than gross production. Energy production from pumped storage is not included in gross or net electricity generation.

Electricity production includes both public and self-producer power plants. Public power plants produce electricity for many users. They may be operated by private, cooperative, or governmental organizations. Self-producer power plants are operated by organizations or companies to produce electricity for internal applications, such as factory operations.

Fuelwood, charcoal, bagasse, animal and vegetal wastes, and all forms of solar energy are excluded from production figures, even when traded commercially.

One petajoule (10^{15} joules) is the same as 0.0009478 Quads (10^{15} British thermal units) and is the equivalent of 163,400 "U.N. standard" barrels of oil or 34,140 "U.N. standard" metric tons of coal. The heat content of various fuels has been converted to coal-equivalent and then petajoule-equivalent values using country- and year-specific conversion factors. For example, a metric ton of bituminous coal produced in Argentina has an energy value of 0.843 metric ton of standard coal equivalent (7 million kilocalories). A metric ton of bituminous coal produced in Turkey has a 1991 energy value of 0.925 metric ton of standard coal equivalent. The original national production data for bituminous coal were multiplied by these conversion factors and then by 29.3076×10^{-6} to yield petajoule equivalents. Other fuels were converted to coal-equivalent and petajoule-equivalent terms in a similar manner.

South Africa refers to the South Africa Customs Union: Botswana, Lesotho, Namibia, South Africa, and Swaziland.

For additional information, refer to the United Nations *1993 Energy Statistics Yearbook*.

Data Table 12.2
Energy Consumption, 1973–93

Sources: United Nations Statistical Division (UNSTAT), *1993 Energy Statistics Yearbook* (UNSTAT, New York, 1995). Gross National Product (GNP): The World Bank, *World Tables*, on diskette (The World Bank, Washington, D.C., 1995).

Commercial energy consumption refers to "apparent consumption" and is defined as domestic production plus net imports, minus net stock increases, and minus aircraft and marine bunkers. *Total* consumption includes energy from solid, liquid, and gaseous fuels, plus primary electricity (see the definition in the Sources and Notes to Table 12.1). Energy consumption *per constant 1987 US$ of GNP* is calculated using GNP data from the World Bank and is a measure of relative energy efficiency. Included under *imports as a percentage of consumption* are imports minus exports. A negative value (in parentheses) indicates that exports are greater than imports.

Traditional fuels includes estimates of the consumption of fuelwood, charcoal, bagasse, and animal and vegetal wastes. Fuelwood and charcoal consumption data are estimated from population data and country-specific per capita consumption figures. These per capita estimates were prepared by the Food and Agriculture Organization of the United Nations (FAO) after an assessment of the available consumption data. Data were supplied by the answers to questionnaires or come from official publications by Bangladesh, Bhutan, Brazil, the Central African Republic, Chile, Colombia, Costa Rica, Cuba, Cyprus, El Salvador, The Gambia, Japan, Kenya, the Democratic People's Republic of Korea, the Republic of Korea, Luxembourg, Malawi, Mauritius, Nepal, Panama, Portugal, the former Soviet Union, Sri Lanka, Sweden, Thailand, and Uruguay. Estimates by the FAO of per capita consumption of nonconiferous fuelwood have ranged from 0.0016 cubic meter per capita per year in Jordan to 0.9783 cubic meter per capita per year in Benin.

Similar estimates were prepared for coniferous fuelwood and for charcoal. Although the energy values of fuelwood and charcoal vary widely, UNSTAT uses standard factors of 0.33 metric ton of coal equivalent per cubic meter of fuelwood and 0.986 metric ton of coal equivalent per metric ton of charcoal.

Bagasse production is based on sugar production data in the *Sugar Yearbook* of the International Sugar Organization. It is assumed that 3.26 metric tons of fuel bagasse at 50 percent moisture are produced per metric ton of extracted cane sugar. The energy of a metric ton of bagasse is valued at 0.264 metric ton of coal equivalent.

A petajoule is one quadrillion (10^{15}) joules. A gigajoule is one billion (10^9) joules. A megajoule is one million (10^6) joules.

Data Table 12.3
Reserves and Resources of Commercial Energy, 1993

Sources: World Energy Council (WEC), *1995 Survey of Energy Resources* (WEC, London, 1995). Hydroelectric technical potential: The World Bank, *A Survey of the Future Role of Hydroelectric Power in 100 Developing Countries* (The World Bank, Washington, D.C., 1984). Hydroelectric installed capacity: United Nations Statistical Division (UNSTAT), *1993 Energy Statistics Yearbook* (UNSTAT, New York, 1995).

Energy resource estimates are based on geological, economic, and technical criteria. Resources are first graded according to the degree of confidence in the extent and location of the resource, based on available geological information, and are then judged on the technical and economic feasibility of their exploitation.

Proved reserves in place represent the total resource that is known to exist in specific locations and in specific quantities and qualities. *Proved recoverable reserves* are the fraction of proved reserves in place that can be extracted under present and expected local economic conditions with existing available technology. Additional energy resources, comprising those that are not currently economic, are not shown in this table.

The coal, oil, and gas sectors of the energy industry each have their own categories for estimating reserves. The WEC attempts to reconcile these categories to fit their cross-sectoral reserve concepts. Each country estimates its resource reserves using its own judgment and interpretation of commonly held concepts. Intercountry comparisons should be made with this caveat in mind. Reserve estimates are not final measured quantities. Those estimates change as exploration, exploitation, and technology advances and as economic conditions change.

There is no internationally accepted standard for categorizing coals of different ranks, although the WEC has used all the information available to do so. Anthracite makes up only a small fraction (3 to 4 percent) of *anthracite/bituminous coals.* Lignite makes up 57 percent (globally) of the proved reserves in place of *subbituminous/lignite coals,* and 63 percent of global proved recoverable reserves.

Crude oil also includes liquids obtained by condensation or extraction from natural gas.

Uranium data refer to known uranium deposits of a size and quality that could be recovered within specified production cost ranges (under $80 per kilogram and under $130 per kilogram) using currently proven mining and processing technologies.

Hydroelectric known exploitable potential refers to that part of a country's annual gross theoretical capacity (the amount of energy that would be obtained if all flows were exploited with 100 percent efficiency) that could be exploited using current technology and under current and expected local economic conditions. This includes both large- and small-scale schemes. Hydroelectric technical potential refers to the annual energy potential of all sites where it is physically possible to construct dams, with no consideration of economic return or adverse effects of site development.

Installed capacity refers to the combined generating capacity of hydroelectric plants installed in the country as of December 31, 1990.

Data Table 12.4
Production, Consumption, and Reserves of Selected Metals, 1980–94

Sources: Production data for 1980, 1985, 1990, and 1994: U.S. Bureau of Mines (U.S. BOM), *Minerals Yearbook 1983, 1986, and Various Years* (U.S. Government Printing Office, Washington, D.C., 1985, 1987, and 1995, respectively).

Consumption data for aluminum, cadmium, copper, lead, nickel, tin, and zinc: World Bureau of Metal Statistics, *World Metal Statistics* (World Bureau of Metal Statistics, Ware, U.K., December 1979, December 1980, December 1985, July 1990, August 1991, September 1991, October 1991, December 1992, and June 1995). Consumption data for mercury: Roskill Information Services Ltd., *Roskill's Metals Databook, 5th Edition, 1984* (Roskill, London, 1984); Roskill Information Services Ltd., *Statistical Supplement to the Economics of Mercury, 4th Edition, 1978* (Roskill, London, 1980); Roskill Information Services Ltd., *The Economics of Mercury, 7th Edition, 1990* (Roskill, London, 1990); and U.S. BOM, *Mineral Industry Surveys, Mercury in 1989* (U.S. Government Printing Office, Washington, D.C., 1989). Consumption data for iron ore and crude steel: International Iron and Steel Institute, *Steel Statistical Yearbook 1985 and 1992* (International Iron and Steel Institute, Brussels, 1985 and 1992), and the United Nations Conference on Trade and Development (UNCTAD), *UNCTAD Commodity Yearbook 1994* (New York, 1995). Reserves and reserve base data: U.S. BOM, *Mineral Commodity Summaries 1993* (U.S.

Government Printing Office, Washington, D.C., 1993).

The U.S. BOM publishes production, trade, consumption, and other data on commodities for the United States as well as for all other countries of the world (depending on the availability of reliable data). These data are based on information from government mineral and statistical agencies, the United Nations, and U.S. and foreign technical and trade literature.

The World Bureau of Metal Statistics publishes consumption data on the metals presented, excluding mercury, iron, and steel. Data on the metals included were supplied by metal companies, government agencies, trade groups, and statistical bureaus. Obviously incorrect data have been revised, but most data were compiled and reported without adjustment or retrospective revisions.

The countries listed represent the top 10 producers of each material in 1992 and the top 10 consumers in 1991.

The *annual production* data are the metal content of the ore mined for *copper, lead, mercury, nickel, tin,* and *zinc. Aluminum* (bauxite) and *iron ore* production are expressed in gross weight of ore mined (i.e., marketable product). Iron ore production refers to iron ore, iron ore concentrates, and iron ore agglomerates (sinter and pellets). *Cadmium* refers to the production of the refined metal. Production of *crude steel,* is defined as the total of usable ingots, continuously cast semifinished products, and liquid steel for castings. The United Nations' definition of crude steel is the equivalent of the term "raw steel" as used by the United States.

Annual consumption of metal refers to the domestic use of refined metals, which include metals refined from either primary (raw) or secondary (recovered) materials. Metal used in a product that is then exported is considered to be consumed by the producing country rather than by the importing country. Data on *mercury* consumption must be viewed with caution; they include estimates on consumption of secondary materials, which are generally not reported. Consumption of *iron ore* is the quantity of iron ore and is calculated as apparent consumption—the net of production plus imports minus exports. Such a value for consumption makes no allowance for stock inventories. This can lead to discrepancies in the published consumption data evident in the latest report by the UNCTAD Intergovernmental Group of Experts on Iron Ore. For example, Brazil had a "reported consumption" (i.e., domestic and imported ores consumed in iron and steel plants, as well as ores consumed for nonmetallurgical uses) of 23.7 million metric tons in 1990, compared to an apparent consumption of 40 mil-

lion metric tons. Apparent consumption of iron ore was chosen because data for reported consumption were only available for a limited number of countries and years. Because different countries report different grades of iron ore, consumption data are not strictly comparable among countries. Because world consumption of iron ore is roughly equal to world production, world production data were used for world consumption totals. Worldwide stock inventories are assumed to be negligible. Consumption of *crude steel* is calculated as apparent consumption. The International Iron and Steel Institute converted imports and exports into crude steel equivalents by using a factor of $1.3/(1 + 0.175c)$, where c is the domestic proportion of crude steel that is continuously cast. Such an adjustment avoids distortion of the export or import share relative to domestic production.

The *world reserve base life index* and the *world reserves life index* are expressed in years remaining. They were computed by dividing the 1992 world reserve base and world reserves by the respective world production rate for 1992. The underlying assumption is constant world production at the 1992 level and capacity.

The reserve base is the portion of the mineral resource that meets grade, quality, thickness, and depth criteria defined by current mining and production practices. The reserve base includes both measured and indicated reserves and refers to those resources that are both currently economic and marginally economic, as well as some of those that are currently subeconomic.

Mineral reserves are those deposits whose quantity and grade have been determined by samples and measurements and could be profitably recovered at the time of the assessment. Changes in geologic information, technology, costs of extraction and production, and prices of mined product can affect the reserve estimates. Reserves do not signify that extraction facilities are actually in place and operative.

Data Table 12.5
Industrial Waste in Selected Countries

Sources: Organisation for Economic Co-Operation and Development (OECD), *Environmental Data Compendium 1993* (OECD, Paris, 1993). Waste definitions: *Basel Convention on the Control of Transboundary Movements of Hazardous Wastes and Their Disposal* (United Nations Environment Programme, 1989) Annex I; and Roger Batstone, James E. Smith, Jr., and David Wilson (eds.), *The Safe Disposal of Hazardous Wastes,* Vol. 1 (The World Bank Technical Paper No. 93, Washington, D.C., 1989), pp. 19–23.

Industrial waste data are collected by various means, and definitions might vary across countries. The OECD generally collects data using questionnaires completed by government representatives. Comparisons should be made cautiously, because (a) definitions vary from country to country, (b) the mix of hazardous materials in each category also varies, (c) these data do not include all industrial or hazardous waste (some data are based only on surveys of particular segments of an industry), and (d) these data do not measure potential toxicity.

Waste generated from surface treatment of metals and plastics includes acids and alkalis (surface metal treatment is the largest source of acid wastes) as well as other toxics. *Waste generated from biocide production* results from the manufacturing and use of insecticides, herbicides, and fungicides (not including those quantities applied correctly, but including spills, residues, etc.). *Waste oil* includes used motor oil, contaminated fuel oils, waste from industrial processes, and waste vegetable oils, among others. *Waste containing PCBs* includes waste from their manufacture, from the scraping of equipment containing PCBs, and from certain hydraulic fluids used in mining equipment and aircraft. *Clinical and pharmaceutical* waste includes waste pharmaceuticals, laboratory chemical residues arising from their production and preparation, and clinical (i.e., infectious) waste from hospitals, medical centers, clinics, and research institutions. Waste from the production and use of *photographic materials* includes waste chemicals from photographic processing. Waste *organic solvents* arise from dry cleaning and metal cleaning, from chemical processes, as well as from the production of numerous manufactured products such as paints, toiletries, thinners, and degreasants. Waste from *paints and pigments* includes waste from the manufacture and use of inks, dyes, pigments, paints, lacquers, and varnishes. Waste from *resins and latex* comes from the production, formulation, and use of resins, latex, plasticizers, glues, and other adhesives.

13. Water and Fisheries

The world's marine ecosystems and the marine fisheries that they support are a vital part of the global food supply. An estimated 950 million people, mostly in developing countries, depend on fish as their primary source of protein. Yet there are continued signs that marine fisheries are in serious trouble. This chapter looks at the causes of the problems—primarily overfishing, but also coastal degradation and a lack of selectivity in fishing techniques—and their biological and social consequences. It also examines the policy failures that have permitted (and in some cases encouraged) overfishing and describes what must be done locally and internationally to put fisheries management on a more sustainable footing.

Discussion then turns from the vast oceans to the far smaller freshwater resources. Fresh water is unevenly distributed over the globe, with abundant supplies available in some localities and much smaller amounts available in others. As human use of these resources for agricultural, industrial, domestic, and municipal purposes continues to expand—and as evidence that many water resources are being used in unsustainable ways accumulates—water experts are raising concerns about the future. Will some regions face critical shortages of water that could undermine human health and economic development?

This chapter looks at the expanded use of freshwater resources. It examines a proposed indicator of future pressures on these resources, the water stress index, and considers its limitations. It also reports on one analysis based on the index that concludes that by the middle of the next century, as much as 18 percent of the world's population could live in countries suffering from water scarcity. The chapter also reports on the potential for improving the efficiency of water use and managing water resources more effectively, measures that could markedly increase the availability of water to meet future needs.

MARINE FISHING TRENDS: TROUBLED WATERS AHEAD

The condition of world fisheries in the 1990s has left little doubt that world fisheries are under great stress. Even though in 1993—the latest year for which figures are available—the global fish harvest from inland and marine sources inched up to a new record high, this seeming abundance masks a serious decline in the productivity of many important fish and shellfish species. One of the few bright spots in the global fish harvest has been the rapid growth of aquaculture, which now accounts for nearly 16 percent of the total harvest and remains the only consistent area of growth [1]. Meanwhile, the twin threats of overfishing and the degradation of coastal ecosystems where the bounty of the sea is spawned have depleted many marine fish stocks, both inshore and in the open ocean. Because the sea still provides 8 of every 10 fish harvested, this biological stress puts at risk the very basis for the future productivity of fisheries. (See Data Table 13.4.)

The social repercussions of a further decline in marine fisheries are expected to be severe. The fishing enterprise directly or indirectly employs some 200 million people worldwide. High unemployment has already hit some areas such as eastern Canada, where the cod fishery has been closed since 1992, idling as many as 40,000 workers [2] [3].

Figure 13.1 Contribution of Fish to Human Diet, 1987–89

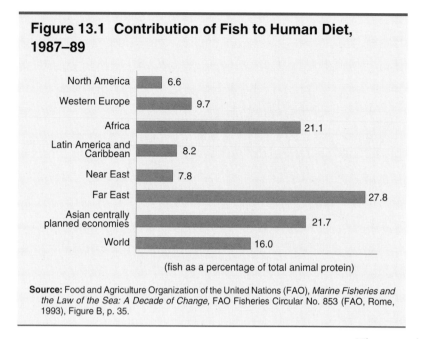

North America — 6.6
Western Europe — 9.7
Africa — 21.1
Latin America and Caribbean — 8.2
Near East — 7.8
Far East — 27.8
Asian centrally planned economies — 21.7
World — 16.0

(fish as a percentage of total animal protein)

Source: Food and Agriculture Organization of the United Nations (FAO), *Marine Fisheries and the Law of the Sea: A Decade of Change,* FAO Fisheries Circular No. 853 (FAO, Rome, 1993), Figure B, p. 35.

Fish in all forms are the source of 16 percent of the animal protein that humans consume (4). (See Figure 13.1.) In the developing world, where fish are a particularly important part of the diet and subsistence fishers still make up a sizable portion of the populace, the potential human costs of the current decline in fisheries are even greater. The prices of most fish species continue to rise as harvests shrink, making fish a less affordable meal among low-income populations. Meanwhile, continued overfishing of near-coastal waters by subsistence and other small-scale fishers, aggravated by competition with larger mechanized fishing vessels, leads to a cycle of smaller catches and increasing damage to the resource base.

The fisheries threat has led to urgent calls for reforming national and international fisheries management, and there now seems to be a consensus among fishing nations that corrective action is both possible and desirable. Although the job of reducing the world fishing fleet (5) and strictly regulating access to fish stocks to let them recover or to keep them healthy may require painful economic and social adjustments, the cost of failing to manage global fisheries sustainably will be far higher.

Trends in the Marine Catch

World fish production comes from three sources: the marine catch, consisting of all species harvested in coastal waters or on the high seas; the inland catch, from lakes and rivers; and aquaculture, both freshwater and marine. Of the total global fish harvest of 101 million metric tons in 1993, 78 percent was caught by the

marine fishing fleet, 6.8 percent was caught inland, and 15.5 percent was raised artificially through aquaculture (6). (See Figure 13.2.) The discussion below concentrates on the marine catch, which is by far the most important component of the world fish harvest.

The marine catch has changed markedly in size and composition over the past 45 years as fishing activity has increased. Between 1950 and 1989, the marine harvest increased nearly fivefold to a high of 86 million metric tons. In 1993, however, it dropped to 84 million metric tons. (Note that although the marine harvest peaked in 1989, the total global fish harvest has continued to climb because of increases in aquaculture production (7) (8).)

The growth in the marine harvest reflects not only the steady growth in the number of fishing vessels and the sophistication of their gear but also the increasing demand of a growing world population. The increase in fishing activity has gradually undermined the health of many marine fish stocks. In 1993, the Food and Agriculture Organization of the United Nations (FAO) estimated that more than two thirds of the world's marine fish stocks were being fished at or beyond their level of maximum productivity. Specifically, FAO numbers show that 25 percent of the stocks for which data are available are either already depleted from overfishing or in imminent danger of serious depletion because of current overharvesting. Another 44 percent of fish

Figure 13.2 Composition of the Global Catch, 1993

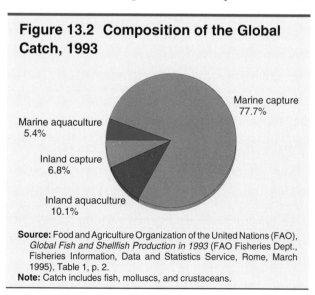

Marine capture 77.7%
Marine aquaculture 5.4%
Inland capture 6.8%
Inland aquaculture 10.1%

Source: Food and Agriculture Organization of the United Nations (FAO), *Global Fish and Shellfish Production in 1993* (FAO Fisheries Dept., Fisheries Information, Data and Statistics Service, Rome, March 1995), Table 1, p. 2.
Note: Catch includes fish, molluscs, and crustaceans.

stocks are being fished at their biological limit, and therefore are also in danger of overexploitation if fishing pressures continue to mount (9).

Regionally, overexploited species run the gamut from fish that inhabit the continental shelves (and their slopes) such as halibut, haddock, cod, hake, redfish, and orange roughy to migratory open-ocean species such as bluefin tuna, albacore, and swordfish. In warmer waters, shrimp have been heavily affected, as have many species of reef fish. Even many shark stocks, which until recently were considered an undesirable bycatch, have experienced sharp drops because of overharvesting and other irresponsible fishing practices such as finning, in which the fins are removed and the rest of the catch is discarded (10) (11).

Overfishing has been more severe in some regions than in others. For example, the northern Atlantic has long been subject to very high fishing pressures, causing steep declines in the stocks of groundfish—particularly cod—that had sustained the fisheries there for centuries. Atlantic cod catches today have plunged to one quarter of their size in the late 1960s (12). (See Figure 13.3.) In 1992, cod stocks in the western Atlantic were found to be at the lowest level ever measured—about 10 percent of their long-term average (13). The northwestern Pacific off the Asian coast is another site of particularly heavy fishing, with 100 percent of the assessed fish stocks exploited at or beyond sustainable limits (14).

Although not all regions are fished this intensively and not all important marine stocks are overfished in any single region, heavy fishing pressure is more the rule than the exception worldwide. In 6 of 11 major Atlantic and Pacific fishing regions, more than 60 percent of all commercial fish stocks either have been depleted or are being fished to their limits (15).

One consequence of the overexploitation of some marine species has been a progressive change in the composition of the global catch to species of lower economic value. As the high-value fish species such as cod, haddock, and hake that once made up the bulk of the commercial catch have declined, the catch of fish such as sardines, anchovies, and pilchard—all small species that are low on the food chain—has increased. These lower-value fish, which have provided nearly all of the growth in marine harvests since the 1970s, are often processed into fish oil and fish meal, which, among other uses, serve as a food source for aquaculture. Currently, about 30 percent of the global catch goes to such nonfood uses (16) (17).

Overfishing is not only due to large-scale industrial fishing fleets but also is caused by small-scale fleets and subsistence fishers in the developing world who fish

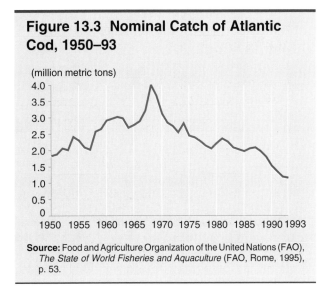

Figure 13.3 Nominal Catch of Atlantic Cod, 1950–93

(million metric tons)

Source: Food and Agriculture Organization of the United Nations (FAO), *The State of World Fisheries and Aquaculture* (FAO, Rome, 1995), p. 53.

close to shore. The small-scale fishing sector employs many more people than the rest of the fishing industry, and, because access to the sea's resources is generally open to all, fishing is frequently a job of last resort in rural areas with few employment alternatives. Small-scale fleets and subsistence fishers are thus responsible for roughly half the total world landings, and most of these fish are used locally for food. Unfortunately, coastal population growth and a lack of other employment opportunities often result in a continual increase in the number of boats working a given area, despite declines in the nearshore catch. The problem of coastal overfishing is sometimes made worse when industrial fishing vessels such as shrimp trawlers work close to shore and compete with small-scale fleets (18) (19).

Open Access, Overcapacity, and Subsidies

Overfishing is a prime cause—though not the only cause—of the decline in marine fisheries. At the heart of the overfishing problem is the issue of open access. Fish stocks have generally been considered common property open to exploitation by anyone with a boat and gear.

As long as fish stocks are plentiful and demand is high, economics dictates that it will be profitable to invest in fishing, and the number of fishers exploiting the resource will continue to increase. Unfortunately, strong demand—or government subsidies meant to encourage development of the fishing industry—may keep the fishing enterprise profitable even after the resource base begins to erode. Indeed, as long as enough fish are caught to cover operating costs, there will be little economic incentive to stop fishing once a vessel is built. Eventually, however, greater and greater effort will be

Table 13.1 Size of the World's Fishing Fleet, 1970 and 1992

Region	Gross Register Tonnage (000 metric tons)		Percent Growth, 1970–92
	1970	1992	
Asia	4,802.3	11,012.5	129
Former Soviet Union	3,996.7	7,765.5	94
Europe	3,097.4	3,018.3	(3)
North America	1,076.9	2,560.0	138
South America	361.5	816.5	126
Africa	244.0	699.1	187
Oceania	37.1	122.3	230
World	**13,615.9**	**25,994.2**	**91**

Source: Food and Agriculture Organization of the United Nations (FAO), *The State of the World's Fisheries and Aquaculture* (FAO, Rome, 1995), pp. 49, 51.

needed to catch the dwindling fish supply, and revenues will fall; by this time, however, there will also be a serious decline in fish stocks (20) (21).

In the 1970s, most nations extended their jurisdiction over coastal waters to 200 miles (322 kilometers) from shore, and many nations began to focus on developing their new national fisheries by subsidizing construction of fishing vessels and fish-processing facilities. The result was significant overcapacity in the world fishing fleet—particularly the industrial fleet. Over the past two decades, the size of the industrial fleet has expanded at a rate that is twice as fast as the rise in catches (22). (Table 13.1 shows that from 1970 to 1992 the size of the fishing fleet more than doubled in every region but Europe and the former Soviet Union.) Today, the global fishing fleet is at least 30 percent larger than it needs to be to fully harvest the available resource (23). This overcapacity, combined with powerful new technologies that have made each new boat more effective at finding and landing fish, has provided a recipe for overexploitation (24).

Not surprisingly, such overcapacity—and the overinvestment that has enabled it—has led to large economic losses in the global fisheries sector for more than a decade. FAO estimates that total expenses for the world fleet exceed total revenues by nearly $50 billion per year. However, since the industrial fishing sector is at once an important employer, a food source, and a source of export earnings, national governments generally try to make up this deficit through subsidies such as investment credits, tax holidays, low-cost loans, and outright grants. The magnitude of these subsidies and their nearly ubiquitous use in both developed and developing nations have been a key factor in the current decline in fisheries. Unfortunately, such subsidies have historically been used with little consideration of the long-term damage to the resource that they foster or the potential alternative uses that these funds might have in national development policies (25) (26) (27).

Coastal Degradation and Discards

Overfishing is not the only factor contributing to the current decline in fisheries. Environmental degradation of coastal areas that is caused by filling and development and by pollution from industrial, municipal, and agricultural sources perhaps represents an even greater long-term threat to aquatic productivity. Conversion of wetlands and pollution of critical areas such as estuaries and bays, which provide spawning, feeding, and nursery areas for many important marine species, are proceeding rapidly in coastal areas as demographic shifts bring a larger share of the population to the coasts (28) (29). (See Chapter 3, "Urban Impacts on Natural Resources.")

The harmful effects of coastal environmental degradation are often felt first by subsistence fishers and small-scale fleets because they ply their trade nearest the shore. In the Philippines, for example, reef fish account for about 20 percent of the inshore catch, much of which is taken for subsistence use. However, silt from unsound agricultural and logging practices, industrial and domestic pollutants, and destructive fishing techniques such as the use of dynamite and poisons have combined to damage some 70 percent of Philippine coral reefs, leading to a loss of reef productivity. Because Filipinos derive nearly half of their protein from fish, this has dealt a blow to local self-sufficiency in many communities (30).

Another reason for the poor condition of global fish stocks is that some 25 percent of the annual marine fish catch is simply discarded because it is considered unusable. Discards include not only undersized fish of the target species but also low-value and nontarget species. The lack of selectivity of current fishing practices and fishing gear leads inevitably to a high level of incidental catch of juvenile fish or other fish without commercial value, as well as considerable numbers of invertebrates, marine mammals, and marine birds.

FAO estimates that from 1988 to 1990, an average of 27 million metric tons of fish per year was discarded (not including discards from subsistence fishing, which tend to be much lower), whereas the usable harvest averaged 77 million metric tons. This means that for every ton of fish or shellfish landed for human consumption, one third of a ton of fish or shellfish is discarded into the sea. Nor does this include the incidental take of marine mammals such as dolphins, whales, and sea turtles, which is conservatively estimated at several hundred thousand individuals annually (31).

Of all fishing activities, shrimp trawling is by far the most indiscriminate and wasteful, accounting for more than one third of all discards. In some cases, shrimp may make up as little as 10 percent of the catch from a shrimp trawl, with the rest of the catch being discarded or sold for fish meal (32) (33). (See Figure 13.4.)

Discarded fish and other creatures often have very high mortality rates. When juvenile fish of a commercially valuable species are discarded and subsequently die, the resulting reduction in potential future catch can translate to billions of dollars of forgone revenue each year, to say nothing of the effects on the health of fish stocks (34).

Decreasing the level of global discards is considered essential if global fish harvests are to be sustained at or near present levels. FAO believes that a concerted effort to develop more selective gear and fishing practices could cut discards by as much as 60 percent by the year 2000 (35).

Managing Fisheries for Recovery and Sustainability

Managing world fisheries so that they return to health and are harvested sustainably will not be easy. Studies suggest that a reduction of 30 to 50 percent in the intensity of fishing—the so-called fishing effort—will be required, which will inevitably translate into the retirement of a large percentage of the global fleet (36).

This downsizing is already proceeding in an ad hoc manner in eastern Canada, the New England states, and the former Soviet Union. More deliberate programs to retire excess capacity—in the form of buyouts of some fishing vessels, for example—will be necessary in most cases. These programs should not simply shift excess capacity from one region to another, as has recently occurred in Canada, where some 65 Canadian vessels from the closed cod fishery were sold to other countries, including Argentina, Chile, Namibia, New Zealand, and South Africa (37).

Reducing or adjusting subsidies will also be important in discouraging new entries and retiring older vessels. Analysts suggest that redirecting at least some of the current fishing subsidies into buyout programs to shrink fleet overcapacity could pay handsome economic dividends as national fleets become more efficient and fish stocks are allowed to produce at their maximum level, raising harvest levels and profits. Short of this approach, however, large-scale programs for so-called disinvestment in fisheries may be difficult to finance, particularly in the developing world. The idea of bank-

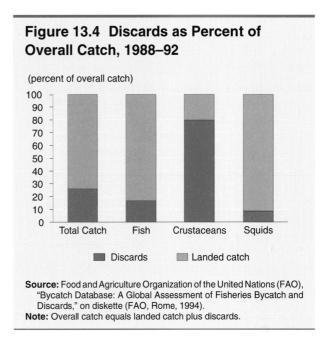

Figure 13.4 Discards as Percent of Overall Catch, 1988–92

(percent of overall catch)

Source: Food and Agriculture Organization of the United Nations (FAO), "Bycatch Database: A Global Assessment of Fisheries Bycatch and Discards," on diskette (FAO, Rome, 1994).
Note: Overall catch equals landed catch plus discards.

rolling such efforts to shrink the industrial fishing sector has not been popular so far with the World Bank and other development banks, despite the economic arguments in its favor (38) (39) (40) (41).

Even if the global fleet is successfully downsized, many experts believe that sustainable management of global fisheries will require some solution to the problem of open access. Otherwise, the fishing effort may not be reduced enough or in a manner that promotes the conservation of stocks.

Determining effective and equitable mechanisms that can be used to limit access to fisheries is certainly the most difficult and contentious problem facing fishery managers today. Some of the options include license limitations that restrict the number of boats allowed in an area; economic disincentives such as harvest taxes or user fees for fishing; cooperative or community management of a defined fishing territory; and individual transferable quotas, which grant fishers exclusive harvest rights to a portion of the sustainable catch of a given stock (with the size of the sustainable catch being set by government regulators) (42).

Individual transferable quotas (ITQs) are being tried in several fisheries around the world with some success. Advantages include relief from the derby-style rush for fish that occurs under more traditional management schemes, in which fleets must compete for limited stocks during a limited fishing season. More important, because these quotas can be bought and sold as private property, they should offer a greater incentive to protect the resource so that the value of the quota can be maintained in the future (43).

This market-based approach, which in essence establishes property rights to a resource that has traditionally been managed as a public good, has potential disadvantages as well. One is the difficulty in fairly apportioning the ITQs at the outset and in ensuring that they are not accumulated over time by a small group of owners who then monopolize the resource. Critics fear that big industry boats with more financial resources will eventually buy up the quotas, squeezing out smaller operators.

Also, ITQs may actually increase the discard problem by encouraging high-grading, a practice in which fishers throw back smaller, previously caught fish and replace them with larger, higher-value fish caught later. A final criticism is that managing fisheries by using ITQs requires a well-developed system of monitoring the catch to make sure that fishers respect their quotas, as well as an ability to make scientifically sound estimates of the sustainable catch. Both of these activities require considerable technical and financial resources not available in every nation (44) (45).

In situations in which subsistence or small-scale fishing is the norm, as in many inshore waters in developing nations, community-based management may be an appropriate means of restricting access. Community-based management involves the formal allocation by a national government of certain defined fish resources to local communities, which then become responsible for further allocating access to the resource among community members. Such systems often follow the lines of traditional communal management of fishing rights practiced by many cultures over the years, allowing local control of the resource within specified areas and limits. Where overfishing has already occurred and the number of fishers is too large, this may have to be accompanied by rural development programs that offer alternative employment for displaced fishers (46) (47).

International Cooperation in Fisheries Management

Although most of the burden of managing fisheries must be shouldered by individual coastal nations acting in their own territorial waters, there is also a significant role to be played by the international community. The high seas—the open oceans that extend beyond the 200-mile (322-kilometer) Exclusive Economic Zones claimed by coastal nations—are still a common resource and have suffered from a lack of international management controls (48). As a result, many fish stocks such as Alaskan pollack in the Bering Sea and turbot in the western Atlantic are gradually being depleted.

A growing concern on the part of fishing nations, however, is the condition of fish stocks that migrate between the territorial waters of nations or that roam the high seas. It is generally acknowledged that these stocks must be managed jointly if they are to be conserved. This strengthening of international resolve was demonstrated in 1992, when a United Nations resolution banning the use of long drift nets on the high seas was adopted. This ban has been implemented successfully worldwide, with very few exceptions (49) (50).

More recently, U.N.-sponsored negotiations resulted in a binding international agreement on the joint management of fish stocks that cross national boundaries or that migrate in the open oceans. The text of the U.N. Conference on Straddling Stocks and Highly Migratory Fish Stocks agreement, which was formally adopted in December 1995, calls for a conservative approach to fisheries management—dubbed the "precautionary approach"—that errs on the side of protecting fish stocks rather than simply responding to declines once they occur. The agreement requires that special efforts be made to monitor fish stocks, and it strengthens inspection and reporting requirements for boats (51) (52). This agreement will be an official companion document to the U.N. Convention on the Law of the Sea, which was negotiated in 1982 and has become conventional law for nearly all fishing nations.

At the same time, in 1995, FAO adopted the voluntary Code of Conduct for Responsible Fisheries, which sets forth principles and standards for fisheries management and development. The Code addresses six general themes: fisheries management, fishing operations, aquaculture development, integration of fisheries into coastal area management schemes, postharvest practices, and trade and fisheries research. Along with this Code, FAO is developing more detailed guidelines to elaborate on each article of the Code in light of the precautionary approach. FAO intends for these guidelines to help the signatories of the Law of the Sea, particularly developing nations, to formulate policies and enact laws that will support sound fisheries management (53) (54) (55).

Fish for the Future

Even the most enlightened conservation measures will take time to bring fish stocks back to health. Many of the more valuable fish species are long-lived, and restoring their numbers may take a decade or longer. Although this will undoubtedly cause painful dislocations in the fishing industry and in local villages worldwide, the benefits are expected to justify the effort. Researchers estimate that rebuilding healthy marine fish stocks could add another 20 million metric tons of high-value fish to the annual harvest (56).

In the meantime, as marine fish stocks recover, global demand for fish is expected to continue its steady growth as the world's population expands. FAO warns that maintenance of the current per capita fish consumption of 13 kilograms per year in the future will require a continued increase in global fish harvests. In the near term, given the state of marine stocks, this additional demand will likely be met through increases in aquaculture production rather than larger marine catches (57) (58).

Aquaculture is already an important resource, particularly in Asia, where it contributes nearly one quarter of the total fish supply. FAO projects that global aquaculture production will need to double over the next 15 years to keep pace with demand. This growth rate is not without its own environmental risks, however, since aquaculture is a known source of water pollution, wetlands loss, and mangrove swamp destruction (59) (60).

Even a rapid, environmentally rational expansion of aquaculture can only act as a complement to better management of marine fisheries. Successful marine fisheries conservation measures are necessary not only to allow a larger global catch but also to keep fish diversity high, to reduce impacts on marine ecosystems, and, ultimately, to maximize sustainable employment in the fisheries sector (61).

FRESHWATER TRENDS: WILL FUTURE NEEDS BE MET?

Despite improvements in the efficiency of water use in many developed countries, the demand for fresh water has continued to climb as the world's population and economic activity have expanded. From 1940 to 1990, withdrawals of fresh water from rivers, lakes, reservoirs, underground aquifers, and other sources increased by more than a factor of four (62). Increases in irrigation and, to a lesser extent, industrial uses of water have been the largest sources of this growing demand. At the same time, contamination by pollutants has seriously degraded water quality in many rivers, lakes, and groundwater sources, effectively decreasing the supply of fresh water (63). The result has been increased pressure on freshwater resources in most regions of the world and a lack of adequate supplies in some localities. Water experts and international institutions warn that water shortages could become critical in some regions. In the absence of significant changes in policy and far

more effective management of water resources, this could pose serious long-term obstacles to sustainable development in many countries (64) (65) (66) (67).

The supply of fresh water in a region is limited by the dynamics of the hydrological cycle, in which sea water evaporates and falls over land as precipitation. The renewable supply of water is defined as the surface water runoff from local precipitation, the inflow from other regions, and the groundwater recharge that replenishes aquifers. Because water can, in principle, be reused many times, the availability of water for human use depends as much on how it is used and how water resources are managed as on any absolute limits. With proper treatment, for example, the water returned to rivers by upstream users is also available to downstream users. Nonetheless, the renewable supply is an important constraint to the sustainable use of water within a region. Apart from human use, water is also needed to sustain the natural ecosystems found in wetlands, rivers, and the coastal waters into which they flow.

Pumping water from underground aquifers faster than they can be recharged or diverting so much water from wetlands or rivers that freshwater ecosystems fail are clearly unsustainable practices. To avoid conflict where water resources are shared, upstream and downstream users must agree on how water is to be allocated. Unfortunately, examples of unsustainable water uses can be found in virtually every region—in the depletion of the Ogallala aquifer in the United States and similar overpumping of other aquifers in parts of North Africa, the Middle East, India, and Southeast Asia; in the diversion of river water from the dying Aral Sea in Kazakhstan and Uzbekistan and from the Florida Everglades; in the excessive withdrawals that are causing intrusions of sea water into deltas and coastal aquifers in China, Viet Nam, and the Gulf of California; in the uncontrolled flow of sewage and fertilizer runoff that is hastening eutrophication in some temperate and tropical lakes and many coastal seas; and in the potential for conflict over water in areas such as the Nile River delta, the Middle East, and Southeast Asia.

Gauging Future Pressures on Water Supplies

If water supplies are finite and water use is rising, what can be said about future pressures on water supplies? In addition, given the enormous geographical variability in water resources, where might these pressures be most severe? One approach to answering these questions is the concept of a *water stress index*, measured as the annual renewable water resources per capita that are available to meet needs for agriculture, industry, and

Table 13.2 Water Stress Index, 1990

Country[a]	Water Resources (cubic meters per capita)
Algeria	690
Bahrain	184
Barbados	195
Burundi	654
Cape Verde	587
Djibouti	19
Israel	461
Jordan	308
Kenya	635
Kuwait	75
Malawi	961
Malta	85
Qatar	103
Rwanda	902
Saudi Arabia	284
Singapore	222
Somalia	980
Tunisia	540
United Arab Emirates	293
Yemen	460

Source: Adapted from Robert Engelman and Pamela LeRoy, *Sustaining Water: An Update* (Population Action International, Washington, D.C., 1995).

Note: a. Includes countries with annual renewable water resources of less than 1,000 cubic meters per capita per year.

domestic use. On the basis of the past experiences of moderately developed countries in arid zones, renewable freshwater resources of 1,000 cubic meters per capita per year have been proposed as an approximate benchmark below which most countries are likely to experience chronic water scarcity on a scale sufficient to impede development and harm human health [68] [69]. By this measure, some 20 countries already suffer from water scarcity [70] [71]. (See Table 13.2.)

The water stress index can also provide a rough guide to future water scarcity. Population Action International has projected future water stress index figures for 149 countries using U.N. population projections and holding renewable water resources constant. It projects that the number of people living in water-scarce countries will rise from 132 million in 1990 to between 653 million (with the low population growth projection) and 904 million (with the high population growth projection) in 2025. By 2050, the population projected to be living in water-scarce countries will rise to between 1.06 billion and 2.43 billion, representing roughly 13 to 20 percent of the projected global population [72] [73]. Africa and parts of western Asia appear particularly vulnerable to increasing water scarcity, but the list of potentially affected countries includes nearly one third of those studied and includes countries in four of the five major continents. (See Table 13.3.) In addition, nations not included in the index because overall they

have adequate water resources may have arid regions where drought and restricted supplies are common. Such regions include northwestern China, western and southern India, large parts of Pakistan and Mexico, and the western coasts of the United States and South America [74] [75] [76]. Thus, the actual population subject to water shortages might be even larger than these estimates.

Such projections must be interpreted cautiously. They do not necessarily imply a future shortage of available water, since that depends on actual use patterns and on the efficiency with which water is used (and reused). Burundi, for example, is potentially a water-scarce country according to the water stress index, but it uses little water for irrigation at present and so has abundant supplies for other purposes. Moreover, efficient management and modern technology can stretch even scarce water supplies much further. Israel, for example, supports its population, its growing industrial base, and intensive irrigation with less than 500 cubic meters per person per year. Even so, Israel's present water use may not be sustainable, since it is overdrawing water from its aquifers and depends on the West Bank for 25 percent of its supplies [77]. National political and economic choices, often driven by market forces, can also alter water use patterns. In Tunisia, for instance, the needs of the coastal areas, which support the bulk of the nation's tourist trade, increasingly cause water to be diverted from agricultural uses and force agriculture toward better irrigation efficiency [78]. If the water stress index, however, is seen as a measure of the potential pressure on water supplies, it suggests that many countries will have to manage water resources far more efficiently than they do now if they are to meet their future needs.

Several additional factors contribute to the potential for regional water shortages by limiting the available supply. Among the most serious is water pollution from a wide variety of industrial, municipal, and agricultural sources. Although there has been significant progress in controlling water pollution in many developed nations over the past three decades, pollution has continued to rise in most developing nations and remains high in the transition economies of Russia and Central Europe, posing a threat to human health and to the health of aquatic ecosystems [79]. One factor is the rapidly growing and industrializing cities of the developing world, where pollution control is still in its infancy and domestic sewage and industrial effluents have left many urban rivers and groundwater sources heavily contaminated. This widening shadow of pollution around major cities has important implications for urban development, exacerbating the already difficult task of extending basic water and sanitation services to the urban poor (80). (See Chapter 2, "Urban Environment and Human Health," and Chapter 3, "Urban Impacts on Natural Resources.")

Managing Water Resources More Effectively

Fortunately, many opportunities exist to improve the efficiency of water use. Irrigation systems, for example, often perform poorly, wasting as much as 60 percent of the total water pumped before it reaches the intended crop (81). Moreover, where drainage is poor, misapplied irrigation waters are a major source of soil waterlogging and salination, which affect an estimated 80 million to 110 million hectares of arable land worldwide (82). More efficient technologies—including drip irrigation systems, lining of irrigation canals, more efficient sprinklers, and better irrigation timing and volume control—are beginning to come into limited use in a few countries and have proved effective at reducing water use. Since agriculture is responsible for some 70 percent of global water use, the potential for water savings through greater efficiency in irrigation is enormous (83). Leaking collection and distribution systems also plague municipal water systems and provide another avenue for significant water savings. (See Chapter 5, "Urban Priorities for Action.") Water usage per unit of industrial production has dropped significantly in the developed world and in a few developing countries in the past two decades. Experience in developed nations also indicates that controlling industrial pollution has a secondary benefit of actually reducing the quantity of water used per unit of industrial output. Thus, pollution control offers one potent and cost-effective means of addressing urban water problems (84).

Although increases in efficiency have been demonstrated in both agriculture and industry in a few countries, they have not yet been widely adopted. A central reason has to do with the economics of water and the failure to adopt and implement appropriate water management policies. A detailed discussion of this subject is beyond the scope of this chapter, but some central points can be mentioned here.

Water is often wasted because it is underpriced (85). Direct and indirect subsidies (especially for agricultural use) are still common in both developed and developing countries. Removing such subsidies and letting water prices rise can provide incentives for conservation and for the investments needed to spread more efficient technologies. Moreover, water often historically allocated for agricultural use may have much higher value in urban and industrial uses. Thus, reallocating

Table 13.3 Projected Water Stress Index, 2050

Country[a]	Projected Water Resources[b] (cubic meters per capita)	
Afghanistan	697	– 1,021
Algeria	247	– 398
Bahrain	72	– 104
Barbados	129	– 197
Burkina Faso	711	– 1,018
Burundi	160	– 229
Cape Verde	176	– 252
Comoros	341	– 508
Cyprus	717	– 1,125
Djibouti	6	– 8
Egypt	398	– 644
Ethiopia	477	– 690
Ghana	816	– 1,105
Haiti	505	– 679
Iran	581	– 891
Israel	192	– 300
Jordan	68	– 90
Kenya	141	– 190
Kuwait	38	– 59
Lebanon	768	– 1,218
Lesotho	596	– 789
Libya	213	– 276
Madagascar	683	– 911
Malawi	236	– 305
Malta	57	– 88
Morocco	468	– 750
Mozambique	948	– 1,337
Nigeria	763	– 1,116
Oman	163	– 235
Peru	756	– 1,125
Qatar	47	– 68
Republic of Korea	964	– 1,488
Rwanda	247	– 351
Saudi Arabia	67	– 84
Singapore	159	– 221
Somalia	223	– 324
South Africa	473	– 658
Syria	454	– 667
Tanzania	728	– 964
Togo	737	– 1,081
Tunisia	221	– 363
Uganda	759	– 1,134
United Arab Emirates	120	– 171
Yemen	90	– 127
Zimbabwe	715	– 1,061

Source: Adapted from Robert Engelman and Pamela LeRoy, *Sustaining Water: An Update* (Population Action International, Washington, D.C., 1995).

Notes: a. Includes countries with projected annual renewable resources of less than 1,000 cubic meters per capita per year.
b. Figures are given for both the low and the high United Nations population growth projections.

water—administratively or through market mechanisms such as trading among users—can also reduce distortions and inefficiencies. Charging user fees for urban and industrial users that fully reflect costs not only can provide incentives for efficient use but also can help to finance the needed infrastructure to expand services to new users. Municipalities in virtually all regions are also experimenting with privatization—transferring management of water systems to private firms, autonomous utilities, or water user associations in hopes of improving management (86). On a regional scale, more attention needs to be given to managing whole watersheds or river basins in an integrated manner.

Water problems have often been seen as local issues, and therefore they have sometimes not garnered sufficient attention by policymakers at a national or international level. Even where comprehensive water plans exist, many of the least-developed countries lack the financial, managerial, and political capacity to implement them. In developed countries, too, opposition to ending subsidies or implementing improved policies often saps the political will for reform (87) (88) (89) (90).

These attitudes may be changing slowly as water supply problems become more pronounced. In recent years, international organizations have increased their efforts to address water management problems, provide basic water services, and identify the need to cooperatively manage shared watersheds and river basins. Nonetheless, more must be done if human needs for reliable supplies of water are to be met in the future.

References and Notes

1. Food and Agriculture Organization of the United Nations (FAO), *Global Fish and Shellfish Production in 1993* (FAO Fisheries Department, Fisheries Information, Data, and Statistics Service, Rome, March 1995), Table 1, p. 2.

2. Mark Clayton, "A Fish Tale? Canada Tries to Save Stocks While Overfishing," *Christian Science Monitor* (March 20, 1995), p. 1.

3. Serge Garcia and C. Newton, "Current Situation, Trends, and Prospects in World Capture Fisheries," paper presented at the Conference on Fisheries Management: Global Aspects, Seattle, Washington, June 1994, p. 4.

4. Food and Agriculture Organization of the United Nations (FAO), *Marine Fisheries and the Law of the Sea: A Decade of Change,* FAO Fisheries Circular No. 853 (FAO, Rome, 1993), pp. 34–35.

5. In addition to shrinking the size of the fleet itself, reducing the overcapacity of the global fishing fleet will also require cutting back a number of fishing-related industries, such as boatyards, processing facilities, and marine suppliers.

6. *Op. cit.* 1.

7. *Op. cit.* 4, p. 4.

8. *Op. cit.* 1.

9. Food and Agriculture Organization of the United Nations (FAO), *The State of World Fisheries and Aquaculture* (FAO, Rome, 1995), p. 8.

10. Food and Agriculture Organization of the United Nations (FAO), "World Review of Highly Migratory Species and Straddling Stocks," FAO Fisheries Technical Paper No. 337 (FAO, Rome, 1994), pp. 30, 34, 41, 52, 56–58.

11. Food and Agriculture Organization of the United Nations (FAO), *Review of the State of World Fishery Resources: Marine Fisheries,* FAO Fisheries Circular No. 884 (FAO, Rome, 1995), pp. 3–63.

12. *Op. cit.* 9, Figure 9, p. 12.

13. *Op. cit.* 11, pp. 3–13.

14. *Op. cit.* 3, p. 13.

15. *Op. cit.* 9, Figure 7, p. 11.

16. *Op. cit.* 3, pp. 5–6, 11.

17. *Op. cit.* 4, pp. 6, 36.

18. *Op. cit.* 4, pp. 44–49.

19. *Op. cit.* 9, pp. 22–23.

20. Joshua John, "Managing Redundancy in Overexploited Fisheries," World Bank Discussion Paper No. 240 (The World Bank, Washington, D.C., 1994), pp. 3–5.

21. *Op. cit.* 4, pp. 20, 23–25, 31–32.

22. Moritaki Hayashi, "United Nations Conference on Straddling Fish Stocks and Highly Migratory Fish Stocks: An Analysis of the 1993 Sessions," in *Ocean Yearbook,* Vol. 11, E. Borgese, N. Ginsburg, and J. Morgan, eds. (University of Chicago Press, Chicago and London, 1994), p. 20.

23. Some estimates of the overcapacity of the global fishing fleet run significantly higher than 30 percent. For example, one economic analysis calculates that the global fishing effort, which is clearly related to global fleet size, is 100 percent greater than it should be to exploit the available resource efficiently. (Source: Francis Christy, Senior Research Officer, IMARIBA, Washington, D.C., 1995, personal communication).

24. *Op. cit.* 3, p. 25.

25. *Op. cit.* 22.

26. *Op. cit.* 3, pp. 25–30.

27. *Op. cit.* 4, pp. 21–22.

28. *Op. cit.* 3, pp. 14–16.

29. *Op. cit.* 4, p. 30.

30. *Op. cit.* 4, pp. 44–47.

31. Dayton Alverson *et al.*, "A Global Assessment of Fisheries Bycatch and Discards," Food and Agriculture Organization of the United Nations (FAO) Fisheries Technical Paper No. 339 (FAO, Rome, 1994), pp. 19, 37, 162.

32. *Ibid.*, p. 47.

33. *Op. cit.* 4, p. 30.

34. *Op. cit.* 31, pp. 37–45, 47, 68, 161.

35. *Op. cit.* 9, p. 21.

36. Serge Garcia, Director, Fisheries Resources Division, Fisheries Department, Food and Agriculture Organization of the United Nations, Rome, June 1995 (personal communication).

37. *Op. cit.* 2.

38. *Op. cit.* 36.

39. Serge Garcia and C. Newton, "Responsible Fisheries: Overview of FAO Policy Developments (1945–1994)," Food and Agriculture Organization of the United Nations (FAO) study paper (FAO, Rome, 1994), p. 12.

40. *Op. cit.* 4, pp. 21–23, 32.

41. Francis Christy, Senior Research Officer, IMARIBA, Washington, D.C., November 1995 (personal communication).

42. Karyn Gimbel, ed., *Limiting Access to Marine Fisheries: Keeping the Focus on Conservation* (Center for Marine Conservation in conjunction with World Wildlife Fund, Washington, D.C., 1994), pp. 11–22.

43. *Ibid.*, pp. 11–74.

44. *Op. cit.* 42, pp. 14–15.

45. Betsy Carpenter, "Not Enough Fish in the Stormy Sea," *U.S. News and World Report* (August 15, 1994), pp. 55–56.

46. *Op. cit.* 20, pp. 9–12.

47. *Op. cit.* 9, pp. 22–23.

48. *Op. cit.* 3, p. 29.

49. *Op. cit.* 22, pp. 20–27.

50. Food and Agriculture Organization of the United Nations (FAO), *Report of the Food and Agriculture Organization Concerning U.N. General Assembly Resolution 49/436 on Large-Scale Pelagic Driftnet Fishing and Its Impact on the Living Marine Resources of the World's Oceans* (FAO, Rome, June 1995), pp. 1–2.

51. The World Conservation Union (IUCN), "The Possibilities of International Law and

Institutions for Sustainable Use of Marine Biodiversity: Focus on Coral Reef Ecosystems," draft version (IUCN, Gland, Switzerland, May 1995), pp. 36–37.

52. Lee Kimball, independent consultant, Washington, D.C., August 1995 (personal communication).

53. *Op. cit.* 9, p. 17.

54. *Op. cit.* 36.

55. *Op. cit.* 51, pp. 38–39.

56. *Op. cit.* 4, p. 32.

57. *Op. cit.* 9, pp. 3–5.

58. *Op. cit.* 1, pp. 1–2.

59. *Op. cit.* 9, pp. 3–5.

60. Food and Agriculture Organization of the United Nations (FAO), *Review of the State of World Fishery Resources: Aquaculture,* FAO Fisheries Circular No. 886 (FAO, Rome, 1995), pp. 3, 24–26.

61. *Op. cit.* 11, pp. 2–3.

62. Igor Shiklomanov, "World Fresh Water Resources," in *Water in Crisis: A Guide to the World's Fresh Water Resources,* Peter H. Gleick, ed. (Oxford University Press, New York, 1993), Table 2.8, p. 20.

63. *Ibid.,* pp. 18, 20–23.

64. United Nations (U.N.) Economic and Social Council, Committee on Natural Resources, *Water Resources: Progress in the Implementation of the Mar del Plata Action Plan and of Agenda 21 on Water-Related Issues* (U.N., New York, January 12, 1994), pp. 4–9.

65. United Nations (U.N.) Economic and Social Council, Commission on Sustainable Development, *Freshwater Resources: Report of the Secretary-General* (U.N., New York, April 22, 1994), pp. 3–5, 15.

66. Peter H. Gleick, ed., *Water in Crisis: A Guide to the World's Fresh Water Resources* (Oxford University Press, New York, 1993).

67. Pierre Najlis, Secretary, Subcommittee on Water Resources, Energy and Natural Resources Branch, Department of Policy Coordination and Sustainable Development, United Nations, New York, July 1995 (personal communication).

68. Malin Falkenmark and Carl Widstrand, "Population and Water Resources: A Delicate Balance," in *Population Bulletin* (Population Reference Bureau, Washington, D.C., 1992), p. 19.

69. Robert Engelman and Pamela LeRoy, *Sustaining Water: Population and the Future of Renewable Water Supplies* (Population Action International, Washington, D.C., 1993), pp. 18–22.

70. *Ibid.*

71. *Op. cit.* 69, p. 8.

72. *Op. cit.* 69.

73. *Op. cit.* 69, p. 8.

74. *Op. cit.* 62, pp. 13–18.

75. *Op. cit.* 69, pp. 24, 33.

76. World Bank, *Water Resources Management* (World Bank, Washington, D.C., 1993), p. 11.

77. *Op. cit.* 69, p. 23.

78. Jean-Marc Faures, Land and Water Division, Food and Agriculture Organization of the United Nations, Rome, October, 1995 (personal communication).

79. The term "transitional economies" lacks a formal definition, but is used here to include the successor states of the former Soviet Union (Armenia, Azerbaijan, the Republic of Belarus, the Republic of Estonia, the Republic of Georgia, the Republic of Kazakhstan, the Kyrgyz Republic, the Republic of Latvia, the Republic of Lithuania, the Republic of Moldova, the Russian Federation, the Republic of Tajikistan, the Republic of Turkmenistan, Ukraine, and the Republic of Uzbekistan) and the countries of Central Europe (Albania, Bulgaria, the Czech Republic, Hungary, Poland, Romania, and the Slovak Republic).

80. Ivanildo Hespanhol and Richard Helmer, "The Importance of Water Pollution Control for Sustainable Development," paper presented at the Symposium on Water Use and Conservation, Amman, Jordan, November 1993, pp. 2–9.

81. Sandra Postel, *Last Oasis: Facing Water Scarcity* (W.W. Norton & Company, New York, 1992), pp. 99–100.

82. *Op. cit.* 64, p. 14.

83. Nikos Alexandratos, ed., *World Agriculture: Towards 2010, An FAO Study* (John Wiley and Sons, Chichester, U.K., and Food and Agriculture Organization of the United Nations, Rome, 1995), p. 354.

84. *Op. cit.* 76, p. 12.

85. *Op. cit.* 76, p. 47.

86. *Op. cit.* 76, pp. 53–55.

87. *Op. cit.* 64, p. 23.

88. Debra Knopman, "Recasting Perceptions of a Water Crisis," in *Water: Our Next Crisis? Proceedings of the Fifth National Conference on Environmental Issues* (Academy of Natural Sciences of Philadelphia, Philadelphia, 1994), pp. 9–35.

89. Peter H. Gleick, "An Introduction to Global Freshwater Issues," in *Water in Crisis: A Guide to the World's Fresh Water Resources,* Peter H. Gleick, ed. (Oxford University Press, New York, 1993), pp. 10–11.

90. *Op. cit.* 76, pp. 21–39.

Data Table 13.1 Freshwater Resources and Withdrawals

	Annual Internal Renewable Water Resources {a}		Annual River Flows		Annual Withdrawals				Sectoral Withdrawals (percent) {b}		
	Total (cubic km)	1995 Per Capita (cubic meters)	From Other Countries (cubic km)	To Other Countries (cubic km)	Year of Data	(cubic km)	Percentage of Water Resources {a}	Per capita (cubic meters)	Domestic	Industry	Agriculture
WORLD	41,022.0	7,176			1987	3,240.00	8	645	8	23	69
AFRICA	3,996.0	5,488			1995	145.14	4	199	7	5	88
Algeria	14.8	**528**	0.4	0.7	1990	4.50	30	180	25 c	15 c	60 c
Angola	184.0	16,618	X	X	1987	0.48	0	57	14 c	10 c	76 c
Benin	25.8	4,770	15.5	X	1994	0.15	1	28	23 c	10 c	67 c
Botswana	14.7	9,886	11.8	X	1992	0.11	1	83	32 c	20 c	48 c
Burkina Faso	28.0	2,713	X	X	1992	0.38	1	40	19 c	0 c	81 c
Burundi	3.6	563	X	X	1987	0.10	3	20	36 c	0 c	64 c
Cameroon	268.0	20,252	0.0	0.0	1987	0.40	0	38	46 c	19 c	35 c
Central African Rep	141.0	42,534	X	X	1987	0.07	0	26	21 c	5 c	74 c
Chad	43.0	6,760	28.0	X	1987	0.18	0	34	16 c	2 c	82 c
Congo	832.0	321,236	610.0	X	1987	0.04	0	20	62 c	27 c	11 c
Cote d'Ivoire	77.7	5,451	1.0	X	1987	0.71	1	66	22 c	11 c	67 c
Egypt	58.1	923	55.5	0.0	1992	56.40	97	956	6 c	9 c	85 c
Equatorial Guinea	30.0	75,000	0.0	X	1987	0.01	0	15	81 c	13 c	6 c
Eritrea	8.8	2,492	6.0	X	X	X	X	X	X	X	X
Ethiopia	110.0	1,998	0.0	X	1987	2.21	2	51	11 c	3 c	86 c
Gabon	164.0	124,242	0.0	X	1987	0.06	0	57	72 c	22 c	6 c
Gambia, The	8.0	7,156	5.0	X	1982	0.02	0	30	7 c	2 c	91 c
Ghana	53.2	3,048	22.9	X	1970	0.30	1	35	35 c	13 c	52 c
Guinea	226.0	33,731	0.0	X	1987	0.74	0	140	10 c	3 c	87 c
Guinea-Bissau	27.0	25,163	11.0	X	1991	0.02	0	17	60 c	4 c	36 c
Kenya	30.2	1,069	10.0	X	1990	2.05	7	87	20 c	4 c	76 c
Lesotho	5.2	2,551	0.0	X	1987	0.05	1	30	22 c	22 c	56 c
Liberia	232.0	76,341	32.0	X	1987	0.13	0	56	27 c	13 c	60 c
Libya	0.6	111	0.0	0.0	1994	4.60	767	880	11 c	2 c	87 c
Madagascar	337.0	22,827	0.0	0.0	1984	16.30	5	1,584	1 c	0 c	99 c
Malawi	18.7	1,678	1.1	X	1994	0.94	5	86	10 c	3 c	86 c
Mali	67.0	6,207	40.0	X	1987	1.36	2	162	2 c	1 c	97 c
Mauritania	11.4	5,013	11.0	X	1985	1.63	14	923	6 c	2 c	92 c
Mauritius	2.2	1,979	0.0	0.0	1974	0.36	16	410	16 c	7 c	77 c
Morocco	30.0	1,110	0.0	0.3	1992	10.85	36	427	5 c	3 c	92 c
Mozambique	208.0	12,997	111.0	0.0	1992	0.61	0	41	9 c	2 c	89 c
Namibia	45.5	29,545	39.3	X	1991	0.25	1	180	29 c	3 c	68 c
Niger	32.5	3,552	29.0	X	1988	0.50	2	69	16 c	2 c	82 c
Nigeria	280.0	2,506	59.0	X	1987	3.63	1	41	31 c	15 c	54 c
Rwanda	6.3	792	X	X	1993	0.77	12	102	5 c	2 c	94 c
Senegal	39.4	4,740	13.0	X	1987	1.36	3	202	5 c	3 c	92 c
Sierra Leone	160.0	35,485	0.0	X	1987	0.37	0	99	7 c	4 c	89 c
Somalia	13.5	1,459	7.5	X	1987	0.81	6	98	3 c	0 c	97 c
South Africa	50.0	1,206	5.2	X	1990	13.31	27	359	17 c	11 c	72 c
Sudan	154.0	5,481	119.0	56.5	1995	17.80	12	633	4 c	1 c	94 c
Swaziland	4.5	5,275	1.9	X	1980	0.66	15	1,171	2 c	2 c	96 c
Tanzania	89.0	2,998	9.0	X	1994	1.16	1	40	9 c	2 c	89 c
Togo	12.0	2,900	0.5	X	1987	0.09	1	28	62 c	13 c	25 c
Tunisia	3.9	443	0.3	0.0	1990	3.08	78	381	9 c	3 c	89 c
Uganda	66.0	3,099	27.0	X	1970	0.20	0	20	32 c	8 c	60 c
Zaire	1,019.0	23,211	84.0	X	1990	0.36	0	10	61 c	16 c	23 c
Zambia	116.0	12,267	35.8	X	1994	1.71	1	186	16 c	7 c	77 c
Zimbabwe	20.0	1,776	5.9	X	1987	1.22	6	136	14 c	7 c	79 c
EUROPE	6,234.6	8,576			1995	455.29	7	626	14	55	31
Albania	21.3	6,190	11.3	X	1970	0.20	1	94	6	18	76
Austria	90.3	11,333	34.0	56.3	1991 d	2.36	3	304	33	58	9
Belarus, Rep	73.8	7,277	21.7	54.9	1989	3.00	5	295	32	49	19
Belgium	12.5	1,236	4.1	8.4	1980	9.03	72	917	11	85	4
Bosnia and Herzegovina	X	X	X	X	X	X	X	X	X	X	X
Bulgaria	205.0	23,378	187.0	X	1988	13.90	7	1,544	3	76	22
Croatia, Rep	61.4	13,660	X	X	X	X	0	X	X	X	X
Czech Rep	58.2	5,653	X	X	1991 d	2.74	5	266	41	57	2
Denmark	13.0	2,509	2.0	11.0	1990	1.20	9	233	30	27	43
Estonia, Rep	17.6	11,490	4.7	X	1989	3.30	21	2,097	5	92	3
Finland	113.0	22,126	3.0	108.0	1991 d	2.20	2	440	12	85	3
France	198.0	3,415	18.0	150.0	1990	37.73	19	665	16	69	15
Germany	171.0	2,096	75.0	X	1991 d	46.27	27	579	11	70	20
Greece	58.7	5,612	13.5	45.2	1980	5.04	9	523	8	29	63
Hungary	120.0	11,864	114.0	120.0	1991 d	6.81	6	661	9	55	36
Iceland	168.0	624,535	0.0	170.0	1991 d	0.16	0	636	31	63	6
Ireland	50.0	14,073	3.0	40.0	1980	0.79	2	233	16	74	10
Italy	167.0	2,920	7.6	X	1990	56.20	34	986	14	27	59
Latvia, Rep	34.0	13,297	16.8	X	1989	0.70	2	262	42	44	14
Lithuania, Rep	24.2	6,541	10.4	X	1989	4.40	19	1,190	7	90	3
Macedonia, former Yugoslav Rep	X	X	X	X	X	X	X	X	X	X	X
Moldova, Rep	13.7	3,093	11.4	12.0	1989	3.70	29	853	7	70	23
Netherlands	90.0	5,805	80.0	86.0	1991 d	7.81	9	518	5	61	34
Norway	392.0	90,385	8.0	392.0	1985	2.03	1	488	20	72	8
Poland, Rep	56.2	1,464	6.8	X	1991 d	12.28	22	321	13	76	11
Portugal	69.6	7,085	31.6	33.9	1990	7.29	10	739	15	37	48
Romania	208.0	9,109	171.0	40.0	1994	26.00	13	1,134	8	33	59
Russian Federation	4,498.0	30,599	227.0	54.0	1991	117.00	3	790	17	60	23
Slovak Rep	30.8	5,753	X	X	1991 d	1.78	6	337	X	X	X
Slovenia, Rep	X	X	X	X	X	X	X	X	X	X	X
Spain	111.3	2,809	1.0	17.0	1991 d	30.75	28	781	12	26	62
Sweden	180.0	20,501	4.0	X	1991 d	2.93	2	341	36	55	9
Switzerland	50.0	6,943	7.5	X	1991 d	1.19	2	173	23	73	4
Ukraine	231.0	4,496	34.4	47.3	1989	34.70	40	673	16	54	30
United Kingdom	71.0	1,219	0.0	67.0	1991 d	11.79	17	205	20	77	3
Yugoslavia, Fed Rep	X	X	X	X	X	X	X	X	X	X	X

	Annual Internal Renewable Water Resources {a}		Annual River Flows		Annual Withdrawals				Sectoral Withdrawals (percent) {b}		
	Total (cubic km)	1995 Per Capita (cubic meters)	From Other Countries (cubic km)	To Other Countries (cubic km)	Year of Data	(cubic km)	Percentage of Water Resources {a}	Per capita (cubic meters)	Domestic	Industry	Agriculture
NORTH & CENTRAL AMERICA	**6,443.7**	**15,369**			**1995**	**608.44**	**9**	**1,451**	**9**	**42**	**49**
Belize	16.0	74,419	X	X	1987	0.02	0	109	10	0	90
Canada	2,901.0	98,462	51.5	2,850.0	1991 d	45.10	2	1,602	18	70	12
Costa Rica	95.0	27,745	X	X	1970	1.35	1	780	4	7	89
Cuba	34.5	3,125	0.0	X	1975	8.10	23	870	9	2	89
Dominican Rep	20.0	2,557	X	X	1987	2.97	15	446	5	6	89
El Salvador	19.0	3,285	X	X	1975	1.00	5	245	7	4	89
Guatemala	116.0	10,922	X	X	1970	0.73	1	139	9	17	74
Haiti	11.0	1,532	X	X	1987	0.04	0	7	24	8	68
Honduras	63.4	11,216	8.0	8.0	1992	1.52	2	294	4	5	91
Jamaica	8.3	3,392	0.0	X	1975	0.32	4	159	7	7	86
Mexico	357.4	3,815	X	X	1991 d	77.62	22	899	6	8	86
Nicaragua	175.0	39,477	X	X	1975	0.89	1	367	25	21	54
Panama	144.0	54,732	X	X	1975	1.30	1	754	12	11	77
Trinidad and Tobago	5.1	3,905	0.0	X	1975	0.15	3	148	27	38	35
United States	2,478.0	9,413	18.9	1,890.0	1990	467.34	19	1,870	13 c	45 c	42 c
SOUTH AMERICA	**9,526.0**	**29,788**			**1995**	**106.21**	**1**	**332**	**18**	**23**	**59**
Argentina	994.0	28,739	300.0	X	1976	27.60	4	1,043	9	18	73
Bolivia	300.0	40,464	X	X	1987	1.24	0	201	10	5	85
Brazil	6,950.0	42,957	1,760.0	X	1990	36.47	1	246	22	19	59
Chile	468.0	32,814	X	X	1975	16.80	4	1,626	6	5	89
Colombia	1,070.0	30,483	X	X	1987	5.34	0	174	41	16	43
Ecuador	314.0	27,400	X	X	1987	5.56	2	581	7	3	90
Guyana	241.0	288,623	X	X	1992	1.46	1	1,812	1	0	99
Paraguay	314.0	63,306	220.0	X	1987	0.43	0	109	15	7	78
Peru	40.0	1,682	X	X	1987	6.10	15	300	19	9	72
Suriname	200.0	472,813	X	X	1987	0.46	0	1,189	6	5	89
Uruguay	124.0	38,920	65.0	X	1965	0.65	1	241	6	3	91
Venezuela	1,317.0	60,291	461.0	X	1970	4.10	0	382	43	11	46
ASIA	**13,206.7**	**3,819**			**1987**	**1,633.85**	**12**	**542**	**6**	**9**	**85**
Afghanistan, Islamic State	50.0	2,482	X	X	1987	26.11	52	1,830	1	0	99
Armenia	13.3	3,687	2.1	5.2	1989	3.80	46	1,145	13	15	72
Azerbaijan	33.0	4,364	20.2	X	1989	15.80	56	2,248	4	22	74
Bangladesh	2,357.0	19,571	1,000.0	X	1987	22.50	1	220	3	1	96
Bhutan	95.0	57,998	X	X	1987	0.02	0	14	36	10	54
Cambodia	498.1	48,590	410.0	X	1987	0.52	0	64	5	1	94
China	2,800.0	2,292	0.0	X	1980	460.00	16	461	6	7	87
Georgia, Rep	65.2	11,942	7.9	20.2	1989	4.00	7	741	21	37	42
India	2,085.0	2,228	235.0	X	1975	380.00	18	612	3	4	93
Indonesia	2,530.0	12,804	X	X	1987	16.59	1	96	13	11	76
Iran, Islamic Rep	117.5	1,746	X	X	1975	45.40	39	1,362	4	9	87
Iraq	109.2	5,340	66.0	X	1970	42.80	43	4,575	3	5	92
Israel	2.2	382	0.5	0.0	1989	1.85	86	408	16 c	5 c	79 c
Japan	547.0	4,373	0.0	X	1990	90.80	17	735	17	33	50
Jordan	1.7	314	0.4	X	1975	0.45	32	173	29	6	65
Kazakhstan, Rep	169.4	9,900	56.0	32.0	1989	37.90	30	2,294	4	17	79
Korea, Dem People's Rep	67.0	2,801	X	X	1987	14.16	21	687	11	16	73
Korea, Rep	66.1	1,469	X	X	1992	27.60	42	632	19	35	46
Kuwait	0.2	103	0.0	X	1974	0.50	X	525	64	32	4
Kyrgyz Rep	61.7	13,003	0.0	38.3	1989	11.70	24	2,729	3	7	90
Lao People's Dem Rep	270.0	55,305	X	X	1987	0.99	0	259	8	10	82
Lebanon	5.6	1,854	0.6	0.9	1975	0.75	16	271	11	4	85
Malaysia	456.0	22,642	X	X	1975	9.42	2	768	23	30	47
Mongolia	24.6	10,207	X	X	1987	0.55	2	273	11	27	62
Myanmar	1,082.0	23,255	X	X	1987	3.96	0	101	7	3	90
Nepal	170.0	7,756	X	X	1987	2.68	2	150	4	1	95
Oman	1.9	892	0.0	X	1975	0.48	24	564	3	3	94
Pakistan	468.0	3,331	170.0	X	1975	153.40	33	2,053	1	1	98
Philippines	323.0	4,779	0.0	X	1975	29.50	9	686	18	21	61
Saudi Arabia	4.6	254	0.0	X	1975	3.60	164	497	45	8	47
Singapore	0.6	211	0.0	X	1975	0.19	32	84	45	51	4
Sri Lanka	43.2	2,354	0.0	X	1970	6.30	15	503	2	2	96
Syrian Arab Rep	53.7	3,662	27.9	30.0	1976	3.34	9	435	7	10	83
Tajikistan, Rep	101.3	16,604	47.9	86.9	1989	12.60	13	2,455	5	7	88
Thailand	179.0	3,045	69.0	X	1987	31.90	18	602	4	6	90
Turkey	193.1	3,117	7.0	69.0	1991 d	33.50	17	585	24 c	19 c	57 c
Turkmenistan, Rep	72.0	17,573	68.9	52.6	1989	22.80	33	6,390	1	8	91
United Arab Emirates	2.0	1,047	0.0	X	1980	0.90	299	884	11	9	80
Uzbekistan, Rep	129.6	5,674	98.1	X	1989	82.20	76	4,121	4	12	84
Viet Nam	376.0	5,044	X	X	1992	28.90	8	414	13	9	78
Yemen, Rep	5.2	359	X	X	1987	3.40	136	335	5	2	93
OCEANIA	**1,614.3**	**56,543**			**1995**	**16.73**	**1**	**586**	**64**	**2**	**34**
Australia	343.0	18,963	0.0	X	1985	14.60	4	933	65	2	33
Fiji	28.6	36,416	0.0	X	1987	0.03	0	42	20	20	60
New Zealand	327.0	91,469	0.0	325.0	1991 d	2.00	1	589	46	10	44
Papua New Guinea	801.0	186,192	X	X	1987	0.10	0	28	29	22	49
Solomon Islands	44.7	118,254	0.0	X	1987	0.00	0	0	40	20	40

Source: Compiled by World Resources Institute.
Notes: a. Annual Internal Renewable Water Resources usually include river flows from other countries. b. Unless otherwise noted, sectoral
withdrawal percentages are estimated for 1987. c. Sectoral percentages date from the year of other annual withdrawal data. d. Data are from the early 1990s, if not otherwise defined.
Regional and world totals may include countries not listed. Total withdrawals may exceed 100 percent due to groundwater drawdowns or river inflows.
0 = zero or less than half the unit of measure; X = not available. For additional information, see Sources and Technical Notes.

Data Table 13.2 Wastewater Treatment

	Wastewater Treatment (Percentage of Population Served)											
	Primary Treatment			Secondary Treatment			Tertiary Treatment			All Treatments		
	1980	1985	1990s	1980	1985	1990s	1980	1985	1990s	1980	1985	1990s
EUROPE												
Austria	10.0	7.0	2.0	25.0	53.0	42.0	3.0	5.0	28.0	38.0	65.0	72.0
Belgium	X	X	X	22.9	X	X	X	X	X	22.9	X	X
Czech Rep	X	X	X	X	47.5	49.6	X	X	X	X	47.5	50.6
Denmark	X	18.0	8.0 a	X	66.0	69.0	X	7.0	21.0 a	X	91.0	98.0 a
Finland	2.0	0.1	X	15.0	10.0	10.0	48.0	62.0	67.0	65.0	72.1	77.0
France	X	X	7.5 a	X	X	X	X	X	X	61.5	64.0	68.3 a
Germany	10.2	7.5	6.5	64.7	70.5	31.5	5.0	6.7	47.6	79.8	84.0	85.6
Greece	X	0.7	0.7	0.5	9.3	10.7	X	X	X	0.5	10.0	11.4
Hungary	7.0	8.0	9.0 a	12.0	17.0	22.0 a	X	X	X	19.0	25.0	31.0 a
Iceland	X	X	2.0	X	X	X	X	X	X	X	X	2.0
Italy	X	X	X	X	X	X	X	X	X	30.0	X	60.7 a
Luxembourg	16.0	14.0	3.2	65.0	69.0	82.2	X	X	5.0	81.0	83.0	90.4
Netherlands	7.0	8.0	0.5	56.0	72.0	83.5	9.0	7.0	9.3	73.0	87.0	93.3
Norway	7.0	8.0	13.0 a	1.0	1.0	1.0 a	26.0	33.0	43.0 a	34.0	42.0	57.0 a
Poland, Rep	X	X	10.8	X	X	26.5	X	X	X	X	X	37.3
Portugal	X	X	9.4 a	X	X	11.4 a	X	X	0.1 a	2.3	3.5	20.9 a
Spain	8.8	13.2	15.0	9.1	15.8	40.1	X	X	0.4	17.9	29.0	59.1
Slovak Rep	X	X	X	27.3	36.4	41.7 a	X	X	X	27.3	36.4	41.7 a
Sweden	1.0	1.0	1.0 a	20.0	11.0	7.0	61.0	82.0	88.0	82.0	94.0	95.0
Switzerland	X	X	X	X	36.0	27.0	X	48.0	64.0	73.0	84.0	91.0
United Kingdom	6.0	6.0	13.6	51.0	52.0	61.5	25.0	25.0	12.3	82.0	83.0	87.4
NORTH & CENTRAL AMERICA												
Canada	14.0	13.0	15.0	25.0	23.0	20.0	25.0	27.0	28.0	64.0	63.0	63.0
Mexico	X	X	X	X	X	19.2	X	X	X	X	X	21.8
United States	15.9	14.2	10.8 a	28.0	31.0	62.0	25.0	28.0	26.7 a	70.0	74.0	71.6 a
ASIA												
Japan	X	X	X	30.0	36.0	50.1	X	X	X	30.0	36.0	50.1
Korea, Rep	X	X	4.0	X	X	39.0	X	X	X	X	X	43.0
Turkey	0.1	0.1	1.3	X	0.2	4.6	X	X	0.5	0.1	0.3	6.3
OCEANIA												
New Zealand	10.0	8.0	X	49.0	80.0	X	X	X	X	59.0	88.0	X

Source: Organisation for Economic Co-Operation and Development.
Notes: a = 1990. X = not available. For additional information, see Sources and Technical Notes.

Data Table 13.3 Marine Fisheries, Yield and State of Exploitation

| | Marine Catch (metric tons) | | | | | | Total Marine Catch {a} (metric tons) | | % of Stocks Fully Fished, Overfished, Depleted, or Recovering in 1992 {b} | Discards (as a % of overall catch) {c} |
| | Marine Fish | | Cephalopods | | Crustaceans | | | | | |
	1981-83	1991-93	1981-83	1991-93	1981-83	1991-93 {b}	1981-83	1991-93 {b}		1988-92
WORLD	**57,918,077**	**67,693,259**	**1,553,445**	**2,720,813**	**3,134,594**	**4,829,607**	**62,606,116**	**75,243,679**	**69**	**24**
ATLANTIC OCEAN	**20,021,612**	**17,952,537**	**462,521**	**1,033,307**	**800,437**	**988,810**	**21,284,570**	**19,974,654**	**X**	**25**
Northwest	1,897,887	1,577,845	51,029	40,365	202,057	305,189	2,150,973	1,923,399	67	19
Northeast	10,282,914	9,270,963	41,737	44,194	211,097	249,000	10,535,747	9,564,156	61	27
Western Central	1,488,739	1,290,928	10,179	20,198	240,278	265,441	1,739,195	1,576,567	37	47
Eastern Central	2,781,365	3,072,082	193,295	219,203	44,844	64,340	3,019,504	3,355,625	85	14
Southwest	1,227,792	1,385,200	155,899	701,456	87,039	90,653	1,470,730	2,177,309	82	27
Southeast	2,342,915	1,355,519	10,383	7,891	15,122	14,187	2,368,421	1,377,598	X	14
PACIFIC OCEAN	**32,561,167**	**42,562,810**	**1,007,483**	**1,485,455**	**1,492,360**	**2,924,635**	**35,061,010**	**46,972,900**	**X**	**24**
Northwest	16,966,580	17,696,934	730,777	887,824	786,514	1,608,874	18,483,871	20,193,632	100	26
Northeast	1,787,664	2,429,484	22,751	19,061	96,162	209,971	1,906,577	2,658,516	50	22
Western Central	4,623,724	6,630,468	157,116	272,053	447,947	867,112	5,228,787	7,769,634	63	27
Eastern Central	1,461,318	1,192,035	22,712	47,582	88,678	80,591	1,572,708	1,320,208	29	33
Southwest	361,883	733,006	71,796	78,525	8,174	7,291	441,853	818,822	45	21
Southeast	7,359,998	13,880,883	2,331	180,410	64,885	150,796	7,427,214	14,212,089	50	15
INDIAN OCEAN	**3,627,006**	**5,957,119**	**32,818**	**132,166**	**405,268**	**616,398**	**4,065,091**	**6,705,683**	**X**	**26**
Western	1,859,183	3,304,919	11,293	72,833	234,900	330,696	2,105,376	3,708,448	X	30
Eastern	1,767,823	2,652,200	21,525	59,333	170,368	285,702	1,959,715	2,997,235	X	22
MEDITERRANEAN AND BLACK SEA	**1,559,733**	**1,163,870**	**50,623**	**69,885**	**34,870**	**49,628**	**1,645,227**	**1,283,383**	**X**	**25**
ANTARCTIC	**148,559**	**56,923**	**0**	**0**	**401,659**	**250,137**	**550,218**	**307,060**	**X**	**10**
ARCTIC	**0**	**0**	**X**	**X**	**X**	**X**	**X**	**X**	**X**	**X**

Source: Food and Agriculture Organization of the United Nations (FAO).

Notes: a. Total catch includes marine fish, cephalopods, and crustaceans only. b. Percentage of marine fish, crustacean, and mollusc stocks assessed by FAO. c. Discards are shown as a percentage of total catch plus discards (overall catch). Marine catch includes aquaculture production.
0 = zero or less than half the unit of measure; X = not available.
For additional information, see Sources and Technical Notes.

Data Table 13.4 Marine and Freshwater Catches, Aquaculture, and Fish Consumption

	Average Annual Marine Catch (000 metric tons) 1991-93	Percent Change Since 1981-83	Average Annual Freshwater Catch (000 metric tons) 1991-93	Percent Change Since 1981-83	Fresh-water Fish	Diad-romous Fish	Marine Fish	Crus-taceans	Molluscs	Total Fish and Shellfish	Other {a}	Per Capita Annual Food Supply Total 1990-92 (kg)	% Change Since 1980-82
WORLD	82,772.1	23	15,930.9	85	8,562.4	1,154.5	362.8	949.3	3,552.0	14,581.1	5,329.5	12.8	18.8
AFRICA	3,244.5	23	1,792.0	35	52.8	1.8	11.5	0.5	2.1	68.8	7.4	7.3	(13.5)
Algeria	88.4	43	0.4	X	0.1	0.0	0.0	0.0	0.0	0.2	X	3.3	10.0
Angola	69.8	(37)	7.0	(7)	X	X	X	X	X	0.0	X	15.0	(8.0)
Benin	8.8	147	31.2	(6)	0.1	X	X	X	X	0.1	X	10.2	(15.5)
Botswana	X	X	1.9	41	X	X	X	X	X	0.0	X	4.2	21.2
Burkina Faso	X	X	7.2	(0)	0.0	X	X	X	X	0.0	X	1.9	35.7
Burundi	X	X	22.0	87	0.1	X	X	X	X	0.1	X	3.7	13.3
Cameroon	59.3	(18)	20.7	3	0.1	X	X	X	X	0.1	X	10.1	(25.7)
Central African Rep	X	X	13.5	4	0.3	X	X	X	X	0.3	X	4.9	(11.4)
Chad	X	X	71.7	72	X	X	X	X	X	0.0	X	4.6	42.3
Congo	19.8	2	22.5	80	0.1	X	X	X	X	0.1	X	33.1	16.4
Cote d'Ivoire	62.1	(13)	18.8	(13)	0.3	X	X	X	X	0.3	X	15.8	(17.6)
Egypt	86.5	207	210.0	70	28.4	X	9.2	X	X	37.6	X	7.3	32.5
Equatorial Guinea	3.2	44	0.4	X	X	X	X	X	X	0.0	X	X	X
Eritrea	2.0 b	X	0.5 b	X	X	X	X	X	X	0.0	X	X	X
Ethiopia	0.1 c	(70)	4.3	24	0.0	X	X	X	X	0.0	X	0.1	0.0
Gabon	22.6	24	2.2	20	0.0	X	X	X	X	0.0	X	27.4	(29.4)
Gambia, The	19.8	122	2.5	(9)	X	X	X	0.0	X	0.0	X	13.7	20.2
Ghana	333.0	64	55.0	32	0.4	X	X	X	X	0.4	X	25.3	16.0
Guinea	35.2	56	3.8	167	0.0	X	X	X	X	0.0	X	8.1	12.0
Guinea-Bissau	5.0	46	0.2	491	X	X	X	X	X	0.0	X	2.2	(36.3)
Kenya	6.1	(11)	176.2	144	0.7	0.3	X	0.1	X	1.2	X	7.3	106.6
Lesotho	X	X	0.0	67	0.0	0.0	X	X	X	0.0	X	1.5	(24.1)
Liberia	4.8	(52)	4.0	0	0.0	X	X	X	X	0.0	X	13.3	(1.2)
Libya	8.5	(28)	0.1	X	0.1	X	X	X	X	0.1	X	2.4	(72.5)
Madagascar	78.6	306	28.4	(29)	0.4	0.0	X	0.3	X	0.7	0.3	7.5	28.6
Malawi	X	X	64.2	9	0.2	X	X	0.0	X	0.2	X	9.5	13.1
Mali	X	X	67.2	(4)	0.0	X	X	X	X	0.0	X	7.4	(30.3)
Mauritania	85.8	42	5.3	(11)	X	X	X	X	X	0.0	X	15.4	34.0
Mauritius	19.7	124	0.1	133	0.0	X	0.0	0.1	0.0	0.1	X	19.2	16.1
Morocco	586.1	46	1.7	64	0.0	0.2	0.3	X	0.1	0.6	X	7.0	9.9
Mozambique	26.3	(28)	4.1	(18)	0.0	X	X	X	X	0.0	X	3.0	(19.6)
Namibia	275.8	2,305	1.1	1,486	0.0	X	X	X	0.0	0.0	1.8	10.6	6.7
Niger	X	X	2.5	(60)	0.0	X	X	X	X	0.0	X	0.5	(65.2)
Nigeria	176.1	15	104.2	(9)	15.3	X	1.2	X	X	16.5	X	4.8	(66.6)
Rwanda	X	X	3.6	220	0.1	X	X	X	X	0.1	X	0.2	(25.0)
Senegal	332.5	48	23.3	56	0.0	X	X	0.0	0.0	0.0	X	21.0	(7.1)
Sierra Leone	48.0	35	13.7	(15)	0.0	X	X	X	X	0.0	X	12.9	(40.3)
Somalia	15.1	54	0.3	(6)	X	X	X	X	X	0.0	X	2.3	59.1
South Africa	584.2	(33)	2.7	193	0.8	1.1	0.0	0.0	1.8	3.7	0.3	9.5	10.0
Sudan	1.5	(29)	30.7	13	0.2	X	X	X	X	0.2	X	0.9	(37.2)
Swaziland	X	X	0.1	37	0.0	X	X	X	X	0.0	X	X	X
Tanzania	51.2	55	282.6	42	0.4	X	X	X	X	0.4	4.9	15.2	27.0
Togo	0.2	107	X	X	0.1	X	X	X	X	0.1	X	12.4	2.8
Tunisia	86.5	35	0.4 b	X	X	0.2	0.7	0.0	0.1	1.0	X	9.9	21.7
Uganda	X	X	241.6	42	0.1	X	X	X	X	0.1	X	14.0	12.9
Zaire	2.1	167	150.3	49	0.7	X	X	X	X	0.7	X	7.7	17.2
Zambia	X	X	66.0	22	3.6	X	X	0.0	X	3.6	X	7.7	(15.1)
Zimbabwe	X	X	21.9	38	0.0	0.1	X	0.0	X	0.2	X	1.5	(43.9)
EUROPE	18,197.9	X	998.8	X	240.0	454.9	20.2	2.3	587.8	1,305.1	4.3	21.0 d	16.4 d
Albania	2.2	(64)	1.3	(59)	0.1	0.0	0.0	X	0.4	0.6	X	2.3	(31.7)
Austria	X	X	4.4	(3)	1.2	2.7	X	0.0	X	3.9	X	9.2	60.8
Belarus, Rep	X	X	14.8	X	X	X	X	X	X	0.0	X	X	X
Belgium	37.2	(23)	0.8	X	0.3	0.5	X	X	X	0.8	X	19.2 e	5.3 e
Bosnia and Herzegovina	X	X	2.8 b	X	X	X	X	X	X	0.0	X	X	X
Bulgaria	27.7	(72)	9.5	(33)	7.2	0.7	X	X	0.0	7.9	X	2.6	(60.4)
Croatia, Rep	26.1 c	X	5.4 c	X	4.9	0.3 c	0.3 c	X	0.2 c	5.7	X	X	X
Czech Rep	X	X	24.4 b	X	22.3 b	0.5 b	X	X	X	22.8	X	X	X
Denmark	1,738.0	(7)	36.3	62	X	41.7	X	X	X	41.7	X	18.8	(0.4)
Estonia, Rep	209.4	X	3.0	X	0.1 c	0.4 c	X	X	X	0.5	X	X	X
Finland	88.8	3	53.8	(23)	0.0	18.2	X	X	X	18.2	X	29.8	7.5
France	768.6	(0)	52.1	137	8.2	44.5	0.4	X	202.0	255.2	0.1	30.7	24.8
Germany	259.9	(50)	49.1	25	14.8	24.9	0.0	X	35.2	74.9	X	20.4	(2.9)
Greece	166.9	80	11.7	26	0.3	2.2	9.1	X	10.3	21.8	0.0	21.7	28.0
Hungary	X	X	27.4	(34)	12.7	0.0	X	X	X	12.7	X	4.0	(7.0)
Iceland	1,447.6	42	0.8	103	X	2.8	0.0	X	X	2.8	X	137.9	60.3
Ireland	278.8	38	1.0	704	X	11.8	X	X	18.8	30.6	X	17.5	10.5
Italy	500.0	1	54.9	26	5.2	39.1	6.0	0.0	104.0	154.4	3.3	21.2	44.4
Latvia, Rep	237.2	X	1.6	X	0.5	0.0 c	X	X	X	0.5	X	X	X
Lithuania, Rep	257.0	X	5.5	X	3.4	0.0 c	X	X	X	3.4	X	X	X
Macedonia, former Yugoslav Rep	X	X	1.6	X	0.7	X	X	X	X	0.7	X	X	X
Moldova, Rep	X	X	5.0	X	X	X	X	X	X	0.0	X	X	X
Netherlands	454.0	(5)	2.8	(16)	1.1	0.7	X	X	57.3	59.1	X	10.4	2.0
Norway	2,425.2	(8)	0.5	50	X	154.8	0.0	X	0.0	154.8	X	X	X
Poland, Rep	412.4	(35)	49.7	87	22.1	4.2	X	X	X	26.2	X	12.6	6.5
Portugal	298.3	17	1.7	X	0.0	1.9	0.4	0.0	4.0	6.2	X	49.1	66.1
Romania	50.2	(70)	34.9	(37)	27.0	X	X	0.0	X	27.0	X	7.5	(12.8)
Russian Federation	5,326.6	X	375.2	X	95.8	1.0 c	0.0 b	0.0 c	0.7 c	97.5	1.4 c	X	X
Slovak Rep	X	X	2.8 b	X	0.8 b	0.8 b	X	X	X	1.6	X	X	X
Slovenia, Rep	2.4 c	X	0.6 c	X	X	X	X	X	X	0.0	X	X	X
Spain	1,283.3	(8)	30.0	11	0.4	19.2	3.5	2.2	148.1	173.5	X	38.8	23.3
Sweden	297.1	17	5.4	42	0.0	5.8	X	0.0	1.2	7.0	X	27.8	(0.1)
Switzerland	X	X	4.0	13	0.1	1.1	X	X	X	1.2	X	13.7	42.2
Ukraine	502.5	X	105.3	X	65.7 c	0.5	0.0 c	X	0.2 c	66.5	X	X	X
United Kingdom	837.2	(4)	15.8	83	0.0	56.8	X	0.0	5.4	62.2	X	19.6	14.6
Yugoslavia, Fed Rep	0.3 c	X	4.5 c	X	1.4	0.0 c	X	X	0.0 c	1.4	X	X	X

	Average Annual Marine Catch		Average Annual Freshwater Catch		Average Annual Aquaculture Production 1991-93 (000 metric tons)							Per Capita Annual Food Supply from Fish and Seafood	
	(000 metric tons) 1991-93	Percent Change Since 1981-83	(000 metric tons) 1991-93	Percent Change Since 1981-83	Fresh-water Fish	Diad-romous Fish	Marine Fish	Crus-taceans	Molluscs	Total Fish and Shellfish	Other {a}	Total 1990-92 (kg)	% Change Since 1980-82
NORTH & CENTRAL AMERICA	**8,246.5**	**17**	**576.2**	**153**	**255.9**	**73.9**	**0.3**	**44.4**	**161.2**	**535.7**	**0.0**	**17.8**	**23.0**
Belize	2.0	42	0.0	(89)	0.0	X	X	0.1	X	0.1	X	5.9	(11.9)
Canada	1,278.5	(4)	51.4	(2)	0.0	36.9	0.0	X	11.4	48.3	0.0	23.3	13.7
Costa Rica	15.8	20	2.1	352	1.4	0.0	X	0.8	0.0	2.2	X	6.5	6.6
Cuba	103.9	(40)	20.3	66	19.3	X	0.0	0.0	0.8	20.0	X	14.4	(24.1)
Dominican Rep	13.0	25	2.1	(31)	0.5	0.0	X	0.4	0.0	0.9	X	7.8	(0.8)
El Salvador	7.6	(42)	4.7	507	0.1	X	0.2	0.2	X	0.4	X	2.2	4.7
Guatemala	3.3	2	4.0	936	0.3	X	X	0.6	0.0	1.0	X	0.8	26.3
Haiti	4.8	(16)	0.5	67	X	X	X	X	X	0.0	X	4.0	12.1
Honduras	21.4	153	0.3	107	0.2	X	X	5.9	X	6.1	X	0.9	(33.3)
Jamaica	7.3	(8)	3.4	2,571	2.7	X	X	0.0	0.0	2.7	X	16.0	(14.3)
Mexico	1,131.9	(10)	167.5	293	12.6	1.3	X	2.7	29.0	45.6	X	10.2	(10.0)
Nicaragua	6.7	39	0.4	10	0.0	X	X	0.1	X	0.1	X	1.0	3.6
Panama	151.9	7	0.4	X	0.2	X	X	3.6	X	3.8	X	12.0	(12.0)
Trinidad and Tobago	12.6	199	X	X	0.0	X	X	0.0	X	0.0	X	11.7	(17.4)
United States	5,319.6	36	318.6	177	218.4	35.8	X	29.6	120.0	403.8	X	22.3	39.1
SOUTH AMERICA	**15,822.5**	**93**	**360.1**	**15**	**37.4**	**66.3**	**0.0**	**117.9**	**7.1**	**228.7**	**51.4**	**8.3**	**1.2**
Argentina	746.7	85	12.1	(8)	X	0.6	X	0.0	0.0	0.6	0.0	6.6	10.0
Bolivia	X	X	5.6	21	0.1	0.2	0.0	X	X	0.3	X	1.1	(52.2)
Brazil	576.9	(10)	213.1	5	24.2	0.7	X	2.7	0.2	27.8	X	6.3	(0.5)
Chile	6,137.0	67	12.4	6,499	X	60.7	0.0	X	6.8	67.5	51.4	22.9	26.2
Colombia	97.9	260	40.2	(15)	10.7	1.5	0.0	7.9	X	20.1	X	2.3	(47.3)
Ecuador	350.2	(31)	3.7	559	1.6	1.1	X	102.1	0.0	104.8	X	10.4	(5.5)
Guyana	39.9	21	0.8	11	0.0	X	X	0.0	X	0.1	X	39.8	0.3
Paraguay	X	X	15.7	359	0.1	X	X	X	X	0.1	X	3.5	200.0
Peru	7,390.4	187	33.3	49	0.4	1.2	X	4.0	0.1	5.6	X	22.1	4.3
Suriname	8.9	182	0.4	202	0.0	X	X	0.0	X	0.0	X	7.0	(59.8)
Uruguay	129.0	(5)	0.5	153	0.0	X	X	0.0	X	0.0	X	5.0	0.0
Venezuela	337.2	74	22.3	38	0.4	0.2	X	1.1	0.1	1.8	0.0	12.5	0.0
ASIA	**36,318.9**	**X**	**12,180.5**	**X**	**7,836.3**	**547.5**	**330.5**	**782.2**	**2,736.0**	**12,232.4**	**5,251.3**	**12.4 d**	**30.1 d**
Afghanistan, Islamic State	X	X	1.2	(19)	X	X	X	X	X	0.0	X	0.1	0.0
Armenia	X	X	4.4	X	1.5	0.3	X	X	X	1.8	X	X	X
Azerbaijan	X	X	38.2	X	X	X	X	X	X	0.0	X	X	X
Bangladesh	283.9	115	684.4	23	197.4	X	X	21.2	X	218.6	X	7.4	3.7
Bhutan	X	X	0.3	37	0.0	X	X	X	X	0.0	X	X	X
Cambodia	34.4	678	78.2	34	7.2	X	X	X	X	7.2	X	12.4	75.9
China	8,668.8	168	6,415.6	303	5,470.3	X	59.2	193.7	1,684.6	7,407.8	3,501.1	10.3	107.4
Georgia, Rep	43.1	X	2.9	X	0.9 c	0.0 c	X	X	X	0.9	X	X	X
India	2,462.0	68	1,738.1	78	1,305.4	0.9	X	42.8	2.0	1,351.1	X	3.9	29.7
Indonesia	2,578.2	71	854.0	66	245.4	151.5	8.6	147.9	X	553.3	95.0	14.5	22.1
Iran, Islamic Rep	231.5	219	86.5	650	27.4	0.7	X	X	X	28.2	X	4.3	161.2
Iraq	3.8	(47)	16.6	(2)	12.6	X	X	X	X	12.6	X	1.0	(61.8)
Israel	3.4	(71)	16.1	15	12.3	0.4	0.9	0.0	X	13.7	X	20.4	26.8
Japan	8,334.6	(22)	186.9	(12)	21.1	93.1	239.4	2.2	454.1	809.9	624.4	75.4	17.3
Jordan	0.0	(92)	0.0	127	0.0	X	X	X	X	0.0	X	2.4	(24.2)
Kazakhstan, Rep	X	X	79.2	X	X	X	X	X	X	0.0	X	X	X
Korea, Dem People's Rep	1,659.7	13	107.3	26	10.7	1.8	X	13.0	53.3	78.8	121.2	42.5	21.4
Korea, Rep	2,560.0	12	37.2	(15)	13.1	4.3	4.0	0.5	330.8	352.7	556.9	58.6	35.3
Kuwait	6.2	(3)	X	X	X	X	0.0	X	X	0.0	X	9.6	(3.4)
Kyrgyz Rep	X	X	1.2	X	X	X	X	X	X	0.0	X	X	X
Lao People's Dem Rep	X	X	29.8	21	12.7	X	X	X	X	12.7	X	6.7	(9.0)
Lebanon	1.8	29	0.1	33	X	0.1	X	X	X	0.1	X	0.4	(36.8)
Malaysia	623.5	(13)	18.2	27	11.2	4.3	1.3	3.3	61.5	81.6	X	24.6	(39.4)
Mongolia	X	X	0.1	(56)	X	X	X	X	X	0.0	X	1.1	10.0
Myanmar	612.3	37	189.7	34	5.1	X	X	0.0	X	5.1	X	15.1	4.6
Nepal	X	X	16.3	278	10.1	X	X	X	X	10.1	X	0.8	187.5
Oman	115.5	23	X	X	X	X	X	0.0	X	0.0	X	X	X
Pakistan	443.4	62	120.0	105	12.9	0.0	X	0.0	X	13.0	X	2.1	23.5
Philippines	1,690.9	34	589.6	7	92.5	186.3	3.6	78.6	36.1	397.2	337.8	32.5	(0.9)
Saudi Arabia	44.3	36	2.1	X	2.2	X	0.2	0.2	X	2.5	X	6.5	(29.1)
Singapore	12.1	(32)	0.0	(94)	X	0.3	0.5	0.4	1.1	2.2	X	X	X
Sri Lanka	187.4	4	20.9	(37)	3.5	X	X	0.7	X	4.2	X	10.8	(28.1)
Syrian Arab Rep	1.5	48	4.0	29	4.2	0.1	X	X	X	4.3	X	0.5	(76.7)
Tajikistan, Rep	X	X	3.8	X	X	X	X	X	X	0.0	X	X	X
Thailand	2,837.0	52	271.9	80	127.0	2.4	0.9	197.4	51.8	379.4	0.1	25.1	32.7
Turkey	408.3	(14)	46.9	35	0.3	6.8	1.5	X	X	8.6	X	6.2	(20.3)
Turkmenistan, Rep	X	X	40.0	X	X	X	X	X	X	0.0	X	X	X
United Arab Emirates	93.3	33	X	X	0.0	X	0.0	0.0	X	0.0	X	25.4	18.5
Uzbekistan, Rep	X	X	26.3	X	18.9 c	0.1 b	X	X	X	18.9	X	X	X
Viet Nam	795.2	65	271.6	42	133.3	X	X	50.7	X	184.0	4.3	13.9	27.5
Yemen, Rep	82.7	31	0.9	X	X	X	X	X	X	0.0	X	X	X
OCEANIA	**821.1**	**84**	**23.3**	**37**	**0.1**	**8.1**	**0.2**	**1.9**	**57.3**	**67.7**	**11.8**	**21.4**	**13.4**
Australia	225.1	42	4.7	170	0.0	5.4	0.2	1.1	9.3	16.2	6.4	17.8	19.5
Fiji	27.0	8	3.8	123	0.1	X	0.0	0.0	0.0	0.1	0.1	41.1	2.3
New Zealand	461.5	152	1.4	244	X	2.7	X	X	47.9	50.6	X	28.4	30.8
Papua New Guinea	11.3	(12)	13.4	2	0.0	0.0	X	X	0.0	0.0	0.0	21.8	(7.0)
Solomon Islands	53.4	36	X	X	X	X	X	0.0	X	0.0	X	55.7	(9.5)

Source: Food and Agriculture Organization of the United Nations.
Notes: a. Includes production of aquatic plants and seaweeds, which are excluded from marine catch; their harvest is to be subtracted as appropriate. b. One year of data. c. Two years of data.
d. Regional total excludes countries of the former Soviet Union. e. Data are for Belgium and Luxembourg.
Total of aquaculture production is included in the country totals for marine and freshwater catches. World and regional totals include countries not listed and unallocated quantities.
0 = zero or less than half the unit of measure; X = not available; negative numbers are shown in parentheses. For additional information, see Sources and Technical Notes.

Sources and Technical Notes

Data Table 13.1
Freshwater Resources and Withdrawals

Sources: Water resources and withdrawal data come from a variety of sources: J. Forkasiewicz and J. Margat, *Tableau Mondial de Donnees Nationales d'Economie de l'Eau, Ressources et Utilisation* (Departement Hydrogeologie, Orleans, France, 1980); J. Margat, Bureau de Recherches Geologiques et Minieres, Orleans, France, April 1988 (personal communication); Alexander V. Belyaev, Institute of Geography, U.S.S.R. National Academy of Sciences, Moscow, September 1989 and January 1990 (personal communication); Peter Gleick, Pacific Institute, Oakland, California, December 1995 (personal communication); withdrawal and sectoral use data for the United States: Wayne B. Solley, Robert R. Pierce, and Howard A. Perlman, "Estimated Use of Water in the United States, in 1990," *U.S. Geological Survey Circular,* No. 1081 (U.S. Geological Survey, Reston, Virginia, 1993); European Communities—Commission, *Environment Statistics 1989* (Office des Publications Officielles des Communautes Europeennes, Luxembourg, 1990), p. 130; Economic Commission for Europe, *The Environment in Europe and North America* (United Nations, New York, 1992), pp. 15–23; United Nations Economic Commission for Europe (ECE), *ECE Environmental Statistical Database,* on diskette, (Statistical Division, UN/ECE, 1995); Organisation for Economic Co-Operation and Development (OECD), *OECD Environmental Data Compendium* (OECD, Paris, in press, 1995); Food and Agriculture Organization of the United Nations (FAO), *Water Resources of African Countries, A Review* (FAO, Rome, 1995), pp. 14–15; desalination data as footnoted: O.K. Buros for the International Desalination Association, *The Desalting ABC's* (Saline Water Conversion Corporation, Riyadh, Saudi Arabia, 1990), p. 5; and population: United Nations Population Division, *World Population Prospects, the 1994 Revision* (United Nations, New York, 1995). Withdrawal data in this table were updated or confirmed from individual country reports when possible. For example, this was accomplished for Egypt, Morocco, South Africa, the Republic of Korea, Viet Nam, Honduras, Brazil, Guyana, and Japan, based on reports prepared by each country for the United Nations Conference on the Environment and Development held in Rio de Janeiro, Brazil, in 1992. In general, data are compiled from published documents (including national, United Nations, and professional literature) and from

estimates of resources and consumption from models using other data, such as area under irrigated agriculture, livestock populations, and precipitation, when necessary.

Annual internal renewable water resources refers to the average annual flow of rivers and groundwater generated from endogenous precipitation. Both estimates of runoff into rivers and recharge of groundwater should be used with caution when comparing different countries because these estimates are based on differing sources and dates. These annual averages also disguise large seasonal, interannual, and long-term variations. When data for *annual river flows from* and *to other countries* are not shown, the internal renewable water resources figure *may* include these flows. These flows could be modified by upstream users. Total outflows from countries are more poorly documented than inflows. When such data are shown they are included in a country's total internal renewable water resources. *Per capita annual internal renewable water resources* data were calculated using 1995 population estimates.

Annual withdrawals as a *percentage of water resources* refer to *total* water withdrawals, not counting evaporative losses from storage basins, as a percentage of internal renewable water resources and river flows from other countries. Water withdrawals also include water from desalination plants in countries where that source is a significant part of all water withdrawals.

Per capita annual withdrawals were calculated using national population data for the year of data shown for withdrawal.

Sectoral withdrawals are classified as *domestic* (drinking water, homes, commercial establishments, public services (e.g., hospitals), and municipal use or provision); *industry* (including water withdrawn to cool thermoelectric plants); and *agriculture* (irrigation and livestock).

Totals may not add because of rounding.

Data Table 13.2
Wastewater Treatment

Source: Organisation for Economic Co-Operation and Development (OECD), *OECD Environmental Data Compendium 1995* (OECD, Paris, 1995, in press).

OECD surveys its members and associates on a variety of environmental questions. Definitions can vary among countries. The *percentage of the population served* is the actual proportion connected to wastewater treatment plants. *Primary treatment* comprises the physical and mechanical processes that re-

move 20 to 30 percent of the biochemical oxygen demand (BOD) and effluents and separates out sludge. *Secondary treatment* is the additional use of biological treatment, such as the use of anaerobic or aerobic microorganisms that remove 80 to 90 percent of BOD. *Tertiary treatment* consists of advanced added chemical or biological-chemical treatments that remove 95 percent or more of BOD. Years given are the closest available. See the source for country details.

Data Table 13.3
Marine Fisheries, Yield and State of Exploitation

Sources: Marine fishery production: Food and Agriculture Organization of the United Nations (FAO), *Fishstat-PC* (FAO, Rome, 1995); state of exploitation: FAO, unpublished data (FAO, Rome, 1995); bycatch: FAO, *The State of World Fisheries and Aquaculture* (FAO, Fisheries Department, Rome, 1995).

FAO divides the world's oceans into 19 marine statistical areas and organizes *annual catch* data by 1,028 "species items"—species groups separated at the family, genus, or species level. "Catch" refers to average landings and does not include discards (see below). *Marine fish* include the following FAO species groupings: flounders, halibuts, soles, etc.; cods, hakes, haddocks, etc.; redfishes, basses, congers, etc.; jacks, mullets, sauries, etc.; herrings, sardines, anchovies, etc.; tunas, bonitos, bill-fishes, etc.; mackerels, snoeks, cutlassfishes, etc.; sharks, rays, chimeras, etc.; and miscellaneous marine fishes. *Cephalopods* include squids, cuttlefishes, octopuses, etc. *Crustaceans* are the total of the following categories: seaspiders, crabs, etc.; lobsters, spiny-rock lobsters, etc.; squat lobsters; shrimps, prawns, etc.; krill, planktonic crustaceans, etc.; and miscellaneous marine crustaceans. Years shown are 3-year averages. *Total marine catch* differs from marine catch in Data Table 13.4 because the following mollusc categories are not included: abalones, winkles, conchs, etc.; oysters; mussels; scallops; clams, cockles, arkshells, etc.; and miscellaneous marine molluscs. Please refer to the Technical Notes for Data Table 13.4 for the definition of nominal fish catch and additional information on FAO's fishery database. Fish catch data presented in this table include harvests from marine aquaculture production. Marine aquaculture provides an insignificant contribution to the total yields of marine fish and cephalopods.

Percentage of stocks fully fished, overfished, depleted, or recovering provides a measure of the degree to which fish stocks within FAO's marine statistical areas were exploited as of 1992. Data refer to all marine stocks for which FAO has data. Exploitation levels were determined by comparing catch levels to estimated maximum sustainable yield (MSY) for each stock. Stocks considered *fully fished* are those with yields within 25 percent of MSY. *Overfished* stocks are those where catch exceeds 25 percent of MSY. *Depleted* stocks are fisheries that have essentially collapsed. *Recovering* stocks are fisheries that have collapsed, where fishers are no longer targeting the species (because such stocks are protected, or, more generally, because catch levels do not justify the level of effort).

Discards as a percentage of overall catch refer to the percentage of overall catch (discards plus landings) during the 1988–92 period that consisted of nontarget or low-value species and undersized fish of targeted species.

Individual countries are charged with collecting catch data and reporting them to FAO. The quality of these estimates varies because many countries lack the resources to adequately monitor catch landings within their borders. In addition, fishers sometimes underreport their catches because they have not kept within harvest limits established to manage the fishery. In some cases, catch statistics are inflated to increase the importance of the fishing industry to the national economy.

Data Table 13.4
Marine and Freshwater Catches, Aquaculture, and Fish Consumption

Sources: Marine, freshwater, and aquaculture catches: Food and Agriculture Organization of the United Nations (FAO), *Fishstat-PC* (FAO, Rome, 1995). Food supply from sea-food: FAO, *Faostat-PC,* on diskette (FAO, Rome, 1995).

Marine and *freshwater catch* data refer to marine and freshwater fish killed, caught, trapped, collected, bred, or cultivated for commercial, industrial, and subsistence use. Crustaceans and molluscs are included. Statistics for mariculture, aquaculture, and other kinds of fish farming are included in the country totals. Quantities taken in recreational activities are excluded. Figures are the national totals averaged over a 3-year period; they include fish caught by a country's fleet anywhere in the world. Catches of freshwater species caught in low-salinity seas are included in the statistics of the appropriate marine area. Catches of diadromous (migratory between saltwater and freshwater) species are shown either in the marine or inland area where they were caught.

Data are represented as nominal catches, which are the landings converted to a live-weight basis, that is, the weight when caught.

Landings for some countries are identical to catches. Catch data are provided annually to the FAO Fisheries Department by national fishery offices and regional fishery commissions. Some countries' data are provisional for the latest year. If no data are submitted, FAO uses the previous year's figures or makes estimates based on other information. For details on data quality, please refer to the Technical Notes to Data Table 13.3.

Years are calendar years except for Antarctic fisheries data, which are for split years (July 1–June 30). Data for Antarctic fisheries are given for the calendar year in which the split year ends.

Aquaculture is defined by FAO as "the farming of aquatic organisms, including fish, molluscs, crustaceans, and aquatic plants. Farming implies some form of intervention in the rearing process to enhance production, such as regular stocking, feeding, and protection from predators, etc. [It] also implies ownership of the stock being cultivated. . . ." Aquatic organisms that are exploitable by the public as a common property resource are included in the harvest of fisheries.

FAO's global collection of aquaculture statistics by questionnaire was begun in 1984; today, these data are a regular feature of the annual FAO survey of world fishery statistics.

FAO's 1,028 "species items" are summarized in six categories. *Freshwater fish* include carps, barbels, and tilapias, among others. *Diadromous fish* include sturgeons, river eels, salmons, trouts, and smelts. *Marine fish* include a variety of species groups such as flounders, cods, redfishes, herrings, tunas, mackerels, sharks, etc. *Crustaceans* include, among others, freshwater crustaceans, crabs, lobsters, shrimps, and prawns. *Molluscs* include freshwater molluscs, oysters, mussels, scallops, clams, and squids. *Other* includes frogs, turtles, and aquatic plants. Data on whales and other mammals are excluded from this table. For a detailed listing of species, please refer to the most recent *FAO Yearbook of Fishery Statistics* (FAO, Rome), which provides notes to data published in *Fishstat-PC.*

Per capita annual food supply from fish and seafood is the quantity of both freshwater and marine fish and fish products available for human consumption. Data on aquatic plants and whale meat are excluded from the totals. The amount of fish and seafood actually consumed may be lower than the figures provided, depending on how much is lost during storage, preparation, and cooking, and on how much is discarded.

14. Atmosphere and Climate

Air pollution continues to be one of the most serious local environmental problems and a continuing threat to human health, especially in urban areas. (See Chapter 2, "Urban Environment and Human Health.") Regionally, acid precipitation and atmospheric transport of a wide range of nutrients and toxic materials damage crops and disturb the acidic balance of lakes and estuaries. Globally, degradation of the stratospheric ozone layer continues. (See Box 14.1.) And rising global concentrations of greenhouse gases such as carbon dioxide and methane increase the risk of climate change.

These examples reflect the impact of growing human populations and expanding industrial activity on the thin layer of air that surrounds the Earth. Scientific research is making rapid progress in understanding the natural systems that govern atmospheric phenomena, the mechanisms by which human activities alter those systems, and the likely future consequences of present human activities. Progress in forging the social and political consensus necessary to deal with these problems and in implementing solutions to them is much slower.

This chapter focuses on global environmental problems concerning the atmosphere. It reports on current emissions of greenhouse gases, on the future emissions implied by a number of scenarios of energy use, and on recent scientific assessments of the likely consequences for the Earth's climate. It contrasts these assessments with the goals of the Framework Convention on Climate Change and discusses the difficulties of stabilizing atmospheric levels of greenhouse gases. It also reports on widely varying estimates of the potential costs—and benefits—of controlling emissions, on recent diplomatic

efforts to strengthen the Climate Convention, and on a recent scientific assessment of whether the climate is actually changing. (See Box 14.2.)

STABILIZING EARTH'S CLIMATE

When most of the world's nations signed the Framework Convention on Climate Change in 1992 at the Earth Summit—the 1992 United Nations Conference on Environment and Development (UNCED)—their goal was to stabilize the atmospheric concentrations of greenhouse gases—primarily carbon dioxide, but also methane, nitrous oxide, and several other heat-trapping gases—at a level that would not dangerously interfere with the Earth's climate system. But the years since UNCED have provided some sobering perspectives on just how difficult attaining this goal may be. Recent projections of global energy use in the next two decades foresee a marked increase in the amount of fossil fuel burned around the world—with a concomitant increase in carbon dioxide emissions. (See Chapter 12, "Energy and Materials.")

At the same time, climate scientists, using computer models, have studied what it will take to stabilize greenhouse gas concentrations at various levels. In general, these studies show that carbon dioxide levels will not stabilize at any desirable level unless emissions—and hence the use of fossil fuels—are cut substantially. The economic costs and benefits of a potential shift toward lower emissions are also slowly coming into sharper focus, providing critical input into the decisions on whether or when to invest in emissions abatement programs.

Even if global policymakers continue to confirm that stabilizing the climate is scientifically and economically

Box 14.1 Protecting the Atmospheric Ozone Layer

January 1, 1996, marked an important milestone in efforts to protect the global environment. On that date, production of the industrial chemicals known as chlorofluorocarbons (CFCs) was to have ceased in developed countries under the provisions of the Montreal Protocol of the Vienna Framework Convention on Ozone-Degrading Substances. Developing countries have a 10-year grace period before they must phase out production as well. The phaseout represents the culmination of diplomatic, scientific, and industrial work to forge an international consensus and to develop alternatives to these environmentally harmful substances.

Another milestone, late in 1995, was the awarding of the Nobel Prize in chemistry to three scientists for their discoveries that trace amounts of gases could profoundly alter the chemistry of the upper atmosphere in ways that could affect Earth's ability to sustain life. The research by Paul Crutzen of Germany and F. Sherwood Rowland and Mario Molina of the United States in the early 1970s showed that both naturally occurring gases such as nitrous oxide and industrial chemicals

such as CFCs could reach the upper atmosphere. There the sun's harsh ultraviolet light degrades these compounds, releasing chlorine and other reactive species that could, the scientists showed, catalyze the destruction of ozone molecules. Since the stratospheric ozone layer absorbs much of the biologically harmful ultraviolet radiation reaching Earth, the scientists warned that increasing concentrations of ozone-degrading gases could cause a global environmental problem, exposing most forms of life to damaging levels of ultraviolet light.

Initially, these conclusions were quite controversial. Subsequent measurements in the atmosphere, however, have confirmed their work and have shown that CFCs and other industrial chemicals are the cause of the huge ozone hole over the Antarctic discovered in 1985 that led to the Montreal Protocol and set in motion current efforts to phase out the production and use of these chemicals.

The scientific discoveries and the world's subsequent actions to eliminate this environmental threat appear to have come just in time to prevent serious and widespread harm. In its citation, the Nobel Committee applauded the three scientists for having "contributed to our salvation from a global environmental problem that could have catastrophic consequences." Even if all governments comply with the Montreal Protocol, however, past emissions will continue to cause ozone degradation for decades to come, and full recovery of the ozone layer is not expected until about 2100. And yet more work remains to be done. Other ozone-depleting substances remain to be controlled, and mechanisms will be needed to assist developing nations in their control efforts [1] [2].

References and Notes

1. Robert F. Service, "Uncovering Threats to the Ozone Layer Brings Rewards," *Science*, Vol. 270, No. 5233 (October 20, 1995), pp. 381–382.

2. Office of Air and Radiation, U.S. Environmental Protection Agency (EPA), and the World Resources Institute, "Protection of the Ozone Layer," EPA Environmental Indicators, EPA 230-N-95-002 (EPA, Washington, D.C., June 1995) pp. 1–4.

justified, they still face the questions of how quickly and how much they should cut, how cuts will be allocated among developed and transition economies [1], and what allowance will be made for the economic and social needs of poorer countries that are in widely different phases of development. These questions provide the basis for present negotiations on how the Climate Convention can be strengthened and post-2000 commitments secured to meet the goals of the Convention without strangling the world economy or penalizing developing nations.

GLOBAL CARBON DIOXIDE EMISSIONS

Present Emissions

In 1992, global emissions of carbon dioxide—the prime greenhouse gas added to the atmosphere as a direct result of human activity—amounted to 26.4 billion metric tons per year, of which 84 percent (22.3 billion metric tons) was from industrial activity. Emissions from industrial activity have climbed 38 percent over the past 20 years. (See Data Tables 14.2 and 14.4.) The United States continues to be the largest source of industrial emissions of carbon dioxide, accounting for nearly 22 percent of global emissions; this is followed by China (11.9 percent), Russia (9.4 percent), and Japan (5 percent). (See Table 14.1.) The countries of the European Union together account for 13 percent of global emissions [2]; the developed countries of the Organisation for Economic Co-Operation and Development (OECD) account for 44.7 percent [3]. (See also Data Tables 14.1 and 14.6.)

National totals, however, represent only part of the picture, because they depend on both population size and the level of industrial activity. Per capita emissions provide a better yardstick for comparing the emissions that result from the average individual's share of national industrial activity, and these figures show widely varying emission patterns. (See Figure 14.1.) Again, the United States had the highest per capita emissions—19.1 metric tons per year—among the nations that were the major sources of global emissions in 1992; per capita emissions in India and China were 4.6 and

Box 14.2 New Scientific Assessment of Global Climate Change

The Intergovernmental Panel on Climate Change (IPCC) is charged with informing governments about the latest scientific understanding of global climate change and the likely effects of increased levels of greenhouse gases in the atmosphere. In early 1996, IPCC released its latest scientific assessment, which updated and refined its earlier findings.

The new report reaffirms IPCC's central estimate of the sensitivity of the global atmosphere to increasing greenhouse gas levels, predicting on the basis of computer models that global temperatures will rise between 1.5° and 4.0° C if the atmospheric concentration of carbon dioxide doubles from its pre-industrial level of 280 parts per million by volume (ppmv) to 560 ppmv. The current level is nearly 360 ppmv. The panel also left unchanged IPCC's earlier

estimates that global mean surface temperatures have increased between 0.3° and 0.6° C and that the global sea level has risen an average of 1.0 to 2.5 millimeters per year over the past century (1).

IPCC revised downward its earlier estimates of how much warming could be expected over the next century to include the effects of aerosols—atmospheric particulates that derive largely from coal-fired power plants and industrial sources and that produce a mild shade effect—and the phaseout of chlorofluorocarbons. Under conditions of moderate population growth and economic expansion and in the absence of any focused international effort to reduce carbon dioxide emissions, computer models suggest that surface temperatures will increase 2.0° C over the next century. Sea levels are projected to rise 0.5 meters by 2100 (2).

IPCC also took its firmest stand to date on whether the global warming observed so far can be attributed to human activities or whether it can still be explained by natural climate variability. The Panel concluded that it is unlikely that the observed temperature changes over the past century are entirely due to natural causes (3).

References and Notes

1. Intergovernmental Panel on Climate Change (IPCC), *IPCC Second Assessment Synthesis of Scientific-Technical Information Relevant to Interpreting Article 2 of the U.N. Framework Convention on Climate Change 1995*, January 1996 draft (World Meteorological Organization/United Nations Environment Programme, Geneva, 1995), pp. 4, 14.

2. *Ibid.*, p. 6.

3. *Op. cit.* 1, p. 4.

11.9 percent, respectively, of the U.S. level. The OECD countries had average per capita emissions of 11.5 metric tons per year in 1992.

Anthropogenic emissions of carbon dioxide add to the complex natural processes of Earth's carbon cycle. Natural sources of carbon dioxide emissions range from volcanic eruptions to the aerobic digestion of decayed vegetation by soil bacteria. Natural sinks for carbon dioxide include regions of expanding forests, peat bogs, seafloor sediments that accumulate shells and other carbonate-rich materials, and, under appropriate conditions, the ocean waters themselves (depending on, among other factors, ocean temperatures, the relative concentrations of carbon dioxide in the atmosphere and ocean, and the amount of mixing in the upper layers of the oceans). As a result of these competing processes, the net accumulation of carbon dioxide in the atmosphere has in recent years amounted to about half of the annual anthropogenic emissions.

Reducing the accumulation of carbon dioxide in the atmosphere depends to a great extent on controlling emissions from the burning of fossil fuels, since these are responsible for roughly 80 percent of yearly carbon dioxide emissions worldwide (the rest come from cement manufacture and from tropical deforestation and other land use changes) (4) (5). Yet fossil fuels still dominate the world energy picture, and this is unlikely to change dramatically in the next 30 years, according to several independent projections of future global energy use (6) (7) (8).

Projecting Future Emissions

Global energy use projections, recently prepared by three different agencies—the International Energy Agency, the U.S. Department of Energy, and the World Energy Council—make use of a number of detailed energy scenarios to look at how carbon dioxide emissions could evolve over the next few decades. The scenarios are built around assumptions about how fast the world economy will expand, how quickly the world's population will grow, the rate of technological advancement, the speed at which new energy-efficient technologies and conservation measures are adopted, and the relative availability and price of fossil, nuclear, and renewable energy sources. These are all important factors influencing both total energy use and carbon dioxide emissions (9). In most cases, the agencies constructed more than one scenario to allow for variation in world economic growth and energy policies. (For an expanded discussion of future energy use scenarios, see Chapter 12, "Energy and Materials.")

These scenarios suggest that in 2010, in the absence of major policy initiatives to curb their use, fossil fuels are likely to be the source of about three quarters of the world's commercial energy, even though the use of renewable energy sources is expected to grow. (Estimates of commercial energy do not include traditional fuels like firewood, crop wastes, and animal dung.) By 2010, the quantity of fossil fuels burned per year is likely

Table 14.1 Fifty Countries with the Highest Industrial Emissions of Carbon Dioxide, 1992

Rank	Country	Total CO$_2$ Emissions (million metric tons)
1	United States	4,881,349
2	China	2,667,982
3	Russian Federation	2,103,132
4	Japan	1,093,470
5	Germany	878,136
6	India	769,440
7	Ukraine	611,342
8	United Kingdom	566,246
9	Canada	409,862
10	Italy	407,701
11	France	362,076
12	Poland	341,892
13	Mexico	332,852
14	Kazakhstan	297,982
15	South Africa	290,291
16	Republic of Korea	289,833
17	Australia	267,937
18	Democratic People's Republic of Korea	253,750
19	Iran	235,478
20	Spain	223,196
21	Saudi Arabia	220,620
22	Brazil	217,074
23	Indonesia	184,585
24	Turkey	145,490
25	Netherlands	139,027
26	Czech Republic	135,608
27	Uzbekistan	123,253
28	Romania	122,103
29	Argentina	117,003
30	Venezuela	116,424
31	Thailand	112,477
32	Belarus	102,028
33	Belgium	101,768
34	Nigeria	96,513
35	Egypt	83,997
36	Algeria	79,172
37	Greece	73,859
38	Pakistan	71,902
39	United Arab Emirates	70,616
40	Malaysia	70,492
41	Iraq	64,527
42	Azerbaijan	63,878
43	Colombia	61,493
44	Norway	60,247
45	Hungary	59,910
46	Sweden	56,796
47	Austria	56,572
48	Bulgaria	54,359
49	Denmark	53,897
50	Singapore	49,790

Source: Carbon Dioxide Information Analysis Center (CDIAC), Oak Ridge National Laboratory, "1992 Estimates of CO$_2$ Emissions from Fossil Fuel Burning and Cement Manufacturing Based on the United Nations Energy Statistics and the U.S. Bureau of Mines Cement Manufacturing Data," ORNL/CDIAC-25, NDP-030 (an accessible numerical database) (Oak Ridge, Tennessee, September 1995).

to be about 35 percent beyond present levels. This estimate is based on moderate projected economic and population growth and is in spite of the fact that, as demand grows, prices could rise (10) (11).

As a direct consequence of this increased burning of fossil fuels, global energy-related carbon dioxide emissions are expected to rise between 30 and 40 percent by 2010 under moderate growth conditions (12) (13). With higher economic growth rates, and therefore higher energy demand, emissions will be greater as well. The World Energy Council's *High Growth* scenario, which assumes particularly robust economic growth in the developing world, shows a 93 percent rise in carbon dioxide emissions by 2020 (14).

Only in the World Energy Council's *Ecologically Driven* scenario do global carbon dioxide emissions scarcely rise between 1990 and 2020. This "what-if" scenario, which is not patterned after current trends in energy use, assumes a determined effort to greatly increase the use of renewable energy sources, reduce coal consumption, and freeze oil use at today's level by switching to greater use of natural gas. (Gas, for an equal amount of energy, emits less carbon dioxide than oil.) More importantly, it assumes a very high level of energy-efficiency improvements, and a concerted effort would undoubtedly be required to implement the improvements (15).

In all scenarios, much of the growth in energy demand and carbon dioxide emissions in the next few decades and beyond comes from the developing world. Although carbon dioxide emissions (under a moderate growth scenario) in 2010 are expected to increase some 24 percent from their 1990 levels in OECD nations, emissions from the developing world are projected to more than double, although from a much smaller base (16). Given current growth trends, developing countries will account for nearly half of global carbon dioxide emissions from industrial sources by 2010; today they are responsible for less than one third (17).

The rapid increases in carbon dioxide emissions in the developing world can be traced to the process of development itself, which generally results in a shift away from the use of traditional fuels toward the use of commercial fuels; an increase in personal income, which leads to the ability to purchase consumer items such as refrigerators, air conditioners, or cars that boost personal energy consumption; and the expansion of energy-intensive industries as economies shift from an agrarian base to a manufacturing and industrial base (18).

China and India, both of which have rapidly expanding economies and high absolute population growth (although at declining rates, especially in China), will likely be responsible for a significant percentage of the growth in global carbon dioxide emissions in the next two decades. The scenarios suggest that by 2010 China and India will account for more than half of all carbon dioxide emissions from the developing world. Indeed, growth in their combined emissions from 1990 to 2010 will exceed the growth in emissions from all OECD countries combined during that period (19) (20). This is due in part to a heavy reliance on coal—the most carbon-rich fuel. (Both China and India have large supplies.) China alone is projected to double its emissions by 2010, but still remain the second largest carbon dioxide emitter in the world behind the United States (21).

Even with the high projected growth in emissions in the developing world, per capita emissions in these areas will still be well below those in the developed world (22) (23). If the rest of the world consumed energy at the same per capita rate as the OECD countries, total world carbon dioxide emissions in 2010 would be roughly triple what is otherwise projected. Moreover, emissions from the developed world are responsible for the overwhelming bulk of excess carbon dioxide in the atmosphere. (See Figure 14.2.) Cumulative emissions from developed and transition countries will represent the majority of excess carbon dioxide until at least the middle of the next century, despite the steep rise in emissions by developing countries.

THE DIFFICULTY OF STABILIZING EMISSIONS

Rising global carbon dioxide emissions work at cross-purposes to the ultimate goal of the Climate Convention: to stabilize greenhouse gas concentrations at a "safe" level that does not alter the climate system in harmful ways. In fact, recent work has made clear how difficult the process of stabilizing atmospheric carbon dioxide concentrations at any reasonable level will be, given the demands of world development.

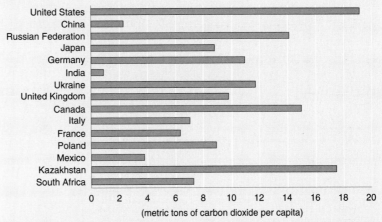

Figure 14.1 Per Capita Carbon Dioxide Releases for the 15 Countries with the Highest Total Emissions by Industrial Sources, 1992

Source: Carbon Dioxide Information Analysis Center (CDIAC), Oak Ridge National Laboratory, "1992 Estimates of CO_2 Emissions from Fossil Fuel Burning and Cement Manufacturing Based on the United Nations Energy Statistics and the U.S. Bureau of Mines Cement Manufacturing Data," ORNL/CDIAC-25, NDP-030 (an accessible numerical database) (Oak Ridge, Tennessee, September 1995).
Note: See Table 14.1 for list of total carbon dioxide emissions for these countries.

Even if global emissions could be held at current levels—an ambitious goal, considering present trends in energy use—the concentration of carbon dioxide in the atmosphere would not stabilize for several hundred years, according to the Intergovernmental Panel on Climate Change (IPCC) (24). (See Figure 14.3.)

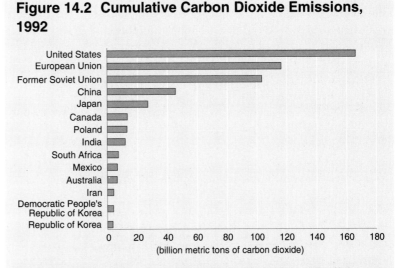

Figure 14.2 Cumulative Carbon Dioxide Emissions, 1992

Source: Carbon Dioxide Information Analysis Center (CDIAC), Oak Ridge National Laboratory, "1992 Estimates of CO_2 Emissions from Fossil Fuel Burning and Cement Manufacturing Based on the United Nations Energy Statistics and the U.S. Bureau of Mines Cement Manufacturing Data," ORNL/CDIAC-25, NDP-030 (an accessible numerical database) (Oak Ridge, Tennessee, September 1995).

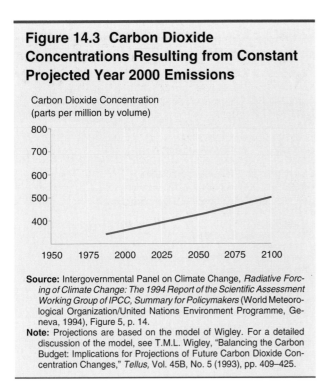

Figure 14.3 Carbon Dioxide Concentrations Resulting from Constant Projected Year 2000 Emissions

Carbon Dioxide Concentration
(parts per million by volume)

Source: Intergovernmental Panel on Climate Change, *Radiative Forcing of Climate Change: The 1994 Report of the Scientific Assessment Working Group of IPCC, Summary for Policymakers* (World Meteorological Organization/United Nations Environment Programme, Geneva, 1994), Figure 5, p. 14.

Note: Projections are based on the model of Wigley. For a detailed discussion of the model, see T.M.L. Wigley, "Balancing the Carbon Budget: Implications for Projections of Future Carbon Dioxide Concentration Changes," *Tellus*, Vol. 45B, No. 5 (1993), pp. 409–425.

The current atmospheric carbon dioxide concentration, which stands at nearly 360 parts per million by volume (ppmv), is about 28 percent greater than that at the beginning of the Industrial Revolution and is growing at an average of 1.5 ppmv per year (0.4 percent per year). Studies by IPCC show that at present emission rates, carbon dioxide concentrations could rise to about 700 ppmv by 2100—more than doubling the preindustrial carbon dioxide level of 280 ppmv—and could continue rising slowly for centuries (25). With the increasing global emissions that are likely with economic development, carbon dioxide levels will climb even faster (26) (27).

What will it take to stabilize atmospheric carbon dioxide concentrations? IPCC calculates that stabilization at today's levels would require that today's carbon dioxide emissions be cut 60 percent and that emissions be maintained at these reduced levels throughout the next century.

The need to curtail emissions to stabilize atmospheric carbon dioxide concentrations is illustrated in Figure 14.4, which shows IPCC's assessment of possible emission profiles over the next three centuries that would lead to the stabilization of carbon dioxide at different levels ranging from 450 to 750 ppmv. As the graph makes clear, stabilization is a long-term process that will take hundreds of years because of the ongoing nature of emissions and the long lifetime of carbon dioxide gas in the atmosphere.

It is important to understand that emissions do not necessarily have to decline immediately to stabilize carbon dioxide concentrations eventually. However, IPCC emphasizes that higher emissions today imply that much sharper cuts in emissions will be needed later on. And, further, the longer that high emissions persist, the greater will be the required cuts in future emissions to stabilize carbon dioxide concentrations at a given level. This is because it is, to a great extent, the cumulative total of emissions over time (the areas under the curves in Figure 14.4) that determines the level at which carbon dioxide stabilizes in the long run, not the particular year-by-year profile of emissions (the shapes of the curves) (28).

The benefits of stabilizing carbon dioxide concentrations depend greatly on the level at which they are stabilized. Stabilization even at today's atmospheric concentration (which would require dramatic changes in world energy use patterns) will not prevent additional greenhouse warming of the atmosphere. It could moderate the pace and magnitude of such warming, however. Stabilization at higher carbon dioxide levels is expected to lead to greater warming. Most scientists active in the field believe that a failure to stabilize carbon dioxide concentrations will lead to progressively rapid and extensive climate change.

ECONOMIC COSTS OF CONTROLLING EMISSIONS

Economic analysis of the costs and benefits of reducing carbon dioxide emissions can help policymakers decide whether emissions should be curtailed and, if so, how much and on what kind of schedule. However, assigning realistic dollar values to these various costs and benefits has proved extremely difficult. In spite of much effort, analyses are still somewhat rudimentary, with results varying from study to study because of differences in background assumptions such as the availability and cost of new energy-efficient technologies or the projected growth in the global economy (and thus the growth in emissions). Estimates depend, in particular, on whether they are based on "top-down" analyses—using aggregate models of the entire macroeconomy to predict large-scale interactions between sectors of the economy—or "bottom-up" analyses—which incorporate detailed studies of engineering costs for various technologies and describe energy consumption in great detail. Nonetheless, IPCC has drawn a number of tentative conclusions from a recent review of these studies.

In general, estimates of the annual costs of holding national carbon dioxide emissions at their 1990 levels run at about 1 to 2 percent of the gross domestic product (GDP) in OECD countries over the long term. Reducing emissions substantially below 1990 levels could cost as much as 3 percent of GDP. Bottom-up studies are more optimistic, suggesting that the costs of reducing emissions 20 percent below 1990 levels within several decades are negligible to negative. In the long term, similar studies suggest, 50 percent reductions in emissions may be possible without increasing the costs of the total energy system (29). Such conclusions are possible, the studies assert, because many energy-efficiency improvements pay for themselves with the savings on energy costs. As much as 10 to 30 percent of current energy demand could be eliminated with off-the-shelf and soon-to-be-available technologies, such as better electric motors, more fuel-efficient cars, and better insulation of dwellings. Realizing these potential savings, however, relies on adopting policy measures such as energy or fuel-efficiency standards for appliances and cars and eliminating market distortions such as low, subsidized energy prices that reduce the economic benefit to the consumer of saving energy (30).

Few comparable studies have been done in developing countries or in the transition economies, but the potential for savings through energy efficiency in these regions may be particularly high, IPCC concludes. Opportunities for absolute reductions in greenhouse gas emissions may exist in the transition economies, where subsidization of energy prices has been substantial and the stock of capital equipment is generally aging and less efficient. In the developing world, however, these "free" emission cuts will fall far short of what would be required to offset the rapid rise in expected emissions associated with economic development (31).

The timing of emission reductions can have a large effect on abatement costs. Under certain circumstances, deferring emission reductions somewhat may save money because the cost per ton of reducing emissions is expected to decline with time. This is because the costs of renewable energy sources such as solar or wind energy are expected to go down. At the same time, new, more efficient industrial processes and consumer products will be coming on line. In addition, when emissions are deferred, capital equipment such as industrial boilers, vehicles, or air-conditioning systems can be turned over naturally at the end of their life cycles rather than being replaced sooner with more efficient, but more expensive, models. The trade-off, of course, is that delaying emissions in the beginning necessitates steeper

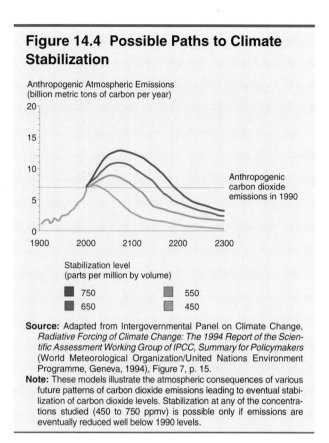

Figure 14.4 Possible Paths to Climate Stabilization

Anthropogenic Atmospheric Emissions
(billion metric tons of carbon per year)

Anthropogenic carbon dioxide emissions in 1990

Stabilization level
(parts per million by volume)

750

650

550

450

Source: Adapted from Intergovernmental Panel on Climate Change, *Radiative Forcing of Climate Change: The 1994 Report of the Scientific Assessment Working Group of IPCC, Summary for Policymakers* (World Meteorological Organization/United Nations Environment Programme, Geneva, 1994), Figure 7, p. 15.
Note: These models illustrate the atmospheric consequences of various future patterns of carbon dioxide emissions leading to eventual stabilization of carbon dioxide levels. Stabilization at any of the concentrations studied (450 to 750 ppmv) is possible only if emissions are eventually reduced well below 1990 levels.

cuts later on or, alternatively, accepting a higher rate of global warming (32) (33).

A key finding from many economic analyses is the important role that research and development can play in lowering the costs of reducing emissions. Vigorous promotion of research and development that focuses on renewable energy sources and energy-efficient technologies can cut the eventual costs of abatement significantly, and is therefore considered a prudent investment even in the near term, particularly if emission cuts are delayed and new technologies are being relied upon to drastically reduce emissions in the future (34) (35) (36).

Economic and some industry assessments also emphasize that cost-effective abatement of carbon dioxide emissions in the next few decades will rely on proper planning and investment today. For instance, infrastructure decisions made now, such as whether to build a traditional coal-fired power plant or to invest in newer, more expensive clean coal technology, can have a large effect on national emission levels. Such decisions will be expensive to reverse later on if steep cuts in emissions are called for. This is especially true for the transition economies and the developing world, because the infrastructure is expected to change more rapidly in these regions. This is one reason why deciding how much and when emissions should be cut is a pressing matter (37).

Box 14.3 The Berlin Climate Summit

In March 1995, the Berlin Climate Summit gave the parties to the Framework Convention on Climate Change their first chance to strengthen the treaty since signing it at the 1992 Earth Summit in Rio de Janeiro. Despite acknowledging the current trends in greenhouse gas emissions and the risks of inaction, however, the first conference of the parties ended without a binding agreement to greatly reduce global emissions in the next century and without agreement from developed nations to make deeper cuts in their emissions.

Even those who are most worried about the growing gap between what is known about climate science and international policy, however, found some comfort in the outcome of the Berlin meeting. Although it is difficult to deal with the politically charged and scientifically complex issue of global warming, delegates did negotiate a specific road map for future negotiations (1). The parties also agreed on a trial period for "activities implemented jointly"—projects undertaken cooperatively by nations to reduce emissions—that will give nations a free hand to experiment so they can learn more about how this mechanism might help achieve the goals of the Climate treaty.

In a decision dubbed the "Berlin Mandate," the parties agreed that existing developed countries' commitments to curb greenhouse gas emissions were not adequate to meet the Convention's goals and set a schedule for negotiating a protocol to toughen them after

1997 (2). In becoming parties to the Climate Convention, developed nations had pledged to try to return their emissions of greenhouse gases not controlled by the Montreal Protocol (the treaty banning the production of ozone-depleting chemicals) to 1990 levels by the year 2000. Referring specifically to this pledge, the Mandate initiates negotiations to "elaborate policies and measures" and "set quantified limitation and reduction objectives within specified time-frames, such as 2005, 2010, and 2020" (3).

The Mandate stipulates that these negotiations will "not introduce any new commitments" for developing countries. As it stands, the Climate Convention requires them to inventory their greenhouse gas emissions and to report on any climate-protecting measures that they take, but not to curb their emissions. This stipulation emerged from 2 weeks of intense negotiations and reflects the strong voice of developing countries. During the first week, India took the lead, and, along with the Philippines, China, Brazil, and Malaysia, drafted a "Green Paper," which became the basis of the Berlin Mandate (4).

The Berlin Mandate also calls on developed countries to make good on their promise of providing financial and technical resources to help developing countries participate in the Climate treaty. The parties decided that the Global Environmental Facility (GEF)—a funding body set up to help finance key environmental projects in developing countries

that may have global environmental benefits—will continue to serve as the Convention's interim financial mechanism for this purpose. The parties also reaffirmed their commitment to technology transfer to help developing nations benefit from continuing improvements in energy technologies.

Because many of the directives hammered out at the Berlin Summit leave considerable room for interpretation, it remains to be seen how far they will take governments toward the Convention's objective of "stabilization of greenhouse gas concentrations at a level that would prevent dangerous anthropogenic interference with the climate system" (5).

To move the parties in this direction, a group of 37 countries with the most to lose from rising sea levels—the Alliance of Small Island States (AOSIS)—pressed for a binding agreement during the Summit requiring developed countries to cut their carbon dioxide emissions to 20 percent below 1990 levels by the year 2005 (6). The AOSIS proposal was not adopted by developed nations, most of which acknowledge that they will have trouble meeting their existing commitment to return to 1990 emission levels, let alone cut an additional 20 percent.

Further complicating the picture is, first, the fact that emissions by developing countries are expected to grow with their economies and, second, that the GEF funding allocated to climate change projects is only a small fraction of the investments that will ultimately

ECONOMIC BENEFITS OF REDUCING EMISSIONS

If setting a price tag on the costs of cutting greenhouse gas emissions is difficult, determining the dollar value of the benefits is even more problematic. The primary benefit of abatement is avoiding the damages associated with global warming, which include coastal inundation from rising sea levels, disruption of rainfall and therefore water use patterns, agricultural effects due to heat stress, and ecosystem damage such as loss of biodiversity and habitat disruption. Other important potential benefits also come from cutting energy-related emissions, however, such as cleaner air, reduced damage to

crops and forests, and less environmental disruption from fossil fuel extraction. These not only have an economic value but are widely accorded a higher and more urgent priority by many countries and communities (38).

Pricing the damages from additional global warming involves many unknowns, since the actual extent and regional distribution of the effects are uncertain. Also, although some effects such as property loss or crop damage are relatively easy to quantify, quantification of damage to environmental amenities such as clean air, functioning ecosystems, or biodiversity has always been troublesome for economists because these are intangibles not traded in the market and their value to human welfare has not been quantified. The long-term and

be required to ensure that these countries develop along paths that minimize their greenhouse gas emissions.

With these challenges in mind, supporters of "joint implementation" welcomed agreement in Berlin on ground rules for a pilot program that would let nations experiment with climate protection activities undertaken jointly by two or more nations. This approach—for example, an offer by a firm in a developed country to finance a renewable energy or reforestation project in a developing country—might be a cost-effective way for developed countries to further curb emissions or increase the sequestration of carbon, while also funneling more money into promoting climate-friendly technologies. The original treaty allowed for joint implementation, but it had not specified how it should work.

Joint implementation was an extremely controversial issue in the negotiations leading up to the Berlin Summit. Critics, including many in developing countries, argued that it would let developed nations abdicate their responsibility to cut their own greenhouse gas emissions while pursuing a cheaper fix elsewhere. Critics also feared that it might supplant the technical and financial assistance promised in the Climate Convention, such as GEF funding. As a result, many developing countries opposed any scheme that would let developed nations use joint implementation projects to meet their commitment to cut emissions to 1990 levels by the year 2000. The parties resolved this issue by

agreeing that no credit would be given to developed nations for any reductions in emissions coming from joint implementation projects during the pilot phase, which they set to end before the year 2000 [7].

Recognizing that the diffusion of low-cost, noncarbon energy technologies is critical for long-term solutions to climate change, governments belonging to the Organisation for Economic Co-Operation and Development announced a Climate Technology Initiative at the Berlin Summit. The Initiative is aimed at accelerating the commercialization of inexpensive renewable energy supply systems.

Technical fixes are only one track, however. As negotiations on a protocol proceed, public support will be crucial. Coal and oil industry lobbyists attending the Summit were vocal in their opposition to strengthening the Climate Convention. Also making their voices heard were natural gas companies offering a high-efficiency energy source with lower carbon emissions than those from fossil fuels; renewable energy companies offering new solutions; insurance industry representatives who have a stake in a stable climate; and a host of groups from outside the environmental community that favor climate protection—from churches and local governments to youth groups and women's groups.

Finally, as more scientific findings are provided, those in the most danger will make the most compelling case for a

strong protocol. Speaking on behalf of AOSIS, Ambassador H.E. Tuiloma Neroni Slade of Samoa expressed his disappointment at the outcome of the Summit and emphasized that "we will continue to play with passion our reluctant role as Earth's early warning system, to continue to raise the alarm, and to raise the heat, on this process" [8].

References and Notes

1. Secretariat, United Nations Framework Convention on Climate Change, *Report of the Conference of the Parties on Its First Session, Held at Berlin from 28 March to 7 April 1995, Part Two: Action Taken by the Conference of the Parties at Its First Session,* FCCC/CP/1995/7/Add. 1 (United Nations, New York, June 6, 1995).

2. Seth Dunn, "The Berlin Climate Change Summit: Implications for International Environmental Law," *International Environment Reporter* (Bureau of National Affairs, Washington, D.C., May 31, 1995), p. 440.

3. *Op. cit.* 1, p. 5.

4. *Op. cit.* 2.

5. United Nations, "United Nations Framework Convention on Climate Change," Article 2 (United Nations Conference on Environment and Development, Rio de Janeiro, Brazil, 1992).

6. *Op. cit.* 2.

7. *Op. cit.* 2, p. 441.

8. H.E. Tuiloma Neroni Slade, "Statement on Behalf of the Alliance of Small Island States," paper presented at the First Conference of the Parties to the United Nations Framework Convention on Climate Change, Berlin, April 7, 1995, p. 1.

uncertain nature of climate change also complicates the pricing of damages, since many of these damages occur in the future and standard economic practice involves discounting these to some lesser, present-day value so that they are comparable to benefits and costs today. The choice of the "discount rate"—the interest rate used to discount the damages—then becomes crucial in estimating the monetary value of the effects from global warming that future generations will suffer [39] [40].

Despite these difficulties, a number of studies have tried to price the damages expected from global warming. These studies generally assume a doubling of the atmospheric carbon dioxide concentration from preindustrial levels, leading to an average 2.5° C warming. Under these conditions, a very limited set of damages

has been estimated at 1 to 1.5 percent of GDP per year in developed countries and 2 to 9 percent of GDP per year in developing countries, with island nations potentially suffering much higher damages [41] [42].

Of course, carbon dioxide concentrations may not stop at a doubling, and warming may continue, in which case additional damage will occur. In fact, they may rise geometrically as warming proceeds. For example, damages from a 10° C rise might reach 6 percent of GDP or more [43]. There is also the risk of a climate catastrophe in which the global climate regime changes quickly in unforeseen and deleterious ways. In this case, the damage could escalate rapidly [44].

Other benefits—both local and regional—of emissions abatement, including air quality improvements, can be quite high. For example, one study estimated that the value of air quality benefits in India from freezing emissions at 1990 levels would actually exceed the costs of the freeze. Likewise, studies in Europe and the United States indicate that such non-climate-related benefits could offset 30 to 100 percent of abatement costs (45). At least some economists who have studied the matter believe that taking into account both climate and other benefits of cutting carbon dioxide and the need to avoid the risk of a climate disaster provide a plausible economic justification for making substantial investments in emissions abatement (46) (47).

NEGOTIATING THE FUTURE

Given the difficulty of stabilizing global atmospheric carbon dioxide concentrations and the benefits of early planning in reducing eventual mitigation costs, many of the nations that signed the Framework Convention on Climate Change have begun to realize that a coordinated international course of action is urgently needed. At the most recent meeting of signatory nations—the first session of the Conference of the Parties that convened in Berlin in March 1995—the participants could not agree upon strict emissions limits, but they did adopt a procedure for negotiating such limits and set a deadline of 1997 for concluding these negotiations. (See Box 14.3.)

Even as the negotiations for a carbon dioxide target and emissions cuts proceed, IPCC has stressed that many of the general outlines of a global carbon dioxide strategy have already begun to take shape, and there are many actions that nations can take immediately. These include:

- Encouraging the adoption of those energy-efficiency improvements that, apart from their greenhouse benefits, are cost-effective in their own right. This implies an active program of policy reforms to en-

courage full-cost pricing of energy, to create efficiency standards, and to implement rebate programs or other financial vehicles to encourage adoption of energy-efficient technologies.

- Supporting expanded research and development of alternative energy sources and energy-efficient technologies, and establishing incentives to encourage the penetration of these into energy markets.

- Specifically promoting policies to encourage the replacement of long-lived energy, transportation, and industrial infrastructures at the end of their life cycles with efficient, low-emission technologies.

- Supporting continued climate research and monitoring so that the mechanism and magnitude of climate change are better understood and so that the effects of climate can be better planned for.

However, even if nations agree to take these actions and the international community is able to negotiate a target for future emission cuts, there is little reason to believe that global action will be quick enough or effective enough in the short term to avoid a rise in atmospheric carbon dioxide concentrations from their present level. The momentum of global development is great, and energy planners point out that it takes time to introduce new technologies and effect large changes in energy systems and infrastructure. Climate scientists estimate that the present burden of greenhouse gases has already committed Earth to an estimated temperature increase of 0.5° to 2.0° C, even if the atmospheric carbon dioxide concentration is stabilized at today's level. Although this does not lessen the urgency of current efforts to decrease future emissions, it does emphasize the need to begin developing adaptation strategies to cope with whatever warming is already under way. It also underscores the fact that global warming is a long-term phenomenon whose mitigation must be seen in a long-term context.

References and Notes

1. The term "transition economies" lacks a formal definition, but it is used here to include the successor states of the former Soviet Union (Armenia, Azerbaijan, the Republic of Belarus, the Republic of Estonia, the Republic of Georgia, the Republic of Kazakhstan, the Kyrgyz Republic, the Republic of Latvia, the Republic of Lithuania, the Republic of Moldova, the Russian Federation, the Republic of Tajikistan, the Republic of Turkmenistan, Ukraine, and the Republic of Uzbekistan) and the countries of Central Europe (Albania, Bulgaria, the Czech Repub-

lic, Hungary, Poland, Romania, and the Slovak Republic).

2. The countries of the European Union include Austria, Belgium, Denmark, Finland, France, Germany, Greece, Ireland, Italy, Luxembourg, the Netherlands, Portugal, Spain, Sweden, and the United Kingdom.

3. The OECD member countries are Australia, Austria, Belgium, Canada, Denmark, Finland, France, Germany, Greece, Iceland, Ireland, Italy, Japan, Luxembourg, Mexico, the Netherlands, New Zealand, Norway, Portu-

gal, Spain, Sweden, Switzerland, Turkey, the United Kingdom, and the United States. Mexico became a member in May 1994. Any discussion of OECD data prior to 1994 does not include data for Mexico.

4. Intergovernmental Panel on Climate Change, *Radiative Forcing of Climate Change: The 1994 Report of the Scientific Assessment Working Group of IPCC, Summary for Policymakers* (World Meteorological Organization/United Nations Environment Programme, Geneva, 1994), Table 1, p. 11.

5. Energy Information Administration, U.S. Department of Energy, *International Energy Outlook, 1995,* Report No. DOE/EIA-0484(95) (U.S. Government Printing Office, Washington, D.C., 1995), p. 18.

6. International Energy Agency, *World Energy Outlook, 1995* (Organisation for Economic Co-Operation and Development, Paris, 1995), p. 2.

7. *Op. cit.* 5, Table 1, p. 5.

8. World Energy Council, *Energy for Tomorrow's World: The Realities, the Real Options, and the Agenda for Achievement* (Kogan Page, London, and St. Martin's Press, New York, 1993), p. 143.

9. Intergovernmental Panel on Climate Change, *1992 Supplement: Scientific Assessment of Climate Change* (World Meteorological Organization/United Nations Environment Programme, Geneva, 1992), p. 11.

10. *Op. cit.* 6, Table A5, p. 301.

11. *Op. cit.* 5, Table 1, p. 5.

12. *Op. cit.* 6, p. 49.

13. *Op. cit.* 5, Table A9, p. 87.

14. *Op. cit.* 8.

15. *Op. cit.* 8, p. 81.

16. *Op. cit.* 6, p. 49.

17. *Op. cit.* 6, p. 49; Table 2.2, p. 50.

18. *Op. cit.* 6, pp. 55–56.

19. *Op. cit.* 6, pp. 50–51.

20. *Op. cit.* 5, Table A9, p. 87.

21. *Op. cit.* 5, Table A9, p. 87.

22. *Op. cit.* 6, p. 4.

23. Intergovernmental Panel on Climate Change (IPCC), *IPCC Synthesis Report,* July 29, 1995 draft (World Meteorological Organization/United Nations Environment Programme, Geneva, 1995), p. 24.

24. Intergovernmental Panel on Climate Change, *Radiative Forcing of Climate Change: The 1994 Report of the Scientific Assessment Working Group of IPCC* (World Meteorological Organization/United Nations Environment Programme, Geneva, 1994), p. 14.

25. *Ibid.,* pp. 5, 11, 14.

26. *Op. cit.* 24, p. 14.

27. *Op. cit.* 9, pp. 10–13.

28. *Op. cit.* 24, pp. 6, 14–16.

29. Intergovernmental Panel on Climate Change, "A Review of Mitigation Cost Studies," Chapter 9 in *Second Assessment Report, Working Group III* (World Meteorological Organization/United Nations Environment Programme, Geneva, 1995), pp. 4–17, 47.

30. *Ibid.,* pp. 5–8, 46.

31. *Op. cit.* 29, pp. 46–47.

32. *Op. cit.* 29, pp. 4–5.

33. *Op. cit.* 23, p. 38.

34. *Op. cit.* 29, pp. 4–5, 33, 46.

35. *Op. cit.* 8.

36. World Energy Council, *New Renewable Energy Resources: A Guide to the Future* (Kogan Page, London, 1994).

37. *Op. cit.* 29, pp. 46–47.

38. Intergovernmental Panel on Climate Change, "The Social Costs of Climate Change: Greenhouse Damage and the Benefits of Control," Chapter 6 in *Second Assessment Report, Working Group III,* April 1995 draft (World Meteorological Organization/United Nations Environment Programme, Geneva, 1995), pp. 5–33.

39. *Ibid.,* pp. 5–6, 52–53.

40. William Cline, *The Economics of Global Warming* (Institute for International Economics, Washington, D.C., 1992), pp. 3–10.

41. *Op. cit.* 38, p. 52.

42. *Op. cit.* 40.

43. *Op. cit.* 38, p. 52.

44. *Op. cit.* 40, p. 34.

45. *Op. cit.* 38, pp. 49–52.

46. Intergovernmental Panel on Climate Change, "Introduction: Scope of the Assessment," Chapter 1 in *Second Assessment Report, Working Group III,* May 31, 1995 draft (World Meteorological Organization/United Nations Environment Programme, Geneva, 1995), pp. 3, 10–13.

47. *Op. cit.* 40.

	Carbon Dioxide Emissions (000 metric tons)						Per Capita Carbon Dioxide Emissions (metric tons)	Bunker Fuels (000 metric tons)
	Solid	Liquid	Gas	Gas Flaring	Cement Manufacture	Total		
WORLD	8,588,416	9,050,080	3,828,880	249,152	626,544	22,339,408	4.10	476,320
AFRICA	271,744	274,430	77,054	65,659	26,905	715,773	X	0
Algeria	3,558	26,165	38,772	7,694	2,982	79,172	3.00	0
Angola	0	1,249	319	2,459	498	4,525	0.44	0
Benin	0	425	0	0	183	612	0.11	0
Botswana	2,173	0	0	0	0	2,173	1.65	0
Burkina Faso	0	557	0	0	0	557	0.07	0
Burundi	15	180	0	0	0	191	0.04	0
Cameroon	4	1,920	0	0	308	2,231	0.18	0
Central African Rep	0	216	0	0	0	216	0.07	0
Chad	0	253	0	0	0	253	0.04	0
Congo	0	3,748	7	169	51	3,972	1.69	0
Cote d'Ivoire	0	6,060	0	0	249	6,309	0.48	0
Egypt	2,524	57,353	16,118	0	8,002	83,997	1.54	0
Equatorial Guinea	0	117	0	0	0	117	0.33	0
Eritrea	X	X	X	X	X	X	X	X
Ethiopia	0	2,744	0	0	161	2,906	0.04	0
Gabon	0	2,154	99	3,261	59	5,569	4.51	0
Gambia, The	0	198	0	0	0	198	0.22	0
Ghana	7	3,265	0	0	509	3,781	0.22	0
Guinea	0	1,026	0	0	0	1,026	0.18	0
Guinea-Bissau	0	209	0	0	0	209	0.22	0
Kenya	297	4,287	0	0	758	5,342	0.22	0
Lesotho	X	X	X	X	X	X	X	X
Liberia	0	275	0	0	4	278	0.11	0
Libya	15	23,721	10,501	4,155	1,129	39,520	8.10	0
Madagascar	4	912	0	0	29	945	0.07	0
Malawi	33	561	0	0	59	652	0.07	0
Mali	0	432	0	0	11	443	0.04	0
Mauritania	15	2,807	0	0	44	2,869	1.36	0
Mauritius	165	1,191	0	0	0	1,356	1.25	0
Morocco	4,869	19,265	48	0	3,166	27,344	1.03	0
Mozambique	161	821	0	0	15	997	0.07	0
Namibia	X	X	X	X	X	X	X	X
Niger	458	616	0	0	11	1,085	0.15	0
Nigeria	180	37,285	9,405	47,896	1,744	96,513	0.84	0
Rwanda	0	421	0	4	29	451	0.07	0
Senegal	0	2,510	0	0	300	2,810	0.37	0
Sierra Leone	0	432	0	0	0	432	0.11	0
Somalia	0	0	0	0	15	15	0.00	0
South Africa	239,138	47,544	0	0	3,613	290,291	7.29	0
Sudan	0	3,338	0	0	125	3,462	0.15	0
Swaziland	267	0	0	0	0	267	0.33	0
Tanzania	0	1,832	0	0	271	2,103	0.07	0
Togo	0	539	0	0	194	733	0.18	0
Tunisia	385	9,746	1,784	22	1,627	13,560	1.61	0
Uganda	0	931	0	0	26	953	0.04	0
Zaire	931	3,151	0	0	99	4,181	0.11	0
Zambia	883	1,411	0	0	187	2,481	0.29	0
Zimbabwe	15,664	2,565	0	0	447	18,675	1.76	0
EUROPE	2,486,141	2,509,400	1,659,895	49,248	161,817	6,866,494	X	120,681
Albania	1,191	2,107	473	0	198	3,968	1.21	0
Austria	12,586	29,217	12,230	0	2,539	56,572	7.29	0
Belarus, Rep	9,541	61,138	30,536	0	813	102,028	9.89	0
Belgium	35,002	42,301	20,709	0	3,752	101,768	10.19	16,147
Bosnia and Herzegovina	8,376	5,646	835	0	198	15,055	3.37	0
Bulgaria	28,685	15,037	8,376	0	2,261	54,359	6.08	0
Croatia, Rep	1,583	8,926	4,822	0	883	16,210	3.33	0
Czech Rep	100,075	19,199	12,359	0	3,979	135,608	13.04	0
Denmark	25,615	22,281	4,386	487	1,129	53,897	10.44	4,701
Estonia, Rep	15,422	3,660	1,506	0	297	20,885	13.19	0
Finland	14,044	20,819	5,668	0	645	41,176	8.21	0
France	71,122	217,931	62,259	0	10,765	362,076	6.34	18,463
Germany	404,681	324,781	129,229	758	18,686	878,136	10.96	0
Greece	30,763	36,299	282	4	6,511	73,859	7.25	0
Hungary	19,720	23,076	16,001	0	1,114	59,910	5.72	0
Iceland	165	1,565	0	0	48	1,777	6.85	0
Ireland	12,652	13,040	4,346	0	813	30,851	8.87	0
Italy	46,716	246,294	94,084	0	20,603	407,701	7.03	0
Latvia, Rep	1,711	7,632	5,240	0	198	14,781	5.53	0
Lithuania, Rep	1,850	12,564	6,599	0	993	22,006	5.86	0
Macedonia, former Yugoslav Rep	0	3,360	491	0	249	4,100	1.98	0
Moldova, Rep	5,166	1,205	6,995	0	846	14,209	3.26	0
Netherlands	30,499	30,466	76,186	205	1,674	139,027	9.16	41,832
Norway	3,085	26,077	4,027	26,425	630	60,247	14.03	0
Poland, Rep	283,213	36,636	16,074	0	5,969	341,892	8.90	0
Portugal	10,974	32,467	0	0	3,737	47,181	4.80	3,580
Romania	39,443	34,738	43,404	0	4,521	122,103	5.24	0
Russian Federation	607,103	683,200	757,682	21,244	33,903	2,103,132	14.11	0
Slovak Rep	15,341	10,475	11,183	0	0	36,999	7	0
Slovenia, Rep	3,103	1,356	641	0	407	5,503	2.75	0
Spain	76,332	120,359	13,275	125	13,110	223,196	5.72	16,045
Sweden	8,603	45,991	934	0	1,268	56,796	6.56	0
Switzerland	810	35,680	4,906	0	2,301	43,701	6.38	0
Ukraine	307,956	108,018	185,424	0	9,944	611,342	11.72	0
United Kingdom	227,974	218,001	114,925	0	5,342	566,246	9.78	19,914
Yugoslavia, Fed Rep	25,040	7,859	3,811	0	1,491	38,197	3.63	0

	Carbon Dioxide Emissions (000 metric tons)						Per Capita Carbon Dioxide Emissions (metric tons)	Bunker Fuels (000 metric tons)
	Solid	Liquid	Gas	Gas Flaring	Cement Manufacture	Total		
NORTH & CENTRAL AMERICA	**1,897,472**	**2,480,550**	**1,262,197**	**18,833**	**56,418**	**5,715,466**	**X**	**67,788**
Belize	0	264	0	0	0	264	1.32	0
Canada	96,891	171,365	132,919	4,463	4,228	409,862	14.99	4,521
Costa Rica	0	3,459	0	0	348	3,807	1.21	0
Cuba	491	27,070	70	0	993	28,623	2.64	0
Dominican Rep	154	9,460	0	0	634	10,248	1.36	0
El Salvador	0	3,213	0	0	341	3,550	0.66	0
Guatemala	0	5,192	18	0	447	5,657	0.59	0
Haiti	0	685	0	0	99	784	0.11	0
Honduras	0	2,733	0	0	326	3,059	0.55	0
Jamaica	176	7,669	0	0	194	8,042	3.26	0
Mexico	13,414	251,101	52,490	2,466	13,381	332,852	3.77	0
Nicaragua	0	2,371	0	0	121	2,495	0.62	0
Panama	180	3,800	114	0	136	4,228	1.69	0
Trinidad and Tobago	0	6,126	11,358	2,931	227	20,643	16.30	0
United States	1,786,167	1,986,042	1,065,227	8,973	34,944	4,881,349	19.13	63,266
SOUTH AMERICA	**67,883**	**375,413**	**116,962**	**17,367**	**27,407**	**605,029**	**X**	**0**
Argentina	2,975	59,097	48,303	4,089	2,539	117,003	3.52	0
Bolivia	0	4,005	1,235	1,121	275	6,632	0.88	0
Brazil	39,875	153,492	8,028	1,674	14,004	217,074	1.39	0
Chile	8,321	21,009	3,836	253	1,319	34,738	2.56	0
Colombia	14,828	35,013	7,332	923	3,393	61,493	1.83	0
Ecuador	0	16,122	238	1,429	1,103	18,888	1.72	0
Guyana	0	835	0	0	0	835	1.03	0
Paraguay	0	2,459	0	0	161	2,620	0.59	0
Peru	861	19,133	894	304	1,085	22,277	0.99	0
Suriname	0	1,982	0	0	26	2,008	4.58	0
Uruguay	4	4,785	0	0	249	5,038	1.61	0
Venezuela	1,019	57,481	47,097	7,573	3,254	116,424	5.75	0
ASIA	**3,660,255**	**2,382,934**	**642,021**	**97,048**	**336,062**	**7,118,317**	**X**	**65,139**
Afghanistan, Islamic State	22	927	363	22	59	1,392	0.07	0
Armenia	377	0	3,569	0	249	4,199	1.21	0
Azerbaijan	73	39,425	22,178	1,905	297	63,878	8.76	0
Bangladesh	649	6,815	9,607	0	147	17,217	0.15	0
Bhutan	48	84	0	0	0	132	0.07	0
Cambodia	0	476	0	0	0	476	0.04	0
China	2,088,011	398,291	30,239	0	151,437	2,667,982	2.27	0
Georgia, Rep	1,652	2,367	9,321	0	498	13,839	2.53	0
India	551,897	161,333	22,420	8,874	24,915	769,440	0.88	2,693
Indonesia	14,883	96,854	39,586	24,648	8,610	184,585	0.95	0
Iran, Islamic Rep	5,514	151,199	47,987	21,735	9,043	235,478	3.81	0
Iraq	0	53,582	5,778	194	4,972	64,527	3.33	0
Israel	13,275	26,297	44	0	1,990	41,605	8.10	0
Japan	317,790	622,294	108,191	0	45,195	1,093,470	8.79	32,371
Jordan	0	10,453	0	0	857	11,311	2.64	0
Kazakhstan, Rep	201,813	57,712	35,475	0	2,982	297,982	17.48	0
Korea, Dem People's Rep	232,767	12,392	0	0	8,588	253,750	11.21	0
Korea, Rep	92,611	166,540	9,435	0	21,248	289,833	6.56	0
Kuwait	0	9,735	5,031	964	249	15,971	8.10	0
Kyrgyz Rep	6,683	4,595	3,602	0	498	15,374	3.41	0
Lao People's Dem Rep	4	271	0	0	0	271	0.07	0
Lebanon	0	10,600	0	0	451	11,051	3.88	0
Malaysia	6,210	42,165	14,411	2,957	4,749	70,492	3.74	0
Mongolia	7,387	1,858	0	0	40	9,281	4.03	0
Myanmar	158	2,063	1,869	99	198	4,386	0.11	0
Nepal	245	916	0	0	136	1,297	0.07	0
Oman	0	4,814	3,532	1,194	498	10,036	6.12	0
Pakistan	8,548	33,995	22,988	2,488	3,884	71,902	0.59	0
Philippines	5,155	41,304	0	0	3,239	49,698	0.77	0
Saudi Arabia	0	124,385	66,047	22,504	7,683	220,620	13.85	0
Singapore	66	48,775	0	0	949	49,790	17.99	30,074
Sri Lanka	4	4,767	0	0	198	4,972	0.29	0
Syrian Arab Rep	4	31,052	3,726	5,881	1,744	42,407	3.19	0
Tajikistan, Rep	304	117	3,400	0	150	3,972	0.70	0
Thailand	15,828	72,804	14,806	0	9,043	112,477	2.02	0
Turkey	59,848	62,658	8,731	0	14,257	145,490	2.49	0
Turkmenistan, Rep	722	19,690	21,497	0	348	42,257	10.96	0
United Arab Emirates	0	18,283	48,955	1,616	1,762	70,616	42.28	0
Uzbekistan, Rep	18,481	22,556	79,230	0	2,982	123,253	5.75	0
Viet Nam	9,226	8,830	4	1,968	1,491	21,522	0.29	0
Yemen, Rep	0	9,658	0	0	425	10,083	0.81	0
OCEANIA	**160,864**	**90,589**	**42,982**	**0**	**2,810**	**297,246**	**X**	**6,493**
Australia	155,603	77,120	32,734	0	2,477	267,937	15.24	6,493
Fiji	55	612	0	0	44	711	0.95	0
New Zealand	5,203	10,442	10,248	0	289	26,179	7.58	0
Papua New Guinea	4	2,253	0	0	0	2,257	0.55	0
Solomon Islands	0	161	0	0	0	161	0.48	0

Source: Carbon Dioxide Information Analysis Center.
Notes: Estimates are of the carbon dioxide emitted, 3.664 times the carbon contained. Emissions from bunker fuels are included in other categories as well.
World totals include countries not listed. 0 = zero or less than half the unit of measure; X = not available.
For additional information, see Sources and Technical Notes.

	Carbon Dioxide Emissions from Land Use Change (000 metric tons)	Methane from Anthropogenic Sources (000 metric tons)					
		Solid Waste	Coal Mining	Oil and Gas Production	Wet Rice Agriculture	Livestock	Total
WORLD	**4,100,000**	**43,000**	**36,000**	**44,000**	**69,000**	**81,000**	**270,000**
AFRICA	**730,000**	**1,700**	**1,700**	**6,000**	**2,400**	**9,000**	**21,000**
Algeria	6,900	140	0	1,400	X	160	1,700
Angola	16,000	34	X	180	8	120	340
Benin	3,200	15	X	X	2	47	65
Botswana	3,200	4	X	X	X	100	110
Burkina Faso	3,400	29	X	X	23	210	260
Burundi	130	5	X	X	8	20	33
Cameroon	28,000	54	X	X	5	200	260
Central African Rep	23,000	12	X	X	3	99	110
Chad	7,100	12	X	X	23	210	240
Congo	14,000	14	X	12	1	4	31
Cote d'Ivoire	15,000	57	X	X	X	51	110
Egypt	X	160	X	150	360	370	1,000
Equatorial Guinea	3,000	2	X	X	X	0	2
Eritrea	X	X	X	X	X	68	68
Ethiopia	8,000	68	X	X	X	1,100	1,200
Gabon	51,000	6	X	240	X	3	250
Gambia, The	130	3	X	X	2	15	20
Ghana	18,000	29	X	X	23	76	130
Guinea	10,000	19	X	X	440	59	520
Guinea-Bissau	1,800	2	X	X	38	19	59
Kenya	1,400	74	X	X	4	460	540
Lesotho	X	4	X	X	X	40	44
Liberia	9,600	12	X	X	15	3	31
Libya	76	42	X	400	X	33	480
Madagascar	21,000	38	X	X	480	350	860
Malawi	11,000	14	X	X	21	37	72
Mali	8,400	27	X	X	66	260	350
Mauritania	1	11	X	X	6	120	140
Mauritius	9	4	X	X	X	2	5
Morocco	4,700	110	9	0	3	230	360
Mozambique	15,000	54	0	X	X	44	98
Namibia	1,800	5	X	X	X	91	96
Niger	X	15	2	X	6	140	160
Nigeria	24,000	3	1	3,600	220	760	4,500
Rwanda	170	4	X	0	2	28	34
Senegal	4,700	32	X	X	16	140	190
Sierra Leone	1,800	15	X	X	120	14	150
Somalia	430	22	X	X	1	510	540
South Africa	14,000	180	1,600	X	1	590	2,400
Sudan	38,000	63	X	X	1	1,000	1,100
Swaziland	370	3	0	X	X	22	25
Tanzania	22,000	68	X	X	190	500	760
Togo	2,100	12	X	X	9	25	45
Tunisia	640	44	X	7	X	81	130
Uganda	5,000	25	X	X	28	200	250
Zaire	280,000	120	1	X	190	81	380
Zambia	34,000	36	0	X	6	110	150
Zimbabwe	5,300	33	47	X	X	150	230
EUROPE	**11,000**	**17,000**	**6,600**	**15,000**	**420**	**14,000**	**53,000**
Albania	X	19	0	2	X	72	92
Austria	X	88	0	15	X	160	260
Belarus, Rep	X	100	X	4	X	410	510
Belgium	X	190	X	X	X	X	190
Bosnia and Herzegovina	X	X	3	X	X	35	38
Bulgaria	X	8,600	10	1	2	120	8,800
Croatia, Rep	X	X	X	28	X	46	73
Czech Rep	X	X	200	3	X	170	380
Denmark	X	25	X	83	X	150	260
Estonia, Rep	X	15	3	X	X	41	59
Finland	X	65	X	X	X	82	150
France	X	290	68	25	21	1,400	1,800
Germany	X	1,400	700	220	X	1,100	3,400
Greece	X	140	11	1	11	170	330
Hungary	X	96	13	65	3	98	270
Iceland	X	5	X	X	X	10	15
Ireland	X	41	0	27	X	450	520
Italy	X	590	0	200	120	620	1,500
Latvia, Rep	X	26	X	X	X	76	100
Lithuania, Rep	X	38	X	X	X	110	150
Macedonia, former Yugoslav Rep	X	X	1	X	X	39	40
Moldova, Rep	X	33	X	X	X	76	110
Netherlands	X	260	X	810	X	350	1,400
Norway	X	64	0	2,200	X	85	2,400
Poland, Rep	X	400	800	54	X	540	1,800
Portugal	X	10	2	X	9	150	170
Romania	X	180	8	280	8	370	840
Russian Federation	X	1,600	2,200	9,700	140	3,800	17,000
Slovak Rep	X	X	230	3	X	84	320
Slovenia, Rep	X	X	2	X	X	33	35
Spain	X	590	180	16	26	570	1,400
Sweden	X	72	0	X	X	130	200
Switzerland	X	20	X	X	X	120	140
Ukraine	X	510	1,300	260	12	1,500	3,600
United Kingdom	X	1,400	790	690	X	1,000	3,800
Yugoslavia, Fed Rep	X	X	8	13	X	160	180

	Carbon Dioxide Emissions from Land Use Change (000 metric tons)	Methane from Anthropogenic Sources (000 metric tons)					
		Solid Waste	Coal Mining	Oil and Gas Production	Wet Rice Agriculture	Livestock	Total
NORTH & CENTRAL AMERICA	190,000	11,000	6,100	8,200	590	9,200	35,000
Belize	980	1	X	X	0	3	4
Canada	X	1,300	390	1,300	X	670	3,600
Costa Rica	14,000	15	X	X	7	110	130
Cuba	3,200	70	X	0	63	240	370
Dominican Rep	4,800	44	X	X	34	130	210
El Salvador	520	23	X	X	3	63	88
Guatemala	21,000	40	X	X	4	120	160
Haiti	470	20	X	X	9	58	88
Honduras	19,000	22	X	X	2	110	130
Jamaica	7,200	11	X	X	X	20	31
Mexico	63,000	610	48	570	16	1,900	3,100
Nicaragua	33,000	25	X	X	27	88	140
Panama	21,000	12	X	X	14	75	100
Trinidad and Tobago	1,200	X	X	290	1	4	300
United States	X	9,200	5,700	6,100	390	5,600	27,000
SOUTH AMERICA	1,800,000	2,200	280	2,200	870	15,000	21,000
Argentina	85,000	260	0	660	26	2,700	3,700
Bolivia	140,000	40	X	120	19	360	540
Brazil	1,100,000	1,300	3	190	350	8,100	9,900
Chile	33,000	100	15	45	5	220	380
Colombia	110,000	160	230	130	230	1,300	2,100
Ecuador	72,000	59	X	110	54	270	490
Guyana	6,900	3	X	X	18	11	31
Paraguay	35,000	23	X	X	4	410	440
Peru	96,000	150	1	29	47	290	520
Suriname	5,100	2	X	X	36	5	42
Uruguay	1,300	24	X	X	29	640	690
Venezuela	170,000	170	34	960	25	770	2,000
ASIA	1,300,000	9,900	20,000	12,000	65,000	30,000	140,000
Afghanistan, Islamic State	1,100	40	X	4	X	160	210
Armenia	X	36	X	X	X	6	42
Azerbaijan	X	61	X	230	X	160	450
Bangladesh	7,700	210	X	83	2,700	860	3,900
Bhutan	4,500	1	X	X	21	14	36
Cambodia	35,000	20	X	X	X	120	140
China	150,000	890	15,000	260	24,000	7,000	47,000
Georgia, Rep	X	45	X	X	X	86	130
India	65,000	2,600	2,200	830	16,000	11,000	33,000
Indonesia	410,000	630	83	2,600	6,400	630	10,000
Iran, Islamic Rep	10,000	350	12	2,000	290	610	3,300
Iraq	24	350	X	53	54	83	540
Israel	X	43	X	0	X	29	73
Japan	X	1,900	84	36	310	1,600	3,900
Jordan	97	35	X	X	X	15	50
Kazakhstan, Rep	X	150	1,300	90	58	920	2,500
Korea, Dem People's Rep	700	130	1,100	X	290	66	1,600
Korea, Rep	1,500	310	140	X	850	88	1,400
Kuwait	X	34	X	140	X	1	170
Kyrgyz Rep	X	27	10	0	1	150	190
Lao People's Dem Rep	37,000	10	X	X	160	99	270
Lebanon	91	23	X	X	X	7	29
Malaysia	210,000	96	2	550	270	38	960
Mongolia	480	13	6	X	X	280	300
Myanmar	130,000	110	0	22	1,700	410	2,300
Nepal	9,000	29	1	X	200	390	610
Oman	X	7	X	130	X	14	150
Pakistan	14,000	55	2	380	860	2,100	3,300
Philippines	110,000	330	1	X	1,400	220	1,900
Saudi Arabia	60	330	X	2,200	X	83	2,600
Singapore	X	65	X	X	X	0	65
Sri Lanka	4,300	29	X	X	480	98	610
Syrian Arab Rep	790	70	X	460	X	88	620
Tajikistan, Rep	X	30	2	1	6	110	150
Thailand	92,000	100	5	130	4,800	490	5,500
Turkey	X	380	32	3	28	690	1,100
Turkmenistan, Rep	X	27	X	880	20	120	1,000
United Arab Emirates	X	35	X	470	X	14	520
Uzbekistan, Rep	X	140	X	610	94	420	1,300
Viet Nam	40,000	140	89	140	3,800	280	4,400
Yemen, Rep	X	X	X	X	X	90	90
OCEANIA	38,000	690	1,400	310	75	3,300	5,800
Australia	X	620	1,400	260	71	2,400	4,800
Fiji	1,400	3	X	X	4	19	25
New Zealand	X	62	10	55	X	880	1,000
Papua New Guinea	35,000	6	X	X	X	7	13
Solomon Islands	1,800	1	X	X	X	1	1

Source: World Resources Institute.

Notes: Estimates are of the carbon dioxide emitted, 3.664 times the carbon contained.
World totals include countries not listed. 0 = zero or less than half the unit of measure; X = not available.
For additional information, see Sources and Technical Notes.

Data Table 14.3 Atmospheric Concentrations of Greenhouse and Ozone-Depleting Gases, 1970–94

Year	Carbon Dioxide (CO2) ppm	Carbon Tetra-chloride (CCl4) ppt	Methyl Chloro-form (CH3CCl3) ppt	CFC-11 (CCl3F) ppt	CFC-12 (CCl2F2) ppt	CFC-113 (C2Cl3F3) ppt	Total Gaseous Chlorine ppt	Nitrous Oxide (N2O) ppb	Methane (CH4) ppb
Preindustrial	280.0 a	0	0	0	0	0	0	285 a	700 a
1970	325.5	X	X	X	X	X	X	X	X
1971	326.2	X	X	X	X	X	X	X	X
1972	327.3	X	X	X	X	X	X	X	X
1973	329.5	X	X	X	X	X	X	X	X
1974	330.1	X	X	X	X	X	X	X	X
1975	331.0	X	X	X	X	X	X	X	X
1976	332.0	X	X	X	X	X	X	X	X
1977	333.7	X	X	X	X	X	X	X	X
1978	335.3	88	58	139	257	X	1,457	298	X
1979	336.7	88	63	147	272	X	1,529	299	X
1980	338.5	90	71	158	289	X	1,622	299	X
1981	339.8	91	76	166	305	X	1,698	299	X
1982	341.0	93	82	175	325	26	1,871	301	X
1983	342.6	94	86	182	341	28	1,945	302	X
1984	344.3	95	89	190	355	31	2,024	303	X
1985	345.7	97	93	200	376	36	2,127	304	X
1986	347.0	98	97	209	394	40	2,222	305	1,600
1987	348.8	100	100	219	411	48	2,321	306	1,611
1988	351.3	101	104	231	433	53	2,432	306	1,619
1989	352.7	101	108	240	452	59	2,531	306	1,641
1990	354.0	102	111	249	469	66	2,626	307	1,645
1991	355.5	102	114	254	483	71	2,691	307	1,657
1992	356.3	101	118	260	496	77	2,762	308	1,673
1993	357.0	101	113	260	502	79	2,768	308	1,671
1994	358.8	101	108	261	509	81	2,774	309	1,666

Source: Carbon Dioxide Information Analysis Center.

Notes: a. Approximately. All estimates are by volume; ppm = parts per million; ppb = parts per billion; and ppt = parts per trillion.
X = not available. For additional information, see Sources and Technical Notes.

Data Table 14.4 World CO2 Emissions from Fossil Fuel Consumption and Cement Manufacture, 1950–92

Year	Carbon Dioxide Emissions (million metric tons) Total	Gas Fuels	Liquid Fuels	Solid Fuels	Cement Manufacture	Gas Flaring	Per Capita Emissions (metric tons)	Bunker Fuels (million metric tons)
1950	6,002	355	1,550	3,946	66	84	2.38	128
1951	6,504	421	1,755	4,166	73	88	2.53	154
1952	6,606	454	1,847	4,129	81	95	2.53	158
1953	6,771	480	1,953	4,148	88	99	2.56	161
1954	6,855	506	2,041	4,115	99	99	2.53	165
1955	7,511	550	2,290	4,452	110	114	2.71	187
1956	8,006	590	2,488	4,694	117	117	2.86	202
1957	8,347	652	2,616	4,825	125	128	2.93	224
1958	8,566	703	2,682	4,924	132	128	2.93	209
1959	9,054	784	2,895	5,093	147	132	3.04	213
1960	9,475	861	3,114	5,199	158	143	3.15	238
1961	9,534	931	3,316	4,968	165	154	3.11	264
1962	9,922	1,015	3,594	4,976	180	161	3.15	275
1963	10,461	1,099	3,858	5,144	187	172	3.26	286
1964	11,051	1,202	4,170	5,283	209	187	3.37	311
1965	11,556	1,286	4,474	5,379	216	202	3.48	322
1966	12,142	1,392	4,855	5,441	231	220	3.55	352
1967	12,531	1,502	5,218	5,331	238	242	3.59	377
1968	13,176	1,630	5,687	5,335	256	267	3.70	399
1969	13,956	1,784	6,134	5,474	271	293	3.85	418
1970	14,964	1,891	6,734	5,730	286	319	4.03	440
1971	15,517	2,030	7,130	5,730	308	322	4.10	465
1972	16,133	2,136	7,530	5,789	326	344	4.18	498
1973	17,005	2,228	8,207	5,818	348	403	4.32	528
1974	17,034	2,264	8,222	5,807	352	392	4.25	502
1975	16,935	2,283	7,808	6,152	348	341	4.14	447
1976	17,913	2,371	8,475	6,291	377	399	4.32	436
1977	18,423	2,367	8,753	6,522	396	381	4.36	440
1978	18,598	2,470	8,731	6,581	425	392	4.32	451
1979	19,632	2,616	9,285	6,932	436	366	4.51	454
1980	19,383	2,660	8,819	7,141	440	326	4.36	458
1981	18,756	2,697	8,321	7,035	443	264	4.14	421
1982	18,613	2,678	7,973	7,266	443	253	4.03	381
1983	18,576	2,686	7,918	7,288	458	231	3.96	363
1984	19,207	2,898	8,006	7,625	469	213	4.03	359
1985	19,848	3,012	7,951	8,200	480	209	4.10	341
1986	20,551	3,078	8,350	8,424	502	198	4.18	359
1987	21,017	3,309	8,387	8,610	524	187	4.18	392
1988	21,841	3,466	8,768	8,838	557	213	4.29	403
1989	22,240	3,598	8,900	8,966	572	205	4.29	403
1990	22,347	3,693	9,090	8,753	572	238	4.21	421
1991	22,614	3,767	9,479	8,500	594	278	4.21	429
1992	22,339	3,829	9,050	8,588	627	249	4.10	476

Source: Carbon Dioxide Information Analysis Center.

Note: Mass of carbon dioxide. Emissions from bunker fuels are included in other categories as well.
For additional information, see Sources and Technical Notes.

Data Table 14.5 Common Anthropogenic Pollutants, 1980–93

	Sulfur Dioxide (000 metric tons)			Nitrogen Oxides (000 metric tons)			Carbon Monoxide (000 metric tons)			Particulate Matter (000 metric tons)			Volatile Organic Compounds (000 metric tons)		
	1980	1990	1993	1980	1990	1993	1980	1990	1993	1980	1990	1993	1980	1990	1993
Albania	(50)	(50)	X	(9)	(9)	X	X	X	X	X	X	X	(30)	X	X
Austria	397	90	71	246	221	182	1,636	1,573	X	79	39	X	374	430	388
Belgium {a}	181	94	94 b	168	172	1,173 b	X	X	272	X	X	X	X	139	X
Bulgaria	1,034	1,030	X	150	150	X	X	X	X	X	X	X	2,594	X	X
Canada	4,643	3,326	3,030 b	1,959	1,999	1,939 b	10,273	X	X	1,907	1,855	X	2,099	2,086	X
Czechoslovakia (former)	3,100	2,564	X	1,204	X	960 b	X	1,291	X	1,350	940	X	X	304	X
Czech Rep	2,257	1,876	1,538 b	X	742	698 b	X	888	1,045 b	X	631	501 b	X	225	205 b
Denmark	448	183	158	273	270	267	X	X	X	X	X	X	197	174	X
Finland	584	260	139 b	264	290	268 b	660	556	X	X	X	X	163	209	X
France	3,348	1,200	1,221 b	1,646	1,487	1,519 b	9,316	10,735	9,759	435	234	228 b	1,975	2,402	2,286
German Dem Rep (former)	4,323	4,755	3,021 b	593	573	478 b	3,409	3,633	2,668 b	2,498	1,960	906 b	886	728	692 b
Germany, Fed Rep (former)	3,166	878	875 b	2,926	2,460	2,426 b	12,013	7,276	6,577 b	691	436	430 b	2,613	2,238	2,073 b
Germany	X	5,633	3,896 b	X	3,033	2,904 b	X	10,909	9,245 b	X	2,396	1,336 b	X	2,966	2,765 X
Greece	400	510	X	217	388	X	X	1,480	X	X	X	X	130	235	X
Hungary	1,633	1,010	827 b	273	238	183 b	1,328	767	836 b	577	205	160 b	(270)	232	136
Iceland	9	8	9	14	24	23	29	31	30	X	X	X	5	6	7 b
Ireland	222	187	X	73	128	X	497	454	X	94	105	X	101	97	X
Italy	3,211	1,682	X	1,585	2,041	X	5,487	9,268	X	433	524	X	696	2,396	X
Japan	1,263	876	X	1,622	1,476	X	X	X	X	174	177	X	X	X	X
Luxembourg	24	10	X	23	15	X	X	X	X	X	X	X	11	X	X
Netherlands	489	204	164	584	575	545	1,616	1,108	899	143	77	52	595	439	411
New Zealand	X	X	X	X	146	X	X	X	X	X	X	X	X	X	X
Norway	141	54	36	184	230	229	886	941	805	25	22	21	174	266	284
Poland	4,100	3,210	2,725	X	1,280	1,120	3,403	2,524	2,109	X	1,975	1,517	700	1,151	779
Portugal	266	286	X	165	216	X	533	1,086	X	119	X	X	92	X	X
Romania	1,800	1,800	X	X	(390)	X	X	X	X	X	X	X	(440)	X	X
Slovak Rep	X	X	374 b	X	X	224 b	X	403	X	X	308	X	X	205	136 b
Spain	3,377	2,205	X	946	1,247	X	3,780	4,950	X	X	X	X	760	1,118	X
Sweden	507	136	101	454	411	399	1,450	X	X	170	X	X	410	531	502 b
Switzerland	126	63	58	196	184	150	711	431	358	28	20	20	311	297	263
Turkey	276	398	X	X	X	512 b	X	X	X	X	X	X	(700)	X	X
United Kingdom	4,903	3,754	3,188	2,395	2,731	2,347	4,895	6,537	5,641	560	460	444	2,442	2,363	2,463
United States	23,780	21,060	20,622 b	21,469	21,373	21,001 b	117,032	83,807	79,092 b	8,992	7,345	7,080 b	25,719	21,477	20,617 b
U.S.S.R. (former) {c}	12,800	8,930	X	3,167	4,407	X	X	X	X	X	X	X	7,000	10,411	X
Belarus, Rep	740	584	X	244	271	X	X	X	X	X	X	X	549	508	X
Ukraine	3,850	2,782	X	X	1,097	X	X	X	X	X	X	X	X	1,369	X
Yugoslavia (former)	1,176	1,480	X	350	420	X	X	X	X	X	X	X	(600)	X	X

Sources: Co-Operative Programme for Monitoring and Evaluation of the Long-Range Transmission of Air Pollutants in Europe (EMEP); the Organisation of Economic Co-Operation and Development; and the United Nations Economic Commission for Europe.
Notes: a. Walloon Region only. b. 1992. c. European part of the U.S.S.R. under the purview of the EMEP.
X = not available. Emissions in parentheses were estimated by EMEP.
For additional information, see Sources and Technical Notes.

Data Table 14.6 Inventories of National Greenhouse Gas Emissions, 1990

	Carbon Dioxide (000 metric tons)			Methane from Anthropogenic Sources (000 metric tons)						Nitrous Oxide (000 metric tons)
	Fossil Fuels	Land Use Change	Net Emissions	Oil and Gas Systems	Agriculture Livestock	Agriculture Other	Waste	Other	Total	
Australia	288,965	130,843	419,808	1,054	3,005	396	1,390	397	6,242	60
Austria	59,200	X	59,200	116	259	X	228	603	1,206	5
Belgium	114,410	X	114,410	X	X	X	X	X	X	X
Canada	457,441	(282)	457,159	1,322	979	0	803	39	3,143	91
Czech Republic	169,514	(2,280)	167,234	463	173	X	150	91	877	41
Denmark	52,100	(2,600)	49,500	22	262	X	122	X	406	10
Finland	54,200	(31,000)	23,200	19	94	X	105	34	252	23
Germany	1,012,443	(20,000)	992,443	1,767	2,043	X	2,397	11	6,218	223
Hungary	71,673	(4,467)	67,206	372	170	3	X	X	545	11
Ireland	30,719	X	30,719	15	603	41	136	X	795	42
Italy	421,000	X	X	X	X	X	X	X	X	X
Japan	1,173,360	(90,000)	1,083,360	125	520	267	465	X	1,377	47
Netherlands	167,000	(120)	166,880	177	508	X	382	X	1,067	60
New Zealand	25,530	(16,716)	8,814	61	1,618	X	433	X	2,112	8
Norway	35,533	(12,200)	23,333	30	91	X	167	1	289	16
Poland	414,930	X	414,930	3,035	1,860	X	820	395	6,110	156
Portugal	42,148	X	42,148	15	163	13	35	X	226	11
Spain	260,654	(4,178)	256,476	758	772	115	494	4	2,143	95
Sweden	61,256	(34,368)	26,888	33	196	X	100	0	329	15
Switzerland	43,600	(5,244)	38,356	11	215	0	48	X	274	29
United Kingdom	584,078	(7,284)	576,794	1,311	1,538	X	1,971	1	4,821	109
United States	4,957,022	(436,000)	4,521,022	8,254	8,088	508	10,150	X	27,000	411

Sources: United Nations General Assembly and national communications.
Notes: 0 = zero or less than half the unit of measure. X = not available. Negative numbers are shown in parentheses.
For additional information, see Sources and Technical Notes.

Sources and Technical Notes

Data Table 14.1
CO₂ Emissions from Industrial Processes, 1992

Source: Carbon Dioxide Information Analysis Center (CDIAC), Environmental Sciences Division, Oak Ridge National Laboratory, "1992 Estimates of CO_2 Emissions from Fossil Fuel Burning and Cement Manufacturing Based on the United Nations Energy Statistics and the U.S. Bureau of Mines Cement Manufacturing Data," ORNL/CDIAC-25, NDP-030 (an accessible numerical database) (Oak Ridge, Tennessee, September 1995).

This table includes data on industrial additions to the carbon dioxide (CO_2) flux from *solid* fuels, *liquid* fuels, *gas* fuels, *gas flaring,* and *cement manufacture.* CDIAC annually calculates emissions of CO_2 from the burning of fossil fuels and the manufacture of cement for most of the countries of the world. Estimates of total and per capita national emissions do not include *bunker fuels* used in international transport because of the difficulty of apportioning these fuels among the countries benefiting from that transport. Emissions from bunker fuels are shown separately for the country where the fuel was delivered.

CDIAC calculates emissions from data on the net apparent consumption of fossil fuels (based on the *World Energy Data Set* maintained by the United Nations Statistical Division), and from data on world cement manufacture (based on the *Cement Manufacturing Data Set* maintained by the U.S. Bureau of Mines). Emissions are calculated using global average fuel chemistry and usage.

Although estimates of world emissions are probably within 10 percent of actual emissions, individual country estimates may depart more severely from reality. CDIAC points out that the time trends from a consistent, uniform time series "should be more accurate than the individual values." Each year, CDIAC recalculates the entire time series from 1950 to the present, incorporating its most recent understanding and the latest corrections to the database. As a result, the carbon emissions estimate data set has become more consistent, and probably more accurate, each year.

Emissions of CO_2 are often calculated and reported in terms of their content of elemental carbon. CDIAC reports them in that way. For this table, their values were converted to the actual mass of CO_2 by multiplying the carbon mass by 3.664 (the ratio of the mass of carbon to that of CO_2).

Solid, liquid, and *gas* fuels are primarily, but not exclusively, coals, petroleum prod-

ucts, and natural gas, respectively. *Gas flaring* is the practice of burning off gas released in the process of petroleum extraction, a practice that is declining. During *cement manufacture,* cement is calcined to produce calcium oxide. In the process, 0.498 metric ton of CO_2 is released for each ton of cement production. *Total* emissions consist of the sum of the CO_2 produced during the consumption of solid, liquid, and gas fuels, and from gas flaring and the manufacture of cement.

Combustion of different fossil fuels releases CO_2 at different rates for the same level of energy production. Burning oil releases about 1.5 times the amount of CO_2 released from burning natural gas; coal combustion releases about twice the CO_2 of natural gas.

It was assumed that approximately 1 percent of the coal used by industry and power plants was not burned, and an additional few percent were converted to nonoxidizing uses. Other oxidative reactions of coal are assumed to be of negligible importance in carbon budget modeling. CO_2 emissions from gas flaring and cement production make up about 3 percent of the CO_2 emitted by fossil fuel combustion.

These data from CDIAC represent the only complete global data set of CO_2 emissions. Individual country estimates, based on more detailed information and a country-specific methodology, could differ. An experts meeting, convened by the Organisation for Economic Co-Operation and Development (OECD) in February 1991, has recommended (*Estimation of Greenhouse Gas Emissions and Sinks,* OECD, Paris, August 1991) that when countries calculate their own emissions of CO_2, they use a more detailed method when these data are available. Such data are currently available for only a few countries (see Data Table 14.6). CDIAC's method has the advantage of calculating CO_2 emissions from a single common data set available for all countries.

Data Table 14.2
Other Greenhouse Gas Emissions, 1991

Sources: Land use change: Food and Agriculture Organization of the United Nations (FAO), Forest Resources Division, *Forest Resources Assessment 1990: Global Synthesis* (FAO, Rome, 1995).

Methane (CH_4) from municipal solid waste: Jean Lerner, personal communication (National Aeronautics and Space Administration Goddard Space Flight Center, Institute for Space Studies, May 1989); and H.G.

Bingemer and P.J. Crutzen, "The Production of CH_4 from Solid Wastes," *Journal of Geophysical Research,* Vol. 92, No. D2 (1987), pp. 2181–2187.

Methane (CH_4) from coal mining: David W. Barns and J.A. Edmonds, *An Evaluation of the Relationship Between the Production and Use of Energy and Atmospheric Methane Emissions* (U.S. Department of Energy, Office of Energy Research, Carbon Dioxide Research Program, No. TR047, April 1990); and the World Energy Council (WEC), *1994 Survey of Energy Resources* (WEC, London, 1995).

CH_4 from oil and gas production and distribution: David W. Barns and J.A. Edmonds, *An Evaluation of the Relationship Between the Production and Use of Energy and Atmospheric Methane Emissions* (U.S. Department of Energy, Office of Energy Research, Carbon Dioxide Research Program, No. TR047, April 1990); Carbon Dioxide Information Analysis Center (CDIAC), Environmental Sciences Division, Oak Ridge National Laboratory, "1991 Estimates of CO_2 Emissions from Fossil Fuel Burning and Cement Manufacturing Based on the United Nations Energy Statistics and the U.S. Bureau of Mines Cement Manufacturing Data," ORNL/CDIAC-25, NDP-030 (an accessible numerical database) (Oak Ridge, Tennessee, September 1995); American Gas Association (AGA), "Natural Gas and Climate Change: The Greenhouse Effect," *Issue Brief 1989–7* (AGA, Washington, D.C., June 14, 1989); A.A. Makarov and I.A. Basmakov, *The Soviet Union: A Strategy of Energy Development with Minimum Emission of Greenhouse Gases* (Pacific Northwest Laboratory, Richland, Washington, 1990); and S. Hobart, David Spottiswoode, James Ball *et al., Methane Leakage from Natural Gas Operations* (The Alphatania Group, London, 1989).

CH_4 from wet rice agriculture: FAO, *FAOSTAT-PC* (FAO, Rome, 1995); Elaine Mathews, Inez Fung, and Jean Lerner, "Methane Emission from Rice Cultivation: Geographic and Seasonal Distribution of Cultivated Areas and Emissions," *Global Biogeochemical Cycles,* Vol. 5, No. 1 (March 1991), pp. 3–24; and U.S. Environmental Protection Agency (U.S. EPA), Office of Policy, Planning, and Evaluation, *International Anthropogenic Methane Emissions: Estimates for 1990* (EPA 230-R-93-010, January 1994), pp. 3-1–3-25.

CH_4 from livestock: Jean Lerner, Elaine Mathews, and Inez Fung, "Methane Emissions from Animals: A Global High-Resolution Data Base," *Global Biogeochemical*

Cycles, Vol. 2, No. 2 (June 1988), pp. 139–156; FAO, *FAOSTAT-PC* (FAO, Rome, 1993); U.S. EPA, Office of Policy, Planning, and Evaluation, *International Anthropogenic Methane Emissions: Estimates for 1990* (EPA 230-R-93-010, January 1994), pp. 2-1–2-44.

CO_2 and CH_4 are the two most important greenhouse gases, and both are still uncontrolled. This data table provides estimates of annual emissions of CO_2 from land use change (i.e., deforestation) and CH_4 emissions by source. Nitrous oxide, tropospheric ozone, and chlorofluorocarbons (CFCs) are also important to the greenhouse effect, but are difficult to estimate—especially the potent CFCs that are rapidly being controlled at national levels by international agreement. Tropospheric ozone has an average lifetime measured in hours and is a product of particular chemical processes involving the precursors CH_4, carbon monoxide, nitrogen oxides, and nonmethane hydrocarbons in the presence of sunlight. Nitrous oxide emissions by country have proved difficult to estimate, in part because significant emissions are poorly understood. Production estimates and emission parameters for CFC-11 and CFC-12 are not available, but production in developing countries will cease on January 1, 1996 (except for some residual production not to exceed 15 percent of 1986 production, to supply developing countries), and recycling mandates have already been imposed.

The Organisation for Economic Co-Operation and Development (OECD) hosted an experts meeting in February 1991 on greenhouse emissions (a final report was published in August 1991, *Estimation of Greenhouse Gas Emissions and Sinks* (OECD, Paris)) to discuss methodologies that countries could use to estimate their own inventories of greenhouse gases (other than CFCs) and to point to areas requiring further research. Although these discussions served to illuminate and define the methods used here, the final published recommendations were directed toward informing governments as to what data they could collect and what kind of basic country-specific (and even ecosystem-specific) research is required if they are to "assess their contribution to greenhouse gas emissions in an international context." The final report of the OECD experts meeting included additional suggested data sets and methods not fully discussed or validated during the meeting (e.g., a suggested source of deforestation data).

The estimates of emissions in this data table can be controversial, but are believed to be accurate estimates of the relative magnitudes of emissions and also the best possible, given the available data sets. The World Resources Institute (WRI) welcomes independent esti-

mates of anthropogenic emissions of greenhouse gases from the countries of the world (see Data Table 14.6). The methods used here were chosen to maximize the use of the available international data so the estimates would be comparable among countries. The international data set on any subject is limited, and so these estimates are also limited. Until most of the countries of the world publish their own independent estimates—based on common methods and scientifically valid parameters—global comparisons will require the use of methods based on the least-common data set. Common methods and parameters were used between countries unless differing, but explicit and published, parameters were available that covered all countries. For example, estimates of CH_4 emissions from coal mining were based on published data on the differing CH_4 content of various coals and their production around the world. More complex calculations—that might have been possible for one or two data-rich countries—are inappropriate for the world as a whole and were not attempted even for those few countries that might have sufficient (and uncontroversial) data. An alternative accounting of national greenhouse gas emissions has recently been published (Susan Subak, Paul Raskin, and David Von Hippel, *National Greenhouse Gas Accounts: Current Anthropogenic Sources and Sinks* (Stockholm Environment Institute, Boston, 1992)) for the year 1988. This approach generally produced results similar to those reported in past volumes of this report and generally followed similar methodologies. WRI has adopted Subak *et al.*'s methodological refinement for estimating CH_4 emissions from solid wastes. Another study, by the U.S. EPA Office of Policy, Planning, and Evaluation, *International Anthropogenic Methane Emissions: Estimates for 1990* (EPA 230-R-93-010, January 1994), provided still more estimates and helped to refine estimates of CH_4 from wet rice cultivation and livestock.

Carbon dioxide emissions from land use change are based on FAO estimates of deforestation and forest biomass for tropical countries. The burning of biomass, per se, does not necessarily contribute to the CO_2 flux. Fire is a natural process, and as long as burning and growth are in balance, there is no net movement of carbon from biomass to the atmosphere. Deforestation, however is defined as the conversion of land from forest to other uses. Carbon released in this process will not be replaced.

The carbon density used to estimate these releases was 45 percent of biomass, and biomass estimates were taken from average forest densities for whole countries as reported by the FAO. These CO_2 emission esti-

mates explicitly include shifting cultivation and the diversion of forest fallow to permanent clearing. They are also consistent and global in scope. They are the most complete estimates available, but are subject to modification should better data become available. Individual countries question these FAO estimates. See Sources and Technical Notes for Data Table 14.1 for further information.

Although, in principle, emissions from land use change should include other gases emitted from the burning of forest land, as well as from the burning of grassland, the conversion of grassland to cropland, the creation of wetlands, and the burning of crop and animal residues, the international data sets needed to estimate these emissions do not exist (OECD experts meeting report). Except for CO_2 emissions from deforestation, then, emissions from biomass burning in general are not available. Grasses or trees that grow back after a fire merely recycle the carbon and do not contribute CO_2 to long-term greenhouse heating.

WRI subtracted elemental carbon permanently sequestered in the soil (an estimated 5 percent of the biomass carbon) and also subtracted the weight of carbon contained in sawlogs and veneer logs (FAO, *FAOSTAT-PC* (FAO, Rome, 1993)), produced in each tropical country from CO_2 releases calculated from land use change. Carbon was estimated as making up 45 percent of the weight of these wood products. This step was taken to approximate the amount of carbon sequestered from the global carbon cycle by the production of durable wooden goods in each country. This is only an estimate because portions of other forest products are also sequestered (e.g., books in libraries, pit props, utility poles), and portions of saw and veneer logs are consumed (e.g., wastewood, disposal of plywood sheets used in concrete form building). This should lead to a small underestimate of total CO_2 emissions because it includes logs from areas not counted as deforested. The methods for estimating emissions from land use change, suggested at the OECD experts meeting, require data and research into processes that do not yet exist. The method used here parallels that found in the work of R.A. Houghton, R.D. Boone, J.R. Fruci *et al.*, "The Flux of Carbon from Terrestrial Ecosystems to the Atmosphere in 1980 Due to Changes in Land Use: Geographic Distribution of the Global Flux," *Tellus*, Vol. 39B, No. 1–2 (1987), pp. 122–139, which has been peer reviewed.

Choices must be made regarding the exact parameters to use in these calculations, but the deforestation and carbon density measures used here are the best general data available. The parameters used for this calculation were based on consistent definitions and common data sources. Even if slightly lower values were used for deforestation and biomass per area, the magnitude of carbon emissions would remain about the same. These estimates are thus a good first approximation to current (i.e., circa 1991) emissions that result from land use change. There is some suggestion that northern temperate and boreal forest areas are net sinks for atmospheric carbon, but this, too, is controversial.

The U.S. EPA Office of Policy, Planning, and Evaluation (*International Anthropogenic Methane Emissions: Estimates for 1990* (EPA 230-R-93-010, January 1994), p. ES-9) estimated that the sources of CH_4 shown in this data table—solid waste, coal production, oil and gas production, wet rice agriculture, and livestock—together make up about 72 percent of total global anthropogenic emissions. The remaining sources are less tractable to reasonable national-level estimates and include biomass burning, liquid wastes, livestock manure, and minor industrial sources.

CH_4 emissions from municipal *solid waste* were calculated by multiplying the 1993 urban population by per capita emission coefficients developed for each country by H.G. Bingemer and P.J. Crutzen in "The Production of CH_4 from Solid Wastes," *Journal of Geophysical Research,* Vol. 92, No. D2 (1987), pp. 2,181–2,187; and by S.D. Piccot *et al.,* in "Evaluation of Significant Anthropogenic Sources of Radiatively Important Trace Gases" (Office of Research and Development, U.S. EPA, Washington, D.C., 1990), cited in OECD, *Estimation of Greenhouse Gas Emissions and Sinks* (OECD, Paris, August 1991), taking into account the proportion landfilled and its degradable organic carbon content. R.J. Cicerone and R.S. Oremland, "Biogeochemical Aspects of Atmospheric Methane," *Global Biogeochemical Cycles,* Vol. 2, No. 4 (December 1988), pp. 299–327, suggest a likely range for annual world emissions from landfills of 30 million to 70 million metric tons. The U.S. EPA Office of Policy, Planning, and Evaluation (*International Anthropogenic Methane Emissions: Estimates for 1990* (EPA 230-R-93-010, January 1994)) estimates total emissions from solid waste at 57 million metric tons using a method substantially similar to that recommended by the OECD, or between 19 million and 39 million metric tons using a specialized regression model. The method used in this table parallels that recommended at the OECD experts meeting.

CH_4 from *coal mining* was estimated using information on the average CH_4 content of anthracite and bituminous coals, subbituminous coals, and lignite mined (WEC) in each country of the world. This latter data set is updated only every 3 years, and so the most

recent year for which the necessary data are available is 1993. Less detailed data sets are available, but are inadequate to the task. This estimate assumed that 100 percent of the CH_4 in extracted coal was emitted, although this is a slight exaggeration. CH_4 is emitted from mines in larger quantities than would be accounted for by the CH_4 content of the coal removed—although in the long run, the CH_4 in an extractable deposit of coal will be emitted, on average, at the rate that it is mined. CH_4 trapped within the rock is released by mining, and this is one of the hazards of underground coal mining. Cicerone and Oremland (*Aspects of Atmospheric Methane*) show a likely range of 25 million to 45 million metric tons of CH_4 emitted annually in the course of mining coal. The U.S. EPA Office of Policy, Planning, and Evaluation (*International Anthropogenic Methane Emissions: Estimates for 1990* (EPA 230-R-93-010, January 1994)) reports its best estimate of total emissions from the "coal fuel cycle" as between 24.4 million and 39.6 million metric tons, and its global average estimate as between 19.4 million and 57 million metric tons. No data set exists that would allow internationally comparable estimates using a methodology suggested by the OECD in its report on the experts meeting.

Substantial quantities of CH_4 are released to the atmosphere in the course of *oil and gas production* and distribution. CH_4 vented in the course of oil production is estimated at 25 percent of the amount that is flared (Gregg Marland, CDIAC (personal communication), 1990). Estimates of CO_2 from gas flaring in Data Table 14.1 also include gas that is vented (see also Barns and Edmonds, p. 3.9). CH_4 emissions from natural gas production were estimated at 0.5 percent of production (Barns and Edmonds, pp. 3.2–3.3). Recent estimates are that no more than 1 percent of CH_4 is lost through leakage from distribution systems in the United States (AGA, "Natural Gas and Climate Change: The Greenhouse Effect"), and no more than 1.7 percent in the former Soviet Union (Makarov and Basmakov, *The Soviet Union: A Strategy for Energy Development with Minimum Emission of Greenhouse Gases*), although careful surveys have not been done. There is reason to believe that pipeline leaks in the former Soviet Union are grossly understated—although the volume of gas produced in the former Soviet Union is sometimes mistakenly overstated—but no other estimates exist. For these estimates, the U.S. experience was extended to Western Europe, Canada was counted as half the U.S. rate, and the Soviet estimate was used for Central Europe and the developing world because their situations were thought to be similar (S. Hobart *et al., Methane Leakage from*

Natural Gas Operations). Cicerone and Oremland (*Aspects of Atmospheric Methane*) suggest a likely range of 25 million to 50 million metric tons of CH_4 emitted because of leaks associated with natural gas drilling, venting, and transmission. The OECD experts meeting developed a general conceptual model of how to estimate emissions from these production and distribution systems, but it was unable to identify data on the factors leading to emissions or any individual data source for this purpose. The U.S. EPA Office of Policy, Planning, and Evaluation (*International Anthropogenic Methane Emissions: Estimates for 1990* (EPA 230-R-93-010, January 1994)) estimates the total emissions from oil and gas production and natural gas processing, transport, and distribution as between 30.3 million and 65.9 million metric tons.

CH_4 produced from the practice of *wet rice agriculture* was calculated based on the area of rice production (as reported by the FAO, *Agrostat-PC,* FAO, Rome, 1993), subtracting those areas devoted to dry (upland), tidal, and deepwater (floating) rice production in each country or, in the case of China and India, in each province (Dana G. Dalrymple, *Development and Spread of High-Yielding Rice Varieties in Developing Countries,* Bureau of Science and Technology, U.S. Agency for International Development, Washington, D.C., 1986; and Robert E. Huke, *Rice Area by Type of Culture: South, Southeast, and East Asia,* International Rice Research Institute, Los Banos, Laguna, Philippines, 1982). This estimate follows the method suggested in the OECD experts meeting report and calculates the number of days of rice cultivation and the percentage of total rice area in each crop cycle by country or, in the case of China and India, by province (Elaine Mathews, Inez Fung, and Jean Lerner, "Methane Emissions from Rice Cultivation: Geographic and Seasonal Distribution of Cultivated Areas and Emissions," *Global Biogeochemical Cycles,* Vol. 5, pp. 3–24).

There are many different studies of CH_4 emissions from wet rice agriculture. In the past, many of these studies had been criticized because they had been undertaken on temperate rices grown in North America or Europe. Recently published studies—based on similar rigorous methods—from subtropical China have dispelled some of that criticism. Studies using similar methodologies from India suggest lower emissions. Country-specific emission factors used here are from a review of the extant literature published by the U.S. EPA Office of Policy, Planning, and Evaluation (*International Anthropogenic Methane Emissions: Estimates for 1990* (EPA 230-R-93-010, January 1994), pp. 3–22). Emission factors for all other countries were derived from the OECD experts meeting report, which recommended using a range of emissions found in a study of China (0.19 to 0.69 gram of CH_4 per square meter per day; H. Schütz, W. Seiler, and H. Rennenberg, presented by H. Rennenberg at the International Conference on Soils and the Greenhouse Effect, August 14–18, 1989, Wageningen, the Netherlands, reported at the OECD experts meeting). The estimate here used the midpoint of that range (0.44 gram of CH_4 per square meter per day), assuming that this range is an unbiased estimate of the normally distributed range of CH_4 emissions. Alternate estimates are possible. Where known, the amount of rainfed wet rice agriculture used emission factors that were 60 percent of those reported for irrigated rice.

A 2-year study in the subtropical rice bowl of China (Szechuan province) produced an estimated median flux (from some 3,000 flux estimates) of about 1.2 grams of CH_4 per square meter per day, and a mean flux of 1.39 grams of CH_4 per square meter per day (M.A.K. Khalil *et al.,* "Methane Emissions from Rice Fields in China," *Environmental Science and Technology,* Vol. 25, No. 5, pp. 979–981). Studies in Europe and North America seem to support the range suggested at the OECD experts meeting. (See the sources for more information.) In general, estimates of CH_4 flux are based on a technique that captures CH_4 produced anaerobically before the growth of the rice plant as well as the bulk of the CH_4 produced that is transported through the rice plant throughout the growing period. Growing periods, temperature, and the type of rice cultivar, fertilizers, and possibly pesticides could influence methanogenesis. In the tropics, using modern varieties of rice, sufficient fertilizer, and adequate water, two or even three rice crops per year are possible.

Rice cultivation uses common techniques in both temperate and tropical climes—even if the cultivars are not well adapted. The preparation of the impoundments wherein wet rice is grown—the creation of a hardpan overlain by soft anaerobic muck—creates similar environmental and chemical regimes wherever it occurs. Nonetheless, variations in water quality, soil, ambient temperature, precision of water control, and presence of cultivated algae or fish could also affect the total flux of CH_4.

Wet rice agriculture is practiced under four main water regimes: irrigated (52.8 percent of the world's total rice area), rainfed (similar to irrigated, 22.6 percent of the total), deep water (often dry in the early part of the season, may be planted to floating rice, 8.2 percent of the world's rice area), and tidal (3.4 percent

of the total area). Cicerone and Oremland (*Aspects of Atmospheric Methane*) suggest a likely range of 60 million to 170 million metric tons for CH_4 emissions associated with wet rice agriculture. The U.S. EPA Office of Policy, Planning, and Evaluation (*International Anthropogenic Methane Emissions: Estimates for 1990* (EPA 230-R-93-010, January 1994)) estimates total global CH_4 emissions at 65 million metric tons.

CH_4 emissions from domestic *livestock* were calculated using FAO statistics on animal populations and published estimates of CH_4 emissions from each type of animal. The animals studied included cattle and dairy cows, water buffalo, sheep, goats, camels, pigs, and caribou. P.J. Crutzen, I. Aselmann, and W. Seiler ("Methane Production by Domestic Animals, Wild Ruminants, Other Herbivorous Fauna, and Humans," *Tellus,* Vol. 38B (1986), pp. 271–284) estimated CH_4 production from animals on the basis of energy intake under several different management methods for several different feeding regimes. These findings were extended and further refined by the U.S. EPA Office of Policy, Planning, and Evaluation (*International Anthropogenic Methane Emissions: Estimates for 1990* (EPA 230-R-93-010, January 1994)). These emission coefficients were then assigned to each country by animal type, based on the specifics of that country's animal husbandry practices and the nature and quality of feed available. Cicerone and Oremland's *Aspects of Atmospheric Methane* shows a likely range of 65 million to 100 million metric tons of CH_4 emissions from enteric fermentation in domestic animals. The U.S. EPA Office of Policy, Planning, and Evaluation (*International Anthropogenic Methane Emissions: Estimates for 1990* (EPA 230-R-93-010, January 1994)) estimates total global emissions of 79.8 million metric tons. Alternate methods of estimation, such as a complex modeling method suggested in the OECD report, are not yet possible because of the lack of basic data.

A major anthropogenic source of CH_4, unaccounted for here, are emissions consequent to the burning of biomass. Extensive biomass burning, especially in the tropics, is believed to release large amounts of CH_4. Cicerone and Oremland (*Aspects of Atmospheric Methane*) put the likely range of those emissions at 50 million to 100 million metric tons. The OECD experts meeting elaborated on the absence of data needed for countries to estimate CH_4 emissions from biomass burning. The U.S. EPA Office of Policy, Planning, and Evaluation (*International Anthropogenic Methane Emissions: Estimates for 1990* (EPA 230-R-93-010, January 1994)) estimates emissions from biomass burning at 48 million metric

tons. In addition, it estimates CH_4 emissions from liquid wastes at 35 million metric tons and emissions from livestock manure at 14 million metric tons.

Other natural sources of CH_4 include wetlands, methane hydrate destabilization in permafrost, termites, freshwater lakes, oceans, and enteric emissions from other animals. Natural sources account for an estimated 25 percent of all CH_4 emissions. Cicerone and Oremland (*Aspects of Atmospheric Methane*) estimate likely ranges of CH_4 emissions at 100 million to 200 million metric tons from natural wetlands, 10 million to 100 million metric tons from termites, 5 million to 25 million metric tons from the oceans, 1 million to 25 million metric tons from fresh water, and possibly 5 million metric tons (potentially rising to 100 million metric tons if temperatures increase in the high arctic) from methane hydrate destabilization. The U.S. EPA Office of Policy, Planning, and Evaluation (*International Anthropogenic Methane Emissions: Estimates for 1990* (EPA 230-R-93-010, January 1994)) citing J. Lelieveld and P.J. Crutzen ("Methane Emissions into the Atmosphere: An Overview," in A.R. van Amstel, ed., *Methane and Nitrous Oxide, Methods in National Emissions Inventories and Options for Control* (Proceedings of an International IPCC Workshop, 3–5 February 1993, Amersfoort, Netherlands, RIVM, Bilthoven, Netherlands, 1993, pp. 17–25)) estimate wetland sources at 125 million metric tons; termite emissions, 30 million metric tons; fresh water and the oceans, 15 million metric tons; and methane hydrate destabilization, 5 million metric tons.

Data Table 14.3
Atmospheric Concentrations of Greenhouse and Ozone-Depleting Gases, 1970–94

Sources: Carbon dioxide: Charles D. Keeling, Scripps Institution of Oceanography, Carbon Dioxide Information Analysis Center (CDIAC), Environmental Sciences Division, Oak Ridge National Laboratory, "Atmospheric CO_2 Concentrations—Mauna Loa Observatory, Hawaii, 1958–1994," ORNL/CDIAC-25, NDP-001/R5 (an accessible numerical database) (Oak Ridge, Tennessee, September 1995); and C.D. Keeling and T.P. Whorf, "Atmospheric CO_2 records from sites in the SIO sampling network," in T.A. Boden, D.P. Kaiser, R.J. Sepanski *et al.,* eds., *Trends '93: A Compendium of Data on Global Change* (ORNL/CDIAC-65, CDIAC, Oak Ridge, Tennessee, 1994), pp. 16–26. Other trace gases: CDIAC, Environmental Sciences Division, Oak Ridge National Laboratory, ORNL/CDIAC-25, DB-1001 (an accessible numerical database); the Internet (ALE/GAGE Monthly Readings at Cape Grim, Tasmania); and originally R.G. Prinn et al., "Atmospheric CFC-11 (CCl₃F), CFC-12 (CCl₂F₂), and N₂O from the ALE-GAGE network," in T.A. Boden et al., eds., *Trends '93: A Compendium of Data on Global Change* (ORNL/CDIAC-65, CDIAC, Oak Ridge, Tennessee, 1994), pp. 396–420.

The trace gases listed here affect atmospheric ozone, contribute to the greenhouse effect, or both. *Carbon dioxide (CO_2)* accounts for about half the increase in the greenhouse effect and is emitted to the atmosphere by natural and anthropogenic processes. See the Technical Notes for Data Tables 14.1 and 14.2 for further details.

Atmospheric CO_2 concentrations are monitored at many sites worldwide; the data presented here are from Mauna Loa, Hawaii (19° 32' N, 155° 35' W). Trends at Mauna Loa reflect global trends, although CO_2 concentrations differ significantly among monitoring sites at any given time. For example, the average annual concentration at the South Pole in 1988 was 2.4 parts per million (ppm) lower than at Mauna Loa.

Annual mean values disguise large daily and seasonal variations in CO_2 concentrations. The seasonal variations are caused by photosynthetic plants storing larger amounts of carbon from CO_2 during the summer than in the winter. Some annual mean values were derived from interpolated data.

Data are revised to correct for drift in instrument calibration, hardware changes, and perturbations to "background" conditions. Details concerning data collection, revisions, and analysis are contained in C.D. Keeling et al., "Measurement of the Concentration of Carbon Dioxide at Mauna Loa Observatory, Hawaii," *Carbon Dioxide Review: 1982,* W.C. Clark, ed. (Oxford University Press, New York, 1982).

Data for all other gases are from values monitored at Cape Grim, Tasmania (45° 41' S, 144° 41' E) under the Atmospheric Lifetime Experiment (ALE) and Global Atmospheric Gases Experiment (GAGE). Although gas concentrations at any given time vary among monitoring sites, the data reported here reflect global trends. Cape Grim generally receives unpolluted air from the Southeast and is the ALE/GAGE station with the longest, most complete data set. Air samples were collected 4 times daily for ALE and 12 times daily for GAGE. The annual values shown here are averages of monthly values calculated by CDIAC. Missing values were interpolated.

Carbon tetrachloride (CCl_4) is an intermediate product in the production of CFC-11 and CFC-12. It is also used in other chemical and pharmaceutical applications and for

grain fumigation. Compared with other gases, CCl_4 makes a small contribution to the greenhouse effect and to stratospheric ozone depletion.

Methyl chloroform (CH_3CCl_3) is used primarily as an industrial degreasing agent and as a solvent for paints and adhesives. Its contribution to the greenhouse effect and to stratospheric ozone depletion is also small.

CFC-11 (CCl_3F), CFC-12 (CCl_2F_2), and *CFC-113 ($C_2Cl_3F_3$)* are potent depletors of stratospheric ozone. Together, their cumulative effect may equal one fourth of the greenhouse contribution of CO_2.

Total gaseous chlorine is calculated by multiplying the number of chlorine atoms in each of the chlorine-containing gases (carbon tetrachloride, methyl chloroform, and the chlorofluorocarbons) by the concentration of that gas.

Nitrous oxide (N_2O) is emitted by aerobic decomposition of organic matter in oceans and soils, by bacteria, by combustion of fossil fuels and biomass (fuelwood and cleared forests), by the use of nitrogenous fertilizers, and through other processes. N_2O is an important depletor of stratospheric ozone; present N_2O levels may contribute one twelfth of the amount contributed by CO_2 toward the greenhouse effect.

Methane (CH_4) is emitted through the release of natural gas and as one of the products of anaerobic respiration. Sources of anaerobic respiration include the soils of moist forests, wetlands, bogs, tundra, and lakes. Emission sources associated with human activities include livestock management (enteric fermentation in ruminants), anaerobic respiration in the soils associated with wet rice agriculture, and combustion of fossil fuels and biomass (fuelwood and cleared forests). CH_4 acts to increase ozone in the troposphere and lower stratosphere; its cumulative greenhouse effect is currently thought to be one third that of CO_2, but on a molecule-for-molecule basis, its effect, ignoring any feedback or involvement in any atmospheric processes, is 11 to 30 times that of CO_2.

Data Table 14.4
World CO_2 Emissions from Fossil Fuel Consumption and Cement Manufacture, 1950–92

Source: Carbon Dioxide Information Analysis Center (CDIAC), Environmental Sciences Division, Oak Ridge National Laboratory, "1992 Estimates of CO_2 Emissions from Fossil Fuel Burning and Cement Manufacturing Based on the United Nations Energy Statistics and the U.S. Bureau of Mines Cement Manufacturing Data," ORNL/CDIAC-25, NDP-

030 (an accessible numerical database) (Oak Ridge, Tennessee, September 1995).

CDIAC calculates world emissions from data on the global production of fossil fuels (based on the World Energy Data Set maintained by the United Nations Statistical Office) and from data on world cement manufacturing (based on the Cement Manufacturing Data Set maintained by the U.S. Bureau of Mines). Emissions are calculated using global average fuel chemistry and usage. These data account for all fuels including "bunker fuels" not accounted for in Data Table 14.1, which are also shown separately. For further information, see the Technical Notes for Data Table 14.1.

Data Table 14.5
Common Anthropogenic Pollutants, 1980–93

Sources: Sulfur and nitrogen emissions: Hilde Sandnes and Helge Styves, *Calculated Budgets for Airborne Acidifying Components in Europe 1985, 1987, 1988, 1989, 1990, and 1991* (Co-Operative Programme for Monitoring and Evaluation of the Long-Range Transmission of Air Pollutants in Europe (EMEP), The Norwegian Meteorological Institute, Technical Report No. 97, 1992), pp. 11–14. Sulfur, nitrogen, carbon monoxide, particulate matter, and volatile organic compounds: Economic Commission for Europe (ECE), *Impacts of Long-Range Transboundary Air Pollution* (ECE Air Pollution Studies 8, United Nations, New York, 1992), pp. 4–5; and Organisation for Economic Co-Operation and Development (OECD), *OECD Environmental Data Compendium 1995* (OECD, Paris, 1995).

Emissions of sulfur in the form of sulfur oxides and nitrogen in the form of its various oxides together contribute to acid rain and adversely affect agriculture, forests, aquatic habitats, and the weathering of building materials. Sulfate and nitrate aerosols impair visibility. These data on anthropogenic sources should be used carefully. Because different methods and procedures may have been used in each country, the best comparative data may be time trends within a country.

Sulfur dioxide (SO_2) is created by natural as well as anthropogenic activities. High concentrations of SO_2 have important adverse health effects, and there is particular concern about its effects on the health of young children, the elderly, and people with respiratory illnesses (e.g., asthma). SO_2 in the presence of moisture contributes to acid precipitation as sulfuric acid.

Anthropogenic *nitrogen oxides* (NO_x) come mainly from industrial sources and contribute to the creation of photochemical smog and the production of tropospheric ozone—an important greenhouse gas. All oxides of nitrogen also contribute to acid precipitation, in the form of nitric acid.

This data table combines data from EMEP, ECE, and OECD to compile as complete a picture as possible of sulfur and nitrogen emissions. EMEP is an activity of the 1979 Convention on Long-Range Transboundary Air Pollution. Data on sulfur and nitrogen emissions are submitted to EMEP and ECE by parties to the 1985 protocol on SO_2 emissions and the 1988 protocol on nitrogen oxide emissions. Parties to these protocols are required to submit preliminary estimates of sulfur and nitrogen emissions by May of the year following the year being estimated, with final estimates due within a year after that. In the event that official data are missing, EMEP interpolates between years for which official data exist. In the event that this is not possible, EMEP will use its own—or others'—emission estimates.

OECD polls its members on emissions with questionnaires that are completed by the relevant national statistical service or designee. OECD does not have any independent estimation capability.

EMEP and ECE report emissions in terms of the elemental content of sulfur, whereas OECD reports its emissions in terms of tons of oxides of sulfur. EMEP and ECE emission estimates were converted to their weight in SO_2. EMEP and OECD report nitrogen emissions in terms of nitrogen dioxide. Please consult the sources for further information.

This data table also reports OECD data for carbon monoxide and particulate matter emissions and combines both EMEP and OECD data to describe the emissions of volatile organic compounds. Differences in definition can limit the comparability of these estimates.

Carbon monoxide (CO), is formed both naturally and from industrial processes, including the incomplete combustion of fossil and other carbon-bearing fuels. Automobile emissions are the most important source of CO, especially in urban environments. CO interferes with oxygen uptake in the blood, producing chronic anoxia leading to illness or, in the case of massive and acute poisoning, even death. CO also scavenges hydroxyl radicals that would otherwise contribute to the removal of methane—a potent greenhouse gas—from the atmosphere.

The health effects of *particulate matter* (PM) are in part dependent on the biological and chemical makeup and activity of the particles. Heavy metal particles or hydrocarbons condensed onto dust particles can be especially toxic. PM arises from numerous anthropogenic and natural sources. Among the

anthropogenic sources are combustion, industrial and agricultural practices, and the formation of sulfates from SO_2 emissions.

In the presence of sunlight, *volatile organic compounds* (VOCs) are, along with oxides of nitrogen, responsible for photochemical smog. Anthropogenic emissions of VOCs arise in part from the incomplete combustion of fuels or the evaporation of fuels, lubricants, and solvents, as well as from the incomplete burning of biomass. These data combine VOC emission data from OECD with VOC data from EMEP.

Data Table 14.6
Inventories of National Greenhouse Gas Emissions, 1990

Sources: Intergovernmental Negotiating Committee for a Framework Convention on Climate Change, *Matters Relating to Commitments—First Review of Information Communicated by Each Party Included in Annex I of the Convention* (United Nations General Assembly, A/AC.237/81, New York, 7 December 1994); and Intergovernmental Negotiating Committee for a Framework Convention on Climate Change, *Matters Relating to Commitments—First Review of Information Communicated by Each Party Included in Annex I of the Convention* (United Nations General Assembly, A/AC.237/WP/1, New York, 6 February 1995). Poland: Ministry of Environmental Protection, Natural Resources, and Forestry, *National Report to the First Conference of the Parties to the United Nations Framework Convention on Climate Change* (Ministry of Environmental Protection, Natural Resources, and Forestry, Warsaw, 1994). Italy: Ministry of Environment and Ministry of Industry, *National Programme for the Limitation of Carbon Dioxide Emissions to the 1990 Levels by the Year 2000* (Ministry of Environment and Ministry of Industry, Rome, 1994).

As part of their responsibilities under the Framework Convention on Climate Change, each "party" listed in Annex I of the Convention must submit (within 6 months of the Convention entering into force) information that includes inventories of national emissions of greenhouse gases other than those controlled by the Montreal Protocol for the Protection of the Ozone Layer. The first of these inventories came due on September 21, 1994. Parties were asked to use guidelines created by the Intergovernmental Panel on Climate Change when preparing their inventories of 1990 emissions, so as to enhance comparability. These inventories are, in fact, detailed estimates of emissions and not inventories as the word is commonly understood. Estimates

of other gas emissions at the national level (e.g., those contained in Data Table 14.5) have been shown to be highly labile due to changes in the understanding of the underlying data, changes in the methods used in estimation, and even changes in the extent of the phenomenon under study. Variations of 30 percent or 40 percent from one estimate of a particular year's emissions to a later estimate of the same year's emissions are not unheard of.

Additional information on the gases contained in this table, and their sources, can be found in the Sources and Technical Notes to Data Table 14.2.

Although estimates of *carbon dioxide* (CO_2) emissions from fossil fuel use and industrial processes are similar in this table and in Data Table 14.1, these inventories differ more extensively from estimates of emissions found in Data Table 14.2. In Data Table 14.2, no attempt was made to estimate sinks for CO_2 as shown in this data table for land use change. Differences also exist between the two data tables in the estimates of methane (CH_4) emissions. These two data tables provide different views of the same phenomenon and together give a better picture than either could alone. Data Table 14.2 provides a global picture with similar methods and a common source for estimation parameters. In contrast, this data table provides national estimates of each nation's own emissions. These inventories use nationally specific details and parameters to come up with these inventory estimates.

CO_2 emissions from *fossil fuels* include emissions from combustion and other industrial processes. CO_2 emissions from *land use change* are estimates of the emissions associated with the clearing of land or increases in forest cover or forest biomass. *Net emissions* sums energy use and negative or positive emissions from forest growth.

Methane emissions from *oil and gas systems* include both emissions from combustion and emissions from venting and leakage from oil and gas production and distribution systems. CH_4 emissions from *livestock* include both enteric fermentation and animal waste. *Other* agricultural sources include wet rice agriculture, CH_4 released from soils, and the burning of agricultural waste and grazing lands. *Waste* includes emissions from landfills and *other* includes emissions from industrial processes and land use change. See the Technical Notes to Data Table 14.2 for further information.

Nitrous oxide (N_2O) is another potent greenhouse gas that is difficult to model. In descending order of importance, the primary sources of N_2O are agriculture, industry, and energy use for transport.

Acknowledgments

World Resources 1996–97 is the product of a unique international collaboration involving many institutions and individuals. Without their advice, support, information, and hard work, this volume could not have been produced.

We are especially grateful for the advice and assistance of our many colleagues at the World Resources Institute (WRI), the United Nations Environment Programme (UNEP), the United Nations Development Programme (UNDP), and the World Bank. Their advice on the selection of material to be covered and their diligent review of manuscript drafts and data tables, often under time pressure, have been invaluable.

Institutions

We wish to recognize and thank the many other institutions that have contributed data, reviews, and encouragement to this project. They include:

The Carbon Dioxide Information Analysis Center (**CDIAC**)
The Earth Council
The Food and Agriculture Organization of the United Nations (**FAO**)
The Global Environmental Monitoring System of UNEP (**GEMS**)
The International Council for Local Environmental Initiatives (**ICLEI**)
The International Federation of Red Cross Societies
The International Food Policy Research Institute (**IFPRI**)
The International Institute for Environment and Development (**IIED**)
The International Labour Organisation (**ILO**)
The National Aeronautics and Space Administration (**NASA**)
The Natural Resources Defense Council (**NRDC**)

The Organisation for Economic Co-Operation and Development (**OECD**)
The Organization of American States (**OAS**)
The Oxford Committee for Famine Relief (**OXFAM**)
The Population Reference Bureau
The United Nations Centre for Human Settlements (**Habitat**)
The United Nations Children's Fund (**UNICEF**)
The United Nations Department of Economic and Social Information and Policy Analysis (**UNDESIPA**)
The United Nations Educational, Scientific, and Cultural Organization (**UNESCO**)
The United Nations Population Division
The United Nations Statistical Division (**UNSTAT**)
The World Conservation Monitoring Centre (**WCMC**)
The World Conservation Union (**IUCN**)
The World Health Organization (**WHO**)

Individuals

Many individuals contributed to the development of this volume by providing expert advice, data, or careful review of manuscripts. While final responsibility for the chapters rests with the *World Resources* staff, the contributions of these colleagues are reflected throughout the book. We are especially grateful to our authors, who performed diligently and then endured patiently our numerous queries and often substantial editorial changes. The outside authors are listed at the end of each chapter. Many of our colleagues at the World Resources Institute contributed to the writing of this volume as well; they are acknowledged below.

Special thanks to Marion Cheatle of UNEP, Michael Cohen of the World Bank, and Ralph Schmidt of UNDP, who coordinated access to pertinent experts at their agencies:

UNEP

Yinka Adebayo, Jacqueline Aloisi de Larderel, Alex Alusa, Michael Atchia, Ali Ayoub, Fritz Balkau, Mona Bjorklund, Monica Borobia, Shahida Ali Butt, Franklin Cardy, Harvey Croze, Arthur Dahl, Anthony K. Edwards, Hiremagalur Gopalan, Ivonne Higuero, Jan Huismans, Jaime Hurtubia, Stejpan Keckes, Sergei Khromov, Chris Kirkcaldy, Hanne T. Laugesen, Mark McFarland, Asenath Omwega, Peter J. Peterson, Jeeny Plahe, Walter Rast, Nelson Sabogal, Mukul Sanwal, Madhava Sarma, Gerhart Schneider, Miriam Schomaker, David Smith, Linda Spencer, Magdalena Steiner, Bai-Mass M. Taal, Jeffrey A. Thornton, Peter Usher, Veerle Vandeweerd, Deborah Vorhies, Kaveh Zahedi, Hamdallah Zedan, Carlos Zulberti.

UNDP

G. Shabbir Cheema, Sakkiko Fukuda-Parr, Thomas B. Johansson, Karen Jorgensen, Eric Kashambuzi, Jonas Rabinovitch, Friedrich Mumm von Mallinckrodt, M. Robertson Work.

World Bank

Carl Bartone, Boris Blazic-Metzner, Eduard Bos, David Cassells, Alison Cave, Mike Collinson, Uttam Dabholkar, Betty Dow, Asif Faiz, John Flora, Colin A. Gannon, Christiaan Grootaert, Kenneth Gwilliam, Rita Hilton, Gordon Hughes, Josef L. Leitmann, Joan Martin-Brown, Alex McCalla, Thomas Merrick, Colin Rees, Zmarak Shalizi, K.C. Sivaramakrishnan, David Steeds, Andrew Steer, Paula Stone, David Williams.

Part I: The Urban Environment

This special section of *World Resources* reflects the collaborative efforts of colleagues at numerous institutions around the world who contributed ideas, data, background papers, and reviews.

Special thanks to Gordon McGranahan of the Stockholm Environment Institute, who played a major role in shaping this section and who gave consistently excellent advice, often on short notice; to Carolyn Stephens of the London School of Hygiene & Tropical Medicine, who coordinated the contributions of many experts on human health and the environment; and to Carl Bartone of the World Bank, Josef Leitmann of the World Bank, and David Satterthwaite of IIED—who graciously responded to our many requests for advice and information. Francisco Mata of the Earth Council coordinated the contribution from ICLEI, as well as several background papers.

These six chapters were written by a team of writers. Outside experts are acknowledged at the end of each chapter. The staff writers were Carolina M. Katz, Robert Livernash, contributing editor Gregory Mock, and Leslie Roberts.

This section profited enormously from the insightful comments provided by our group of special advisors, who painstakingly reviewed every chapter: Mike Douglass, University of Hawaii at Manoa; David Foster, U.S. Agency for International Development (U.S. AID); Hilda Herzer, Centro Estudios Sociales y Ambientales; Gordon McGranahan, Stockholm Environment Institute; Jay Moor, Habitat; Jonas Rabinovitch, UNDP; Carole Rakodi, University of Wales, College of Cardiff; Raquel Rolnik, Instituto Polis; David Satterthwaite, IIED; Carolyn Stephens, London School of Hygiene & Tropical Medicine.

We are especially grateful to the individuals who contributed background papers: Jeff Abbott, Habitat for Humanity International; Jonathan Baker, Scandinavian Institute of African Studies; Kalyan Biswas, Government of West Bengal; Jose Antonio Borello, CEUR; Ernst Brugger, Fundacion para el desarrollo sostenible en America Latina (FUNDES); Horacio Eduardo Caride, IIED-AL; Josef Leitmann, the World Bank; Tanvi Nagpal, WRI; Greg Newhouse, California Energy Commission; David Pearce, Centre for Social and Economic Research on the Global Environment (CSERGE); Jaime Ravinet, Mayor of Santiago, Chile; Ossama S. Salem, Centre for Environment and Development in the Arab Region and Europe (CEDARE).

U.S. Agency for International Development

Again, we wish to thank our colleagues at U.S. AID for their financial support of this special section, as well as the comments on each chapter: Orestes Anastasia, John Austin, John Borrazzo, Laurie DeFreese, J. Paul E. des Rosiers, Lindsay Elmendorf, David Foster, Viviann Gary, Jack Gisiger, Joanne Grossi, Al van Huyck, Peter M. Kimm, Michael Lippe, Robert MacLeod, Ivan Puchalt, Tamara Rickman, Liz Satow, Steven Sharp, David Wallinga, John Wilson, Bill Yaeger.

Urban Environment Reviewers

We are grateful to the following individuals for their thoughtful comments on this special section: Richard H. Adams, Jr., IFPRI; Abdlatif Y. Al-Hamad, Arab Fund for Economic and Social Development; Deborah Bleviss, International Institute for Energy Conservation; Ilona Blue, South Bank University; Ellen Brennan, United Nations Population Division; J. Alan Brewster, WRI; Ernst Brugger, FUNDES; Jeb Brugmann, ICLEI;

Sandy Cairncross, London School of Hygiene & Tropical Medicine; Fantu Cheru, American University; Tasneem Chowdhury, York University; Kathy Courrier, WRI; Devra Davis, WRI; Ximena de la Barra, UNICEF; Harry Dimitriou, University of Hong Kong; Ian Douglas, University of Manchester; Marc Dourojeanni, Inter-American Development Bank; Jochen Eigen, Habitat; Oscar Figueroa, Catholic University; Keith Florig, Resources for the Future; Tom Fox, WRI; Robert M. Friedman, H. John Heinz III Center for Science, Economics, and the Environment; Christine Furedy, York University; Ralph Gakenheimer, Massachusetts Institute of Technology; Greg Goldstein, WHO; Hermann Habermann, UNSTAT; Peter Hall, University College London; Marjorie Harper, Natural Resources Conservation Service; Carl Haub, Population Reference Bureau; Larry Heligman, United Nations Population Division; Judith A. Hermanson, Cooperative Housing Foundation; Guenter O. Karl, Habitat; John Kasarda, University of North Carolina at Chapel Hill; Gary Kraus, National Academy of Sciences; Xia Kunbao, China National Environmental Protection Agency; Vinay Lall, Society for Development Studies; Diana Lee-Smith, Mazingira Institute; Todd Litman, Victoria Transport Policy Institute; Jim MacKenzie, WRI; Claudia Marcondes, University of Toronto; Jos Maseland, Habitat; Patricia L. McCarney, University of Toronto; Steve McCoy-Thompson, International City/County Management Association (ICMA); A.J. McMichael, London School of Hygiene & Tropical Medicine; Robert H. McNulty, Partners for Livable Communities; Dinesh Mehta, National Institute of Urban Affairs; Jonathan Miller, U.S. EPA; Eric Miller, University of Toronto; Luc Mougeot, International Development Research Centre; Ricardo Neves, Instituto de Tecnologia para o Cidadao; Stephen B. Olsen, University of Rhode Island; Bart Ostro, California Environmental Protection Agency; Horst Otterstetter, Pan American Health Organization; Mary Paden, WRI; David Pearce, CSERGE; Eduardo Perez, Environmental Health Project; Walt Reid, WRI; Robert Repetto, WRI; Andrew Robertson, National Oceanic and Atmospheric Administration (NOAA); Dale Rothman, University of British Columbia; Lee Schipper, University of California at Berkeley; Dieter Schwela, WHO; David Sheer, International Management and Development Group, Ltd.; Jac Smit, Urban Agriculture Network; Elisabeth Sommerfelt, Demographic and Health Survey; Richard Stren, Centre for Urban and Community Studies; M.S. Swaminathan, M.S. Swaminathan Research Foundation; Geetam Tiwari, India Institute of Technology; Dan Tunstall, WRI; Michael P. Walsh; Greg Watters, WHO;

John Whitelegg, Eco-Logica Ltd.; R. Wirasinha, WHO; Nicholas You, Habitat.

Part II: Global Conditions and Trends and Data Tables

Basic Economic Indicators

Principal author: Dale S. Rothman of the Sustainable Development Research Institute at the University of British Columbia, with a contribution by Allen L. Hammond.

Reviewers and other contributors include: Christian Averous, OECD; J. Alan Brewster, WRI; Herman Daly, University of Maryland; Anne Forrest, Environmental Law Institute; Tom Fox, WRI; F. Mehran, ILO; Walt Reid, WRI; Robert Repetto, WRI; Beven Stein, OECD; David Stern, Boston University.

Population and Human Development

Principal authors: Robert Livernash of the World Resources staff and Joe Palca of National Public Radio.

Reviewers and other contributors include: J. Alan Brewster, WRI; Col. Donald S. Burke, Walter Reed Army Institute of Research; Giovanni Andrea Cornia, UNICEF; Bob Engelman, Population Action International; Paul R. Epstein, Cambridge Hospital; Faid El Boustani, UNESCO; Tom Fox, WRI; Joseph-Alfred Grinblat, U.N. Population Division; Hermann Habermann, UNSTAT; Carl Haub, Population Reference Bureau; Larry Heligman, UNDESIPA; Donald A. Henderson, The Johns Hopkins University; Gerald T. Keusch, Tufts University School of Medicine; Frank Lostumbo, National Council for International Health; Geraldo Nascimento, UNESCO; Walt Reid, WRI; Gita Sen, Indian Institute of Management; Mary Wilson, Mount Auburn Hospital.

Forests and Land Cover

Principal author: Dirk Bryant of the World Resources staff, with a contribution by Bruce Cabarle of WRI.

Reviewers and other contributors include: J. Alan Brewster, WRI; Nigel Dudley, Equilibrium; Philip M. Fearnside, Instituto Nacional de Pesquisas da Amazonia (INPA); Curtis Flather, U.S. Department of Agriculture; Tom Fox, WRI; David Gordon, Pacific Environment and Resources Center; Alan Grainger, University of Leeds; Richard A. Houghton, Woods Hole Research Institute; Lynn Huntsinger, University of California, Berkeley; Alexander V. Korotkov, FAO; J.P. Lanly, FAO;

Julia Morris, U.S. Department of Agriculture; Walter Parham, China Tropical Lands Project; Walt Reid, WRI; K.D. Singh, FAO; Nigel Sizer, WRI; Lisa Tracy, Pacific Environment and Resource Center; Bruce Wilcox, Institute for Sustainable Development.

Food and Agriculture

Principal author: Robert Livernash of the World Resources staff, with contributions by former WRI staff May Mercado Peters and Steven McCann.

Reviewers and other contributors include: Nikos Alexandratos, FAO; William Bender; Bob Blake, WRI; Tom Fox, WRI; Peter Hazell, IFPRI; Francesco Pariboni, FAO; David Pimentel, Cornell University; Per Pinstrup-Andersen, IFPRI; Walt Reid, WRI; Neill Schaller, Wallace Institute for Alternative Agriculture; Gary H. Toenniessen, Rockefeller Foundation; S. Zarqa, FAO.

Biodiversity

Principal author: Dirk Bryant of the World Resources staff.

Reviewers and other contributors include: Tundi Agardy, World Wildlife Fund; Devin M. Bartley, FAO; Chris Bleakley, Great Barrier Reef Marine Park Authority; J. Alan Brewster, WRI; Brian Groombridge, WCMC; Richard Neal, Southwest Fisheries Science Center; John B. Pearce, NOAA; Walt Reid, WRI.

Energy and Materials

Principal author: Eric Rodenburg of the World Resources staff; with contributions by Jim MacKenzie of WRI, Roger Dower of WRI, and Gregory Mock of the World Resources staff.

Reviewers and other contributors include: Christian Averous, OECD; J. Alan Brewster, WRI; Colin Campbell; Joy Dunkerley; Tom Fox, WRI; Hermann Habermann, UNSTAT; Mary J. Hutzler, U.S. Department of Energy; Anatoly Konevsky, UNSTAT; Walt Reid, WRI; Michael Schomberg, World Energy Council; Kirk Smith, Hawaii East-West Center.

Water and Fisheries

Principal authors: Gregory Mock and Dirk Bryant of the World Resources staff.

Reviewers and other contributors include: J. Alan Brewster, WRI; Francis T. Christy, IMARIBA; Adele Crispoldi, FAO; Bob Engelman, Population Action International; Jean Marc Faures, FAO; Tom Fox, WRI; Serge Garcia, FAO; Peter Gleick, The Pacific Institute;

Andreas Kahnert, U.N. Economic Commission for Europe; Richard Neal, Southwest Fisheries Science Center; John B. Pearce, NOAA; Walt Reid, WRI; Robert Repetto, WRI; Aaron Zazueta, WRI.

Atmosphere and Climate

Principal authors: Gregory Mock and Eric Rodenburg of the World Resources staff, with a contribution by Liz Cook of WRI.

Reviewers and other contributors include: Christian Averous, OECD; Thomas A. Boden, CDIAC; Roger Dower, WRI; John Harte, University of California at Berkeley; Mary J. Hutzler, U.S. Department of Energy; Michael Jefferson, World Energy Council; Andreas Kahnert, U.N. Economic Commission for Europe; Michael MacCracken, Office of the U.S. Global Change Research Program; Walt Reid, WRI; Michael Schomberg, World Energy Council.

Production Staff

A talented team of editorial, production, and publishing experts accomplished the enormous task of preparing this volume for printing. We thank them for their dedication, hard work, and high professional standards. In addition to the World Resources staff, they include:

Additional Factchecking and Research: Nicole Schofer, Stephen J. Latham, Steven McCann, Peter Grimes

Copyeditors: Michael Hayes, Michael Edington

Index: Bland Blackford

Cover design: Pamela Reznick, Reznick Design

Photographs: Theresa de Salis and Mark Edwards, Still Pictures

Maps: Daniel Nielsen

Mechanical Production: EPI, Rockville, MD

We are especially grateful to WRI Librarian Beth Behrendt for assisting us with research and materials.

It has been a privilege to work with so many outstanding individuals throughout the world in producing *World Resources 1996–97*.

Leslie Roberts, Editor-in-Chief

The World Resources Institute (WRI) is an independent center for policy research and technical assistance on global environmental and development issues. WRI's mission is to move human society to live in ways that protect Earth's environment and its capacity to provide for the needs and aspirations of current and future generations. Because people are inspired by ideas, empowered by knowledge, and moved to change by greater understanding, WRI provides—and helps other institutions provide—objective information and practical proposals for policy and institutional change that will foster environmentally sound, socially equitable development.

WRI's particular concerns are with globally significant environmental problems and their interaction with economic development and social equity at all levels. WRI focuses on: the global commons, where the cumulative weight of human activities is undermining the integrity of environmental systems; U.S. policies, since the United States is the world's largest producer, consumer, and polluter, as well as a trend-setter for many nations; and developing countries, where natural resource deterioration is dimming development prospects and swelling the ranks of the poor and hungry.

In all of its policy research and work with institutions, WRI tries to build bridges between ideas and action, meshing the insights of scientific research, economic and institutional analyses, and practical experience with the need for open and participatory decision-making. In pursuit of its mission, WRI researches policy, gathers and disseminates information, strengthens institutions, builds technical capacities, and communicates information to government and private sector decision-makers, NGOs, and educators. However diverse, these paths aim in the same direction. In short, WRI analyzes obstacles in the path to sustainability, recommends ways to surmount them, and promotes the understanding and implementation of these recommendations.

WRI's work is carried out by a 115-member interdisciplinary staff, strong in the social and natural sciences and augmented by a network of advisors, collaborators, international fellows, and partner institutions in more than 50 countries. WRI is an independent, not-for-profit corporation that receives financial support from private foundations, governmental and intergovernmental institutions, private corporations, and interested individuals.

UNEP

United Nations Environment Programme

United Nations Avenue, Gigiri
P.O. Box 30552
Nairobi, Kenya

Executive Director
Elizabeth Dowdeswell

Deputy Executive Director
Reuben Olembo

Regional and Liaison Offices

Latin America and the Caribbean:
UNEP Regional Office for Latin America and the Caribbean
Boulevard de los Virreyes No. 155
Col. Lomas Virreyes, P.O. Box 10-793
1100 Mexico City, Mexico

Europe:
UNEP Regional Office for Europe
Geneva Executive Centre
15 Chemin des Anêmones, Case Postale 356
1219 Châtelaine, Geneva, Switzerland

Africa:
UNEP Regional Office for Africa
UNEP Headquarters
United Nations Avenue, Gigiri
P.O. Box 30552
Nairobi, Kenya

North America:
UNEP Regional Office for North America
Room DC2-0803
2 United Nations Plaza
New York, N.Y. 10017 U.S.A.

West Asia:
UNEP Regional Office for West Asia
1083 Road No. 425
Jufair 342, P.O. Box 10880
Manama, Bahrain

Asia and the Pacific:
UNEP Regional Office for Asia and the Pacific
United Nations Building
Rajadamnern Avenue
Bangkok 10200 Thailand

Cairo:
UNEP Arab League Liaison Office
31 Abdel Moneim Riad, Dokki, P.O. Box 212
Cairo, Egypt

Other Outposted Offices
International Register for Potentially Toxic Chemicals
Programme Activity Centre (IRPTC/PAC)
Geneva Executive Centre
15 Chemin des Anêmones, Case Postale 356
1219 Châtelaine, Geneva, Switzerland

UNEP Industry and Environment Programme Activity Centre (IE/PAC)
Tour Mirabeau
39-43 Quai Andre Citroen, F-75739
Paris Cedex 15, France

UNEP International Environmental Technology Centre (IETC)
Osaka Office
2-110 Ryokichi koen
Tsurumi-ku, Osaka a538, Japan

UNEP/Department of Humanitarian Affairs (DHA)
Geneva/Relief Coordination Branch
Palais des Nations
8-14 avenue de la Paix
1211 Geneva 10, Switzerland

The United Nations Environment Programme (UNEP) was established in 1972 and given by the United Nations General Assembly a broad and challenging mandate to stimulate, coordinate, and provide policy guidance for sound environmental action throughout the world. Initial impetus for UNEP's formation came out of the largely nongovernmental and antipollution lobby in industrialized countries. This interest in pollutants remains, but right from the early years, as perceptions of environmental problems broadened to encompass those arising from the misuse and abuse of renewable natural resources, the promotion of environmentally sound or sustainable development became a main purpose of UNEP.

From the global headquarters in Nairobi, Kenya, and seven regional and liaison offices worldwide, UNEP's staff of some 320 scientists, lawyers, administrators, and information specialists carry out UNEP's program, which is laid down and revised every two years by a Governing Council of representatives from its 58 member states. These members are elected on a staggered basis for four years by the United Nations General Assembly.

UNEP's mission is to provide leadership and encourage partnership in caring for the environment by inspiring, informing, and enabling nations and peoples to improve their quality of life without compromising that of future generations. Broadly, UNEP's program aims to stimulate action on major environ-

mental problems, promote environmentally sound management at both national and international levels by encouraging the application of assessment results, and make such actions and findings known to the public—from scientists and policymakers to industrialists and schoolchildren. The program is run in cooperation with numerous other United Nations agencies, governments, intergovernmental organizations, nongovernmental organizations and specialized institutions.

From the 1996–97 biennium, UNEP is strengthening its regional delivery and adopting a more integrated approach. Activities are now grouped under five programme areas: sustainable management and use of natural resources; sustainable production and consumption; a better environment for human health and well-being; globalization and the environment; global and regional servicing and support. The programme is implemented through three divisions: Programme; Environment Information and Assessment; Policy and External Relations.

The Division of Environment Information and Assessment works with a wide range of partners to keep under review and report on the state of the world environment, provide early warning of environmental threats, develop harmonised methodologies and tools for policy relevant assessments, improve access to information for environmental decision making and enhance developing countries' capabilities to use information.

United Nations Development Programme

1 U.N. Plaza
New York, New York 10017 U.S.A.

Administrator
James Gustave Speth

Associate Administrator
Rafeeuddin Ahmed

Regional Bureau for Asia and the Pacific
Assistant Administrator and Director
Ntay Htun

Regional Bureau for Arab States
Assistant Administrator and Director
Saad Alfarargi

Regional Director for Europe and the Commonwealth of
Independent States
Anton Kruiderink

Regional Bureau for Latin America and the Caribbean
Assistant Administrator and Director
Fernando Zumbado

Regional Bureau for Africa
Assistant Administrator and Director
Ellen Johnson Sirleaf

Bureau for Programme and Policy Support
Assistant Administrator and Director
Anders Wijkman

Bureau for Resources and External Affairs
Assistant Administrator and Director
Normand Lauzon

The United Nations Development Programme (UNDP) is the world's largest multilateral source of grant funding for development cooperation. It was created in 1965 through a merger of two predecessor programmes for United Nations technical cooperation. Its funds, which totaled US$1.9 billion in 1995, come from yearly voluntary contributions from member States of the UN or its related agencies.

Through a network of 136 offices worldwide, UNDP works with 175 governments to build developing countries' capacities for sustainable human development. To execute the programmes and projects it supports, it draws upon developing countries' national technical capacities, as well as the expertise of over 30 international and regional agencies and non-governmental organizations.

People are at the centre of all UNDP activities, which focus on four priority areas: poverty elimination; creation of jobs and sustainable livelihoods; advancement of women; and protection and regeneration of the environment. Within this context, UNDP is frequently asked to assist in promoting sound governance and market development, and to support the rebuilding of societies in the aftermath of war and humanitarian emergencies. Global and interregional programmes address worldwide problems, including food security and HIV/AIDS.

Fifty-eight per cent of UNDP's total resources are allocated for the countries designated as "least-developed" by the UN General Assembly. Eighty-seven per cent of UNDP's country programme funds go to countries with annual per capita GNPs of $750 or less.

A *Human Development Report*, published yearly for UNDP since 1990 and drafted by a team of independent consultants, assists the international community in developing new, practical and pragmatic concepts, measures and policy instruments for promoting more people-oriented development.

Environment is one of the main themes for UNDP's 1992-96 programming cycle. Environmental objectives are therefore included in 87 per cent of the country programmes approved for this period and virtually all activities are screened for their environmental impact. Programmes to build capacities for sustainable development and natural resource management are supported in such sectors as food security, forestry, water and sanitation, energy and urban development.

UNDP assisted developing country governments and local NGOs and grassroots organizations in preparing for the 1992 United Nations Conference on Environment and Development (UNCED). As a follow-up to UNCED, it is (i) assisting the developing countries in integrating environmental concerns into development plans, and (ii) providing support in strengthening capacity for management of environment and sustainable development programmes as called for in AGENDA 21, UNCED's blueprint for action. For this purpose UNDP launched "Capacity 21", which became fully operational in June 1993. By December 1994, Austria, Canada, Denmark, Finland, France, Germany, Italy, Japan, Netherlands, Norway, Sweden, Switzerland, the United Kingdom, the United States and the US Environmental Protection Agency had pledged a total of $50.3 million and further support was expected.

Forty-one new national UNDP posts for sustainable development officers were established in early 1994. The new national staff members will advocate the integration of environmental considerations into UNDP-supported activities, and promote and support specific initiatives such as Capacity 21 and the Global Environment Facility (GEF).

The World Bank

The World Bank Group is a partner in opening markets and strengthening economies. Its goal is to improve the quality of life and expand prosperity for people everywhere, especially the world's poorest.

A first-rate financial standing and access to the world's capital markets enable the Bank to invest broadly in societies—from health, education, and the environment to infrastructure and policy reform.

The World Bank Group of institutions includes:

- The International Bank for Reconstruction and Development (IBRD), founded in 1944, is the single largest provider of development loans to middle-income developing countries and a major catalyst of similar financing from other sources. The IBRD funds itself primarily by borrowing on international capital markets.

- The International Development Association (IDA), founded in 1960, assists the poorest countries by providing interest-free credits with 35- to 40-year maturities. IDA is funded primarily by governments' contributions.

- The International Finance Corporation (IFC) supports private enterprises in the developing world through providing loan and equity financing, and through a range of advisory services.

- The Multilateral Investment Guarantee Agency (MIGA) offers investors insurance against noncommercial risk and helps developing country governments attract foreign investment.

- The International Center for the Settlement of Investment Disputes (ICSID) encourages the flow of foreign investment to developing countries through arbitration and conciliation facilities.

Over its 52-year history the World Bank has become a global partnership in which more than 179 countries have joined together for common goals: to improve the quality of life for people throughout the world and to meet the challenge of sustainable development.

The World Bank Group
1818 H Street, N.W.
Washington, D.C. 20433 U.S.A.

Executive Directors:
Khalid H. Alyahya
Khalid M. Al-Saad
Marc-Antoine Autheman
Ali Bourhane
Andrei Bugrov
Marcos C. de Paiva
Huw Evans
Fritz Fischer
Jean-Daniel Gerber
Leonard Good
Eveline Herfkens
Ruth Jacoby
Bimal Jalan
Abdul Karim Lodhi
Leonard Mseka
Peter W.E. Nicholl
Atsuo Nishihara
Julio Nogues
Franco Passacantando
Jan Piercy
Walter Rill
Pasugswad Suwan
Jorge Terrazas
Li Yong

Officers:
James D. Wolfensohn, *President*
Rachel Lomax, *Vice President and Chief of Staff*
Jessica Einhorn, *Managing Director*
Richard Frank, *Managing Director*
Gautam S. Kaji, *Managing Director*
Caio Koch-Weser, *Managing Director*
Sven Sandstrom, *Managing Director*

Index

A

Abidjan, Cote d'Ivoire, *4–5*
  bus lanes and high speed buses, 94
Accra, Ghana
  causes of death, 34
  household environmental indicators, *46*
  mortality rates by socioenvironmental zones, *49*
  and Sao Paulo, Brazil, 49–51
  urban market gardens, *5*
Acid precipitation, 279, 315
  forest degradation, 23
Acquired immune deficiency syndrome (AIDS). *see* Diseases, AIDS
Action for Security Health for All (ASHA), Delhi, India, *38*
Administrative capacity, energy management, 273
Administrative legal resources, 125
Aedes aegypti mosquito
  dengue fever, 41
  extended range, *182*
Aedes albopictus mosquito, dengue fever, 41
Africa
  see also East Africa; sub-Saharan Africa
  AIDS, 177–78, 180
  cholera, 180
  crop yields, 232
  food shortages, 227
  migration, 7
  population projection, 175
  tropical forests, 205, 211
  tuberculosis, 180
  urbanization trends, 3
African cities, fertility rates, *4*
African Housing Board, 137
Age, by country, *192–93*
Agenda 21, *144*
Agricultural growth
  and biodiversity, *232*
  land and water resources, *232*
Agricultural inputs, *240–41*
Agricultural production
  developing countries, *228*
  and food, *238–39*
  growth rates, 227
  and loss of genetic stocks, 234
  and soil degradation, 234
Agricultural research, *230*

Agricultural research and extension service, developing countries, 236
Agriculture
  and environment, *232*
  and food, 225
  and greenhouse gases, *232*
  international assistance, 236
  and water use, 303
Agronomic practices, improvement, 234
Agronomy, teaching of, 234
Aguablanca, Cali, Colombia, *138–39*
AIDS (acquired immune deficiency syndrome). *see* Diseases, AIDS
Air basin management districts, 113–14
Air basins, and air pollution, 113
Air pollution, 81, 279, 282, 315
  see also Ambient air pollution; Indoor air pollution; Urban air pollution
  and air basins, 113
  cleaner fuels, 97
  and deforestation, xiv
  domestic sources, 42–44
  and economic growth, 113
  and energy consumption, 85
  and forest health, 210
  and income level, 18
  lead, 6
  Los Angeles, 68–69
  and motor vehicles, 82, 86
  nickel smelters, *206*
  particulates and lead, *104*
  priorities for action, 113–16
  in selected cities, *154*
  temperature extremes, 18
  traffic congestion, *20, 24*
  and two-stroke engines, 98
  and two-wheel vehicles, 98
  urban, 1
  in urban areas, x
  and urban sprawl, 59
  voluntary substitute emissions reduction measures, 69
Air pollution sources
  energy generation, 113
  industry, 113
  transportation, 113
Air quality standards
  monitoring and enforcement, 114
  World Health Organization (WHO), 66, *66*
Air and water pollution controls, costs and benefits, *110–11*
Algal blooms, Guatemalan coast, 256

Aligarh City, India, natural resource extraction, 62
Alliance of Small Island States (AOSIS), sea levels, *322*
Aluminum, *290–91*
Amazonian forests, 212
Ambient air pollution, 45
  electric power plants, 18
  and motor vehicles, 45
Amphibians, threatened species, *266–67*
Anopheles stephensi mosquito, malaria, 41
Antarctic, ozone hole, *316*
Aquaculture, 295–97
  as an environmental risk, 301
  Asia, 301
  and mangrove degradation, 254
  supplementing marine fish stock, 301
Aquifer, overextraction, 7
Aquifers, 301
  depletion, 64
Arab NGO Network, *144*
Aral Sea, water diversion, 301
Archer, Dennis, 17
Asbestos-related lung disease, Bombay, India, 45
Asia
  see also East Asia; South Asia
  aquaculture, 301
  bicycling, *95*
  cholera, 180
  chronic undernutrition, 236
  coastal ecosystems, 248
  energy demand, 278
  food production, 225
  marine biodiversity, *252*
  migration, 7
  motor vehicles, 82–83
  population projection, 175
  tropical forests, 205, 211
  urbanization trends, 3
  wastepickers, 112
Asian Coalition for Housing Rights, *144*
Aswan Dam, and Nile River, 254
Athens, Greece, traffic bans, 93
Atmosphere, and climate, 315–337
Australia
  Great Barrier Reef Marine Park, 259
  marine biodiversity, *252*
Australian Institute of Marine Science, 253
Azidothymidine. *see* AZT (azidothymidine)
AZT (azidothymidine), 187

B

Baare, Anton, *51*
Badshah, Akhtar, *133*
Baltic Sea, eutrophication, 71
Bangkok, Thailand
  garbage collection, 130
  gridlock, *85*
  hazardous wastes, 23
  land subsidence, 64
  lead pollution, 47
  pollution reduction recommendations, *104*
  traffic congestion reduction recommendations, *104*
Banks, 138, 143
Basti sevikas, Delhi, India, 39
Beaches and sand dunes, and construction, 61
Berkeley, California
  multinucleated urban regions, 119
  wastepickers, 113
Berlin Climate Summit, 322
Berlin Mandate, 322
  developing countries, 322
Bhopal, India, Union Carbide factory accident, 15
Bicycling, 81, 83, 88, *90–91, 95–96, 97*
Biodiversity, 247–60
  see also Marine biodiversity
  and agricultural growth, 232
  coral reefs, 253
  and infectious disease, *183*
  and logging, *208–09*
Biodiversity assessment, United Nations Environment Programme (UNEP), 247–48
Biological production, coastal ecosystems, 58
Biomass fuel, 278
Biomass fuels, developing countries, 63
Biomass loss, and forest degradation, 208
Bioregional management, 259
Birds, threatened species, *264–65*
Birth rates
  by country, *192–93*
  urbanization, 58
Black Death. *see* Plague, bubonic
Black Sea, pollution and overfishing, 254
Bombay, India, asbestos-related lung disease, 45
Boston, Long Range Water Supply Program (LRWSP), 109
Brazilian Institute of Municipal Administration, extension service, 130
Brazilian rosewood (*Dalbergia nigra*), 212
Bribery, *209*
Bronx Center, *141*
Bronx, New York, citizen participation, *141*
Brown Agenda, 19–24
  definition, 19
Brown, Lester, 228
"Brownfield" sites
  definition, *16*
  and urban containment policies, 118
Brugmann, Jeb, *129*
Brundtland Commission, 145
Buenos Aires, Argentina, Programa Alimentario Integral y Solidario (PAIS), 135

Built environment, and human health, 187
Bus lanes and high speed buses, 94
Business training, *139*

C

Cadmium, *290–91*
Cairo, Egypt, Zabbaleen, 135
Cajamarca, Peru
  and decentralized government, *128*
  Provincial Sustainable Development Plan, *128*
Calcutta, India, wastewater treatment, 110
Cali, Colombia, housing program, *138–39*
California Air Resources Board (CARB), 68–69
California Clean Air Act, 69
Canada, forests, 204
Cancer, and socioeconomic status, 48
Carbon dioxide emissions, 67, 70, *280–81,* 315–19, *319, 331*
  see also Greenhouse gas emissions
  anthropogenic and natural, 317
  concentrations, *320*
  and consumer purchase power, 318
  costs of control, 320
  developing countries, 318–19
  effects upon measure of national wealth, *160*
  from fossil fuel consumption and cement manufacture, *330*
  industrial, *318,* 326–27
  stabilization of concentrations, 320
  technologies, 321
  transition countries, 319
  United States, 316
Carbon dioxide releases, per capita, *319*
Carbon monoxide, 44, 86, 90, *111, 331*
Carbon storage capacity, *232*
Caribbean, coastal ecosystems, 253
Caribbean countries, urbanization, 3
Cartegena, Colombia, sewage system, 106
Carvajal Foundation, Cali, Colombia, *138–39*
Causes of death
  chronic diseases, 34
  communicable diseases, 34
  developed countries, 180
  developing countries, 34, 179, *180*
CDC. *see* Centers for Disease Control and Prevention
Cement manufacture and fossil fuel consumption, carbon dioxide emissions, *330*
Center for African Settlement Studies and Development, *144*
Centers for Disease Control and Prevention (CDC)
  biosafety level-4 containment facilities, 187
  identification of Ebola virus, 181
Central Europe
  population, 175
  urban poverty, 12
Centro Internacional de Mejoramiento de Maiz y Trigo (CIMMYT), *230*
Cereals production
  growth rates, 227
  yields, 228, *238–39*
Chagas' disease, and triatomine bugs, 41
Chattanooga, Tennessee
  air pollution, 142

  participatory planning, *142*
Chatterjee, Rachel, 26
Chernobyl nuclear accident
  as a factor in illness and birth defects, 178
  forest degradation, *206*
Chesapeake Bay
  erosion control, *73*
  eutrophication, 71, 74
  overharvesting, 255
  regional coastal zone management, 73–74
Chesapeake Bay Program, initiatives, 74–75
Child labor, urban poor, 14
Child mortality, 177
  Abidjan, Cote d'Ivoire, *5*
  as an indicator of human well-being, 173
  diarrheal disease, 21
  food contamination, 40
  infectious and parasitic disease, *181*
  Jakarta, Indonesia, *6*
  urban areas, 36
  urban-rural, *32*
  urbanization, 31
Children
  biological and social risks, 35
  intestinal disorders, 36
  and poverty, 14
  respiratory infections, 36
  and solid waste, 44
Children's health, 36, 42, *133*
  AIDS, 184
  Delhi, India, 38
  and education, *196–97*
  exposure to lead, 47, *104*
  immunization, *196–97*
  indoor air pollution, 22
  lead exposure, 15, 20, 24
  nutrition, 236
  in urban areas, 17
  urban violence, 36
  vaccinations, *32*
  wastepicking, *112*
China
  coal gasification plants, 115
  forests, 204–05
  reliance on coal, 319
  roundwood imports, 206
  sulfur dioxide, 67
  Three Gorges Project, 279
Chlorine, and wastewater, 72
Chlorofluorocarbons (CFCs), *316*
Cholera, 110–11
Chronic and degenerative diseases
  as causes of death, 34
  social factors, 32
Ciliwung River, Jakarta, Indonesia, *7*
Cisneros, Henry, 13
Cities
  see also Compact cities; Megacities; Urban areas; Urbanization
  "ecological footprint," 58
  and education, 174
  and environment, 1–27
  and environment protection, 13
  greater than 750,000 population, *150–51*
  greater than 500,000 residents, *61*
  and health, 174
  income, 17–18
  and incomes of residents, 174
  inequality among residents, 14
  inner-city problems, 13
  neighborhoods, 33, 39
  see also Inner-city neighborhoods

opportunities, ix, 2, 25, 58
political accountability, *126*
pollution, ix
population of largest, *9*
priorities for action, x
resource consumption, ix
social environment, x
and sustainable development, 26, *26*, 58, 145
as "transnational spaces for economic activity," 11
vulnerable groups, 14, 35–37
wetland conversion, 62
Cities of wealth
  composition of waste, 70
  consumption and waste generation, 57, 62, 70
  natural resource extraction and depletion, 62
  regional and global environmental effects, 18
  and sustainable development, 145
Citizen participation, 140
  Bronx, New York, *141*
City and community, and environmental sustainability, 125–45
City indicators, India, *154*
City location, and environmental impact, 59
City size and wealth, household environmental problems, *46*
City-wide problems, urban environment, 44–47
Clean Air Act, enforcement, 142
"Clean" production, manufacturing, 18
Climate
  and atmosphere, 315–337
  and energy, xiii
  human influence, xiv
  and infectious diseases, *182*
  protection, *323*
  research and monitoring, 324
  stabilization, 315, *321*
Climate change, 257, 315, 320
  global warming, *317*
  scientific assessment, *317*
Climate changes, *208*, *281*
  greenhouse gas emissions, 273, 279
Climate convention, 316
Climate Technology Initiative, *323*
Climate treaty, *322*
Climatic conditions, and occupational hazards, 45
CO2 Reduction Program, International Council for Local Environmental Initiatives (ICLEI), *129*
Coal, *288–89*, 318
  ash, 279
  gasification plants, 115
  industry lobbyists, *323*
  mining, 63
Coal- and oil-fired power plants, pollution reduction, 114
Coastal degradation, 295
  discards, 298
Coastal development, and habitat loss, 254
Coastal ecosystems, 247
  biological production, 58
  Caribbean, 253
  current conditions, 253
  and development, 248, *249*
  factors in decline of, 253
  indicators of risk, 248
  Indo-Western Pacific, 253

marine biodiversity, 248
and marine biological productivity, 251
threatened by urbanization and tourism, *61*
threats to, 248–49
urban impacts, 58
urban land conversion, 60
Coastal erosion
  and shoreline development, 61
  Tangiers, Morocco, *62*
Coastal habitats, ecosystems at risk, xiv
Coastal and marine ecosystems, 260
Coastal pollution, watershed protection, 27
Coastal urban centers, 60
Coastal wetlands, conversion and degradation, 253
Coastlines
  land reclamation, 61
  potential threats, *250*
  study of, 61
  urban encroachment, 59
Coasts, conversion of, 60
Coasts and coastal waters
  pollution, 298
  population pressures, 254
Code of Conduct for Responsible Fisheries, 300
Collection of solid waste, 135
Collective action, neighborhood and community issues, 135
Commodity indexes, world, *170*
Commodity prices, world, *170*
Communicable diseases, as causes of death, 34
Communities and citizens, and urban environmental management, 125
Community action, Honduras, *134*
Community banks, Nigeria, *143*
Community and city, and environmental sustainability, 125
Community credit programs, 140
Community development, nongovernmental organizations (NGOs), *133*
Community inputs, urban redevelopment, *141*
Community involvement, 52
  Abidjan, Cote d'Ivoire, *5*
  environmental initiatives, *128–29*
  environmental planning and decisionmaking, 131
  in environmental solutions, 105
  Jakarta, Indonesia, *7*
  Karachi, Pakistan, 106
  urban environmental challenge, 25
  water and sanitation, 106–07
Community management, elements of success, 134
Community membership
  and environmental improvement, 135
  and household stability, 135
Community mobilization, urban poor, 125, *132–33*
Community networks, *132–33*, 135
Community organizations, 137
Community perceptions
  and health solutions, *51*
  of urban health risks, *50*
Community planning and management, women's role in, 136

Community-based development, financial resources, 140
Community-level approach, environmental management, 131
Community-oriented strategies, water and sanitation, xi
Commuter journeys
  and road systems, 84
  and transit systems, 84
Compact cities, 26
  and transportation, 88
Compost plants, 135
Condominial wastewater collection system, 106, *108*
Conference of the Parties (to the Berlin Climate Summit), 324
Consensus building, and public participation, *129*
Conservation
  and marine endemism, *252*
  marine species, *252*
Construction materials manufacturers, *138*
Consultative Group on International Agricultural Research (CGIAR), *230*, 234
Consumer purchase power, and carbon dioxide emissions, 318
Consumption, urban areas, 58, 62–65
Contaminated sediments, cost of clean-up, 72
Contraception, and fertility rates, 175–76
Convention on Biological Diversity, 211, 260
Convention on International Trade in Endangered Species (CITES), 259
  Wild Fauna and Flora, 212
Cooperation of local and regional governments, 120
Cooperative Housing Foundation (CHF), Tegucigalpa, Honduras, 139
Copenhagen, Denmark, bicycling, *97*
Copper, *290–91*
Coral reefs
  biodiversity, 253
  bleaching of, 249, 253
  degradation and destruction, 253, 255
  disease, 257
  and marine biodiversity, 251
  Philippines, 298
  pollution damage to, *7*
Cost of clean-up, contaminated sediments, 72
Cost recovery, 103
  water and sewer, 108–09
Cost-effective waste management, urban areas, 58
Costs and benefits, water and air pollution controls, *110–11*
Cote d'Ivoire, gross domestic product, *4*
Crop production and total land use, developing countries, *230*
Crop yields, 231–32
  Africa, 232
  cereal, *233*
  Latin America, 232
  postharvest losses, 234
  South Asia, 232
Cropland, *216–17*
  by country, *240–41*

continuous cropping, 233
developing countries, 230
expansion, 230
management of, 233
as percent of Earth's land surface, 201
rehabilitation, 234
Cropland expansion
Latin American, 231
sub-Saharan Africa, 231
Crutzen, Paul, *316*
Curitiba, Brazil
integrated transportation and land use, 88
integrated transportation network, *120*

D

Dam construction, and infectious disease,
183
Data needs, of municipalities, 103
Decentralization
Cajamarca, Peru, *128*
Quito, Ecuador, 131
Deforestation, 63
see also Forest degradation and destruction;
Forests, defoliation
and air pollution, xiv
definition, 203
effects upon measure of produced assets, *160*
Europe, 210
Middle East, 204, 210
North Africa, 204, 210
Deforestation rate
by country, *204*
tropical forests, *205, 209*
Delhi, India
Action for Security Health for All (ASHA), *38*
housing, 40
tax collection, 130
transportation, *90–91*
urban poverty, *38*
Dependency ratio, urban-rural, *150–51*
Depression, and urbanization, 31
Detroit
infant mortality, *16*
national redevelopment grant, *17*
suburban flight, *16*
Developed countries
see also specific countries
causes of death, 32, 179, *180*
chronic and degenerative diseases, 32
dependence on imported energy, 274
fertility rate, 174
forest degradation, 201
forested area, 201
indoor air pollution, 114
infant mortality, 179
life expectancy, 177
national wealth, *160*
population trends, 3, *174, 175*
threats to public health, 31–32
toxic wastes, 24
urban consumption and waste generation, *57*
urban environments, ix
urban-to-urban migration, 3
water management, 109
Developing countries
see also specific countries
agriculture research and extension service,
236
air pollution, 86
Berlin Mandate, *322*
biomass fuels, 63

carbon dioxide emissions, 318–19
causes of death, 34, *180*
causes of urban problems, 18
cereals, 227
crop production and total land use, *230*
croplands, 230
empowerment of women, 176
energy consumption, 273–75
fertility rate, 174
food security, *229*
food yield, *226*
forest degradation, 201
grain imports projected, 236
growth in crop yields, *227*
health, 178
housing, 15
indoor air pollution, 22, 114
industrial pollution, 164
industry location, 66
infant mortality, 179
institutional capacity, 110
jurisdictional complexity, 27
land transformation, 201
life expectancy, 32, 177
local governments, 126
maize, 227, *227*
mosquitos and flies, 41
national wealth, *160*
political accountability in major cities, *126*
population growth, 1, 3
population trends, 173, *174*
risks of occupational hazards, 45
solid and hazardous wastes, 23
solid waste management, 112
strengthening local governments, 126–31
toxic waste, 24
traffic accidents, 47, 87
urban environments, x
urban expansion, 59
urban growth, 4, *4*
urban poor, 1–2
urban transportation, 81
urbanization, 1
water pollution, 302
water and sanitation, 19
Development, and coastal ecosystems, 248,
249
Development assistance, and external debt,
168–69
Diarrhea, *111, 181*
Dioxins, 256
Disease Intelligence Unit, World Health Organization (WHO), *43*
Disease surveillance, 186–87
Pan American Health Organization, 187
World Health Organization, 187
Disease transmission
hospital-acquired infections, 185
international travel and commerce, 185
overcrowding, 184
Diseases
see also Infectious disease
AIDS, 4, 37, 177–78, 180, 184–85
break-bone fever. *see* Diseases, dengue
cancer, 179
cholera, *43*, 180–81, *183*, 186
chronic diseases as a cause of death, 179
communicable diseases, 180
cryptosporidiosis, 186
dengue, 180, 184–85
diarrheal diseases, 180
diphtheria, *20*, 184, 186
eastern equine encephalitis, *183*

emerging or reemerging, 180–81
hantavirus, 181–82, *182*
heart disease, 179
hemorrhagic fever, 181
hepatitis, *20*
HIV, 180, 184
influenza, 185
Japanese encephalitis, *182*
Lyme disease, *183*
malaria, *43*, 180, *182, 183*
measles, 186
nosocomial infections, 185
occupational, 45
plague, 181, *182*, 185
polio, 180
Rift Valley fever, 183
smallpox, 180, 185
tuberculosis (TB), *20*, 180, 184–85
vector-borne, *182*
West Nile fever, *182*
yellow fever, 180
Disposable diapers, and solid waste, 44
Dolphins, die-offs, 249, 256
Douglass, Mike, 145
Drainage channels, and flood control, *121*
Drinking, and socioeconomic status, 48
Drinking water, safe
see also Freshwater; Groundwater; River basins; Water
access to, x, 1, *152–53*
Drug abuse, and urbanization, x, 31
Duckweed, and wastewater treatment, 110

E

Earth Summit, *128, 144*, 211, 315
East Africa, marine biodiversity, *252*
East Asia
education of women, 176
fertility rate, 175
genuine savings, *160*
East Calcutta, India, wetland loss, 62
Eastern Europe, urban poverty, 12
Ebola virus, 181
"Ecological footprint," of cities, 58
Economic costs, urban environmental degradation, 24
Economic development
environmental Kuznets curves, 163
and global environmental goals, 213
Economic efficiency, 103
Economic growth
access to jobs, 84
and air pollution, 113
energy demand, 277–78
and environmental degradation, 25
and environmental protection, 2, 25
and environmental quality, 159, 162–65
rural-urban trade links, 84–85
and social dislocation and alienation, 134
and social and economic inequities, 134
Economic incentives, and zoning, *121*
Economic indicators
alternative methods of measurement, 159
genuine saving, *160*
human capital, *160*
natural capital, *160*
produced assets, *160*
wealth, *160*

Economic inequality, and gross domestic product, 162

Economic opportunity
and environmental improvement, *5*
urbanization, 3

Economic policy instruments, solid waste collection, 112

Economic productivity, and human health, *104*

Economic rationale, pollution prevention, 116

Economic and regulatory instruments
industrial effluents, 111
urban environment, 104
urban pollution control, *106*

Economic sustainability
see also Sustainable development
conventional economic indicators, 161

Economist's (The) Big Mac ™ index, purchase power parity, *162*

"ECOPROFIT Label," pollution reduction incentive, *129*

Ecosystem based units, and land use planning, 121

Ecosystem change, and infectious disease, *182–83*

Ecosystem diversity, 251

Ecosystems at risk, coastal habitats, xiv

Education
and children's health, *196–97*
females, *32*

Education of women, and population growth, 176

Educational opportunities, urban, 10

Efficient use of resources, and minimization of waste, 145

El Molino, Mexico City, 135

El Nino/Southern Oscillation (ENSO) events
cholera, 186
vector-borne disease, *182*

Electric buses, 142

Electric power plants, ambient air pollution, 18

Electric vehicles, *69*

Elizabeth, New Jersey, *33*

Emission standards
enforcement, 24
Jakarta, Indonesia, 7
and taxes, *104*

Emissions
abatement, 315, 323
control, 324
projections, 317
stabilization, 319
of various transportation modes, *93*

Emissions reductions
economic benefits, 322–24
timing, 321

Endangered species. *see* Threatened and endangered species

Energy
alternative fuels, 97
and climate, xiii
commercial reserves and resources, *288–89*
conservation, 115, 145
demand, 273, 277–78, 282
efficiency, 58, *280–81*, 282
fuel consumption, 82
and materials, 273–82

patterns of use, 62–63
policies, 115, 273, 278, *281*, 282, 324
prices, *281*
pricing, 324
subsidies, 273, 282
sustainable supply, *280*
technologies, *322–23*, 324
trends, 273

Energy consumption, *274, 286–87*
and air pollution, 85
biomass, 278
commercial, *275*
constraints, 279, 282
developing countries, 273
environmental costs, 279
industrialization, 273
and land use planning, 119
projections, *280–81*
taxes, 282
and urban sprawl, 59

Energy consumption and production, 273
commercial, *284–85*
patterns, 114, 274, 282
pollution, 273
transition countries, 274, *274*

Energy demand, and greenhouse gas emissions, 2

Energy generation, and air pollution, 113

Energy infrastructure, 279, 282

Energy production and distribution facilities
investment capital, 273, 279, 282
privatization, 273
technology, 273

Energy resources, 275–77
alternative sources, 324
environmental constraints, 273
geological constraints, 273
natural gas, 276
other sources, 277–79
petroleum, 275, 278
renewable, xiii, 273, 278–79, *280*, 318, *323*
solid fuel (coal, lignite, peat), 276
urban impacts on, 63

Energy sector emissions
decisions made at national level, 114
reduction of, 114–15

Energy-driven equipment, technology, 273

ENSO. *see* El Nino/Southern Oscillation events

Environment
see also Urban environment
and agriculture, *232*
and cities, 1–27
definition, *33*
and urban form, 118

Environment protection, and cities, *13*

Environmental costs, and energy consumption, 279

Environmental damage prevention, 121

Environmental degradation
and agricultural production, 229
and urban poor, 15

Environmental degradation, irreversible, examples, 164

Environmental deterioration, and globalization, 7

Environmental education, 140

Environmental health risks, Quito, Ecuador, 38

Environmental impact
and city location, 59

poor cities, 57
of urban poor, 18
of urban wealthy, 18
wealthy cities, 57

Environmental improvement
and commercial enterprises, 134
and community membership, 135
and household security, 135
and housing security, 15

Environmental improvements, marketing opportunity, 142

Environmental indicators, by income level of country, *19*

Environmental initiatives
community involvement, *128–29*
local, *128–29*

"Environmental justice," and urban poor, 15

Environmental Kuznets curves
carbon dioxide emissions, 165
economic development, 163

Environmental laws and regulations, spatial planning law, Jakarta, 7

Environmental management
administrative legal resources, 125
community-level approach, 131
and income generation, 134
integrating into life of urban poor, 134–35
jurisdictional complexity, 26
political will, 125
public support, 125
in very large cities, 16
women's role in, 136

Environmental priorities, methods of establishing, *142*

Environmental protection
and economic growth, 2, 25
expenditures in urban areas, 58

Environmental quality, and economic growth, 159, 164

Environmental sustainability
city and community, 125
cost-effectiveness, 142
urban populations, xi

"Epidemiological transition," 32

Equity, among races, genders, nations and regions, 173

Erosion control, 235
Chesapeake Bay, 73

Estuarine ecosystems, mangroves and seagrass, 251

Estuary hydrology, and shoreline development, 61

Ethanol, 97

Europe
coastal ecosystems, 248
deforestation, 210

Eutrophication, 71, 254, 256
Baltic Sea, 71
Chesapeake Bay, 71, 74
Hong Kong, 76

Exclusive economic zone (EEZ), 260

Extension service, Brazilian Institute of Municipal Administration, 130

External debt
and development assistance, *168–69*
sub-Saharan Africa, 225

F

Family planning, *132–33*
   costs, 176
   programs, 176
Family planning programs, and population trends, 173
FAO assessment summary, forests, *203*
Favela dwellers, Rio de Janeiro, Brazil, 60
Fecal-oral route diseases, and sanitation, 41
Fertility rates
   by country, *192–93*
   and contraception, 175
   as a critical indicator of demographic stability, 173
   and population trends, 173
   urban-rural, *32*
   and urbanization, 174
Fertilizers
   consumption, 232, *240–41*
   organic, 233
Financial resources, community-based development, 140
Fish
   conservation measures, 300
   in human diet, *296*
   international management controls, 300
   mercury content, 7
   prices, *296*
   threatened species, *266–67*
Fish and shellfish
   contamination, 186
   declining catches, 71–72
   nurseries, 254
Fish stocks, *252*
   decline, 249–51, 298
   monitoring, 300
Fisheries
   Code of Conduct for Responsible Fisheries, 300
   open access, 297
   overcapacity, 297
   productivity, 228
   and urban sewage, 72
   and water, 295–304
Fisheries management, 295
   international cooperation, 300
   for recovery and sustainability, 299
Fishing
   aquarium market, 253
   ban on drift nets, 300
   blast fishing, 255, 298
   catch regulations, 260
   community-based management, 300
   discards, 298, *299*
   finning, 296
   fleet reduction, 299
   global catch, *296*
   inspection and reporting requirements for boats, 300
   marine mammals, 298
   overexploitation, 255
   overfishing, 295–96
   policy failures, 295
   quotas, 258, 299–300
   shrimp trawling, 299
   subsidies, 297–99
   trawling, 255
   unemployment, 295
   wasteful practices, 298
   world's fishing fleet, *298*
Flood control, 60

and drainage channels, *121*
Florida Everglades, water diversion, 301
Florida Keys National Marine Sanctuary, 254
Food
   access to, 236
   and agricultural production, *238–39*
   handling and storage practices, 41
   regulation and inspection, 41
Food and agriculture
   production and trade, 225–26
   recent trends, 225–27
   yields, 226–27
Food and Agriculture Organization of the United Nations (FAO), 228, 296, 300
   Forest Resources Assessment, 201
   forests, *206*
Food aid
   development projects, 227
   and food trade, *244–45*
Food contamination, 40–41
   and child mortality, 40
Food production, 228
   Asia, 225
   growth, 229
   Latin America, 225
   and population growth, 229
   rice hybrids, *230*
   and social disintegration, 228
   and soil erosion, 228
   South Asia, 229
   Soviet Union (former), 225
   sub-Saharan Africa, 229
   temperate zone nations, 228
   trends, 225, *226*
   water scarcity, 228
Food production potential, World Bank study, 228
Food security, 228, 235–36
   chronic undernutrition, 236
   and civil strife, 236
   developing countries, *229*
   overfishing, xii
   soil erosion and degradation, xii
   sub-Saharan Africa, 225
   and urban expansion, 60
Food trade, and food aid, *244–45*
Food yield, developing countries, *226*
Forest, definition, 203
Forest condition
   measures of, 208
   and satellite imagery, 210–11
Forest cover
   changes in extent and distribution, 203
   land area, *202*
   North America, 205
   original (prehistoric), 205
   tropical, 165
   uniformity, 210
Forest degradation and destruction
   acid precipitation, 23
   biomass loss, 208
   Chernobyl nuclear power plant accident, *206*
   developed countries, 201
   developing countries, 201
   forecast, 164–65
   habitat fragmentation, 208–09
   industrial emissions, *206*
   logging, *206*
   and microclimate changes, *209*
   permafrost zone, *206*
Forest management

   criteria and indicators for sustainability, 212
   fire suppression, 210
   institutional and legal structures, *207*
   non-European Montreal process, 212
   Pan-European Helsinki process, 212
   Russian Federation, *206–07*
   sustainability, xiv, 201, 213
Forest regions, by country, *202*
Forest resources, *218–19*
Forest Resources Assessment, Food and Agriculture Organization (FAO), 201
Forest Stewardship Council (FSC), 213
Forested area, developed countries, 201
Forests
   see also Deforestation; Tropical forests
   boreal, *206*, 212
   defoliation, *210*
   efficient use of, 213
   European, *210*
   FAO assessment summary, *203*
   and land cover, 201–21
   natural, *218–19*
   naturalness, 208
   noneconomic values and trade, 213
   plantation area, *205*
   policy instruments, 211
   and pollution, 201
   protection laws, *209*
   Siberian, *206*
   state of, 201
   temperate, 204–05, *206*, 209–10, 212
   their role and value, 201
   and trade, 212
   and woodland, *216–17*
Fossil fuels, 273, 279
   and carbon dioxide, 317
   consumption and production, xiii
Fossil fuels consumption, and cement manufacture, *330*
Framework Convention on Climate Change, *129*, 211, 315, *322*, 324
Freshwater management, international cooperation, 304
Freshwater supplies, 302
   management of shared watersheds and river basins, xii
   policies that conserve, xii
   water pricing, xii

G

"Garbage Purchase" program, trash collection, *121*
"Garbage That Is Not Garbage," recycling, *121*
Gender, and human development, *176*
Genuine Progress Indicator, *160*
Genuine savings, definition, 161
Geothermal fuel, *284–85*
GLASOD (a survey of soil degradation), International Soil Reference and Information Center, 233
Global climate change, xiv
Global Climate Convention, xiv, *281*
Global Environment Facility (GEF), *322*
Global environmental goals, and economic development, 213
Global warming, 86, 211, 279, *322*
   adaption strategies, 324
   climate change, 317

damages, 322
and infectious disease, *182*
and marine biodiversity, 257
policy responses to, *323*
rate of, *321*
threat to coastal cities, 70
and wetlands, 257
Globalism, and exacerbation of inequities, 11
Globalization, and environmental deterioration, 11
Governments at all levels, and urban environmental management, 125
Government's role, in urban environmental management, 125
Grain imports projected, developing countries, 236
Graz, Austria, pollution reduction, *129*
Great Barrier Reef Marine Park Authority, 258
"Green performance" ratings, of manufacturing facilities, 116
Green Revolution, 226
Greenbelts, 118
Greenhouse gas emissions, xiv, 57–58, 67, 70, 86, 282, 315, *317*, 319, 322, *322–23*, *328–29*
and agriculture, *232*
climate change, 273, 279
concentration stabilization, *322*
and energy demand, 2
national inventories, *331*
Greenhouse and ozone-depleting gases, atmospheric concentrations, *330*
Greenhouse warming, *115*, 320
Gridlock, 81, 85, *85*
Grocery stores, *139*
Gross domestic product (GDP), *166–67*
in constant 1985 international dollars, *164*
Japan, *164*
as measure of economic progress, 159, 161
United States, *164*
Gross national product (GNP), *166–67*
as measure of economic progress, 159
Groundwater, extraction, *232*
Guatemala City
Chinautla water supply, 107
solid and hazardous wastes, 23
Guerrero, Rodrigo, *139*

H

Habitat destruction, 260
Habitat fragmentation, and forest degradation, 208–09
Habitat II (United Nations Conference on Human Settlements), ix
Habitat International Coalition, 140, *144*
Habitat loss
and coastal development, 254
marine species, 254
Hamilton-Wentworth, Canada, public consultation process, *128*
Harvesters, *240–41*
Havana, bicycling, 95
Hazardous wastes, 23
Bangkok, Thailand, 23
Health

and an aging population, 175
and built environment, 187
and economic productivity, *104*
expenditures, *194–95*
and human development, 178
and industrialization, 187
occupational exposures to hazards, 45
and relative inequality, 49
self-help initiatives, 132–33, 137, *139*
and social marginalization, 48
and socioeconomic inequities, 32
and socioeconomic status, 48
trends, 178
and urban physical environment, 37
urban poor, 15
and urban poverty, 38
and urban social environment, 48–51
and urbanization, 187
women, 17, 22, 36–37, *38*, 42, *132–33*
Health inequalities, urban population, 35
Health profiles
differences among cities, 32
urban dwellers, 32
Health risks
Kansas City, Missouri, 35
London, 35
New York City, 35
for urban children, 35–36
for urban women, 36–37
Health services
mobile health training teams, *133*
preventive, 178, 186
urban, 10
Health solutions, and community perceptions, *51*
"Health transition," 32
Health of urban dwellers, multisectoral strategies, 52
Healthy Cities Project, *144*
Heart disease, and socioeconomic status, 48
Helsinki Declaration of Action for Environment and Health in Europe, 48
Hepatitis, *110–11*
Higher plants, threatened species, *264–65*
HIV (human immunodeficiency virus). *see* Diseases, HIV
Honduras, community action, *134*
Hong Kong, 75–76
land reclamation, 75
water pollution, 75–76
Housefly, and sanitation, 41
Household environmental indicators
Accra, Ghana, *46*
Jakarta, Indonesia, *46*
Sao Paulo, Brazil, *46*
Household environmental management, income-generating activities, 135
Household environmental problems
megacities, *46*
wealth and city size, *46*
Household and neighborhood problems, 39–44
Household security, and environmental improvement, 135
Household stability, and community membership, 135
Housing
Delhi, India, 40
favelas (squatter settlements) of Rio de Janeiro, Brazil, 11

jhuggi-jhopri settlements, *91*
jhuggies, 38
kampung villages of Jakarta, 6
katchi abadi, *132*
over-water settlements, 15
squatter settlements, 4, 15, *38*, 60
urban housing, 40
for urban poor, 15
Housing security
and environmental improvement, 15
and urban poor, 15
Human behavior, and disease, 183–84
Human capital, as an economic indicator, *160*
Human demographics and behavior, and disease, 183–84
Human development
definition, 176
and education of women, 176
indicators by gender and opportunity, 176
and population, 173–87
trends, 176
Human Development Index, *160*, 176
Human Development Report, 173
Human health
and urban environment, 31
urban poverty, 31
Human immunodeficiency virus (HIV). *see* Diseases, HIV
Human and social capital
degradation of, 159
as a measure of economic well-being, 159
Human well-being, and urbanization, 1
Hydrocarbon emissions, *68*
Hydrocarbons, 86, 90
Hydroelectric power, *288–89*
Hydrological cycle, 301
Hydrology of wetlands and estuaries, and shoreline development, 61–62
Hydropower, *284–85*
environmental and social opposition, 278–79
Hyundai Corporation, clear-cutting, *206*

I

ICP. *see* International Comparison Project
Incineration, of solid waste, 70
Income
of cities, 17–18
of urban households, 18
Income generation, and environmental management, 134–35
Income level of cities, air pollution, 18
Income level of country
access to safe water, *19*
air pollution, *19*
environmental indicators, *19*
municipal wastes, *19*
Increased income, and urban environmental indicators, 163
India
city indicators, *154*
household connections to utilities, *154*
household income by cities, *154*
plague epidemic, 42
population by cities, *154*
reliance on coal, 319
social development by cities, *154*
transportation paradigm, *90–91*

Indian National Family Health Survey, 1992-93, 175

India's National Institute for Communicable Diseases, plague research unit, *43*

Individual transferable quotas (ITQs), 299–300
  see also Fishing, quotas

Indo-Western Pacific, *252*
  coastal ecosystems, *253*

Indoor air pollution, 22, 114
  children's health, 22
  cigarette smoking, 114
  developed countries, 114
  developing countries, 114
  low quality fuels, 22
  and pest control, 41
  rural environments, 42
  sick building syndrome, 44
  smoke from cookstoves, 36, 114
  smoky household fires, 42–43
  strategies to reduce, 114
  women, 22

Indore, India, drainage improvement project, *50*

Industrial air pollution, 113
  see also Air pollution
  carbon dioxide, *318, 326–27*
  forest degradation, *206*

Industrial pollution, 58
  developing countries, 164
  and effluent taxes, *106*
  emission permits, *106*
  metal plating operations, 72
  pulp mills, 72
  refineries, 72
  sewer fees, *106*
  tanneries, 72
  and urban runoff, 72

Industrial solvents, *68*

Industrial waste management options, 115–16

Industrial wastes
  Hong Kong, 76
  in selected countries, *292*
  and wastewater treatment, 111

Industrialization
  and energy consumption, 273
  and human health, 187
  and urbanization, 3

Industry and commerce, advantages of urbanization, 10

Infant health, exposure to lead, 47

Infant mortality, *194–95*
  see also Child mortality
  Abidjan, Cote d'Ivoire, *5*
  Detroit, *16*
  influencing factors, 179
  Jakarta, Indonesia, 6
  Manila, Philippines, 35
  urban areas, 36
  urbanization, 31, 179

Infectious disease, 179–83
  see also Diseases
  access to health care and sanitation, 180
  drug development, 187
  drug resistance, 185
  microbial adaptation and change, 185
  and overcrowding, 184, 186
  and sanitation, 186
  vaccines, 185, 187
  waterborne illnesses, 186

Information clearinghouses, pollution prevention, 116

Information sources on urban areas, 149

Infrastructure
  replacement decisions, 321
  transportation, 119
  water and sanitation, 110

Infrastructure costs, urban sprawl, 59

Inner cities
  public transportation, *16*
  urban poverty, 12

Inner-city neighborhoods, *33*
  see also Cities, neighborhoods
  Elizabeth, New Jersey, *33*

Institute for Chemical Engineering, Graz University of Technology, *129*

Institute for Sustainable Development (ISD), 205

Institutional capacity, developing countries, 110

Institutional and legal structures, forest management, 207

Institutional structure, and political power, 126–27

Insurance industry, stable climate, *323*

Integrated approaches, resource protection, 73

Integrated coastal zone management, 259

Integrated Coastal Zone Management (ICZM), 73

Integrated transportation and land use planning, Curitiba, Brazil, *120–21*

InterAction Council of Former Heads of State and Government, 212

Intergovernmental Panel on Climate Change (IPCC), xiv, *317*

Intergovernmental Panel on Forests, 212

International agreements, marine resources protection, 259

International Cities for Climate Protection Campaign, *129*

International Civil Aviation Organization, quarantine measures, *43*

International Comparison Project (ICP), purchasing power parity, *162*

International Convention on the Prevention of Pollution from Ships (MARPOL), MARPOL Protocol, 259

International cooperation
  chlorofluorocarbons (CFCs), *316*
  climate protection, *323*
  criteria for sustainable management of tropical forests, 212
  emissions control, 324
  fisheries management, 300
  freshwater management, 304
  International Comparison Project (ICP), *162*

International Council for Local Environmental Initiatives (ICLEI), 115, *144*
  Urban CO$_2$ Reduction Program, *129*

International Drinking Water Supply and Sanitation Decade, 19, 105

International Energy Agency (IEA), 278, *280–81*

International Food Policy Research Institute (IFPRI), 236

International Monetary Fund, purchasing power parity, *162*

International Soil Reference and Information Center, GLASOD (a survey of soil degradation), 233

International Tropical Timber Agreement (ITTA), 212–13

International Tropical Timber Organization (ITTO), sustainable management of tropical forests, 212

International Union of Local Authorities, *144*

International urban environment programs, *144*

Iron ore, *290–91*

Irrigation, *240–41*, 301, 303
  expansion, 231
  improvements, 234
  and salinization of soil, 231

Island nations, and global warming, 323

Izmir, Turkey, pollution control, *107*

J

Jacksonville, Florida, city-county consolidation, *16*

Jakarta Bay
  coral reefs, 7
  mercury contamination, 72

Jakarta, Indonesia, 6–7
  household environmental indicators, *46*
  kampung villages, 6
  natural resource extraction, 62

Japan, per capita gross domestic product (GDP), *164*

K

Kampung Improvement Project, Jakarta, Indonesia, 7

Kampung villages, Jakarta, Indonesia, 6

Kane, Hal, 228

Kansas City, Missouri, health risks, 35

Karachi, Pakistan
  community involvement and participation, 106
  Orangi Pilot Project, 106, *132–33*

Kathmandu, Nepal, nongovernmental organizations, 137

Kenya
  demographics and health, *10*
  urban-rural population, *10*

Kikwit, Zaire
  hemorrhagic fever, 181
  reemerging disease, 180

Kochcice, Poland, wastewater treatment, 110

Krakow, Poland, lung cancer, *20*

Kuznets curves. *see* Environmental Kuznets curves

L

La Paz, Bolivia, *2*
  Squatter settlement, *118*

Labor force, and population growth, *190–91*

Lagoons, *253*

Land

see also Cropland; Rangelands
area under forest cover, *202*
for housing, 117
resources protection, 117
Land area and use, *216–17*
Land conservation, dense settlement patterns, 58
Land conversion, 58–62
aquaculture, *232*
urban impacts on, 57
Land cover, and forests, 201–21
Land degradation, overgrazing, 233
Land and housing tenure, and security, 136
Land ownership, *latifundia* land system of Brazil, 11
Land reclamation
coastlines, 61
Hong Kong, 75
San Francisco Bay, 61
Singapore, 61
Land redistribution
land banking, 117
land readjustment, 117
land sharing, 117
land tenure security, 117
Land subsidence, 64, *64*
Bangkok, Thailand, 64
Jakarta, Indonesia, 7
Land transformation, developing countries, 201
Land use
"brownfield" sites, *16*
greenbelts, 118
priorities for action, 116–21
and transportation, 87–88, 119
and transportation strategy, 87–88
urban growth boundaries, 118
watersheds, 254
Land use changes, Sao Paulo, Brazil, *60*
Land use patterns, and urban form, 116
Land use planning
by region, 120
and ecosystem based units, 121
and energy consumption, 119
siting and density of urban industries, 118
and transportation, *120–21*
and urban densities, 118–19
and urban environment, 116
Land use planning laws, *209*
Land and water resources, agricultural growth, *232*
Landfills, for deposit of solid waste, 70
Large marine ecosystem (LME), 259
Latin America
cholera, 180
crop yields, 232
cropland expansion, 230–31
education of women, 176
energy demand, 278
fertility rate, 175
food production, 225
tropical forests, 205, 211
urban poverty, 12
urbanization, 3
Laws. *see* Environmental laws and regulations
Lead, 20, 22–24, 38, 45, 47, 86, *104*
air pollution in selected cities, *154*
as a commodity, *290–91*
Lead pollution, Bangkok, Thailand, 47

Legalizing settlements, tenure and provision of services, 137
Leicester, England, national grant for inner-city cleanup, *16*
Leishmaniasis, and sand flies, 41
Lerner, Jaime, *120*
Life expectancy
as an indicator of human well-being, 173
by country, *192–93*
developed countries, 177
developing countries, 32, 177
Jakarta, Indonesia, 6
trends, 177–78
trends in Russia, 178
urban, 10
and urbanization, 31
and water and sanitation, *105*
women, 176
Light rail transit, 94
Lignite, *104*
Lima, Peru, water prices, 20
Linear material flows, manufacturing, 18
Literacy
female, 176, *196–97*
male, *196–97*
Livestock production
feed consumption, *242–43*
populations of animals, *242–43*
Local Agenda 21
developing local indicators, *128*
United Nations Conference on Environment and Development (UNCED), *128*
Local government personnel
building technical and professional competences, 127, 130
training, 130
Local governments, *138*
components of strong institutional capacity, 126
developing countries, 126
generating revenue, 127
and industry, 131
and nongovernmental organizations, 131
and parastatal service companies, *129*
and partnerships, 127, 130–31
primary responsibilities, 126
and privatization, 130–31
and urban environment, 125–27
Local Initiative Facility for Urban Environment (LIFE), *144*
Logging, *209, 218–19*
and biodiversity, *208–09*
clear-cutting, *206*
and economically vulnerable countries, *208–09*
forest degradation, *206*
technologies, *206–07*
London, health risks, 35
Los Angeles, air pollution, 68–69

M

Mabogunje, Akin L., *143*
Madras, India, scavengers, 112–13
Mahila Mandals, Delhi, India, *39*
Mahogany (*Swietenia macrophylla*), 212
Maize, *230*
developing countries, 227, *227*

Making the Land Use-Transportation-Air Quality Connection, One Thousand Friends of Oregon, *92*
Males, mortality in Russia, 177
Mammals, threatened species, *264–65*
Mangrove areas, location, *255*
Mangroves, 253–54, 301
degradation and destruction, 253–54
extent and loss, *256*
Manila, Philippines, wastepicking, *112*
Manila, Philippines, infant mortality, 35
Manufacturing
"clean" production, 18
linear material flows, 18
Marine biodiversity, 247, 249–54, 260, *268–69*
Asia, *252*
Australia, *252*
coastal ecosystems, 248
East Africa, *252*
and global warming, 257
Pacific Islands, *252*
pressures on, 254
tools for protecting, 258
Marine biological productivity
and coastal ecosystems, 251
definition, 251
Marine catch, trends, *296*
Marine debris, 257
Marine ecosystems
and human survival, 249
and regional warming, 257
Marine endemism, and conservation, *252*
Marine fish catch, 253
Marine fish stocks, 301
Marine fisheries, yield and state of exploitation, *309*
Marine fishing trends, 295
Marine and freshwater catches, aquaculture, and fish consumption, *310–11*
Marine habitat loss, urbanization, 248, 254
Marine mammals, 249
pollution, 256
threatened and endangered species, 255
Marine parks, Hong Kong, 76
Marine pollution, major sources, 257
Marine populations and species, trends, 250
Marine protected areas (MPAs), *252*, 258–59
assessment, 258
potentially threatened, *250*
Marine resources management, inadequate institutional structures, 254
Marine resources protection, international agreements, 259
Marine species
conservation priorities, *252*
documenting extinction, 251
extent and variety, 250
habitat loss, 254
introduction, 257
loss of breeding habitat, 251
overexploitation, 255
pollution susceptibility, 251
richness and conservation, *252*
spawning grounds, 251
Marine species introduction, 257
see also Species introduction

Marketing opportunity, environmental improvements, 142

MARPOL Protocol, International Convention on the Prevention of Pollution from Ships (MARPOL), 259

Materials, and energy, 273–82

Maternal mortality, 194–95

Mathare Slum Upgrading Scheme, Nairobi, Kenya, 5

Megacities, 6, 8
  defined, 8
  household environmental problems, 46
  population and growth rate, 9
  water shortages, 63

Melrose Commons, Nos Quedamos Committee, 141

Menon, Subhadra, 52

Mercury, 290–91

Mercury contamination
  Jakarta Bay, 72
  Minamata Bay, 72

Mercury content in fish, 7

Metal plating operations, industrial pollution, 72

Metals, production, consumption, reserves, 290–91

Methane, 232, 315
  from anthropogenic sources, 328–29, 331

Metropolitan Environmental Improvement Program (MEIP), 144

Mexico City
  air pollution, 20, 24, 67
  El Molino, 135
  Metropolitan Commission for the Protection of Air Quality, 131
  water supply, 64–65

Microclimate changes, and forest degradation, 209

Microenterprise system, 139

Microenterprises, Ndolo, Zambia, 5

Middle East, deforestation, 204, 210

Migration
  AIDS, 184
  diversity among migrants, 11
  infectious disease, 181
  and natural population increase, 11
  rural-to-urban, 7
  urban, 4
  urban-to-urban, 3

Minamata Bay, mercury contamination, 72

Minimization of waste, and efficient use of resources, 145

Mining
  land degradation, 279
  water pollution, 279

Mites, and scabies, 41

Mixed farming systems, 235

Mobility, urban dwellers, 81

Moisture conservation, 235

Molina, Mario, 316

Monitoring and enforcement
  air quality standards, 114
  regulatory tools, 106–07

Monrovia, Liberia, food contamination, 41

Montreal Protocol, 322
  Vienna Framework Convention on Ozone-Degrading Substances, 316

Mortality
  see also child mortality, infant mortality, maternal mortality
  causes of death, 179–80, 179–80
  infectious and parasitic disease, 181
  and nutrition, 194–95
  and population trends, 173
  roadway death rates, 87

Mortality rates, traffic accidents, 47

Mortality rates by socioenvironmental zones
  Accra, Ghana, 49
  Sao Paulo, Brazil, 49

Mosquitos and flies, developing countries, 41

Motor vehicles
  see also Transportation, modes of
  and air pollution, 86, 97–98
  and ambient air pollution, 45
  growth in ownership, 82–83, 83
  improved efficiency, 82
  inspection and maintenance, 97–98
  taxes and pollution fees, 89, 92
  transportation, 81
  two and three wheel, 82–83, 90
  urban air pollution, 22, 86

Multifamily kitchens, community networks, 135

Multisectoral strategies, for improving health of urban dwellers, 52

Municipal governments
  and energy consumption patterns of residents, 114
  participatory planning processes, 131
  and taxes, 127
  their role in pollution prevention, 116

Municipal partnerships, 103

Municipal revenue sources, selected countries, 127

Muungano Women's Group, Nairobi, Kenya, 136–37

Mycobacterium tuberculosis, 184
  see also Diseases, tuberculosis

N

Nairobi, Kenya, 14
  Mathare Slum Upgrading Scheme, 5
  Muungano Women's Group, 136–37

National governments
  and energy policies, 115
  national technical assistance programs, 130

National wealth
  see also Wealth
  composition of, 160
  developed countries, 160
  developing countries, 160
  and genuine saving, 160–61

Natural areas, protection of, 262–63

Natural capital, effects upon national wealth, 160

Natural gas, 276, 281, 288–89

Natural resource extraction
  Aligarh City, India, 62
  Jakarta, Indonesia, 62

Natural resource extraction and depletion, urban impacts on, 57–58, 62–65

Natural resources
  degradation or depletion, 164
  management of, 236
  urban impacts on, 57

Natural sinks for carbon dioxide, 317

Ndolo, Zambia, microenterprises, 5

Neighborhood and community issues, collective action, 135

Neighborhoods. see Cities, Neighborhoods; Inner-city neighborhoods

Netherlands, bicycling, 96

Networks, community, 132–33, 135

Neves, Ricardo, 96

New York City, 2
  health risks, 35

Newark, New Jersey, recycling industries, 16

Nickel, 290–91

Nigeria, community banks, 143

Nile River, and Aswan Dam, 254

Nitrogen oxide emissions, 86

Nitrogen oxides, 20, 66, 68–69, 111, 331

Nitrous oxide, 232, 316

Nobel Committee, 316

Nobel Prize in chemistry, 316

Noise pollution, 81, 86–87
  and human hearing, 87
  oceans and seas, 255
  and psychological well-being, 87

Non-European Montreal process, forest management, 212

Noncommunicable diseases, and social environment, 48

Nongovernmental organizations (NGOs), 140, 144, 213
  Abidjan, Cote d'Ivoire, 5
  Action for Security Health for All (ASHA), 38
  community development, 133
  environmental initiatives, 128
  informal waste collection, 112
  Kathmandu, Nepal, 137
  and local governments, 131
  Orangi Pilot Project, 132–33
  partnerships with, 137–40
  and urban environmental management, 125
  as watchdogs for industrial pollution problems, 116

Nonmotorized transportation, bicycles and pedestrians, 96

Nonmotorized vehicles
  links with public transportation, 95–96
  and pedestrians, 95–96

Nordic countries, policies for women's empowerment, 176

North Africa, deforestation, 204, 210

North America
  forest cover, 205
  travel patterns, 84
  urban poverty, 12
  vision of future, 142

Nos Quedamos Committee, Melrose Commons, 141–42

Nuclear fuel, 279

Nuclear power, 280, 284–85
  uranium reserves, 277

Nutrient recycling, 235

Nutrition, xiii
  and mortality, 194–95

O

Occupational hazards
  and climatic conditions, 45
  in urban environment, 45

Ocean temperatures
   amnesic shellfish poisoning, *183*
   and infectious disease, *182–83*
Oceans and seas
   access to fish stocks, 296
   international management controls, 300
   noise pollution, 255
   northern Atlantic, 296
   sea level, *317, 322, 322*
   upwellings, 251, 255
   vent communities, 251
Ogallala aquifer, United States, 301
Oil, *288–89, 318*
   see also Petroleum
   dependence, 275
Oil industry lobbyists, *323*
One Thousand Friends of Oregon, Making
   the Land Use-Transportation-Air Quality
   Connection, *92*
Ontario, Canada, urban expansion, 59
Opportunities for people, 173
   and human development, 176
Orangi Pilot Project, Karachi, Pakistan,
   106, *132–33*
Organisation for Economic Co-Operation
   and Development (OECD), 274, *323*
   motor vehicles, 82
   sewage, 21
   solid and hazardous wastes, 23
Organochlorines, 256
Our Common Future, World Commission
   on Environment and Development, 145
Ozone, *66, 67, 68–69*
   and plant damage, 67
Ozone damage to U.S., cost of, *20, 24*
Ozone hole, Antarctic, *316*
Ozone layer (stratospheric), *315, 316*
Ozone-depleting chemicals, phaseout, ix
Ozone-depleting and greenhouse gases, at-
   mospheric concentrations, *330*

P

Pacific Islands, marine biodiversity, *252*
Palca, Joe, 187
Pan American Health Organization, disease
   surveillance, 187
Pan-European Helsinki process, forest man-
   agement, 212
Paper production, *220–21*
Parastatal service companies, and local gov-
   ernments, *129*
Participatory planning
   Chattanooga, Tennessee, *142*
   municipal governments, 131
Particulate emissions, *86, 111, 331*
   air pollution, *104*
   air pollution in selected cities, *154*
   and premature death, 46
Partnerships
   local governments, 127, 130–31
   nongovernmental organizations (NGOs),
      137–40
   for solid waste collection, 112
Pastureland, *216–17*
Patnaik, Rajesh, *51*
Pedestrians
   and nonmotorized vehicles, 95–96

traffic accidents, 47
Penn World Table, purchasing power parity,
   162
Perkasie, Pennsylvania, solid waste manage-
   ment, 113
Perth, Australia, urban sprawl, *84*
Pest control
   and indoor environmental health threats, 41
   roundwood imports, *206*
Pests
   introduced tree, *206, 210*
   urban areas, 41
Petroconsultants S.A., *276–77*
Petroleum
   see also Oil
   energy resources, 275, 278
   reserves, *275, 276*
Petroleum resources, production, *276–77*
Philippines, coral reefs, 298
Phoenix, solid waste collection, 113
Photovoltaic cells, 279
Plague, bubonic (Black Death), *42*
Plague epidemic
   causes for reemergence, *42*
   cost, *43*
   India, *42–43*
Plague, pneumonic, *42*
Plantation areas, *218–19*
   uniformity, 210
Plantation cover, 208
Policy options, urban environment, 104
Policymaking, definition of environment, *33*
Political accountability in major cities, de-
   veloping countries, *126*
Political power, and institutional structure,
   126–27
Political will, 103
   energy management, 273
Political will of local leaders, 125, 127
Pollutants, anthropogenic, *331*
Pollution, 81
   see also Air pollution; Industrial pollution;
      Noise pollution
   costs of, *104*
   energy production and consumption, 273
   and forests, 201
   marine mammals, 256
   and sedimentation, 255–57
   taxes, 273
   transition economies of Central and Eastern
      Europe, *20*
Pollution control, 260
   Quezon City, Philippines, *129*
   water resources management, 303
Pollution emissions, forecast, *164–65*
Pollution prevention, 103, 145
   as the best solution, 109
   economic rationale, 116
   and industrial emissions, 115
   information clearinghouses, 116
   municipal governments' role, 116
   water, 109
Pollution reduction incentive, "ECO-
   PROFIT Label," *129*
Pollution susceptibility, marine species, 251
Polychlorinated biphenyls (PCBs), 256
Poorest countries, chronic undernutrition,
   225
Population

and human development, 173–87
   regional differences, 175
   regional trends, *175*
   urban population by region, 9
Population Action International, 302
Population growth
   developing countries, 1, 3
   energy demand, 277–79
   and food production, 229
   and labor force, *190–91*
   policies that influence fertility rates, xii
Population growth, xi
Population increase, and migration, 11
Population projection, United States, 175
Population trends, 173–74
   as an indicator of future demands on re-
      sources, 173
   developed countries, 3
   in developed and transitional economies, 173
   and projections, *174*
   urbanization, 174
Portland, Oregon, 98
   bus service, 92
   urban growth boundaries, 92
Ports, and species introduction, 248
Poverty
   and children, 14
   and diphtheria, 184
   and the environment, 25
   and tuberculosis, 184
   and urban economy, 131–34
   in the urban environment, x
   and urban social environment, 48
   and women, 14
Poverty data, by country, *150–51*
Poverty and poor people
   population trends, 173
   women, 176
PPP. *see* Purchasing power parity
Practical Farmers of Iowa, 234
Prague, Czechoslovakia, causes of death, 34
Premature death, and particulate air pollu-
   tion, 46
Primorsky region, biodiversity, *206*
Private enterprises, and urban environ-
   mental management, 125
Private sector, role in solid waste manage-
   ment, 113
Privatization
   energy production facilities, 273
   and local governments, 130–31
   water resource management, 304
Productivity, and traffic congestion, 24
Property tax, 127, 130
Psychosocial illnesses, and urbanization, 31
Public consultation process, Hamilton-
   Wentworth, Canada, *128*
Public health measures, breakdown in, 186
Public participation, and consensus building, *129*
Public transit
   buses, 94
   improving service, 94–95
   privatization, 94–95
   rail transit, 94
Public transportation
   inner city, 16
   and job opportunities, 16
   transportation, modes of, 81

Public transportation lines, and urban growth, 119
Public-Private Partnerships Programme, 144
Pulp mills, industrial pollution, 72
Purchasing power parity (PPP), 166–67
  The Economist's Big Mac ™ index, 162
  definition, 161
  developing countries, 163
  International Comparison Project (ICP), 162
  and market exchange rates, 162
  Penn World Table, 162

Q

Quarantine measures, International Civil Aviation Organization, 43
Quezon City, Philippines, pollution control, 129
Quito, Ecuador
  decentralization, 131
  environmental health risks, 38

R

Rabinovitch, Jonas, 121
Radioactive waste, 256
Rangelands, 232
  see also Pastureland
  overgrazing, 233
  productivity, 228
Rapid transit, 94
Recycling, 135
  in cities, 58
  organic wastes, 135
  solid waste management, 113
  and wastepickers, 51
  water, 109
Red Cross, hemorrhagic fever, 181
Red tides, 249
Refineries, industrial pollution, 72
Regional coastal zone management, Chesapeake Bay, 73–74
Regional land use planning, 120
Regional warming, and marine ecosystems, 257
Regulations. see Environmental laws and regulations
Regulatory tools
  monitoring and enforcement, 106
  urban pollution control, 106
Relative inequality
  and health, 49
  and self-perception, 49
Reptiles, threatened species, 266–67
Research
  energy-efficient technologies, 321
  renewable energy sources, 321
Resource consumption
  urban areas, xi
  and wealth, 2
Resource protection, integrated approaches, 73
Revenue generation, local government, 127
ReVision 2000, Chattanooga, Tennessee, 142
Rice, 227, 230
Rio de Janeiro, Brazil
  favela dwellers, 60

urban poor, 59
water, access to, 37
Risk behaviors, and socioeconomic status, 48
River basins, 304
Road maintenance fees, 89
Road systems
  and commuter journeys, 84
  road pricing, 87–89
Rolesprom, 207
Roots and tubers, yield by country, 238–39
Roundwood imports
  China, 206
  pest control, 206
  United States, 206
Roundwood production, 220–21
Rowland, F. Sherwood, 316
Rural growth rate, by country, 150–51
Russia
  see also Soviet Union (former); Transition countries
  causes of death, 177–78
  health care services, 178
  life expectancy trends, 177
Russian Federation
  forest management, 206–07
  forests, 204, 206–07
  population projection, 175
  timber industry, 207

S

Samarga River watershed, 206
San Francisco Bay
  land reclamation, 61
  wetland conversion, 62
San Miguel Teotongo, Mexico, Union de Vecinos de San Miguel Teotongo (UVST), 137
Sand flies, and leishmaniasis, 41
Sanitary revolution, 37
Sanitation
  access to, 152–53
  and fecal-oral route diseases, 41
  and housefly, 41
  latrines, 40
  low-cost, 132
Sanitation, adequate, access to, by income level of country, 19
Santiago, Chile
  costs and benefits of water and air pollution controls, 110–11
  wastewater disposal, 21
Sao Paulo, Brazil
  and Accra, Ghana, 49–51
  bike paths and lanes, 96
  causes of death, 34
  household environmental indicators, 46
  land use changes, 60
  mortality rates by socioenvironmental zones, 49
  urban expansion, 59
Satellite imagery, and forest condition, 210–11
Scabies, and mites, 41
Scavengers, reducing health risks to, 51
Scavengers, human
  see also Wastepickers
  Abidjan, Cote d'Ivoire, 5

Hanoi, Viet Nam, 12
Schistosomiasis, and snails, 41
School of architecture, partnership with, 138
Seagrass beds, 253
Seals, die-offs, 249, 256
Seattle, 98
  social marginalization, 48
Seawall construction, 61
Security, land and housing tenure, 136
Sedimentation, and pollution, 255–57
Self-perception, and relative inequality, 49
Senegal, charcoal production, 63
Settlement patterns, land conservation, 58
Sewage, 72
  see also Urban sewage
  Organisation for Economic Co-Operation and Development (OECD), 21
Sewage system, Cartegena, Colombia, 106
Sewage-borne pathogens, 72
Sewers, 4
  condominial, 106
  and storm water, 72
  United States, 21
Shoreline development
  coastal erosion, 61–62
  and hydrology of estuaries, 61
Siberia
  forests, 206–07
  Nelma-Sukpai Road, 206
Sick building syndrome, indoor air pollution, 44
Singapore
  area licensing scheme, 89
  land reclamation, 61
Single parent households, urban poor, 135
"Sirdo," recycling organic wastes, 135
Slade, Tuiloma Neroni, 323
Smil, Vaclav, 228
Smoke, air pollution in selected cities, 154
Smokestacks, 115
Smoking, and socioeconomic status, 48
Snails, and schistosomiasis, 41
Social dislocation and alienation, and economic growth, 134
Social and economic inequities, and economic growth, 134
Social environment
  and health, 48–51
  and noncommunicable diseases, 48
Social impact, urbanization, 31
Social inequities
  access to jobs, 87
  transportation, 81, 87
  travel costs, 87
  urban areas, x
Social instability, and unemployment, 48
Social marginalization
  behavior changes, 48
  and health, 48
  Seattle, 48
Social stability, threats to, 25
Socioeconomic inequities, and health, 32
Socioeconomic status
  and cancer, 48
  and drinking, 48
  and health, 48
  and heart disease, 48

and risk behaviors, 48
and smoking, 48
Soil degradation, 63, 232–34
and agricultural production, 234
salinization, 232
survey, 233
Soil erosion, 208, 232
Solid and hazardous wastes, 23
Guatemala City, 23
Tokyo Bay, 23
wastepickers, 23
Solid waste, 44, 70–71
see also Waste disposal
and children, 44
and disposable diapers, 44
generated, 70
incineration, 6
reducing generation of, 113
trash collection, 5
and wastepickers, 44, 112–13, 135
Solid waste collection, 1, 7, 70
see also Trash collection
economic policy instruments, 112
informal waste collection, 112
partnerships for, 112
Solid waste management, x–xi, 111–12
developing countries, 112
partnerships with nongovernmental organizations, 112
partnerships with private sector, 113
pay-per-bag systems, 113
privatization, 113
recycling, 70, 113
and urban consumption, 111
and urban poor, 111
Solid wastes, nontoxic, 257
South Asia
crop yields, 232
food security, 225
national wealth, 160
urban poverty, 12
Southcoast Air Quality Management District, California, 68
Southeast Asia, fertility rate, 175
Southern California Edison, 69
Soviet Union (former)
see also Russia; Russian Federation; Transition countries
food production, 225
forest cover, 205
life expectancy, 177
population, 175
Species
estimated total numbers, 248
habitat loss, 60
introduction, 248–49
Squatter housing, as a percent of total housing stock, 117
Squatter settlements
see also Housing, squatter settlements
access to jobs, 134
Balaju, 137
La Paz, Bolivia, 118
Steel, crude, 290–91
Sub-Saharan Africa
AIDS, 177
chronic undernutrition, 236
cropland expansion, 231
external debt, 225
food production, 229
food security, 225
genuine saving, 160

Suburban flight
Detroit, 16
United States, 59, 87
Sulfur dioxide, 20, 45, 66, 104, 206, 331
air pollution in selected cities, 154
China, 67
Sulfur emissions, 66
Sulfur oxides, 111
Suriname
and ecotourism, 208
forests, 208
Suriname's Forest Service, 209
Sustainability, criteria and indicators for for-
est management, 212
Sustainable Cities Programme, 144
Sustainable development, 206
see also Economic sustainability
and cities, 58, 145
and cities of wealth, 145
definition, 145
equitable distribution of income, 162
Sustainable solutions, cities, 26, 26
Sustainable transportation systems, 87
nonmotorized transportation, 96

T

Tangiers, Morocco, coastal erosion, 62
Tanneries, industrial pollution, 72
Target, 2000, 213
Tax collection, Delhi, India, 130
Taxes
and emission standards, 104
energy consumption, 282
industrial effluents, 106
and municipalities, 127
pollution, 273
property tax, 127, 130
Technologies
cost effectiveness, 103
energy, 322–23
energy-efficient, 324
for reducing carbon dioxide emissions, 321
water and sanitation, 105–07
Technology
energy production facilities, 273
energy-driven equipment, 273
Tegucigalpa, Honduras, Cooperative Housing Foundation (CHF), 139
Temperature, and disease vectors, 182
Temperature extremes, air pollution, 18
Thermal vents. see Oceans and seas, vent
communities
Threatened and endangered species, 211–12
Amur leopard, 206
causes of extinction, 247
hot spots, 252
mammals, birds, and higher plants, 264–65
marine mammals, 255
reptiles, amphibians, and fish, 266–67
Siberian tiger, 206
Three Gorges Project, China, 279
Timber Working Group, 212–13
Tin, 290–91
Tiwari, Geetam, 91
Tokyo Bay, solid and hazardous wastes, 23
Tolls. see Road systems, road pricing
Toronto, Urban CO2 Reduction Project, 115

Toxic wastes
developed countries, 24
developing countries, 24
Tractors, 240–41
Trade
and forests, 212
and noneconomic values of forests, 213
Traffic accidents, 87
developing countries, 47, 87
mortality rates, 47
pedestrians, 47, 87, 90
Traffic congestion, 82, 85, 104
air pollution, 20, 24
motor vehicles, x
and productivity, 24
Traffic jams, losses due to, 25
Transit systems, and commuter journeys, 84
Transition countries of Central and Eastern
Europe
carbon dioxide emissions, 319
energy consumption, 274
energy consumption and production, 274
industrial activity, 18
life expectancy, 177
pollution and health, 20
population trends, 175
reduction in greenhouse gas emissions, 321
and urban poverty, 12
and water pollution, 302
Transportation
see also Urban transportation
and air pollution, 113
frequency of travel, 83
full cost pricing, 88–89
and income, 83
infrastructure, 119
and land use, 88, 119, 120–21
length of trips, 83
managing travel demands, 87–93
parking controls, 93
"smart" cards, 89
and social inequities, 87
traffic bans, 93
urban areas, x
Transportation demands, and urban form,
88
Transportation infrastructure, 93
Transportation, modes of
bicycling, 81, 83, 88, 90–91, 95–96, 96
capacity, cost, and emissions of various, 93
dolmus minibuses, 95
electric cars, 97
jeepneys, 95
kabu-kabus, 95
motor scooters and motorcycles, 90
passenger cars, 82
see also Motor vehicles
public transportation, 81
rickshaws, 90
two-stroke motorcycles, 104
walking, 81, 83, 88, 96
Transportation patterns, and urban density,
83
Transportation strategies
flexible work hours, 104
improving traffic management, 104
and land use, 87–88
up-grading bus service, 104
Trash collection
"garbage purchase" program, 121
urban areas, 44

Travel and commerce, and infectious diseases, 185
Travel patterns, and urban form, 83–84
Triatomine bugs, and chagas' disease, 41
Tropical forests, 205, 210–12
    Africa, 205, 211
    Asia, 205, 211
    condition of, 210
    deforestation, 205, *209*
    degradation and conversion, *211*
    Latin America, 205, 211
    plantation area, *205*
    rainforests, 205, *208*
Typhoid, *110–11*

U

Ultraviolet light, *316*
UNCED. *see* Earth Summit
UNDP. *see* United Nations Development Programme
Unemployment, and social instability, 48
UNEP. *see* United Nations Environment Programme
UNEP Conference on Protection of the Marine Environment from Land-Based Activities, 260
Union Carbide factory accident, Bhopal, India, 15
United Nations, 140, 300
    see also U.N.
United Nations Centre for Human Settlements (Habitat), *144*
    urban data collected, 149
United Nations Children's Fund (UNICEF), 139
    urban data collected, 149
United Nations Conference on Environment and Development (UNCED). *see* Earth Summit
United Nations Conference on Human Settlements, ix
United Nations Conference on Straddling Stocks and Highly Migratory Fish Stocks, 260, 300
United Nations Convention on the Law of the Sea, 259–60, 300
United Nations Convention to Combat Desertification, 233
United Nations Development Programme (UNDP), 140, *144*
    Human Development Index, *160*
    Human Development Report, 173
United Nations Environment Programme (UNEP)
    biodiversity assessment, 247–48
    Regional Seas agreements, 259
    urban data collected, 149
United Nations Population Division, urban data collected, 149
United States
    see also U.S.
    carbon dioxide emissions, 316
    deforestation, 204
    Ogallala aquifer, 301
    per capita gross domestic product (GDP), *164*
    population projection, 175
    roundwood imports, *206*
    sewers, 21

suburban flight, 59, 87
    urban sprawl, 9
Unleaded gasoline, 97
Upwellings, oceans and seas, 251
Ural region, forests, *206*
Uranium, *288–89*
    reserves, 277
Urban air pollution, 22–23, 66–70
    see also Air pollution
    and motor vehicles, 86
    respiratory diseases, 22
Urban area, variously defined, *8*
Urban areas
    see also Cities; Urbanization
    air pollution, 1
    cost-effective waste management, 58
    energy efficiency, 58
    environmental protection expenditures, 58
    natural features, 18
    pests, 41
    priorities for action, 103–21
    water management practices, 63
    water pollution, 1, 302
Urban CO₂ Reduction Project, International Council for Local Environmental Initiatives, 115
Urban consumption
    and solid waste management, 111
    waste disposal, 57
Urban containment policies, and "brownfields," 118
Urban densities, and land use planning, 118–19
Urban density, and transportation patterns, 83
Urban development, and urban land use planning, 60
Urban dwellers
    health profiles, 32
    mobility, 81
    multisectoral strategies for improving health, 52
Urban economy
    interconnections, 134
    and poverty, 131
Urban employment opportunities, 11–12
Urban encroachment, coastlines, 59
Urban environment, ix
    city-wide problems, 44–47
    definition, 32
    economic costs of degradation, 24
    economic and regulatory instruments, 104
    factors effecting improvement, 163
    and human health, 31
    and land use planning, 116
    and local governments, 125–27
    occupational hazards, 45
    policy options, 104
Urban environmental challenge, 25–27
    community involvement, 25
Urban environmental management
    government's role, 125
    stakeholders, 125
Urban environmental problems, 15–24
    associated with economic growth or affluence, 1, 7
    associated with poverty, 1, 7
    determinants of, 16
    exposure to lead, 47
    priorities, 25, 103
    solutions, 25

Urban expansion
    developing countries, 59
    and food security, 60
    and fragile ecosystems, x
    Ontario, Canada, 59
    Sao Paulo, Brazil, 59
Urban form
    compact cities, 88
    dispersion, 83–84
    and environment, 118
    greenbelts, greenways and urban growth boundaries, 88
    and land use patterns, 116
    and manufacturing practices, 84
    mixed land use model, 88
    multinucleated urban regions, 119
    suburbs, 84
    and transportation demands, 88
    and travel patterns, 83–84
Urban growth
    boundaries, 92, 118
    by region, *3*
    causes of, 10–12
    contributors to, 11
    and public transportation lines, 119
    rates, *150–51*
Urban growth patterns, 3–10
    and infrastructure development, 9
    suburbanization, 9
    urban fringe, *4*, 9
    urban sprawl, 9
Urban health
    differences among cities, 32, *33*, 34
    differences within cities, 35–37
Urban health risks, community perceptions, *50*
Urban impacts
    coastal ecosystems, 58
    energy resources, 63
    land conversion, 57–58
    natural resource extraction and depletion, 57–58, 62–65
    natural resources, 57
    waste disposal, 57–58
Urban indicators, *150–51*
Urban land conversion, coastal ecosystems, 60
Urban land use planning, and urban development, 60
Urban Management Programme (UMP), 140, *144*
Urban managers, need for data, 103
Urban market gardens, Accra, Ghana, *5*
Urban migration, and AIDS, 184
Urban parks and plazas, urban renewal, *140*
Urban physical environment, and health, 37
Urban pollution, need for policy intervention, 70
Urban pollution control
    combined approach, *106–07*
    economic instruments, *106*
    regulatory tools, *106*
Urban poor
    access to clean drinking water, 1
    child labor, 14
    community mobilization, 125, *132–33*
    Detroit, *16*
    developed countries, 12–13, 15
    developing countries, 1, *4*
    employment opportunities, 11
    and environmental degradation, 15

and "environmental justice," 15
homelessness, 14
housing, 14–15
and housing security, 15
impact on environment, 57–58
informal transit, 95
participative planning, 131
problems of, x
and road pricing, 89
single parent households, 135
smoky fuels, *44*
and solid waste management, 111
transportation costs, 87, 91
and water subsidies, 108
Urban population
    by country, *150–51*
    by region, *3*
    cities of over one million, *9*
    health inequalities, 35
Urban poverty, 12–14
    Central Europe, 12
    Delhi, India, *38*
    Eastern Europe, 12
    environmental implications, 14
    ethnic minorities, 12
    and health, 38
    human health, 31
    industrial Europe, 12
    inner cities, 12
    isolation of poor minorities, *13*
    and the *latifundia* land system of Brazil, 11
    Latin America, 12
    North America, 12
    South Asia, 12
Urban priorities, access to water and sanitation, 105
Urban redevelopment
    community inputs, *141*
    displacement of residents, *141*
Urban renewal, urban parks and plazas, *140*
Urban runoff, and industrial pollution, 72
Urban sewage, 72
    cost of treatment, 109–10
    and fisheries, 72
    lower cost options, 110
    water pollution, 109
Urban social environment
    and health, 48–51
    and poverty, 48
Urban sprawl, 88
    air pollution, 59
    energy consumption, 59
    infrastructure costs, 59
    low density development, 59
    Perth, Australia, *84*
    transportation, 81, *84*
Urban transportation, 81–99
    see also Transportation
    cost of infrastructure, 84
    costs, 84, 87
    developing world, 81
    patterns of, *83*
    strategies and tools, 87–99
Urban transportation trends, 82–84
    impacts of, 84
Urban unemployment in developed countries, causes of, 12
Urban violence, children's health, 36
Urban wastes, 65
Urban wealthy, environmental impact, 18
Urban-rural health statistics, by selected countries, *32*

Urbanization
    see also Cities; Urban areas
    benefits, 1, 10
    birth rates, 58
    child mortality, 31
    depression, 31
    developing countries, 1
    drug abuse, x, 31
    and economic growth, 10
    economic opportunities, 3
    economies of scale, 10
    and fertility, 174
    and human health, 187
    and human well-being, 1
    and industrialization, 3
    infant mortality, 31
    infectious disease, 181
    and life expectancy, 31
    psychosocial illnesses, 31
    regional governance, *13*
    scale of change, 4
    social impact, 31
    urban violence, 31, 35
Urbanization, trends in, by region, *3*
U.S., *see also* United States
U.S. Department of Energy (DOE), *280–81*
U.S. Department of Energy's (DOE) Energy Information Administration, 278
U.S. Environmental Protection Agency, 33, 68

V

Vehicle pollution, reduction of, 97
Vent communities, oceans and seas, 251
Vienna Framework Convention on Ozone-Degrading Substances, Montreal Protocol, *316*
Violence, in urban environments, x
Vision, 2000, 142
Vistula River, coal mining, 63
Volatile organic compounds (VOCs), *111*, *331*

W

Walking. *see* Transportation, modes of, walking
Waste disposal
    see also Solid waste
    surface and groundwater contamination, 70
    urban consumption, 57
    urban impacts, 57
Waste management, urban areas, 58
Wastepickers
    see also scavengers, human
    protective gear for, 113
    and recycling, *51*
    solid and hazardous wastes, 23
    and solid waste, 44, 112
    solid waste reduction, 135
    "unions" or "cooperatives," 112
    Urban Ore, 113
Wastewater
    and chlorine, 72
    disposal, 21–22
    treatment, *308*
Wastewater disposal, Santiago, Chile, 21
Wastewater treatment, *308*
    Calcutta, India, 110

and duckweed, 110
and industrial wastes, 111
Kochcice, Poland, 110
and wetlands, 110
Water
    see also Drinking water, clean; Freshwater; Piped water
    efficient use of, 234
    and fisheries, 295–304
    irrigation, 301
    metering, *65*
    patterns of use, 302, 322
    piped, *4*, 7, 108
    pricing, 63, *65*, 109, 234, 303
    promoting conservation, 109
    recycling, 109
    renewable supply, 301
    resources and withdrawals, *306–07*
    shortages, 301
    subsidies, 303
    trends, 301
Water, access to, 40
    Rio de Janeiro, Brazil, *37*
Water and air pollution controls, costs and benefits, *110–11*
Water conservation
    demand management, 109
    Long Range Water Supply Program (LRWSP), 109
Water, contaminated, and hygiene, 39
Water demand, industrial uses, 301
Water diversion, 254
    Aral Sea, 301
    Florida Everglades, 301
Water management practices, urban areas, 63
Water pollution, 5, 71–73, 301
    Hong Kong, 75–76
    industrial effluents, *107*, 111
    industrial waste, 6
    reduction, 109
    surface water, *104*
    and transition economies, 302
    urban areas, 1, 15, 18
    urban sewage, 109
Water prices, 108
    Guatemala City, 107
    Lima, Peru, 20
Water resources management, x, 303
    economics of water, 303
    irrigation, 303
    municipal water systems, 303
    pollution control, 303
    privatization, 304
    regional management, 304
    treatment of industrial effluents, xii
Water, safe, access to, by income level of country, *19*
Water and sanitation, 39–40, 105–11, 137
    access to, 20–21, *22*
    adopting appropriate technology and standards, 105–07
    community involvement, 106–07
    condominial sewers, 106, *108*
    developing countries, 19
    human feces, 39
    infrastructure, 110
    International Drinking Water Supply and Sanitation Decade, 19
    and life expectancy, *105*
    operation and maintenance, 107
    priorities for action, 105–13

strategies to improve coverage, 105
water losses, 108
women, 107
Water and sanitation services, *4*
Water scarcity, 295, 302
   and food production, 228
   and water quality, 64
Water and sewage, user fees, 130
Water and sewer, cost recovery, 108
Water shortages, megacities, 63
Water stress index, 301, *302–03*
Water subsidies, and urban poor, 108
Water supplies, future pressures, 301
Water supply, 63–65
   arid regions, 302
   Mexico City, *64–65*
   unaccounted for, 66
Water supply and sanitation, x–xi
Water systems, inefficient, 63
Water use, and agriculture, 303
Watershed protection, coastal pollution, 27
Watersheds, 304
   land use, 254
   siltation of, *208*
Wealth
   see also National wealth
   differences between high income and develop-
      ing countries, *160*
   and resource consumption, 2
Wealth and city size, household environmental problems, *46*
Wetland conversion
   cities, 62
   San Francisco Bay, 62
Wetland loss, East Calcutta, India, 62
Wetlands, 66, 301
   conversion, 298
   draining, 61
   flood protection, 62
   and global warming, 257
   as nurseries and habitats, 251

and wastewater treatment, 110
Wheat, *227, 232, 234*
Wind power, *284–85*
Women
   biological and social risks, 35
   as community decisionmakers, 39
   competing roles, *136*
   as decisionmakers, 136, 176
   education, 32
   education of and population growth, 176
   employment of, *133,* 137
   empowerment, *38*
   exposure to smoke from cookstoves, 36
   as heads of poor households, 14
   health, 17, 36–37, *38,* 42, *132–33*
   as health care providers, *39*
   life expectancy, 176
   literacy, 176, *196–97*
   Mahila Mandals, 39
   as managers of household and community, *39*
   policies for empowerment, 176
   and poverty, 14, 176
   professional or organizational networks, 137
   role in community planning and manage-
      ment, 136
   role in environmental management, 52, 105,
      136
   role in family health, 52
   vulnerability to disease, 36
   wages of compared to men, 176
   water and sanitation, 107
Women in environment, Kathmandu Nepal,
   137
Women's status
   access to credit, 177
   and population trends, 173, 176
Women's Work Centers (WWCs), Karachi,
   Pakistan, *133*
Wood production and trade, *220–21*
World Bank, 140, *144,* 258
   food production potential, 228
   purchasing power parity, *162*
   urban pollution and traffic congestion, *104*

water and air pollution, *110–11*
wealth and genuine savings indicators, *160*
"World cities," 10–11
World Commission on Environment and
   Development, *Our Common Future,* 145
World Commission on Forests and Sustain-
   able Development (WCFSD), 212
World Conference on Women 1995
   declaration of women's rights, 177
   empowerment of women, 176
World Conservation Union (IUCN) Com-
   mission on National Parks and Protected
   Areas, 258
World Energy Council (WEC), 278, *280–81*
World Health Organization (WHO), 140,
   144
   air quality standards, 66, *66*
   Disease Intelligence Unit, *43*
   Disease surveillance, 187
   hemorrhagic fever, 181
   urban data collected, 149
   *World Health Report 1995: Bridging the
      Gaps,* 178
World Resources Institute studies
   coastlines, xiv, 61
   Suriname, *208–09*
   threats to coastal ecosystems, 247

Z

Zabbaleen, Cairo, Egypt, 135
Zegras, Christopher, 99
Zinc, *290–91*
Zoning
   and economic incentives, *121*
   to encourage high residential densities along
      transit corridors, *92*

World Resources Database Index

The *World Resources* electronic database is IBM-PC compatible. Most variables are presented in annual or 5-year time series for up to 152 countries. An asterisk (*) indicates nontypical data files. A plus sign (+) indicates files brought forward unchanged from a previous version of the database. The database is provided in industry standard ".wk1" files that can be used by any spreadsheet or database management software. Data sources and technical notes are included. **To order,** call 1-800-822-0504 or 410-516-6963, fax 410-516-6998, or write to: WRI Publications, P.O. Box 4852, Hampden Station, Baltimore, MD USA 21211.

Basic Economic Indicators

Gross national product (GNP) (current US$); Atlas methodology, 1970–93
GNP per capita (current dollars); Atlas methodology, 1970–93
GNP (constant market prices, US$); 1971–93
Gross domestic product (GDP) (constant US$); 1971–93
GDP per capita (current dollars)
GDP (PPP) (international dollars)
GDP (PPP) per capita (international dollars)
Average annual growth rate of GNP, 1980–93
Average annual growth rate of GDP, 1980–93
Average annual growth rate of GDP (PPP), 1980–92
GDP (current local currency), 1970–93
Distribution of GDP (current local currency):
  Agricultural share, 1971–93
  Industrial share, 1971–93
Services share, 1971–93
Conversion factors (current local to U.S. currency), 1970–92+
Official development assistance (ODA) (current US$), 1982–93
Total external debt (current US$), 1970–93
Disbursed long-term public debt (current US$), 1970–93
Total debt service (current US$), 1970–93
Total exports of goods and services (current US$), 1970–93
Total imports of goods and services (current US$), 1970–93
Current borrowing (current US$), 1970–93
Selected world commodity indexes and prices (constant 1990 US$), 1975–94 *

Population and Human Development

Total population, 1950–2025
Population growth rate, 1950–2025
Total economically active population, 1950–2005+
Labor force growth rate, 1981–2000
Crude birth rate, 1950–2025
Life expectancy:
  Both sexes, 1950–2025
  Females, 1950–2025+
  Males, 1950–2025+
Total fertility rate, 1950–2025
Total population over age 65, 1950–2025
Total population under age 15, 1950–2025
Crude death rate, 1950–2025
Infant mortality, 1950–2025
Under-5 mortality rate, 1960–93
Maternal mortality rate
Child malnutrition:
  Wasting
  Stunting
Per capita average calories available

Safe drinking water—urban (1980 and 1990)
Urban connections to water:
  House pipe
  Public standpipe
  Borehole and pump
  Other
Safe drinking water—rural (1980 and 1990)
Sanitation services—urban (1980 and 1990)
Urban connections to sanitation services:
  House to sewer
  Septic system
  Wet latrine
  Other
Sanitation services—rural (1980 and 1990)
Total expenditures for health
Adult female literacy (1970 and 1990)
Adult male literacy (1970 and 1990)
Gross primary school enrollment:
  Female
  Male
Births attended by trained personnel
Oral rehydration therapy use
Low birth-weight infants
Percent of 1-year-olds immunized against:
  TB
  DPT
  Polio
  Measles
Couples using contraception

Land Cover and Settlements

Land area, 1961–93
Population density, 1961–95
Domesticated land as a percentage of land area
Cropland area, 1961–93
Permanent pasture area, 1961–93
Forest and woodland area, 1961–93
Other land area, 1961–93

Total urban population, 1950–2025
Total rural population, 1950–2025
Average annual population change:
  Urban, 1965–95
  Rural, 1965–95
Number of cities with at least 750,000 inhabitants
Percentage of population residing in cities with at least 750,000 inhabitants, 1950–2000+
Number of people residing in cities with at least 750,000 inhabitants, 1950–2000+
Dependency ratio:
  Urban
  Rural
People in absolute poverty:
  Total
  Urban
  Rural
Total labor force+
Percentage of labor force in:
  Agriculture+
  Industry+
  Services+
Habitat indicators — selected Indian cities*

Food and Agriculture

Index of agricultural production:
  Total, 1961–94
  Per capita, 1960–94
Index of food production:
  Total, 1960–94
  Per capita, 1960–94
Production of cereals, 1961–94
Area harvested for cereals, 1961–94
Production of roots and tubers, 1961–94
Area harvested for roots and tubers, 1961–94
Total cropland area, 1961–93
Total irrigated land, 1961–93
Total fertilizers consumed, 1961–93
Pesticide consumption
Total tractors in use, 1961–93
Total harvesters in use, 1961–93
Total number of cattle, 1961–94
Total number of sheep, 1961–94
Total number of goats, 1961–94
Total number of pigs, 1961–94
Total number of horses, 1961–94
Total number of mules, 1961–94
Total number of asses, 1961–94
Total number of buffaloes, 1961–94
Total number of camels, 1961–94
Total number of chickens, 1961–94
Grain fed to livestock, 1960–94
Total cereal imports, 1961–93
Total cereal exports, 1961–93
Total pulse imports, 1961–93
Total pulse exports, 1961–93
Total edible oil imports, 1961–93
Total edible oil exports, 1961–93
Total cereal donations, 1971–92

Total cereal receipts, 1971–92
Total edible oil donations, 1971–92
Total edible oil receipts, 1971–92
Total milk donations, 1971–92
Total milk receipts, 1971–92

Forests

Extent of natural forest, 1980 and 1990
Extent of other wooded land, 1980 and 1990
Annual deforestation total forest:
  Extent
  Percent
Annual logging of closed broadleaf forest:
  Extent
  Percent of closed forest
  Percent of which is primary forest
Plantations:
  Extent
  Annual change
Protected forest
Rain forest:
  Extent, 1980 and 1990+
  Percent annual change+
Moist deciduous forest:
  Extent, 1980 and 1990+
  Percent annual change+
Hill and montane forest:
  Extent, 1980 and 1990+
  Percent annual change+
Dry deciduous forest:
  Extent, 1980 and 1990+
  Percent annual change+
Very dry forest:
  Extent, 1980 and 1990+
  Percent annual change+
Desert forest:
  Extent, 1980 and 1990+
  Percent annual change+
Roundwood production, total, 1961–93
Fuel and charcoal, production, 1961–93
Industrial roundwood, production, 1961–93
Sawnwood, production, 1961–93
Panels, production, 1961–93
Paper, production, 1961–93
Exports, roundwood, 1961–93
Imports, roundwood, 1961–93

Biodiversity

Protected areas under IUCN category (cat.) I-V:
  Number
  Total area
  Percent of land area
Protected areas under IUCN cat. I-III:
  Number
  Total area
Protected areas under IUCN cat. IV and V:
  Number
  Total area
Protected areas under IUCN cat. I–V of at least 100,000 ha in size:

Number+
Total area+
Percent of total
Protected areas under IUCN cat. I–V of at least 1 million ha in size:
  Number+
  Total area+
  Percent of total
Resource and anthropological reserves (IUCN cat. VI–VIII):+
  Number+
  Total area+
Biosphere reserves:
  Number
  Total area
World heritage sites:
  Number
  Total area
Wetlands of international importance:
  Number
  Total area
Marine and coastal protected areas:
  Number
  Total area
Extent of mangroves
Extent of coral reefs
Number of mammal species:
  All
  Endemic
  Threatened
  Per 10,000 square km
Number of bird species:
  All
  Endemic
  Threatened
  Per 10,000 square km
Number of higher plant species:
  All
  Endemic
  Threatened
  Per 10,000 square km
Number of reptile species:
  All
  Endemic
  Threatened
  Per 10,000 square km
Number of amphibian species:
  All
  Endemic
  Threatened
  Per 10,000 square km
Number of freshwater fish species:
  All
  Threatened
Number of coastal species:
  Fish
  Turtles
  Mammals
  Threatened mammals

Energy and Materials

Commercial energy production:
   Total, 1950–92
   Solid fuel, 1950–92
   Liquid fuel, 1950–92
   Gaseous fuel, 1950–92
   Geothermal and wind, 1950–92
   Hydro, 1950–92
   Nuclear, 1950–92
Commerical energy consumption:
   Total, 1950–92
   Per capita, 1950–92
   Per constant 1987 U.S. dollars of GNP, 1970–92
Imports 1970–92
Exports 1970–92
Traditional fuels consumption, total 1970–92
Anthracite and bituminous coals:
   Reserves in place
   Recoverable reserves
Subbituminous and lignite coals:
   Reserves in place
   Recoverable reserves
Crude oil—recoverable reserves
Natural gas—recoverable reserves
Uranium:
   Recoverable at less than US$80 per kg
   Recoverable at less than US$130 per kg
Hydroelectric:
   Known exploitable potential
   Installed capacity
Production, bauxite*
Consumption, aluminum*
Production, cadmium*
Consumption, cadmium*
Production, copper*
Consumption, copper*
Production, lead*
Consumption, lead*
Production, mercury*
Consumption, mercury*
Production, nickel*
Consumption, nickel*
Production, tin*
Consumption, tin*
Production, zinc*
Consumption, zinc*
Production, iron ore*
Consumption, iron ore*
Production, steel crude*
Consumption, steel crude*
Waste generated (metric tons):*
   From surface treatment of metals and plastics*
   From biocide production (metric tons)*

Waste—oil (metric tons)*
Waste—containing PCBs (metric tons)*
Waste—clinical and pharmaceutical (metric tons)*
Waste from production and use of (metric tons):*
   Photographic materials*
   Organic solvents*
   Paints and pigments*
   Resins and latex*

Water and Fisheries

Annual internal renewable water resources:
   Total
   Per capita
Annual river flows:
   From other countries
   To other countries
Year of data: annual withdrawal
Annual withdrawal:
   Total
   Percent of water resources
   Per capita
Sectoral withdrawal:
   Domestic
   Industry
   Agriculture
Percent of population served by:
   Primary wastewater treatment (OECD countries)*
   Secondary wastewater treatment (OECD countries)*
   Tertiary wastewater treatment (OECD countries)*
   All wastewater treatment (OECD countries)*
Annual marine catch, by region, 1970–93
Annual freshwater catch, 1970–93
Annual aquaculture production:
   Freshwater fish, 1984–93
   Diadromous fish, 1984–93
   Marine fish, 1984–93
   Crustaceans, 1984–93
   Molluscs, 1984–93
   Total fish and shellfish, 1984–93
   Other, 1984–93
Per capita annual food supply from fish and fishery products
Length of coastline
Maritime area:
   Shelf to 200 meter depth
   Exclusive economic zone
Regional marine catch 1981–93:*
   Marine Fish*
   Cephalopods*
   Crustaceans*

Total*
Percent of stocks under stress*
Percent discarded*

Atmosphere and Climate

Carbon dioxide emissions from industrial sources:
   Solid fuels, 1970–92
   Liquid fuels, 1970–92
   Gas fuels, 1970–92
   Gas flaring, 1970–92
   Cement manufacture, 1970–92
   Total, 1970–92
   Per capita, 1970–92
Carbon dioxide emissions from:
   Bunker fuels
   Land-use change
Methane emissions from:
   Solid waste
   Coal mining
   Oil and gas production
   Wet rice agriculture
   Livestock
   Total
Atmospheric concentrations of greenhouse and ozone depleting gases:*
   Carbon dioxide, 1965–94*
   Carbon tetrachloride, 1975–94*
   Methyl chloroform, 1975–94*
   CFC-11, 1975–94*
   CFC-12, 1981–94*
   CFC-113, 1983–94*
   Total gaseous chlorine, 1975–94*
   Nitrous oxide, 1975–94*
   Methane, 1965–94*
World carbon dioxide emissions from fossil fuels:*
   Total, 1955–92*
   Solid fuels, 1955–92*
   Liquid fuels, 1955–92*
   Gas fuels, 1955–92*
   Gas flaring, 1955–92*
   Cement manufacture, 1955–92*
   Per capita, 1955–92*
Sulfur emissions, 1970–93*
Nitrogen emissions, 1970–93*
Common anthropogenic pollutants:*
   Carbon monoxide, 1980–93*
   Particulate matter, 1980–93*
   Hydrocarbons, 1980–93*
Inventories of national greenhouse gas emissions*
Air pollution in selected cities*